Microeconomics and Behaviour

Second Southern African edition

Microeconomics and Behaviour

Second Southern African edition

Pierre de Villiers & Robert H Frank

McGraw Hill Education

London Boston Burr Ridge, IL Dubuque, IA Madison, WI New York San Francisco
St. Louis Bangkok Bogotá Caracas Kuala Lumpur Lisbon Madrid Mexico City
Milan Montreal New Delhi Santiago Seoul Singapore Sydney Taipei Toronto

Microeconomics and Behaviour
Pierre de Villiers, Robert H Frank
ISBN-13 9780077167929
ISBN-10 0077167929

Published by McGraw-Hill Education
Shoppenhangers Road
Maidenhead
Berkshire
SL6 2QL
Telephone: 44 (0) 1628 502 500
Fax: 44 (0) 1628 770 224
Website: www.mheducation.co.uk

British Library Cataloguing in Publication Data
A catalogue record for this book is available from the British Library

Library of Congress Cataloging in Publication Data
The Library of Congress data for this book has been applied for from the Library of Congress

Content Acquisitions Manager: Thomas Hill
Product Developer: Laura Rountree
Content Product Manager: Alison Davis
Digital Controller: Sarah Fleming
Marketing Manager: Geeta Kumar

Text Design by HL Studios
Cover design by Adam Renvoize
Printed and bound in Great Britain by Ashford Colour Press Ltd

ISBN-13 9780077167929
ISBN-10 0077167929

Dedication

To my wife, Natalie, who is my inspiration.

Brief Table of Contents

Detailed Table of Contents

About the Author

A. P. (Pierre) de Villiers is associate professor in the Department of Economics at the University of Stellenbosch, where he teaches mainly in microeconomics, mathematics for economists, and economics of education. He graduated with a BComm degree at the University of Stellenbosch, and majored in economics, accountancy and mathematics. He then completed a master's degree in economics before doing his higher education diploma. For the next five years he was a schoolteacher at Swellendam High School, and received a merit award from the then Cape Province Education Department for outstanding performance as a teacher.

He then joined the Department of Economics at Stellenbosch University as a lecturer. Education remained close to his heart, and he completed his PhD with a dissertation concerning the efficiency (or the lack of it) of the South African school system. He published a couple of articles with topics related to the school system in South Africa. He broadened his scope and also published in topics dealing with management structures in firms, and the economic consequences of HIV/AIDS and crime on the South African economy. For the last couple of years he has shifted his focus to higher education, especially the financing of higher education and how to make it affordable for potential students from disadvantaged communities.

He has been involved in several research reports. He completed research projects for, the National Financial Aid Scheme of South Africa, *inter alia*, the Department of Education in Western Cape, the Department of Transport in Western Cape, the Fiscal Incidence Project of the Treasury, the Council of Higher Education and Media 24. He was also involved with the writing of textbooks both for the school system and for higher education. At Stellenbosch University he has twice received the vice-chancellor's award for outstanding teaching performance.

Robert H. Frank is the Henrietta Johnson Louis Professor of Management and Professor of Economics at the Johnson Graduate School of Management at Cornell University, where he also teaches principles of microeconomics in the College of Arts and Sciences. His 'Economic View' column appears monthly in *The New York Times*. His research has focused on rivalry and cooperation in economic and social behaviour. His books on these themes have been translated into 18 languages.

He is past president of the Eastern Economic Association, a co-recipient of the 2004 Leontief Prize for Advancing the Frontiers of Economic Thought, and a recipient of the Merrill Scholars Program Outstanding Educators Citation. At the Johnson School, he was awarded the Russell Distinguished Teaching Award in 2004 and the Apple Distinguished Teaching Award in 2005.

Preface

My goal in writing *Microeconomics and Behaviour* was to produce an intellectually challenging text that would be both accessible and engaging for students, especially given the diversity of the Southern African student population. Two typical errors are made with standard microeconomics textbooks. Some focus so much on accessibility that not enough theory is covered, or it is not covered in enough depth. Others are too technical, with the focus more on mathematics for the sake of mathematics rather than on economics. With this text I believe a balance between these two approaches has been struck. The more technical work is covered in boxes within the chapters, and lecturers can decide the level at which they want to include mathematical applications in their courses. This is an important issue, given the diversity of technical knowledge of students in Southern African higher education institutions. Lecturers can use this text with minimal use of mathematics or they can include the more technical material, but I do not think any part of the work is too technical for the average student to understand.

This book was written with the conviction that economic theory and analytical tools are complements, not substitutes. I believe that students who are exposed to analytical tools without dealing properly with economic theory rarely learn to appreciate our discipline. They seem unable to 'think like an economist'. By contrast, those students who are properly exposed to economic theory, and learn that quantitative techniques supplement it and can be used to simulate real-life situations or test economic theories, learn to like economics.

Microeconomics and Behaviour develops the basic analytical tools with patience and attention to detail. At the same time it incorporates the use of real-life examples and applications to make students familiar with the way economists think, and to learn the same skills in the process of going through these applications.

Economic naturalism

One of the problematic issues of our subject is that it is not an exact science like the natural sciences. When you put a piece of magnesium on the water it always leads to exactly the same chemical reaction. With economics, this is not the case. People do not always behave in the same way or in a rational way. So one day, when oranges are on special offer, you cannot provide them quickly enough for your customers, whereas on another occasion consumers do not want to touch cut-price fruit as they think it is too old or possibly defective. Most economic problems are not positive ones that can be solved with statistics or facts; they are normative problems, where someone must make a value judgement. For example, what inflation rate should be set in Southern Africa? Most students will answer that it should be between 3 and 6 per cent, just because it is the official policy of the South African Reserve Bank. But a low inflation rate depresses economic growth, which results in the creation of fewer job opportunities in a country with an unemployment rate of almost 30 per cent. Surely a case can be made for stimulating economic growth to create more jobs, even if it leads to slightly higher inflation rates? It is not that either of these policies is wrong. It is just that the executive committee of the Reserve Bank judged that a lower inflation rate was the best option.

Economic naturalism involves analysing this type of real-life situation. We use numerous examples of situations that have intrigued students over the years, and teach them to use microeconomic tools to solve the problems they are confronted with. For example, why do airline companies charge those passengers who buy their tickets at the last minute the highest prices? Why are child safety seats required in cars in many countries but not in aeroplanes? Why do female models earn so much more than male models? Why does the highest-paid male movie star earn so much more than the highest-paid female movie star? Why does the top tennis player in the world earn so much more than the twentieth-ranked player, who is almost as good? Why does an almost new car sell for so much less than a new car? By guiding students through these everyday situations, they learn to appreciate that economics is not only textbook theory but has many applications in the real world, and indeed is used extensively in practice.

Problem solving

We think all economists agree that, in order to understand price theory, it is important to solve problems. *Microeconomics and Behaviour* has been written with this in mind. Each chapter contains worked examples and exercises for the student to tackle on their own, the answers to which are provided at the end of the chapter. At the end of each chapter are also many carefully chosen problems drawn from familiar contexts. Students relate better to the concrete than to the abstract, and this approach has proven to be effective. The way in which examples and exercises are covered in the chapters provides the groundwork to prepare students for the end-of-chapter problems. These problems place students in the position of having to make irrational choices, which helps them to better understand the normative nature of economic problems and to recognize the errors of judgement that many consumers make.

Changes for the second Southern African edition

This text is not written with a specific institution in mind. Therefore it covers more topics than any one institution will typically include in its microeconomics course. The chapters included in this text cover the topics that our market research has indicated most institutions cover in their courses. Although no institution is likely to cover all of the chapters, we recommend that most are included in a course at second-year level.

For this edition, we used feedback from institutions adopting the textbook and other reviewers to determine which new topics to include and which to scrap. The second Southern African edition is now developing independently of the original textbook written for American students. Future editions will incorporate events that have taken place since the publication of this edition, and data will be updated where new information has become available.

Although the original American edition by Robert Frank provided an excellent theoretical structure, with good practical applications, the whole text for the first edition was thoroughly revised, and the examples, exercises and applications were adjusted with the Southern African audience in mind. However, certain foreign examples were retained (or new ones added) because the Southern African economy operates in a global environment. In my opinion, this is the biggest plus point of this edition. The typical Southern African student will be able to relate to (almost) all of the examples and exercises used in the text.

The presentation of this edition remains the same as the first. Quantitative material is provided within the text itself; technical details are presented in boxes. This approach demonstrates to students that economic theory and quantitative techniques are complementary and not two distinct disciplines. However, care has been taken not to include mathematics for mathematics' sake; rather, it is included only where it complements theory. By treating the mathematics in this way, lecturers are free to skip the more technical material or to include all of the mathematics in their courses.

In this new Southern African edition the latest available economic information has been included and examples updated or changed to make them more relevant or realistic. New economic naturalists have also been added to enhance the text's Southern African flavour. In most chapters essay style questions have been added in response to review feedback.

The following changes have been made. In Part 1, Chapter 2 includes new sections dealing with consumer and producer surplus and how to convert nominal prices into real prices. Graphs and a discussion have also been added to illustrate the tax burden concept.

Part 2 deals with consumer behaviour. In Chapters 3 and 4, the sequence of the discussions has been altered to help students navigate these key areas of microeconomics. Various graphs have now been updated to reflect changes in the ICC. The text addresses the difference between the Hicks and Slutsky approaches to income and substitution effects resulting from a price change, and a section dealing with income elasticity and the effect on tax income is also included. Chapter 5 now includes different options for insuring against risk.

Part 3 deals with the firm, and market structures. In Chapter 7, new tables and graphs have been added to illustrate the relationship between TP, AP and MP and returns to scale with isoquants. A section highlighting the difference between diminishing returns, returns to scale, economies of scale and economies of scope has also been included for this new edition. In Chapter 8, better distinctions have been made between accounting and economic costs as well as between sunk cost and fixed costs. A new section dealing with the minimum efficient scale of production has also been added. In Chapter 9, greater attention has been paid to why we still explain economic actions using rather unrealistic perfectly competitive markets. This chapter also includes a discussion on the differences between allocative and productive efficiency. In Chapter 10, Southern African competition policy and the efficiency loss resulting from a monopoly have been updated. The Hirschman–Herfindahl Index has also been added. In Chapter 11, the structure of the chapter has been changed to help with student understanding of oligopoly models. Concentration indexes were also added in the discussion on the Southern African situation.

Part 4 deals with factor markets. In Chapter 12, new content addressing the value of the marginal product of labour, a firm hiring labour in a competitive market and minimum wage has been added and illustrated using data concerning trade unions and other labour-related statistics.

Part 5 deals with externalities, public goods and welfare. In Chapter 14, new information concerning the ecological footprint has been included, while Chapter 16 now includes new sections on competitive equilibrium in consumption and taxes as a source of efficiency.

Pierre de Villiers
October 2014

Acknowledgements

Our thanks go to the following reviewers for their comments at various stages in the text's development:

Amanda Fitschen, *University of South Africa*
Barry Povey, *University of Cape Town*
Busani Moyo, *University of South Africa*
Corne van Walbeek, *University of Cape Town*
Ephias Makaudze, *University of Western Cape*
Karlien Kitching, *University of the Free State*
Marcel Kholer, *University of Kwa-Zulu Westville*
Michael Sale, *Nelson Mandela Metropolitan University*
Narain Sinha, *University of Botswana*
Ralitza Dobreva, *University of Kwa-Zulu Westville*
Requier Wait, *North West University*

We would also like to thank Marcel Kholer for the material which he has provided for this textbook and its accompanying online resources.

Every effort has been made to trace and acknowledge ownership of copyright and to clear permission for material reproduced in this book. The publishers will be pleased to make suitable arrangements to clear permission with any copyright holders whom it has not been possible to contact.

Guided Tour

Chapter preview

This is an innovative feature, which poses a problem or questions that the material developed in the chapter will enable the student to answer.

Chapter preview

In this chapter we'll explore wh
mally function so smoothly, and w
direct allocation are sometimes p
early part of the chapter will loc
ply and demand analysis. First, w
usual descriptive features of supp
analysis covered in the introducto
we'll see that, for given attributes
sellers, the unregulated competitiv
the best attainable outcome, in the

are downward sloping: th
rises as
uct falls
called t
Althoug
Chapter
cally p
curve t
such ex
never e

Law of demand The empirical observation that, when the price of a product falls, people demand larger quantities of it.

The demand curve (DD)
given by the following equa

Key terms

These are key terms, which students will need to familiarize themselves with. They are highlighted throughout each chapter, and explained for easy reference.

Economic naturalist sections

Examples and applications are drawn from everyday experience; they enable the student to identify with the material.

Economic naturalist 1

Why is airline food so bad?

Many people complain about airline
Indeed, if any serious restaurant
to serve such food, it would quic
bankrupt. Our complaints seem to
or granted that airline meals should be just as go
he ones we eat in restaurants. But why should
he cost–benefit perspective says that airlines
ncrease the quality of their meals if and only if th
fit would outweigh the cost. The benefit of bette
s probably well-measured by what passengers wo
villing to pay for it, in the form of higher ticket pri
restaurant-quality meal could be had for, say, a
R80 increase in fares, most people would probab

Example 1.2

Should I go surfing today or work

Assume you study at the Nelson M
your campus. From experience y
for the day is R80 (which include
of going surfing. You must also t
will forgo by heading for the beac
professor's research assistant. Th
ing to do it for free. The question
Here, the cost of surfing is no
opportunity cost of the lost earni

Exercises and examples

These prepare the student for the end-of-chapter problems by taking them through a sequence of carefully crafted examples and exercises within each chapter.

'The next step' sections

These are sections within certain chapters that include additional material on the specific topic discussed. They are clearly marked, and the lecturer can decide whether to include or exclude them.

'The next step'

Using calculus to maximi

With calculus we can solve th
budget allocation problem wi
recourse to the geometry of indiff
Let $U(X, Y)$ be the consumer's
tion; and suppose M, P_X and P_Y de
the price of X and the price of Y,
Formally, the consumer's alloca
can be stated as follows:

Summary

- Our task in this chapter was t
basic model of rational consu
all its variants, this model t
ers' preferences as given, and
will try to satisfy them in the
way possible.
- The first step in solving the co
eting problem is to summariz
er's preferences. Here, we
preference ordering by which

Chapter summary

Chapter summaries are written in a narrative format that carefully summarizes the material covered in the chapter.

Problems

Each chapter ends with a set of problems that range in difficulty from routine to highly challenging.

Problems

1 Assume that tea and lem
ments, and that coffee
substitutes:
  a How, if at all, will the impo
  tive ceiling price on tea a
  lemons? Explain.
  b How, if at all, will the impo
  tive ceiling price on tea a

Answers to in-chapter

2.1 $4Q^* = 12 - 2Q^*$, which yiel
$P^* = 4Q^* = 8$, or $P^* = 12 - 2Q$
2.2 At a price of R90/lobster, the
ded is 500 lobsters/day (600
the quantity supplied is 1
$\left(\frac{1}{0.9}(90)\right)$, making excess d

Answers to in-chapter exercises

All the answers to the in-chapter exercises are provided at the end of each chapter. Variations and extensions of these exercises are echoed in the end-of-chapter problems, which enable students to approach them with greater confidence. Answers to the problems are available in the *Instructor's Manual*.

Mc Graw Hill Education

connect®
ECONOMICS

McGraw-Hill Connect Economics is a learning and teaching environment that improves student performance and outcomes whilst promoting engagement and comprehension of content.

You can utilize publisher-provided materials, or add your own content to design a complete course to help your students achieve higher outcomes.

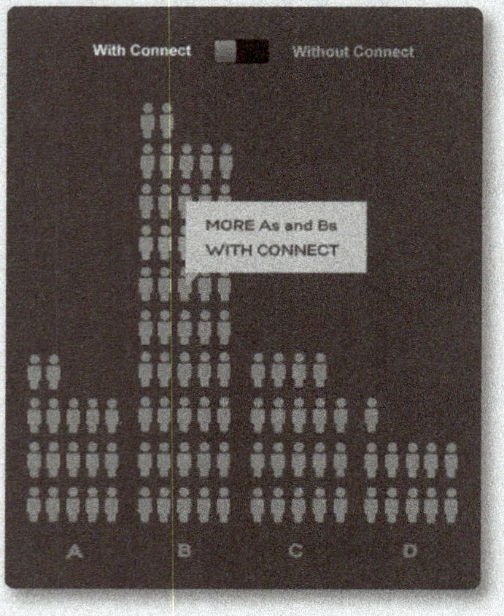

PROVEN EFFECTIVE

INSTRUCTORS

With McGraw-Hill Connect Plus Economics, instructors get:

- Simple **assignment management**, allowing you to spend more time teaching.
- **Auto-graded** assignments, quizzes and tests.
- **Detailed visual reporting** where students and section results can be viewed and analysed.
- Sophisticated **online testing** capability.
- A **filtering and reporting** function that allows you to easily assign and report on materials that are correlated to learning outcomes, topics, level of difficulty, and more. Reports can be accessed for individual students or the whole class, as well as offering the ability to drill into individual assignments, questions or categories.
- **Instructor materials** to help supplement your course.

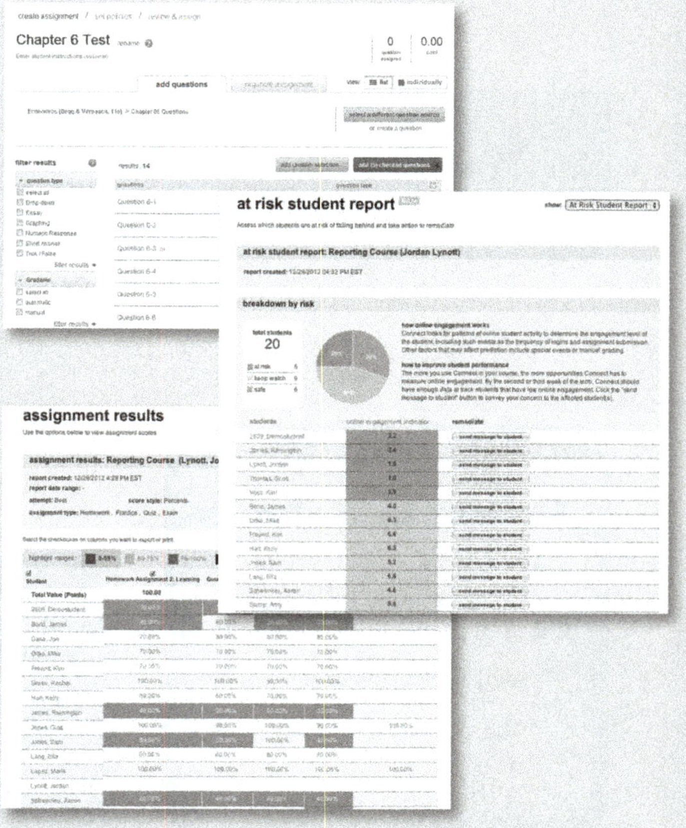

Get Connected. Get Results.

STUDENTS

With McGraw-Hill Connect Plus Economics, students get:

Assigned content

- Easy **online access** to homework, tests and quizzes.
- **Immediate feedback** and 24-hour tech support.

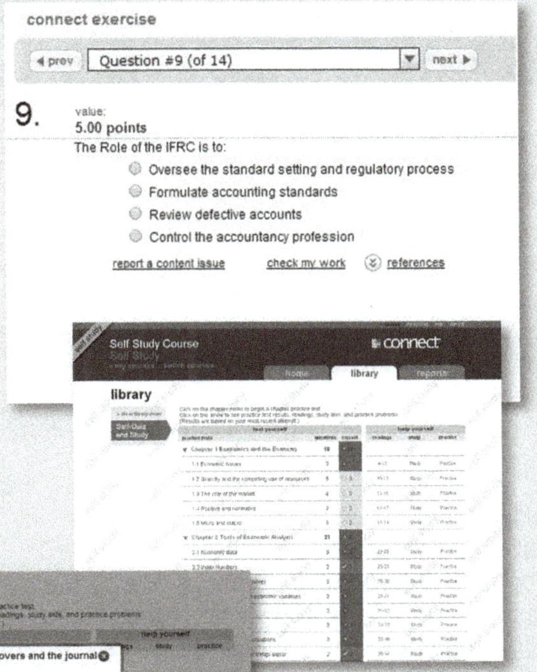

Self-Quiz and Study

- **Practice tests** help you to easily identify your strengths and weakness and create a clear revision plan.
- **Study tools** – including specific readings, animated graphs, vignettes and summaries give you extra practice on individual topics.

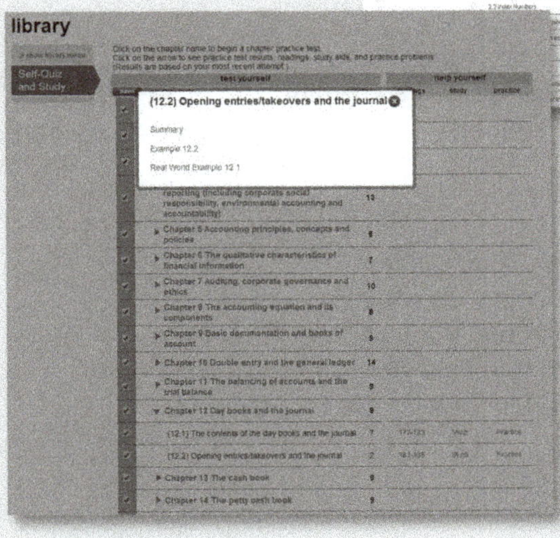

If your instructor is **not** prescribing Connect as part of your course, you can still access a full range of student support resources on our Self Study platform at http://connect.mcgraw-hill.com/selfstudy.

Self Study

ACCESS OPTIONS

connect® |ECONOMICS

Is an online assignment and assessment solution that offers a number of powerful tools and features that make managing assignments easier, so faculty can spend more time teaching. With Connect Economics, students can engage with their coursework anytime and anywhere, making the learning process more accessible and efficient.

Graphing Tools

Enable students to develop their graphical ability, calculating and plotting data as part of basic and complex questions. Auto graded graphing questions are available throughout the assignable and student self-study content and can provide immediate feedback. Students can also access animated graphs as part of their Study Tools, giving them the chance to visualise and understand key concepts step-by-step.

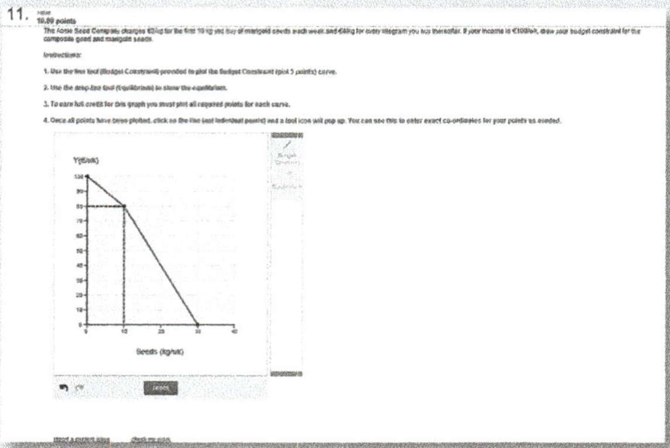

Calculation questions

Test students' mathematical understanding, allowing them additional practice and further opportunity to develop their problem solving skills. The questions are auto-graded so faculty can spend more time teaching.

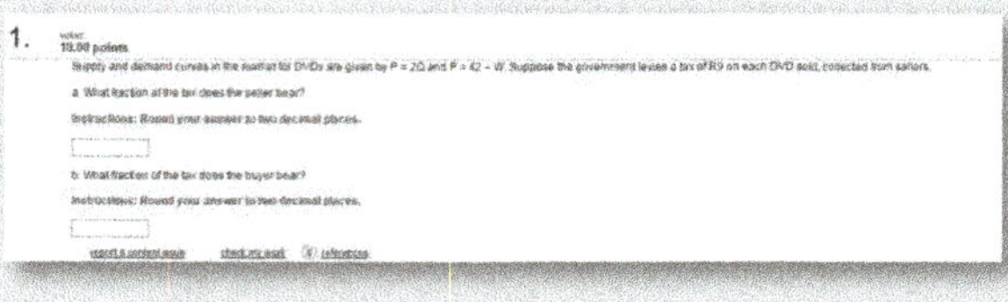

Algorithmic problem sets

Provide repeated opportunities for students to practise and master concepts with multiple versions of each problem. Or use the algorithmic problems in class testing to provide each student with a different version than that seen by their peers.

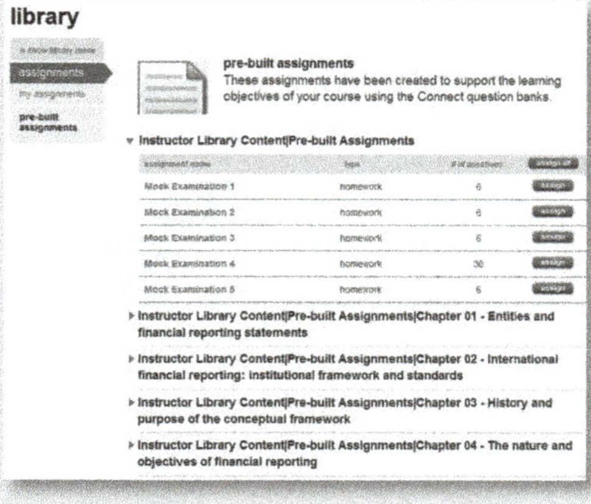

Pre-built assignments

Assign all of the autogradable end of chapter material as a ready-made assignment with the simple click of a button.

McGraw Hill Education

connect® ECONOMICS

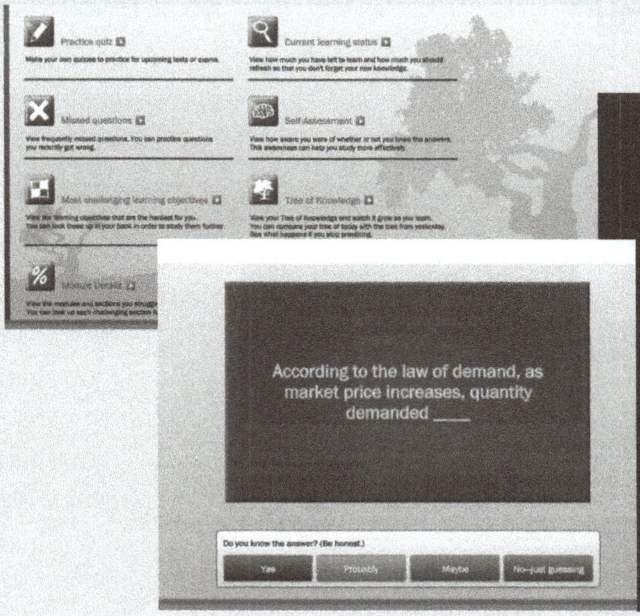

LearnSmart™

LearnSmart is the most widely used and intelligent adaptive learning resource that is proven to strengthen memory recall, improve course retention and boost grades. Distinguishing what students know from what they don't, and honing in on concepts they are most likely to forget, LearnSmart continuously adapts to each student's needs by building an individual learning path so students study smarter and retain more knowledge. Real-time reports provide valuable insight to instructors, so precious class time can be spent on higher-level concepts and discussion.

Online Learning Centre

Online **LearningCentre**

Lecturer support – Helping you to help your students

In addition to the assignments, questions, problems and activities McGraw-Hill Education provides within Connect, we also offer a host of resources to support your teaching:

- **Faster course preparation** – time-saving support for your module
- **High-calibre content to support your students** – resources written by your academic peers, who understand your need for rigorous and reliable content
- **Flexibility** – edit, adapt or repurpose; test in Connect or through EZ Test Online – the choice is yours

The materials created specifically for lecturers adopting this textbook include:

- *Lecturer's Manual* to support your module preparation, with case notes, guide answers, teaching tips and more
- *PowerPoint presentations* to use in lecture presentations, which include dynamic graphs. These are available in English and Afrikaans.
- *Image library* of artwork from the textbook
- Additional *test bank* resources to encourage your students to develop their understanding and practise what they learn

To request your password to access these resources, contact your McGraw-Hill Education representative or visit:

www.mheducation.co.uk/textbooks/devilliers2

Test Bank available in McGraw-Hill EZ Test Online

A test bank of hundreds of questions is available to lecturers adopting this book for their module. For flexibility, this is available for adopters of this book to use through Connect or through the EZ Test Online website. For each chapter you will find:

- A range of multiple choice, true or false, short-answer or graphing questions
- Questions identified by type, difficulty and topic to help you select those that best suit your needs
- Available in both English and Afrikaans

McGraw-Hill EZ Test Online is:

- **Accessible** anywhere with an internet connection – your unique login provides you access to all your tests and material in any location
- **Simple** to set up and easy to use
- **Flexible**, offering a choice from question banks associated with your adopted textbook or allowing you to create your own questions
- **Comprehensive**, with access to hundreds of banks and thousands of questions created for other McGraw-Hill titles
- **Compatible** with Blackboard and other course management systems
- **Time-saving** – students' tests can be immediately marked and results and feedback delivered directly to your students to help them to monitor their progress

To register for this FREE resource, visit **www.eztestonline.com**

Part 1

Introduction

Part contents

In these first two chapters we review material from the introductory microeconomics course. For most students this will be revision or a short recap of what you did last year. Chapter 1 applies the principles of cost–benefit analysis to a variety of choices familiar from experience. Its goal is to give you an intuitive feel for what it means to 'think like an economist'.

Chapter 2 develops basic supply and demand analysis, our analytical tool for explaining the prices and quantities of goods traded in markets. We shall see that, although unregulated markets may not always yield outcomes we like, they often produce the best results attainable under the circumstances. By contrast, governmental efforts to help the poor by regulating prices and quantities often produce undesired side effects. We shall see that programmes which increase their income are a better way to assist the poor.

Chapter 1

Thinking like an economist

Much of microeconomics entails the study of how people choose under conditions of scarcity. Some people may react to this description by saying that the subject is only relevant in developing countries, because material scarcity is largely a thing of the past in developed countries.

This reaction, however, takes too narrow a view of scarcity, for there are *always* important resources in short supply. At his death, Aristotle Onassis was worth several billion euros. He had more money than he could possibly spend, and used it for such things as finely crafted whale ivory footrests for the barstools on his yacht. And yet he confronted the problem of scarcity much more than most of us will ever have to. Onassis was the victim of *myasthenia gravis*, a debilitating and progressive neurological disease. For him, the scarcity that mattered was not money but time, energy and the physical skill needed to carry out ordinary activities.

Time is a scarce resource for everyone, not just the terminally ill. In deciding which movies to see, for example, it is time, not the price of admission, which constrains most of us. With only a few free nights available each month, seeing one movie means not being able to see another, or not being able to have dinner with friends.

Time and money are not the only important scarce resources. Consider the economic choice you confront when a friend invites you to a buffet brunch. You must decide how to fill your plate. Even if you are not rich, money would be no object, since you can eat as much as you want for free. Nor is time an obstacle, since you have all afternoon, and would enjoy spending it in the company of your friend. The important scarce resource here is the capacity of your stomach. You can only eat so much before you become sick. Eating another waffle necessarily means having less room for more scrambled eggs. The fact that no money changes hands here does not make your choice any less an economic one.

Every choice involves important elements of scarcity. Sometimes the most relevant scarcity will involve money, but not always. Coping with scarcity is the essence of the human condition. Indeed, were it not for the problem of scarcity, life would be stripped of much of its intensity. For someone with an infinite lifetime and limitless material resources, hardly a single decision would ever matter.

In this chapter we examine some basic principles of microeconomic theory, and see how an economist might apply them to a wide variety of choices involving scarcity. Later chapters develop the theory more formally. For now, our only goal is to get an intuitive feel for that distinctive mind-set known as 'thinking like an economist'. And the best way to do that is to work through a series of problems familiar from actual experience.

The cost–benefit approach to decisions

Many of the choices economists study can be posed as the following question:

Should I do activity x?

For the choice confronting a moviegoer, '… do activity x?' might be, for example, '… see the latest movie in the *Iron Man* series tonight?' For the person attending the buffet brunch, it might be '… eat another waffle?' Economists answer such questions by comparing the costs and benefits of doing the activity in question. The decision rule we use is disarmingly simple. If $C(x)$ denotes the costs of doing x and $B(x)$ denotes the benefits, it is

If $B(x) > C(x)$, do x; otherwise don't.

To apply this rule, we must define and measure costs and benefits. Monetary values are a useful common denominator for this purpose, even when the activity has nothing directly to do with money. We define $B(x)$ as the maximum rand amount you would be willing to pay to do x. Often $B(x)$ will be a

Example 1.1

Should I turn down my stereo?

You have settled into a comfortable chair and are listening to your stereo when you realize that the next two tracks on the CD are ones you dislike. If you had a programmable player, you would have programmed it not to play them. But you don't, and so you must decide whether to get up and turn the music down, or stay put and wait it out.

The benefit of turning it down is not having the songs you don't like blare away at you. The cost, in turn, is the inconvenience of getting out of your chair. If you are extremely comfortable, and the music is only mildly annoying, you will probably stay put. But if you haven't been settled for long, or if the music is really bothersome, you are more likely to get up.

Even for simple decisions like this, it is possible to translate the relevant costs and benefits into a monetary framework. Consider first the cost of getting out of your chair. If someone offered you 1 cent to get up out of a comfortable chair, and there was no reason other than the cent to do it, would you take the offer? Most people would not. But if someone offered you R1000, you would be on your feet in an instant. Somewhere between 1 cent and R1000 lies your **reservation price**, the minimum amount it would take to get you out of the chair.

Reservation price of activity x The price at which a person would be indifferent between doing x and not doing x.

To see where the threshold lies, imagine a mental auction with yourself in which you keep boosting the offer by small increments from 1 cent until you reach the point at which getting up is barely worthwhile. Where this point occurs will obviously depend on circumstance. If you are rich, it will tend to be higher than if you are poor, because a given amount of money will seem less important; if you feel energetic, it will be lower than if you feel tired; and so on. For the sake of discussion, suppose your reservation price for getting out of the chair turns out to be R100. You can conduct a similar mental auction to determine the maximum sum you would be willing to pay someone to turn the music down. This reservation price measures the benefits of turning the music down; let us suppose it turns out to be R75.

In terms of our formal decision rule, we then have x 'turn my stereo down', with $B(x) = \text{R}75 < C(x) = \text{R}100$, which means that you should remain in your chair. Listening to the next two songs will be unpleasant, but less so than getting up would be. A reversal of these cost and benefit figures would imply a decision to get up and turn the music down. If $B(x)$ and $C(x)$ happened to be equal, you would be indifferent between the two alternatives.

hypothetical magnitude, the amount you would be willing to pay if you had to, even though no money will change hands. $C(x)$, in turn, is the value of all the resources you must give up in order to do x. Here too $C(x)$ need not involve an explicit transfer of money.

For most decisions, at least some of the benefits or costs will not be readily available in monetary terms. To see how we proceed in such cases, consider the following simple decision.

The role of economic theory

The idea that anyone might actually calculate the costs and benefits of turning down a stereo may sound absurd. Economists have been criticized for making unrealistic assumptions about how people behave, and outsiders are quick to wonder what purpose is served by the image of a person trying to decide how much he would pay to avoid getting up from his chair.

There are two responses to this criticism. The first is that economists don't assume that people make such calculations explicitly. Rather, many economists argue, we can make useful predictions by assuming that people act *as if* they made such calculations. This view was forcefully expressed by Nobel laureate Milton Friedman, who illustrated his point by looking at the techniques expert pool players use.[1] He argued that the shots they choose, and the specific ways they attempt to make them, can be predicted extremely well by assuming that players take careful account of all the relevant laws of Newtonian physics. Of course, few expert pool or snooker players have had formal training in physics, and hardly any can recite such laws as 'the angle of incidence equals the angle of reflection'. Nor are they likely to know the definitions of 'elastic collisions' and 'angular momentum'. Even so, Friedman argued, they would never have become expert players in the first place *unless* they played as dictated by the laws of physics. Our theory of pool or snooker player behaviour assumes, unrealistically, that players know the laws of physics. Friedman urged us to judge this theory not by how accurate its central assumption is, but by how well it *predicts* behaviour. And on this score it performs very well indeed.

Like good snooker players, we must also develop skills for coping with our environments. Many economists, Friedman among them, believe that useful insights into our behaviour can be gained by assuming that we act as if governed by the rules of rational decision making. Using trial and error we eventually absorb these rules, just as snooker players absorb the laws of physics.

Professional snooker players may not know all the formal laws of Newtonian physics, but the quality of their play suggest that they have a deep understanding of it. ©iStock.com/SrdjanPav.

A second response to the charge that economists make unrealistic assumptions is to concede that behaviour does often differ from the predictions of economic models. Thus, as economist Richard Thaler puts it, we often behave more like novice than expert snooker players – ignoring bank shots and having no idea about putting the proper spin on the cue ball to position it for the next shot. Considerable evidence supports this second view.

But even where economic models fail on descriptive grounds, they often provide useful guidance for decisions. That is, even if they don't always predict how we *do* behave, they may often give useful insights into how to achieve our goals more efficiently. If novice snooker players have not yet internalized the relevant physical laws, they may nonetheless consult those laws for guidance about how to improve. Economic models often play an analogous role with respect to ordinary consumer and business decisions. Indeed, this role alone provides a compelling reason for learning economics.

Common pitfalls in decision making

Some economists are embarrassed if an outsider points out that much of what they do boils down to an application of the principle that we should perform an action if and only if its benefits exceed its

[1] Milton Friedman, 'The methodology of positive economics', *Essays in Positive Economics*, University of Chicago Press, Chicago, 1953.

costs. That just doesn't sound like enough to keep a person with a PhD busy all day! There is more to it, however, than meets the eye. People who study economics quickly discover that measuring costs and benefits is as much an art as a science. Some costs seem almost deliberately hidden from view. Others may seem relevant but, at closer look, turn out not to be.

Economics teaches us how to identify the costs and benefits that really matter. An important goal of this book is to teach you to become a better decision-maker. A good starting point is to examine some common pitfalls in decision making. The relevant economic principles are simple and commonsensical, but many people ignore them.

Pitfall 1: Ignoring implicit costs

One pitfall is to overlook costs that are not explicit. If doing activity x means not being able to do activity y, then the value to you of doing y (had you done it) is an **opportunity cost of activity x**. Many people make bad decisions because they tend to ignore the value of such forgone opportunities. This insight suggests that it will almost always be instructive to translate questions such as 'Should I do x?' into ones such as 'Should I do x or y?' In the latter question, y is simply the most highly valued alternative to doing x. Examples 1.2 and 1.3 help drive this important point home.

> **Opportunity cost of activity x** The value of all that must be sacrificed to do x.

The fact that you liked the research job (in Examples 1.2 and 1.3) just well enough to have been willing to do it for free is another way of saying there were no psychic costs associated with doing it. This is important, because it means that by not doing the job you would not have been escaping something unpleasant. Of course, not all jobs fall into this category. Suppose instead that your job is to scrape plates in the campus cafeteria for the same pay, R90/day, and that the job is so unpleasant that you would be unwilling to do it for less than R60/day. Assuming your manager at the dining hall permits you to take a day off whenever you want, let us now reconsider your decision about whether to go surfing or rather scrape plates when you can take a day off.

As Example 1.3 makes clear, costs and benefits are reciprocal. Not incurring a cost is the same as getting a benefit. By the same token, not getting a benefit is the same as incurring a cost.

Obvious as this sounds, it is often overlooked. A case in point was a foreign graduate student who got his degree some years ago and was about to return to his home country. The trade regulations of his nation permitted people returning from abroad to bring back a new automobile without having to pay the normal 50 per cent import tariff. The student's father-in-law asked him to bring him back a new R300 000 Toyota, and sent him a cheque for exactly that amount. This put the student in a quandary. He had been planning to bring back a Toyota and sell it in his home country. Because, as noted, new cars face a 50 per cent import tax, such a car would sell at a dealership there for R450 000. The student estimated that he could easily sell it privately for R420 000, which would net him an R120 000 gain. Thus the opportunity cost of giving the car to his father-in-law for R300 000 was going to be R120 000! Not getting this big benefit was a big cost. In the end, it was one the student elected

Example 1.2

Should I go surfing today or work as a research assistant?

Assume you study at the Nelson Mandela Metropolitan University and there is a great surf spot near your campus. From experience you know that a day at the beach is worth R120 to you. The charge for the day is R80 (which includes bus fare and other expenses). However, this is not the only cost of going surfing. You must also take into account the value of the most attractive alternative you will forgo by heading for the beach. Suppose the best alternative is your new job as your Economics professor's research assistant. The job pays R90 per day, and you like it just well enough to be willing to do it for free. The question you face is, 'Should I go surfing or work as a research assistant?'

Here, the cost of surfing is not just the explicit cost of the surfing package (R80) but also the opportunity cost of the lost earnings (R90). The total cost is therefore R170, which exceeds the benefits of R120. Since $C(x) > B(x)$, you should stay on campus and work for your professor. Someone who ignored the opportunity cost of the forgone earnings would decide incorrectly to go surfing.

Example 1.3

Should I go surfing today or scrape plates?

There are two equivalent ways of looking at this decision. One is to say that one benefit of going surfing is not having to scrape plates. Since you would never be willing to scrape plates for less than R60/day, avoiding that task is worth that amount to you. Going surfing thus carries the indirect benefit of not scraping plates. When we add that indirect benefit to the R120 direct benefit of the surfing, we get $B(x) = \text{R}180$. In this view of the problem, $C(x)$ is the same as before, namely, the R80 surfing expenditure plus the R90 opportunity cost of the lost earnings, or R170. So now $B(x) > C(x)$, which means you should go surfing.

Alternatively, we could have viewed the unpleasantness of the plate-scraping job as an offset against its salary. From this approach, we would subtract R60/day from your R90/day earnings and say that the opportunity cost of not working is only R30/day. Then $C(x) = \text{R}80 + \text{R}30 = \text{R}110 < B(x) = \text{R}120$, and again the conclusion is that you should go surfing.

It makes no difference in which of these two ways you handle the valuation of the unpleasantness of scraping plates. It is critically important, however, that you do it either one way or the other. Don't count it twice!

Example 1.4

Should I work first or go to university first?

University costs are not limited to tuition fees, housing, food, books, supplies and the like. They also include the opportunity cost of earnings forgone while studying. Earnings increase with experience. Thus the more experience you have, the more you must forgo to attend university. This opportunity cost is therefore lowest when you are right out of high school.

On the benefit side, one big gain of a university education is sharply higher earnings. The sooner you graduate, the longer you will reap this benefit. Another benefit is the pleasantness of going to university as opposed to working. In general, the kinds of jobs people hold tend to be less unpleasant (or more pleasant), the more education they have. By going to university right away, you thus avoid having to work at the least pleasant jobs. For most people, then, it makes sense to go to university first and work afterwards. Certainly it makes more sense to attend university at age 20 than at age 50.

A common exception involves people who are too immature right out of high school to reap the benefits of university work, who often do better by taking a gap-year and work a year or two before university.

The university example is a perfect illustration of Friedman's argument about how to evaluate a theory. High school leavers don't decide when to attend university on the basis of sophisticated calculations involving opportunity costs. On the contrary, most start right out of high school simply because that is what most of their peers do. It is the thing to do.

But this begs the question of how it got to *be* the thing to do. Customs do not originate out of thin air. A host of different societies have had centuries to experiment with this decision. If there were a significantly better way of arranging the learning and working periods of life, some society would have long since discovered it. Our current custom has survived because it is efficient. People may not make explicit calculations about the opportunity cost of forgone earnings, but they often behave *as if* they do.[2]

As simple as the opportunity cost concept is, it is one of the most important in microeconomics. The art in applying the concept correctly lies in being able to recognize the most valuable alternative that is sacrificed by the pursuit of a given activity.

[2] This does not mean that all customs necessarily promote efficiency. For example, circumstances may have changed in such a way that a custom that promoted efficiency in the past no longer does so. In time, such a custom might change. Yet many habits and customs, once firmly entrenched, are very slow to change.

to bear, because he valued keeping peace in the family even more. As the cost–benefit principle makes clear, the best decision is not always the one that leaves you with the most money in your pocket.

Pitfall 2: Failing to ignore sunk costs

An opportunity cost may not seem to be a relevant cost, when in reality it is. On the other hand, sometimes an expenditure may seem relevant when in reality it is not. Such is often the case with *sunk costs* – costs that are beyond recovery at the moment a decision is made. Unlike opportunity costs, these costs *should be* ignored. Not ignoring them is a second pitfall in decision making. The principle of ignoring sunk costs emerges clearly in the following example.

In Example 1.5, note the role of the assumption that, costs aside, you are indifferent between the two modes of transport. If you had preferred one mode to the other, we would also have had to weigh that preference. For example, if you were willing to pay R810 to avoid the hassle of driving, the real cost of driving would be R2600, not R1 790, and you should take the bus.

Exercises such as the one here are sprinkled throughout the text to help you make sure that you understand important analytical concepts. You will master microeconomics more effectively if you do these exercises as you go along.

Exercise 1.1

How, if at all, would your answer to the question in Example 1.5 be different if the worth of avoiding the hassle of driving were R200 and you average one R250 traffic ticket for every 400 km you drive?

As a check, the answers to the in-chapter exercises are at the end of each chapter. Naturally, the exercises will be much more useful if you work through them ***before*** *consulting the answers.*

Although our cost–benefit decision rule fails the test of prediction in this experiment, its message for the rational decision-maker stands unchallenged. The two groups logically *should* have behaved the same. The only difference between them, after all, is that patrons in the refund group have lifetime incomes that are

Example 1.5

Should I drive to Bloemfontein or take the bus?

You must take three employees of your firm on a 1000-km trip from Cape Town to Bloemfontein. Except for the cost, you are completely indifferent between driving and taking the bus. The bus fare is R550 per person. You don't know how much it would cost to drive your car, so you call AA of SA for an estimate. The AA tells you that, for your make of car, a typical 10000-km driving year involves the following costs:

Insurance	R11 100
Interest	15000
Fuel and oil	13000
Maintenance	4900
Total	R44000

Suppose you calculate that these costs come to R4.40/km, and use this figure to compute that the 1000-km trip will cost the four of you R4400 by car. And since this is more than the R2200 bus fare, you decide to take the bus.

If you decide in this fashion, you fall victim to the sunk cost pitfall. Insurance and interest payments do not vary with the number of kilometres you drive each year. Both are sunk costs, and will be the same whether or not you drive to Bloemfontein. Of the costs listed, fuel and oil and maintenance are the only ones that vary with kilometres driven. These come to R17900 for each 10000 kilometres you drive, or R1.79/km. At R1.79/km it costs you only R1790 to drive to Bloemfontein, and since this is less than the bus fare, you should drive.

Example 1.6

The pizza experiment

A local pizza parlour offers an all-you-can-eat lunch for R100. You pay at the door, then the waiter brings you as many slices of pizza as you like. Thaler performed this experiment: an assistant served as the waiter for one group of tables.[3] The 'waiter' selected half the tables at random and gave everyone at those tables a R100 refund before taking orders. Diners at the remaining tables got no refund. He then kept careful count of the number of slices of pizza each diner ate. What difference, if any, do you predict in the amounts eaten by these two groups?

Diners in each group confront the question 'Should I eat another slice of pizza?' Here, the activity x consists of eating one more slice. For both groups, $C(x)$ is exactly zero: even members of the group who did not get a refund can get as many additional slices as they want at no extra charge. Because the refund group was chosen at random, there is no reason to suppose that its members like pizza any more or less than the others. For everyone, the decision rule says keep eating until there is no longer any extra pleasure in eating another slice. Thus $B(x)$ should be the same for each group, and people from both groups should keep eating until $B(x)$ falls to zero.

By this reasoning, the two groups should eat the same amount of pizza, on average. The R100 admission fee is a sunk cost and should have no influence on the amount of pizza one eats. *In fact, however, the group that did not get the refund consumed substantially more pizza.*

R100 higher than the others'. Such a trivial difference should have no effect on pizza consumption. Members of the no-refund group seemed to want to make sure they 'got their money's worth'. In all likelihood, however, this motive merely lead them to overeat.[4]

What's wrong with being motivated to 'get your money's worth'? Absolutely nothing, as long as the force of this motive operates *before* you enter into transactions. Thus it makes perfectly good sense to be lead by this motive to choose one restaurant over an otherwise identical competitor that happens to cost more. Once the price of your lunch has been determined, however, the get-your-money's-worth motive should be abandoned. The satisfaction you get from eating another slice of pizza should then depend only on how hungry you are and on how much you like pizza, not on how much you paid. Yet people often seem not to behave in this fashion. The difficulty may be that we are not creatures of complete flexibility. Perhaps motives that make sense in one context are not easily abandoned in another.

Exercise 1.2

Jim wins a ticket from a radio station to see the Basadi Women of Jazz band perform at an outdoor concert in Gaberone. Malusi has paid R240 for a ticket to the same concert. On the evening of the concert there is a tremendous thunderstorm. If Jim and Malusi have the same tastes, which of them will be more likely to attend the concert, assuming that each decides on the basis of a standard cost–benefit comparison?

Pitfall 3: Measuring costs and benefits as proportions rather than absolute rand amounts

When a boy asks his mother 'Are we almost there yet?' how will she answer if they are 15 km from their destination? Without some knowledge of the context of their journey, we cannot say. If they are near the end of a 500-km journey, her

[3] See Richard Thaler, 'Toward a positive theory of consumer choice', *Journal of Economic Behavior and Organization*, 1980, vol. 1, pp. 39–60. Prices have been changed to apply it to South Africa.

[4] An alternative to the 'get-your-money's-worth' explanation is that R100 is a significant fraction of the amount of cash many diners have available to spend *in the short run*. Thus members of the refund group might have held back in order to save room for the dessert they could now afford to buy. To test this alternative explanation, the experimenter could give members of the no-refund group a R100 cash gift earlier in the day and then see whether the amount of pizza consumed by the two groups still differed.

answer will almost certainly be yes. But if they have just embarked on a 25-km journey, she will say no.

Contextual clues are important for a variety of ordinary judgements. Thinking about distance as a percentage of the total amount to be travelled is natural and informative. Many also find it natural to think in percentage terms when comparing costs and benefits. But as the following pair of simple examples illustrates, this tendency often causes trouble.

When using the cost–benefit test, you should express costs and benefits in absolute rand terms. Comparing percentages is not a fruitful way to think about decisions like these.

Pitfall 4: Failure to understand the average-marginal distinction

So far we have looked at decisions about whether to perform a given action. Often, however, the choice is not whether to perform the action but the extent to which it should be performed. In this more complex case, we can apply the cost–benefit principle by reformulating the question. Instead of asking 'Should I do activity x?', we repeatedly pose the question 'Should I increase the level by which I am currently engaging in activity x?'

To answer this question, we must compare the benefit and cost of an *additional unit* of activity. The cost of an additional unit of activity is

Exercise 1.3

You are holding a discount coupon that will entitle you to a fare reduction on only one of the two trips you are scheduled to take during the coming month. You can either get R750 off the normal R2800 airfare return ticket from Johannesburg to Cape Town, or you can get R1000 off the normal R11 500 airfare to London. On which trip should you use your coupon?

Example 1.7a

Should you drive to Game to save R40 on a R240 cordless kettle?

You are about to buy a cordless kettle at the nearby campus store for R240 when a friend tells you that the very same kettle is on sale at Game for only R200. If Game is a 15-minute drive away, where would you buy the kettle? (If it fails under warranty, you must send it to the manufacturer for repair, no matter where you bought it.)

Example 1.7b

Should you drive downtown to save R40 on a R8000 plasma television?

You are about to buy a new television at the nearby campus store for R8040 when a friend tells you that the very same set is on sale at Game for only R8000. If Game is a 15-minute drive away, where would you buy the television? (Again, repairs under warranty would entail sending the television to the manufacturer in each case.)

There is no uniquely correct answer to either of these questions, both of which ask whether the benefit of driving to Game is worth the cost. Most people say the trip would definitely be worth making for the cordless kettle, but definitely not worth making for the plasma television. When pressed to explain, they say driving yields a 16.7 per cent saving on the radio but only a 0.05 per cent saving on the plasma television.

These percentages, however, are irrelevant. In each case the benefit of driving to Game is exactly the R40 saving from the lower purchase price. What is the cost of driving to Game? Some might be willing to make the drive for as little as R20, while others might not be willing to do it for less than R100. But whatever the number, it should be the same in both cases. So your answers to the questions just posed should be the same. If you would be willing to make the drive for, say, R30, then you should buy both the cordless kettle and the television at Game. But if your reservation price for making the drive is, say, R120, then you should buy both appliances at the nearby campus store.

Marginal cost The increase in total cost that results from carrying out one additional unit of an activity.
Marginal benefit The increase in total benefit that results from carrying out one additional unit of an activity.

called the **marginal cost** of the activity, and the benefit of an additional unit is called its **marginal benefit**.

The cost–benefit rule tells us to keep increasing the level of an activity as long as its marginal benefit exceeds its marginal cost. But, as Example 1.8 shows, people often fail to apply this rule correctly.

To illustrate, suppose the marginal cost of launching a boat and crew is constant at R1000 per boat per day. Then Archie should launch a fourth boat only if doing so will add at least R1000 in daily revenue from his total fish catch. The mere fact that the current average revenue is R2000 per boat simply doesn't tell us what the marginal benefit of launching the fourth boat will be.

Suppose, for example, that the relationship between the number of boats launched and the daily total revenue is as described in Table 1.1. With three boats per day, the average benefit per boat would then be R2000, just as indicated above. If Archie launched a fourth boat, the average daily revenue would fall to R1600 per boat, which is still more than the assumed marginal cost of R1000. Note, however, that in the second column the total revenue from four boats is only R400 per day more than the total revenue from three boats. That means that the marginal revenue from launching the fourth boat is only R400. And since that is less than its marginal cost (R1000), launching the fourth boat makes no sense.

Table 1.1 How total cost varies with the number of boats launched

Number of boats	Daily total benefit (R)	Daily average benefit (R/boat)
0	0	0
1	3000	3000
2	4800	2400
3	6000	2000
4	6400	1600

The following example illustrates how to apply the cost–benefit principle correctly in this case.

Exercise 1.4

If the marginal cost of launching each boat had not been R1000 but R1500, how many boats should Archie have launched?

The cost–benefit principle tells us that *marginal* costs and benefits – measures that correspond to the *increment* of an activity under consideration – are the relevant ones for choosing the level at which to pursue the activity. Yet many people compare the *average* cost and benefit of the activity when making such decisions. As Example 1.8 should have made clear,

Example 1.8

Should Archie launch another boat?

Archie manages a small fishing fleet of three boats in Hout Bay. His current daily cost of operations, including boat rentals and fishermen's wages, is R3000, or an average of R1000 per boat launched. His daily total revenue, or benefit, from the sale of fish is currently R6000, or an average of R2000 per boat launched. Archie decides that since his cost per boat is less than his revenue per boat, he should launch another boat. Is this a sound decision?

To answer this question, we must compare the marginal cost of launching a boat with its marginal benefit. The information given, however, tells us only the **average cost** and **average benefit** of launching a boat – which are, respectively, one-third of the total cost of three boats and one-third of the total revenue from three boats. Knowing the average benefit and average cost per boat launched does not enable us to decide whether launching another boat makes economic sense. For although the average benefit of the three boats launched thus far *might* be the same as the marginal benefit of launching another boat, it might also be either higher or lower. The same statement holds true regarding average and marginal costs.

Average cost The average cost of undertaking n units of an activity is the total cost of the activity divided by n.
Average benefit The average benefit of undertaking n units of an activity is the total benefit of the activity divided by n.

Example 1.9

How many boats should Archie launch?

The marginal cost of launching a boat and crew is again constant at R1000 per day. If total daily revenue from the catch again varies with the number of boats launched as shown in Table 1.1, how many boats should Archie launch?

Archie should keep launching boats as long as the marginal benefit of doing so is at least as great as the marginal cost. With marginal cost constant at R1000 per launch, Archie should thus keep launching boats as long as the marginal benefit is at least R1000.

Applying the definition of marginal benefit to the total benefit entries in the second column of Table 1.1 yields the marginal benefit values in the third column of Table 1.2. (Because marginal benefit is the change in total benefit that results when we change the number of boats by one, we place each marginal benefit entry midway between the rows showing the corresponding total benefit entries.) For example, the marginal benefit of increasing the number of boats from one to two is R1800, the difference between the R4800 total revenue with two boats and the R3000 with one.

Table 1.2 How marginal benefit varies with the number of boats launched

Number of boats	Daily total benefit (R)	Daily marginal benefit (R/boat)
0	0	
		3000
1	3000	
		1800
2	4800	
		1200
3	6000	
		400
4	6400	

however, increasing the level of an activity may not be justified, even though its average benefit at the current level is significantly greater than its average cost.

Comparing the R1000 marginal cost per boat with the marginal benefit entries in the third column of Table 1.2, we see that the first three launches satisfy the cost–benefit test, but the fourth does not. Archie should thus launch three boats.

Using marginal benefit and marginal cost graphically

The examples just discussed entail decisions about an activity that could take place only on specific levels – no boats, one boat, two boats, and so on. The levels of many other activities, however, can vary continuously. One can buy petrol, for example, in any quantity one wishes. For activities that are continuously variable, it is often convenient to display the comparison of marginal benefit and marginal cost graphically.

The invisible hand

One of the most important insights of economic analysis is that the individual pursuit of self-interest is often not only *consistent* with broader social objectives, but actually even *required* by them. Wholly unaware of the effects of their actions, self-interested consumers often act as if driven by what Adam Smith called an *invisible hand* to produce the greatest social good. In perhaps the most widely quoted passage from *The Wealth of Nations*, Smith wrote:

> It is not from the benevolence of the butcher, the brewer, or the baker that we expect our dinner, but from their regard of their own interest. We address ourselves not to their humanity, but to their self-love, and never talk to them of our necessities, but of their advantage.

Exercise 1.5

If Susan's marginal benefit curve is as given in Fig. 1.1, how many minutes should Susan speak with David each month if the long-distance rate falls to 30 cents per minute?

Smith observed that competition among sellers fostered attempts to develop better products,

Example 1.10

How much should Susan talk to David each month?

Susan has a Callmore telephone plan for which the charge is 60 cents per minute for a long-distance call to her boyfriend, David. (Fractional minutes are billed at the same rate, so a 30-second call would cost her 30 cents.) The value to Susan, measured in terms of her willingness to pay, of an additional minute of conversation with David is shown on the *MB* curve in Fig. 1.1. How many minutes should she spend on the phone with David each month?

The downward slope of the *MB* curve reflects the fact that the value of an additional minute declines with the total amount of conversation that has occurred thus far. (As we shall see in Chapter 3, it is a common pattern that the more someone has of a good, the less value he or she assigns to having additional units of it.) The *MC* curve in the diagram measures the cost of each additional minute, assumed to be constant at R0.60. The optimal quantity of conversation is the quantity for which these two curves cross – namely, 400 minutes per month. If Susan speaks with David for less than that amount, the marginal benefit from adding another minute would exceed the marginal cost, so she should talk longer. But if they speak for more than 400 minutes per month, the amount she would save by speaking less would exceed the benefit she would sacrifice, which means they should speak less.

Figure 1.1 The optimal quantity of conversation

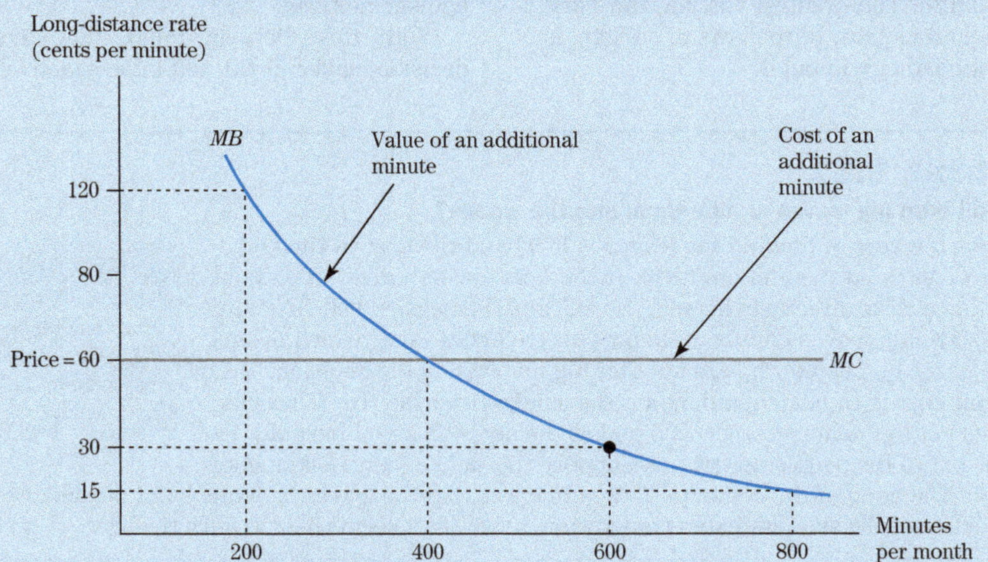

The optimal amount of conversation is the quantity for which the marginal benefit of conversation is just equal to its marginal cost.

and cheaper ways of producing them. The first to succeed in those attempts enjoyed higher profits than their rivals, but only temporarily. As others copied the new products and methods, their offerings put inevitable downward pressure on prices. Smith's insight, in a nutshell, was that, although sellers were seeking only to promote their own advantage, the ultimate beneficiaries were consumers.

Modern economists sometimes lose sight of the fact that Smith did not believe that *only* selfish motives are important. In his earlier treatise, *The Theory of Moral Sentiments*, for example, he wrote movingly about the compassion we feel for others:

> How selfish soever man may be supposed, there are evidently some principles in his nature, which interest him in the fortune of others, and render their happiness necessary to him, though he derives nothing from it, except the pleasure of seeing it. Of this kind is pity or compassion, the emotion which we feel for the misery of others, when we either see it, or are made to conceive it in a very lively manner. That we often derive sorrow from the sorrow of others, is a matter of fact too obvious to require any instances to prove it; for this sentiment, like all the other original passions of human nature, is by no means confined to the virtuous and humane, though they perhaps may feel it with the most exquisite sensibility. The greatest ruffian, the most hardened violator of the laws of society, is not altogether without it.

Smith was well aware, moreover, that the outcome of unbridled pursuit of self-interest is sometimes far from socially benign. As the following example illustrates, the invisible hand mechanism breaks down when important costs or benefits accrue to people other than the decision-makers themselves.

External costs and benefits often motivate laws that limit individual discretion. (External costs and benefits will be our focus in Chapter 14.) Many communities, as a result of high pollution rates especially in urban areas and in an effort to live *greener*, now have laws prohibiting the burning of leaves within city limits. Such laws may be viewed as a way of making the costs and benefits seen by individuals more nearly resemble those experienced by the community as a whole. With a law against burning leaves in effect, the potential leaf burner weighs the penalty of breaking the law against the cost of hauling the leaves. Most people conclude it is cheaper to haul them.

Would parents want their daughter or son to marry *Homo economicus*?

Many economists and other behavioural scientists remain sceptical about the importance of duty and other unselfish motives. They feel that the larger material pay-offs associated with selfish behaviour so strongly dominate other motives that, as a first approximation, we may safely ignore non-egoistic motives.

With this view in mind, the stereotypical decision-maker in the self-interest model is often

Example 1.11

Should I burn my leaves or haul them into the woods?

Suppose the cost of hauling the leaves is R100 and the cost to the homeowner of burning them is only R10. If the homeowner cares only about costs that accrue directly to herself, she will burn her leaves. The difficulty is that burning leaves entails an important **external cost**, which means a cost borne by people who are not directly involved in the decision. This external cost is the damage done by the smoke from the fire. That cost accrues not to the homeowner who makes the decision about burning the leaves, but to the people downwind. Suppose the smoke damage amounts to R150. The good of the community then requires that the leaves be hauled, not burned. From the perspective of the self-interested homeowner, however, it seems best to burn them.[5]

External cost of an activity A cost that falls on people who are not directly involved in the activity.

[5] Of course, if the homeowner interacts frequently with the people downwind, self-interest may still dictate hauling the leaves, to preserve goodwill for future interactions. But where the people downwind are anonymous strangers, this motive will operate with less force.

given the label *Homo economicus*, or 'economic man'. *Homo economicus* does not experience the sorts of sentiments that motivate people to vote or to return lost wallets to their owners with the cash intact. On the contrary, personal material costs and benefits are the only things he cares about. He does not contribute voluntarily to private charities or public television stations, he keeps promises only when it pays to do so and, if the pollution laws are not carefully enforced, he disconnects the catalytic converter on his car to save on fuel. And so on.

Obviously, many people do not fit the me-first caricature of the self-interest model. They donate bone marrow to strangers with leukaemia. They endure great trouble and expense to see justice done, even when it will not undo the original injury. At great risk to themselves they pull people from burning buildings, and jump into icy rivers to rescue people who are about to drown. Soldiers throw their bodies atop live grenades to save their comrades.

To be sure, selfish motives are important. When a detective investigates a murder, for example, his first question is, 'Who stood to benefit from the victim's death?' When an economist studies a government regulation, she wants to know whose incomes it enhances. When a member of parliament proposes a new spending project, the political scientist tries to discover which of his constituents will be its primary beneficiaries.

Our goal in much of this text is to understand the kinds of behaviour to which selfish motives give rise in specific situations. But throughout this process it is critical to remember that the self-interest model is not intended as a prescription for how to conduct your own affairs. On the contrary, we shall see in later chapters that *Homo economicus* is woefully ill-suited to the demands of social existence as we know it.

Being a purely self-interested person entails a degree of social isolation that is not only bad for the soul but may also be bad in financial terms. To succeed in life, even in purely material terms, people must form alliances and relationships of trust. Later chapters present specific examples of how unselfish motives confer material rewards on those who hold them. For the present, however, bear in mind that the self-interest model is intended only to capture one part of human behaviour, albeit an important one.

The economic naturalist

Studying biology enables people to observe and marvel at many details of life that would otherwise escape them. For the naturalist, a walk in a quiet forest becomes an adventure. In much the same way, studying microeconomics enables someone to become an 'economic naturalist', a person who sees the mundane details of ordinary existence in a sharp new light. Each feature of the man-made landscape is no longer an amorphous mass but the result of an implicit cost–benefit calculation. Following are some examples of economic naturalism.

Many of us respond warmly to the maxim, 'Anything worth doing is worth doing well.' After all, it encourages a certain pride of workmanship that is often sadly lacking. Economic naturalist 1.1 makes clear, however, that if the maxim is interpreted literally, it does not make any sense. To do something well requires time, effort and expense. But these are scarce resources. To devote them to one activity makes them unavailable for another. Increasing the quality of one of the things we do thus necessarily means reducing the quality of others – yet another application of the concept of opportunity cost. Every intelligent decision must be mindful of this trade-off.

Everything we see in life is the result of some such compromise. For Louis Oosthuizen, playing championship golf rules out becoming a professional tennis player. Yet this obviously does not mean he shouldn't spend any time playing tennis. It just means that he should hold himself to a lower standard there than on the golf course.

The reasoning in Economic naturalist 1.2 also helps make clear why many manual transmissions now have six forward speeds when 50 years ago most had only three (and many automatic transmissions only two). The benefit of adding an extra speed, again, is that it increases fuel economy. The value of this benefit, in rand terms, thus depends directly on the price of fuel. The price of petrol relative to other goods is much higher than it was 50 years ago, which helps explain why transmissions have more speeds than they used to.

Positive questions and normative questions

In California, logging companies are currently cutting down some of the few remaining stands of virgin redwood to supply contractors with timber to build homes. Near Sequoia the redwoods are the biggest trees (in volume) in the world, and north of San Francisco the coastal redwoods are the tallest trees in the world. Many of the trees being cut down by logging companies are more than 2000 years old, a national treasure that will never be replaced. To the logging companies, however, they are worth more as timber than as monuments to the past. Whether the remaining stands of virgin redwood ought to be protected is in the end a **normative question** – a question involving our values. A normative question is a question about what *ought* to be or *should* be. By itself, economic analysis cannot answer such questions. The problem is that there isn't one correct answer to a normative question. A society that reveres nature and antiquity may well decide the fate of the redwoods differently from one that holds other values, even though members of both societies are in complete agreement about all the relevant economic facts and theories. Economic analysis is on firmer ground when it comes to answering **positive questions** – questions about what the consequences of specific policies or institutional arrangements will be. If we ban the cutting of virgin redwoods, what will happen to the price of timber? What substitute building materials are likely to be developed, and at what cost? How will employment in the logging and housing industries be affected? These are all positive economic questions, and the answers to them are clearly relevant to our thinking about the underlying normative question. The advantage of positive questions is that correct answers can be determined based on the relevant statistics or data.

Normative question A question about which policies or institutional arrangements lead to the best outcomes.

Positive question A question about the consequences of specific policies or institutional arrangements.

Suppose the Minister of Finance is considering introducing a 'supertax' on everybody earning more than R500 000 per annum, and he contacts you about the number of taxpayers who will be affected by it. This is a positive economic problem that can easily be solved by just contacting SARS. However, most economic problems are normative. For example, what is the ideal inflation rate for South Africa next year? One could argue that a low inflation rate is good for stability, and it ensures that South African products are not outpriced on international markets. However, one could also argue that the economy should rather be stimulated to create more jobs, but the downside of such a policy is that it might lead to higher inflation rates. Both arguments have their merit, and in this case it will be Gill Marcus, the Governor of the South

Economic naturalist 1.1

Why is airline food so bad?

Many people complain about airline food. Indeed, if any serious restaurant dared to serve such food, it would quickly go bankrupt. Our complaints seem to take for granted that airline meals should be just as good as the ones we eat in restaurants. But why should they? The cost–benefit perspective says that airlines should increase the quality of their meals if and only if the benefit would outweigh the cost. The benefit of better food is probably well-measured by what passengers would be willing to pay for it, in the form of higher ticket prices. If a restaurant-quality meal could be had for, say, a mere R80 increase in fares, most people would probably be delighted to pay it. The difficulty, however, is that it would be much more costly than that to prepare significantly better meals at 39 000 feet in a tiny galley with virtually no time. It could be done, of course. An airline could remove 20 seats from the plane, install a modern, well-equipped kitchen, hire extra staff, spend more on ingredients, and so on. But these extra costs would be more like R500 per passenger than R50. For all our complaints about the low quality of airline food, few of us would be willing to bear this extra burden. Research by the German airline Lufthansa in 2010 indicated that people's ability to taste sweet and salty flavours diminishes by as much as 30 per cent at high altitude and low humidity inside airline cabins. The sad result is that airline food is destined to remain of low quality.

©groveb.

Economic naturalist 1.2

Why do manual transmissions have six forward gears, automatics only five?

The more forward gears a car's transmission has, the better its fuel economy will be. The additional gears act like the 'overdrive' of cars of the 1940s, conserving fuel by allowing cars to cruise at highway speeds at lower engine revolutions. Most cars in current production offer six forward gears on their manual transmissions, but only four of five on their automatics (although some of the more expensive cars now come out with six-gear automatic gearboxes). Since fuel economy is obviously a good thing, why limit the number of gears on automatics?

The reason is that fuel economy is not our only objective. We also want to keep the total production cost (and thus the price) of the car within limits. Automatic transmissions are more complex than manual ones, and the cost of adding an extra gear is accordingly much greater in automatics. The benefits of adding an extra gear, by contrast, are the same in both cases. If car-makers follow the rule 'Add an extra gear if the additional benefit outweighs the additional cost', then automatics will have fewer gears than manuals. That is why a six-gear automatic gearbox is only found in the more expensive models for which the buyers are less price-sensitive and are thus willing to pay the extra cost.

African Reserve Bank, who will have the final say on the matter of which monetary policy the bank introduces.

Microeconomics and macroeconomics

Our focus in this chapter is on issues confronting the individual decision-maker. As we proceed, we'll also consider economic models of groups of individuals – for example, the group of all buyers or all sellers in a market. The study of individual choices and the study of group behaviour in individual markets both come under the rubric of microeconomics. Macroeconomics, by contrast, is the study of broader aggregations of markets. For example, it tries to explain the national unemployment rate, the overall price level, and the total value of national output.

Economists are much better at predicting and explaining what happens in individual markets than in the economy as a whole. When prominent economists disagree in the press or on television, the issue is more likely to be macroeconomic than microeconomic in nature. But even though economists still have trouble with macroeconomic questions, macroeconomic analysis is undeniably important. After all, recessions and inflation disrupt millions of lives.

Economists increasingly believe that the key to progress in macroeconomics lies in more careful analysis of the individual markets that make up broader aggregates. As a result, the distinction between micro and macro has become less clear in recent years.

Summary

- Microeconomics entails the study of choice under scarcity. Scarcity is ever-present, even when material resources are abundant. There are always important limitations on time, energy, and the other things we need to pursue our goals.
- Much of the economist's task is to try to answer questions of the form 'Should I do activity x?' The approach to answering them is disarmingly simple. It is to do x if, and only if, its costs are smaller than its benefits. Not incurring a cost is the same as gaining a benefit.
- The cost–benefit model sometimes fails to predict how people behave when confronted with everyday choices. The art of cost–benefit analysis lies in being able to specify and measure the relevant costs and benefits, a skill many decision-makers lack. Some costs, such as sunk costs, often seem relevant but turn out not to be. Others, such as implicit costs, are sometimes ignored, even though they are important. Benefits too are often difficult to measure. Experience has taught that becoming aware of the most common

pitfalls helps most people become better decision-makers.

- When the question is not whether to perform an activity but rather at what level to perform it, marginal analysis draws our attention to the importance of marginal benefits and marginal costs. We should increase the level of an activity whenever its marginal benefit exceeds its marginal cost.
- The principles of rational choice are by no means limited to formal markets for goods and services. Indeed, some form of implicit or explicit cost–benefit calculation lies behind almost every human action, object and behaviour. Knowledge of the underlying principles casts our world in a sharp new light, not always flattering, but ever a source of stimulating insight.

Questions for review

1 What is your opportunity cost of reading a novel this evening?

2 Your roommate is thinking of dropping out of university this semester. If his tuition payment for this semester is non-refundable, should he take it into account when making his decision?

3 Give three examples of activities accompanied by external costs or benefits.

4 Why is the opportunity cost of attending university higher for a 50 year old than for a 20 year old?

5 Why should sunk costs be irrelevant for current decisions?

6 How can the cost–benefit model be useful for studying the behaviour of people who do not think explicitly in terms of costs and benefits?

Problems

1 Nozipho has a flexible summer job. She can work every day but is allowed to take a day off any time she wants. Her friend Vusi suggests they go to Gold Reef City on Tuesday. The admission charge for the park is R180 per person, and it will cost them R60 each for petrol and parking. Nozipho loves amusement parks, and a day at the park is worth R540 to her. However, Nozipho also enjoys her job so much that she would actually be willing to pay R120 per day to do it.

a If Nozipho earns R120 if she works, should she go to the amusement park?

b If Nozipho earns R180?

c If Nozipho earns R240?

2 Tom is a mushroom farmer. He invests all his spare cash in additional mushrooms, which grow on otherwise useless land behind his barn. The mushrooms double in size and value during their first year, after which time they are harvested and sold at a constant price per kilogram. Tom's friend Dick asks Tom for a loan of R2000, which he promises to repay after one year. How much interest will Dick have to pay Tom in order for Tom to be no worse off than if he had not made the loan?

3 The meal plan of the cafeteria at the University of Western Cape lets students eat as much as they like for a fixed fee of R7200 per semester. The average student there eats 150 kg of food per semester. The cafeteria at the University of Cape Town charges students R7200 for a book of meal tickets that entitles the student to eat 150 kg of food per semester. If the student eats more than 150 kg, she pays extra; if the student eats less, she gets a refund. If students are rational, at which university will average food consumption be higher?

4 You are planning a 1000-km trip to Durban. Except for cost, you are indifferent between driving and taking the luxury bus. Bus fare is R1320. Operating your car during a typical

10 000-km driving year involves the following costs:

Insurance	R11 000
Interest	16 500
Fuel and oil	11 000
Tyres	1210
Licence and registration	550
Maintenance	5390
Total	R45 650

Should you drive or take the bus?

5 Gert and Elsa have rented a banquet hall to celebrate their wedding anniversary. Fifty people have already accepted their invitation. The caterers will charge R200 per person for food and R60 per person for drinks. The band will cost R4000 for the evening, and the hall costs R3400. Now Gert and Elsa are considering inviting 10 more people. By how much will these extra guests increase the cost of their party?

6 You loan a friend R5000, and at the end of one year she writes you a cheque for R5000 to pay off this loan. If the annual interest rate on your savings account is 8 per cent, what was your opportunity cost of making this loan?

7 Bill and Joe live in Germiston. At 14:00 Bill goes to the local Computicket branch and buys a R70 ticket to a soccer game to be played that night between Kaizer Chiefs and Orlando Pirates in Soweto's FNB Stadium (Soccer City), which is a 50-km drive away. Joe plans to attend the same game, but doesn't purchase his ticket in advance, because he knows from experience that it is always possible to buy just as good a seat at the arena. At 16:00 a heavy, unexpected thunderstorm begins, making the prospect of the drive to Soweto much less attractive than before. If both Bill and Joe have the same tastes and are rational, is one of them more likely to attend the game than the other? If so, say who and explain why. If not, explain why not.

8 Two types of radar weather-detection device are available for commercial passenger aircraft: the 'state-of-the-art' machine, and another that is significantly less costly, but also less effective. The Airport Company of South Africa (ACSA) has hired you for advice on whether all passenger planes should be required to use the state-of-the-art machine. After careful study, your recommendation is to require the more expensive machine only in passenger aircraft with more than 200 seats. How would you justify such a recommendation to an ACSA member who complains that all passengers have a right to the best weather-detecting radar currently available?

9 A group has chartered a bus to Polekwane. The driver costs R900, the bus costs R4500 and tolls will cost R675. The driver's fee is non-refundable, but the bus may be cancelled a week in advance at a charge of only R450. At R162 per ticket, how many people must buy tickets so that the trip need not be cancelled?

10 Residents of your city are charged a fixed weekly fee of R120 for refuse collection. They may put out as many refuse bags as they wish. The average household puts out three bags per week. Now, suppose your city changes to a 'tag' system whereby paper, glass, etc. must be put in separate bags. Each bag of refuse must have a tag affixed to it. The tags cost R20 each. What effect will the introduction of the tag system have on the total quantity of refuse collected?

11 Suppose that random access memory (RAM) can be added to your computer at a cost of R750 per terabyte. Suppose also that, because your computer has insufficient memory, the value to you of an additional terabyte of memory, measured in terms of your willingness to pay, is R6000 for the first terabyte and then falls by one-half for each additional terabyte. Draw a graph of marginal cost and marginal benefit. How many terabytes of memory should you purchase?

12 Suppose that in Problem 11 the cost of RAM falls to R375 per terabyte. How many terabytes of memory should you purchase now? Suppose additionally that your benefit for an additional terabyte of memory rises to R12 000 for the first terabyte, again falling by one-half for each additional terabyte. How many terabytes of memory should you purchase now, with both the lower price and the larger benefit?

*13 Dana has purchased a R200 ticket to a rock concert. On the day of the concert she is invited to a welcome-home party for a friend returning from abroad. She cannot attend both the concert and the party. If she had known about the party before buying the ticket, she would have chosen the party over the concert. *True or false:* It follows that if she is rational, she will go to the party anyway. Explain.

***14** Yesterday you were unexpectedly given a free ticket to a Muse concert scheduled for 1 April. The market price of this ticket is R300, but the most you could sell it for is only R180. Today you discover that Lady Gaga will be giving a concert that same evening. Tickets for the Lady Gaga concert are still available at R300. Had you known before receiving your Muse ticket yesterday that Lady Gaga would be coming, you definitely would have bought a ticket to see her, not Muse. *True or false:* From what we are told of your preferences, it follows that if you are a rational utility maximizer, you should attend the Lady Gaga concert. Explain.

***15** Mr Buyani recently faced a choice between being (a) an economics professor, which pays R480 000/yr, or (b) a safari leader, which pays R400 000/yr. After careful deliberation, Buyani took the safari job, but it was a close call. 'For a rand more,' he said, 'I'd have gone the other way.'

Now Buyani's brother-in-law approaches him with a business proposition. The terms are as follows:

- Buyani must resign his safari job to work full time in his brother-in-law's business.
- Buyani must give his brother-in-law an interest-free loan of R800 000, which will be repaid in full if and when Buyani leaves the business. (Buyani currently has much more than R800 000 in the bank after he received a payment from his provident fund when he resigned from his previous job.)
- The business will pay Buyani a salary of R560 000/yr. He will receive no other payment from the business.

The interest rate is 10 per cent per year. Apart from salary considerations, Buyani feels that working in the business would be just as enjoyable as being an economics professor. For simplicity, assume there is no uncertainty regarding either Buyani's salary in the proposed business or the security of his monetary investment in it. Should Buyani join his brother-in-law and, if so, how small would Buyani's salary from the business have to be to make it *not* worthwhile for him to join? If not, how large would Buyani's salary from the business have to be to make it worthwhile for him to join?

***16** You have just purchased a new Ford Focus 1.6 Trend 4dr for R250 000, but the most you could get for it if you sold it privately is R187 500. Now you learn that Volkswagen is offering its Jetta 1.6 TDI Comfordline, which normally sells for R312 500, at a special sale price of R250 000. If you had known before buying the Focus that you could buy a Jetta at the same price, you would definitely have chosen the Jetta. *True or false:* From what we are told of your preferences, it follows that if you are a rational utility maximizer, you should definitely not sell the Focus and buy the Jetta. Explain.

Answers to in-chapter exercises

1.1 Someone who gets a R250 traffic ticket every 400 km driven will pay R625 in fines, on average, for every 1000 km driven. Adding that figure to the R200 hassle cost of driving, and then adding the R1790 fuel and oil and maintenance costs, we have R2615. This is more than the R2200 bus fare, which means taking the bus is best.

1.2 The R240 Malusi paid for his ticket is a sunk cost. At the moment he must decide whether to attend the concert. For both Jim and Malusi, therefore, the costs and benefits

* Problems marked with an asterisk (*) are more difficult.

should be the same. If the benefit of seeing the concert outweighs the cost of sitting in the rain, they should go. Otherwise they should stay at home.

1.3 You should use your coupon for the London trip, because it is more valuable to save R1000 than to save R750, irrespective of the total price of the airline ticket.

1.4 Two boats. Referring to Table 1.2, note that if marginal cost is R1500, it now pays to launch the second boat (marginal benefit = R1800) but not the third, because marginal benefit is then only R1200.

1.5 At 30 cents per minute, Susan should talk for 600 minutes per month, because at that point marginal cost equals marginal benefit.

Chapter 2

Supply and demand

2008 saw oil prices increase to record levels, above $160 per barrel, sparking off much research to produce alternative energy sources at more affordable prices. Research into both electric cars and different means of using fossil fuels in current engines received a huge stimulus from this. However, after the financial crisis in the United States, and with many countries experiencing recession, the price of oil dropped to below $60 within two months. Why? This was demand and supply in action. With the US and the Eurozone in recession, their demand for oil decreased. Similarly, the main trading partners of these countries also experienced economic problems, because their export markets suddenly decreased substantially. With economic activities worldwide slowing down, the international demand for oil decreased. With people expecting this situation to last for at least a year or two, the future demand for oil also decreased. The result was a drop in the price of oil to levels that had been experienced more than three years before the financial crisis. However, in the meantime economies recovered worldwide and by 2014 the oil price had risen to approximately $120 per barrel.

The world had last seen such a dramatic increase in the oil prices in the 1970s. South Africa experienced further problems then because the policy of apartheid meant that it could not buy oil on the open market. This made the country even more vulnerable. Not only were prices very high for the oil that it *could* buy, but oil was also not available in sufficient quantities. The government introduced measures to ensure that South Africans consumed less petrol. The petrol price increased substantially, and speed limits were reduced to 80 km/h on the open road and 50 km/h in urban areas. Petrol stations were forced to close between 19:00 and 07:00. Only people with a special permit were allowed to buy petrol during those hours, and only at certain designated petrol stations. Motorists were also rationed in terms of the amount of petrol that they could buy per occasion. A special permit was even needed to buy petrol for lawnmowers! Some petrol stations also ran out of supplies, which made the people waiting for petrol very angry. Fewer South Africans went on holiday, because doing so was very expensive and driving from Mussina to Cape Town at 80 km/h, for example, was not very enjoyable. Shifting to more economical diesel cars was not an option because the diesel engines of passenger cars were not as refined as we have become accustomed to today. They were also not fitted with turbo boosters and were very 'lazy'. Because they made a lot of noise, they were also very uncomfortable to drive.

The South African government's system of price controls and allocations tried to accomplish a task that is usually relegated to markets. These programmes typically produce confusion and conflict. South Africans did consume less petrol, but this reduction was accompanied by unhappiness, and a feeling that they were being treated unfairly. Of course, the unfettered market can itself produce outcomes that people don't like, but rarely does it fail to allocate available supplies in a smooth, efficient manner.

Chapter preview

In this chapter we'll explore why markets normally function so smoothly, and why attempts at direct allocation are sometimes problematic. The early part of the chapter will look at basic supply and demand analysis. First, we'll review the usual descriptive features of supply and demand analysis covered in the introductory course. Next, we'll see that, for given attributes of buyers and sellers, the unregulated competitive market yields the best attainable outcome, in the sense that any other combination of price and quantity would put at least some buyers or sellers in a worse situation. We will also briefly look at consumer and producer surplus that indicates that some consumers are actually paying less than what they are willing to pay for a product and that certain producers receive a higher price than the one at which they would be willing to supply their products.

Despite the efficiency feature of the market economy, market outcomes often do not command society's approval. Perhaps the biggest shortcoming of the market-driven economy is that it benefits you only if you have money. Concern for the well-being of the poor has motivated the governments of almost every country to intervene in a variety of ways – for instance, by adopting laws that peg prices above or below their equilibrium levels. Such laws, we shall see, almost always generate harmful, if unintended, consequences.

A generally more efficient solution to the problems of the poor is to boost their incomes directly. The law of supply and demand cannot be repealed by the legislature. But legislatures can alter the underlying forces that govern the shape and position of supply and demand schedules.

Finally, we shall explore supply and demand analysis as a useful device for understanding how taxes affect equilibrium prices and quantities. In particular, it helps dispel the myth that a tax is paid primarily by the party on whom it is directly levied; rather, the burden of a tax falls most heavily on whichever side of the market is least able to avoid it.

Supply and demand curves

Our basic tool for analysing market outcomes is supply and demand analysis, already familiar to most of you from your introductory course. Let us begin with the following working definition of a market:

Market: A market is any place or situation where buyers and sellers or their agents make contact to negotiate prices and quantities of a good or service to be traded.

Some markets are confined to a single specific time and location. For example, all the participating buyers and sellers (or at least their designated representatives) gather together in the same place for an antiques auction. Other markets span vast geographic territory, and most participants in them never meet or even see one another. The Johannesburg Stock Exchange is such a market. The Internet, where we nowadays do most of our market research if we want to buy a specific product, provides access to markets of this type for almost any good.

Sometimes the choice of market definition will depend on the bias of the observer. In antitrust cases, for example, current policy prohibits mergers between companies whose combined share of the market would exceed a given threshold. Accordingly, government prosecutors who oppose a merger will often try to define markets as narrowly as possible, thereby making the combined market share as large as possible. The merging companies, by contrast, tend to view their markets in much broader terms, which naturally makes their combined market share smaller. In South Africa, for example, the Competition Tribunal fined Pioneer Foods Group R500 million with regard to the bread price-fixing scandal. In 2012 Telkom was fined R449 million for abusing its dominance in the telecommunications market between 1999 and 2004. The construction group

Murray & Roberts received a fine of R309 million in 2013 as a result of its historical anti-competitive practices. In 2013 Walmart had great difficulty in convincing the Competition Tribunal that its R16.5 billion bid to take over 51 per cent of Massmart would not be detrimental to South African consumers or lead to job losses. In the same year the Tribunal prohibited the merger between US multinational Pioneer Hi-Bred International and South Africa's Pannar Seed. In general, as in these cases, the best market definition will depend on the purpose of the party concerned.

Over the years, economists have increasingly recognized that even subtle product differences matter a great deal to some consumers, and the trend in analysis has been towards ever-narrower definitions of goods and markets. Two otherwise identical products are often classified as separate if they differ only with respect to the times or places they are available. An umbrella on a sunny day, for example, is in this sense a very different product from an umbrella during a downpour. And the markets for these two products behave very differently indeed. On a hot summer day low-quality umbrellas may sell for as little as R20, but those same umbrellas may fetch a price of R35 on rainy days.

To make our discussion concrete, let us consider the workings of a specific market – say, the market for 1 kg lobsters in Paternoster, on 20 December 2014. Remember that we call them lobsters in the sea, crayfish in fresh water, but on the West Coast they just talk of *kreef*. For this market, our task is to explain both the price of lobsters and the quantity traded. We begin with the basic *demand curve*, a simple mathematical relationship that tells us how many lobsters buyers wish to purchase at various possible prices (*ceteris paribus* – holding all else constant). The *DD* curve depicted in Fig. 2.1, for example, tells us that 400 lobsters will be demanded at a price of R120 each, 100 at a price of R300, and so on.

If a visitor from outer space was told only that lobsters sell for R180 each, he would have no way of knowing whether they were cheap or expensive. In 1900 a R180 lobster would have been out of reach of all but the wealthiest consumers. In 2014, in contrast, lobsters would be considered a bargain at that price. Unless otherwise stated, the price on the vertical axis of the demand curve diagram will refer to the **real price** of the good, which means its price relative to the prices of all other goods and services. Thus the prices on the vertical axis of Fig. 2.1 represent lobster prices on 20 December 2014, and the context within which those prices are interpreted by buyers is the set of prices of all other goods on that same date.

Real price of a product Its price relative to the prices of other goods and services.

Figure 2.1 The demand curve for lobsters in Paternoster, 20 December 2014

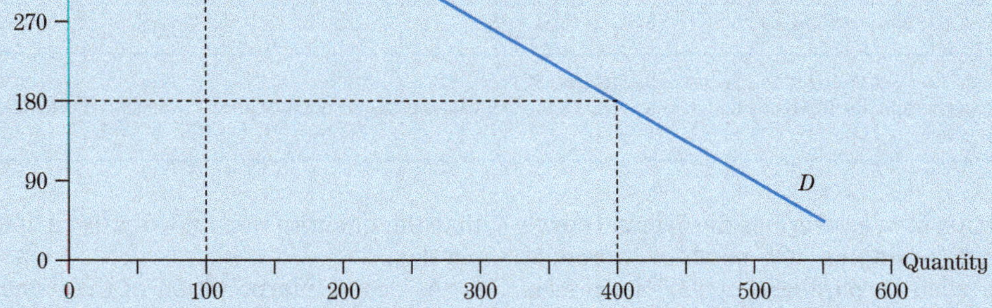

The demand curve tells us the quantities buyers will wish to purchase at various prices. Its key property is its downward slope: when price falls, the quantity demanded increases. This property is called the *law of demand*.

Example 2.1

How to convert nominal prices to real prices

How did the price of a 20-pack of cigarettes change over the last 50 years? One way to answer that question is to look at the nominal prices of cigarettes and to conclude that there was a massive increase from only R0.19 per packet of 20 cigarettes in 1960 to R23.24 in 2012. However, when we convert all the prices to 2012 rand values, the picture looks quite different. In real terms, prices just slightly more than doubled from R11.62 in 1960 to R23.24 in 2013. To convert nominal prices to real prices we use the following formula: real price of X_t = (Nominal price of X_t/CPI$_t$) × 100. For example, the nominal price of a packet of cigarettes in 2000 was R8.02 and the consumer price index was 53.03. To convert the nominal price to real prices: (8.02/53.03) × 100 = R15.12. This is the cost of cigarettes in terms of the buying power of a rand in 2012.

Prices of a packet of 20 cigarettes in South Africa: 1961–2012

Year	Retail price per packet of 20 cigarettes (rand)	CPI	Real retail price per packet of 20 cigarettes in 2012 prices (rand)*
1961	0.19	1.64	11.62
1965	0.19	1.80	10.76
1970	0.22	2.01	10.42
1975	0.32	3.23	9.83
1980	0.49	5.73	8.56
1985	0.84	11.03	7.62
1990	1.65	22.48	7.34
1995	3.48	38.39	9.06
2000	8.02	53.03	15.12
2005	12.53	67.02	18.70
2006	13.51	69.12	19.54
2007	14.91	73.39	20.32
2008	16.27	80.65	20.17
2009	18.60	86.38	21.53
2010	20.96	90.09	23.26
2011	22.15	94.68	23.40
2012	23.24	100	23.04

Source: Statistics South Africa and Treasury Budget Review.

*You may get marginally different values if you calculate the real values using the nominal and CPI values in this table due to rounding issues.

The discussion above describes the demand curve as a schedule telling us how much of a product consumers wish to purchase at various prices. This is called the *horizontal interpretation* of the demand curve. For instance, at a price of R450 per lobster, the demand curve in Fig. 2.1 tells us that the quantity demanded will be 100 lobsters per day.

A second interpretation of the demand curve (*vertical interpretation*) is to start with quantity on the horizontal axis and then read the marginal buyer's reservation price on the vertical axis. Thus when the quantity of lobsters sold is 400 per day, the demand curve in Fig. 2.1 tells us that the marginal buyer's reservation price is R180 per lobster.

The demand curve shown in Fig. 2.1 happens to be linear, but demand curves in general need not be. The key property assumed of them is that they are downward sloping: the quantity demanded rises as the price of the product falls. This property is often called the **law of demand**. Although we shall see in Chapter 4 that it is theoretically possible for a demand curve to be upward sloping, such exceptions are virtually never encountered in practice.

Law of demand
The empirical observation that, when the price of a product falls, people demand larger quantities of it.

The demand curve (*DD*) in Fig. 2.1 can also be given by the following equation:

$$P_D = 540 - 0.9Q_D \qquad (2.1)$$

In other words, if the demand is 400 lobsters per day,

$$\begin{aligned} P_D &= 540 - (0.6 \times 400) \\ &= 180 \end{aligned} \qquad (2.2)$$

Keep in mind that, as economists, we actually make a mathematical blunder by putting price on the y-axis and quantity on the x-axis. Normally in mathematics the dependent variable is on the y-axis and the independent variable is on the x-axis. Remember that, when $y = f(x)$, the standard equation of a linear curve is $y = mx + c$. With the above-mentioned demand curve of our lobster example, $Q = f(P)$: in other words, quantity is the dependent variable and price the independent variable, and not the other way round as it may look on the graph. However, it became economic convention to draw it like this, and in this textbook we shall stick to this convention.

As we shall see in more detail in Chapter 4, there are normally two independent reasons why the quantity demanded falls when price rises. One is that many people switch to other substitutes. Thus, when lobster gets more expensive, some consumers may switch to crab, others to meat or poultry. A second reason is that people are not *able* to buy as much as before. When price goes up, it is not possible to buy as much as before unless we purchase less of something else. The buying power of our money decreases if prices increase.

The demand curve for a good is a summary of the various cost–benefit calculations that buyers make with respect to the good. The question each person faces is, 'Should I buy the product?' (and usually, 'If so, how much of it?'). The cost side of the calculation is simply the price of the product (and implicitly, the other goods or services that could be bought with the same money or the opportunity cost of that money). The benefit side is the satisfaction provided by the product. The negative slope of the demand schedule tells us that the cost–benefit criterion will be met for fewer and fewer potential buyers as the price of the product rises.

On the seller's side of the market, the corresponding analytical tool is the supply schedule. A hypothetical schedule for our lobster market is shown as line *SS* in Fig. 2.2. Again, the linear form (straight line) of this particular schedule is not a characteristic feature of supply schedules generally. What these schedules do tend to have in common is their upward slope: the quantity supplied rises as the price of a product rises. This property can be called the **law of supply**. For a supplier to be willing to sell a product, its price must cover the marginal cost of producing or acquiring it. As we shall see in detail in Chapter 7, the cost of producing additional units often tends to rise as more units are produced, especially in the short run.

Law of supply
The empirical observation that, when the price of a product rises, firms offer more of it for sale.

In our lobster market the reasons for this are clear. Suppliers harvest the lobsters closest to shore first, and then work their way further offshore as they try to enlarge their catch. The more lobsters they try to harvest, the further they have to go, the more equipment and people they have to use, and hence the more it costs.

Another factor contributing to the upward slope of the supply curve is substitution on the part of fishermen. A typical example on the West Coast will be that, as the price of lobsters increases, more producers switch to lobsters rather than continue to fish for snoek.

Like demand curves, supply curves can be interpreted either horizontally or vertically. Under the horizontal interpretation, we begin with a price, and then go over to the supply curve to read the quantity that sellers wish to sell at that price on the horizontal axis. For instance, at a price of R180 per lobster, sellers in Fig. 2.2 wish to sell 200 lobsters per day.

Under the vertical interpretation, we begin with a quantity, and then go up to the supply curve to read the corresponding marginal cost on the vertical axis. For example, if sellers in Fig. 2.2

Figure 2.2 The supply curve of lobsters in Paternoster, 20 December 2014

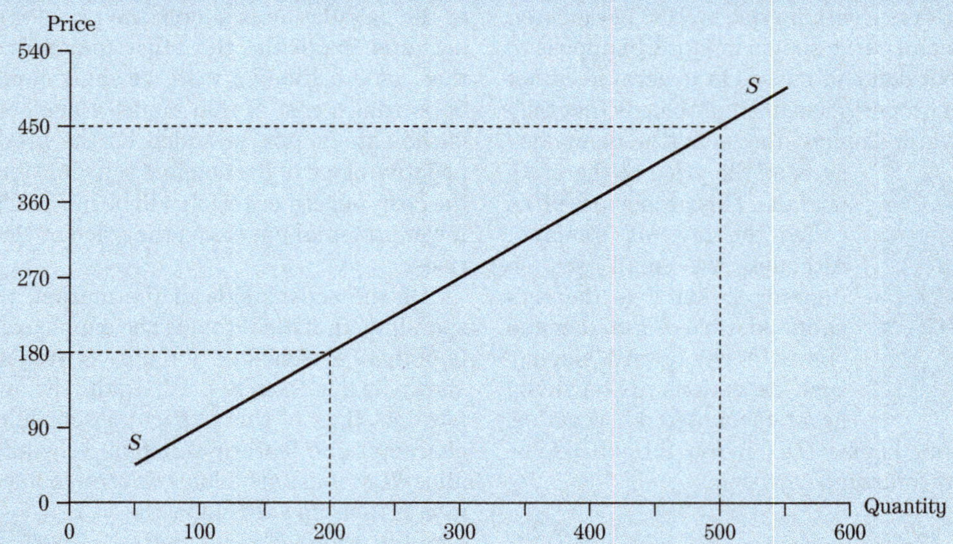

The upward slope of the supply schedule reflects the fact that costs tend to rise when producers expand production in the short run.

are currently supplying 500 lobsters per day, the opportunity cost of the last lobster supplied by the marginal seller would be R450. In other words, the supply curve tells us that the marginal cost of delivering the 500th lobster is R450. (Recall from your first year's economics course that the *MC* curve is the supply curve of a firm. We shall touch on that again in Chapter 7.) If someone could deliver a 501st lobster for less than R450, he or she would have had an incentive to do so, in which case the quantity of lobster supplied at a price of R450 would not have been 500 per day to begin with. Using similar reasoning, when the quantity of lobsters supplied is 200 per day, the marginal cost of delivering another lobster must be R180.

An alternative way of describing the supply schedule is to call it the set of price–quantity pairs for which suppliers are satisfied. The term 'satisfied' has a technical meaning here, which is that any point on the supply schedule represents the quantity that suppliers want to sell, *given the price they face*. They would obviously be happy to get even higher prices for their offerings. But for any given price, suppliers would consider themselves worse off if forced to sell either more or less than the corresponding quantity on the supply curve. If, for example, the price of lobsters in Fig. 2.2 were R180, suppliers would not be satisfied selling either more or fewer than 200 lobsters a day. A supply curve thus gives the quantities at different prices that producers are *willing* to sell at different prices, not what they are actually supplying. As we shall discuss in the next section, they operate on only one point on the supply curve.

The demand schedule is also a set of price–quantity pairs for which buyers are satisfied in precisely the same sense. At any given price, they would consider themselves worse off if forced to purchase either more or less than the corresponding quantity on the demand schedule. A demand curve gives the quantities that consumers are *willing* to buy and not what they are actually buying. As is the case with supply, consumers operate on only one point on the supply curve.

The supply curve (*SS*) in Fig. 2.2 can also be given by the following equation:

$$P_S = 0.9Q_S \tag{2.3}$$

In other words, if the supply is 200 lobsters per day:

$$\begin{aligned} P_S &= 0.9 \times 200 \\ &= 180 \end{aligned} \tag{2.4}$$

Determinants of demand and supply

Before we discuss the equilibrium in the market, let us first summarize. The factors that influence the demand for a product are called the *determinants of demand*. In the next few chapters we investigate in detail the forces that determine the shape and position of market demand curves. For the moment, let's discuss a few whose roles are intuitively clear.

Determinants of demand

Price

If the price of a product increases, people will normally demand fewer units of that good. On the other hand, a decrease in the price of a good will increase the quantity demanded for it. As was explained, this is the reason why a demand curve is negatively sloped.

Incomes

Normally the quantity demanded of a good at any price rises with income. Goods that have this property are called *normal goods*. So-called *inferior goods* (such as black-and-white televisions) are the exception. For such goods, the quantity demanded at any price falls when income increases. As income increases consumers abandon these goods in favour of higher-quality substitutes (such as LED televisions, or even HD plasma screens) if they can afford to.

Tastes

Tastes vary across people and over time. In Southern Africa we are used to sitting on padded furniture, whereas in many Eastern societies like China and Japan people are conditioned to favour sitting cross-legged on the floor. The demand for armchairs in South Africa and other Western societies is greater than in the East. By the same token, the demand for skirts with hemlines above the knee tends to vary sharply from one decade to another, and in certain cultures such garments are even prohibited. Tastes vary over time as different products are in fashion. As a result of the continuous change in consumer preferences, the demand for certain products will vary over time.

Prices of substitutes and complements

Complementary goods are normally consumed together. For some people bacon and eggs constitute their typical breakfast. For them, a sharp increase in the price of bacon leads not only to a reduction in the quantity of bacon demanded but also to a reduction in the demand for eggs. An increase in the price of one good decreases the demand for the other good. Other examples are printers and printer cartridges and DVDs and DVD players. Substitutes, on the other hand, satisfy the same want of consumers. If you are hungry, you can eat a hamburger or a chickenburger. Therefore an increase in the price of hamburgers will lead to an increase in the demand for chickenburgers. If the price of a product is increased, this will lead to an increase in the demand for substitute products. Other examples include butter and margarine and tea and coffee.

Expectations

Expectations about future income and price levels also affect current purchase decisions. For example, someone who expects higher future income is likely to spend more today than an otherwise identical person who expects lower future income. (After all, with higher expected future income, the need to save diminishes.) Similarly, people will often accelerate their current purchases of goods whose prices are expected to rise in the months to come.

Population

In general, the number of people who buy a product grows as the number of potential buyers grows. Thus, in cities with growing populations, the demand for housing increases from year to year, whereas it tends to fall in rural areas with declining populations. An increase in population will not necessarily increase demand, though. Frequently we find in Southern Africa that the poor have the largest families, but this actually makes their poverty worse. If an increase in population is not accompanied by a simultaneous increase in buying power, demand will not necessarily increase.

Figure 2.3 graphically displays some of the factors that shift demand curves. We shall revisit these factors in more detail in Chapters 4 and 8.

Determinants of supply

Price

If the price of a product increases, producers will normally supply more units of that good. On the other hand, a decrease in the price of a good will decrease the quantity supplied of that good. As we have discussed, this is the reason why a supply curve is positively sloped.

Technology

The quantity that suppliers are willing to offer at any price depends primarily on their costs of

Figure 2.3 Determinants of demand that shift demand curves

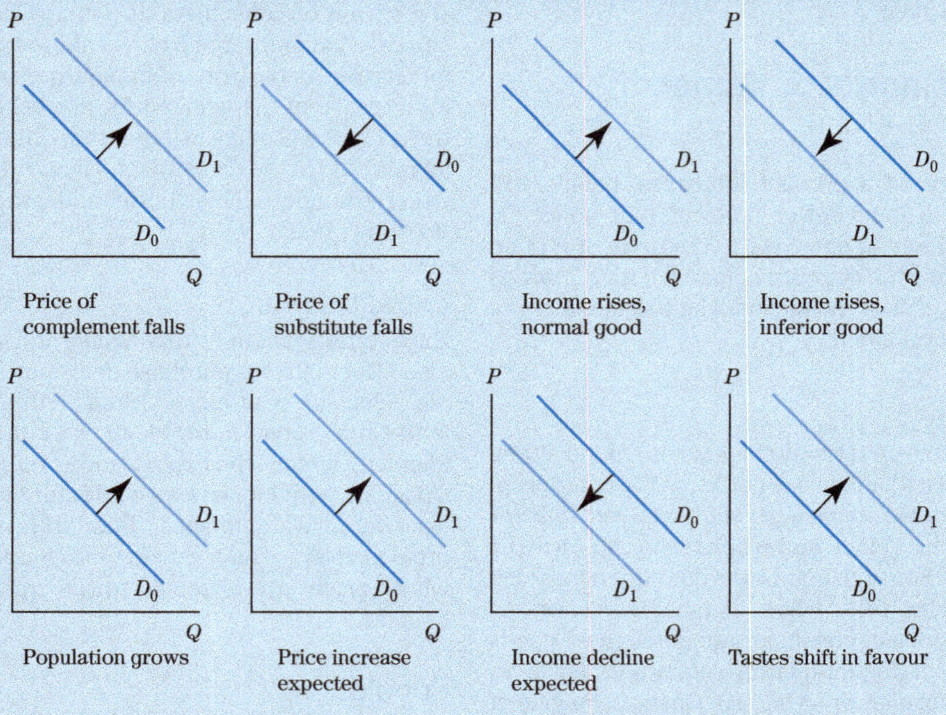

Prices of substitutes and complements, incomes, population, expectation of future price, income changes and tastes all influence the position of the current demand curve for a product.

production. These costs, in turn, are closely linked to technology. For instance, the discovery of a more efficient lobster trap will reduce the cost of harvesting lobsters, which results in a rightward shift in the supply schedule.

Factor prices

A supplier's costs also depend on the payment it must make to its *factors of production*: labour, capital, natural resources, and so on. If the price of lobster boats rises, the cost of fuel goes up, or if the wage paid to lobstermen increases, the supply schedule for lobsters shifts to the left.

The number of suppliers

The more firms that can supply a good, the greater will be the quantity supplied of it at any given price. The supply schedule of touch-screen mobile phones has shifted sharply to the right as more and more companies have begun producing them.

Expectations

Suppliers take expected changes in prices into account in their current production decisions. For example, if you are a cattle farmer in Limpopo, and there is an outbreak of foot-and-mouth disease in the Western Cape, it makes sense to anticipate an increase in beef prices in the future, because the epidemic will decrease future supply. Then it makes sense for you to withhold current supplies of mature livestock to take advantage of the higher expected future prices.[1]

Weather

For some products, particularly agricultural ones, nature has significant effects on the supply schedule. In years of drought, for example, the supply schedule for many foodstuffs shifts to the left. Similarly, heavy rainfall during harvest time can also decrease the supply of agricultural goods.

Figure 2.4 shows the effects of some factors that shift supply schedules.

[1] Note that supply is the quantity offered for sale at various prices at a specific point in time, not necessarily current production (when suppliers are able to store inventory). Hence the ranchers reduce sales of cattle in the current period, since they can sell them in a later period when prices are higher.

Figure 2.4 Determinants of supply that shift supply schedules

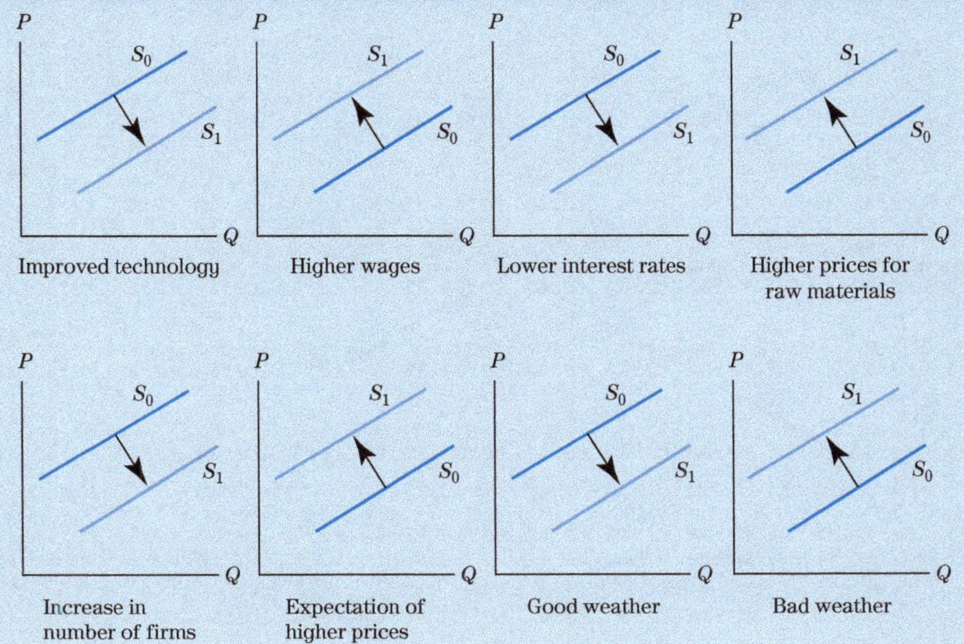

Technology, input prices, the number of firms, expectations about future prices and the weather all affect the position of the supply schedule for a given product.

Neither of the preceding lists of supply and demand shifters is meant to be exhaustive.

Changes in demand versus changes in the quantity demanded

When economists use the expression *change in demand*, they mean a shift in the entire demand curve. Thus, when the average income level of buyers increases, the demand curve shifts to the right – there is a change in demand. When we say *change in the quantity demanded*, we mean a movement along the demand curve. When the price of a good falls, for example, the result is an increase in the quantity demanded not an increase in demand.

Analogous interpretations attach to the expressions *change in supply* and *change in the quantity supplied*. These terminological distinctions are important for clear communication, both in classroom discussion and in exams. Make sure you know the difference, as my experience with previous generations of students is that they tend to get confused.

Equilibrium quantity and price

With both the supply and demand schedules in hand, we can describe the *equilibrium quantity and price* of lobsters. It is the price–quantity pair at which both buyers and sellers are satisfied, or where the supply and demand curves intersect. Put another way, it is where the quantity supplied by producers equals the quantity demanded by consumers at the same price. Figure 2.5 depicts the equilibrium in our lobster market, at which a total of 300 lobsters is traded at a price of R180 each.

Recall that the demand and supply schedules were given by the following equations:

$$P_D = 540 - 0.9Q_D \qquad (2.5)$$

$$P_S = 0.9Q_S \qquad (2.6)$$

In equilibrium $P_D = P_S$, and therefore

$$540 - 0.9Q = 0.9Q$$

(In equilibrium $Q_D = Q_S$, so we can ignore the subscripts.)

$$-1.8Q = -540$$

$$Q = 300$$

Figure 2.5 Equilibrium in the lobster market

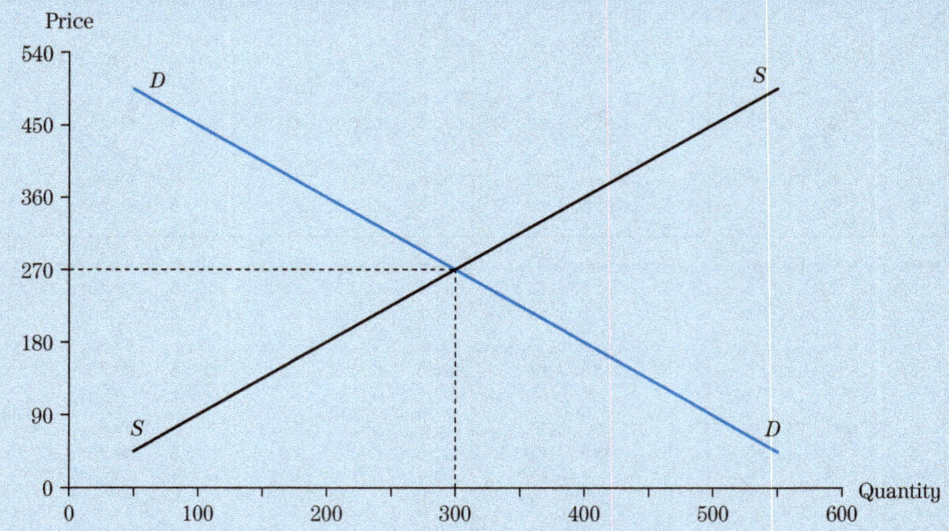

The intersection of the supply and demand curves represents the price–quantity pair at which all participants in the market are 'satisfied': buyers are buying the quantity they want to buy at that price, and sellers are selling the quantity they want to sell.

By substituting $Q = 300$ in the demand or supply equations, we get

$$P = 540 - (0.9 \times 300)$$
$$= 270$$

or

$$P = 0.9 \times 300$$
$$= 270$$

We can also rewrite the equations:

$$0.9Q_D = 540 - P_D \tag{2.7}$$

$$Q_D = 600 - \frac{1}{0.9}P_D$$

and

$$Q_S = \frac{1}{0.9}P_S$$

In equilibrium $Q_D = Q_S$, and therefore

$$600 - \frac{1}{0.9}P_D = \frac{1}{0.9}P_S$$

(We can ignore the subscripts, because $P_D = P_S$ in equilibrium.)

$$-\frac{2}{0.9}P = -600$$
$$P = 270$$

Substitute this in either the demand equation

$$Q_D = 600 - \left(\frac{1}{0.9} \times 270\right)$$
$$= 300$$

or the supply equation

$$Q_S = \frac{1}{0.9} \times 270$$
$$= 300$$

to get an equilibrium quantity of 300.

Obviously, the algebraic solution gives the same answer as the one portrayed in Fig. 2.5. Remember that, when we solve for two variables in two linear equations, we calculate where these two functions intersect. The algebraic approach has the further advantage that it is much quicker and easier to calculate than having to produce accurate drawings of the demand and supply schedules.

Exercise 2.1

Find the equilibrium price and quantity in a market whose supply and demand curves are given by $P = 4Q_S$ and $P = 12 - 2Q_D$, respectively.

If we were at any price–quantity pair other than the one in Fig. 2.5 ($P =$ R270 and $Q = 300$), either buyers or sellers – or both – would be dissatisfied in the sense described above. If for some reason the price happened to lie above the R270 equilibrium level, sellers would tend to be the ones who were frustrated. At a price of R360, for example, buyers would purchase only 200 lobsters, whereas sellers would offer 400 (see Fig. 2.6). The demand of buyers would be satisfied at a price of R360, but sellers would not be satisfied. A situation in which price exceeds its equilibrium value is called one of **excess supply**, or *surplus*. At R360, there is an excess supply of 200 (400 – 200) lobsters.

Excess supply The amount by which quantity supplied exceeds quantity demanded at a specific price.

If, by contrast, the price happened to lie below the equilibrium price of R270, then buyers would be the ones dissatisfied. At a price of R180, for example, they would want to purchase 400 lobsters, whereas suppliers would be willing to sell only 200. A situation in which price lies below its equilibrium value is referred to as one of **excess demand**, or *shortage*. At a price of R180 in this lobster market, there is an excess demand of 200 lobsters. At the market equilibrium price of R270, both excess demand and excess supply are exactly zero.

Excess demand The amount by which quantity demanded exceeds quantity supplied at a specific price.

Exercise 2.2

At a price of R90 in this hypothetical lobster market, how much excess demand for lobsters will there be? How much excess supply will there be at a price of R450?

Adjustment to equilibrium

When price differs from the equilibrium price, trading in the marketplace will be constrained – by the behaviour of buyers if the price lies above equilibrium, by the behaviour of sellers if below. At any price other than the equilibrium price, one side or the other of the market is dissatisfied. At prices above equilibrium, for example, sellers are not selling as much as they want to. The

Figure 2.6 Excess supply and excess demand in the lobster market

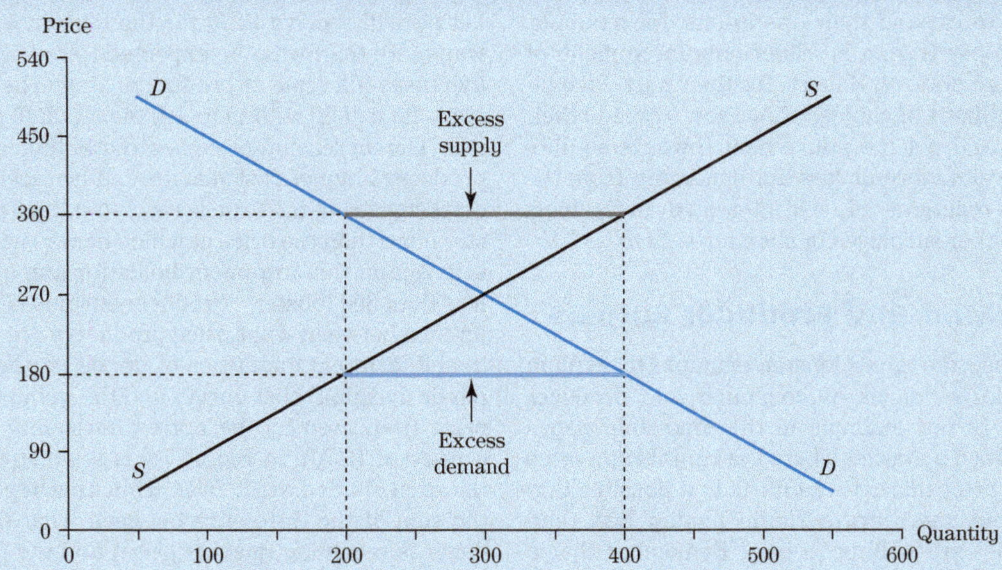

When price exceeds the equilibrium level, there is excess supply, or surplus. When price is below the equilibrium level, there is excess demand, or shortage.

impulse of a dissatisfied seller is to reduce the price. Remember last year's rag when you were responsible for the hamburger stall at your residence? Everything was coming to an end and you still had hamburgers left. What did you do? Yes, you acted in an economically rational manner and reduced the price to get rid of them! In the seafood business, the rule of thumb is 'sell it or smell it'. At a price of R360 each, 200 lobsters are being sold, but another 200 go unclaimed. Each seller reasons, correctly, that if he were to cut his price slightly, while others remained at R360, he could move all his unsold lobsters. Buyers will abandon sellers who charge R360 in favour of those who charge only R330. But then the deserted sellers themselves have a motive for cutting price. And if all sellers cut price to R330, each will again have a large quantity of unsold lobsters. Downward pressure on price will persist as long as there remain any dissatisfied sellers – that is, until the price falls to its equilibrium value of R270.

When the price is below R270, buyers are dissatisfied. Under these conditions, sellers will realize that they can increase their prices and still sell as much as they wish to. This upward pressure on price will persist until the price reaches its equilibrium value. Put another way, consumers will start bidding against each other in the hope of seeing their demands satisfied.

An extraordinary feature of this equilibrating process is that no one consciously plans or directs it. The actual steps that consumers and producers must take to move towards equilibrium are often indescribably complex. Suppliers looking to expand their operations, for example, must choose from a bewilderingly large menu of equipment options. Buyers, for their part, face literally millions of choices about how to spend their money. And yet the adjustment towards equilibrium results more or less automatically from the natural reactions of self-interested individuals facing either surpluses or shortages.

Consumer and producer surplus

Let us use the same lobster example to explain the basic principles of consumer and producer surplus. In our example in the preceding pages we assumed a market where the equilibrium price in the lobster market was R270. Is it possible that some consumers are actually paying less than what they are willing to pay? Remember that a demand curve is the locus of price–quantity combinations that consumers are *willing* to buy. If only one lobster was supplied, consumers would be willing to pay almost R540 in order to get it. In other words, they are paying R270 less per lobster than what they are willing to pay. If, say, 50 lobsters were supplied, consumers would be willing to pay R495 per lobster. How do we know that? Their demand curve tells us what they are willing to pay for different quantities and we can see it in Fig. 2.7. In this case, they will pay R225 more per lobster than the going market price. The same argument as above holds for any quantity less than 300 lobsters. Up to that amount, consumers will always be willing to pay more than the going market price of R270 per lobster. This is exactly what consumer surplus is – the difference between what consumers are willing to pay (their demand curve) and the going market price (in our example, R270, which can be presented by the dotted horizontal line). In Fig. 2.7, this is indicated by the dark blue area, *ABE*. It is the sum of the differences between what consumers are willing to pay for each product and the market price. If the market is in equilibrium at point *E*, many consumers are actually paying less than what they are willing to pay for lobsters.

We can explain producer surplus in the same way. Can you still remember the definition of a supply curve? From your first year course, you'll recall that the supply curve is equal to the marginal cost curve of the producer. In other words, the supply curve is the locus of price–quantity combinations that a producer is willing to supply. When he catches only one lobster, there are basically no costs involved and he is almost willing to give it away for free. However, in this market he will receive R270 for the lobster, which is way more than what he expected to receive. If he increases his scale of production and sells 50 lobsters, he will be willing to sell them at R45 per lobster. The increasing price is directly linked to the producer's higher cost structure. If he receives the market price of R270, he is receiving R245 per lobster more than the price at which he was willing to sell. Again, this argument holds for any quantity less than 300 lobsters. Producer surplus is the difference between what price producers are willing to sell different quantities of goods at (their supply or marginal cost curve) and the going market price (indicated by the dotted horizontal line at a price of R270). In Fig. 2.7, this is illustrated by the grey shaded area, *BCE*. This area represents the sum of the difference between what the producer is receiving (market price) and the price at which he is willing to sell (supply curve) for each product.

Figure 2.7 Consumer and producer surplus in the lobster market

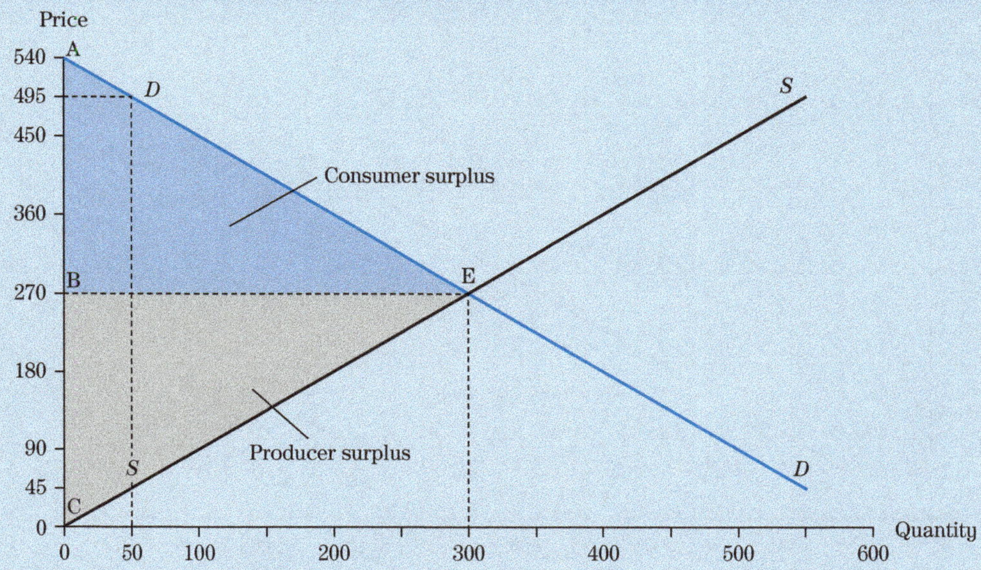

Consumer surplus is what the consumers pay less than what they are willing to pay and producer surplus is what producers receive more that what they are willing to sell for.

Some welfare properties of equilibrium

Given the attributes – tastes, abilities, knowledge, incomes, and so on – of buyers and sellers, the equilibrium outcome has some attractive properties. Specifically, we can say that no reallocation can improve some people's position without harming the position of at least some others. *If price and quantity take anything other than their equilibrium values, however, it will always be possible to reallocate so as to make at least some people better off without harming others.*

Sticking with the lobster example, suppose price is R180, with suppliers therefore offering only 200 lobsters. As indicated in Fig. 2.8, the vertical interpretation of the demand curve tells us that, when only 200 lobsters are available, buyers are willing to pay R360. Similarly, the vertical interpretation of the supply curve tells us that, when 200 lobsters a day are supplied, the marginal cost of delivering another lobster is only R180. When the value to the buyer of the last lobster caught (R360) is higher than the cost of harvesting it (R180), there is room to make a deal to put both parties in a better situation.

Suppose, for example, a dissatisfied buyer were to offer a supplier R225 for a lobster. The supplier would gladly sell an additional lobster at this price (since, at 200 lobsters, an additional lobster costs only R180 to harvest). This transaction would improve the buyer's position by R135 (the difference between the R360 value he attaches to the lobster and the R225 he paid for it). It would also improve the seller's position by R45 (the difference between the R225 he got and the R180 cost of harvesting the extra lobster). No one suffers any harm from this transaction (except the extra lobster!), and the participants reap R180 of additional benefit from it (R135 for the buyer, R45 for the seller). A similar argument can be made concerning any other price below the equilibrium value. For any such price, it is always possible to make some people better off without hurting others.

What if the price had been higher than the equilibrium price to begin with? Suppose price is R360, with trading therefore limited by buyers' demands for 200 lobsters. (Again, see Fig. 2.8.) Now a dissatisfied seller can propose a transaction that will make both the seller and some buyers better off. Suppose, for example, a seller offers an additional lobster for sale for R315. Since buyers value additional lobsters at R360, whoever buys it will be better off by R45. And since lobsters cost only R180 to harvest, the seller will be better off by R135. Again, no one is injured by this transaction and, again, the two parties gain a total of R180.

Figure 2.8 An opportunity for improvement in the lobster market

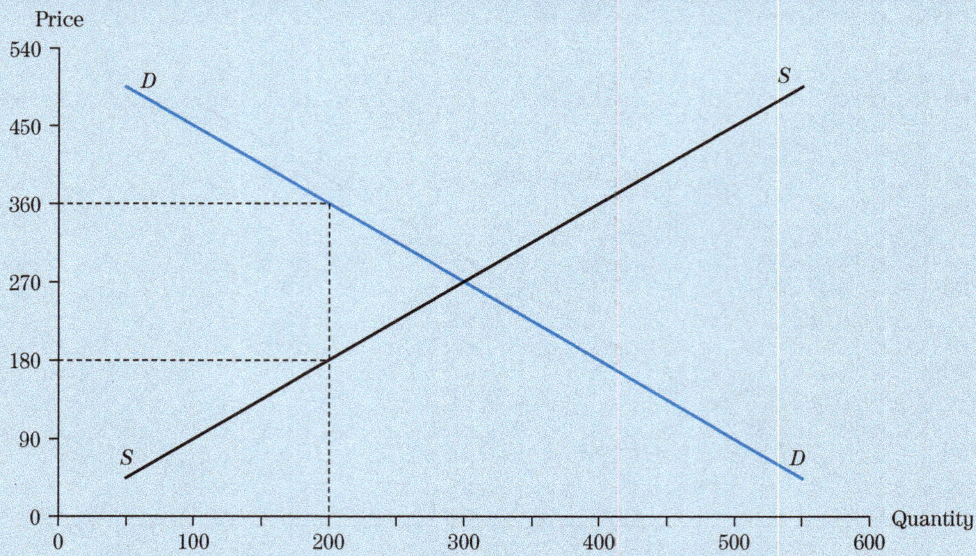

When the quantity traded in the market is below (or above) the equilibrium quantity, it is always possible to reallocate resources in such a way that some people are made better off without harming others. Here, a dissatisfied buyer can pay a seller R225 for an additional lobster, thus making both parties better off.

Thus, no matter whether price starts out above or below its equilibrium value, a mutually beneficial transaction will always be possible. We'll examine the welfare properties of the market system in much greater detail in later chapters. But for now, suffice it to say that the equilibrium price and quantity constitute the best outcome attainable, given the initial attributes and endowments of buyers and sellers.

Free markets and the poor

The fact that market equilibrium is efficient in the sense just described does not mean that it is necessarily desirable in any absolute sense. All markets may be in perfect equilibrium, for example in Southern African countries, and yet many people will lack sufficient income to purchase even the bare necessities of life, such as food, clothing and housing. Saying market equilibrium is efficient does not challenge the notion that being poor is difficult, often even painful. Efficiency says merely that, *given the low incomes of the poor*, free exchange enables them to do the best they can with the money they have. One can hold this view and still believe it desirable to provide public assistance to poor people.

Concern for the well-being of the poor motivates most societies to try to intervene in the economy by regulating prices and/or quantities. The difficulty is that these interventions often produce unintended harmful consequences. However, as will be discussed in Chapter 14, certain goods and services, such as low-cost housing or medical services for the poor, won't be provided if the government does not intervene in the economy. Many critics of the market system complain that it is unfair to ration goods and services by asking how much (poor) people are willing to pay for them, but as Example 2.2 clearly illustrates, serious contradictions plague alternative schemes of allocation. Consider again our hypothetical lobster market. Suppose we are concerned that the equilibrium price of R270 will exclude many deserving poor persons from experiencing the pleasure of a lobster dinner. If we then adopt a system that periodically gives free lobsters to the poor, wouldn't such a system represent a clear improvement in the eyes of any person who feels compassion for the poor?

The answer, as in Example 2.2, is that for the same cost we can do even better. When a poor person, or indeed even a rich person, does not buy lobster because the price is too high, she is saying, in effect, that she would prefer to spend her money on other things. If we gave her a lobster, what would she want to do with it? In an ideal world, she would immediately sell it to someone willing to pay the R270 equilibrium price for it. We

Example 2.2

Denied boarding compensation

What are the efficiency and distributional implications of handling excess demand for seats on overbooked flights through a first-come, first-served policy as opposed to an auction mechanism?

One would expect that, if you paid R11 000 for a return airline ticket from Johannesburg to London and reserved a specific seat, you would show up. Surprisingly, this is not the case and this is the reason why commercial airlines frequently issue more reservations than there are seats on a flight without experiencing any difficulty at all. In this way, they try to ensure that they fly with full aeroplanes. Occasionally, however, 330 passengers will show up for a flight on the Airbus A340-600 with a capacity of only 319 seats. How do they deal with this problem?

Initially, airlines dealt with overbooked flights by boarding passengers on a first-come, first-served basis. This solution gives insufficient weight to the interests of passengers with pressing needs who may arrive at the airport a little late. With this problem clearly in mind – too many people showing up for a flight – the airline is now required to call for volunteers to abandon their seats in return for either a cash payment or an in-kind payment, such as a free air ticket. In most countries, this type of practice is now compulsory and enforced by law.

The advantage of the current practice is that it allows passengers to decide for themselves how pressing their schedules are. People with important meetings could simply refuse to volunteer. The last time I flew back from New York, I was offered $800 to fly via South America, but since I had pre-arranged commitments I could not take advantage of the offer. However, enough passengers volunteered to ensure that our aeroplane was no longer overbooked. In comparison with the first-come, first-served solution, this ruling promises a better outcome for all passengers because the preferences of passengers are taken into consideration.

Initially this ruling was met by opposition from consumer-action groups, who objected to it on the grounds that it was unfair to low-income passengers as they would almost always be the ones to wait for the next flight. However, by volunteering such passengers signal that the cash payment is *worth* the wait and they will thus gain from the agreement.

Why is an auction a better way to allocate seats on an overbooked flight than first-come, first-served? ©iStock.com/InkkStudios

know there will be such persons, because some of the lobsters that would have been bought for R270 were instead given to the poor. The poor person's sale of the lobster to one of these people will bring about a clear improvement for both parties – for the buyer, or else he would not have bought it, and for the seller, because the lobster is worth less than R270 to her.

The practical difficulty, as we shall see in detail in later chapters, is that it would take time and effort for our hypothetical poor person to find a buyer for the lobster. In the end, she would probably eat it herself. True enough, she might enjoy her lobster dinner. But, by her own reckoning, she would have enjoyed the R270 even more.

The problem is the same with petrol price controls that are introduced to protect the poor from sharply higher prices. As was seen in the 1970s, their effect was to induce a host of behaviours that helped neither rich nor poor.

Despite statements to the contrary by critics of the market system, people are highly responsive to energy prices when they make decisions about how to spend their incomes. If petrol costs R18.50/litre, for example, many people will be tempted to form car pools or purchase fuel-efficient cars, even though they would do neither if price were only R9.50/litre. Whether a long trip is considered worth taking also clearly depends on the price of petrol. This was clearly illustrated in South Africa in 2008, when petrol prices increased sharply from less than R7.50/litre to more than R11.50/litre in six months, and the tourism industry experienced a sharp decrease in the number of tourists. Although the price dropped to R8.70/litre in 2011, it again increased in 2014, to above R14.00; people are currently thus much more sensitive to changes in fuel prices than was the case six years ago.

Regardless of whether fuel is in short supply, it is in everyone's interest – rich or poor – to use it for the activities they value most. A policy that does not take this into account involves particularly high costs when fuel is scarce. Selling petrol for less than the equilibrium price is just such a policy. It encourages people to use petrol in wasteful ways.

Rent controls

As an old saying goes, the surest way to destroy a city, short of dropping a nuclear bomb on it, is to pass a rent control law. Such laws, like so many others, are motivated by an honest concern for the well-being of low-income citizens. In Southern Africa this may sound like an ideal measure to ensure that rich property owners do not exploit the poor, but the economic consequences of such laws are no less damaging for being unintended.

Basic supply and demand analysis is again all we need to see clearly the nature of the difficulties. In Stellenbosch, students are of the opinion that flats are very expensive to rent. Assume that Fig. 2.9 depicts the supply and demand schedules of bachelor flats for students. The equilibrium rent in this market would be R4200/mth, and at this level there would be 2400 flats rented. Suppose that Stellenbosch city council has passed a law that holds rents at R_c = R2800/mth, or R1400 below the market-clearing value. R_c in this example constitutes a **price ceiling** for rents, a *maximum* level

Figure 2.9 Rent controls in the market for flats

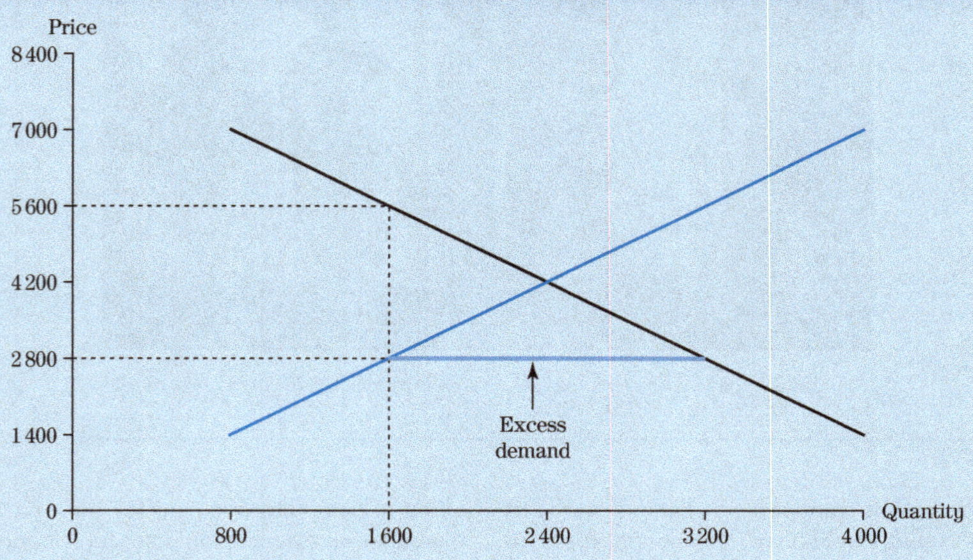

With the rent control level set at R2800 a month, there is an excess demand of 1600 flats a month.

Price ceiling
Maximum level above which the price of a good is not permitted by law to rise.

beyond which rents are not permitted to rise. At R2800/mth, students would like to rent 3200 flats, but suppliers are willing to offer only 1600. There is an excess demand of 1600 units. And if the rent control level remains fixed at R2800/mth, excess demand will grow over time as population grows and inflation reduces the value of money.

In an unregulated market, the immediate response would be rents rising sharply. But here the law prevents them from rising above R_c. Yet the pressures of excess demand can make themselves felt in other ways. One way is owners spending less on maintaining their rental units because they are not receiving the minimum price for which they are willing to rent them. If there are two renters knocking at the door of each vacant apartment, clogged drains, peeling paint, broken thermostats and the like are not apt to receive prompt attention. If one takes into account that bachelor flats on campus sell for about R1.1 million, this situation isn't surprising.

Why are rent-controlled apartments less well-maintained than unregulated units? ©iStock.com/pidjoe

The most serious difficulty is that, with an offering of only 1600 flats per month, we see in Fig. 2.9 that renters would be willing to pay as much as R5600/mth for a flat (again, the vertical interpretation of the demand curve). This pressure almost always finds ways, legal or illegal, of expressing itself. In areas where rent control is introduced, such as New York City, it is not uncommon to see 'finder's fees' or 'key deposits' as high as several thousand dollars. Owners who cannot ask a price determined by market forces for their flat also have the option of converting it to an apartment block, which enables them to sell their asset for a price much closer to its true economic value.

Even when rent-controlled apartment owners do not hike their prices in these various ways, serious misallocations result. A student steadfastly remains in her flat after graduation and getting a job because it is cheaper than alternative dwellings not covered by rent control. It would be better for all concerned if she relinquished that space to a needy student, but under rent controls she has no economic incentive to do so.

At the market-clearing price of R4200 per month, flat-owners will be willing to rent out 2400 units; under rent control, they will rent out only 1600. Some students ('insiders') gain by paying a lower monthly rent, but it may be the case that 800 students ('outsiders') may not find flats to rent. Some students gain with this ruling, but others lose out.

Exercise 2.3

In the market for apartments described in Fig. 2.9, what would happen if the rent control level were set at R5600/mth?

Example 2.3

The effects of lowering rent control

Suppose the rent control is lowered (strengthened) to R1400/mth. What is the excess demand, and how does it compare with the excess demand when rents were limited (more loosely) to R2800/mth?

At R1400/mth, buyers would like to rent 4000 apartments, but suppliers are willing to offer only 800. Thus there is an excess demand of 3200 units. The excess demand is greater than the excess demand of 1600 units at the R2800/mth rent control.

In response to the kinds of problem described above, some rent-control programmes have been modified to allow landlords to raise rents when a tenant moves out of an apartment. Such changes reduce, but do not eliminate, misallocations. And they may even create new problems. For example, a landlord who knows that a tenant's departure would permit a rent increase may take any available lawful steps to make the tenant's life unpleasant if he remains.

There are more effective ways to help poor people than to give them cheap petrol, rent-controlled apartments or free lobsters. One would be to give them additional income and let them decide for themselves how to spend it. Chapter 16 examines some of the practical difficulties involved in transferring additional purchasing power into the hands of the poor. In brief, the most pressing problem is that it is hard to target cash at the genuinely needy without attracting others who could fend for themselves. There are no simple or easy solutions. However, given the enormous losses caused by policies that keep prices below their equilibrium levels, these issues deserve our most serious attention.

Price supports

Rent controls are an example of a price ceiling that prevents the price from rising to its equilibrium level. For many agricultural products, the government's policy has been to impose not ceilings but *price supports*, or **price floors**, which keep prices *above* their equilibrium levels. In contrast to price ceilings, which required merely the announcement of a level beyond which prices could not rise, price supports require the government to become an active buyer in the market.

Price floor A minimum price for a good, established by law, and supported by government's offer to buy the good at that price.

Dairy farmers have been through a difficult time and many stopped farming or switched to other types of agricultural product. At the turn of the century, there were about 7500 dairy farmers in South Africa; by 2014, there were fewer than 2 000. According to Tom Tucker, chairman of the Milk Producers Organisation, an economically viable dairy farming unit consists of at least 600 milk cows and requires about R60 million. This may be one of the reasons why the number of dairy farmers has decreased to the extent described above. Let us assume that your father is one of those surviving dairy farmers and that he has a farm in the Free State. Figure 2.10 depicts the demand and supply schedules of milk in the Free State, with a price support level of P_S = R16.00/litre in this market. Because P_S is above the equilibrium price, there is an excess supply of 200 kilolitres/day. To maintain the price at P_S = R16.00/litre, the government must purchase 200 kilolitres/day. Otherwise, farmers would face powerful incentives to cut their prices.

An important purpose of farm price supports is to ensure that prices are high enough to provide

Figure 2.10 A price floor in the milk market

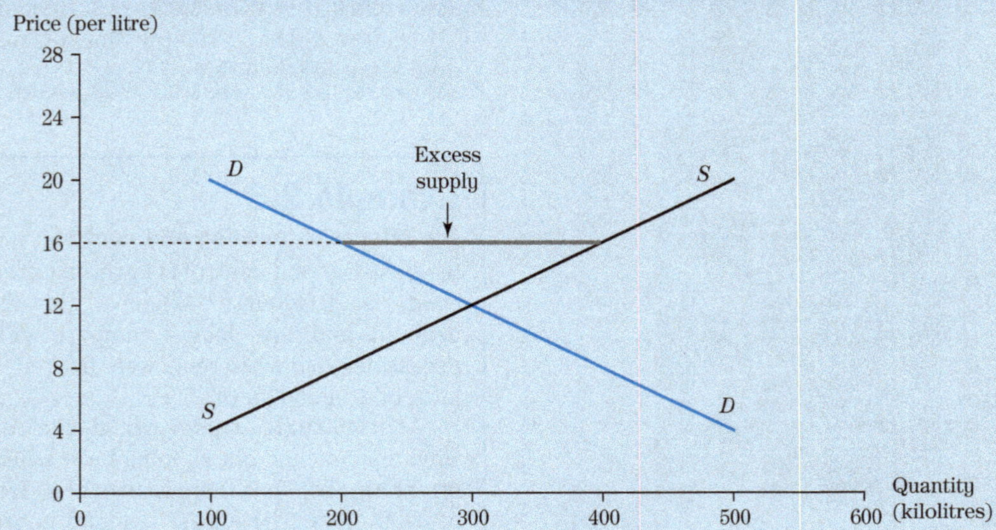

For a price support to have any impact, it must be set above the market-clearing price. Its effect is to create excess supply, which the government then purchases.

adequate incomes for farm families. In practice, however, the supports have proved a costly and inefficient instrument. One problem is the disposition of the surplus bought by the government. To produce this surplus requires valuable labour, capital, fertilizer and other inputs. Yet often it is simply left to decay in government storage bins. Another difficulty is that much of the surplus is produced by large corporate farms, whose owners have no need of support. For every rand that price supports put into the hands of a needy family farmer, several more go into the coffers of prosperous agribusinesses. Price supports also raise the food bills of all families, and often raise the prices of goods not directly supported. (See Example 2.4, later in this chapter.) If society wants to subsidize small family farms, there are more efficient and direct means than agricultural price supports.

The government could also regulate the price of milk, and fix it at R16.00/litre. The result of this would be that supply would outstrip demand by 200 kilolitres/day (as explained above). Consumers would buy 100 kilolitres less than would be the case in the competitive market, where 300 kilolitres would be sold at a price of R12.00/litre. Some consumers would thus not be able to afford milk, because of the high price, but certain sellers would also not find a market for their product. As we have seen with price ceilings, price floors also involve winners and losers, and the losers may be the poorer farmers. Price regulation frequently has unintended negative side effects.

The rationing and allocative functions of prices

Prices serve two important and distinct functions. First, they ration existing supplies of goods. Scarcity is the universal feature of economic life. Without the problem of scarcity it would not be necessary for us to study economics! Equilibrium prices curtail excessive claims of consumers by rationing scarce supplies to the users who place the highest value on them. This is the **rationing function of price**. It is a short-run function, in the sense that its focus is the distribution of output that already exists.

Rationing function of price The process whereby price directs existing supplies of a product to the users who value it most highly.

The second function of price is that of a signal to direct productive resources among the different sectors of the economy. In industries in which there is excess demand, firms are able to charge more than they need to cover their costs of production and make excessive profits. The resulting profits act as a carrot that lures additional resources into these industries. On the other hand, losses act as the stick that drives resources out of those industries in which there is excess supply. This is the so-called **allocative function of price**. It is a long-run function in the sense that its focus is to induce resources to migrate from industries with excess supply to those with excess demand. Remember, it is the possibility of making profits that ensures that markets operate efficiently, by directing resources to those industries where the most profit can be made. However, it has a negative side, in that the lack of a profit motive will prevent resources from being directed to those industries that supply goods and services to the poor.

Allocative function of price The process whereby price acts as a signal that guides resources away from the production of goods whose prices lie below cost towards the production of goods whose prices exceed cost.

In our example above, rent controls subvert both functions of the price mechanism. The rationing function is undercut by the alternative mechanisms that distribute flats with little regard for the value people place on them. The underlying needs of renters are relegated to secondary status. Both luck and the people you happen to know are often decisive. Artificially low rents undercut the allocative function of price by sending a false signal to investors about the need for additional housing. Under rent controls, apartment builders earn less than they could by investing their money elsewhere. The cruel irony is that the pressing need in many communities with rent controls is for more low-income housing units, not fewer – which is precisely what the market would produce on its own if the poor were given more money.

Predicting and explaining changes in price and quantity

To predict or explain changes in equilibrium prices and quantities, we must predict or account for the shifts in the relevant supply and/or demand schedules. When supply and demand curves have the conventional slopes, the following propositions about equilibrium prices and quantities will hold:

- An increase in demand will lead to an increase in both the equilibrium price and the quantity.

- A decrease in demand will lead to a decrease in both the equilibrium price and the quantity.
- An increase in supply will lead to a decrease in the equilibrium price and an increase in the equilibrium quantity.
- A decrease in supply will lead to an increase in the equilibrium price and a decrease in the equilibrium quantity.

There is no point in memorizing this list, since each proposition can be easily derived by shifting the relevant curve in a standard supply–demand diagram.

These simple propositions permit us to answer a variety of questions.

Exercise 2.4

What will happen to the equilibrium price and quantity in the fresh seafood market if: (1) a scientific report is issued saying that fish contains mercury, which is toxic to humans; and (2) the price of diesel (used to operate fishing boats) falls significantly?

How do taxes affect equilibrium prices and quantities?

In the previous section we looked at how rent control and support programmes affect markets.

Economic naturalist 2.1

Why do the prices of some goods, like avocado pears, go down during the months of heaviest consumption while others, like accommodation in Sun City, go up?

When confronting any problem like this, we must first decide whether there was a change in the determinant of demand or supply. Once we have identified that, we can easily solve the problem with a simple graph of demand and supply curves. The answer to the question above is that the seasonal consumption increase is the result of a supply increase in the example of avocado pears, and a demand increase in the example of accommodation in Sun City. As shown in Fig. 2.11, these shifts produce the observed seasonal relationships between equilibrium prices and quantities. (The subscripts *w* and *s* in Fig. 2.11 are used to denote winter and summer values, respectively.) When supply of avocado pears increases in winter, the increase in the equilibrium quantity occurs concurrently with a decrease in the equilibrium price. When demand for Sun City accommodation increases in summer, the increase in the equilibrium quantity occurs concurrently with an increase in the equilibrium price.

Figure 2.11 Two sources of seasonal variation

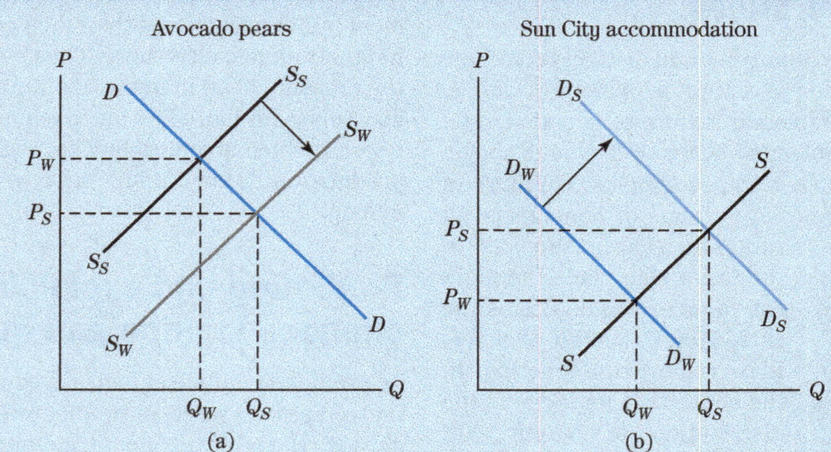

The quantity of avocado pears consumed is highest in winter and, of Sun City accommodation, is highest in summer. (a) The prices of avocado pears are at their lowest during the winter because the quantity increase is the result of increased supply. (b) Sun City accommodation prices are at their highest in summer because the quantity increase is the result of an increase in demand.

Example 2.4

If soya bean are one of the ingredients in cattle feed, how does a price support programme in the soya bean market affect the equilibrium price and quantity of beef?

The price support programme raises the price of soya beans, with a resulting increase in the price of cattle feed. This causes a leftward shift in the supply schedule for beef (see Fig. 2.12), which results in an increase in the equilibrium price and a reduction in the equilibrium quantity of beef.

Figure 2.12 The effect of soya bean price supports on the equilibrium price and quantity of beef

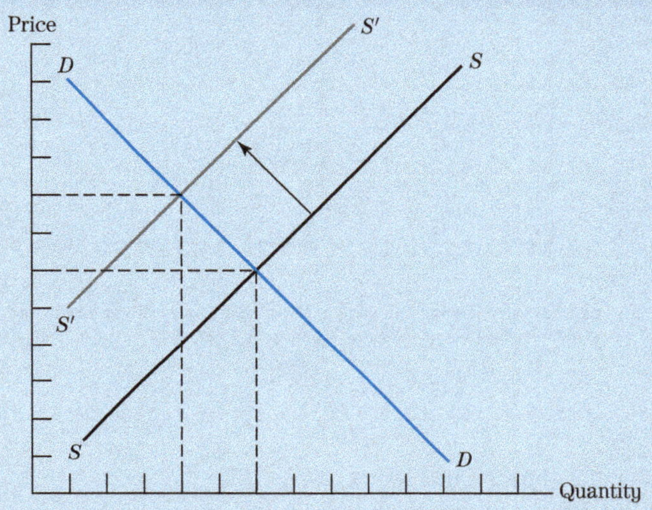

By raising the price of soya beans, an input used in beef production, the price supports produce a leftward shift in the supply curve of beef. The result is an increase in the equilibrium price and a reduction in the equilibrium quantity.

Now we are going to use supply and demand analysis to analyse the effects of various taxes. We shall consider only a constant tax per unit of output. For example, how will the equilibrium price and quantity of a product be affected if a tax of $T = 10$ is levied on each unit sold by the producer? There are two equivalent ways to approach this question. The first is to suppose that the tax is levied on the seller. In Fig. 2.13, the line SS denotes the original supply schedule. At a price of $P_0 = 25$, sellers were willing to supply Q_0 units of output. When a tax $T = 10$ is levied on sellers, the market price would have to be $P_0 + 10 = 35$ for them to get the same net payment that they used to receive when the price was $P_0 = 25$. At a price of 35, then, suppliers will offer the same amount of output they used to offer at a price of 25. The same procedure can be repeated for every other point on the original supply curve to derive the new supply curve. The resulting after-tax supply schedule is the original supply schedule shifted vertically upwards by the amount of the tax ($T = 10$ in our example).

In Fig. 2.14, DD represents the demand curve facing the sellers who have been taxed $T = 10$ per unit of output. The initial equilibrium is at a price of P^* and quantity traded of Q^*. The effect of the tax is to cause the equilibrium quantity to fall from Q^* to Q_1^*. The price paid by the buyer rises from P^* to P_1^*; and the price, net of the tax, received by the seller falls to $P_1^* - 10$.

The seller thus receives less per product after the introduction of the tax, although the price of the product has increased. However, the seller does not pay the full burden of the tax. Total tax per product is equal to the vertical distance between the two supply curves. Tax per product is thus equal to $P_1^* - (P_1^* - 10)$. Consumers pay the increase in the market price, in other words $P_1^* - P^*$, but the rest of the tax $[P^* - (P_1^* - 10)]$

Figure 2.13 A tax of $T = 10$ levied on the seller shifts the supply schedule upwards by T units

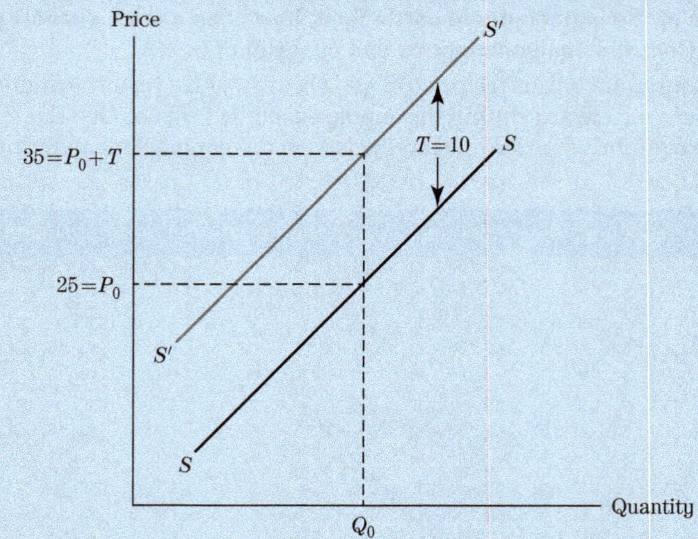

The original supply schedule tells us what price suppliers must charge in order to cover their costs at any given level of output. From the seller's perspective, a tax of $T = 10$ units is the same as a unit-cost increase of 10 units. The new supply curve thus lies 10 units above the old one.

must be paid by the seller. The burden of the tax is thus divided between the buyer and the seller.

Algebraically, the seller's share of the tax, denoted t_s, is the reduction in the price the seller receives, divided by the tax:

$$t_s = \frac{P^* - (P_1^* - T)}{T} \tag{2.8}$$

Similarly, the buyer's share of the tax, t_b, is the increase in price (including tax) divided by the tax:

Figure 2.14 Equilibrium prices and quantities when a tax of $T = 10$ is levied on the seller

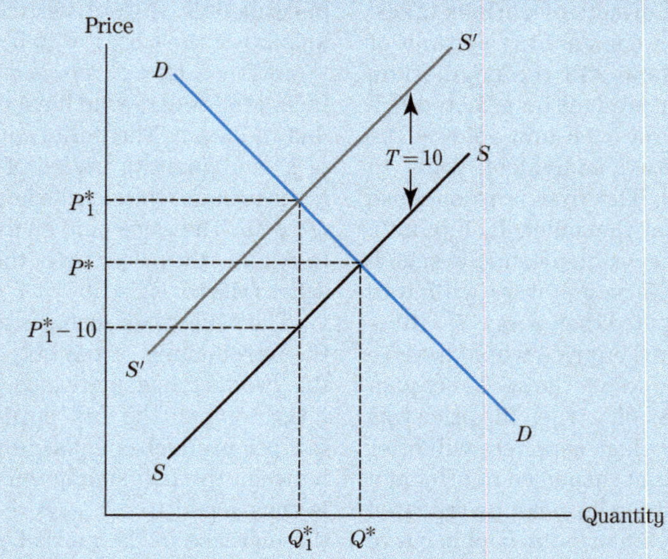

The tax causes a reduction in equilibrium quantity from Q^* to Q_1^*. The new price paid by the buyer rises from P^* to P_1^*. The new price received by the seller falls from P^* to $P_1^* - 10$.

Figure 2.15 The elasticity of demand and supply determines the burden of tax

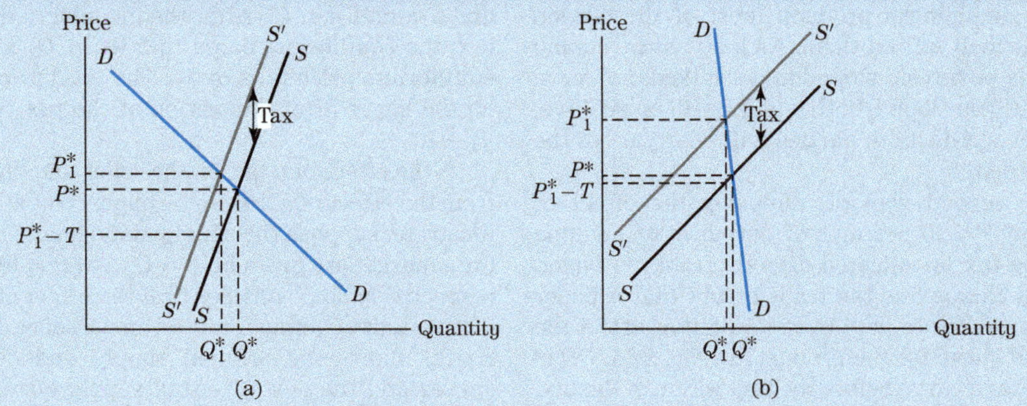

(a) If supply is inelastic relative to demand, producers will pay the burden of tax. (b) If demand is inelastic relative to supply, consumers will pay the burden of tax.

$$t_b = \frac{P_1^* - P^*}{T} \tag{2.9}$$

Exercise 2.5

Verify that $t_s + t_b = 1$.

In general, t_b and t_s depend on the shapes of the supply and demand schedules. If, for example, supply is highly unresponsive to changes in price (inelastic), t_b will be close to zero and t_s close to 1. This is illustrated in Fig. 2.15(a), where $P_1^* - P^*$ is much smaller than $P^* - (P_1^* - T)$. Conversely, if demand is highly unresponsive to price (inelastic), t_b will be close to 1 and t_s close to zero. This can clearly be seen in Fig. 2.15(b). Here, $P_1^* - P^*$ is much bigger than $P^* - (P_1^* - T)$. These claims amount to a statement that a tax tends to fall most heavily on the side of the market that can least escape it. If buyers have no substitute products to which they are prepared to turn, the lion's share

Figure 2.16 The effect of a tax of $T = 10$ levied on the buyer

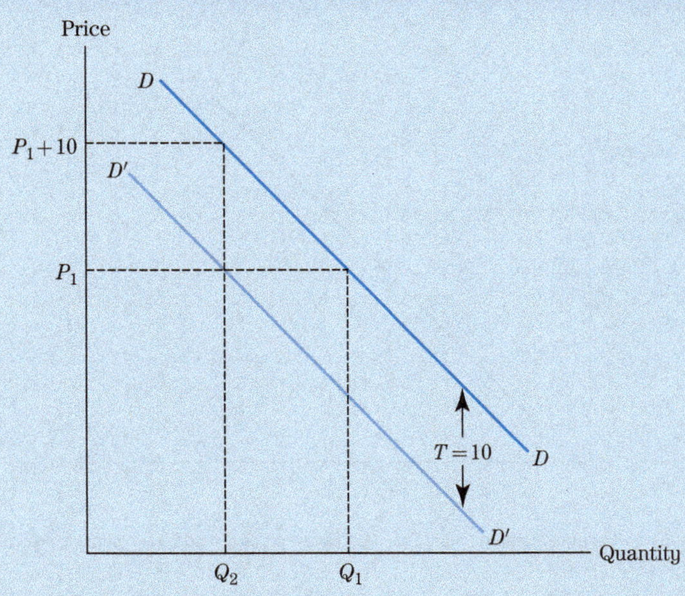

Before the tax, buyers would buy Q_1 units at a price of P_1. After the tax, a price of P_1 becomes $P_1 + 10$, which means buyers will buy only Q_2. The effect of the tax is to shift the demand curve downwards by 10 units.

of the tax will be passed on to them by suppliers. But if suppliers have no alternative other than to go on supplying a product, most of the burden of a tax will fall on them. As long as the supply curve is positively sloped and the demand curve is negatively sloped, both t_s and t_b will be positive; in other words, both parties will bear part of the tax burden.

The second way of analysing the effect of a tax of $T = 10$ per unit of output is to imagine that the tax is collected directly from the buyer. A good example is the transfer tax that a buyer of a house has to pay. How would that affect the demand curve for the product? In Fig. 2.16, *DD* is the demand curve before the imposition of the tax. At a price of P_1, buyers would demand a quantity of Q_1. After imposition of the tax, the total amount that buyers have to pay if the product price is P_1 will be $P_1 + 10$. Accordingly, the quantity they demand (afford) falls from Q_1 to Q_2. In like fashion, we can reckon the quantity demanded at any other price after imposition of the tax. *D′D′* is the resulting after-tax demand curve in Fig. 2.16. It is the original demand curve translated downwards by 10 units.

If *SS* in Fig. 2.17 denotes the supply schedule for this market, we can easily trace out the effects of the tax on the equilibrium price and quantity. The initial equilibrium is at a price of P^* and a quantity of Q^*. After the introduction of the tax, the equilibrium quantity falls to Q_2^* and the equilibrium price falls to P_2^*. The total price paid by the buyer after imposition of the tax rises to $P_2^* + 10$.

Is the effect of a tax on the seller any different from the effect of a tax on the buyer? Not at all. To illustrate, suppose the supply and demand curves for a market are given by $P = Q_S$ and $P = 10 - Q_D$, respectively, and consider first the effect of a tax of 2 per unit of output imposed on the seller. Figure 2.18(a) shows the original supply and demand curves and the new after-tax supply curve, *S′S′*. The original equilibrium price and quantity are both equal to 5. After the introduction of the tax, the new equilibrium price to the buyer is 6 and the quantity is 4. The price received by sellers is 4 (6 minus tax of 2).

Now, consider a tax of 2 per unit of output imposed on the buyers. Figure 2.18(b) shows the original supply and demand curves and the new after-tax demand curve, *D′D′*. Note that the effects on price and quantity are exactly the same as in the case of the tax levied on sellers shown in (a).

Figure 2.17 Equilibrium prices and quantities after imposition of a tax of $T = 10$ paid by the buyer

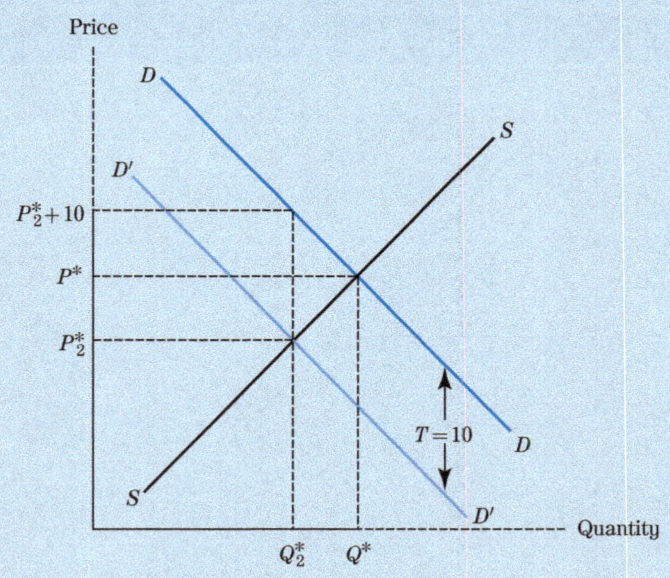

The tax causes a reduction in equilibrium quantity from Q^* to Q_2^*. The new price paid by the buyer rises from P^* to $P_2^* + 10$. The new price received by the seller falls from P^* to P_2^*.

Figure 2.18 A tax on the buyer leads to the same outcome as a tax on the seller

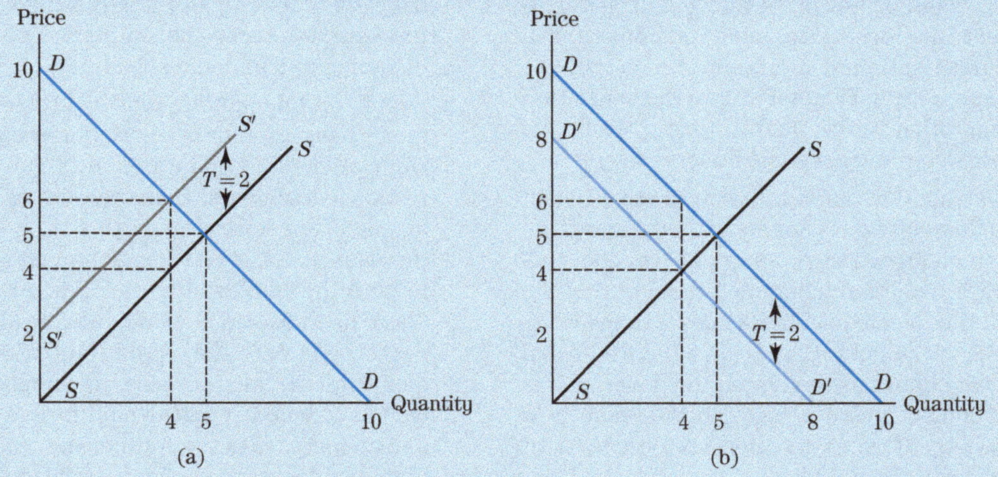

The price received by sellers (net of the tax), the price paid by buyers (including tax) and the equilibrium quantity will all be the same when the tax is collected from sellers (a) as when it is collected from buyers (b).

Exercise 2.6

Consider a market whose supply and demand curves are given by $P = 4Q_S$ and $P = 12 - 2Q_D$, respectively. How will the equilibrium price and quantity in this market be affected if a tax of 6 per unit of output is imposed on sellers? If the same tax is imposed on buyers?

When tax revenues must be raised, many political leaders find it expedient to propose a sales tax on corporations, because 'they can best afford to pay it'. But careful analysis of the effects of a sales tax shows that its burden will be the same whether it is imposed on buyers or on sellers. The *legal incidence of the tax* (whether it is imposed on buyers or on sellers) has no effect on the *economic incidence* of the tax (the respective shares of the tax burden borne by buyers and sellers). Economically speaking, the entity from which the tax is actually collected is thus a matter of complete indifference. However, this does not mean that buyers and sellers always share the burden of taxes equally. Their respective shares may be highly unequal.

Exercise 2.7

True or false? The steeper the demand curve for a good relative to the supply curve for that good, the greater the proportion of a tax on that good that will fall on buyers. Explain.

Summary

- The supply curve is generally an upward-sloping line that tells us what quantity sellers are willing to offer at any given price. The demand curve is a downward-sloping line that tells us what quantity buyers are willing to buy at any given price. In an unregulated market, the equilibrium price and quantity are determined by the intersection of these two curves.
- If price is above its equilibrium, there will be dissatisfied sellers, or excess supply. This condition motivates sellers to cut their prices. In contrast, when prices are below equilibrium, there will be dissatisfied buyers, or excess demand. This condition motivates sellers to charge higher prices. The only stable outcome is the one in which excess demand and excess supply are exactly zero.

- Given the attributes of buyers and sellers, the equilibrium price and quantity represent the best attainable outcome (or a Pareto-optimum situation, which will be dealt with in Chapter 16), in the sense that any other price–quantity pair would be worse for at least some buyers or sellers.
- The fact that market outcomes are efficient in this sense does not mean they necessarily command society's approval. On the contrary, we often mentioned the fact that the market mechanism does not serve the interests of the poor. Concern for the well-being of the poor has motivated the governments of almost every society to intervene in a variety of ways to alter the outcomes of market forces.
- Sometimes these interventions take the form of laws that peg prices above or below their equilibrium levels. Such laws often generate harmful, mostly unintended, consequences. Rent controls, for example, interfere with both the rationing and allocative functions of the price mechanism. They lead to black-marketeering, and a rapid deterioration of the stock of rental housing. By the same token, price support laws in agriculture tend to enrich large corporate farms while doing little to ease the plight of the small family farm. In almost every instance, it is possible to design an alternative intervention that is better in every respect.
- If the difficulty is that the poor have too little money, the solution is to discover ways of boosting their incomes directly. Legislatures cannot repeal the law of supply and demand. But legislatures do have the capacity to alter the underlying forces that govern the shape and position of supply and demand schedules.
- Supply and demand analysis is the economist's basic tool for predicting how equilibrium prices and quantities will change in response to changes in market forces. Four simple propositions guide this task: (1) an increase in demand will lead to an increase in both the equilibrium price and quantity; (2) a decrease in demand will lead to a decrease in both the equilibrium price and quantity; (3) an increase in supply will lead to a decrease in the equilibrium price and an increase in the equilibrium quantity; and (4) a decrease in supply will lead to an increase in the equilibrium price and a decrease in the equilibrium quantity.
- Incomes, tastes, the prices of substitutes and complements, expectations and population are among the factors that shift demand schedules. Supply schedules, in turn, are governed by such factors as technology, input prices, the number of suppliers, expectations and, for agricultural products, the weather.
- Consumers do not always pay what they are willing to pay for products. Consumer surplus is the difference between what consumers are willing to pay and what they actually pay. In the same vein, producer surplus is the difference between what producers receive at the market price and the amount that they are willing to sell the products for.

Questions for review

1 What is the difference between 'scarcity' and 'shortage'?

2 What would the supply curve look like for a good that is not scarce? Assuming the good is useful, what would its demand curve look like? Explain why a positive price for a commodity implies that it is scarce.

3 Give two examples of actions taken by the administration of your university whose effect is to prevent specific markets from reaching equilibrium. What evidence of excess supply or excess demand can you cite in these examples?

4 What is the difference between 'a reduction in supply' and 'a reduction in the quantity supplied'?

5 Identify each of the following as (1) a change in demand or (2) a change in the quantity demanded:

a Grape consumption falls because of a consumer boycott.

b Grape consumption falls because of a tax on grape producers.

c Grape consumption rises because of a good harvest.

d Grape consumption rises because of a change in tastes.

6 When there is excess supply, why is any single seller able to sell all she wants to by offering only a small reduction below the current market price?

7 Give an example of a market in which the allocative function of price is not very important.

8 Suppose you are a government official and need to collect revenue by taxing a product. For political reasons, you want the burden of the tax to fall mostly on consumers, not firms (who have been substantial contributors to your campaign fund). What should you look for when picking a product to tax?

9 Which would a rational poor person be more likely to accept, and why?

a A R500 000 Mercedes (immediate resale value = R300 000).

b R350 000 cash.

Problems

1 Assume that tea and lemons are complements, and that coffee and tea are substitutes:

a How, if at all, will the imposition of an effective ceiling price on tea affect the price of lemons? Explain.

b How, if at all, will the imposition of an effective ceiling price on tea affect the price of coffee? Explain.

2 The market for DVDs has supply and demand curves given by $P_S = 2Q_S$ and $P_D = 168 - Q_D$, respectively:

a How many units will be traded at a price of R150? At a price of R100? Which participants will be dissatisfied at these prices?

b What quantity of DVDs at what price will be sold in equilibrium?

c What is the total revenue from DVD sales when the market is in equilibrium?

3 Computer hardware and software are complements. Discuss the effects on the equilibrium price and quantity:

a In the software market, when the price of computer hardware falls.

b In the hardware market, when the price of computer software rises.

4 Suppose a newly released study shows that battery-powered toys harm a child's development and recommends that parents adjust their purchasing behaviour accordingly. Use diagrams to show the effect on price and quantity in each of the following markets:

a The market for battery-powered toys.

b The market for alkaline or rechargable batteries.

c The market for yo-yos (which do not require batteries).

5 Using diagrams, show what changes in price and quantity would be expected in the following markets under the scenarios given:

a *Crude oil*: As petroleum reserves decrease, it becomes more difficult to find and recover crude oil.

b *Air travel*: Worries about air safety cause travellers to shy away from air travel.

c *Rail travel*: Worries about air safety cause travellers to shy away from air travel.

d *Hotel rooms in Dubai*: Worries about air safety cause travellers to shy away from air travel.

e *Milk*: A genetically engineered hormone enables large milk producers to cut production costs.

6 For each scenario in Problem 5, state whether the effect is a change in demand or just a change in quantity demanded.

7 Suppose demand for seats at soccer games is $P = 1900 - (1/50)Q$ and supply is fixed at $Q = 90\,000$ seats:

a Find the equilibrium price and quantity of seats for a soccer game (using both algebra and a graph).

b Suppose the government intervenes and sets the price of tickets at R50. How many consumers will be dissatisfied (how large is excess demand)?

c Suppose the next game is between major rivals Orlando Pirates and Kaizer Chiefs (one of the most important games on the soccer calendar), and so demand jumps to $P = 2100 - (1/50)Q$. How many consumers will be unable to get tickets for the big game if prices are not allowed to increase above R50?

d How do the distortions of this price ceiling differ from the more typical case of upward-sloping supply?

8 The demand for apartments is $P = 12\,000 - Q$ and supply is $P = Q$ units. The government imposes rent control at $P = \text{R}3000\text{/mth}$. Suppose demand grows in the market to $P = 14\,000 - Q$:

a How is excess demand affected by the growth in demand for apartments?

b At what price would the government have to set the rent control to keep excess demand at the same level as prior to the growth in demand?

9 Suppose demand is $P = 600 - Q$ and supply is $P = Q$ in the soya bean market, where Q is tonnes of soya beans per year. The government sets a price support at $P = \text{R}500\text{/}$ tonnes and purchases any excess supply at this price. In response, as a long-run adjustment, farmers switch their crops from corn to soya beans, expanding supply to $P = (1/2)Q$.

a How does excess supply with the larger supply compare with excess supply prior to the farmers' switching of crops?

b How much more does the government have to spend to buy up the excess supply?

10 How would the equilibrium price and quantity change in the market depicted below if the marginal cost of every producer were to increase by R2/kg? (*Hint*: Recall the vertical interpretation of the supply curve discussed in Chapter 1.)

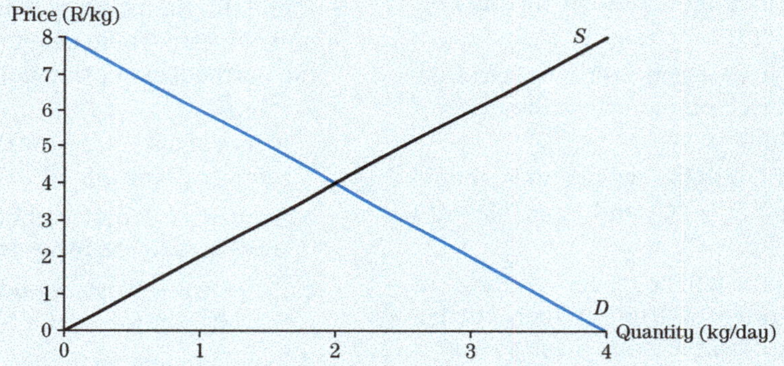

11 The demand curve of a firm that is currently selling 6 units is $P = 20 - 2Q_D$. Explain what consumer surplus means and calculate its size in this case.

12 The government, fearful that a titanium shortage could jeopardize national security, imposes a tax of R2/g on the retail price of this rare metal. It collects the tax from titanium sellers. The original supply and demand schedules for titanium are as shown in the diagram. Show, in the same diagram, how the short-run equilibrium price and quantity of titanium will be affected by the tax. Label all important points clearly.

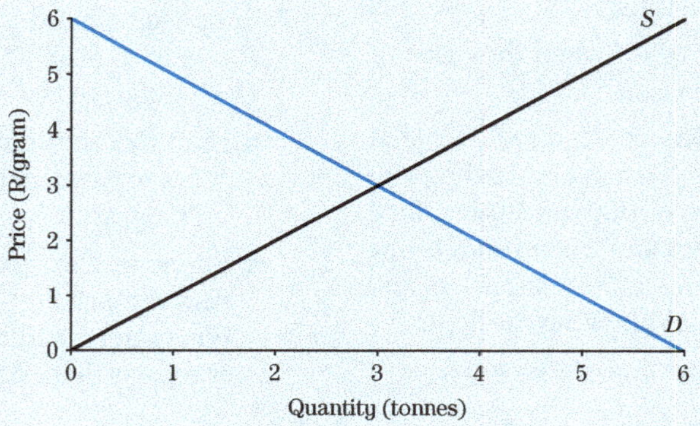

13 In the market for titanium described in Problem 12 (with no tax), suppose that a price floor of R4/g results in sales of only 2 tonnes/yr (with no tax). Describe a transaction that will make some buyers and sellers better off without harming others.

14 Suppose the titanium market in Problem 12, with a tax of R2/g, experiences growth in the demand for titanium because of new-found medical uses. The new demand curve is $P = 8 - Q$. Find the change in government tax revenue resulting from the heightened demand for titanium.

15 Suppose instead that the titanium market in Problem 13, with no tax but a price floor at R4/g, suffers a reduction in supply because of dwindling titanium reserves. The new supply curve is $P = 2 + Q$. How does excess supply change as a result of the reduction in supply? Is the price floor still binding (does it cause price to rise from its equilibrium level)?

16 Suppose that the demand and supply for DVD packs are given by the figure below:

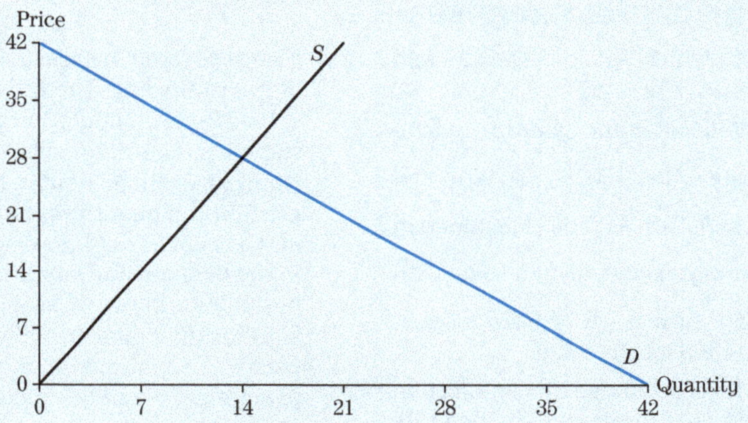

Assume further that the state government levies a tax of R9 on each DVD pack sold, collected from sellers.

- **a** What quantity of DVDs will be sold in equilibrium?
- **b** What price do buyers pay?
- **c** How much do buyers now spend in total?
- **d** How much money goes to the government?
- **e** Show the above results graphically.

17 For the tax described in Problem 16:

- **a** What fraction of the tax does the buyer bear?
- **b** What fraction of the tax does the seller bear?

18 Suppose the Minister of Trade and Industry has to decide whether to impose a quota or an import tax on imported Korean cars, and that you must advise him. You can choose between a 'voluntary' import quota on Korean cars sold in South Africa or the imposition of a higher import tax (tariff). Assuming the tariff is in the form of a constant tax T per Korean car sold in South Africa, and that T is chosen to produce the same quantity reduction as the quota, what will your advice to the Minister be?

19 Suppose that medical research studies have established that charred meat grilled over hot coals causes cancer. Since the government cannot easily regulate home cooking methods, it decides to place a 100 per cent tax at the retail level on charcoal briquettes to discourage the consumption of barbecued meat. Suppose daily demand for charcoal is $P = 120 - 2Q$ and supply is $P = 30 + Q$, where P is in rands per bag and Q is the number of 10 kg bags of charcoal sold weekly:

- **a** What are the before-tax and after-tax prices of charcoal?
- **b** What are the before-tax and after-tax quantities of charcoal?
- **c** How is the tax divided between sellers and buyers?

20 Supply is $P = 4Q$ and demand is $P = 20$, where P is price in rands per unit and Q is units of output per week:

- **a** Find the equilibrium price and quantity (using both algebra and a graph).

b If sellers must pay a tax of $T = \text{R}4\text{/unit}$, what happens to the quantity exchanged, the price buyers pay and the price sellers receive (net of the tax)?

c How is the burden of the tax distributed across buyers and sellers, and why?

21 Repeat Problem 20, but instead suppose the buyer pays the tax, demand is $P = 28 - Q$ and supply is $P = 20$.

22 Discuss the determinants of demand and supply and explain how they will affect demand and supply.

23 Explain how the burden of a tax levied on a product is distributed between the producer and consumers. Use graphs to illustrate your answer.

Answers to in-chapter exercises

2.1 $4Q^* = 12 - 2Q^*$, which yields $Q^* = 2$ and $P^* = 4Q^* = 8$, or $P^* = 12 - 2Q^* = 8$.

2.2 At a price of R90/lobster, the quantity demanded is 500 lobsters/day $\left(600 - \frac{1}{0.9}(90)\right)$ and the quantity supplied is 100 lobsters/day $\left(\frac{1}{0.9}(90)\right)$, making excess demand equal to 400 lobsters/day. At a price of R450/lobster, excess supply is 400 lobsters/day.

2.3 A rent control level set above the equilibrium price has no effect. The rent will settle at its equilibrium value of R4200/mth.

2.4 The report on mercury shifts the demand curve to the left. The fall in the price of diesel shifts the supply curve to the right. As shown in the diagrams below, the equilibrium price will go down – (a) and (b) – but the equilibrium quantity may go either up (b) or down (a). Without knowing the exact change in the demand and supply schedules, it is not possible to know what will happen with the equilibrium quantity. When given the mathematical equations of the demand and supply curves, it can be calculated precisely.

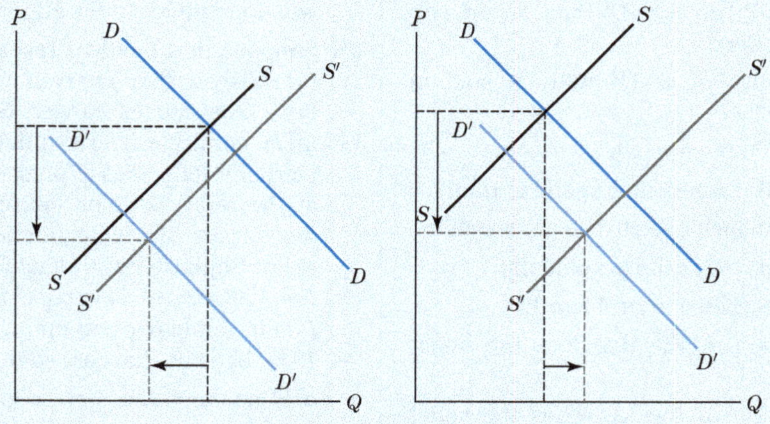

Exercise Answer 2.4

2.5
$$t_s + t_b = \frac{p^* - (p_1^* - T)}{T} + \frac{p_1^* - p^*}{T}$$
$$= \frac{P^* - (P_1^* - T) + (P_1^* - P^*)}{T}$$
$$= \frac{T}{T}$$
$$= 1$$

2.6 The original equilibrium price and quantity (when equating $4Q = 12 - 2Q$) are given by $P^* = 8$ and $Q^* = 2$, respectively. The supply curve with the tax is given by $P = 6 + 4Q_S$ (because the supply curve shifts vertically up by 6 units). Letting P' and Q' denote the new equilibrium values of price and quantity, we now have $6 + 4Q' = 12 - 2Q'$, which yields $Q' = 1$, $P' = 10$, where P' is the price paid by buyers. $P' - 6 = 4$ is the price received by sellers. Alternatively, the demand curve with a tax of 6 levied on buyers is given by $P = 6 - 2Q_D$ (because the demand curve shifts vertically down by 6 units), and we have $4Q' = 6' - 2Q'$, which again yields $Q' = 1$. $P'' = 4$, where P'' is the price received by sellers. $P'' + T = P'' + 6 = 10$ is the price paid by buyers.

2.7 True.

Buyer's share of tax with $D' = (a - P^*)/T$

Buyer's share of tax with $D = (b - P^*)/T$

Clearly with the steeper demand curve (D') more of the tax is paid by the seller than with demand curve D.

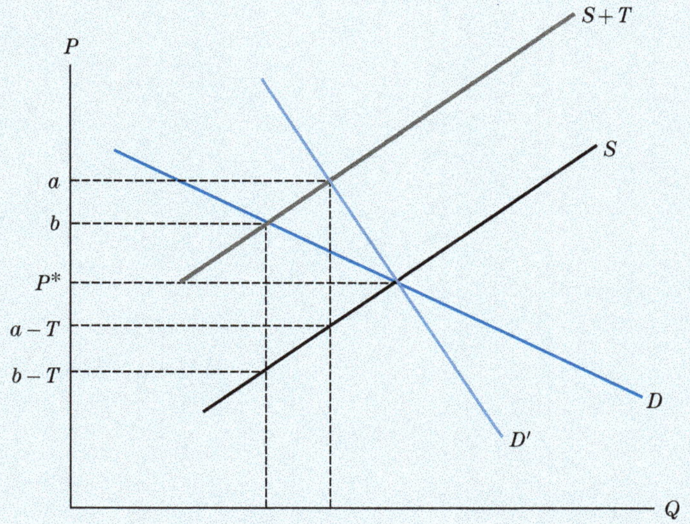

Part 2

The theory of consumer behaviour

Part contents

The next four chapters develop the theory of consumer behaviour. Chapter 3 is of special importance because it lays out the economic theory of how people with limited resources choose between competing alternatives. The methods and tools developed in this chapter recur throughout the remainder of the book, and indeed throughout all of economics. Chapter 4 shows how the theory of rational individual choice can be used to derive individual and market demand curves.

Chapter 5 shows how the rational choice model can be extended to cover choices that involve uncertainty or incomplete information. Finally, Chapter 6 looks at a variety of circumstances in which ordinary people tend to make irrational choices. Experience shows that being aware of this tendency helps people make better decisions.

Chapter

3

Rational consumer choice

Bruce Springsteen has sold 65 million albums in the USA and more than 120 million worldwide, received 20 Grammy Awards, two Golden Globes and an Academy Award. You have never seen a live performance by him. You have just received your monthly allowance via an electronic payment, and are on your way to the local music store to buy a ticket for a performance of Bruce Springsteen & the E Street Band in the FNB Stadium in Soweto. The price of a ticket is R400. In scenario 1, you draw cash at an ATM but lose the R400 on your way to the store. In scenario 2, you buy the ticket but lose it on your way home. Try to imagine your frame of mind in each scenario.

- **a** Would you proceed to buy the ticket in scenario 1?
- **b** Would you return to buy another ticket in scenario 2?

Similar questions[1] were recently put to a large class of undergraduates who had never taken an economics course. In response to the first question, 54 per cent answered yes, saying they would buy the ticket after losing the R400. But only 32 per cent answered yes to the second question – 68 per cent said they would *not* buy another ticket after losing the first one. There is, of course, no 'correct' answer to either question. The events described will have more of an impact, for example, on a poor consumer than on a rich one. Yet a moment's reflection reveals that your behaviour in one scenario logically should be exactly the same as in the other. After all, in both scenarios, the only economically relevant change is that you now have R400 less to spend than before. This might well mean that you will want to give up having the ticket; or it could mean saving less or giving up some other good that you would have bought. But your choice should not be

[1] These questions are patterned after similar questions posed by decision theorists Daniel Kahneman and Amos Tversky (see Chapter 6).

affected by the particular way in which you happened to become R400 poorer. In both scenarios the cost of the ticket is R400, and the benefit you will receive from attending the show is also the same. You should either buy the ticket in both scenarios, or not buy it in both. And yet, as noted, many people would choose differently in the two scenarios.

Chapter preview

Our task in this chapter is to set forth the economist's basic model for answering questions such as the ones posed above. This model is known as the theory of *rational consumer choice*. It underlies all individual purchase decisions, which in turn add up to the demand curves we worked with in the preceding chapter.

Rational choice theory begins with the assumption that consumers enter the marketplace with well-defined preferences. Taking prices as given, their task is to allocate their incomes to best serve these preferences. Three steps are required to carry out this task. Step 1 is to describe all the combinations of goods that the consumer wants to consume. In the process the consumer must be able to rank her preferences in some order of importance or in what order she prefers to satisfy them. Step 2 is to determine the various combinations of goods the consumer is *able* to buy. These combinations depend on both her income level and the prices of the goods. Step 3 is to select from among the feasible combinations the particular one that she *prefers* to all others. Formal development of these two elements of the theory will occupy our attention throughout this chapter. We begin with consumer preferences before we set off to describe the set of possibilities that will be determined by prices and income.

Consumer preferences

For simplicity, let us begin by considering a simplistic world with only two goods: shelter and food. A **preference ordering** enables the consumer to rank different bundles of goods in terms of their desirability or order of preference. Consider two bundles, A and B. For concreteness, suppose that A contains 4 m^2/wk of shelter and 2 kg/wk of food, whereas B has 3 m^2/wk of shelter and 3 kg/wk of food. Knowing nothing about a consumer's preferences, we can say nothing about which of these bundles he will prefer. A has more shelter but less food than B. Someone who spends a lot of time at home would probably choose A, whereas someone with a rapid metabolism might be more likely to choose B.

Preference ordering A ranking of all possible consumption bundles in order of preference.

In general, we assume that, for any two such bundles, the consumer is able to make one of three possible statements: (1) A is preferred to B; (2) B is preferred to A; (3) A and B are equally attractive. The preference ordering enables the consumer to rank different bundles, but not to make more precise quantitative statements about their relative desirability. Thus the consumer might be able to say that he prefers A to B, but not that A provides twice as much satisfaction as B.

Preference orderings often differ widely among consumers. One person will like Rachmaninoff, another Johnny Clegg. Despite these differences, however, most preference orderings share several important features. More specifically, economists generally assume four simple properties of preference orderings: *completeness*, *more-is-better*, *transitivity* and *convexity*. These properties allow us to construct the concise analytical representation of preferences we need for the budget allocation problem.

Completeness

A preference ordering is *complete* if it enables the consumer to rank all possible combinations of goods and services. Taken literally, the completeness assumption is never satisfied, for there are many goods we know too little about to be able to evaluate. It is nonetheless a useful simplifying assumption for the analysis of choices among bundles of goods with which consumers are familiar. Its real intent is to rule out instances like the one portrayed in the fable of Buridan's ass. The hungry animal was unable to choose between two bales of hay in front of him, and starved to death as a result.

More-is-better

The more-is-better property means simply that, other things being equal, more of a good is preferred to less. We can, of course, think of examples of more of something making us worse rather than better off (as with someone who's been drinking too much during rag in the beginning of the year). But these examples usually contemplate some sort of practical difficulty, such as having a self-control problem or being unable to store a good for future use. As long as people can freely store or dispose of goods they don't want, having more of something can't make them worse off.

As an example of the application of the more-is-better assumption, consider two bundles: A, which has 12 m^2/wk of shelter and 10 kg/wk of food, and B, which has 12 m^2/wk of shelter and 11 kg/wk of food. The assumption tells us that B is preferred to A because it has more food and no less shelter. Obviously, the consumer will also choose an alternative bundle if it contains more units of both goods.

Transitivity

If you like steak better than hamburger and hamburger better than hot dogs, you are probably someone who likes steak better than hot dogs. To say that a consumer's preference ordering is transitive means that, for any three bundles A, B and C, if he prefers A to B and B to C, then he always prefers A to C. For example, suppose A is (4, 2), B is (3, 3) and C is (2, 4). If you prefer (4, 2) over (3, 3) and (3, 3) over (2, 4), then you must prefer (4, 2) over (2, 4). The preference relationship is thus assumed to be like the relationship used to compare people's heights. If Eben Etzebeth is taller than Bakkies Botha and Bakkies is taller than Pieter-Steph du Toit, we know that Eben must be taller than Pieter-Steph.

Not all comparative relationships are transitive. Some seasons, the Natal Sharks defeat the Blue Bulls, and the Blue Bulls defeat the Stormers, but that doesn't tell us that the Natal Sharks will necessarily defeat the Stormers.

Transitivity is a simple consistency property, and applies as well to the relation 'equally attractive as' and to any combination of it and the 'preferred to' relation. For example, if A is equally attractive as B and B is equally attractive as C, it follows that A is equally attractive as C. Similarly, if A is preferred to B and B is equally attractive as C, it follows that A is preferred to C.

The transitivity assumption can be justified as eliminating the potential for a 'money pump' problem. To illustrate, suppose you prefer A to B and B to C, but you also prefer C to A, so that your preferences are intransitive. If you start with C, you would trade C for B, trade B for A and then trade A for C. This cycle could continue forever. If in each stage you were charged a tiny fee for the trade, you would eventually transfer all your money to the other trader. Clearly, such preferences are problematic.

As reasonable as the transitivity property sounds, we shall see examples in later chapters of behaviour that seems inconsistent with it. But it is an accurate description of preferences in most instances. Unless otherwise stated, we shall adopt it.

Convexity

Mixtures of goods are preferable to extremes. If you are indifferent between two extreme bundles A and B (i.e. some of the one and nothing of the other), your preferences are convex if you prefer a bundle that contains half of A and half of B (or any other mixture) to either of the original bundles. For example, suppose you are indifferent between A = (4, 0) and B = (0, 4). If your preferences are convex, you will prefer the bundle (2, 2) to each of the more extreme bundles. This property conveys the sense that we like balance in our mix of consumption goods.

Indifference curves

Let us consider some implications of these assumptions about preference orderings. Most important, they enable us to generate a graphical description of the consumer's preferences. To see how, consider first the bundle A in Fig. 3.1, which has 12 m^2/wk of shelter and 10 kg/wk of food. The more-is-better assumption tells us that all bundles to the northeast of A are preferred to A, and that A, in turn, is preferred to all those to the southwest of A. Thus the more-is-better assumption tells us that Z, which has 28 m^2/wk of shelter and 12 kg/wk of food, is preferred to A, and that A, in turn, is preferred to W, which has only 6 m^2/wk of shelter and 4 kg/wk of food.

Now consider the set of bundles that lie along the line joining W and Z. Because Z is preferred to A and A is preferred to W, it follows that, as we move from Z to W, we must encounter a bundle that is equally attractive as A. (The intuition behind this claim is the same as the intuition that tells us that if we climb on any continuous path on a mountainside from one point at 500 m above sea level to another at 1000 m, we must pass through every intermediate altitude along the way.) Let B denote the bundle that is equally attractive as A, and suppose it contains 17 m^2/wk of shelter and 8 kg/wk of food. (The exact amounts of each good in B will of course depend on the specific consumer whose preferences we are talking about.) The more-is-better assumption also tells us that there will be only one such bundle on the straight line between W and Z. Points on that line to the northeast of B are all better than B; those to the southwest of B are all worse.

Figure 3.1 Generating equally preferred bundles

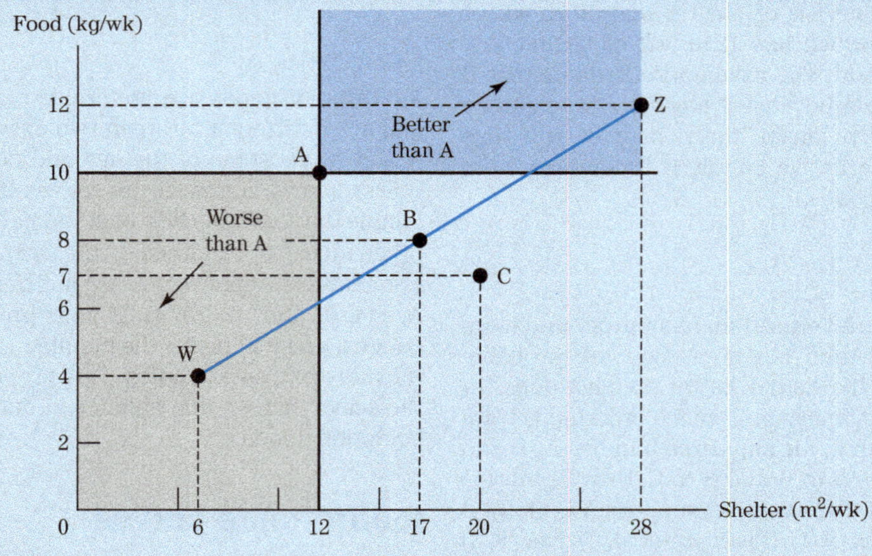

Z is preferred to A because it has more of each good than has A. For the same reason, A is preferred to W. It follows that, on the line joining W and Z, there must be a bundle B that is equally attractive as A. In similar fashion, we can find a bundle C that is equally attractive as B.

In precisely the same fashion, we can find another point – call it C – that is equally attractive as B. C is shown as the bundle (20, 7), where the specific quantities in C again depend on the preferences of the consumer under consideration. By the transitivity assumption, we know that C is also equally attractive as A (since C is equally attractive as B, which is equally attractive as A).

We can repeat this process as often as we like, and the end result will be an **indifference curve**, a set of bundles all of which are equally attractive as the original bundle A, and hence also equally attractive as one another. This set is shown as the curve labelled I_0 in Fig. 3.2. It is called an indifference curve because the consumer is indifferent among all the bundles that lie along it. Any two combinations of goods on an indifference curve give exactly the same satisfaction to the consumer. (Remember that we draw an indifference curve for an *individual consumer*, and not for the community as a whole.)

Indifference curve A set of bundles among which the consumer is indifferent.

An indifference curve also permits us to compare the satisfaction implicit in bundles that lie along it with those that lie either above or below it. It permits us, for example, to compare bundle C (20, 7) to bundle K (23, 4), which has less food and more shelter than has C. We know that we are indifferent between C and D (25, 6) because both bundles lie on the same indifference curve. D, in turn, is preferred to K because of the more-is-better assumption: it has 2 m^2/wk more shelter and 2 kg/wk more food than has K. Transitivity, finally, tells us that since C is equally attractive as D and D is preferred to K, C must be preferred to K.

By analogous reasoning, we can say that bundle L is preferred to A. *In general, bundles that lie above an indifference curve are all preferred to the bundles that lie on it. Similarly, bundles that lie on an indifference curve are all preferred to those that lie below it.*

The completeness property of preferences implies that there is an indifference curve that passes through every possible bundle. That being so, we can represent a consumer's preferences with an **indifference map**, an example of which is shown in Fig. 3.3. This indifference map shows just four of the infinitely many indifference curves that, taken together, yield a complete description of the consumer's preferences.

Indifference map A representative sample of the set of a consumer's indifference curves, used as a graphical summary of her preference ordering.

Figure 3.2 An indifference curve

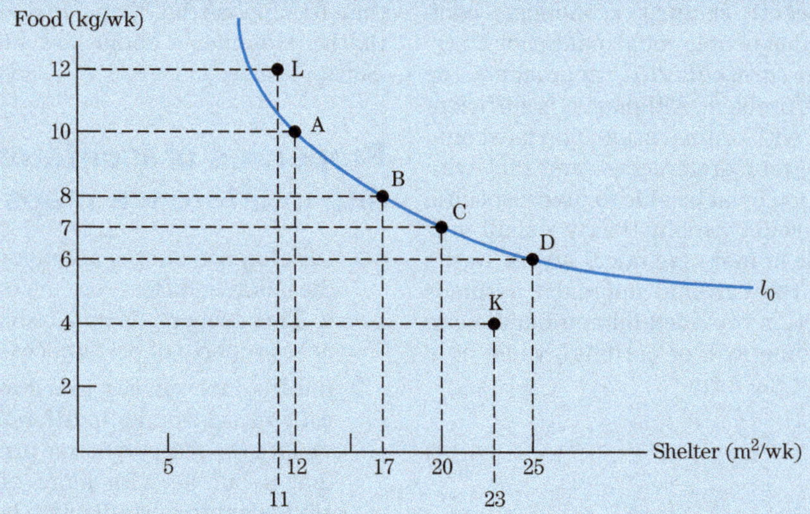

An indifference curve is a set of bundles that the consumer considers equally attractive. Any bundle, such as L, that lies above an indifference curve is preferred to any bundle on the indifference curve. Any bundle on the indifference curve, in turn, is preferred to any bundle, such as K, that lies below the indifference curve.

The numbers $I_1, \ldots, I_4$ in Fig. 3.3 are index values used to denote the order of preference that corresponds to the respective indifference curves. Any index numbers would do equally well provided they satisfied the property $I_1 < I_2 < I_3 < I_4$. In representing the consumer's preferences, what really counts is the *ranking* of the indifference curves, not the particular numerical values we assign to them.

Cardinal versus ordinal utility

In our discussion so far we have assumed that people are able to rank each possible bundle in an order of preference. This is called the *ordinal utility* approach, and does not require that people be able to make quantitative statements about how much they like various bundles. Thus it assumes that a consumer will always be able to say whether he prefers A to B, but that he may not

Figure 3.3 Part of an indifference map

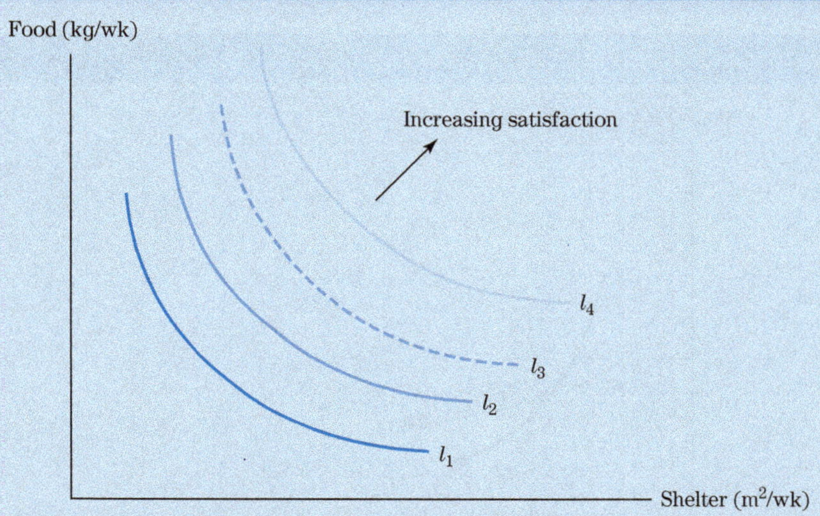

The entire set of a consumer's indifference curves is called the consumer's indifference map. Bundles on any indifference curve are less preferred than bundles on a higher indifference curve, and more preferred than bundles on a lower indifference curve.

be able to make such statements as 'A is 6.43 times as good as B'.

In the nineteenth century, economists commonly assumed that people could make such statements. This is the *cardinal utility* approach to the consumer choice problem. Although it is sufficient if you know that with ordinal utility you must only be able to rank your preferences, and that with cardinal utility you must be able to give a specific value to your level of satisfaction, we shall now briefly discuss it in more technical terms. In the two-good case, the cardinal approach assumes that the satisfaction provided by any bundle can be assigned a numerical, or cardinal, value by a utility function of the form

$$U = U(X,Y) \tag{3.1}$$

where X and Y are the two goods.

The concept of the indifference map was first discussed by Francis Edgeworth, who derived it from a cardinal utility function in the manner described above. It took the combined insights of Vilfredo Pareto, Irving Fisher and John Hicks to establish that Edgeworth's apparatus was not uniquely dependent on a supporting cardinal utility function. As we will see, the only aspect of a consumer's preferences that matters is the shape and location of her indifference curves. Consumer choice turns out to be completely independent of the labels we assign to these indifference curves, provided only that higher curves correspond to higher levels of utility.

Modern economists prefer the ordinal approach because it rests on much weaker assumptions than the cardinal approach. That is, it is much easier to imagine that people can rank different bundles than to suppose that they can make precise quantitative statements about how much satisfaction each provides.

Properties of indifference curves and indifference maps

1 Indifference curves are ubiquitous. Any bundle has an indifference curve passing through it. This property is ensured by the completeness property of preferences.

2 Indifference curves are downward sloping. An upward-sloping indifference curve would violate the more-is-better property by saying that a bundle with more of both goods is equivalent to a bundle with less of both.

3 Indifference curves (from the same indifference map) cannot cross. To see why, suppose that two indifference curves did, in fact, cross as in Fig. 3.4. The following statements would then have to be true:

- Utility at E is equal to utility at D (because they both lie on indifference curve I_1).
- Utility at D is equal to utility at F (because they both lie on indifference curve I_2).
- Utility at E is equal to utility at F (by the transitivity assumption).

But we also know that F is preferred to E (because more is better). Because it is not possible for the statements *utility at E is equal to utility at F* and *utility at F is greater*

Figure 3.4 Why two indifference curves do not cross

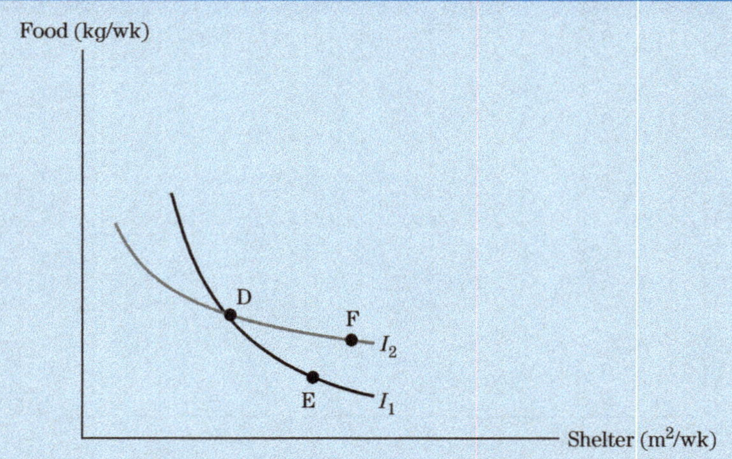

If indifference curves were to cross, they would have to violate at least one of the assumed properties of preference orderings.

Figure 3.5 The marginal rate of substitution

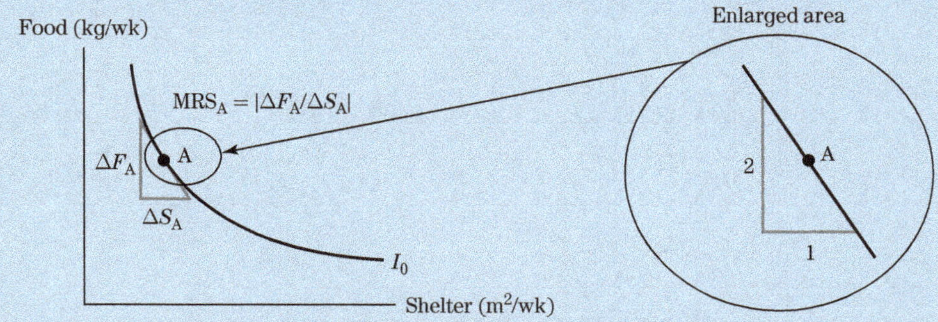

The MRS at any point along an indifference curve is defined as the absolute value of the slope of the indifference curve at that point. In the figure it is the amount of food the consumer must be given to compensate for the loss of 1 unit of shelter.

than utility at E to be true simultaneously, the assumption that two indifference curves cross thus implies a contradiction. The conclusion is that the original proposition must be true, namely, that two indifference curves cannot cross.

4 Indifference curves become less steep as we move downwards and to the right along them. As discussed below, this property is implied by the convexity property of preferences. As we shall explain in the next section, this is the result of the diminishing marginal rate of substitution (MRS).

Trade-offs between goods

An important property of a consumer's preferences is the rate at which she is willing to exchange, or 'trade off', one good for another. This rate is represented at any point on an indifference curve by the **marginal rate of substitution (MRS)**, which is defined as the absolute value of the slope of the indifference curve at that point. In the left panel of Fig. 3.5, for example, the marginal rate of substitution at point A is given by the absolute value of the slope of the tangent to the indifference curve at A, which is the ratio $\Delta F_A/\Delta S_A$.[2] (The notation ΔF_A means 'small change in food from the amount at point A'.) If we take ΔF_A units of food away from the consumer at point A, we have to give her ΔS_A additional units of shelter to make her just as well off as before. The right panel of the figure shows an enlargement of the region surrounding bundle A. If the marginal rate of substitution at A is 2, this means that the consumer must be given 2 kg/wk of food to make up for the loss of 1 m^2/wk of shelter to keep his level of satisfaction unchanged.

Marginal rate of substitution (MRS) At any point on an indifference curve, the rate at which the consumer is willing to exchange the good measured along the vertical axis for the good measured along the horizontal axis; equal to the absolute value of the slope of the indifference curve.

The slope of an indifference curve, or MRS, tells us the rate at which we can substitute food for shelter without changing total satisfaction. Put another way, the slope of the budget constraint is the marginal cost of shelter in terms of food, and the MRS is the marginal benefit of shelter in terms of food.

The convexity property of preferences tells us that, along any indifference curve, the more a consumer has of one good, the more she must be given of that good before she will be willing to give up a unit of the other good. Stated differently, MRS declines as we move downwards to the right along an indifference curve. Indifference curves with diminishing rates of marginal substitution are thus convex when viewed from the origin.

In Fig. 3.6, note that at bundle A food is relatively plentiful, and the consumer would be willing to sacrifice 3 kg/wk of it in order to obtain an additional square metre of shelter. Her MRS at A is 3. At C, the quantities of food and shelter are more balanced, and there she would be willing to give up only 1 kg/wk of food to obtain an additional square metre of shelter. Her MRS at C is 1. Finally, note that food is relatively scarce at D, and there

[2] More formally, the indifference curve may be expressed as a function $Y = Y(X)$, and the MRS at point A is defined as the absolute value of the derivative of the indifference curve at that point: $MRS = |dY(X)/dX|$.

Figure 3.6 Diminishing marginal rate of substitution

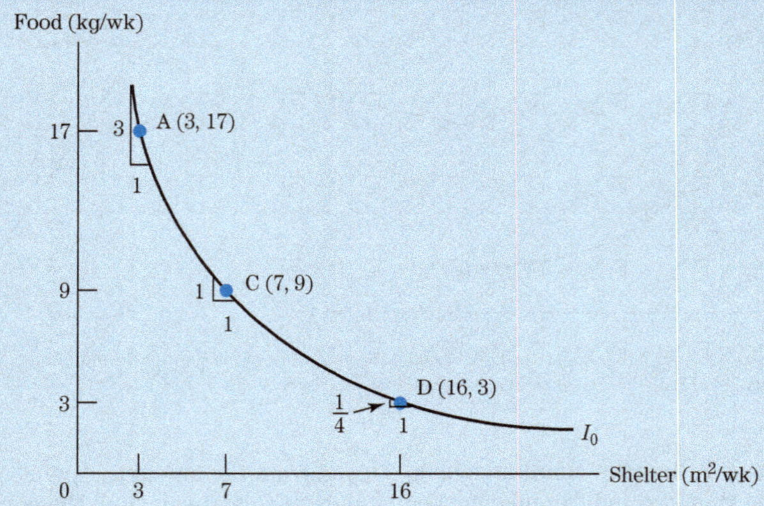

The more food the consumer has, the more she is willing to give up to obtain an additional unit of shelter. The marginal rates of substitution at bundles A, C and D are 3, 1 and $\frac{1}{4}$, respectively.

she would be willing to give up only $\frac{1}{4}$ kg/wk of food to obtain an additional unit of shelter. Her MRS at D is $\frac{1}{4}$.

Intuitively, diminishing MRS means that consumers like variety. We are usually willing to give up goods we already have a lot of to obtain more of those goods we now have only a little of. It is also linked to the fact that the marginal utility of a good decreases as more of that good is consumed.

Using indifference curves to describe preferences

To get a feel for how indifference maps describe a consumer's preferences, let us see how indifference maps can be used to portray differences in preferences between two consumers. Suppose, for example, that both Poppie and Sarah like sushi, but that Sarah likes apples much more than does Poppie. This difference in their tastes is captured by the different slopes of their indifference curves in Fig. 3.7. Note in Fig. 3.7(a), which shows Poppie's indifference map, that Poppie would be willing to exchange 1 kg of sushi for 1 kg of apples at bundle A. But at the corresponding bundle in Fig. 3.7(b), which shows Sarah's indifference map, we see that Sarah would trade 2 kg of sushi for 1 kg of apples. Their difference in preferences shows up clearly in this difference in their marginal rates of substitution of sushi for apples.

The opportunity set or budget constraint

Up till now we have only looked at what the consumer would want to consume, but now we are going to take into account what the consumer can afford to buy. For simplicity, we are again considering a world with only two goods, shelter and food. A **bundle** of goods is the term used to describe a particular combination of shelter, measured in square metres (m^2) per week, and food, measured in kilograms (kg) per week. In Fig. 3.8, one bundle (bundle A) consists of 5 m^2/wk of shelter and 7 kg/wk of food, while another (bundle B) consists of 3 m^2/wk of shelter and 8 kg/wk of food. In general, (S_0, F_0) will denote the bundle with S_0 m^2/wk of shelter and F_0 kg/wk of food. By convention, the first number of the pair in any bundle represents the good measured along the horizontal axis, and the second one the good on the vertical axis. In the previous section we focused on whether A will be preferred to B, or vice versa. Here we are interested in whether we can afford those bundles.

> **Bundle** A particular combination of two or more goods.

Note that the units on both axes are *flows*, which means physical quantities per unit of time – kilograms per week, square metres per week. Consumption is always measured as a flow. It is important to keep track of the time dimension

Figure 3.7 People with different tastes

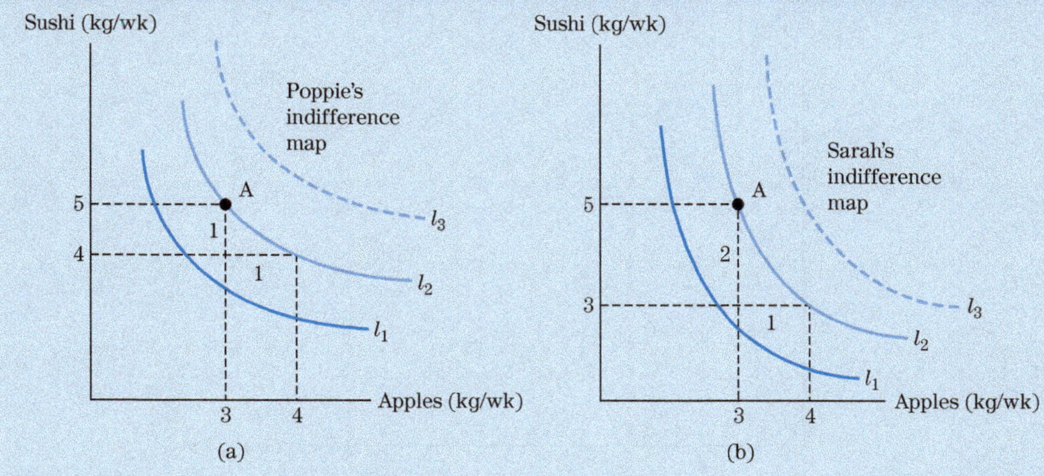

Relatively speaking, Poppie is a sushi lover and Sarah an apple lover. This difference shows up in the fact that, for any given bundle, Poppie's marginal rate of substitution of sushi for apples is smaller than Sarah's.

because without it there would be no way to evaluate whether a given quantity of consumption was large or small. (Suppose all you know is that your food consumption is 2 kg. If that's how much you eat each day, it's a lot. But if that's all you eat in a month, you're not likely to survive for long.)[3]

Suppose the consumer's income is $M =$ R2000/wk, all of which she spends on some combination of food and shelter. (Note that income is also a flow.) Suppose further that the prices of shelter and food are $P_S =$ R100/m^2 and $P_F =$ R200/kg, respectively. If the consumer spent all her income on shelter, she could buy $M/P_S =$ (R2000/wk) ÷ (R100/m^2) = 20 m^2/wk. That is, she could buy the bundle consisting of 20 m^2/wk of shelter and 0 kg/wk of food, denoted (20, 0). Thus 20 m^2/wk is the maximum amount of shelter the consumer can buy with an income of R2000/wk. Alternatively, suppose the consumer spent all her income on food. She would then get the bundle consisting of $M/P_F =$ (R2000/wk) ÷ (R200/kg), which is 10 kg/wk of food and 0 m^2/wk of shelter, denoted (0, 10). Therefore, 10 kg/wk is the maximum amount of food the consumer can purchase with an income of R2000/wk.

In Fig. 3.9 these polar cases are labelled K and L, respectively. The consumer is also able to purchase any other bundle that lies along the straight line that joins points K and L. (Verify, for example, that the bundle (12, 4) lies on this same line.) This line is the budget constraint, and is known as the **budget line** (labelled B in the diagram). This line represents the maximum combinations of the two goods that the consumer can afford. No combination of goods that lies to the right of the budget line can be afforded.

> **Budget line** The set of all bundles that exactly exhaust the consumer's income at given prices. Also called the *budget constraint.*

Recall from your school maths that the slope of a straight line is $(\Delta Y/\Delta X)$. Here, note that the slope of the budget constraint is its vertical intercept divided by its horizontal intercepts: $(10\text{ kg/wk})/20\text{ m}^2/\text{wk} = -\frac{1}{2}\text{ kg/m}^2$. The minus sign signifies that the budget line falls as it moves to the right – that it has a negative slope. More generally, if M denotes the consumer's weekly income, and P_S and P_F denote the prices of shelter and food, respectively, the horizontal and vertical intercepts will be given by (M/P_S) and (M/P_F), respectively. Thus the general formula for the slope of the budget constraint is given by $-(M/P_F)/(M/P_S) = -P_S/P_F$, which is simply the negative of the price ratio of the two goods (in other words, the price of the product on the x-axis divided by the price of the product on the y-axis). Given their respective prices, it is the rate at which food can be exchanged for shelter. Thus, in Fig. 3.9, 1 kg of food can be exchanged for 2 m^2 of shelter. In the language of opportunity cost from Chapter 1, we

[3] The flow aspect of consumption also helps us alleviate any concern about goods not being divisible. If you consume 1.5 kg/mth, then you consume 18 kg/year, which is a whole number.

Figure 3.8 Two bundles of goods

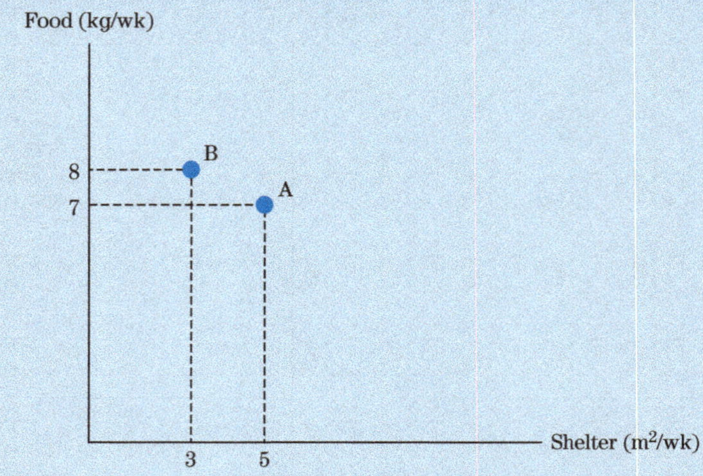

A bundle is a specific combination of goods. Bundle A has 5 units of shelter and 7 units of food. Bundle B has 3 units of shelter and 8 units of food.

would say that the opportunity cost of an additional square metre of shelter is $P_S/P_F = \frac{1}{2}$ kg of food.

In addition to being able to buy any of the bundles along her budget constraint, the consumer is also able to purchase any bundle that lies within the *budget triangle* bounded by it and the two axes. D is one such bundle in Fig. 3.9. Bundle D costs R1300/wk, which is well below the consumer's income of R2000/wk. The bundles on or within the budget triangle are also referred to as the **affordable set**, or *feasible set*. Bundles like E that lie outside the budget triangle are said to be *infeasible* or *unaffordable*. At a cost of R2800/wk, E is simply beyond the consumer's reach.

Affordable set Bundles on or below the budget line; bundles for which the required expenditure at given prices is less than or equal to the income available.

If S and F denote the quantities of shelter and food, respectively, the budget constraint must satisfy the following equation:

$$P_S S + P_F F = M \tag{3.2}$$

Figure 3.9 The budget line, or budget constraint

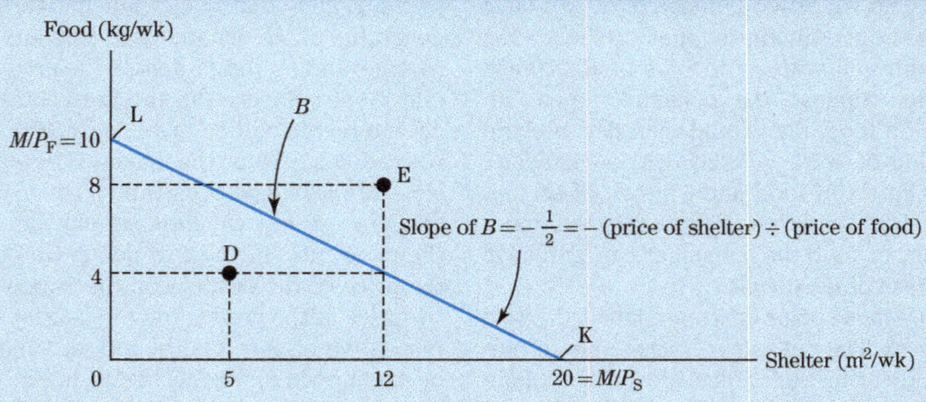

Line B describes the set of all bundles the consumer can purchase for given values of income and price. Its slope is the negative of the price of shelter divided by the price of food. In absolute value, this slope is the opportunity cost of an additional unit of shelter – the number of units of food that must be sacrificed in order to purchase one additional unit of shelter at market prices.

Figure 3.10 The effect of a rise in the price of shelter

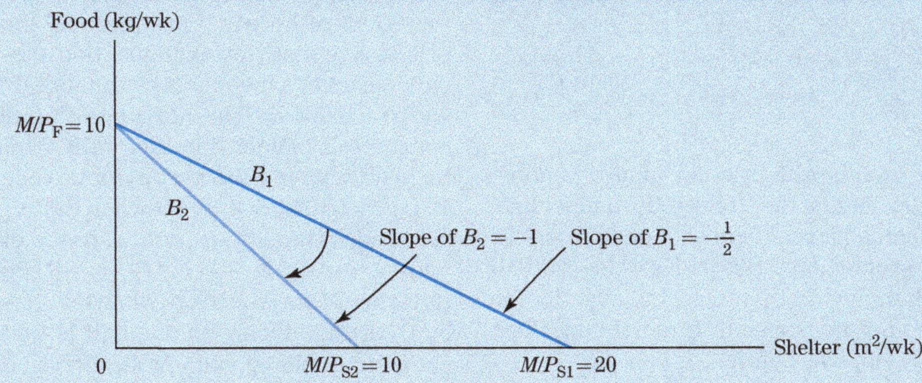

When shelter goes up in price, the vertical intercept of the budget line remains the same. The original budget line rotates inwards about this intercept.

which says simply that the consumer's weekly expenditure on shelter ($P_S S$) plus her weekly expenditure on food ($P_F F$) must add up to her weekly income (M). To express the budget constraint in the manner conventionally used to represent the formula for a straight line, we solve Eq. 3.2 for F in terms of S, which yields

$$F = \frac{M}{P_F} - \frac{P_S}{P_F} S \qquad (3.3)$$

Equation 3.3 is another way of seeing that the vertical intercept of the budget constraint is given by M/P_F and its slope by $-(P_S/P_F)$. The equation for the budget constraint in Fig. 3.9 is $F = 10 - \frac{1}{2}S$.

Budget shifts due to price or income changes

Price changes

The slope and position of the budget line are fully determined by the consumer's income and the prices of the respective goods. Change any one of these factors and we have a new budget constraint. Figure 3.10 shows the effect of an increase in the price of shelter from $P_{S1} = \text{R}100/\text{m}^2$ to $P_{S2} = \text{R}200/\text{m}^2$. Since both weekly income and the price of food are unchanged, the vertical intercept of the consumer's budget constraint stays the same. The rise in the price of shelter rotates the budget line inwards about this intercept, as shown in the diagram.

Note in Fig. 3.10 that, even though the price of food has not changed, the new budget line, B_2, curtails not only the amount of shelter the consumer can buy but also the amount of food.[4]

Exercise 3.1

Show the effect on the budget line B_1 in Fig. 3.10 of a fall in the price of shelter from R100/m^2 to R80/m^2.

In Exercise 3.1 you saw that a fall in the price of shelter (which is on the horizontal axis) again leaves the vertical intercept of the budget line unchanged. This time the budget line rotates outwards. Note also in Exercise 3.1 that, although the price of food remains unchanged, the new budget line enables the consumer to buy bundles that contain not only more shelter but also more food than she could afford on the original budget line. In general, if the product on the x-axis becomes more expensive, the budget line becomes steeper, but if the price of the product on the x-axis decreases, the budget line becomes flatter.

The following exercise illustrates how changing the price of the good on the vertical axis affects the budget constraint.

[4] The single exception to this statement involves the vertical intercept (0, 10), which lies on both the original and the new budget constraints.

Exercise 3.2

Show the effect on the budget line B_1 in Fig. 3.10 of a rise in the price of food from R200/kg to R400/kg.

When we change the price of only one good, we necessarily change the slope of the budget line, $-P_S/P_F$. The same is true if we change both prices by different proportions. But as Exercise 3.3 will illustrate, changing both prices by exactly the same proportion gives rise to a new budget line with the same slope as before.

Exercise 3.3

Show the effect on the budget line B_1 in Fig. 3.10 of a rise in the price of food from R200/kg to R400/kg and a rise in the price of shelter from R100/m^2 to R200/m^2.

Note from Exercise 3.3 that the effect of doubling the prices of both food and shelter is to shift the budget line to the left and parallel to the original budget constraint. The important lesson of this exercise is that the slope of a budget line tells us only about *relative prices*, and nothing about prices in absolute terms. When the prices of food and shelter change in the same proportion, the opportunity cost of shelter in terms of food remains the same as before. If the price of both goods increases by the same *percentage* the budget line shifts parallel to the left, and when both prices decrease by the same *percentage* the budget line shifts parallel to the right.

Income changes

The effect of a change in income is much like the effect of an equal proportional change in all prices. Suppose, for example, that our hypothetical consumer's income is cut by half, from R2000/wk to R1000/wk. The horizontal intercept of the consumer's budget line then falls from 20 m^2/wk to 10 m^2/wk, and the vertical intercept falls from 10 kg/wk to 5 kg/wk, as shown in Fig. 3.11. Thus the new budget line, B_2, is parallel to the old, B_1, each with a slope of $-\frac{1}{2}(P_S/P_F) = -$R1 000/R2 000). In terms of its effect on what the consumer can buy, cutting income by one-half is thus no different from doubling each price. Precisely the same budget line results from both changes.

Exercise 3.4

Show the effect on the budget line B_1 in Fig. 3.11 of an increase in income from R2000/wk to R2400/wk.

Exercise 3.4 illustrates that an increase in income shifts the budget line parallel outwards. As in the case of an income reduction, the slope of the budget line remains the same.

Budgets involving more than two goods

In the examples discussed so far, we simplified the world to one where only two different goods existed. The reality is not so simple. In its most general form, the consumer budgeting problem can be posed as a choice between not two but N different goods, where N can be an indefinitely

Figure 3.11 The effect of cutting income by half

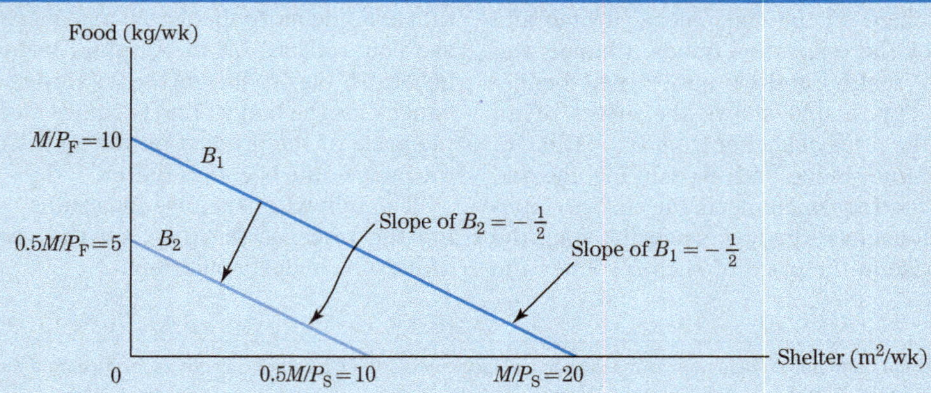

Both horizontal and vertical intercepts fall by half. The new budget line has the same slope as the old, but is closer to the origin.

large number. With only two goods ($N = 2$), the budget constraint is a straight line, as we just saw. With three goods ($N = 3$), it is a plane. When we have more than three goods, the budget constraint becomes what mathematicians call a *hyper plane*, or *multidimensional plane*. However, we are not very good at visualizing surfaces that have more than three dimensions.

The nineteenth-century economist Alfred Marshall proposed a disarmingly simple solution to this problem. It is to view the consumer's choice as being one between a particular good – call it X – and an amalgam of other goods, denoted Y. This amalgam is generally called the **composite good**. By convention, the units of the composite good are defined so that its price is R1.00 per unit. This convention enables us to think of the composite good as the amount of income the consumer has left over after buying good X. Equivalently, it is the amount the consumer spends on goods other than X. For the moment, all the examples we consider will be ones in which consumers spend all their incomes. In Chapter 4 we shall use the rational choice model to analyse the decision to save.

Composite good
In a choice between a good X and numerous other goods, the amount of money the consumer spends on those other goods.

To illustrate how the composite good concept is used, suppose the consumer has an income of RM/wk, and the price of X is P_X. The consumer's budget constraint may then be represented as a straight line in the X, Y plane, as shown in Fig. 3.12. Because the price of a unit of the composite good is R1.00, a consumer who devotes all his income to it will be able to buy M units. All this means is that he will have RM available to spend on other goods if he buys no X. Alternatively, if he spends his entire income on X, he will be able to purchase the bundle (M/P_X, 0). Since the price of Y is assumed to be R1.00/unit, the slope of the budget line is simply $-P_X$.

As before, the budget line summarizes the various combinations of bundles that exhaust the consumer's income. Thus the consumer can have X_1 units of X and Y_1 units of the composite good in Fig. 3.12, or X_2 and Y_2, or any other combination that lies on the budget line.

Kinked budget lines

The budget constraints we have worked with so far could be illustrated with straight lines. When relative prices are constant, the opportunity cost of one good in terms of any other is the same, no matter what bundle of goods we already have. But sometimes budget constraints are kinked lines. To illustrate, consider the following example of quantity discounts.

Exercise 3.5

Suppose Eskom charges R0.75/kWh for the first 1000 kWh of power purchased by a residential consumer each month, but R1.50/kWh each for all additional kilowatt-hours. For a residential consumer with a monthly income of R6000, graph the budget constraint for electric power and the composite good. What if the rate jumps to R1.50/kWh for *all* kilowatt-hours if power consumption in a month exceeds 1 000 kWh (where the higher rate applies to all, not just the additional, kilowatt-hours)?

Figure 3.12 The budget line with the composite good

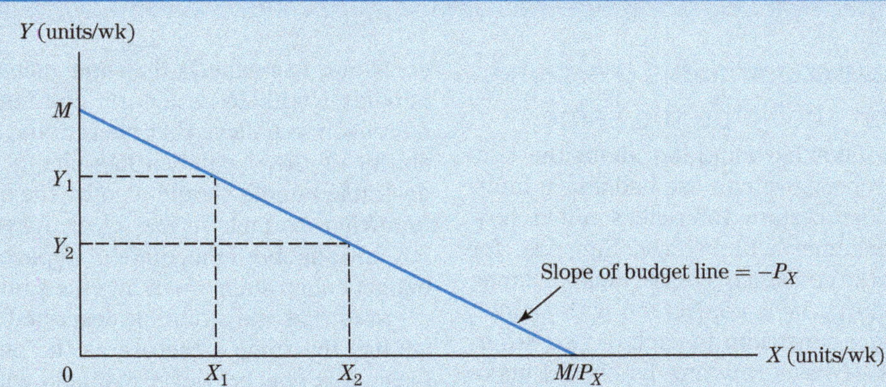

The vertical axis measures the amount of money spent each week on all goods other than X.

Example 3.1

Assume Eskom charges R1.50 per kilowatt-hour (kWh) for the first 1000 kWh of power purchased by a residential customer each month, but only R0.75/kWh for all additional kWh. For a residential customer with a monthly income of R6000, graph the budget constraint for electric power and the composite good.

If the consumer buys no electric power, he will have R6000/mth to spend on other goods. Thus the vertical intercept of his budget constraint is (0, 6000). As shown in Fig. 3.13, for each of the first 1000 kWh he buys, he must give up R1.50, which means that the slope of his budget constraint starts out at −1.5. At 1000 kWh/mth the price falls to R0.75/kWh, which means that the slope of his budget constraint from that point rightwards is only $-\frac{3}{4}$ (or −0.75).

Note that along the budget constraint shown in Fig. 3.13, the opportunity cost of electricity depends on how much the consumer has already purchased. Consider a consumer who now uses 1020 kWh each month, and is trying to decide, because of the high crime rates in South Africa, whether to leave his front porch light on all night, which would result in additional consumption of 20 kWh/mth. Leaving his light on will cost him an extra R15/mth. Had his usual consumption been only 980 kWh/mth, however, the cost of leaving the front porch light on would have been R30/mth. On the basis of this difference, we can predict that people who already use a lot of electricity (more than 1000 kWh/mth) should be more likely than others to leave their porch lights burning at night.

Figure 3.13 A quantity discount gives rise to a non-linear budget constraint

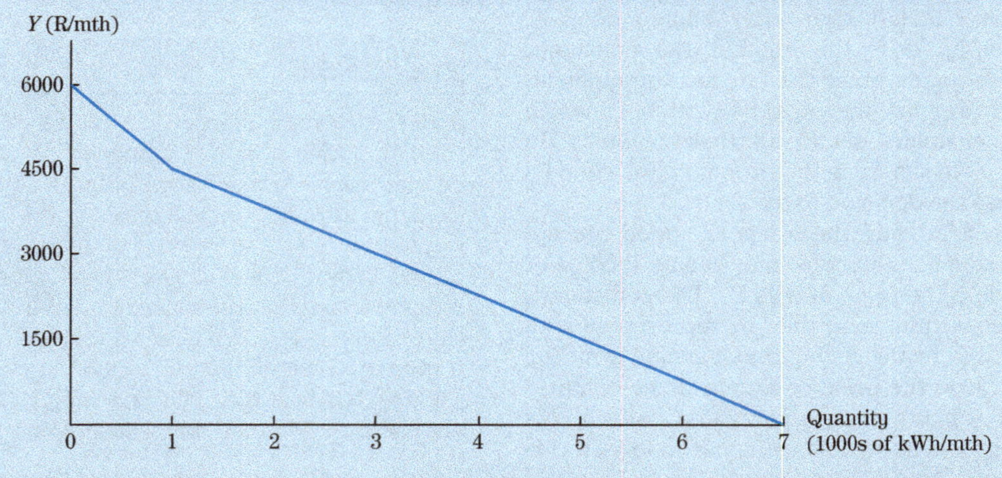

Once electric power consumption reaches 1000 kWh/mth, the opportunity cost of additional power falls from R1.50/kWh to R0.75/kWh.

If the budget constraint is the same, the decision should be the same

Even without knowing anything about the consumer's preferences, we can use budgetary information to make certain inferences about how a rational consumer will behave. Suppose, for example, that the consumer's tastes do not change over time, and that he is confronted with exactly the same budget constraint in each of two different situations. If he is rational, he should make exactly the same choice in both cases. After all, if the budget constraint is the same as before, the consumer has exactly the same menu of possible bundles available as before; and since we have no reason to believe that his ranking of the desirability of these bundles has changed, the most desirable bundle should also be the same. As the following example makes clear, however, it may not always be immediately apparent that the budget constraints are in fact the same.

Note that the situation described in Example 3.2 has the same structure as the one described in the lost concert ticket example with which we began this chapter. It too is one in which the decision should be the same in both instances, because

Example 3.2

On one occasion, Godfrey fills his car's tank with petrol on the evening before his departure to the Chobe Game Reserve. He awakens to discover that a thief has siphoned out all but 1 litre from his 56 litre tank. On another occasion, he plans to stop for petrol on his way out the next morning before he departs to Chobe Game Reserve. He awakens to discover that he has lost R770 from his wallet. If petrol sells for R14/litre and the round trip will consume 40 litres, how, if at all, should Godfrey's decision about whether to take the trip to Chobe differ in the two cases? (Assume that, monetary costs aside, the inconvenience of having to refill his tank is negligible.)

Suppose Godfrey's income is RM/mth. Before his loss, his budget constraint is B_1 in Fig. 3.14. In both instances described, his budget constraint at the moment he discovers his loss will shift inwards to B_2. If he does not take the trip, he will have M – R770 available to spend on other goods in both cases. And if he does take the trip, he will have to purchase the required petrol at R14/litre in both cases. No matter what the source of the loss, the remaining opportunities are exactly the same. If Godfrey's budget is tight, he may decide to cancel his trip. Otherwise, he may go, despite the loss. But because his budget constraint and tastes are the same in the lost-cash case as in the stolen-petrol case, it would not be rational for him to take the trip in one instance but not in the other.

Figure 3.14 Budget constraints following theft of petrol, loss of cash

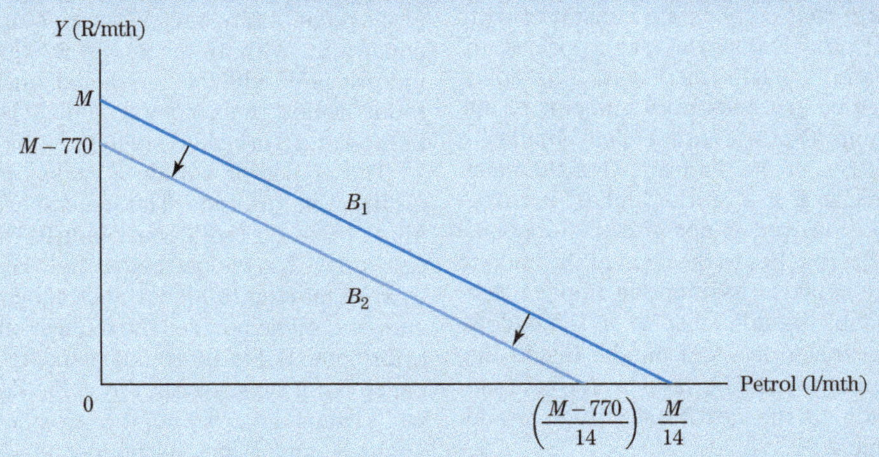

A theft of R770's worth of petrol has exactly the same effect on the budget constraint as the loss of R770 in cash. The bundle chosen should therefore be the same, irrespective of the source of the loss.

the budget constraint and preferences are the same in each.

Although the rational choice model makes it clear that the decisions *should* be the same if the budget constraints and preferences are the same, people sometimes choose differently. The difficulty is often that the way the different situations are described sometimes causes people to overlook the essential similarities between them. For instance, in Example 3.2 many people erroneously conclude that the cost of taking the trip is higher in the stolen-petrol case than in the lost-money case, and so they are less likely to take the trip in the former instance. Similarly, many people are less inclined to buy the concert ticket after losing the first one than after having lost R400, because they think, incorrectly, that the ticket would cost more under the lost-ticket scenario. As we have seen, however, the amount that will be saved by not buying the ticket or by not taking the trip is exactly the same under each scenario.

To recapitulate briefly, the budget constraint or budget line summarizes the combinations of bundles that the consumer is able to buy. Its position is determined jointly by income and prices. From the set of feasible bundles, the consumer's task is to pick the particular one she likes best. To identify this bundle, we need some means of summarizing the consumer's preferences over all possible bundles she might consume. We now turn to this task.

The best feasible bundle

We now have the tools we need to determine how the consumer should allocate his income between two goods. The indifference map tells us how the various bundles are ranked in order of preference. The budget constraint, in turn, tells us which bundles are affordable. The consumer's task is to put the two together and choose the most preferred or **best affordable bundle**. (Recall from Chapter 1 that it is sufficient to assume that people make decisions *as if* they were thinking in terms of indifference curves and budget constraints, just as expert pool players choose between shots as if they knew all the relevant laws of Newtonian physics.)

Best affordable bundle The most preferred bundle of those that are affordable.

Let us again consider the choice between food and shelter that confronts a consumer with an income of $M = \text{R}2000/\text{wk}$ facing prices of $P_F = \text{R}200/\text{kg}$ and $P_S = \text{R}100/\text{m}^2$. Figure 3.15 shows this consumer's budget constraint and part of his indifference map. Of the five labelled bundles – A, D, E, F and G – in the diagram, G is the most preferred, because it lies on the highest indifference curve. G, however, is not affordable, nor is any other bundle that lies to the right of the budget line. The more-is-better assumption implies that the best affordable bundle must lie *on* the budget constraint, not inside it. (Any bundle inside the budget constraint would be less preferred than one just slightly to the northeast, which would also be affordable.)

Where exactly is the best affordable bundle located along the budget constraint? We know that it cannot be on an indifference curve that lies partly inside the budget constraint. On the indifference curve I_1, for example, the only points that are even candidates for the best affordable bundle are the two that lie on the budget constraint, namely, A and E. But A cannot be the best affordable bundle because it is equally attractive as D, which in turn is less desirable than F by the more-is-better assumption. So, by transitivity, A is less desirable than F. For the same reason, E cannot be the best affordable bundle.

Since the best affordable bundle cannot lie on an indifference curve that lies partly inside the budget line, and since it must lie on the budget line itself, we know it has to lie on an indifference curve that intersects the budget line only once. In Fig. 3.15 that indifference curve is the one labelled I_2, and the best affordable bundle is F, which lies at the point of tangency between I_2 and the budget constraint. With an income of R2000/wk and facing prices of R100/m^2 for shelter and R200/kg for food, the best this consumer can do is buy 6 kg/wk of food and 8 m^2/wk of shelter.

The choice of bundle F makes perfect sense on intuitive grounds. The consumer's goal, after all, is to reach the highest indifference curve he can, given his budget constraint. His strategy is to keep moving to higher and higher indifference curves until he reaches the highest one that is still affordable. For indifference maps for which a tangency point exists, as in Fig. 3.15, the best bundle will always lie at the point of tangency. Although points A and E on the budget line are possible

Figure 3.15 The best affordable bundle

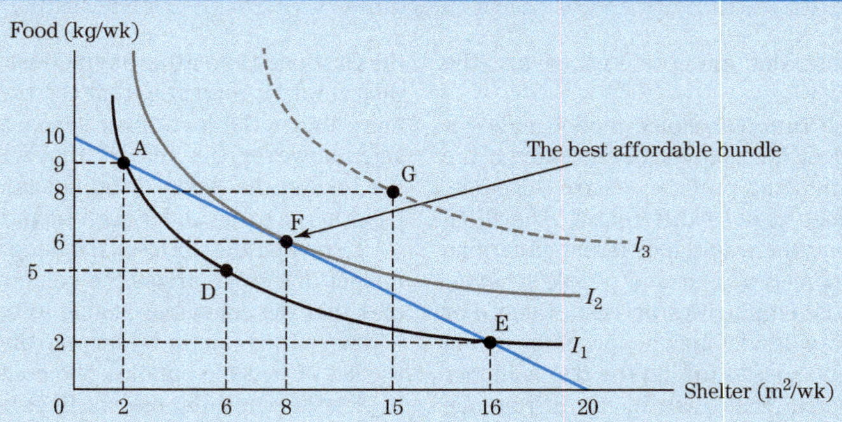

The best the consumer can do is to choose the bundle on the budget constraint that lies on the highest attainable indifference curve. Here, that is bundle F, which lies at a tangency between the indifference curve and the budget constraint.

points to consume, point F costs the same but lies on a higher indifference curve (meaning a higher level of satisfaction).

In Fig. 3.15, note that the marginal rate of substitution (which is the slope of the indifference curve) at F is exactly the same as the absolute value of the slope of the budget constraint. This will always be so when the best affordable bundle occurs at a point of tangency (and is applicable only at that point). The condition that must be satisfied in such cases is therefore

$$\text{MRS} = \frac{P_S}{P_F} \tag{3.4}$$

The right-hand side of Eq. 3.4 represents the opportunity cost of shelter in terms of food. Thus, with $P_S = \text{R}100/\text{m}^2$ and $P_F = \text{R}200/\text{kg}$, the opportunity cost of an additional square metre of shelter is $\frac{1}{2}$kg of food. The left-hand side of Eq. 3.4 is $|\Delta F/\Delta S|$, the absolute value of the slope of the indifference curve at the point of tangency. It is the amount of additional food the consumer must be given in order to compensate him fully for the loss of 1 m^2 of shelter. In the language of cost–benefit analysis discussed in Chapter 1, the slope of the budget line represents the opportunity cost of shelter in terms of food, whereas the slope of the indifference curve represents the benefits of consuming shelter as compared with consuming food. Since the slope of the budget line is $-\frac{1}{2}$ in this example, the tangency condition tells us that $\frac{1}{2}$kg of food would be required to compensate for the benefits given up with the loss of 1 m^2 of shelter.

If the consumer were at some bundle on the budget line for which the two slopes were not the same, then it would always be possible for him to purchase a better bundle. To see why, suppose he were at a point where the slope of the indifference curve (in absolute value) is less than the slope of the budget constraint (also in absolute value), as at point E in Fig. 3.15. Suppose, for instance, that the MRS at E is only $\frac{1}{4}$. This tells us that the consumer can be compensated for the loss of 1 m^2 of shelter by being given an additional $\frac{1}{4}$ kg of food. But the slope of the budget constraint tells us that, by giving up 1 m^2 of shelter, he can purchase an additional $\frac{1}{2}$kg of food. Since this is $\frac{1}{4}$kg more than he needs to remain equally satisfied, he will clearly be better off if he purchases more food and less shelter than at point E. The opportunity cost of an additional kilogram of food is less than the benefit it confers.

Exercise 3.6

Suppose that the marginal rate of substitution at point A in Fig. 3.15 is 1.0. Show that this means the consumer will be better off if he purchases less food and more shelter than at A.

Corner solutions

The best affordable bundle need not always occur at a point of tangency. In some cases, there may simply *be* no point of tangency – the MRS may be everywhere greater, or smaller, than the slope of the budget line. In this case we get a **corner solution**, like the one shown in Fig. 3.16, where M, P_F and P_S are again given by R2000/wk, R200/kg and R100/m^2, respectively.

Corner solution In a choice between two goods, a case in which the consumer does consume only one of the goods.

Figure 3.16 A corner solution

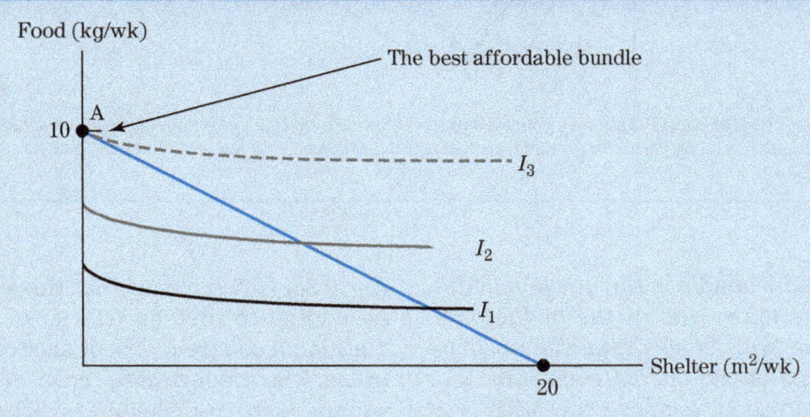

When the MRS of food for shelter is always less than the slope of the budget constraint, the best the consumer can do is to spend all his income on food.

Example 3.3

Itumeleng Khune spends his entire soft drink budget on Coke and Pepsi, and cares only about total sugar content. If Pepsi has twice the sugar content of Coke, and if Pepsi costs R15.00/litre and Coke costs R11.25/litre, how will Itumeleng spend his soft drink budget of R225/wk?

For Itumeleng, Pepsi and Coke are *perfect substitutes*, which means that his indifference curves will be linear. The blue line in Fig. 3.17 is the set of all possible Pepsi–Coke combinations that provide the same satisfaction as the bundle consisting of 0 litres of Pepsi per week and 30 litres of Coke per week. Since each litre of Pepsi has twice the sugar content of a litre of Coke, all bundles along this line contain precisely the same amount of sugar. The grey line closest to the origin is the indifference curve for bundles equivalent to bundle (0, 10), and the second grey line is the indifference curve corresponding to (0, 20). Along each of these indifference curves, the marginal rate of substitution of Coke for Pepsi is always 2/1: that is, 2 litres of Coke for every litre of Pepsi.

In the same diagram, Itumeleng's budget constraint is shown as B (the black line). The slope of his indifference curves is -2, and of his budget line is $-\frac{4}{3}$. The best affordable bundle is the one labelled A, a corner solution in which he spends his entire budget on Pepsi. This makes intuitive sense in the light of Itumeleng's peculiar preferences: he cares only about total sugar content, and Pepsi provides more sugar per rand than does Coke. If the Pepsi–Coke price ratio P_P/P_C had been 3/1 (or any other amount greater than 2/1), Itumeleng would have spent all his income on Coke. That is, we would again have had a corner solution, only this time on the vertical axis. Only if the price ratio had been exactly 2/1 might we have seen Itumeleng spend part of his income on each good. In that case, any combination of Coke and Pepsi on his budget constraint would have served equally well.

Figure 3.17 Equilibrium with perfect substitutes

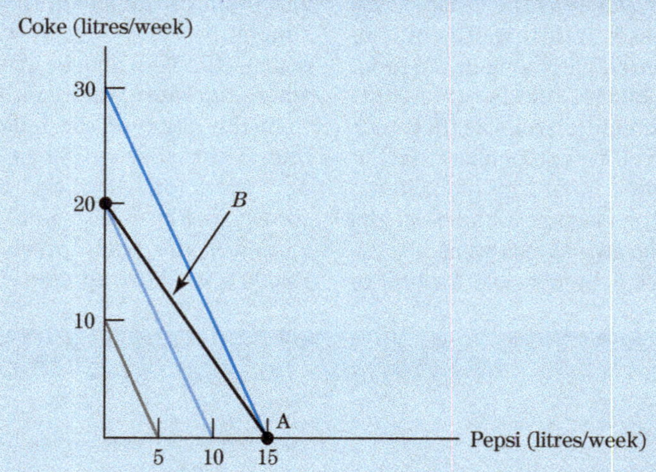

Here, the MRS of Coke for Pepsi is 2 at every point. Whenever the price ratio P_P/P_C is less than 2, a corner solution results in which the consumer buys only Pepsi. On the budget constraint B, the consumer does best to buy bundle A.

The best affordable bundle is the one labelled A, and it lies at the upper end of the budget constraint. At A, the MRS is less than the absolute value of the slope of the budget constraint. For the sake of illustration, suppose the MRS is at A – 0.25, which means that this consumer would be willing to give up 0.25 kg of food to get an additional square metre of shelter. But at market prices the opportunity cost of an additional square metre of shelter is 0.5 kg of food. He increases his satisfaction by continuing to give up shelter for more food until it is no longer possible to do so. Even though this consumer regards shelter as a desirable commodity, the best he can do is to spend all his income on food. Market prices are such that he would have to give up too much food to make the purchase of even a single unit of shelter worthwhile.

The indifference map in Fig. 3.16 satisfies the property of diminishing marginal rate of substitution – moving to the right along any indifference curve, the slope becomes smaller in absolute terms. But because the slopes of the indifference curves start out smaller than the slope of the budget constraint here, the two never reach equality.

Indifference curves that are not strongly convex are characteristic of goods that are easily substituted for one another. Corner solutions are more likely to occur for such goods, and indeed are almost certain to occur when goods are perfect substitutes. (See Example 3.3.) For such goods the MRS does not diminish at all; rather, it is everywhere the same. With perfect substitutes, indifference curves are straight lines. If they happen to be steeper than the budget constraint, we get a corner solution on the horizontal axis; if less steep, we get a corner solution on the vertical axis.

Most of the time we shall deal with problems that have *interior solutions* – that is, with problems where the best affordable bundle will lie at a point of tangency. An interior solution, again, is one where the MRS is exactly the same as the slope of the budget constraint.

Exercise 3.7

Suppose Albert always uses exactly two pats of butter on each piece of toast. If toast costs R1.50/slice and butter costs R3.00/pat, find Albert's best affordable bundle if he has R180/mth to spend on toast and butter. Suppose Albert starts to watch his cholesterol level, and therefore alters his preference to using exactly one pat of butter on each piece of toast. How much toast and butter would Albert then consume each month?

Indifference curves when there are more than two goods

In the examples thus far, the consumer cared about only two goods. Where there are more than two, we can construct indifference curves by using the same device we used earlier to represent multi-good budget constraints. We simply view the consumer's choice as being one between a particular good X and an amalgam of other goods Y, which is again called the composite good. As before, the composite good is the amount of income the consumer has left over after buying the good X.

In the multi-good case we may thus continue to represent the consumer's preferences with an indifference map in the XY plane. Here, the indifference curve tells us the rate at which the consumer will exchange the composite good for X. As in the two-good case, equilibrium occurs when the consumer reaches the highest indifference curve attainable on his budget line.

An application of the rational choice model

As the following example makes clear, the composite good construct enables us to deal with more general questions than we could in the two-good case.

The analysis in Example 3.4 raises the question of why the government did not just give poor people cash grants in the first place. The ostensible reason is that the government wanted to help poor people buy food, not luxury items, or even cigarettes and alcohol. And yet if most participants would have spent at least as much on food as they received in stamps, not being able to use stamps to buy other things is a meaningless restriction. For instance, if someone would have spent R1875 on food anyway, getting R1250 in food stamps simply lets him take some of the money he would have spent on food and spend it instead on whatever else he chooses.

On purely economic grounds, there is thus a strong case for replacing the food stamp programme with a much simpler programme of cash grants to the poor. At the very least, this would eliminate the cumbersome step of requiring grocers to redeem their stamps for cash.

As a political matter, however, it is easy to see why government might have set things up the way it did. Many taxpayers would be distressed to see their tax rands used to buy illicit substances. If the food stamp programme prevents even a tiny minority of participants from spending more on such goods, it spares many political difficulties.

Example 3.4 calls our attention to a problem that applies not just to the food stamp programme

Example 3.4

Is it better to give poor people cash or food stamps?

One objective of the food stamp programme is to alleviate hunger. Under the terms of the programme, people whose incomes fall below a certain level are eligible to receive a specified quantity of food stamps. For example, a person with an income of R5000/mth might be eligible for R1250/mth worth of stamps. These stamps can then be used to buy R1250/mth worth of food. Any food he buys in excess of R1250/mth he must pay for in cash. Stamps cannot be used to purchase cigarettes, alcohol or various other items. The government gives food retailers cash for the stamps they accept.

The cost to the government for the consumer in the example given was R1250 – the amount it had to reimburse the store for the stamps. Would the consumer have been better off had he instead been given R1250 directly in cash?

We can try to answer this question by investigating which alternative would get him to a higher indifference curve. Suppose Y denotes the composite good and X denotes food. If the consumer's income is R5000/mth and P_X is the price of food, his initial equilibrium is the bundle J in Fig. 3.18. The effect of the food stamp programme is to increase the total amount of food he can buy each month from R5000/P_X to R6250/P_X. In terms of the maximum amount of food he can buy, the food stamp programme is thus exactly the same as a cash grant of R1250.

Where the two alternatives differ is in terms of the maximum amounts of other goods he can buy. With a cash grant of R1250, he has a total monthly income of R6250, and this is, of course, the maximum amount of non-food goods (the composite good) he can buy. His budget constraint in this case is thus the line labelled AE in Fig. 3.18.

Figure 3.18 Food stamp programme vs. cash grant programme

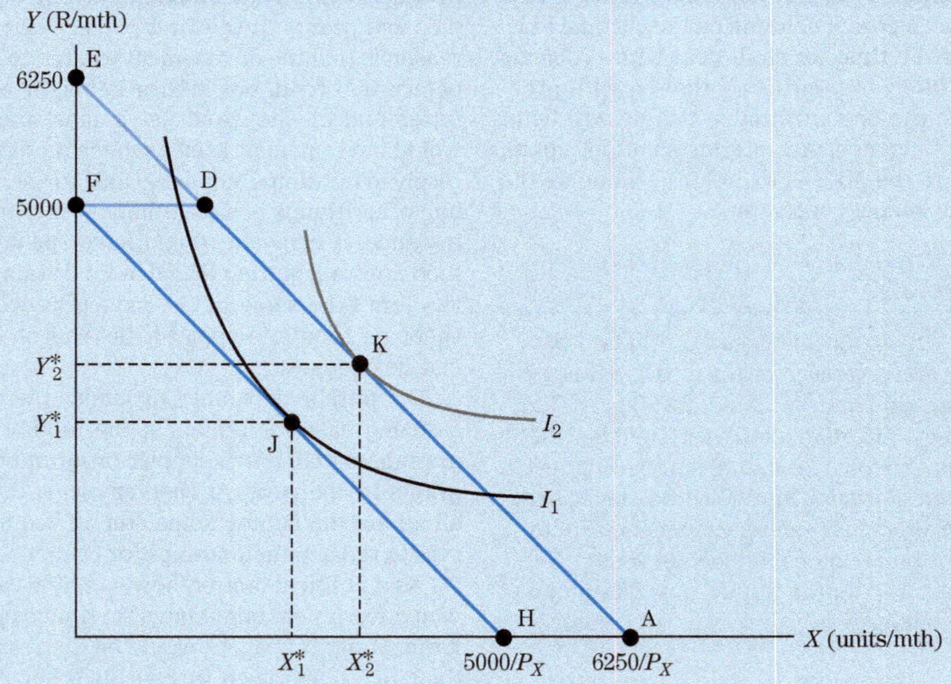

By comparison with the budget constraint under a cash grant (AE), the budget constraint under food stamps (ADF) limits the amount that can be spent on non-food goods. But for the consumer whose indifference map is shown, the equilibrium bundles are the same under both programmes.

With the food stamp programme, by contrast, the consumer is not able to buy R6250/mth of non-food goods, because his R1250 in food stamps can be used only for food. The maximum amount of non-food goods he can purchase is R5000. In Fig. 3.18, his budget constraint under the food stamp programme is labelled ADF. For values of Y less than R5000, it is thus exactly the same as his budget constraint under the cash grant programme. For values of Y larger than R5000, however, his budget constraint under the food stamp programme is completely flat.

Note that the consumer whose indifference curves are shown in Fig. 3.18 buys exactly the same bundle – namely, bundle K – under both programmes. The effect of the food stamp programme here is precisely the same as the effect of the cash grant. In general, this will be true whenever the consumer with a cash grant would have spent more on food anyway than the amount of food stamps he would have received under the food stamp programme.

Figure 3.19 depicts a consumer for whom this is *not* the case. With a cash grant, he would choose the bundle L, which would put him on a higher indifference curve than he could attain under the food stamp programme, which would lead him to buy bundle D. Note that bundle D contains exactly R1250 worth of food, the amount of food stamps he received. Bundle L, by contrast, contains less than R1250 worth of food. Here, the effect of the food stamp programme is to cause the recipient to spend more on food than he would have if he had instead been given cash.

The face value of the food stamps most participants receive is smaller than what they would spend on food. For these people, the food stamp programme leads, as noted, to exactly the same behaviour as a pure cash grant programme.

Figure 3.19 Where food stamps and cash grants yield different outcomes

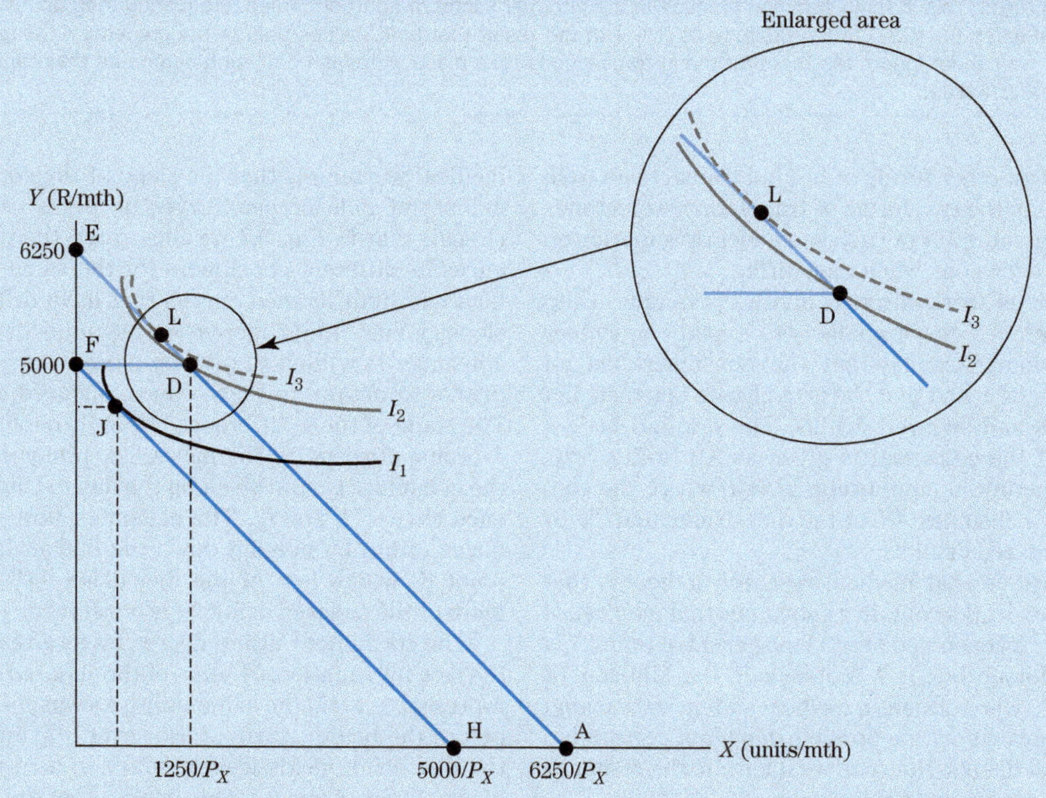

For the consumer whose indifference map is shown, a cash grant would be preferred to food stamps, which force him to devote more to food than he would choose to spend on his own.

Economic naturalist 3.1

Why do some people pay in kind instead of cash/credit card?

In some instances people may be willing to pay in kind rather than in cash for certain services rendered. Although cash/credit card/EFT transactions are more common than payment in kind, the latter is frequently encountered. Let us take the situation portrayed in the cartoon. Why would the mechanic be willing to service the dentist's car in exchange for braces for his daughter? It is not rare for people to have cash-flow problems even though they may have a lot of assets. It may thus be possible that, although the mechanic has a garage as an asset, he may be short of cash to pay for braces for his daughter. Seeing that braces can cost up to R20000, it may be highly likely. Even if he is a member of a medical aid scheme it will not help much because such schemes cover very little of those type of costs. They can also both benefit from this arrangement in another way: because it is payment in kind no invoices are made out and the mechanic does not have to pay tax on the income from the service rendered and the dentist also does not have to pay taxes on the braces provided.

©iStock.com/savas keskiner

By paying in kind both participants in the transaction gain. It has to be said that many cash transactions these days are also not backed by invoices and the suppliers of these services can put the money in their pockets without paying taxes. This is fairly common practice in the informal sector in Southern Africa. Frequently they do not apply general sales tax (GST) to the customer's bill, with the result that both parties gain in the process. Although it is illegal, we cannot ignore the fact that many transactions take place with cash or in-kind payments that cannot be traced afterwards.

but to all other forms of in-kind transfers as well: although the two forms of transfer are sometimes equivalent, gifts in cash seem clearly superior on those occasions when they differ.

Let us work through another example using indifference curve analysis to explain consumer behaviour. Assume that the consumer has an income of Y and that she is to choose between diet drinks and sugared drinks. The original budget line of the consumer is given as AB in Fig. 3.20, and the initial equilibrium is at J, where the consumer consumes D_1^* of the diet drinks and S_1^* of the sugared drinks.

Assume that medical research indicates that the diet drinks contain a substance that may cause cancer if consumed over a long period of time. This is endorsed by Dr A Motsoaledi, the Minister of Health, who releases a medical statement warning the public about the possible danger of consuming the diet drinks. How can we illustrate the response of the consumer to this warning?

The first result is that J no longer represents maximum satisfaction, even though it may be obtainable by the consumer. The result of the medical warning is that the slope of the consumer's set of indifference curves becomes steeper. (Recall that in Fig. 3.7 we illustrated the preferences of different consumers for the same products with indifference curves that have different slopes.) The MRS_{DS} increases, meaning that the consumer is willing to give up more cans of diet drinks to obtain an extra can of sugared drink. The slope of the indifference curve through point J, or any other point, increases. The preference of the consumer is now given by the dashed indifference curves I_1' and I_2'. The consumer now maximizes utility by moving down the budget line to point K, where less of the diet drink (D_2^*) and more of the sugared drink S_1^* is consumed.

The consumer's utility decreases as a result of the new information. S_1^* units of the sugared drink represent exactly the same utility as was the case before the health warning. However, D_1^* units of the diet drink yields less satisfaction as a result of the threat of cancer. This implies that the indifference curve I_1' represents a lower level of satisfaction than the original indifference curve I_2. The result of the health warning is that the consumer

Figure 3.20 How a health risk may alter consumer behaviour

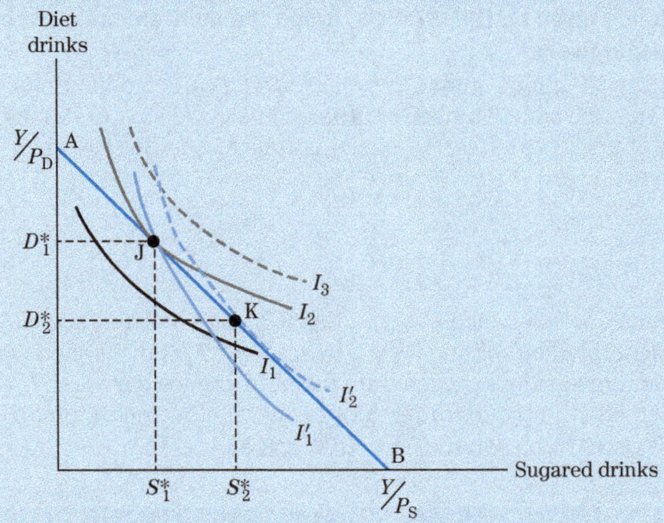

If consumers are faced with a product that may negatively affect their health, they will consume less of the good that may cause illness.

consumes less of the unhealthier product and their satisfaction level decreases.

This application of indifference curve analysis gives us an indication of how government can react to products that are not illegal to consume, but which have a health risk attached to them. In South Africa the government has reacted to the increased risk of lung cancer caused by smoking by requiring the manufacturers of cigarettes to put a health warning on the outside of every pack of cigarettes. Statistics indicate that this has had the desired effect and that, in total, South Africans are smoking less. This is an example of how government can cost-effectively change consumer behaviour.

The utility function approach to consumer choice

Another approach that economists use to represent the consumer's preferences is by means of a *utility function*. For each possible bundle of goods, a utility function yields a number that represents the amount of satisfaction provided by that bundle. Suppose, for example, that Tom consumes only food and shelter, and that his utility function is given by $U(F, S) = FS$, where F denotes the number of kilograms of food, S the number of square metres of shelter he consumes per week and U his satisfaction, measured in 'utils' per week.[5] If $F = 4$ kg/wk and $S =$ 3 m^2/wk, Tom will receive 12 utils/wk of utility, just as he would if he consumed 3 kg/wk of food and 4 m^2/wk of shelter. By contrast, if he consumed 8 kg/wk of food and 6 m^2/wk of shelter, he would receive 48 utils/wk.

The utility function is analogous to an indifference map, in that both provide a complete description of the consumer's preferences. In the indifference curve framework we can rank any two bundles by seeing which one lies on a higher indifference curve. In the utility function framework we can compare any two bundles by seeing which one yields a greater number of utils. Indeed, as the following example illustrates, it is straightforward to use the utility function to construct an indifference map.

In the indifference curve framework, the best attainable bundle is the bundle on the budget

[5] The term 'utils' represents an arbitrary unit. As we shall see, what is important for consumer choice is not the actual number of utils that various bundles provide, but the ranking of the bundles based on their associated utilities.

Example 3.5

If Tom's utility function is given by $U(F, S) = FS$, graph the indifference curves that correspond to 1, 2, 3 and 4 utils, respectively.

In the language of utility functions, an indifference curve is all combinations of F and S that yield the same level of utility – the same number of utils. Suppose we look at the indifference curve that corresponds to 1 unit of utility – that is, the combinations of bundles for which $FS = 1$. Solving this equation for S, we have

$$S = \frac{1}{F} \tag{3.5}$$

which is the indifference curve labelled $U = 1$ in Fig. 3.21. The indifference curve that corresponds to 2 units of utility is generated by solving $FS = 2$ to get $S = 2/F$, and it is shown by the curve labelled $U = 2$ in Fig. 3.21. In similar fashion, we generate the indifference curves to $U = 3$ and $U = 4$, which are correspondingly labelled in the diagram. More generally, we get the indifference curve corresponding to a utility level of U_0 by solving $FS = U_0$ to get $S = U_0/F$.

Figure 3.21 Indifference curves for the utility function $U = FS$

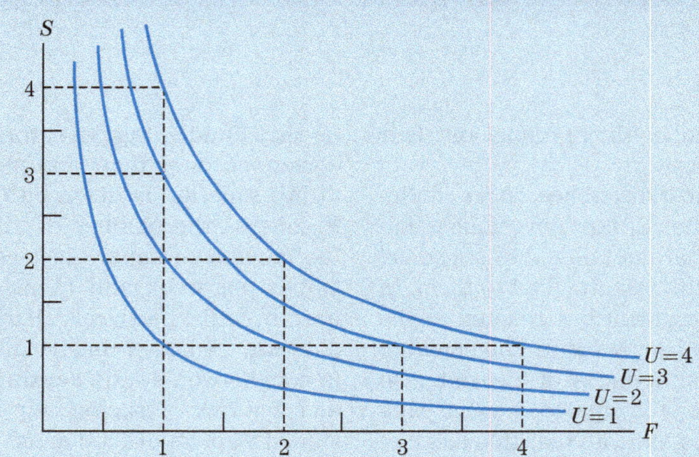

To get the indifference curve that corresponds to all bundles that yield a utility level of U_0, set $FS = U_0$ and solve for S to get $S = U_0/F$.

line that lies on the highest indifference curve. Analogously, the best attainable bundle in the utility function framework is the bundle on the budget constraint that provides the highest level of utility. In the indifference curve framework, the best attainable bundle occurs at a point of tangency between an indifference curve and the budget constraint. At the optimal bundle, the slope of the indifference curve, or MRS, equals the slope of the budget constraint. Suppose food and shelter are again our two goods, and P_F and P_S are their respective prices. If $\Delta S/\Delta F$ denotes the slope of the highest attainable indifference curve at the optimal bundle, the tangency condition says that $\Delta S/\Delta F = P_F / P_S$. What is the analogous condition in the utility function framework?

Marginal utility Change in total utility if an extra unit of the good is consumed.

To answer this question, we must introduce the concept of **marginal utility** (the marginal utility of a good is the rate at which total utility changes with consumption of the good), which is the rate at which total utility changes as the quantities of food and shelter change. More specifically, let MU_F denote the number of additional utils we get for each additional unit of food, and MU_S denote the number of additional utils we get for each additional

Figure 3.22 Utility along an indifference curve remains constant

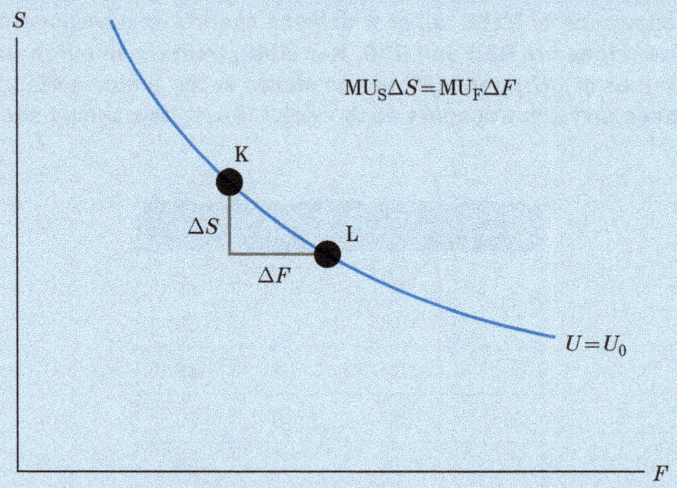

In moving from K to L, the loss in utility from having less shelter, $MU_S \cdot \Delta S$, is exactly offset by the gain in utility from having more food, $MU_F \cdot \Delta F$.

unit of shelter. In Fig. 3.22, note that bundle K has ΔF fewer units of food and ΔS more units of shelter than bundle L. Thus, if we move from bundle K to bundle L, we gain $MU_F \cdot \Delta F$ utils from having more food, but we lose $MU_S \cdot \Delta S$ utils from having less shelter.

Because K and L lie on the same indifference curve, we know that both bundles provide the same level of utility. Thus the utility we lose from having less shelter must be exactly offset by the utility we gain from having more food. This tells us that

$$|MU_F \cdot \Delta F| = |MU_S \cdot \Delta S| \tag{3.6}$$

Dividing Eq. 3.6 by $MU_S \cdot \Delta F$ gives

$$\frac{MU_F}{MU_S} = \frac{\Delta S}{\Delta F} \tag{3.7}$$

Suppose that the optimal bundle lies between K and L, which are very close together, so that ΔF and ΔS are both very small. As K and L move closer to the optimal bundle, the ratio $\Delta S/\Delta F$ becomes equal to the slope of the indifference curve at that bundle, which Eq. 3.7 tells us is equal to the reverse ratio of the marginal utilities of the two goods. And since the slope of the indifference curve at the optimal bundle is the same as that of the budget constraint, the following condition must also hold for the optimal bundle:

$$\frac{MU_F}{MU_S} = \frac{P_F}{P_S} \tag{3.8}$$

Equation 3.8 is the condition in the utility function framework that is analogous to the $MRS = P_F/P_S$ condition in the indifference curve framework.

If we cross-multiply terms in Eq. 3.8 we get an equivalent condition that has a very straightforward, intuitive interpretation:

$$\frac{MU_F}{P_F} = \frac{MU_S}{P_S} \tag{3.9}$$

Example 3.6

Suppose that the marginal utility of the last rand John spends on food is greater than the marginal utility of the last rand he spends on shelter. For example, suppose the prices of food and shelter are R10/kg and R20/m^2, respectively, and that the corresponding marginal utilities are 6 and 4. Show that John cannot possibly be maximizing his utility.

If John bought 1 m^2/wk less shelter, he would save R20/wk and would lose 4 utils. But this would enable him to buy 2 kg/wk more food, which would add 12 utils, for a net gain of 8 utils.

Example 3.7

Mary has a weekly allowance of R150, all of which she spends on newspapers (*N*) and magazines (*M*), whose respective prices are R15 and R30. Her utility from these purchases is given by *U*(*N*) + *V*(*M*). If the values of *U*(*N*) and *V*(*M*) are as shown in the table, is Mary a utility maximizer if she buys 4 magazines and 2 newspapers each week? If not, how should she reallocate her allowance?

N	*U(N)*	*M*	*V(M)*
0	0	0	0
1	18	1	30
2	30	2	48
3	39	3	60
4	45	4	66
5	48	5	69

For Mary to be a utility maximizer, extra utility per rand must be the same for both the last newspaper and the last magazine she purchases. However, since the second newspaper provides 0.8 additional utils per rand spent, which is four times the 0.2 utils per rand she gets from the fourth magazine, Mary is not a utility maximizer.

N	*U(N)*	*MU(N)*	$MU(N)/P_N$	*M*	*U(M)*	*MU(M)*	$MU(M)/P_M$
0	0			0	0		
		12	1.2			20	1.0
1	12			1	20		
		8	0.8			12	0.6
2	20			2	32		
		6	0.6			8	0.4
3	26			3	40		
		4	0.4			4	0.2
4	30			4	44		
		2	0.2			2	0.1
5	32			5	46		

To see clearly how she should reallocate her purchases, let us rewrite the table to include the relevant information on marginal utilities. From this table, we see that there are several bundles for which $MU_N/P_N = MU_M/P_M$, namely: 3 newspapers and 2 magazines; or 4 newspapers and 3 magazines; or 5 newspapers and 4 magazines. The last of these bundles yields the highest total utility (114 utils) but costs R195, and hence is beyond Mary's budget constraint. The first, which costs only R105, is affordable, but so is the second, which costs exactly R150 and yields higher total utility than the first (105 utils vs. 87 utils). With 4 newspapers and 3 magazines, Mary gets 0.4 utils per rand from her last purchase in each category. Her total utility is 105 utils, which is 9 more than she got from the original bundle.

In words, Eq. 3.9 tells us that the ratio of marginal utility to price must be the same for all goods at the optimal bundle. This means that the marginal utility per last rand spent on all goods must be the same. The following examples illustrate why this condition must be satisfied if the consumer has allocated his budget optimally.

In Example 3.4, note that if all Mary's utility values were doubled, or cut by half, she would still do best to buy 4 newspapers and 3 magazines each week. This illustrates the claim that consumer choice depends not on the absolute number of utils associated with different bundles, but instead on the ordinal ranking of the utility levels associated with different bundles. If we double all the utils associated with various bundles, or cut them by half, the ordinal ranking of the bundles will be preserved, and thus the optimal bundle will remain the same. This will also be true if we take the logarithm of the utility function, the square root of it, or add 5 to it, or transform it in any other way that preserves the ordinal ranking of different bundles.

'The next step'

Using calculus to maximize utility

With calculus we can solve the consumer's budget allocation problem without direct recourse to the geometry of indifference maps. Let $U(X, Y)$ be the consumer's utility function; and suppose M, P_X and P_Y denote income, the price of X and the price of Y, respectively. Formally, the consumer's allocation problem can be stated as follows:

Maximize $U(X, Y)$ subject to

$$P_X X + P_Y Y = M \tag{3.10}$$

The method of Lagrangian multipliers

As noted earlier, the function $U(X, Y)$ itself has no maximum; it simply keeps on increasing with increases in X or Y. The maximization problem defined in Eq. 3.10 is called a *constrained maximization problem*, which means that we want to find the values of X and Y that produce the highest value of U *subject to the constraint that the consumer spends only as much as his income.* We shall examine two different approaches to this problem.

One way of making sure that the budget constraint is satisfied is to use the method of *Lagrangian multipliers.* In this method we begin by transforming the constrained maximization problem in Eq. 3.10 into the following unconstrained maximization problem:

$$\underset{X,Y,\lambda}{\text{Maximize}}\ \mathcal{L} = U(X,Y) - \lambda(P_X X + P_Y Y - M) \tag{3.11}$$

The term λ is called a Lagrangian multiplier, and its role is to ensure that the budget constraint is satisfied. The first-order conditions for a maximum of $\mathcal{L}$ are obtained by taking the first partial derivatives of $\mathcal{L}$ with respect to X, Y and λ and setting them equal to zero:

$$\frac{\partial \mathcal{L}}{\partial X} = \frac{\partial U}{\partial X} - \lambda P_X = 0 \tag{3.12}$$

$$\frac{\partial \mathcal{L}}{\partial Y} = \frac{\partial U}{\partial Y} - \lambda P_Y = 0 \tag{3.13}$$

and

$$\frac{\partial \mathcal{L}}{\partial \lambda} = M - P_X X - P_Y Y = 0 \tag{3.14}$$

The next step is to solve Eqs 3.12–3.14 for X, Y and λ. The solutions for X and Y are the only ones we really care about here. The role of the equilibrium value of λ is to guarantee that the budget constraint is satisfied. Note in Eq. 3.14 that setting the first partial derivative of $\mathcal{L}$ with respect to λ equal to zero guarantees this result.

Specific solutions for the utility-maximizing values of X and Y require a specific functional form for the utility function. We shall work through an illustrative example in a moment. But first note that an interesting characteristic of the optimal X and Y values can be obtained by dividing Eq. 3.12 by Eq. 3.13 to get

$$\frac{\partial U / \partial X}{\partial U / \partial Y} = \frac{\lambda P_X}{\lambda P_Y} = \frac{P_X}{P_Y} \tag{3.15}$$

Equation 3.15 is the utility function analogue to Eq. 3.4 from the text, which says that the optimal values of X and Y must satisfy MRS $= P_X/P_Y$. The terms $\partial U/\partial X$ and $\partial U/\partial Y$ from Eq. 3.15 are called the *marginal utility of X* and the *marginal utility of Y*, respectively. In words, the marginal utility of a good is the extra utility obtained per additional unit of the good consumed. Equation

Figure 3.23 The optimal bundle when $U = XY$, $P_x = 6$, $P_y = 3$ and $M = 60$.

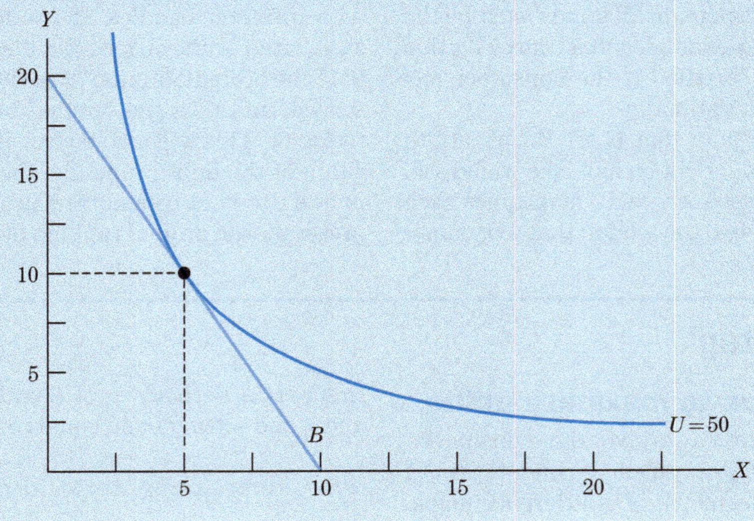

3.15 tells us that the ratio of these marginal utilities is simply the marginal rate of substitution of Y for X.

If we rearrange Eq. 3.15 in the form

$$\frac{\partial U/\partial X}{P_X} = \frac{\partial U/\partial Y}{P_Y} \quad (3.16)$$

another interesting property of the optimal values of X and Y emerges. In words, the left-hand side of Eq. 3.16 may be interpreted as the extra utility gained from the last rand spent on X. Equation 3.16 is thus the calculus derivation of the result shown earlier in Eq. 3.9.

An example

To illustrate the Lagrangian method, suppose that $U(X, Y) = XY$, and that $M = 60$, $P_X = 6$ and $P_Y = 3$. Our unconstrained maximization problem would then be written as

$$\text{Max}\,\mathcal{L} = XY - \lambda(6X + 3Y - 60) \quad (3.17)$$

The first-order conditions for a maximum of $\mathcal{L}$ are given by

$$\frac{\partial L}{\partial X} = \frac{\partial(XY)}{\partial X} - 6\lambda = Y - 6\lambda = 0 \quad (3.18)$$

$$\frac{\partial L}{\partial Y} = \frac{\partial(XY)}{\partial Y} - 3\lambda = X - 3\lambda = 0 \quad (3.19)$$

and

$$\frac{\partial L}{\partial \lambda} = 60 - 6X - 3Y = 0 \quad (3.20)$$

Dividing Eq. 3.18 by Eq. 3.19 and solving for Y, we get $Y = 2X$; substituting this result into Eq. 3.20 and solving for X, we get $X = 5$, which in turn yields $Y = 2X = 10$. Thus (5, 10) is the utility-maximizing bundle.[6]

An alternative method

There is an alternative way of making sure that the budget constraint is satisfied, one that involves less cumbersome notation than the Lagrangian approach. In this alternative method we simply solve the budget constraint for Y in terms of X and substitute the result wherever Y appears in the utility function. Utility then becomes a function of X alone, and we can *maximize* it by taking its first derivative with respect to X and equating that to zero.[7] The value of X that solves that equation is the optimal value of X, which can then be substituted

[6] Assuming that the second-order conditions for a local maximum are also met.
[7] Here, the second-order condition for a local maximum is that $d^2U/dX^2 < 0$.

back into the budget constraint to find the optimal value of Y.

To illustrate, again suppose that $U(X, Y) = XY$, with $M = 60$, $P_X = 6$ and $P_Y = 3$. The budget constraint is then $6X + 3Y = 60$, which solves for $Y = 20 - 2X$. Substituting this expression back into the utility function, we have $U(XY) = X(20 - 2X) = 20X - 2X^2$. Taking the first derivative of U with respect to X and equating the result to zero, we have

$$\frac{dU}{dX} = 20 - 4X = 0 \tag{3.21}$$

which solves for $X = 5$. Plugging this value of X back into the budget constraint, we discover that the optimal value of Y is 10. So the optimal bundle is again (5, 10), just as we found using the Lagrangian approach. For these optimal values of X and Y, the consumer will obtain $(5) \times (10) = 50$ units of utility.

Both algebraic approaches to the budget allocation problem yield precisely the same result as the graphical approach described in the text. Note in Fig. 3.23 that the $U = 50$ indifference curve is tangent to the budget constraint at the bundle (5, 10).

Summary

- Our task in this chapter was to set forth the basic model of rational consumer choice. In all its variants, this model takes consumers' preferences as given, and assumes they will try to satisfy them in the most efficient way possible.
- The first step in solving the consumer budgeting problem is to summarize the consumer's preferences. Here, we begin with a preference ordering by which the consumer is able to rank all possible bundles of goods. This ranking scheme is assumed to be complete and transitive, and to exhibit the more-is-better property. Preference orderings that satisfy these restrictions give rise to indifference maps, or collections of indifference curves, each of which represents combinations of bundles among which the consumer is indifferent. Reference orderings are also assumed to exhibit a diminishing marginal rate of substitution, which means that, along any indifference curve, the more of a good a consumer has, the more he must be given to induce him to part with a unit of some other good. The diminishing MRS property accounts for the characteristic convex shape of indifference curves.
- The second step in solving the budgeting problem is to identify the set of bundles of goods the consumer is able to buy. The consumer is assumed to have an income level given in advance, and to face fixed prices. Prices and income together define the consumer's budget constraint, which, in the simple two-good case, is a downward-sloping line. Its slope, in absolute value, is the ratio of the two prices. It is the set of all possible bundles that the consumer might purchase if he spent his entire income.
- The budget constraint tells us what combinations of goods the consumer can afford to buy. To summarize the consumer's preferences over various bundles, we use an indifference map. In most cases, the best affordable bundle occurs at a point of tangency between an indifference curve and the budget constraint. At that point, the marginal rate of substitution is exactly equal to the rate at which the goods can be exchanged for one another at market prices. In some rare instances the optimum consumption bundle may be where only one of the goods is consumed.

Questions for review

1 If the prices of all products are rising at 20 per cent per year, and your employer gives you a 20 per cent salary increase, are you better off, worse off or equally well off in comparison with your situation a year ago?

2 *True or false*: If you know the slope of the budget constraint (for two goods), you know the prices of the two goods. Explain.

3 *True or false*: The downward slope of indifference curves is a consequence of the diminishing marginal rate of substitution.

4 Construct an example of a preference ordering over Coke, Coke Zero and Diet Pepsi that violates the transitivity assumption.

5 Explain in your own words how the slope of an indifference curve provides information about how much a consumer likes one good relative to another.

6 Explain why a consumer will often buy one bundle of goods even though he prefers another.

7 Why are corner solutions especially likely in the case of perfect substitutes?

8 *True or false*: If the indifference curve map is concave to the origin, then the optimal commodity basket must occur at a corner equilibrium, except possibly when there are quantity discounts.

9 If Ralph were given R100, he would spend none of it on tuna fish. But when asked, he claims to be indifferent between receiving R100 worth of tuna fish and a R100 note. How can this be?

Problems

1 The Acme Seed Company charges R30/kg for the first 10 kg you buy of marigold seeds each week, and R15/kg for every kilogram you buy thereafter. If your income is R1500/wk, draw your budget constraint for the composite good and marigold seeds.

2 Repeat Problem 1, except now the price for every kilogram after 10 kg/wk is R60/kg.

3 Smith likes cashews better than almonds, and likes almonds better than walnuts. He likes pecans equally well as macadamia nuts, and prefers macadamia nuts to almonds. Assuming his preferences are transitive, which does he prefer:

   a Pecans or walnuts?

   b Macadamia nuts or cashews?

4 Originally P_X is R120 and P_Y is R80. *True or false*: If P_X increases by R18 and P_Y increases by R12, the new budget line will be shifted inwards and parallel to the old budget line. Explain.

5 Martha earns R1875 each week and cannot borrow money. She buys fish fingers and the composite good. Suppose that fish fingers cost R31.25 per packet and the composite good costs R1 per unit.

   a Sketch Martha's budget constraint.

   b What is the opportunity cost, in terms of packets of fish fingers, of an additional unit of the composite good?

6 In Problem 5, suppose that in an inflationary period the price of the composite good increases to R1.50 per unit, but the price of fish fingers remains the same.

   a Sketch the new budget constraint.

   b What is the opportunity cost of an additional unit of the composite good?

7 In Problem 6, suppose that Martha demands a pay rise to fight inflation. Her boss raises her salary to R2812.50/wk.

   a Sketch the new budget constraint.

   b What is the opportunity cost of an additional unit of the composite good?

8 Picabo, a professional skier, spends her entire income on skis and bindings. She wears out one pair of skis for every pair of bindings she wears out.

   a Graph Picabo's indifference curves for skis and bindings.

   b Now draw her indifference curves, on the assumption that she is such an aggressive skier that she wears out two pairs of skis for every pair of bindings she wears out.

9 Suppose Picabo in Problem 8 has R36000 to spend on skis and bindings each year. Find her best affordable bundle of skis and bindings under both of the preferences described in the previous problem. Skis are R4800/pair and bindings are R2400/pair.

10 For Alexi, coffee and tea are perfect substitutes: one cup of coffee is equivalent to one cup of tea. Suppose Alexi is a housewife and has R1200/mth to spend on these beverages, and tea costs R12.00/cup whereas coffee costs R16.00/cup. Find Alexi's best affordable bundle of tea and coffee. How much could the price of a cup of tea rise without harming her standard of living?

11 Eve likes apples but doesn't care about pears. If apples and pears are the only two goods available, draw her indifference curves.

12 Johan Cronje likes food but because he is such a good athlete he hates cigarette smoke. The more food he has, the more he would be willing to give up to achieve a given reduction in cigarette smoke. If food and cigarette smoke are the only two goods, draw Johan's indifference curves.

13 If you were president of a conservation group, which rate structure would you prefer Eskom to use: the one described in Example 3.1, or one in which all power sold for R1.20/kWh? (Assume that each rate structure would exactly cover the company's costs.)

14 Pretty Yende, a famous opera singer, spends all her income attending plays, and movies and likes plays exactly four times as much as she likes movies.

a Draw her indifference map.

b Pretty earns R1600/wk. If theatre tickets cost R160 each and movie tickets cost R40 each, show her budget line and highest attainable indifference curve. How many plays will she see?

c If theatre tickets are R160 and movie tickets are R50, how many plays will she attend?

15 Sketch:

a A typical person's indifference curves between garbage and the composite good.

b Indifference curves for the same two commodities for Oscar the Grouch on *Sesame Street*, who loves garbage and has no use for the composite good.

16 Boris budgets R9/day for his coffee with Cremora. He likes it only if it is prepared with 4 parts coffee, 1 part Cremora. Coffee costs R1/teaspoon, Cremora R0.50/teaspoon. How much coffee and how much Cremora will Boris buy per week? How will your answers change if the price of coffee rises to R3.25/teaspoon? Show your answers graphically.

17 The Western Cape Education Department for Basic Education wants to support education, but does not want to support religion. To this end, it gives the Islamic Al Azhar High School in Cape Town R2 million, with the stipulation that this money be used for secular purposes only. The accompanying graph shows Al Azhar High School's pre-government gift budget constraint and best attainable indifference curve for secular and non-secular expenditures. How would the school's welfare differ if the gift came without the secular-use restriction?

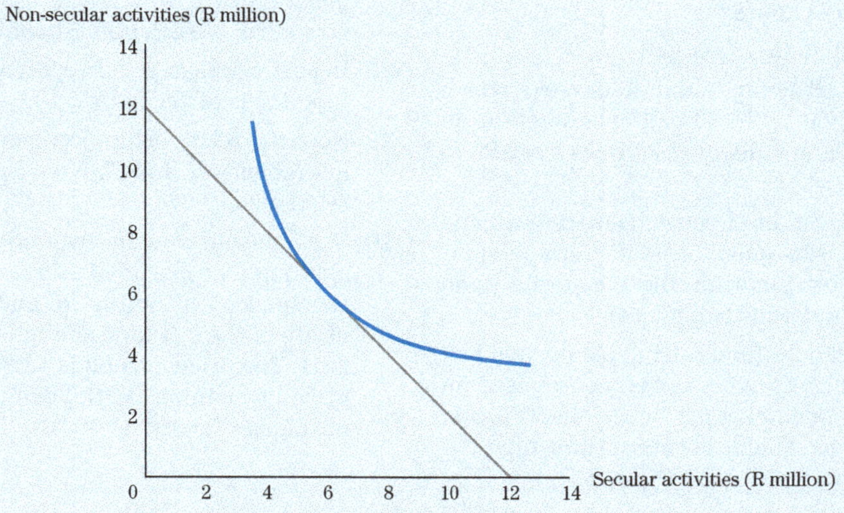

Problem 17

18 Telkom offers an optional package for international calling whereby each month the subscriber gets the first 50 minutes of international calls free, the next 100 minutes at R2.50/min and any additional time at the normal rate of R5.00/min. Draw the budget constraint for international phone calls and the composite good for a subscriber with an income of R4000/mth.

19 For the Telkom subscriber in Problem 18, what is the opportunity cost of making an additional 30 minutes of calls if he currently makes:

a 30 minutes of calls each month?

b 130 minutes of calls each month?

20 You have the option of renting a car on a daily basis for R700/day or on a weekly basis (6 or 7 days) for R3500/wk. Draw your budget constraint for a budget of R6300/trip.

a Find your best affordable bundle if your travel preferences are such that you require exactly R2450 worth of other goods for each day of rental car consumption.

b Alternatively, suppose you view a day of rental car consumption as a perfect substitute for R612.50 worth of other goods.

21 Howard said that he was exactly indifferent between consuming four slices of pizza and one beer versus consuming three slices of pizza and two beers. He also said that he prefers a bundle consisting of one slice of pizza and three beers to either of the first two bundles. Do Howard's preferences exhibit diminishing marginal rates of substitution?

22 Neotel, South Africa's latest telecommunications firm, has offered you a choice between the following billing plans for local calls outside business hours:

- Plan A: Pay R0.75 per call
- Plan B: Pay an initial R30/week, which allows you up to 30 calls per week at no charge; any calls over 30/week cost R0.75 per call.

If your budget for phone calls is R180/wk and the composite good costs R1, graph your budget constraints for the composite good and calls under the two plans.

***23** At your school's fund-raising picnic, you pay for soft drinks with tickets purchased in advance – one ticket per bottle of soft drink. Tickets are available in sets of three types:

- Small: R30 for 3 tickets
- Medium: R40 for 5 tickets
- Large: R50 for 8 tickets

If the total amount you have to spend is R120, and fractional sets of tickets cannot be bought, graph your budget constraint for soft drinks and the composite good that costs R10 per unit.

***24** Consider two very up-market Italian restaurants located in identical towns 2000 km apart. The restaurants are identical in every respect but their tipping policies. At one, there is a flat R150 service charge, but no other tips are accepted. At the other, a 15 per cent tip is added to the bill. The average food bill at the first restaurant, exclusive of the service charge, is R1000. How, if at all, do you expect the amount of food eaten in the two restaurants to differ?

***25** Mr R. Mogoba, a retired university administrator, consumes only grapes and the composite good $Y (P_Y = \text{R}1)$. His income consists of R100 000/yr from his retirement fund, plus the proceeds from whatever he sells of the 2000 bushels of grapes he harvests annually from his vineyard. Last year, grapes sold for R20/bushel, and Mogoba consumed all 2000 bushels of his grapes in addition to 10 000 units of Y. This year the price of grapes is R30/bushel, while P_Y remains at R1. If his indifference curves have the conventional shape, will this year's consumption of grapes be greater than, smaller than or the same as last year's? Will this year's consumption of Y be greater than, smaller than or the same as last year's? Explain.

26 Tom spends all his R150 weekly income on two goods, X and Y. His utility function is given by $U(X, Y) = XY$. If $P_X = 2$ and $P_Y = 5$, how much of each good should he buy?

27 Repeat Problem 26, except now Tom's utility function is given by $U(X, Y) = X^{1/2}Y^{1/2}$.

28 Note the relationship between your answers in Problems 26 and 27. What accounts for this relationship?

29 Sue consumes only two goods, food and clothing. The marginal utility of the last rand she spends on food is 18, and the marginal utility of the last rand she spends on clothing is 11. The price of food is R1.80/unit, and the price of clothing is R1.90/unit. Is Sue maximizing her utility?

* Problems marked with an asterisk (*) are more difficult.

30 Albert has a weekly allowance of R102, all of which he spends on used CDs (C) and DVD rentals (D), whose respective prices are R24 and R18. His utility from these purchases is given by $U(C) + V(D)$. If the values of $U(C)$ and $V(D)$ are as shown in the table, is Albert a utility maximizer if he buys 2 CDs and rents 3 DVDs each *week? If not, how should he reallocate his allowance?*

C	$U(C)$	D	$V(D)$
0	0	0	0
1	60	1	105
2	100	2	165
3	120	3	195
4	140	4	210

31 When you were born your parents bought an education savings plan in your name. Use indifference curve analysis to illustrate how your situation at university will change if the funds from that plan become available to you. Distinguish between a situation where it is stipulated that you may use the money only to buy education and a situation where you can spend it on anything.

Answers to in-chapter exercises

3.1

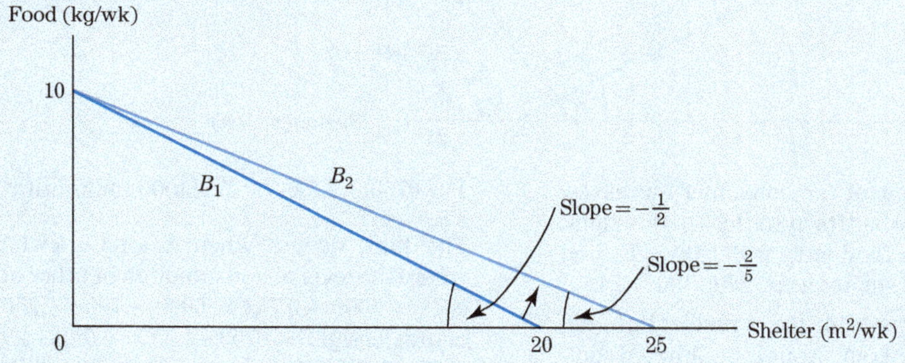

When the price of shelter becomes cheaper, the budget line becomes flatter. Intersection on the shelter axis: 2000/80 = 25.

3.2

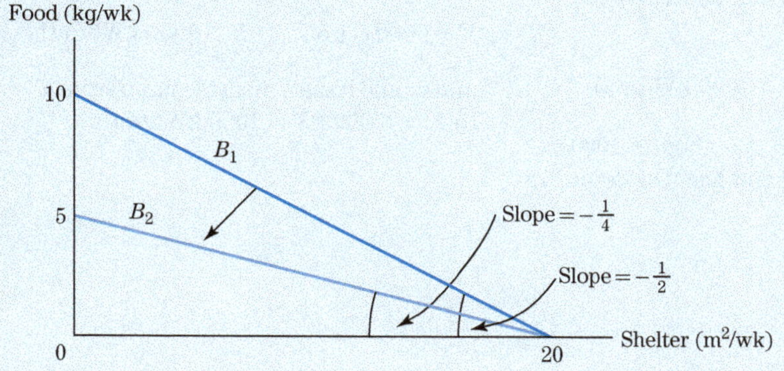

When the price of food increases, the budget line becomes flatter. Intersection on the food axis: 2000/400 = 5.

3.3

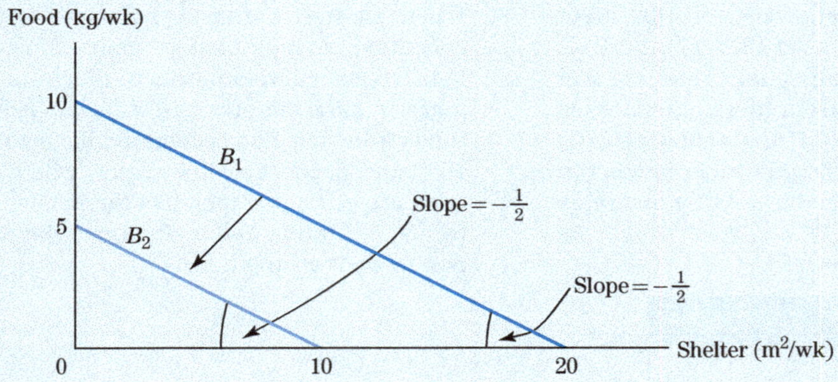

When the prices of both goods increase by the same percentage, the budget line shifts to the left, but the slope of the budget line stays unchanged.

3.4

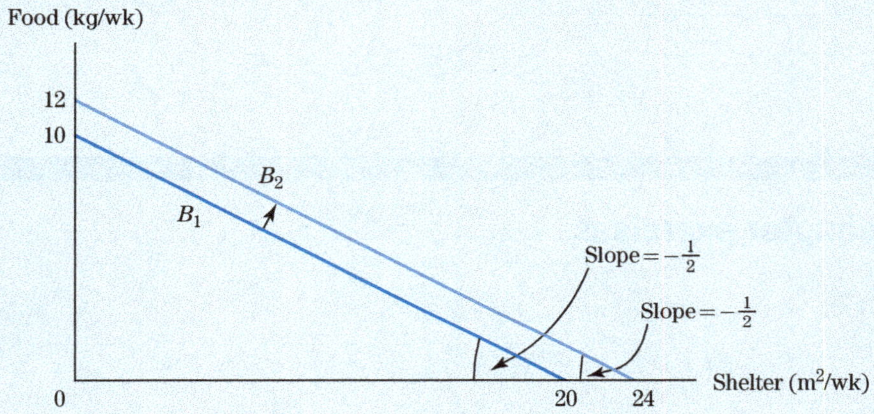

When the income of the consumer increases, the budget line shifts parallel to the right. Intersection on food axis: 2400/200 = 12, and intersection on shelter axis: 2400/100 = 24.

3.5 The budget constraint for a residential consumer with Eskom would be kinked outwards, as the initial rate for the first 1000 kWh/mth is lower (see figure at the top of page 91.) For power consumption X up to 1000 kWh/mth, the budget constraint has a slope at the lower rate, R0.75/kWh:

$$Y = 6000 - 0.75X \qquad 0 \leq X \leq 1000 \text{ kWh/mth}$$

For power consumption X above 1000 kWh/mth, the budget constraint has a slope at the higher rate, R1.50/kWh:

$$Y = 6750 - 1.5X \qquad X > 1000 \text{ kWh/mth}$$

The kink occurs when $X = 1000$ kWh/mth, where the level of consumption of other goods is $Y = 6000 - 0.75X = 6000 - 750 = 5250$ or, equivalently, $Y = 6750 - 1.5X = 6750 - 1500 = 5250$. If the rate were instead R1.00/kWh for all kWh that exceeded 1000 kWh/mth, then the budget constraint for $X > 1000$ kWh/mth would be

$$Y = 6000 - 1.5X \qquad X > 1000 \text{ kWh/mth}$$

and would have a discrete jump from $Y = 5250$ to $Y = 4500$ at $X = 1000$ kWh/mth.

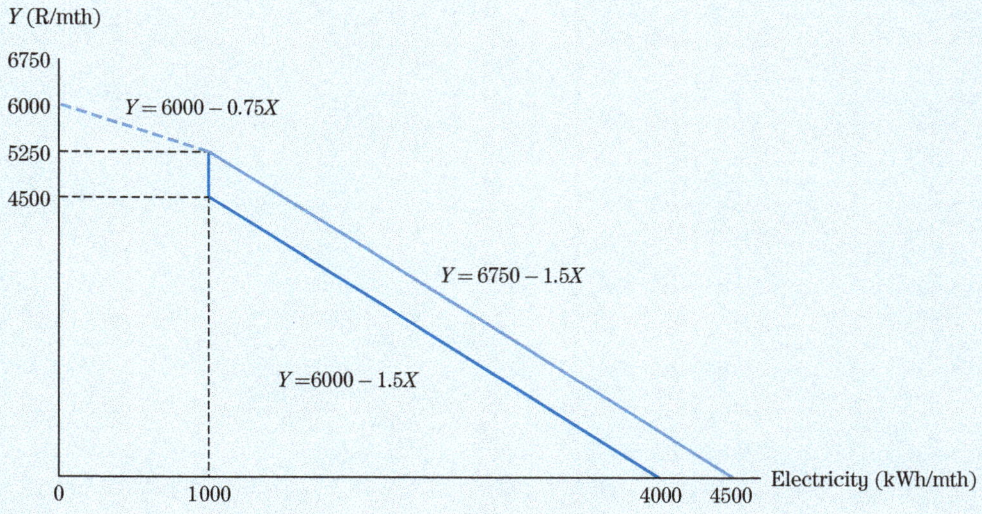

3.6 At bundle A, the consumer is willing to give up 1 kg of food to get an additional square metre of shelter. But at the market prices it is necessary to give up only $\frac{1}{2}$ kg of food to buy an additional square metre of shelter. It follows that the consumer will be better off than at bundle A if he buys 1 kg less of food and 2 m^2 more of shelter.

3.7 Albert's budget constraint is $1.5T = 180 - 3B$, thus $T = 120 - 2B$. Albert's initial preferences are for two pats of butter for every slice of toast: $B = 2T$. Substituting this equation into his budget constraint yields $T = 120 - 4T$, or $5T = 120$, which solves for $T = 24$ slices of toast, and thus $B = 48$ pats of butter each month. Albert's new preferences are for one pat of butter for every slice of toast: $B = T$. Substituting this equation into his budget constraint yields $T = 120 - 2T$, or $3T = 120$, which solves for $T = 40$ slices of toast, and thus $B = 40$ pats of butter each month.

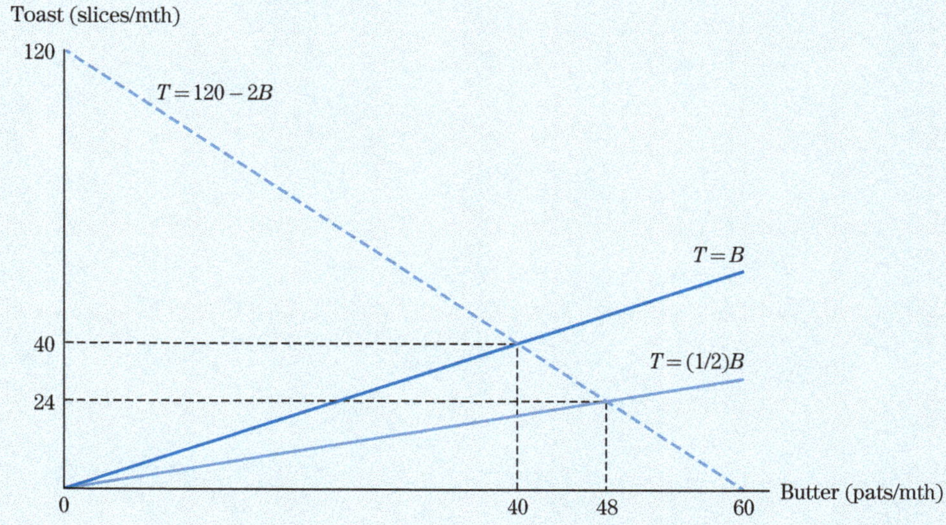

Chapter 4

Individual and market demand

A kilogram of salt costs R4.00 at the grocery store where I shop. My family and I use the same amount of salt at that price as we would if it instead sold for R2.00/kg or even R10.00/kg. I also consume about the same amount of salt now as I did as a graduate student (or even less because I have to watch my cholesterol levels) when my income was less than one-tenth of what it is today.

Salt is an unusual case. The amounts we buy of many other goods are much more sensitive to price and income. However, if I consider investing in property the situation is completely different. If I decide to buy a four-bedroom apartment in Stellenbosch where I live I may get a good buy at around R2.25 million. However, if I consider buying property in London to entrench me against the depreciating rand, the situation is different. A four-bedroom apartment in Ealing, on the outskirts of London, will sell for about £1 million, but the same apartment in the city centre may put me back £10 million! Clearly, I won't be able to buy in London the same type of property that I can afford in South Africa.

Chapter preview

Viewed within the framework of the rational choice model, my behaviour with respect to salt and housing purchases is perfectly intelligible. Our focus in this chapter is to use the tools from Chapter 3 to shed additional light on why, exactly, the responses of various purchase decisions to changes in income and price differ so widely. In Chapter 3 we saw how changes in prices and incomes affected the budget constraint. Here we shall see how changes in the budget constraint affect actual purchase decisions. More specifically, we shall use the rational choice model to generate an individual consumer's demand curve for a product, and employ our model to construct a relationship that summarizes how individual demands vary with income.

We shall see how the total effect of a price change can be decomposed into two separate effects: (1) the substitution effect, which denotes the change in the quantity demanded that results because the price change alters the attractiveness of substitute goods; and (2) the income effect, which denotes the change in quantity demanded that results from the change in purchasing power (or real income) caused by the price change.

Next we shall show how individual demand curves can be added to yield the demand curve for the market as a whole. A central analytical concept we shall develop in this chapter is the price elasticity of demand, a measure of the responsiveness of purchase decisions to small changes in price. We shall also consider the income elasticity of demand, a measure of the responsiveness of purchase decisions to small changes in income. And we shall see that, for some goods, the distribution of income, not just its average value, is an important determinant of market demand. A final elasticity concept in this chapter is the cross-price elasticity of demand, which is a measure of the responsiveness of the quantity demanded of one good to small changes in the prices of another good. Cross-price elasticity is the criterion by which pairs of goods are classified as being either substitutes or complements.

Network externalities will then be discussed. Here we will deal with the snob and bandwagon effects. The chapter will be concluded with a discussion of the intertemporal consumption bundles. We shall discuss how the consumer decides what to consume now and what will be consumed in the future.

The effects of changes in price

The price–consumption curve

Recall from Chapter 2 that a market demand curve tells us how much of a good the market as a whole wants to purchase at various prices (in other words, what consumers are *willing* to buy). Suppose we want to generate a demand schedule for a good – say, housing – not for the market as a whole, but for only a single consumer. Holding income, preferences and the prices of all other goods constant, how will a change in the price of housing affect the amount of housing the consumer buys? To answer this question, we begin with this consumer's indifference map, plotting housing on the horizontal axis and the composite good Y on the vertical axis. Suppose the consumer's income is R2400/wk and the price of the composite good is again R1 per unit. The vertical intercept of her budget constraint will then be 2400. The horizontal intercept will be $2400/P_S$, where P_S denotes the price of housing. Figure 4.1 shows four budget constraints that correspond to four different prices of housing: R480/m^2, R240/m^2, R120/m^2 and R80/m^2. The corresponding best affordable bundles contain 2.5, 7, 15 and 20 m^2/wk of housing, respectively. If we were to repeat this procedure for indefinitely many prices, the resulting points of tangency would trace out the line labelled PCC in Fig. 4.1.

Figure 4.1 The price–consumption curve

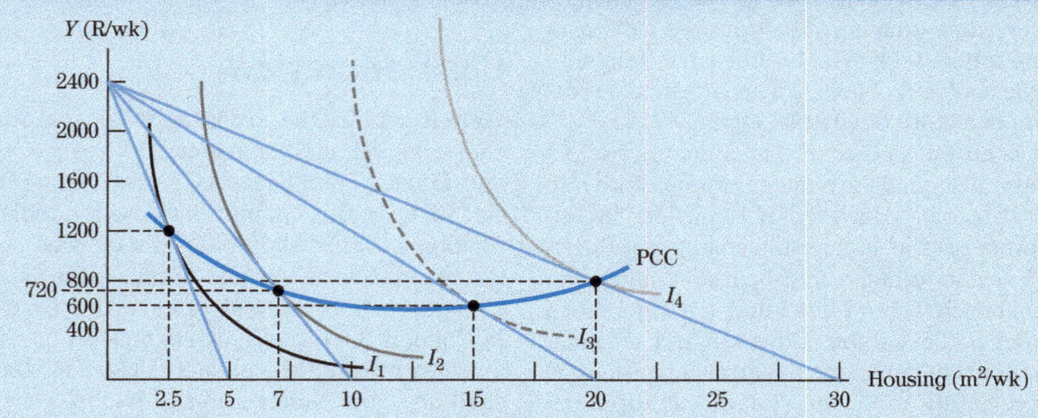

Holding income and the price of Y fixed, we vary the price of housing. The set of optimal bundles traced out by the various budget lines is called the price–consumption curve, or PCC.

Table 4.1 A demand schedule

Price of housing (R/m^2)	Quantity of housing demanded (m^2/wk)
480	2.5
240	7
120	15
80	20

To derive the individual's demand curve for housing from the PCC in Fig. 4.1, begin by recording the quantities of housing that correspond to the housing prices on each budget line.

Price–consumption curve (PCC) Holding income and the price of *Y* constant, the PCC for a good *X* is the set of optimal bundles traced on an indifference map as the price of *X* varies.

This line is called the **price–consumption curve,** or **PCC**.

For the particular consumer whose indifference map is shown in Fig. 4.1, note that each time the price of housing falls, the budget constraint rotates outwards, enabling the consumer to purchase not only more housing but also more of the composite good. And each time the price of housing falls, this consumer chooses a bundle that contains more housing than in the bundle chosen previously. Note, however, that the amount of money spent on the composite good may either rise or fall when the price of housing falls. Thus the amount spent on other goods falls when the price of housing falls from R480/m^2 to R240/m^2, but rises when the price of housing falls from R120/m^2 to R80/m^2. Below, we shall see why this is a relatively common purchase pattern.

The individual consumer's demand curve

An individual consumer's demand curve tells us the quantities the consumer will buy at various prices. All the information we need to construct the individual demand curve is contained in the price–consumption curve. The first step in going from the PCC to the individual demand curve is to record the relevant price–quantity combinations from the PCC (where the consumer is in equilibrium) in Fig. 4.1, as in Table 4.1.

The next step is to plot the price–quantity pairs from Table 4.1, with the price of housing on the vertical axis and the quantity of housing on the horizontal axis. With a sufficient number of price–quantity pairs, we generate the individual's demand curve, shown as *DD* in Fig. 4.2. Note carefully that in moving from the PCC to the individual

Figure 4.2 An individual consumer's demand curve

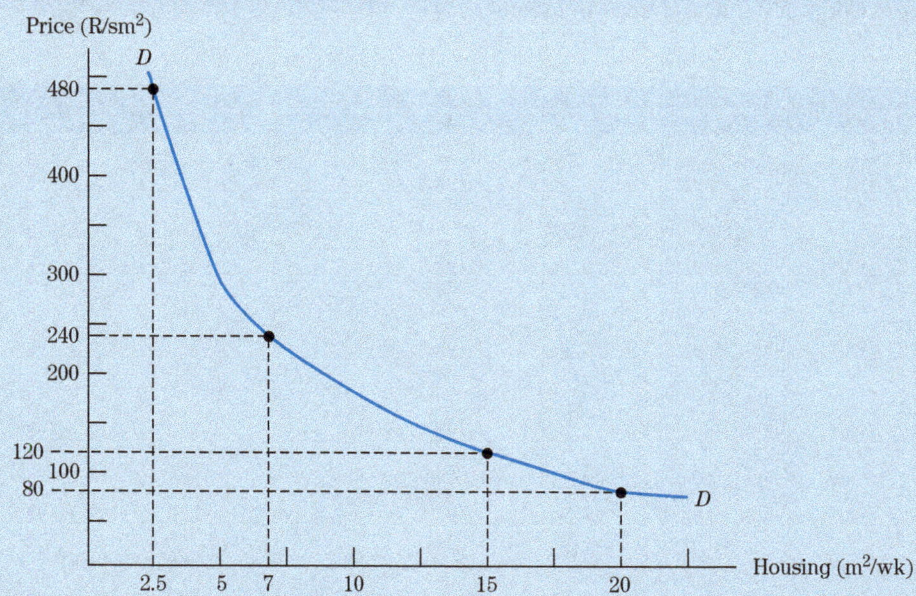

The individual demand curve is a relationship that tells us how much the consumer will purchase at different prices. Remember that it is only an indication of what the consumer is willing to do, because one can only operate on one point on the demand curve at a given time.

demand curve, we are moving from a graph in which both axes measure quantities to one in which price is plotted against quantity.

The effects of changes in income

The income–consumption curve

The PCC and the individual demand schedule are two different ways of summarizing how a consumer's purchase decisions respond to variations in price. Analogous devices exist to summarize responses to variations in income. The income analogue to the PCC is the **income–consumption curve**, or **ICC**. To generate the PCC for housing, we held preferences, income and the price of the composite good constant while tracing out the effects of a change in the price of housing. In the case of the ICC, we hold preferences and relative prices constant, and trace out the effects of changes in income.

Income–consumption curve (ICC)
Holding the prices of *X* and *Y* constant, the ICC for a good *X* is the set of optimal bundles traced on an indifference map as income varies.

In Fig. 4.3, for example, we hold the price of the composite good constant at R1 per unit and the price of housing constant at R200/m^2, and examine what happens when income takes the values R800/wk, R1200/wk, R2000/wk and R2400/wk. Recall from Chapter 3 that a change in income shifts the budget constraint parallel to itself. As before, to each budget there corresponds a best affordable bundle. The set of best affordable bundles is denoted as ICC in Fig. 4.3. For the consumer whose indifference map is shown, the ICC happens to be a straight line, but this need not always be the case.

The Engel curve

The analogue to the individual demand curve in the income domain is the individual **Engel curve**. It takes the quantities of housing demanded from the ICC and plots them against the corresponding values of income. Table 4.2 shows the income–housing pairs for the four budget constraints shown in Fig. 4.3. If we were to plot indefinitely many income–consumption pairs for the consumer shown in Fig. 4.3, we would trace out the line *EE* shown in Fig. 4.4, which is the Engel curve.

Engel curve
A curve that plots the relationship between the quantity of *X* consumed and income.

Note that on the vertical axis of the ICC we measure the amount the consumer spends each week on all goods other than housing. On the vertical axis of the Engel curve, by contrast, we measure the consumer's total weekly income.

Note also that, as was true with the PCC and individual demand curves, the ICC and Engel curves contain essentially the same information. The advantage of the Engel curve is that it allows

Figure 4.3 An income–consumption curve

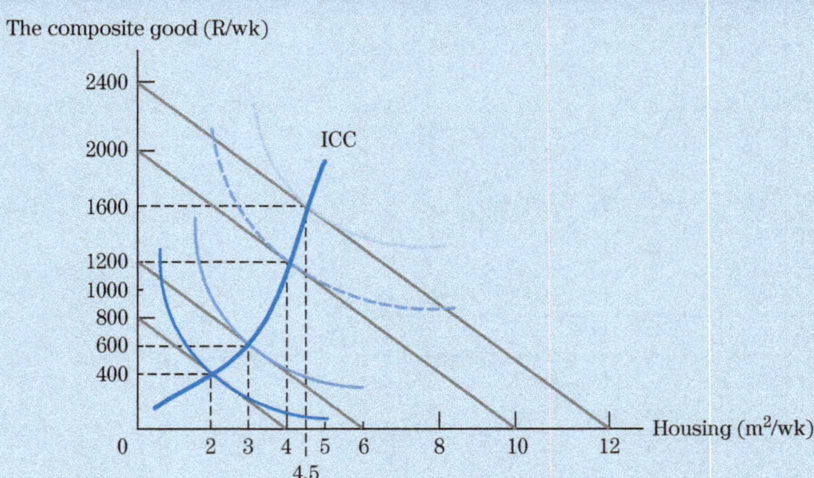

As income increases, the budget constraint moves outwards. Holding preferences and relative prices constant, the ICC traces out how these changes in income affect consumption. It is the set of all tangencies as the budget line moves outwards.

Table 4.2 Income and quantity of housing demanded

Income (R/wk)	Quantity of housing demanded (m²/wk)
800	2
1200	3
2000	4
2400	4.5

us to see at a glance how the quantity demanded varies with income.

Normal and inferior goods

Note that the Engel curve in Fig. 4.5(a) is upward sloping, implying that the more income a consumer has, the more tenderloin steak he will buy each week. Most things we buy have this property, which is the defining characteristic of a **normal good**. Goods that do not have this property are called **inferior goods**. For such goods, an increase in income leads to a reduction in the quantity demanded. Figure 4.5(b) is an example of an Engel curve for an inferior good. The more income a person has, the less maize porridge he will buy each week.

Normal good One whose quantity demanded rises as income rises.

Inferior good One whose quantity demanded falls as income rises.

Why would someone buy less of a good following an increase in his income? Instead of eating maize porridge for breakfast each morning, the consumer may prefer to eat more expensive breakfast cereals or bacon and eggs each day. For such a consumer, maize porridge is an inferior good.

For any consumer who spends all her income, it is a matter of simple arithmetic that not all goods can be inferior. After all, when income rises, it is mathematically impossible to spend less on all goods at once. Thus, whereas maize porridge is an inferior good for many consumers, there are probably very few people for whom 'food' is inferior.[1] It is important to remember that when a product is inferior it has nothing to do with the quality of the product. It is only an indication of how the quantity the consumer buys differs if income changes. A good may be inferior for certain consumers but a normal good for others. Black-and-white televisions, for example, may be an inferior good for the rich but a normal good for the poor.

The income and substitution effects of a price change

In Chapter 2 we saw that a change in the price of a good affects purchase decisions for two reasons. Consider the effects of a price increase. (The effects

Figure 4.4 An individual consumer's Engel curve

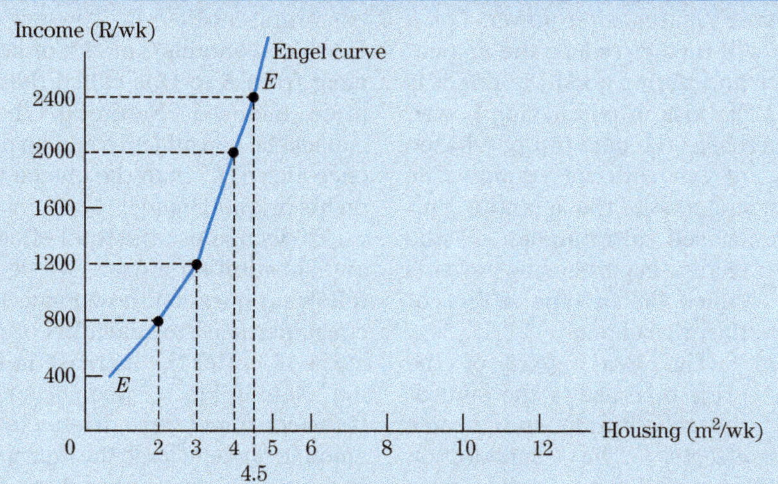

Holding preferences and relative prices constant, the Engel curve tells us how much housing the consumer will purchase at various levels of income.

[1] Another useful way to partition the set of consumer goods is between so-called *necessities* and *luxuries*. A good is defined as a luxury for a person if he spends a larger proportion of his income on it when his income rises. A necessity, by contrast, is one on which he spends a smaller proportion of his income when his income rises. (More on this distinction follows.)

Figure 4.5 The Engel curves for normal and inferior goods

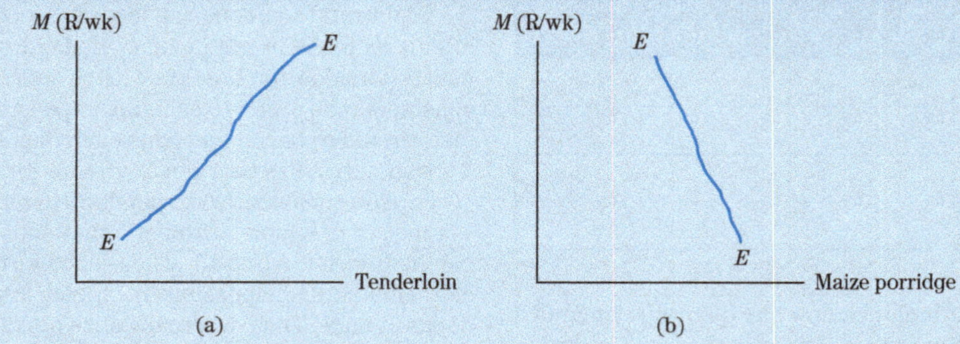

(a) This Engel curve is for a normal good. The quantity demanded increases with income. (b) This Engel curve for maize porridge has the negative slope characteristic of inferior goods. As the consumer's income grows, he switches from maize porridge to more desirable food such as breakfast cereals, or bacon and eggs.

of a price reduction will be in the opposite direction.) When the price of a good rises, close substitutes become more attractive (affordable) than before. For example, when the price of rice increases, wheat becomes more attractive. This is the so-called **substitution effect** of a price increase. Note that in this section the Hicks method will be used. 'The next step' section later explains the difference between this method and the Slutsky approach.

Substitution effect That component of the total effect of a price change that results from the associated change in the relative attractiveness of other goods.

The second effect of a price increase is to reduce the consumer's purchasing power. For a normal good this will further reduce the amount purchased, but for an inferior good the effect is just the opposite. The loss in purchasing power, taken by itself, increases the quantity purchased of an inferior good. The change in the quantity purchased attributable to the change in purchasing power is called the **income effect** of the price change.

Income effect That component of the total effect of a price change that results from the associated change in real purchasing power.

The *total effect* of the price increase is the sum of the substitution and income effects. The substitution effect is always the same for normal and inferior goods: when price goes up, quantity demanded goes down – and vice versa. The direction of the income effect depends on whether the good is normal or inferior. For normal goods, the income effect works in the same direction as the substitution effect: when price goes up, the fall in purchasing power causes the quantity demanded to fall, and when price goes down, the rise in purchasing power causes the quantity demanded to rise. For inferior goods, by contrast, the income and substitution effects work against one another.

The substitution, income and total effects of a price change can be seen most clearly when displayed graphically. Let us begin by depicting the total effect of a price increase. In Fig. 4.6 the consumer has an initial income of R2400/wk, and the initial price of housing is R120/m^2. This gives rise to the budget constraint labelled B_0, along which the optimal bundle is A, which contains 10 m^2/wk of housing. Now let the price of housing increase from R120/m^2 to R480/m^2, resulting in the budget constraint labelled B_1. The new optimal bundle is D, which contains 2 m^2/wk of housing. The movement from A to D is called the *total effect* of the price increase. Naturally, the price increase causes the consumer to end up on a lower indifference curve (I_1) than the one he was able to attain on his original budget (I_0).

To decompose the total effect into the income and substitution effects, we begin by asking the following question: how much income would the consumer need to reach his original indifference curve (I_0) after the increase in the price of housing? Note in Fig. 4.7 that the answer is R4800/wk. If the consumer were given a total income of that amount, it would undo the injury caused by the loss in purchasing power resulting from the increase in the price of housing. The budget constraint labelled B' is purely hypothetical, a device constructed for the purpose at hand. It has the same slope as the new budget constraint (B_1), namely −480, and is just far enough out to be tangent to the original indifference curve, I_0. With the budget

Figure 4.6 The total effect of a price increase

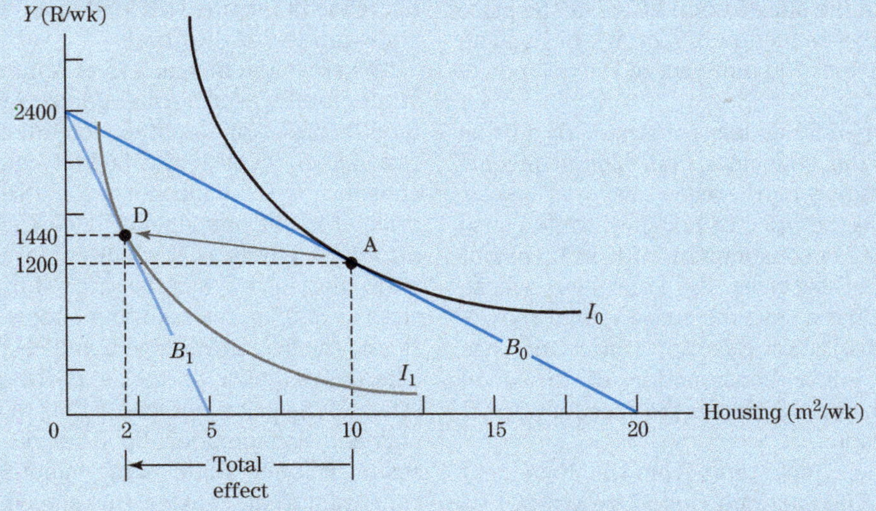

With an income of R2400/wk and a price of housing of R120/m², the consumer chooses bundle A on the budget constraint B_0. When the price of housing rises to R480/m², with income held constant at R2400/wk, the best affordable bundle becomes D. The movement from 10 to 2 m²/wk of housing is called the total effect of the price increase.

Figure 4.7 The substitution and income effects of a price change for a normal good

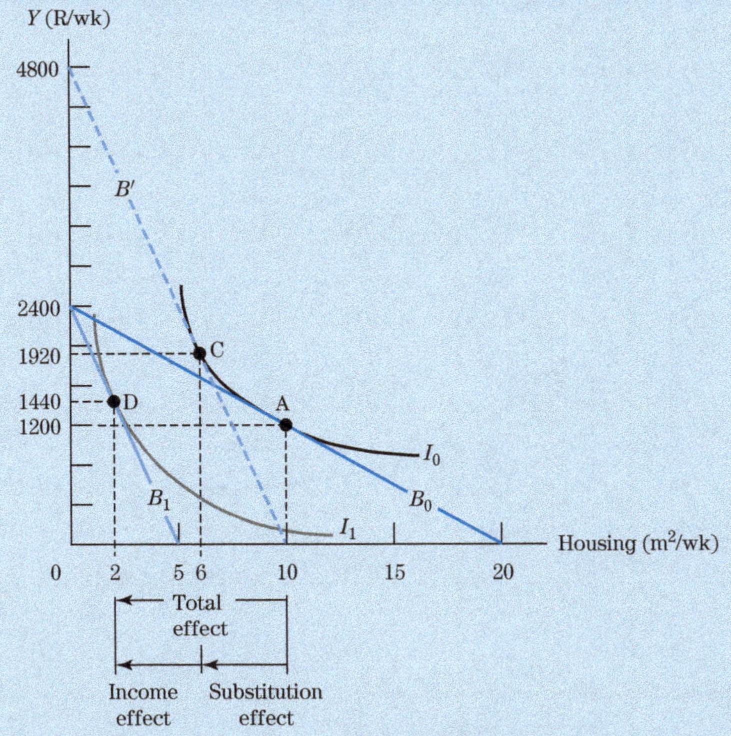

To get the substitution effect, slide the new budget B_1 outwards parallel to itself until it becomes tangent to the original indifference curve, I_0. The movement from A to C gives rise to the substitution effect, the reduction in housing due solely to the fact that housing is now more expensive relative to other goods. The movement from C to D gives rise to the income effect. It is the reduction in housing that results from the loss in purchasing power implicit in the price increase.

constraint B' the optimal bundle is C, which contains 6 m²/wk of housing. The movement from A to C gives rise to the substitution effect of the price change – here, a reduction of 4 m²/wk of housing and an increase of 720 units/wk of the composite good.

The hypothetical budget constraint B' tells us that, even if the consumer had enough income to reach the same indifference curve as before, the increase in the price of housing would cause him to reduce his consumption of it in favour of other goods and services. For consumers whose indifference curves have the conventional convex shape, the substitution effect of a price increase will always reduce consumption of the good whose price increased. This is the case for normal and inferior goods.

The income effect stems from the movement from C to D. The particular good shown in Fig. 4.7 happens to be a normal good. The hypothetical movement of the consumer's income from R4800/wk to R2400/wk accentuates the reduction of his consumption of housing, causing it to fall from 6 m²/wk to 2 m²/wk. This movement is in line with the definition of a normal good – a decrease in income will lead to a decrease in the consumption of the good.

Whereas the income effect reinforces the substitution effect for normal goods, the two effects tend to offset one another for inferior goods. In Fig. 4.8, B_0 depicts the budget constraint for a consumer with an income of R480/wk who faces a price of maize porridge of R20/kg. On B_0 the best affordable bundle is A, which contains 12 kg/wk of maize porridge. When the price of maize porridge rises to R40/kg, the resulting budget constraint is B_1 and the best affordable bundle is now D, which contains 9 kg/wk of maize porridge. The total effect of the price increase is thus to reduce maize porridge consumption by 3 kg/wk. Budget constraint B' once again is the hypothetical budget constraint that enables the consumer to reach the original indifference curve at the new price ratio. Note that the substitution effect (the change in maize porridge consumption associated with movement from A to C in Fig. 4.8) is to reduce the

Figure 4.8 Income and substitution effects for an inferior good

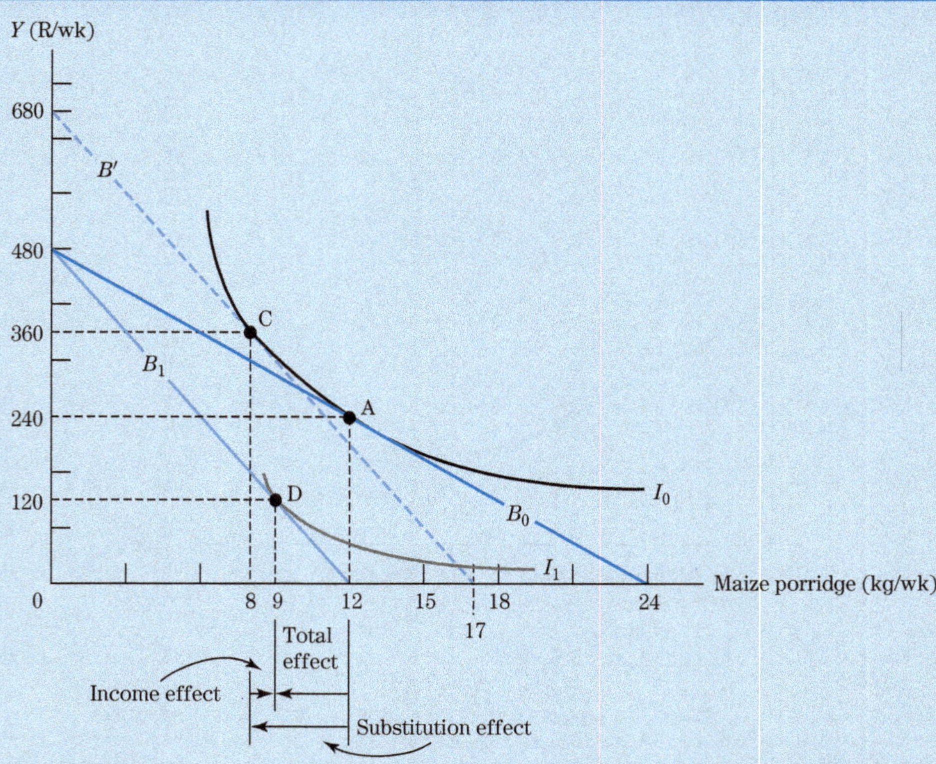

By contrast to the case of a normal good, the income effect acts to offset the substitution effect for an inferior good. Note that the decrease in consumption as a result of the substitution effect is greater than the increase in consumption as a result of the income effect. The total effect is thus in the direction of the substitution effect.

quantity of maize porridge consumed by 4 kg/wk – that is, to reduce it by more than the value of the total effect. The income effect by itself (the change in maize porridge consumption associated with the movement from C to D) actually increases maize porridge consumption by 1 kg/wk. The income effect thus works in the opposite direction to the substitution effect for an inferior good such as maize porridge.

Giffen goods

A **Giffen good** is one for which the total effect of a price increase is to increase, not reduce, the quantity purchased. Since the substitution effect of a price increase is always to reduce the quantity purchased, the Giffen good must be one whose income effect offsets the substitution effect. That is, the Giffen good must be an inferior good – so strongly inferior, in fact, that the income effect is actually larger than the substitution effect.

> **Giffen good** One for which the quantity demanded rises as its price rises.

A much-cited example of a Giffen good was the potato during the Irish potato famine of the nineteenth century. The idea was that potatoes were such a large part of poor people's diets to begin with, that an increase in their price had a severely adverse effect on the real value of purchasing power. Having less real income, many families responded by cutting back on meat and other more expensive foods, and buying even more potatoes (see Fig. 4.9.) Or so the story goes. Modern historians dispute whether the potato ever was really a Giffen good.

Figure 4.9 The demand curve for a Giffen good

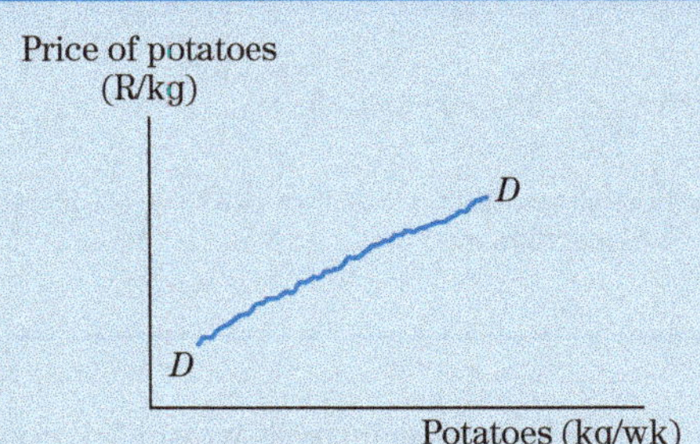

If a good is so strongly inferior that the income effect of a price increase dominates the substitution effect, the demand curve for that good will be upward sloping. Giffen goods are a theoretical possibility, but are seldom, if ever, observed in practice.

Whatever the resolution of this dispute, the potato story does illustrate the characteristics that a Giffen good would logically have to possess. First, it would not only have to be inferior but also account for a large share of the consumer's budget. Otherwise, an increase in its price would not create a significant reduction in real purchasing power. (Doubling the price of salt, for example, does not make anyone appreciably poorer.) The second characteristic required of a Giffen good is that it has a relatively small substitution effect, one small enough to be overwhelmed by the income effect. In practice, it is extremely unlikely that a good will satisfy both requirements and we do not encounter Giffen goods in reality.

Example 4.1 tells us that, if the price of ski bindings goes up relative to the price of skis, people will not alter the proportion of skis and bindings they purchase. But because the price increase lowers their real purchasing power (that is, because it limits the quantities of both goods they can buy), they will buy fewer units of ski equipment. The income effect thus causes them to lower their consumption of both skis and bindings by the same proportion.

Exercise 4.1

Do Example 4.1 (on page 102) with the assumption that pairs of skis and pairs of bindings are perfect two-for-one complements. (That is, assume that Paula wears out two pairs of skis for every pair of bindings she wears out.)

Exercise 4.2

Starting from the original price in Example 4.2 (on page 103), what will be the income and substitution effects of an increase in the price of tea to R22.50/cup?

Consumer responsiveness to changes in price

We began this chapter with the observation that, for certain goods, such as salt, consumption is highly insensitive to changes in price, whereas for others, such as housing, it is much more sensitive. The principal reason for studying income and substitution effects is that they help us understand such differences.

Consider first the case of salt. When analysing substitution and income effects, there are two

Example 4.1

Income and substitution effects for perfect complements

Suppose skis and bindings are perfect, one-for-one complements and Paula spends all her equipment budget of R12 000/yr on these two goods. Skis and bindings each cost R2000. What will be the income and substitution effects of an increase in the price of bindings to R4000 per pair? (First draw in the indifference curves and then add the budget lines.)

Since our goal here is to examine the effect on two specific goods (skis and bindings), we proceed by devoting one axis to each good and dispense with the composite good. The indifference curves are L-shaped, going through the points (1, 1), (2, 2), (3, 3), etc. The original budget line, B_0, is a linear curve cutting the skis axis at 6 and the binding axis at 6. The optimal bundle is denoted as A in Fig. 4.10. Paula buys three pairs of skis per year and three pairs of bindings. When the price of bindings rises from R2000 per pair to R4000 per pair, we get the new budget line B_1, and the resulting optimal bundle D, which contains two pairs of skis per year and two pairs of bindings. An equipment budget of R18 000/yr is what the consumer would need at the new price to attain her original indifference curve (I_0). (To get this figure, slide B_1 out until it hits I_0, then calculate the cost of buying the bundle at the vertical intercept – here, nine pairs of skis per year at R2000 per pair.) Note that because perfect complements have right-angled indifference curves, the budget B' results in an optimal bundle C that is exactly the same as the original bundle A. For perfect complements, the substitution effect is zero. So, for this case, the total effect of the price increase is exactly the same as the income effect of the price increase.

Figure 4.10 Income and substitution effects for perfect complements

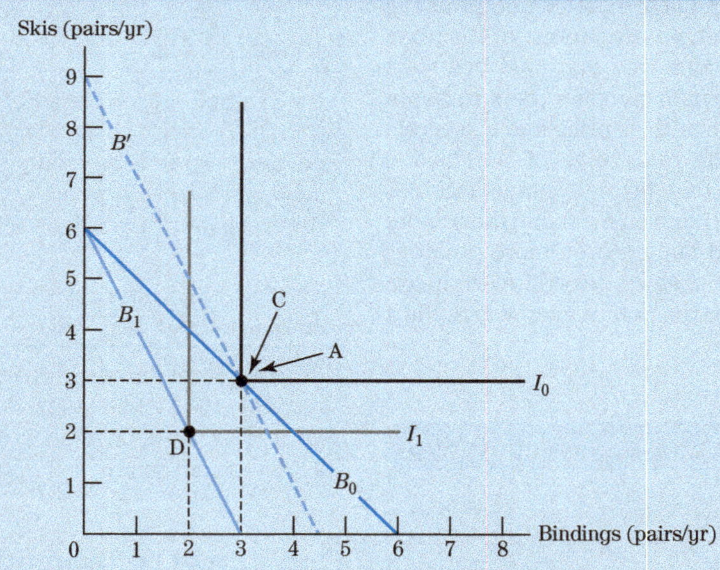

For perfect complements, the substitution effect of an increase in the price of bindings (the movement from A to C) is equal to zero. The income effect (the movement from A to D) and the total effect are one and the same.

salient features to note about salt. First, for most consumers, it has no close substitutes. If someone were forbidden to shake salt onto his steak, he might respond by shaking a little extra pepper, or even by squeezing some lemon juice onto it. But for most people, these alternatives would fall considerably short of the real thing. Salt's second prominent feature is that it occupies an almost imperceptibly small share of total expenditure. An extremely heavy user of salt might consume a kilogram every

Example 4.2

Income and substitution effects for perfect substitutes

Suppose Pam considers tea and coffee to be perfect one-for-one substitutes and spends R180/wk on these two beverages. Coffee costs R15/cup, whereas tea costs R18/cup. What will be the income and substitution effects of an increase in the price of coffee to R22.50/cup?

The indifference curves are straight lines like I_0 and I_1. The original budget line intersects the tea axis at 10 and the coffee axis at 12. Pam will initially demand 12 cups of coffee per week and no cups of tea (point A in Fig. 4.11), since each good contributes equally to her utility, but tea is more expensive (budget line B_0 and indifference curve I_0). When the price of coffee rises, Pam switches to consuming only tea, buying 10 cups per week and no coffee (point D: steeper budget line B_1 and indifference curve I_1). Pam would need a budget of R216/wk to afford 12 cups of tea (point C), which she likes as well as the 12 cups of coffee she originally consumed. The substitution effect is from (12, 0) to (0, 12) and the income effect from (0, 12) to (0, 10), with the total effect from (12, 0) to (0, 10). With perfect substitutes, the substitution effect can be very large: for small price changes (near the MRS), consumers may switch from consuming one good to consuming only the other.

Figure 4.11 Income and substitution effects for perfect substitutes

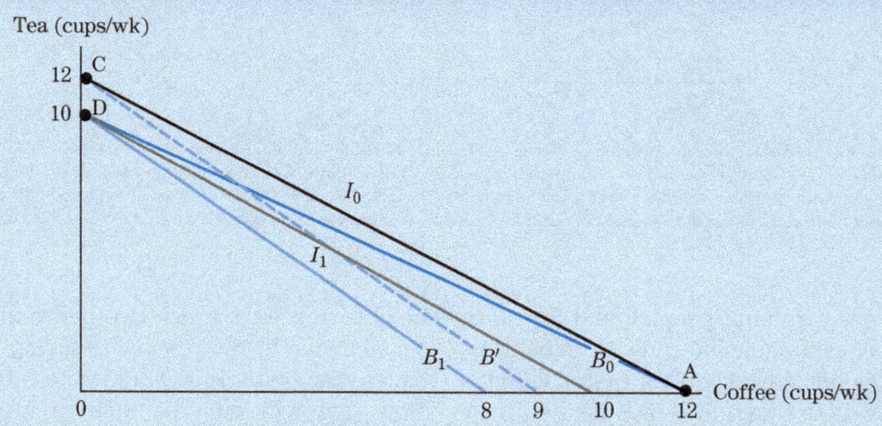

For perfect substitutes, the substitution effect of an increase in the price of coffee (the movement from A to C) can be very large.

month. If this person's income were R18000/mth, a doubling of the price of salt – say, from R6/kg to R12/kg – would increase the share of his budget accounted for by salt from 0.00033 to 0.00067. For all practical purposes, the income effect for salt is negligible.

In Fig. 4.12, the fact that salt has no close substitutes is represented by indifference curves with a nearly right-angled shape. Salt's negligible budget share is captured by the fact that the cusps of these indifference curves occur at extremely small quantities of salt.

Suppose, as in Fig. 4.12, that the price of salt is originally R6/kg, resulting in the equilibrium bundle A in the enlarged region, which contains 0.5002 kg/mth of salt. A price increase to R12/kg results in a new equilibrium bundle D with 0.5 kg/mth of salt. The income and substitution effects are measured in terms of the intermediate bundle C. Geometrically, the income effect is small because the original tangency occurred so near the vertical intercept of the budget constraint. When we are near the pivot point of the budget constraint, even a very large rotation produces only a small movement. The substitution effect, in turn, is small because of the nearly right-angled shape of the indifference curves.

Let us now contrast salt with housing. The two salient facts about housing are that: (1) it accounts for a substantial share of total expenditures (more

Figure 4.12 Income and substitution effects of a price increase for salt

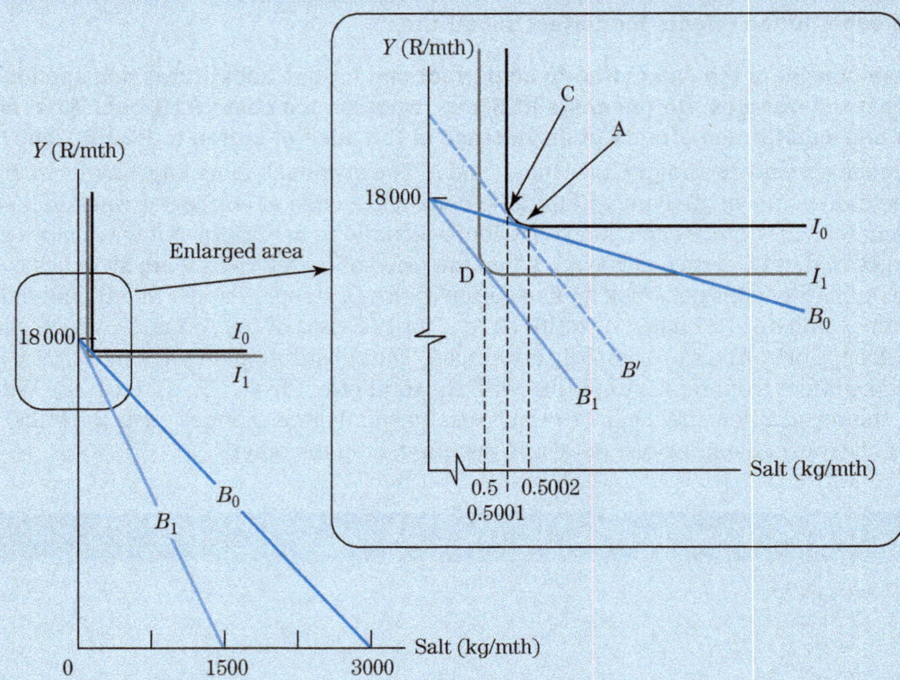

The total effect of a price change will be very small when (1) the original equilibrium bundle lies near the vertical intercept of the budget constraint, and (2) the indifference curves have a nearly right-angled shape. The first factor causes the income effect (the reduction in salt consumption associated with the movement from C to D) to be small; the second factor causes the substitution effect (the reduction in salt consumption associated with the movement from A to C) to be small.

than 30 per cent for many people); and (2) most people have considerable latitude to substitute other goods for housing. The first factor is highlighted by the fact that many people living in Johannesburg, for example, can afford to live in apartments larger than the ones they now occupy, yet they prefer to spend what they save in rent on restaurant meals, theatre performances and the like. Another substitution possibility is to consume less conveniently located housing. Someone who works in Johannesburg city centre can live near her job and pay high rent; alternatively, she can live in one of the suburbs and pay considerably less. Or she can choose an apartment in a less fashionable neighbourhood or one not quite as close to public transport. The point is that there are many different options for housing, and the choice among them depends strongly on income and relative prices.

Let us assume in Fig. 4.13 that you get a good job, earn R200 000/yr and the initial price of housing is R1000/m^2. The resulting budget constraint is B_0, and the best affordable bundle on it is A, which contains 100 m^2/yr of housing. You will thus be able to afford a nice two-bedroom apartment. An increase in the price of housing to R4000/m^2 causes the quantity demanded to fall to 20 m^2/yr. Now you will only be able to afford a small bachelor's flat. The smooth convex shape of the indifference curves represents the high degree of substitution possibilities between housing and other goods, and accounts for the relatively large substitution effect (the fall in housing consumption associated with the movement from A to C). Note also that the original equilibrium bundle, A, was far from the vertical pivot point of the budget constraint. In contrast to the case of salt, here the rotation in the budget constraint caused by the price increase produces a large movement in the location of the relevant segment of the new budget constraint. Accordingly, the income effect for housing (the fall in housing consumption associated with the movement from C to D) is much larger than for salt. With both a large substitution and a large income effect working together, the total effect of an increase in the price of housing (the fall in housing consumption associated with the movement from A to D) is very large.

Figure 4.13 Income and substitution effects for a price-sensitive good

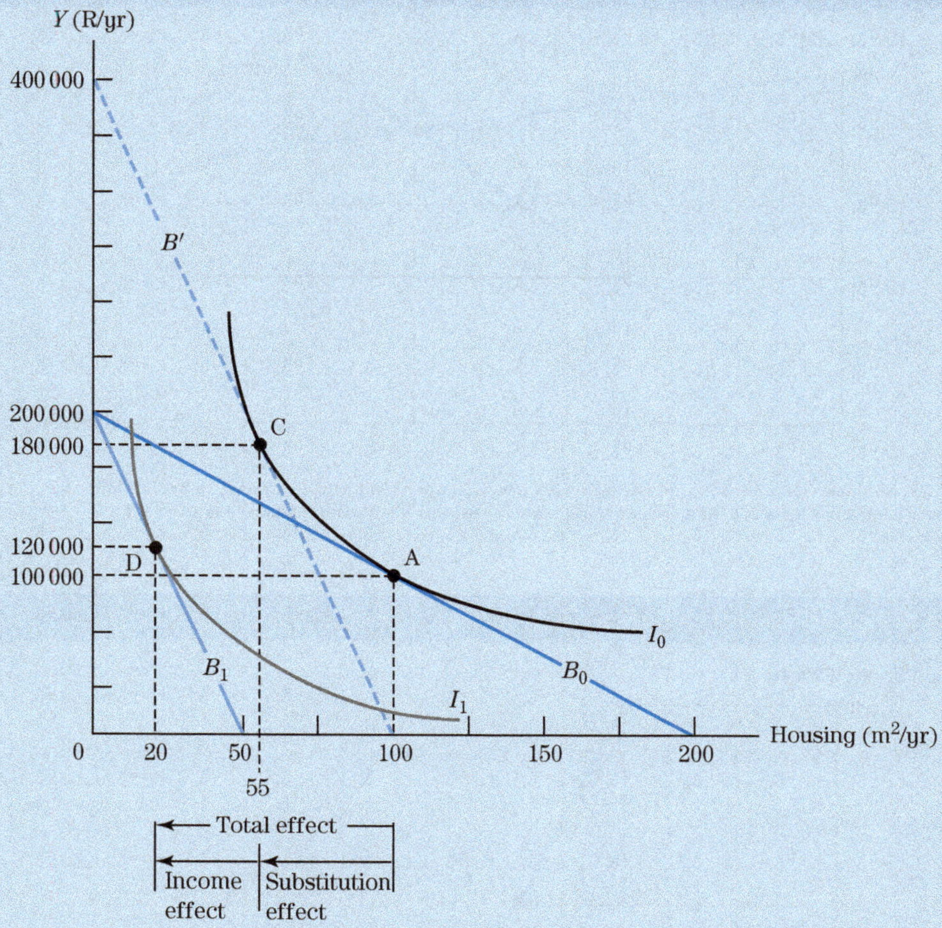

Because housing occupies a large share of the budget, its income effect tends to be large. And because it is practical to substitute away from housing, the substitution effect also tends to be large. The quantities demanded of goods with both large substitution and large income effects are highly responsive to changes in price.

Example 4.3

Deriving the individual demand curve for perfect complements

James views car washes and petrol as perfect complements in a 1:40 ratio, requiring one car wash for every 40 litres of petrol. Petrol costs R15/litre, and James has R5 760/mth to spend on petrol and car washes (see Fig. 4.14). Construct James' demand curve for car washes by considering his quantity demanded of car washes at various prices (such as R120, R360 and R840; see Fig. 4.15).

James' preferences dictate that his optimal bundle must satisfy $P = 40W$, as his indifference curves are L-shaped. James' budget constraint is $15P + P_W W = 5760$ (where P is petrol and not price), or $P = 384 - 0.67P_W W$. Substituting $P = 40W$, his budget constraint is $600W + P_W W = 5760$, which implies $(600 + P_W)W = 5760$. At $P_W = 120$, $W = 8$; at $P_W = 360$, $W = 6$; and at $P_W = 840$, $W = 4$, as summarized in Table 4.3.

Figure 4.14 A price increase for car washes

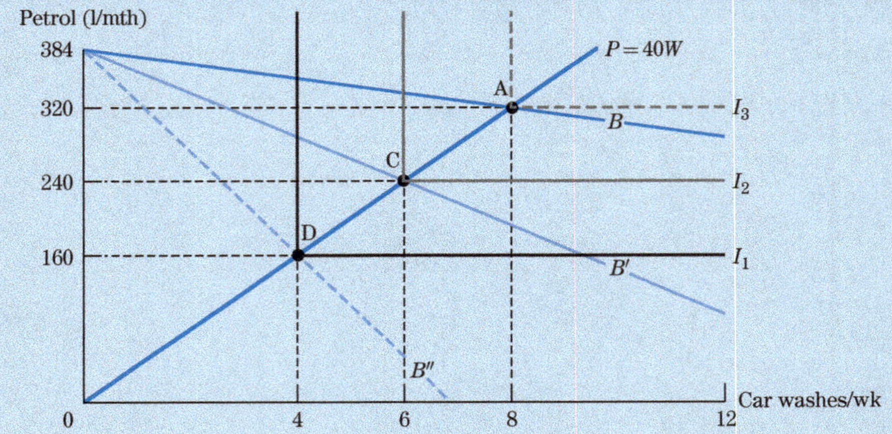

With R5760/mth, James buys 8 washes/mth when the price is R120/wash (budget constraint *B*), 6 washes/mth when the price is R360/wash (budget constraint *B*′) and 4 washes/mth when the price is R840/wash (budget constraint *B*′).

Figure 4.15 James' demand for car washes

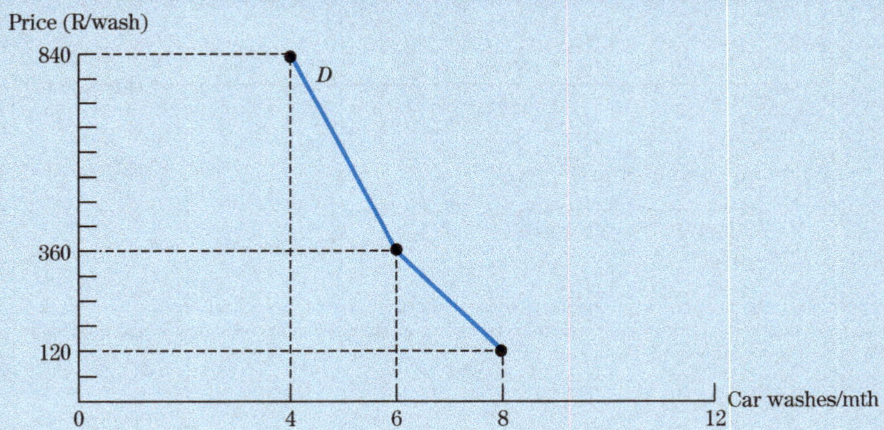

The quantity of car washes James demands at various prices forms his demand curve for car washes.

Table 4.3 A demand schedule for car washes

Price of car wash (R/wash)	Quantity of car washes demanded (washes/mth)
120	8
360	6
840	4
5160	1

'The next step'

The Slutsky approach to the income and substitution effects of a price change

We have discussed the fact that a price change in the price of a product involved a movement along the original indifference curve as well as a movement to a different indifference curve. What happens to the demand for housing when we change the price of housing? We divided the change into a substitution effect (the change in quantity demanded while utility stays the same) and an income effect (the change in quantity demanded while utility changes as a result of a change in real income, but the relative price of housing remains unchanged). The change in housing as the result of a unit change in the price of housing (keeping utility constant) is given by

$$\partial H/\partial P_{X\,(U\,=\,U^*)} \quad (4.1)$$

The total change in the quantity demanded of housing due to a unit change in its price is

$$dH/dP_X = \partial H/\partial P_{X\,(U\,=\,U^*)} + (\partial H/\partial I)(\partial I/\partial P_X) \quad (4.2)$$

From the budget constraint of the consumer $I = P_X X + P_Y Y$, it follows by differentiation that

$$\partial I/\partial P_X = X \quad (4.3)$$

Equation 4.3 tells us how much additional income will be needed after the price change to leave the consumer just as well off as he was before. It has become customary to write the income effect as a negative (reflecting a decrease in purchasing power); thus Eq. 4.2 changes to

$$dH/dP_X = \partial H/\partial P_{X\,(U\,=\,U^*)} - X(\partial X/\partial I) \quad (4.4)$$

In this format it is known as the Slutsky equation. The first term is the substitution effect, indicating the change in the quantity of housing demanded while keeping utility fixed. The second term is the income effect: the change in purchasing power resulting from the price change times the change in demand resulting from a change in purchasing power.

The Slutsky approach can be illustrated with the aid of Fig. 4.16. Assume the consumer is initially in equilibrium at E, where H_1 units of housing are consumed and Y_1 are spent on other goods. As housing becomes cheaper the new budget line will shift from AB to AB'. Slutsky reduces the consumer's income until the consumer can just afford the original bundle. The compensated budget line of Slutsky moves inward, parallel to AB' until it goes through the original consumption bundle at point E. This gives the budget line AB' and enables the consumer to reach a higher level of utility, I_2, at point E^*. This movement along the compensated budget line $C'D'$ from point E to E^* is the substitution effect. The shift of the budget line from $C'D'$ to AB' coupled with the movement from E^* to E' represents the income effect of the price decrease in housing.

Figure 4.16 Slutsky approach to the substitution and income effects of a price decrease for a normal good

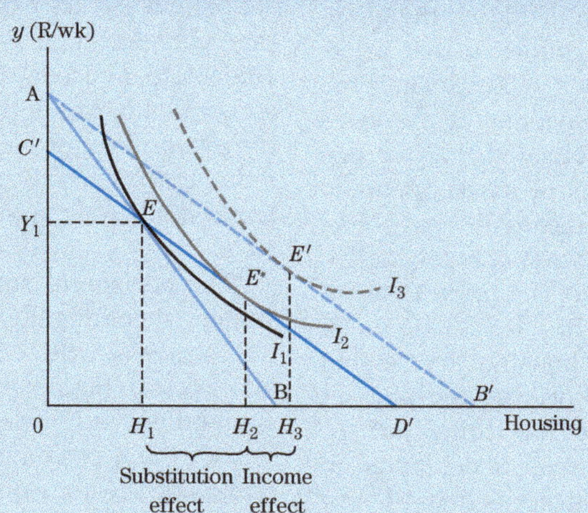

To get the substitution effect, slide the new budget line AB' parallel to the left until it goes through the original consumption point E. The movement from E to E^* gives rise to the substitution effect, the change in consumption of housing linked to the same real income, but a different set of prices. The shift from E^* to E' is the income effect of the price decrease in housing.

Figure 4.17 Generating market demand from individual demands

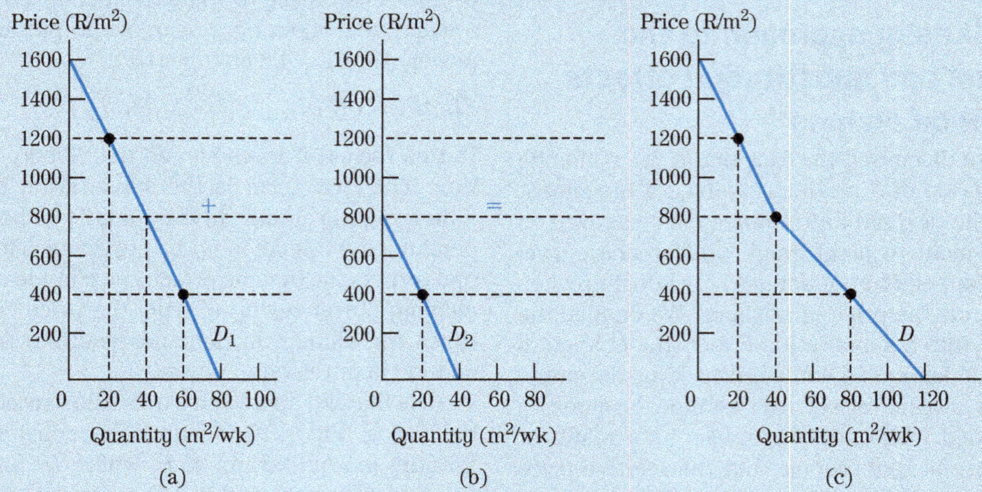

The market demand curve (D in panel c) is the horizontal sum of the individual demand curves, D_1 (panel a) and D_2 (panel b).

Market demand: aggregating individual demand curves

Having seen where individual demand curves come from, we are now in a position to see how individual demand curves may be aggregated to form the market demand curve. Consider a market for a good – for the sake of concreteness, again housing – with only two potential consumers. Given the demand curves for these consumers, how do we generate the market demand curve? In Fig. 4.17(a) and (b), D_1 and D_2 represent the individual demand curves for consumers 1 and 2, respectively. To get the market demand curve, we begin by calling out a price – say, R400/m² – and adding the quantities demanded by each consumer at that price. This sum, 60 m²/wk + 20 m²/wk = 80 m²/wk, is the total quantity of housing demanded at the price R400/m². We then plot the point (80, 400) as one of the quantity–price pairs on the market demand curve D in Fig. 4.17(c). To generate additional points on the market demand curve, we simply repeat this process for other prices. Thus the price R800/m² corresponds to a quantity of 40 + 0 = 40 m²/wk on the market demand curve for housing. Proceeding in like fashion for additional prices, we trace out the entire market demand curve. Note that for prices above R800/m², consumer 2 demands no housing at all, and so the market demand curve for prices above R800 is identical to the demand curve for consumer 1.

The procedure of announcing a price and adding the individual quantities demanded at that price is called *horizontal summation*. It is carried out the same way whether there are only two consumers in the market or many millions. In both large and small markets, the market demand curve is the horizontal summation of the individual demand curves. Do not get confused by the kink in the demand curve. It is because consumer 2 has no demand above a price of R800. Take time to go through this simple example again if you feel a bit unsure about Fig. 4.17(c) and convince yourself that it is just the horizontal summation of the other two demand curves.

In Chapter 2 we saw that it is often easier to generate numerical solutions when demand and supply curves are expressed algebraically rather than geometrically. Similarly, it will often be convenient to aggregate individual demand curves algebraically rather than graphically. When using the algebraic approach, a common error is to add individual demand curves vertically instead of horizontally. A simple example makes this danger clear.

The horizontal summation of individual consumers' demands into market demand has a simple form when the consumers in the market are all identical. Suppose n consumers each have the demand curve $P = a - bQ_i$. To add up the quantities for the n consumers into market demand, we rearrange the consumer demand curve to express quantity alone on one side $Q_i = a/b - (1/b)P$. (If we multiply the demand equation by n when P is the dependent variable, we are adding the curves vertically!) Then market demand is the sum of

Example 4.4

Disa and Hsieh are the only consumers in the market for beach chairs in a small town, Qumbu, in the Transkei. Their demand curves are given by $P = 300 - 20Q_d$ and $P = 300 - 30Q_h$, where Q_d and Q_h are the quantities demanded by Disa and Hsieh, respectively. What is the market demand curve for beach chairs in their town?

When we add demand curves horizontally, we are adding **quantities**, not prices. Thus it is necessary first to solve the individual demand equations for the respective quantities in terms of price. This yields $Q_d = 15 - (P/20)$ for Disa and $Q_h = 10 - (P/30)$ for Hsieh. If the quantity demanded in the market is denoted by Q, we have

$$\begin{aligned} Q &= Q_d + Q_h \\ &= [15 - (P/20)] + [10 - (P/30)] \\ &= 25 - (P/12) \end{aligned}$$

Solving back for P, we get the equation for the market demand curve: $P = 300 - 12Q$. We can easily verify that this is the correct market demand curve by adding the individual demand curves graphically, as in Fig. 4.18.

A common pitfall is adding the demand functions as originally stated. Here, this would yield $P = 600 - 5Q$, which is obviously not the market demand curve we are looking for.

Figure 4.18 The market demand curve for beach chairs

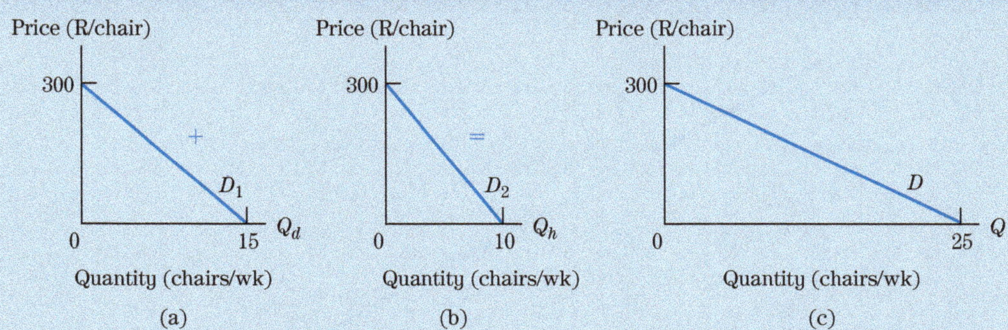

When adding individual demand curves algebraically, be sure to solve for quantity first before adding.

the quantities demanded, Q_i, by each of the n consumers:

$$\begin{aligned} Q &= nQ_i \\ &= n\left(\frac{a}{b} - \frac{1}{b}P\right) \\ &= \frac{na}{b} - \frac{n}{b}P \end{aligned} \quad (4.5)$$

We can then rearrange market demand, $Q = na/b - n(P/b)$, to get it back in the form of price alone on one side: $P = a - (b/n)Q$. It intuites that each one unit demanded by the market is $1/n$ unit for each consumer. These calculations suggest a general rule for constructing the market demand curve when consumers are identical. If we have n individual consumer demand curves $P = a - bQ_i$, then the market demand curve is

$$P = a - \left(\frac{b}{n}\right)Q$$

Exercise 4.3

Write the individual demand curves for housing in Fig. 4.17 in algebraic form, and then add them algebraically to generate the market demand curve for housing. (*Caution*: Note that the formula for quantity along D_2 is valid only for prices between 0 and 800.)

Example 4.5

Suppose a market has 10 consumers, each with demand curve $P = 10 - 5Q_i$, where P is the price in rands per unit and Q_i is the number of units demanded per week by the ith consumer (Fig. 4.19). Find the market demand curve.

First, we need to rearrange the representative consumer demand curve $P = 10 - 5Q_i$ to have quantity alone on one side:

$$Q_i = 2 - \tfrac{1}{5}P \tag{4.6}$$

Then we multiply by the number of consumers, $n = 10$:

$$\begin{aligned} Q &= nQ_i \\ &= 10Q_i \\ &= 10\left(2 - \tfrac{1}{5}P\right) \\ &= 20 - 2P \end{aligned} \tag{4.7}$$

Finally, we rearrange the market demand curve $Q = 20 - 2P$ to have price alone on one side, $P = 10 - \frac{1}{2}Q$, to return to the slope-intercept form.

Figure 4.19 Market demand with identical consumers

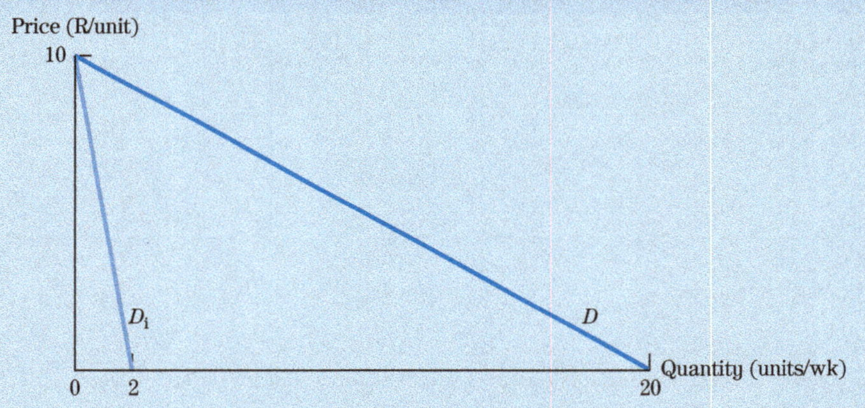

When 10 consumers each have demand curve $P = 10 - 5Q_i$, the market demand curve is the horizontal summation $P = 10 - \frac{1}{2}Q$ with the same price intercept and one-tenth the slope.

Exercise 4.4

Suppose a market has 30 consumers, each with the demand curve $P = 120 - 60Q_i$, where P is price in rands per unit and Q_i is the number of units demanded per week by the ith consumer. Find the market demand curve.

Price elasticity of demand

An analytical tool of central importance is the **price elasticity of demand**. It is a quantitative measure of the responsiveness of purchase decisions to variations in price, and as we shall see in both this and later chapters, it is useful for a variety of practical problems. Price elasticity of demand is defined as the percentage change in the quantity of a good demanded that results from a 1 per cent change in price.

Price elasticity of demand The percentage change in the quantity of a good demanded that results from a 1 per cent change in its price.

For example, if a 1 per cent rise in the price of housing caused a 2 per cent reduction in the quantity of housing demanded, then the price elasticity of demand for housing would be −2. The price elasticity of demand will always be negative (or zero), because price changes always move in the opposite direction to changes in quantity demanded. It is important to remember that we work with *percentage changes* and not the changes in absolute values.

The demand for a good is said to be *elastic* with respect to price if its price elasticity is less than −1 (or the absolute value of the price elasticity of demand is greater than 1). The example of housing mentioned in the preceding paragraph would thus be a good for which demand is elastic with respect to price. This means that the percentage change in quantity demanded is greater than the percentage change in price. The demand for a good is *inelastic* with respect to price if its price elasticity is greater than −1 (absolute value smaller than 1) and *unit elastic* with respect to price if its price elasticity is equal to −1 (absolute value equal to 1). These definitions are portrayed graphically in Fig. 4.20; Fig. 4.20(a) shows normal calculated values and Fig. 4.20(b) absolute values. As economists we normally use the absolute values to comment on the elasticity of demand for a product, although it is not wrong to work with the calculated negative values.

When interpreting actual demand data, it is often useful to have a more general definition of price elasticity that can accommodate cases in which the observed change in price does not happen to be 1 per cent. Let P be the current price of a good; let Q be the quantity demanded at that price; and let ΔQ be the change in the quantity demanded that occurs in response to a very small change in price, ΔP. The price elasticity of demand at the current price and quantity will then be given by

$$\varepsilon = \frac{\Delta Q / Q}{\Delta P / P} \qquad (4.8)$$

The numerator on the right side of Eq. 4.8 is the proportional change in quantity. The denominator is the proportional change in price. Equation 4.8 is exactly the same as our earlier definition when ΔP happened to be a 1 per cent change in current price. The advantage is that the more general definition also works when ΔP is any other small percentage change in current price.

A geometric interpretation of price elasticity

Another way to interpret Eq. 4.8 is to rewrite it as

$$\varepsilon = \frac{\Delta Q}{\Delta P}\frac{P}{Q} \qquad (4.9)$$

Equation 4.9 suggests a simple interpretation in terms of the geometry of the market demand curve. When ΔP is small, the ratio $\Delta P/\Delta Q$ is the slope of the demand curve, which means that the ratio $\Delta Q/\Delta P$ is the reciprocal of that slope. Thus the price elasticity of demand may be interpreted as the product of the ratio of price to quantity and the reciprocal of the slope of the demand curve:

$$\varepsilon = \frac{P}{Q}\frac{1}{\text{slope}} \qquad (4.10)$$

Equation 4.10 is called the *point-slope method* of calculating price elasticity of demand. By way of illustration, consider the demand curve for housing shown in Fig. 4.21. Because this demand curve is linear, its slope is the same at every point, namely, −2. The reciprocal of this slope is $-\frac{1}{2}$. The price elasticity of demand at point A is therefore given by the ratio of price to quantity at A (1200/200) multiplied by the reciprocal of the slope at A ($-\frac{1}{2}$), so we have

$$\varepsilon = \frac{1200}{200} \times \frac{-1}{2}$$
$$= -3$$

Figure 4.20 Three categories of price elasticity

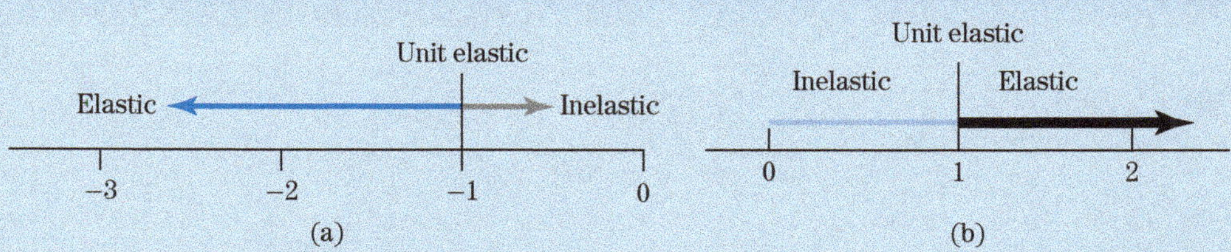

(a) Normal calculated values; (b) absolute values. With respect to price, the demand for a good is elastic if its price elasticity is less than −1, inelastic if its price elasticity exceeds −1 and unit elastic if its price elasticity is equal to −1.

When the market demand curve is linear, as in Fig. 4.21, several properties of price elasticity quickly become apparent from this interpretation. The first is that the price elasticity is different at every point along the demand curve. More specifically, we know that the slope of a linear demand curve is constant throughout, which means that the reciprocal of its slope is also constant. The ratio of price to quantity, by contrast, takes a different value at every point along the demand curve. As we approach the vertical intercept, it approaches infinity. It declines steadily as we move downwards along the demand curve, finally reaching a value of zero at the horizontal intercept.

A second property of demand elasticity is that it is never positive. As noted earlier, because the slope of the demand curve is always negative, its reciprocal must also be negative; and because the ratio P/Q is always positive, it follows that the price elasticity of demand – which is the product of these two – must always be a negative number (except at the horizontal intercept of the demand curve, where P/Q, and hence elasticity, is zero). As mentioned before, economists normally ignore the negative sign of price elasticity and refer simply to its absolute value. When a good is said to have a 'high' price elasticity of demand, this will always mean that its price elasticity is large in absolute value, indicating that the quantity demanded is highly responsive to changes in price. Similarly, a good whose price elasticity is said to be 'low' is one for which the absolute value of elasticity is small, indicating that the quantity demanded is relatively unresponsive to changes in price.

A third property of price elasticity at any point along a straight-line demand curve is that it will be inversely related to the slope of the demand curve. The steeper the demand curve, the less elastic is demand at any point along it. This follows from the fact that the reciprocal of the slope of the demand curve is one of the factors used to compute price elasticity. Just do not make the mistake of thinking that by looking at the slope of a demand curve you know whether it is elastic or inelastic. It all depends on the scale of the axes. A steep demand curve can also be drawn as a flatter curve by just changing the scale on the axes.

Another way to calculate price elasticity is to use calculus. The demand curve in Fig. 4.21 is a linear function, and thus in the format $y = mx + c$ (or $P = mQ + c$). In Fig. 4.21, c will take the value 1 600, and we know that the slope is -2. The standard format of the demand equation is $P = -2Q + 1\,600$. To use calculus, we have to rewrite the demand equation in the format $Q = f(P)$. Our demand function then becomes

$$Q = 800 - \frac{P}{2} \qquad (4.11)$$

Recall that the formula for price elasticity is $\varepsilon = (\Delta Q/\Delta P) \cdot (P/Q)$. We also know that $\Delta Q/\Delta P$ is

Figure 4.21 The point-slope method

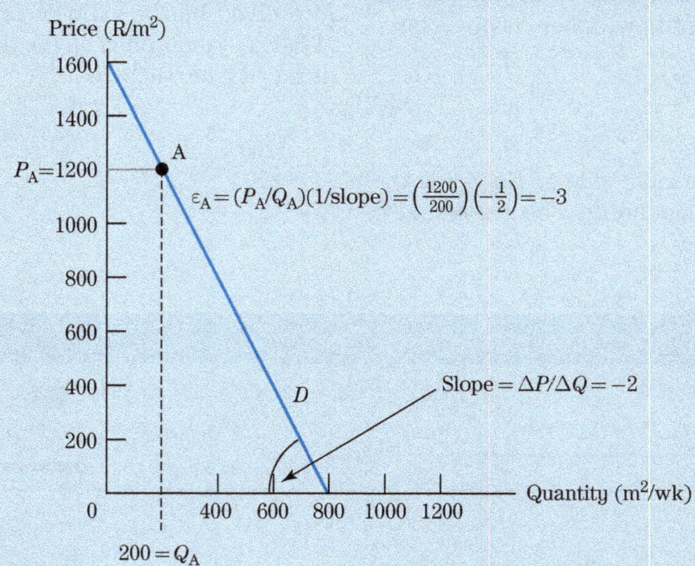

The price elasticity of demand at any point is the product of the price–quantity ratio at that point and the reciprocal of the slope of the demand curve at that point. The price elasticity at A is thus (1200/200) × (−1/2) = −3.

the slope of the function, which is also the first-order derivative of the demand function. The price elasticity can thus also be written as (and this is the formula that we always use)

$$\varepsilon = \frac{dQ}{dP}\frac{P}{Q} \tag{4.12}$$

The price elasticity at point A is thus $-0.5 \times (1200/200) = -3$.

Exercise 4.5

Use the point-slope method (Eq. 4.10 or 4.12) to determine the elasticity of the demand curve $P = 32 - Q$ at the point where $P = 24$.

Two polar cases of demand elasticity are shown in Fig. 4.22. In Fig. 4.22(a), the horizontal demand curve, with its slope of zero, has an infinitely high price elasticity at every point. Such demand curves are often called *perfectly elastic* and, as we shall see, are especially important in the study of competitive firm behaviour. In Fig. 4.22(b), the vertical demand curve has a price elasticity everywhere equal to zero. Such curves are called *perfectly inelastic.*

Although it is theoretically possible, it is almost impossible for any demand curve to be perfectly inelastic at all prices. Beyond some sufficiently high price, income effects must curtail consumption, even for seemingly essential goods with no substitutes, such as surgery for malignant tumours. Even so, the demand curve for many such goods and services will be perfectly inelastic over an extremely broad range of prices (recall the salt example discussed earlier in this chapter).

The unit-free property of elasticity

Another way of measuring responsiveness to changes in price is to use the slope of the demand curve. Other things being equal, we know for example that the quantity demanded of a good with a steep demand curve will be less responsive to changes in price than will one with a less steep demand curve.

Since the slope of a demand curve is much simpler to calculate than its elasticity, it may seem natural to ask, 'Why bother with elasticity at all?' One reason is that the slope of the demand curve is sensitive to the units we use to measure price and quantity, whereas elasticity is not. By way of illustration, notice in Fig. 4.23(a) that, when the price of petrol is measured in R/litre, the slope of the demand curve at point C is −0.02. By contrast, in Fig. 4.23(b), where price is measured in R/100 g, the slope at C is −0.00015625. In both cases, however, note that the price elasticity of demand at C is −3. This will be true no matter how we measure price and quantity, and most people find it much more informative to know that a 1 per cent cut in price will lead to a 3 per cent increase in the quantity demanded than to know that the slope of the demand curve is −0.00015625.

Some representative elasticity estimates

As the entries in Table 4.4 show, the price elasticities of demand for different products often differ

Figure 4.22 Two important polar cases

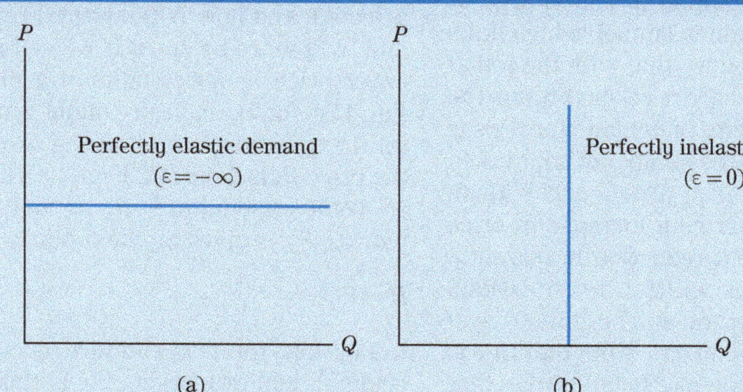

(a) The price elasticity of the demand curve is equal to −∞ at every point. Such demand curves are said to be perfectly elastic.
(b) The price elasticity of the demand curve is equal to 0 at every point. Such demand curves are said to be perfectly inelastic.

Figure 4.23 Elasticity is unit-free

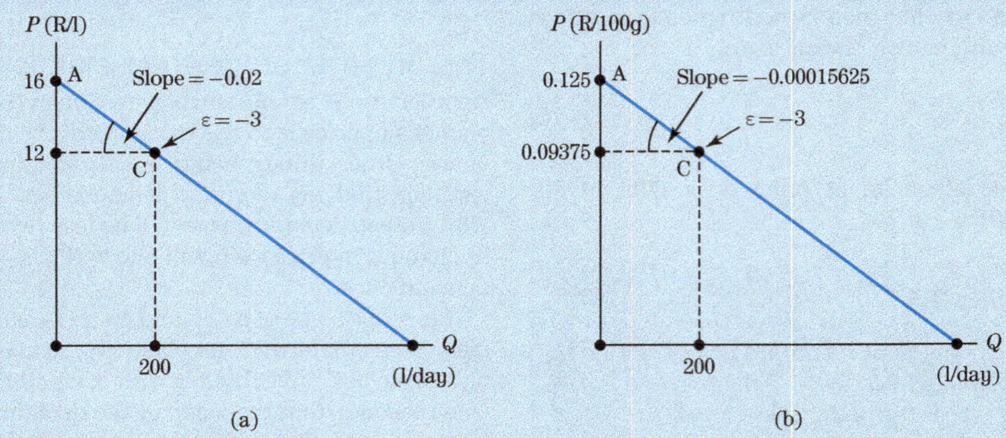

The slope of the demand curve at any point depends on the units in which we measure price and quantity. The slope at point C when we measure the price of petrol in rands per litre (a) is much larger than when we measure the price in rands per 100 grams (b). The price elasticity at any point, by contrast, is completely independent of units of measure.

substantially. Unless indicated otherwise, these elasticities are for South Africa. The low elasticity of the demand for electricity in the agricultural sector indicates that this sector is heavily dependent on electricity, irrespective of the price of electricity. On the other hand, in the industry they are much more sensitive to changes in the price of electricity and will try to adjust technology to use less electricity. Income effects for green peas are likely to be small, even for low-income consumers, yet the price elasticity of demand for green peas is more than 33 times larger than for water. The difference is that there are many more close substitutes for green peas than for water. Later in this chapter we investigate in greater detail the factors that affect the price elasticity of demand for a product.

Elasticity and total expenditure

Suppose you are the administrator in charge of setting tolls for the Huguenot Tunnel, which links Paarl and Worcester. Suppose that with the toll at R40/trip, 20 000 trips per day are taken through the tunnel. If the price elasticity of demand for trips is −2.0, what will happen to the number of trips taken per day if you raise the toll by 10 per cent? With an elasticity of −2.0, a 10 per cent increase in price will produce a 20 per cent reduction in quantity. Thus the number of trips will fall to 16 000/day. Total income at the higher toll will be (16 000 trips/day) × (R44/trip) = R704 000/day. Note that this is smaller than the total income of R800 000/day that occurred under the R40 toll. Remember that the total expenditure of motorists is equal to the total income of the operators of the tunnel. As a general rule, we can say that total expenditure of consumers will equal the total revenue of producers (or the suppliers of a service).

Now suppose that the price elasticity had been not −2.0 but −0.5. How would the number of trips and total expenditure then be affected by a 10 per cent increase in the toll? This time the number of trips will fall by 5 per cent, to 19 000/day, which means that total income will rise to (19 000 trips/day) × (R44/trip) = R836 000/day. If your goal as an administrator is to increase the total revenue collected from the tunnel toll, you need to know something about the price elasticity of demand before deciding whether to raise the toll or lower it.

This example illustrates the important relationships between price elasticity and total income (or expenditure). The questions we want to be able to answer are of the form, 'If the price of a product changes, how will total spending on the product be affected, and how will my total revenue change?' and 'Will more be spent if we sell more units at a lower price or fewer units at a higher price?' In Fig. 4.24, for example, we might want to know how total expenditures on housing are affected when the price falls from R1200/m^2 to R1000/m^2.

Total expenditure, R, at any quantity–price pair (Q, P), is given by the product

$$R = PQ \tag{4.13}$$

In Fig. 4.24, total expenditure by consumers at the original quantity–price pair is thus (R1200/m^2) × (400 m^2/wk) = R480 000/wk. Geometrically, it is the sum of the two shaded areas E and F. Following the price reduction, the new total expenditure is

Table 4.4 Price elasticity estimates for selected products

Good or service	Price elasticity
Green peas (Africa)	−6.7
Avocados (Africa)	−2.9
Mangoes (Africa)	−7.7
Electricity (industry)	−0.9
Electricity (agriculture)	−0.2
Alcoholic beverages	−0.6
Cell phones	−2.6
Demand for credit	−0.3
Cigarettes	−0.6
Water	−0.2
Marijuana	−1.0
Air travel business (Canada)	−0.4
Air travel leisure (Canada)	−1.3

(R1000/m^2) × (600 m^2/wk) = R600 000/wk, which is the sum of the shaded areas F and G. These two total expenditures have in common the shaded area F. The change in total expenditure is thus the difference in the two shaded areas E and G. The area E, which is (R200/m^2) × (400 m^2/wk) = R80 000/wk, may be interpreted as the reduction in expenditure caused by selling the original 400 m^2/wk at the new, lower price. G, in turn, is the increase in expenditure caused by the additional 200 m^2/wk of sales. This area is given by (R1000/m^2) × (200 m^2/wk) = R200 000/wk. Whether total expenditure rises or falls thus boils down to whether the gain from additional sales exceeds the loss from lower prices. Here, the gain exceeds the loss by R120 000, so total expenditure (or total revenue) rises by that amount following the price reduction.

If the change in price is small, we can say how total expenditure will move if we know the initial price elasticity of demand. Recall that one way of expressing price elasticity is the percentage change in quantity divided by the corresponding percentage change in price. If the absolute value of that quotient exceeds 1, we know that the percentage change in quantity is larger than the percentage change in price. And when that happens, the increase in expenditure from additional sales (in other words, your additional income as a seller) will always exceed the reduction from sales of existing units at the lower price. In Fig, 4.24, note that the elasticity at the original price of R1200 is −3.0, which confirms our earlier observation that the price reduction lead to an increase in total expenditure. Suppose, on the contrary, that price elasticity is less than unity. Then the percentage change in quantity will be smaller than the corresponding percentage change in price, and the additional sales will not compensate for the reduction in expenditure from sales at a lower price. Here, a price reduction will lead to a reduction in total expenditure as well as in the total revenue of the producer.

Exercise 4.6

For the demand curve in Fig. 4.24 (on page 116), what is the price elasticity of demand when P = R400/m^2? What will happen to total expenditure (or income of the sellers) on housing when price falls from R400/m^2 to R300/m^2?

The general rule for small price reductions, then, is this:

> A price reduction will increase total revenue if and only if the absolute value of the price elasticity of demand is greater than 1.

Parallel reasoning leads to an analogous rule for small price increases:

> An increase in price will increase total revenue if and only if the absolute value of the price elasticity is less than 1.

Some of these short-run elasticity estimates represent the midpoint of the corresponding range of estimates.

Sources: D. Hallam, P. Liu, G. Lavers, P. Pilkauskas, G. Rapsomanikis and J. Claro, *The Market for Non-traditional Agricultural Exports*, FAO Commodities and Trade Technical Paper 3, 2004; A. B. Van As, C.D.H. Parry and M. Blecher, 'The alcohol injury fund', *South African Medical Journal Forum*, 2003, vol. 93, no. 11, pp. 828–829; F. Gasmi, M. Ivaldi and L. R. Virto, *An Empirical Analysis of Cellular Demand in South Africa*, Institut d'Économie Industrielle (IDEI) Working Paper no. 531, 2008 (available at http://idei.fr/doc/wp/2008/cellular_demand.pdf); D. Karlon and J. Ziman, *Elasticities of Demand for Consumer Credit*, Yale University Economic Growth Center Discussion Paper 926, 2005; Abt Associates, *Illicit Drugs: Price Elasticity of Demand and Supply*, 2005; W.H. Boshoff, *Price Elasticity and Other Factors Shaping Cigarette Demand in South Africa 1996–2006*, Stellenbosch Economic Working Paper 14/07, 2007; R. Inglessi-Lotz and J.M. Blignaut, 'Estimating the price elasticity of demand for electricity by sector in South Africa', *South African Journal of Management Sciences*, vol. 14, no. 4, 2011; D.W. Gillen, W.G. Morrison and C. Steward, *Air Travel Demand Elasticities: Concepts, Issues and Measurement*, Canadian Department of Finance, 2008.

Figure 4.24 The effect on total expenditure of a reduction in price

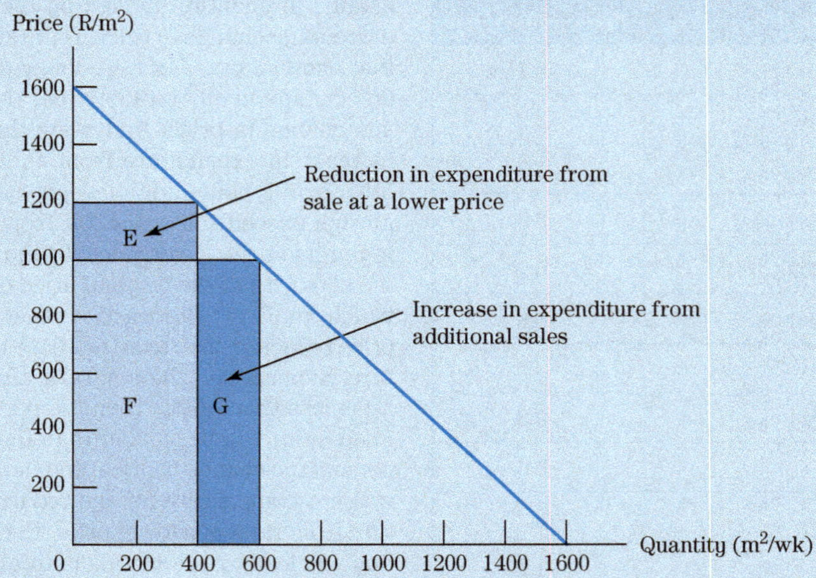

When price falls, people spend less on existing units (E). But they also buy more units (G). Here, G is larger than E, which means that total expenditure rises.

Figure 4.25 Demand and total expenditure

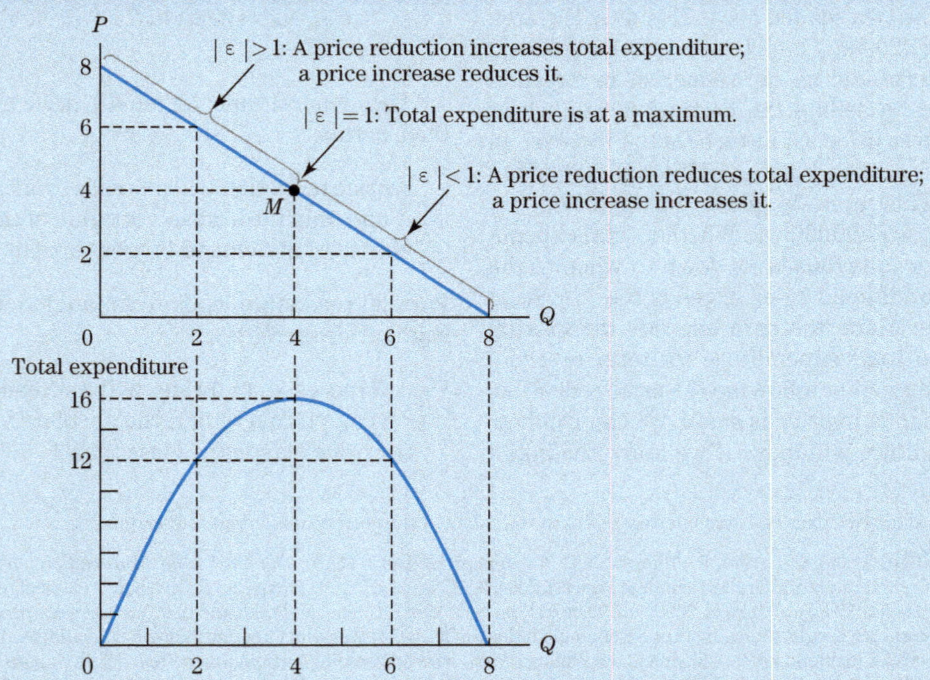

When demand is elastic, total expenditure of consumers changes in the opposite direction from a change in price. When demand is inelastic, total expenditure and price both move in the same direction. At the midpoint of the demand curve (M), total expenditure is at a maximum.

These rules are summarized in the top panel of Fig. 4.25, where M is the midpoint of the demand curve.

The relationship between elasticity and total expenditure is spelled out in greater detail in the relationship between the top and bottom panels of Fig. 4.25. The top panel shows a straight-line demand curve. For each quantity, the bottom panel shows the corresponding total expenditure. As indicated in the bottom panel, total expenditure starts at zero when Q is zero, and increases to its maximum value at the quantity corresponding to the midpoint of the demand curve (point M in the top panel). At that quantity, price elasticity is unity. Beyond that quantity, total expenditure declines with output, reaching zero at the horizontal intercept of the demand curve. If a firm operates on the elastic part of the demand curve, it will have to decrease price to increase its income. If it operates on the inelastic part of the demand curve, an increase in price will lead to an increase in total revenue. Recall that, although the slope of a straight-line demand curve is always the same on any point on that curve, the price elasticity of demand changes as you move along the curve.

Elasticity and tax income

If government wants to levy a tax on a product it is important that it knows whether the demand for that product is elastic or inelastic. This can be illustrated with Fig. 4.26, where the demand in Fig. 4.26(a) is inelastic and the demand in Fig. 4.26(b) is elastic. Also assume that the initial market equilibrium price in both markets is P_0. Now an equal tax is levied in both markets, shifting the supply curves vertically up with the size of the tax. It is clear that the consumers in the inelastic market are going to pay the burden of the tax and clearly more than in the elastic market ($P_1 > P_3$). Government is also going to collect more income in the inelastic market than in the elastic market (area P_1ABP_2 > area P_3CDP_4). The deadweight loss (which will be discussed in more detail in Chapters 10 and 11) is also smaller in the inelastic market than in the elastic market (area ABE < area CDE). The implication is thus very simple. If the government wants to levy a tax on a product, it makes more sense to do it in a market where the elasticity of demand is inelastic.

Determinants of price elasticity of demand

What factors influence the price elasticity of demand for a product? Our earlier discussion of substitution and income effects suggests primary roles for the following factors.

Substitution possibilities

The substitution effect of a price change tends to be small for goods with no close substitutes. Consider, for example, the vaccine against rabies. People who have been bitten by rabid animals have no substitute for this vaccine, so demand for it is highly inelastic. We saw that the same was true for a good such as salt. But consider now the demand

Figure 4.26 Implication of levying a tax in markets with different demand elasticities

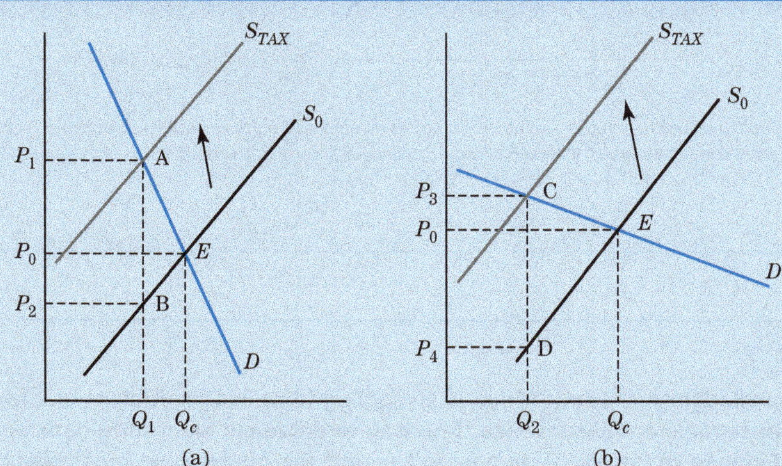

When a tax is levied on a product, the consumers pay more of the tax in an inelastic market ($P_1 - P_0 > P_3 - P_0$), the government gather more revenue (area P_1ABP_2 > area P_3CDP_4) and the dead-weight loss is also smaller (area ABE < area CDE).

Example 4.6

The market demand curve for bus rides in a small community is given by $P = 15 - (Q/100)$, where P is the fare per ride and Q is the number of rides each day. If the price is R7.50/ride, how much revenue will the transit system collect each day? What is the price elasticity of demand for rides? If the system needs more revenue, should it raise or lower price? How would your answers have differed if the initial price had been not R7.50/ride but R10?

Total revenue for the bus system is equal to total expenditure by riders, which is the product PQ. First, we solve for Q from the demand curve and get $Q = 1500 - 100P$. When P is R7.50/ride, Q will be 750 rides/day, and the resulting total revenue will be R5625/day. To compute the price elasticity of demand, we can use the formula $(dQ/dP)(P/Q)$. Here, $dQ/dP = -100$ and P/Q takes the value $7.50/750 = 1/100$. Price elasticity is thus the product $-100 \times (1/100) = -1$. With a price elasticity of unity, total revenue attains its maximum value. If the bus company either raises or lowers its price, it will earn less than it does at the current price.

At a price of R7.50, the company was operating at the midpoint of its demand curve. If the price had instead been R10, it would be operating above the midpoint. More precisely, it would be halfway between the midpoint and the vertical intercept (point K in Fig. 4.27). Quantity would be only 500 rides/day, and price elasticity would have been -2 (computed, for example, by multiplying the price–quantity ratio at K, $10/500 = 0.02$, by the derivative of the demand curve, -100). Operating at an elastic point on its demand curve, the company could increase total revenue by cutting its price.

Figure 4.27 The demand for bus rides

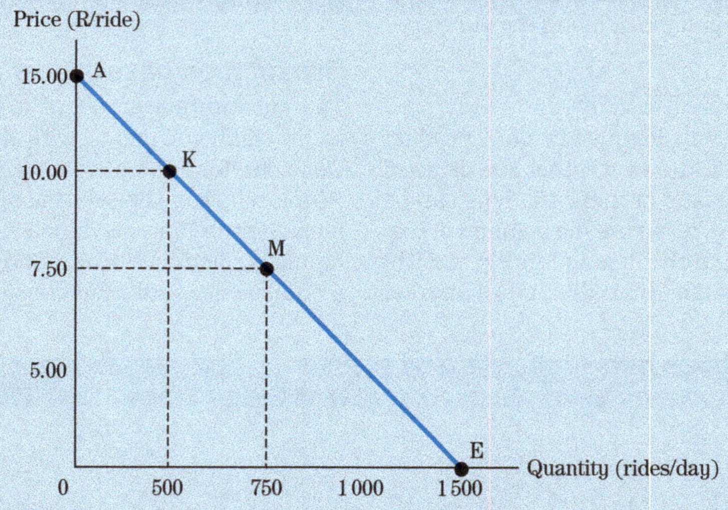

At a price of R7.50/ride, the bus company is maximizing its total revenues. At a price of R10/ride, demand is elastic with respect to price, and so the company can increase its total revenues by cutting its price.

Example 4.7

It is common knowledge that South Africa is struggling to provide sufficient electricity for all South African households and businesses. One way to decrease electricity consumption is for the Minister of Finance to introduce an energy tax, but the government must also consider a rebate programme to return the tax revenues to households. The purpose of the energy tax is

not to use it as a source of income for the government, but merely to discourage the use of electricity. What would be the effect of such a policy?

Let us assume the price elasticity of demand is −0.5. Assume further that the average consumer consumes 1200 units of electricity, that the price of electricity is R10 per unit and that the consumer's annual income is R90 000. Figure 4.28 shows the effect of the energy tax. The original budget line is AB and the consumer is in equilibrium at point C, where 1200 units of electricity are consumed. This means that the consumer is spending R12 000 on electricity and R78 000 on other goods.

A tax of R5 per unit of electricity is now introduced. This will increase the price of electricity by 50 per cent, shifting the budget line to AD. As a result of a price elasticity of −0.5, a 50 per cent increase in the price of electricity will decrease consumption by 25 per cent, from 1200 to 900 units. The point of equilibrium of the consumer is now point E on a lower indifference curve U_1.

The rebate programme is introduced to partly offset the higher tax burden on the consumer. The average tax paid by the consumer is R4500 (900 units multiplied by R5 per unit), and a rebate of R4500 is introduced. The effect of the rebate is that the budget line shifts upwards by R4500, to FJ. This budget line is parallel to AD. The income elasticity of electricity is 0.3. The R4500 tax rebate represents a 5 per cent increase in income (R4500/R90 000 = 0.05). We would thus expect the rebate to increase consumption by 1.5 per cent (0.3 times 5 per cent), from 900 to 913.5 units. The consumer will eventually be in equilibrium at point H on a higher utility level than at point E (the indifference curve going through point H was omitted to simplify the figure).

The net effect of the energy tax and the tax rebate is that the average consumer will be slightly worse off after it is introduced, because point H lies on a lower indifference curve than point C. It is, however, on a higher level of satisfaction than point E, where the consumer would operate if only the energy tax was introduced. Without putting the consumer in a much worse position, the government has achieved what it wanted – to decrease the consumption of electricity from 1200 units to 913.5 units.

Figure 4.28 Effect of an energy tax with a rebate

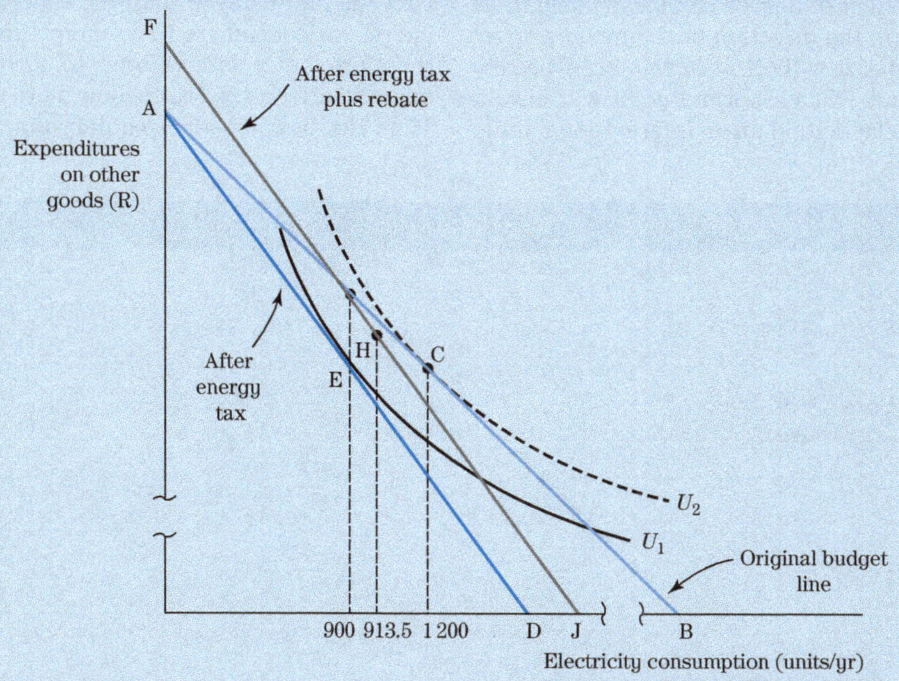

An energy tax with a tax rebate will put the average consumer in a slightly worse position, while the consumption of electricity will decrease.

for a particular brand of salt, say, Cerebos. Despite the advertising claims of salt manufacturers, one brand of salt is a more-or-less perfect substitute for any other.

Because the substitution effect between specific brands is large, a rise in the price of one brand should sharply curtail the quantity of it demanded. In general, the absolute value of price elasticity will rise with the availability of attractive substitutes.

Budget share

The larger the share of total expenditures accounted for by the product, the more important will be the income effect of a price change. Goods such as salt, rubber bands, cellophane wrap and a host of others account for such small shares of total expenditures that the income effects of a price change are likely to be negligible. For goods such as housing and higher education, by contrast, the income effect of a price increase is likely to be large. In general, the smaller the share of total expenditure accounted for by a good, the less elastic will demand be.

Direction of income effect

A factor closely related to the budget share is the direction – positive or negative – of its income effect. Whereas the budget share tells us whether the income effect of a price change is likely to be large or small, the direction of the income effect tells us whether it will offset or reinforce the substitution effect. Thus a normal good will have a higher price elasticity than an inferior good, other things being equal, because the income effect reinforces the substitution effect for a normal good, but offsets it for an inferior good.

Time

Our analysis of individual demand did not focus explicitly on the role of time. But it too has an important effect on responses to changes in price. Consider the oil price increases of recent years. One possible response is simply to drive less. But many auto trips cannot be abandoned, or even altered, very quickly. A person cannot simply stop going to work, for example. He can cut down on his daily commute by joining a car pool, using public transport if it is available or purchasing a house closer to where he works. He can also curtail his petrol consumption by trading in his current car for one that is more economical. But all these steps take time, and as a result the demand for petrol will be much more elastic in the long run than in the short run.

The short- and long-run effects of a supply shift in the market for petrol are contrasted in Fig. 4.29. Initially, the market is in equilibrium at A where price is R15.00/litre and 6 million litres are consumed per day. Assume that this equilibrium is disturbed by a supply reduction from *S* to *S*′. In the short run, the effect is for price to rise to P_{SR} = R20.00/litre and for quantity to fall to $Q_{SR} = 5$ million litres/day. The long-run demand curve is more elastic than the short-run demand curve. As consumers have more time to adjust, therefore, price effects tend to moderate while quantity effects tend to become more pronounced. Thus the new long-run equilibrium in Fig. 4.29

Figure 4.29 Price elasticity is greater in the long run than in the short run

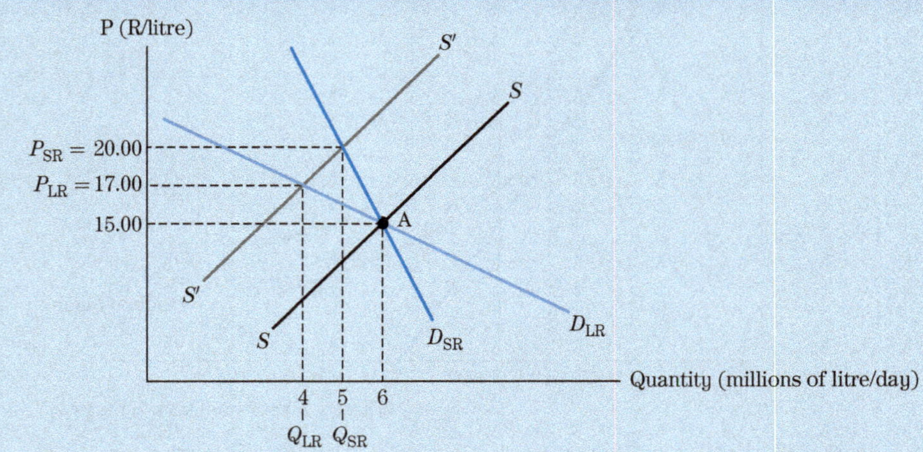

The more time people have, the more easily they can switch to substitute products. The price effects of supply alterations are therefore always more extreme in the short run than in the long run.

occurs at a price of P_{LR} = R17.00/litre and a quantity of Q_{LR} = 4 million litres/day.

We see an extreme illustration of the difference between short-run and long-run price elasticity values in the case of natural gas used in households. In a study in the USA, it was found that the price elasticity for this product is only −0.1 in the short run but a whopping −10.7 in the long run![2] This difference reflects the fact that, once consumers have chosen appliances to heat and cook with, they are virtually locked in for the short run. People aren't going to cook their rice for only 10 minutes just because the price of natural gas has gone up. In the long run, however, consumers can and do switch between fuels when there are significant changes in relative prices.

The constant elasticity demand curve

The demand curves discussed so far have been linear, for which, as noted, price elasticity declines as we move down the demand curve. Not all demand curves have this property, however; on the contrary, there are others for which price elasticity can remain constant or even rise with movements down the demand curve. The *constant elasticity demand curve* is the name given to a demand curve for which elasticity does not vary with price and quantity. Whereas the linear demand curve has the general form $P = a - bQ$, the constant elasticity demand curve is instead written

$$P = \frac{k}{Q^{1/\varepsilon}} \tag{4.14}$$

where k and ε are positive numbers, the specific values of which determine the exact shape and position of the curve.[3] An example with $k = 2$ and $\varepsilon = 1$ is shown in Fig. 4.30.

Let us examine some points on the curve pictured in Fig. 4.30 and verify that they do indeed have the same price elasticity. Consider first the point $P = 2$, $Q = 1$, and calculate price elasticity as the product of the ratio P/Q and the reciprocal of the slope of the demand curve. To calculate the slope of the demand curve, we need to calculate the ΔQ that occurs in response to a very small ΔP near the point (1, 2). Suppose, for example, we use a price change of +0.001. If $P = 2.001$, we can solve from the demand curve (that is, from the equation $P = 2/Q$) to get the corresponding $Q = 2/2.001 = 0.9995$. Thus $\Delta Q = 0.9995 - 1 = -0.0005$, and the slope of the demand curve at (1, 2) may be calculated as $\Delta P/\Delta Q$, or $0.001/(-0.0005) = -2$. The reciprocal of the slope is $-\frac{1}{2}$, and so the price elasticity is $2\left(-\frac{1}{2}\right) = -1$. We can also do this with calculus. If $k = 2$ and $\varepsilon = 1$, the equation is $P = 2/Q$ and $Q = 2/P$, which implies $dQ/dP = -2/P^2$. At the point (1, 2), the price elasticity is $(-2/2^2)(2/1) = -1$.

Figure 4.30 A constant elasticity demand curve

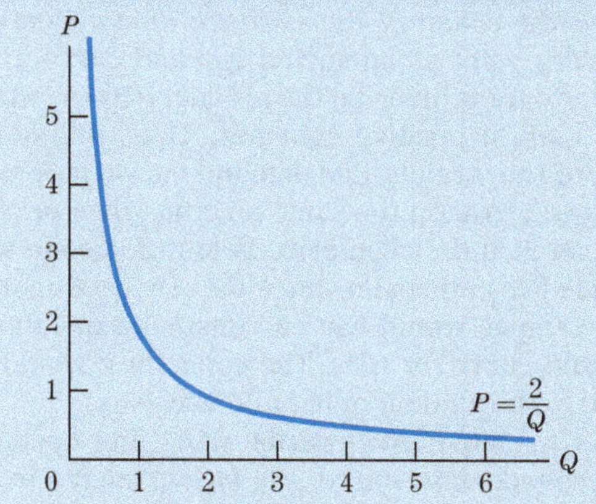

Whereas the price elasticity along a linear demand curve declines as quantity increases, it remains the same along a constant elasticity demand curve.

Consider now the point (2, 1). Again using a ΔP of 0.001, we get a new Q of $2/1.001 = 1.998$, or a ΔQ of -0.002. Thus the slope of the demand curve at (2, 1) is $0.001/(-0.002) = -\frac{1}{2}$ and its reciprocal is −2. The price elasticity at (2, 1) is therefore $\left(\frac{1}{2}\right)(-2)$, or again −1. Once again with calculus we get the same answer: $(-2/1^2)(1/2) = -1$.

Exercise 4.7

Try several other points along the demand curve in Fig. 4.30 and verify that the price elasticity in every instance is equal to −1. [The answer at the end of the chapter uses the points (0.5, 4) and (4, 0.5).]

[2] H.S. Houthakker and L. Taylor, *Consumer demand in the United States: Analyses and Projections*, 2d edn, Cambridge, MA: Harvard University Press, 1970.

[3] Using the formal definition of elasticity, it is easy to show that the elasticity at any price–quantity pair along this demand curve is $-\varepsilon$:

$$\frac{P}{Q}\frac{dQ(P)}{dP} = \frac{k/Q^{1/\varepsilon}}{Q}\frac{1}{(-1/\varepsilon)kQ^{-1/\varepsilon-1}} = -\varepsilon$$

The demand curve given by $P = k/Q$ is a special case of the constant elasticity demand curve, called the *constant expenditure demand curve.* At every point along such a demand curve, total expenditure is given by the product $PQ = k$, where k is again a positive constant. Thus, unlike the case of the straight-line demand curve, here people spend exactly the same amount when price is high as they do when price is low. Someone who spends her entire allowance on CDs each month, for example, would have a constant expenditure demand curve for CDs. The constant k would be equal to the amount of her allowance.

As we move downwards along any constant elasticity demand curve ($P = k/Q^{1/\varepsilon}$), the fall in the ratio P/Q is exactly counterbalanced by the rise in the reciprocal of the slope. A constant elasticity demand curve with $\varepsilon > 1$ has the property that a price cut will always increase total expenditures. For one with $\varepsilon < 1$, by contrast, a price cut will always reduce total expenditures.

Exercise 4.8

What happens to total expenditure when price falls from 4 to 3 along the demand curve given by $P = 4/Q^{1/2}$?

Segment ratio method

The price elasticity at a given point along a straight-line demand curve may be given one other useful geometric interpretation. Suppose we divide the demand curve into two segments AC and CE, as shown in Fig. 4.31. The price elasticity of demand (in absolute value) at point C, denoted by $|\varepsilon_c|$, will then be equal to the ratio of the two segments:[4]

$$|\varepsilon_c| = \frac{CE}{AC} \tag{4.15}$$

Equation 4.15 is called the *segment ratio* for calculating price elasticity of demand.

Knowing that the price elasticity of demand at any point along a straight-line demand curve is the ratio of two line segments greatly simplifies the task of making quantitative statements about it. Consider the demand curve shown in the top panel of Fig. 4.32. At the midpoint of that demand curve (point M), for example, we can see at a glance that the value of price elasticity is -1. One-quarter of the way down the demand curve (point K in Fig. 4.32) the elasticity is -3; three-quarters of the way down (point L) it is $-\frac{1}{3}$; and so on. The bottom panel of Fig. 4.32 summarizes the relation between the position on a straight-line demand curve and the price elasticity of demand.

Figure 4.31 The segment ratio method

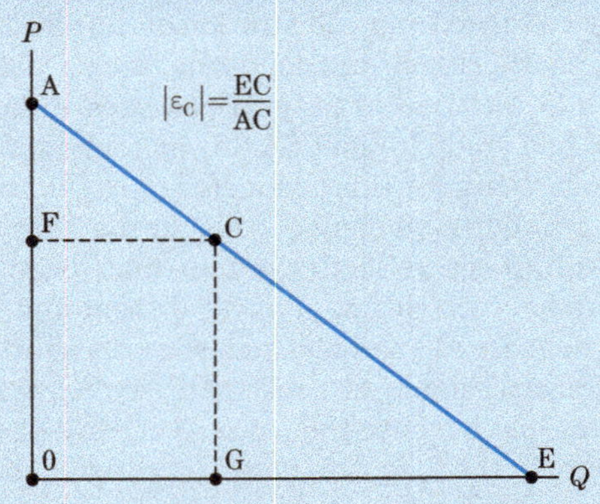

The absolute value of price elasticity at any point is the ratio of the two demand curve segments from that point. At point C, the absolute value of the price elasticity of demand is equal to CE/AC.

The dependence of market demand on income

As we have seen, the quantity of a good demanded by any person depends not only on its price but also on the person's income. Since the market demand curve is the horizontal sum of individual demand curves, it too will be influenced by consumer incomes. In some cases, the effect of income on market demand can be accounted for completely if we know only the average income level in the market. This would be the case, for example, if all consumers in the market were alike in terms of preference, and all had the same income.

In practice, however, a given level of average income in a market will sometimes give rise to different market demands, depending on how income is distributed. A simple example helps make this point clear.

[4] To see why this is so, we can make use of some simple high school geometry. First, note that the reciprocal of the slope of the demand curve in Fig. 4.31 is the ratio GE/GC, and that the ratio of price to quantity at point C is GC/FC. Multiplying these two, we get $|\varepsilon_c| = (GE/GC)(GC/FC) = GE/FC$. Now note that the triangles AFC and CGE are similar, which means that the ratios of their corresponding sides must be the same. In particular, it means that the ratio GE/FC, which we just saw is equal to the price elasticity of demand at point C, must also be equal to the ratio CE/AC. And this, of course, is just the result we set out to establish.

Figure 4.32 Elasticity at different positions along a straight-line demand curve

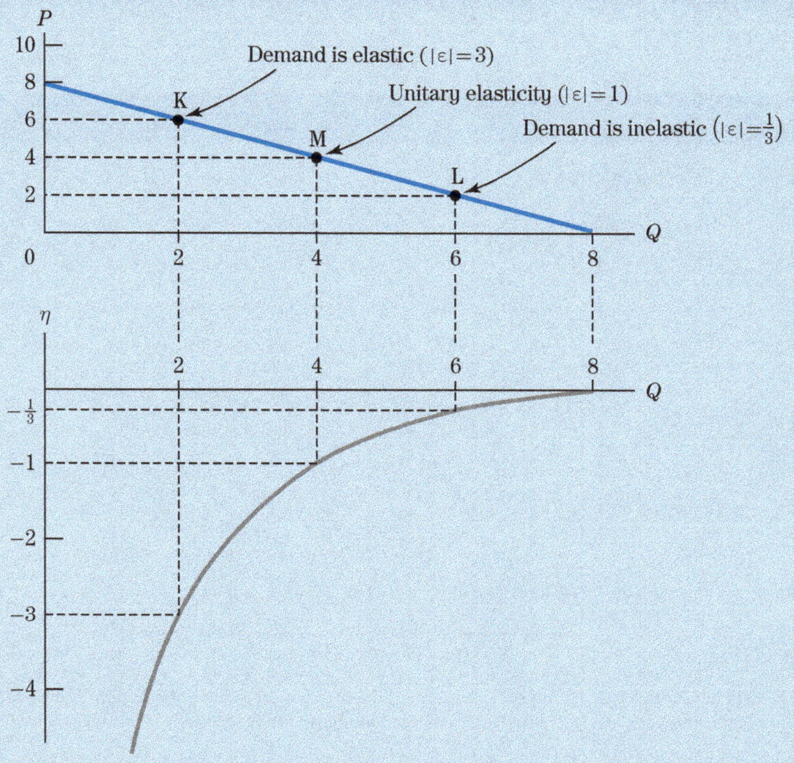

Using the segment ratio method, the price elasticity at points K, M and L (top panel) can be calculated in an instant.

The dependence of market demands on the distribution of income is important to bear in mind when the government considers policies to redistribute income. A policy that redistributes income from rich to poor, for example, is likely to increase demand for goods such as food and reduce demand for luxury items, such as jewellery and foreign travel.

Demand in many other markets is relatively insensitive to variations in the distribution of income. In particular, the distribution of income is not likely to matter much in markets in which individual demands tend to move roughly in proportion to changes in income.

Engel curves at the market level are schedules that relate the quantity demanded to the average

Example 4.8

Two consumers, A and B, are in a market for food. Their tastes are identical, and each has the same initial income level, R1800/wk. If their individual Engel curves for food are as given by *EE* in Fig. 4.33, how will the market demand curve for food be affected if A's income goes down by 50 per cent while B's goes up by 50 per cent?

The non-linear shape of the Engel curve pictured in Fig. 4.33 is plausible, considering that a consumer can eat only so much food. Beyond some point, increases in income should have no appreciable effect on the amount of food consumed. The implication is that B's new income (R2700/wk) will produce an increase in his consumption (2 kg/wk) that is smaller than the reduction in A's consumption (4 kg/wk) caused by A's new income (R900/wk).

What does all this say about the corresponding individual and market demand curves for food? Identical incomes and tastes give rise to identical individual demand curves, denoted by D_A and D_B in Fig. 4.34. Adding D_A and D_B horizontally, we get the initial market demand curve, denoted by D. The nature of the individual Engel curves tells us that B's increase in demand will be smaller than

A's reduction in demand following the shift in income distribution. Thus, when we add the new individual demand curves (D'_A and D'_B), we get a new market demand for food (D') that lies to the left of the original demand curve.

Figure 4.33 The Engel curve for food of A and B

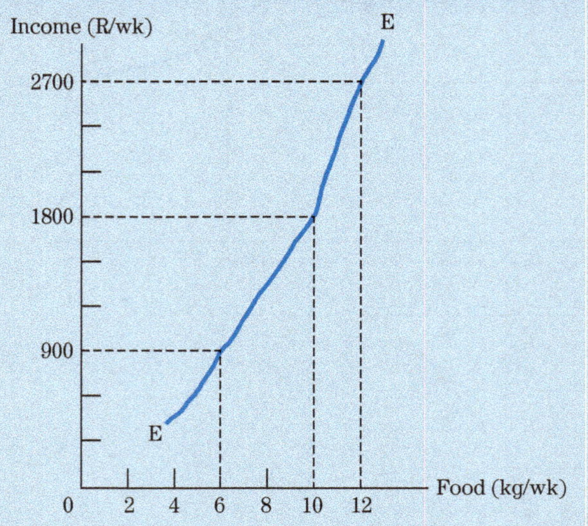

When individual Engel curves take the non-linear form shown, the increase in food consumption that results from a given increase in income will be smaller than the reduction in food consumption that results from an income reduction of the same amount.

Figure 4.34 Market demand sometimes depends on the distribution of income

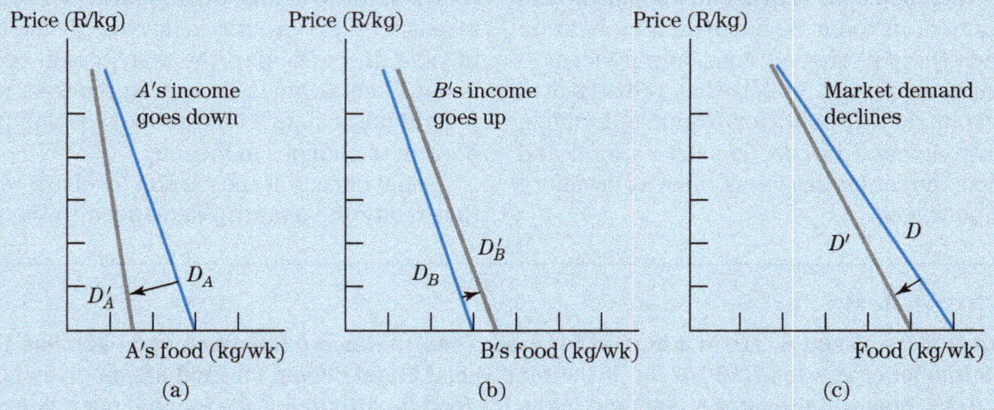

A given increase in income produces a small demand increase for B (panel b); an income reduction of the same size produces a larger demand reduction for A (panel a). The redistribution from A to B leaves average income unchanged but reduces market demand (panel c).

income level in the market. The existence of a stable relationship between average income and quantity demanded is by no means certain for any given product, because of the distributional complication just discussed. In particular, note that we cannot construct Engel curves at the market level by simply adding individual Engel curves horizontally. Horizontal summation works as a way of generating market demand curves from individual demand curves because all consumers in the market face the same market price for the product. But when incomes differ widely from one consumer to

Figure 4.35 An Engel curve at the market level

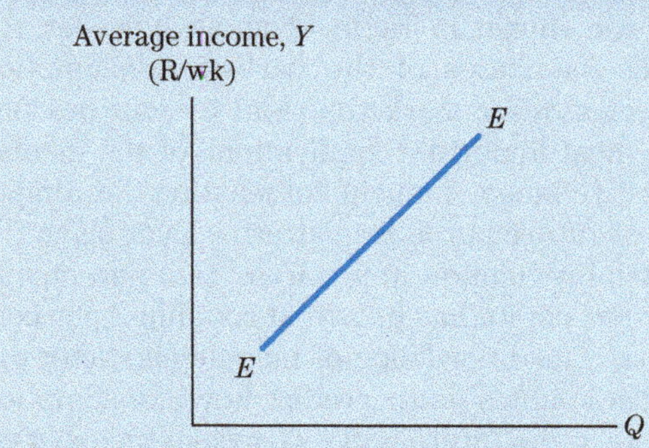

The market Engel curve tells what quantities will be demanded at various average levels of income.

another, it makes no sense to hold income constant and add quantities across consumers.

As a practical matter, however, reasonably stable relationships between various aggregate income measures and quantities demanded in the market may nonetheless exist. Suppose such a relationship exists for the good X and is as pictured by EE in Fig. 4.35, where Y denotes the average income level of consumers in the market for X, and Q denotes the quantity of X. This locus is the market analogue of the individual Engel curves discussed earlier.

Income elasticity of demand The percentage change in the quantity of a good demanded that results from a 1 per cent change in income.

If a good exhibits a stable Engel curve, we may then define its **income elasticity of demand**, a formal measure of the responsiveness of purchase decisions to variations in the average market income. Denoted by η, it is given by a formula analogous to the one for price elasticity:

$$\eta = \frac{\Delta Q/Q}{\Delta Y/Y} \tag{4.16}$$

where Y denotes average market income and ΔY is a small change therein. We can also use calculus to calculate income elasticity of demand:

$$\eta = \frac{dQ}{dY}\frac{Y}{Q} \tag{4.17}$$

Goods for which a change in income produces a less than proportional change in the quantity demanded at any price, thus have an income elasticity less than 1. Such goods are called *necessities*, and their income elasticities must lie in the interval $0 < \eta < 1$. Food and water are commonly cited examples. *Luxuries* are those goods for which $\eta > 1$. Common examples are expensive jewellery and foreign travel. Inferior goods are those for which $\eta < 0$. Goods for which $\eta = 1$ will have Engel curves that are straight lines through the origin, as pictured by the locus EE in Fig. 4.36(a). The market Engel curves for luxuries, necessities and inferior goods, where these exist and are stable, are pictured in Fig. 4.36(b).

The income elasticity formula in Eq. 4.18 is easier to interpret geometrically if we rewrite it as

$$\eta = \frac{Y}{Q}\frac{\Delta Q}{\Delta Y} \tag{4.18}$$

Figure 4.36 Engel curves for different types of goods

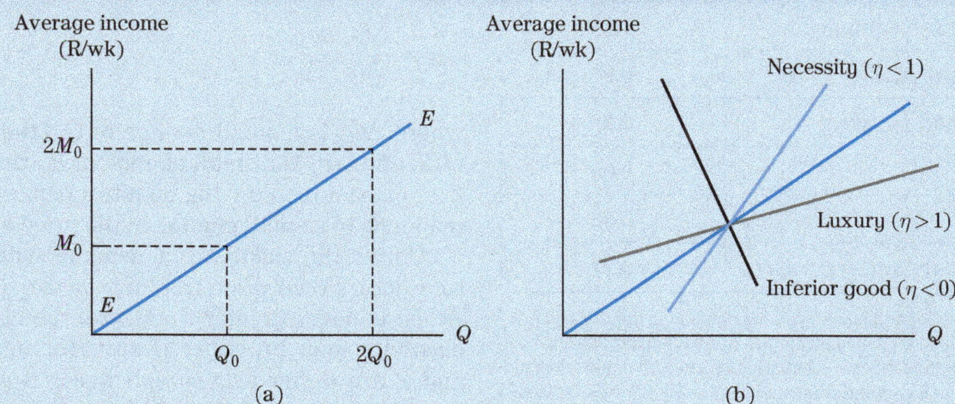

(a) The good whose Engel curve is shown has an income elasticity of 1. For such goods, a given proportional change in income will produce the same proportional change in quantity demanded. Thus when average income doubles, from M_0 to $2M_0$, the quantity demanded also doubles, from Q_0 to $2Q_0$. (b) The Engel curves show that consumption increases more than in proportion to income for a luxury and less than in proportion to income for a necessity, and it falls with income for an inferior good.

The first factor on the right side of Eq. 4.18 is simply the ratio of income to quantity at a point along the Engel curve. It is the slope of the straight line from the origin to that point.

The second factor is the reciprocal of the slope of the Engel curve at that point. If the slope of the ray exceeds the slope of the Engel curve, the product of these two factors must be greater than 1 (the luxury case). If the ray is less steep, η will be less than 1 but still positive, provided the slope of the Engel curve is positive (the necessity case). Thus, in distinguishing between the Engel curves for necessities and luxuries, what counts is not the slopes of the Engel curves themselves, but how they compare with the slopes of the corresponding rays. Finally, if the slope of the Engel curve is negative, η must be less than zero (the inferior case).

Application: forecasting economic trends

If the income elasticity of demand for every good and service were 1, the composition of GDP would be completely stable over time (assuming technology and relative prices remained unchanged). Each year, the proportion of total spending devoted to food, travel, clothing, and indeed to every other consumption category, would remain unchanged.

Table 4.5 Income elasticities of demand for selected products

Good or service	Income elasticity
Health	1.49
Education	1.43
Transport	1.38
Recreation and entertainment	1.34
Furniture and equipment	1.13
Housing and fuel	0.91
Clothing and footwear	0.89
Food	0.65
Crude oil	0.43
Personal care and services	– 0.74

Sources: S. Mukhopadhyay, 'Consumer demand in South Africa', Trade and Industrial Policy Strategies Annual Forum, 2002; E. Ziramba, 'Price and income elasticities of crude oil import demand in South Africa: A cointegration analysis', *Energy Policy*, 2010, vol 38, pp. 7844–7849.

As the entries in Table 4.5 show, however, the income elasticities of the various consumption categories differ markedly. And therein lies one of the most important applications of the income elasticity concept, namely, forecasting the composition of future purchase patterns. Ever since the industrial revolution in the West, real purchasing power per capita has grown at roughly 2 per cent per year. Our knowledge of income elasticity differences enables us to predict how consumption patterns in the future will differ from the ones we see today.

Thus, if the elasticities are correct, a growing share of the consumer's budget will be devoted to goods such as health products, vehicles and education, whereas ever-smaller shares will go to clothing, footwear and personal care and services.

Cross-price elasticities of demand

Cross-price elasticity of demand The percentage change in the quantity of one good demanded that results from a 1 per cent change in the price of the other good.

The quantity of a good purchased in the market depends not only on its price and on consumer incomes, but also on the prices of related goods. **Cross-price elasticity of demand** is the percentage change in the quantity demanded of one good caused by a 1 per cent change in the price of the other good. More generally, for any two goods, X and Z, the cross-price elasticity of demand may be defined as follows:[5]

$$\varepsilon_{XZ} = \frac{\Delta Q_X / Q_X}{\Delta P_Z / P_Z} \tag{4.19}$$

where ΔQ_X is a small change in Q_X, the quantity of X, and ΔP_Z is a small change in P_Z, the price of Z. ε_{XZ} measures how the quantity demanded of X responds to a small change in the price of Z.

Unlike the elasticity of demand with respect to a good's own price (the *own-price elasticity*), which is never greater than zero, the cross-price elasticity may be either positive or negative. X and Z are defined as *complements* if $\varepsilon_{XZ} < 0$. If $\varepsilon_{XZ} > 0$, they are *substitutes*. Thus a rise in the

[5] In calculus terms, the corresponding expression is given by $\varepsilon_{XZ} = (P_Z/Q_X)(dQ_X/dP_Z)$.

price of bacon will reduce not only the quantity of bacon demanded, but also, because bacon and eggs are complements, the demand for eggs. A rise in the price of coffee, by contrast, will tend to increase the demand for tea. Another good example is the cross-price elasticity of demand for music. Sales of digital music downloads have been soaring with the growth of broadband and falling prices for downloads. As a result, sales of traditional music CDs are declining at a steep rate. Estimates of the cross-price elasticity of demand for the meat market in South Africa are shown in Table 4.6. Except for the cross-price elasticity of pork and chicken, and vice versa, all have positive signs. This is what one would expect of substitute products. Cross-price elasticities can also be used to define a market, but more on that when we get to Chapters 9–11 where different market structures will be discussed.

Although the basic principles applied to calculating the different forms of elasticity are very simple, we frequently do not have all the data necessary to calculate it accurately. Therefore, there is not much information available concerning the elasticities of different products in reality. The results that are available are normally done at a national level. Obviously individual firms have undertaken research to calculate these elasticities for the products that they produce. The results of these studies are not freely available because they do not want their competitors to gain insight into their own research.

Table 4.6 Cross-price elasticities for selected pairs of products

Good	Good with price change	Cross-price elasticity
Pork	Beef	+0.38
Pork	Chicken	−0.17
Pork	Mutton	+0.10
Beef	Pork	+0.05
Beef	Chicken	+0.09
Beef	Mutton	+0.02
Mutton	Beef	+0.06
Mutton	Chicken	+0.17
Mutton	Pork	+0.04
Chicken	Beef	+0.14
Chicken	Pork	−0.04
Chicken	Mutton	+0.09

Source: From P.R. Taljaard, *Econometric Estimation of Demand for Meat in South Africa*, unpublished thesis submitted for MSc degree, University of the Free State, 2003.

Exercise 4.9

Would the cross-price elasticity of demand be positive or negative for the following pairs of goods: (a) apples and oranges; (b) airline tickets and the price of petrol; (c) computer hardware and software; (d) pens and paper; (e) pens and pencils?

Network externalities

Up till now we have assumed that one consumer's demand for a good is independent of another's. However, one person's demand for a good may be determined by the number of other people also buying the good. If this is the case, we say that a *network externality* exists. This effect can be positive or negative. If a typical consumer demands more of a product because more people are buying it, we talk about a *positive externality*. If for the same reason the typical customer demands less of the good, we say that a *negative externality* exists.

One example of a positive externality is the bandwagon effect – the desire to have a good because almost everybody else has it. This is frequently the case with children's toys, or clothes that everybody wants because they have the right label. This is illustrated in Fig. 4.37. On the horizontal axis we measure the sales of some fashionable good (Billabong T-shirts, for example) in thousands per month. Assume that consumers think only 20000 people are buying the good; they will have little incentive to buy the good to be in style. Some will still buy it (depending on the price), but only for its *intrinsic value*. Demand is then given by D_{20} on the assumption that there are no externalities.

Suppose that consumers think that 40000 people are buying the good: they will find it more attractive to buy the good, and the demand curve will shift to the right. The demand curve is now D_{40}, which is to the right of D_{20}. In exactly the same way, if consumers think 60000 people are buying the good, the demand curve will be D_{60}, which is to the right of D_{40}. The more people consumers

Figure 4.37 Positive network externality: the bandwagon effect

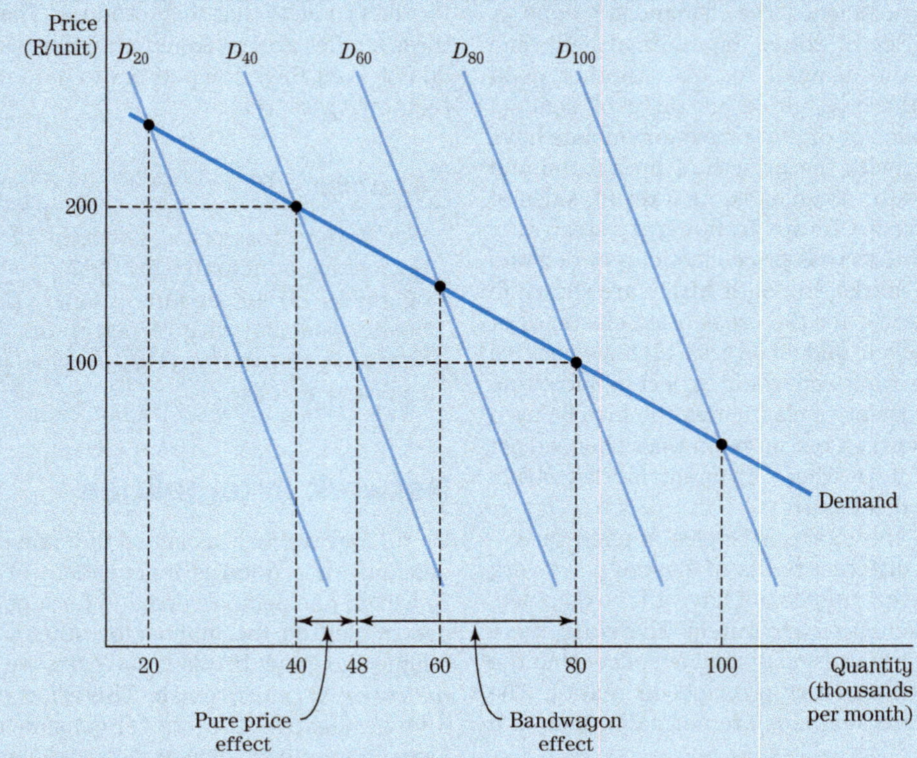

The bandwagon effect makes the individual demand grow in response to the growth in purchases by other consumers.

believe are buying the good, the further to the right the demand curve will shift.

Over time consumers will get a good idea of how many people are actually buying the good, but this number will be determined by the price. In Fig. 4.37 we can see that, if the price is R200, 40000 people will buy the good. In this case the relevant demand curve is D_{40}. In the same way, if the price is R100, 80000 people will buy the good, and the relevant demand curve will be D_{80}. The market demand curve is constructed by joining the points on D_{20}, D_{40}, D_{60}, D_{80} and D_{100} that correspond to quantities 20000, 40000, 60000, 80000 and 100000. The market demand curve is more elastic than curves D_{20}, and so on. Let us now examine why that is the case.

What happens when the price drops from R200 to R100 with demand curve D_{40}? If there was no bandwagon effect, quantity would increase from 40000 to 48000. This is known as the *pure price effect*, which is based on the intrinsic value of the good. As more people buy the good it becomes more fashionable to buy it, and more people want to buy it. The increase from 48000 to 80000 is known as the *bandwagon effect*. As more people buy the good, everybody wants to jump on the bandwagon and own the good.

Positive externalities can also arise for other reasons. If you are the only person with a CD player, it will not make economic sense for manufacturers to manufacture CDs. Without them the CD player will be of no use to you. The more people who own players, the more economical it will become to manufacture CDs, and the greater will be the value of the player to you. The same applies to cell phones and computers. As media of communication they are of little use if you cannot send SMS texts or emails to other people because they do not own cell phones or computers. If you are the only person on Facebook it will not make sense to provide such a facility. From the above it is clear that the behaviour of other consumers does influence you and play a role in your consumption decisions.

Another example of network externalities occurs when the consumer does not want to buy

Economic naturalist 4.1

Why has the nature of outdoor braai appliances in South Africa changed so much in the last decade?

South Africa is a nation that is fond of its braai with something cold in the hand. However, traditionally it was a braai around an open fire and later built-in braais. When George Stephan designed the first kettle-shaped barbeque grill in 1951 in Chicago there was not much of a demand for such a product in South Africa. Initially, very few Webers were sold in South Africa. Over time people started to realize that it is actually a convenient way to prepare meat. More people are living in flats nowadays without proper braai facilities. A Weber is very convenient if you only have a small balcony where you can braai. If the wind is blowing, your meat won't get ash blown on it and you cannot accidentally start a bush fire. There is much less smoke involved, which is in line with the trend of living 'greener'. Nowadays it is thus nothing strange to see a group of people enjoying a braai around a Weber. (It's been suggested that, because using a Weber involves less work, there's more time to drink!) You can pick up a fairly nice Weber braai for about R1700, which isn't overly expensive.

Traditional Charcoal grill
©Tetra Images/Alamy

The story doesn't end here, though. Jan Scanell, Mr Braai of South Africa, has a full-time job promoting braais all over South Africa. Although officially 24 September is Heritage Day, Scanell has kidnapped that date as National Braai Day and more people actually celebrate that! An increasing number of people now see braai as an art form and spend lots of money on it accordingly. The Weber Summit – the state of the art – sells for about R40 000. It has a flush-mounted side burner, an infrared rotisserie burner, a sear burner, snap-jet ignition system, separate spit and fork storage, stainless steel cooking plates, working surfaces and rod cooking grates. It works on gas, which means producing cleaner air and avoiding using coal-fired electricity. Furthermore, the average income of the South African family increased from R48 385 in 2001 to R103 204 in 2011. However, the average income of a white household in South Africa, the typical Weber Summit buyer, increased from R193 820 in 2001 to R365 134 during the same period.[6] This means that more South Africans than before can now afford the luxury of a Weber Summit.

a good because too many other people already own it – the so-called *snob effect*. The quantity demanded of a 'snob good' is higher, the fewer the people who own it. Very rare works of art, specially designed sports cars, exclusive SUV cars and made-to-measure clothing are all examples of snob goods. The fewer the people who own these goods, the higher will be the prestige (or snob value) attached to buying them.

The snob effect is illustrated in Fig. 4.38. D_2 is the demand curve if consumers believe that only 2000 people own the good. If consumers believe that 4000 people own the good, it is less exclusive. The snob value attached to the good will be less, the quantity demanded will be lower and demand curve D_4 will apply. If consumers believe that 6000 people own the good, demand will be even less, and demand curve D_6 will apply. Over time consumers will learn how many people actually own the good. We get the market demand curve by joining the points on D_2, D_4, D_6... that correspond to the quantities 2000, 4000, 6000....

The snob effect makes market demand less elastic. To illustrate, let us assume that the price is R300 000 and 2000 people are buying the good. What will happen if the price drops to R150 000? Without the snob effect, the quantity demanded would increase to 14 000 (along D_2). However, as a snob good its value is reduced as more people own it. The snob effect results in demand being reduced by 8000 units, resulting in a net increase of 4000 units after the decrease in price (a movement along the market demand curve). For certain

[6] http://www.pewresearch.org/fact-tank/2013/12/06/chart-of-the-week-how-south-africa-changed-and-didnt-over-mandelas-lifetime/; Drew Desilver, 'Chart of the week: How South Africa changed, and didn't, over Mandela's lifetime', Pew Research Center, 6 December 2013.

Figure 4.38 Negative network externality: the snob effect

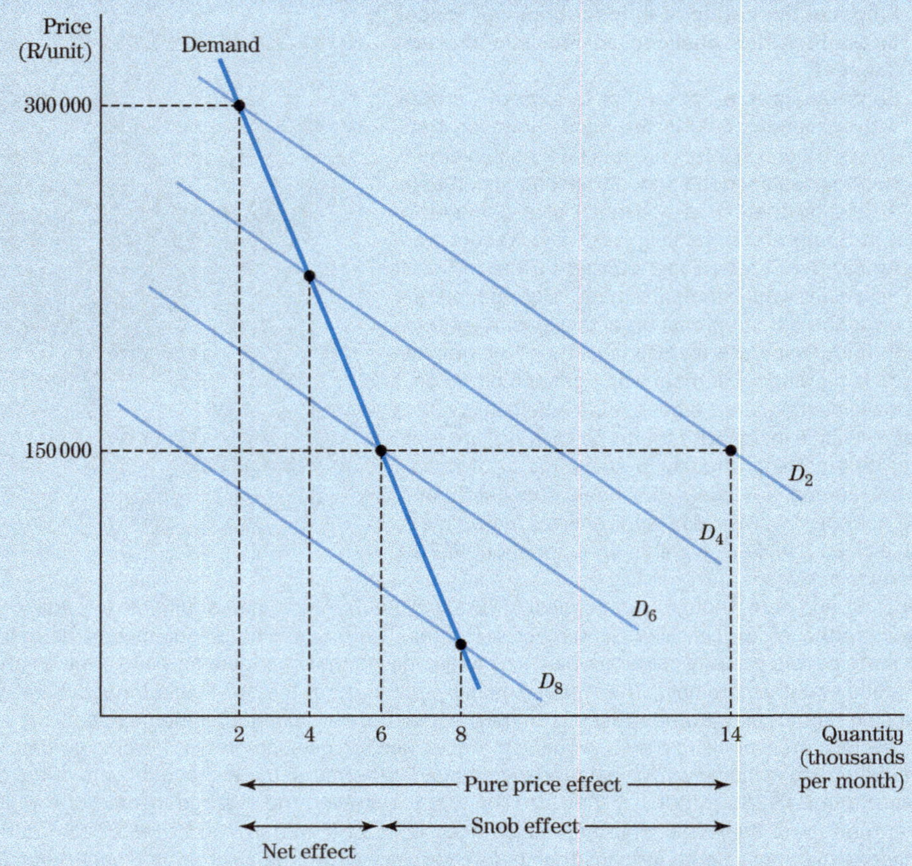

The snob effect makes individual demand decrease in response to the growth in purchases by other consumers.

goods the whole advertising campaign is designed to create a snob effect or exclusiveness. Rolex watches are a good example. After Chad le Clos took the gold in the 200-metre butterfly at the London Olympics 2012, beating Michael Phelps, one of the greatest athletes of all time, he was featured in a couple of articles in South African magazines, wearing – you guessed it – a Rolex watch. The firm's goal was to make demand for the product less elastic, so that it could increase prices and still sell the good.

Intertemporal consumption bundles

People may either consume all their income now or save part for the future. How would rational consumers distribute their consumption over time? To keep the analysis manageable, suppose there are only two time periods, *current* and *future*. In the standard, or *atemporal*, choice model in Chapter 3, the alternatives were different goods that could be consumed in the current period – apples now versus oranges now, and so on. In our simple *intertemporal choice model*, the alternatives instead will be *current consumption* (C_1) versus *future consumption* (C_2). Each of these is an amalgam – the functional equivalent of the composite good (see Chapter 3). For simplicity, we set aside the question of how to apportion current and future consumption among specific consumption goods.

In the atemporal choice model, any bundle of goods can be represented as a point in a simple two-dimensional diagram. We use an analogous procedure in the intertemporal choice model. In Fig. 4.39, for example, current consumption of R6000 combined with future consumption of R6000 is represented by the bundle E. Bundle D represents current consumption of R3000 and future consumption of R9000.

The intertemporal budget constraint

Suppose you receive R50000 income now and R60000 in the future. Suppose also that, if you deposit some of your current income in a bank, you can receive your principal plus 20 per cent in the future period. Similarly, if you wish to borrow against your future income, you may receive R1 now for every R1.20 you must repay in the future (see Fig. 4.40). To construct your intertemporal budget constraint, first note that you can always merely consume your income in each period, so $C_1 = \text{R}50000$ and $C_2 = \text{R}60000$ must be a point on your intertemporal budget constraint. Another option is to deposit all R50000 (maximum lending) and thus receive $1.2 \times \text{R}50000 = \text{R}60000$ in addition to your R60000 future income for $C_2 = \text{R}120000$ future consumption with no current consumption ($C_1 = 0$). Yet another option is to borrow R60000/1.2 = R50000 (maximum borrowing) in addition to your R50000 current income for $C_1 = \text{R}100000$ current consumption with no future consumption ($C_2 = 0$). The equation for your intertemporal budget constraint is $C_2 = \text{R}120000 - 1.2C_1$ or, equivalently, $1.2C_1 + C_2 = \text{R}120000$.

In general, suppose you receive M_1 of your income in the first period and M_2 in the second, and can either borrow or lend at interest rate r. What is the most you can consume in the future period? Maximum future consumption occurs when you set all your current income aside for future use. Setting aside M_1 in the current period at the interest rate r means your deposit will grow to $M_1(1 + r)$ by the future period. So the most you can possibly consume in the future is that amount plus your future income, or $M_1(1 + r) + M_2$.

What is the most you could consume in the current period? The answer is your current income plus the maximum amount you can borrow against your future income. The most you can borrow against a future income of M_2 is called the **present value** of M_2, denoted by PV(M_2). It is the amount that, if deposited today at interest rate r, would be worth exactly M_2 in the future period. Accordingly, we can find the present value of M_2 by solving $\text{PV}(M_2)(1 + r) = M_2$ for PV(M_2):

> **Present value** The present value of a payment of X rands T years from now is $X/(1 + r)^T$, where r is the annual rate of interest.

$$\text{PV}(M_2) = \frac{M_2}{1+r} \tag{4.20}$$

For example, if M_2 were R110000 and the interest rate were 10 per cent (that is, $r = 0.10$), the present value of M_2 would be R110000/1.1 = R100000. Present value is a simple equivalence relationship between sums of money that are payable at different points in time. If $r = 0.10$, then R100000 today will be worth R110000 in the future. By the same token, R110000 in the future is worth R100000 today when the interest rate is 10 per cent.

It is not necessary, of course, to borrow or save the maximum amounts possible. The consumer

Figure 4.39 Intertemporal consumption bundles

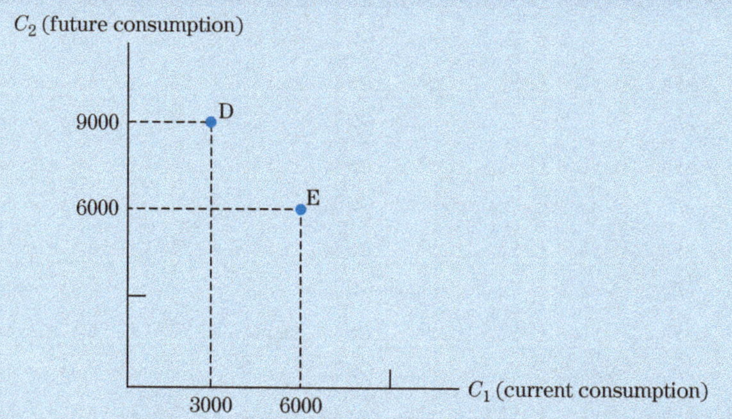

Alternative combinations of current and future consumption are represented as points in the $C_1 - C_2$ plane. By convention, the horizontal axis measures current consumption; the vertical axis, future consumption.

Figure 4.40 The intertemporal budget constraint

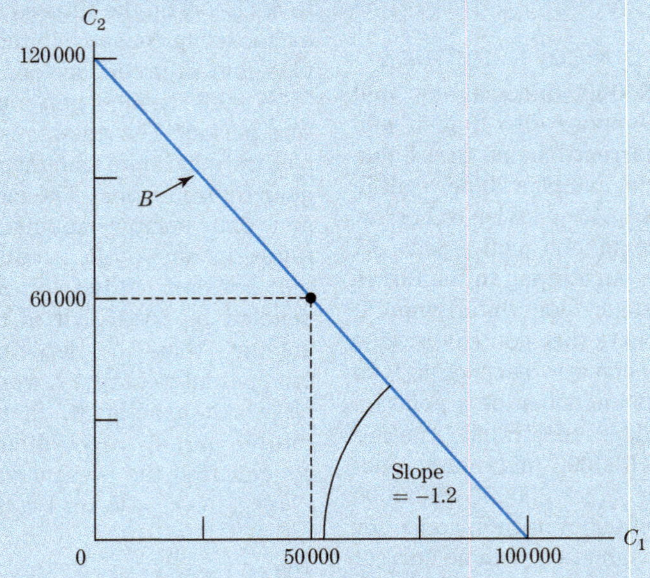

For every rand by which current consumption is reduced, it is possible to increase future consumption by R1.20.

who wishes to shift some of her future income into the current period can borrow any amount up to the maximum at the rate of $1/(1 + r)$ rands today for every rand given up in the future. Or she can save any amount of her current income and get back $(1 + r)$ rands in the future for every rand not consumed today. The intertemporal budget constraint, shown as B in Fig. 4.41, is thus again the straight line that joins the maximum current consumption and maximum future consumption

Figure 4.41 Intertemporal budget constraint with income in both periods, and borrowing or lending at rate r

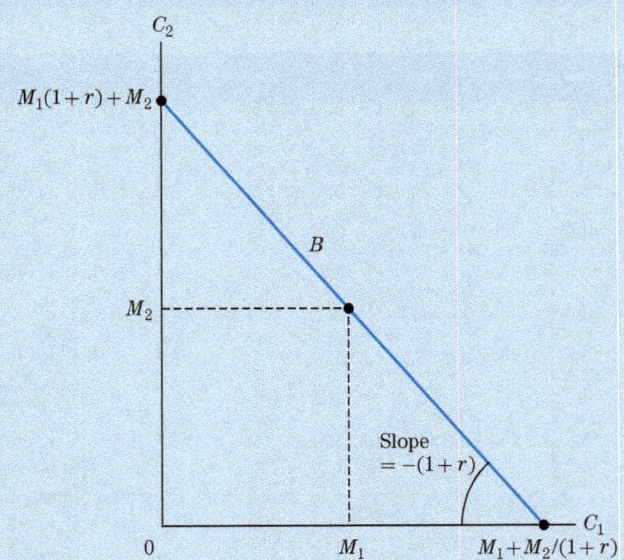

The opportunity cost of R1 of present consumption is $(1 + r)$ rands of future consumption. The horizontal intercept of the intertemporal budget constraint is the present value of lifetime income, $M_1 + M_2/(1 + r)$.

points. And its slope will again be $-(1 + r)$. As in the atemporal model, here too the slope of the budget constraint may be interpreted as a relative price ratio. This time it is the ratio of the prices of current and future consumption. Current consumption has a higher price than future consumption because of the opportunity cost of the interest forgone when money is spent rather than saved. It is conventional to refer to the horizontal intercept of the intertemporal budget constraint as the *present value of lifetime income.*

Exercise 4.10

You have R50 000 of current income and R42 000 of future income. If the interest rate between the current and future period is 5 per cent, what is the present value of your lifetime income? What is the maximum amount you could consume in the future? What is the equation describing your intertemporal budget constraint?

Figure 4.42 An intertemporal indifference map

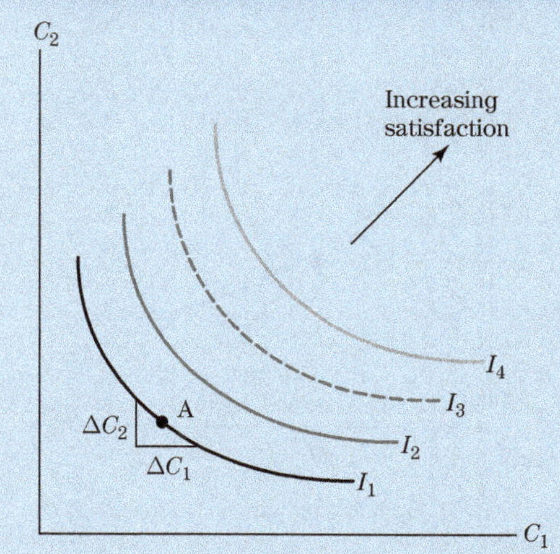

As in the atemporal model, movements to the north-east represent increasing satisfaction. The absolute value of the slope of an indifference curve at a point is called the marginal rate of time preference (MRTP) at that point. The MRTP at A is $|\Delta C_2/\Delta C_1|$.

As in the atemporal case considered in Chapter 3, the intertemporal budget constraint is a convenient way of summarizing the consumption bundles that someone is *able* to buy. And again, as before, it tells us nothing about which particular combination a person will *choose* to buy.

Intertemporal indifference curves

To discover which bundle the consumer will select from those that are feasible, we need some convenient way of representing the consumer's preferences over current and future consumption. Here again the analytical device is completely analogous to one we used in the atemporal case. Just as a consumer's preferences over two current consumption goods may be captured by an indifference map, so too may his preferences over current and future goods be represented in this fashion. In Fig. 4.42 the consumer is indifferent between the bundles on I_1, which are less desirable than those on I_2, and so on.

The absolute value of the slope of the intertemporal indifference curve at any point is the marginal rate of substitution between future and current consumption. At point A in Fig. 4.42 it is given by $|\Delta C_2/\Delta C_1|$, and this ratio is also referred to as the **marginal rate of time preference (MRTP)** at A. (One can also determine it with calculus by calculating $|dC_2/dC_1|$.) If $|\Delta C_2/\Delta C_1| > 1$ at A, the consumer is said to exhibit *positive time preference* at that point. This means that he requires more than 1 unit of future consumption to compensate him for the loss of a unit of current consumption. If $|\Delta C_2/\Delta C_1| < 1$ at a point, he is said to exhibit *negative time preference* at that point. Such a person is willing to forgo 1 unit of current consumption in return for less than 1 unit of future consumption. Finally, if $|\Delta C_2/\Delta C_1| = 1$ at a point, the consumer is said to have *neutral time preference* at that point. With neutral time preference, present and future consumption trade off against one another at the rate of 1 to 1.

Marginal rate of time preference (MRTP) The number of units of consumption in the future a consumer would exchange for 1 unit of consumption in the present.

As in the atemporal case, it appears justified to assume that the marginal rate of time preference declines as one moves downwards along an indifference curve. The more current consumption a person already has, the more he will be willing to give up in order to obtain an additional unit of future consumption. For most of us, then, the question of whether time preference is positive, negative or neutral will be a matter of where we happen to be on our indifference maps. The heir of a wealthy family who is unable to borrow against the R5 billion he is due to inherit in two years' time very likely has a strongly positive time preference. By contrast, the primitive farmer whose food stocks are perishable

Figure 4.43 The optimal intertemporal allocation

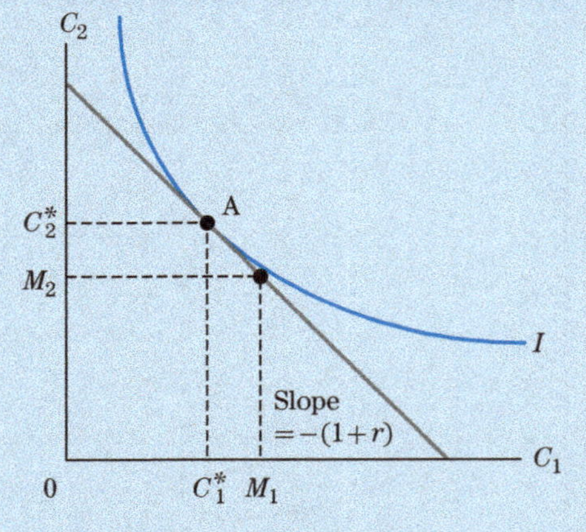

As in the atemporal model, the optimal intertemporal consumption bundle (bundle A) lies on the highest attainable indifference curve. Here, that occurs at a point of tangency.

Figure 4.44 Patience and impatience

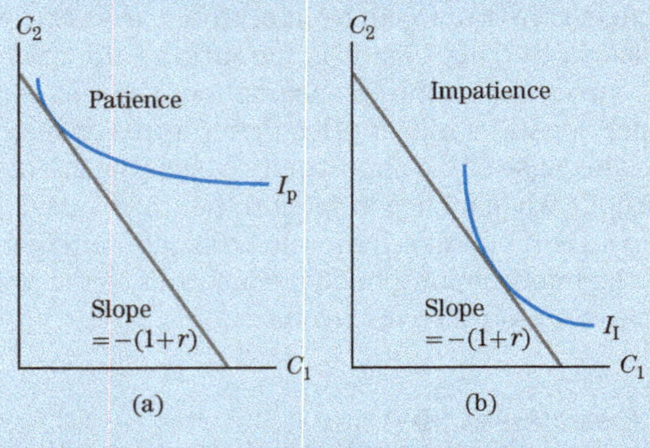

(a) The patient consumer postpones the bulk of consumption until the future period. (b) The impatient consumer consumes much more heavily in the current period. But in equilibrium, the marginal rate of time preference $(1 + r)$ is the same for both types of consumers.

is likely to have a negative time preference in the wake of having harvested a bumper crop.

The optimal allocation between current and future consumption is determined exactly as in the atemporal model. The consumer selects the point along his budget constraint that corresponds to the highest attainable indifference curve. If the intertemporal indifference curves have the conventional convex shape, we ordinarily get a tangency solution like the one shown in Fig. 4.43. If the MRTP is everywhere larger than (or everywhere smaller than) the slope of the budget constraint, corner solutions result, just as in the atemporal case.

Note in Fig. 4.43 that the marginal rate of time preference at the optimal bundle (C_1^*, C_2^*) is positive because the absolute value of the slope of the budget constraint is $1 + r > 1$. In the example pictured in the diagram, the consumer has the same income in each time period, but consumes slightly more in period 2.

The optimal allocation will of course be different for different consumers. The optimum shown in Fig. 4.44(a), for example, is for a consumer whose preferences are much more heavily tilted in favour of future consumption. The one shown in Fig. 4.44(b), by contrast, is for a consumer who cares much more about present consumption. But in each case note that the slope of the indifference curve at the optimal point is the same. As long as consumers can borrow and lend at the interest rate r, the marginal rate of time preference at the optimal bundle will be $(1 + r)$ (except, of course, in the case of corner solutions). For interior solutions positive time preference is the rule, regardless of the consumer's preferences.

It is conventional to assume that both current and future consumption are normal goods. Thus an increase in the present value of lifetime income, all other factors being constant, will cause both current and future consumption to rise.

Example 4.9

You have current income of R100 000 and future income of R154 000, and can borrow and lend at the rate $r = 0.1$. Under these conditions you consume exactly your income in each period. True or false: an increase in r to $r = 0.4$ will cause you to save some of your current income.

Line B in Fig. 4.45 is the original budget constraint. Its horizontal intercept is the present value of lifetime income when $r = 0.1$: R100 000 + R154 000/1.1 = R240 000. Its vertical intercept is future income plus $(1 + r)$ times current income: R154 000 + (1.1) (R100 000) = R264 000. The optimal bundle occurs at A, by assumption, which implies that the MRTP at A is 1.1. When the interest rate rises to 0.4, the intertemporal budget constraint becomes B'. Its horizontal intercept is R100 000 + R154 000/1.4 = R210 000. Its vertical intercept is R154 000 + (1.4) (R100 000) = R294 000. Because the MRTP at A is less than the absolute value of the slope of the budget constraint B', it follows that the consumer will be better off by consuming less now and more in the future than he did at A. The new bundle is shown at D in Fig. 4.45.

Figure 4.45 The effect of a rise in the interest rate

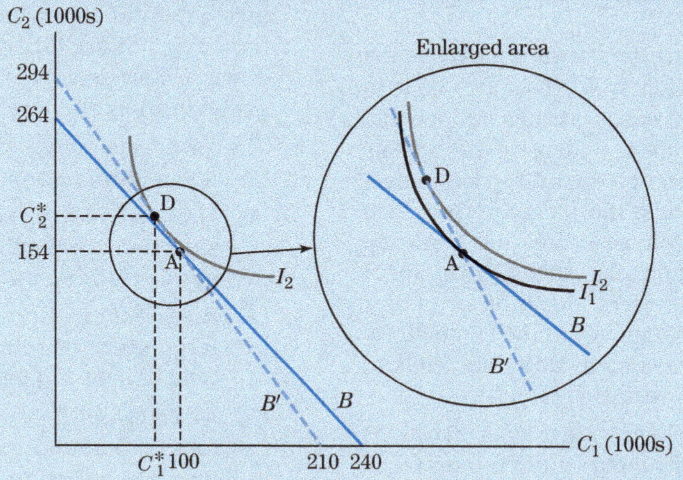

When the interest rate goes up, the intertemporal budget constraint rotates about the current endowment point. If the current endowment point (A) was optimal at the lower interest rate, the new optimal bundle (D) will have less current consumption and more future consumption.

Summary

- Our focus in this chapter was on how individual and market demands respond to variations in prices and incomes. To generate a demand curve for an individual consumer for a specific good *X*, we first trace out the price–consumption curve in the standard indifference curve diagram. The PCC is the line of optimal bundles observed when the price of *X* varies, with the price of the other good, income and preferences held constant. We then take the relevant price–quantity pairs from the PCC and plot them in a separate diagram to get the individual demand curve.
- The income analogue to the PCC is the income–consumption curve, or ICC. It too is constructed using the standard indifference curve diagram. The ICC is the line of optimal bundles traced out when we vary the consumer's income, holding preferences and relative prices constant. The Engel curve is the income analogue to the individual demand curve. We generate it by retrieving the relevant income–quantity pairs from the ICC and plotting them in a separate diagram.
- Normal goods are those the consumer buys more of when income increases, and inferior goods are those the consumer buys less of as income rises.
- The total effect of a price change can be decomposed into two separate effects:

(1) the substitution effect, which denotes the change in the quantity demanded that results because the price change makes substitute goods seem either more or less attractive; and

(2) the income effect, which denotes the change in quantity demanded that results from the change in real purchasing power caused by the price change.

The substitution effect always moves in the opposite direction from the movement in price: price increases always reduce the quantity demanded, and price reductions always increase the quantity demanded. For normal goods, the income effect also moves in the opposite direction from the price change, and thus tends to reinforce the substitution effect. For inferior goods, the income effect moves in the same direction as the price change, and thus tends to undercut the substitution effect.

- Goods for which purchase decisions respond most strongly to price tend to be ones that have large income and substitution effects that work in the same direction. For example, a normal good that occupies a large share of total expenditures, and for which there are many direct or indirect substitutes, will tend to respond sharply to changes in price. For many consumers housing is a prime example of such a good. The goods least responsive to price changes will be those that account for very small budget shares, and for which substitution possibilities are very limited. For most people salt has both of these properties.
- There are two equivalent techniques for generating market demand curves from individual demand curves. The first is to display the individual curves graphically and then to add them horizontally. The second is algebraic, and proceeds by first solving the individual demand curves for the respective Q values, then adding those values, and finally solving the resulting sum for P.
- A central analytical concept in demand theory is the price elasticity of demand, a measure of the responsiveness of purchase decisions to small changes in price. It is defined as the percentage change in quantity demanded that is caused by a 1 per cent change in price. Goods for which the absolute value of elasticity exceeds 1 are said to be elastic; those for which it is less than 1, inelastic; and those for which it is equal to 1, unit elastic.
- Another important relationship is the one between price elasticity and the effect of a price change on total expenditure. When demand is elastic, a price reduction will increase total expenditure; when inelastic, total expenditure falls when the price goes down. When demand is unit elastic, total expenditure is at a maximum.
- The price elasticity of demand depends largely on four factors:

  (1) *Substitutability.* The more easily consumers may switch to other goods, the more elastic demand will be.

  (2) *Budget share.* Goods that account for a large share of total expenditures will tend to have higher price elasticity.

  (3) *Direction of income effect.* Other factors remaining the same, inferior goods will tend to be less elastic with respect to price than normal goods.

  (4) *Time.* Habits and existing commitments limit the extent to which consumers can respond to price changes in the short run. Price elasticity of demand will tend to be larger, the more time consumers have to adapt.
- Changes in the average income level in a market generally shift the market demand curve. The income elasticity of demand is defined analogously to price elasticity. It is the percentage change in quantity that results from a 1 per cent change in income. Goods whose income elasticity of demand exceeds zero are called normal goods; those for which it is less than zero are called inferior; those for which it exceeds 1 are called luxuries; and those for which it is less than 1 are called necessities. For normal goods, an increase in income shifts market demand to the right, and for inferior goods, an increase in income shifts demand to the left. For some goods, the distribution of income, not just its average value, is an important determinant of market demand.
- The cross-price elasticity of demand is a measure of the responsiveness of the quantity demanded of one good to a small

change in the price of another. It is defined as the percentage change in the quantity demanded of one good that results from a 1 per cent change in the price of the other. If the cross-price elasticity of demand for X with respect to the price of Z is positive, X and Z are substitutes; and if negative, they are complements. In remembering the formulae for the various elasticities – own price, cross-price and income – many people find it helpful to note that each is the percentage change in an effect divided by the percentage change in the associated causal factor.

- The intertemporal choice model is analogous to the atemporal choice model in Chapter 3. In the two-dimensional case it begins with a commodity graph that depicts current and future consumption levels of a composite good. The consumer's initial endowment is the point, (M_1, M_2), which corresponds to current and future income. If the consumer can borrow and lend at the rate r, his intertemporal budget constraint is then the line passing through the endowment point with a slope of $-(1 + r)$. The opportunity cost of a unit of current consumption is $1 + r$ units of future consumption. The horizontal intercept of the intertemporal budget constraint is the present value of all current and future income, which is also called the present value of lifetime wealth.
- The consumer's intertemporal preferences are represented on an indifference map with the same properties as in the atemporal case. A consumer is said to exhibit positive, neutral or negative time preference at a point if his marginal rate of time preference (the absolute value of the slope of his indifference curve) at that point is greater than 1, equal to 1 or less than 1, respectively. In the case of interior solutions, equilibrium occurs at a tangency between the intertemporal budget constraint and an indifference curve. Because the slope of the intertemporal budget constraint exceeds 1 when $r > 0$, consumers exhibit positive time preference in equilibrium, irrespective of the shape of their indifference curves.

Questions for review

1. Why does the quantity of salt demanded tend to be unresponsive to changes in its price?
2. Why is the quantity of education demanded in private universities much more responsive than is salt to changes in price?
3. Draw Engel curves for both a normal good and an inferior good.
4. Give two examples of what are, for most students, inferior goods.
5. Can the price–consumption curve for a normal good ever be downward sloping?
6. To get the market demand curve for a product, why do we add individual demand curves horizontally rather than vertically?
7. Summarize the relationship between price elasticity, changes in price and changes in total expenditure or income.
8. Why don't we measure the responsiveness of demand to price changes by the slope of the demand curve, instead of using the more complicated expression for elasticity?
9. For a straight-line demand curve, what is the price elasticity at the revenue-maximizing point?
10. Do you think a university education at a specific university has a high or a low price (tuition) elasticity of demand?
11. How can changes in the distribution of income across consumers affect the market demand for a product?
12. If you expected a long period of declining GDP, what kinds of company would you invest in?
13. *True or false*: For a budget spent entirely on two goods, an increase in the price of one will necessarily decrease the consumption of both, unless at least one of the goods is inferior. Explain.

14 Mike spends all his income on tennis balls and football tickets. His demand curve for tennis balls is elastic. *True or false*: If the price of tennis balls rises, he consumes more tickets. Explain.

15 *True or false*: If each individual in a market has a straight-line demand curve for a good, then the market demand curve for that good must also be a straight line. Explain.

16 Suppose your budget is spent entirely on two goods: bread and butter. If bread is an inferior good, can butter be inferior as well?

17 Bus services are generally more energy efficient than cars, yet the trend over the past 30 years has been a decline in the proportion of commuters taking buses, despite an increase in real energy prices. Why?

18 Explain why 1 plus the interest rate in the intertemporal choice model is analogous to the relative price ratio in the consumer choice model discussed in Chapter 3.

Problems

1 Sam spends R45/wk on orange juice and apple juice. Orange juice costs R15/glass and apple juice costs R7.50/glass. Sam views 1 cup of orange juice as a perfect substitute for 3 cups of apple juice. Find Sam's optimal consumption bundle of orange juice and apple juice each week. Suppose the price of apple juice rises to R15/glass, while the price of orange juice remains constant. How much additional income would Sam need to afford his original consumption bundle? Put orange juice on the vertical axis and apple juice on the horizontal axis of your graph.

2 Bruce has the same income and faces the same prices as Sam in Problem 1, but he views 1 cup of orange juice as a perfect substitute for 1 cup of apple juice. Find Bruce's optimal consumption bundle. How much additional income would Bruce need to be able to afford his original consumption bundle when the price of apple juice doubles?

3 Maureen has the same income and faces the same prices as Sam and Bruce, but Maureen views 1 cup of orange juice and 1 cup of apple juice as perfect complements. Find Maureen's optimal consumption bundle. How much additional income would Maureen need to afford her original consumption bundle when the price of apple juice doubles?

4 The market for matches has 10 potential consumers, each having an individual demand curve $P = 101 - 10Q_i$, where P is price in rands per box and Q_i is the number of boxes demanded per week by the ith consumer. Find the market demand curve using algebra. Draw an individual demand curve and the market demand curve. What is the quantity demanded by each consumer, and in the market as a whole, when matches are priced at $P = \text{R}1.00$/box?

5 a For the demand curve $P = 60 - 0.5Q$, find the elasticity at $P = 10$.

b If the demand curve shifts parallel to the right, what happens to the elasticity at $P = 10$?

6 Consider the demand curve $Q = 100 - 50P$:

a Draw the demand curve, and indicate which portion of the curve is elastic, which portion is inelastic and which portion is unit elastic.

b Without doing any additional calculation, state at which point of the curve will producers maximize their income, and then explain the logic behind your answer.

7 Suppose the demand for driving through the Huguenot Tunnel is given by $Q = 200\,000 - 2000P$:

a If the toll (P) is R50, how much revenue is collected?

b What is the price elasticity of demand at this point?

c Could the tunnel authorities increase their revenues by changing their price?

8 Consumer expenditures on safety are thought to have a positive income elasticity. For example, as incomes rise, people tend to buy safer

cars (larger cars with side air bags); they are more likely to fly on trips rather than drive; they are more likely to get regular health tests; and they are more likely to get medical care for any health problems the tests reveal. Is safety a luxury or a necessity?

9 Professors Adams and Brown make up the entire demand side of the market for summer research assistants in the economics department. If Adams' demand curve is $P = 50 - 2Q_A$ and Brown's is $P = 50 - Q_B$, where Q_A and Q_B are the hours demanded by Adams and Brown, respectively, what is the market demand for research hours in the economics department?

10 Suppose that, at a price of R400, 300 tickets are demanded for a sought-after performance at the Grahamstown art festival. Now the price rises to R600, and 280 tickets are demanded. Assuming the demand for tickets is linear, find the price elasticities at the quantity–price pairs (300, 400) and (280, 600).

11 The monthly market demand curve for calculators among engineering students is given by $P = 100 - Q$, where P is the price per calculator in rands and Q is the number of calculators purchased per month. If the price is R30, how much revenue will calculator makers receive each month? Find the price elasticity of demand for calculators. What should calculator makers do to increase revenue?

12 What price maximizes total expenditure along the demand curve $P = 27 - Q^2$?

13 The Spur stand at the Rand Easter Show faces a daily demand curve of $Q = 1800 - 15P$, where P is the price of a bag of one dozen hot dogs in rands, and Q is the number of hot dog bags purchased each day.

- **a** If the vendor has been selling 300 bags of hot dogs each day, how much revenue has he been collecting?
- **b** What is the price elasticity of demand for hot dog bags?
- **c** The vendor decides that he wants to generate more revenue. Should he raise or lower the price of his hot dogs?
- **d** At what price would he achieve maximum total revenue?

14 Rank the absolute values of the price elasticities of demand at points A, B, C, D and E on the following three demand curves:

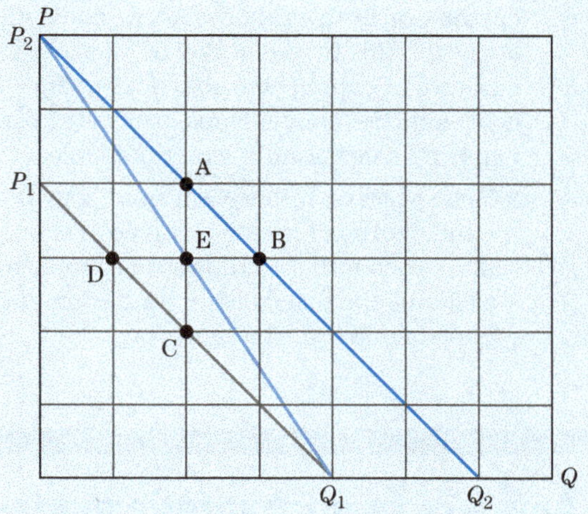

15 Draw the Engel curves for the following goods: food, Hawaiian vacations, peanuts, budget sports trainers.

16 Is the cross-price elasticity of demand positive or negative for the following pairs of items?

- **a** Tennis rackets and tennis balls
- **b** Bread and jam
- **c** Hot dogs and hamburgers

***17** In 2014, X cost R3 and sold 400 units. That same year, a related good, Y, cost R10 and sold 200 units. In 2015, X still cost R3 but sold only 300 units, while Y rose in price to R12 and sold only 150 units. Other things remaining the same, and assuming that the demand for X is a linear function of the price of Y, what was the cross-price elasticity of demand for X with respect to Y in 2014?

***18** Smith cannot tell the difference between rice and wheat, and spends all her food budget of R240/wk on these foodstuffs. If rice costs R30/kg, draw Smith's price–consumption curve for wheat, and the corresponding demand curve.

19 Kathy earns R55 000 in the current period, and will earn R60 000 in the future period. What is the maximum interest rate that would allow her to spend R105 000 in the current period? What is the minimum interest rate that would allow her to spend R120 500 in the future period?

***20** Suppose the local espresso bar in the new shopping mall makes the following offer: people who supply their own 250 ml carton of milk can buy a cup of cappuccino for only R15 instead of R25. Customers can buy 250 ml

* Problems marked with an asterisk (*) are more difficult.

cartons of milk in the adjacent convenience store for R5. In the wake of this offer, the quantity of cappuccino sold goes up by 60 per cent, and the convenience store's total revenue from sales of milk exactly doubles.

a *True or false*: If there is a small, but significant, degree of hassle involved in supplying one's own milk, it follows that the absolute value of the price elasticity of demand for cappuccino is 3. Explain.

b *True or false*: It follows that demand for the convenience store's milk is elastic with respect to price. Explain.

21 Use indifference curve analysis to explain how the market demand curve is determined.

22 Use indifference curve analysis to explain how the Engel curve of a product is determined. Comment on the type of good based on the shape of your Engel curve.

Answers to in-chapter exercises

4.1 On Paula's original budget, B_0, she consumes at bundle A (4 pairs of skis and 2 pairs of bindings). On the new budget, B_1, she consumes at bundle D. (To say that D has 1.5 pairs of bindings per year means that she consumes 3 pairs of bindings every 2 years.) As was the case in Example 4.1, the substitution effect of the price increase (the movement from A to C) is zero.

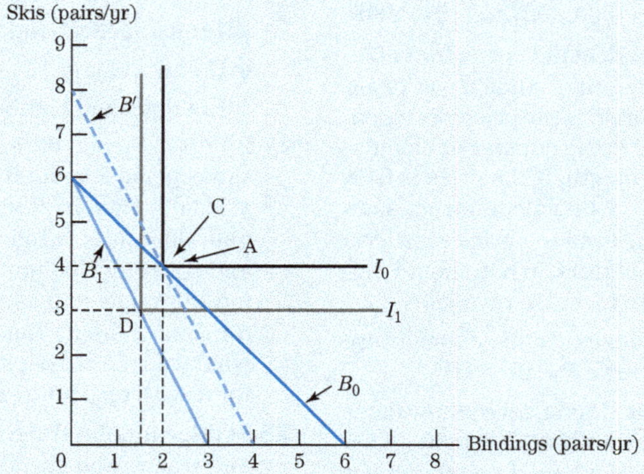

4.2 The income effect, substitution effect and total effects are all zero because the price change does not alter Pam's optimal consumption bundle. She will continue to consume 12 cups of coffee and no tea.

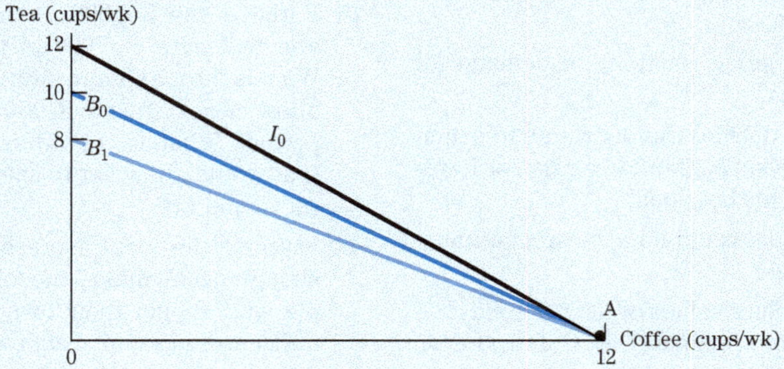

4.3 The formulae for D_1 and D_2 are $P = 1600 - 20Q_1$ and $P = 800 - 20Q_2$, respectively. For the region in which $0 \leq P \leq 800$, we have $Q_1 = 80 - (P/20)$ and $Q_2 = 40 - (P/20)$. Adding, we get $Q_1 + Q_2 = Q = 120 - (P/10)$; thus $P = 1200 - 10Q$ for $0 \leq P \leq 800$. For $800 < P \leq 1600$, the market demand curve is the same as D_1, namely, $P = 1600 - 20Q$.

4.4 First, we need to rearrange the representative consumer demand curve $P = 120 - 60Q_i$ to have quantity alone on one side:

$$Q_i = 2 - \tfrac{1}{60}P$$

Then we multiply by the number of consumers, $n = 30$:

$$\begin{aligned} Q &= nQ_i \\ &= 30Q_i \\ &= 30\left(2 - \tfrac{1}{60}P\right) \\ &= 60 - \tfrac{1}{2}P \end{aligned}$$

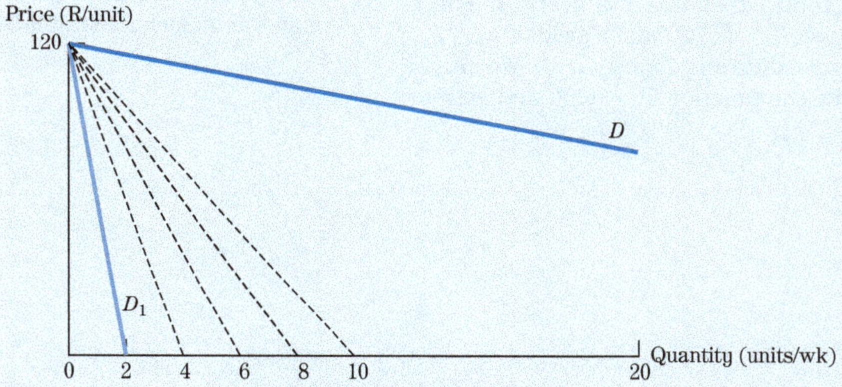

Exercise Answer 4.4

Finally, we rearrange the market demand curve $Q = 60 - \frac{1}{2}P$ to have price alone on one side, $P = 120 - 2Q$, to return to the slope–intercept form. The market demand curve will intersect the quantity axis at 60 units.

4.5 Since the slope of the demand curve is −1, we have $\varepsilon = P/Q$. At $P = 24$, $Q = (32 - 24) = 8$, and so $\varepsilon = -P/Q = -\frac{24}{8} = -3$.

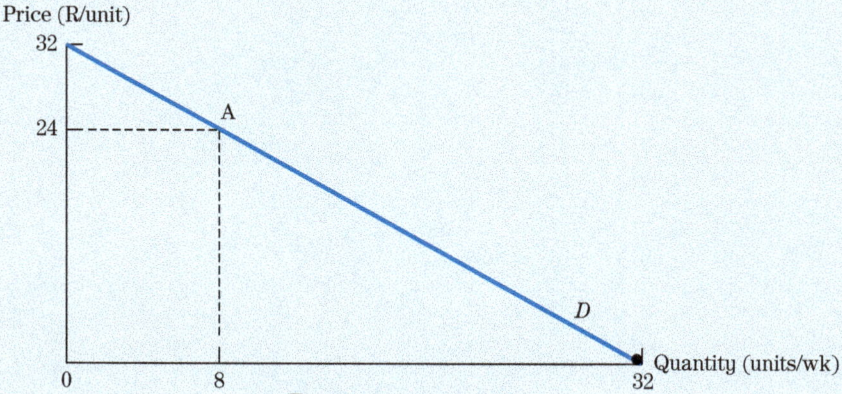

Exercise Answer 4.5

We can also do it with calculus. If $P = 32 - Q$, then $Q = 32 - P$. $\varepsilon = -1\left(\frac{24}{8}\right) = -3$.

4.6 Elasticity when $P = \text{R}400/\text{m}^2$ is $-1\ (400/1200) = -\frac{1}{3}$, so a price reduction will reduce total expenditure. At $P = 400$, total expenditure (or income of the seller) is R480 000/wk, which is more than the R390 000/wk of total expenditure at $P = 300$.

4.7 First consider the point (0.5, 4). If we again let ΔP be 0.001, so that the new P is 4.001, the resulting Q is $2/4.001 = 0.499875$, which means that ΔQ is −0.000125. Price elasticity is therefore equal to $(4/0.5)(-0.000125/0.001) = -1$. With calculus the calculation is

$$\varepsilon = \frac{-2}{4^2} \times \frac{4}{0.5} = -1$$

Now consider the point (4, 0.5). If we again let ΔP be 0.001, so that the new P is 0.501, the resulting Q is $2/0.501 = 3.992$, which means that ΔQ is -0.008. Price elasticity is therefore equal to (0.5/4) $(-0.008/0.001) = -1$. Once again we can calculate elasticity with calculus:

$$\varepsilon = \frac{-2}{0.5^2} \times \frac{0.5}{4} = -1$$

4.8 For $P = 4$, we have $4 = 4/\sqrt{Q}$, which yields $Q = 1$, so total expenditure is $4(1) = 4$. For $P = 3$, we have $3 = 4/\sqrt{Q}$, which yields $Q = \frac{16}{9}$, so total expenditure is $(3)(\frac{16}{9}) = \frac{16}{3}$. We can also rewrite the function $Q = 16/p^2$, and elasticity at $P = 4$ is $\varepsilon = \frac{-32}{4^3} \times \frac{4}{1} = -2$.

But when $\varepsilon = -2$, we know that total expenditure rises with a decrease in price.

4.9 Substitutes, such as a, b and e, have positive cross-price elasticity (an increase in the price of one good raises quantity demanded of the other good). Complements, such as c and d, have negative cross-price elasticity (an increase in the price of one good lowers quantity demanded of the other good).

4.10 PV = R50000 + R42000/1.05 = R90000. Maximum future consumption = 50000(1.05) + R42000 = R94500. The equation for your intertemporal budget constraint is $C_2 = \text{R}94500 - 1.05C_1$.

Chapter 5

The economics of information and choice under uncertainty

When a toad and his rival vie for the same mate, each faces an important strategic decision. Should he fight for her or set off in search of another? To fight is to risk injury, but to continue searching entails costs as well. At the very least, it will consume time. And there is no guarantee that the next potential mate will not herself be the object of some other toad's affections.

Each toad's assessment of the other's fighting capabilities plays an important role in this decision. If one's rival is considerably larger, the likelihood of prevailing will be low and the likelihood of injury high, so it will be prudent to continue searching. Otherwise, it may pay to fight.

Many of these decisions must be made at night, when it is hard to see, so toads have found it expedient to rely on various non-visual clues. The most reliable is the pitch of the rival's croak. In general, larger toads have longer and thicker vocal cords, and hence a deeper croak. Hearing a deep croak in the night, a toad may reasonably infer that a big toad made it. Indeed, experiments have shown that the common toad is much more likely to be intimidated by a deep croak than by a high-pitched one.[1]

Chapter preview

Information is an important input for decision making, not only for toads, but also for consumers

[1] See John Krebs and Richard Dawkins, 'Animal signals: Mind reading and manipulation', in J. Krebs and N. Davies (eds), *Behavioral Ecology: An Evolutionary Approach*, 2nd edn, Sunderland, MA: Sinauer Associates, 1984, pp. 380–402.

and firms. Our models in previous chapters assumed perfect information. In practice, however, we are often woefully ill-informed. Our concern in the first part of this chapter is with the question of how we gather and evaluate relevant information. Because many of the issues that will concern us arise in simple form in the context of the toad's problem, it provides a convenient starting point for our discussion. We shall see that the principles that govern communication between toads help us understand such diverse issues as product warranties, hiring practices and even how people choose partners in personal relationships. We shall also examine statistical discrimination, the process by which people use group characteristics to help estimate the characteristics of specific individuals.

Although the quality of decisions can often be improved by the intelligent gathering of information, it is almost impossible to acquire all potentially relevant information. Our task in the second part of this chapter is to expand the consumer choice model of Chapter 3 to accommodate decisions made under uncertainty.

The economics of information

Communication between potential adversaries

The problems of communication between parties whose goals are potentially in conflict are fundamentally different from those involving parties with common goals. Toads searching for mates obviously fall into the former category, as in general will any two parties to an economic exchange. The seller, for example, sometimes has an incentive to overstate the quality of his product. The buyer, likewise, often has an incentive to understate the amount she is willing to pay for it. This is something we all see or encounter frequently in the real world. The seller wants to sell the product at a price that is higher than the value of the product while the buyer wants to feel she bought a bargain.

The streetwise shopper knows to be wary of inflated claims about product quality. But how exactly does she distinguish a good product from a bad one? How, similarly, does a producer persuade a potential rival that he will cut his price sharply if the rival enters his market? What does a statement like 'I will cut my price' mean? Since the producer has an incentive to utter such statements whether true or not, they convey no information.

We do know, however, that adversaries can communicate information that has strategic value. Toads, after all, are able to broadcast information of this sort. But they do not do it merely by saying 'I am a big toad.' The big toad's implicit claim is credible only because of the physical barriers that prevent the small toad from uttering a deep croak. The toad's croak is an example of a signal: a means of conveying information.

The toad example illustrates two important properties of **signalling** between potential adversaries: (1) signals must be costly to fake; and (2) if some individuals use signals that convey favourable information about themselves, others will be forced to reveal information even when it is considerably less favourable. Each principle is important for understanding how economic agents gather and interpret information. Let's begin by stating each principle in terms of its application in the toad example, and then examine its application in a variety of economic contexts.

Signalling Communication that conveys information.

The costly-to-fake principle

For a signal between adversaries to be credible, it must be costly (or, more generally, difficult) to fake. If small toads could costlessly imitate the deep croak that is characteristic of big toads, a deep croak would no longer be characteristic of big toads – but they cannot. Therefore the deepness of a croak emerges as a reliable signal.

This **costly-to-fake principle** has clear application to signals between people. It is at work, for example, in the following episode from Joe McGinnis' *Fatal Vision*, screened a couple of years ago. Captain Jeffrey MacDonald, an Army Green Beret physician, has been told he's suspected of having killed his wife and daughters. The Army has assigned him a military defence attorney. Meanwhile, however, MacDonald's mother recruits Bernard Segal, a renowned private attorney from Philadelphia, to defend her son. When Segal calls MacDonald in Fort Bragg, North Carolina, to introduce himself, his first question concerns MacDonald's Army attorney:

Costly-to-fake principle For a signal to an adversary to be credible, it must be costly to fake.

> 'Are his shoes shined?'
>
> 'What?' MacDonald sounds incredulous. Here he is, all but accused of having murdered his

> own wife and children, and his first conversation with the Philadelphia lawyer who presumably has been hired to set things right, concerns the other lawyer's shoes.
>
> Segal repeats the question. 'And this time,' he says later, 'I could almost hear Jeff smiling over the phone. That was when I first knew I had a client who was not only intelligent but who caught on very quickly. He said, no, as a matter of fact, the lawyer's shoes were kind of scruffy. I said, "Okay in that case, trust him. Co-operate with him until I can get down there myself." The point being, you see, that if an Army lawyer keeps his shoes shined, it means he's trying to impress the system. And if he was trying to impress the system in that situation – the system being one which had already declared a vested interest, just by public announcement of suspicion, in seeing his client convicted – then he wasn't going to do Jeff any good. The unshined shoes meant maybe he cared more about being a lawyer.'

The condition of the attorney's shoes was obviously not a perfect indication of his priorities in life. Yet they did provide at least *some* reason to suspect that he wasn't just an Army lackey. Any attorney who wore scruffy shoes merely to convey the impression that he wasn't looking to get ahead in the Army actually *wouldn't* get ahead. So the only people who can *safely* send such a signal are those who really do care more about their roles as attorneys.

Some economic applications of the costly-to-fake principle follow.

Product quality assurance

Certain agricultural products are graded according to, for example, size, and consumers know exactly what they will get if they buy jumbo-sized eggs. If you buy a second-hand car, only time will tell whether it was a good buy. If you invest in your education, it will take a very long time before you will know whether it was a good investment. Unfortunately, in the economy many products are so complex that consumers cannot inspect their quality directly. In such cases, firms that offer high quality need some means of communicating this fact to potential buyers; otherwise they will not be able to charge high enough prices to cover their added costs.

One way to solve this problem is for the firm to develop a reputation for delivering high quality. But conditions will not always allow a firm to do this. Consider the case of sidewalk vendors who sell sunglasses on the streets of Cape Town. This business has no headquarters, no costly capital equipment and no loyal customers to worry about – indeed, no sunk costs of any kind. Even if a vendor had supplied quality products on the same street corner for years that would provide no assurance that he would still be in business tomorrow. In short, a firm with no obvious stake in the future has an inherently difficult time persuading potential customers it will make good on its promises.

The incentives are different for a firm with extensive sunk costs. If such a firm goes out of business, it loses the value of substantial investments that cannot be liquidated. Accordingly, the material interests of these firms favour doing everything they can to remain in business. And if buyers know that, they can place much greater trust in the promise of a high-quality product. If such a firm charged a price commensurate with high quality and then delivered shoddy merchandise, it would get too little repeat business to survive, and would thus have incurred its sunk costs in vain.

These observations suggest a reason for believing that heavily advertised products will in fact turn out to have higher quality, just as their slogans proclaim. An extensive national advertising campaign is a sunk cost, its value lost for ever if the firm goes out of business. Having made such an investment, the firm then has every incentive to deliver. That firms believe many consumers have spotted this pattern is evidenced by the fact that they often say 'as seen on national TV' in their magazine or newspaper ads.

Choosing a trustworthy employee

In many situations employees have an opportunity to cheat their employers. The firm needs a signal that identifies a prospective employee as trustworthy. For example, perhaps trustworthy people generally enjoy working in volunteer charitable organizations, which untrustworthy people instead tend to consider highly burdensome. In such cases, the groups people decide to join will convey statistically reliable information about their character.

This notion seems borne out in the procedure by which some professional couples in Johannesburg recruit carers for their children. The care of children is one of those tasks in which trustworthiness is of obvious importance. The very reason for needing someone else to look after them, after all, is that you are not there to do so yourself. Bitter experience has apparently persuaded many Johannesburgers that the local labour market is not a good place to recruit people.

The solution many of these couples have adopted is to advertise for carers in newspapers of rural areas such as the Karoo. The couples have discovered that people raised in the Karoo or other small towns are trustworthy to a degree that the average Johannesburger is not. The signal works because someone who merely wanted to *appear* trustworthy would find it unpalatable, if not impossible, to stay in these rural areas after they had completed their school career. Like the deepness of a toad's croak as a signal of its size, residing in rural areas (away from the city lights) is a good signal of trustworthiness because it would be so costly for an opportunistic person to simulate.

Choosing a hard-working, smart employee

As a final illustration of the costly-to-fake principle, consider a degree that was gained with distinction from an elite university. Employers are looking for people who are smart, and willing to work hard. There are obviously a great many people in the world who have both these traits yet do not have an elite degree. Even so, employers are reasonably safe in assuming that a person who has such a degree is both smart and hardworking, for it is not obvious how anyone without that combination of traits could go about gaining an elite degree with distinction.

No one really questions the fact that the graduates of elite institutions generally turn out to be productive employees. But there is a lively debate indeed about the causality of the influence. People who think education does indeed increase productivity point to the fact that the graduates of elite institutions earn significantly higher salaries. Sceptics caution that the entire differential cannot be attributed to the quality of their education because the students at the best institutions were undoubtedly more productive to begin with.

The full-disclosure principle

A second important principle illustrated by the toad example can be called the **full-disclosure principle**, which says that if some individuals stand to benefit by revealing a favourable value, others will be forced to disclose their less favourable values. This principle helps answer the initially puzzling question of why the smaller toads bother to croak at all. By croaking, they tell other toads how small they are. Why not just remain silent and let them wonder?

Full-disclosure principle Individuals must disclose even unfavourable qualities about themselves lest their silence be taken to mean that they have something even worse to hide.

Suppose all toads with croaks pitched higher than some threshold do, in fact, remain silent. Imagine an index from 0 to 10 that measures the pitch of a toad's croak, with 10 being the highest and 0 the lowest; and suppose, arbitrarily, that toads with an index value above 6 keep quiet (see Fig. 5.1).

It is easy to see why any such pattern would be inherently unstable. Consider a toad with an index of 6.1, just above the cut-off. If he remains silent, what will other toads think? From experience, they will know that *because* he is silent, his croak must be pitched higher than 6. But how much higher?

Lacking information about this particular toad, they cannot say exactly. But they can make

Figure 5.1 The information implicit in silence

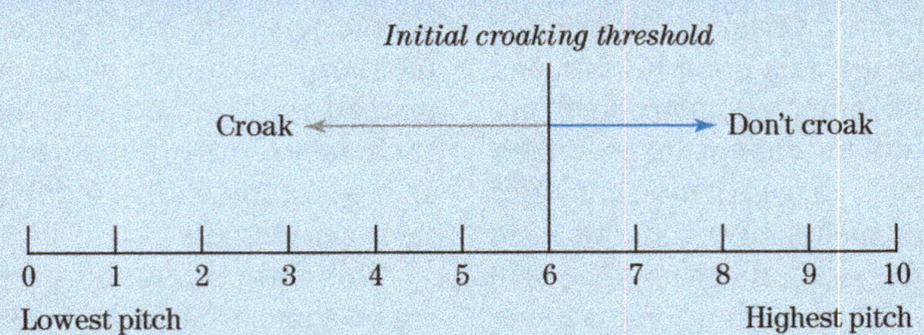

If only those toads with a pitch below 6.0 bother to croak, toads who remain silent reveal that their pitch is, on average, significantly higher than 6.0.

an educated statistical guess. Suppose toads are uniformly scattered along the pitch scale. This means that, if we pick a toad at random from the entire population of toads, the pitch of its croak will be equally likely to take any value along the pitch scale. With the croaking threshold at 6, however, a toad who remains silent will be systematically different from a randomly selected toad. In particular, experience will tell us that the average index for toads who remain silent is 8 (halfway between 6 and 10). Any toad with an index less than 8 will, by the fact of his silence, create the impression that he is smaller than he really is. Our toad with an index of 6.1 would therefore do far better to croak than not.

Thus, if the threshold for remaining silent is 6, it will pay all toads with an index less than 8 to croak. If they do, of course, the threshold will shift from 6 to 8. But a threshold of 8 will not be stable either. With the cut-off at that level, it will pay all toads with an index less than 9 to croak. *Any* threshold less than 10 is for similar reasons destined to unravel. This process does not happen because the small toads want to call attention to their smallness by croaking; rather, they are forced to do so in order to keep from appearing smaller than they really are. This asymmetry of information means that the silent toad knows exactly how big he is, whereas his rival can only make an informed guess.

Product warranties

Information asymmetries help explain, for example, why the producer of a low-quality product might disclose that fact by offering only very limited warranty coverage. The asymmetry here is that producers know much more than consumers about how good their products are. The firm that knows it has the best product has a strong incentive to disclose that information. A credible means of doing so is a liberal guarantee.

Once this product appears with its liberal guarantee, consumers immediately know more than before, not only about *its* quality, but also that the ones without guarantees cannot be of the same high quality. Lacking any other information, this means consumers will underestimate the quality of those products that are just slightly inferior to the best product.

Consider the situation confronting the producer of the second-best product. If it continues to offer no guarantee, consumers will think its product is worse than it really is. Accordingly, this producer will do better to offer a guarantee of its own. But because of its product's slightly lower quality, the terms of its guarantee cannot be quite so liberal as those for the best product.

With the second-best product now guaranteed, the class of remaining unguaranteed products is of still lower average quality than before. The unravelling process is set in motion, and in the end all producers must either offer guarantees or live with the knowledge that consumers rank their products lowest in quality. The terms of the guarantees will in general be less liberal, the lower is a product's quality. Producers clearly do not want to announce their low quality levels by offering stingy warranty coverage. Their problem is that failure to do so would make consumers peg their quality levels even lower than they really are.

This does not mean that guarantees work perfectly in the real world. Many of us have experienced a product's breakdown just after its guarantee has expired. Similarly, products may break down at more regular intervals than the producer foresees, and this can cause serious financial problems for the producer. Another problem with guarantees is that they mean something only as long as the producing firm is still in operation. If a consumer buys a product, and it breaks down before the guarantee expires, but the producer has gone out of business, the guarantee means nothing. For example, say a couple of years ago you bought a Karrimor backpack with a lifetime guarantee. Although it serves you well on numerous hikes, this year two of its zips broke. In the meantime Karrimor has gone out of business, so your lifetime guarantee is worthless. Guarantees are thus just a signal and not a solution to the information problem.

The standard service plan for new cars in South Africa at the beginning of 2011 was a three-year/60 000 km guarantee, normally linked with a warranty guarantee of three years/100 000 km. Some manufacturers, such as Mercedes-Benz, then offered a six-year/120 000 km maintenance plan, and Volvo extended this warrantee to seven years/140 000 km on certain models. Now most car manufacturers offer a 120 000 km maintenance plan and some even provide a 120 000 km service plan too.

Regulating the employment interviewer

Another illuminating application of the full-disclosure principle is the difficulty it poses for government policies that try to restrict the amount of information corporations can demand of job applicants. Consider, for example, the legislation that prohibits employers from asking about marital status and plans for having children. Before the enactment of this legislation, employers routinely solicited such information, particularly from female job candidates. The information helps predict the likelihood of withdrawal from the labour force, and the employer's motive in asking for it was to avoid investing in the hiring and training of workers who would not stay long. Since the demographic information is costly to fake (few people would refrain from marrying in order to appear less likely to drop out of the labour force), it can be a signal between parties whose interests might be in conflict.

To achieve this, however, it is not sufficient merely to prohibit employers from asking about demographic categories. If a woman realizes, for example, that her own particular categories place her in the most favoured hiring category, she has an incentive to *volunteer* information about them. This sets up the familiar unravelling process whereby all but the least-favourable information will eventually be volunteered by job candidates. The candidate who fails to volunteer information, however unfavourable, is simply assumed to be in the least-favourable category.

People and things belong to categories, some of which are, by consensus, better than others. To be trustworthy is better than to be untrustworthy, hard-working better than lazy, and so on. The general message of the full-disclosure principle is that lack of evidence that something resides in a favoured category will often suggest that it belongs to a less-favoured one. Stated in this form, the principle seems transparently simple. And yet its implications are sometimes far from obvious.

The lemons principle

As the following Economic naturalist illustrates, the full-disclosure principle helps resolve the long-standing paradox of why new cars usually lose a large fraction of their market value the moment they are driven from the showroom.

Economic naturalist 5.1

Why do 'almost new' used cars sell for so much less than brand new ones?

A new car purchased on Monday for R340 000 might sell for only R270 000 as a used car the following Friday. The explanation for this large price reduction clearly cannot be that the car has suffered physical depreciation of more than 20 per cent in less than a week.

Economists struggled for years to make sense out of this curious pattern of events. In an uncomfortable departure from their characteristic professional posture, some even speculated that consumers held irrational prejudices against used cars. Berkeley economist George Akerlof, however, suggested that mysterious superstitions might not be necessary. In his famous 'The market for "lemons"', one of the most widely cited economics papers in the past several decades, he offered an ingenious alternative explanation (which became the first clear statement of the full-disclosure principle).[2]

Why do used cars sell for such big discounts?
©istock.com/adrian beesley

Akerlof began with the assumption that new cars are, roughly speaking, of two basic types: good ones and 'lemons'. The two types look alike. But the owner of each car knows from experience which type hers is. Since prospective buyers cannot tell which type is which, good cars and lemons (those that we say, tongue in cheek, were built on a Friday afternoon before a long weekend) must sell for the same price. We are tempted to think the common price will be a weighted average of the respective values of the two types, with the weights being the proportions accounted for by each type. In the new-car market, in fact, this intuition proves roughly correct.

[2] George Akerlof, The market for "lemons": Quality uncertainty and the market mechanism', *Quarterly Journal of Economics*, 1970, vol. 3, pp. 488–500.

In the used-car market, however, things work out differently. Since good cars are worth more to their owners than lemons are to theirs, a much larger fraction of the lemons finds its way quickly into the used-car market. As used-car buyers notice the pattern, the price of used cars begins to fall. This fall in price then reinforces the original tendency of owners of good cars not to sell. In extreme cases, the *only* used cars for sale will be lemons.

Akerlof's insight was to realize that the mere fact that a car was for sale constituted important information about its quality. This is not to say that having a lemon is the only reason that prompts people to sell their cars. Even if it were just a minor reason, however, it would still keep the owner of a good car from getting full value for it in the second-hand market. And that may be all that is needed to initiate the by now familiar unravelling process. Indeed, trouble-free cars rarely find their way into the used-car market except as a result of heavy pressure from external circumstances ('Emigrating, must sell my Volvo station wagon' or 'Injured hand, must sell my manual BMW and buy an automatic car').

Akerlof's explanation thus vindicates our intuition that physical depreciation is an insufficient reason for the sharp price differential between new and used cars. The gap is much more plausibly understood as a reflection of the fact that cars offered for sale, taken as a group, are simply of lower average quality than cars not offered for sale.

The stigma of the newcomer

The full-disclosure principle also suggests why it might once have been more difficult than it is now to escape the effects of a bad reputation by moving. In the current environment, where mobility is high, a dishonest person would be attracted to the strategy of moving to a new location each time he got caught cheating. In generally stable environments, movers, like used cars, were suspect. Nowadays, however, there are so many *external* pressures to move that the mere fact of being a newcomer carries almost no such presumption.

Choosing a relationship

Most people want partners who are kind, caring, healthy, intelligent, physically attractive, and so on. Information about physical attractiveness may be gathered at a glance. But many of the other traits people seek in a partner are difficult to observe, and people often rely on behavioural signals that reveal them. To be effective, such signals must be costly to fake. Someone who is looking for, say, a highly disciplined partner might thus do well to take special interest in people who run marathons in less than three hours.

Conspicuous consumption as ability signalling

Suppose you have been unjustly accused of a serious crime, and are looking for an attorney to represent you. And suppose your choice is between two lawyers who, so far as you know, are identical in all respects except for their standard of consumption. One wears a threadbare polyester suit off the rack

Economic naturalist 5.2

Why is coyness often an attractive attribute?

1930s comedian and film star Groucho Marx stated that he wouldn't join any club that would have him as a member. To follow a similar strategy in the search for a relationship would obviously result in frustration. There may be good reasons for avoiding a seemingly attractive searcher who is too eager. Such a posture will often suggest unfavourable traits that are difficult to observe. The properties of effective signals thus make it clear why coyness, within limits, is so adaptive.

The same properties also have implications for the institutional arrangements under which people search for partners. Modern urban life coupled with heavy work schedules make it hard for people to meet one another. In response, commercial dating services offer to match people with ostensibly similar interests and tastes. Such services have become increasingly popular over the last two decades with the development of the internet. Participants in these services are thus spared the time and expense of getting to know people with whom they have few interests in common. And yet while marriages often result from commercial dating services, many people have found them a bad investment. The apparent reason is that, without meaning to, they act as a screening device that identifies people who have trouble initiating their own relationships. People who participate in dating services are indeed easier to meet, just as the advertisements say. But signalling theory says that, on average, they may be less worth meeting.

and arrives at the courthouse in a 15-year-old, rust-eaten Toyota sedan. The other wears an impeccably tailored sharkskin suit and drives a new R2 million BMW 760iL. Which one would you hire?

Conspicuous consumption The buying of expensive services and products in order to flaunt your wealth and impress others.

Our simple signalling principles suggest that the latter attorney is probably a better bet. The reason is that a lawyer's level of ability in a competitive market is likely to be mirrored closely by his income, which in turn will be positively correlated with his consumption. There is obviously no guarantee that the lawyer who spends more on consumption will have higher ability. But, as in other situations involving risk, here too people must be guided by the laws of probability. And these laws say unequivocally to choose the better-dressed lawyer.

For important decisions involving people we do not know well, even weak signals of ability are often decisive. First impressions count for a lot during job interviews, because we never get a second chance to make a first impression. Placement counsellors have always stressed the importance of quality attire and a good address in the job search process. Even when the employer *knows* how good an applicant is, she may still care a great deal about how that person will come across to others. This will be especially true in jobs that involve extensive contact with outsiders who do *not* know how good the employee is.

Judging from their spending behaviour, many single people seem to believe that their marriage prospects hinge critically on what clothes they wear and what cars they drive. At first glance this seems curious, because by the time most people marry, they presumably know one another well enough for such things not to count for much. Even so, many potential mates have been rejected at the outset for seeming 'unsuitable'.

The importance of consumption goods as signals of ability will be different for different occupations. Earnings and the abilities that count most among professors are not strongly correlated, and they can continue driving old cars or wearing jeans to work. But it might be a big mistake for an aspiring investment banker to drive such a car and not be properly dressed in the presence of her potential clients.

Choice under uncertainty

No matter how much time and energy we spend gathering information, we must make most choices without complete knowledge about the relevant alternatives. The choice between, say, going on a

Economic naturalist 5.3

Why do residents of De Aar spend less on their professional wardrobes than their counterparts in Johannesburg?

As in the case of an investment banker hoping to attract new clients, it is clear that a person's incentive to spend additional money on conspicuous consumption goods will be inversely related to the amount and reliability of independent information that other people have about her abilities. The more people know about someone, the less she can influence their assessments of her by rearranging her consumption in favour of observable goods. This may help explain why consumption patterns in small towns, which have highly stable social networks, are so different from those in big cities. The wardrobe a professional person 'needs' in De Aar, for example, costs less than half as much as the one that same person would need in Johannesburg. Similarly, because the reliability of information about a person increases with age, the share of income devoted to conspicuous consumption should decline over time. The more mature spending patterns of older people may say as much about the declining pay-offs to ability signalling as they do about the increasing wisdom of age.

Note that conspicuous consumption as an ability signal confronts us with a dilemma. The concept of a tasteful wardrobe, like the notion of a fast car, is inescapably relative. To make a good first impression, it is not sufficient to wear clothes that are clean and mended. We must wear something that looks better than what most others wear. This creates an incentive for everyone to save less and spend more on clothing. But when *everyone* spends more on clothing, relative appearance remains unchanged. Conspicuous consumption is thus essentially a *positional good*, one whose attractiveness depends on how it compares with goods in the same category consumed by others. In the familiar stadium metaphor, all spectators leap to their feet to get a better view of an exciting play, only to find the view no better than if all had remained seated. Here, too, the aggregate outcome of individually rational behaviour is markedly different from what people hoped.

As a group, it might pay to spend much less on conspicuous consumption and to save much more for retirement. But if conspicuous consumption strongly influences estimates of ability, it may not pay any individual, acting alone, to take this step.

hiking trail or buying a new 3D Blu-ray player can be made more intelligently if we consult sources such as the South African Weather Service and *Consumer Reports*. And yet, in the end, we simply cannot rule out the possibility of bad weather or defective computer chips. Such risks are a prominent feature of many of our most important decisions. Our task in the remainder of this chapter is to enlarge the basic consumer choice model in Chapter 3 to accommodate them.

Probability and expected value

When choosing a university to attend, a person to marry, an occupation to pursue or even a movie to see, there are likely to be important characteristics you are uncertain about at the moment of choice. Sometimes your choice is between two alternatives that are equally risky (the choice, for example, between two blind dates!); at other times, it will be between a little-known alternative and a relatively familiar one (for instance, the decision whether to transfer to another university for your honours degree or to stay where you are).

Economic decisions made under uncertainty are essentially gambles. We have a variety of intuitions about what makes for an attractive gamble, and many of these intuitions carry over into the realm of economic choices. To illustrate, consider the following series of gambles involving the toss of a fair coin:

- *Gamble 1.* If the coin comes up heads, you win R2000; if tails, you lose R10. This is a gamble you are unlikely ever to be offered in a profit-making casino. The winning outcome is 200 times larger than the losing outcome, and the two outcomes are equally likely. Only people whose religious faith proscribes gambling would consider turning this gamble down, and even for them the choice might be difficult.
- *Gamble 2.* If heads, you win R4000; if tails, you lose R2000. With a winning outcome only twice as large as the losing outcome, this bet is obviously less attractive than the first, but it too would be accepted by many people.

Finally, consider a third gamble. It is the same as the second, except that the pay-offs are multiplied by 100.

- *Gamble 3.* If heads, you win R200 000; if tails, you lose R100 000; losers are allowed to pay off their loss in small monthly payments spread out over 20 years. If put to the test, most people would refuse this bet, even though its pay-offs are in exactly the same proportion as those in gamble 2. It is the task of a theory of choice under uncertainty to explain this pattern of behaviour.

Expected value The sum of all possible outcomes, weighted by their respective probabilities of occurrence.

One important property of a gamble is its **expected value**, a weighted average of all its possible outcomes, where the weights are the respective probabilities. The probability that a fair coin will come up heads when tossed is 1/2. One way of interpreting this statement is to say that it means that, if a fair coin were tossed a very large number of times, it would come up heads half the time, tails the other half of the time. Thus the three bets described above have expected values of

$$EV_1 = \left(\frac{1}{2}\right)R2000 + \left(\frac{1}{2}\right)(-R10) = R995 \tag{5.1}$$

$$EV_1 = \left(\frac{1}{2}\right)R4000 + \left(\frac{1}{2}\right)(-R2000) = R1000 \tag{5.2}$$

and

$$EV_3 = \left(\frac{1}{2}\right)R200\ 000 + \left(\frac{1}{2}\right)(-R100\ 000) = R50\ 000 \tag{5.3}$$

where the notation EV_i denotes the expected value of gamble i, where $i = 1, 2, 3$.

A gamble is clearly more attractive if it has a positive expected value rather than a negative one. But from the way most people respond to these three hypothetical gambles, it is clear that having a positive expected value is by no means sufficient to make a gamble attractive. On the contrary, gamble 3 has the highest expected value of the three, yet is the one least likely to be accepted. By contrast, gamble 1, which has the lowest expected value, is the one most likely to be chosen.

Now, the lesson is obviously not that having a higher expected value is a bad thing in itself. Rather, it is that, in addition to the expected value of a gamble, most people also consider how they feel about each of its possible outcomes. The feature that makes gamble 3 so unattractive to most people is that there is a 50–50 chance of the extremely unpleasant outcome of losing R100 000.

Gamble 2 also contains an unpleasant possibility, namely, a 50–50 chance of losing R2000. But this is an outcome many people feel they could live with. Gamble 1 is by far the easiest choice for most people, because its positive outcome is large enough to make a difference, whereas its negative outcome is too small to really matter.

The von Neumann–Morgenstern expected utility model

The formal economic theory of choice between uncertain alternatives was advanced by John von Neumann, a distinguished mathematician at the Institute for Advanced Study, and Oskar Morgenstern, a Princeton economist. Its central premise is that people choose the alternative that has the highest **expected utility**. Their theory of expected utility maximization assumes a utility function U, which assigns a numerical value to the satisfaction associated with different outcomes. The expected utility of a gamble is the expected value of utility over all possible outcomes.

Expected utility The expected utility of a gamble is the expected value of utility over all possible outcomes.

For the sake of simplicity we shall consider the outcome of a gamble to be defined uniquely by the amount of total wealth to which it corresponds. For example, if a consumer with an initial wealth level of 10 000 accepted gamble 1 above and won, the outcome would be total wealth of 10 000 + 2000 = 12 000, and the consumer's utility would be U(12 000). If he lost, his wealth would be 10 000 − 10 = 9990, and his utility U(9990). More generally, if M_0 is the consumer's initial wealth level, the expected utility of accepting the first gamble would be

$$EU_1 = \left(\frac{1}{2}\right)U(M_0 + 2000) + \left(\frac{1}{2}\right)U(M_0 - 10) \quad (5.4)$$

If you refuse gamble 1, your expected utility will simply be the utility of the wealth level M_0, namely, $U(M_0)$. Faced with this choice, the von Neumann–Morgenstern expected utility criterion tells you to accept the gamble if and only if EU_1 is larger than $U(M_0)$.

Risk averse Preferences described by a utility function with diminishing marginal utility of wealth.

Persons whose utility functions are concave in total wealth are said to be **risk averse**, which means that they would always refuse a gamble whose expected value is zero. Gambles with an expected value of zero are called **fair gambles**.

Fair gamble A gamble whose expected value is zero.

Consider, for example, a gamble G in which you win R75 if the coin comes up heads, but lose R75 if tails. The expected value of this gamble is (1/2)75 + (1/2)(−75) = 0, so it is a fair gamble. For a person with an initial wealth level of 100 and utility function given by $U = U(M)$, the expected utility of this gamble is

$$\begin{aligned} \mathrm{EU_G} &= 0.5U(100 + 75) + 0.5U(100 - 75) \\ &= 0.5U(175) + 0.5U(25) \end{aligned} \quad (5.5)$$

For any fair gamble, the expected value of your wealth if you accept the gamble is the same as the certain value of your wealth if you refuse the gamble. Here, the expected value of wealth when you take the gamble is equal to 100. If you refuse the gamble, you will have a certain wealth level of 100, which yields utility equal to U(100). Expected utility theory says that, if $\mathrm{EU_G} > U(100)$ you should accept the gamble; otherwise, you should refuse it.

The expected utility of a gamble has a straightforward geometric interpretation. We first construct the chord that joins the points on the utility function that correspond to losing and winning the gamble, respectively (that is, the points A and C in Fig. 5.3). For the utility function shown in Fig. 5.3, the expected utility of the gamble is equal to 0.5(45) + 0.5(95) = 70. Note that this value corresponds to the point on the chord between A and C that lies directly above the expected value of wealth under the gamble (100). Note that the expected utility of refusing the gamble is simply U(100) = 80, which is clearly larger than the expected utility of the gamble itself.

Indeed, it is clear from Fig. 5.3 that a risk-averse person will refuse not only fair gambles but even some that have positive expected value. For this particular utility function shown, all gambles that result in an expected value of final wealth less than 130 yield a lower expected utility than that of standing pat with the initial wealth level 100.

The gambles we have considered so far have been ones decided by the toss of a coin. With probability 1/2, a good outcome occurred; with probability 1/2, a bad outcome. In general, however, the probability of winning a gamble can be any number between 0 and 1. But as the following example and exercise illustrate, the expected utility of a gamble may still be interpreted as a point on the chord joining the winning and losing endpoints, even when the probability of winning is something other than 1/2.

Exercise 5.1

Graph the utility function in Example 5.2 (on page 155) for $0 < M < 50$. Locate the points on the utility function that correspond to the winning and losing outcomes of the gamble in Example 5.2. Draw the chord between these two points, labelling the winning endpoint C and the losing endpoint A. What fraction of AC must you move from C before reaching the expected utility of the gamble?

The general rule illustrated by Exercise 5.1 is that, if the probability of winning is p and the probability of losing is $1 - p$, then the expected utility lies a fraction of $1 - p$ to the left of point C, the winning endpoint of the chord joining the winning and losing points on the utility function.

One intuitive rationale for the assumption that most people are risk averse is that increments to total wealth yield diminishing marginal utility – which, again, means that the more wealth a consumer has, the smaller will be the increase in her utility caused by a one-unit increase in wealth. Most of us are comfortable with the idea that an extra R1000 means more to a person if her total wealth is R20 000 than it would if her total wealth were R1 million. Note

Example 5.1

Suppose Ramaphosa's utility function is given by $U(M) = \sqrt{M}$. If Ramaphosa has an initial wealth of 110 000, which of the above gambles has the highest expected utility?

The three expected utilities are given by

$$EU_1 = \left(\frac{1}{2}\right)\sqrt{112\,000} + \left(\frac{1}{2}\right)\sqrt{109\,990}$$
$$= 333.155$$

$$EU_2 = \left(\frac{1}{2}\right)\sqrt{114\,000} + \left(\frac{1}{2}\right)\sqrt{108\,000}$$
$$= 333.136$$

and

$$EU_3 = \left(\frac{1}{2}\right)\sqrt{310\,000} + \left(\frac{1}{2}\right)\sqrt{10\,000}$$
$$= 328.388$$

so gamble 1 is the most attractive of the three for Ramaphosa.

The key insight of the theory is that the expected values of the outcomes of a set of alternatives need not have the same ranking as the expected utilities of the alternatives. Differences in these orderings arise because utility is often a non-linear function of final wealth. In the empirically most common case, utility is assumed to be a concave function of total wealth, which means that the utility function has the characteristic profile shown in Fig. 5.2. More formally, a function $U(M)$ is said to be concave if, for any pair of values M_1 and M_2, the function lies above the chord joining the points $[M_1, U(M_1)]$ and $[M_2, U(M_2)]$. The utility function $U = \sqrt{M}$ is a concave function of M. A utility function that is concave in M is also said to exhibit **diminishing marginal utility** of wealth. Marginal utility is simply the slope of the utility function, and a utility function with diminishing marginal utility is one whose slope declines as M increases. Intuitively, the meaning of diminishing marginal utility of wealth is that the more wealth a consumer has, the smaller will be the increase in his utility caused by a one-unit increase in wealth.

Diminishing marginal utility For a utility function defined by wealth, one in which marginal utility declines as wealth increases.

Figure 5.2 A concave utility function

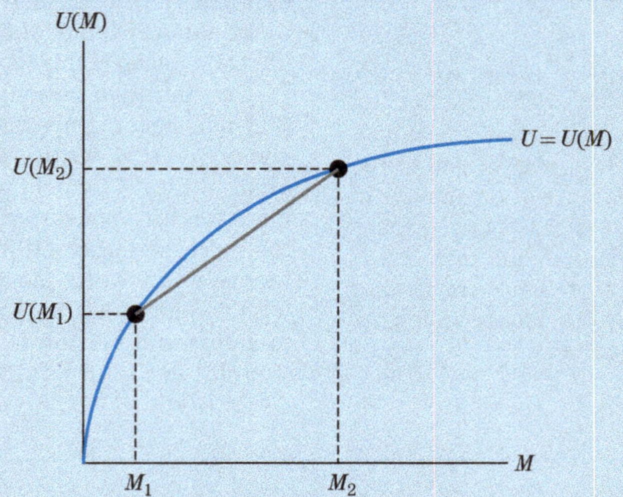

Any arc of a concave utility function lies above the corresponding chord.

Figure 5.3 A risk-averse person will always refuse a fair gamble

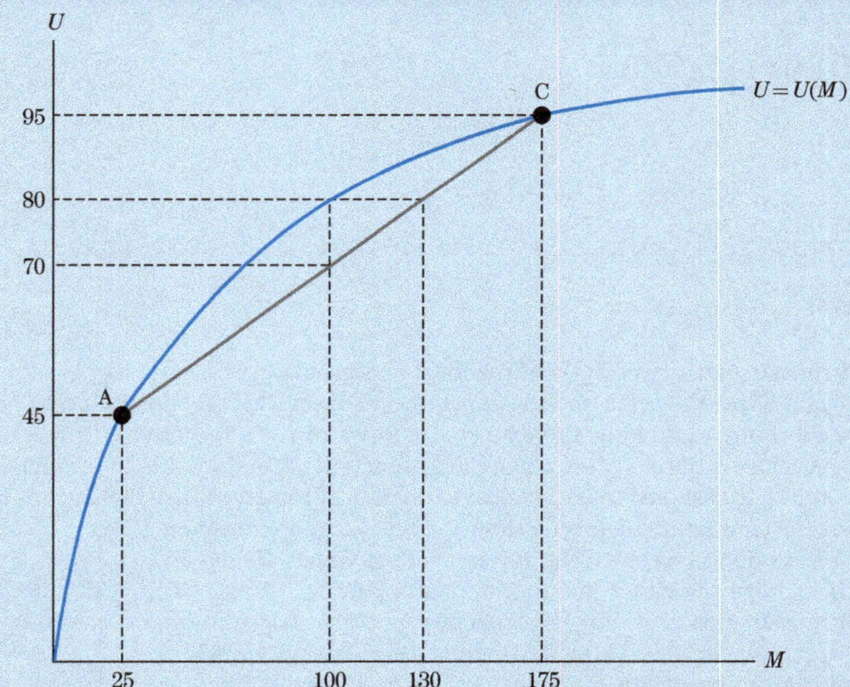

The expected utility of a gamble lies on the chord joining points A and C. If the probability of winning is 1/2, the expected utility lies halfway between A and C. Since a point on the arc of a concave function always lies above the corresponding point on the chord, the expected utility of a fair gamble will always be less than the utility of refusing the gamble.

Example 5.2

Your utility function is $U = \sqrt{M}$ and your initial wealth is 360. Will you accept a gamble in which you win 130 with probability 2/3 and lose 110 with probability 1/3?

The expected utility of the gamble is given by

$$
\begin{aligned}
EU_G &= \left(\frac{2}{3}\right)\sqrt{360+130} + \left(\frac{1}{3}\right)\sqrt{360-110} \\
&= 20.028
\end{aligned}
$$

If you refuse the gamble, your utility will be $\sqrt{360} = 18.974$, which is smaller than 20.028, so you should accept the gamble.

that this intuition is equivalent to saying that the utility function is concave in total wealth – which in turn implies that a given gain in wealth produces a smaller gain in utility than the loss that would be caused by a comparable loss in wealth.

Whether people are risk averse is of course an empirical question. We do know that people who, for example, climb sheer rock faces are not risk averse some of the time. Indeed, most of us are not risk averse at least some of the time (as, for example, when we play roulette in a casino or buy a Lotto ticket or enjoy any other game of chance with negative expected value).

Consider a person with an initial wealth of M_0 who is confronted with a gamble that pays B with probability 1/2 and $-B$ with probability 1/2. If this person is a **risk seeker**, her utility function will look like the one pictured in Fig. 5.4. It is *convex* in total wealth, which implies that the expected utility of accepting a fair gamble, EU_G, will be larger than the utility of refusing it, $U(M_0)$. Geometrically, a convex utility function is one whose slope increases with total wealth.

Risk seeking Preferences described by a utility function with increasing marginal utility of wealth.

Figure 5.4 The utility function of a risk-seeking person is convex in total wealth

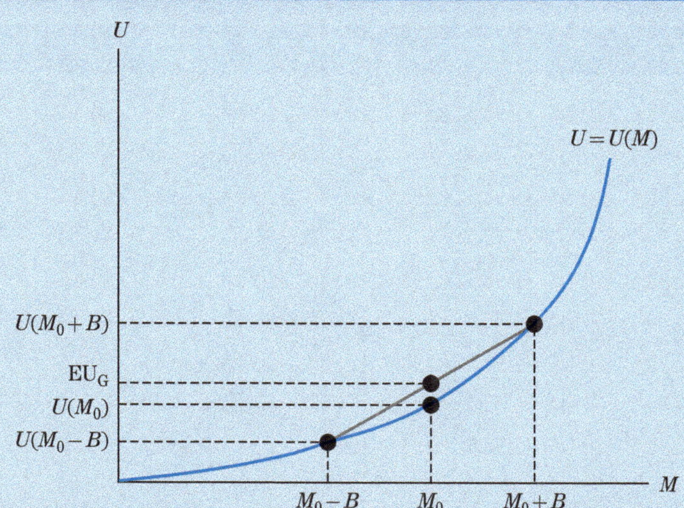

Any arc of a convex function lies below the corresponding chord. For a risk seeker, the expected utility of a fair gamble, EU_G, will always exceed the utility of refusing the gamble, $U(M_0)$.

Exercise 5.2

Consider a person with an initial wealth level of 5000 who faces a chance to win 1000 with probability 1/2 and to lose 1000 with probability 1/2. If this person's utility function is given by $U(M) = M^2$, will she accept this gamble?

Risk neutral Preferences described by a utility function with constant marginal utility of wealth.

A person is said to be **risk neutral**, finally, if he is generally indifferent between accepting or refusing a fair gamble. The utility function of a risk-neutral person will be linear, like the one shown in Fig. 5.5.

Exercise 5.3

Consider a person with initial wealth of 5000 who faces a chance to win 1000 with probability 1/2 and to lose 1000 with probability 1/2. If this person's utility function is given by $U(M) = M$, will she accept this gamble?

The gambles we have considered thus far have had only two outcomes. In general, however, a gamble can have any number of possible outcomes. The expected value of a gamble with more than two outcomes is, as before, a weighted sum of the possible outcomes, where the weights are again the respective probabilities. For example, a gamble with three possible outcomes, B_1, B_2 and B_3, which occur with probabilities p_1, p_2 and p_3, respectively, has an expected value of $p_1B_1 + p_2B_2 + p_3B_3$. Because the probabilities must add up to 1, we know that $p_3 = 1 - p_1 - p_2$. The expected utility of this gamble is therefore $p_1U(B_1) + p_2U(B_2) + (1 - p_1 - p_2)U(B_3)$.

Exercise 5.4

Suppose one in every four new laptops is defective. The defective ones, however, cannot be identified except by those who own them. Consumers are risk neutral and value non-defective laptops at R20 000 each. Computers do not depreciate physically with use. If used laptops sell for R6000, how much do new ones sell for?

As the preceding example clearly illustrates, information that helps reduce uncertainty has economic value. And this is reflected in the fact that we employ vocational testing services, guidance counsellors and a variety of other professionals to generate just this type of information. This is exactly the reason why many of you went to vocational guidance officers before coming to university, so that they could guide you to take the course most suitable for your personality and abilities.

Figure 5.5 Risk neutrality

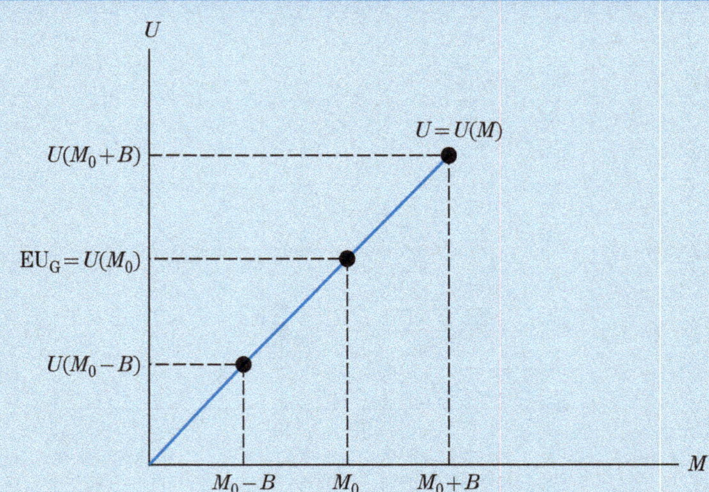

A risk-neutral consumer is indifferent between accepting or refusing a fair gamble because the expected utility of accepting, EU_G, is the same as the certain utility of refusing, $U(M_0)$.

Example 5.3

Suppose it is known that some fraction z of all laptops are defective. The defective ones, however, cannot be identified except by those who own them. Consumers are risk neutral and value non-defective laptops at R25 000 each. Computers do not depreciate physically with use. New laptops sell for R15 000 and used ones for R5000. What is z?

Because of the lemons principle, we know that all used laptops for sale must be defective. (The owners of non-defective laptops could not sell them for what they are worth in the used market, so they hold on to them.) Accordingly, the price of a used computer is the same as the value of a new defective one. (Recall that being used, by itself, doesn't cause the machines to depreciate.) Because consumers are risk neutral, the price of a new laptop – R15 000 – is simply a weighted average of the values of non-defective and defective computers, where the weights are the respective probabilities. Thus we have

$$R15\,000 = R5000z + R25\,000\,(1 - z) \quad (5.6)$$

which solves for $z = 1/2$.

Example 5.4

Boipelo has a von Neumann–Morgenstern utility function given by $U = 1 - 1/M$, where M is the present value of her lifetime income. If Boipelo becomes a teacher, she will make $M = 5$ with probability 1. If she becomes an actress, she will make $M = 400$ if she becomes a star, but only $M = 2$ if she fails to become a star. The probability of her becoming a star is 0.01. Nelson is an infallible judge of acting talent. After a brief interview, he can state with certainty whether Boipelo will become a star if she chooses to pursue a career in acting. What is the most she would be willing to pay for this information?

To answer this question, we must first calculate Boipelo's expected utility if she lacks access to Nelson's information. If she were to become a teacher, she would have a lifetime income of 5 with probability 1, so her expected utility would be simply

$$U_T = 1 - \frac{1}{5} = 0.8$$

If instead she pursued an acting career, her expected utility would be

$$\begin{aligned} EU_A &= 0.01\left(1 - \frac{1}{400}\right) + 0.99\left(1 - \frac{1}{2}\right) \\ &= 0.505 \end{aligned}$$

Because her expected utility is higher by becoming a teacher rather than an actress, she will become a teacher and have an expected utility of 0.8.

Now suppose she has access to an interview with Nelson that will reveal with certainty whether she would become a star if she pursued an acting career. And suppose the charge for this interview is P, where P is measured in the same units as M (see Fig. 5.6).

The clear advantage of having the information Nelson provides is that, if he says she would succeed as an actress, she can then avail herself of that lucrative, but otherwise too risky, career path. If Nelson says she would not succeed, however, she can choose teaching with no regrets. Her expected utility if she pays P for the interview is given by

$$EU_I = 0.01\left(1 - \frac{1}{400 - P}\right) + 0.99\left(1 - \frac{1}{5 - P}\right) \quad (5.7)$$

Figure 5.6 The value of reducing uncertainty

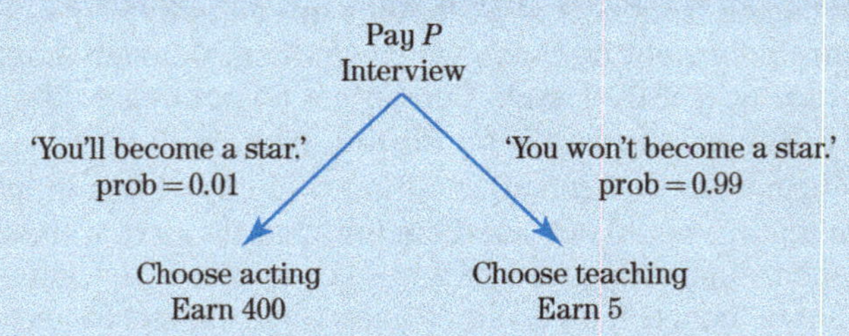

Under the assumed pay-offs, the expected utility of becoming an actress is less than the expected utility of becoming a teacher. But because a successful actress earns so much more than a teacher, information about whether an acting career would be successful has obvious economic value.

To find the maximum amount that Nelson can charge for an interview, we set EU_I equal to Boipelo's expected utility if she lacks information, and solve for P (recall that if she lacks information she becomes a teacher and gets $U_T = 0.8$):

$$\begin{aligned} EU_I &= 0.01\left(1 - \frac{1}{400 - P}\right) + 0.99\left(1 - \frac{1}{5 - P}\right) \\ &= U_T \\ &= 0.8 \end{aligned} \tag{5.8}$$

As an exercise, you can verify that a P value of approximately 0.0494 solves this equation. For any price less than that, Boipelo should pay Nelson for his evaluation. But if Jacob charges more than 0.0494, Boipelo should skip the interview and become a teacher.

Example 5.5

Rashaad, who was injured by a defective product, is weighing the decision of whether to sue the manufacturer. His utility function is given by $U(M) = 1 - (1/M)$, where M is his total wealth. His total wealth if he does not sue is $M_0 = 7$. If he sues, he could win, with probability 0.5, in which case he would receive a damage award of 5. If he loses, he will receive nothing in damages. Suppose the opportunity cost of the time required for a lawyer to file a suit on Rashaad's behalf is 2. Will Rashaad file a suit if he has to pay the lawyer a fee of 2? Can a risk-neutral lawyer offer Rashaad a fee schedule whose expected value is sufficient to cover the lawyer's opportunity cost (that is, whose expected value is at least 2) and which simultaneously will induce Rashaad to sue? If so, describe such a fee schedule.

From the perspective of Rashaad and his lawyer, the economic cost of filing a suit is 2, the opportunity cost of the lawyer's time. The expected benefit of filing the suit is the probability of winning (0.5) times the damage award if he wins (5), or 2.5. Thus the expected value of filing the lawsuit is $2.5 - 2.0 = 0.5 > 0$. But the question for Rashaad is not whether filing the suit has positive expected value, but rather whether it will increase his expected utility. If Rashaad sues and pays his lawyer 2, his total wealth (net of the lawyer's fee) will be $7 + 5 - 2 = 10$ if he wins and $7 - 2 = 5$ if he loses. His expected utility if he files suit will thus be $0.5[1 - (1/10)] + 0.5[1 - (1/5)] = 0.85$. If he does not sue, his wealth will be 7 for sure, which means his utility will be $1 - (1/7) = 0.86 > 0.85$. Thus if he has to pay his lawyer a fee of 2, he will not sue.

Rashaad's aversion to risk prevents him from filing a suit that has positive expected value. Luckily for him, his lawyer happens to be risk neutral. This means the lawyer can design a fee schedule under which the lawyer assumes all the risk of an unsuccessful filing. What would such a fee schedule look like?

Let F_1 be the lawyer's fee if Rashaad sues and wins, and F_2 be the fee if Rashaad sues and loses. Because Rashaad is risk averse, the best possible fee structure from his perspective would be one in which his income is the same irrespective of the suit's outcome:

$$7 + 5 - F_1 = 7 - F_2 \tag{5.9}$$

Is his lawyer willing and able to offer such a fee schedule? Risk neutrality means that the lawyer will be content to accept the case provided the expected value of his fee is enough to cover the opportunity cost of his time, which is assumed to be 2. So we have

$$0.5F_1 + 0.5F_2 = 2 \tag{5.10}$$

Equations 5.9 and 5.10 solve for $F_1 = 4.5$ and $F_2 = -0.5$.

The negative value of F_2 means that if Rashaad files suit and loses, his lawyer will actually pay Rashaad 0.5. Thus, no matter what the outcome of the suit, Rashaad ends up with $M = 7.5$ under the proposed fee schedule, or 0.5 more than if he did not sue. (Note that 0.5 is exactly the expected value of the lawsuit.) Thus if Rashaad's lawyer offers him the proposed fee schedule, he will sue because his expected utility if he does so, $U = (1 - 1/7.5) = 0.87$, will be higher than if he does not sue (0.86), even if he loses the case.

This example illustrates the principle that, in transactions involving risk, a risk-neutral seller can make the transaction more attractive to a risk-averse buyer by acting, in effect, as an insurance company.

Exercise 5.5

In Example 5.5, find the values of F_1 and F_2 that would have made Rashaad indifferent between filing a suit and not filing it.

The answer to the question asked in Exercise 5.5 is called the **certainty equivalent value** of the gamble associated with filing the lawsuit. The certainty equivalent value of a gamble is the sum of money for which an individual would be indifferent between receiving that sum and taking the gamble.

Certainty equivalent value The sum of money for which an individual would be indifferent between receiving that sum and taking the gamble.

Exposure to risk is an undesirable thing for risk-averse consumers, enough so that they are often willing to sacrifice substantial resources in order to reduce it. Thus the certainty equivalent value of a gamble is less than the expected value of a gamble for risk-averse consumers. As you showed in Exercise 5.5, the consumer in Example 5.5 would have been willing to accept an expected value lower by 0.5 rather than run the risk of having to absorb the full cost of an unsuccessful lawsuit.

Insuring against bad outcomes

When the risks that different consumers confront are *independent* of one another (that is, when the likelihood of a bad outcome happening to one consumer is independent of the likelihood of one happening to another), it will often be possible for consumers to act collectively to achieve a result they all prefer.

Risk pooling

Recall gamble 3 considered earlier in this chapter, in which you could flip a coin and win R200 000 if it came up heads, but lose R100 000 if it came up tails. Although this is obviously a much better than fair gamble (its expected value is R50 000), most people would be reluctant to accept it because it would be so difficult to deal with a loss of R100 000. But suppose you could join 9999 other people in an agreement under which you each accept the gamble, then pool the resulting gains and losses and share them equally. Would you enter that agreement?

You'd be almost crazy not to, because with 10 000 independent flips of a fair coin, the number of heads will lie between 4900 and 5100 more than 95 per cent of the time. The upside is that, if you join the agreement, not only is the expected value of your share of the winnings R50 000 (the same as if you gambled alone), but also, more importantly, your share of the winnings is extremely likely to be close to R50 000. The only way you could lose money under this agreement would be if 10 000 flips of a fair coin came up tails more than two-thirds of the time. The odds of that happening are so remote that you really don't need to worry about it.

Law of large numbers A statistical law that says that if an event happens independently with probability p in each of N instances, the proportion of cases in which the event occurs approaches p as N grows larger.

Risk sharing, or *risk pooling*, works because of a statistical property called the **law of large numbers**. This law says that if an event happens independently with probability p for each of a large number of individuals, then the *proportion* to whom it happens in a given year will rarely deviate significantly from p. Suppose the event is that of a fire destroying a private home, and that it happens with probability 0.002 for each home in a given year. For a small collection of individual homes, the proportion destroyed by fire can vary sharply from year to year. But in a sample of, say, 2 000 000 homes, we can be reasonably sure that the number destroyed by fire in a given year will be very close to 4000 (so that the proportion destroyed, 4000/2 000 000, would be 0.002).

For individuals, or even small groups of individuals, accidental losses pose a problem of inherent uncertainty. But for a large group of individuals, the proportion of people who will have accidents is extremely stable and predictable. And this property of the law of large numbers makes it possible for people to reduce their risk exposure through pooling arrangements.

Another method of risk sharing is the practice of joint ownership of business enterprises. When a new business starts, two things can happen. The business can succeed, in which case its owners earn a lot of money. Alternatively – and much more likely – it can fail, in which case they lose all or part of their initial investments. Starting a business is thus a gamble, much like any other. Consider a business venture that requires an initial investment of R1 000 000. Suppose that with probability 1/2 you will lose this initial investment, and with probability 1/2 you will not only get it back but also earn a dividend of R2 000 000. It is clear that, although the expected value of this enterprise is positive (namely, R500 000), many people would find it unacceptably risky. But if 1000 people pooled their resources and shared the investment, the venture would suddenly look exactly like gamble 2 – each person would stand to lose R1000 with probability 1/2 or gain R2000 with probability 1/2. Without changing the business venture itself at all, it has suddenly become attractive to a great many more people. Partnerships, joint stock companies, racehorse syndicates and a host of other similar institutional arrangements enable people to translate unacceptably large risks into much more palatable small ones.

Another example of collective action to reduce uncertainty is the operation of insurance markets. A car accident that causes death or serious injury can easily result in a court judgement of several million rands against the driver. The likelihood of such a bad outcome is remote, but the consequences are so dire that few families could bear them. Private insurance companies offer a means for consumers to share this risk. By contributing a monthly premium of several hundred rands each, the policyholders create a pool of revenues that is large enough to settle the small handful of judgements awarded each year. Because of the law of large numbers, insurance companies can predict very accurately how much revenue they will need to cover their benefit claims. In effect, each party accepts a sure small loss (its insurance premium) in return for a guarantee of not having to bear a much larger one.

For the average consumer, insurance for sale in a private marketplace will always be an unfair gamble, in the specific sense defined earlier. To see why, note first that if an insurance company paid out exactly the same amount in benefits as it collected in premiums, then buying insurance would be a fair gamble – the amount a policyholder got back in benefits would be equal, on average, to the amount she paid in premiums. But a private insurance company must collect more in premiums than it pays out in benefits because it must also cover its costs of sales agents, bookkeepers, claims investigators and the rent of the company's offices. That most people prefer a small unfair gamble (buying insurance) to a much larger fair one (taking their chances without insurance) is often cited as evidence that most people are risk averse.

Options

An option is a contract that a person buys to complete a transaction over a specified time period going into the future. Let's explain it with a simple example. Assume you want to buy a car and there are two sellers. One will sell the car on an *as seen* basis. If you buy it and it's a lemon, you're stuck with it. The second seller will offer you a 30-day money-back guarantee. If you buy the car and for some reason it does not fulfil your expectations, you have the option to return it within 30 days and to get your money back. The value of this option means you are willing to pay more for the second car than the first – you are willing to pay to reduce your risk.

Typically, an option must include details of the underlying transaction, such as what is being bought or sold, at what price, where the transaction will take place and other relevant information. In the car example, the option will state that resale of the car will be at the original purchase price and that the offer holds for 30 days after the initial transaction takes place. Options should also specify during which period an option may be exercised. A third attribute of an option is the price – sometimes it's explicit and directly quoted; sometimes, as in the car example, it is implicit because it's part of a larger transaction. The car will be more expensive if it is sold with such an option.

Because the transaction that underlies an option will occur sometime in the future, it is subject to many uncertainties. If the car that you bought has no problems, the transaction will have little value. After 30 days the car will still be worth what you paid for it and the option to resell the car at its original price will have no value. However, you may experience engine or gearbox problems and then the option is of much more value to you. You could also discover that the car is worth more than you thought and then it is very unlikely that you will sell it back.

It is useful to see the value of the transaction option in two dimensions: (1) the expected value of the transaction and (2) the variability of the value of the transaction. The greater the value of the expected value of the transaction, the greater will be the value of an option to undertake the transaction. If you don't expect much trouble with your car, the resale option has little value. Suppose you believe a 50 per cent chance exists that the car will need R5000 worth of repairs during the first 30 days and a 50 per cent chance that it will not. Reselling the car when it needs repair means you make R5000, but reselling it when it does not need repair yields nothing. The expected value of the option is then $0.5(5000) + 0.5(0) =$ R2500. However, if you think there's a 50–50 chance that the car will need R10 000 worth of repairs, the expected value of the transaction will be R5000. Now you will be willing to pay more for the resale option.

The more variable the potential value of a transaction, the more valuable will be the option to undertake it or not. If you believe again that there is a 50/50 chance that the car will need R5000 repairs within 30 days, that means the expected value is R2500. Consider now the situation whereby you believe a 50–50 chance exists that the car will need R10 000 worth of repairs or that it is worth R5000 more than you anticipated. Half the time the transaction will yield R10 000 because you can resell the car that needs repair. However, half the time the transaction will have a negative value because you will sell the car for R5000 less than you discovered it is worth. The expected value of the transaction is now $0.5(10\,000) + 0.5(-5000) =$ R2500. The expected value of both scenarios is the same.

However, the option for resale in the second case is more valuable. Remember that you need not exercise the option after you see how the car works out. In the first case, 50 per cent of the time the transaction is worth R5000 because you can sell it for R5000 more than it is worth. And 50 per cent of the time you will discover that the transaction is worthless because you can sell the car for what it is worth. So you will most probably not opt for the resale and the expected value after the uncertainty is resolved is still R2500. In the second case, the transaction is worth R1 0000 50 per cent of the time after the uncertainty has been resolved because you can sell the car for R10 000 more than it is worth. The other 50 per cent of the time the transaction is again worthless because you will never sell a car worth R5000 more than is being offered. Therefore the expected value of the transaction is now R5000 $[0.5(10\,000) + 0.5(0)]$ – considerably more than in the less variable case.

The reservation price for insurance

What is the most a consumer would pay for insurance against a loss? Suppose a risk-averse consumer with an initial wealth of 1750 has the utility function $U(M)$, as shown in Fig. 5.7. If he faces the prospect of a loss of 1500 with probability 1/3, his expected utility is $(1/3)\ U(250) + (2/3)U(1750) = (1/3)(45) + (2/3)\ (90) = 75$. (See Fig. 5.7, and note that his expected utility lies on the chord joining A and C at the point directly above $M = 1250$, his expected wealth without insurance.) Now suppose this consumer could buy an insurance policy that completely covered the loss. What is the most he would be willing to pay for such a policy? In Fig. 5.7, we see

Figure 5.7 The reservation price for insurance

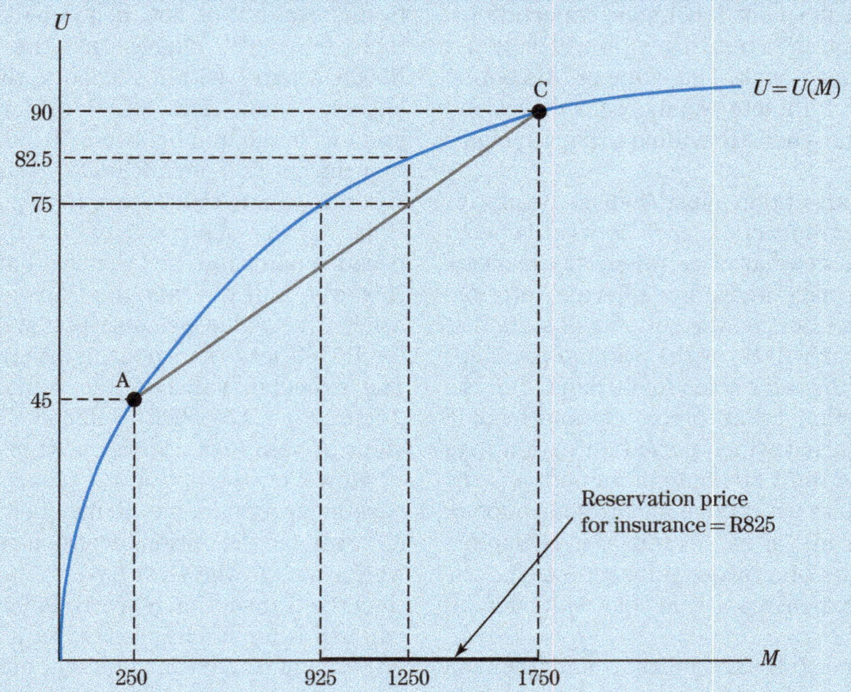

The consumer's initial wealth is 1750, and he faces a loss of 1500 with probability 1/3. His expected utility is 75. Because he gets the same expected utility from a certain wealth level of 925, he would be willing to pay as much as 1725 – 925 = 825 for insurance against the loss.

that if he paid R825 for it, his utility would be $U(1750 - 825) = U(925) = 75$, whether or not a loss occurred. Since this is exactly the same as his expected utility if he did not buy the policy, he would be indifferent between buying and not buying it. His *reservation price* for the policy, the most he would be willing to pay for it, is thus 825. Note that 1750 – 825 = 925 is the *certainty equivalent value* of gambling on getting 1750 – 1500 with probability 1/3 and 1750 with probability 2/3. If I is the actual price of the insurance, and is less than 825, then the consumer will buy the policy and get consumer surplus from it of $825 - I$.

Adverse selection

When a trading opportunity is presented to a heterogeneous group of potential traders, those who accept it will be different – and often worse – on average, than those who do not. For example, the used cars that are for sale are of lower quality than the used cars that are not for sale; and the participants in dating services are generally less worth meeting than non-participants. Both illustrate the lemons principle, and are also sometimes referred to as examples of **adverse selection**.

Adverse selection The process by which the less-desirable potential trading partners volunteer to exchange.

Adverse selection is the process by which 'undesirable' members of a population of buyers or sellers are more likely to participate in a voluntary exchange. Adverse selection is especially relevant to insurance markets. To remain in business, an insurance company must have revenues from premiums that cover the claims it pays out plus its administrative expenses. Its premiums therefore must closely reflect the likelihood of claims being filed and not all potential consumers are equally likely to file claims. In the car accident insurance case, for example, some drivers are several times more likely to have accidents than others.

If insurance companies could identify the most risky drivers, they could adjust their premiums accordingly. To some extent, of course, they attempt to do precisely that, charging higher rates for drivers with a history of accidents or even for those having no prior insurance history. These adjustments are imperfect because some people who have not been in an accident may be much more at risk than many drivers with blemished records.

Competitive pressure in the insurance market will in general force premiums to reflect the average level of risk for policies in a given category. This means that drivers who know they are much riskier than average face an attractive price on insurance. The other side of this coin, however, is that the same premium is unattractive to drivers who know they are much less risky than average. The result is that many of the least risky drivers will be induced to self-insure – that is, to forgo buying insurance and simply take their chances. And when that happens, the average riskiness of the drivers who do buy insurance goes up, which necessitates a rise in premiums. This increase, in turn, makes the insurance even less attractive to less risky drivers, inducing still more of them to self-insure. In the end, all but the worst drivers may be excluded from participation in the insurance market. This is an unfortunate outcome for many careful drivers, who would gladly pay an insurance premium that was anywhere close to the expected value of their losses.

Moral hazard

Another phenomenon with important implications for insurance markets is **moral hazard**, which occurs when insurance creates incentives for people to behave in inefficient or even fraudulent ways. Consider the case of Vernon, also called 'Nub City', a small town in Florida in the USA given that nickname by insurance investigators who were sceptical about its curious pattern of accident claims. This town was the focus of the 1981 documentary *Vernon, Florida* directed and produced by Errol Morris. In the early 1960s this small town with 750 residents was responsible for two-thirds of all loss-of-limb related claims in the USA. Over 50 people in the town had suffered 'accidents' involving the loss of various appendages and one investigator commented that 'somehow they always shoot off parts they seem to need least'.[3]

Moral hazard
Incentives that lead people to file fraudulent claims, or to be negligent in their care of goods insured against theft or damage.

Because the amount an insurance company charges in premiums must be sufficient to cover the amount it pays out in claims, fraudulent insurance claims cause premiums to be higher than they otherwise would be. But moral hazard also causes insurance premiums to rise for reasons unrelated to fraud. Many people whose cars are insured, for example, are less likely to take simple steps to reduce the likelihood of their being damaged or stolen. Similarly, someone whose house is insured against fire damage is less likely for that reason to install a sprinkler system that would limit fire damage. Taking precautions is costly, and people who know their losses are fully covered by insurance are less likely to take them.

Statistical discrimination

As noted above, car insurance companies often try to tailor their rates to the driving records of individual policyholders. In addition, most companies charge different rates to people with identical driving records if they happen to belong to groups with significantly different average risk. Perhaps the most conspicuous example is the extremely high rate for single male drivers under 25 years of age. The average accident rate for drivers in this group is much higher than for any other demographic category. Even so, plenty of males under 25 are exceptionally good drivers. There are surely several such people in your class and you may also be one. The difficulty is that insurance companies cannot identify these good drivers without incurring substantial costs.

In urban areas in South Africa, many car insurance companies charge different rates depending on what part of a city you live in. Their rationale is that traffic congestion, theft, vandalism, uninsured drivers, and other factors that influence claims, differ greatly from neighbourhood to neighbourhood. The awkward result, however, is that people who live just 500 metres from one another sometimes end up paying substantially different insurance rates.

Many have complained that such rate differentials are inherently unfair. But before judging the insurance companies, it is important to understand what would happen to one that abandoned these differentials. Suppose, for example, that a company decided to sell insurance at the same price to all drivers with clean records. If it retained its current list of policyholders, this

[3] John Farrier, *How Vernon, Florida Became Known as 'Nub City'*, 17 March 2012. http:www.neatorama.com.

would mean lowering its current rates for people in unsafe neighbourhoods, teenage boys and other high-risk groups, and raising them for everyone else. But why should older drivers from safe neighbourhoods then remain with the company? They could save by switching to a company that had stuck with the old rate structure, and many of them would surely do so. By the same token, members of high-risk groups who now hold policies with other companies would have a strong incentive to switch to the one with the new rate structure. In the end, the company would be left with only policyholders from high-risk groups. The company could stick with its new programme of charging the same rate for everyone, but that rate would have to be high enough to cover the claims generated by the highest-risk group of all.

Recognizing this problem, some pressure groups are campaigning for laws that would prohibit group insurance rating. The argument is that if *all* companies are forced to offer a single rate, members of low-risk groups cannot escape rate increases by switching to other companies. The difficulty with this approach, however, is that the government cannot force private insurance companies to provide insurance against their will. As a result, many companies will pull out of those areas that are costliest to serve, leaving their former customers to fend for themselves.

Application: always self-insure against small losses

As noted earlier, insurance provided in private markets will have negative expected value because of the resources used by the company to administer its policies. The phenomenon of adverse selection provides another reason to self-insure when the size of the potential loss is manageable. It says that insurance premiums must be large enough to cover the cost of serving the typical policyholder, who will have a greater risk of losses than the average person. Still another reason why insurance premiums exceed the expected value of the average person's losses is the problem of moral hazard.

Despite the fact that insurance premiums must cover administrative expenses, adverse selection and the costs of moral hazard, most of us still find it prudent to insure against major losses, such as damage to our homes by fire. But many people also insure against a host of much smaller losses.

Buying insurance against minor losses violates the principle that you should always pick the alternative with the highest expected outcome when only small outcomes are at stake. Car collision insurance policies typically offer a choice of the amount of each claim to leave uncovered – the 'deductible provision'. If you choose the R3500 deductible provision, for example, your insurance policy will cover all but the first R3500 of any damage claim. Policies with this provision are cheaper than those without, because the company not only does not have to pay the first R3500 in damages, but also avoids the trouble and expense of processing numerous small damage claims. Because of this additional cost reduction, the amount you expect to save in premiums is larger than the extra amount you expect to spend on repairs. And the higher the deductible provision you choose, the greater the expected savings will be. Rather than insure fully against collision damage, it thus makes much more sense to choose a large deductible provision, and deposit the savings in an interest-bearing account.

How large a deductible provision? The larger the better, subject to the proviso that you have enough resources on hand to take care of the uncovered portion of any damage claim. Indeed, for many middle- and upper-income consumers, and for those with older cars that are not worth very much, the most sensible strategy is not to buy car collision insurance at all. Relative to the alternative of buying collision insurance, going without collision insurance is a better-than-fair gamble, and if you are wealthy enough to withstand the worst outcome, you should take it.

Caution: always consider insuring against major losses

If a major loss is defined as one that will deprive you of a significant fraction of your lifetime wealth, you should probably insure against such losses. You should carry major medical insurance, with deep coverage against both catastrophic illness and loss of income from disability; you should carry a personal liability insurance policy against the possibility of a ruinous court judgement; if you live on a flood plain, you should carry flood insurance; and so on. Ironically, however, many people leave these life-shattering risks uncovered, while at the same time insuring themselves fully against the possible theft of their microwave ovens.

The winner's curse

When Northwestern University psychologist Max Bazerman was teaching at Boston University some years ago, he and his colleague William Samuelson performed the following experiment in their microeconomics classes.[4] First they placed \$8 worth of coins in a clear glass jar. After giving their students a chance to examine the jar carefully, they then auctioned it off – coins and all – to the highest bidder. They also asked each student to submit a written estimate of the value of the coins in the jar.

On average, students behaved conservatively, with respect both to their bids and to the estimates they submitted. Indeed, the average estimate was only \$5.13, about one-third less than the actual value of the coins. Similarly, most students dropped out of the bidding well before the auction price reached \$8.

Yet the size of the winning bid in any auction depends not on the behaviour of the *average* bidder, but on the behaviour of the *highest* bidder. In 48 repetitions of this experiment, the top bid averaged \$10.01, more than 20 per cent more than the coins were worth. Bazerman and Samuelson thus made almost \$100 profit at the collective expense of their winning bidders.

At that price, the winners may consider it an important lesson learned cheaply. The stakes were higher when oil company executives were taught the same lesson in the early 1970s. For the first time, the federal government conducted an auction of potentially valuable oil leases in the Gulf of Mexico. Companies had no experience of bidding on such leases, but they did have access to standard geological methods for estimating their value. In hindsight, we can now see that the oil leases fetched prices that were too high. The winning bidders – who paid prices in the millions for their leases – would have earned a much higher return on their investments had they deposited the same money in a savings account.

The general principle that the winning bid for an item often exceeds its true value is known as the *winner's curse*. The startling thing about the winner's curse is that it does not require anyone to use a biased estimate of the value of the prize. The problem is that all estimates involve at least some element of randomness. An estimate is said to be *unbiased* if, on average, it is equal to the true value. Temperature forecasts, for instance, are unbiased: they are too high on some days and too low on others, but their long-run average values track actual temperatures almost perfectly. By the same token, even if each bidder's estimate is unbiased, it will on some occasions be too high, and on others too low. And the winner of the auction will, of course, be the bidder whose estimate happens to be too high by the greatest margin.

A fully rational bidder will take into account the fact that the winning bid tends to be too high. Referring again to the coin auction, suppose that someone's best estimate of the value of the coins in the jar is \$9. Knowing that the winning bid will tend to be too high, he can then protect himself by adjusting his bid downwards. If other bidders are fully rational, they too will adjust their bids, and the identity of the winning bidder should be the same as before.

How big should the downward adjustment be? A moment's reflection makes it clear that the more bidders there are, the larger the adjustment should be. Suppose the true value of the good being auctioned is R5000. To illustrate what is meant by an unbiased estimate, imagine that each potential bidder draws a ball from an urn containing 201 balls consecutively numbered from 4900 to 5100. (Once its number is inspected, each ball is returned to the urn.) The expected value of the number on any given ball is 5000, no matter how many bidders there are. But the expected value of the *highest* number drawn will increase with the number of bidders. (If a million people drew balls from such urns, it is almost certain that someone would get 5100, the maximum possible value; but if only five people drew, the highest number would be much smaller, on average.) Accordingly, the more bidders there are, the more you should adjust your estimate downwards.

To illustrate the mechanics of the adjustment process, consider an auction in which the true value of the item for sale is 0.5, and in which each bidder uses an estimate that is uniformly distributed between 0 and 1. This estimate is equally likely to take any value between 0 and 1, so it has an expected value of 0.5, which means it is unbiased (see Fig. 5.8).

If there were only one bidder at this auction, the expected value of the highest estimate would be 0.5, and so there would be no need for him to make an adjustment. If there were N bidders, however, what would be the expected value of the highest estimate? Suppose we put the N estimates in ascending order and call them $X_1, X_2, \ldots, X_N$, so that X_N denotes the highest of the N estimates. Since the estimates all come from a uniform distribution, the expected values of $X_1, X_2, \ldots, X_N$ will be evenly spaced along the interval. As noted, when

[4] For a more detailed account of this experiment, see David Warsh, 'The winner's curse', *Boston Globe*, 17 April 1988.

Figure 5.8 An unbiased estimate with a uniform distribution

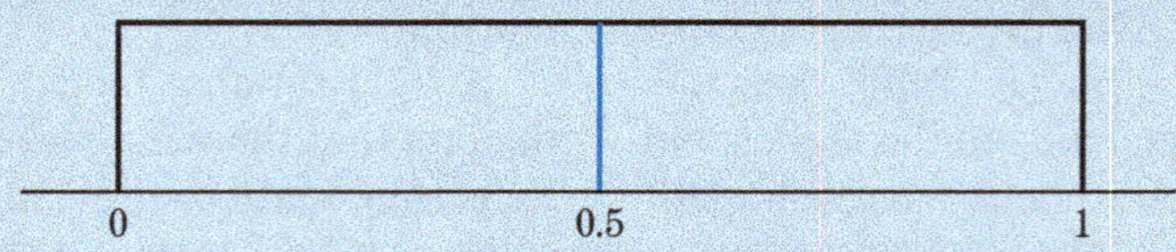

Each potential bidder has an estimate of the value of the resource that is equally likely to take any value between 0 and 1. The true value of the resource is the average value of these estimates, which is 0.5.

Figure 5.9 The expected value of the highest estimate $N = 1, 2, 3$ and 4

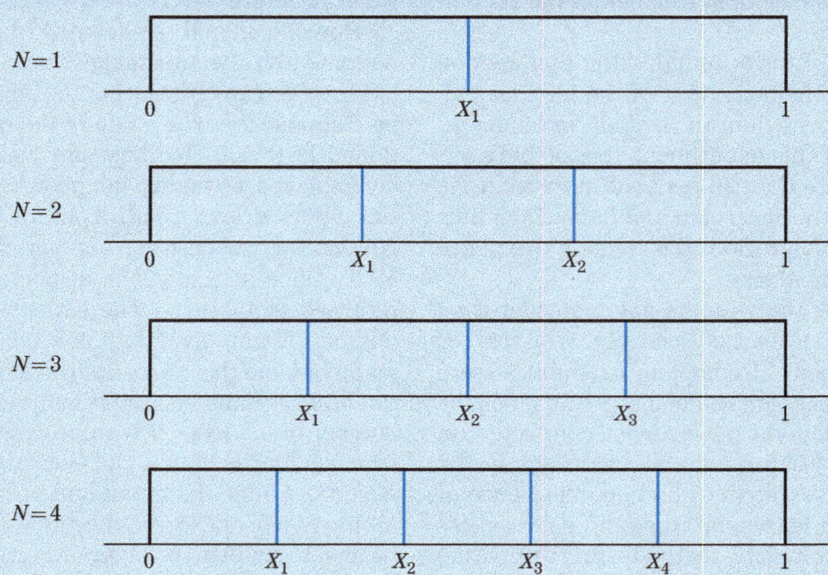

When more people make estimates of the value of a resource, the expected value of the highest estimate increases. When the estimates are uniformly distributed on the interval (0, 1), the largest of N estimates (X_N) has an average value of $N/(N + 1)$.

$N = 1$ we have only X_1, and its expected value, 0.5, lies right in the middle of the interval.

What about when $N = 2$? Now our two estimates are X_1 and X_2, and their expected values are as shown in the second panel of Fig. 5.9. This time the highest estimate has an expected value of 2/3. In the third panel, note that the highest of three estimates has an expected value of 3/4. In the bottom panel, finally, the highest of four estimates has an expected value of 4/5. In general, the highest of N estimates will have an expected value of $N/(N + 1)$.[5]

If the estimates were all drawn from a uniform distribution on (0, C), not on (0, 1), the expected value of the highest estimate would be $CN/(N + 1)$.

As a practical matter, do bidders really adjust their behaviour to eliminate the winner's curse? An evolutionary argument can be made to the

[5] The random variables $X_1, \ldots, X_N$ are known as the 'order statistics' of a sample of size N. To find the expected value of X_N, note first that X_N is less than any value z if and only if each of the N sampled values is less than z. For the uniform distribution on (0, 1), the probability of that event is simply z^N. This is the cumulative distribution function of X_N. The probability density function of X_N is therefore $d(z^N)/d_z$, or Nz^{N-1}. The expected value of X_N is thus given by

$$\int_0^1 zNz^{N-1}dz = \frac{N}{N+1}$$

Example 5.6

Suppose 50 people are bidding for an antique clock, and each has an unbiased estimate of the true value of the clock that is drawn from a uniform distribution on the interval (0, *C*), where *C* is unknown. Your own estimate of the value of the clock is R15 000. How much should you bid?

Your answer is to adjust your estimate so that if it happens to be the highest of the 50, you will not bid more, on average, than the true value of the clock, which is $C/2$. The expected value of the highest of 50 estimates is $(50/51)C$, so if your estimate of 15 000 happens to be the highest, you have, on average,

$$(50/51)C = 15\,000 \quad (5.11)$$

which solves for $C = 15\,300$. This is your adjusted estimate of the value of C on the assumption that yours was the highest of the 50 unadjusted estimates. Since the true value of the clock is $C/2$, you should therefore bid only R7650.

effect that there will be an automatic tendency for this to happen. The idea is that bidders who fail to adjust their estimates downwards will end up losing money each time they win an auction, and will eventually go bankrupt. Those who survive may not understand the winner's curse at all. They may simply be people who happen for other reasons to bid cautiously.

Exercise 5.6

If there had been only four bidders in Example 5.6, how much should you have bid?

When extremely large sums of money are at stake, and bankruptcy is a real possibility, the evolutionary argument has obvious force. However, some economists suggest that it will not apply in all circumstances. Even when a person pays too much for something at auction, it is often possible to recoup the loss by putting forth additional effort. In such cases, the person will regret having paid too much, but his economic survival will not be at stake – only his leisure time and peace of mind. In this case, it is the careless optimists who ignore the winner's curse and win all the auctions. They then scramble to stay on their feet – and actually many of them ultimately manage to do so. Their utility, however, is lower than if they had not won the auctions. The irony is that they may nonetheless drive out the more realistic bidders from many markets.

I've known about the winner's curse for years, and yet I still bid whatever I think something is worth whenever I attend an antiques auction. Am I being irrational? The answer depends on

Example 5.7

Suppose you are the economic adviser for a firm that heard about a profitable Project Mthombo by PetroSA to extend its sustainability. The firm must decide whether to acquire PetroSA, whose only asset is a gas field that has a net value *X* under its current management. The owners of PetroSA know the exact value of *X*, but your company knows only that *X* is a random number that is uniformly distributed between 0 and 100. Your company's superior management means that PetroSA's gas field would be worth 1.5*X* in its hands. What is the highest value of *P* that you can bid and still not expect to take a *loss* if your company acquires PetroSA?

If your company bids P, and X is greater than P, then PetroSA will refuse the offer and the deal is off. Your company earns zero profit in that case. If PetroSA accepts your company's offer, then we know that $X < P$. Since X is uniformly distributed between 0 and 100, the expected value of X, given that $X < P$, is $P/2$. This means that the expected value of PetroSA's gas field to your company is 1.5 times that, or $0.75P$. If your company bids P and PetroSA accepts, then your company's expected profit will be $0.75P - P = -0.25P$. So, for any positive P, your company expects to lose $0.25P$ if PetroSA accepts its offer. Your company's best strategy is therefore not to bid at all.

what I intend to do with the things I end up buying. Many of the participants at the auctions I attend are dealers, and I would indeed be irrational if I were a dealer and failed to adjust my estimates. But I am not a dealer. I keep whatever I buy for my own use. Since each item is unique, the issue of whether I could purchase it more cheaply elsewhere doesn't come up. For me, the only test my bid has to pass is whether the item is worth that amount to me.

Summary

- Potential parties to an economic exchange often have many common goals, but in an important respect they must be viewed as adversaries. In product and labour markets, both buyers and sellers face powerful incentives to misrepresent their offerings.
- For messages between potential adversaries to be credible, they must be costly to fake. A firm with extensive sunk costs, for example, can communicate credibly that it offers a reliable product because, if it fails to satisfy its customers, it stands to lose a lot of money. By contrast, a street vendor, for whom the costs of going out of business are very low, has a more difficult time persuading buyers he offers high quality.
- Messages between potential adversaries must also satisfy the full-disclosure principle, which means that, if one party is able to disclose favourable information about itself, others will feel pressure to disclose parallel information, even if it's considerably less favourable. The producer of a low-quality product does not *want* to signal his product's inferior status by offering only limited warranty coverage. But unless he does so, many buyers will make an even less favourable assessment.
- Cars that are offered for sale in the second-hand market are of lower quality than those that are not for sale; participants in dating services are often less worth meeting than others; and so on. These are illustrations of the lemons principle.
- The analytical tool for dealing with choice under uncertainty is the von Neumann–Morgenstern expected utility model. This model begins with a utility function that assigns a numerical measure of satisfaction to each outcome, where outcomes are defined in terms of the final wealth to which they correspond. The model says that a rational consumer will choose between uncertain alternatives so as to maximize her expected utility.
- The ordering of the expected values of a collection of gambles is often different from the ordering of the expected utilities of those gambles. The differences arise because of non-linearities in the utility function. The concave utility function, any arc of which always lies above the corresponding chord, leads to risk-averse behaviour. Someone with such a utility function will always refuse a fair gamble, which is defined as one with an expected value of zero. A person with a convex utility function, any arc of which lies below the corresponding chord, is said to be a risk seeker. Such a person will always accept a fair gamble. A person with a linear utility function is said to be risk neutral, and is always indifferent between accepting and refusing a fair gamble.
- Because of adverse selection, firms are under heavy competitive pressure to find out everything they possibly can about potential buyers and employees. This pressure often results in statistical discrimination. In insurance markets, people from groups with different accident rates often pay different premiums, even though their individual driving records are identical.
- Insurance purchased in private markets is generally an unfair gamble, not only because of the administrative costs included in insurance premiums, but also because of adverse selection and moral hazard. The fact that most people nonetheless buy substantial amounts of insurance is taken as evidence of risk aversion.

Questions for review

1 Why must a signal between potential adversaries be costly to fake?

2 Explain why, despite the potential adversarial relationship between sellers and buyers, commercial advertising nonetheless transmits information about product quality.

3 What practical difficulty confronts laws that try to regulate what questions can be asked of job applicants during employment interviews?

4 How does statistical discrimination affect the distribution of insurance premiums within a group?

5 How does statistical discrimination affect the average insurance premium paid by members of different groups?

6 Why is it intuitively plausible to assume that most people are risk averse?

7 Give some examples of behaviour that seem inconsistent with the assumption of risk aversion.

8 Explain, in your own words, why it makes sense to self-insure against minor losses.

9 Give some examples in which people do not self-insure against minor losses.

Problems

1 Suppose the messiness of apartments is measured on a scale from 0 to 100, with 0 the cleanest and 100 the messiest. Suppose also that the distribution of apartments by messiness is as shown in the diagram. That is, suppose 10 per cent of the apartments lie between 0 and 20, 20 per cent between 20 and 40, and so on.

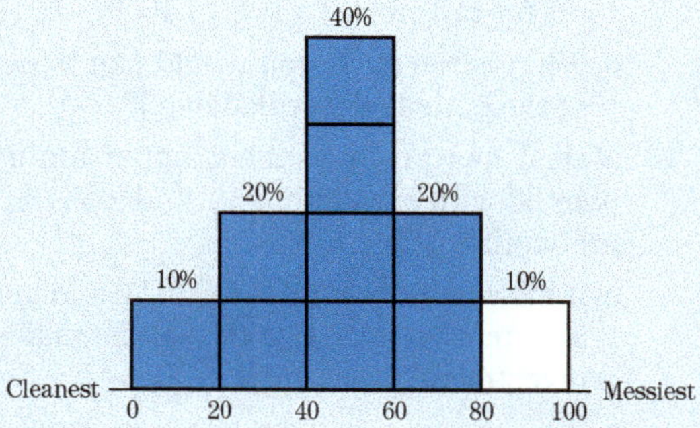

Suppose, finally, that all parents tried to teach their children never to let anyone in to see their apartments if they were over 80 on the messiness scale. If such a rule of thumb were widely observed, what would be your best estimate of the messiness index of someone who said, 'You can't come in now, my place is a mess'? In a world in which everyone makes use of all available information, would you expect this rule of thumb to be stable? What do you conclude from the fact that people really do sometimes refuse admission on the grounds that their apartments are too messy?

2 Explain in detail what will happen to an insurance company that charges teenage boys the same rates for car insurance as it charges its other customers.

3 It is known that some fraction d of all new cars is defective. Defective cars cannot be identified as such except by the people who own them. Each consumer is risk neutral, and values a non-defective car at R270 000. New cars sell for R180 000 each and used ones for R45 000. If cars do not depreciate physically with use, what is d?

4 A new motorcycle sells for R108 000, and a used one sells for R12 000. If there is no depreciation, and risk-neutral consumers know that 20 per cent of all new motorcycles are defective, how much do consumers value a non-defective motorcycle?

5 The exhaust system on your 1986 Pulsar needs to be replaced, and you suspect that the price of a new exhaust system is the same as what you would get if you tried to sell the car. If you know that the car is otherwise okay, what relevance does Akerlof's model of lemons have to your decision about whether to purchase a new exhaust system?

6 What grounds are there for assuming that a randomly chosen social worker is less likely to cheat you at cards than a randomly chosen person?

7 At the turn of this century, most banks required managers to have a high school

certificate. Even though the tasks currently performed by managers in most banks can still be performed by persons who have mastered the high school curriculum, many banks now require that their managers have university degrees. Assuming that the real costs of university education are lower now than at the turn of the century, and that these costs are lower for persons of higher ability, construct an explanation for why banks might have raised their hiring standards.

8 What is the expected value of a random toss of a (fair and six-sided) dice?

9 A fair coin is flipped twice, and the following pay-offs are assigned to each of the four possible outcomes:

H–H: win 20; H–T: win 9; T–H: lose 7; T–T: lose 16.

What is the expected value of this gamble?

10 Suppose your utility function is given by $U = \sqrt{M}$, where M is your total wealth. If M has an initial value of 16, will you accept the gamble in the preceding problem?

11 A special Lotto is offered to commemorate Mandela's birth date and you win the jackpot worth R20 million! You now look at alternative ways to invest it. A broker phones you with some information you requested on certain junk bonds. If the company issuing the bonds posts a profit this year, it will pay you a 40 per cent interest rate on the bond. If the company files for bankruptcy, you will lose all you invested. If the company breaks even, you will earn a 10 per cent interest rate. Your broker tells you there is a 50 per cent chance that the company will break even and a 20 per cent chance that it will file for bankruptcy. Your other option is to invest in a risk-free government bond that will guarantee 8 per cent interest for 1 year.

a What is the expected interest rate for the junk bond investment?

b Which investment will you choose if your utility function is given by $U = M^2$?

c Which investment will you choose if your utility function is given by $U = \sqrt{M}$?

12 Suppose your current wealth, M, is R1000 and your utility function is $U = M^2$. You have a lottery ticket that pays R100 with a probability of 0.25 and R0 with a probability of 0.75. What is the minimum amount for which you would be willing to sell this ticket?

13 Your father's utility function is $\sqrt{M}$. His current wealth is R7 000 000. There is a 0.00001 probability that his legal liability in a car accident will reduce his wealth to R0. What is the most he would pay for insurance to cover this risk?

14 A farmer's hens lay 10 000 eggs/day, which he sells for R2 each, his sole source of income. His utility function is $U = \sqrt{M}$, where M is his daily income. Each time the farmer carries in eggs from the hen house, there is a 50 per cent chance he will fall and break all the eggs. Assuming he assigns no value to his time, is he better off by carrying all the eggs in one trip or by carrying 5000 in each of two trips? (*Hint*: There are three possibilities when he takes two trips: 10 000 broken eggs, 5 000 broken eggs and no broken eggs. What is the probability of each of these outcomes?)

15 Your current wealth level is $M = 5300$ and you are forced to make the following wager: if a fair coin comes up heads, you get 1500; if it comes up tails, you lose 1300. Your utility function is $U = \sqrt{M}$.

a What is the expected value of this gamble?

b What is its expected utility?

c How would your answers change if the pay-off for tails fell to a loss of 1500?

d What is the most you would pay to get out of the gamble described in (c)?

16 Malusi has an investment opportunity that pays 33 with probability 1/2 and loses 30 with probability 1/2.

a If his current wealth is $M = 111$, and his utility function is $U = \sqrt{M}$, will he make this investment?

b Will he make it if he has two equal partners? (Be sure to calculate the relevant expected utilities to at least two decimal places.)

17 John has a von Neumann–Morgenstern utility function given by $U = \sqrt{M}$, where M is his income. If he becomes an economics professor, he will make $M = 121$/yr with probability 1. If he becomes an attorney, he will make $M = 1600$/yr if he becomes a partner in a big law firm that is registered on the Johannesburg Stock Exchange, but only

$M = 64$/yr if he fails to make partner. The probability of his becoming a partner is 0.2. Smith is an infallible judge of legal talent. After a brief interview, he can state with certainty whether John will become a partner. What is the most John would be willing to pay for this information? (Set up the relevant equation. You don't need to solve it.)

*18 In the preceding problem, assuming that conducting the interview is costless, is Smith getting the highest possible expected income for himself by charging John the same fee regardless of the outcome of the interview?

*19 There are two groups of equal size, each with a utility function given by $U(M) = \sqrt{M}$, where $M = 100$ is the initial wealth level for every individual. Each member of group 1 faces a loss of 36 with probability 0.5. Each member of group 2 faces the same loss with probability 0.1.

a What is the most a member of each group would be willing to pay to insure against this loss?

b In part (a), if it is impossible for outsiders to discover which individuals belong to which group, will it be practical for members of group 2 to insure against this loss in a competitive insurance market? (For simplicity, you may assume that insurance companies charge only enough in premiums to cover their expected benefit payments.) Explain.

c Now suppose that the insurance companies in part (b) have an imperfect test for identifying which persons belong to which group. If the test says that a person belongs to a particular group, the probability that he really does belong to that group is $x < 1.0$. How large must x be in order to alter your answer to part (b)?

*20 There are two groups, each with a utility function given by $U(M) = \sqrt{M}$, where $M = 144$ is the initial wealth level for every individual. Each member of group 1 faces a loss of 44 with probability 0.5. Each member of group 2 faces the same loss with probability 0.1.

a What is the most a member of each group would be willing to pay to insure against this loss?

b If it is impossible for outsiders to discover which individuals belong to which group, how large a share of the potential client pool can the members of group 1 be before it becomes impossible for a private company with a zero-profit constraint to provide insurance for the members of group 2? (For simplicity, you may assume that insurance companies charge only enough in premiums to cover their expected benefit payments, and that people will always buy insurance when its price is equal to or below their reservation price.) Explain.

*21 Given a choice between A (a sure win of 100) and B (an 80 per cent chance to win 150 and a 20 per cent chance to win 0), Errol picks A. But when he is given a choice between C (a 50 per cent chance to win 100 and a 50 per cent chance to win 0) and D (a 40 per cent chance to win 150 and a 60 per cent chance to win 0), he picks D. Show that Errol's choices are inconsistent with expected utility maximization.

22 A class of 100 students is participating in an auction to see who gets a large jar of R5 coins. Each student has an unbiased estimate of the total value of the coins. If these estimates are drawn from the interval (0, C), where C is not known, and your own estimate is R150, how much should you bid?

23 Suppose you are the economic adviser for a firm that is trying to decide whether to acquire the Bumbler Oil Company, whose only asset is an oil field that has a net value of X under its current management. The owners of Bumbler know the exact value of X, but your company knows only that X is a random number that is uniformly distributed between 0 and 100. Your company's superior management means that Bumbler's oil field would be worth $X + 40$ in its hands.

a What is the most your company can bid and not expect to take a loss?

b Assuming your company is the only bidder, what bid maximizes your company's expected profits?

* Problems marked with an asterisk (*) are more difficult.

Answers to in-chapter exercises

5.1 The expected utility of the gamble corresponds to point D, which lies one-third of the way from C to A.

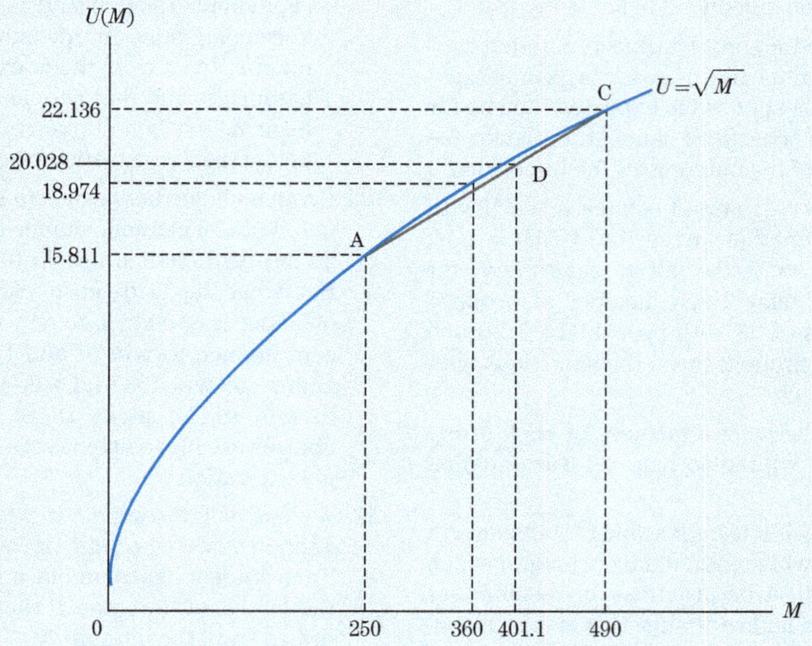

5.2 If she accepts the gamble, her expected utility is given by $EU_G = (1/2)(6000^2) + (1/2)\ (4000^2) =$ 26 000 000. Her utility if she refuses the gamble is only $5000^2 = 12\,500\,000$, and so she should accept the gamble.

5.3 If she accepts the gamble, her expected utility is given by $EU_G = (1/2)(6000) + (1/2)\ (4000) =$ 5000. Her utility if she refuses the gamble is also 5000, and so she is indifferent between accepting and refusing the gamble.

5.4 As in Example 5.3, the key step here is to see that the only used laptops for sale will be defective. As a result of the lemons principle, the owner of a good laptop could not sell it for what it is worth in the second-hand market. So if the value of a defective laptop is R6000, then the value of a new laptop to a risk-neutral buyer must be (1/4)(R6000) + (3/4)(R20000) = R16 500.

5.5 Rashaad would be indifferent between filing the suit and not filing it under a fee schedule for which his income, including damage awards and net of lawyer's fees, would be exactly 7 no matter how the suit was decided. That happens when $F_1 = 5$ and $F_2 = 0$. In this case, the expected value of Rashaad's lawyer's fee would be $0.5(5) + 0.5(0) = 2.5$, or 0.5 more than the opportunity cost of the lawyer's time. Under this fee structure, the lawyer would capture the entire expected value of the lawsuit.

5.6 With four bidders, the expected value of the largest estimate is $(4/5)C$. Equating this to 15 000, and solving, we get $C = 18\,750$, and so you should bid 9375.

Chapter 6

Cognitive limitations and consumer behaviour

The University of Cape Town has two sets of faculty tennis courts, one outdoor, one indoor. Membership in the outdoor facility is available for a fixed fee per season, with no additional charge based on actual court use. Assume the indoor facility, by contrast, has not only a seasonal fee but also a R100 per hour charge for court time. The higher charges of the indoor facility reflect the additional costs of heating, electricity and building maintenance. The indoor facility opens in early April, when the Cape weather can be anything from bright sunshine and mild temperatures to blowing sleet and heavy rains. The outdoor courts remain open, weather permitting, until early May.

Demand for the indoor facility is intense, and people who want to play regularly must commit themselves to reserving a specific hour each week. Having done so, they must pay for the hour whether or not they use it. During good weather almost everyone prefers to play on the outdoor courts, which are nestled below Table Mountain and have stunning views.

Here is the problem. You are committed to pay for an indoor court at 15:00 on Saturday 20 April, the only hour you are free to play that day. It is a warm, sunny autumn afternoon. Where should you play, indoors or out?

Surprisingly, many of my non-economist friends baulk upon hearing that playing on the outdoor courts is the only sensible thing to do. 'But we've already paid for the indoor court,' they invariably complain. However, when asked, 'If both courts cost the same, which would you choose?' they immediately respond, 'Outdoors.' I then explain to them that both courts *do* cost the same – because our fee for the hour will be R100 no matter where we play – indeed, even if we do not play at all. The R100 is a sunk cost, and should have no effect on our decision. Yet, even at this point, many people seem to feel uncomfortable about wasting the indoor court we have paid for.

The alternative, however, is to waste an opportunity to play outdoors, which we all agree is something even more valuable!

Eventually, most people come round to the notion that it is more sensible to abandon the indoor court, even though it is paid for, and play outdoors on sunny autumn days. The rational choice model says unequivocally that this is what we should do. But it does not seem to be the natural inclination of most people. On the contrary, in the absence of a prodding economist, most people who have paid for an indoor court end up using it, even on the most pleasant days.

Chapter preview

Sometimes motives other than self-interest might be important to lead people to behave in ways that may be regarded as irrational. But, irrational or not, behaviours such as tipping in restaurants or returning lost wallets to their owners are undertaken without regret. If a rationalist were to point out that there is no way a waiter in a distant city could retaliate for not having been left a tip, most of us would respond, 'So what?' We would not suddenly regret having left tips all our lives.

Our focus in this chapter is on irrational behaviour of an altogether different sort, behaviour that is the result of failure to see clearly how best to achieve a desired result. Failure to ignore the sunk costs of the indoor tennis court is one example. People often *do* want to alter their behaviours once their consequences become clear to them.

In addition to failing to ignore sunk costs, we shall see that people violate the prescriptions of rational choice models in a variety of other systematic ways. We shall examine several behavioural models of choice that often do a much better job of predicting actual decisions than the rational choice model. They tell us, for instance, that we often *do* tend to ignore sunk costs, not that we *should* ignore them.

The rational choice model says we can make better decisions by ignoring sunk costs, and most people, on reflection, strongly agree. The value of behavioural models is that they call our attention to situations in which we are likely to make mistakes. They are an important tool for helping us avoid common pitfalls in decision making.

Bounded rationality

The late Nobel laureate Herbert Simon was among the first to impress upon economists that human beings are incapable of behaving like the rational beings portrayed in standard rational choice models. Simon was a pioneer in the field of artificial intelligence, and stumbled upon this realization in the process of trying to instruct a computer to 'reason' about a problem. He discovered that, when we ourselves confront a puzzle, we rarely reach a solution in a neat, linear fashion. Rather, we search in a haphazard way for potentially relevant facts and information, and usually quit once our understanding reaches a certain threshold. (Those of you who have completed a 3000-piece puzzle will know this to be exactly the way you go about it.) Our conclusions are often inconsistent, even flatly incorrect. But, much of the time, we come up with serviceable solutions. In Simon's terms, we are 'satisficers', not maximizers.

Subsequent economists have taken Simon's lead and developed a sophisticated literature on decision making under incomplete information. We now realize that when information is costly to gather, and cognitive processing ability is limited, it is not even rational to make fully informed choices of the sort portrayed in simple models. Paradoxically, it is irrational to be completely well-informed!

Other research, strongly influenced by cognitive psychologists Daniel Kahneman and Amos Tversky, demonstrates that even with transparently simple problems, people often violate the most fundamental axioms of rational choice. Choosing whether to play tennis indoors or outdoors is a good example. The relevant facts in this problem could hardly be any simpler, and yet, as noted, people consistently choose irrationally. Such examples, Kahneman and Tversky showed, are by no means isolated. On the strength of this work, Kahneman was awarded the Nobel Prize in Economics in 2002, an honour that Tversky undoubtedly would have shared had it not been for his untimely death in 1996.

One of the most cherished tenets of the rational choice model is that wealth is fungible. Fungibility implies, among other things, that our total wealth, not the amount of money we have in any particular account, determines what we buy. Kahneman and Tversky, however, provided a vivid experimental demonstration to the contrary.[1] They told

[1] See Amos Tversky and Daniel Kahneman, 'The framing of decisions and the psychology of choice', *Science*, 1981, vol. 211, pp. 453–458. The values used in the text were converted to rands to make the experiment more applicable to the Southern African audience.

one group of people to imagine that, having earlier purchased tickets for R350, they arrive at the theatre to discover they have lost them. Members of a second group are told to picture themselves arriving just before the performance to buy their tickets, when they find each of them has lost R350 on the way to the theatre. People in both groups are then asked whether they will continue with their plans to attend the performance. In the rational choice model, the forces governing this decision are the same for both groups. Losing a R350 ticket should have precisely the same effect as losing R350 in cash. (Recall from Chapter 3 the rule that, if tastes and budget constraints are the same, decisions should also be the same.) And yet, in repeated trials, most people in the lost-ticket group say they would not attend the performance, whereas an overwhelming majority – 88 per cent – in the lost-money group say they would.

Kahneman and Tversky explained that people apparently organize their spending into separate 'mental accounts' for food, housing, entertainment, general expenses, and so on. People who lose their tickets act as though they debit R350 from their mental entertainment accounts, whereas those who lose R350 debit their general expense accounts. For people in the former group, the loss makes the apparent cost of seeing the show rise from R350 to R700, whereas for those in the second it remains R350.

The rational choice model makes it clear that the second group's assessment is the correct one. And on reflection most people do, in fact, agree that losing a ticket is no better reason not to see the performance than losing R350 in cash.

The asymmetric value function

The rational choice model says that people should evaluate events, or collections of events, in terms of their overall effect on total wealth. Suppose A is the event that you receive an unexpected gift of R1500 and B is the event that you return from vacation to find a R1200 invoice from the city council for the repair of a broken water pipe on your property. According to the rational choice model, you should regard the occurrence of these two events as a good thing because their net effect is a R300 increase in your total wealth.

Kahneman and Tversky found, however, that people seem to weigh each event separately, and attach considerably less importance to the gain than to the loss – so much less that many people actually refuse to accept pairs of events that would increase their overall wealth!

In the rational choice model, this of course can never happen. Confronted with the two events A and B described above, a person with an initial wealth of M_0 knows exactly how to react. The combined effect of A (a R1500 gain) and B (a R1200 loss) is to increase her wealth to $M_0 + 300$. And since utility is an increasing function of total wealth, the two events taken together cause utility to increase from U_0 to U_1, as shown in Fig. 6.1.

Kahneman and Tversky proposed that people evaluate alternatives not with the conventional utility function, but instead with a *value function* that is defined over *changes* in wealth. One important property of this value function is that it is much steeper in losses than in gains. In Fig. 6.2, for example, note how it assigns a

Figure 6.1 Utility of a pair of events that increases total wealth

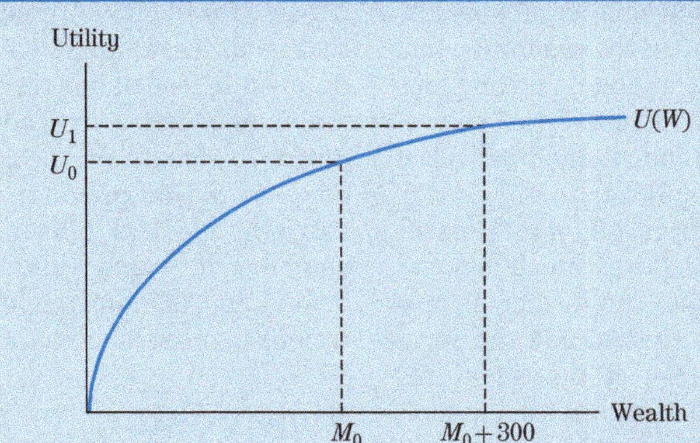

Under the rational choice model, any combination of events that increases total wealth will also increase total utility.

Figure 6.2 The Kahneman–Tversky value function

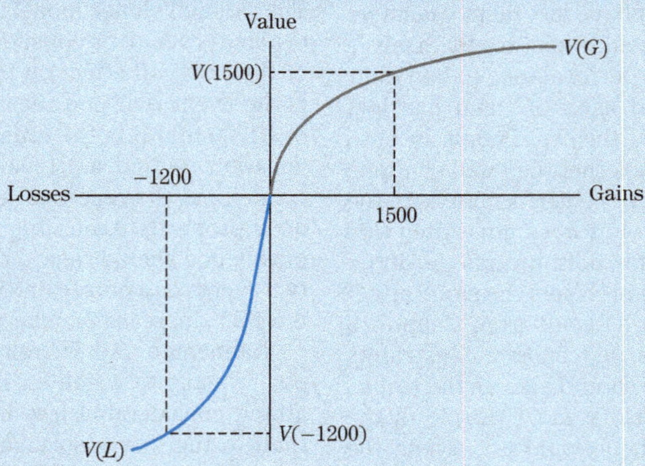

Unlike the traditional utility function, the value function is defined over *changes* in total wealth. It is steeper in losses than in gains, concave in gains and convex in losses.

much larger value, in absolute terms, to a loss of R1200 than to a gain of R1500. Note also that the value function is concave in gains and convex in losses. This property is the analogue of diminishing marginal utility in the traditional model. It says that the impact of incremental gains or losses diminishes as the gains or losses become larger.

Kahneman and Tversky emphasized that their value function is a purely descriptive device. They are trying to summarize regularities in the ways people actually seem to make choices. They make no claim that people *should* choose in the ways predicted by their value function.

According to Kahneman and Tversky, people typically evaluate each item in a collection of events separately, and then make decisions on the basis of the sum of the separate values. In this example, $V(1500)$ is much smaller, in absolute terms, than $V(-1200)$. Because the algebraic sum of the two is less than zero, anyone who employs this decision mechanism will refuse the pair of opportunities A and B, even though their net effect is to increase total wealth by R300.

To summarize: people treat gains and losses asymmetrically, giving the latter much heavier weight in their decisions than the former. People also evaluate events first and then add the separate values together. The first of these features does not necessarily imply irrational behaviour. There is nothing inconsistent, after all, about feeling that a loss causes more pain than the happiness caused by a gain of the same magnitude. What *does* often appear irrational is the second step – treating each event separately, rather than considering their combined effect.

Another example helps illustrate this point. Assume that a state's proposed new medical insurance plan is introduced. Further assume that the old plan paid 100 per cent of all covered medical expenses, and the premium was approximately R7500/yr per family. The new plan has a R3000 deductible feature – people must pay the first R3000 in medical expenses each year, but once that threshold is reached, the insurance again pays 100 per cent. The premium for the new plan is R3750/yr, half that of the old plan. Assume that employees have the option of staying with the old plan or switching to the new.

Seen through the lens of the rational choice model, the new plan dominates the old. The R3750 savings in premiums is more than enough to compensate for the R3000 deductible feature. Families that incur less than R3000/yr in medical expenses do even better under the new plan. Nonetheless, many employees are adamant regarding their desire to remain on the old plan. If some people code the R3750 premium savings and the R3000 extra in medical bills as separate events, the asymmetric value function predicts just such behaviour. As indicated in Fig. 6.3, the R3000 loss weighs in more heavily than the R3750 gain.

Sunk costs

Another basic principle of the rational choice model is that sunk costs should be ignored when making decisions. In the tennis example at the beginning

Figure 6.3 Rejection of a dominant insurance plan

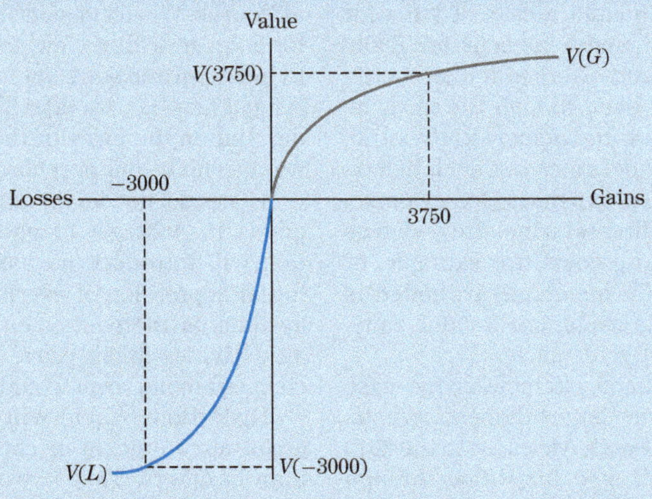

Because the saving in premiums (R3 750) is larger than the largest possible increase in uncovered expenses (R3 000), the new plan is necessarily better than the old. But if people code gains and losses separately, they may nonetheless refuse to switch to the new policy.

of this chapter, we saw that it is this principle, not sunk cost, which is sometimes ignored. Richard Thaler, author of the all-you-can-eat pizza experiment discussed in Chapter 1, argues that such examples are not isolated: that people in fact show a general tendency not to ignore sunk costs. Recall that, in the experiment, diners whose admission charges were refunded ate substantially fewer slices of pizza than others. He offered several other vivid illustrations of this pattern.

One is a thought experiment in which you are asked first to imagine that you have bought a pair of fashionable shoes for R2500, only to discover that they are painfully tight. They improve slightly after being broken in, but still cause considerable discomfort. Do you continue wearing these shoes or give them away? Would your response be any different if you had not bought the shoes but instead had received them as a gift?

Under the rational choice model, it should not matter whether you bought the shoes or were given them. Either way, you own them now, and the only question is whether the discomfort they cause is serious enough to discontinue wearing them. People in both categories should be equally likely to discontinue wearing the shoes. Contrary to this prediction, however, people are much more likely to say they would abandon the shoes if they had received them as a gift. Having shelled out R2500 apparently makes many people determined to endure them.

One final sunk cost example. Suppose you have just paid R300 for tickets to the African Cup of Nations final to be played tonight in the FNB stadium 130 km north of your home. Suddenly it starts raining heavily, and the roads north, while passable, are flooded in places. Do you still go to the game? Would your answer have been different if, instead of having bought the tickets, you had received them for free? Thaler finds that most people who bought the tickets would go, whereas most of those who were given them say they would stay at home. According to the rational choice model, of course, the decision should be the same in either case. If your anticipated pleasure from seeing the game exceeds the expected hassle of the drive, you should go; otherwise stay at home. Neither element in this cost–benefit calculation should depend on how you obtained the tickets.

Out-of-pocket costs versus opportunity costs

Thaler suggested that our tendency not to ignore sunk costs may be given a simple interpretation in terms of the Kahneman–Tversky value function. In terms of the tennis example, failure to play on the outdoor courts on a nice day is coded mentally as a forgone gain, whereas not playing on the R100 indoor court you have already paid for is coded as a loss. Even though the gain is larger than the loss here, the greater steepness of the value function in the loss domain creates a bias in favour of the indoor court.

Much the same interpretation is supported by a number of other plausible examples. Consider a person who in 1982 bought a case of wine for R10/bottle. Today the same wine sells for R300/bottle. His wine merchant offers him R200/bottle for it, and he refuses, even though the most he would pay for the same wine today is R140/bottle. The rational choice model rules out such behaviour. But if out-of-pocket expenses (for example, for the purchase of additional wine) are coded as losses, while opportunity costs (for example, of not selling the wine to the merchant) are coded as forgone gains, then the asymmetric value function allows for just such a response.

An even more common example is the case of tickets to premium entertainment events. Category 4 tickets (for South Africans) to the 2010 World Cup soccer final sold for R1050 through official channels, but in the open market went for prices as high as R7000. Thousands of fans used their R1050 tickets to attend the game, thus passing up the opportunity to sell them for R7000. Very few of these fans, however, would have spent R7000 on buying a ticket for the game.

Thaler offered the parallel example of the man who would refuse to mow his neighbour's lawn for R120, yet mows his own identical lawn, even though his neighbour's son would be willing to mow it for him for only R60. This behaviour, as well as the behaviour of the World Cup soccer fans, is also consistent with the notion that out-of-pocket expenses are coded as losses, opportunity costs as forgone gains.

Affective forecasting errors

Choosing intelligently between a pair of alternatives often requires only an accurate prediction of how each will affect us right away. For example, in choosing between rice and potatoes for dinner, we need only predict which one will be more satisfying that evening. Most people are reasonably good at this.

In many other cases, intelligent choice requires that we predict not only which alternative will be more satisfying at the moment, but also how the experience of each would evolve over time if chosen. Yet adaptation typically receives little attention when people confront purchase decisions.[2] For the most part, we estimate the attractiveness of a good or activity by trying it and seeing how it affects us. When considering whether to pay extra for a house with a view, for instance, we sit in its living room and stare out for a while; when considering a new car, we take it for a test drive; and so on. And on the basis of these initial impressions, we then make our purchase decisions.

If we do not adapt differently over time for goods in different categories, ignoring adaptation will introduce no bias. For example, if the initial impression of every activity overstated its eventual attractiveness by a factor of, say, three, all activities might prove disappointing, but our choices among them would not be distorted.

Distortions surely will result, however, if we adapt more quickly or completely in some areas than in others. Thus if we choose among potential experiences in accordance with how strongly we react to them initially, the logical implication is that we shall invest too heavily in experiences whose attractiveness declines steeply over time, and too little in those whose attractiveness declines less steeply, or even grows, over time. The psychologists Leaf Van Boven and Thomas Gilovich found that people tend to adapt much more quickly to the consumption of goods than to the consumption of experiences.[3] Thus although most people experience a rush of satisfaction when they first acquire a 55-inch FHD LED television or a spacious SUV, these feelings almost invariably tend to decay rapidly. Once we become accustomed to the bigger TV or the more spacious vehicle, their favourable features fade into the background. We are no longer conscious of them.

In contrast, the time profiles of our reactions to increases in many other forms of consumption have essentially the opposite configuration. For example, our subjective experience of vigorous exercise or of trying to play a musical instrument may even be mildly unpleasant at first, but for most people these experiences become more pleasurable as additional time passes. To the extent that we ignore our tendencies to adapt differently in different spheres, we spend too much on some goods, too little on others.

Consider, for example, a man trying to decide whether to trade in his Toyota Fortuner for a new Porsche 911 Carrera Cabriolet. He could meet the

[2] For a discussion, see George Loewenstein and David Schkade, 'Wouldn't it be nice? Predicting future feelings', in D. Kahneman, E. Diener and N. Schwartz (eds), *Well-being: The Foundations of Hedonic Psychology*, New York: Russell Sage Foundation, 1999, pp. 85–105.

[3] See Leaf Van Boven and Thomas Gilovich, 'To do or to have? That is the question', *Journal of Personality and Social Psychology*, 2003, vol. 85, December, pp. 1193–1202.

payments on the new car by working an additional Saturday each month, which in his case would mean not spending that Saturday with his friends or family. The rational choice model suggests that he will work the extra Saturday if the satisfaction afforded by the Porsche outweighs the satisfaction provided by the company of his friends and family. But never having owned a Porsche, he cannot be sure how that experience would affect him. Nor can he know how things would evolve if he continued to spend the extra Saturday with friends. In both cases, he must make rough guesses about the future.

Introspection may provide reasonably good estimates of how these experiences will affect his satisfaction in the short run. But in the problem at hand, the relevant short-run and long-run effects are likely to be different. Because the Porsche is much faster and handles much better than his Toyota, his test drive will provide an initial thrill. Over time, however, he will grow accustomed to the new car's capabilities, and its capacity to stimulate will decay. The contribution to subjective well-being of additional time spent with friends will have a markedly different time profile. As relationships continue over time, the satisfaction they provide tends to increase rather than diminish.

In the long run, then, extra time spent with friends might well prove to be the better choice. Yet the short-run increment in satisfaction might easily be higher with the new car. And because these short-run effects are the most vivid and readily available sources of information at the moment of decision, they may bias choice in favour of the car.

Failure to take adaptation into account has similar implications for the decision about how much to save. Here the problem stems from how the amount we consume at one point in time affects our ability to derive pleasure from a given consumption level later on. By way of illustration, consider the following hypothetical choice between two different consumption profiles that could be financed from the same stream of lifetime earnings. In each case, suppose that you and all others in your age cohort will earn a salary of R300 000 each and every year from age 21 until retirement at age 65. In one instance, suppose you and the others spend exactly your salaries of R300 000 each year, as shown by the consumption level profile labelled A in Fig. 6.4. Alternatively, suppose you and the others start out by saving R60 000 a year (or, to put it another way, suppose you start out by consuming only R240 000 a year), then gradually diminish your rate of saving until, by middle age, you begin drawing down your savings in ever-larger amounts to finance additional consumption. If we ignore, for simplicity, the fact that your savings will generate interest, and ignore the effect of inflation on your real income, this pattern yields the rising consumption profile labelled B in Fig. 6.4. Note that, although profile B starts out R60 000 lower than profile A and ends up R60 000 higher, total lifetime consumption is the same on each profile. Which one would you choose (assuming that in either case you will receive the same generous pension during retirement)?

When asked a similar question, almost 80 per cent of a sample of more than 200 Stellenbosch

Figure 6.4 Static and rising consumption profiles

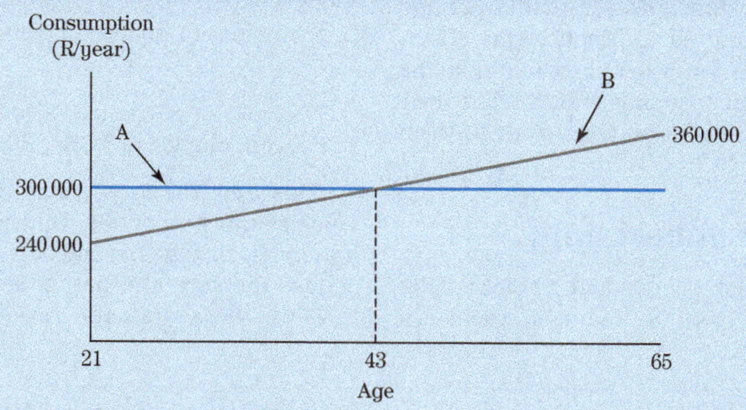

Which consumption profile would you choose: A, in which everyone consumes R300 000 every year, or B, in which everyone starts out consuming R240 000 a year and ends up consuming R360 000? When asked this question, a large sample of undergraduates voiced a strong preference for B.

second-year students chose B, the rising consumption profile. Evidence suggests that this profile will in fact be the more satisfying of the two.[4] Here again, the idea is that our evaluations of almost everything – including material living standards – depend on our frames of reference. One frame of reference is to compare what we currently have to what others have. But since everyone is assumed to follow the same consumption profile in this example, this comparison adds nothing of interest. A second frame of reference involves comparing what we currently have with what we ourselves had in the recent past, and it is this frame of reference that proves decisive for the problem at hand. For example, someone who consumes R300 000 this year is more likely to be satisfied with her standard of living if she had consumed R270 000 last year than if she had consumed R330 000. People who consume too much too soon thus establish a more demanding frame of reference within which their later consumption must be evaluated.

The more we save during the early course of the life cycle, the steeper, and hence more satisfying, our consumption profiles will be. As obvious as this might seem, however, many of us never consciously consider the extent to which our current spending habits affect our evaluations of future living standards. To the extent that we ignore this relationship, we shall tend to save too little and may make costly – and avoidable – errors.

Perhaps the most vivid example of failure to account for future adaptation is the drug abuser's failure to anticipate increasing tolerance to his drug of choice. Thus a cocaine abuser typically launches on his downward spiral in the expectation that repeated ingestion of the drug will yield the same rush of euphoria he experienced on his first trial.

He quickly discovers, however, that larger and larger doses are required to produce this effect. We may be sure that fewer people would take the first steps along this miserable trajectory if their patterns of future adaptation were clear to them at the outset.

Choice under uncertainty

The standard model of rational choice under uncertainty is the von Neumann–Morgenstern expected utility model discussed in Chapter 5. This model provides valuable *guidance* about how best to choose between uncertain alternatives. But Kahneman and Tversky showed that it does not always provide a good *description* of the way people actually decide.[5] To illustrate, they presented a series of choices to a group of volunteer subjects. They began with the following problem, which elicited responses that were perfectly consistent with the expected utility model.

Problem 1

Choose between

A: A sure gain of R2880 (84 per cent)

and

B: A 25 per cent chance of getting R12 000 and a 75 per cent chance of getting R0 (16 per cent).

The numbers in parentheses indicate the percentage of subjects who picked each alternative. Here, most people chose the sure gain of R2880, even though the expected value of the lottery, at R3000, was R120 higher. To verify that this pattern is consistent with the expected utility model, let U denote a subject's utility function, defined by total wealth, and let M denote her initial wealth in rands. Then the expected utility of choice A is $U(M + 2880)$, whereas the expected utility of choice B is $0.25U(M + 12\,000) + 0.75U(M)$. If utility is a concave function of total wealth (that is, if people are risk averse), we see in Fig. 6.5 why A might easily have been more attractive than B.

Subjects were then asked to consider an apparently very similar problem.

Problem 2

Choose between

C: A sure loss of R9000 (13 per cent)

and

D: A 75 per cent chance of losing R12 000 and a 25 per cent chance of losing R0 (87 per cent).

This time the lottery has the same expected value as the sure option. Under the expected utility model, risk-averse subjects therefore ought to choose the sure alternative once again. But this time we see a dramatic reversal. Almost seven

[4] See D.C. Shin, 'Does rapid economic growth improve the human lot?', *Social Indicators Research*, 1980, vol. 8, pp. 199–221; and Robert Frank and Robert Hutchens, 'Wages, seniority, and the demand for rising consumption profiles', *Journal of Economic Behavior and Organization*, 1993, vol. 21, pp. 251–276.

[5] See Amos Tversky and Daniel Kahneman, 'Judgement under uncertainly: heuristics and biases', *Science*, 1974, vol. 185, pp. 1124–1131. The example was simplified into rand terms for the Southern African audience.

Figure 6.5 A risk-averse person will usually prefer a sure gain to a lottery with slightly higher expected value

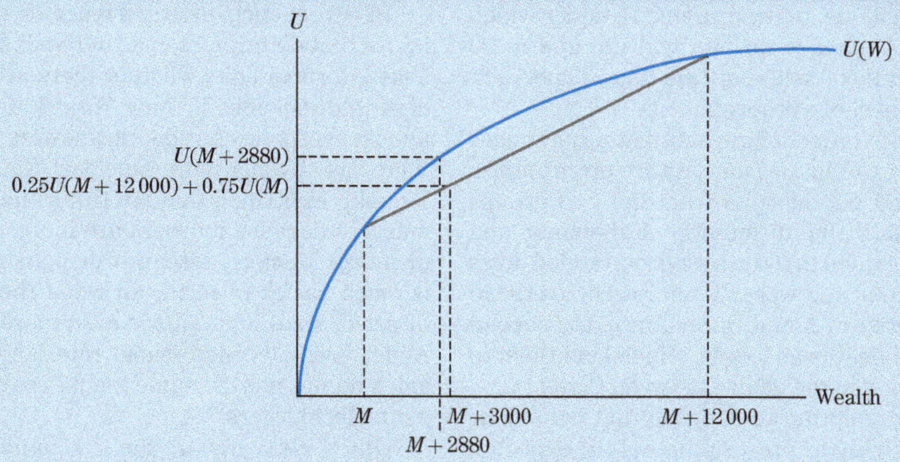

If the utility function is sufficiently concave, $U(M + 2880)$ will exceed the expected utility of a gamble with positive expected value, $0.25U(M + 12000) + 0.75U(M)$.

times as many people chose the lottery as chose the sure loss of R9000.

Finally, the subjects were asked to consider the following problem.

Problem 3

Choose between

E: A 25 per cent chance of getting R2880 and a 75 per cent chance of losing R9000 (0 per cent)

and

F: A 25 per cent chance of getting R3000 and a 75 per cent chance of losing R9000 (100 per cent).

Viewed in isolation, the responses to Problem 3 are completely unsurprising. The lottery in E is simply worse in every way than the one in F, and only someone who wasn't paying attention would have chosen E. But note that lottery E is what we get when we combine choices A and D from Problems 1 and 2; and that, similarly, lottery F is the result of combining choices B and C from the two earlier problems. In the first two problems, the combination of B and C was chosen by fewer subjects (3 per cent) than any other, whereas the combination of A and D was by far the most popular (chosen by 73 per cent of all subjects) – even though the combination of A and D is strictly dominated by the combination of B and C. Such findings, needless to say, pose a sharp challenge to the expected utility model.

Kahneman and Tversky argued that the observed pattern is exactly what would have been predicted using their asymmetric value function. In Problem 1, for example, note that the choice is between a certain gain and a lottery whose possible outcomes are non-negative. Since the value function is concave in gains, and since the expected value of the lottery is only slightly larger than the sure alternative, it predicts the choice of the latter.

In Problem 2, by contrast, the choice is between a certain loss, on the one hand, and a lottery, each of whose outcomes is a loss, on the other. Since the value function is convex in losses, it predicts risk-seeking behaviour with respect to such a choice, and this, of course, is just what we saw. Because Problem 3 forced people to amalgamate the relevant gains and losses, subjects were easily able to see that one pair of alternatives dominated the other, and chose accordingly.

It is tempting to suppose that violations of the expected utility model occur only when the problem is sufficiently complicated that people have difficulty computing what the model prescribes. But Kahneman and Tversky showed that even the simplest of decisions can be influenced by framing the alternatives differently.

For example, they asked a group of subjects to choose between various policy responses to a rare disease that would claim 600 lives if we did nothing. One group was asked to choose either programme A, which would save exactly 200 lives with certainty, or programme B, which would save 600 lives with probability 1/3 and zero lives with probability 2/3. Here, 72 per cent of all subjects chose programme A. A second group was asked to choose either programme C, under which exactly 400 people will die, or programme D, under which there is a 1/3 chance no one will die and a 2/3 chance that all 600 will die. This time, 78 per cent of all subjects chose programme D.

A moment's reflection reveals that programmes A and C are exactly the same, as are programmes B and D. And yet subjects from the two groups chose dramatically differently. Kahneman and Tversky explained that the first group coded 'lives saved' as gains, and were therefore risk averse in choosing between A and B. Similarly, the second group coded deaths as losses, which lead them to be risk seeking in the choice between C and D.

It is also tempting to suppose that behaviour inconsistent with the prescriptions of the expected utility model is confined largely to situations involving novice decision-makers, or situations where little of importance is at stake. Kahneman and Tversky found, however, that even experienced physicians make similarly inconsistent recommendations about treatment regimens when the problems are framed differently. The moral is that we are all well-advised to be cautious when making decisions under uncertainty.

Judgemental heuristics and biases

As the examples considered so far make clear, people often make irrational decisions even when they have the relevant facts at their fingertips. Yet another difficulty confronting the rational choice model is that we often draw erroneous inferences about what the relevant facts are. More importantly, many of the errors we make are systematic, not random. Kahneman and Tversky identified three particularly simple heuristics, or rules of thumb, that people use to make judgements and inferences about the environment.[6] Let us consider each of the three heuristics in turn.

Availability

We often estimate the frequency of an event, or class of events, by the ease with which we can summon examples from memory. Much of the time, there is a close positive correlation between the ease with which we can do so and the true frequency of occurrence. It is easier, after all, to recall examples of things that happen often.

But frequency of occurrence is not the only factor that determines ease of recall. If people are asked, for example, whether there are more murders than suicides in New York State each year, almost everyone confidently answers yes. And yet there are always more suicides! Kahneman and Tversky explained that we think there are more murders because murders are more 'available' in memory. Memory research demonstrates that it is much easier to recall an event the more vivid or sensational it is. This is even more so in South Africa, with its high crime rate, and where suicides do not get the same media coverage as, for example, murders.

Other elements in the mechanics of memory can also affect the availability of different events. Ask yourself, for example, whether there are more words in the English language that start with the letter *r* than words that have *r* as their third letter. Most people answer confidently that many more words start with *r*, but in fact many more words have *r* as their third letter. We store words in memory much as they are stored in a dictionary – alphabetically, beginning with the first letter. We know plenty of words with *r* as their third letter, but it is no easier to remember them than it is to find them in a dictionary.

Events also tend to be more available in memory if they have happened more recently. A large body of research indicates that people tend to assign too much weight to recent information when making assessments about relative performance. In cricket, for example, a player's lifetime batting average against a certain bowler is the best available predictor of how he will do against that bowler in his next innings. It is apparently not uncommon, however, for a captain not to use a specific bowler against a batsman he has performed poorly against in the last couple of times out, even though he has bowled him out many times during the last couple of years. The problem is that the captain estimates the player's performance by examples of it that spring easily to mind. And the most recent examples are the easiest ones to think of.

Economically, the availability bias is important because we often have to estimate the relative performance of alternative economic options. Managers of companies, for example, must weigh the merits of different employees for promotion.

[6] See Amos Tversky and Daniel Kahneman, 'Judgement under uncertainly: heuristics and biases', *Science*, 1974, vol. 185, pp. 1124–1131. The example was simplified into rand terms for the Southern African audience.

The most effective managers will be those who guard against the natural tendency to put too much weight on recent performance.

Representativeness

Kahneman and Tversky also discovered an interesting bias in the way we attempt to answer questions of the form 'What is the likelihood that object A belongs to class B?'

For example, suppose Steve is a shy person, and we want to estimate the likelihood that he is a librarian rather than a salesperson. Most people are eager to respond that Steve is much more likely to be a librarian, because shyness is thought to be a representative trait of librarians, but rather an unusual one for salespeople. Such responses are often biased, however, because the likelihood of belonging to the category in question is influenced by many other important factors besides representativeness.

Let's use an example to explain this. Suppose that 80 per cent of all librarians are shy, but only 20 per cent of all salespeople. Suppose further that there are nine salespeople in the population for every librarian. Under these reasonable assumptions, if we know that Steve is shy and that he is either a librarian or a salesperson, what is the probability that he is a librarian? The relevant numbers for answering this question are displayed in Fig. 6.6. There, we see that even though a much larger proportion of librarians are shy, there are more than twice as many shy salespersons as there are shy librarians. The reason, of course, is that there are so many more salespeople than librarians. Out of every 100 people here, 26 of them are shy – 18 salespersons and 8 librarians. This means that the odds of a shy person being a librarian are only 8/26, or just under one-third. Yet most people who confront this example are reluctant to say that Steve is a salesperson, because shyness is so unrepresentative of salespersons.

Exercise 6.1

Suppose 90 per cent of all librarians are shy, but only 20 per cent of all salespersons are, and that there are four times as many salespersons as librarians. What is the likelihood that a randomly chosen shy person is a librarian, given that he is either a salesperson or a librarian?

Another example of the representativeness bias is the statistical phenomenon known as the *regression effect*, or *regression to the mean*. Suppose a standard IQ test is administered to 100 people, and that the 20 who score highest have an average score of 122, or 22 points above the average for the population. If these same 20 people are then tested a second time, their average score will almost always be substantially smaller than 122. The reason is that there is a certain amount of randomness in performance on IQ tests, and the people who did best on the first test are likely to include disproportionately many whose

Figure 6.6 Distribution by type – librarians and salespersons

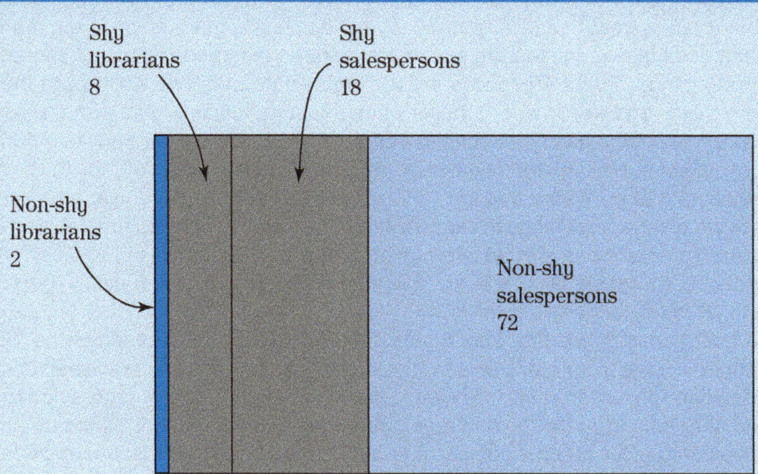

Even though shyness is more representative of librarians than of salespersons, a shy person is much more likely to be a salesperson than a librarian. The reason is that there are many more salespersons than librarians.

performances happened to be better than usual on that particular test.

We have substantial first-hand experience with regression effects in our daily lives (for example, the sons of unusually tall fathers tend to be shorter than their fathers). Kahneman and Tversky noted, however, that we often fail to make adequate allowance for it in our judgements because, they conjectured, we feel intuitively that an output (for example, an offspring) should be representative of the input (for example, the parent) that produced it.

Psychologists have long demonstrated that praise and other forms of positive reinforcement are much more effective than punishment or blame for teaching desired skills. Quite independently of whether a person is praised or blamed, a good performance is likely to be followed by a poorer one and a bad performance by a better one. Someone who praises good performances is therefore likely to conclude, erroneously, that praise perversely *causes* worse performance. Conversely, someone who denigrates poor performance is likely to spuriously take credit for the improvement that in fact results from regression effects. The co-movements of praise, blame and performance would convince all but the most sophisticated analyst that blame works and praise doesn't. Managers who are trying to elicit the most effective performances from their employees can ill afford to make this mistake.

Anchoring and adjustment

In one common estimation strategy, known as 'anchoring and adjustment', people first choose a preliminary estimate – an anchor – and then adjust it in accordance with whatever additional information they have that appears relevant. Kahneman and Tversky discovered that this procedure often leads to biased estimates, for two reasons. First, the initial anchor may be completely unrelated to the value to be estimated. And second, even when it is related, people tend to adjust too little from it.

To demonstrate the anchoring and adjustment bias, Kahneman and Tversky asked a sample of students to estimate the percentage of African countries that are members of the United Nations. Each person was first asked to spin a wheel that generated a number between 1 and 100. The student was then asked whether her estimate was higher or lower than that number. And, finally, the student was asked for her numerical estimate of the percentage. The results were nothing short of astonishing. Students who got a 10 or below on the spin of the wheel had a median estimate of 25 per cent, whereas the corresponding figure for those who got a 65 or above was 45 per cent. Each student surely *knew* that the initial random number had no possible relevance for estimating the percentage of African nations that belong to the UN. Nonetheless, the numbers had a dramatic effect on the estimates they reported.

Economic naturalist 6.1

In cricket, why does the rookie of the year often have a mediocre second season?

When the Proteas went to Australia in 2012, Faf du Plessis got a place in the team for the second test as a result of injuries in the touring squad. He grabbed the opportunity and scored a very good 78 runs in the first innings. South Africa was set the impossible target of 430 to win the test with 150 overs left in the match and was in deep trouble when it lost its fourth wicket with the score on only 45. Then Faf came in and played a heroic innings of 110 runs in 466 minutes to force a very unlikely draw. In the four innings against Australia and two against New Zealand he scored 443 runs at an average of 110.8. His impressive form lead to him being appointed captain of the T20 team, and in four tests he scored 179 runs at an average of 89.5. With the start of the next season he played six innings in the test team, but scored only 99 runs at an average of 19.8. In six T20 internationals he scored only 39 runs at an average of only 6.5. The decline in Faf's performance fits a pattern observed in cricket and other professional sports, in which the rookie of the year typically performs at a much lower level in the next season. What explains this pattern?

The phenomenon in question is called the 'sophomore jinx'. A related phenomenon is the '*Sports Illustrated* jinx', which holds that an athlete whose picture appears on the cover of that magazine one week is destined to do poorly the next. Both these supposed jinxes, however, are easily explained as the result of regression to the mean. Someone gets to be rookie of the year only after having had an extraordinarily good season. Similarly, athletes appear on the cover of *Sports Illustrated* only after an unusually strong performance. Their subsequent performance, even if still well above average, will almost inevitably fall below the standard that earned them their accolades. Fortunately, Faf adjusted well and in the 2013/14 season had a test batting average of 66.5 and in the T20 internationals he averaged 69.3.

In another illustration, two groups of high school students were asked to estimate the product of eight numbers within five seconds. The first group was given this expression:

$$8 \times 7 \times 6 \times 5 \times 4 \times 3 \times 2 \times 1$$

while the second group was given exactly the same numbers in reverse order:

$$1 \times 2 \times 3 \times 4 \times 5 \times 6 \times 7 \times 8$$

The time limit prevents most students from performing the entire calculation (which would lead to the correct answer of 40 320). What many of them apparently do is perform the first few multiplications (their anchor), and then project an estimate of the final result. For both groups of students these anchors turn out not to be very appropriate, and the projections turn out to be grossly insufficient. The resulting bias displays exactly the predicted pattern: the median estimate for the first group was 2250, whereas for the second group it was only 512.

An important economic application of the anchoring and adjustment bias is in estimating the failure rates of complex projects. Consider, for example, starting a new business. To succeed, it is necessary that each of a large number of events happen. Satisfactory financing must be obtained, a workable location found, a low-cost production process designed, sufficiently skilled labour hired, an effective marketing campaign implemented, and so on. The enterprise will fail if any one of these steps fails. When many steps are involved, the failure rate is invariably high, even when each step has a high probability of success. For example, a programme involving 10 steps, each with a success rate of 90 per cent, will fail 65 per cent of the time. When estimating failure rates for such processes, people tend to anchor on the low failure rate for the typical step, from which they make grossly insufficient adjustments. The anchoring and adjustment bias may thus help explain why the overwhelming majority of new businesses fail.

The psychophysics of perception

Yet another pattern in the way we perceive and process information has importance in economic applications. It derives from the so-called **Weber–Fechner law** of psychophysics. Weber and Fechner set out to discover how large the change in a stimulus had to be before we could perceive the difference in intensity. Most people, for example, are unable to distinguish a 100-watt light bulb from a 100.5-watt light bulb. But how large does the difference in brightness have to be before people can reliably identify it?

Weber–Fechner law The property of perception whereby the just noticeable difference in a stimulus tends to be proportional to the value of the stimulus.

Weber and Fechner found that the minimally perceptible difference is roughly proportional to the original intensity of the stimulus. Thus the more intense the stimulus is, the larger the difference has to be, in absolute terms, before we can tell the difference.

Thaler suggested that the Weber–Fechner law seems to be at work when people decide whether price differences are worth worrying about. Suppose, for example, you are about to buy a 28-litre microwave oven in a store for R1099 when a friend informs you that the same microwave oven is selling for only R949 in another store only 10 minutes away. Do you go to the other store? Would your answer have been different if you had been about to buy a 46-inch 3D LED television for R12 999 and your friend told you the same set was available at the other store for only R12 849? Thaler found that most people answer yes to the first question and no to the second.

In the rational choice model, it is inconsistent to answer differently for the two cases. A rational person will travel to the other store if and only if the benefits of doing so exceed the costs. The benefit is R150 in both cases. The cost is also the same for each trip, whether it is to buy a microwave oven or a television. If it makes sense to go in one case, it also makes sense in the other.

The difficulty of actually deciding

In the rational choice model, there should be no difficult decisions. If the choice between two alternatives is a close call – that is, if the two alternatives are predicted to yield approximately the same utility – then it should not make much difference which is chosen. But if one of the options clearly has a higher expected utility, the choice should again be easy.

In reality, of course, we all know that difficult decisions are more the rule than the exception. The difficulty is most pronounced when the alternatives differ along dimensions that are hard to compare. If the three things we care about in a car

Figure 6.7 Choosing between two apartments

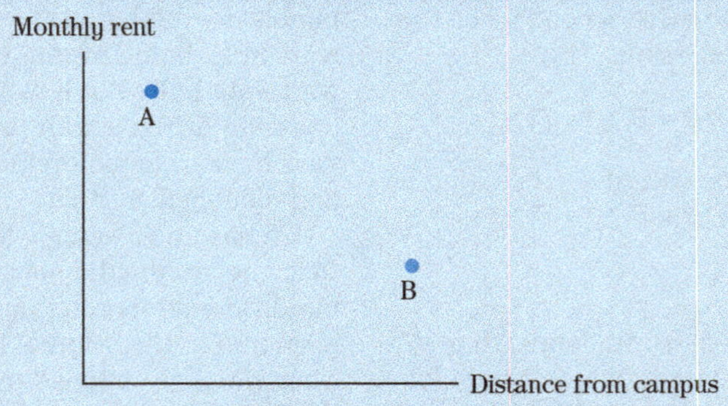

By suitably manipulating the monthly rents and distances from campus, it is possible to get a group of students to split 50–50 in their choices between A and B.

are, say, comfort, fuel economy and safety, it will be easy to decide between two cars if one is safer and more comfortable and has better fuel economy than the other. But what if one is much more comfortable and has much worse fuel economy? In principle, we are supposed to have indifference curves that tell us the rate at which we would be willing to trade one characteristic for the other. In practice, however, it is just not so easy. It is not uncommon for people to dwell on the possibility that they will regret whichever choice they make. ('If I pick the more comfortable car, what will happen if I then get transferred to a job that requires a long daily commute?')

Such difficulties appear to cast doubt on a fundamental axiom of rational choice theory, namely, that choices should be independent of irrelevant alternatives. This axiom can be illustrated by the following story.

A man comes into a delicatessen and asks what kinds of sandwiches are available. The attendant answers that they have roast beef and chicken. The patron deliberates for a few moments, and finally asks for a roast beef sandwich. The attendant says, 'Oh, I forgot to mention, we also have tuna.' To this, the patron responds, 'Well, in that case I guess I'll have chicken.' According to the rational choice model, the availability of tuna should matter only if it is the alternative the patron most prefers. There is no intelligible basis for its availability to cause a switch from roast beef to chicken.

In collaboration with Itamar Simonson, Tversky performed some intriguing experiments that suggest choice may not, in fact, always be independent of irrelevant alternatives.[7] One of their examples is the choice between apartments that differ along two dimensions, monthly rent and distance from campus. From a student's point of view, an apartment is more attractive the closer it is to campus and the lower is its monthly rent. A group of students was asked to choose between two apartments like the pair shown in Fig. 6.7. Notice in the figure that neither apartment dominates the other. A is more expensive, but B is further from campus. We expect that students who are relatively more concerned about rent will choose apartment B, while those who care primarily about commuting time will pick A. By manipulating the distance and rent, it is easy to get a group of students to divide roughly 50–50 between the two apartments.

So far, no surprises. But now the researchers add a third apartment, C, to the list of choices, giving us the set depicted in Fig. 6.8. Notice that C is *dominated* by B – that is, it is both further from campus *and* more expensive than B. In terms of the rational choice model, it is a classic example of an irrelevant alternative. Faced with the choice A, B or C, no rational consumer would ever choose C. And indeed, in actual experiments, hardly anyone ever does.

The surprise is that options like C turn out to affect people's choices between the remaining options. Simonson and Tversky discovered that when an apartment like C is added to the pair A and B, the effect is to shift people's choices substantially in favour of B. Before C was available, students divided 50–50 between A and B. Once C

[7] See Itamar Simonson and Amos Tversky, 'Choice in context: Tradeoff contrast and extremeness aversion', *Journal of Marketing Research*, 1992, vol. 29, August, pp. 281–295.

Figure 6.8 Adding an irrelevant alternative

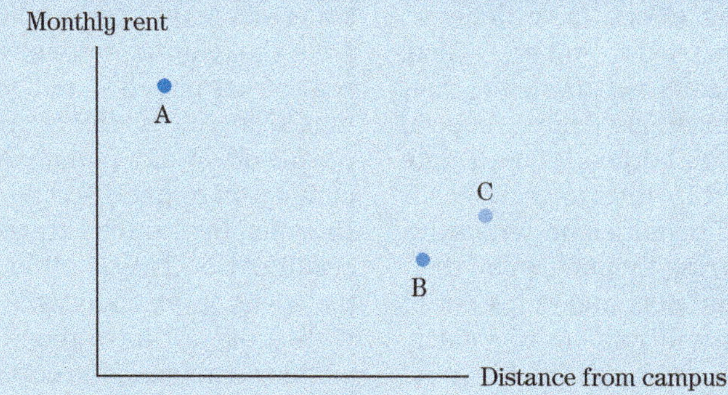

was added, however, more than 70 per cent of the students chose B, the option that dominates C.

Many people apparently find the original choice between A and B a difficult one to make. The appearance of C gives them a comparison they can make comfortably, namely, that between B and C. The researchers hypothesized that this creates a 'halo effect' for B, which makes it much more likely to be chosen over A. Perhaps a similar effect might cause the availability of tuna to cause someone to switch his decision from roast beef to chicken. Whatever the reason for such behaviour, it clearly violates the axiom that choice is independent of irrelevant alternatives and is clearly not rational behaviour.

The self-control pitfall

Another reason why behaviour doesn't always track the predictions of simple rational choice models is that people often have difficulty carrying out plans they believe to be in their own

Economic naturalist 6.2

Why do real estate agents often show clients two houses that are nearly identical, even though one is both cheaper and in better condition than the other?

As in the examples just discussed, the fact that one house dominates another may endow the first house with a halo that makes it more attractive relative to houses that are better than it on at least some dimensions. For example, an agent might have a client who is having difficulty making up her mind between a Greek revival house and a Cape Dutch house. By showing the client a similar Cape Colonial that is priced higher and is less well-maintained than the first, she might clinch the sale in favour of the dominant Cape Colonial. Again, people seem to dislike choosing between alternatives that are difficult to compare. Experienced real estate agents often avoid this problem by giving their clients an opportunity to focus on an easy choice.

©Dennies MacDonald/Alamy

©Natalia Brats lawsky/age fotostock

Why might a real estate agent bother showing a dominated alternative?

interests. Thomas Schelling notes, for example, that most cigarette smokers say they want to quit.[8] Many of them, with great effort, have done so. Many more, however, have tried to quit and failed.

Fearing they will be tempted to spend their savings, people join 'Christmas clubs', special accounts that prohibit withdrawals until late autumn; they buy whole-life insurance policies, which impose substantial penalties on withdrawals before retirement. Fearing they will spoil their dinners, they put the salted nuts and chips out of easy reach; fearing they will gamble too much, they limit the amount of cash they take to Grand West Casino. Fearing they will stay up too late watching TV, they move the television out of the bedroom.

The moral of the burgeoning self-control literature is that *devising* a rational intertemporal consumption plan is only part of the problem. There is also the task of *implementing* it. But here, too, rational deliberation can help us avoid some of the most important pitfalls. The consumer who has just given up smoking, for example, can predict that he will desperately want a cigarette if he goes out drinking with his friends on Friday nights. And he can also insulate himself from that temptation by committing himself to alternative weekend activities for the next month or so. By the same token, the person who wants to shield herself from the temptation to spend too much may have part of her pay diverted automatically into a savings account, and this is precisely what millions of people do. Today many people are tempted to get club cards to get discounts at specific shops, and financial institutions are too willing to give people credit cards. This is all in an effort to make people spend more than what they would have done if they did not have those cards. Therefore some people do not take the cards that shops offer them, and only pay cash to avoid this pitfall.

These issues once again highlight the distinction between the positive and normative roles of the rational choice model discussed in Chapter 1. Thus, because the rational choice model takes no account of self-control problems and the like, it will sometimes fail to predict how people actually behave. But note carefully that this does not mean that the model, even in its narrowest form, is wrong or useless. For here, as in other instances, it can play the important normative role of guiding people towards better decisions, ones that accord more fully with their real objectives.

Summary

- Numerous examples of behaviour contradict the predictions of the standard rational choice model. People often fail to ignore sunk costs. They play tennis indoors when, by their own account, they would prefer to play outside. They behave differently when they lose a ticket than when they lose an equivalent amount of cash. Psychologists argue that such behaviour is the result of limitations in human cognitive capacity.
- An important class of departure from rational choice appears to result from the asymmetric value function described by Kahneman and Tversky. In contrast to the rational choice model, which uses a utility function defined by total wealth, Kahneman and Tversky's descriptive theory uses a value function defined by changes in wealth. Unlike the traditional model, it gives losses much heavier decision weight than gains. This feature makes decisions extremely sensitive to how alternatives are framed. For example, if a loss is combined with a slightly larger gain, the net effect typically receives a positive evaluation, as it would under the rational choice model. But Kahneman and Tversky suggest that, when gains and losses occur as discrete events, people tend to evaluate their effects separately, in which case the impact of the loss tends to outweigh that of the larger gain.
- Another source of suboptimal decisions is failure to anticipate how we will adapt to different consumption experiences over time. In choosing between two goods, people tend to favour the alternative that provides greater satisfaction at

[8] See Thomas Schelling. *Choice and consequence*, Cambridge, MA: Harvard University Press, 1984.

the moment of decision. Evidence suggests, however, that the satisfaction provided by some goods and activities tends to decay quickly over time, whereas for others it decays less quickly, or even increases. The upshot is a tendency to spend too much on goods and activities in the former category, and too little on those in the latter.

- Decisions under uncertainty also often violate the prescriptions of the expected utility model. Here, too, the asymmetric value function provides a consistent description of several important patterns. People tend to be risk averse in the domain of gains, but risk seeking in the domain of losses. The result is that subtle differences in the framing of the problem can shift the mental reference point used for reckoning gains and losses, which in turn can produce radically different patterns of choice.
- Another important departure from rational choice occurs in the heuristics, or rules of thumb, that people use to make estimates of important decision factors. The availability heuristic says that one way in which people estimate the frequency of a given class of events is by the ease with which they can recall relevant examples. People tend to overestimate the frequency of vivid or salient events, and of other events that are especially easy to retrieve from memory.
- Another important heuristic is representativeness. People estimate the likelihood that an item belongs to a given class by how representative it is of that class. We saw that this often leads to substantial bias, because representativeness is only one of many factors that govern this likelihood. Shyness may indeed be a trait representative of librarians, but because there are so many more salespeople than librarians, it is much more likely that a randomly chosen shy person is a salesperson than a librarian.
- Anchoring and adjustment is a third heuristic that often leads to biased estimates of important decision factors. This heuristic says that people often make numerical estimates by first picking a convenient (but sometimes irrelevant) anchor and then adjusting from it (usually insufficiently) on the basis of other potentially relevant information. This procedure often causes people to underestimate the failure rate of projects with many steps. Such a project fails if any one of its essential elements fails, which means that even if the failure rate of each element is extremely low, a project with many elements is nonetheless very likely to fail. This may help explain the naive optimism of people who start new businesses.
- Another departure from rational choice relates to the psychophysics of perception. Psychologists have discovered that the barely perceptible change in any stimulus is proportional to its initial level. This seems to also hold true when the stimulus in question is the price of a good or service. People think nothing of driving across town to save R150 on a R1100 microwave oven, but would never dream of doing so to save R150 on a R13 000 TV.
- Departures from rational choice may also occur because people simply have difficulty choosing between alternatives that are hard to compare. The rational choice model assumes that we have complete preference orderings, but in practice it often seems to require a great deal of effort for us to decide how we feel about even very simple alternatives.
- Finally, departures from rational choice may occur because people lack sufficient willpower to carry out plans they believe to be in their own interests. In such instances, people may try to place tempting, but inferior, alternatives out of reach.
- Behavioural models of choice often do a much better job of predicting actual decisions than the rational choice model. It is important to remember, however, that the behavioural models claim no normative significance. That is, the mere fact that they predict, for example, that people often *do* ignore sunk costs should not be taken to mean that people *should* ignore them. The rational choice model says we can make better decisions by ignoring sunk costs, and most people, on reflection, strongly agree. In this respect, behavioural models of choice are an important tool for helping us avoid common pitfalls in decision making.

Questions for review

1 Suppose you were the owner of a small business and were asked the maximum you would be willing to pay in order to attend a course in the traditional theory of rational choice. In which case would your answer be larger: (a) if it were known that people always behave in strict accordance with the predictions of rational choice theory; or (b) if it were known that people's behaviour, yours included, often departs systematically from the predictions of rational choice theory?

2 Why is it rational to make decisions with less than complete information?

3 Distinguish between (a) the best decision and (b) the decision that leads to the best possible outcome.

4 Is there anything irrational about weighing gains less heavily than losses?

5 The policy of one school was to punish students for being late, whereas the corresponding policy in an otherwise identical school was to reward students for being on time. If effectiveness is measured by behaviour on the day following punishment or reward, which policy would seem to be more effective? Is this standard of effectiveness a good one?

Problems

1 Suppose your happiness is given by a Kahneman–Tversky value function like the one shown in the diagram. You have decided to put the most favourable spin on the various combinations of events that occur in your life. For each of the following pairs of events, will you be happier if you consider their effects separately or if you first combine them and consider only their net effect?

a A gain of R5000 and a loss of R500

b A gain of R500 and a loss of R5000

c A gain of R5000 and a gain of R6000

d A loss of R5000 and a loss of R6000

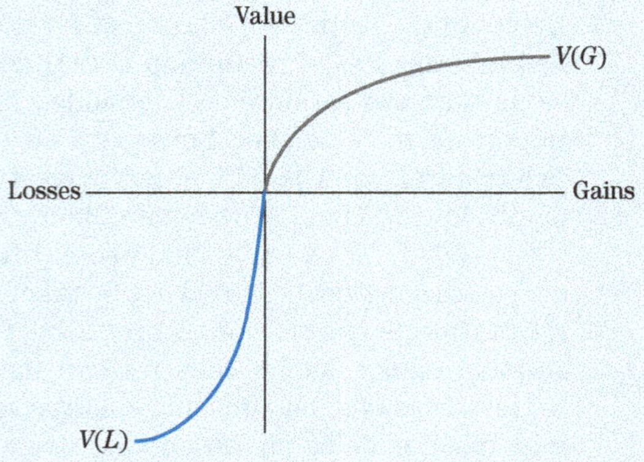

2 Brand Pretorius has hired you as a consultant to give them marketing advice about how to sell its new Toyota Land Cruiser 3.0 Diesel TX Auto. On the basis of the material covered in this chapter, suggest two specific marketing strategies for Brand to consider.

3 Give two examples of how the framing of alternatives tends to produce systematic effects on people's choices.

4 Studies have shown that in the Mannenberg Plains crime rates fall in the years following increased police patrols. Does this pattern suggest that the increased patrols are the *cause* of the crime reductions?

5 Chillyboy is a gourmet. He makes it a point never to visit a restaurant a second time unless he has been served a superb meal on his first visit. He is puzzled at how seldom the quality of his second meal is as high as the first. Should he be?

6 Sherlock Holmes the detective fancies himself a shrewd judge of human nature. In careful tests it has been discovered that he is right 80 per cent of the time when he says that a randomly chosen suspect is lying. Sherlock Holmes says that Jones is lying. The polygraph expert, who is right 100 per cent of the time, says that 40 per cent of the subjects interviewed by Sherlock Holmes are telling the truth. What is the probability that Jones is lying?

7 A witness testifies that the taxicab that struck and injured Bryan in a dark alley was green. On investigation, the attorney for Green Taxi Company discovers that the

witness identifies the correct colour of a taxi in a dark alley 80 per cent of the time. There are two taxi companies in town, Green and Blue. Green operates 15 per cent of all local taxis. The law says that the Green Taxi Company is liable for Bryan's injuries if and only if the probability that it caused them is greater than 0.5. Is the Green Taxi Company liable? Explain.

8 Last week your travel agent called to tell you that she had found a great fare, R10 540, for your trip to the United Kingdom later this month. This fare was almost R3000 below the APEX (advance purchase excursion) fare. You told her to book it immediately, and went around the department telling everyone about your great bargain. An hour later she called you back and told you that the reservation agent at South African Airways had made a mistake, and that the quoted fare did not exist. Your agent said she would hunt around and do the best she could for you. A few days later she found a ticket consolidator who could book you on the same South African Airways flight for R12 070, a figure still well below what you originally had expected to pay. This time you didn't go around the department bragging about your bargain. How might the material in this chapter be used to shed light on your behaviour?

9 In planning your next vacation, you have narrowed your choices down to two packages offered by your travel agent, a week in Londolozi for R28 000 or a week in Mauritues for R20 000. You are indifferent between these choices. You see an ad in the travel section of the newspaper for a week in Londolozi, with accommodation identical to that offered by your agent, for R31 000. According to the theory of rational choice, should the information in the newspaper ad influence your vacation plans? Explain.

10 Mary will drive across town to take advantage of a 40 per cent-off sale on a R400 blouse, but will not do so to take advantage of a 10 per cent-off sale on a R10 000 TV. Assuming that her alternative is to pay list price for both products at the department store next to her home, is her behaviour rational?

11 Rafael is the best tennis player in the world, but is having difficulty choosing between two tennis rackets, A and B. As shown in the diagram, B has more power than A, but less control. According to the rational choice model, how will the availability of a third alternative – racket C – influence Rafael's final decision? If Rafael behaves like most ordinary decision-makers in this situation, how will the addition of C to his choice set matter?

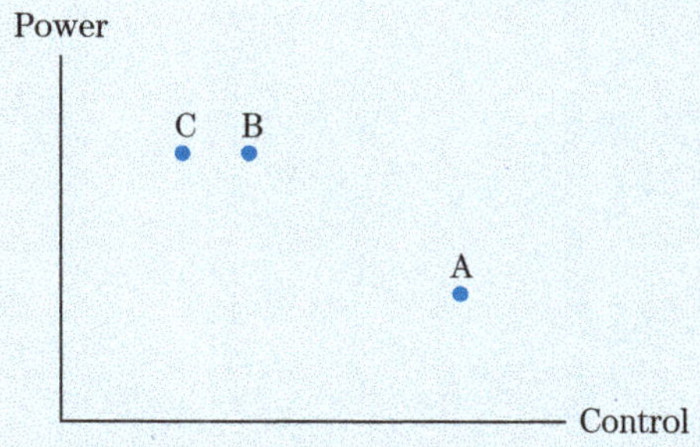

12 In the autumn, Robinson Crusoe puts 50 coconuts from his harvest into a cave just before a family of bears goes in to hibernate. As a result, he is unable to get the coconuts out before the bears emerge the following spring. Coconuts spoil at the same rate no matter where he stores them, and yet he continues this practice each year. Why might he do this?

Answer to in-chapter exercise

6.1 If there are four times as many salespersons as librarians, then there will be 80 salespersons for every 20 librarians. Of the 80 salespersons, 20 per cent, or 16, will be shy. Of the 20 librarians, 90 per cent, or 18, will be shy. Thus the likelihood that a shy person is a librarian is $18/(18 + 16) = 0.53$.

Part 3

The theory of the firm and market structure

Part contents

The economic theory of the firm assumes that the firm's primary goal is to maximize profits. Profit maximization requires the firm to expand its output whenever the benefit of doing so exceeds the cost. Our agenda in the first two chapters of Part 3 is to develop the cost side of this calculation. Chapter 7 begins with the theory of production, which shows how labour, capital and other inputs are combined to produce output. Making use of this theory, Chapter 8 then describes how the firm's costs vary with the amount of output it produces.

The next three chapters consider the benefit side of the firm's calculation under four different forms of market structure. Chapter 9 looks at the perfectly competitive firm, for which the benefit of selling an extra unit of output is exactly equal to its price. Chapter 10 examines the monopoly firm, or sole supplier of a good for which there are no close substitutes. For such a firm, the benefit of selling an extra unit of output is generally less than its price, because it must cut its price on existing sales in order to expand its output. Chapter 11 looks at two intermediate forms of market structure: monopolistic competition and oligopoly. In making decisions about output levels, monopolistically competitive firms behave just like monopolists. By contrast, the oligopolist must take account of strategic responses of its rivals when it calculates the benefits of expanding output.

Chapter 7

Production

Many people think of production as a highly structured, often mechanical process whereby raw materials are transformed into finished goods. And, without doubt, a great deal of production – such as a mason's laying bricks for the walls of a house – is of roughly this sort. Economists emphasize, however, that production is also a much more general concept, encompassing many activities not ordinarily thought of as such. We define it as *any activity that creates present or future utility.*

Thus the simple act of telling a joke constitutes production. The well-known comedian Marc Lottering explains why no South Africans were involved in the 9/11 incidents. 'Two of us would have forgotten our passports at home ... Three of us would have overweight luggage.' Once a joke is told, it leaves no more tangible trace than a pleasant memory. But under the economic definition of production, Marc Lottering is as much a production worker as the artisan whose chisel and lathe mould a willow tree log into a Kookaburra cricket bat. The person who delivers a singing telegram is also engaged in production; so is the doctor who gives a child a tetanus shot; the lawyer who draws up someone's will; the people who collect garbage on Wednesday mornings; and even the economists who write about production.

Chapter preview

In our discussions on consumer choice during the preceding chapters, an existing menu of goods and services was taken for granted. But where do these goods and services come from? In this chapter we shall see that their production involves a decision process very similar to the one we examined in earlier chapters. Whereas our focus in earlier chapters was on the economic decisions that underlie the demand side of the market relationship, our focus in the next seven chapters is on the economic decisions that underlie the supply side.

In this chapter we describe the production possibilities available to us for a given state of technology and resource endowments. We want to know how output varies with the application of productive inputs in both the short run and the long run.

Answers to these questions will set the stage for our efforts in the next chapter to describe how firms choose among technically feasible alternative methods of producing a given level of output.

The input–output relationship, or production function

There are several ways to define production. One definition, mentioned above, is that it is any activity that creates present or future utility. Production may be equivalently described as a process that transforms inputs (factors of production) into outputs. Among the inputs used in production, economists have traditionally included land, labour, capital and the more elusive category called entrepreneurship. To this list, it has become increasingly common to add such factors as knowledge or technology, organization and energy.

Production function The relationship that describes how inputs such as capital and labour are transformed into output.

A **production function** is the relationship by which inputs are combined to produce output. Schematically, it may be represented as the box in Fig. 7.1. Inputs are fed into it and output is discharged from it. The box implicitly embodies the existing state of technology, which has been improving steadily over time. Thus a given combination of productive inputs will yield a larger number of cars with today's technology than with the technology of 1990.

A production function may also be thought of as a cooking recipe. It lists the ingredients and tells you, say, how many pancakes you will get if you manipulate the ingredients in a certain way.[1]

Yet another way of describing the production function is to cast it in the form of a mathematical equation. Consider a production process that employs two inputs, capital (K) and labour (L), to produce meals (Q). The relationship between K, L and Q may be expressed as

$$Q = F(K, L) \tag{7.1}$$

where F is a mathematical function that summarizes the process depicted in Fig. 7.1. It is no more than a simple rule that tells how much Q we get when we employ specific quantities of K and L. By way of illustration, suppose the production function for meals is given by $F(K, L) = 2KL$, where K is measured in equipment-hours per week, L is measured in person-hours per week and output is measured in meals per week. We can use a worker (L) and a frying pan as equipment (K) to produce these meals. For example,

Figure 7.1 The production function

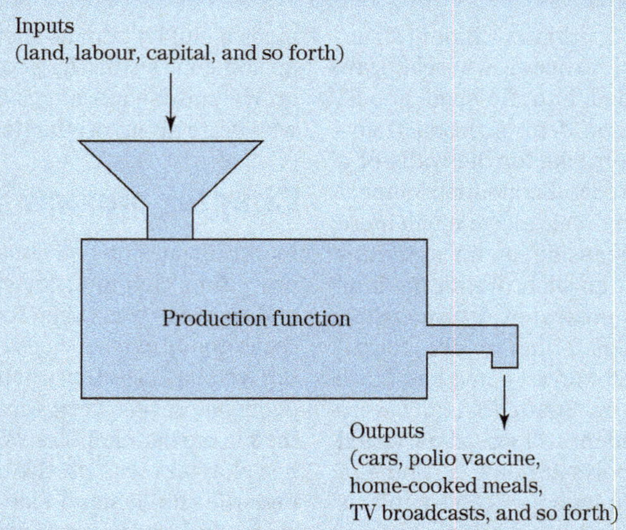

The production function transforms inputs such as land, labour, capital and entrepreneurship into output. The box in the diagram embodies the existing state of technological knowledge. Because knowledge has been accumulating over time, we get more output from a given combination of inputs today than we would have in the past.

[1] In some recipes the ingredients must be mixed in fixed proportions. Other recipes allow substitution between ingredients, as in a pancake recipe that allows milk and oil to be substituted for eggs. Production functions can be of either of these two types.

Table 7.1 The production function $Q = 2KL$

		Labour (person-hours/wk)				
		1	2	3	4	5
Capital (equipment-hours/wk)	1	2	4	6	8	10
	2	4	8	12	16	20
	3	6	12	18	24	30
	4	8	16	24	32	40
	5	10	20	30	40	50

The entries in the table represent output, measured in meals per week, and are calculated using the formula $Q = 2KL$.

2 equipment-hr/wk combined with 3 person-hr/wk would yield $2(2)(3) = 12$ meals/wk with this particular production function. The relationship between K, L and weekly output of meals for the production function $Q = 2KL$ is summarized in Table 7.1. If we use a different production function we will get totally different values in the table.

Intermediate products

Capital (as embodied, for example, in the form of stoves and frying pans) and labour (as embodied in the services of a chef) are clearly by themselves insufficient to produce meals. Raw foodstuffs are also necessary. The production process described by Eq. 7.1 is one that transforms raw foodstuffs into the finished product we call meals. In this process, foodstuffs are *intermediate products*, which many economists treat as inputs like any others. For the sake of simplicity we shall ignore intermediate products in the examples we discuss in this chapter. But this feature could be built into all these examples without changing any of our essential conclusions.

Fixed and variable inputs

The production function tells us how output will vary if some or all of the inputs are varied. In practice, there are many production processes in which the quantities of at least some inputs cannot be altered quickly. The FM radio broadcast of Bok Radio, a fairly new regional radio station in the Western Cape devoted to promoting South African music, is an example of such a process. To carry it out, complex electronic equipment is needed, and also a music library and a large transmission tower. Compact discs can be purchased in a matter of hours; but it may take weeks to acquire the equipment needed to launch a new station, and months or even years to purchase a suitable location and construct a new transmission tower, or to get a licence that will permit you to undertake the broadcasting.

The **long run** for a particular production process is defined as the shortest period of time required to alter the amounts of *every* input. The **short run**, by contrast, is defined as that period during which one or more inputs cannot be varied. An input whose quantity can be altered in the short run is called a **variable input**. One whose quantity cannot be altered – except perhaps at prohibitive cost – within a given time period is called a **fixed input**. In the long run all inputs are variable inputs, by definition, and nothing is fixed any more. In the Bok Radio broadcast example, CDs are variable inputs in the short run, but the broadcast tower is a fixed input. If sufficient time elapses, however, even it becomes a variable input. In some production activities, such as those of a street-corner hot dog stand, even the long run does not involve an extended period of time. We begin in the next section by considering short-run production, and then we move on to long-run production in the following section.

Long run The shortest period of time required to alter the amounts of all inputs used in a production process.

Short run The longest period of time during which at least one of the inputs used in a production process cannot be varied.

Variable input An input that can be varied in the short run.

Fixed input An input that cannot vary in the short run.

Production in the short run

Consider again the production process described by $Q = F(K, L) = 2KL$, the simple two-input production function described in Table 7.1. And suppose we are concerned with production in the short run – here, a period of time in which the labour input is variable but the capital input is fixed, say, at the value $K = K_0 = 1$. With capital held constant, output becomes, in effect, a function of only the variable input, labour: $F(K, L) = 2K_0L = 2L$. This means we can plot the production function in a two-dimensional diagram, as in Fig. 7.2(a). For this particular $F(K, L)$, the short-run production function is a straight line through the origin, whose slope is two times the fixed value of K: thus $\Delta Q/\Delta L = 2K_0$. In Fig. 7.2(b), note that the short-run production rotates upwards to $F(K_1, L) = 6L$ when K rises to $K_1 = 3$.

Figure 7.2 A specific short-run production function

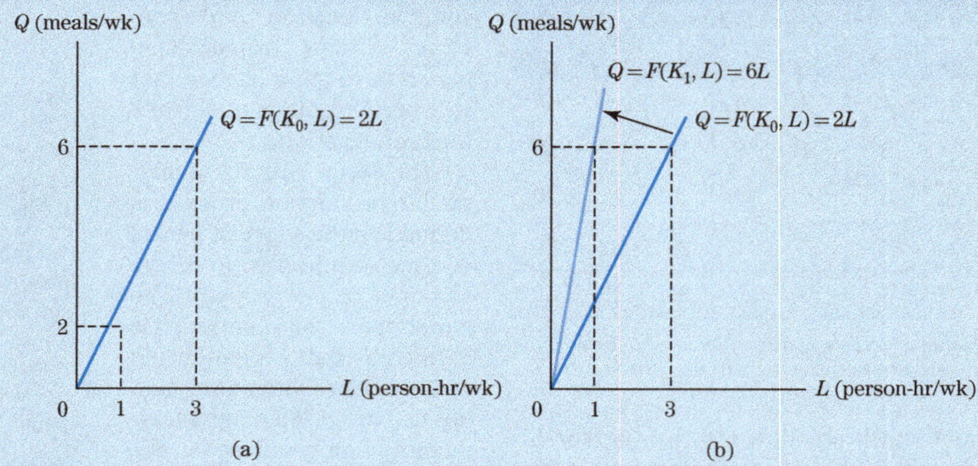

Panel (a) shows the production function $Q = 2KL$, with K fixed at $K_0 = 1$. Panel (b) shows how the short-run production function shifts when K is increased to $K_1 = 3$.

Exercise 7.1

Graph the short-run production function for $F(K,L) = \sqrt{K}\sqrt{L}$ when K is fixed at $K_0 = 4$.

As you saw in Exercise 7.1, the graphs of short-run production functions will not always be straight lines. The short-run production function shown in Fig. 7.3 has several properties that are commonly found in production functions observed in practice. First, it passes through the origin, which is to say that we get no output if we use no variable input. Second, initially the addition of variable inputs augments output at an increasing rate: moving from 1 to 2 units of labour yields 10 extra

Figure 7.3 Another short-run production function

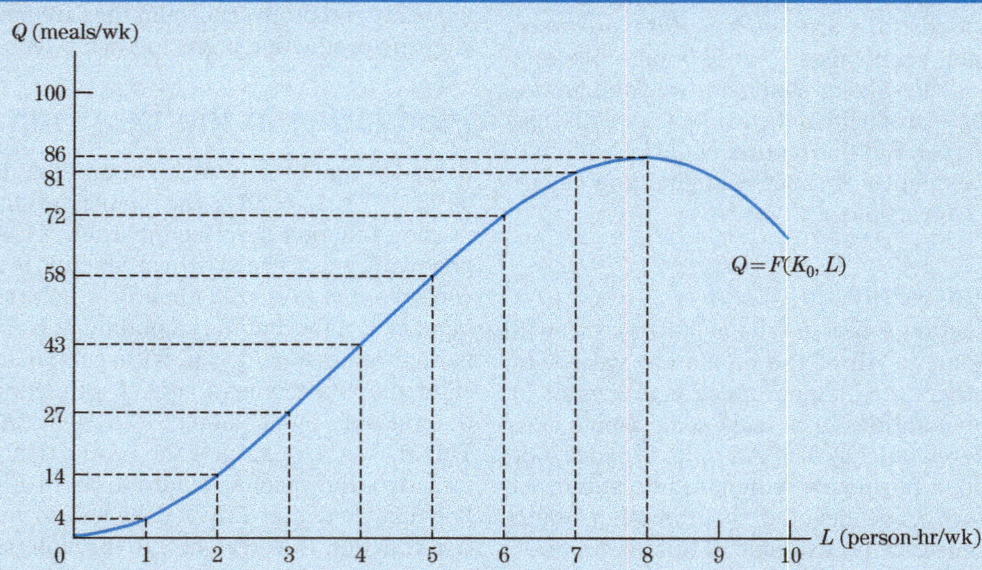

The curvilinear shape shown here is common to many short-run production functions. Output initially grows at an increasing rate as labour increases. Beyond $L = 4$ output grows at a diminishing rate with increases in labour, and beyond $L = 8$ total output decreases.

units of output, while moving from 2 to 3 units of labour gives 13 additional units. Finally, the function shown in Fig. 7.3 has the property that beyond some point ($L = 4$ in the diagram), additional units of the variable input give rise to smaller and smaller increments in output. Thus the move from 5 to 6 units of labour yields 14 extra units of output, whereas the move from 6 to 7 units of labour yields only 9. For some production functions, the level of output may actually decline with additional units of the variable input beyond some point, as happens here when we use more than 8 units of labour. With a limited amount of capital to work with, additional workers may eventually begin to get in one another's way. Theoretically total product can thus decrease in very specific circumstances, but it is seldom experienced in reality.

The property whereby output initially grows at an increasing rate may stem from the benefits deriving from the division of tasks and specialization of labour. With one employee, all tasks must be done by the same person, whereas with two or more employees, tasks may be divided, and employees may perform their dedicated tasks better. (Similar logic applies to specializing in one task within any period of time.) Workers thus become masters in the limited part of the production process in which they are involved.

The final property noted about the short-run production function in Fig. 7.3 – that beyond some point, output grows at a diminishing rate with increases in the L variable input – is known as the **law of diminishing returns** (or the law of diminishing marginal product). And although it too is not a universal property of short-run production functions, it is extremely common. The law of diminishing returns is a short-run phenomenon. Formally, it may be stated as follows:

Law of diminishing returns If other inputs are fixed, the increase in output resulting from an increase in the variable input must eventually decline.

> As equal amounts of a variable input are sequentially added while all other inputs are held fixed, the resulting *increments* to output will eventually diminish.

Employing the logic of Economic naturalist 7.1, the British economist Thomas Malthus argued in 1798 that the law of diminishing returns implied eventual misery for the human race. The difficulty is that agricultural land is fixed and, beyond some point, the application of additional labour will yield ever-smaller increases in food production. The inevitable result, as Malthus saw it, is that population growth will drive average food consumption down to the starvation level.

Whether Malthus' prediction will be borne out in the future remains to be seen. But he would never have imagined that food production per capita would grow more than 20-fold during the ensuing two centuries. Note carefully, however,

Economic naturalist 7.1

Why can't the population of the entire world be fed from a handful of grain?

The law of diminishing returns suggests that no matter how much labour, fertilizer, water, seed, capital equipment and other inputs were used, only a limited amount of grain could be grown with the seeds shown in the photo. With so few seeds available, increases in other inputs would quickly cease to have any effect on total output. Unlike the story in the Bible when the two fishes and five loaves of bread increased multifold when Jesus handed the food out to the people, this is not the way it works in reality.

©Pixtal/AGE fotostock

Figure 7.4 The effect of technological progress in food production

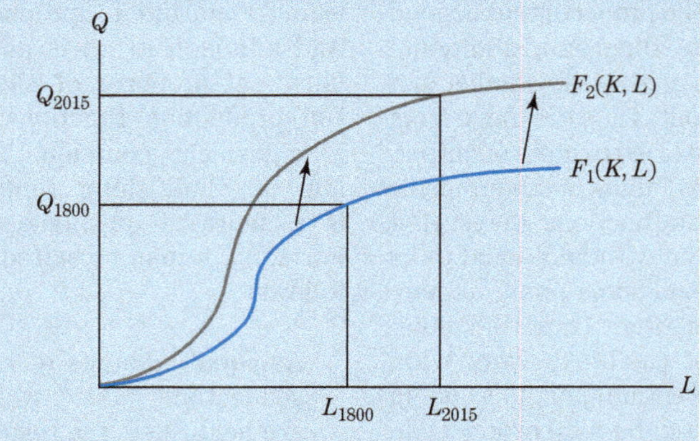

F_1 represents the production function for food in the year 1800. F_2 represents the corresponding function for 2015. The effect of technological progress in food production is to cause F_2 to lie above F_1. Even though the law of diminishing returns (marginal product) applies to both F_1 and F_2, the growth in food production between 1800 and 2015 has more than kept pace with the growth in labour inputs over the same period.

that the experience of the last 200 years does not contradict the law of diminishing returns. What Malthus did not foresee was the explosive growth in agricultural technology, which has far outstripped the effect of a fixed supply of land. Still, the ruthless logic of Malthus' observation remains. No matter how advanced our technology, if population continues to grow, it is just a matter of time before limits on arable land spell persistent food shortages. Another factor coming into play is that more and more agricultural land is used for housing and factories.

The world's population has grown rapidly during the years since Malthus made his prediction, from 978 million in 1800 to 7.209 billion in 2014. During the twentieth century alone, world population increased from 1.65 billion to 6 billion and since 1970 has doubled. In both China (1.4 billion) and India (1.3 billion) there are more people today than the world population in 1798. Are we in fact doomed to eventual starvation? Perhaps not. As the late economist Herbert Stein once famously remarked, 'If something can't go on for ever, it won't.' It is predicted that the world's population will surpass 9 billion by 2042, but certain population specialists now predict that it will peak by the year 2070 and then begin to decline.[2] Later predictions by the United Nations indicate that world population will stabilize at just above 10 billion.[3] If we don't blow ourselves up in the meantime, there is thus a good chance that we shall escape the dire fate that Malthus predicted.

Technological improvements in production are represented graphically by an upward shift in the production function. In Fig. 7.4, for example, the curves labelled F_1 and F_2 are used to denote the agricultural production functions in 1800 and 2015, respectively. The law of diminishing returns applies to each of these curves, and yet the growth in food production has kept pace with the increase in labour input during the period shown.

Total, marginal and average products

Short-run production functions such as those shown in Figs 7.3 and 7.4 are often referred to as **total product curves**. They relate the total amount of output to the quantity of the variable input. Also of interest in many applications is the *marginal product* of a variable input. It is defined as *the change in the*

Total product curve A curve showing the amount of output as a function of the amount of variable input.

[2] See Wolfgang Lutz, Warren Sanderson and Sergei Sherbov, 'The end of world population growth', *Nature*, 2001, vol. 412, 2 August, pp. 543–545.

[3] Worldometers. Real time world statistics. http://www.worldometers.info/world-population/.

Table 7.2 Example of total product, average product and marginal product

Labour	Total product	Average product	Marginal product
0	0	0	0
1	2	2	2
2	14	7	12
3	27	9	13
4	43	10.75	16
5	58	11.6	15
6	72	12	14
7	80	11.43	6
8	86	10.75	0

total product that occurs in response to a unit change in the variable input (all other inputs held fixed). A business manager trying to decide whether to hire or fire another worker has an obvious interest in knowing what the **marginal product** of labour is.

Marginal product Change in total product resulting from a one-unit change in the variable input.

To refresh our memories and to explain the correlation between total product, average product and marginal product, we will use Table 7.2 as our reference point. Normally we write the marginal values between the values of the labour units, but to keep our discussion simple we will write it on the same line in the table.

Marginal product is equal to the change in total product for a one-unit increase in the variable input. More formally, if ΔL denotes a small change in the variable input, and ΔQ denotes the resulting change in output, then the marginal product of L, denoted MP_L, is defined as

$$MP_L = \frac{\Delta Q}{\Delta L} \quad (7.2)$$

Geometrically, the marginal product at any point is simply the *slope* of the total product curve at that point, as shown in the top panel of Fig. 7.5.[4] For example, the marginal product of labour when $L = 2$ is $MP_{L=2} = 12$. Likewise, $MP_{L=4} = 16$ and $MP_{L=7} = 6$ for the total product curve shown in Fig. 7.5. Note, finally, that MP_L is negative for values of L greater than 8.

The marginal product curve itself is plotted in the bottom panel in Fig. 7.5. Note that it rises at first, reaches a maximum at $L = 4$, and then declines, finally becoming negative for values of L greater than 8. Note also that the maximum point on the marginal product curve corresponds to the inflection point on the total product curve, the point where its curvature switches from convex (increasing at an increasing rate) to concave (increasing at a decreasing rate). This is the point where the slope of the total product curve reaches a maximum value. Note also that the marginal product curve reaches zero at the value of L at which the total product curve reaches a maximum. This is because the slope of the total product curve is zero (horizontal line) at that point of production.

As we shall see in greater detail in later chapters, the importance of the marginal product concept lies in the fact that decisions about running an enterprise most naturally arise in the form of decisions about *changes*. Should we hire another engineer or accountant? Should we reduce the size of the maintenance staff? Should we install another copier? Should we lease another delivery truck?

To answer such questions intelligently, we must compare the benefit of the change in question with its cost – in other words, we must compare the changes in the marginal values. And, as we shall see, the marginal product concept plays a pivotal role in the calculation of the benefits when we alter the level of a productive input. Looking at Fig. 7.5, we may identify a range of values of the variable input that a rational manager would never employ. In particular, as long as labour commands a positive wage, such a manager would never want to employ the variable input in the region where its marginal product is negative ($L > 8$ in Fig. 7.5). Equivalently, he would never employ a variable input past the point where the total product curve reaches its maximum value (where $L = 8$ and $MP_L = 0$ or the slope of TP is zero).

[4] Remember that the slope of a function is also the first-order derivative of that function. Therefore the formal definition of the marginal product of a variable input is given by $MP(L) = \partial F(K, L)/\partial L$.

Figure 7.5 The marginal product of a variable input

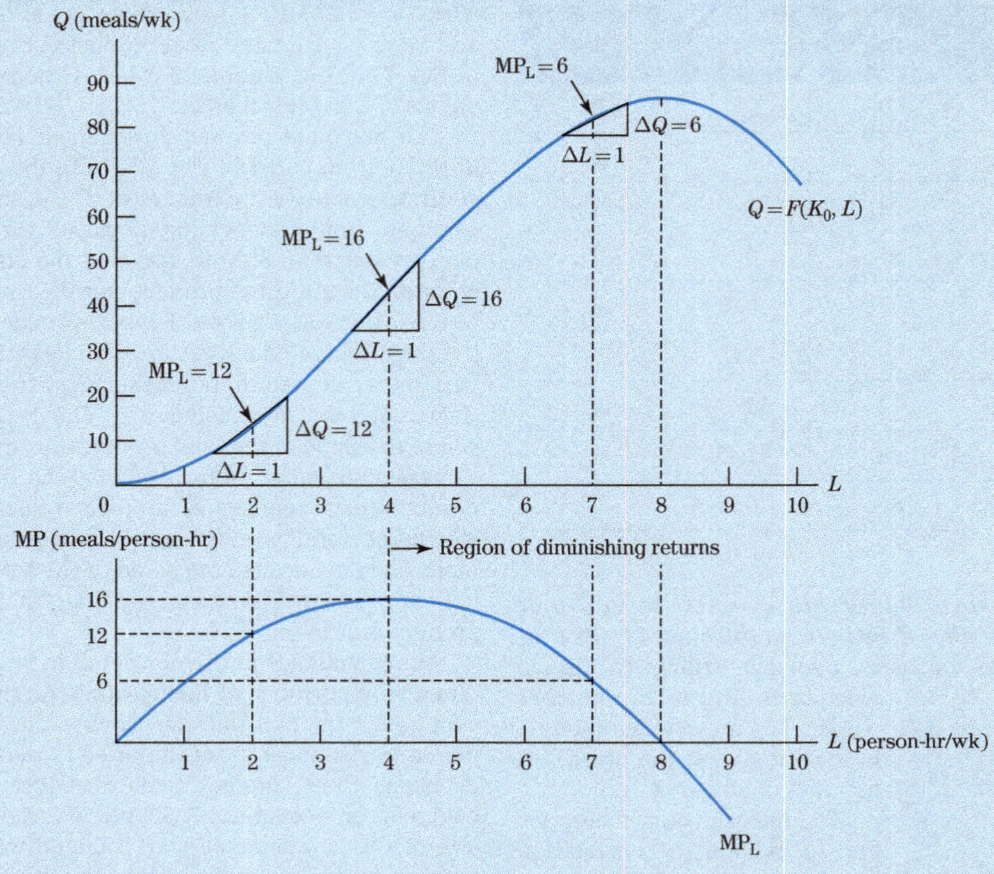

At any point, the marginal product of labour, MP_L, is the slope of the total product curve at that point (top panel). For the production function shown in the top panel, the marginal product curve (bottom panel) initially increases as labour increases. Beyond $L = 4$, however, the marginal product of labour decreases as labour increases. For $L > 8$ the total product curve declines with L, which means that the marginal product of labour is negative in that region.

Exercise 7.2

What is the marginal product of labour when $L = 3$ in the short-run production function shown in Fig. 7.2(a)? When $L = 1$? Does this short-run production function exhibit diminishing returns to labour?

Average product Total product divided by the number of units of the variable input used in the production process.

The **average product** of a variable input is defined as the total product divided by the quantity of the variable input used in the production process. Denoted by AP_L, it is thus given by

$$AP_L = \frac{Q}{L} \tag{7.3}$$

When the variable input is labour, the average product is also called *labour productivity.*

Geometrically, the average product is the slope of the line joining the origin to the corresponding point on the total product curve. Three such lines, R_1, R_2 and R_3, are drawn to the total product curve shown in the top panel in Fig. 7.6. The average product at $L = 2$ is the slope of R_1, which is $\frac{14}{2} = 7$. Note that R_2 intersects the total product curve in two places: first, directly above $L = 4$, and then directly above $L = 8$. Accordingly, the average products for these two values of L will be the same, namely, the slope of R_2, which is $\frac{43}{4} = \frac{86}{8} = 10.75$. R_3 intersects (or is tangent to) the total product curve at only one point, directly above $L = 6$. The average product for $L = 6$ is thus the slope of R_3, $\frac{72}{6} = 12$. R_3 is the line with the steepest slope that touches the total product curve. Any line from the origin with a steeper slope will miss the total product curve completely. When you employ six workers ($L = 6$), average product is thus a maximum.

Exercise 7.3

For the short-run production function shown in Fig. 7.2(a), what is the average product of labour at $L = 3$? At $L = 1$? How does average product compare with marginal product at these points?

The relationships among total, marginal and average product curves

Because of the way the total, marginal and average products are defined, systematic relationships exist among them. The top panel in Fig. 7.6 shows a total product curve, and three of the rays whose slopes define the average product of the variable input. The steepest of the three rays, R_3, is tangent to the total product curve at $L = 6$. Its slope, $\frac{72}{6} = 12$, is the average product of labour at $L = 6$. The marginal product of labour at $L = 6$ is defined as the slope of the total product curve at $L = 6$, which happens to be exactly the slope of R_3, since R_3 is tangent to the total product curve. Thus $AP_{L=6} = MP_{L=6}$, as shown in the bottom panel by the fact that the AP_L curve intersects the MP_L curve for $L = 6$. Also note that MP_L intersects AP_L at the maximum turning point of AP_L.

For values of L less than 6, note in the top panel in Fig. 7.6 that the slope of the total product curve is larger than the slope of the ray to the

Figure 7.6 Total, marginal and average product curves

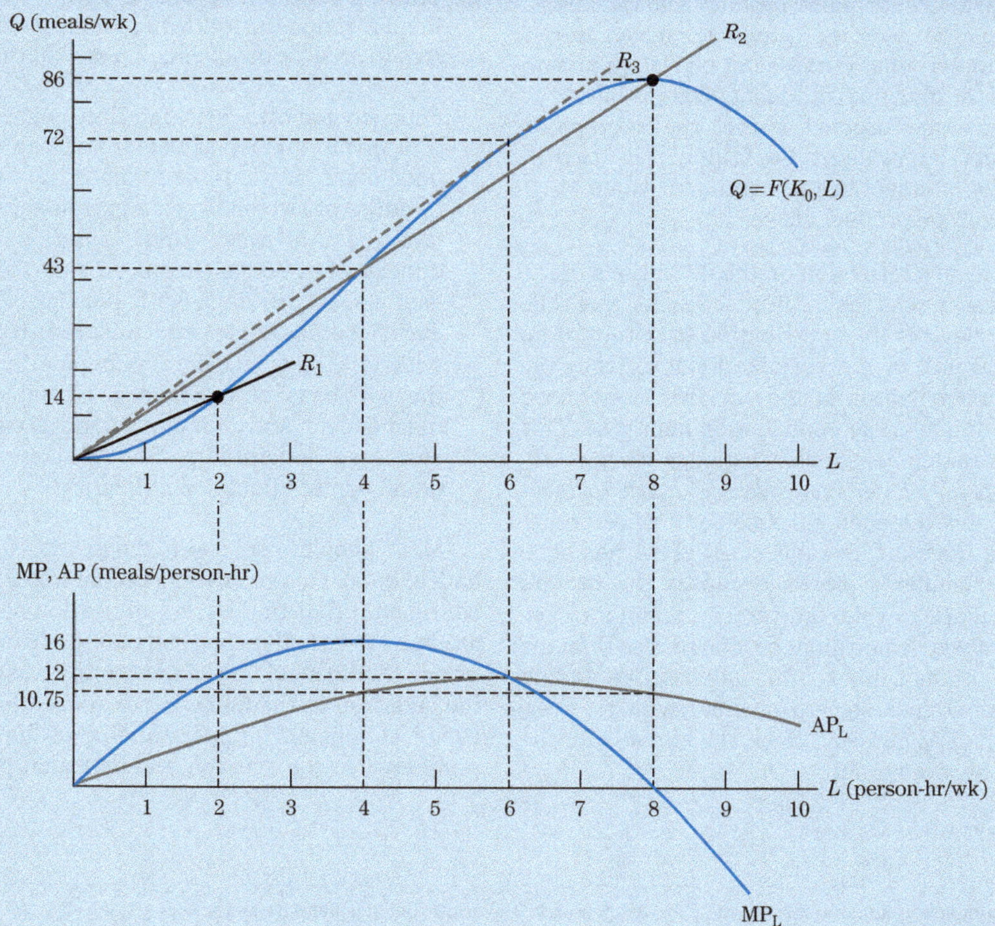

The average product at any point on the total product curve is the slope of the ray to that point. For the total product curve shown in the top panel, AP_L rises up to $L = 6$, then declines if more labour is employed. At $L = 6$, $MP_L = AP_L$. For any $L < 6$, $MP_L > AP_L$, and for any $L > 6$, $MP_L < AP_L$.

corresponding point. Thus, for $L < 6$, $MP_L > AP_L$, as reflected in the bottom panel. This implies that AP_L will increase. Note also in the top panel that, for values of L greater than 6, the slope of the total product curve is smaller than the slope of the ray to the corresponding point. This means that for $L > 6$ we have $AP_L > MP_L$, as shown in the bottom panel in Fig. 7.6. This implies that AP_L will decrease.

Note finally in Fig. 7.6 that, for extremely small values of L, the slope of the ray to the total product curve becomes indistinguishable from the slope of the total product curve itself. This tells us that, for $L = 0$, average and marginal products are the same, which is reflected in the bottom panel in Fig. 7.6 by the fact that the two curves emanate from the same point.[5]

The relationship between the marginal and average product curves may be summarized as follows:

> When the marginal product curve lies above the average product curve, the average product curve must be rising; and when the marginal product curve lies below the average product curve, the average product curve must be falling. The two curves intersect at the maximum value of the average product curve.

A moment's reflection on the definitions of the two curves makes the intuitive basis for this relationship clear. If the contribution to output of an additional unit of the variable input exceeds the average contribution of the variable inputs used thus far, the average contribution must rise. This effect is analogous to what happens when a student with an 85 per cent average mark for economics joins the economics society, whose other members have an average mark of 64 per cent: the new member's presence causes the group's average mark to rise. Conversely, adding a variable input whose marginal product is less than the average product of existing units is like adding a new economics society member with an average mark of 52 per cent. Here, the effect is for the existing average to fall.[6]

Exercise 7.4

Consider a short-run production process for which $AP_{L=10} = 7$ and $MP_{L=10} = 12$. Will $AP_{L=10.1}$ be larger or smaller than $AP_{L=10}$ for this process?

The practical significance of the average–marginal distinction

The distinction between average and marginal products is of central importance to anyone who must allocate a scarce resource between two or more productive activities. How should the resource be allocated in order to maximize total output? Many people incorrectly think that as long as average product is increasing one should expand production. The following examples make clear the issues posed by this problem, and the general rule required to solve it.

Read through the following scenario carefully, and try to answer the question posed at the end.

> Suppose you own a fishing fleet consisting of a given number of boats, and can send your boats in whatever numbers you wish to either of two ends of an extremely wide lake, east or west. Under your current allocation of boats, the ones fishing at the east end return daily with 1000 kg of fish each, whereas those in the west return daily with 1200 kg each. The fish populations at the two ends of the lake are completely independent, and your current yields can be sustained indefinitely. Should you alter your current allocation of boats?

Most people, especially those who have not had a good course in microeconomics, answer confidently that the current allocation should be altered. Specifically, they say that the fishing fleet owner should send more boats to the west side of the lake. Yet, as the following example illustrates, even a rudimentary understanding of the distinction between the average and marginal products

[5] For the production function shown, that point happens to be the origin, but in general it need not be.

[6] Mathematically, the result that MP intersects AP at the maximum value of AP can be shown by noting that the necessary condition for a maximum of AP is that its first partial derivative with respect to L be zero:

$$\frac{\partial(Q/L)}{\partial L} = \frac{L(\partial Q/\partial L) - Q}{L^2} = 0$$

from which it follows that $\partial Q/\partial L = Q/L$.

Example 7.1

In the fishing fleet scenario just described, suppose the relationship between the number of boats sent to each end and the number of kilograms caught per boat is as summarized in Table 7.3. Suppose further that you have four boats in your fleet, and that two currently fish the east end while the other two fish the west end. (Note that all of the information given is consistent with the facts outlined in the scenario.) Should you move one of your boats from the east end to the west end?

From the entries in Table 7.3, it follows that your total output under the current allocation is 4400 kg of fish per day (1000 kg from each of the two boats at the east end, 1200 kg from each of the two at the west end). Now suppose we do what you intuitively felt is the best thing to do and transfer one boat from the east end to the west end, which means you now have three boats in the west and only one in the east. From the figures in Table 7.3, we see that your total output will now be only 4300 kg per day, or 100 kg per day less than under the current allocation. So no, you should not move an extra boat to the west end. Well, the other alternative is to send one of the west end boats to the east end. Loss of a boat from the west end would reduce the total daily catch at that end by 1100 kg (the difference between the 2400 kg caught by two boats and the 1300 kg that would be caught by one), which is more than the extra 1000 kg you would get by having an extra boat at the east end. The current allocation of two boats to each end is optimal.

Table 7.3 Average product, total product and marginal product (kg/day) for two fishing areas

Number of boats	East end			West end		
	AP	TP	MP	AP	TP	MP
0	0	0		0	0	
			1000			1300
1	1000	1000		1300	1300	
			1000			1100
2	1000	2000		1200	2400	
			1000			900
3	1000	3000		1100	3300	
			1000			700
4	1000	4000		1000	4000	

The average catch per boat is constant at 1000 kg per boat for boats sent to the east end of the lake. The average catch per boat is declining as the number of boats sent to the west end increases.

of a productive resource makes it clear that this response is not justified.

Example 7.1 is an instance of an important class of problem in which managers must decide how to allocate an input across several alternative processes used for producing a given product. *The general rule for allocating an input efficiently in such cases is to allocate the next unit of the input to the production activity where its marginal product is highest.* This form of the rule applies to resources, such as boats, that are not perfectly divisible, and also to cases in which the marginal product of a resource is always higher in one activity than in another (see Example 7.2). For a resource that is perfectly divisible, and for activities for which the marginal product of the resource is not always higher in one than in the others, the rule is to *allocate the resource so that its marginal product is the same in every activity.*

Many people, however, 'solve' these kinds of problem by allocating resources to the activity with the highest *average* product, or by trying to equalize *average* products across activities. The

Example 7.2

This is the same as the fishing fleet in Example 7.1, except that now the marginal product of each boat sent to the west end of the lake is equal to 1200 kg/day.

The difference between this example and Example 7.1 is that this time there is no drop-off in the rate at which fish are caught as more boats are sent to the west end of the lake. So this time the average product of any boat sent to the west end is identical to its marginal product. And since the marginal product is always higher for boats sent to the west end, the optimal allocation is to send all four boats to that end. If all four boats are sent to the west end of the lake, the total catch will be 4800 kg, an increase of 400 kg compared to the original allocation of two boats to each side.

reason why this particular wrong answer has appeal is that people often focus on only part of the relevant production process. By sending only two boats to the west end, the average catch at that end is 200 kg per day greater than the average catch per boat at the east end. But note that, if you send a third boat to the west end, that boat's contribution to the total amount of fish caught at the west end will be only 900 kg per day (the difference between the 3300 kg caught by three boats and the 2400 kg caught by two). What people often tend to overlook is that the third boat at the west end catches some of the fish that would otherwise have been caught by the first two.

As the figures in Table 7.3 illustrate, the opportunity cost of sending a third boat to the west end is the 1000 kg of fish that will no longer be caught at the east end. But since that third boat will add only 900 kg to the daily catch at the west end, the best that can be done is to keep sending two boats to each end of the lake. The fact that either of the two boats currently fishing at the east end could catch 100 kg per day more by moving to the west end is no cause for concern to a fishing fleet owner who understands the distinction between average and marginal products.

Exercise 7.5

Explain why we cannot necessarily conclude that you should bowl more medium-fast balls in the following scenario.

You are a cricket bowler who bowls two different kinds of ball: medium-fast balls and spin balls. Your team statistician tells you that, at the current rate at which you employ these different types of ball, batsmen hit 0.275 runs against each of your medium-fast balls, but only 0.200 against each spin ball. Should you alter your current mix of balls bowled?

Example 7.1 produced what economists call an *interior solution* – one in which each of the production activities is actually employed. But not all problems of this sort have interior solutions. As the next example will make clear, one activity sometimes dominates the other.

Example 7.3

Suppose that from the last seconds you devoted to Problem 1 on your economics exam you earned 4 extra marks, while from the last seconds devoted to Problem 2 you earned 6 extra marks. The total number of marks you earned on these two questions was 20 and 12, respectively, and the total time you spent on each was the same. The total number of marks possible on each problem was 40. How – if at all – should you have reallocated your time between problems?

The rule for efficient allocation of time spent on exams is the same as the rule for efficient allocation of any resource: the marginal product of the resource should be the same in each activity. From the information given, the marginal product of your time spent on Problem 2 was higher than the marginal product of your time spent on Problem 1. Even though the average product of your time spent on Problem 1 was higher than on Problem 2, you would have scored more marks if you had spent a few seconds less on Problem 1 and a few seconds more on Problem 2.

Cases such as the one illustrated in Example 7.2 are by no means unusual. But by far the more common, and more interesting, production decisions are the ones that involve interior solutions such as the one we saw in Example 7.1, where some positive quantity of the productive input must be allocated to each activity.

'The next step'

Application: the average–marginal distinction

Suppose that when your tennis opponent comes to the net, your best response is either to lob (hit the ball over his head) or to pass (hit the ball out of reach on either side). Each type of shot is more effective if it catches your opponent by surprise. In 2014 Roger Federer hired the services of Stefan Edberg to get his tennis career back on track. Federer, arguably one of the best players of all time, basically played his shots from the baseline and seldom came to the net. Edberg, on the other hand, played a serve-and-volley game. Only time will tell whether getting Edberg on his coaching team and playing more aggressively as a result is a wise move on the part of Federer.

The following example is similar to the scenario faced by Federer and Edberg. Suppose someone who lobs all the time will win a given point only 10 per cent of the time with a lob, but that someone who virtually never lobs will win the point on 90 per cent of the rare occasions when he does so. Similarly, suppose someone who tries passing shots all the time wins any given point only 30 per cent of the time with a passing shot, but someone who virtually never tries to pass wins 40 per cent of the time when he does try. Suppose, finally, that the rate at which each type of shot becomes less effective with use declines linearly with the proportion of times a player uses it. What is the best proportion of lobs and passing shots to use when your opponent comes to the net?[7]

The pay-offs from the two types of shot are summarized graphically in Fig. 7.7. Here, the 'production' problem is to produce the greatest possible percentage of winning shots when your opponent comes to the net. $F(L)$ tells you the percentage of points you will win with a lob as a function of the proportion of times you lob (L). $F(L)$ is thus, in effect, the average product of L. $G(L)$ tells you the percentage of points you will win with a passing shot, again as a function of the proportion of times you lob. The negative slope of $F(L)$ reflects the fact that lobs become less effective the more you use them. Similarly, the positive slope of $G(L)$ says that passing shots become more effective the more you lob. Your problem is to choose L^*, the best proportion of times to lob (and, for that matter, also the best proportion of times to play a passing shot).

To find the optimal value of L, we must first discover how the percentage of total points won, denoted by P, varies with L. For any value of L, P is simply a weighted average of the percentages won with each type of shot. The weight used for each type of shot is simply the proportion of times it is used. Noting that $(1 - L)$ is the proportion of passing shots when L is the proportion of lobs, we have

$$P = LF(L) + (1 - L)G(L) \qquad (7.4)$$

The expression $LF(L)$ is the percentage of total points won on lobs. $(1 - L)G(L)$, similarly, is the percentage of total points won on passing shots. From Fig. 7.7 we see that the algebraic formulae for $F(L)$ and $G(L)$ are given by $F(L) = 90 - 80L$ and $G(L) = 30 + 10L$. Substituting these relationships into Eq. 7.4 gives

$$P = 30 + 70L - 90L^2 \qquad (7.5)$$

which is plotted in Fig. 7.8. The value of L that maximizes P turns out to be $L^* = 0.389$, and the corresponding value of P is 43.61 per cent.[8]

Note in Fig. 7.9 that, at the optimal value of L, the likelihood of winning with a lob is

[7] This example was suggested by Harvard psychologists Richard Herrnstein and James Mazur, in 'Making up our minds: A new model of economic behavior', *The Sciences*, 1987, November/December, pp. 40–47.

[8] The calculus-trained student can find L^* without having to plot P as a function of L simply by solving

$$\frac{dp}{dL} = 70 - 180L = 0$$

which yields $L^* = \frac{7}{18} = 0.389$, which, upon substitution into Eq. 7.5, yields $P = 43.61$.

almost twice as high (58.9 per cent) as that of winning with a passing shot (33.9 per cent). Many people seem to find this state of affairs extremely uncomfortable – so much so that they refuse to have anything to do with it. In extensive experimental studies, Harvard psychologists Richard Herrnstein and James Mazur found that people tend to divide their shots not to maximize their overall chances of winning, but to equate the *average product* of each type. Note in Fig. 7.10 that this occurs when $L = 2/3$, at which point the percentage of points won with either shot is 36.7. At this value of L, however, the *marginal product* of a passing shot will be much higher than for a lob, because it will strongly increase the effectiveness of all your *other* lobs. (Of course, an extra passing shot will also reduce the effectiveness of your other passing shots, but by a much smaller margin.)

The situation here is analogous to the allocation example involving the fishing boats mentioned earlier in the chapter. There is no more reason to want the average return to each

Figure 7.7 Effectiveness versus use: lobs and passing shots

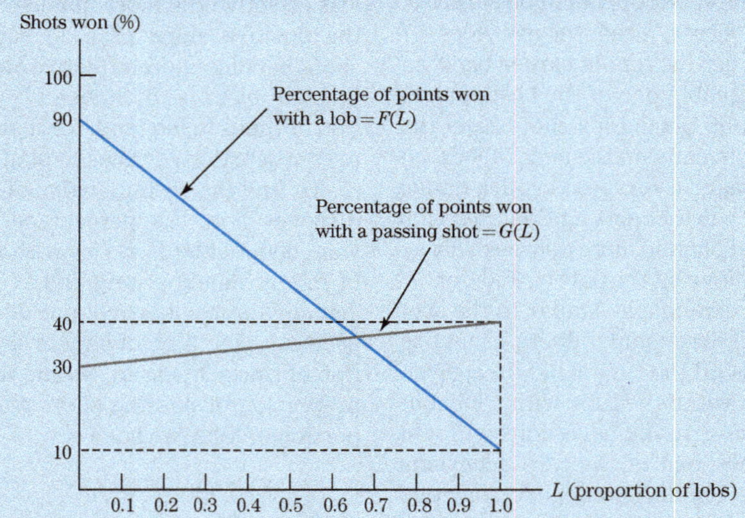

Figure 7.8 The optimal proportion of lobs

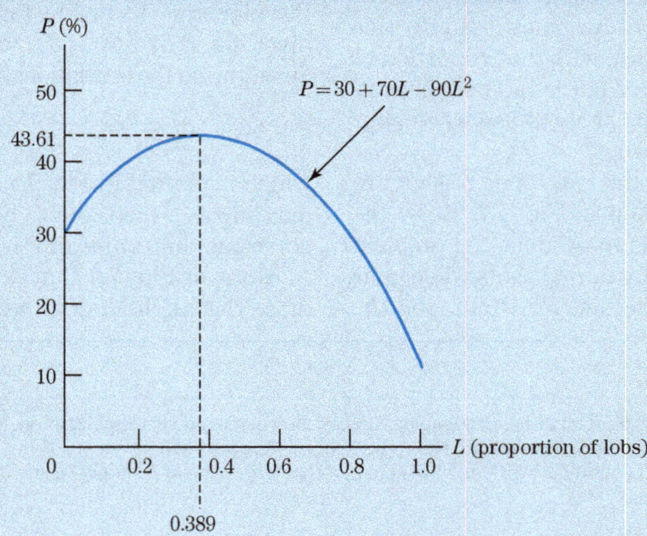

tennis shot to be the same than there is to want the average product on each end of the lake to be the same. And yet the tendency to equate average rather than marginal products is a very common pitfall, one that even experienced maximizers have to be on their guard against. (Whether Federer and Edberg will make all these technical calculations to alter Federer's style of play is, however, doubtful.) Let us consider one final example.

Figure 7.9 At the optimizing point, the likelihood of winning with a lob is much greater than of winning with a passing shot

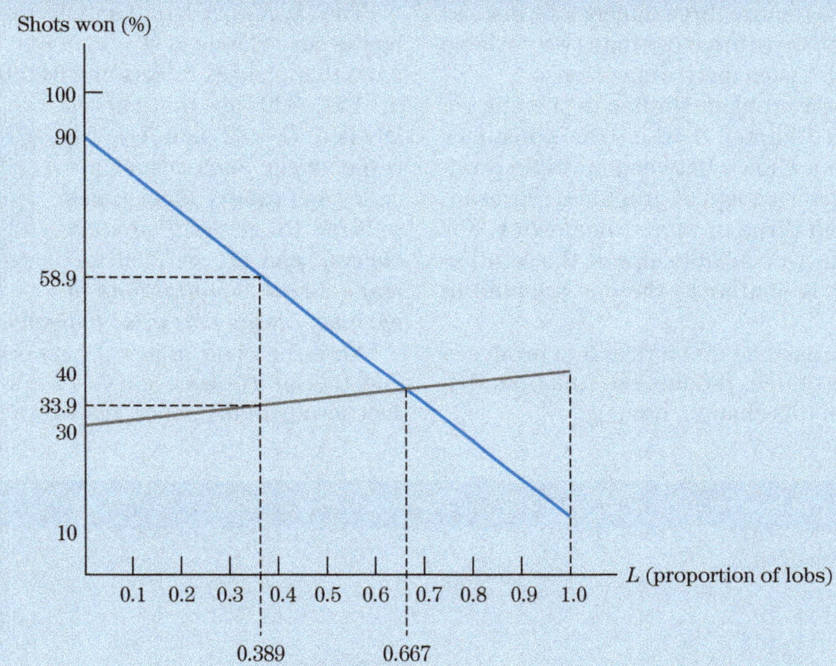

Example 7.4

True or false? The best rugby coach is the one who always chooses the player who will gain the most metres if he receives the ball.

If you answered 'true', you have not been paying attention. The best coach is the one who selects the best mix of plays, just as the best tennis player is the one who selects the best mix of shots. In the Super Rugby series, passing plays gain almost twice as many metres, on average, as individual running plays. Why don't coaches attack with their backline more frequently? Because the passing game loses effectiveness if it is used too frequently, and increases the risk of making handling errors. From the big difference in average gains for the two types of play, it is apparent that most coaches are aware that running the ball with the backline is necessary to gain more metres. But many ostensibly expert commentators seem completely oblivious to this point. Trailing by 4 points with 20 seconds to go with a scrum halfway in the opponents' half, a team is more likely to score a try if it passes the ball. However, a team will win more games over the long run if it nonetheless uses a running play attitude in this situation every once in a while. The Brumbies over the years are an excellent example of the effectiveness of playing a passing (running) game. If a team decides to run with the ball (instead of driving with the forwards), but fail to score or make a handling error, both the fans in the stands and the announcers in the booth may feel that it was an idiotic decision.

Production in the long run

The examples discussed thus far have involved production in the short run, where at least one productive input cannot be varied. In the long run, by contrast, all factors of production are by definition variable. In the short run, with K held fixed in the production function $Q = F(\bar{K}, L)$, we were able to describe the production function in a simple two-dimensional diagram. With both K and L variable, however, we now require three dimensions instead of two. And when there are more than two variable inputs, we require even more dimensions.

This creates a problem similar to the one we encountered in Chapter 3 when the consumer was faced with a choice between multiple products: we are not very adept at graphical representations involving three or more dimensions. For production with two variable inputs, the solution to this problem is similar to the one adopted in Chapter 3.

To illustrate, assume that a firm that produces tablets has the same production function discussed earlier in this chapter, namely:

$$Q = F(K, L) = 2KL \quad (7.6)$$

and suppose we want to describe all possible combinations of K and L that give rise to a particular level of output – say, $Q = 16$ tablets. To do this, we solve $Q = 2KL = 16$ for K in terms of L, which yields

$$K = \frac{8}{L} \quad (7.7)$$

The (L, K) pairs that satisfy Eq. 7.7 are shown by the curve labelled $Q = 16$ in Fig. 7.10. The (L, K) pairs that yield 32 tablets and 64 tablets are shown in Fig. 7.10 as the curves labelled $Q = 32$ and $Q = 64$, respectively. Such curves are called **isoquants** (sometimes referred to as *equal product curves*), and are defined formally as *all combinations of variable inputs that yield a given level of output.*[9]

Isoquant The set of all variable input combinations that yield a given level of output.

Note the clear analogy between the isoquant and the indifference curve of consumer theory. Just as an indifference map provides a concise

Figure 7.10 Part of an isoquant map for the production function $Q = 2KL$

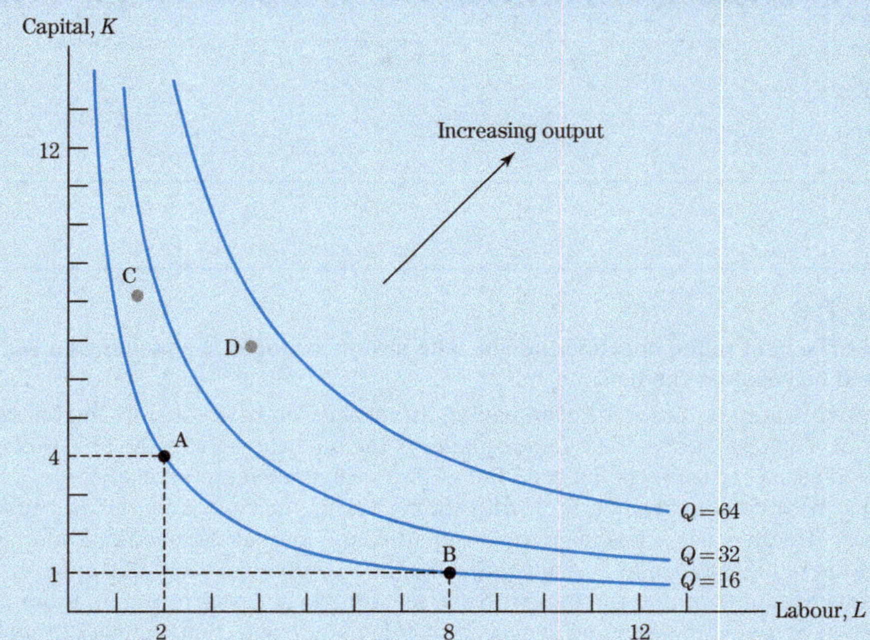

An isoquant is the set of all (L, K) pairs that yield a given level of output. For example, each (L, K) pair on the curve labelled $Q = 32$ yields 32 tablets. The isoquant map describes the properties of a production process in much the same way as an indifference map describes a consumer's preferences.

[9] 'Iso' comes from the Greek word for 'same', which also appears, for example, in the meteorological term 'isobars', meaning lines of equal barometric pressure.

representation of a consumer's preferences, an *isoquant map* provides a concise representation of a production process.

On an indifference map, movements to the northeast correspond to increasing levels of satisfaction. Similar movements on an isoquant map correspond to increasing levels of output. A point on an indifference curve is preferred to any point that lies below that indifference curve, and less preferred than any point that lies above it. Likewise, any input bundle on an isoquant yields more output than any input bundle that lies below that isoquant, and less output than any input bundle that lies above it. Thus bundle C in Fig. 7.10 yields more output than bundle A but less output than bundle D.

The only substantive respect in which the analogy between isoquant maps and indifference maps is incomplete is the significance of the labels attached to the two types of curve. From Chapter 3 recall that the actual numbers assigned to each indifference curve were used to indicate only the relative rankings of the bundles on different indifference curves. The number we assign to an isoquant, by contrast, corresponds to the actual level of output we get from input bundles along that isoquant. With indifference maps we are free to relabel the indifference curves in any way that preserves the original ranking of bundles. But with isoquant maps the labels are determined uniquely by the production function. Make sure you do not get confused between indifference curves and isoquants. Although the curves appear to look the same, with indifference curves one has two consumer goods on the axes, but with isoquants it is two inputs. Make sure if you get questions in tests or exams that you never have products on the axes if you work with production. This is something students frequently get wrong.

'The next step'

Some examples of production functions

In this section we shall examine two of the many different production functions that are commonly used in economic analysis.

The Cobb–Douglas production function

Perhaps the most widely used production function of all is the Cobb–Douglas, which in the two-input case takes the form

$$Q = mK^{\alpha}L^{\beta} \tag{7.8}$$

where α and β are numbers between 0 and 1, and m can be any positive number.

To generate an equation for the Q_0 isoquant, we fix Q at Q_0 and then solve for K in terms of L. In the Cobb–Douglas case, this yields

$$K = \left(\frac{m}{Q_0}\right)^{-1/\alpha}(L)^{-\beta/\alpha} \tag{7.9}$$

For a particular Cobb–Douglas function $Q = K^{1/2}L^{1/2}$, the Q_0 isoquant will be

$$K = \frac{Q_0^2}{L} \tag{7.10}$$

A portion of the isoquant map for this particular Cobb–Douglas production function is shown in Fig. 7.11.

The number assigned to each particular isoquant in Fig. 7.11 is exactly the level of output to which it corresponds. For example, when we have 2 units of K and 2 units of L, we get $Q = \sqrt{2}\sqrt{2} = 2$ units of output. Recall from Chapter 3 that the numbers we used to label the indifference curves on an indifference map conveyed information only about *relative* levels of satisfaction. All that was required of our indexing scheme in that context was that the *order* of the numbers we assigned to the indifference curves reflect the proper ranking of the corresponding satisfaction levels. With isoquants,

Figure 7.11 Isoquant map for the Cobb–Douglas production function $Q = K^{1/2}L^{1/2}$

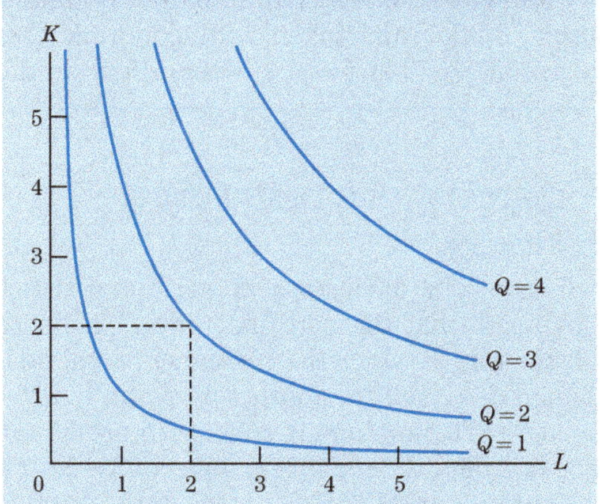

the situation is altogether different. We have, in effect, no choice about what labels to assign to them.

Calculus-trained students can easily verify the following expressions for the marginal products of labour and capital in the Cobb–Douglas case:

$$MP_K = \frac{\partial Q}{\partial K} = \alpha m K^{\alpha-1} L^{\beta} \quad (7.11)$$

and

$$MP_L = \frac{\partial Q}{\partial L} = \beta m K^{\alpha} L^{\beta-1} \quad (7.12)$$

The Leontief, or fixed-proportions, production function

The simplest among all production functions that are widely used is the *Leontief*, named for the Nobel laureate Wassily Leontief, who devised it. For the two-input case, it is given by

$$Q = \min(aK, bL) \quad (7.13)$$

If you are unfamiliar with this curious functional form, its interpretation is simply that Q is equal to either aK or bL, whichever is smaller. Suppose, for example, that $a = 2$, $b = 3$, $K = 4$ and $L = 3$. Then $Q = \min(2 \times 4, 3 \times 3) = \min(8, 9) = 8$. The isoquant map for $Q = \min(2K, 3L)$ is shown in Fig. 7.12.

To see why the Leontief is also called the fixed-proportions production function, note first in Fig. 7.12 that, if we start with 3 units of K and 2 units of L, we get 6 units of output. If we then add more L – so that we have, say, 3 units of L instead of 2 – we still get only $Q = \min(2 \times 3, 3 \times 3) = \min(6, 9) = 6$ units of output. By the same token, adding more K when we are at $K = 3$ and $L = 2$ will not lead to any additional output. In the Leontief case, K and L are used most effectively when $aK = bL$ – in the example at hand, when $2K = 3L$. In Fig. 7.12, the locus of points for which $2K = 3L$ is shown as the linear function (straight line) $K = \left(\frac{3}{2}\right)L$. It is along this ray that the cusps of all the right-angled isoquants of this Leontief production function will lie.

Figure 7.12 Isoquant map for the Leontief production function $Q = \min(2K, 3L)$

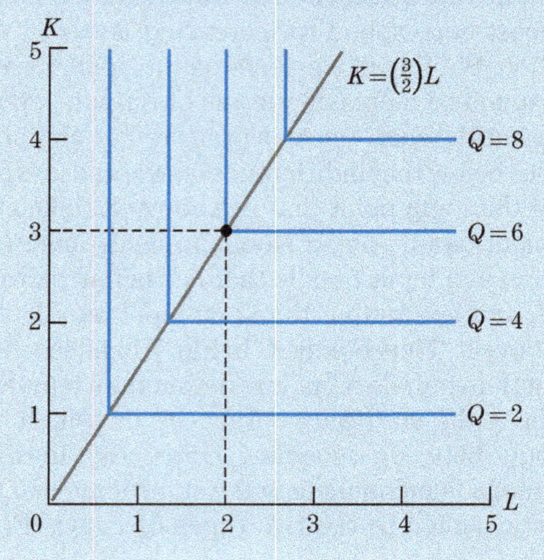

Recall from Chapter 3 that, in the case of perfect complements, the indifference curves had the same right-angled shape as the isoquants for the Leontief production function. This meant that the MRS was infinite on the vertical arm of the indifference curve, zero on the horizontal arm and undefined at the cusp. For exactly parallel reasons, the MRTS (see the section below, where the MRTS is explained) in the Leontief case will be infinite on the vertical arm of the isoquant, zero on the horizontal and undefined at the cusp.

The marginal rate of technical substitution

Recall from our discussion of consumer theory in Chapter 3 that the marginal rate of substitution is the rate at which the consumer is willing to exchange one good for another along an indifference curve. The analogous concept in production theory is called the **marginal rate of technical substitution**, or **MRTS**. It is the rate at which one input can be exchanged for another without altering total output. In Fig. 7.13, for example, the MRTS at A is defined as the absolute value of the slope of the isoquant at A, $|\Delta K/\Delta L|$.

Marginal rate of technical substitution (MRTS) The rate at which one input can be exchanged for another without altering the total level of output.

In consumer theory, we assumed that the marginal rate of substitution diminishes with downward movements along an indifference curve. For most production

Figure 7.13 The marginal rate of technical substitution

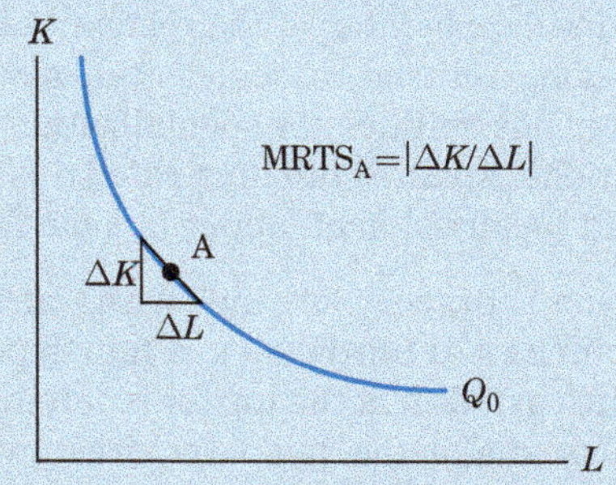

The MRTS is the rate at which one input can be exchanged for another without altering total output. The MRTS at any point is the absolute value of the slope of the isoquant that passes through that point. If ΔK units of capital are removed at point A, and ΔL units of L are added, output will remain the same at Q_0 units of cell phones.

functions the MRTS displays a similar property. Holding output constant, the less we have of one input, the more we must add of the other input to compensate for a one-unit reduction in the first input.

A simple but important relationship exists between the MRTS at any point and the marginal products of the respective inputs at that point. In a small neighbourhood of point A in Fig. 7.13, suppose we reduce K by ΔK and augment L by an amount ΔL just sufficient to maintain the original level of output. If MP_K denotes the marginal product of capital at A, then the reduction in output caused by the loss of ΔK is equal to $MP_K \cdot \Delta K$. Using MP_L to denote the marginal product of L at A, it follows similarly that the gain in output resulting from the extra L is equal to $MP_L \cdot \Delta L$. Finally, since the reduction in output of cell phones from having less K is exactly offset by the gain in output of cell phones from having more L, it follows that

$$MP_K \cdot \Delta K = MP_L \cdot \Delta L \tag{7.14}$$

Dividing by $MP_K \cdot \Delta L$, we get

$$\frac{MP_L}{MP_K} = \frac{\Delta K}{\Delta L} \tag{7.15}$$

which says that the MRTS at A is simply the ratio of the marginal product of L to the marginal product of K. This relationship will have an important application in the next chapter, where we shall take up the question of how to produce a given level of output at the lowest possible cost.

Exercise 7.6

Given a firm's current level of capital and labour inputs, the marginal product of labour for its production process is equal to 3 units of output. If the marginal rate of technical substitution between K and L is 9, what is the marginal product of capital?

In consumer theory, the shape of the indifference curve tells us how the consumer is willing to substitute one good for another. In production theory, an essentially similar story is told by the shape of the isoquant. Figure 7.14 illustrates the extreme cases of inputs that are perfect substitutes (a) and perfect complements (b). Figure 7.14(a) describes a production process in which cars and petrol are combined to produce trips.

Figure 7.14 Isoquant maps for (a) perfect substitutes and (b) perfect complements

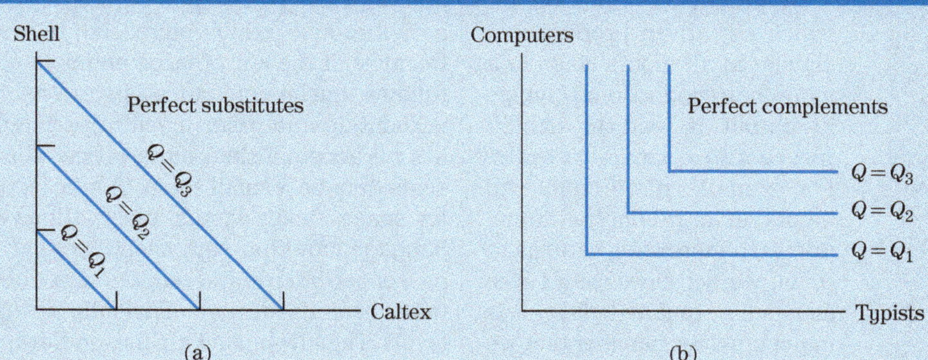

In panel (a), we get the same number of trips from a given total quantity of petrol, no matter how we mix the two brands. Shell and Caltex are perfect substitutes in the production of car journeys. In panel (b), computers and typists are perfect complements in the process of typing letters.

The input of petrol comes in two brands, Shell and Caltex, which are perfect substitutes for one another. We can substitute 1 litre of Shell petrol for 1 litre of Caltex petrol and still produce the same number of trips as before. The MRTS between Shell and Caltex remains constant at 1 as we move downwards along any isoquant. One reason for this is that the price of petrol is regulated in South Africa, so the price of the two brands of petrol will be the same. Therefore we will have no preference for one brand relative to the other.

Figure 7.14(b) describes a production process for typing letters using the two inputs of computers and typists. In this process, the two inputs are perfect complements. Here, inputs are most effectively combined in fixed proportions. Having more than one computer per typist doesn't augment production nor does having more than one typist per computer.

Returns to scale

A question of central importance for the organization of industry is whether production takes place most efficiently at large scale rather than small scale (where 'large' and 'small' are defined relative to the scale of the relevant market). This question is important because the answer dictates whether an industry will end up being served by many small firms or only a few large ones.

The technical property of the production function used to describe the relationship between scale and efficiency is called *returns to scale*. The term tells us what happens to output when all inputs are increased by exactly the same proportion. Because returns to scale refer to a situation in which all inputs are variable, *the concept of returns to scale is an inherently long-run concept.*

Increasing returns to scale The property of a production process whereby a proportional increase in every input yields a more than proportional increase in output (percentage increase in output is larger than the percentage increase in inputs).

A production function for which any given proportional change in all inputs leads to a more than proportional change in output is said to exhibit **increasing returns to scale**. For example, if we double all inputs in a production function with increasing returns to scale, we get more than twice as much output as before. It is important to remember that we work with percentage changes in inputs and outputs and not changes in absolute quantities. As we shall see in Chapters 10 and 11, such production functions generally give rise to conditions in which a small number of firms supply most of the relevant market.

Increasing returns to scale often result from the greater possibilities for specialization in large organizations. Adam Smith illustrated this point by describing the division of labour in a pin factory:[10]

> One man draws out the wire, another straightens it, a third cuts it, a fourth points it, a fifth grinds it at the top for receiving the head; to make the head requires two or three distinct operations. ... I have seen a small manufactory ... of this kind where only ten men were employed ... [who] could, when they exerted themselves, make among them about twelve pounds of pins in a day. There are in a pound upwards of four thousand pins of middling size. Those ten persons, therefore, could make among them upwards of forty-eight thousand pins in a day. Each person, therefore, making a tenth part of forty-eight thousand pins might be considered as making four thousand eight hundred pins in a day. But if they had all wrought separately and independently ... they could not each of them have made twenty, perhaps not one pin in a day.

The airline industry is often cited as one with increasing returns to scale. Industry professionals have long stressed that having a large number of flights helps an airline fill each flight by feeding passengers from its incoming flights to its outgoing flights. Perhaps some of you have experienced a flight from OR Tambo International Airport to an international destination like London being delayed because the airline waited for its domestic flight from Cape Town to arrive so it could take a lot of those passengers on board. Local airport activities also exhibit increasing returns to scale. Because of the law of large numbers, moreover, it follows that maintenance operations, flight crew scheduling and other inventory-related activities are all accomplished more efficiently on a large scale than on a small scale. Similarly, ticket-counter space, ticket agents, reservations equipment, baggage-handling equipment, ground crews and passenger-boarding facilities are all resources that are utilized more efficiently at high activity levels. The low-budget airlines in Europe are good examples of greater efficiency when resources are used more optimally. There, your flight is

[10] Adam Smith, *The wealth of nations*, New York: Everyman's Library, 1910 (1776), Book 1, p. 5.

Figure 7.15 Returns to scale illustrated with isoquants

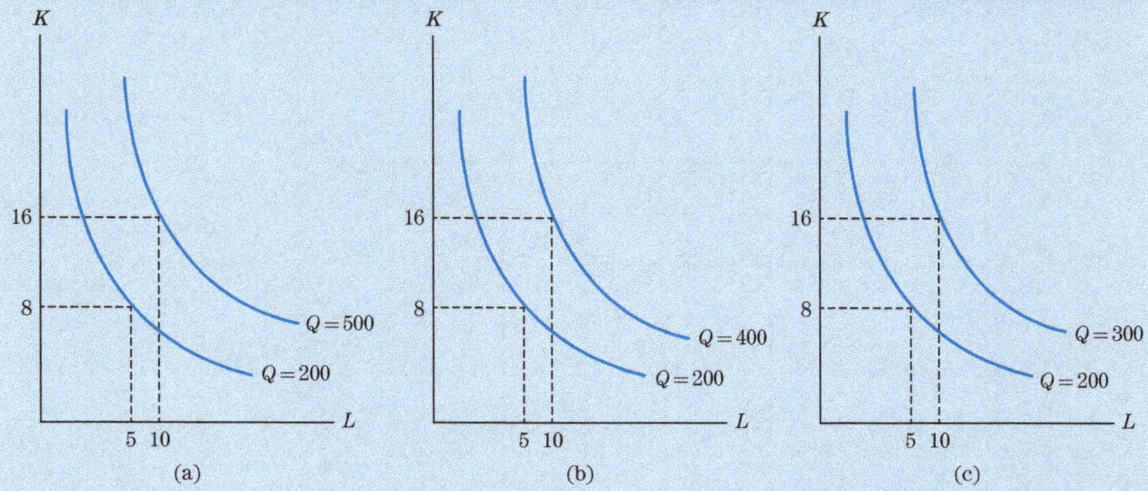

If inputs increase by 100 per cent and outputs by more than 100 per cent, we have increasing returns to scale (a). If inputs increase by 100 per cent and outputs also by 100 per cent, we have constant returns to scale (b). If inputs increase by 100 per cent and outputs by less than 100 per cent, we have decreasing returns to scale (c).

frequently delayed because the incoming plane is used for the outgoing flight! Increasing returns to scale constitute the underlying explanation for why the industry has been moving towards ever-larger airlines in the last decade or two and why the Airbus A380 is in such high demand.

This can be illustrated with isoquants too. Suppose you use 5 units of labour and 8 units of capital to produce 200 Kindles per day, as illustrated in Fig. 7.15(a). Suppose we double both our inputs, but from the graph it is clear that outputs increased by 150 per cent. Outputs clearly increased by a higher percentage than inputs, demonstrating increasing returns to scale.

Constant returns to scale The property of a production process whereby a proportional increase in every input yields an equal proportional increase in output (percentage increase in output is the same as the percentage increase in inputs).

A production function for which a proportional change in all inputs causes output to change by the same proportion is said to exhibit **constant returns to scale**. In such cases, doubling all inputs results in a doubling of output. In industries in which production takes place under constant returns to scale, large size is neither an advantage nor a disadvantage.

This situation is illustrated in Fig. 7.15(b). When we use 8 units of capital and 5 units of labour we once again produce 200 Kindles per day. When we double both our inputs our outputs also doubled, to 400 Kindles per day. If both inputs and outputs increase by the same percentage, we call it constant returns to scale.

Decreasing returns to scale The property of a production process whereby a proportional increase in every input yields a less than proportional increase in output (percentage increase in output is smaller than the percentage increase in inputs).

Finally, a production function for which a proportional change in all inputs causes a less than proportional change in output is said to exhibit **decreasing returns to scale**. Here, large size is a handicap, and we do not expect to see large firms in an industry in which production takes place with decreasing returns to scale. As we shall see in Chapter 9, the constant and decreasing returns cases often enable many sellers to co-exist within the same narrowly defined markets.

Once again it can be illustrated with isoquants. In Fig. 7.15(c) we once again produce 200 Kindles per day when we use 5 units of labour and 8 units of capital. However, when we double both our inputs, our output only increases by 50 per cent, to 300 Kindles per day. This figure illustrates decreasing returns to scale.

A production function need not exhibit the same degree of returns to scale over the entire range of output. On the contrary, there may be increasing returns to scale at low levels of output, followed by constant returns to scale at intermediate levels

Figure 7.16 Returns to scale shown on the isoquant map

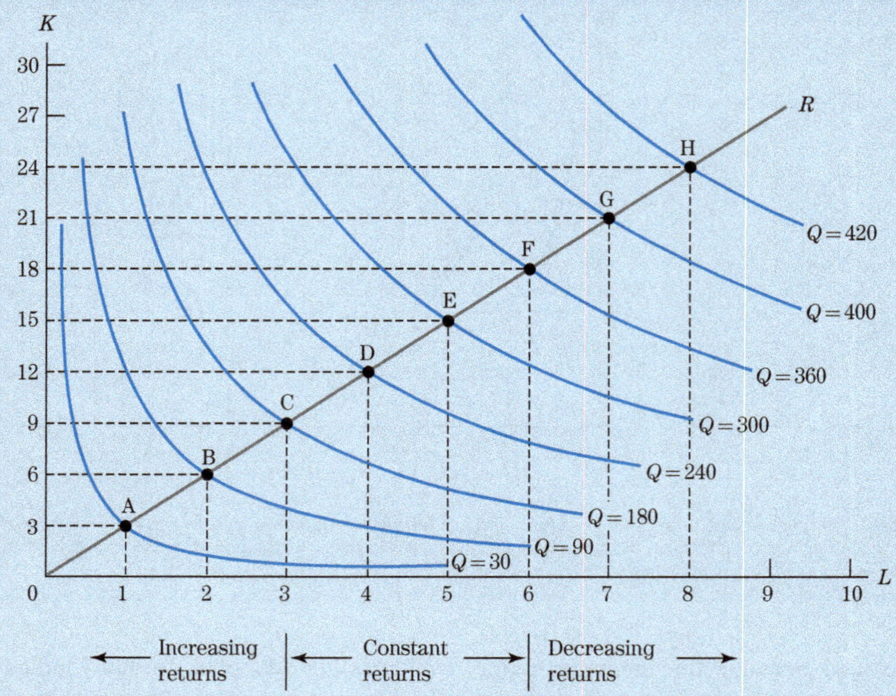

In the region from A to C, this production function has increasing returns to scale: proportional increases in input yield more than proportional increases in output. In the region from C to F, there are constant returns to scale: inputs and output grow by the same percentage in this region. In the region northeast of F, there are decreasing returns to scale: proportional increases in both inputs yield less than proportional increases in output.

of output, followed finally by decreasing returns to scale at high levels of output. This will be explained in the next section with the aid of Fig. 7.16.

Before we move on to that, let us briefly revise four different, but closely related, concepts. *Diminishing returns* is a short-run phenomenon and refers to the decrease in marginal product of the variable input while the other input(s) remain constant. *Returns to scale* refers to the long run and measures what happens with output if all inputs are increased by x per cent. If output increases by less than x per cent, we have decreasing returns to scale, if it also increases by x per cent it is constant returns to scale, and if it increases by more than x per cent we have increasing returns to scale. *Economies of scale* refer to the fact that in the long run a firm can decrease its average cost per product by increasing its scale of production. *Economies of scope* are related to economies of scale. The difference is that economies of scope refer to the lowering of a firm's average costs as a result of producing two or more products (and not merely one, as is the case with economies of scale). Make sure you are certain about the above-mentioned differences because students sometimes get confused with these terms.

'The next step'

A mathematical definition of returns to scale

Mathematically, to increase all inputs in the same proportion means simply to multiply all inputs by the same number $c > 1$. By way of illustration, consider the production function we discussed earlier in this chapter, $Q = F(K, L) = 2KL$. For this particular function, when we multiply each input by c we get

$$\begin{aligned} F(cK,cL) &= 2(cK)(cL) \\ &= c^2 2KL \\ &= c^2 F(K,L) \end{aligned} \tag{7.16}$$

The result of multiplying each input by c in this production function is thus to multiply the original output level by c^2. Output thus grows more than in proportion to input growth in this case (with proportional growth, we would have had output equal to $cF(K, L)$), so this production function has increasing returns to scale. Thus, for example, if $c = 2$ (a doubling of each input), we get $F(2K, 2L) = 2(2K)(2L) = 4(2KL)$, a quadrupling of output.

Drawing on these observations, the definitions of our three cases may be summarized as follows:

Increasing returns:

$$F(cK, cL) > cF(K, L) \tag{7.17}$$

Constant returns:

$$F(cK, cL) = cF(K, L) \tag{7.18}$$

and

Decreasing returns:

$$F(cK, cL) < cF(K, L) \tag{7.19}$$

Try the following two exercises to ensure you cement your ability to apply these definitions to specific examples.

Exercise 7.7

Does the production function $Q = \sqrt{K}\sqrt{L}$ have increasing, constant *or* decreasing returns to scale?

Exercise 7.8

Does the production function $Q = K^{1/3}L^{1/3}$ have increasing, constant or decreasing returns to scale?

In the case of the Cobb–Douglas production function, $Q = mK^{\alpha}L^{\beta}$, Eqs 7.17–7.19 imply a simple relationship between the parameters α and β and the degree of returns to scale. Specifically, if $\alpha + \beta > 1$, there are increasing returns to scale; $\alpha + \beta = 1$ means constant returns to scale; and $\alpha + \beta < 1$ means decreasing returns to scale. To illustrate for the constant-returns case, suppose $Q = F(K, L) = mK^{\alpha}L^{\beta}$, with $\alpha + \beta = 1$. Then we have

$$F(cK, cL) = m(cK)^{\alpha}(cL)^{\beta} \tag{7.20}$$

which reduces to

$$\begin{aligned} c^{(\alpha+\beta)}mK^{\alpha}L^{\beta} &= cmK^{\alpha}L^{\beta} \\ &= cF(K, L) \end{aligned} \tag{7.21}$$

which, according to Eq. 7.18, is the defining characteristic of constant returns to scale.

Showing returns to scale on the isoquant map

A simple relationship exists between a production function's returns to scale and the spacing of its isoquants.[11] Consider the isoquant map in Fig. 7.16. As we move outward into the isoquant map along the ray labelled R, each input grows by exactly the same proportion. The particular production function whose isoquant map is shown in the diagram exhibits increasing returns to scale in the region from A to C. Note, for example, that when we move from A to B, both inputs double while output goes up by 300 per cent; likewise, when we move from B to C, both inputs grow by 50 per cent while output grows by 100 per cent. In the region from C to F, this same production function exhibits constant returns to scale. Note, for example, that when we move from D to E, both inputs grow by 25 per cent and output also grows by 25 per cent. Also as we move from E to F, inputs as well as outputs increase by 20 per cent. Finally, the production function whose isoquant map is shown in Fig. 7.16 exhibits decreasing returns to scale in the region to the northeast of F. Thus, when we move from F to G, both inputs increase by 16.7 per cent whereas output grows by only 11.1 per cent and, as we move from G to H, both inputs increase by 14.2 per cent but output by only 5 per cent.

[11] The discussion in this section applies to *homothetic* production functions, an important class of production functions defined by the property that the slopes of all isoquants are constant at points along any ray.

The distinction between diminishing returns and decreasing returns to scale

It is important to bear in mind that decreasing returns to scale have nothing whatsoever to do with the law of diminishing returns. Decreasing returns to scale refer to what happens when *all* inputs are varied by a given proportion. The law of diminishing returns, by contrast, refers to the case in which one input varies while all others are held fixed. As an empirical generalization, it applies with equal force to production functions having increasing, constant or decreasing returns to scale. The law of diminishing returns is a short-run concept when only one input is variable, while returns to scale is a long-run concept when all outputs are variable.

The logical puzzle of decreasing returns to scale

If the production function $Q = F(K, L)$ is a complete description of the corresponding production process, it is difficult to see how any production function could ever exhibit decreasing returns to scale in practice. The difficulty is that we ought to be able to duplicate the process used to produce any given level of output, and thereby achieve constant returns to scale. To illustrate, suppose first that $Q_0 = F(K_0, L_0)$. If we now want to produce $2Q_0$ units of output, we can always do so by repeating what we did the first time – namely, combining K_0 and L_0 to get Q_0 and adding that to the Q_0 we already have. Similarly, we can get $3Q_0$ by carrying out $F(K_0, L_0)$ three times in succession. Simply by carrying out the process again and again, we can get output to grow in the same proportion as inputs, which means constant returns to scale. And for reasons similar to those discussed above in relation to the airline industry, it will often be possible to do even better than that.

In cases in which it is not possible to at least double our output by doubling both K and L, we seem forced to conclude that there must be some important input besides K and L that we are failing to increase at the same time. This input is variously referred to as 'organization' or 'communication', the idea being that when a firm gets past a certain size, it somehow starts to become out of control. Others claim that it is the shortage of managerial or entrepreneurial resources that creates bottlenecks in production. If there is indeed some unmeasured input that is being held fixed as we expand K and L, then we are still in the short run, by definition. And there is no reason to expect to be able to double our output by doubling only *some* of our inputs.

Economic naturalist 7.2

Why do more and more businesses use pre-fabricated units for housing and industrial premises?

Kwikspace, South Africa's largest manufacturer of pre-fabricated units, was established more than 40 years ago. Over time its business has grown substantially. Why this change over time?

Kwikspace provides mobiles, rentals, offices, classrooms, remote camps and clinics all over Africa. Apart from pre-fabricated units it also customizes containers to individual client's needs; the completed units are simply placed on a cement foundation. By making standardized units the company reaps economies of scale and can produce them relatively cheaply. The other advantage is that the units can be built in a much shorter time span than conventional units. For example, Kwikspace claims it can deliver a whole school in only 24 days. Between November 2013 and January 2014, the company created 55 rental units for labourers at the Tumela Mine in Thabazimbi. According to Kwikspace's CEO, Shaun McCormack, its ability to deliver quickly in remote areas is one of the company's biggest advantages in comparison to traditional building methods. As a result, Kwikspace is also involved in a project for Mota-Engil, providing two pre-fabricated camps for the 100 workers employed in rebuilding the Great East Road (T4) from Luangwa Bridge to Nyomba. Another advantage of these units is that they can be removed after project completion.

Businesses thus favour pre-fabricated units for two reasons: much greater economies of scale are possible in their construction, making them cheaper; and they can be delivered and erected within a very short space of time.

Summary

- Production is any activity that creates current or future utility. A production function summarizes the relationship between inputs and outputs. The short run is defined as that period during which at least some inputs are fixed. In the two-input case, it is the period during which one input is fixed, the other variable. Normally we assume that it is labour that is variable in the short run.
- The marginal product of a variable input is defined as the change in output brought forth by using one additional unit of the variable input, all other inputs held fixed. The law of diminishing returns says that, beyond some point, the marginal product declines with additional units of the variable input.
- The average product of a variable input is equal to the total output divided by the quantity of the variable input used in the production process. Whenever marginal product lies above average product, the average product will increase with increases in the variable input. Conversely, when marginal product lies below average product, average product will decline with increases in the variable input.
- An important practical problem is that of how to allocate an input across two productive activities to generate the maximum possible output. In general, two types of solution are possible. A corner solution occurs when the marginal product of the input is always higher in one activity than in the other. In that case, the best thing to do is concentrate all the input in the activity where it is more productive.
- An interior solution occurs whenever the marginal product of the variable input, when all of it is placed in one activity, is lower than the marginal product of the first unit of the input in the other activity. In this case, the output-maximizing rule is to distribute the input across the two activities in such a way that its marginal product is the same in both. The pitfall to be on guard against is the tendency to equate not marginal but average products in the two activities.
- The long run is defined as the period required for all inputs to be variable. The actual length of time that corresponds to the short and long runs will differ markedly in different cases. In the two-input case, all the relevant information about production in the long run can be summarized graphically by the isoquant map. The marginal rate of technical substitution is defined as the rate at which one input can be substituted for another without altering the level of output. The MRTS at any point is simply the absolute value of the slope of the isoquant at that point. For most production functions the MRTS will diminish as we move downwards to the right along an isoquant.
- A production function is said to exhibit constant returns to scale if a given proportional (percentage) increase in all inputs produces the same proportional (percentage) increase in output, decreasing returns to scale if a given proportional increase in all inputs results in a smaller proportional increase in output, and increasing returns to scale if a given proportional increase in all inputs causes a greater proportional increase in output. Production functions with increasing returns to scale are also said to exhibit economies of scale. Returns to scale constitute a critically important factor in determining the structure of industrial organization.

Questions for review

1 List three examples of production that a non-economist might not ordinarily think of as production.

2 Give an example of production in which the short run lasts at least 1 year.

3 Why should a person in charge of hiring productive inputs care more about marginal products than about average products?

4 A wag remarked in 2014 before the general election that, when a certain politician moved

from Johannesburg to Port Elizabeth, the average IQ level in both cities went up. Interpret this remark in the context of the average–marginal relationships discussed in the chapter.

5 How is an isoquant map like an indifference map? In what important respect do the two constructs differ?

6 Distinguish between diminishing returns to a variable input and decreasing returns to scale.

7 *True or false*: If the marginal product is decreasing, then the average product must also be decreasing. Explain.

8 A factory adds a worker and subsequently discovers that the average product of its workers has risen. *True or false*: The marginal product of the new worker is less than the average product of the plant's workers before the new employee's arrival.

9 Currently, 2 units of labour and 1 unit of capital produce 1 unit of output. If you double both the inputs (4 units of labour and 2 units of capital), what can you conclude about the output produced under constant returns to scale? Decreasing returns to scale? Increasing returns to scale?

Problems

1 Graph the short-run total product curves for each of the following production functions if K is fixed at $K_0 = 4$:

a $Q = F(K, L) = 2K + 3L$

b $Q = F(K, L) = K^2L^2$

2 Do the two production functions in Problem 1 obey the law of diminishing returns?

3 Suppose the marginal product of labour is currently equal to its average product. If you were one of 10 new workers the firm was about to hire, would you prefer to be paid the value of your average product or the value of your marginal product? Would it be in the interests of an employer to pay you the value of your average product?

4 The following table provides partial information on total product, average product and marginal product for a production function. Using the relationships between these properties, fill in the missing cells.

<table>
<tr><th>Labour</th><th>Total product</th><th>Average product</th><th>Marginal product</th></tr>
<tr><td>0</td><td></td><td>0</td><td></td></tr>
<tr><td>1</td><td>180</td><td></td><td rowspan="2">140</td></tr>
<tr><td>2</td><td></td><td></td></tr>
<tr><td>3</td><td>420</td><td></td><td></td></tr>
<tr><td>4</td><td></td><td>120</td><td></td></tr>
</table>

5 The Johannesburg Police Department must decide how to allocate police officers between West Johannesburg and Hillbrow. Measured in arrests per day, the average product, total product and marginal product in each of these two areas are given in the table below. Currently, the police department allocates 200 police officers to Hillbrow and 300 to West Johannesburg. If police can be redeployed only in groups of 100, how, if at all, should the police department reallocate its officers to achieve the maximum number of arrests per day?

Number of police	West Johannesburg			Hillbrow		
	AP	TP	MP	AP	TP	MP
0	0	0		0	0	
			40			45
100	40	40		45	45	
			40			35
200	40	80		40	80	
			40			25
300	40	120		35	105	
			40			15
400	40	160		30	120	
			40			5
500	40	200		25	125	

6 Suppose a crime wave hits West Johannesburg, so that the marginal product and average

product of police officers are now 60 arrests per day for any number of police officers. What is the optimal allocation of 500 police officers between the two areas now?

7 A firm's short-run production function is given by

$$Q = \tfrac{1}{2}L^2 \text{ for } 0 \leq L \leq 2$$

and

$$Q = 3L - \tfrac{1}{4}L^2 \text{ for } 2 < L \leq 7$$

a Sketch the production function.

b Find the maximum attainable production. How much labour is used at that level?

c Identify the ranges of L utilization over which the marginal product of labour is increasing and decreasing.

d Identify the range over which the marginal product of labour is negative.

8 Each problem on an exam is worth 20 marks. Suppose that from the last seconds you devoted to Problem 10 on the exam you earned 2 extra marks, while from the last seconds devoted to Problem 8 you earned 4 extra marks. The total numbers of marks you earned on these two problems were 8 and 6, respectively, and the total time you spent on each was the same. How – if at all – should you have reallocated your time between them?

9 Suppose capital is fixed at 4 units in the production function $Q = KL$. Draw the total, marginal and average product curves for the labour input.

*10 Do the following production functions have increasing, decreasing or constant returns to scale? Which ones fail to satisfy the law of diminishing returns?

a $Q = 4K^{1/2}L^{1/2}$

b $Q = aK^2 + bL^2$

c $Q = \min(aK, bL)$

d $Q = 4K + 2L$

e $Q = K^{0.5}L^{0.6}$

f $Q = K_1^{0.3}K_2^{0.3}L^{0.3}$

*11 What is the marginal product of labour in the production function $Q = 2K^{1/3}L^{1/3}$ if K is fixed at 27?

(This problem is most easily solved using the calculus definition of marginal product.)

12 Can the Cobb–Douglas production function be used to portray a production process in which returns to scale are increasing at low output levels and are constant or decreasing at high output levels?

13 Suppose that a firm with the production function

$$Q = \min(2K, 3L)$$

is currently using 6 units of capital and 5 units of labour. What are the marginal products of K and L in this case?

14 Identify the regions of increasing, constant and decreasing returns to scale on the isoquant map shown.

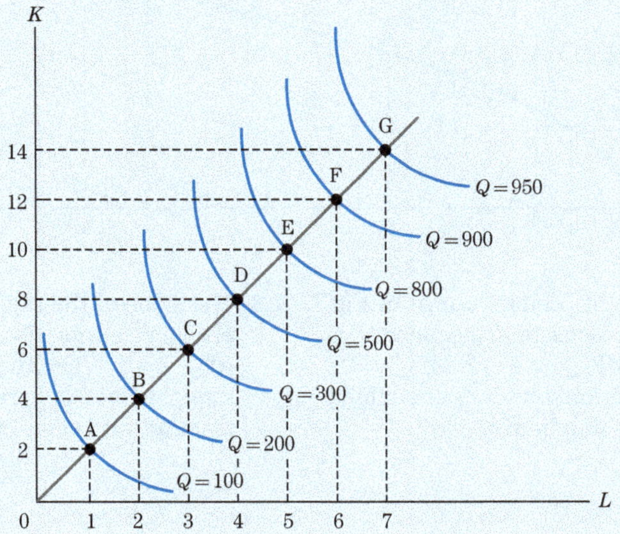

* Problems marked with an asterisk (*) are more difficult.

15 When Paul Samuelson switched from physics to economics, Robert Solow is said to have remarked that the average IQ in both disciplines went up. A bystander responded that Solow's claim must be wrong, because it implies that the average IQ for academia as a whole (which is a weighted average of the average IQ levels for each discipline) must also have gone up as a result of the switch, which is clearly impossible. Was the bystander right? Explain.

16 Suppose you are a cricket bowler with two types of ball, a medium-fast and a spin ball. Your opponents' batting averages against these two types of ball are as shown in the diagram below. If your goal is to minimize your opponents' overall batting average, what is the optimal proportion of medium-fast balls? At this proportion, what are opponents' batting averages against the two types of ball that you bowl?

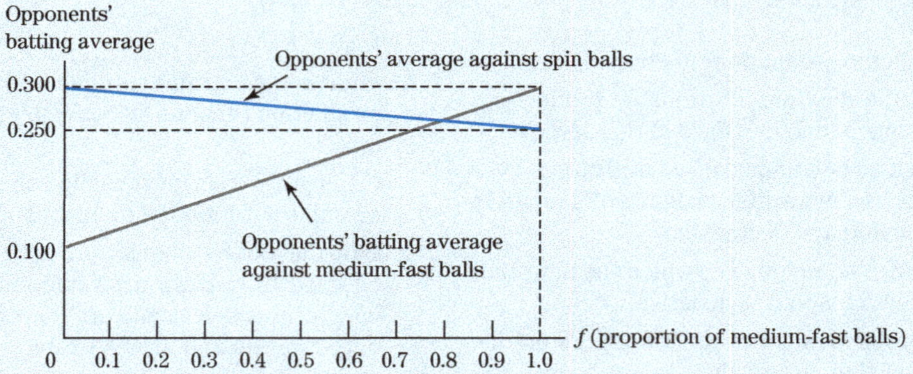

Answers to in-chapter exercises

7.1 For $K = 4$, $Q = \sqrt{4}\sqrt{L} = 2\sqrt{L}$.

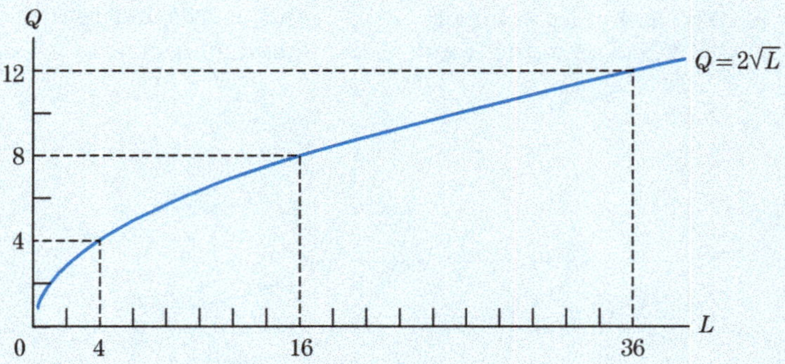

7.2 The slope of the total product curve in Fig. 7.2(a) is 2 for all values of L because it is a straight line. So $MP_{L=3} = 2$ and $MP_{L=1} = 2$. The production function thus does not exhibit diminishing returns to labour.

7.3 The slope of the ray to any point on the total product curve is 2, so $AP_{L=3} = 2$ and $AP_{L=1} = 2$. When the total product curve is a straight line, as here, $AP_L = MP_L$ and is constant for all values of L.

7.4 Because $AP_{L=10} < MP_{L=10}$, AP will rise when L increases, and so $AP_{L=10.1} > AP_{L=10}$.

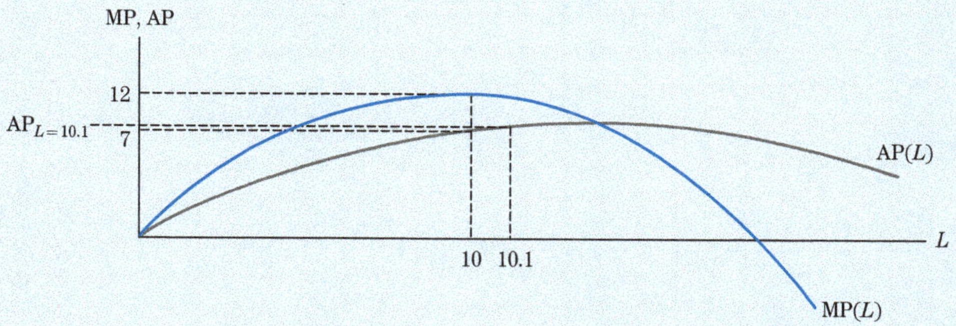

7.5 We cannot say that the bowler should bowl more medium-fast balls without first knowing how a change in the proportion of different type of ball bowled would alter the effectiveness of both types of ball. In particular, bowling more medium-fast balls may decrease the effectiveness not only of the additional medium-fast balls bowled, but of all other medium-fast balls as well. And if this loss exceeds the gain from switching from spin bowling to medium-fast balls, more medium-fast balls should not be bowled.

7.6 From the relationship $MP_L/MP_K = MRTS$, we have $3/MP_K = 9$, which yields $MP_K = \frac{1}{3}$.

7.7 $F(K,L) = \sqrt{K}\sqrt{L}$, so $F(cK,cL) = \sqrt{cK}\sqrt{cL} = \sqrt{c^2}\sqrt{K}\sqrt{L} = cF(K,L)$, and so it has constant returns to scale.

7.8 $F(K, L) = K^{1/3}L^{1/3}$, so $F(cK, cL) = (cK)^{1/3}(cL)^{1/3} = c^{2/3}K^{1/3}L^{1/3} = c^{2/3}F(K, L) < cF(K, L)$, and so it has decreasing returns to scale.

Chapter 8

Costs

If you have had the opportunity to drive through South Africa, you may have come across some of the beautiful passes that were built by Italian prisoners of war. Examples are the Tradoux Pass, between Barrydale and Suurbraak, and the Montagu Pass, between Oudtshoorn and George, to name just two. Once the right of way was cleared and the culverts and bridges laid in, the next step was to spread gravel over the roadbed. The Italian prisoners of war squatted by the side of the road in the blazing sun, tapping away at large rocks with their hammers. In a 12-hour day, each worker would produce a small mound of gravel, not enough to cover even one running metre of roadbed. But there were a lot of people working, and eventually the job was done.

©Design Pics/LSM Photo

Today we don't hire people to hammer rocks into gravel by hand. Instead, we have huge machines that pulverize several tonnes of rock each minute. The reason for this difference may seem obvious to many of us – but for the wrong reason. We may think that at the time of the Second World War South Africa was much poorer than today, and could not afford the expensive equipment used in developed nations. But this explanation is wrong. When the passes were built, there was an abundant supply of very cheap labour, and it made sense to build the passes with manual labour, even if we had had vast surplus revenues in our national treasury, because labour was very cheap relative to capital equipment then. That is why the Chinese economy is currently using lots of labour instead of machines, because labour is very cheap and available in abundant quantities in China. However, in a country such as the USA, where labour is more expensive, more machines will be used in the production process.

Chapter preview

In this chapter our goal is to translate the theory of production developed in Chapter 7 into a coherent theory of costs. In Chapter 7 we established the relationship between the quantities of inputs employed and the corresponding level of output. Here, we shall forge the link between the quantity of output produced and the cost of producing it.

Our first step will be to tackle the question of how costs vary with output in the short run. This question turns out to be more involved than it sounds, for there are seven different types of cost to keep track of – total cost, variable cost, fixed cost, marginal cost, average total cost, average variable cost and average fixed cost. This array sounds bewildering at first, but the links between the different cost concepts are actually clear and simple. And each turns out to be important for the study of firm behaviour, our principal concern in the chapters to follow.

Of even greater importance for the structure and conduct of industry is the question of how costs vary with output in the long run. Here, we shall begin with the question of how to produce a given level of output – say, a kilometre of road – at the lowest possible cost. A given quantity can be produced in many ways: we need to find the cheapest way, the most appropriate method for existing factor prices. The answer to this question enables us to explore how costs are related to returns to scale in production.

Costs in the short run

Remember from your first-year course that in Economics we make a distinction between economic and accounting costs. Accounting costs are equal to the exact amount paid in expenses when producing a good or providing a service. When we calculate economic costs we must also take into account the opportunity cost. Remember that the opportunity cost of an activity is equal to the value of the next-best activity that you now can no longer afford. Another important aspect to remember from your first-year course in Economics is that profit for the entrepreneur is included in the cost curves of the firm.

To see how costs vary with output in the short run, it is convenient to begin with a simple production example of the sort we discussed in Chapter 7. Suppose Katlego's Cleaners washes bags of laundry using labour (L) and capital (K). Labour is purchased in the open market at a wage rate $w =$ R150/person-hr.[1] We assume that capital is fixed in the short run. The relationship between the variable input and the total number of bags washed per hour is summarized in Table 8.1. Note that output initially grows at an increasing rate with additional units of the variable input (as L grows from 0 to 4 units), and then grows at a diminishing rate (as L grows from 4 to 8 units).

The total cost of producing the various levels of output is simply the cost of all the factors of production employed. If Katlego owns his own capital, its implicit rental value is an opportunity cost – the money Katlego could have earned if he had sold his capital and invested the proceeds in, say, a government bond (see Chapter 1). Suppose Katlego's capital is fixed at 120 machine-hr/hr, the rental value of each of which

Table 8.1 The short-run production function for Katlego's Cleaners

Quantity of labour (person-hr/hr)	Quantity of output (bags/hr)
0	0
1	4
2	14
3	27
4	43
5	58
6	72
7	81
8	86

The entries in each row of the right-hand column tell us the quantity of output produced by the quantity of variable input in the corresponding row of the left column. This production function initially exhibits increasing, then diminishing, returns to the variable input.

[1] A person-hour is one person working for 1 hour. In Chapter 12 we shall consider how input prices are determined. For the present, we simply take them as given.

is $r =$ R3.75/machine-hr,[2] for a total capital rental of R450/hr. This cost is a **fixed cost (FC)**, which means that it does not vary in the short run as the level of output varies. More generally, if K_0 denotes this fixed amount of capital and r is its rental price per unit, we have

Fixed cost (FC) Cost that does not vary with the level of output in the short run (the cost of all fixed factors of production).

$$FC = rK_0 \tag{8.1}$$

Other examples of fixed cost might include property taxes, insurance payments, interest on loans and other payments to which the firm is committed in the short run, and which do not vary as the level of output varies. Business managers often refer to fixed costs as *overhead costs*. Because fixed costs are independent of production activities, they can only be avoided if the firm shuts down and exits the industry.

Sunk costs are sometimes confused with fixed costs. As explained above, fixed costs do not vary with output. Factory costs for a firm are the same whether it produces 1 or 1000 goods. Sunk costs are those that the firm has already paid, which cannot be recovered. The cost of the factory is a fixed cost, but not a sunk cost because it can be sold if the firm wants to. Let us explain sunk cost using a simple example. Suppose the firm is the only producer in the world of a very specific product that requires highly specialized tools to manufacture. If the firm goes out of business it cannot sell those tools because there will be no demand for them. The cost is already paid for and it cannot be recovered. These are thus sunk costs. Some sunk costs are actually also fixed costs. Take, for example, the insurance that you pay on your building. It is a fixed cost, but also a sunk cost because you cannot recover it even if you sell the building.

Variable cost (VC) Cost that varies with the level of output in the short run (the cost of all variable factors of production).

Variable cost (VC) is defined as the total cost of the variable factors of production at each level of output. To calculate VC for any given level of output in this example, we simply multiply the amount of labour needed to produce that level of output by the hourly wage rate. Thus the variable cost of 27 bags/hr is (R150/person-hr) × (3 person-hr/hr) = R450/hr. More generally, if L_1 is the quantity of labour required to produce an output level of Q_1 and w is the hourly wage rate, we have

$$VC_{Q_1} = wL_1 \tag{8.2}$$

Note the explicit dependence of VC on output in the notation on the left-hand side of Eq. 8.2, which is lacking in Eq. 8.1. This is to emphasize that variable cost depends on the output level produced, whereas fixed cost does not.

Total cost (TC) All economic costs of production: the sum of variable cost and fixed cost.

Total cost (TC) is the sum of FC and VC. If Katlego wishes to wash 43 bags/hr, the total cost of doing so will be R450/hr + (R150/person-hr) × (4 person-hr/hr) = R700/hr. More generally, the expression for total cost of producing an output level of Q_1 is written

$$\begin{aligned} TC_{Q_1} &= FC + VC_{Q_1} \\ &= rK_0 + wL_1 \end{aligned} \tag{8.3}$$

Table 8.2 shows fixed, variable and total cost for corresponding output levels for the production function given in Table 8.1. The relationships among the various cost categories are most clearly seen by displaying the information graphically, not in tabular form. The short-run production function from Table 8.1 is plotted in Fig. 8.1. Recall from Chapter 7 that the initial region of

Table 8.2 Outputs and costs

Q	FC	VC	TC
0	450	0	450
4	450	150	600
14	450	300	750
27	450	450	900
43	450	600	1050
58	450	750	1200
72	450	900	1350
81	450	1050	1500
86	450	1200	1650

The fixed cost of capital is R450/hr, and the cost per unit of the variable factor (L) is R150/hr. Total cost is calculated as the sum of fixed cost and variable cost.

[2] A machine-hour is one machine working for 1 hour. To say that Katlego's capital is fixed at 120 machine-hr/hr means that he has 120 machines that can operate simultaneously.

upward curvature ($0 \leq L \leq 4$) of the production function corresponds to increasing returns to the variable input. Beyond the point $L = 4$, the production function exhibits diminishing returns to the variable input.

Graphing the total, variable and fixed cost curves

Not surprisingly, the shape of the variable cost curve is systematically related to the shape of the short-run production function. The connection arises because the production function tells us how much labour we need to produce a given level of output, and this quantity of labour, when multiplied by the wage rate, gives us variable cost. Suppose, for example, we want to plot the variable cost of producing 58 units of output. (See Figs 8.1 and 8.2.) We first note from the production function shown in Fig. 8.1 that 58 units of output require 5 units of labour, which, at a wage rate of R150/person-hr, gives rise to a variable cost of $(5)(150) = 750$/hr. So, in Fig. 8.2, the output level of 58 is plotted against a variable cost of R750/hr. Similarly, note from the production function that 43 units of output require 4 units of labour, which, at the R150 wage rate, gives rise in Fig. 8.2 to a variable cost of R600/hr. In like fashion, we can generate as many additional points on the variable cost curve as we choose.

Of particular interest is the relationship between the curvature of the production function and that of the variable cost curve. Note in Fig. 8.1 that $L = 4$ is the point at which diminishing returns to the variable factor of production set in. For values of $L < 4$, there are increasing returns to L, which means that increments in L produce successively larger increments in Q in that region. Put another way, in this region a given increase in output, Q, requires successively smaller increments in the variable input, L. As a result, variable cost grows at a diminishing rate for output levels less than 43. For example, if the variable input labour increases by 100 per cent from 2 to 4 units, output increases by 207 per cent (from 14 units to 43 units). This is reflected in Fig. 8.2 by the concave shape of the variable cost curve for output levels between 0 and 43.

Once L exceeds 4 in Fig. 8.1, we enter the region of diminishing returns. Here, successively larger increments in L are required to produce a given increment in Q. In consequence, variable cost grows at an increasing rate in this region. For example, if the variable input labour increases by 33.3 per cent from 6 to 8 units, output increases by only 19.4 per cent, from 72 to 86 units. This is reflected in the convex shape of the variable cost curve in Fig. 8.2 for output levels in excess of 43.

Because fixed costs do not vary with the level of output, their graph is simply a horizontal line. Figure 8.2 shows the fixed, variable and total cost curves (FC, VC and TC) for the production function shown in Fig. 8.1. Note in the figure that the variable cost curve passes through the origin, which means simply that variable cost is zero when we

Figure 8.1 Output as a function of one variable input

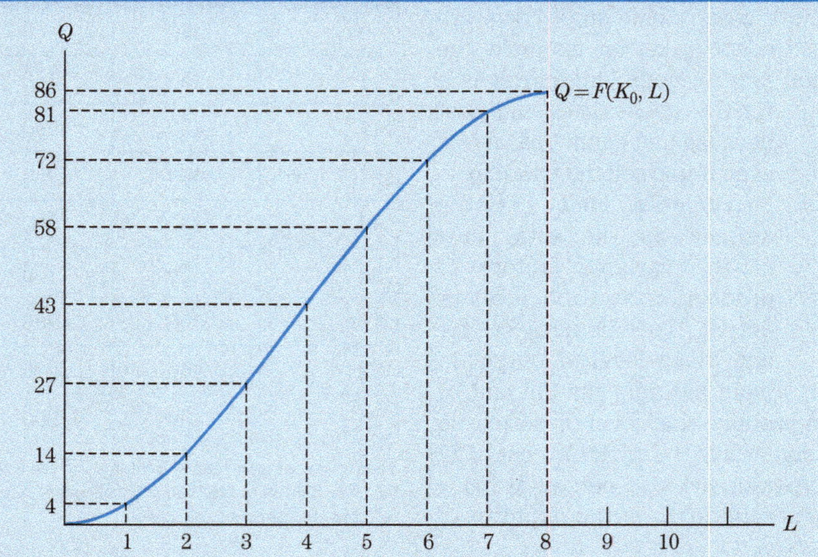

This production process shows increasing returns to the variable input up to $L = 4$, and diminishing returns thereafter.

Figure 8.2 The total, variable and fixed cost curves

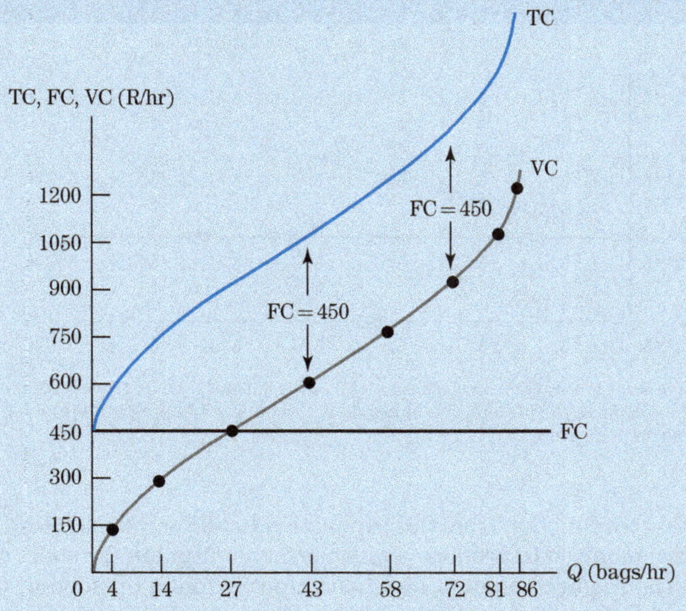

These curves are for the production function of Katlego's Cleaners, shown in Fig. 8.1. The variable cost curve passes through the origin, which means that the variable cost of producing zero units of output is equal to zero. The TC curve, which is the sum of the FC and VC curves, is parallel to the VC curve and lies FC = 450 units above it.

Example 8.1

Suppose the production function is given by $Q = 3KL$, where K denotes capital and L denotes labour. The price of capital is R20/machine-hr, the price of labour is R240/person-hr and capital is fixed at 4 machine-hr/hr in the short run. Graph the TC, VC and FC curves for this production process.

Unlike the production process shown in Fig. 8.1, the process in this example is one in which there are everywhere constant returns to the variable factor of production. As shown in Fig. 8.3, output here is strictly proportional to the variable input.

Figure 8.3 The production function $Q = 3KL$, with $K = 4$

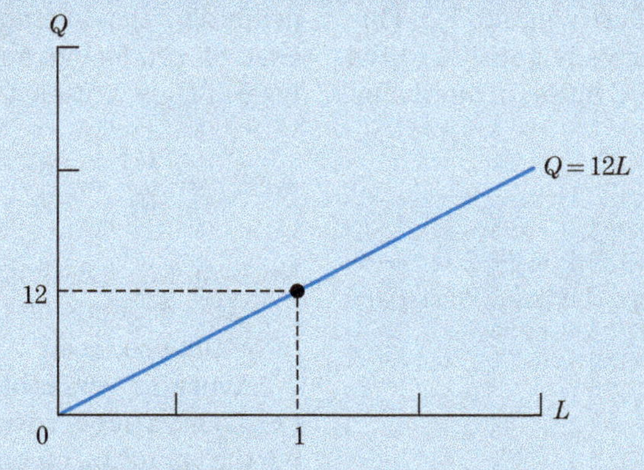

This short-run production function exhibits constant returns to L over the entire range of L. There is neither a region of increasing returns nor a region of diminishing returns to L.

Figure 8.4 The total, variable and fixed cost curves for the production function $Q = 3KL$

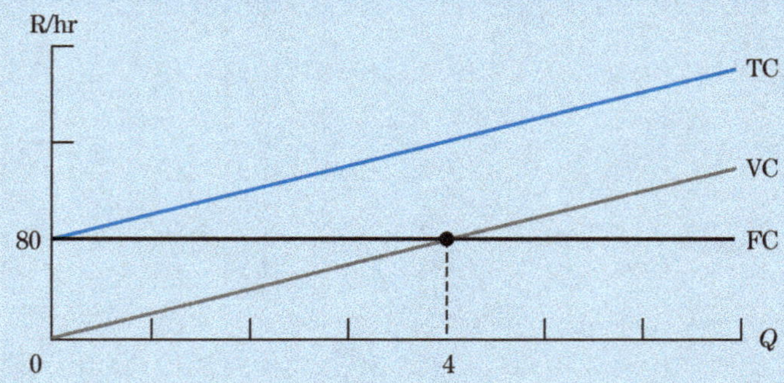

With K fixed at 4 machine-hr/hr in the short run and a price of K of $r =$ R20/machine-hr, fixed costs are R80/hr. To produce Q units of output per hour requires $Q/12$ person-hr/hr of labour. With a price of labour of R240/person-hr, variable cost is R20Q/hr. Total cost is R80/hr + R20Q/hr.

To derive the total cost function from this production function, we must first discover how much capital and labour are required to produce a given level of output in the short run. Since K is fixed at 4 machine-hr/hr, the required amount of labour input is found by solving $Q = 3KL = 3(4)L$ for $L = Q/12$. The total cost of producing Q units of output per hour is therefore given by

$$\begin{aligned} TC(Q) &= (\text{R}20/\text{machine-hr})(4 \text{ machine-hr/hr}) \\ &\quad + (\text{R}240/\text{person-hr})(\tfrac{Q}{12} \text{ person-hr/hr}) \\ &= \text{R}80/\text{hr} + \text{R}20Q/\text{hr} \end{aligned} \tag{8.4}$$

The R80/hr expenditure on capital constitutes fixed cost. Variable cost is total cost less fixed cost, or

$$VC_Q = 20Q \tag{8.5}$$

The total, variable and fixed cost curves are plotted in Fig. 8.4.

produce no output. The total cost of producing zero output is equal to fixed costs, FC. Note also in the figure that the vertical distance between the VC and TC curves is everywhere equal to FC. This means that the total cost curve is parallel to the variable cost curve and lies FC units (in our example 450 units) above it.

Exercise 8.1

Same as Example 8.1 except the price of capital $r =$ R40/machine-hr.

Other short-run costs

Average fixed cost (AFC) is fixed cost divided by the quantity of output. For the production function shown in Table 8.1 and Fig. 8.1, for example, the average fixed cost of washing 58 bags/hr is (R450/hr) ÷ 58 bags/hr) = R7.76/bag. More generally, the average fixed cost of producing an output level of Q_1 is written as

Average fixed cost (AFC) Total fixed cost divided by the quantity of output.

$$AFC_{Q_1} = \frac{FC}{Q_1} = \frac{rK_0}{Q_1} \tag{8.6}$$

Note in Eq. 8.6 that, unlike FC, AFC depends on the level of output produced.

Average variable cost (AVC) is variable cost divided by the quantity of output. If Katlego washes 72 bags/hr, his AVC will be (R150/person-hr) × (6 person-hr/hr) ÷ 72 bags/hr = R12.50/bag.

Average variable cost (AVC) Total variable cost divided by the quantity of output.

The average variable cost of producing an output level Q_1 may be written as

$$\text{AVC}_{Q_1} = \frac{\text{VC}_{Q_1}}{Q_1} = \frac{wL_1}{Q_1} \quad (8.7)$$

Average total cost (ATC) Total cost divided by the quantity of output. What a product costs on average to produce.

Average total cost (ATC) is total cost divided by the quantity of output. And since total cost is the sum of total fixed cost and total variable cost, it follows that ATC is the sum of AFC and AVC. For example, the ATC of washing 58 bags/hr is (R450/hr) ÷ (58 bags/hr) + (R150/person-hr) × (5 person-hr/hr) ÷ (58 bags/hr) = R7.76/bag + R12.93/bag = R20.69/bag. The average total cost of producing Q_1 units of output is given by

$$\begin{aligned}\text{ATC}_{Q_1} &= \text{AFC}_{Q_1} + \text{AVC}_{Q_1} \\ &= \frac{rK_0 + wL_1}{Q_1}\end{aligned} \quad (8.8)$$

Marginal cost (MC) Change in total cost that results from a one-unit change in output. The additional production cost of the last unit produced.

Marginal cost (MC), finally, is the change in total cost that results from producing an additional unit of output.[3] In going from 58 to 72 bags/hr, for example, total costs go up by R150/hr, which is the cost of hiring the extra worker needed to achieve that increase in output. Since the extra worker washes an extra 14 bags/hr, the marginal cost of the additional output in per-bag terms is (R150/hr) ÷ (14 bags/hr) = R10.71/bag. More generally, if Q denotes the change in output from an initial level of Q_1, and ΔTC_{Q_1} denotes the corresponding change in total cost, marginal cost at Q_1 is given by

$$\text{MC}_{Q_1} = \frac{\Delta\text{TC}_{Q_1}}{\Delta Q}\left(\text{or } \frac{\text{dTC}}{\text{d}Q}\right) \quad (8.9)$$

Because fixed cost does not vary with the level of output, the change in total cost when we produce Q additional units of output is the same as the change in variable cost. Thus an equivalent expression for marginal cost is

$$\text{MC}_{Q_1} = \frac{\Delta\text{VC}_{Q_1}}{\Delta Q} \quad (8.10)$$

where VC_{Q_1} represents the change in variable cost when we produce Q units of additional output.

Graphing the short-run average and marginal cost curves

Since FC does not vary with output, average fixed cost declines steadily as output increases. Suppose McGraw-Hill's fixed costs in producing this textbook were approximately R600 000. If only 1000 copies were produced, its average fixed cost would be R600/book. But if the publisher produces 10 000 copies, AFC will fall to R60/book. McGraw-Hill's best-selling economics principles text, by Campbell McConnell and Stanley Brue, is considerably longer than this book, and yet its average fixed cost comes to little more than R10/book. The process whereby AFC falls with output is often referred to as *spreading overhead costs.*

For the fixed cost curve FC shown in the top panel in Fig. 8.5, the corresponding average fixed cost curve is shown in the bottom panel as the curve labelled AFC. As output shrinks towards zero, AFC grows without bounds, and it falls ever closer to zero as output increases. At very high production levels it will strive towards zero, but will be just bigger than zero. Note that the units on the vertical axis of the AFC curve are rands per unit (R/unit) of output, and that the vertical axis of the FC curve, by contrast, is measured in rands per hour (R/hr).

Geometrically, average variable cost at any level of output Q, which is equal to VC/Q, may be interpreted as the slope of a ray to the variable cost curve at Q. Notice in the top panel in Fig. 8.5 that the slope of a ray to the VC curve declines with output up to the output level Q_2; thereafter it begins to increase. The corresponding average variable cost curve, shown in the bottom panel in Fig. 8.5, therefore reaches its minimum value at Q_2, the output level at which the ray R_2 is tangent to the variable cost curve. Beyond that point, the AVC curve increases with output.

The graph of the ATC curve is generated in an analogous fashion. For any level of output, ATC is the slope of the ray to the total cost curve at that output level. For the total cost curve in the top panel in Fig. 8.5, the corresponding ATC curve is plotted in the bottom panel of the diagram. Note that the minimum point on ATC in the bottom panel occurs at Q_3, the output level for which the ray R_1 is tangent to the TC curve in the top panel.

[3] In calculus terms, the definition of marginal cost is simply $\text{MC}_{Q_1} = \text{dTC}_{Q_1}/\text{d}Q$.

Figure 8.5 The marginal, average total, average variable and average fixed cost curves

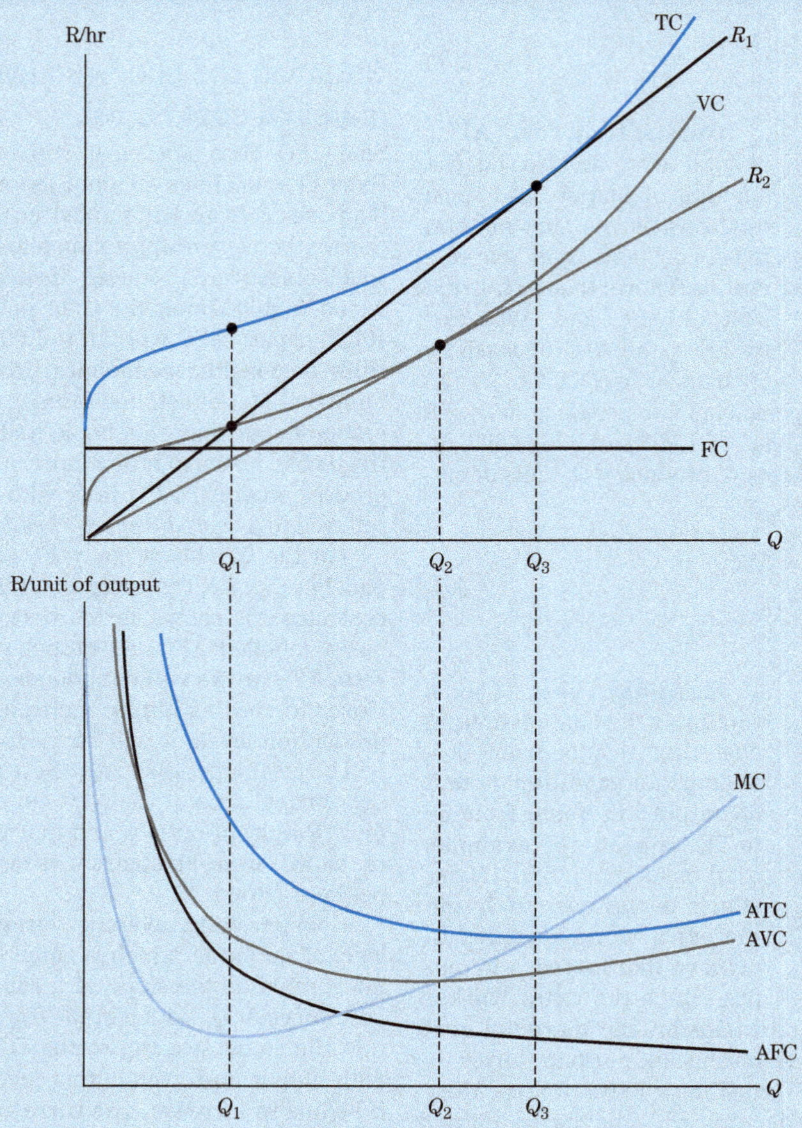

The MC curve intersects the ATC and AVC curves at their respective minimum turning points.

Example 8.2

Construct a table showing average fixed cost, average variable cost, average total cost and marginal cost using the information in Table 8.1 for Katlego's Cleaners. Then graph these average costs.

We calculate average fixed cost as fixed cost divided by quantity (AFC = FC/Q), average variable cost as variable cost divided by quantity (AVC = VC/Q) and average total cost as total cost divided by quantity (ATC = TC/Q). We calculate marginal cost by finding the difference in total cost and dividing by the difference in quantity MC = TC/Q to fill in the table below. The average cost curves are illustrated in Fig. 8.6.

Outputs and costs				
Q	AFC	AVC	ATC	MC*
0	∞	–	∞	
				27.50
4	112.50	37.50	150.00	
				15.00
14	32.14	21.43	53.57	
				11.54
27	16.67	16.67	33.34	
				9.38
43	10.47	13.95	24.42	
				10.00
58	7.76	12.93	20.69	
				10.71
72	6.25	12.50	18.75	
				16.67
81	5.56	12.96	18.52	
				30.0
86	5.23	13.95	19.18	

*The marginal cost entries are placed between the lines of the table to indicate that each entry represents the cost per bag of moving from the preceding output level to the next.

Figure 8.6 Quantity versus average costs

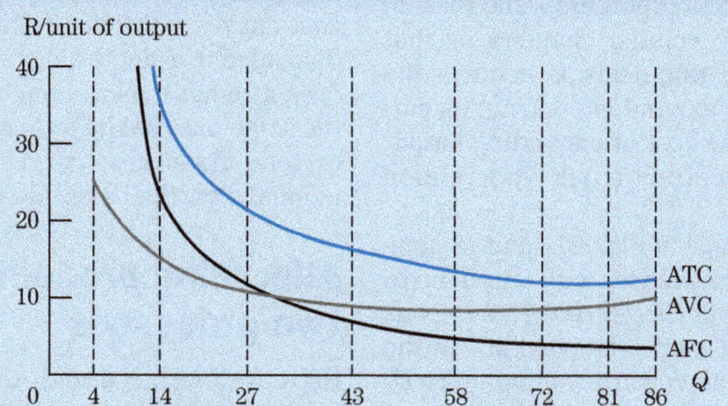

ATC is the sum of AVC and AFC. AFC is declining for all values of *Q*.

Recall that, because TC = FC + VC, it follows that ATC = AFC + AVC (simply divide both sides of the former equation by output). This means that the vertical distance between the ATC and AVC curves at any level of output will always be the corresponding level of AFC. Thus the vertical distance between ATC and AVC approaches infinity as output declines towards zero, and shrinks towards zero as output grows towards infinity. Note also in Fig. 8.5 that the minimum point on the AVC curve occurs for a smaller unit of output than does the minimum point on the ATC curve. Because AFC declines continuously, ATC continues falling even after AVC has begun to turn upwards. Between Q_2 and Q_3 the magnitude of the decrease in AFC is greater than the increase in AVC, but at production levels greater than Q_3 the magnitude in the increase in AVC is greater than the decrease in AFC.

Exercise 8.2

If FC takes the value 20, what is the vertical distance between the ATC and AVC curves in Fig. 8.5 when $Q = 10$?

In terms of its role in the firm's decision regarding how much output to produce, by far the most important of the seven cost curves is the *marginal cost curve.* Remember that marginal cost at any level of output may be interpreted as the slope of the total cost curve at that level of output (or the first-order derivative of the total cost curve relative to variable input – normally labour – that the firm uses in the production process). The reason, as we shall see in the coming chapters, is that the firm's typical operating decision involves the question of whether to expand or contract its current level of output. The cost of expanding output (or the savings from contracting) is by definition equal to marginal cost.

Notice in the top panel in Fig. 8.5 that the slope of the total cost curve decreases with output up to Q_1, and rises with output thereafter.[4] This tells us that the marginal cost curve, labelled MC in the bottom panel, will be downward sloping up to Q_1 and upward sloping thereafter. Q_1 is the point at which diminishing returns set in for this production function, and diminishing returns are what account for the upward slope of the short-run marginal cost curve.

At the output level Q_3 the slope of the total cost curve is exactly the same as the slope of the ray to the total cost curve (the ray labelled R_1 in the top panel in Fig. 8.5). This tells us that marginal cost and average total cost will take precisely the same value at Q_3. To the left of Q_3 the slope of the total cost curve is smaller than the slope of the corresponding ray, which means that marginal cost will be smaller than average total cost in that region. For output levels in excess of Q_3 the slope of the total cost curve is greater than the slope of the corresponding ray, so marginal cost will be larger than average total cost for output levels larger than Q_3. These relationships are reflected in the average total cost and marginal cost curves shown in the bottom panel in Fig. 8.5. Notice that the relationship between the MC and AVC curves is qualitatively similar to the relationship between the MC and ATC curves. One common feature is that MC intersects each curve at its minimum point. Both average cost curves have the additional property that, *when MC is less than average cost (either ATC or AVC), the average cost curve must be decreasing with output; and when MC is greater than average cost, average cost must be increasing with output.*

Producing an additional unit whose cost exceeds the average (either total or variable) cost incurred thus far has the effect of pulling the average cost up. Conversely, an extra unit whose cost is less than the average will necessarily pull down the average.

Finally, note in the bottom panel in Fig. 8.5 that the units on the vertical axis of the marginal cost curve diagram are again rands per unit (R/unit) of output, the same as for the three short-run average cost curves. All four of these curves can thus be displayed in a single diagram. But you must never, *ever*, attempt to place any of these four curves on the same axes as the total cost, total variable cost or total fixed cost curves. The units measured along the vertical axes are simply not compatible.

Allocating production between two processes

Here, we are faced with the problem of dividing a given production quota between two production processes in such a way as to produce the quota at the lowest possible cost. Let Q_T be the total amount to be produced, and let Q_1 and Q_2 be the amounts produced in the first and second processes,

[4] A point at which the curvature change is called an *inflection point.*

Example 8.3

Suppose output is given by the production function $Q = 3KL$, where K denotes capital and L denotes labour. The price of capital is R20/machine-hr, the price of labour is R240/person-hr and capital is fixed at 4 units in the short run (this is the same production function and input prices as in Example 8.1). Graph the ATC, AVC, AFC and MC curves.

Recall from Example 8.1 that the total cost curve for this process is given by

$$TCQ = 80 + 20Q \tag{8.11}$$

Marginal cost is the slope of the total cost curve, which here is equal to R20/unit of output:

$$MC_Q = \frac{\Delta TC_Q}{\Delta Q} \text{ or } \frac{dTC}{dQ} = 20 \tag{8.12}$$

Average variable cost is given by VC_Q/Q, which is also R20/unit of output:

$$AVC_Q = \frac{20Q}{Q} = 20 \tag{8.13}$$

When marginal cost is constant, as in this production process, it will always be equal to AVC.

Average fixed cost is given by

Figure 8.7 Cost curves for a specific production process

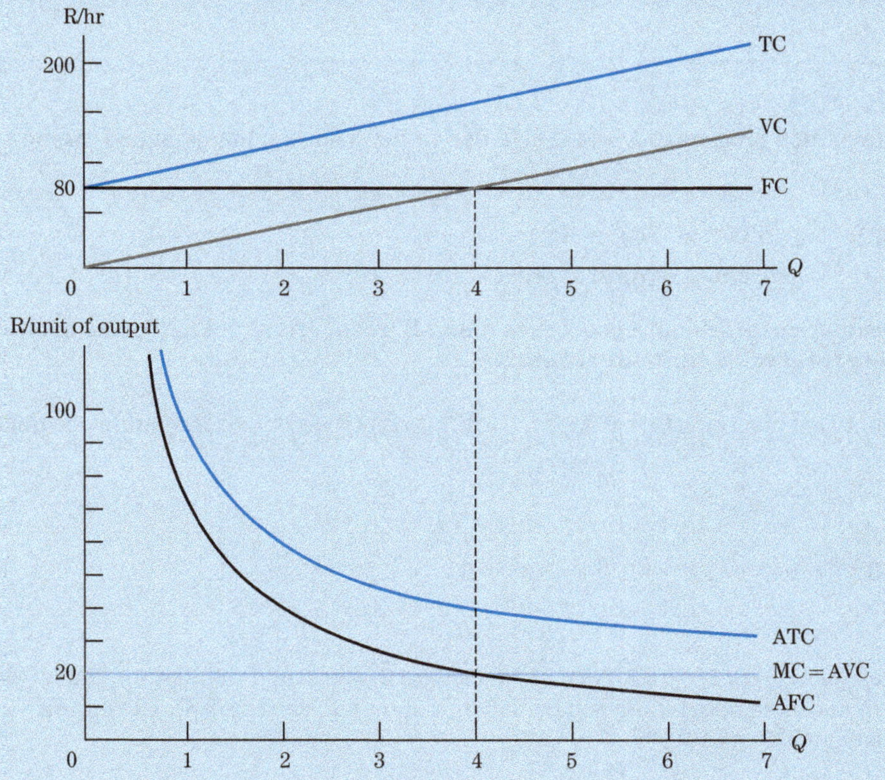

For production processes with constant marginal cost, average variable cost and marginal cost are identical. Marginal cost always lies below ATC for such processes.

$$\text{AFC}_Q = \frac{80}{Q} \tag{8.14}$$

and average total cost is given by

$$\text{AFC}_Q = 20 + \frac{80}{Q} \tag{8.15}$$

in this example. The marginal and average cost curves are as shown in the bottom panel in Fig. 8.7, where the top panel reproduces the corresponding total, variable and fixed cost curves.

respectively. And suppose the marginal cost in either process at very low levels of output is lower than the marginal cost at Q_T units of output in the other (which ensures that both processes will be used).[5]

The values of Q_1 and Q_2 that solve this problem will then be the ones that result in equal marginal costs for the two processes.

To see why, suppose the contrary: that is, suppose that the cost-minimizing allocation resulted in higher marginal cost in one process than in the other. We could then shift one unit of output from the process with the higher marginal cost to the one with the lower. Because the result would be the same total output as before, but at a lower total cost, the initial division could not have been the cost-minimizing one.

In Chapter 7 we saw that two production processes could have equal marginal products even though their average products differed substantially. Here, too, it is possible for two production processes to have equal marginal costs even though their average costs differ markedly.

Example 8.4

Suppose production processes A and B give rise to the following marginal and average total cost curves:

$\mathbf{MC^A = 12Q^A}$, $\mathbf{ATC^A = 16/Q^A + 6Q^A}$,

$\mathbf{MC^B = 4Q^B}$, $\mathbf{ATC^B = 240/Q^B + 2Q^B}$,

where the superscripts denote processes A and B, respectively. What is the least costly way to produce a total of 32 units of output?

The minimum-cost condition is that $MC^A_{Q^A} = MC^B_{Q^B}$ with $Q^A + Q^B = 32$. Equating marginal costs, we have

$$12Q^A = 4Q^B \tag{8.16}$$

Substituting $Q^B = 32 - Q^A$ into Eq. 8.16, we have

$$12Q^A = 128 - 4Q^A \tag{18.17}$$

which solves for $Q^A = 8$. $Q^B = 32 - 8 = 24$ takes care of the remaining output, and at these output levels marginal cost in both plants will be R96/unit of output (see Fig. 8.8). The line $MC^T = 3Q^T$ is the horizontal sum of MC^A and MC^B.[6]

[5] Suppose the marginal cost at $Q = Q_T$ using production function A were less than the marginal cost at $Q = 0$ for production process B: $MC^A_{Q_T} < MC^B_0$. Then the cheapest way of producing Q_T would be to use only process A.

[6] MC^T is found by solving $Q^T = Q^A + Q^B = MC/12 + MC/4 = MC/3$ for $MC^T = 3Q^T$.

The average total cost values that correspond to this allocation are $ATC^A = R50$/unit of output and $ATC^B = R58$/unit of output. From the average total cost curves we can deduce total cost curves in this example (just multiply ATC by Q).[7] They are given by $TC^A = 16 + 6(Q^A)^2$ and $TC^B = 240 + 2(Q^B)^2$. The cost-minimizing allocation results in $TC^A = R400$ and $TC^B = R1392$, illustrating that the cost-minimizing allocation does not require equality of total costs either.

Figure 8.8 The minimum-cost production allocation

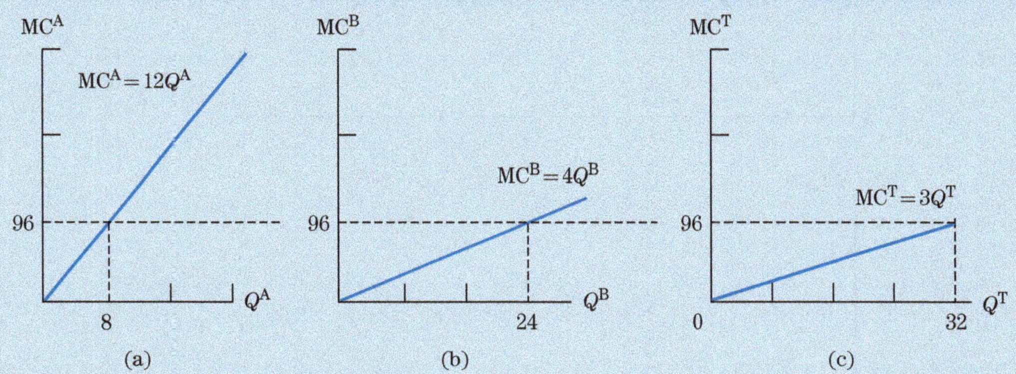

To produce a given total output at minimum cost, it should be allocated across production activities so that the marginal cost of each activity is the same.

Exercise 8.3

Same as Example 8.4 except the total output is 12.

The relationships between MP, AP, MC and AVC

In Chapter 7 we saw that the marginal product curve cuts the average product curve at the maximum value of the AP curve. And in this chapter we have seen that the marginal cost curve cuts the average variable cost curve at the minimum value of the AVC curve.

There is a direct link between these relationships. To see the connection, note first that from the definition of marginal cost we have $MC = \Delta VC/\Delta Q$. When labour is the only variable factor, $\Delta VC = \Delta wL$, so that $\Delta VC/\Delta Q$ is equal to $\Delta wL/\Delta Q$. If wage rates are fixed, this is the same as $w\Delta L/\Delta Q$. And since $\Delta L/\Delta Q$ is equal to 1/MP, it follows that

$$MC = \frac{w}{MP} \tag{8.18}$$

In similar fashion, note from the definition of average variable cost that $AVC = VC/Q = wL/Q$, and since L/Q is equal to 1/AP, it follows that

$$AVC = \frac{w}{AP} \tag{8.19}$$

From Eq. 8.18 we see that the minimum value of marginal cost corresponds to the maximum value of MP. Likewise, it follows from Eq. 8.19 that the minimum value of AVC corresponds to the maximum value of AP. The top panel in Fig. 8.9 plots the AP and MP curves as functions of L. The bottom panel uses Eqs 8.18 and 8.19 to plot the corresponding MC and AVC curves as functions of L. (Normally, the MC and AVC curves are plotted as functions of Q. The value of Q that corresponds to a given value of L in the bottom panel may be calculated by multiplying L by the corresponding value of AP_L.) Note that the MP curve in the top panel takes its maximum value at $L = L_1$, and that the minimum value of the MC curve in the bottom panel occurs at the output level (Q_1) that corresponds to $L = L_1$. Note also that the AP curve in the top panel takes its maximum value at $L = L_2$, and that the minimum value of the AVC curve in

[7] Note that $MC^A = dTC^A/dQ^A = d[16 + 6(Q^A)^2]/dQ^A = 12Q^A$ and $MC^B = dTC^B/dQ^B = d[240 + 2(Q^B)^2]/dQ^B = 4Q^B$.

Figure 8.9 The relationships between MP, AP, MC and AVC

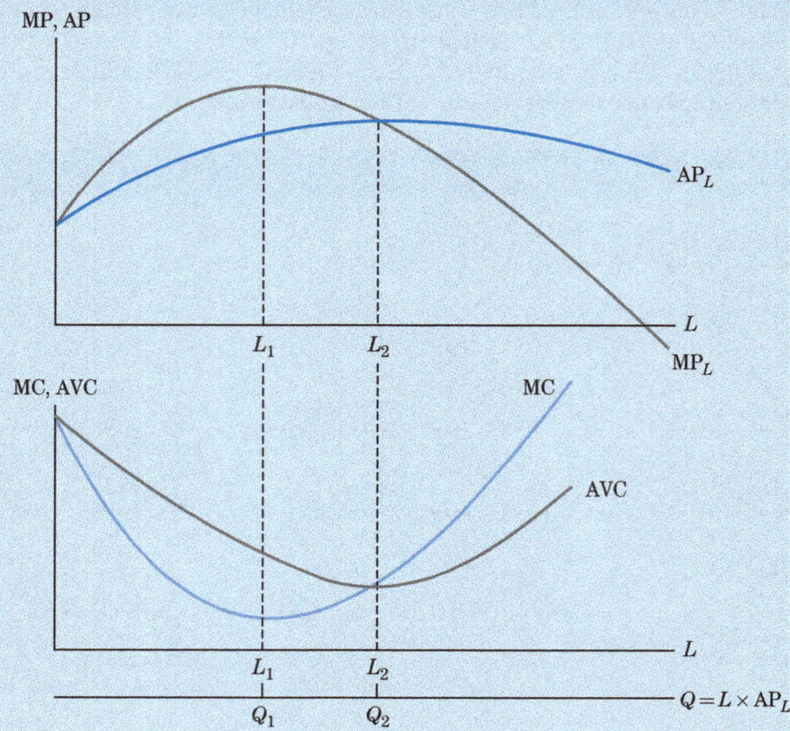

Normally, the MC and AVC curves are plotted with Q on the horizontal axis. In the bottom panel they are shown as functions of L. The value of Q that corresponds to a given value of L is found by multiplying L times the corresponding value of AP_L. The maximum value of the MP curve, at $L = L_1$, top panel, corresponds to the minimum value of the MC curve, at $Q = Q_1$, bottom panel. Similarly, the maximum value of the AP curve, at $L = L_2$, top panel, corresponds to the minimum value of the AVC curve, at $Q = Q_2$, bottom panel.

the bottom panel occurs at the output level (Q_2) that corresponds to $L = L_2$.

Exercise 8.4

For a production function at a given level of output in the short run, the marginal product of labour is greater than the average product of labour. How will marginal cost at that output level compare with average variable cost?

Costs in the long run

In the long run all inputs are variable by definition. If the manager of the firm wishes to produce a given level of output at the lowest possible cost, and is free to choose any input combination she pleases, which one should she choose? As we shall see in the next section, the answer to this question depends on the relative prices of capital and labour.

Choosing the optimal input combination

Irrespective of the structure of an industry the objective of most producers is to produce any given level and quality of output at the lowest possible cost. Equivalently, the producer wants to produce as much output as possible from any given expenditure on inputs.

Let us begin with the case of a firm that wants to maximize output from a given level of expenditure. Suppose it uses only two inputs, capital (K) and labour (L), whose prices, measured in rands per unit of input per day, are $r = 40$ and $w = 80$, respectively. What different combinations of inputs can this firm purchase for a total expenditure of $C =$ R4000/day? Notice that this question has the same structure as the one we encountered in the theory of consumer behaviour in Chapter 3 ('With an income of M, and facing prices of P_X and P_Y, what combinations of X and Y can the

Figure 8.10 The isocost line

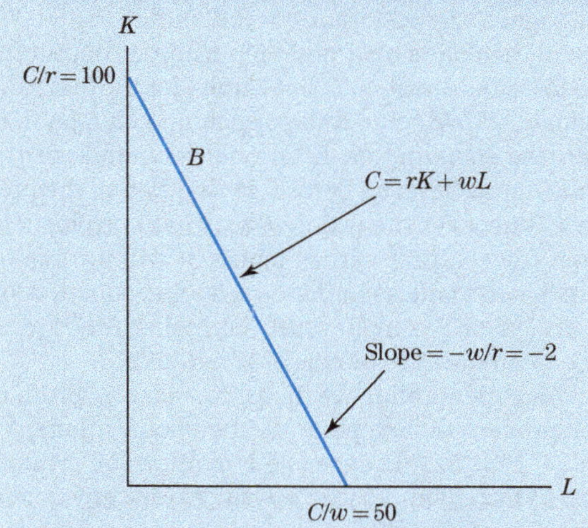

For given input prices ($r = 40$ and $w = 80$ in the diagram), the isocost line is the locus of all possible input bundles that can be purchased for a given level of total expenditure C (R4000 in the diagram). The slope of the isocost line is the negative of the input price ratio, $-w/r$.

Figure 8.11 The maximum output for a given expenditure

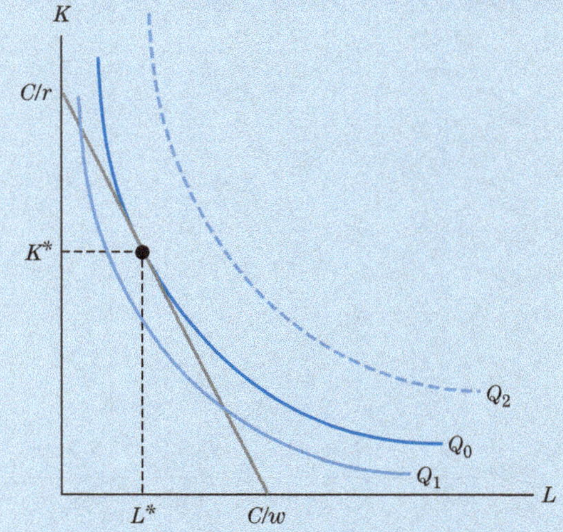

A firm that is trying to produce the largest possible output for an expenditure of C will select the input combination at which the isocost line for C is tangent to an isoquant.

consumer buy?'). In the consumer's case, recall that the answer was easily summarized by the budget constraint. The parallel information in the case of the firm is summarized by the **isocost line** (also known as the *equal cost curve*), shown in Fig. 8.10 for the example given. Any of the input combinations on the locus labelled B can be purchased for a total expenditure of R4000/day. Analogously to the budget constraint case, the slope of the isocost line is the negative of the ratio of the input prices, $-w/r$.

Isocost line A set of input bundles, each of which costs the same amount.

Exercise 8.5

If $w = 30$ and $r = 60$, draw the isocost lines that correspond to total expenditure of R900 and R1800 per unit of time.

The analytic approach to finding the maximum output that can be produced for a given cost turns out to be similar to that for finding the optimal consumption bundle. Just as a given level of satisfaction can be achieved by any of a multitude of possible consumption bundles (all of which lie on the same indifference curve), so too can a given amount of output be produced by any of a host of different input combinations (all of which lie on the same isoquant). In the consumer case, we found the optimum bundle by superimposing the budget constraint onto the indifference map and locating the relevant point of tangency (except in the case of corner solutions). Here, we superimpose the isocost line onto the isoquant map. In Fig. 8.11, the tangency point (L^*, K^*) is the input combination that yields the highest possible output (Q_0) for an expenditure of C.

As noted, the problem of producing the largest output for a given expenditure is solved in essentially the same way as the problem of producing a given level of output for the lowest possible cost. The only difference is that in the latter case we begin with a specific isoquant (the one that corresponds to the level of output we are trying to produce), and then superimpose a map of isocost lines, each corresponding to a different cost level. In our first exercise, cost was fixed and output varied; this time, output is fixed and costs vary. As shown in Fig. 8.12, the least-cost input bundle (L^*, K^*) corresponds to the point of tangency between an isocost line and the specified isoquant (Q_0). One can produce a production quantity of Q_0 with input combinations that correspond to points A or B, but that will then be at a cost of C_3. By producing at point C the same quantity is produced (Q_0), but at the lowest cost possible (C_2). At a cost lower than C_2 (C_1, for example), it is impossible to produce a quantity of Q_0.

Figure 8.12 The minimum cost for a given level of output

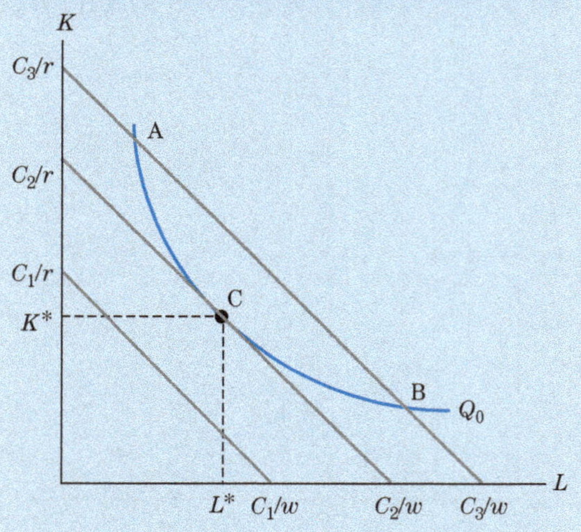

A firm that is trying to produce a given level of output, Q_0, at the lowest possible cost will select the input combination at which an isocost line is tangent to the Q_0 isoquant.

Recall from Chapter 7 that the slope of the isoquant at any point is equal to $-MP_L/MP_K$, the negative of the ratio of the marginal product of L to the marginal product of K at that point. (Recall also from Chapter 7 that the absolute value of this ratio is called the marginal rate of technical substitution, MRTS.) Combining this with the result that minimum cost occurs at a point of tangency with the isocost line (whose slope is $-w/r$), it follows that

$$\frac{MP_{L^*}}{MP_{K^*}} = \frac{w}{r} \tag{8.20}$$

where K^* and L^* again denote the minimum-cost values of K and L. Cross-multiplying, we have

$$\frac{MP_{L^*}}{w} = \frac{MP_{K^*}}{r} \tag{8.21}$$

Note first that MP_{L^*} is simply the extra output obtained from an extra unit of L at the cost-minimizing point. w is the cost, in rands, of an extra unit of L. The ratio MP_{L^*}/w is thus the extra output we get from the last rand spent on L. Similarly, MP_{K^*}/r is the extra output we get from the last rand spent on K. In words, Eq. 8.21 tells us that, when costs are at a minimum, the extra output we get from the last rand spent on an input must be the same for all inputs used in the production process.

It is easy to show why, if that were not the case, costs would not be at a minimum. Suppose, for example, that the last units of both labour and capital increased output by 80 units ($MP_L = MP_K = 80$). And again, suppose that $r =$ R40 and $w =$ R80. We would then have obtained only 1 unit of output for the last rand spent on L, but 2 units for the last rand spent on K. We could reduce spending on L by R80, increase spending on K by only R40, and get the same output level as before, saving R40 in the process. Whenever the ratios of marginal products to input prices differ across inputs, it will always be possible to make a similar cost-saving substitution in favour of the input with the higher MP/P ratio (except in the case of corner solutions).

More generally, we may consider a production process that employs not two but N inputs, X_1, X_2, . . . , X_N. In this case the condition for production at minimum cost is a straightforward generalization of Eq. 8.21:

$$\frac{MP_{X_1}}{P_{X_1}} = \frac{MP_{X_2}}{P_{X_2}} = \cdots \frac{MP_{X_N}}{P_{X_N}} \tag{8.22}$$

Exercise 8.6

Suppose capital and labour are perfect complements in a ratio of one-to-one. That is, suppose that $Q = \min(L, K)$. Currently, the wage is $w = 5$ and the rental rate is $r = 10$. What is the minimum cost and method of producing $Q = 20$ units of output? Suppose the wage rises to $w' = 20$. If we keep total cost the same, what level of output can now be produced, and what method of production (input mix) is used?

Exercise 8.7

Repeat the previous exercise, but now suppose capital and labour are perfect substitutes in a ratio of one-to-one:

$Q = K + L$

The relationship between optimal input choice and long-run costs

Given sufficient time to adjust, the firm can always buy the cost-minimizing input bundle that corresponds to any particular output level and relative input prices. To see how the firm's costs vary with output in the long run, we need only compare the costs of the respective optimal input bundles.

Economic naturalist 8.1

Why are grapes harvested by hand in South Africa but by machine in the United States?

As we all know, the economy of the United States is much more advanced than the economy of South Africa. In general, the technology used in the USA is also much more advanced than the technology used in South Africa. The literacy rate (the percentage of people older than 15 who can read and write) in the USA is 99 per cent; in South Africa it is only 93 per cent. In 2013 GDP per capita in the USA was $52 839, while it was only $11 525 in South Africa. Almost 40 per cent of Americans aged 15–64 have a higher education qualification; only 4.3 per cent of South Africans have such a qualification. For that reason, there is an abundant supply of illiterate and semi-skilled workers in South Africa. Labour in the USA is thus also more expensive than in South Africa and it is more economical to make use of machines to harvest grapes. The typical vineyard in the USA is also larger than its equivalent in South Africa and can thus benefit from economies of scale. Although a few rich farmers in South Africa use harvesting machines, by far the majority of farmers still use workers to harvest the grapes.

Linked to all of the above-mentioned factors we can add that the official unemployment rate in South Africa is about 25 per cent. There are thus many casual workers that farmers use as temporary staff during harvest time but not the rest of the year. Their pay is relatively low and only legislation ensures that they receive at least the minimum wage. However, it cannot be denied that the strikes held by farm workers in the De Doorns area in 2013 made farmers more willing to use machines instead of labour for harvesting. In 2014 the cost of a Gregoire G175 V (not the state of the art machine) amounted to about R3.5 million, which put it beyond the financial means of most vineyard owners in South Africa. Therefore most grapes in South Africa are still harvested using manual labour not machines.

©iStock.com/JoseLOrtin

©Ingram Publishing

Machines and labour used to harvest grapes

Economic naturalist 8.2

Why do unions support minimum wage laws so strongly?

South African labour unions have historically been among the most outspoken proponents of minimum wage legislation. They favour not only a higher minimum wage but also broader coverage. Yet almost all members of, for example, Cosatu, Nehawu or Numsa already earn substantially more than the minimum wage, and so are not directly affected by changes in the legislation. Why, then, do these unions devote such great effort and expense to lobbying in favour of minimum wages?

One reason might be that their members are genuinely concerned about the economic well-being of workers less fortunate than themselves. No doubt many do feel such concern. But there are other disadvantaged groups – many of them even more deserving of help than low-wage workers – on whose behalf the unions might also have lobbied. Why doesn't Cosatu work just as hard, for example, trying to get extra benefits for homeless children or the physically disabled?

An understanding of the condition for production at minimum cost helps answer these questions. It is frequently so that union workers tend to be more skilled than non-union workers. Unskilled labour and skilled labour are substitutes for one another in many production processes, giving rise to isoquants shaped something like the one shown in Fig. 8.13. Which mix of the two skill categories the firm chooses to use will depend strongly on relative prices. Figure 8.13 shows the least costly mix for producing $Q = Q_0$ both before and after the enactment of the minimum wage statute. The wage rate for skilled labour is denoted by w. The pre-legislation price of unskilled labour is w_1, which rises to w_2 after enactment of the law. The immediate effect is to increase the absolute value of the slope of the isocost line from $-w_1/w$ to $-w_2/w$, causing the firm to increase its employment of skilled labour from S_1 to S_2, and simultaneously reducing its employment of unskilled (non-union) labour from U_1 to U_2.

Figure 8.13 The effect of a minimum wage law on employment of skilled labour

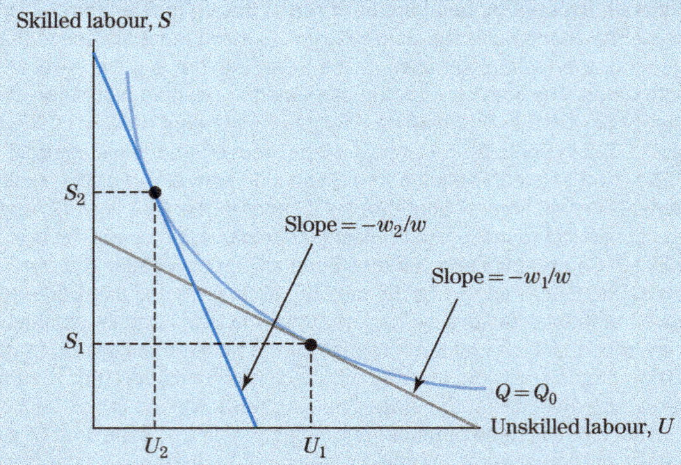

Unskilled labour and skilled labour are substitutes for one another in many production processes. When the price of unskilled labour rises, the slope of the isocost line rises, causing many firms to increase their employment of skilled (unionized) labour.

©iStock.com/Georg Winken

Why do union members, who earn substantially more than the minimum wage, favour increasing the minimum wage?

Although most union workers are not affected directly by the minimum wage laws, these laws have the indirect consequence of increasing the demand for union labour.[8] Even if unions lacked their avowed concern for the well-being of unskilled, largely non-union workers, there would thus be little mystery as to why unions devote so much of their resources in support of extensions of minimum wage legislation.

The curve labelled *EE* in Fig. 8.14 shows the firm's **output expansion path**. It is the set of cost-minimizing input bundles when the input price ratio is fixed at w/r. Thus, when the price of K is r and the price of L is w, the cheapest way to produce Q_1 units of output is to use the input bundle S, which contains K_1^* units of K and L_1^* units of L and costs TC_1. The bundle S is therefore one point on the output expansion path. In like fashion, the output level Q_2 is associated with bundle T, which has a total cost of TC_2; Q_3 is associated with U, which costs TC_3; and so on. According to the theory of firm behaviour, the long-run expansion path is the analogue to the income

[8] Note that this example assumes that the firm will produce the same level of output after the minimum wage hike as before. As we shall see in the next chapter, however, the firm will generally produce less output than before. If the output reduction is large enough, it could offset the firm's switch to skilled labour.

Economic naturalist 8.3

Why would a bathroom equipment manufacturer bake the image of a housefly onto the centre of its ceramic urinals?

The substitution of capital for labour is sometimes motivated not by a change in factor prices, but by the introduction of new ideas. We can explain this with an example of the 'official toilet project' initiated by Jos van Bedaf, then head manager of cleaning for Schiphol airport in Amsterdam.[9] His problem was that the airport men's rooms, which were used by more than 100000 patrons a year, had a tendency to become messy and smelly, despite frequent cleanings. Mr van Bedaf's solution was not to intensify the efforts of maintenance crews, but to make a minor change in the restroom equipment. Specifically, he requested that his sanitation equipment manufacturer supply the airport with urinals with the image of a housefly baked onto the centre of each fixture's glazed ceramic surface. His theory was that the presence of this target would cause patrons to be much more accurate in their use of the facilities. The result? Dramatically cleaner facilities and a 20 per cent reduction in cleaning costs. A national newspaper in the Netherlands rated the Schiphol facilities first on a list of clean restrooms. Today the flies are no longer 'at work' in the men's restrooms, they've been replaced by golf flags and patrons have to 'sink their putt'.

Figure 8.14 The long-run expansion path

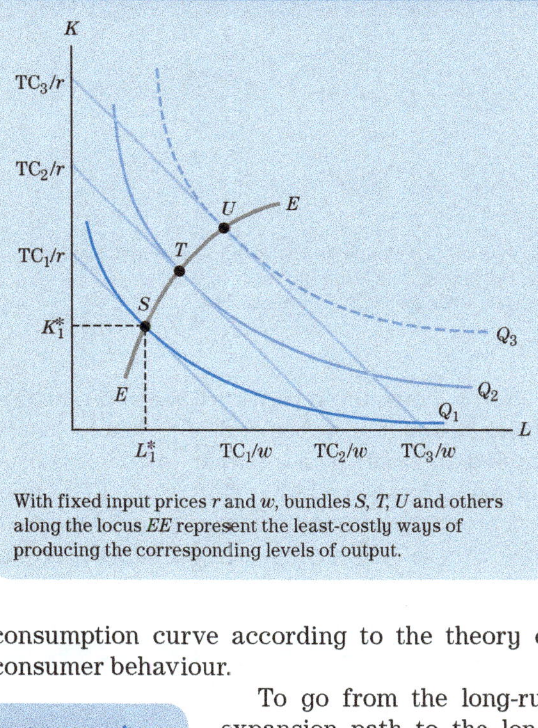

With fixed input prices r and w, bundles S, T, U and others along the locus EE represent the least-costly ways of producing the corresponding levels of output.

consumption curve according to the theory of consumer behaviour.

Output expansion path The locus of tangencies (minimum cost input combinations) traced out by an isocost line of given slope as it shifts outwards into the isoquant map for a production process.

To go from the long-run expansion path to the long-run total cost curve, we simply plot the relevant quantity–cost pairs from Fig. 8.14. Thus the output level Q_1 corresponds to a long-run total cost of TC_1, Q_2 to TC_2, and so on. The result is the curve labelled LTC in the top panel in Fig. 8.16. In the long run there is no need to distinguish between total, fixed and variable costs, since all costs are variable and nothing is fixed any more.

The LTC curve will always pass through the origin, because in the long run the firm can liquidate all of its inputs. If the firm elects to produce no output, it need not retain, or pay for, the services of any of its inputs. The shape of the LTC curve shown in the top panel looks very much like that of the short-run total cost curve shown in Fig. 8.2. But this need not always be the case, as we shall presently see. For the moment, though, let us take the shape of the LTC curve in the top panel in Fig. 8.15 as given, and ask what it implies for the long-run average and marginal cost curves.

Analogously to the short-run case, long-run marginal cost (LMC) is the slope of the long-run total cost curve:

$$LMC_Q = \frac{\Delta LTC_Q}{\Delta Q}\left(\text{or } \frac{dLTC}{dQ}\right) \quad (8.23)$$

In words, LMC is the cost to the firm, in the long run, of expanding its output by one unit.

Long-run average cost (LAC) is the ratio of long-run total cost to output:

$$LAC_Q = \frac{LTC_Q}{Q} \quad (8.24)$$

The bottom panel in Fig. 8.15 shows the LAC and LMC curves that correspond to the LTC curve shown in the top panel. The slope of the LTC curve is diminishing up to the output level Q_1 and increasing thereafter, which means that the LMC curve takes its minimum value at Q_1. The slope of

[9] This example is based on Stefan Verhagen, 'Fly in the pot', *Cornell Business*, 21 April 1992.

Figure 8.15 The long-run total, average and marginal cost curves

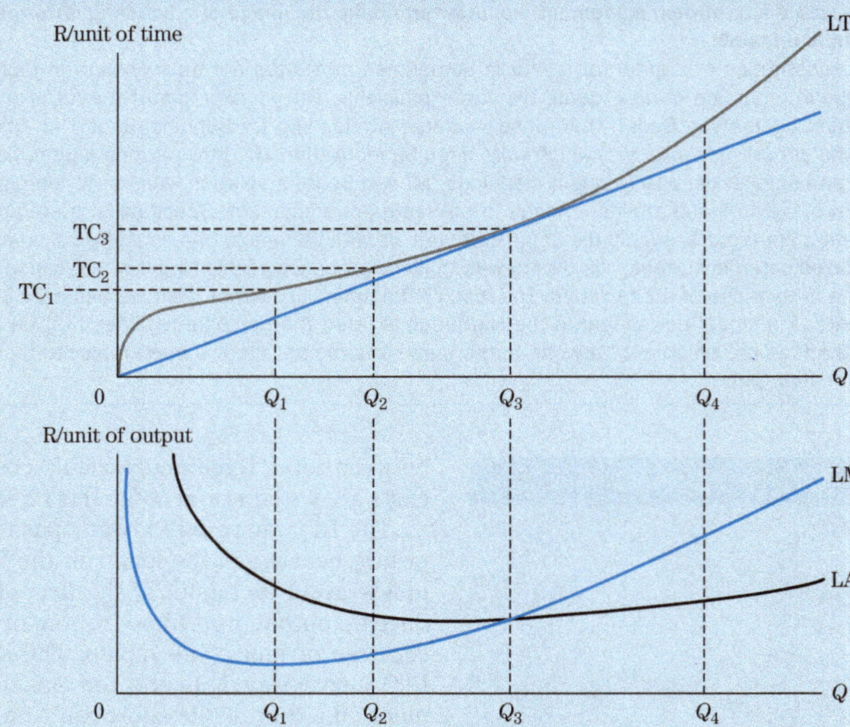

In the long run, the firm always has the option of ceasing operations and ridding itself of all its inputs. This means that the long-run total cost curve (top panel) will always pass through the origin. The long-run average and long-run marginal cost curves (bottom panel) are derived from the long-run total cost curves in a manner completely analogous to the short-run case.

LTC and the slope of the ray to LTC are the same at Q_3, which means that LAC and LMC intersect at that level of output. And again as before, the traditional average–marginal relationship holds: LAC is declining whenever LMC lies below it, and rising whenever LMC lies above it.

For a constant returns to scale production function, doubling output exactly doubles costs. Tripling all inputs triples output and triples costs, and so on. As shown in Fig. 8.16(a), the LTC curve for a production function with constant returns to scale is therefore a straight line through the origin.

Figure 8.16 The LTC, LMC and LAC curves with constant returns to scale

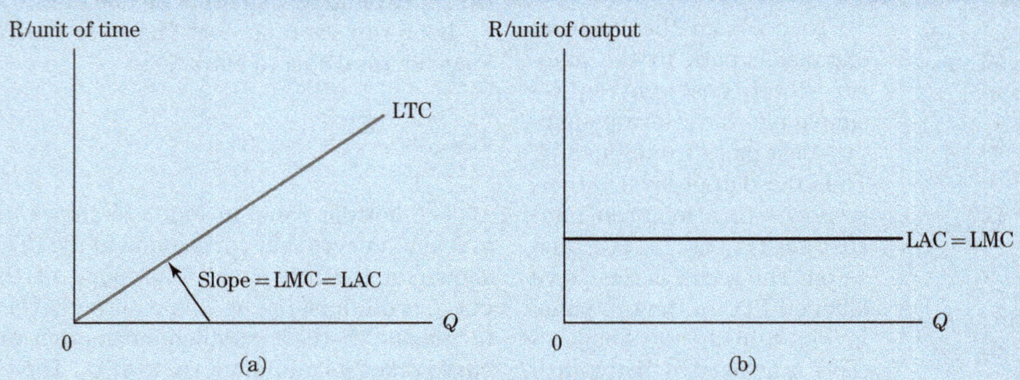

(a) With constant returns, the long-run total cost curve is a straight line. (b) Long-run marginal cost is constant and equal to long-run average cost.

Figure 8.17 The LTC, LAC and LMC curves for a production process with decreasing returns to scale

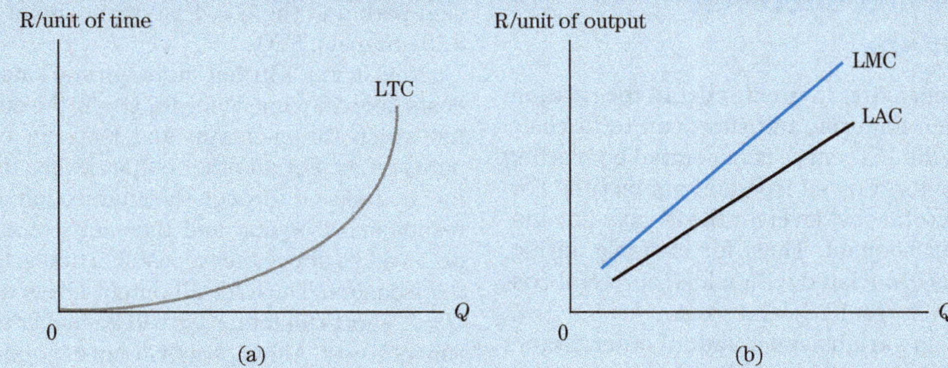

Under decreasing returns, a certain percentage increase in all inputs will lead to a smaller percentage increase in output, and additional units of production will become more expensive to produce.

Because the slope (or the first-order derivative) of LTC is constant, the associated LMC curve is a horizontal line, and is exactly the same as the LAC curve (Fig. 8.16(b)).

When the production function has decreasing returns to scale, a certain percentage increase in all inputs will lead to a smaller percentage increase in output, and additional units of production will become more expensive to produce. The LTC, LMC and LAC curves for a production function with decreasing returns to scale are shown in Fig. 8.17. For the particular LTC curve shown in Fig. 8.17(a), the associated LAC and LMC curves happen to be linear (Fig. 8.17(b)), but this need not always be the case. The general property of the decreasing returns case is that it gives rise to an upward-curving LTC curve and upward-sloping LAC and LMC curves. Remember that, when LAC is increasing, it implies that LMC lies above it.

Consider, finally, the case of increasing returns to scale. Here, a certain percentage increase in all inputs will lead to a larger percentage increase in output, and total cost will increase at a decreasing rate, as shown in Fig. 8.18(a). The accompanying LAC and LMC curves are shown in Fig. 8.18(b). The distinguishing feature of the LAC and LMC curves under increasing returns to scale is not the linear form shown in this particular example, but the fact that they are downward sloping.

The production processes whose long-run cost curves are pictured in Figs 8.16, 8.17 and 8.18 are 'pure cases', exhibiting constant, decreasing and increasing returns to scale, respectively, over their entire ranges of output. As discussed in Chapter 7, however, the degree of returns to scale of a production function need not be the same over the whole range of output.

Figure 8.18 The LTC, LAC and LMC curves for a production process with increasing returns to scale

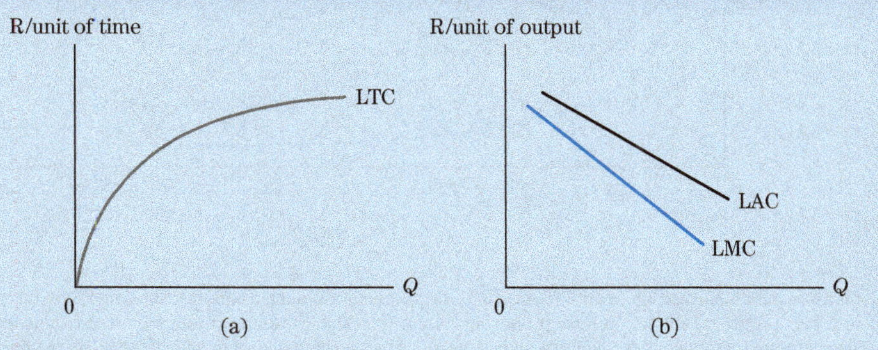

With increasing returns, a certain percentage increase in all inputs will lead to a smaller percentage increase in output, and additional units of production will get cheaper to produce.

The relationship between long-run and short-run cost curves

Let us consider first in greater detail the relationship between long-run and short-run total costs. Recall that the LTC curve is generated by plotting the Q value for a given isoquant against the corresponding total cost level for the isocost line tangent to that isoquant. Thus, for example, in Fig. 8.19 $Q = 1$ is associated with a long-run total cost of LTC_1, $Q = 2$ with LTC_2, and so on.

When K is variable, as it and all other factors are in the long run, the expansion path is given by the line $0E$. Now suppose, however, that K is fixed at K_2^*, the level that is optimal for the production of $Q = 2$. The short-run expansion path will then be the horizontal line through the point $(0, K_2^*)$, which includes the input bundles X, T and Z. The short-run total cost of producing a given level of output – say, $Q = 1$ – is simply the total cost associated with the isocost line that passes through the intersection of the short-run expansion path and the $Q = 1$ isoquant (point X in Fig. 8.19), namely, STC_1.

Note in Fig. 8.19 that short-run and long-run total costs take the same value for $Q = 2$, the output level for which the short-run and long-run expansion paths cross. For all other output levels, the isocost line that passes through the intersection of the corresponding isoquant and the short-run expansion path will lie above the isocost line that is tangent to the isoquant. Thus, for all output levels other than $Q = 2$, short-run total cost will be higher than long-run total cost. Although a firm can expand along the long-run expansion path in the long run, it may be forced to expand along the more expensive short-run expansion path in the short run.

The short-run and long-run total cost curves that correspond to the isoquant map of Fig. 8.19 are shown in Fig. 8.20. Note in Fig. 8.19 that the closer output is to $Q = 2$, the smaller the difference will be between long-run and short-run total

Figure 8.19 The short-run and long-run expansion paths

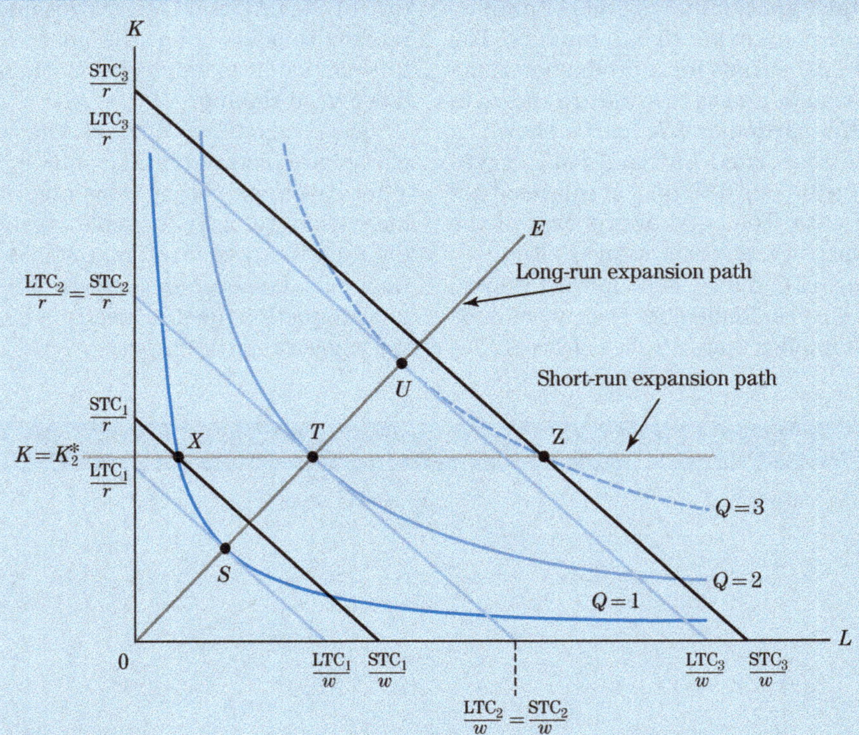

The long-run expansion path is the line $0E$. With K fixed at K_2^* the short-run expansion path is a horizontal line through the point $(0, K_2^*)$. Because K_2^* is the optimal amount of K for producing 2 units of output, the long-run and short-run expansion paths intersect at T. The short-run total cost of producing a given level of output is the cost associated with the isocost line that passes through the intersection of the relevant isoquant and the short-run expansion path. Thus, for example, STC_3 is the short-run total cost of producing 3 units of output.

Figure 8.20 The LTC and STC curves associated with the isoquant map in Fig. 8.19.

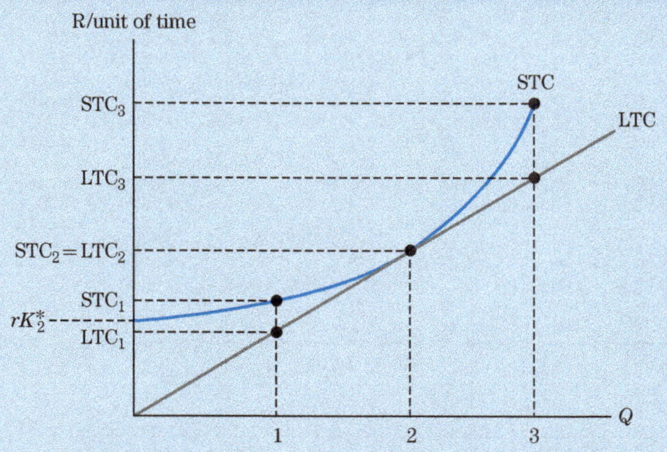

As Q approaches 2, the level of output for which the fixed factor is at its optimal level, STC_Q approaches LTC_Q. The two curves are tangent at $Q = 2$.

cost. This property is reflected in Fig. 8.20 by the fact that the STC curve is tangent to the LTC curve at $Q = 2$: the closer Q is to 2, the closer STC_Q is to STC_2. Note also in Fig. 8.20 that the STC curve intersects the vertical axis at rK_2^*, the fixed cost associated with K_2^* units of K.

The production process whose isoquant map is shown in Fig. 8.19 happens to be one with constant returns to scale. Accordingly, its long-run average and marginal cost curves will be the same horizontal line, as illustrated in Fig. 8.21. The position of this line is determined by the slope of the LTC curve in Fig. 8.20. The associated ATC curve will be U-shaped and tangent to the LAC curve at $Q = 2$, as shown in Fig. 8.21.

There are short-run cost curves not just for $K = K_2^*$, but for every other level of the fixed input as well. For example, the short-run average cost curve when K is fixed at (the optimal amount of K for producing $Q = 3$) is shown in Fig. 8.21 as the curve labelled $ATC_{K=K_3^*}$. Like the ATC curve associated with K_2^*, it too is U-shaped, and is tangent to the LAC curve at $Q = 3$. The ATC curves will in general be U-shaped and tangent to the LAC curve at the output level for which the level of the fixed input happens to be optimal.

One way of thinking about the LAC curve is as an 'envelope' containing all the short-run average total cost (ATC) curves. Suppose the ATC curves that correspond to 10 000 different levels of K were drawn in a diagram like Fig. 8.22. If we then took a string and moulded it to the outer contour of these ATC curves, it would trace out the shape of the LAC curve. In Fig. 8.22, note that for the output level at which a given ATC is tangent to the LAC, the long-run marginal cost (LMC) of producing that level of output is the same as the short-run marginal cost (SMC). Thus $LMC(Q_1) = SMC(Q_1)$, $LMC(Q_2) = SMC(Q_2)$ and $LMC(Q_3) = SMC(Q_3)$. Note also that each point along a given ATC curve, except for the tangency point, lies above the corresponding point on the LAC curve. Note, finally, that at the minimum point on the LAC curve in Fig. 8.22 ($Q = Q_2$), the long-run and short-run marginal and average costs all take exactly the same value.

When the LAC curve is U-shaped, note that the tangencies between it and the associated ATC curves do not in general occur at the minimum points on the ATC curves. The lone exception is the ATC curve that is tangent to the minimum point of the U-shaped LAC (ATC_2 in Fig. 8.22). On the downward-sloping portion of the LAC curve the tangencies will lie to the left of the minimum points of the corresponding ATC curves (like ATC_1), and on the upward-sloping portion of the LAC curve the tangencies will lie to the right of the minimum points (like ATC_3).

Note also in Fig. 8.22 that the SMC curves are always steeper than the LMC curve. The reason is implicit in our discussion of why LMC and SMC are nearly the same in a neighbourhood of the tangency points. Starting at a tangency point – say, at Q_1 in Fig. 8.22 – suppose we want to produce an extra unit of output in the short run. To do so, we shall have to move from an input mix that is optimal to one that contains slightly more L and slightly less K than would be optimal for

Figure 8.21 The LAC, LMC and two ATC curves associated with the cost curves from Fig. 8.20

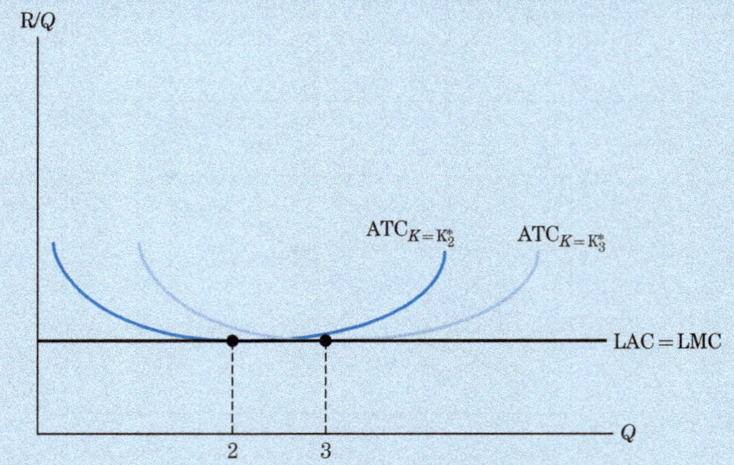

Short-run average cost is tangent to long-run average cost at the same output level for which the corresponding LTC and STC curves are tangent.

producing $Q_1 + 1$ in the long run. So the cost of that extra unit will be higher in the short run than in the long run, which is another way of saying $SMC_{Q_1+1} > LMC_{Q_1+1}$.

The production level at which the firm reaches the minimum turning point of its LAC curve is also known as the minimum efficient scale (MES). In theory, this means that if a firm reaches that production level while servicing half of the market there will be room in the market for only two firms that operate efficiently. Normally the MES is not a specific output level, but rather a range of

Figure 8.22 The family of cost curves associated with a U-shaped LAC curve

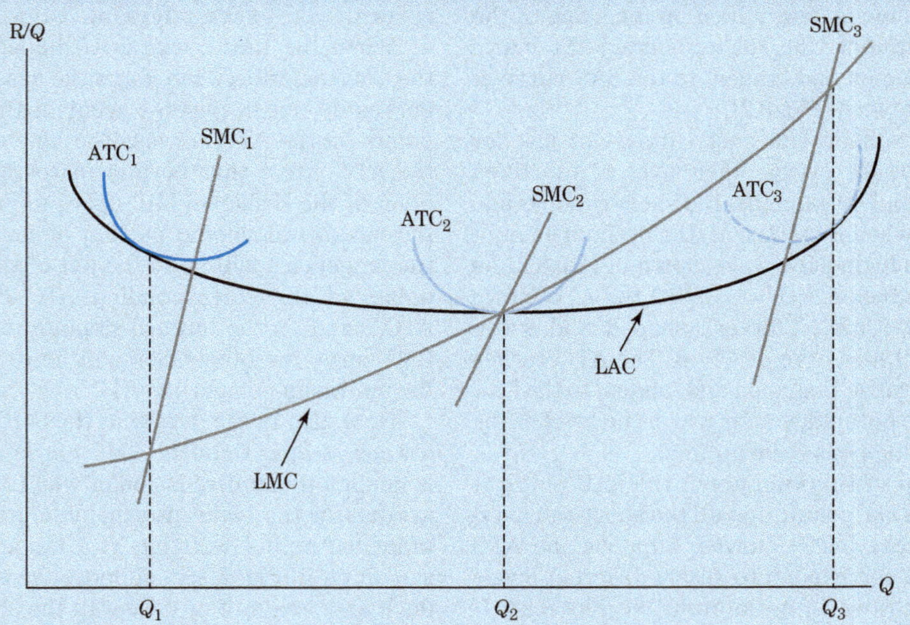

The LAC curve is the 'outer envelope' of the ATC curves. LMC = SMC at the Q value for which the ATC is tangent to the LAC. At the minimum point on the LAC, LMC = SMC = ATC = LAC.

output levels at which the firm experiences constant returns to scale.

The MES depends on the nature of production in an industry. In industries where the ratio of fixed costs to variable costs is high, there is plenty of scope to reduce unit cost by increasing production volume. This is likely to be a concentrated industry (few firms) and economies of scale operate as a barrier to entry for new firms. If the MES is only a small percentage of market demand, a competitive industry will likely exist, with room for many firms. In a natural monopoly the situation is slightly different. Such a firm services the whole market while it still operates on the negatively-sloped part of its LAC. By becoming bigger, its average production costs decrease. In such an industry there is room for only one firm.

Now suppose that we start at Q_1 and want to produce 1 unit of output less than before. To do so, we shall have to move to an input bundle that contains less L and more K than would be optimal for producing $Q_1 - 1$. In consequence, our cost savings will be smaller in the short run than they would be in the long run, when we are free to adjust both L and K. This tells us that $\text{LMC}_{Q_1-1} > \text{SMC}_{Q_1-1}$. To say that LMC exceeds SMC whenever output is less than Q_1, but is less than SMC when output is greater than Q_1, is the same thing as saying that the LMC curve is less steep than the SMC curve at Q_1.

Some intuition about the ATC–LAC relationship for a given ATC curve is afforded by noting that to the left of the ATC–LAC tangency the firm has 'too much' capital, with the result that its fixed costs are higher than necessary; and that to the

'The next step'

The calculus approach to cost minimization

Using the Lagrangian technique discussed in Chapter 3, we can show that the equality of MP/*P* ratios (Eq. 8.22) emerges as a necessary condition for the following cost-minimization problem:

$$\min_{K,L}(P_K K + P_L L) \text{ subject to } F(K, L) = Q_0 \tag{8.25}$$

To find the values of K and L that minimize costs, we first form the Lagrangian expression:

$$\mathcal{L} = P_K K + P_L L - \lambda[F(K, L) - Q_0] \tag{8.26}$$

The first-order condition for a minimum is given by

$$\frac{\partial \mathcal{L}}{\partial K} = P_K - \frac{\lambda \partial F}{\partial K} = 0 \tag{8.27}$$

$$\frac{\partial \mathcal{L}}{\partial L} = P_L - \frac{\lambda \partial F}{\partial L} = 0 \tag{8.28}$$

and

$$\frac{\partial \mathcal{L}}{\partial \lambda} = Q_0 - F(K, L) = 0 \tag{8.29}$$

Dividing Eq. 8.27 by Eq. 8.28 and rearranging terms, we have

$$\frac{\partial F / \partial K}{P_K} = \frac{\partial F / \partial L}{P_L} \tag{8.30}$$

which is the result of Eq. 8.21. (As an exercise, derive the same result by finding the first-order conditions for a maximum level of output subject to a cost limit of C.)

An alternative to the Lagrangian technique is to solve the production function constraint in Eq. 8.25 for K in terms of L, and then substitute the result back into the expression for total cost. To illustrate this alternative approach, consider the following example.

Example 8.5

For the production function $F(k, L) = \sqrt{K}\sqrt{L}$ with $P_K = 4$ and $P_L = 2$, find the values of K and L that minimize the cost of producing 2 units of output.

Our problem here is minimizing $4K + 2L$ subject to $F(K, L) = \sqrt{K}\sqrt{L} = 2$. Here, the production function constraint is $Q = 2 = \sqrt{K}\sqrt{L}$, which yields $K = 4/L$. So our problem is minimizing $4(4/L) + 2L$ with respect to L. The first-order condition for a minimum is given by

$$\frac{d[(16/L) + 2L]}{dL} = 2 - \frac{16}{L^2} = 0 \quad (8.31)$$

which yields $L = 2\sqrt{2}$. Substituting back into the production function constraint, we have $K = 4/(2\sqrt{2}) = 2/\sqrt{2}$.

right of the tangency the firm has 'too little' capital, so that diminishing returns to labour drive its costs up. Only at the tangency point does the firm have the optimal quantities of both labour and capital for producing the corresponding level of output. Also note that, to the left of Q_2, the firm is experiencing increasing returns to scale because the LAC decreases as the firm increases its output. At Q_2 (the minimum turning point of LAC) the firm experiences constant returns to scale. However, if more than Q_2 is produced, the firm is experiencing decreasing returns to scale, and the average cost per product increases as more units of output are produced.

Exercise 8.8

Consider a production function $Q = F(K, L)$ for which only two values of K are possible. These two values of K give rise to the ATC curves shown in the diagram. What is the LAC curve for this firm?

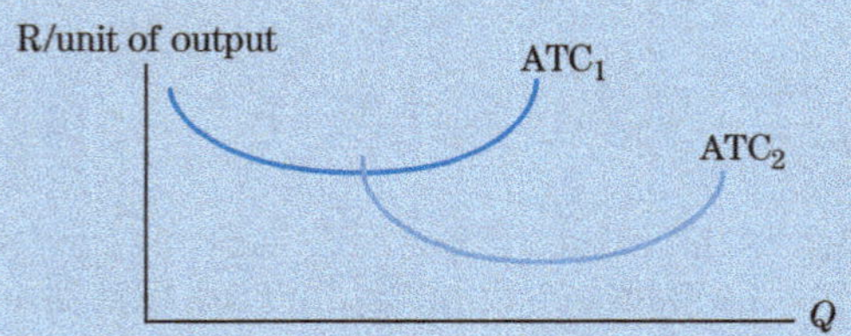

The learning curve versus economies of scale

We have already discussed the concept of economies of scale. A firm experiences economies of scale when all inputs are increased by a certain percentage, which results in a larger percentage increase in outputs. This implies that the average cost per product decreases as production levels increase.

From our discussion so far it may seem that a large firm will necessarily have lower long-run average cost than a smaller firm as a result of economies of scale in production. However, in some firms long-run average cost may decline because workers adapt to new technology, or just because they work smarter. A firm's marginal and average costs may decline for the following reasons:

- When workers first undertake a task it may take them a long time. As they become familiar with it, their speed increases.
- Managers of the production process learn by their mistakes and, over time, plan the whole production process better to increase efficiency.
- Engineers may streamline their product designs to save time without increasing defects. Better, specialized tools and more effective plant organization may also lower production cost.
- Some suppliers of the materials used in the production process may also become more efficient, pass this on via lower prices, and thus lower costs for the manufacturer.

As a result of all the above-mentioned factors, over time firms 'learn' more about the production process, thus enabling them to decrease average production cost. Figure 8.23 illustrates this learning experience in the form of a *learning curve*. The horizontal axis measures the cumulative number of machines produced, and the vertical axis the hours of labour needed to produce these machines. Initially, the workers take about 80 hours to produce one machine lot, but as they become more accustomed to the production process they can produce the machines at a much faster rate. However, when about 300 machine lots are produced, the entire learning effect will be complete.

If the production process is relatively new, and production cost is high at low levels and relatively low at high levels, this would indicate learning effects and not economies of scale. When the learning effect is at play, the firm can decrease its production cost irrespective of the scale of the firm's production. However, if the firm knows it enjoys economies of scale, it should expand its production to very large lots to take advantage of the lower cost associated with size.

Figure 8.23 The learning curve

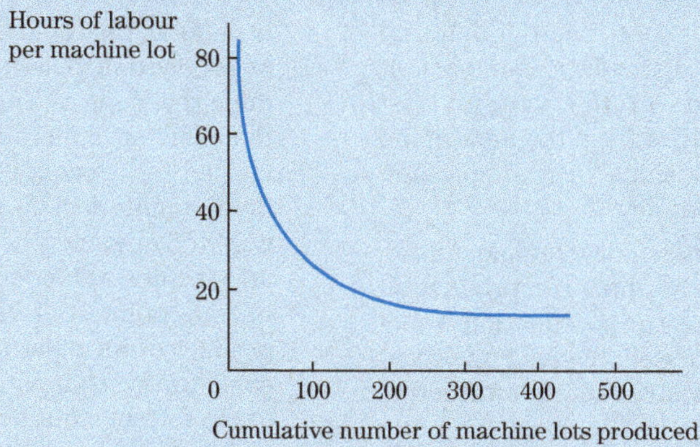

The learning curve indicates the relationship between a firm's cumulative output and the extent to which the labour needed to produce it falls as cumulative output increases.

The difference between these two concepts is clearly illustrated in Fig. 8.24. Because the ATC_1 curve is downward sloping it illustrates the cost structure of a firm that enjoys economies of scale. If the firm increases its output, it will move from A to B along ATC_1 as a result of economies of scale. In other words, to decrease average production cost per unit of output the firm has to increase its production levels. The learning effect, however, has a different effect on the cost structure. In Fig. 8.24, this is illustrated by a move from A on ATC_1 to C on ATC_2. By working 'smarter' a firm can decrease its average production cost per unit of output at *all* levels of output. The learning effect shifts the average cost curve of a firm downwards as production cost at all levels of production decreases. With older, well-established firms one would not expect to see much of a learning effect at work to lower their cost structures; it would be more common for them to experience economies of scale. However, for new firms entering the economy one would expect the learning effect to lower their cost structures, rather than them experiencing economies of scale. As firms become more established, the learning effect tends to wear off, but as new technology or production processes are introduced, they may experience it once again.

Figure 8.24 Economies of scale versus learning effect

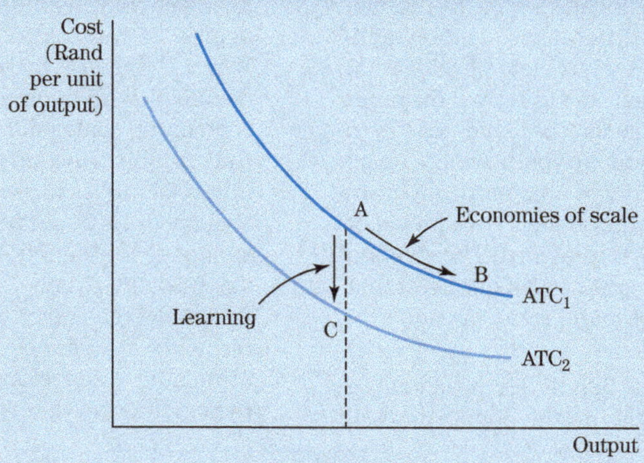

A firm's average production cost decreases as a result of a growth in production resulting from economies of scale (movement from A to B) or the learning effect (movement from A to C).

Summary

- Because students experience the material on cost curves as difficult, it is important to remember that all the various cost curves can be derived from the underlying production relationships in a simple and straightforward manner.
- Short-run cost curves, for example, all follow directly from the short-run production function. All short-run production functions we have discussed involved one fixed factor and one variable factor, but the theory would be exactly the same for more than one fixed input. Short-run total costs are decomposed into fixed and variable costs, which correspond, respectively, to payments to the fixed and variable factors of production. Because of the law of diminishing returns, beyond some point we require ever larger increments of the variable input to produce an extra unit of output. The result is that short-run marginal cost, which is the slope of the short-run total cost curve, is increasing with output in the region of diminishing returns. Diminishing returns are also responsible for the fact that short-run average total and variable cost curves – which are, respectively, the slopes of the rays to the short-run total and variable cost curves – eventually rise with output. Average fixed costs always take the form of a rectangular hyperbola, approaching infinity as output shrinks towards zero, and falling towards zero as output grows increasingly large.
- The problem of allocating a given production quota to two different production facilities is similar to the problem of allocating an available input across two different facilities. In the latter case, the goal is to maximize the amount of output that can be produced with a given amount of input. In the former, it is to produce a given level of output at the lowest total cost. The solution is to allocate the production quota so that the marginal cost is the same in each production process.
- The optimal input bundle for producing a given output level in the long run will depend on the relative prices of the factors of production. These relative prices determine the slope of the isocost line, which is the locus of input bundles that can be purchased for a given total cost. The optimal input bundle will be the one that lies at the point of tangency between an isocost line and the desired isoquant. At the cost-minimizing point, the ratio of the marginal product of an input to its price will be the same for every input. Put another way, the extra output obtained from the last rand spent on one input must be the same as the extra output obtained from the last rand spent on any other input.
- These properties of production at minimum cost help us understand why methods of production often differ sharply when relative factor prices differ sharply. We saw, for example, that it helps explain why developing countries often use labour-intensive techniques while their industrial counterparts choose much more capital-intensive ones, and why labour unions often lobby on behalf of increased minimum wages, even though virtually all of their members earn more than the minimum wage to begin with.
- For a given level of output, long-run total costs can never be larger than short-run total costs, for the simple reason that we have the opportunity to adjust all inputs in the long run but only some of them in the short run. The slope of the long-run average cost curve is a direct reflection of the degree of returns to scale in production. When there are increasing returns, LAC declines with output. With decreasing returns, by contrast, LAC rises with output. And, finally, constant returns in production give rise to a horizontal LAC curve. A U-shaped LAC curve is one that corresponds to a production process that exhibits first increasing, then constant and finally decreasing returns to scale. No matter what its shape, the LAC curve will always be an envelope containing the corresponding family of ATC curves, each of

which will be tangent to the LAC curve at one, and only one, point. At the output levels that correspond to these points of tangency, LMC and the corresponding SMC will be the same.

- The relationship between market structure and long-run costs derives from the fact that survival in the marketplace requires firms to incur the lowest costs possible using available production technologies.

Questions for review

1 What is the relationship between the law of diminishing returns and the curvature of the variable cost curve?

2 What is the relationship between the law of diminishing returns and the slope of the short-run marginal cost curve?

3 In which production process is fixed cost likely to be a larger percentage of short-run total costs: book publishing or landscape gardening?

4 Why does the short-run MC curve cut both the ATC and AVC curves at their minimum points?

5 If the LAC curve is rising beyond some point, what can we say about the degree of returns to scale in production?

6 Why should the production of a fixed amount of output be allocated between two production activities so that the marginal cost is the same in each?

Problems

1 The Preservation Embalming Company's cost data have been partially entered in the table below. Following the sudden and unexpected death of the company's accountant, you are called on to fill in the missing entries.

Bodies embalmed	Total cost	Fixed cost	Variable cost	ATC	AVC	AFC	MC
0	24			–	–	–	
1							16
2			50				
3	108						
4							52
5					39.2		
6				47			

2 Sketch the short-run TC, VC, FC, ATC, AVC, AFC and MC curves for the production function

$Q = 3KL$

where K is fixed at 2 units in the short run, with $r = 3$ and $w = 2$.

3 When the average product of labour is the same as the marginal product of labour, how will marginal cost compare with average variable cost?

4 A firm has access to two production processes with the following marginal cost curves:

$MC_1 = 0.8Q_1$ and $MC_2 = 4 + 0.4Q_2$

a If it wants to produce 16 units of output, how much should it produce with each process? (Round to two decimals.)

b If it wants to produce 8 units of output?

5 A firm uses two inputs, K and L, in its production process and finds that no matter how much output it produces or how input prices vary, it always minimizes its costs by buying only one or the other of the two inputs. Draw this firm's isoquant map.

6 A firm finds that no matter how much output it produces or how input prices vary, it always minimizes its costs by buying half as many units of capital as of labour. Draw this firm's isoquant map.

7 A firm purchases capital and labour in competitive markets at prices of $r = 120$ and $w = 80$, respectively. With the firm's current input mix, the marginal product of capital is 240 and the marginal product of labour is 360. Is this firm minimizing its costs? If so, explain how you know. If not, explain what the firm ought to do.

8 A firm has a production function $Q = F(K, L)$ with constant returns to scale. Input prices are $r = 2$ and $w = 1$. The output-expansion path for this production function at these input prices is a straight line through the origin. When it produces 5 units of output, it uses 2 units of K and 3 units of L. How much K and L will it use when its long-run total cost is equal to 70?

9 A firm with the production function $Q = F(K, L)$ is producing an output level Q^* at minimum cost in the long run. How will its short-run marginal cost when K is fixed compare with its short-run marginal cost when L is fixed?

10 A firm employs a production function $Q = F(K, L)$ for which only two values of K are possible, K_1 and K_2. Its ATC curve when $K = K_1$ is given by $ATC_1 = Q^2 - 4Q + 6$. The corresponding curve for $K = K_2$ is $ATC_2 = Q^2 - 8Q + 18$. What is this firm's LAC curve?

11 If a firm's LMC curve lies above its SMC curve at a given level of output, what will be the relationship between its ATC and LAC curves at that output level?

*12 A firm has the long-run total cost function

$$LTC(Q) = 2Q^3 - 40Q^2 + 440Q$$

Derive expressions for long-run average cost and marginal cost, and sketch these curves.

*13 For the long-run total cost function

$$LTC(Q) = Q^2 + 10$$

sketch ATC, AVC, AFC and MC.

*14 A firm produces output with the production function

$$Q = \sqrt{K}\sqrt{L}$$

where K and L denote its capital and labour inputs, respectively. If the price of labour is 1 and the price of capital is 4, what quantities of capital and labour should it employ if its goal is to produce 2 units of output?

*15 Sketch LTC, LAC and LMC curves for the production function given in Problem 2. Does this production function have constant, increasing or decreasing returns to scale?

*16 Suppose that a firm has the following production function:

$$Q(K,L) = 2L\sqrt{K}$$

a If the price of labour is 2 and the price of capital is 4, what is the optimal ratio of capital to labour?

b For an output level of $Q = 1000$, how much of each input will be used?

17 A firm with the production function

$$Q(K,L) = 2\sqrt{KL}$$

is currently utilizing 8 units of labour and 2 units of capital. If this is the optimal input mix, and if total costs are equal to 16, what are the prices of capital and labour?

18 For a firm with the production function

$$Q(K, L) = 3\ln K + 2\ln L$$

find the optimal ratio of capital to labour if the price of capital is 4 and the price of labour is 6.

19 A computer company's cost function, which relates its average cost of production AC to its

* These problems are most easily solved using the calculus definition of marginal cost.

cumulative output in thousands of computers, Q, and its plant size in terms of thousands of computers produced per year, q (within the production range of 10 000 to 50 000 computers), is given by

$AC = 10000 - 0.1Q + 0.3q$

a Is there a learning curve effect?

b Are there economies of scale?

c During its existence, the firm has produced a total of 40 000 computers, and is producing 10 000 computers this year. Next year it plans to increase production to 12 000 computers. Will its average cost of production increase or decrease? Explain.

Answers to in-chapter exercises

8.1 The variable cost curve is the same as before; the FC and TC curves are shifted upwards by 80 units. (See the following graph.)

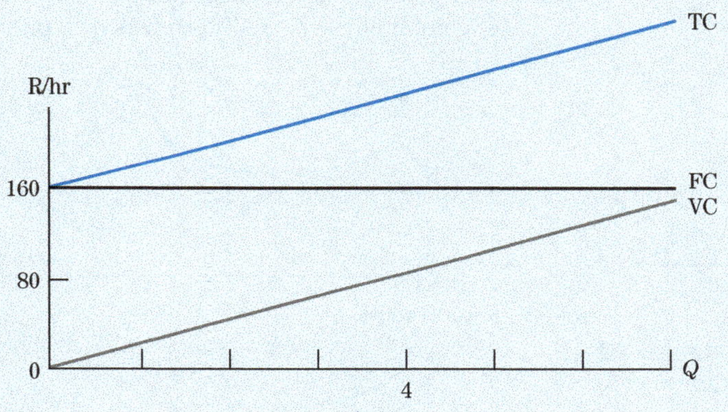

8.2 The vertical distance between the ATC and AVC curves is AFC. So we have $ATC_{10} - AVC_{10} = FC/10 = 20/10 = 2$.

8.3 Equating marginal costs, we have $12Q_A = 4Q_B$. Substituting $Q_B = 12 - Q_A$ yields $12Q_A = 48 - 4Q_A$, which solves for $Q_A = 3$. $Q_B = 12 - 3 = 9$ takes care of remaining output, and at these output levels marginal cost in both plants will be R36/unit of output.

8.4 When marginal product lies above average product, marginal cost lies below average variable cost (see Fig. 8.9).

8.5

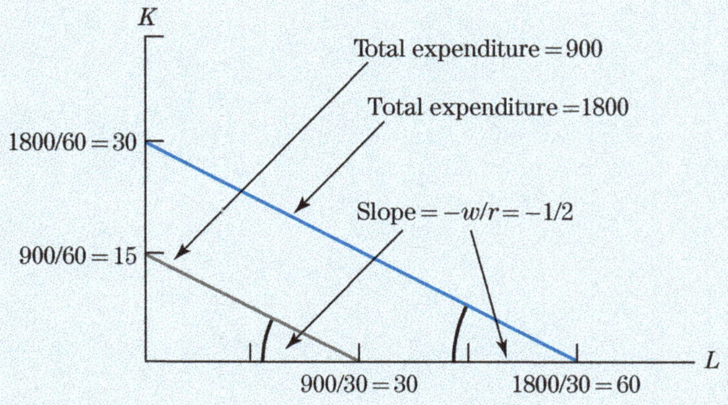

8.6 To produce 20 units of output, we shall need $L = K = 20$. As $r = 10$ and $w = 5$, costs are

$$C = 10K + 5L = 200 + 100 = 300$$

which may be rewritten as $K = 30 - \frac{1}{2}L$ in slope-intercept form. When the wage rises to $w = 20$, keeping costs at $C = 300$ requires that we find the point at which $K = L$ on the new isocost curve:

$$C = 10K + 20L = 300$$

which may be rewritten as $K = 30 - 2L$ in slope-intercept form. Setting $K = L$, we have

$$10K + 20L = 300 = 10L + 20L = 300 = 30L = 300, \text{ so } L = 10.$$

Thus $L = K = 10$, and we produce $Q = 10$.

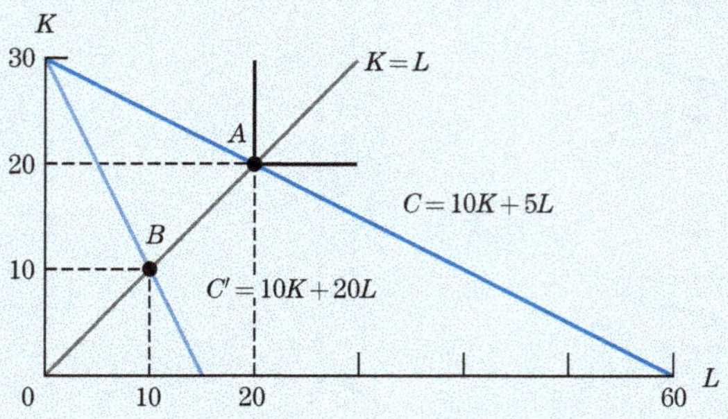

8.7 To produce 20 units of output, we shall need $L = 20$ or $K = 20$. Since $r = 10$ and $w = 5$, costs are

$$C = \min\{10K, 5L\} = \min\{200, 100\} = 100$$

When the wage rises to $w = 20$, keeping costs at $C = 100$ implies that

$$Q = \max\left\{\frac{100}{r}, \frac{100}{w}\right\} = \max\{10, 5\} = 10$$

Thus we use no labour ($L = 0$), all capital ($K = 10$) and produce $Q = 10$.

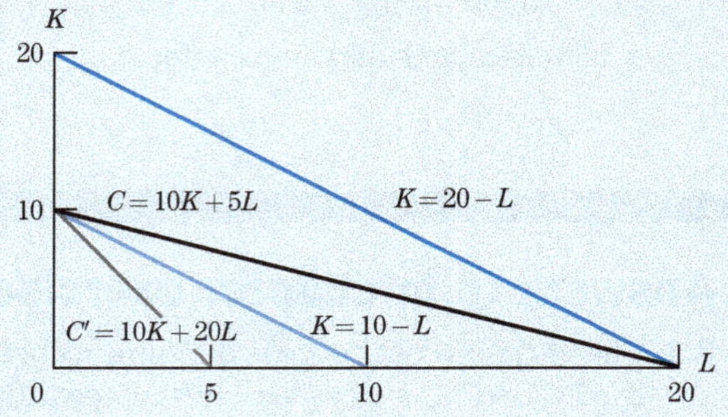

8.8 The LAC curve (bottom panel) is the outer envelope of the two ATC curves (top panel).

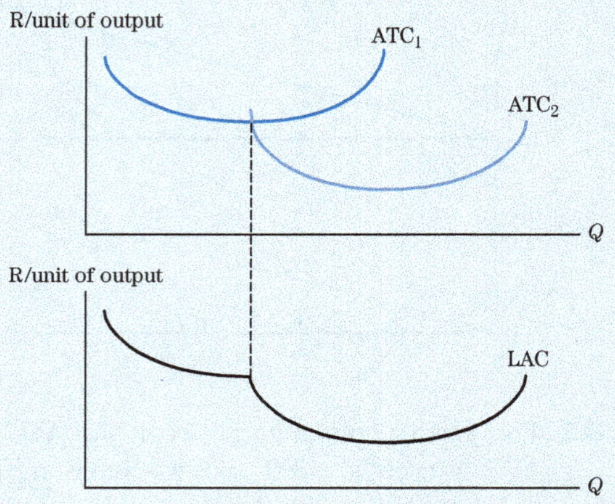

Chapter 9

Perfect competition

Imagine yourself a member of the Eastern Cape government. You have been asked to vote for a bill whose purpose is to alleviate poverty among small farmers in the province. Such farmers rent their farmland from landowners, and are allowed to keep the proceeds from the sale of the crops they grow. Because of limited rainfall, their crops are usually meagre, resulting in very low incomes for the average worker. The bill under consideration would authorize public funds to construct an irrigation system that would double the crop yields on the land in the province.

You strongly favour the objective of the bill, and are about to vote in favour of it when you meet with your legal adviser, an intern who majored in economics at the University of Botswana. She urges you in the strongest possible terms not to vote for the bill. She concedes that the project would double crop yields, and she too is sympathetic to the goal of providing improved conditions for small farmers. Even so, she insists that the bill would have little or no long-run effect on the earnings of farmers. Your adviser has given you sound advice on similar matters in the past, and you decide to hear her out.

Chapter preview

In this chapter we shall develop the analytical tools necessary for our hypothetical state legislator to assess his adviser's advice, including a model of price and output determination in perfectly competitive markets. Our first step will be to characterize the competitive firm's objective as that of earning the highest possible profit. This is clearly not the only goal a firm might pursue, but we shall see several reasons why firms might often behave as if profit were all they cared about.

We shall then consider the four conditions that define a perfectly competitive market (that you most probably covered in your first-year course):

- the existence of a standardized product
- price-taking behaviour on the part of firms

- perfect long-run mobility of factors of production
- perfect information on the part of consumers and firms

It turns out that none of these conditions is likely to be satisfied in practice for any industry. Nonetheless, we shall see that the economic model of perfect competition often generates useful insights, even when its structural preconditions are only approximately satisfied. Remember that the usefulness of an economic model is judged by how well it predicts future events in the economy and the model of perfect competition is a very useful model to predict economic behaviour.

Next, using the cost curves discussed in Chapter 8, we shall derive the necessary condition for profit maximization in the short run. The rule calls for the firm to produce an output level at which its short-run marginal cost is equal to the price of the product (MC = P) and in perfect competition this is also where it equals marginal revenue. We shall see that implementation of this rule fortunately does not require that firms have a detailed understanding of the economist's concept of marginal cost.

From the individual firm's supply decision, we shall move to the issue of industry-wide supply. The technique for generating the industry supply schedule turns out to be closely analogous to the one for aggregating individual demand curves into a market demand curve: we simply add the individual firms' supply curves horizontally.

The industry short-run supply and demand curves interact to determine the short-run market price, which forms the basis for output decisions by individual firms. We shall see that a firm's short-run profitability acts as a signal governing the movement of resources into and out of the industry – more specifically, that profits prompt resources to enter while losses prompt them to leave. Because we assume that there is no set-up cost or closure cost when firms enter or exit the market, these signals will result in firms either entering or exiting the industry.

We shall see that, in the long run, if tastes and technology are unchanging, a competitive industry whose firms have U-shaped LAC curves will settle at an equilibrium price equal to the minimum value of the LAC curve. And we shall also see that, under certain conditions, it will not be possible in such a market for anyone to enter into additional transactions that would benefit some people without at the same time harming some others.

The goal of profit maximization

In studying not only perfect competition but also a variety of other market structures, economists traditionally assume that the firm's central objective is to maximize profit. Two things must be said about this assumption. The first is to clarify just what is meant by the term 'profit', and the second is to explain why it often makes sense to assume that firms try to maximize it.

Profit – or, more precisely, *economic profit* – is defined as the difference between total revenue and total cost, where total cost includes all costs – both explicit and implicit – associated with resources used by the firm. This definition is significantly different from the one used by accountants (and what you will use in Accountancy if you take it as a subject) and many other non-economists, which does not subtract opportunity or implicit costs from total revenue. *Accounting profit* is simply total revenue less all explicit costs incurred.

To illustrate the distinction, suppose a firm produces 100 units of output per week by using 10 units of capital and 10 units of labour. Suppose the weekly price of each factor is R100/unit, and the firm owns its 10 units of capital. If output sells for R25/unit, the firm's total revenue will be R2500/wk. To calculate the week's economic profit, we subtract from R2500 the R1000 spent on labour (an explicit cost) and the R1000 opportunity cost of capital (an implicit cost), which leaves R500. (Under the assumption that the firm could have rented its capital to some other firm at the weekly rate of R100/unit, the R1000 opportunity cost is simply the earnings forgone by using the capital in its own operation.) The week's accounting profit for this firm, by contrast, is R1500, the difference between the R2500 total revenue and the R1000 out-of-pocket expenditure for labour.

Accounting profit may be thought of as the sum of two components:

- *normal profit*, which is the opportunity cost of the resources owned by the firm (in this example, R1000)
- *economic profit*, as defined above (here, R500)

Economic or abnormal profit is profit over and above the normal profit level associated with a specific industry.

The importance of the distinction between accounting and economic profits is driven home forcefully by the following example.

Example 9.1

Cullen Rupert runs a putt-putt golf course in Manaba Beach, Kwazulu Natal. He rents the course and equipment from a large recreational supply company, and supplies his own labour. His monthly earnings, net of rental payments, are R12 000, and he considers working at the golf course just as attractive as his only other alternative, working as a grocery clerk for R12 000/mth.

Now Cullen learns that his Uncle Johan has given him some land in Durban (the parcel bounded by the streets shown in Fig. 9.1). The land has been cleared, and Cullen discovers that a construction company is willing to install and maintain a putt-putt golf course on it for a payment of R60 000/mth. Cullen also commissions a market survey, which reveals that he would collect R900 000/mth in revenue by operating a putt-putt golf course there. (After all, there are many more potential golfers and tourists in Durban than in Manaba Beach.) After deducting the R60 000/mth payment to the construction company, this would leave him with R840 000/mth free and clear. Given these figures, and assuming that the cost of living is the same in Durban as in Manaba Beach, should Cullen, a profit maximizer, switch his operation to Durban?

Since he is a profit maximizer, he should switch to Durban only if his economic profit there will be higher than in Manaba Beach. Suppose, however, that Cullen is unfamiliar with the concept of economic profit, and instead compares his accounting profits in the two locations.

In Manaba Beach his accounting profit is R12 000/mth, the amount he has left over after paying all his bills. In Durban the corresponding figure will be R840 000/mth. On this comparison, he would not even think twice and would quickly forsake Manaba Beach for Durban.

If he compares economic profits, however, he will reach precisely the opposite conclusion. In Manaba Beach his economic profit is zero once we account for the opportunity cost of his labour. (He could have earned R12 000/mth as a grocery clerk, exactly the amount of his accounting profit.) To calculate what his economic profits would be in Durban, we must deduct from his R840 000/mth accounting profits – not only the R12 000 monthly opportunity cost of his labour, but also the opportunity cost of his land. Few locations in South Africa command higher land prices than next to the 'golden mile' in Durban. Suppose we conservatively estimate that Cullen's land would sell for R150 000 000 in today's real estate market, and suppose that the interest rate is 1 per cent/mth. The opportunity cost of devoting the land to a putt-putt golf course will then be (0.01) R150 000 000) = R1 500 000/mth, which makes his monthly economic profit in Durban R840 000 – R12 000 – R1 500 000 = –R672 000. Thus, if we assign any reasonable value to the opportunity cost of his land, it will obviously be better for Cullen to sell or rent it to someone else and remain in Manaba Beach. The reason why real estate is so expensive is that people can build skyscrapers on it and charge high rents to a multitude of tenants. To build a putt-putt golf course on the golden mile in Durban would be like wearing diamonds on the soles of your shoes.

Figure 9.1 Potential site for a putt-putt golf course in Durban

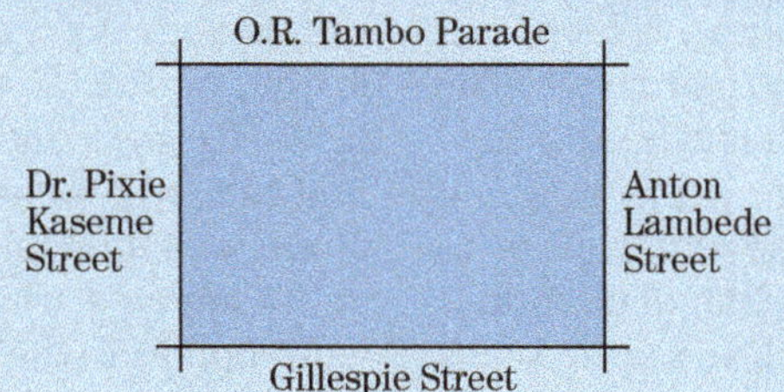

Let's turn now to the assumption of profit maximization. To predict what any entity – a firm, person, committee or government – will do under specific conditions, some sort of assumption must be made about its goals. After all, if we know where people want to go, it's much easier to predict what they'll do to get there. Economists assume that the goal of firms is to maximize economic profit; then they try to discover what specific behaviours promote that goal.

Exercise 9.1

In Example 9.1, how low would the monthly interest rate have to be before Cullen should relocate to Durban?

Numerous challenges to the profit-maximization assumption have been raised. Some critics say the firm's goal is to maximize its chances of survival; others believe that it wants to maximize total sales or total revenues to increase its market share; and some even claim that firms don't try to maximize anything at all.

One reason for such scepticism is that there are many examples whereby the managers of firms appear unqualified to take the kinds of actions required for maximizing profit. It is important to understand, however, that the assumption of profit maximization is not refuted by the existence of incompetent managers. On the contrary, a case can be made that, even in a world in which the actions of firms are initially random, a long-run tendency for profit-maximizing behaviour will eventually dominate.[1]

The argument is analogous to Charles Darwin's theory of evolution by natural selection, and it goes roughly as follows. First, in a world of random action, some firms will, purely by chance, come much closer than others to profit-maximizing behaviour. The former firms will have greater surplus revenues at their disposal, which will enable them to grow faster than their rivals. The other side of this coin is that firms whose behaviour deviates most sharply from profit maximization are those most likely to be bankrupt or to leave the industry. In the animal kingdom, food is an essential resource for survival, and profit plays a parallel role in the competitive marketplace. Those firms with the highest profits are often considerably more likely to survive. The evolutionary argument concludes that, over long periods of time, behaviour will tend towards profit maximization purely as a result of selection pressures in the competitive environment.

But the forces in support of profit maximization are not limited to the unintentional pressures of natural selection. They also include the actions of people who are very consciously pursuing their own interests. Bankers and other moneylenders, for example, are eager to keep their risks to a minimum, and for this reason they prefer to do business with highly profitable firms. In addition to having more internal resources, such firms thus have easier access to external sources of capital to finance their growth. Another important force supporting profit-maximizing behaviour is the threat of an outside takeover. The price of shares of stock in a firm is based on the firm's profitability (more on this point in Chapter 13), with the result that shares of stock of a nonprofit-maximizing firm will often sell for much less than their potential value. This creates an opportunity for an outsider to buy the stock at a bargain price and then drive its price upwards by altering the firm's behaviour.

Another pressure in favour of profit maximization is that the owners of many firms compensate their managers in part by giving them a share of the firm's profits. This provides a clear financial incentive for managers to enhance profitability whenever opportunities arise for them to do so.

Let us note, finally, that the assumption of profit maximization does not imply that firms conduct their operations in the most efficient conceivable manner at all times. In the world we live in there are many unintelligent, incompetent managers and not every task in the firm can be assigned to the most competent person in the universe. In a sensible world, the most important tasks will be carried out by the best managers, and the less important tasks by less competent ones. So the mere fact that we often observe firms doing silly things does not establish that they are not maximizing profits. To maximize profits means simply to do the best one can under the circumstances, and that will sometimes mean having to muddle along with uninspired managers.

Taken as a whole, the foregoing observations lend support to the assumption of profit maximization. We might even say that they place the burden of proof on those who insist that firms do not maximize profits. But they obviously do not establish

[1] See, for example, Armen Alchian, 'Uncertainty, evolution, and economic theory', *Journal of Political Economy*, 1950, vol. 58, no. 3, pp. 211–221.

conclusively that firms always pursue profit at the expense of all other goals. This remains an empirical question, and in the chapters to come we shall see some evidence that firms sometimes fall short. Even so, the assumption of profit maximization is a good place to begin our analysis of firm behaviour, and there is no question but that it provides useful insights into how firms respond to changes in market conditions.

The four conditions for perfect competition

To predict how much output a competitive firm will produce, economists have developed the *theory of perfect competition.* Four conditions define the existence of a perfectly competitive market. Let us consider each of them in turn.

1. *Firms sell a standardized product.* In a perfectly competitive market, the product sold by one firm is assumed to be a perfect substitute for the product sold by any other. Interpreted literally, this is a condition that is rarely if ever satisfied. Connoisseurs of fine wines, for example, insist that they can tell the difference between wines made from the same variety of grape grown on estates only a few hundred metres apart. It is also difficult to speak of a market for even such a simple commodity as shirts, because shirts come in so many different styles and quality levels. If we define the market sufficiently narrowly, however, it is sometimes possible to achieve a reasonable degree of similarity among the products produced by competing firms. For instance, 'Oom Sarel peaches' may not be exactly the same on different farms, but they may be close enough that most buyers don't care very much which farm they come from (and when we buy peaches we normally don't know their provenance). The assumption is that products are homogeneous, and no firm can thus raise its price above the price of its competitors without losing some of its business. In a world of homogeneous products, brand names means nothing because all products are the same.
2. *Firms are price takers.* This means that the individual firm treats the market price of the product as given. More specifically, it must believe that the market price will not be affected by how much output it or its competitors produce. This condition is likely to be satisfied when the market is served by a large number of firms, each of which produces a negligible fraction of total industry output. The actions of any one single firm will have no effect on the market price. But a large number of firms is not always necessary for price-taking behaviour. Even with only two firms in the market, for example, each may behave as a price taker if it believes that other firms stand ready to enter its market at a moment's notice. The assumption of price taking refers to consumers too. Each consumer consumes such a small percentage of total consumption that no one consumer can influence the market price by altering her consumption levels. Therefore, consumers are also price takers at the going market price.
3. *Free entry and exit, with perfectly mobile factors of production in the long run.* One implication of this condition is that, if a firm perceives a profitable business opportunity at a given time and location, it will be able to hire the factors of production required to take advantage of it. Similarly, if its current venture no longer appears attractive in relation to alternative business ventures, it is free to discharge its factors of production, which will then move to industries in which opportunities are more readily available. Of course, no one believes that resources are perfectly mobile. Labour, in particular, is not likely to satisfy this condition. People buy homes, make friends, enrol their children in school and establish a host of other commitments that make it difficult to move from one place to another. Nonetheless, the perfect mobility assumption is often reasonably well satisfied in practice, especially if we take into account that it is not always necessary for labour to move geographically in order for it to be mobile in an economic sense. In the electronic era many workers don't travel to work every day, but make contact with their employers via the internet. This makes labour more mobile now than, say, two decades ago. This assumption means that buyers can easily move from one supplier to another, and that any supplier can easily enter or exit a market. There are no restrictions such as acquiring of licences, ownership of specific raw materials or patent rights (that give rise to monopolies, as discussed in Chapter 10) that prohibit firms from entering certain industries.

4 *Firms and consumers have perfect information.* A firm has no reason to leave its current industry if it has no way of knowing about the existence of more profitable opportunities elsewhere. Similarly, a consumer has no motive to switch from a high-priced product to a lower-priced product of identical quality unless she knows about the existence of the latter. The world is sufficiently complex that relevant features of the product will inevitably be hidden from view. As a practical matter, the assumption of perfect information is usually interpreted to mean that people can acquire most of the information that is most relevant to their choices without great difficulty. Even this more limited condition will fail in many cases. As we saw in Chapter 6, when discussing consumer behaviour, people often have the relevant information right at their fingertips and yet fail to make sensible use of it. These observations notwithstanding, we shall see that the state of knowledge is often sufficient to provide a reasonable approximation to the perfect information condition. Although we are still a far cry from perfect information in practice, the development of electronic media means that we now know more about what's happening in any part of the world than ever before. However, consumers still do not know about all possible consumption opportunities and producers about all possible production opportunities and available technology.

To help assess whether the assumptions underlying the model of perfect competition are hopelessly restrictive, it is useful to compare them with assumptions that underlie the physicist's model of objects in motion. If you have taken a high school physics course, then you know (or once knew) that a force applied to an object on a frictionless surface causes that object to accelerate at a rate inversely proportional to its mass. Thus a given force applied to a 10 kg object will cause that object to accelerate at twice the rate we observe when the same force is applied to a 20 kg object.

To illustrate this theory, physics teachers show us DVDs of what happens when various forces are applied to a hockey ball atop a large artificial turf surface. They understand perfectly well that there is an easily measured amount of friction between the ball and the artificial turf. But they are also aware that the friction levels are so low that the model still provides reasonably accurate predictions.

In the kinds of situation we are most likely to encounter in practice, friction is seldom as low as between a hockey ball and an artificial turf surface. This will be painfully apparent to you, for example, if you have just taken a fall from your Yamaha Scrambler on an asphalt road. But even here the physicist's laws of motion apply, and we can make adjustments for friction in order to estimate just how far a fallen rider will slide. And even where the model cannot be calibrated precisely, it tells us that the rider will slide further the faster he was going when he fell, and that he will slide further if the pavement is wet, or covered with sand or gravel, than if it is clean and dry. Anyone who's watched a MotoGP race and seen Valentino Rossi fall as he comes round a corner at 250 km/h, skid on the tarmac and then just wipe the dirt from his clothing as he comes to a standstill will know that protective clothing decreases friction with the road substantially. Without such garments, many more bikers would have died over the years.

Similar issues are involved in the economic model of perfect competition. We have to be honest and say bluntly that no such thing as a perfectly competitive market exists in reality. One of the main criticisms of this market structure is that it leaves no room for innovation and advertising – the pillars of a profit-making enterprise. Product homogeneity is also regarded as totally unrealistic because brand names are very important in reality. The assumption of perfect information is also far removed from what we actually experience. With perfect information, risk would be a thing of the past and no firm would ever go out of business. Unfortunately this ideal world does not exist. So you can quite rightly ask why we still spend time in this course on such an unrealistic market structure.

However, the market for certain agricultural products comes close to satisfying the four conditions described above. The Johannesburg Stock Exchange is another good example of a near-perfect competitive market. This does not prevent certain investors from losing a lot of money when they buy or sell shares at the wrong time. Street food vendors are another good example of a near-perfect competitive market. Their products are homogeneous, consumers are free to buy at any vendor and entry/exit barriers for sellers are basically non-existent.

The predictions of the competitive model in these cases are in many ways as precise as those of the physicist's model applied to the hockey ball on the artificial turf surface. Despite criticisms levelled at it, this model has a remarkable ability to explain what economic impact a certain event will have. So the competitive model can tell us something useful if we interpret it with care.

Before we move on, it is important to bear in mind that, when an economic model is evaluated, one must always remember the assumptions within which the model is operating. Always judge it within its framework of assumptions, because the assumptions are necessary to simplify the real world. It is necessary to build a model that is simple enough to use, and not so complicated that nothing can be derived from it. Another important point in judging a model is to look at how well it predicts how the economy will adjust if an economic variable(s) changes.

The short-run condition for profit maximization

The first question we want our model of competitive firm behaviour to be able to answer is, 'How does a firm choose its output level in the short run if it wants to maximize its profit?' It will choose that level of output for which the difference between total revenue and total cost is the largest.

Consider a firm with the short-run total cost curve labelled TC in the top panel in Fig. 9.2. Like many of the firms we discussed in Chapter 8, this firm experiences first increasing, then decreasing, returns to its variable input, which produces the familiar pattern of curvature in its total cost curve. We also assume that fixed cost is equal to R3000. Suppose this firm can sell its output at a price of P_0 = R180/unit. Its total revenue per week will then be R180/unit of output times the number of units of output sold each week. For example, if the firm sells no output, it earns zero total revenue; if it sells 10 units of output per week, it earns R1800/wk; if it sells 20 units/wk, it earns R3600/wk; and so on. So for the perfectly competitive firm, which can sell as much or as little output as it chooses at a constant market price, total revenue is exactly proportional

Figure 9.2 Revenue, cost and economic profit

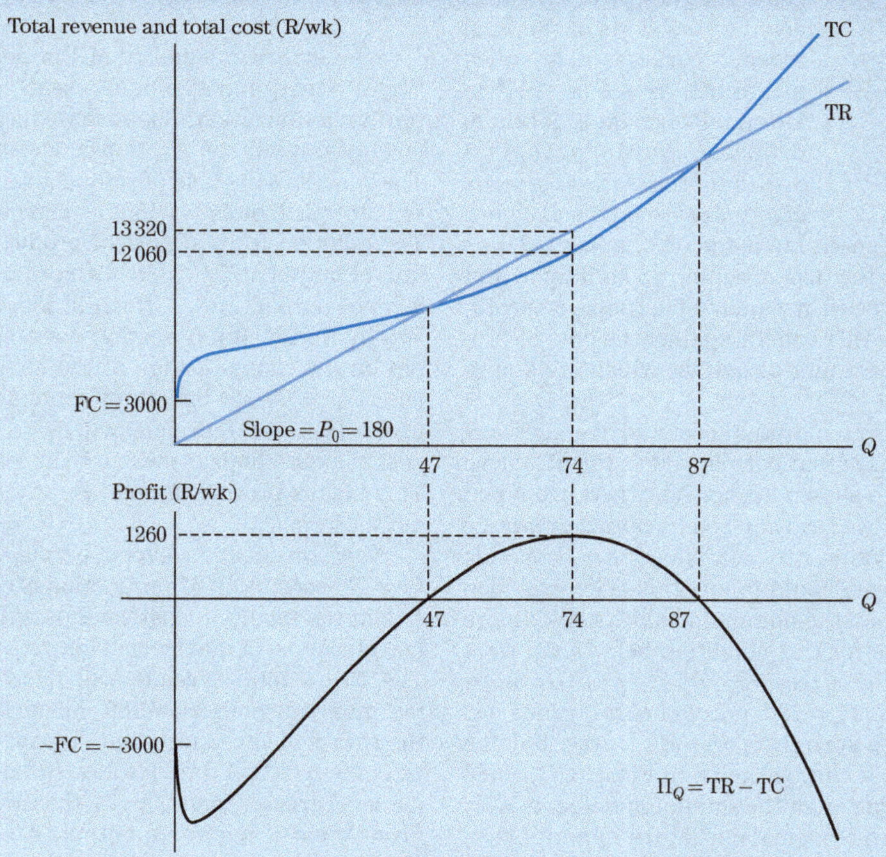

The total revenue curve is the ray labelled TR in the top panel. The difference between it and total cost (TC in the top panel) is economic profit (Π_Q in the bottom panel). At $Q = 0$, $\Pi_Q = -FC = -3000$. Economic profit reaches a maximum (R1260/wk) for $Q = 74$.

to output. For the firm in this example, the total revenue curve is a linear function through the origin with a slope of $P_0 = 180$, and labelled TR in the top panel in Fig. 9.2.

The bottom panel in Fig. 9.2 plots the difference between TR and TC, which is the curve labelled Π_Q. Here, Π_Q is positive for output levels between $Q = 47$ and $Q = 87$, and reaches a maximum at $Q = 74$. For output levels less than 47 or greater than 87, the firm makes economic losses, which is simply another way of saying that its economic profits are negative for those values of Q.

In the bottom panel in Fig. 9.2, note also that the vertical intercept of the profit curve is equal to −R3000/wk, the negative of the firm's fixed cost. When the firm produces no output, it earns no revenue but must still pay its fixed costs, so its profit when $Q = 0$ is simply −FC. If there were no positive output level for which the firm could earn higher profit than −FC, its best option would be to produce zero output in the short run.

The maximum profit point can also be characterized in terms of the relationship between output price and short-run marginal cost. Output price, which is equal to the slope of the total revenue curve, is also called **marginal revenue (MR)**.[2] Marginal revenue is formally defined as *the change in revenue that occurs when the sale of output changes by one unit.* In the cost–benefit language of Chapter 1, MR is the benefit to the firm of selling an additional unit of output. If the firm wants to maximize its profit, it must weigh this benefit against the cost of producing an extra unit of output, which is its marginal cost.

Marginal revenue (MR) The change in total revenue that occurs as a result of a one-unit change in sales.

The short-run marginal cost and average variable cost curves that correspond to the TC curve in Fig. 9.2 are shown in Fig. 9.3, where we again suppose that the firm can sell its output at a price of $P_0 = \text{R}180$/unit. To maximize its economic profit, the firm should follow this rule: Provided P_0 is larger than the minimum value of AVC (more on the reason for this condition below), *the firm should produce a level of output for which marginal revenue, $P_0 = 180$, is equal to marginal cost on the rising portion of the MC curve.* For the particular cost curves shown in Fig. 9.3, $P_0 = 180$ is indeed larger than the minimum value of AVC, and is equal to marginal cost at the quantity level $Q^* = 74$. The requirement that marginal revenue intersect marginal cost on the rising portion of marginal cost implies that marginal revenue intersects marginal cost from above. Thus marginal revenue lies below marginal cost past this point of intersection, and the firm has no incentive to expand output beyond this point. The additional cost to produce an extra unit of output will be more than the additional income that the firm will earn if it sells that unit at the market price of R180. In the short run, profit is thus maximized when firms produce and sell the amount of products whereby marginal cost equals marginal revenue (MC = MR).

As the following exercise demonstrates, the definitions of MR and MC tell us something about the relative values of the slopes of the TR and TC curves at the maximum-profit point in Fig. 9.2.

Exercise 9.2

How do the slopes of the TC and TR curves compare at $Q = 74$ in Fig. 9.2? (You can do this exercise with derivatives as well.)

Why is 'price (equal to MR in perfect competition) = marginal cost' a necessary condition for profit maximization? Suppose we pick some other level of output, say Q_1, that is less than $Q^* = 74$. The benefit to the firm of selling an additional unit of output will be $P_0 = \text{R}180$ (its marginal revenue). The addition to total cost of producing an extra unit of output at Q_1 will be its marginal cost at the level of output, MC_{Q_1}, which in Fig. 9.3 is clearly less than R180. It follows that, for any level of output on the rising portion of the MC curve to the left of $Q^* = 74$, the benefit of expanding (as measured by marginal revenue) will be greater than the cost of expanding (as measured by marginal cost). This means profit will increase when we expand output from Q_1.

Now consider any level of output to the right of $Q^* = 74$, such as Q_2. If production is contracted by 1 unit, the resulting cost savings will be equal to marginal cost at that level of output, namely MC_{Q_2}. The firm's total revenue will decrease with its marginal revenue, $P_0 = 180$. Since $MC_{Q_2} > \text{R}180$, the firm will save more than it loses when it contracts output by 1 unit. It follows that, for any output level greater than $Q^* = 74$, the firm's profit will grow when it contracts output. Another way of

[2] As we shall see in the next chapter, output price and marginal revenue are *not* the same for a monopolist if profits are maximized.

Figure 9.3 The profit-maximizing output level in the short run

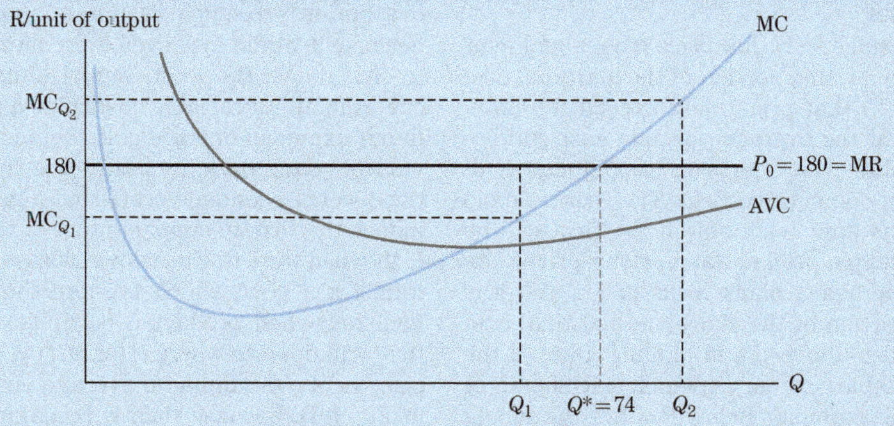

A necessary condition for profit maximization is that price equals marginal cost on the rising portion of the marginal cost curve. Here, this happens at the output level $Q^* = 74$.

putting this, is that the firm's profit will decrease if it expands production beyond 74 units. The only output level at which the firm cannot earn higher profit by either expanding or contracting is $Q^* = 74$, the level for which the cost of any move is exactly equal to its benefit.

One can reach the same conclusion by using derivatives. The firm's problem is maximizing the difference between total revenue and total cost: $\Pi = PQ - TC_Q$, where TC_Q is the short-run total cost of producing Q units of output. The first-order condition for a maximum is given by

$$\frac{d\Pi}{dQ} = P - \frac{dTC_Q}{dQ} = P - MC_Q = 0$$

which gives the condition $P = MC_Q$. The second-order condition for a maximum is given by

$$\frac{d^2\Pi}{dQ^2} = \frac{-dMC_Q}{dQ} < 0$$

or

$$\frac{dMC_Q}{dQ} > 0$$

which tells us why we must be at a point on the rising portion of the marginal cost curve. This is the same as saying that MC = MR at equilibrium, because $P = MC$ when a firm maximizes its output in a perfectly competitive market.

The shutdown condition

Recall that the rule for short-run profit maximization is to set price equal to marginal cost, provided price exceeds the minimum value of average variable cost. Why must price be greater than the minimum point of the AVC curve? The answer is that, unless this condition is met, the firm will do better to shut down – that is, to produce no output – in the short run. To see why, note that the firm's *average revenue (AR)* per unit of output sold is simply the price at which it sells its product. (When price is constant for all levels of output, average revenue and marginal revenue are the same).[3] If average revenue is less than average variable cost, the firm is taking a loss on each unit of output it sells. The firm's total revenue (average revenue times quantity) will be less than its total variable cost (AVC times quantity), and this means that it would do better by not producing any output at all. Shutting down in this context means simply producing zero output in the short run. The firm will resume production if price again rises above the minimum value of AVC, the trigger point for its **shutdown condition**.

Shutdown condition If price falls below the minimum of average variable cost, the firm should shut down in the short run.

As we saw in Fig. 9.2, a firm that produces zero output will earn economic profit (in actual fact, losses) equal to the negative of its fixed costs. If the price of its product is less than the minimum value of its

[3] Note that $AR = TR/Q = PQ/Q = P$. Only in perfect competition are the demand curve (D), the price curve (P), the average revenue curve (AR) and the marginal revenue curve (MR) the same horizontal line at the going market price.

average variable costs, it would experience even greater economic losses if it produced a positive level of output.

The two rules – (1) that price must equal marginal cost on a rising portion of the marginal cost curve, and (2) that price must exceed the minimum value of the average variable cost curve – together define the short-run supply curve of the perfectly competitive firm. The firm's supply curve tells us how much output the firm will be willing to supply/produce at various prices. As shown by the heavy black locus in Fig. 9.4, it is the rising portion of the short-run marginal cost curve that lies above the minimum value of the average variable cost curve (which is R120/unit of output in this example). Below $P = 120$, the supply curve coincides with the vertical axis, indicating that the firm supplies zero output when price is less than min AVC. For prices above 120, the firm will supply the output level for which $P = \text{MC}$. For example, prices of 140 and 200 will cause this firm to supply 64 and 78 units of output, respectively. The competitive firm acts here as both a price taker and a profit maximizer: taking the market price as given, it chooses the level of output that maximizes economic profit at that price.

Note in Fig. 9.4 that the firm supplies positive output whenever price exceeds min AVC, and recall that average variable cost is less than average total cost, the difference being average fixed cost. It follows that no matter how small is AFC, there will be a range of prices that lie between the AVC and ATC curves. For any price in this range the firm supplies the level of output for which P (or MR) = MC, which means that it will lose money, because P is less than ATC. For example, the firm whose cost curves are shown in Fig. 9.4 cannot cover all its costs at a price of R140. Even so, its best option is to supply 64 units of output per week, because it would lose even more money if it were to shut down. By producing 64 units the firm is covering all its variable costs plus a portion (R20 in our example) of fixed cost. Being able to cover variable costs does not assure the firm of a positive level of economic profit, but it is sufficient to induce the firm to supply output in the short run. If the firm were to close down, losses would equal total fixed cost, which is more than the losses incurred when producing 64 units. Obviously a firm will operate where P (or MR) = MC when the price is above minimum average cost (like R200 in Fig. 9.4), because then it is making economic profits.

Note also in Fig. 9.4 that the firm's short-run supply curve is upward sloping. This is because the relevant portion of the firm's short-run marginal cost curve is upward sloping, which, in turn, is a direct consequence of the law of diminishing returns (which we discussed in Chapter 7).

The short-run supply curve for a competitive industry

The short-run supply curve for a competitive industry is generated in a manner analogous to the one we used to generate the market demand curve in Chapter 4. In this case we simply announce a price and then add together the amounts each firm wishes to supply at that price. The resulting sum is industry supply at that price. Additional points on the industry supply curve are generated by

Figure 9.4 The short-run supply curve of a perfectly competitive firm

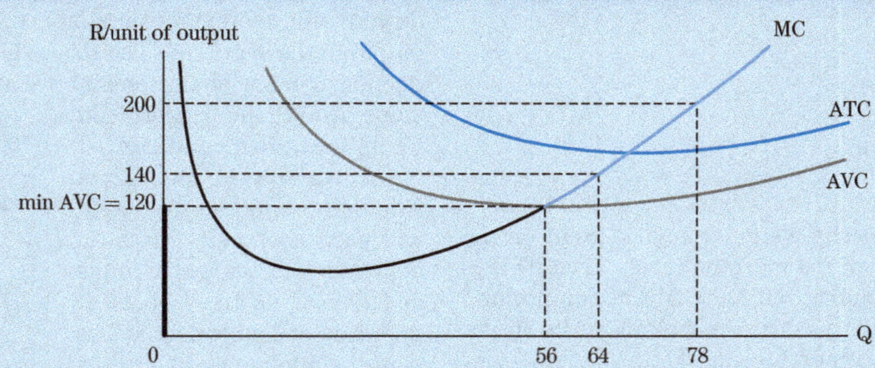

When price lies below the minimum value of average variable cost (here, R120/unit of output), the firm will make losses at every level of output, and will keep its losses to a minimum by producing zero. For prices above min AVC, the firm will supply that level of output for which P(or MR) = MC on the rising portion of its MC curve.

pairing other prices with the sums of individual firm supplies at those prices.

Figure 9.5 illustrates the procedure for one of the simplest cases, an industry consisting of only two firms. At a price of R20/unit of output, only firm 1 (panel a) wishes to supply any output, and so its offering, $Q_1 = 2$ units of output per week, constitutes the entire industry supply at $P = 2$ (panel c). At $P = 30$, firm 2 enters the market (panel b) with an offering of $Q_2 = 4$. Added to firm 1's offering at $P = 30$ (namely, $Q_1 = 3$), the resulting industry supply at $P = 30$ is $Q = 7$ (panel c). In like fashion, we see that industry supply at $P = 70$ is $Q = 7 + 8 = 15$. In Chapter 4 we saw that the market demand curve is the horizontal summation of the individual consumer demand curves. Here, we see that the market supply curve is the *horizontal summation* of the individual firm's supply curves.

The horizontal summation of an individual firm's supplies into industry supply has a simple form when the firms in the industry are all identical. Suppose n firms each have supply curve $P = c + dQ_i$. To add up the quantities for the n firms into industry supply, we rearrange the firm supply curve $P = c + dQ_i$ to express quantity alone on one side: $Q_i = -(c/d) + (1/d)P$. Then industry supply is the sum of the quantities supplied Q_i by each of the n firms:

$$Q = nQ_i$$
$$= n\left(-\frac{c}{d} + \frac{1}{d}P\right)$$
$$= -\frac{nc}{d} + \frac{n}{d}P$$

We can then rearrange industry supply $Q = (n/d)P - (nc/d)$ to get it back in the form of price alone on one side: $P = (d/n)Q + c$. Intuitively, each one unit supplied by the industry is $1/n$ unit for each firm to supply. These calculations suggest a general rule for constructing the industry supply curve when firms are identical. If we have n individual firm supply curves $P = dQ_i + c$, then the industry supply curve is $P = (d/n)Q + c$. If you get supply functions in the format $P = f(Q)$ that you must add together, it is important to remember to rearrange the functions in the format $Q = f(P)$, add them together and then rearrange the functions back in the format $P = f(Q)$ before you draw the function. If you don't do it this way, you will add the functions *vertically*, which is incorrect.

Exercise 9.3

Suppose an industry has 30 firms, each with supply curve $P = 90Q_i + 20$. What is the industry supply curve?

Short-run competitive equilibrium

The individual competitive firm must choose the most profitable level of output to produce in response to a given price. But where does that price come from? As we saw in Chapter 2, it comes from the intersection of the supply and demand curves for the product. Recall that, at the

Figure 9.5 The short-run competitive industry supply curve

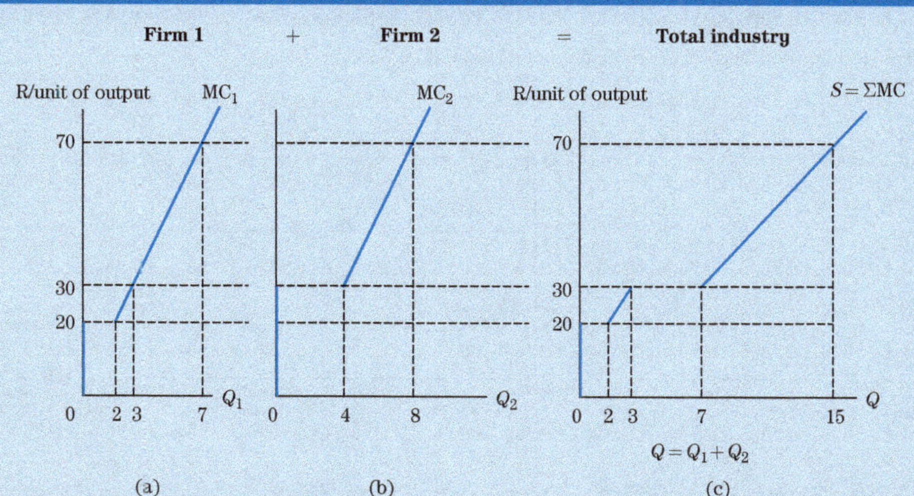

To get the industry supply curve (panel c), we simply add the individual firm supply curves (panels a and b) horizontally.

Example 9.2

Suppose an industry has 200 firms, each with supply curve $P = 1000Q_i + 100$. What is the industry supply curve?

First, we need to rearrange the representative firm supply curve $P = 1000Q_i + 100$ to have quantity alone on one side:

$$Q_i = \frac{1}{1000}P - \frac{1}{10}$$

Then we multiply by the number of firms, $n = 200$:

$$\begin{aligned} Q &= nQ_i = 200Q_i \\ &= 200\left(\frac{1}{1000}P + \frac{1}{10}\right) \\ &= \frac{1}{5}P - 20 \end{aligned}$$

Finally, we rearrange the industry supply curve $Q = \frac{1}{5}P - 20$ to have price alone on one side, $P = 5Q + 100$, to return to the slope-intercept form.

equilibrium price, sellers are selling the quantity they wish to sell and buyers are buying the quantity they wish to buy.

In Fig. 9.6(a), the curve labelled D is the market demand curve for a product sold in a perfectly competitive industry. The curve labelled S is the corresponding short-run industry supply curve, the horizontal summation of the relevant portions of the individual short-run marginal cost curves (those that lie above the respective minimum values of AVC). These two curves intersect to establish the short-run competitive equilibrium price, here denoted by $P^* =$ R200/unit of output. $P^* = 200$, in turn, is the price on which individual firms base their output decisions.

The conditions confronting a typical firm are shown in Fig. 9.6(b). The demand curve facing this firm is a horizontal line at $P^* = 200$. This means that it can sell as much or as little as it chooses at the market price of R200/unit. If a firm charged more than R200, it would sell no output at all, because buyers would switch to a competing firm

Figure 9.6 Short-run price and output determination under pure competition

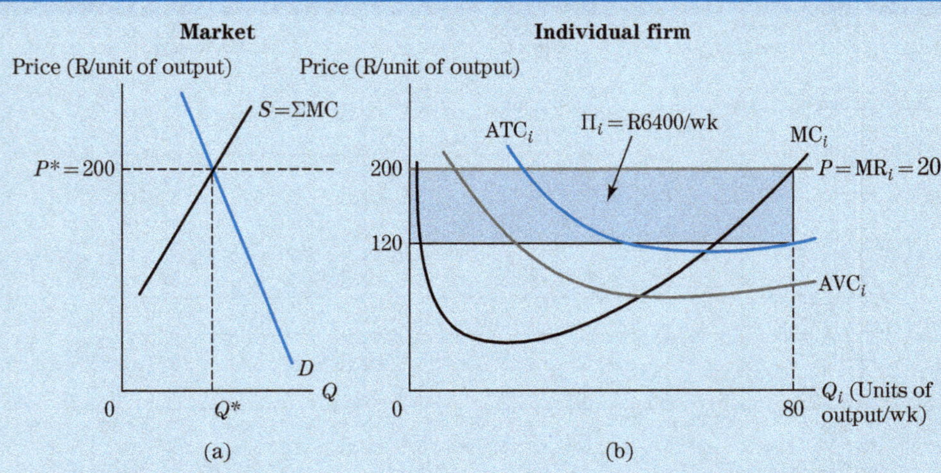

The short-run supply and demand curves intersect to determine the short-run equilibrium price, $P^* = 200$ (panel a). The firm's demand curve is a horizontal line at $P^* = 200$ (panel b). Taking $P^* = 200$ as given, the firm maximizes economic profit by producing 80 units/wk, for which it earns an economic profit of $\Pi_i =$ R6400/wk (the shaded rectangle in panel b).

that sells for R200. Remember that we assume perfect information, so consumers will know this is the only firm that charges more than the market price of R200. A firm could charge less than R200, of course, but would have no motive to do so if its objective was to maximize economic profit, since it can already sell as much as it wants to at R200. The result is that, even though the market demand curve is downward sloping, the demand curve facing the individual firm is perfectly elastic. (Recall from the definition of price elasticity in Chapter 4 that a horizontal demand curve has infinite price elasticity, which is what 'perfectly elastic' means.)

In Fig. 9.6(b), the representative firm maximizes its profit by equating P^* $(MR) = \text{R200/unit}$ to marginal cost at an output level of $Q_i^* =$ 80 units/wk. At that output level, its total revenue is $P^*Q^* = \text{R16 000/wk}$ and its total costs are $ATC_{Q_i^*}Q_i^* = (\text{R120/unit})(80 \text{ units/wk}) = \text{R9 600/wk}$. Its economic profit is the difference between total revenue and total cost, R16 000/wk – R9600/wk = R6400/wk, and is represented by the shaded rectangle denoted Π_i. Equivalently, profits can be calculated as the difference between price (R200/unit) and average total cost (R120/unit) times the quantity sold (80 units/week).

Recall that the opportunity cost of resources owned by the firm constitutes part of the cost included in its average total cost curve. This is why we say that total revenues over and above total costs constitute economic profit. If the firm's revenue were exactly equal to its total cost, it would earn only a normal profit – which is to say, zero economic profit.

Similarly, a price equal to average total cost implies that total cost equals total revenue, and the firm earns zero economic profit. Bear in mind that, in a perfect competitive market structure, price is also equal to average cost. Thus price equal to the minimum average total cost can be called the *break-even point* – the lowest price at which the firm will not suffer negative economic profits in the short run.

The situation portrayed in Fig. 9.6 is one in which the short-run equilibrium price enables the firm to make a positive economic profit. Another possibility is that the short-run supply and demand curves will intersect at an equilibrium price that is sufficiently high to induce firms to supply output, but not high enough to enable them to make economic profits. This situation is illustrated in Fig. 9.7, which is a graphical representation of Table 9.1. In Fig. 9.7(a), supply and demand in the industry intersect at a price $P^* = \text{R100/unit}$ of output, which lies above the minimum value of the AVC curve of the firm shown in the right panel, but below that firm's ATC curve at the profit-maximizing level of output, $Q_i^* = 60$ units of output per week. The result is that the firm makes an economic loss of $P^*Q_i^* - ATC_{Q_i^*}Q_i^* = (\text{R60} \times \text{R100}) - (\text{R120} \times \text{R60}) =$ $-\text{R1 200/wk}$. This loss is shown in Fig. 9.7(b) by the

Figure 9.7 A short-run equilibrium price that results in economic losses

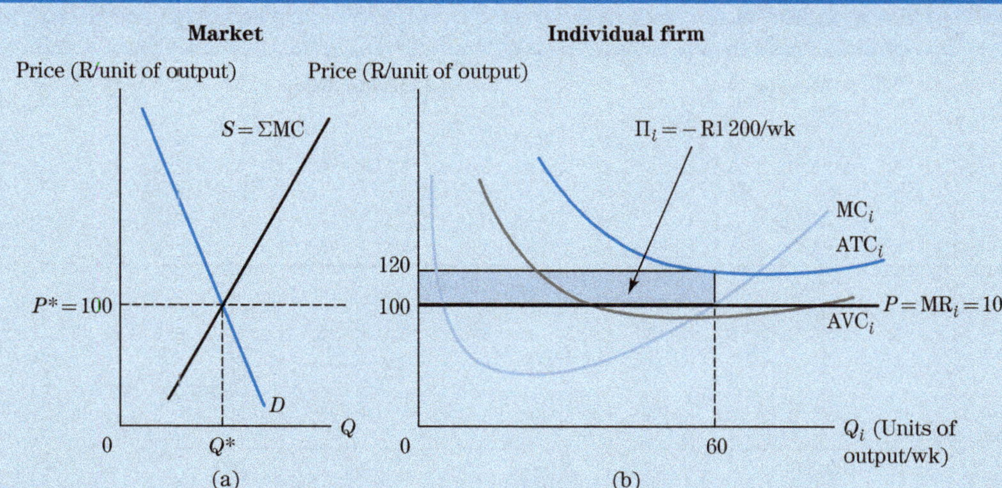

The short-run supply and demand curves sometimes intersect to produce an equilibrium price $P^* = \text{R100/unit}$ of output (panel a) that lies below the minimum value of the ATC curve for the typical firm (panel b), but above the minimum point of its AVC curve. At the profit-maximizing level of output (in this case, minimum losses), $Q_i^* = 60$ units/wk, the firm earns an economic loss of $\Pi_i = -\text{R1200/wk}$.

Table 9.1 Economic profits versus economic losses

Q	ATC	MC	$\Pi(P=200)$	$\Pi(P=100)$
40	140	60	2400	−1600
60	120	100	4800	−1200
80	120	200	6400	−1600
100	150	310	5000	−5000

At a price of 200 the firm earns economic profits, but at a price of 100 it suffers economic losses.

shaded rectangle labelled Π_i. Note that this loss is less than −TFC, the value of economic profit when output is zero. Thus it makes sense to produce even when economic profit falls below zero in the short run. When price is above the minimum value of average total cost, equating MR to MC gives us the production level at which the firm will maximize its profits. If, however, the price falls below minimum average total cost, equating MR and MC gives the production volume that will minimize the firm's losses.

Exercise 9.4

If the short-run marginal and average variable cost curves for a competitive firm are given by $MC = 2Q$ and $AVC = Q$, how many units of output will the firm produce at a market price of $P = 12$? At what level of fixed cost will this firm earn zero economic profit?

The efficiency of short-run competitive equilibrium

Allocative efficiency A condition in which all possible gains from exchange are realized.

One of the most attractive features of competitive markets is the fact that they result in **allocative efficiency**, which means that they fully exploit the possibilities for mutual gain through exchange. To illustrate, let us consider the short-run equilibrium pictured in Fig. 9.8(a), and suppose that the cost curves pictured in Fig. 9.8(b) are the same for each of 1000 firms in the industry.

In a competitive market in the short run, consumers give firms money, which firms use to buy variable inputs to produce the output that goes to consumers. To say that the competitive equilibrium leaves no room for further mutually beneficial exchange is the same as saying that there is no way for any producer and consumer to agree to a private transaction at any price other than R100. Of course, consumers would gladly pay less than R100 for an additional unit of output. But since R100 is equal to the value of the resources required to produce another unit (MC_i in Fig. 9.8(b)), no firm would be willing to respond. Firms, for their part, would gladly produce an extra unit of output if the price were higher than R100. But with 100 000 units of output already in the market, there are no consumers left who are willing to pay more than R100 (Fig. 9.8(a)). At the short-run competitive equilibrium

Figure 9.8 Short-run competitive equilibrium is efficient

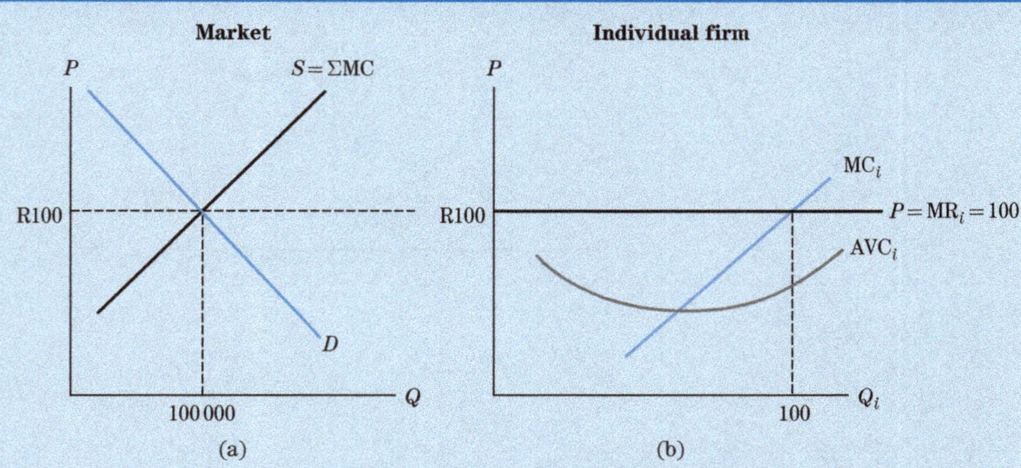

At the equilibrium price and quantity, the value of the additional resources required to make the last unit of output produced by each firm (MC in panel b) is exactly equal to the value of the last unit of output to buyers (the demand price in panel a). This means that further mutually beneficial trades do not exist.

price and quantity, the value of the resources used to produce the last unit of output (as measured by short-run marginal cost) is exactly equal to the value of that unit of output to consumers (as measured by the price they are willing to pay for it). Firms may wish that prices were higher and consumers may complain that prices are too high already, but the two parties have no incentive to trade at any price other than the equilibrium price.

Producer surplus

To say that a competitive market is efficient is to say that it maximizes the net benefits to its participants. In policy analysis, it is often useful to estimate the actual amount by which people and firms gain from their participation in specific markets. Suppose, for example, that a government of a poor developing country knows it can open up new markets for seafood by building a road from its coast to an interior region. If its goal is to use the country's resources as efficiently as possible, its decision about whether to build the road will depend on whether the benefits people and firms reap from these new markets exceed the cost of building the road.

In Chapter 2 we discussed the concept of consumer surplus as a measure of the benefit to the consumer of engaging in a market exchange. An analogous measure exists for producers. Economists call it **producer surplus**, and it measures how much better off the firm is as a result of having supplied its profit-maximizing level of output. It may seem tempting to say that the firm's producer surplus is simply its economic profit, but surplus and profit often differ. To see why, first recall that, in the short run, if the firm produces nothing, it will sustain a loss equal to its fixed cost. If the price exceeds the minimum value of AVC, however, it can do better by supplying a positive level of output. How much better? The firm's gain compared with the alternative of producing nothing is the difference between total revenue and total variable cost at the output level where $P = \text{MC}$. Now recall that economic profit is the difference between total revenue and total cost, and that total cost differs from variable cost by fixed cost: it follows that producer surplus is the sum of economic profit and fixed cost.[4] Diagrammatically, it is the area of the shaded rectangle shown in Fig. 9.9(a). In the short run, producer surplus is thus larger than economic profit, because the firm would lose more than its economic profit if it were prevented from participating in the market. In the long run, all costs are variable. So producer surplus is the same as economic profit in the long run.

Producer surplus The rand amount by which a firm benefits from producing a profit-maximizing level of output.

Figure 9.9 Two equivalent measures of producer surplus

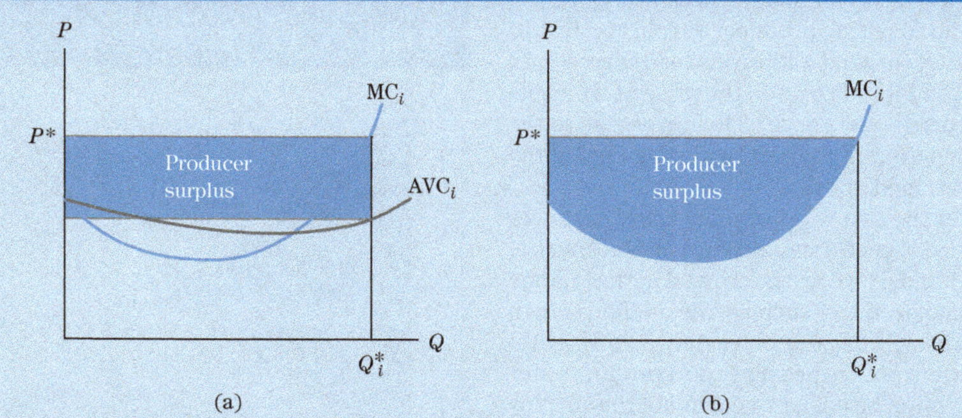

The difference between total revenue and total variable cost is a measure of producer surplus, the gain to the producer from producing Q_i^* units of output rather than zero. It can be measured as the difference between $P^*Q_i^*$ and $\text{AVC}_{Q_i^*}Q_i^*$ (shaded rectangle, panel a), or as the difference between $P^*Q_i^*$ and the area under the marginal cost curve (upper shaded area, panel b).

[4] If $\Pi = \text{TR} - \text{TC}$ and $\text{TC} = \text{VC} + \text{FC}$, then producer surplus $= \text{TR} - \text{VC} = \text{TR} - \text{TC} + \text{FC} = \Pi + \text{FC}$.

Figure 9.10 Aggregate producer surplus when individual marginal cost curves are upward sloping throughout

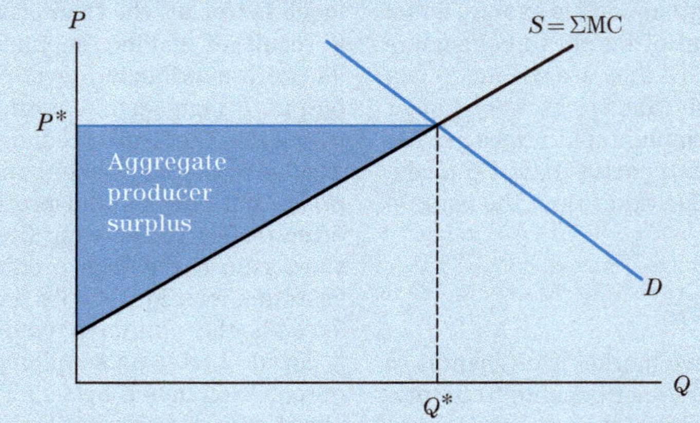

For any quantity, the supply curve measures the minimum price at which firms would be willing to supply it. The difference between the market price and the supply price is the marginal contribution to aggregate producer surplus at that output level. Adding these marginal contributions up to the equilibrium quantity Q^*, we get the shaded area, which is aggregate producer surplus.

Figure 9.9(b) shows an equivalent way of representing producer surplus. The alternative measure makes use of the fact that variable cost at any level of output is equal to the area under the marginal cost curve (below the shaded area in Fig. 9.9(b)). To see why this is so, note that the variable cost of producing 1 unit of output is equal to marginal cost at 1 unit, MC_1; VC for 2 units is the sum of MC_1 and MC_2, and so on – so that $VC_Q = MC_1 + MC_2 + \ldots + MC_Q$, which is the area under the MC curve. Hence the difference between total revenue and total variable cost may also be expressed as the upper shaded area in Fig. 9.9(b). Another way to define producer surplus is the difference between what the producer receives per product (P^* in Fig. 9.9(b)) and the price at which he is willing to sell (MC curve). This gives rise to the same shaded area in Fig. 9.9(b) as when using the method described above.

Which of the two ways of measuring producer surplus is most useful will depend on the specific context at hand. If we are interested in the change in an existing producer surplus, the method shown in Fig. 9.9(b) will usually be easier to work with. But when we want to measure total producer surplus, it will often be easier to calculate the surplus using the method shown in Fig. 9.9(a).

To measure aggregate producer surplus for a market, we simply add the producer surplus for each firm that participates. In cases where each firm's marginal cost curve is upward sloping for the bulk of its range, aggregate producer surplus will be well approximated by the area between the supply curve (quantities that all producers together are willing to sell at different prices) and the equilibrium price line, P^*, as shown in Fig. 9.10.

Recall from Chapter 2 that a rough approximation of consumer surplus for the market as a whole is given by the area between the demand curve and the equilibrium price line, as indicated by the shaded upper triangle in Fig. 9.11. The total benefits from exchange in the marketplace can be measured by the sum of consumer and producer surpluses.

Figure 9.11 The total benefit from exchange in a market

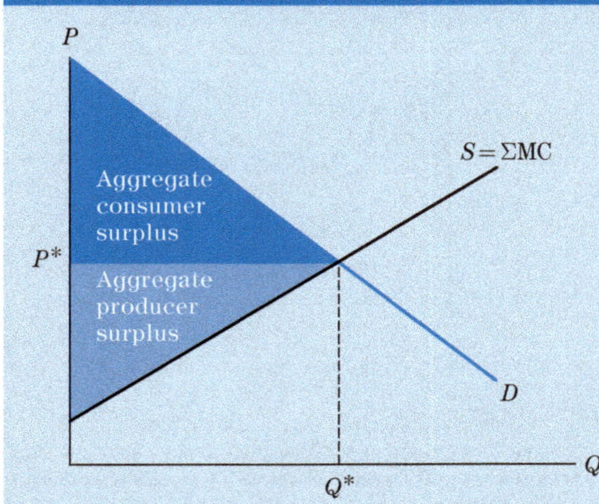

The sum of aggregate producer surplus (shaded lower triangle) and consumer surplus (shaded upper triangle) measures the total benefit from exchange.

Example 9.3

Suppose there are two types of firework user: careless and careful. Careful users never get hurt, but careless ones sometimes injure not only themselves but also innocent bystanders. The short-run marginal cost curves of each of the 1000 firms in the firework industry are given by MC = 100 + Q, where Q is measured in kilograms of cherry bombs per year, and MC is measured in rands per kilogram of cherry bombs. The demand curve for fireworks by careful users is given by $P = 500 - 0.001Q$ (same units as for MC). Legislators would like to continue to permit careful users to enjoy fireworks. But since it is logistically impossible to distinguish between the two types of user, they have decided to outlaw fireworks altogether. How much better off would consumers and producers be if legislators had the means to affect a partial ban? Use the consumer and producer surplus approach.

If the entire firework market is banned completely, the total of consumer and producer surplus will be zero. So to measure the benefits of a partial ban, we need to find the sum of consumer and producer surplus for a firework market restricted to careful users. To generate the supply curve for this market, we simply add the marginal cost curves of the individual firms horizontally. The marginal cost of an individual firm is given as $P = 100 + Q$, implying $Q = P - 100$. For the entire industry, $Q = 1000P - 100\,000$, which converts to $P = 0.001Q + 100$, the curve labelled S in Fig. 9.12. The demand curve for careful users would intersect S at an equilibrium price of R300 and an equilibrium quantity of 200 000 kg/yr.

By outlawing the sale of fireworks altogether, legislators eliminate producer and consumer surplus values given by the areas of the two shaded triangles in Fig. 9.12, which add up to R40 000 000/yr. In the language of cost–benefit analysis, this is the cost imposed on producers and careful users. The benefit of the ban is whatever value the public assigns to the injuries prevented (net of the cost of denying careless users the right to continue). It is obviously no simple matter to put a rand value on the pain and suffering associated with fingers blown off by cherry bombs. In Chapter 12 we shall discuss how rough estimates have been attempted in similar situations. But even in the absence of a formal quantitative measure of the value of injuries prevented, the public can ask itself whether the forgone surplus of R40 000 000/yr is a reasonable price to pay.

Figure 9.12 Producer and consumer surplus in a market consisting of careful firework users

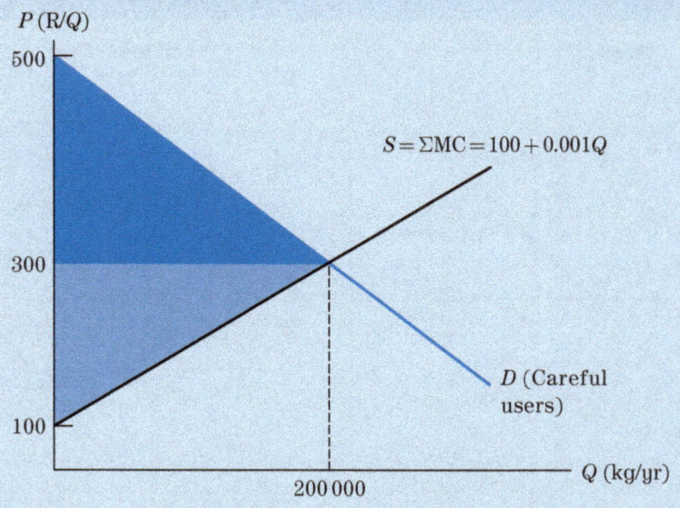

The upper shaded triangle is consumer surplus (R20 000 000/yr). The lower shaded triangle is producer surplus (R20 000 000/yr). The total benefit of keeping this market open is the sum of the two, or R40 000 000/yr.

Exercise 9.5

What would the sum of consumer and producer surplus be in Example 9.3 if the demand curve for careful users were instead given by $P = 300 - 0.001Q$?

Adjustments in the long run

The firm's objective, in both the long run and the short run, is to earn the highest economic profit it can. In the preceding section we saw that a firm will sometimes find it advantageous to continue supplying output in the short run, even though it is making economic losses. In the long run, however, a firm would prefer to go out of business if it could not earn at least a normal profit in its current industry.

Suppose that industry supply and demand intersect at the price level $P = 100$, as shown in Fig. 9.13(a). The cost curves for a representative firm are shown in Fig. 9.13(b). At $Q = 200$, the price of R100/unit of output exceeds ATC_1 in time period 1, with the result that the firm earns economic profit of R6000 in each time period. This profit is indicated by the shaded rectangle.

The situation depicted in Fig. 9.13 is inherently unstable. The reason for this is that positive economic profit creates an incentive for outsiders to enter the industry. Recall that the average total cost curves already include the opportunity cost of the capital that a firm requires to do business. This means that an outsider can buy everything needed to duplicate the operations of one of the existing firms in the industry, and in the process earn an economic profit of R6000 in each time period.

As additional firms enter the industry, their short-run marginal cost curves are added to those of existing firms, which shifts the industry supply curve to the right. If only one firm entered the industry, there would be no significant effect on price. And with price virtually the same as before, each firm in the industry would continue to earn economic profits of R6000 in each time period. These profits will continue to act as a carrot to lure additional firms into the industry, and the accumulating rightward supply shift will gradually cause price to fall.

Figure 9.14(a) portrays the rightward shift in industry supply that results from a significant amount of entry. The new supply schedule, S', intersects the demand schedule at $P = 80$, and this lower price is the new price on which firms must base their decisions. Firms can readjust their capital stocks, and in Fig. 9.14(b) this gives rise to the short-run cost curves ATC_2 and SMC_2. Note that the adjustment by existing firms to the lower price level shifts each of their short-run marginal cost curves to the left. The profit-maximizing level of output for $P = 80$ is $Q = 180$, which results in an

Figure 9.13 A price level that generates economic profit

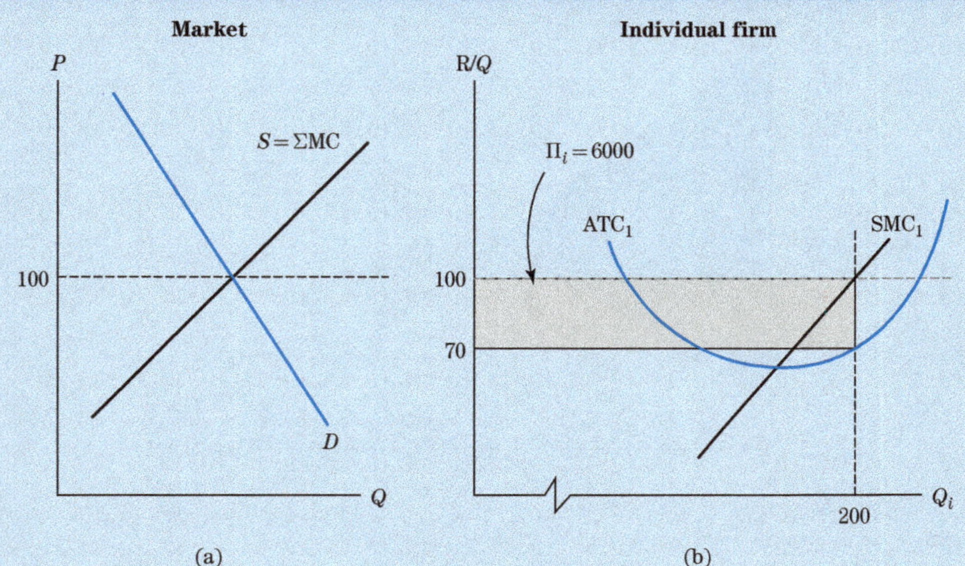

At the price level $P = $ R100/unit, the firm has adjusted its plant size so that $SMC_1 = 100$. At the profit-maximizing level of output, $Q = 200$, the firm earns an economic profit equal to R6000 in each time period, indicated by the area of the shaded rectangle.

Figure 9.14 A step along the path towards long-run equilibrium

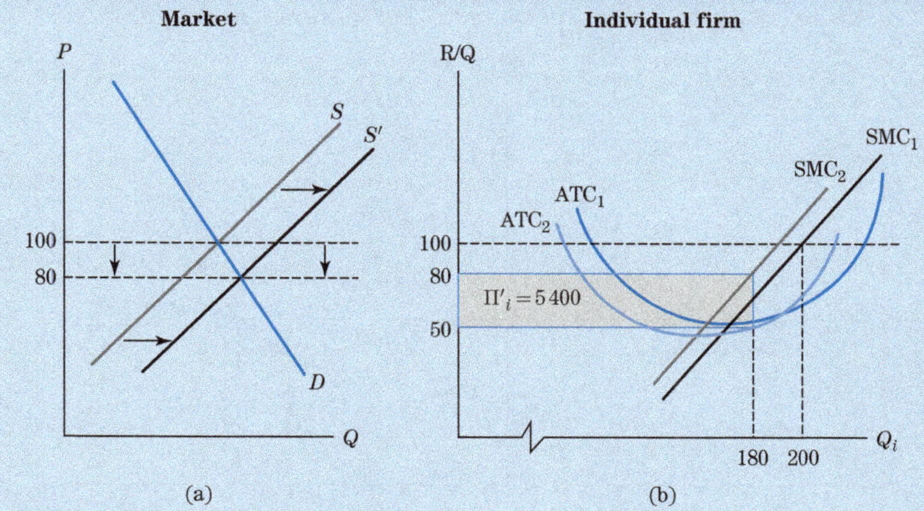

Entry of new firms causes supply to shift rightwards, lowering price from 100 to 80. The lower price causes existing firms to adjust their capital stocks downwards, giving rise to the new short-run cost curves ATC_2 and SMC_2. As long as price remains above short-run average cost (here, $ATC_2 = 50$), economic profits will be positive ($\Pi = R5400$ in time period 3), and incentives for new firms to enter will remain.

economic profit of R5400 in each time period, as indicated by the shaded rectangle.

Even after the adjustments described above take place, new and existing firms in the industry continue to earn positive economic profits. Although the new profit level is lower than before, it still acts as an incentive for additional entry into the industry. Further entry sets off yet another round of adjustment as described above, and for industries whose firms have U-shaped long-run average cost curves this will continue until: (1) price reaches the minimum point on the LAC curve (P^* in Fig. 9.15(b)); and (2) all firms have moved to the capital stock size that gives rise to a short-run average total cost curve that is tangent to the LAC curve at its minimum point (ATC^* in Fig. 9.15(b)). Note in Fig. 9.15(b) that, once all firms have reached this position, economic profit for each will be zero. This is the long-run competitive equilibrium position for the industry. Once it is reached, there will be no further incentive for new firms to enter the industry, because existing firms will all be earning an economic profit of zero. As was discussed earlier, this is known as the *break-even point* for a firm. However, it is important to remember that, although economic profits are zero, firms still make normal profits because they are included in the cost curves. Therefore there are also no incentives for existing firms to exit the market because they are making normal profits.

Suppose we had instead started our discussion with a situation in which price was below the minimum value of ATC. In that case, existing firms would be earning negative economic profits (that is, economic losses), which would be an incentive for some of them to leave the industry. The exodus would shift the supply curve leftwards, causing an increase in price, and movements by existing firms to adjust their capital stocks upwards. This process would continue until all firms had once again settled into the long-run equilibrium position portrayed in Fig. 9.15(b) and were all earning normal profit but zero economic profit.

How efficient is this long-run equilibrium situation? Allocative efficiency is when the economy produces only those type of goods and services that are more desirable in society and also in high demand. This means that goods will be traded when price is equal to marginal cost. In Fig. 9.15 it is clear that this is the case when the economy is in long-run equilibrium. The social surplus is also maximized because there is no deadweight loss. This will become clear when the deadweight loss of a monopoly is discussed in the next chapter. Productive efficiency means that it must be a production point on your production possibility frontier (PPF). This also implies that production takes place at the minimum point on a firm's average cost curve. This is also the case with perfect competitive equilibrium.

Figure 9.15 The long-run equilibrium under perfect competition

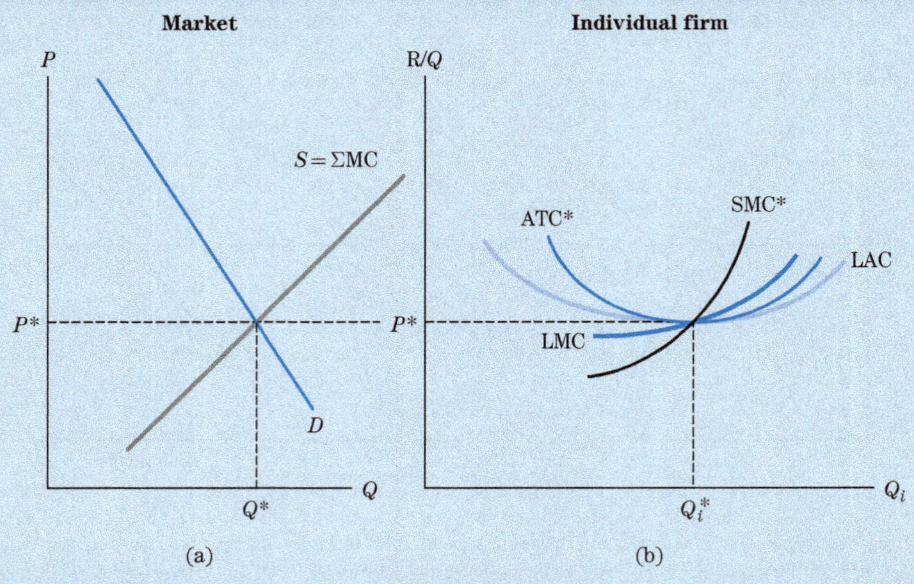

If price starts above P^*, entry keeps occurring and capital stocks of existing firms keep adjusting until the rightward movement of the industry supply curve causes price to fall to P^*. At P^* the profit-maximizing level of output for each firm is Q_i^*, the output level for which $P^* = SMC^* = LMC = ATC^* = LAC$. Economic profits of all firms are equal to zero.

The profit motive

As Adam Smith saw clearly more than two centuries ago, it is the self-interest motive – in particular, the carrot of economic profit or the stick of economic losses – that drives competitive industries to their respective long-run equilibrium positions. As Smith described the actions of an industrialist,

> he intends only his own security; and by directing that industry in such a manner as its produce may be of the greatest value, he intends only his own gain; and he is in this, as in many other cases, lead by an invisible hand to promote an end which was no part of his intention. Nor is it always the worse for the society that it was no part of it. By pursuing his own interest, he frequently promotes that of the society more effectually than when he really intends to promote it.[5]

The market mechanism co-ordinates a huge volume of activities. Near Stellenbosch University's student residences is a 24/7 McDonald's. At 03:00 any student can take a few steps outside and purchase a fresh cup of coffee or something to eat. No students had to instruct the manager of McDonald's to be open all night or told him where to buy paper cups or potatoes for chips. A security firm will sell new remote controls for the security gates at a nearby housing complex. The butcher's shop has fresh lamb chops and beef steaks on Fridays and Saturdays, and a truck arrives each morning at dawn carrying fresh snoek caught in the waters near Saldanha. At only a few hours' notice, several airlines stand ready to carry passengers to Johannesburg, Durban, Gaberone or even New York. All this activity – and much, much more – takes place without any central co-ordination at all, the result of a multitude of economic agents each striving to earn an economic profit.

Whatever other faults it may have, the market system cannot be accused of producing products that people don't want to buy. In the market system the consumer is sovereign, and firms that fail to provide what consumers want face economic extinction.[6] The question of whether central plans are more efficient than market incentives was a hotly debated issue until their demise in the late

[5] Adam Smith, *The Wealth of Nations*, Chapter 2 (http://www.online-literature.com/view.php/wealth_nations/24?term = invisible%20hand).

[6] The late Harvard economist John Kenneth Galbraith challenged this view. We shall consider his arguments in Chapter 11.

1980s, and today even controlled economies all over the globe have introduced market-like incentives in a desperate attempt to revive their lagging production figures.

This is not to say that competitive markets lead to the best possible outcome in every instance. On the contrary, in later chapters we shall see that market systems fall short in a variety of ways. Although markets are efficient at producing what people demand in the marketplace, a serious drawback of capitalism is that it only looks after you if you have money. Much-needed goods such as housing for the poor won't be supplied in such a market because the risks are too high and the profit incentive too small; firms and financial institutions don't want to get involved.

Application: the cost of extraordinary inputs

The irrigation project

We are in a position now to return to the question with which we began this chapter, namely, whether a state-supported irrigation system that doubles crop yields will raise the incomes of poor farmers. Recall that the farmers in question live in the Eastern Cape and rent their farm parcels from landowners.

First, let's consider the current situation, in which no irrigation system exists. Farmers here may be viewed as the operators of small competitive firms. They rent land, supply their own labour and keep the proceeds from selling their maize in a market so large that their own offerings have no appreciable effect on the price of maize, which is, say, R200/bushel. For the sake of simplicity, let us ignore the cost of seed, tools and other minor inputs.

Suppose that an individual farmer can farm 40 hectares, and that without irrigation the land will yield 30 bushels of maize per hectare per year. His total revenue from the sale of his maize will then be R240 000/yr, from which he must deduct the rent for his land. How will that rent be determined?

Suppose the alternative to working as a farmer is to work in a factory for R120 000/yr, and that factory work is generally regarded as neither more nor less pleasant than farming. If the land rent were only, say, R100 000/yr for a 40 ha parcel, then all workers in the county would prefer farming to working in factories because their net earnings would be R140 000 instead of R120 000. Assuming that there are many more factory workers than could farm the county's limited supply of farmland, there would be excess demand for farm parcels at a rental price of R100 000/yr. Factory workers would bid against one another, and the bidding would continue until the rental price for a 40 ha parcel reached R120 000/yr. At that price, a farmer would have R120 000 left over from the sale of his crops, which would leave him indifferent between the options of farming and factory work. The land rent could never exceed R120 000 for long under these conditions, for if it did, net farm incomes would fall below R120 000/yr, and everyone would want factory work instead of farming.

Now let's see what happens with the introduction of the irrigation project. With maize yields now 60 bushels/ha instead of 30, a 40 ha farm will produce R480 000 in annual total revenue instead of R240 000. If the land rent remained at R120 000/yr, a farmer would earn R360 000/yr instead of R120 000. Indeed, it was the prospect of such a dramatic rise in farm incomes that attracted so much support for the irrigation bill in the first place. One can forgive non-economists for reasoning like this, but we as economists know better.

What supporters of the bill have failed to recognize is that land rents will not remain at R120 000/yr after the introduction of the irrigation system. Needless to say, factory workers would bid vigorously for an opportunity to rent a farm parcel that would raise their income from R120 000 to R360 000/yr. In the face of this bidding pressure, the rental price of farmland will continue to rise until it reaches a level of R360 000/yr. (If it were only R340 000, for example, a factory worker could switch to farming and raise his annual income from R120 000 to R140 000.) Once the annual rent for a 40 ha parcel reaches R360 000, the balance between farm and factory opportunities is restored.

Recall that our hypothetical state legislator's aide recommended against the irrigation project, on the grounds that it would not raise the incomes of farmers in the long run. She perceived correctly that the beneficiaries of the state-supported irrigation project would be not the impoverished farmers, but the owners of the land. These owners already have high incomes so no social purpose is served by spending tax money on increasing their incomes further. Obviously the irrigation project would still be attractive if the costs were less than the value of the extra maize that resulted (MR > MC). Remember that, as economists, we do not let our emotions get the better of us; rather, we use facts or empirical evidence to prove our argument.

An efficient manager

Suppose one firm is like all others except that it employs an extraordinarily efficient manager. This manager is so efficient that the firm earns R10 000 000 of economic profit each year in an industry in which the economic profit of the other firms hovers close to zero. Because this manager receives the same salary as all other managers, the firm that employs her incurs much lower costs than all other firms in the industry. However, this situation creates a strong incentive for some other firm to bid this manager away by offering her a higher salary.

Suppose a new firm offered her a dramatic increase of R6 000 000 on her current annual salary, and she accepted. Despite paying the new manager an abnormally high salary (compared with what other managers in the industry receive), the firm would then earn an economic profit of R4 000 000/yr. That's not as good as an economic profit of R10 000 000/yr, but it is R4 000 000/yr better than the normal profit her original employer will earn without her.

Still other firms would have an incentive to offer even more for this manager. Theory tells us that the bidding should continue until the cost savings for which she is responsible are entirely incorporated into her salary – that is, until her salary is R10 000 000/yr higher than the salary of an ordinary manager. And once her salary is bid up to that level, the firm that hires her will no longer enjoy a cost advantage over the other firms in the industry. The existence of such competitive bidding for inputs makes it plausible to assume that all firms in a competitive industry have roughly the same average total costs in equilibrium.

Exercise 9.6

Suppose all firms in an industry have 'competent' managers and earn zero economic profit. The manager of one of the firms suddenly leaves, and the firm finds that only incompetent applicants respond when the position is advertised at the original salary of R2 000 000/yr (which is the going rate for competent managers in this industry). Under an incompetent manager paid this salary, the firm will experience an economic loss of R800 000/yr. At what salary would it make sense for this firm to hire an incompetent manager?

The long-run supply curve for a competitive industry

We saw that the short-run supply curve for a perfectly competitive industry is the horizontal summation of the short-run marginal cost curves of all the individual firms. But the corresponding long-run supply curve for a competitive industry is not the horizontal summation of the long-run marginal cost curves of individual firms. Our task in the next sections is to derive the long-run supply curve for competitive industries operating under a variety of different cost conditions.

Long-run supply curve with U-shaped LAC curves

What does the long-run supply curve look like in an industry in which all firms have identical U-shaped LAC curves? Suppose, in particular, that these LAC curves resemble the one labelled LAC_i in Fig. 9.16(b). Suppose the demand curve facing the industry is initially that labelled D_1 in Fig. 9.16(a). Given this demand curve, the industry will be in long-run equilibrium when each firm installs the capital stock that gives rise to the short-run marginal cost curve labelled SMC_i in Fig. 9.16(b). The number of firms in the industry will adjust so that the short-run supply curve, denoted S_{SR} in Fig. 9.16(a), intersects D_1 at a price equal to the minimum value of LAC_i. Because all firms make zero economic profit (although they make normal profit), existing firms have no incentive to leave the industry and those firms outside the industry have no incentive to join the industry. Therefore this situation portrays a long-run equilibrium point.

Now suppose demand shifts rightwards from D_1 to D_2, intersecting the short-run industry supply curve at price P_2. The short-run effect will be for each firm to increase its output from $Q^*_{i_1}$ to $Q^*_{i_2}$ (where SMR = SMC), which will lead to an economic profit measured by the shaded rectangle in Fig. 9.16(b). These abnormal profits will lure additional firms into the industry until the rightward supply shift (to S^* in Fig. 9.16(a)) again results in a price of min LAC. The long-run response to an increase in demand, then, is to increase industry output by increasing the number of firms in the industry. As long as the expansion of industry output does not cause the prices of capital, labour or other inputs to rise, there will be no long-run increase in the price of the product.

If we started from a situation of long-run equilibrium, but demand had shifted to the left from

Figure 9.16 The long-run competitive industry supply curve if demand increases

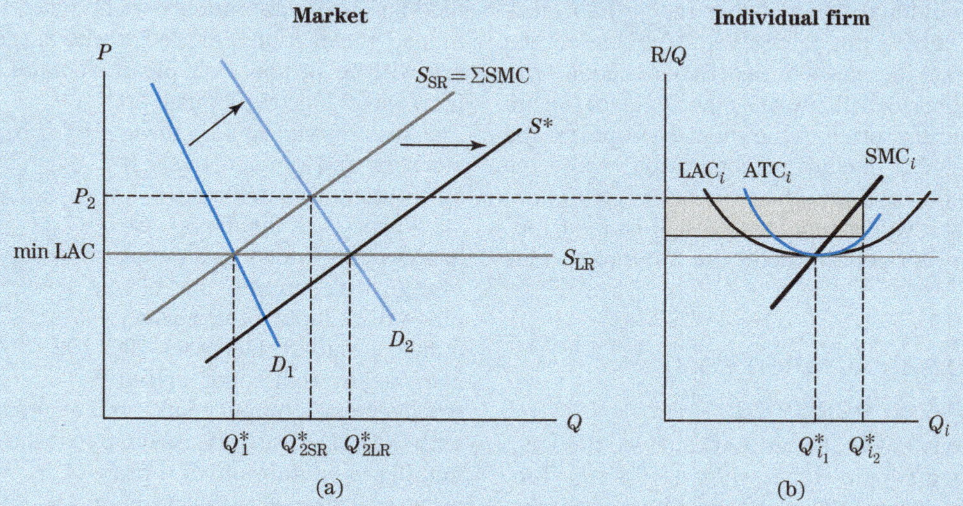

When firms are free to enter or leave the market, price cannot depart from the minimum value of the LAC curve in the long run. If input prices are unaffected by an increase in industry output, the long-run supply curve is S_{LR}, a horizontal line at the minimum value of LAC.

D_1, a parallel story would have unfolded as portrayed in Fig. 9.17: price would have fallen in the short run to P_2, firms would have adjusted their offerings and would then sell $Q_{i_2}^*$, and that would lead to a resulting economic loss, as indicated by the shaded rectangle in Fig. 9.17(b). These losses would induce some firms to leave the industry. The exodus would shift industry supply to the left (eventually to S^*) until price had again risen to min LAC. Here, again, the long-run response to a shift in demand is accommodated by a change in the number of firms. With U-shaped LAC curves, there is no tendency for a fall in demand to produce a long-run decline in price.

Figure 9.17 The long-run competitive supply curve if demand decreases

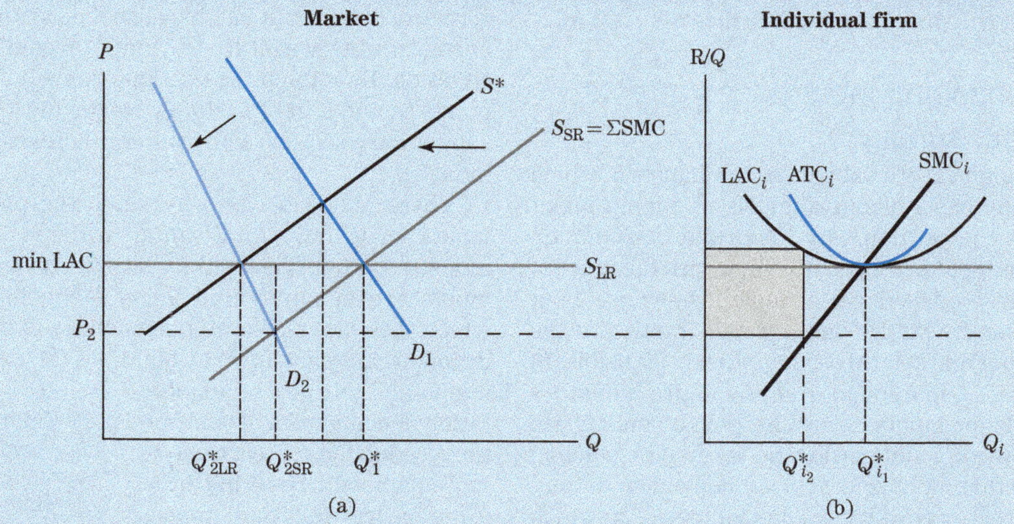

When firms are free to enter or leave the market, price cannot depart from the minimum value of the LAC curve in the long run. If input prices are unaffected by a decrease in industry output, the long-run supply curve is S_{LR}, a horizontal line at the minimum value of LAC.

This type of industry is also known as a *constant cost industry*. Irrespective of the size of the market, individual firms always reach their minimum cost at the same price level. Whether demand in the market increases or decreases, the long-run equilibrium price will always move back to the initial equilibrium price (which will be equal to the minimum AVC) that was in operation before the change in demand and the long-run supply curve for a constant cost industry with U-shaped LAC curves is a horizontal line at the minimum value of the LAC curve.

Industry supply when each LAC curve is horizontal

As in the case of U-shaped LAC curves, the long-run industry supply curve when each firm's LAC curve is horizontal will again be a horizontal line (again assuming that input prices do not change with changes in industry output). But there is one salient difference between the two cases: when firms have identical U-shaped LAC curves, we can predict that each firm will produce the quantity that corresponds to the minimum point on its LAC curve. We thus get an industry composed of firms that all produce the same level of output.

With horizontal LAC curves, by contrast, there is simply no unique minimum-cost point. LAC is the same at any level of output, which leads to an indeterminacy not present in the earlier case. We just cannot predict what the size distribution of firms will look like in the case of horizontal LAC curves. All we can say with confidence is that price in the long run will gravitate towards the value of LAC.

How changing input prices affects long-run supply

In our analysis of cost curves in Chapter 8, which forms the basis of our analysis of supply under perfect competition, an important assumption was that input prices do not vary with the amount of output produced. For a single firm whose input purchases constitute only a small fraction of the total input market, this assumption is plausible. In many cases, moreover, even the entire industry's demands for inputs constitute only a small share of the overall input market. So we may reasonably assume that input prices do not depend on output.

But there are at least some industries in which the volume of inputs purchased constitutes an appreciable share of the entire input market. The market for commercial airliners, for example, consumes a significant share of the total amount of titanium sold each year. In such cases, a large increase in industry output will often be accompanied by significant increases in input prices. If an industry uses highly skilled workers, these workers will be in short supply if demand for them increases. This will push up the price (wages) of these workers, and increase the cost structure in this industry.

Pecuniary diseconomy A rise in production cost that occurs when an expansion of industry output causes a rise in the prices of inputs.

When that happens, we have what is known as a **pecuniary diseconomy**, a bidding-up of input prices when industry output increases. It also means that input prices will decrease if output contracts. Let us explain this with the aid of Fig. 9.18. Assume that the market is initially in equilibrium at a price of P_1, where that price level is equal to the minimum LAC_1. If demand in the market increases to D_2, the market price will increase to P_2. But because production volumes in the market have increased, the cost structure in the increasing-cost industry will increase from LAC_1 to LAC_2. It is clear from Fig. 9.18(b) that firms are making economic profits, and that this is not a stable long-run equilibrium situation.

The abnormal profits that existing firms are making in this industry will draw new firms into it. The result is that the supply curve in the market will shift to the right. In Fig. 9.18(a), this is indicated by a move from S_{SR} to S^*. New firms will enter the market up to the point where the market price is driven down to equal the minimum value of the LAC_2 curve. Once again, firms are making zero economic profit but, because they are making normal profits, we return to a long-run equilibrium situation. By joining the two long-run equilibrium points (A and B in Fig. 9.18(a)), we get the long-run supply curve S_{LR} of a firm in an increasing-cost industry.

There are also cases in which the prices of inputs may fall significantly with expanding industry output. This will happen, for example, if inputs are manufactured using technologies in which there are substantial economies of scale. A dramatic increase in road building, for example, might facilitate greater exploitation of economies of scale in the production of earthmoving equipment, resulting in a lower price for that input. Such cases are called **pecuniary economies**, and give rise to a downward-sloping long-run industry supply curve.

Pecuniary economy A fall in production cost that occurs when expansion of industry output causes a drop in the prices of inputs.

Figure 9.18 Long-run supply curve for an increasing-cost industry

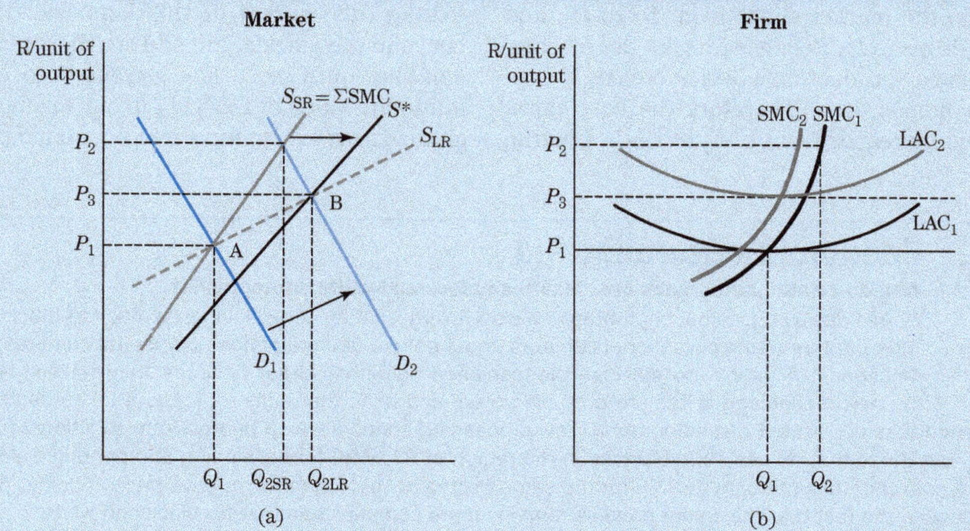

When input prices rise with industry output, each firm's LAC curve will also rise with industry output (b). Thus the firm's LAC curve when industry output is Q_2 lies above its LAC curve when industry output is Q_1 (b). Firms will still gravitate to the minimum points on their LAC curves, but because this minimum point depends on industry output, the long-run industry supply curve (S_{LR} in panel a) will now be upward sloping.

Competitive industries in which falling input prices lead to downward-sloping supply curves are called *decreasing-cost industries.*

Once again, we can illustrate this with the aid of a graph. Assume the industry is initially in long-run equilibrium at a price of P_1 and that each firm is producing Q_1 units. Because this price is equal to the minimum value of the LAC_1 curve, all firms are making zero economic profit (as portrayed in Fig. 9.19).

Figure 9.19 Long-run supply curve for a decreasing-cost industry

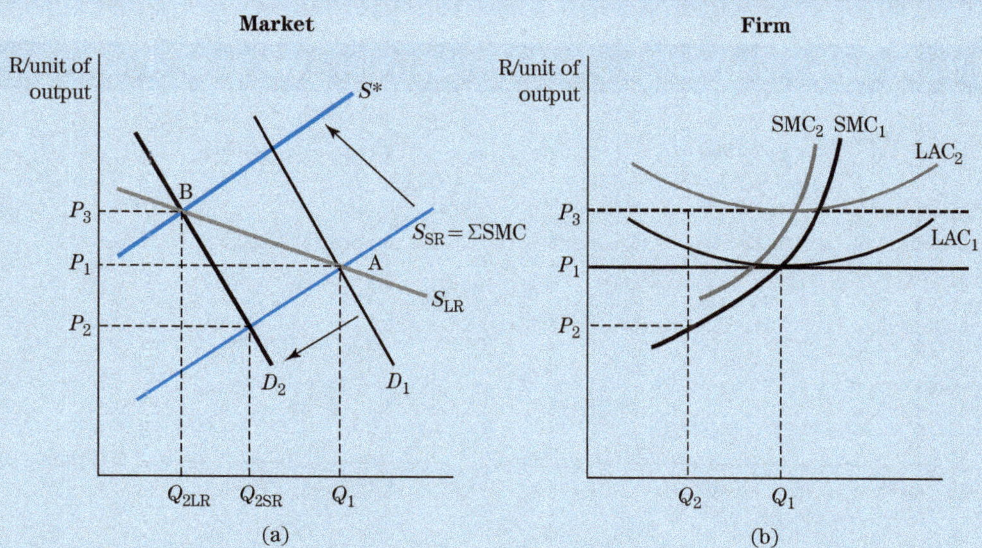

When input prices decrease with industry output, each firm's LAC curve will also rise with industry output if production volume decreases (panel b). Thus the firm's LAC curve when industry output is Q_2 lies above its LAC curve when industry output is Q_1 (panel b). Firms will still gravitate to the minimum points on their LAC curves, but because this minimum point depends on industry output, the long-run industry supply curve (S_{LR}, panel a) will now be downward sloping.

Let us now assume that there is a *decrease* in the demand for that good in the market. The demand in the market shifts from D_1 to D_2, and the price drops to P_2. Because this is a decreasing-cost industry, production costs increase if production volumes drop. Therefore the cost curve of the firm increases from LAC_1 to LAC_2. Clearly, all individual firms are making an economic loss when they produce Q_2, and this will result in firms exiting this market. If this happens, the supply curve in the market will shift to the left. This will continue until price has increased to equal the minimum value of LAC_2 (P_3 in our example). Once again, firms are making zero economic profit and

Economic naturalist 9.1

Why do colour photographs cost less than black-and-white photographs?

When I was a boy, colour photographs were a luxury, costing several times as much as black and white. Today, rather than conventional cameras, most people use their phones or digital cameras. However, thousands of people do still use old-fashioned cameras, either because they haven't adapted to the new technology or they're a bit *old school* and think that editing photos afterwards is somehow cheating and takes the art out of photography. Few processing shops develop photos from traditional rolls of film nowadays, but those that do can charge prices in the region of R119.99 for developing and printing a 24-exposure roll of black-and-white film but only R69.99 for the same in colour. This fall in the relative price of colour photos has occurred despite the fact that the colour process remains more complex than that for black and white.

If colour processing is more complex than black and white, why does it cost less? The answer lies in part in the economies of scale possible in the production of the machinery used to make both types of print. When colour photography was in its infancy, film was expensive and the colours tended to fade rapidly, so most people used black and white. The high volume of black-and-white photo processing, in turn, made it possible to produce processing machines cheaply as a result of economies of scale. As the price of colour film declined over time and its quality improved, so more people chose to use it, and demand for colour-processing equipment gradually grew. Economies of scale in the production of processing equipment then lead to a fall in the cost of an important input for colour printmaking – a pecuniary economy. Simultaneously, the decline in production of black-and-white processing equipment lead to an increase in its price – a pecuniary diseconomy. This outcome can be directly linked to the change in demand – shifting from black-and-white to colour prints.

The resulting changes in the equilibrium prices and quantities of the two types of print are roughly as shown in Fig. 9.20. Note that the relative positions of the two supply curves are the same for both years. This means that the printmaking industry would be willing to supply any given total quantity of black-and-white prints for a lower price than for the same quantity of colour prints in both years. It is the change in demand patterns, together with downward-sloping supply curves in both markets, that explains the observed reversal in relative prices.

Figure 9.20 Pecuniary economies and the price of colour and black-and-white photos

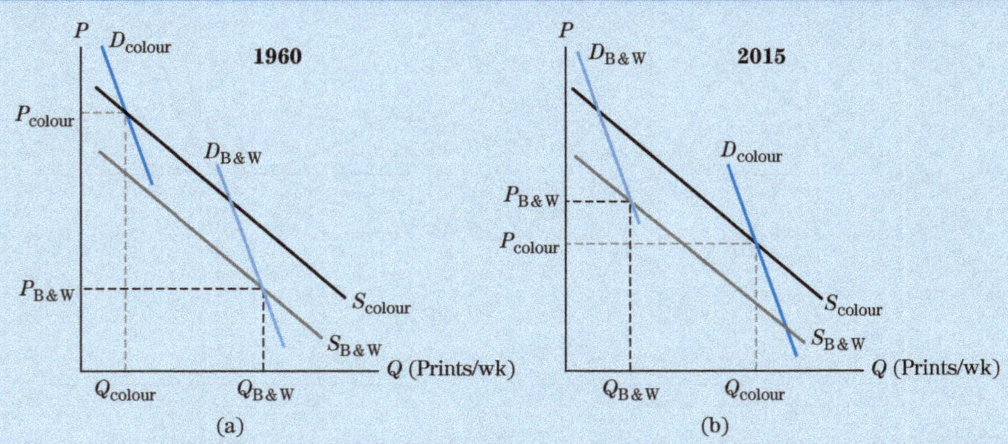

As a result of economies of scale in the production of equipment used to process film, the long-run supply curves of both colour and black-and-white prints are downward sloping. In 1960, when the quality of colour film was poor, most people demanded black and white, resulting in lower prices. Today, by contrast, demand for colour is much greater than for black and white. The result is that colour prints are now less expensive than black and white, even though colour-processing equipment remains more complicated.

there will be no incentive for new firms to enter this market. However, existing firms won't exit because they are making normal profits. By joining the two long-run equilibrium points (A and B), we get the negatively-sloped S_{LR} of the market.

Irrespective of whether demand increases or decreases, with a decreasing-cost industry the long-run supply curve will always be negatively sloped and with an increasing-cost industry the supply curve will always have be positively sloped. Practise on your own to ensure you can show a decrease in demand of an increasing-cost industry and an increase in demand of a decreasing-cost industry.

The elasticity of supply

In Chapter 4 we defined the price elasticity of demand as a measure of the responsiveness of the quantity demanded to variations in price. An analogous concept exists for measuring the responsiveness of the quantity supplied to variations in price. Naturally, it is called the **price elasticity of supply**. Suppose we are at point A on the industry supply curve shown in Fig. 9.21, where a change in price of ΔP gives rise to a change ΔQ in the quantity supplied. The price elasticity of supply, denoted ε^s, is then given by

Price elasticity of supply The percentage change in quantity supplied that occurs in response to a 1 per cent change in product price.

$$\varepsilon^s = \frac{\Delta Q}{\Delta P}\frac{P}{Q} \left(\text{or } \frac{dQ}{dP}\frac{P}{Q} \text{ if you use derivatives}\right) \quad (9.1)$$

As in the case of elasticity of demand, supply elasticity has a simple interpretation in terms of the geometry of the industry supply curve. When ΔP is small, the ratio $\Delta P/\Delta Q$ is the slope of the supply curve, which means that the ratio $\Delta Q/\Delta P$ is the reciprocal of that slope. Thus the price elasticity of supply may be interpreted as the product of the ratio of price to quantity and the reciprocal of the slope of the supply curve:

$$\varepsilon^s = \frac{P}{Q}\frac{1}{\text{slope}} \quad (9.2)$$

As a result of the law of diminishing returns, the short-run competitive industry supply curve will always be upward sloping, which means that the short-run elasticity of supply will always be positive. For industries with a horizontal long-run supply curve, the long-run elasticity of supply is infinite. Output can be expanded indefinitely without a change in price. As a result of pecuniary economies and diseconomies, long-run competitive industry supply curves may also be either downward or upward sloping in specific cases. The corresponding long-run elasticities of supply in these cases will be either negative or positive.

As noted earlier, most industries employ only a relatively small share of the total volume of inputs traded in the marketplace, which means that modest variations in industry output should have no significant effect on input prices in most industries. In practical applications of the competitive model, therefore, most economists adopt the working hypothesis that long-run supply curves are horizontal. Of course, this hypothesis can always

Figure 9.21 The elasticity of supply

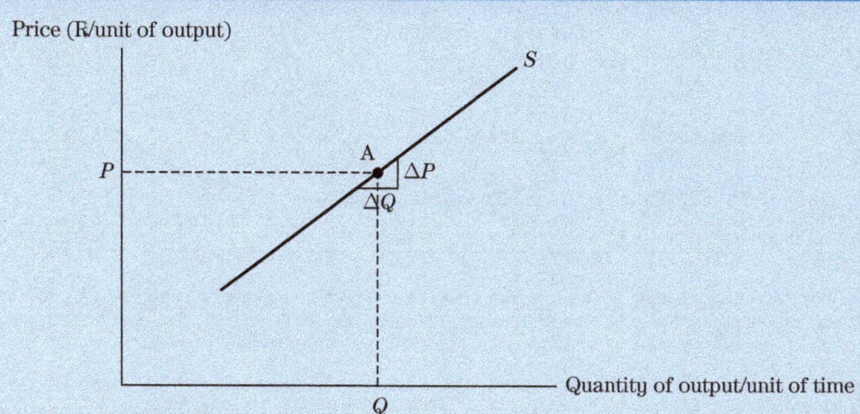

At point A, the elasticity of supply is given by $\varepsilon^s = \frac{\Delta Q}{\Delta P}\frac{P}{Q}$ or $\frac{dQ}{dP}\frac{P}{Q}$. Because the short-run supply curve is always upward sloping, the short-run elasticity of supply will always be positive. In the long run, elasticity of supply can be positive, zero or negative.

be modified when there is evidence that pecuniary economies or diseconomies are important.

Applying the competitive model

As noted earlier in the chapter, economists recognize that no industry strictly satisfies the four requirements for perfect competition – a standardized product, firms as price takers, perfect factor mobility and perfect information. For practical purposes, the important question is how far an industry can fall short of these conditions before the general tendencies of the competitive model fail to apply. Unfortunately, there are no hard-and-fast rules for making this judgement. In industries where entry and exit are especially easy – such as the airline industry – a firm may behave as a price taker even in a market in which it is the only competitor.[7] In industries in which entry and exit are more difficult, even the existence of a relatively large number of established firms does not guarantee price-taking behaviour. In the short run, especially, firms may be able to work out tacit agreements to restrain price competition even when there are abnormal profits.

Despite this difficulty, experience has shown that many of the most important long-run properties of the competitive model apply in most industries, with the notable exception of those in which the government erects legal barriers to entry (for example, by requiring a government licence in order to participate in a market, as is the case in the airline industry).

By way of illustration, let's consider three brief applications that highlight some of the insights afforded by the perfectly competitive model.

Price supports as a device for saving family farms

In 1998 there were 100000 commercial farmers in South Africa and that figure declined to just over 36000 (mostly white) in 2013, while the number of subsistence/emerging farmers remained stagnant at about 450000. Since 1990 more than 700000 jobs in agriculture have been lost.[8] This change is obviously not the result of a dramatic decline in food consumption. Rather, it is one of the many consequences of vastly more productive methods of farming resulting from increasing mechanization.

As farm machinery has grown larger, become more sophisticated and more expensive, the size of land parcels at which long-run average cost curves cease declining has grown ever larger. Where family farms of fewer than 100 ha were once common in South Africa, large corporate farms with several thousand hectares have become increasingly common.

In terms of the competitive model developed in this chapter, the family farm may be thought of as a firm whose capital stock gives rise to the short-run cost curves denoted ATC_F and SMC_F in Fig. 9.22. The corresponding cost curves for the corporate farm are denoted ATC_C and SMC_C. Competition has the effect of driving the long-run equilibrium price towards P^*, the minimum point on the LAC

Figure 9.22 Cost curves for family and corporate farms

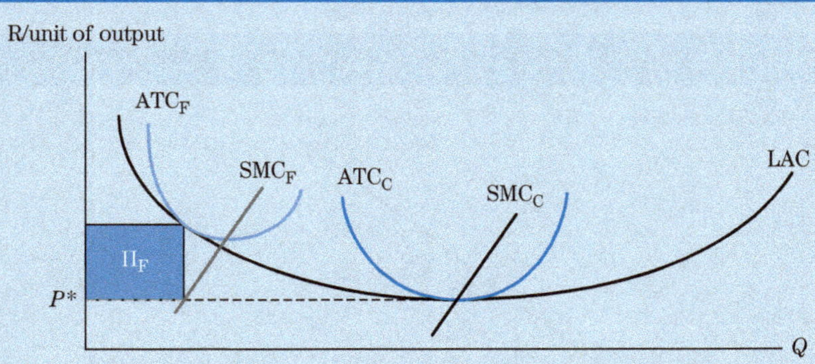

With the availability of modern farming methods, large farms have much lower unit costs than small ones. A price that covers cost for large corporate farms will produce large economic losses for family farms.

[7] At a limited number of large airports, entry is difficult even in the airline industry. For these airports to accommodate carriers, new capacity will have to be built, which could take years or even decades.

[8] Information taken from Andrew Makenete, 'Bio energy: Enhancing agricultural production and South African food security', paper presented at the EMRC Agribusiness Forum, 17 June 2009; and Mamphela Ramphele, 'Loss of farmers worrisome', Land Divided Conference, 24 March 2013.

curve. At P^* corporate farms earn a normal profit while family farms, with their higher costs, make economic losses of Π_F, as measured by the shaded rectangle in Fig. 9.22.

Despite the intense determination of many family farmers to remain on the land, large losses are simply not sustainable over a period of many years. Because farmers get very emotional about land that has been in the family for many years, struggling farmers frequently remain on their farms well past the time where they are able to earn a profit equal to the opportunity cost of their land. Many remain even long after they have ceased to earn the opportunity cost of their own labour. And a substantial number hang on by borrowing away most of the value of their only significant asset, their farmland. But credit cannot be extended without limit, and in the absence of government intervention, the long-run tendency has been for family farmers to leave the industry, selling whatever land they still own to the more efficient corporate farms.

Contrary to the stylized assumptions of the model of perfect competition, this process of resource mobility is far from perfect. Family farming is a way of life, one that people do not readily abandon when the terms of trade turn against them. There is great sympathy among South Africans for the plight of family farmers. We don't like to witness scenes on the nightly news of families huddled tearfully together as the auctioneer sells off the last of their possessions. We appreciate that these families have worked hard all their lives in an era when many others earn their living by selling crack or robbing convenience stores. The current state of affairs makes it even more difficult for emerging (mostly black) farmers to survive in these harsh conditions. What programmes can the government put in place to help farmers survive?

Price supports for agricultural products are one option the government can choose. The details of these types of support programme are highly complex, but for the purpose of our analysis it will suffice to say that the government announces a price for a given product and then stands ready to buy whatever private buyers fail to purchase. Normally the farmer receives the difference between a specified target price and the actual market price. With these types of programme it is possible that the price consumers pay may be lower than what the unregulated equilibrium price would have been.

Sad to say, where these type of programme were introduced, they failed miserably. Sadder still, even the most cursory understanding of competitive market dynamics would have made it clear that this outcome is inevitable. To illustrate, suppose the price support is set at P_G in a market in which the unsupported price would have been P^*. In Fig. 9.23, we see that the short-run effect is to cause family farms to increase their output to Q_F, and to cause corporate farms to increase theirs to Q_C. At these output levels family farms will still make an economic loss, indicated by the blue rectangle labelled Π_F in Fig. 9.23, whereas corporate farms now earn an economic profit, indicated by the shaded rectangle Π_C.

In the short run, to the extent that the new loss is smaller than the previous loss suffered by family farmers, the price support has had the intended effect of helping the family farmer. But the relief

Figure 9.23 The short-run effect of agricultural price supports

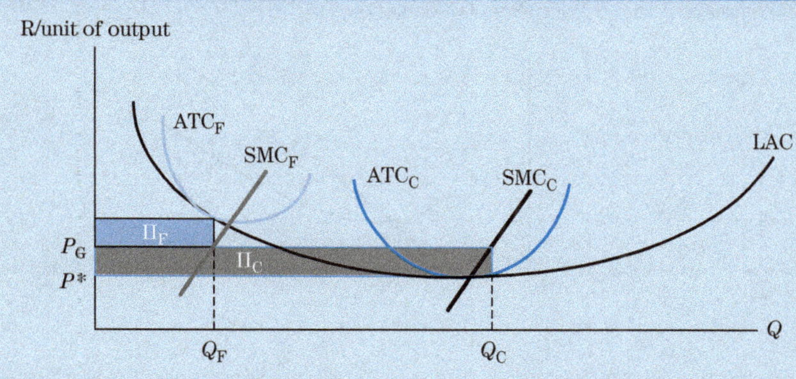

Price supports initially reduce the losses of family farms, while creating economic profits for corporate farms. In the long run, however, they serve only to bid up land prices.

is destined to be transitory. To see why, note first that the same price support that reduces the short-run losses of family farms also generates positive profits for corporate farms. We know, however, that positive profits are not sustainable in an industry with freedom of entry. They will lure outsiders to bid for farmland so that they too may earn more than a normal rate of return. The effect of this bidding will be to cause land prices to rise to the point where corporate farms no longer earn economic profits. But with land prices higher than before, the cost curves of all farms, corporate and family, shift upwards (not drawn in Fig. 9.23). For owners, some of the sting of these economic losses is mitigated by the greater implicit value of their land. But for the many farm families who rent their land, there is no such compensation.

As technology continues to advance, and with it the scale of the most efficient farms, the stage is now set for another round of distress for family farms, and the attendant pressure to increase the government price support level. A treadmill has been set in motion whereby the price support keeps escalating, only to set off another round of escalation in land prices. As a policy for protecting the long-term economic viability of family farms, the agricultural price support programme could hardly have been more ill conceived.

Economists are not in a position to tell government whether trying to preserve the existence of the family farm is a worthwhile goal. That is a political question, and in South Africa this is further complicated by the effort of government to redistribute land and increase the number of black commercial farmers. But given that the government has decided to pursue this objective, economists can provide advice regarding what policies are most likely to be effective. The price support system is doomed to fail because of the competitive bidding for land that it induces. Its long-run effect is to drive up the price of land, while doing little to ensure the survival of small family farms. A much more direct and efficient way to aid family farmers would be to reduce their income taxes, or, in the case of more extreme need, to give them outright cash grants.

The illusory attraction of taxing business

As noted in Chapter 2, political leaders often find it easier to propose new taxes on business than to collect additional taxes from individuals. Proposals to tax business usually include statements to the effect that 'wealthy corporations can better afford to pay extra taxes than can struggling workers'. But, as we saw in Chapter 2, a tax placed on the product sold by an industry will in general be passed on, at least in part, to consumers.

Let us examine a perfectly competitive industry in which individual firms have identical U-shaped LAC curves like the one labelled LAC_i in Fig. 9.24(b). In the most common case, moderate variations in the industry's output will have no appreciable effect on its input prices, with the result that the long-run supply curve for this industry will be a horizontal line at the minimum point of LAC_i (the curve labelled S_{LR} in Fig. 9.24(a)). If D is the market demand curve, then the equilibrium price will be P^*.

Figure 9.24 The effect of a tax on the output of a perfectly competitive industry

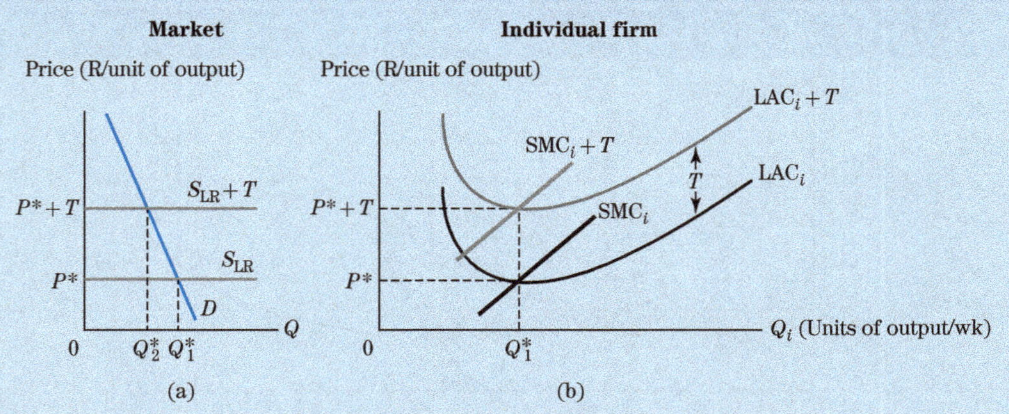

A tax of T rands per unit of output raises the LAC and SMC curves by T rands (b). The new long-run industry supply curve (S_{LR} + T) is again a horizontal line at the minimum value of LAC (a). Equilibrium price rises by T rands (a), which means that 100 per cent of the tax is passed on to consumers.

Economic naturalist 9.2

Why did 18-wheel cargo trucks suddenly begin using airfoils in the mid-1970s?

Before 1970, the profile of the typical 18-wheel semi-tractor-trailer truck resembled a match box. The broad, flat expanse of the top of the trailer was directly exposed to the force of the oncoming wind, which at highway speeds was substantial. But 93 octane petrol at the coast cost only 7.5 cents/litre in 1970, and so running the engine a little harder incurred a quite small penalty at that time.

The oil crisis in the early 1970s saw the price of oil increase from $3 per barrel in 1970 to more than $40 per barrel in 1980. In response, fuel prices also increased, from about 7 cents/litre in 1970 to more than 50 cents/litre by the early 1980s. As a result, the penalty imposed by the shape of the trailer became much more important – so much so that entrepreneurs devised ways of reducing it. One of the most successful innovations was the simple airfoil that now adorns the cab of virtually every large truck on the road, as shown in the photograph below. Its purpose is to deflect the wind from the top of the trailer. The profile of today's semi is still no aerodynamic masterpiece, but truckers estimate that the reduced wind resistance increases their mileage by 15 per cent at highway speeds.

The truckers who were first to install the airfoils did so at a time when the industry price level was determined by the higher costs of running trucks that lacked them. As a result, these early adopters earned economic profits from their efforts. As time passed, however, more and more trucks began to sport the devices, and the industry price level gradually declined in response to the lower costs they made possible. Today it is rare to see an 18-wheeler that lacks an airfoil, and by now it is safe to assume that the resultant cost savings have been fully reflected in lower trucking rates. The result is that the owner of a truck must now install an airfoil merely to be able to earn a normal rate of profit. Those who fail to install them pay the penalty of earning economic losses.

©iStock.com/kevinjanco

Why did airfoils suddenly appear on large trucks in the mid-1970s?

The price of diesel was only R5.37/litre in January 2007 at the Reef, but it increased to R11.27/litre in August 2008. Once again, truck owners had to be innovative to try to save costs in order to undercut their competitors. Many tracking devices were installed in the vehicles (although this was obviously also for safety reasons) to monitor their movement more closely. Vehicles' engines were also fitted with governors that prevented them from driving faster than a specified speed, to try to force the drivers to save as much fuel as possible. Fortunately for the transport industry the price of diesel dropped considerably, to R6.55/litre in mid-2009, as a result of the financial crisis that started in the USA and the ensuing global recession. However, when the US economy began to recover in 2013/14 the rand depreciated sharply, by more than 30 per cent, and, although the price of oil is currently relatively low, at about $115 per barrel, we are paying almost R16/litre.

These increases in fuel and diesel prices forced firms to look at more efficient ways to transport their goods. MAN, who developed the first commercial vehicle diesel engines more than 100 years ago, launched the TGS WW range of extra-heavy duty trucks in 2010, powered by the MAN D26 common-rail diesel engine. In 2012, the new MAN TGS Efficient Line range of long-haul trucks undertook a gruelling 2400 km economy run around the country to prove that significant fuel savings can be achieved via the fitment of various cost-effective components. According to MAN's executive chairman, Geoff du Plessis, the economy run proved that a 7.8 per cent saving in diesel can be achieved by its TGS Efficient Line truck-tractors, with a concomitant reduction in carbon emissions of 2.63 kg for every litre of diesel saved.

Now suppose a tax of T rands is collected on each unit of output sold in the market. The effect of this tax is to shift the LAC and SMC curves of each firm upwards by T rands (Fig. 9.24(b)). The new long-run industry supply curve is again a horizontal line at the minimum value of the LAC curve – this time the curve $S_{LR} + T$ in Fig. 9.24(a). The effect of the tax is to increase the price of the product by exactly T rands. Industry output contracts from Q_1^* to Q_2^* (Fig. 9.24(a)), and this contraction is achieved by firms leaving the industry.

Thus we see that, for competitive industries whose firms have U-shaped LAC curves, and whose input prices are fixed (the most empirically relevant case), the burden of a tax on output falls entirely on consumers. As we shall see in later chapters, there are a variety of legitimate reasons for taxing the output of specific industries. But the claim that corporations have more money than do people is simply not one of these reasons. Claims to the contrary are fraudulent, and an economically literate population would be unlikely to re-elect politicians who defended taxing business on these grounds.

If constant-cost competitive industries are able to pass on 100 per cent of taxes to buyers, why do industry lobbyists oppose taxes so strongly? Note in Fig. 9.24 that one effect of a tax is to reduce total industry output. This reduction is achieved by some firms going out of business. Bankruptcy is never a pleasant experience for the owners of a firm, and on this account it is far from surprising that industry trade associations are so strongly opposed to new taxes.

The adoption of cost-saving innovations

The economist's emphasis on the competitive firm as a price taker sometimes creates the impression that competitive firms do little more than passively respond to impersonal price signals served up by the environment. This impression is deeply misleading. While it is true, for example, that an individual trucker can do little to affect trucking rates set in the open market, there is a great deal he can and must do to ensure his continued survival.

The short-run response to the dramatic fuel price increase of the 1970s (which repeated itself in 2007–2009 and again in South Africa in 2013–2014) automatically lead to just the sorts of adjustment predicted by the competitive model: short-term losses, exit from the industry, gradually rising prices and a gradual restoration of profitability for surviving firms. But the change in the environment also created opportunities that some firms actively exploited to their own advantage. A case in point is illustrated in Economic naturalist 9.2.

The lesson of this Economic naturalist is that the entrepreneur who earns economic profits is the one who adopts cost-saving innovations ahead of the competition. It is the search for such innovations that keeps even the price-taking firm from being merely a passive reactor to economic forces beyond its control.

Summary

- The assumed objective of the firm is to maximize its economic profit. Economic profit is the difference between total revenue and cost – both explicit and implicit – of all resources used in production. Economic profit is not to be confused with accounting profit, which is the difference between total revenue and the explicit cost of resources used.
- The economic model of perfect competition assumes a standardized product, price-taking behaviour on the part of the firms, perfect mobility of resources and perfect information on the part of buyers and firms. In this sense, it is similar to the physicist's model of motion on frictionless surfaces. Both models describe idealized conditions that are rarely if ever met in practice, and yet each generates useful predictions for and explanations of events we observe in the real world.
- The rule for profit maximization in the short run is to produce the level of output for which price (also equal to marginal revenue) is equal to short-run marginal cost on the rising portion of that curve. If price falls below the minimum value of average variable cost, the firm will shut down. The individual firm's short-run supply curve is thus the rising portion of its short-run marginal cost curve that lies above the minimum point of its average variable cost curve.
- The short-run industry supply curve is the horizontal summation of the individual

firms' supply curves. It intersects the industry demand curve to determine the short-run equilibrium price. The individual competitive firm's demand curve is a horizontal line at the equilibrium price. If that price happens to lie above the minimum value of the long-run average cost curve, each firm will earn positive economic profit. If price is less than that value, each will suffer economic losses.

- Long-run adjustments consist not only of alterations in the size of existing firms' capital stocks, but also of entry and exit of firms. Where firms have identical U-shaped LAC curves, the long-run equilibrium price will be the minimum value of that LAC curve, and each firm will produce the corresponding quantity.
- Both long-run and short-run equilibrium positions are efficient in the sense that the value of the resources used in making the last unit of output is exactly equal to the value of that output to the buyer; in other words, it exhausts all possibilities for mutually beneficial exchange. The long-run equilibrium has two additional attractive features: (1) output is produced at the lowest possible unit cost; and (2) the seller is paid only the cost of producing the product. No economic profit is extracted from the buyer.
- Under perfect competition with constant input prices, the long-run industry supply curve is a horizontal line, not only when LAC curves are horizontal but also when they are U-shaped. When input prices are an increasing function of industry output, the industry supply curves in both cases will be upward sloping. When input prices decline with industry output, the competitive industry supply curve will be downward sloping.
- The effect of competition for the purchase of unusually high-quality inputs is to raise the price of those inputs until they no longer enable the firm that employs them to earn an economic profit. This is an extremely important part of the long-run adjustment process, and failure to account for it lies behind the failure of many well-intended economic policies.
- Even price-taking firms must actively seek out means of reducing their costs of doing business. To the early adopters of cost-saving innovations goes a temporary stream of economic profit, while late adopters must suffer through periods of economic losses.

Questions for review

1 What is the difference between economic profit and accounting profit, and how does this difference matter for actual business decisions?

2 Under what conditions will we expect firms to behave as price takers even though there are only a small number of other firms in the industry?

3 Would the market for dry cleaning be perfectly competitive in large cities such as Johannesburg or London? Why or why not? How about in a small city such as Athens, Port Elizabeth or Ohio?

4 A firm's total revenue curve is given by $\text{TR} = aQ - 2Q^2$. Is this a perfectly competitive firm? Explain why or why not.

5 Does the fact that a business manager may not know the definition of marginal cost contradict the theory of perfect competition?

6 *True or false*: If marginal cost lies below average fixed cost, the firm should shut down in the short run. Explain.

7 What do economists mean when they say that short-run competitive equilibrium is efficient?

8 *True or false*: In a constant-cost industry, a tax of a constant, fixed amount on each unit of output sold will not affect the amount of output sold by a perfectly competitive firm in the long run. Explain.

9 Suppose all firms in a competitive industry are operating at output levels for which price is equal to long-run marginal cost. *True or*

false: This industry is necessarily in long-run equilibrium.

10 *True or false*: Consumer surplus is the area between the demand curve and the price line. For a perfectly competitive firm, the demand curve equals the price line. Thus a perfectly competitive industry produces no consumer surplus.

11 Why are pecuniary economies and diseconomies said to be the exception rather than the rule?

12 Would you expect a firm that adopts cost-saving innovations faster than 80 per cent of all firms in its industry to earn economic profits? If so, will there be any tendency for these profits to be bid away?

Problems

1 A competitive firm has the cost structure described in the following table. Graph the marginal cost, average variable cost and average total cost curves. How many units of output will it produce at a market price of 32? Calculate its profits and show them in your graph.

Q	ATC	AVC	MC
1	44	4	8
2	28	8	16
4	26	16	32
6	31	24	48
8	37	32	64

2 If the short-run marginal and average variable cost curves for a competitive firm are given by $SMC = 2 + 4Q$ and $AVC = 2 + 2Q$, how many units of output will it produce at a market price of 10? At what level of fixed cost will this firm earn zero economic profit?

3 Each of 1000 identical firms in the competitive peanut butter industry has a short-run marginal cost curve given by

$$SMC = 4 + Q$$

If the demand curve for this industry is

$$P = 10 - \frac{2Q}{1\,000}$$

what will be the short-run loss in producer and consumer surplus if an outbreak of aflatoxin suddenly makes it impossible to produce any peanut butter?

4 Assuming the aflatoxin outbreak in Problem 3 persists, will the long-run loss in producer and consumer surplus be larger than, smaller than or the same as the short-run loss?

5 A perfectly competitive firm faces a price of 10 and is currently producing a level of output at which marginal cost is equal to 10 on a rising portion of its short-run marginal cost curve. Its long-run marginal cost is equal to 12. Its short-run average variable cost is equal to 8. The minimum point on its long-run average cost curve is equal to 10. Is this firm earning an economic profit in the short run? Should it alter its output in the short run? In the long run, what should this firm do?

6 All firms in a competitive industry have long-run total cost curves given by

$$LTC_Q = Q^3 - 10Q^2 + 36Q$$

where Q is the firm's level of output. What will be the industry's long-run equilibrium price? (*Hint*: Use either calculus or a graph to find the minimum value of the associated long-run average cost curve.) What will be the long-run equilibrium output level of the representative firm?

7 Same as Problem 6, except now

$$LTC_Q = Q^2 + 4Q$$

Could any firm actually have this particular LTC curve? Why or why not?

8 The marginal and average cost curves of taxis in Soweto are constant at R20.00/km. The demand curve for taxi trips in Soweto is given by $P = 100 - 0.0001Q$, where P is the fare, in rands per km, and Q is measured in km per year. If the industry is perfectly competitive, and each cab can provide exactly 10 000 km/yr of service, how many cabs will there be in equilibrium, and what will be the equilibrium fare?

9 Now suppose that the city council of Soweto decides to curb congestion in the downtown area by limiting the number of taxis to 60. Applicants participate in a lottery, and the

60 winners get a medallion, which is a permanent licence to operate a taxi in Soweto. What will the equilibrium fare be now? How much economic profit will each medallion holder earn? If medallions can be traded in the marketplace, and the rate of interest is 10 per cent/yr, how much will the medallions sell for? (*Hint*: How much money would you have to deposit in a bank to earn annual interest equal to the profit made by a taxi medallion?) Will the person who buys a medallion at this price earn a positive economic profit?

10 Eddy is like all other managers in a perfectly competitive industry except in one respect: because he has great people skills, workers are willing to work for him for half the going wage rate. All other firms in the industry have short-run total cost curves given by

$STC_Q = M + 100Q + wQ^2$

where M is the salary paid to ordinary managers and w is the going wage rate for the industry. If all firms in the industry face an output price of 280, and if $w = 20$, how much more will Eddy be paid than the other managers in the industry?

11 You are the owner-manager of a small competitive firm that manufactures house paints. You and your 1000 competitors have total cost curves given by

$TC = 8 + 2Q + 2Q^2$

and the industry is in long-run equilibrium. Now you are approached by an inventor who holds a patent on a process that will reduce your costs by half at each level of output.

a What is the most you would be willing to pay for the exclusive right to use this invention?

b Would the inventor be willing to sell at that price?

12 In the short run, a perfectly competitive firm produces output using capital services (a fixed input) and labour services (a variable input). At its profit-maximizing level of output, the marginal product of labour is equal to the average product of labour.

a What is the relationship between this firm's average variable cost and its marginal cost? Explain.

b If the firm has 10 units of capital and the rental price of each unit is R40/day, what will be the firm's profit? Should it remain open in the short run?

13 A firm in a competitive industry has a total cost function of $TC = 0.2Q^2 - 5Q + 30$, whose corresponding marginal cost curve is $MC = 0.4Q - 5$. If the firm faces a price of 6, what quantity should it sell? What profit does the firm make at this price? Should the firm shut down?

14 The demand for petrol is $P = 50 - 0.002Q$ and the supply is $P = 2 + 0.004Q$, where P is in rands and Q is in litres. If a tax of R10/litre is placed on petrol, what is the incidence of the tax? What is the lost consumer surplus? What is the lost producer surplus? Round your answers to two decimals.

15 Suppose that bicycles are produced by a perfectly competitive, constant-cost industry. Which of the following will have a larger effect on the long-run price of bicycles: (1) a government programme to advertise the health benefits of bicycling, or (2) a government programme that increases the demand for steel, an input in the manufacture of bicycles that is produced in an increasing-cost industry?

16 Suppose a representative firm in a perfectly competitive, constant-cost industry has a cost function $TC = 4Q^2 + 100Q + 100$.

a What is the long-run equilibrium price for this industry?

b If market demand is given by the function $Q = 1000 - P$, where P denotes price, how many firms will operate in this long-run equilibrium?

c Suppose the government grants a lump-sum subsidy to each firm that manufactures the product. If this lump-sum subsidy equals 36, what would be the new long-run equilibrium price for the industry?

17 The domestic supply and demand curves for Rooibos tea bags are given by $P = 10 + Q$ and $P = 100 - 2Q$, respectively, where P is the price in rands per 1 kg pack and Q is the quantity in millions of kilogram packs per year. South Africa produces and consumes only a trivial fraction of world Rooibos tea output, and the current world price of R30/kg is unaffected by events in the South African market. Transportation costs are also negligible.

a How much will South African consumers pay for Rooibos tea bags, and how many bushels of tea per year will they consume?

b How will your answers to part (a) change if the government decides to levy a tariff of R20/kg? What is consumer surplus and producer surplus after the imposition of the tariff?

c What total effect on domestic producer and consumer surplus will the tariff have? How much revenue will the tariff raise?

18 There are about 29 million sheep in South Africa, 75 per cent of which are concentrated in the Eastern Cape, Northern Cape and the Free State. A researcher at the University of Witwatersrand has discovered a drug that weakens the fibres of a sheep's wool just above its skin. The drug sharply reduces the cost of shearing sheep because the entire coat pulls off easily in one piece. The global wool market is reasonably close to perfect competition in terms of both product and factor sides. Trace out all the effects of the introduction of this new drug.

19 You are operating in a decreasing-cost industry. Explain with the aid of graphs how the long-run supply curve in this industry is determined.

Answers to in-chapter exercises

9.1 Let r^* be the monthly interest rate for which Cullen's economic profit would be zero. Then r^* must satisfy

$$R900\,000 - R60\,000 - R12\,000 - r^*(R150\,000\,000) = 0$$

which yields $r^* = 0.00552$, or 0.552 per cent/mth. Cullen should relocate only if the interest rate is lower than r^*.

9.2 Marginal cost is the slope of the total cost curve (or dTC/dQ), and marginal revenue is the slope of the total revenue curve (or dTR/dQ). At the maximum profit point, $Q^* = 74$, the slopes of these two curves are exactly the same (or dTC/dQ = dTR/dQ, thus MC = MR).

9.3 First, we need to rearrange the representative firm supply curve $P = 20 + 90Q_i$ to have quantity alone on one side:

$$Q_i = \frac{1}{90}P - \frac{2}{9}$$

Then we multiply by the number of firms, $n = 30$:

$$Q = nQ_i = 30Q_i$$
$$= 30\left(\frac{1}{90}P - \frac{2}{9}\right)$$
$$= \frac{1}{3}P - \frac{20}{3}$$

Finally, we rearrange the industry supply curve $-\frac{1}{3}P - \frac{20}{3}$ to have price alone on one side, $P = 3Q + 20$, to return to slope-intercept form.

9.4 Short-run profit maximization for a perfectly competitive firm occurs at the quantity where price equals marginal cost, $P = \text{MC}$, provided $P > \min \text{AVC}$ (otherwise, the firm shuts down). Since marginal cost is $\text{MC} = 2Q$, the market price $P = 12$ equals marginal cost $12 = 2Q$ at quantity $Q = 6$. Note that, here, min AVC = 6. We can express profits (with fixed costs separated out) as $\Pi = (P - \text{AVC})Q - \text{FC}$. Since average variable cost is $\text{AVC} = Q = 6$, the firm would earn economic profits of

$$\Pi = (12 - 6)6 - \text{FC} = 36 - \text{FC}$$

Thus, with fixed cost FC = 36, the firm would earn zero economic profits.

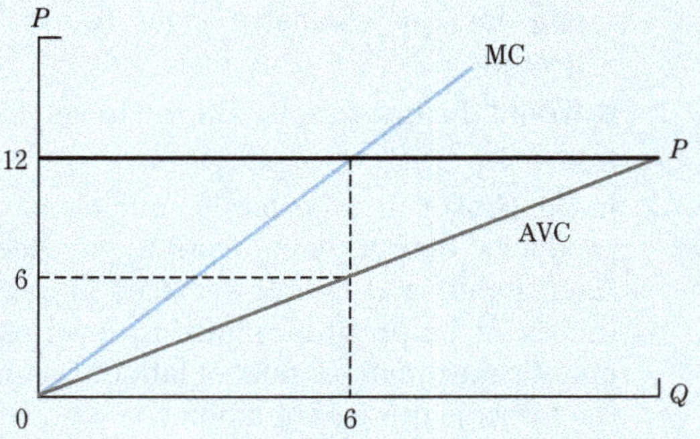

9.5 Total surplus is equal to the sum of the two shaded triangles shown on page 293, which is R1 000 000/yr.

9.6

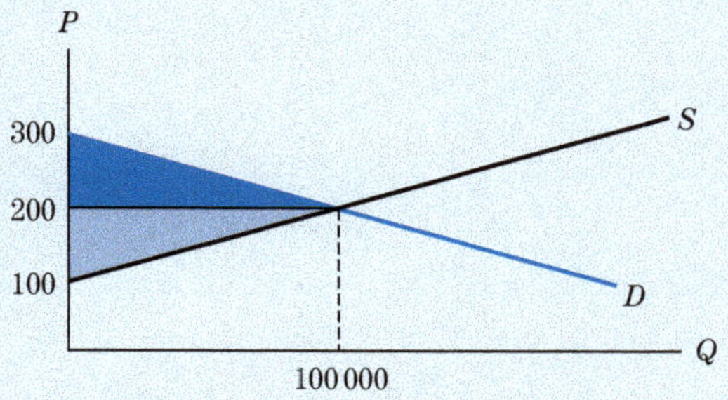

$$CS = \frac{1}{2}(300 - 200)\ 100\,000 = 5\,000\,000$$

$$PS = \frac{1}{2}(200 - 100)\ 100\,000 = 5\,000\,000$$

Chapter 10

Monopoly

Frequently, movie theatres charge different admission prices to moviegoers who belong to different groups. In the city where your university is located, different prices may apply to students, adults and families belonging to a movie club. Some theatres sell ten-packs of movie tickets at a lower unit price than single tickets bought just before the show. And people who attend movies in the morning or afternoon sometimes pay much less than those who attend evening showings. Frequently Ster-Kinekor, South Africa's main supplier of movie theatres, also offers free shows to children who belong to the movie club and go to the movies before the evening shows begin. None of these practices would be expected under our model of perfect competition, which holds that all buyers pay a single price for a completely standardized product.

The same theatre operators that charge different ticket prices to different groups follow quite another practice when it comes to the sale of concession items. Here, the law of one price almost always prevails. Students, adults, senior citizens, Supersport league soccer players, the clergy, trade union members – everybody pays exactly the same price for their popcorn. The same observation applies to the prices of soft drinks and chocolates. These prices, however, are usually much higher than we see for the same items sold in grocery stores and other retail establishments, and certainly far higher than any reasonable measure of the marginal cost of providing them. Normally specials are offered that appear to make buying all three goods the best buy, irrespective of whether you actually want them all.

Both behaviours – charging differential admission prices, on the one hand, and uniformly high concession prices, on the other – are, as we shall see, perfectly consistent with what the economic model predicts about the single seller of a good or service.

Chapter preview

In this chapter, our task will be to examine the market structure that least resembles perfect competition – namely, *monopoly*, a market served by a single seller of a product with no close substitutes. We shall discuss five factors that lead to this market structure:

- control over key inputs
- economies of scale
- patents
- network economies
- government licences

We shall then see that the monopolist's rule for maximizing profits in the short run is the same as that used by perfectly competitive firms. The monopolist will expand output if the gain in revenue exceeds the increase in costs (MR > MC), and will contract output if the loss in revenue is smaller than the reduction in costs. In other words, the monopolist will produce and sell where MR = MC.

Next, we shall examine the monopolist's behaviour when confronted with the option of selling in several separate markets. Here again, the logic of cost–benefit analysis will provide a convenient framework for analysing the firm's decision about whether to alter its current behaviour.

Our next step will be to examine the efficiency properties of the standard monopoly equilibrium. Unlike the perfectly competitive case, the monopoly equilibrium does not exhaust the potential gains from exchange. In general, the value to society of an additional unit of output will exceed the cost to the monopolist of the resources required to produce it. This finding has often been interpreted to mean that monopoly is less efficient than perfect competition. But this interpretation, we shall see, is of only limited practical significance because the conditions that give rise to monopoly are rarely compatible with those required for perfect competition.

The policy focus of this chapter centres on the question of how the government should treat natural monopolies – markets characterized by downward-sloping long-run average cost curves. We shall consider five policy alternatives:

- state ownership
- private ownership with government price regulation
- competitive bidding by private firms for the right to be the sole provider of a service
- vigorous enforcement of antitrust laws designed to prevent monopoly finally
- a completely laissez-faire, or hands-off, policy

Because problems are inherent in each alternative, the best policy generally will be different in different circumstances.

Defining monopoly

Monopoly is a market structure in which a single seller of a product with no close substitutes serves the entire market. This definition could hardly appear any simpler, and yet it turns out to be exceedingly difficult to apply in practice. Consider the example of movie theatres with which the chapter began. Is a local movie house a monopoly under our definition? In South Africa the cinema world is dominated by Ster-Kinekor and Nu Metro. In smaller cities there will be only one cinema, and only one showing of a given film at a given time. Whether it is a monopoly obviously depends on what we mean by a close substitute. If, for example, the theatre is currently showing *Rio 2*, there are likely to be a variety of close substitutes for its product. Indeed, quite a number of films featuring animated animals are released each year, and the potential patrons of such films generally do not have to look far if they are dissatisfied with the films available at any particular theatre.

But what about a theatre that is in the midst of an exclusive six-month, first-run engagement of the latest film in *The Hobbit* series? For fans of this series, there is really no close substitute. Those who want to see it while the excitement level surrounding its release is still high have only one seller to deal with.

The key feature that differentiates the monopoly from the competitive firm is the price elasticity of demand facing the firm. For the perfectly competitive firm, recall, price elasticity is infinite. If a competitive firm raises its price only slightly, it will lose all its sales. A monopoly, by contrast, has significant control over the price it charges.

Empirically, one practical measure for deciding whether a firm enjoys significant monopoly power is to examine the cross-price elasticity of demand for its closest substitutes. In one famous antitrust case in the USA, the DuPont Corporation was charged with having an effective monopoly on the sale of cellophane. Even though the company sold more than 80 per cent of all cellophane traded, it was able to defend itself against this charge by arguing that the cross-price elasticities between cellophane and its close substitutes – at the time, mainly waxed paper and aluminium foil – were sufficiently high to justify lumping all these flexible-wrap products into a single market. DuPont sold less than 20 per cent of total industry output under this broader market definition. In a controversial decision, the court deemed that percentage small enough to sustain effective competition.

This is not to say, however, that cross-price elasticity provides a clear, unambiguous measure that distinguishes a product with close substitutes from one without. While there may not be anything quite like the latest movie in *The Hobbit* series, there have always been lots of alternative ways to entertain oneself for two hours. However, for the person whose heart is set on seeing *The Hobbit* movie, the theatre operator is a monopolist; for the person merely in search of a good movie, by contrast, the same theatre operator faces stiff competition. The difference between perfect competition and monopoly often boils down to the question of which of these two types of buyer is more numerous. As in so many other cases in economics, the task of distinguishing between competition and monopoly remains as much an art as a science.

Note carefully that the distinction between monopoly and competition does not lie in any difference between the respective price elasticities of the market demand curves for the two cases. On the contrary, the market price elasticity of demand for products supplied by competitive firms is often much smaller than the price elasticity of demand facing a monopolist. For example, the price elasticity of demand is smaller for wheat than for Trellidor security gates, even though wheat is produced under nearly perfectly competitive conditions whereas Trellidor's patents make it the only legal SABS-approved seller in most of its markets in South Africa. The important distinction between monopoly and competition is that the demand curve facing the individual competitive firm is horizontal, whereas the monopolist's demand curve is simply the downward-sloping demand curve for the entire market.

South Africa has a number of firms that operate as monopolies or very close to monopolies: Telkom in the telecommunications industry, Transnet in rail transport, Eskom in the provision of electricity, SA Breweries in the supply of beer and MultiChoice in the broadcasting industry. In late 2013, MultiChoice introduced BoxOffice, a service whereby movies can be rented from the comfort of your own home, without the hassle of going to the video store. Only time will tell whether this move will put video shops out of business. If that does happen, MultiChoice will operate a monopoly in the provision of home entertainment movies.

Five sources of monopoly

How does a firm come to be the only one that serves its market? Economists discuss five factors, any one or a combination of which can enable a firm to become a monopoly. We also make a distinction between technical and legal barriers to entry that prevent other firms from entering the industry. The first four factors discussed below – namely, exclusive control over important inputs, economies of scale, patents and network economies – are technical barriers. Government licences or franchises are examples of legal barriers to entry. Although we do not discuss them, intellectual property rights can also be regarded as a legal barrier to entry. Let's now consider these factors in turn.

Exclusive control over important inputs

French company, Perrier (now owned by Nestlé), sells bottled mineral water. It spends millions of euros each year advertising the unique properties of this water, which are the result, it says, of a once-in-eternity confluence of geological factors that created its mineral spring. In the Western Cape, Sonaqua also offers mineral water. For some people, telling the difference between Sonaqua and Perrier is challenging. But others feel differently, and for many of them there is simply no satisfactory substitute for Perrier. Perrier's monopoly position with respect to these buyers is the result of its exclusive control over an input that cannot easily be duplicated.

De Beers' once exclusive control of global raw diamond supply had established a similar monopoly position. However, synthetic diamonds have now improved in quality to such an extent that occasionally they fool even an experienced jeweller. That said, for many buyers preference for a stone that was actually mined from the earth is not simply based on its greater hardness and refractive brilliance. They want real diamonds, and de Beers was the company that could provide them. Over time, however, de Beers' influence has diminished as other producers, especially from Russia, Canada and Australia, began distributing diamonds outside the established de Beers channel. While de Beers effectively controlled more than 80 per cent of the world diamond market in 1990, its share has now diminished to about 40 per cent.

Exclusive control of key inputs is not a guarantee of permanent monopoly power. The preference for real diamonds, for example, is based largely on the fact that mined diamonds have historically been genuinely superior to synthetic ones. But assuming that synthetic diamonds eventually do become completely indistinguishable from real ones, there will no longer be any basis for this preference. And as a result, de Beers' control over the supply of mined diamonds will cease to confer monopoly power. New ways to produce existing products are constantly being devised, and the exclusive input that generates today's monopoly is likely to become obsolete tomorrow.

Economies of scale

A market with declining long-run average costs will probably be served by, a single firm. If two firms attempted to serve such a market, with each producing only part of the total output sold, each would have higher average costs than if one of them alone served the market. In Fig. 10.1(a), for example, note that a single firm can produce an industry output of Q^* at an average cost of LAC_{Q^*}, whereas with two firms sharing the same market, average cost rises to $LAC_{Q^*/2}$. Markets characterized by declining long-run average cost curves are for this reason often referred to as **natural monopolies**. Such a firm serves the whole market while it is operating on the negatively-sloped part of its LAC curve. A frequently cited example is the provision of local telephone landlines. In South Africa, Neotel, the second landline operator, received its licence to trade only in 2008. Basically, Eskom provides most electricity in South Africa via its coal and nuclear plants, and those firms generating electricity by means of solar power or wind turbines have great difficulty entering the industry.

Natural monopoly
An industry whose market output is produced at the lowest cost when production is concentrated in the hands of a single firm.

Consider now the LAC curve shown in Fig. 10.1(b). The minimum point on this curve occurs at the output level Q_0. The output level Q_0 may be called the *minimum efficient scale*: the level of production required for LAC to reach its minimum level. If Q_0 constitutes a substantial share of industry output – more than, say, 20 per cent – the industry will tend to be dominated by a small handful of firms. As in the natural monopoly case, a large number of small firms would be unlikely to survive in such a market, since each would have much higher average costs than larger firms. By contrast to the natural monopoly case, however, the upturn in the LAC beyond Q_0 will make it difficult for a single firm to serve the entire market. Markets served by firms with LACs like the one shown in Fig. 10.1(b) are likely to be 'highly concentrated', which means that a small number of firms will tend to account for the lion's share of all output sold. This is referred to as an *oligopolistic market structure*. The South African economy has many examples of a few firms dominating certain industries.[1]

Patents

Most countries protect inventions through some sort of patent system. A patent typically confers the right to exclusive benefit from all exchanges involving the invention to which it applies. There are costs as well as benefits to patents. On the cost side, the monopoly it creates usually leads, as we shall see, to higher prices for consumers. On the

Figure 10.1 Natural monopoly and concentrated industries

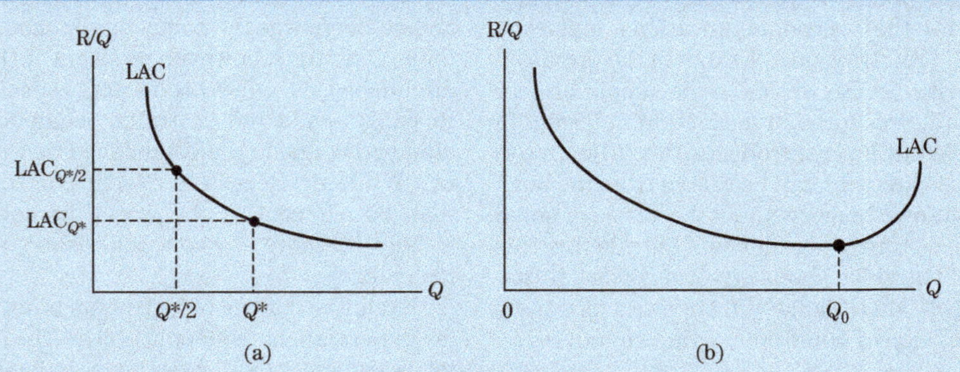

(a) When the LAC curve is always declining, irrespective of the level of production, it is always cheaper for a single firm to serve the entire industry. (b) U-shaped LAC curves whose minimum points occur at a substantial share of total market output are characteristic of markets served by only a small handful of firms.

[1] For a more detailed discussion of this topic, see, for example, J. Fedderke and W. Szalontai, *South African Manufacturing Industry Structure and its Implications for Competition Policy*, School of Economics, University of Cape Town, Working Paper Number 111, 2008.

benefit side, the patent makes possible a great many inventions that would not otherwise occur. Although some inventions are serendipitous, most are the result of long-term effort and expense in sophisticated research laboratories. If a firm were unable to sell its product for a sufficiently high price to recoup these outlays, it would have no economic reason to undertake research and development in the first place. Without a patent, competition would force price down to marginal cost, and the pace of innovation would be slowed dramatically. The protection from competition afforded by a patent is what makes it possible for the firm to recover its costs of innovation.

In South Africa, the life of a patent is 20 years from the date of filing the completed application, and it must be renewed annually, usually from the fourth year. There is no such thing as a 'worldwide patent'. Most South Africans provisionally register their South African patents, and a search is then conducted, usually by the Austrian Patent Office, throughout the 141 member countries bound by the terms of the Patent Cooperation Treaty to investigate the patentability of the invention before patenting proceeds. For a firm to have 'worldwide' patent protection, the patent must be registered in all 152 signatory countries to the Paris Convention individually, or in each country in which patent protection is required. Many feel that patent lifespan is too short, and it can be argued that it should be extended in the prescription drug industry, where the testing and approval process often consumes all but a few years of the current patent period.

Network economies

On the demand side of many markets, a product becomes more valuable as greater numbers of consumers use it. A vivid early illustration was the defeat on the part of VHS technology of the competing Beta format in home video recorders in the 1980s. The attraction of VHS over the initial versions of Beta was that it permitted longer recording times. Beta later corrected this deficiency, and on most important technical dimensions became widely regarded by experts as superior to VHS. Yet the initial sales advantage of VHS proved insuperable. Once the fraction of consumers owning VHS passed a critical threshold, the reasons for choosing it became compelling – variety and availability of tape rentals, access to repair facilities, the capability to exchange tapes with friends, and so on. With the arrival of DVDs, video tapes became outdated. Once again, there were many formats on the market: DVD ± R, DVD ± RW, DVD RAM and later HD DVDs. No one format was totally superior to the others, and sales were very evenly spread between them. With the arrival of Blu-ray discs in 2009, this situation is changing because their quality is far superior. Taken together with large high definition TV screens, surround-sound entertainment systems and even 3D technology, the superior quality of Blu-ray discs is reason enough for consumers to buy Blu-ray recorders. Once a certain threshold is reached, this new technology will, like VHS, win the race in the next generation of home entertainment.

In extreme cases, such network economies function like economies of scale as a source of natural monopoly. Microsoft's Windows operating system, for example, achieved its dominant market position on the strength of powerful network economies. Because Microsoft's initial sales advantage gave software developers a strong incentive to write for the Windows format, the inventory of available software in the Windows format is now vastly larger than for any competing operating system. And although general-purpose software, such as word-processing programs and spreadsheets, continues to be available for multiple operating systems, specialized professional software and games usually appear first in the Windows format, and often only in that format. This software gap has given people a good reason for choosing Windows, even if, as in the case of many Apple Macintosh users, they believe a competing system is otherwise superior. The end result is that more than 90 per cent of the world's personal computers now run the Microsoft's Windows operating system. If that's not a pure monopoly, it comes awfully close. And every couple of years Microsoft updates the operating programs a little, forcing users to buy the new software so as to ensure compatibility with other users.

Government licences or franchises

In many markets the law prevents anyone but a government-licensed firm doing business. In the first edition of this book, I mentioned being happy that fast-food restaurants are restricted in the world-famous Kruger National Park. Surely people visit national parks to experience life in the wild. In 2013 it was decided that certain fast-food operators would be allowed to do business in the park and the first eateries opened in 2014 in Lower Sabie, Olifants and Letaba rest camps. These were then followed by new restaurants in Pretoriuskop, Skukuza and Satara. However, not just any old fast-food operator is free to open its doors. The Parks Board negotiated with several companies and then granted exclusive licences to these operators to serve a particular camp. In such cases, the government licence, as a source of monopoly, is really a scale economy acting in another form because not enough demand exists to create a market for multiple operators.

Government licences are also required in a variety of other markets, such as for taxis, where scale economies do not seem to be an important factor. Following a switch from typical 10-seater minibuses (which were frequently rather run down and unroadworthy) to bigger and newer minibuses, the South African government intervened directly to regulate this industry to a larger extent. At most, such regulation had limited success.

Government licences are sometimes accompanied by strict regulations that spell out what the licensee can and cannot do. When the government grants an exclusive licence to a restaurant chain, for example, it often requires the chain to charge prices that are no more than, say, 10 per cent higher than those it charges in its unregulated outlets. In other cases, the government simply charges an extremely high fee for the licence, virtually forcing the licensee to charge premium prices. This is the practice of some airport authorities, who essentially auction their terminal counter space to the highest bidders. Your annoyance at having to pay R15 for a can of Coke in OR Tambo Airport should thus more properly be focused on the Airport Company of South Africa (ACSA) than on the vendor.

By far the most important of the five factors explaining enduring monopolies is economies of scale. Production processes change over time, which makes exclusive control over important inputs only a transitory source of monopoly. Patents too are inherently transitory. Network economies, once firmly entrenched, can be as persistent a source of natural monopoly as economies of scale. Strictly speaking, network economies work through the demand side of the market by affecting what buyers are willing to pay for a product. But they may be equivalently conceptualized on the supply side as yet another feature of product quality. The more people who own the product, the higher is its effective quality level. It may thus be said of a product which benefits from network economies that any given quality level can be produced at lower cost as sales volume increases. Viewed in this way, network economies are just another form of economies of scale in production, and that's how we shall view them in the discussion that follows. Government licences can persist for extended periods, but many of these licences are themselves merely an implicit recognition of scale economies that would lead to monopoly in any event.

Information as a growing source of economies of scale

Students today can barely believe the effort previously involved in sourcing information; a world without the internet is almost unimaginable to them. Typing essays and theses on manual typewriters, without memory or easy means of correction, seems almost more unreal than science fiction. The personal computer changed all that. In 1984, at the dawn of the personal computing age, approximately 80 per cent of the cost of a personal computer was accounted for by its hardware, and only 20 per cent by its software. Only six years later, those percentages were exactly reversed. Now all but a tiny fraction of the total cost involved in bringing a personal computer to market is associated in one way or another with the production of information. Although this transformation has been especially dramatic in the case of personal computers, similar changes have been occurring for most other products as well.

The distinctive feature about information is that virtually all costs associated with its production are fixed – in contrast to hardware, for which a large share of production costs are roughly proportional to the volume of production. The upshot is that the production of information-rich products is often characterized by enormous economies of scale.

Because the concept of economies of scale refers to the long run by definition, the preceding paragraph's reference to economies of scale and fixed costs in the same breath might seem inconsistent. After all, fixed costs are expenditures associated with fixed inputs and, as we saw in Chapter 7, no inputs are fixed in the long run.

As a practical matter, however, large one-time costs, including product research and other costs associated with generating information, are often incurred before a product is launched. Typically these costs never recur, even during a product life cycle spanning several decades. Strictly speaking, these costs are not fixed since the inputs used for generating the information could be varied in principle. Yet when the product is launched, there is simply no economic reason for varying them. So for practical purposes these costs are essentially fixed. In any case, the important point is that the firm's long-run average cost curve is likely to be downward sloping whenever a substantial share of its total cost is associated with initial investment in information.

A good practical example is the microprocessor that powers personal computers and a growing array of other products. The fixed investment required to produce the latest Intel chip is roughly R20 billion. Once the chip has been designed and the manufacturing facility built, however, the marginal cost of producing each chip is only a few cents. It is hardly a surprise, therefore, that Intel currently supplies more than 80 per cent of all microprocessors sold today.

Economies of scale have always been an important feature of the modern industrial landscape. But as more and more of the value embedded in products consists of information, the importance of economies of scale can only increase.

With this brief overview of the causes of monopoly in mind, let us turn now to the consequences of monopoly. In order to do so, we shall proceed in much the same fashion as applied to our study of the competitive firm. That is, we shall examine the firm's output decision, and ask whether it leads to a situation in which all possible gains from exchange are exhausted. The answer is generally, no. But in formulating a government policy to improve on the results of unregulated monopoly, we shall see that it is critical to understand the original source of monopoly.

The profit-maximizing monopolist

As in the competitive case, we assume that the monopolist's goal is to maximize economic profit. And again as before, in the short run this means choosing the level of output for which the difference between total revenue and short-run total cost is greatest. The case for this motive is less compelling than in the case of perfect competition. After all, the monopolist's survival is less under siege than its competitors', and so the evolutionary argument for profit maximization applies with less force in the monopoly case. Nonetheless, we shall explore the behaviours that follow from the monopolist's goal of profit maximization.

The monopolist's total revenue curve

The key difference between the monopolist and the perfect competitor is the way in which total, and hence marginal, revenue varies with output. Recall from Chapter 9 that the demand curve facing the perfect competitor is simply a horizontal line at the short-run equilibrium market price (determined in the industry) – call it P^*. The competitive firm is a price taker, typically because its own output is too small to have any discernible influence on the market price. Under these circumstances, the perfectly competitive firm's total revenue curve is a ray with slope P^*, as shown in Fig. 10.2.

Now consider a monopolist with the downward-sloping demand curve $P = 800 - \frac{1}{5}Q$ pictured in the top panel in Fig. 10.3. For this firm, too, total revenue is the product of price and quantity. At point A on its demand curve, for example, it sells 1000 units of output per week at a price of R600/unit, giving a total revenue of R600 000/wk. At B, it sells 2000 units at a price of R400, so its total revenue at B will be R800 000/wk, and so on. The difference between the monopolist and the competitor is that, for the monopolist to sell a larger amount of output, it must cut its price – not only for the marginal unit but for all preceding units too. As we saw in Chapter 4, the effect of a downward-sloping demand curve is that total revenue is no longer proportional to output sold. As in the competitive case, the monopolist's total revenue curve (middle panel in Fig. 10.3) passes through the origin because, in each case, selling no output generates no revenue. But as price falls, total revenue for the monopolist does not rise linearly with output. Instead, it reaches a maximum value at the quantity corresponding to the midpoint of the demand curve (B in the top panel), after which it again begins to fall. The corresponding values of the price elasticity of demand are shown in the bottom panel in Fig. 10.3. Note that total revenue

Figure 10.2 The total revenue curve for a perfect competitor

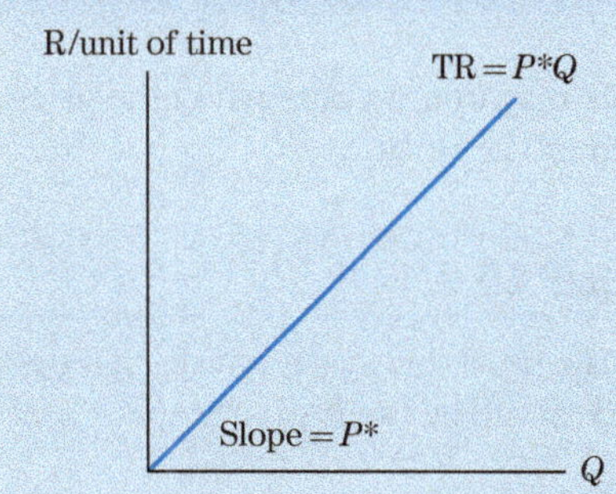

Price for the perfect competitor remains at the short-run equilibrium level P^*, irrespective of the firm's output. Its total revenue is thus the product of P^* and the quantity it sells: $TR = P^*Q$.

Figure 10.3 Demand, total revenue and elasticity

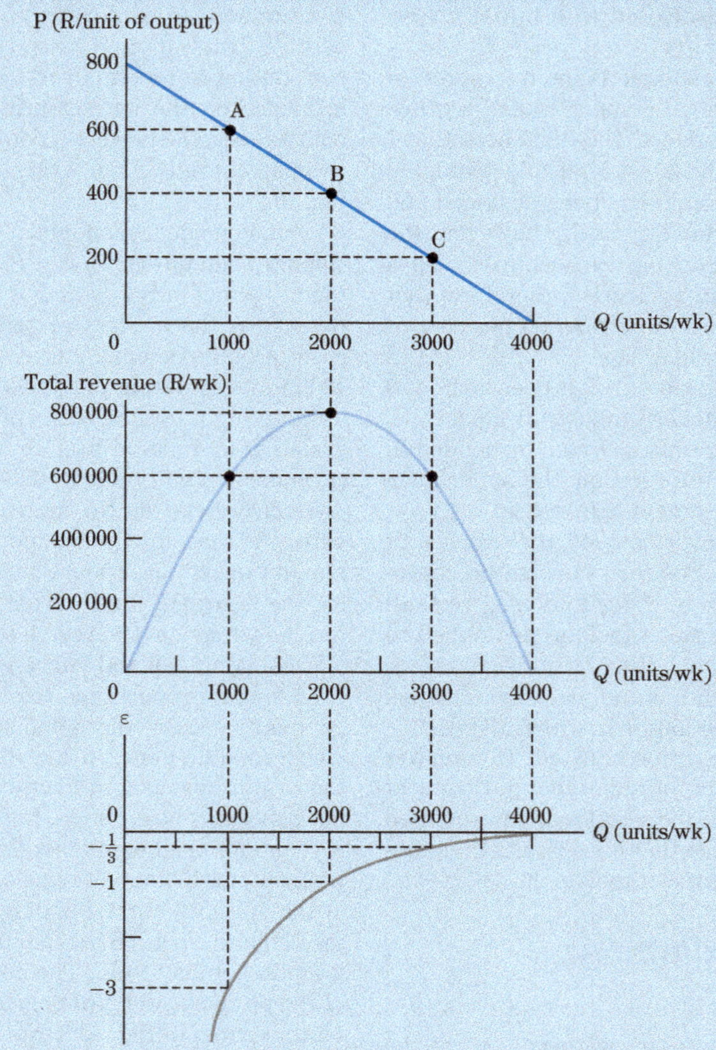

For the monopolist to increase sales, it is necessary to cut price (top panel). Total revenue rises with quantity, reaches a maximum value and then declines (middle panel). The quantity level for which the price elasticity of demand is unity corresponds to the midpoint of the demand curve, and at that value total revenue is maximized.

reaches its maximum value when the price elasticity of demand is unity.

Exercise 10.1

Sketch the total revenue curve for a monopolist whose demand curve is given by $P = 100 - 2Q$.

The top panel in Fig. 10.4 portrays the short-run total cost curve and total revenue curve for a monopolist facing the demand curve shown in Fig. 10.3. Economic profit, plotted in the bottom panel, is positive in the interval from $Q = 450$ to $Q = 3050$, and is negative elsewhere. The maximum profit point occurs at $Q^* = 1750$ units/wk, which lies to the left of the output level for which total revenue is at a maximum ($Q = 2000$).

Notice in Fig. 10.4 that, at the production level where the vertical distance between the short-run total cost and total revenue curves is greatest (when $Q = 1750$), the slope of the total revenue curve is equal to the slope of the total cost curve. Suppose this were not the case. For example, suppose that at the maximum-profit point the total cost curve was steeper than the total revenue

Figure 10.4 Total cost, revenue and profit curves for a monopolist

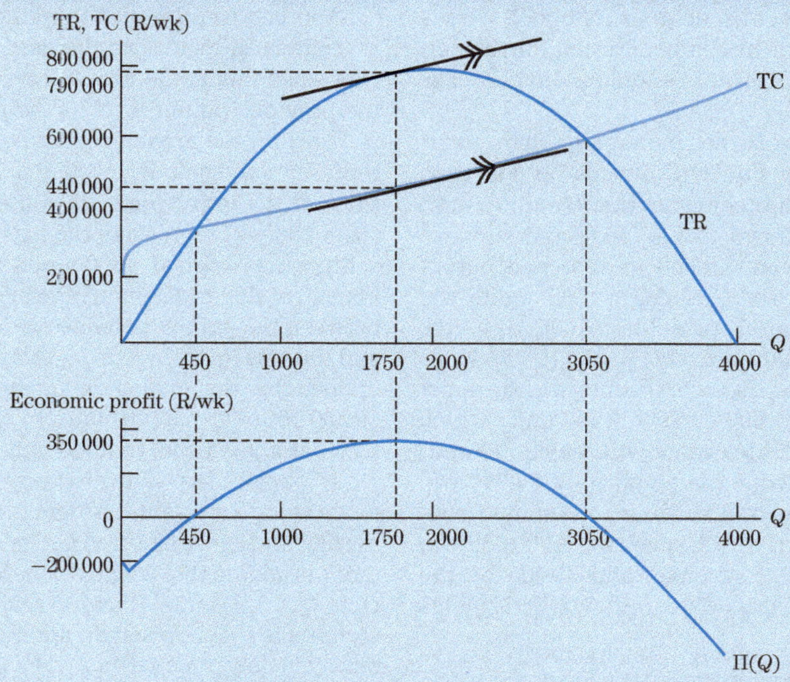

Economic profit [Π(Q) in the bottom panel] is the vertical distance between total revenue and total cost (TR and TC in the top panel). Note that the maximum profit point, $Q^* = 1750$, lies to the left of the output level at which TR is at a maximum ($Q = 2000$).

curve. It would then be possible to earn higher profits by producing less output, because costs would go down by more than the corresponding reduction in total revenue. Conversely, if the total cost curve was less steep than the total revenue curve, the monopolist could earn higher profits by expanding output because total revenue would go up by more than total cost.

Marginal revenue

The slope of the total cost curve at any level of output is by definition equal to marginal cost at that output level. By the same token, the slope of the total revenue curve is the definition of marginal revenue. In derivative terms, the slope of the total cost curve is dTC/dQ, and the slope of the total revenue curve is dTR/dQ. As in the case of the perfectly competitive firm, we can think of marginal revenue as the change in total revenue when the sale of output changes by 1 unit. More precisely, suppose ΔTR_Q is the change in total revenue that occurs in response to a small change in output, ΔQ. Marginal revenue, denoted MR_Q, is then given by

$$MR_Q = \frac{\Delta TR_Q}{\Delta Q} \qquad (10.1)$$

Using this definition, a profit-maximizing monopolist in the short run will choose that level of output Q^* for which

$$MC_{Q^*} = MR_{Q^*} \left(\text{or } \frac{dTC}{dQ} = \frac{dTR}{dQ} \right) \qquad (10.2)$$

provided marginal revenue intersects marginal cost from above. Equation 10.2 defines the **optimality condition for a monopolist**. The monopolist wants to sell all units for which marginal revenue exceeds marginal cost, so marginal revenue should lie above marginal cost prior to the intersection. (For some cost structures, marginal cost may decline initially and then increase, leading to two intersections of marginal cost and marginal revenue and that is the reason why marginal revenue must intersect marginal cost from above.)

Optimality condition for a monopolist
A monopolist maximizes profit by choosing the level of output at which marginal revenue equals marginal cost.

Recall that the analogous condition for the perfectly competitive firm is to choose the output level for which price and marginal cost are equal. Recalling that marginal revenue and price (P) are exactly the same for the competitive firm (when such a firm expands output by one unit, its total revenue goes up by P), we see that the profit-maximizing condition for the perfectly competitive firm is simply a special case of Eq. 10.2.

In the case of the monopoly firm, marginal revenue per unit will always be less than price.[2] To see why, consider the demand curve $P = 800 - 0.2Q$ shown in Fig. 10.5, and suppose that the monopolist wishes to increase output from $Q_0 = 1000$ to $Q_0 + \Delta Q = 1500$ units/wk. His total revenue from selling 1000 units/wk is (R600/unit)(1000 units/wk) = R600 000/wk. To sell an additional $\Delta Q = 500$ units/wk, he must cut his price to R600 − ΔP = R500/unit, which means his new total revenue will be (R500/unit)(1500 units/wk), which is equal to R750 000/wk. To calculate marginal revenue, we simply subtract the original total revenue, R600 000/wk, from the new total revenue, and divide by the change in output, $\Delta Q = 500$ units/wk. This yields

$$MR_{Q_0=1000} = \frac{(\text{R}750\,000/\text{wk} - \text{R}600\,000/\text{wk})}{(500\text{ units/wk})} = \text{R}300/\text{unit}$$

which is clearly less than the original price of R600/unit.

Another useful way of thinking about marginal revenue is to view it as the gain in revenue from new sales minus the loss in revenue from selling the previous output level at the new, lower price. In Fig. 10.5, the area of rectangle B (R250 000/wk) represents the gain in revenue from the additional sales at the lower price. The area of rectangle A (R100 000/wk) represents the loss in revenue from selling the original 1000 units/wk at R500/unit instead of R600. Marginal revenue is the difference between the gain in revenue from additional sales and the loss in revenue from sales at a lower price, divided by the change in quantity. This yields (R250 000/wk − R100 000/wk) / (500 units/wk), which is again equal to R300/unit.

To explore how marginal revenue varies as we move along a straight-line demand curve, consider the demand curve pictured in Fig. 10.6, and suppose that the monopolist wishes to increase output from Q_0 to $Q_0 + \Delta Q$ units. His total revenue from selling Q_0 units is P_0Q_0. To sell an additional ΔQ units he must cut his price to $P_0 - \Delta P$, which means his new total revenue will be $(P_0 - \Delta P) \cdot (Q_0 + \Delta Q)$, which is equal to $P_0Q_0 + P_0\,\Delta Q - \Delta PQ_0 - \Delta P\Delta Q$.

Figure 10.5 Changes in total revenue resulting from a price cut

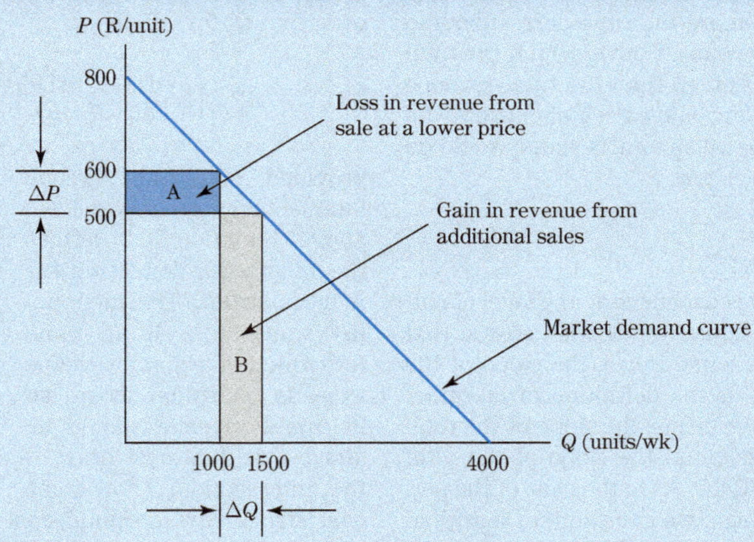

The area of rectangle A (R100 000/wk) is the loss in revenue from selling the previous output level at a lower price. The area of rectangle B (R250 000/wk) is the gain in revenue from selling the additional output at the new, lower price. Marginal revenue is the difference between these two areas (R250 000 − R100 000 = R150 000/wk) divided by the change in output (500 units/wk). Here, MR equals R300/unit, which is less than the new price of R500/unit.

[2] There is actually one exception to this claim, namely, the case of the perfectly discriminating monopolist, discussion of which follows.

To calculate marginal revenue, simply subtract the original total revenue, P_0Q_0, from the new total revenue, and divide by the change in output, ΔQ. This leaves

$$MR_{Q_0} = P_0 - \left(\frac{\Delta P}{\Delta Q}\right)Q_0 - \Delta P$$

which is clearly less than P_0 (the original price). As ΔP approaches zero, the expression for marginal revenue thus approaches[3]

$$MR_{Q_0} = P_0 - \frac{\Delta P}{\Delta Q}Q_0 \qquad (10.3)$$

Equation 10.3 makes intuitive sense if we think of ΔQ as being a one-unit change in output: P_0 would then be the gain in revenue from the sale of that extra unit, and $(\Delta P/\Delta Q) \cdot Q_0 = \Delta PQ_0$ would be the loss in revenue from the sale of the existing units at the lower price. We see again in Eq. 10.3 that marginal revenue is less than price for all positive levels of output.

The fact that area B is larger than area A in Fig. 10.6 means that marginal revenue is positive at Q_0. Once output moves past the midpoint (M in Fig. 10.6) on a straight-line demand curve (like Q_1 in Fig. 10.6), however, the marginal revenue of a further expansion to $Q_1 + \Delta Q$ will be negative. Thus the area of rectangle C is larger than the area of rectangle D in Fig. 10.6, which means that marginal revenue at output level Q_1 is less than zero.

Marginal revenue and elasticity

Yet another useful relationship links marginal revenue to the price elasticity of demand at the corresponding point on the demand curve. Recall from Chapter 4 that the price elasticity of demand at a point (Q, P) is given by

$$\varepsilon = \frac{\Delta Q}{\Delta P}\frac{P}{Q}\left(\text{or } \frac{dQ}{dP}\frac{P}{Q}\right) \qquad (10.4)$$

In Eq. 10.4, the terms ΔQ and ΔP have opposite signs because the demand curve is downward sloping. By contrast, recall that the ΔQ and ΔP terms in Eq. 10.3, which also represent changes in P and Q as we move along the demand curve, are both positive. Suppose we redefine ΔQ and ΔP from Eq. 10.4 so that both of these terms are positive. That equation then becomes

$$|\varepsilon| = \frac{\Delta Q}{\Delta P}\frac{P}{Q} \qquad (10.5)$$

Figure 10.6 Marginal revenue and position on the demand curve

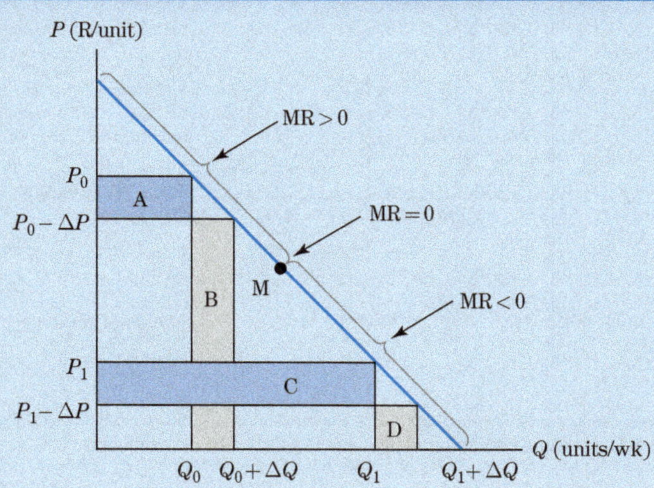

When Q is to the left of the midpoint (M) of a straight-line demand curve (for example, $Q = Q_0$), the gain from added sales (area B) outweighs the loss from a lower price for existing sales (area A). When Q is to the right of the midpoint (for example, $Q = Q_1$), the gain from added sales (area D) is smaller than the loss from a lower price for existing sales (area C). At the midpoint of the demand curve, the gain and the loss are equal, which means marginal revenue is zero.

[3] Note that when ΔP shrinks towards zero, the corresponding ΔQ does so as well. Because ΔP and ΔQ are both positive here, the ratio $\Delta P/\Delta Q$ is simply the negative of the slope of the demand curve.

The purpose of making both ΔQ and ΔP positive is to be able to relate Eq. 10.5 back to Eq. 10.3. If we now solve Eq. 10.5 for $\Delta P/\Delta Q = P/(Q|\varepsilon|)$ and substitute into Eq. 10.3, we get

$$MR_Q = P\left(1 - \frac{1}{|\varepsilon|}\right) \quad (10.6)$$

Equation 10.6 tells us that the less elastic is demand with respect to price, the more price will exceed marginal revenue.[4] It also tells us that, in the limiting case of infinite price elasticity, marginal revenue and price are exactly the same. (Recall from Chapter 9 that price and marginal revenue are the same for the competitive firm, which faces a horizontal, or infinitely elastic, demand curve.)

Graphing marginal revenue

Equation 10.6 also provides a convenient way to plot the marginal revenue values that correspond to different points along a demand curve. To illustrate, consider the straight-line demand curve in Fig. 10.7 ($P = 800 - 0.2Q$ or $Q = 4000 - 5P$), which intersects the vertical axis at a price value of $P = 800$. The elasticity of demand is infinite at that point, which means that $MR_0 = 800(1 - 1/|\varepsilon|) = 800$ Although marginal revenue will generally be less than price for a monopolist, the two are exactly the same when quantity is zero. The reason is that at zero output there are no existing sales for a price cut to affect.

Now suppose we move, say, one-quarter of the way down the demand curve to point A, (1000, 600). At that point, $|\varepsilon| = 3$. Thus we have $MR_{1000} = (600)(1 - \frac{1}{3}) = 400$. Halfway down the demand curve, at point B, (2000, 400), $|\varepsilon| = 1$, which gives us $MR_{2000} = (400)(1 - \frac{1}{1}) = 0$. This confirms our earlier finding (Chapter 4) that total revenue is at a maximum at the midpoint of a straight-line demand curve, where elasticity is unity. Recall that MR is the slope of TR, and where the TR function has its maximum turning point the slope of the TR function will be zero and therefore MR is also zero at that point.

Finally, consider point C, (3000, 200), which is three-quarters of the way down the demand curve. Here, $|\varepsilon| = \frac{1}{3}$, so we have $MR_{3000} = (200)[1 - (1/\frac{1}{3})] = (200)(-2) = -400$. Thus, at

Figure 10.7 The demand curve and corresponding marginal revenue curve

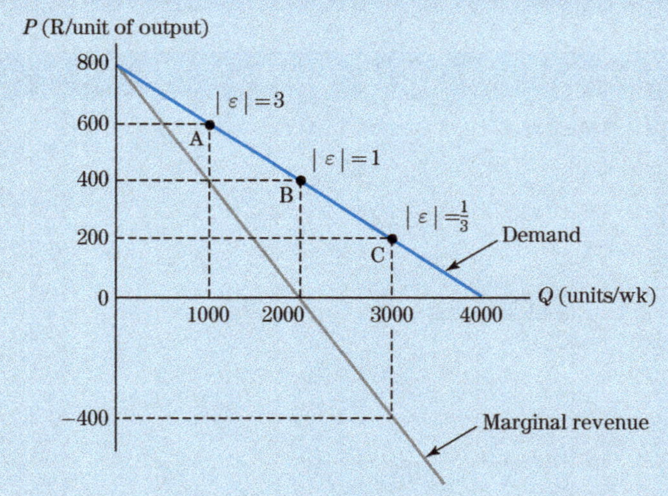

For the case of a straight-line demand curve, the corresponding marginal revenue curve is also a straight line. It has the same vertical intercept as the demand curve, and its horizontal intercept is half that of the demand curve.

[4] Equation 10.6 can be derived using calculus as follows:

$$MR = \frac{dTR}{dQ} = \frac{d(PQ)}{dQ} = P + Q\frac{dP}{dQ} = P\left(1 + \frac{QdP}{PdQ}\right)$$

$$= P\left(1 + \frac{1}{\varepsilon}\right) = P\left(1 + \frac{1}{|\varepsilon|}\right)$$

$Q = 3000$, the effect of selling an extra unit of output is to reduce total revenue by R400/wk.

Filling in additional points in the same fashion, we quickly see that the marginal revenue curve associated with a straight-line demand curve is itself a straight line, one whose slope is twice that of the demand curve. The marginal revenue curve cuts the horizontal axis just below the midpoint of the demand curve, and for all quantities larger than that marginal revenue is negative. Note that all points to the right of the midpoint of the demand curve have price elasticity values of less than 1 in absolute value. The fact that marginal revenue is negative in this region thus fits our observation from Chapter 4 that a cut in price will reduce total revenue whenever demand is inelastic with respect to price.

Exercise 10.2

Sketch demand and marginal revenue curves for a monopolist whose market demand curve is given by $P = 100 - 2Q$.

Graphical interpretation of the short-run profit-maximization condition

Recall from Chapter 9 the graphical representation of the maximum-profit point for the competitive firm in the short run. An analogous graphical representation exists for the monopolist. Consider a monopolist with the demand, marginal revenue and short-run cost curves pictured in Fig. 10.9. The profit-maximizing level of output for this firm is Q^*, the one for which the marginal revenue and marginal cost curves intersect. At that quantity level, the monopolist can charge a price of P^*, and by so doing will earn an economic profit equal to the shaded rectangle labelled Π. Obviously the monopolist can ask a price at the level where the MR and MC curves intersect, but will be stupid to do so. This is how a monopoly differs from a perfectly competitive market – the monopolist can influence the market price. At quantity Q^*, the market is willing to pay P^* (and we know this from the demand curve that tells us what consumers are willing to pay), and therefore the monopolist can ask that price and maximize its profit.

Example 10.1

Find the marginal revenue curve that corresponds to the demand curve $P = 12 - 3Q$.

The marginal revenue curve will have the same intercept as and twice the slope of the demand curve, which gives us $MR = 12 - 6Q$, as plotted in Fig. 10.8.

The general formula for a linear demand curve is $P = a - bQ$, where a and b are positive numbers. Then $TR = aQ - bQ^2$. But we know that $MR = dTR/dQ = a - 2bQ$. Clearly, the slope of the marginal revenue curve ($2b$) is double the slope of the demand curve (b).

Figure 10.8 A specific linear demand curve and the corresponding marginal revenue curve

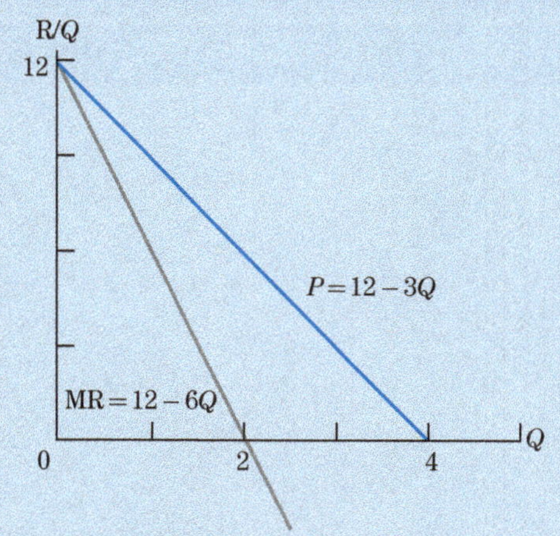

The marginal revenue curve has the same vertical intercept and twice the slope of the corresponding linear demand curve.

Figure 10.9 The profit-maximizing price and quantity for a monopolist

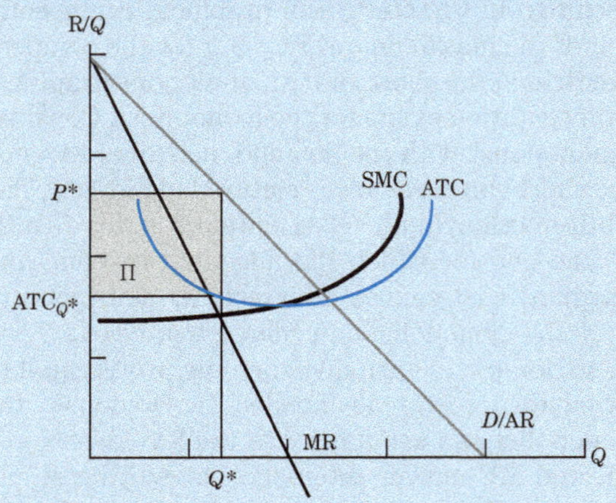

Maximum profit occurs at the output level Q^*, where the gain in revenue from expanding output (or loss in revenue from contracting output), MR, is exactly equal to the cost of expanding output (or the savings from contracting output), SMC. At Q^*, the firm charges P^* and earns an economic profit of Π.

Note in Fig. 10.10 that the monopolist's fixed cost was irrelevant to the determination of the profit-maximizing output level and price. This makes sense intuitively because fixed cost has no bearing on the gains and losses that occur when output changes.

Exercise 10.3

How would the profit-maximizing price and quantity change in Example 10.2 if the monopolist's total cost curve were instead given by $TC = 6400 + 400Q$? The associated marginal cost curve is $MC = 400$.

A profit-maximizing monopolist will never produce on the inelastic portion of the demand curve

If a monopolist's goal is to maximize profits, it follows directly that it will never produce

Example 10.2

A monopolist faces a demand curve of $P = 1000 - 20Q$ and a short-run total cost curve of $TC = 6400 + 200Q$. How much will the monopolist sell, and how much economic profit will it earn at that price?

The marginal revenue curve for this demand curve is $MR = 1000 - 40Q$. Marginal cost is the slope (or first-order derivative) of the total cost curve, which is constant at 200 in this example. Setting MR = MC, we have $1000 - 40Q = 200$, which yields the profit-maximizing quantity, $Q^* = 20$. Plugging $Q^* = 20$ back into the demand curve, we get the profit-maximizing price, $P^* = 600$. This solution is shown graphically in Fig. 10.10, which also displays the average total cost curve for the monopolist. Note that, at Q^*, the ATC is 520, which means the monopolist earns an economic profit of $600 - 520 = 80$ on each unit sold. With $Q^* = 20$, this makes for a total economic profit of 1600.

Figure 10.10 The profit-maximizing price and quantity for specific cost and demand functions

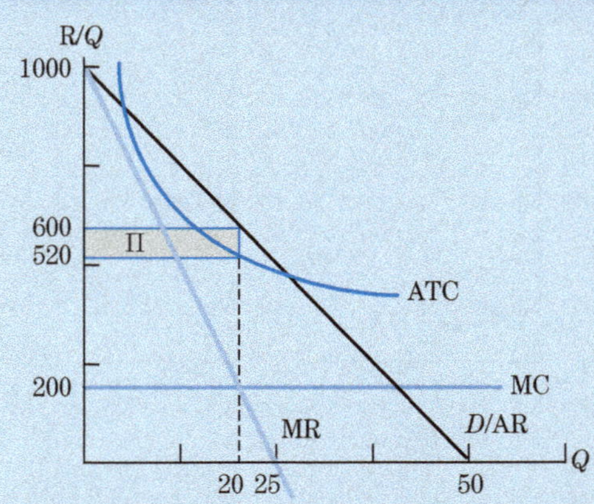

an output level on the inelastic portion of its demand curve. If it were to increase its price at such an output level, the effect would be to increase total revenue. The price increase would also reduce the quantity demanded, which, in turn, would reduce the monopolist's total cost. Since economic profit is the difference between total revenue and total cost, profit would necessarily increase in response to a price increase from an initial position on the inelastic portion of the demand curve. The profit-maximizing level of output must therefore lie on the elastic portion of the demand curve, where further price increases would cause both revenue and costs to go down.

The profit-maximizing mark-up

The profit-maximization condition MR = MC can be combined with Eq. 10.6, which says $MR = P[1 - (1/|\varepsilon|)]$, to derive the profit-maximizing mark-up for the monopolist:

$$\frac{P - MC}{P} = \frac{1}{|\varepsilon|} \tag{10.7}$$

which is the difference between price and marginal cost, expressed as a fraction of the profit-maximizing price. For example, if the price elasticity of demand facing a monopolist were equal to −2, the profit-maximizing mark-up would be $\frac{1}{2}$, which implies that the profit-maximizing price is twice marginal cost. Equation 10.7 tells us that the profit-maximizing mark-up is small if demand is elastic and vice versa. In the limiting case of infinitely elastic demand, the profit-maximizing mark-up is zero (which implies $P = MC$), the same as in the perfectly competitive case.

Measuring monopoly power

For a firm operating in a perfectly competitive market, price equals marginal cost; for the monopoly, however, price exceeds marginal cost. To measure monopoly power, we examine the extent to which the profit-maximizing monopolist price exceeds marginal cost. In particular, we use the mark-up of price minus marginal cost to price ratio. This measure of monopoly power was introduced by Abba Lerner in 1934. This is known as the *Lerner index of monopoly power*, and can be written as $L = (P - MC)/P$. The value of the Lerner index ranges from 0 to 1. With perfect competition, $P = MC$ and $L = 0$. The larger the value of L, the greater the degree of monopoly power.

We can also express the Lerner index in terms of the price elasticity of demand. Because we know that $(P - MC)/P = -1/\varepsilon$, we can write the Lerner index as $L = -1/\varepsilon$. Considerable monopoly power does not necessarily mean that the monopolist is making high profits. Profit is dependent on average cost relative to price, and it is possible that a firm with more monopoly power can earn lower profits than a firm with less monopoly power because of higher average costs.

For example, assume that the demand curve of the profit-maximizing monopoly is given by $Q = 11 - \frac{1}{5}P$, and that SMC = 5. We can rewrite the equation as $P = 55 - 5Q$, and thus $MR = 55 - 10Q$. To determine P and Q at the profit-maximizing values, we set $55 - 10Q(MR) = 5(MC)$. This solve for $Q = 5$ and $P = 30$. We know that

$$\varepsilon = \frac{dQ}{dP}\frac{P}{Q} = -\frac{1}{5} \times \frac{30}{5} = -\frac{6}{5}$$

Therefore,

$$L = -\frac{1}{s} = \frac{5}{6}$$

The monopolist's shutdown condition

In the case of the perfectly competitive firm, we saw that it paid to shut down in the short run whenever the price fell below the minimum value of average variable cost (AVC). The analogous condition for the monopolist is if there exists no quantity for which the demand curve lies above the average variable cost curve. The monopolist whose demand/average revenue, marginal revenue, SMC and AVC curves are shown in Fig. 10.11, for example, has no positive level of output for which price exceeds AVC, and so she does best by ceasing production in the short run. She will then sustain a short-run economic loss equal to her fixed costs, but she would do even worse at any positive level of output.

Another way of stating the shutdown condition for a monopolist is to say that she should cease production whenever average revenue is less than average variable cost at every level of output. Average revenue is simply another name for price – the value of P along the monopolist's demand curve.[5]

[5] More formally, note that average revenue = $TR/Q = PQ/Q = P$.

Figure 10.11 also illustrates the important point that MR = MC is a necessary, but not sufficient, condition for maximum profit. Note in the figure that marginal revenue is equal to marginal cost at the output level Q_0. Why isn't this the maximum-profit point? Recall that, in the case of the perfectly competitive firm, the maximum-profit condition called for price to equal marginal cost on a rising portion of the marginal cost curve, above the minimum point on the AVC curve. A somewhat different condition applies in the case of the monopolist. In Fig. 10.11, note that at Q_0 the MR curve intersects the MC curve from below.[6] This means not only that Q_0 is not the maximum-profit point, but also that it actually corresponds to a lower profit level than any of the other output levels nearby. For example, consider an output level just less than Q_0. At any such output level the gains from contracting output (MC) will exceed the losses (MR), so the firm does better to contract from Q_0. Now consider an output level just slightly larger than Q_0. For such an output level, the gains from expanding (MR) exceed the costs (MC), so the firm does better to expand. Thus, when the firm is at Q_0, it can earn higher profits by either contracting or expanding. Q_0 is called a *local minimum profit point*.[7]

Note also in Fig. 10.11 that the MR curve intersects the MC curve for a second time at the output level Q_1. This time the intersection occurs from above, and you can easily show, as an exercise, that Q_1 yields higher profits than any of the other output levels close by. (The argument runs exactly parallel to that in the preceding paragraph.) We refer to points like Q_1 as *local maximum profit points*. But, although Q_1 yields more profit than any nearby output level, the firm fails to cover its average variable cost at the level of output, and so does better simply to produce nothing at all. The point Q^* we saw earlier, in Fig. 10.9, is both a local maximum profit point and a global maximum profit point, the latter designation indicating that no other output level, including zero, yields higher profit. For a monopolist, a global maximum profit point might occur either on the rising or on the falling portion of the MC curve. But it must be at a point where the MR curve intersects the MC curve from above, and the slope of the MR curve is therefore steeper than the slope of the MC curve.

To recapitulate briefly, we have seen that the monopolist behaves like a perfectly competitive firm in the sense that each chooses an output level by weighing the additional benefits of expanding (or contracting) output against the corresponding costs. For both the perfect competitor and the monopolist, marginal cost is the relevant measure of the cost of expanding output. Fixed costs are

Figure 10.11 A monopolist who should shut down in the short run

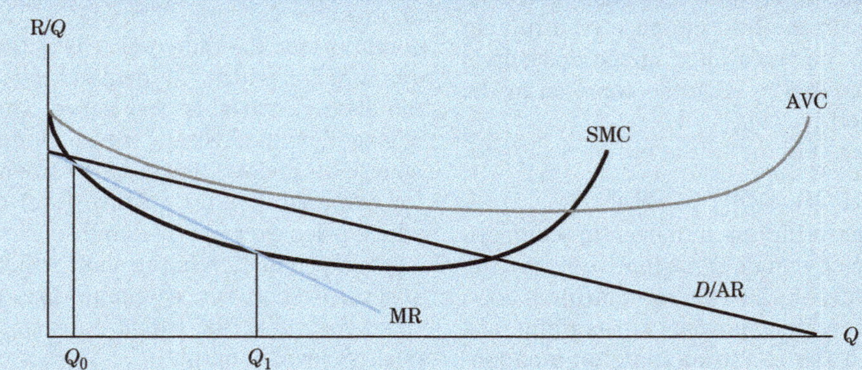

Whenever average revenue (the price value on the demand curve) is lower than average variable cost for every level of output, the monopolist does best to cease production in the short run.

[6] To 'intersect from below at Q_0' means that, as Q approaches Q_0 from the left, MR lies below MC and then crosses MC when $Q = Q_0$.

[7] The second-order condition for maximum profit is given by

$$\frac{d(MR - MC)}{dQ} = \frac{dMR}{dQ} - \frac{dMC}{dQ} = 0$$

which says simply that the slope of the marginal revenue curve must be less than the slope of the marginal cost curve.

Exercise 10.4

Find the optimal price and quantity for the monopolist described by the information in the following table.

Q	P	MR	SMC	AVC
0	100	100	150	150
15	86	71	71	107
25	75	50	41	84
34	66	33	33	72
50	50	0	63	63

irrelevant for short-run output decisions in both cases. For both the monopolist and the perfect competitor, the benefits of expanding output are measured by their respective values of marginal revenue. For the competitor, marginal revenue and price are one and the same. For the monopolist, by contrast, marginal revenue is less than price. The firm in a competitive market maximizes profit by expanding output until marginal cost equals price. The monopolist also maximizes profit by expanding output until marginal cost equals marginal revenue, but asks a price that consumers are willing to pay (reflected in the demand curve). The monopolist thus chooses a lower output level than if she had used the competitor's criterion. Both the monopolist and the perfect competitor do best to shut down in the short run if price is less than average variable cost for all possible levels of output.

A monopolist has no supply curve

As we saw in Chapter 9, the competitive firm has a well-defined supply curve. It takes market price as given, and responds by choosing the output level for which marginal cost and price are equal. For the individual firm, its supply curve is the positively-sloped part of the MC curve equal to and larger than the minimum AVC. At the industry level, a shifting demand curve will trace out a well-defined industry supply curve, which is the horizontal summation of the individual firm supply curves.

There is no similar supply curve for the monopolist. The reason for this is that the monopolist is not a price taker, which means that there is no unique correspondence between price and marginal revenue when the market demand curve shifts. Thus a given marginal revenue value for one demand curve can correspond to one price, while the same value of marginal revenue for a second demand curve corresponds to a different price. As a result, it is possible to observe the monopolist producing Q_1^* and selling at P^* in one period, and then selling Q_2^* at P^* in another period.

To illustrate, consider a monopolist with a demand curve of $P = 1000 - 10Q$ and with the same cost curves as in Example 10.2, namely, $\text{TC} = 6400 + 200Q$ so $\text{MC} = 200$. The marginal revenue curve for this monopolist is given by $\text{MR} = 1000 - 20Q$, and equating MR to MC yields a profit-maximizing output level of $Q^* = 40$. The corresponding profit-maximizing price is $P^* = 600$. Note that this is the same as the profit-maximizing price we saw for the monopolist in Example 10.2, even though the demand curve here lies to the right of the one in Example 10.2.

When the monopolist's demand curve shifts, the price elasticity of demand at a given price generally will also shift. But these shifts need not occur in the same direction. When demand shifts rightwards, for example, elasticity at a given price may either increase or decrease, and the same is true when demand shifts leftwards. The result is that there can be no unique correspondence between the price a monopolist charges and the amount it chooses to produce. And hence we say that the monopolist has no supply curve; rather, it has a supply rule, which is to equate marginal revenue and marginal cost and to produce the quantity where this is the case.

Adjustments in the long run

In the long run, the monopolist is of course free to adjust all inputs, just as is the competitive firm. What is the optimal quantity in the long run for a monopolist with a given technology? The best the monopolist can do is to produce the quantity for which long-run marginal cost is equal to marginal revenue. In Fig. 10.12, that will mean choosing a capital stock that gives rise to the short-run average and marginal cost curves labelled ATC* and SMC*. For that level of capital stock, the short-run marginal cost curve passes through the intersection of the long-run marginal cost and marginal revenue curves. Q^* will be the profit-maximizing quantity in the long run, and it will sell at a price of P^*. For the conditions pictured in Fig. 10.12, the long-run economic profit level, Π, will be

Figure 10.12 Long-run equilibrium for a profit-maximizing monopolist

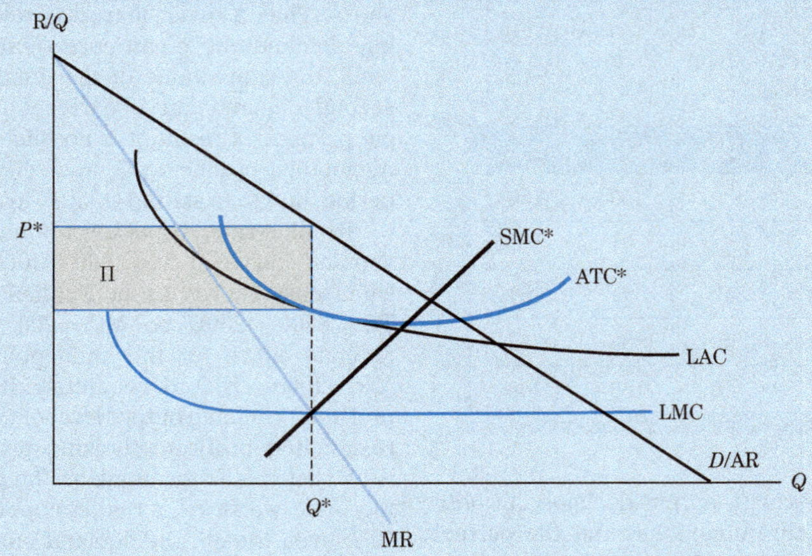

The profit-maximizing quantity in the long run is Q^*, the output level for which LMC = MR. The profit-maximizing price in the long run is P^*. The optimal capital stock in the long run gives rise to the short-run marginal cost curve SMC*, which passes through the intersection of LMC and MR.

positive, and is indicated by the area of the shaded rectangle.

As we saw in Chapter 9, economic profits tend to vanish in the long run in perfectly competitive industries. This tendency will sometimes be present for a monopoly. To the extent that the factors that gave rise to the firm's monopoly position come under attack in the long run, there will be downward pressure on its profits. For example, competing firms may develop substitutes for important inputs that were previously under the control of the monopolist. Or, in the case of patented products, competitors may develop close substitutes that do not infringe on existing patents, which are in any event only temporary.

In other cases, however, there may be a tendency for monopoly profits to persist. The firm shown in Fig. 10.12, for example, has a declining long-run average cost curve, which means that it may enjoy a persistent cost advantage over potential rivals. In such natural monopolies, economic profits may be highly stable over time. (Recall that we discussed the cost structure of a natural monopoly with the aid of Fig. 10.1 at the beginning of the chapter). And the same, of course, may be true for a firm whose monopoly comes from having a government licence. Persistent economic profits are indeed one of the major policy concerns regarding monopoly, as we shall discuss later in the chapter.

Price discrimination

Our discussion thus far has assumed that the monopolist sells all its output at a single price. In reality, however, monopolists often charge different prices to different buyers, a practice that is known as *price discrimination*. The movie theatre discount tickets discussed at the beginning of this chapter constitute one example. In the following sections we analyse how the profit-maximizing monopolist behaves when it is possible to apply different prices to different buyers. When price discrimination is possible, a monopolist can transfer some of the gains from consumers into its own profits. However, we shall see that not all the higher profits under price discrimination come at the expense of consumers. Efficiency is enhanced as the monopolist expands output towards the level at which demand intersects marginal cost.

Sale in different markets

Suppose the monopolist has two completely distinct markets in which it can sell its output, for instance the market for students and the market for the general public. It can actually also be the only supplier in the domestic market for its product, and the only one in a foreign market as well. If it is a profit maximizer, what prices should it charge and what quantities should it sell in each market?

Suppose the demand and marginal revenue curves for the two markets are as given in Figs 10.13(a) (the student market) and 10.13(b) (the market for the general public). It is the same as saying that the demand for the general public is given by the function: $P_p = 225 - 0.005Q_P$ and for students by $P_S = 125 - 0.00125Q_S$. Also assume that TC = $500000 + 0.001Q^2$, with the resulting $MC = 0.002Q$. First, note that if the monopolist is maximizing profit, its marginal revenue should be the same in each market. (If it weren't, it could sell one unit less in the market with lower MR and one unit more in the market with higher MR, thereby increasing its profit.) Given that MR in the two markets must be the same, the profit-maximizing total quantity will be the one for which this common value is the same as marginal cost. Graphically, the solution is to add the marginal revenue curves horizontally across the two markets, and produce the level of output for which the resulting curve intersects the marginal cost curve. Remember that we first have to re-specify the demand functions in the format $Q = f(P)$ before we can add them. This means that the demand functions become $Q_P = 45000 - 200P_P$ and $Q_S = 100000 - 800P_S$ to give market demand $Q = 145000 - 1000P$, and to draw the curve we re-specify it as $P = 145 - 0.001Q$; with the resulting $MR = 145 - 0.002Q$. In Fig. 10.13(c), the optimal total output is indicated by $Q = 36250$ units. $Q = 21000$ of it is sold in the market for the general public at a price of R148.75, and the remaining $Q = 15250$ in the student market, at a price of R98.75.

Exercise 10.5

Suppose a monopolist sells in two separate markets, with demand curves given by $P_1 = 100 - Q_1$ and $P_2 = 200 - Q_2$, respectively. If her total cost curve is given by $TC = 5 + 20Q$ (for which the associated marginal cost curve is given by $MC = 20$), what quantities should she sell and what prices should she charge in the two markets?

Note in Exercise 10.5 that the monopolist who sells in two markets charges a higher price in the market where demand is less elastic with respect to price.[8] Charging different prices to buyers in

Figure 10.13 The profit-maximizing monopolist that sells in two markets

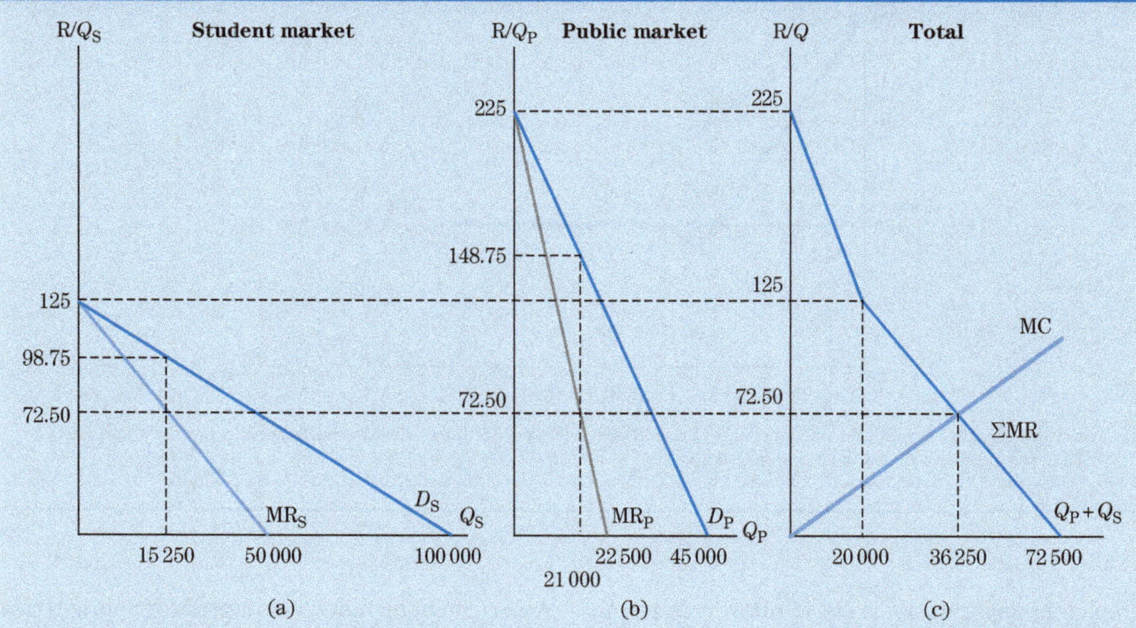

For a monopolist that sells in two markets, the profit-maximizing output level is where the SMR curve intersects the MC curve, here $Q = 36250$. Marginal revenue in each market will be the same when $Q_S = 15250$ and $Q_P = 21000$ are sold in the market for students and the market for the general public, respectively.

[8] This result follows from Eq. 10.6, which says that $MR = P(1 - 1/|\varepsilon|)$. Setting $MR_1 = MR_2$ yields $P_1/P_2 = (1 - 1)/|\varepsilon_2|)/(1 - 1/|\varepsilon_1|)$; hence the higher price will be charged to customers with the lower price elasticity of demand.

Example 10.3

A monopolist has marginal costs $MC = 10Q$ and home market demand $P_H = 300 - 10Q$. The monopolist can also sell to a foreign market at a constant price $P_F = 120$. Find and graph the quantity produced, quantity sold in the home market, quantity sold in the foreign market and price charged in the home market. Explain why the monopolist's profits would fall if it were to produce the same quantity but sell more in the home market.

The linear demand curve $P = 300 - 10Q$ has associated marginal revenue $MR = 300 - 20Q$. The profit-maximizing level of output for a monopolist selling to segmented markets occurs where $\sum MR = MC$. The horizontal sum of the marginal revenues across markets is the home marginal revenue function MR_H up to home output where $MR_F = MR_H$, and then the foreign marginal revenue function $MR_F = 120$ for any further units (see Fig. 10.14). Total marginal revenue equals marginal cost at $MR_F = MC$, which solves for $Q = 12$. Marginal cost for this level of output equals home marginal revenue at $300 - 20Q_H = 120$, so $Q_H = 9$ with the remaining units sold abroad:

$$Q_F = Q - Q_H = 12 - 9 = 3$$

In the home market, the monopolist charges

$$P_H = 300 - 10Q_H = 300 - 90 = 210$$

Any further units sold at home would yield marginal revenue less than 120. Since sales to the foreign market yield a constant marginal revenue of 120, shifting sales to the home market would decrease profits as a result of the lost marginal revenue for each unit shifted.

Figure 10.14 A monopolist with a perfectly elastic foreign market

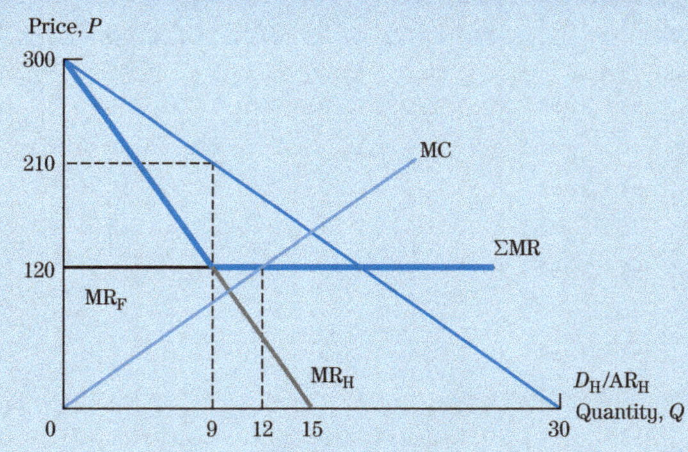

The curve $\sum MR$ follows MR_H as long as $MR_H \geq MR_F$, and then follows MRF. The profit-maximizing output level is where the $\sum MR$ curve intersects the MC curve, here $Q^* = 12$.

completely separate markets is often referred to as *third-degree price discrimination*. There is no special significance to the term 'third-degree' beyond the fact that this type of price discrimination happened to have been the third one that appeared in an early taxonomy.

Examples of third-degree price discrimination abound. This textbook, for instance, is an American book that was adapted for South African students, but to a large extent is the same as the American version. However, this version and other international student editions sell for much less than the US version. Because the incomes of students are generally much lower in foreign markets (such as South Africa) than in the United States, the price elasticity of demand tends to be much higher in foreign than in US markets. The price that maximizes profits in the US market would discourage most students in developing countries from buying it.

Notice also that price discrimination is feasible only when it is impossible, or at least impractical, for buyers to trade among themselves. If students in other countries could trade with those in South Africa, for example, it would not be possible to sell fuel for R10.50/litre in Maseru and R16.50/litre in Bloemfontein. Entrepreneurial students would buy petrol at R10.50 abroad and sell it to South African students for, say, R13.50; others, hoping to get in on the action, would cut price even further, and eventually the price differential would vanish. Buying at a low price from one source and reselling at a higher price is often called **arbitrage**. Where arbitrage is practical, large price differentials for a single product cannot persist. Arbitrage ensures, for example, that the price of gold in London can never differ significantly from the price of gold in New York.

Arbitrage The purchase of something for costless risk-free resale at a higher price.

Intertemporal price discrimination

With this type of price discrimination your market is split into two: initially, you ask a high price; later, you lower it. This is what we typically see in the electronic market with the release of the latest computers, iPads, advanced digital cameras, HD plasma televisions and cell phones. Another good example is the premiere screening of the latest movie, which costs more than later screenings.

In Fig. 10.15 D_E is the inelastic demand curve of those consumers who do not want to wait to buy the product. D_L is the demand of the group that is willing to wait for a certain time period and buy the product later. The strategy is to initially ask a high price of P_E and sell it mainly to those consumers on D_E. Over time, after the first group of buyers has bought the product, the price is lowered to P_L, and mostly consumers on D_L will then buy the product. In the process the firm can increase its profits. Initially its profits will be equal to the rectangle P_0ADP_E in the inelastic market and later it will reap a profit equal to the area P_0BCP_L in the more price-sensitive market.

Textbooks are another good example. Frequently the hardcover version is sold at a high price, and then the cheaper paperback copy is released a year or two later. Many people think that the paperback version is cheaper as a result of lower production costs. Once a book has been edited and typeset, the marginal cost of printing another copy, whether hardcover or paperback, is very low indeed. The reason why the paperback is selling at a lower price is that the high-demand customers have already bought the hardback

Figure 10.15 Intertemporal price discrimination

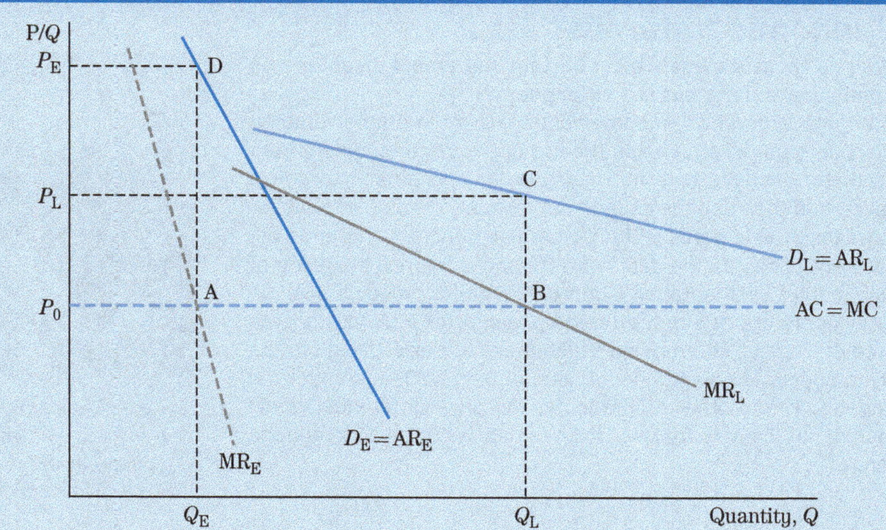

Consumers are divided into groups by charging different prices over time. Initially, the product is sold at a high price to consumers with inelastic demand; later, the price is dropped for the masses with more elastic demand.

Economic naturalist 10.1

Why do some doctors and lawyers offer discounts to people with low incomes?

In medicine, law, dentistry and other professions, many practitioners set their fees on a sliding scale – in effect, selling their services to low-income consumers at significant discounts. This practice is often said to stem from professionals' concerns about the economic hardships confronting the poor. Such concerns are no doubt often heartfelt. But note also that the services offered by these professionals are normal goods, which means that the demand curves of low-income customers lie well below those of their wealthier counterparts. Sliding-scale fees may thus also be viewed as attempts by professionals to increase their profits by tailoring their prices to elasticity differences among different groups of buyers. It has already been pointed out that a similar pattern is observed in the market for movie tickets, in which it is common for theatre owners to set lower prices for students, movie club members and other groups believed to have higher price elasticities of demand.

edition, and the customers now buying the book have more elastic demand.

Peak-load pricing

Peak-load pricing is less an effort to capture consumer surplus and more a means of increasing efficiency. In the tourism industry there are definite seasonal periods, when rates are higher, and then more affordable rates out of season. In South Africa the football World Cup in 2010 was a good example: accommodation and airline fees skyrocketed for the duration of the tournament. For example, the cost of flights between Cape Town and Johannesburg for the duration of the tournament at least doubled. Why do businesses charge higher fees during times of high demand and lower prices during times of low demand? We shall explain this phenomenon with the aid of the provision of electricity, for which demand varies greatly over the course of a day. Typically, demand is higher during the day when businesses are in operation. However, residential demand reaches a peak during 18:00–20:00, when people return from work, prepare food, put on the washing machine and tumble dryer, watch television, and so on. This is one reason why South Africa experienced blackouts in certain regions during times of peak demand.

We shall assume that a uniform price is charged, and that the marginal cost of producing electricity by Eskom is given by SMC in Fig. 10.16. We work within an environment where all generators, transmission lines and so on have already been built, and so we do not need to consider

Economic naturalist 10.2

Why do theatre owners offer certain customers discounts on admission tickets but not on popcorn?

Arbitrage is practical in some cases but not in others. Student discounts on tickets enable theatre operators to segment their markets, because it is not possible for one person to see a movie at a low price and then sell the experience to someone else at a higher price. By the same token, it is practical for lawyers and doctors to charge different people different prices on the basis of differences in price elasticity of demand. But such market segmentation is more difficult for products such as popcorn. If theatre operators attempted to sell popcorn for R15 to students and for R30 to adults, some enterprising student would seize the arbitrage opportunity, selling popcorn to disgruntled adults for only R20. And under the pressure of competition from other arbitrageurs, the price differential would fall until it was barely sufficient to make it worth the students' while to engage in the transaction.

©Photo Alto/Superstock
Why do theatre owners give certain customers discounts on tickets but not on snacks?

capital expenditure. We also assume that the demand varies in two periods: D_{op} during the off-peak period and D_{pp} during the peak period. Now assume that NERSA (National Energy Regulator of South Africa) expects Eskom to sell electricity at a price of P, which is just high enough to cover average costs in the peak and off-peak periods. At this price, Eskom will provide Q_{op} during the off-peak period, but what will be the most profitable quantity to produce in the long run? In the peak period it would like to produce Q_{FP}, where MC = MR (= P). This means that a shortage would develop in the short run. NERSA wants Eskom to provide Q_{pp} at a price of P, but because marginal revenue (also P) is less than marginal cost it will not be in Eskom's interest to supply it. It means that Eskom will not have the incentive to produce the correct quantities demanded in the market. In the off-peak period, it will not produce at its efficient production level; in the peak period, it will not supply enough electricity. Unfortunately electricity cannot be stored. So Eskom cannot produce Q_{FP} in the off-peak period, store the electricity, keep on producing Q_{FP} in the peak period and use the surplus produced in the off-peak period to supplement production in the peak period.

With peak-load pricing different prices are charged during peak and off-peak periods. The price in each period will be where SMC intersects the relevant demand curve. Eskom will thus supply Q'_{op} at a price of P_2 during the off-peak period, and Q'_{pp} at a price of P_1 during the peak period. With this new price structure consumers will have an incentive to use electricity more economically, and shift their use of electricity from peak periods to off-peak periods. With the dual-price system the use of electricity in off-peak periods increases from Q_{op} to Q'_{op}. Use in the peak period decreases from Q_{pp} to Q'_{pp}.

If production in the peak period is reduced from Q_{pp} to Q'_{pp}, costs fall by the area under the SMC over this range, and benefits fall by the area under the demand curve D_{pp}. Costs fall more than benefits, so there is a net gain, indicated by the blue shaded triangle between D_{pp} and SMC. In the same fashion, benefits rise more than costs if consumption is increased in the off-peak period (Q_{op} to Q'_{op}) indicated by the grey shaded area between D_{op} and SMC. If we assume that total output of electricity remains unchanged ($Q_{op} - Q'_{op} = Q_{pp} - Q'_{pp}$), and that NERSA ensures that Eskom makes zero economic profit, the efficiency gain will be realized by

Figure 10.16 Peak-load pricing

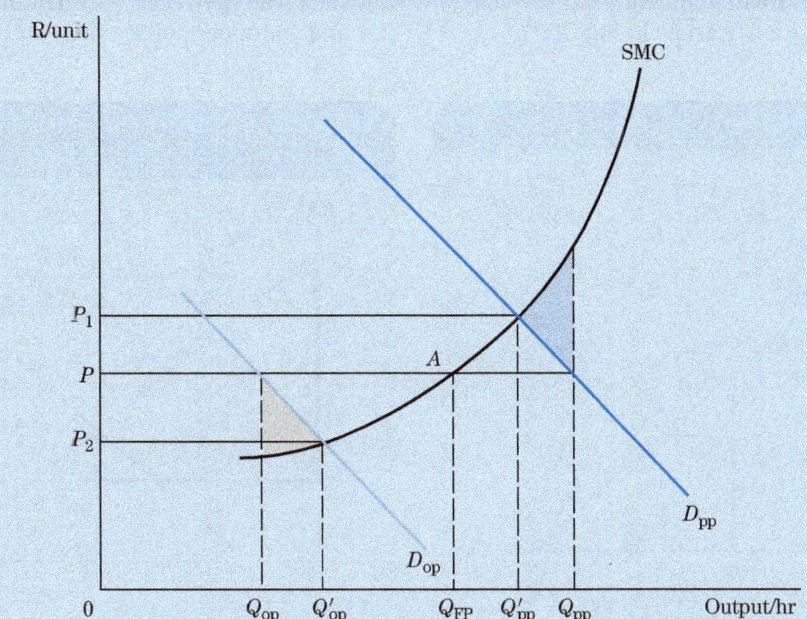

Demand for certain goods and services varies sharply during particular times of the day or year. Charging a higher price during peak periods is more profitable for the firm than charging the same price at all times.

the consumers of electricity. The total cost of producing electricity is reduced, and if prices are set to just cover costs, revenues from consumers also fall. In the long run there is an added advantage of peak-load pricing. Under uniform pricing Eskom must have capacity to produce Q_{pp} in peak periods, but with peak-load pricing it has only to supply Q'_{pp}. Eskom will thus save in terms of building generating facilities, and these cost savings also represent an efficiency gain of peak-load pricing.

The perfectly discriminating monopolist

First-degree price discrimination is the term used to describe the largest possible extent of market segmentation. To illustrate, suppose a monopolist has N potential customers, each one of whom has a downward-sloping demand curve like that labelled D_i in Fig. 10.17. What is the most revenue the monopolist could extract from the sale of Q' units of output to such a customer? If the monopolist had to sell all units at the same price, the best he could do would be to charge P', which would yield total revenue of $P'Q'$. But if he can charge different prices for different units of output, he can do much better. For example, he can sell the first Q_1 units at a price of P_1, the next $Q_2 - Q_1$ units at a price of P_2, and so on. If the intervals into which the monopolist can partition the product are arbitrarily small, this form of pricing will augment total revenue by the area of the shaded triangle in Fig. 10.17.

Had the monopolist been forced to charge a single price for all units, that shaded triangle would have been consumer surplus. When he is able to charge different prices for each unit, however, the monopolist captures all the consumer surplus. The consumer pays the maximum he would have been willing to pay for each unit, and as a result receives no surplus. This is exactly the reason why firms engage in price discrimination. They can increase their profit by charging different prices and converting the consumer surplus into profit for the firm.

How much output will a profit-maximizing, perfectly discriminating monopolist produce? As always, the rule is to equate marginal revenue to marginal cost. Figure 10.18 portrays the demand, short-run marginal and average total cost curves for a perfectly discriminating monopolist. But what is the marginal revenue curve for this monopolist? It is exactly the same as his demand curve. Because he can discriminate perfectly, he can lower his price to sell additional output without having to cut price on the output originally sold. Price and marginal revenue are one and the same, just as in the case of perfect competition. The best this firm can do is to produce Q^* units of output, each of which it sells at the highest price each of its buyers is willing to pay (and that we know is reflected by the demand curve of the monopolist).

There are two salient points of comparison between the perfectly discriminating monopolist and the monopolist who cannot discriminate

Figure 10.17 Perfect price discrimination

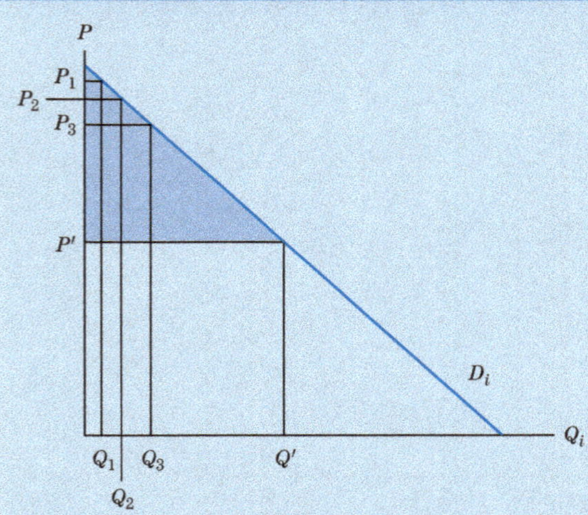

If the monopolist can sell each unit of output at a different price, he will charge the maximum the buyer is willing to pay (according to the demand curve) for each unit. In this situation, the monopolist captures all the consumer surplus.

Figure 10.18 The perfectly discriminating monopolist

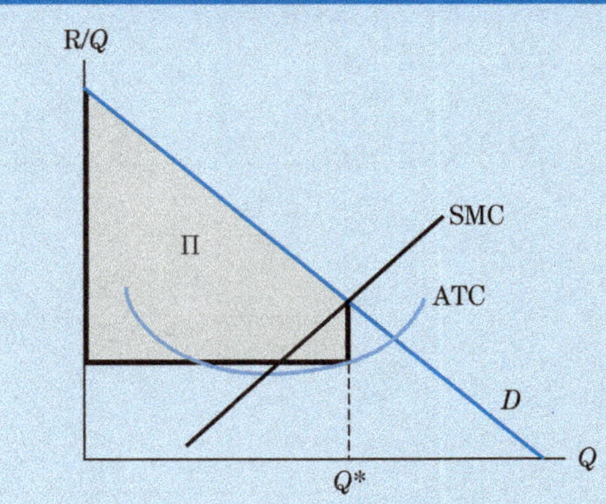

The marginal revenue curve for the monopolist who can discriminate perfectly is exactly the same as his demand curve. The profit-maximizing output is Q^*, the one for which the SMC and demand curves intersect. Economic profit (Π) is given by the shaded area.

at all. The first is that the perfect discriminator produces a higher level of output, because he need not be concerned with the effect of a price cut on the revenue from output produced thus far. He can cut price for the people who would not otherwise buy, and maintain higher prices for those who are willing to pay them.

A second important difference is that positive consumer surplus generally exists under the non-discriminating monopolist, but none under the perfect discriminator. Because the non-discriminator must charge the same price to all buyers, there is pressure on him not to set his price too high. If he sets it at the level the least elastic demanders are willing to pay, he will lose the patronage of all the others. As a result, the monopolist will not do this, and the least elastic demanders end up paying a price well below their respective reservation prices – hence the consumer surplus.

Perfect price discrimination is a never-attained theoretical limit. If a customer's demand curve were tattooed on his forehead, it might be possible for a seller to tailor each price to extract the maximum possible amount from every buyer (also known as their *reservation price*). But, in general, the details of individual demand are only imperfectly known to the seller. Merchants often estimate individual elasticity on the basis of information known about groups to which the individual belongs. A catalogue merchant, for example, may print special editions with higher prices for mailing to high-income areas such as Sandton or Constantia.

Perhaps the closest thing we see to an in-depth assessment of individual elasticities is in the behaviour of merchants in bazaars in the Middle East. The shrewd camel trader in Cairo has had many years of experience in trying to assess how much a buyer with a given demographic and psychological profile is willing to pay. His stock in trade is to interpret the incongruous gesture, the furtive eye movement. But even here, the wily buyer may know how to conceal his eagerness to own the camel. Shrewd Turkish carpet dealers in the Grand Bazaar in Istanbul lure potential customers into their shops, offer them tea (and compliments!), and all the time observe their body language to try to determine what they're willing to pay.

Second-degree price discrimination

Yet another form of price discrimination on the part of sellers is posting, not a single price, but a schedule along which price declines with the quantity bought. Thus many electricity suppliers employ *declining tail-block rate structures* by which the first, say, 300 kilowatt-hours per month are billed at 10 cents, the next 700 at 8 cents and all quantities over 1000 kilowatt-hours/mth at 5 cents each. In South Africa the tail-block rate structure works in exactly the opposite way. Here, you pay a tariff of, say, 60 cents per kilowatt-hours per month for the first 800 kilowatt-hours used, the next 1500 kilowatt-hours are 90 cents each, and for electricity used in excess of 2300 kilowatt-hours per month you pay 110 cents per unit. Such rate structures are a form of *second-degree price discrimination*.

Figure 10.19 illustrates the effect of such a rate structure for a consumer with the demand curve labelled D_i. In comparison with the alternative of charging a price of P_3 for every unit, the quantity discount scheme increases the consumer's total payment by an amount equal to the shaded area.

Second-degree price discrimination is like first-degree price discrimination in that it tries to extract consumer surplus from each buyer to make profit for the monopolist. The two principal differences are these:

- the same rate structure is available to every consumer under second-degree schemes, which means that they make no attempt to tailor charges to elasticity differences among buyers

Figure 10.19 Second-degree price discrimination

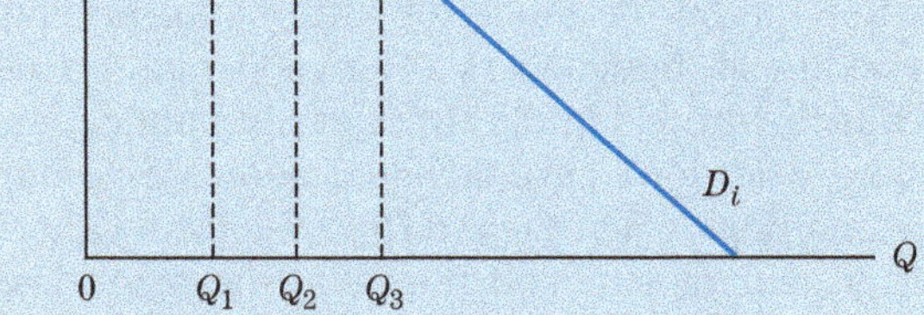

The seller offers the first block of consumption (0 to Q_1) at a high price (P_1), the second block (Q_1 to Q_2) at a lower price (P_2), the third block (Q_2 to Q_3) at a still lower price (P_3), and so on. Even though second-degree price discrimination makes no attempt to tailor rates to the characteristics of individuals or specific groups, it often enables the monopolist to capture a substantial share of consumer surplus (the shaded area).

- the limited number of rate categories tends to limit the amount of consumer surplus that can be captured under second-degree schemes

First-degree schemes get the whole triangle, whereas Fig. 10.19 shows that second-degree schemes capture only part of it.

The hurdle model of price discrimination

Every seller would like to practise perfect price discrimination. The difficulty, as noted earlier, is that sellers lack the information on individual demand curves necessary to do so. Yet another important form of price discrimination consists of a technique whereby the firm induces the most elastic buyers to identify themselves. This is the *hurdle model of price discrimination*. The basic idea is that the seller sets up a hurdle of some sort, and makes a discount price available to those buyers who elect to jump over it. The logic is that those buyers who are most sensitive to price will be more likely than others to jump the hurdle.

One example of a hurdle is a rebate coupon included in the product package. Here, jumping over the hurdle means taking the coupon with you when you go shopping and presenting it to the teller in order to claim the discount. The firm's hope is that people who don't care much about price will be less likely than others to bother going through this process. If so, then people whose demands are less elastic end up paying the 'regular' price, while those with more elastic demands pay the lower discount price. It is becoming easier to overcome this hurdle in the electronic era, where everything can be carried out online. However, the same basic principle applies, that the less price-sensitive buyers (or most of them) will not make the effort.

It is a rare product indeed whose seller does not use the hurdle model of differential pricing. For example, booksellers offer only high-priced hardback editions in the first year of publication. Buyers who don't care strongly about price buy these editions when they're first released. Others wait a year or two and then buy the much less expensive paperback edition. Here, the hurdle is having to endure the wait. Appliance sellers offer regular 'scratch-'n'-dent' sales at which machines with trivial cosmetic imperfections are sold for less than half their regular price. Here, there are two common hurdles: having to find out when and where the sale takes place, and having to put up with a scratch or dent (which most of the time will be out of sight). In South Africa, airlines such as Kulula and Mango offer 'supersaver' discounts of up to half off the regular coach fare. Here also there are two common hurdles: having to make reservations a fairly long time in advance, and having to stay over (say) more than two nights. Many retailers include discount coupons in their newspaper ads. Here, the hurdles are having to read the ads, clip the coupons and get to the store before they expire. Some sellers post signs behind the counter saying 'Ask about our special low price'. Here, the hurdle is merely having to do the asking. But even this trivial hurdle can be remarkably effective, because many well-heeled buyers would find asking about a special price too unseemly even to contemplate.

None of these schemes perfectly segregates high-elasticity from low-elasticity buyers. For instance, there are some people who wait for the August sales to buy winter clothing, even though they would buy just as many garments if the sales weren't offered. But, on the whole, the hurdles seem to function much as intended. A perfect hurdle would be one that imposed only a negligible cost on the buyers who jumped it, yet perfectly separated buyers according to their elasticity of demand. Analytically, the effect of such a hurdle is portrayed in Fig. 10.20, where P_H represents the 'regular' price and P_L represents the discount price. With a perfect hurdle, none of the people who pay the discount price has a reservation price greater than or equal to the regular price, which means that all of them would have been excluded from the market had only the regular price been available.

Figure 10.20 A perfect hurdle

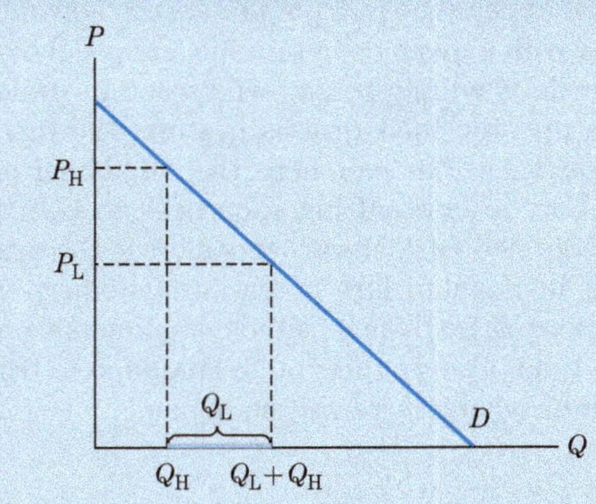

When a hurdle is perfect, the only buyers who become eligible for the discount price (P_L) by jumping it are those who would not have been willing to pay the regular price (P_H). A perfect hurdle also imposes no significant costs on those who jump it.

The hurdle model need not be limited to the two-price version depicted in Fig. 10.20. On the contrary, many sellers have developed it into a highly complex art form, involving literally dozens of price–hurdle combinations. On its Cape Town–Durban route alone, for example, South African Airways offers a number of different fares (which may also vary from day to day), each with its own set of restrictions. But no matter how simple or complex the scheme may be, its goal is the same – to give discounts to customers who would not otherwise buy the product. The so-called low-cost airlines such as Mango and Kulula in South Africa and airlines such as Ryanair, easyJet and Vueling in Europe frequently make use of this type of pricing policy.

The hurdle model is like first-degree price discrimination in that it tries to tailor prices to the elasticities of individual buyers. The principal difference is that, even in its most sophisticated form, the hurdle model cannot hope to capture all the consumer surplus.

The efficiency loss from monopoly

Recall from Chapter 9 the claim that perfect competition leads to an efficient allocation of resources. This claim was based on the observation that in long-run competitive equilibrium there are no possibilities for additional gains from exchange. The value to buyers of the last unit of output is exactly the same as the market value of the resources required to produce it. Remember that, in a competitive market, price equals marginal cost. This is also known as allocative efficiency. Productive efficiency is attained when a certain good is produced at minimum cost, given the level of production of other goods. Productive efficiency will be at the minimum value of average total costs (where ATC and MC intersect), but monopolies may not demonstrate productive efficiency as a result of X-inefficiencies, such as organizational slack, unused capacity or using more resources than needed because of a lack of competition. The principal–agent problem can explain this. Shareholders (the principals) elect directors (agents) to act on their behalf. However, managers may take actions to maximize their own welfare (for example, hiring extra staff to reduce their workload) that increase unit costs.

How does the long-run equilibrium under monopoly measure up by the same criteria? Not very well, it turns out. To illustrate, consider a monopolist with increasing marginal costs, and the demand structure shown in Fig. 10.21. To compare equilibrium under perfect competition and monopoly, we value the welfare of consumers and producers equally. In the perfectly competitive market, Q_c will be sold at a price of P_c where demand equals supply. Consumer surplus will be the triangle HFP_c, and the producer surplus will be the triangle OFP_c. Price is equal to MC and they operate at the minimum turning point of LAC. As we explained in Chapter 9, it means the equilibrium situation in a perfectly competitive market is both allocative and productive efficient.

The profit-maximizing quantity for this monopolist is Q_m (where MR = MC), which he will sell at a price of P_m (according to the demand curve that tells us what buyers are willing to pay). Note that, at Q_m, the value of an additional unit of output to buyers is P_m, which is greater than the cost of producing an additional unit, MC. This means that the single-price monopolist does not exhaust all possible gains from exchange and is thus not allocative efficient. Because the firm is not operating at the minimum point of LAC, it is also productive inefficient. All possible gains from exchange can be achieved only by asking different prices of every consumer. With the single-price monopolist, what happens to consumer and producer surplus? With the price increasing from P_c to P_m, the consumer surplus is now only triangle HGP_m, while producer surplus simultaneously increases to area OEGP_m. Consumer surplus (or the welfare of the consumers) decreases by areas A and B. Producer surplus (or the welfare of the producer) increases by area A, but decreases by area C. Area A is lost by consumers (in the form of consumer surplus), but is gained by the producer (in the form of higher income) and the welfare of the community at large remains unchanged. Triangles B and C are welfare lost by consumers and producers, respectively, and represent a net loss in the welfare of the community. This loss (the area of triangles A plus B in Fig. 10.21) is called the *deadweight loss from monopoly* and results from inefficiencies arising from a lack of competition.

Suppose the reason for having a monopoly is that the firm enjoys patent protection for its product. Can we now say that the welfare loss from having a single-price monopoly is equal to the lost consumer and producer surplus measured in Fig. 10.21? Before answering, we must first ask, 'What is the alternative to the current situation?' If it is a society without patent protection, we might well never have got the product in the first place, so it hardly makes sense to complain that, compared

Figure 10.21 The welfare loss from a single-price monopoly

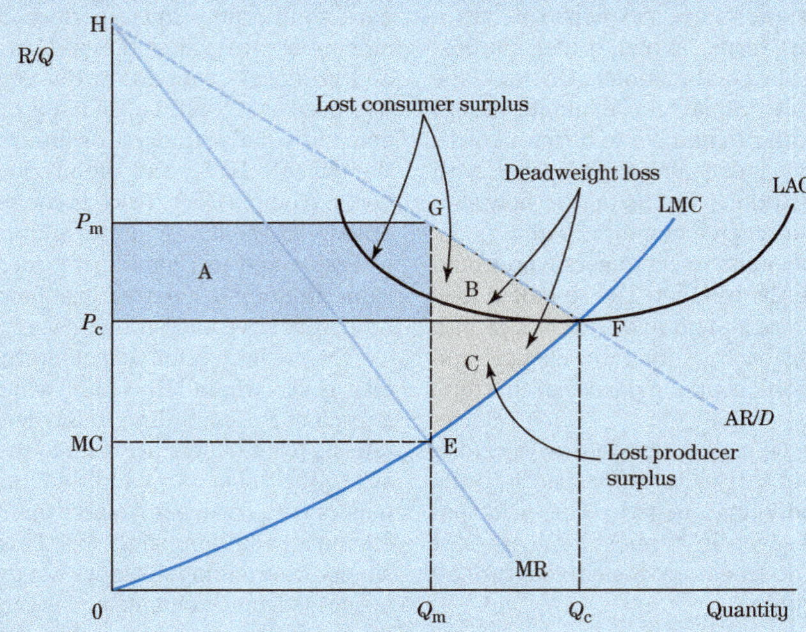

A monopolist who charges a single price to all buyers will produce Q_m and sell at P_m. A competitive industry operating under the same cost conditions would produce Q_c and sell at P_c. In comparison with the perfectly competitive outcome, single-price monopoly results in a loss of consumer surplus equal to the area of A + B. Since the monopolist earns A but loses C, the cost to society is B + C – called the deadweight loss from monopoly.

with pure competition, monopoly produces a welfare loss. True enough, the patent-protected single-price monopoly does not exhaust all possible gains from trade. But with the patent-protected monopoly, we do get a consumer surplus plus producer surplus of OEGH, whereas we might have got nothing at all without the patent protection.

Public policy towards natural monopoly

These observations make it clear that the relevant question is not whether monopoly is efficient in comparison with some unattainable theoretical ideal, but how it compares with the alternatives we actually confront. This question is nowhere more important than in the case of natural monopoly.

To keep the analysis simple, we assume that the competitive market and the monopolist have the same cost curves. This is portrayed in Fig. 10.22. And suppose the demand and marginal revenue curves for a single-price monopolist producing with this technology are as shown in Fig. 10.22. The theoretical ideal allocation for this market would be to produce a quantity of Q_c and sell it at marginal cost, which here is equal to P_c. By contrast, the single-price monopoly will operate where MC = MR and produces only Q_m and sells it for P_m.

There are basically two objections to the equilibrium price–quantity pair of the single-price natural monopoly: (1) the fairness objection, which is that the producer earns an economic profit (Π); and (2) the efficiency objection, which is that price is above marginal cost, resulting in lost consumer surplus (S).

Policymakers may respond in a variety of ways to the fairness and efficiency objections. The five options considered below account for the most important alternatives.

State ownership and management

Efficiency requires that price be equal to marginal cost. The difficulty this creates is that, for natural monopoly, marginal cost is below average total cost. Because private firms are not able to charge prices less than average cost and remain in business in the long run, the single-price firm has no alternative but to charge more than marginal cost. An option for getting around this particular difficulty is to have the state take over the industry. The attractive feature of this option is that the

Figure 10.22 A natural monopoly

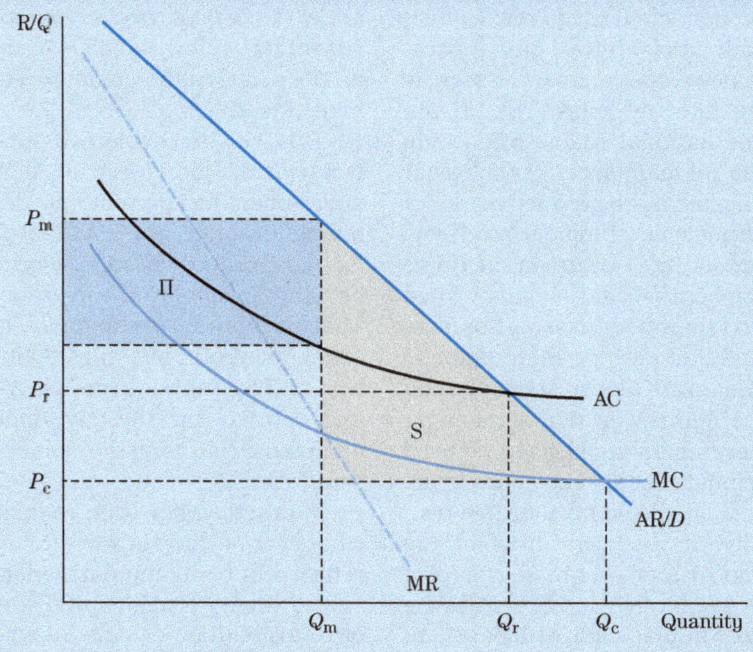

The two main objections to single-price natural monopoly are that it earns economic profit (Π) and that it results in the loss of consumer surplus (*S*).

government is not bound, in the way a private firm is, to earn at least a normal profit. It would thus be able to set a price equal to marginal cost, and absorb the resulting economic losses out of general tax revenues.

But there are also unattractive features of state ownership. Foremost among them is the fact that it often seems to weaken incentives for cost-conscious, efficient management. As the late Harvard University economist Harvey Leibenstein emphasized, an organization's costs depend not just on its technology, but also on the vigour with which it pursues efficiency. In Leibenstein's phrase, an organization that does not act energetically to curb costs is said to exhibit **X-inefficiency**.[9]

X-inefficiency A condition in which a firm fails to obtain maximum output from a given combination of inputs.

X-inefficiency is by no means the exclusive province of government. In widely varying degrees, it is found in private firms too. Leibenstein argued that the extent to which X-inefficiency is a problem will depend on economic incentives, which suggests a theoretical reason for believing that it is likely to be more widespread in government or semi-state-owned firms. When a private firm cuts a rand from its costs, its profit goes up by a rand. By contrast, when the person in charge of a government agency cuts a rand from her agency's budget, the effect is merely to shrink her fiefdom.

Several noted scholars have argued that the goal of most bureaucrats is to maximize their operating budgets.[10] This is not to deny that bureaucrats are for the most part sincere, dedicated public servants. But it is perhaps only human nature for a bureaucrat to think that her particular agency has the most important mission in government, and to lobby accordingly on its behalf.

Below we shall consider some evidence that bears on the relative efficiency of state-managed and private firms. Each spring in the cities in the Western Cape, for example, municipal road crews repair the potholes left by winter while, at the same time, other road surfaces such as the N1 and/or toll roads are being repaired by private

[9] Harvey Leibenstein, 'Allocative efficiency vs. X-efficiency', *American Economic Review*, June 1966, pp. 392–415.

[10] See, for example, William Niskanen, *Bureaucracy and Representative Government*, Aldine-Atherton, Chicago, 1971; and Philip Black *et al.*, *Public Economics for South African Students*, Oxford University Press, Cape Town, 2011. But for a contrasting view, see Albert Breton and Ronald Wintrobe, *The Logic of Bureaucratic Conduct*, Cambridge University Press, Cambridge, 1982.

companies. The contrast between the two groups is often striking. It is common to see seven members of an eight-man municipal road crew leaning on their shovels smoking cigarettes, giving occasional advice to the newcomer among them as he lazily tamps asphalt into the holes. The private crews who work the national roads, often only half as large, usually fill many more potholes per day and are generally just more productive.

Another illuminating case study on the effects of state management is the Department of Home Affairs. Try to remember the last time you visited the DHA in person to renew your passport or identity document. Would you ever go there again if you didn't have to? If you are like most people, you came away with the impression that a manager of even very modest talents could have devised some way of performing that service more expeditiously. We may safely speculate that few people would elect to live in a society in which the Department of Home Affairs was in charge of a substantial share of productive activity. Because the security measures in place in the department do not comply with international standards, from 2009 onwards South Africans visiting the UK need a visa as well as a passport. The department was warned beforehand of the need to tighten security measures but failed to comply with the standards laid down by the UK.

Despite the X-inefficiency problem, state-operated natural monopoly may be the best solution in some cases.[11] But there are other policy alternatives that offer many of the same benefits with fewer apparent costs.

State regulation of private monopolies

One such alternative is to leave ownership in private hands, while providing guidelines or regulations that limit pricing discretion. The stereotypical example of this approach is public regulation of private companies that provide electricity, water and telephone services. In South Africa this was also the case, and it is only in the last couple of years that some of these services have been privatized.

The main form of government price regulation normally employed is *rate-of-return regulation*, in which prices are set to allow the firm to earn a predetermined rate of return on its invested capital. Ideally, this rate of return would allow the firm to recover exactly the opportunity cost of its capital, which is to say, it would ideally be the same as the competitive rate of return on investment.

This can be explained for natural monopolies with the aid of Fig. 10.22. Assuming that the government has perfect knowledge, it will set the maximum price at P_r. At that price the monopolist will produce Q_r, and the price per product will be exactly equal to the average cost per product. That means that the monopolist will make zero economic profit, but still stay in business because it is making normal profits. A price of P_r is the lowest price that the government can lay down while ensuring that the monopolist still stays in business.

In practice, however, regulatory commissions can never be certain what the competitive rate of return will be in any particular period. It is difficult to value a firm's capital stock so that the rate of return can be calculated with a fair degree of accuracy. Another problem is deciding on the fair rate of return for a specific industry. If the rate the government sets lies below the competitive rate of return, the firm will have an incentive to reduce the quality of its service and will eventually go out of business. By contrast, if regulators set too high a rate of return, prices will be higher than necessary, and the firm will earn an extra-normal profit. Neither of these outcomes is attractive, but regulatory commissions have traditionally decided that the problems caused by an insufficient rate of return are far more serious than those caused by an excessive one.

Harvey Averch and Leland Johnson were the first to empirically explore in detail the consequences of a regulatory rate of return set higher than the cost of capital.[12] Their conclusion, in a nutshell, is that this practice gives the firm an incentive to substitute capital for other inputs in a way that inflates the cost of doing business. If the regulated utility's goal is to maximize profit, the behavioural path it will follow is to make its *rate base* – the invested capital on which it earns the allowed rate of return – as large as possible. If the regulated monopolist can borrow capital at 12 per cent/yr and is allowed to earn 15 per cent/yr on each rand invested, it can clear R30 000 of

[11] See Elliott D. Sclar, *You Don't Always Get What You Pay For*, Cornell University Press, Ithaca, NY, 2000.

[12] Harvey Averch and Leland Johnson, 'Behavior of the firm under regulatory constraint', *American Economic Review*, December 1962, pp. 1052–1069. See also R.M. Spann, 'Rate of return regulation and efficiency in production: An empirical test of the Averch–Johnson thesis', *Bell Journal of Economics*, Spring 1974, pp. 38–52.

extra profit for every extra R1 000 000 of borrowed funds it invests.

At least two important distortions follow from the discrepancy between the allowed rate of return and the actual cost of capital. The first we may call the *gold-plated water cooler effect*. It refers to the fact that the regulated monopolist has an incentive to purchase more capital equipment than is actually necessary to produce any given level of output. Faced with a choice between buying a regular water cooler, for example, and a more expensive gold-plated one, the regulated monopolist has an incentive to opt for the latter. To illustrate, suppose that the allowed rate of return on capital were 15 per cent a year and the actual cost of capital only 12 per cent. If a gold-plated water cooler costs R10 000 more than a regular one, the monopolist would then earn R300 higher profit each year by installing the more expensive water cooler. Regulatory commissions try to prevent the purchase of unnecessary equipment, but the complexities of day-to-day operations are too great to allow every decision to be monitored carefully.

A second distortion induced by rate-of-return regulation is peculiar to the monopolist who serves more than one separate market, and we may call it the *cross-subsidy effect*. Because the allowed rate of return exceeds the cost of capital, such a monopolist has an incentive to sell below cost in the more elastic market, and cross-subsidize the resulting losses by selling above cost in the less elastic market. The idea is that the below-cost price in the elastic market boosts sales by more than the above-cost price in the less elastic market curtails them. The resulting increase in output increases the requirement for capital to produce it, and hence increases the profits allowed by regulation.

To illustrate, consider the regulated monopolist whose demand and cost curves for two markets are shown in Fig. 10.23. (Assume constant long-run average and marginal costs.) The ATC curves are constructed to include the allowed rate of profit, which exceeds the cost of capital. Thus, when the monopolist is earning zero profit in terms of the cost curves shown in Fig. 10.23, he is really earning

$$\Pi = (r^{a} - r^{c})K \qquad (10.8)$$

where r^{a} is the allowed rate of return, r^{c} is the actual cost of capital and K is the size of the total capital stock. To maximize profit, the monopolist thus wants to make K as big as possible, which in turn means making the sum of the outputs sold in the two markets as large as possible. To do that, he will set MR = MC in the market with the less elastic demand (market 1 in panel a) and use the profits earned in that market (Π_1) to subsidize a price below average cost in the market with more elastic demand (market 2 in panel b). The aim, again, is to boost sales in the latter market by more than they

Figure 10.23 Cross-subsidization to boost total output

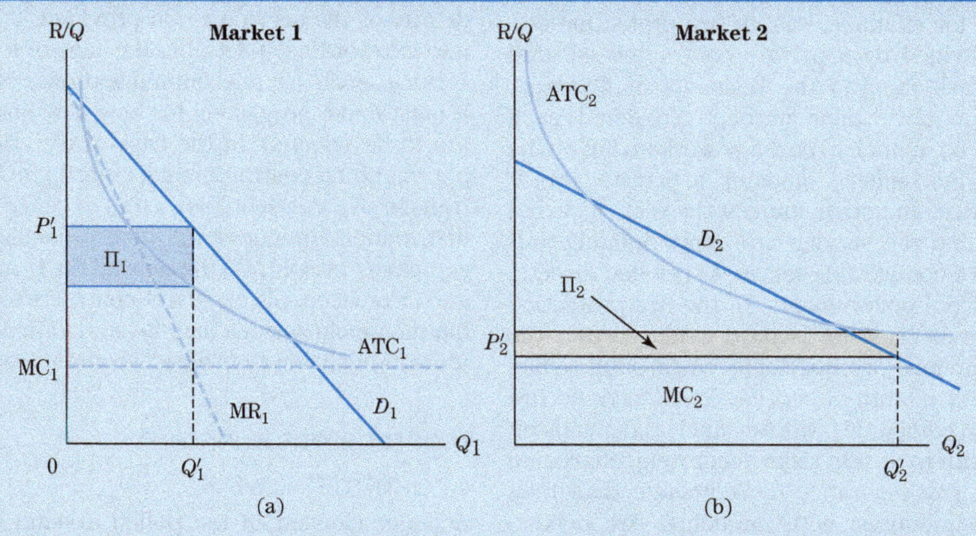

A regulated monopolist is generally allowed to earn a rate of return that exceeds the actual cost of capital, which provides an incentive to acquire as much capital as possible. To increase output (and thereby to increase the required capital stock), the monopolist can sell above cost in his less elastic market (market 1 in panel a) and use the resultant profits ($\Pi_1 > 0$) to subsidize the losses ($\Pi_2 < 0$) sustained by selling below cost in his more elastic market.

are curtailed in the former. By selling the largest possible output, the monopolist is able to employ the largest possible capital stock, and thereby is able to earn the largest possible profit.

Regulatory pitfalls have not prevented governments in virtually every part of the world from continuing to intervene in the price and output decisions of important natural monopolies such as electric utilities and local telephone services. Whether these interventions do more good than harm, in purely economic terms, remains an unsettled question. But they clearly seem to serve an important psychological function on behalf of a public that feels understandably uncomfortable about not having a buffer between itself and the sole supplier of a critical good or service.

Exclusive contracting for a natural monopoly

In the title of a widely quoted article, UCLA economist Harold Demsetz asked the disarmingly simple question, 'Why regulate monopoly?'[13] His point was that, even though cost conditions may dictate that a market be served by a single supplier, there can still be vigorous competition to see who gets to be that supplier. In Demsetz's proposal, the government would specify in detail the service it wanted provided – fire protection, garbage collection, postal delivery, whatever – and then call for private companies to submit bids to supply the service. And to the lowest bidder goes the contract.

This scheme has been tried with success in developed countries. The city of Scottsdale, Arizona, for example, has its fire protection services provided by a private contractor selected in this fashion. And the residents of Oakland, California, have their garbage collected each week not by municipal garbage workers but by the Oakland Scavenger Company, a private, profit-seeking firm. In both instances, the costs incurred in providing the service are approximately half the cost of comparable services provided directly by municipal governments. In the fire protection case, moreover, there is hard evidence that the cost reductions are not achieved through reductions in the quality of service. Profit-seeking fire insurance companies, whose survival depends on their ability to assess risks accurately, charge no more for fire insurance in Scottsdale than they do in communities with municipal fire departments. The advantage of private contracting for the provision of natural monopoly services is that it takes production out of the hands of bureaucrats, who are often not very good at keeping costs down.

Twenty years ago food and cleaning services in your student residences were provided by workers who were employed by your institution. Nowadays all (or most of) those services have been contracted out to private companies that provide the same service at relatively more affordable rates. Other services, such as the upkeep of gardens and general maintenance, have also been contracted out to private firms. These are just a few examples of services around you that are now provided – more efficiently – by private firms. The difference is that these firms must make a profit to survive, whereas in the past the employees of your institution were not required to generate profits.

The political scientist Elliott Sclar cautions, however, that the advantages of contracting for public services are often more apparent than real (see footnote 11). Most contracts with private suppliers, for example, contain contingency clauses that allow higher fees in the event of unforeseen changes in circumstances. The government employees who monitor the implementation of private contracts may be unable to keep these extra fees under tight control. Added to this is the problem of corruption. Public contracts in practice may often go not to the firm that submits the lowest bid but to the one that pays the highest bribe.

Even if we ignore these problems, private contracting may not be an attractive option in many cases. Because the contract must specify the details of the service to be provided, it must go into extraordinary detail in the case of a complex service, such as telecommunications. Moreover, it must make provisions for how new contractors are to be selected. In the case of electricity supply, changing contractors necessarily involves the transfer of a vast, complex array of generation and distribution equipment. At what price should this equipment be sold? By the time all the i's are dotted and t's crossed, the exclusive contracts for providing monopoly service may be so detailed as to be indistinguishable from direct economic regulation.

Vigorous enforcement of antitrust laws

A major element in the policy arsenal for dealing with monopoly is the nation's antitrust laws.

[13] Harold Demsetz, 'Why regulate monopoly?', *Journal of Law and Economics*, April 1968, pp. 55–65.

Legislation usually makes creating a monopoly illegal and subsequently deals with mergers that will lead to substantially less competition.

In South Africa both of these issues (monopolistic behaviour, whereby the firm abuses its market power, and mergers that may lead to less competition) are included in the Competition Act No. 89 of 1998.[14] This new Act replaced the Competition Board with the Competition Authority and established the Competition Commission, the Competition Tribunal and the Competition Appeal Court. The Competition Commission has the power to disallow small and intermediate mergers, and makes recommendations on larger mergers referred to the Competition Tribunal. From an economist's perspective, the main goal of competition policy should be to enhance allocation efficiency. In the South African case, the Act included other goals such as employment creation, expansion of opportunities for South Africans in world markets, equality of opportunities for small and medium-sized enterprises and promotion of a greater spread of ownership.

The latest change in competition policy in South Africa resulted from the Competition Amendment Act No. 1 of 2009. This Act introduced measures such as criminal sanctions against directors and managers who participate in cartel conduct, or tacitly consent to such conduct; a market inquiry provision to inquire into the state of competition in a particular market; and leniency provisions that protect whistleblower firms or individuals.

In the case of industries with declining long-run average cost curves, the cost of production will be much higher if we are served by many firms rather than by only a few. The most vigorous supporters of the antitrust laws insist that the laws will not impede the formation of natural monopolies. But, as we shall see in Chapter 11, they may substantially lengthen the timeframe within which economies of scale are fully realized.

One response to this difficulty would be to apply antitrust laws to preventing only those mergers where significant cost savings would not be realized. It is, however, very difficult for the government to distinguish one type of case from another. In many cases it is almost impossible to quantify the advantages and disadvantages of a merger, and in certain cases it is very difficult even to define the market (e.g. radio broadcasting). Competition policy is thus still a very hotly debated issue, surrounded by uncertainty.

In South Africa, competition authorities use the Hirschman–Herfindahl Index (HHI) to evaluate the potential effects of a merger on market concentration (Chapter 11 explains the HHI in more detail). The increase in concentration as measured by the HHI can be calculated by doubling the product of the market shares of the merging firms. For example, the merger of firms with market shares of 5 and 10 per cent of the market, respectively, will lead to an increase in the HHI of 100 ($5 \times 10 \times 2 = 100$). In calculating the HHI before the merger, the market shares of the merging firms are squared individually: ($a^2 + b^2$). After the merger, the sum of those market shares must be squared: $(a + b)^2 = a^2 + 2ab + b^2$. The increase in HHI is thus 2ab.

If the pre-merger HHI is below 1000 the market is considered unconcentrated. Mergers resulting in unconcentrated markets are unlikely to have adverse competitive effects and normally require no further analysis. A pre-merger HHI of between 1000 and 1800 means the market is moderately concentrated. If a merger raises the HHI by more than 100 points in these type of industries, it raises significant competitive concerns. In pre-merger industries with an HHI of above 1800, a merger that leads to an increase in the HHI of more than 50 points raises significant competitive concerns. If a merger in this type of industry will increase the HHI by more than 100 points, it is presumed that the merger is likely to create or enhance market power.

A laissez-faire policy towards natural monopoly

As a fifth and final alternative for dealing with natural monopoly, let us consider the possibility of laissez-faire, or doing nothing – just letting the monopolist produce whatever quantity it chooses and selling it at whatever price the market will bear. The obvious objections to this policy are the two we began with, namely, the fairness and efficiency problems. In this section, however, we shall see that there may be at least some circumstances in which these problems are of only minimal importance.

Consider, in particular, a natural monopolist that uses the hurdle model of differential pricing.

[14] For a detailed discussion of competition policy in South Africa, see Nicola Theron, 'The economics of competition policy: Merger analysis in South Africa', *South African Journal of Economics*, December 2001, vol. 69, no. 4, pp. 614–658.

'The next step'

This can also be explained with the aid of derivatives. For the single-price monopolist, the profit function is given by

$$\Pi_1 = (A - BQ)\,Q - F - MQ$$

which yields a profit-maximizing quantity of $Q' = (A - M)/2B$, and a corresponding price of $P' = (A + M)/2$.

The profit function for the two-price monopolist, by contrast, is given by

$$\Pi_2 = (A - BQ_H)\,Q_H + (A - BQ_H - BQ_L)\,Q_L - F - M(Q_H + Q_L)$$

The first-order conditions for a maximum are given by

$$\frac{\partial \Pi_2}{\partial Q_H} = A - 2BQ_H - BQ_L - M = 0$$

and

$$\frac{\partial \Pi_2}{\partial Q_L} = A - BQ_H - 2BQ_L - M = 0$$

which can be solved for

$$Q_H = \frac{A - M}{3B} = Q_L$$

$$P_L = \frac{A + 2M}{3}$$

$$P_H = \frac{2A + M}{3}$$

To keep the discussion simple, let's suppose constant average and marginal costs, and that the monopolist charges a regular price and also a discount price, the latter available to customers who clear some hurdle, such as mailing in a rebate form. How does the presence of this differential pricing device affect the fairness and efficiency objections to natural monopoly?

Consider first the efficiency objection. Recall that the problem is that the single-price monopolist charges a price above marginal cost, which excludes many potential buyers from the market, ones who value the product more highly than the value of the resources required to produce it.

For illustrative purposes, let's examine a natural monopolist with a total cost curve given by $F + MQ$ and a linear demand curve given by $P = A - BQ$. Figure 10.24(a) shows the demand (average revenue), marginal revenue and marginal cost curves for such a monopolist. If the monopolist is a single-price profit maximizer, it will produce Q_m and sell for P_m. But if it is able to charge one price to the buyers along the upper part of the demand curve and a lower price to all other buyers (Fig. 10.24(b)), its profit-maximizing strategy will be to sell Q_H at price P_H and Q_L at price P_L.

Note that the efficiency loss associated with the two-price monopolist (lost consumer surplus,

Figure 10.24 The efficiency losses from single-price and two-price monopoly

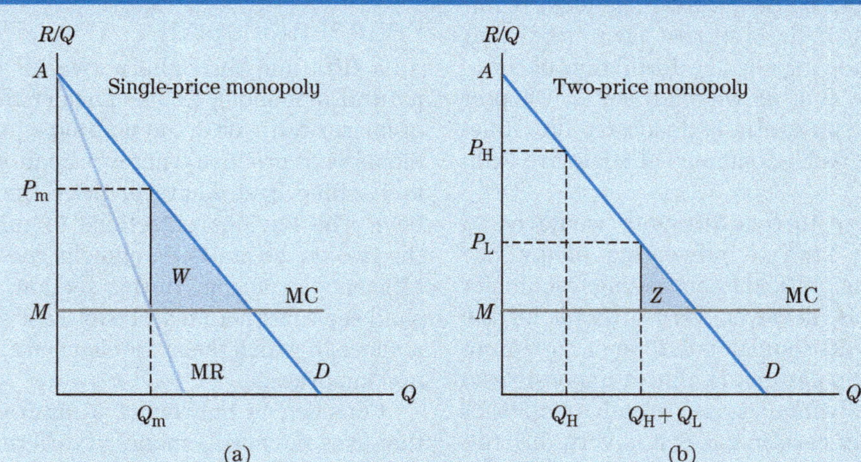

By being able to offer a discount price to the most elastic portion of the demand curve, the two-price monopolist (panel b) expands the market, thereby causing a much smaller efficiency loss (area *Z*, panel b) than in the case of the single-price monopolist (area *W*, panel a).

which is the area of triangle Z in Fig. 10.24(b)) is much smaller than the corresponding loss for the single-price monopolist (the area of triangle W in Fig. 10.24(a)).

In general, the more finely the monopolist can partition its market under the hurdle model, the smaller the efficiency loss will be. As noted earlier, it is common in most firms to see not one but a whole menu of different discount prices, each with a different set of restrictions (the deeper the discount, the more stringent the restriction). Given the wide latitude many firms have to expand their markets through hurdle pricing, the efficiency problem of natural monopoly will often be of only secondary importance.

What about the fairness problem? First, what is this problem? The popular perception of it is that the monopolist transfers resources from people who desperately need them (namely, poor consumers) to others who have more than they need to begin with (namely, wealthy shareholders). We shall see below that, defined in this particular way, the problem is sometimes less serious than it appears.

The more general question of what constitutes a fair distribution of society's resources is a deeply philosophical one, which, although very relevant in the South African situation, is well beyond the scope of our discussion here. At the very least, however, we can say that no firm is entitled to acquire, through force or coercion, the power to extract excessive resources from other persons. But suppose the monopolist has become the lone seller in the market through completely benevolent means. This is not implausible. As a natural monopolist, its costs are by definition lower than if other firms also served the same market. And perhaps the firm's cheerful and courteous service has also helped entrench this position. Does it then create an injustice by charging prices in excess of marginal cost?

Certainly consumers would be happier to pay only the marginal cost of production. But marginal cost is less than average cost in a natural monopoly, and so it is not possible for everyone to pay marginal cost and have the supplier remain in business. At best, some consumers can pay prices close to marginal cost, but others will have to pay substantially more. Even so, if the monopolist is earning an economic profit, we know that buyers are paying more, on average, than the cost of the resources required to serve them. How can this be defended in the name of fairness?

Earlier we saw that hurdle pricing makes the monopoly allocation more efficient. It would be an exaggeration to say that the same hurdle model makes the existence of monopoly profits seem completely fair. But it does help mitigate some of the most serious objections to them.

Consider first the source of a given rand of monopoly profit. From which buyers does this rand come? It is straightforward to show that it cannot have come from the discount price buyer. Typical discount prices range from 15 to 50 per cent off the so-called regular price, and seldom do more than half of all buyers pay the discount price. Taking an illustrative case in which the discount is 30 per cent and half of all buyers receive it, we see that the monopolist's revenue would fall by 15 per cent if everyone paid the discount price. Very few firms would remain profitable in the face of a 15 per cent decline in total revenue.

It follows that, if the monopolist is earning economic profit, the source of that profit is the buyer who pays the regular price. The fact that this buyer could have paid a discount price if he had been willing to jump the requisite hurdle tells us that the burden imposed on him is no greater than the trouble of jumping the hurdle. This is obviously not the same as saying that the regular-price buyer makes a voluntary charitable contribution to the monopolist. But it does take at least some of the sting out of the notion that the monopolist's customers are being cruelly victimized.

So much for the source of monopoly profit. What about its disposition? Who gets it? If we assume a corporate income tax rate of 28 per cent, 28 cent of each rand of monopoly profits goes via SARS to the South African Treasury. The remainder is paid out to shareholders, either directly through dividends or indirectly by reinvesting it into the company. Granted, the average income of shareholders is greater than that of citizens as a whole. But there are also many low-income shareholders in South Africa. Most employee pension and provident funds, for example, are partly invested in the stock market, as are the private insurance holdings of many low-income individuals. So a sizeable fraction of any rand of monopoly profit will wind up in the hands of low-income shareholders.

But to take the worst possible case from a distributional point of view, let us suppose that what's left of the rand of monopoly profit goes entirely to the wealthiest resident of Houghton. Assume that she pays a marginal personal income tax rate of 40 per cent on the 72 cents that the government hasn't already taken through corporate taxation, leaving 43 cents. Value-added tax will claim an additional 6 cents, leaving only 37 cents in the hands of our wealthy shareholder.

To summarize, then, the source of a rand in monopoly profit is the regular-price buyer, someone who could have paid a discount price had he but taken a little extra trouble. Of that rand, 57 cents goes to the national Treasury and another 6 cents is paid in value-added tax. The disposition of almost two-thirds of the rand is thus subject to governmental control. The remainder becomes income in the hands of shareholders, at least some of whom have low incomes to begin with. So it is by no means clear that the economic profit associated with natural monopoly creates distributional inequities of the sort commonly perceived.

Hurdles, of course, are seldom perfect. Inevitably they screen out some buyers who will not buy at the regular price. And, much of the time, real resources must be expended in order to jump over these hurdles. Mailing in a rebate coupon may not take a lot of time, but the time it takes could certainly be better spent. And in at least some cases, tax avoidance will keep the government from collecting as much as the tax tables specify.

So what are we to conclude from this brief analysis of the five policy options for dealing with natural monopoly? The short answer is that each has problems. None completely eliminates the difficulties that arise when a single seller serves the market. Sometimes the least-costly solution will be competitive contracting; at other times, it will be direct state ownership. Regulation will continue to play a role in specific industries, particularly the traditional public utilities. And despite their many shortcomings, antitrust laws serve the public well by discouraging price-fixing and other anti-competitive practices. But in some cases, particularly those in which the monopolist has devised means of richly segmenting the market, the best option may be simply not to intervene at all.

Does monopoly suppress innovation?

One of the most enduring topics of conversation among economic conspiracy buffs is the notion that monopolists deprive consumers of a spectrum of enormously valuable technological innovations. Who has not heard, for example, of how the light bulb manufacturers have conspired to prevent revolutionary new designs for long-lasting light bulbs from reaching the market? To some degree this issue was addressed in South Africa by the introduction of energy-saving light bulbs when Eskom was struggling to supply enough electricity in 2007. The higher costs of energy-saving bulbs were in some sense bypassed when South Africans were allowed to exchange their normal light bulbs for energy-saving bulbs – for free. As more people switched to energy-saving bulbs so production costs decreased as a result of economies of scale; these bulbs are now cheaper in real terms than they were in 2007. Also, as fewer people used conventional bulbs their prices increased quite considerably.

Is the suppression of innovation yet another cost of monopoly that we ought to have considered in our analysis of public policy options? As Example 10.4 will make clear, the logic of profit maximization suggests that monopolists may not always be so eager to suppress innovation. This example does not imply that the monopolist's incentives to introduce innovations will always and everywhere be the same as those of a competitive firm. But it should caution us against uncritical acceptance of claims that monopolists always deprive consumers of the benefits of the latest available technology.

Advantages and disadvantages of monopolies

To conclude this chapter, let's just briefly look at the advantages and disadvantages of monopolies. One of the disadvantages is that a monopoly leads to higher prices and lower output compared with perfect competition. Under perfect competition price is equal to marginal cost (as explained in Chapter 9), but with a monopoly the price is always higher than marginal cost. Because of the lack of competition there is a possibility that the consumer may be exploited, because she is unable to purchase an alternative. However, public perception that a monopolist can charge any price it wants is not true. If it charges a price above consumers' reservation prices, nobody will buy its goods. Although it is true that the consumer may be exploited in a monopolistic market, the monopolist cannot charge any price, and only limited exploitation can occur. A lack of competition may lead to the monopolist experiencing higher cost curves. Whereas a firm in a competitive market must use the most efficient production techniques to stay in business, the monopolist is frequently sheltered by barriers to entry, and that is why we frequently find X-inefficiencies in the monopolistic market. The abnormal profits of the monopolist may lead to an unequal distribution of income, and cause unhappiness. The scale of this problem depends on the size of the monopolist. Few people will be concerned about the monopoly profits of the village store, but people may get very excited about

Example 10.4

Suppose current light bulbs have an expected life of 1000 hours. Now the light bulb monopolist discovers how to make a bulb that lasts 10 000 hours at the same per-bulb cost of production. Will the monopolist introduce the new bulb?

Suppose we measure the quantity produced by the monopolist not as light bulbs *per se*, but as the number of bulb-hours of lighting services. Thus, if the cost of producing the current design is, say, R10.00/bulb-hr, then the cost of the new design is only R1.00/bulb-hr. In Fig. 10.25, D represents the market demand curve for lighting and MR the associated marginal revenue curve.

Note that the profit-maximizing price and quantity for the current design, whose marginal cost is R10/bulb-hr, are P_1 and Q_1, respectively. For the new design, whose marginal cost is R1/bulb-hr, the profit-maximizing price and quantity are P_2 and Q_2. The monopolist's profit under the current design is the area of the rectangle ABCE. For the new design, the corresponding profit value is the shaded area of the rectangle FGHK. And because the monopolist's profit is higher under the new design, it has every incentive to make that design available. As mentioned above, the energy-saving light bulbs we use in South Africa have a much longer lifespan than traditional tungsten bulbs. However, the production costs of the former are currently considerably higher than those of the latter. As a result, tungsten light bulbs sell for a price in the region of R100 per 5-bulb pack compared to about R200 for energy-saving bulbs in the same size pack.

Figure 10.25 Does monopoly suppress innovation?

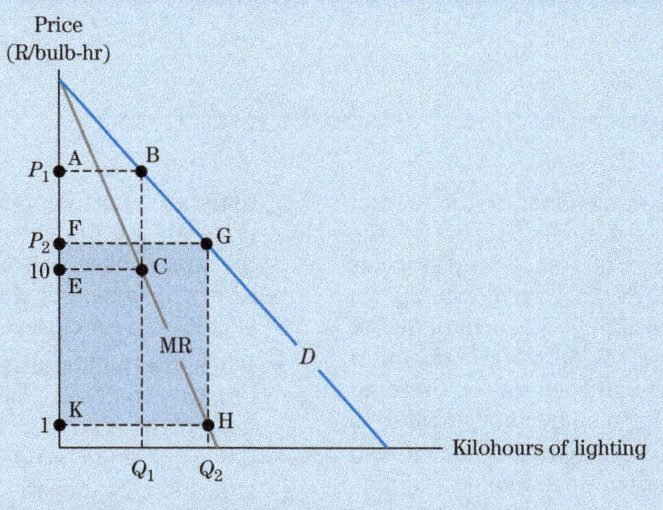

The cost of producing the new, efficient light-bulb, at R1.00/bulb-hr, is only one-tenth the cost of producing the current design, R10/bulb-hr. Because the monopolist's profits with the efficient design (area FGHK) exceed its profits with the current design (area ABCE), it will offer the new design.

the monopoly profits of giant national and international firms. However, 2009 saw widespread unrest in South Africa in response to xenophobic attacks on foreigners who monopolized business activities in the townships – an exceptional situation in which people did become excited about monopolistic activities on a small scale.

One of the advantages of monopoly profit is that it enables the monopoly to invest in research and development. This can lead to the development of new technology that may actually lower the cost structure of firms. This type of firm is also frequently better adapted to industries in which huge capital investment is needed, such as pharmaceuticals. The capital-intensive nature of activities in this industry mean that the pharmaceutical industry is typically dominated by a few big firms with substantial market power. The size of monopolies may lead to economies of scale, and these savings may be passed on to consumers in the form of lower prices. For all practical purposes, Eskom is the only electricity supplier in South Africa. Although the economy is now expanding following the end of the recession, requiring new electricity plants to ensure the country doesn't experience power shortages, building such plants is very expensive and Eskom thus maintains its monopoly position. Allowing more electricity suppliers to enter the South African market will make the cost of generating electricity increase because country is too small to accommodate more firms and not all of them will experience economies of scale. However, it does not mean that alternative energy sources like solar power or wind turbines should not be allowed to also supply the national grid. Although a firm may be a monopoly in the local market (e.g. Iscor), it may face stiff competition in the international market.

Globalization in the form of international competition will force the local monopoly to operate efficiently, otherwise it will be driven out of its local market by a more efficient foreign firm. It may also be the case that a firm became a monopoly because it was very efficient and successful (Google, for example) and drove inefficient firms out of the market. One has to remember that not all monopolies are run inefficiently just because they are big.

It is important to bear in mind that not all monopolies are necessarily bad. The size of big monopolists makes certain research and patenting possible that would not be feasible in a competitive market. Facing fierce competition, firms cannot afford to spend too much time and money on research and development. However, we cannot ignore the fact that certain monopolies misuse their market power and charge excessive prices, which is why governments keep an eye on them to ensure consumers aren't exploited. Price regulation and/or antitrust legislation are intended to achieve just this. Whether a monopoly is good or bad depends on the size of the firm, and on the specific market conditions in which it operates. Each monopoly has to be judged on its own merit.

Summary

- Monopoly is the name given to the market structure in which a single firm serves the entire market. Five factors, acting alone or in combination, give rise to monopoly: (1) control over key inputs; (2) economies of scale; (3) patents; (4) network economies; and (5) government licences. In the long run, by far the most important of these is economies of scale, in part because it also helps explain network economies and government licences.
- Because the monopolist is the only seller in the market, its demand curve is downward sloping. Unlike the perfect competitor, which can sell as much as it chooses at the market price, the monopolist must cut price in order to expand its output. The monopolist's rule for maximizing profits is the same as that used by perfectly competitive firms: it is to expand output if the gain in revenue (marginal revenue) exceeds the increase in costs (marginal cost), and to contract if the loss in revenue is smaller than the reduction in costs. The pivotal difference is that marginal revenue is less than price for the monopolist, but equal to price for the perfect competitor. However, the monopolist will also produce at that level of production where marginal cost is equal to marginal revenue.
- When the monopolist can sell in several separate markets, he distributes output among them so that marginal revenue is the same in each. Here again, the familiar logic of cost–benefit analysis provides a convenient framework for analysing the firm's decision about whether to alter its current behaviour.
- Unlike the perfectly competitive case, the monopoly equilibrium generally does not exhaust the potential gains from exchange. In general, the value to society of an additional unit of output will exceed the cost to the monopolist of the resources required to produce it. This finding has often been interpreted to mean that monopoly is less efficient than perfect competition. But this interpretation is of only limited practical significance, because the conditions that give rise to monopoly – in particular,

economies of scale in production – are rarely compatible with those required for perfect competition.

- Our policy focus in this chapter was on the question of how the government should treat natural monopolies – markets characterized by downward-sloping long-run average cost curves. We considered five policy alternatives: (1) state ownership; (2) private ownership with government price regulation; (3) competitive bidding by private firms for the right to be the sole provider of a service; (4) vigorous enforcement of antitrust laws designed to prevent monopoly; and finally (5) a complete laissez-faire, or hands-off, policy. Problems arise with each of these alternatives, and the best policy will in general be different in different circumstances. The laissez-faire stance is most attractive in markets where the monopolist is able to employ the hurdle model of differential pricing. Allowing buyers to decide for themselves whether to become eligible for a discount price softens both the efficiency and fairness objections to natural monopoly.

Questions for review

1 What five factors give rise to monopoly? In the long run, why are economies of scale the most important factor?

2 If South Africa has hundreds of cement producers but a small town has only one, is this cement producer a monopolist? Explain.

3 When is marginal revenue less than price for a monopolist? Explain.

4 Why does a profit-maximizing monopolist never produce on an inelastic portion of the demand curve? Would a revenue-maximizing monopolist ever produce on the inelastic portion of the demand curve?

5 Why is an output level at which MR intersects MC from below never the profit-maximizing level of output?

6 What effect will the imposition of a 50 per cent tax on economic profit have on a monopolist's price and output decisions? (*Hint*: Recall that the assumed objective is to choose the level of output that maximizes economic profit.)

7 Suppose the elasticity of demand is $\varepsilon = -3$. By how much will a profit-maximizing monopolist's price exceed marginal cost? How does this mark-up of price over marginal cost compare with perfect competition?

8 *True or false*: A lump-sum tax on a monopolist will always increase the price charged by the monopolist and lower the quantity of output sold.

9 *True or false*: If a monopolist faces a perfectly horizontal demand curve, the deadweight loss to the economy is zero.

10 What forces work against X-inefficiency in privately-owned monopolies?

11 How does the hurdle method of price discrimination mitigate both the efficiency and fairness problems associated with monopoly?

Problems

1 You are a self-employed profit-maximization consultant specializing in monopolies. Five single-price, profit-maximizing monopolies are currently seeking your advice, and although the information they have supplied to you is incomplete, your expert knowledge allows you to go back and make a definite recommendation in each case. Select one of the following recommendations for each firm in the short run:

a Remain at the current output level.

b Increase output.

c Reduce output.

d Shut down.

e Go back and recalculate your figures because those supplied can't possibly be right.

Firm	*P*	MR	TR	*Q*	TC	MC	ATC	AVC	Your recommendation
A	3.90	3.00		2000	7400	2.90		3.24	
B	5.90			10 000		5.90	4.74	4.24	
C		9.00	44 000	4000		9.00	11.90	10.74	
D	35.90	37.90		5000		37.90	35.90		
E	35.00		3990	1000	3300		At min. value	23.94	

2 A monopolist has a demand curve given by $P = 100 - Q$ and a total cost curve given by $\text{TC} = 16 + Q^2$. Find the monopolist's profit-maximizing quantity and price. How much economic profit will the monopolist earn?

3 Now suppose the monopolist in Problem 2 has a total cost curve given by $\text{TC} = 32 + Q^2$. The corresponding marginal cost curve is still $\text{MC} = 2Q$, but fixed costs have doubled. Find the monopolist's profit-maximizing quantity and price. How much economic profit does the monopolist earn?

4 Now suppose the monopolist in Problem 2 has a total cost curve given by $\text{TC} = 16 + 4Q^2$. Find the monopolist's profit-maximizing quantity and price. How much economic profit does the monopolist earn?

5 Now suppose the monopolist in Problem 2 also has access to a foreign market in which he can sell whatever quantity he chooses at a constant price of 60. How much will he sell in the foreign market? What will his new quantity and price be in the original market?

6 Now suppose the monopolist in Problem 2 has a long-run marginal cost curve of $\text{MC} = 20$. Find the monopolist's profit-maximizing quantity and price. Find the efficiency loss from this monopoly.

7 Suppose a perfectly discriminating monopolist faces market demand $P = 100 - 10Q$ and has constant marginal cost $\text{MC} = 20$ (with no fixed costs). How much does the monopolist sell? How much profit does the monopolist earn? What is the maximum per-period licence fee the government could charge the firm and have the firm still stay in business?

8 The demand by children for showings at a local movie theatre has a constant price elasticity equal to −4. The demand curve for all other people attending the movie theatre has a constant price elasticity equal to −2. If the marginal cost per person attending the theatre is R21 per showing, how much should the theatre charge members of each group?

9 During the Iran–Iraq war, the same arms merchant often sold weapons to both sides of the conflict. In this situation, different prices could be offered to the two sides because there was little danger that the country offered the lower price would sell arms to its rival to profit on the difference in prices. Suppose a French arms merchant has a monopoly of Exocet air-to-sea missiles and is willing to sell them to both sides. Iraq's demand for Exocets is $P = 4000 - 0.5Q$ and Iran's is $P = 3000 - Q$, where P is in millions of rand. The marginal cost of Exocets is $\text{MC} = Q$. What price will be charged to each country?

10 If you have ever gone grocery shopping on a weekday afternoon, you have probably noticed some elderly shoppers going slowly down the aisles checking their coupon book for a coupon that matches some of their purchases. How is this behaviour explained by the hurdle model of price discrimination?

11 A monopolist's price is R100. At this price the absolute value of the elasticity of demand is 2. What is the monopolist's marginal cost?

12 Suppose the government imposed a price ceiling on a monopolist (an upper bound on the price the monopolist can charge). Let $\bar{P}$ denote the price ceiling, and suppose the monopolist incurs no costs in producing output. *True or false*: If the demand curve faced by the monopolist is inelastic at the price $\bar{P}$, then the monopolist would be no better off if the government removed the price ceiling.

13 The *Business Day*, a profit-maximizing newspaper, faces a downward-sloping demand schedule for advertisements. When advertising for itself in its own pages (for example, an ad saying 'Read Richard Haslop in Friday's edition'), is the opportunity cost of a given-size ad simply the price it charges its outside advertisers? Explain.

***14** Crazy Harry, a monopolist, has a total cost curve given by $TC = 5Q + 15$. He sets two prices for his product: a regular price P_H and a discount price P_L. Everyone is eligible to purchase the product at P_H. To be eligible to buy at P_L, however, it is necessary to present a copy of the latest Crazy Harry newspaper ad to the salesperson. Suppose the only buyers who present the ad are those who would not have been willing to buy the product at P_H.

a If Crazy Harry's demand curve is given by $P = 20 - 5Q$, what are the profit-maximizing values of P_H and P_L?

b How much economic profit does Harry make?

c How much profit would he have made if he had been forced to charge the same price to all buyers?

d Are buyers better or worse off as a result of Harry's being able to charge two prices?

15 An author has signed a contract in which the publisher promises to pay her R25 000 plus 20 per cent of gross receipts from the sale of her book. *True or false*: If both the publisher and the author care only about their own financial return from the project, then the author will prefer a higher book price than will the publisher.

16 A film director has signed a contract in which the production studio promises to pay her R10 000 000 plus 5 per cent of the studio's rental revenues from the film, all of whose costs of production and distribution are fixed. *True or false*: If both the director and the studio care only about their own financial return from the project, then the director will prefer a lower film rental price than will the studio.

17 Name the factors that give rice to monopoly.

18 Discuss the different strategies that governments can use to treat monopolies.

19 Discuss the difference between the long run equilibrium in a perfectly competitive market and a monopoly. Use a graph to illustrate your answer. In your answer you must refer to allocative and productive efficiency as well as welfare loss.

Answers to in-chapter exercises

10.1

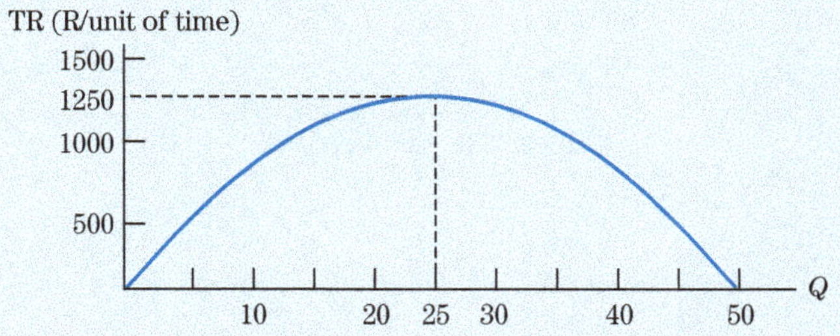

* This problem is most easily solved using calculus.

10.2 $TR = P.Q = 100Q - 2Q^2$ and $MR = 100 - 4Q$.

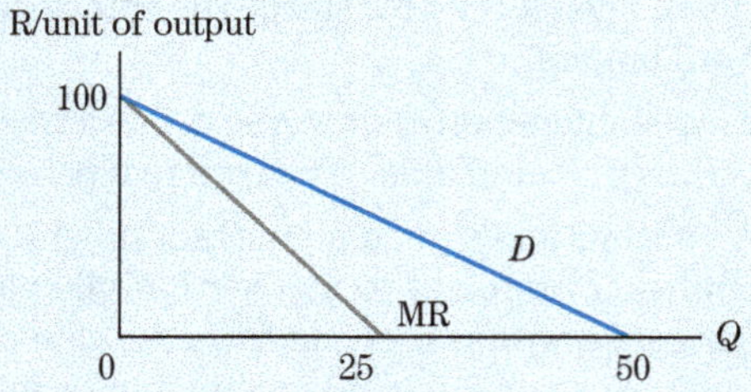

10.3 $MC = 400 = 1000 - 40Q = MR$, which solves for $Q^* = 15$, $P^* = 1000 - 20Q^* = 700$.

10.4 The profit-maximizing level of output for a single-price monopolist occurs where MR = MC. Marginal revenue equals marginal cost at both $Q = 15$ and $Q = 34$, but at $Q = 34$ marginal revenue intersects marginal cost from above and thus is the maximal level. However, even at $Q = 34$, price does not cover average variable cost ($66 = P < AVC = 72$). The average variable cost curve lies everywhere above the demand curve (see figure), so the firm can do no better than earn profits equal to negative fixed costs. Thus the optimal quantity is $Q = 0$: the firm should shut down!

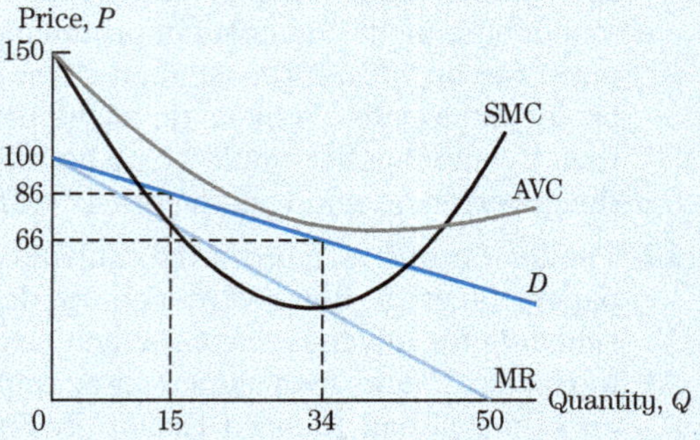

10.5 $MR_1 = 100 - 2Q_1$ (left panel) and $MR_2 = 200 - 2Q_2$ (centre panel), so the horizontal summation of the ΣMR curves is given by MR (right panel). The profit-maximizing quantity is 130, 40 of which should be sold in market 1 and the remaining 90 in market 2. The profit-maximizing prices are $P_1^* = 60$ and $P_2^* = 110$.

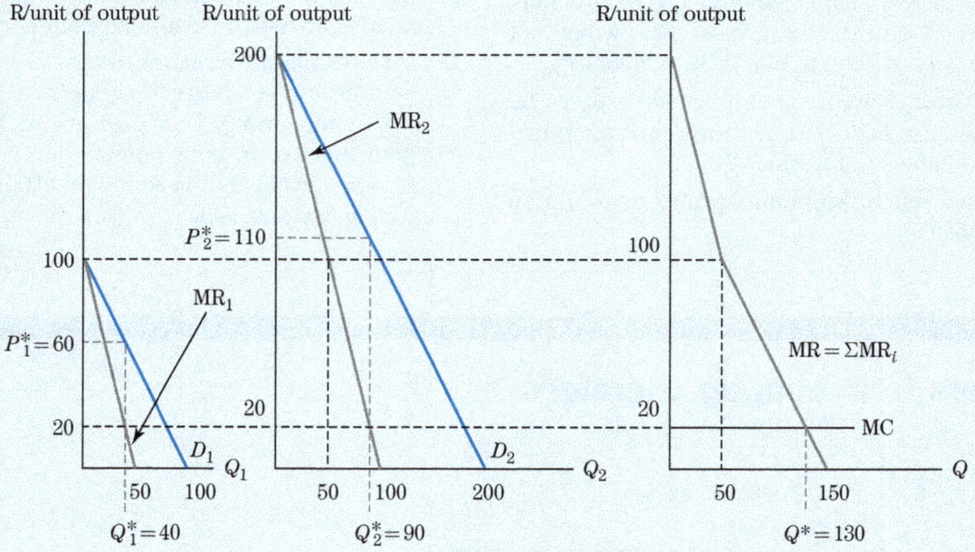

Exercise Answer 10.5

Chapter 11

Imperfect competition: a game-theoretic approach

Three lawyers and three economists meet one morning as they arrive at OR Tambo Airport to catch the Gautrain to Midrand, where they are scheduled to attend the annual meeting of the Law and Economics Association. Each lawyer buys a one-way ticket. To their surprise, however, they notice that the economists standing in the adjacent ticket line buy only a single ticket among them. 'What are they up to?' one of the lawyers wonders aloud to his colleagues as the six men take their seats on the train.

Shortly after the train pulls out, the lawyers notice the conductor punching tickets in the carriage ahead. At this point, the three economists quickly crowd into one of the toilets at the back of the carriage. Presently, the conductor comes by and collects each lawyer's ticket and, on his way to the next carriage, knocks on the door of the occupied toilet, saying 'Tickets, please.' The door opens a crack, and a hand reaches out to present a ticket, which the conductor dutifully punches and returns.

Four days later, the men arrive at Midrand for their return journey. Inspired by the economists, the lawyers buy only a single ticket, cackling to themselves at their cleverness. But this time they are puzzled to notice that the economists don't buy any tickets at all.

The six men board the train, and at first sight of the approaching conductor, the three lawyers hurriedly sequester themselves in one of the toilets. At this, the three economists get up and proceed to the rear of the car. Two of them go into the other toilet while the third knocks on the door of the lawyers' toilet, saying, 'Tickets, please.' One of the lawyers holds his ticket out of the door, which the economist collects and then joins his colleagues in the other toilet.

Chapter preview

As the parable of the lawyers and economists illustrates, the pay-off to an action often depends not only on the action itself, but also on how it relates to actions taken by others in the same environment. In previous chapters we viewed economic decision-makers as confronting an environment that is essentially passive. In the perfectly competitive environment of Chapter 9, for example, firms were assumed to ignore the actions of their adversaries. And in the monopoly environment of Chapter 10 the firm simply had no rivals to worry about. Both perfect competition and monopoly represent idealized forms. They are useful for generating insights into general tendencies but are rarely, if ever, encountered in practice. Our task in this chapter is to describe and explore the hybrid forms of industrial organization we deal with on a daily basis – namely, oligopoly and monopolistic competition.

Let us explain the collusive behaviour of firms with a practical example. When the World Cup soccer tournament was staged in South Africa in 2010, airline companies knew there would be a high demand for tickets. They could decide to collude – and charge everyone higher prices – or to compete fiercely on low-price tickets. Clearly they opted for the collusive option. A British Airways return flight from Cape Town to London for the duration of the World Cup cost about R17 000, on Virgin Atlantic Airways R16 800 and on SAA R16 000. A month after the World Cup the same flights with the same airlines cost R9000, R10 100 and R8400, respectively. Even today you can fly to London and back for a little over R10 000. Domestic fares for the duration of the World Cup increased to such a degree that the Competition Board of South Africa launched an enquiry. In a controversial decision, the airlines were not prosecuted.

The cost of hotel accommodation also increased substantially during the World Cup. The Bay Hotel in Camps Bay more than doubled its price for a suite, from R5760 to R12 825 per night (an increase of 122 per cent!). If no other hotel followed suit, the Bay Hotel would find itself with lots of empty rooms. However, the accommodation industry also colluded (formally or informally) and hotels duly increased their prices. For example, the Cullinan Hotel in Cape Town increased its rate per double room from the normal R1416 to R2446, the Abbey Manor increased its price for a grand room from R1380 to R2750 per night and the TAJ Hotel increased the price of its superior rooms from R2560 to R3540. Because all role players increased their prices, it left foreign visitors with little option but to pay the higher prices. These are good examples of the action of certain role players in a market influencing the behaviour of other players in that market. Important local events like the Comrades marathon, Argus cycling race, Currie Cup final or the Absa Premier League final also motivate hotels tend to increase their prices but not on the scale seen during the World Cup.

We shall begin the chapter by analysing the behaviour of oligopolists, comparing several simple models in which firms make alternative assumptions about the behaviour of their rivals. In these models we still assume that products are homogeneous. We shall then apply these concepts when discussing some elementary concepts of game theory. After considering a traditional model of monopolistic competition (where the assumption of product homogeneity is relaxed), we shall discuss a simple spatial model of monopolistic competition in which customers have particular locations or product characteristics that they most prefer. In this situation, we shall see, firms tend to compete most intensively for the buyers of products that are most similar to their own.

Some specific oligopoly models

If a firm is considering a change in its output level or selling price, there are many possible assumptions it could make about the reactions of its rivals. It could assume, for example, that its rivals will continue producing at their current levels of output. Alternatively, it could assume that they will continue to charge their current prices. Or it could assume that they will react in various specific ways to its own price and output changes. In the sections that follow, we explore the implications of each alternative assumption. In dealing with duopoly models, each will first be explained with the aid of a numerical example. After completion of each model a general algebraic method will be explained. We will do it in this way because some students find it difficult to follow the argument with the general algebraic functions and we first want you to work through a model with numerical values.

The Cournot model

We begin with the simplest case, the so-called **Cournot model**, in which each firm

Cournot model Oligopoly model in which each firm assumes that rivals will continue producing at their current *output* levels.

assumes that its rivals will continue producing at their current levels of output. Named for the French economist Auguste Cournot, who introduced it in 1838, this model describes the behaviour of two firms that sell bottled water from mineral springs. A two-firm oligopoly is called a *duopoly*, and the Cournot model is sometimes referred to as the *Cournot duopoly model*, although its conclusions can easily be generalized to more than two firms.

The central assumption of the Cournot model is that each duopolist treats the other's *output* as a fixed number, one that will not respond to its own production decisions. This is a weak form of interdependence, indeed, but we shall see that even it leads to an outcome in which the behaviour of each firm substantially affects its rival.

Suppose the total market demand curve for mineral water is given by $P = 204 - 2Q$; where Q_1 is the output of firm 1 and Q_2 the output of firm 2. We can rewrite the demand function as $P = 204 - 2(Q_1 + Q_2)$. Cournot also assumed that the water could be produced at zero marginal cost, but this assumption is merely for convenience. Essentially similar conclusions would emerge if each firm experienced constant positive marginal cost. When you work through Exercise 11.1 later in this chapter, in which we deal with positive marginal cost, try to convince yourself that working with positive or zero *MC* is basically the same thing.

Let us look first at the profit-maximization problem facing firm 1. Given its assumption that firm 2's output is fixed at Q_2, the demand curve for firm 1's water is given by $P_1 = (204 - 2Q_2) - 2Q_1$, which is rewritten to emphasize the fact that firm 1 treats Q_2 (the production volume of firm 2) as given.

As we see from the demand curve above, we get the demand curve for firm 1 by subtracting $2Q_2$ from the vertical intercept of the market demand curve. The idea is that firm 2 has skimmed off the first $2Q_2$ units of the market demand curve, leaving firm 1 the remainder to work with.

If Q_2 were equal to zero, firm 1 would have the entire market demand curve to itself, as indicated by D in Fig. 11.1. If Q_2 is positive, we get firm 1's demand curve by shifting the vertical axis of the demand diagram rightward by Q_2 units. Firm 1's demand curve is that portion of the original demand curve that lies to the right of this new vertical axis, and for this reason it is sometimes called a *residual demand curve*. It intersects the quantity axis at $Q_1 = (204 - 2Q_2)/2$. If Q_2 is equal to zero, it means the demand curve intersects the quantity axis at 102. The associated marginal

Figure 11.1 The profit-maximizing Cournot duopolist

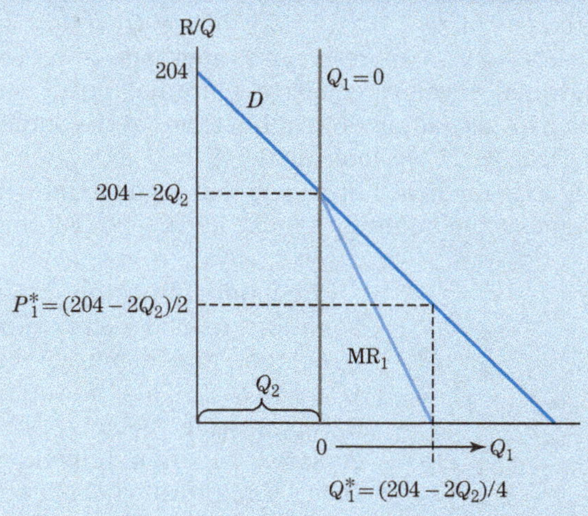

The Cournot duopolist's demand curve is obtained by shifting the vertical axis rightwards by the amount produced by the other duopolist (Q_2 in the diagram equal to 34 in this numerical example). The portion of the original market demand curve that lies to the right of this new vertical axis is the demand curve facing firm 1 if market demand is $P = 204 - 2Q$.

revenue curve is labelled MR_1. We know that the MR curve is the first-order derivative of TR and $TR_1 = PQ_1$. So we multiply our demand function by Q_1 and calculate the first-order derivative to get $MR_1 = (204 - 2Q_2) - 4Q_1$. Marginal revenue for firm 1 is the same as the original demand curve, but with double the slope. Firm 1's rule for profit maximization is the same as for any other firm that faces a downward-sloping demand curve, namely, to equate marginal revenue and marginal cost. Marginal cost in this example is assumed to be zero, so the profit-maximizing level of output for firm 1 is that level for which its marginal revenue curve takes the value of zero.

The equilibrium output for a Cournot duopoly can be deduced from the residual demand diagram. Given that firm 2 is producing Q_2, firm 1 maximizes its profits by producing where marginal revenue is zero (and equals marginal cost). Because marginal revenue has twice the slope as demand, marginal revenue intersects zero marginal cost at half the distance from the $Q_1 = 0$ axis to the horizontal intercept of the demand curve. As a result of symmetry (the two firms are identical, so they must behave the same), $Q_2 = Q_1$, which means that each of the three segments shown on the horizontal axis in Fig. 11.1 has the same length. And this implies that each firm produces output equal to one-third of the distance from the origin to the horizontal intercept of the demand curve. The demand curve $P = 204 - 2Q$ has a horizontal intercept of $Q = 102$ (204/2): hence $Q_1 = Q_2 = 34$ [204/(3 × 2)]. A more general approach is to set marginal revenue equal to marginal cost, and solve for the output of firm 1 in terms of the output of firm 2:[1] If we look at the $Q_1 = 0$ axis as the R/Q axis for firm 1, it means that its demand will intersect the quantity axis at $[(204 - 2Q_2)/2]$ and $Q_1^* = \frac{204-2Q_2}{4}$.

Reaction function A curve that shows the profit-maximizing level of output for one oligopolist for each amount supplied by another.

Economists call this equation firm 1's **reaction function**, and denote it by $Q_1^* = R_1(Q_2)$. This notation is suggestive because the reaction function tells how firm 1's quantity will react to the quantity level offered by firm 2.

Because the Cournot duopoly problem is completely symmetrical, firm 2's reaction function has precisely the same structure and we can write Q_2 as a function of Q_1. The reaction curve of firm 2 is thus given by $Q_2^* = R_2(Q_1) = \frac{204-2Q_1}{4}$.

The two reaction functions are plotted in Fig. 11.2. To illustrate the workings of the reaction function concept, suppose firm 1 initially produced a quantity of Q_1^0. Firm 2 would then produce the level of output that corresponds to Q_1^0 on its reaction function. Firm 1 would respond to that output level by picking the corresponding point on its own reaction function. Firm 2 would then respond by picking the corresponding point on its reaction function, and so on. The end result of this process is a stable equilibrium at the intersection of the two reaction functions. When both firms are producing 34 units of output, neither wants to change. Algebraically, the equilibrium level of output for firm 1 can be determined by substituting $Q_1^* = Q_2^*$ into the reaction curve. And when we solve $Q_1^* = \frac{204-2Q_2}{4}$, we know that $Q_1^* = Q_2^*$ and we can substitute Q_2 with Q_1 so that $Q_1^* = \frac{204-2Q_1}{4}$; $\frac{3}{2}Q_1^* = 51$, which yields $Q_1^* = 34$. It implies that $Q_2^* = 34$. These output levels thus constitute a Nash equilibrium for the Cournot duopolists.

Figure 11.2 Reaction functions for the Cournot duopolists

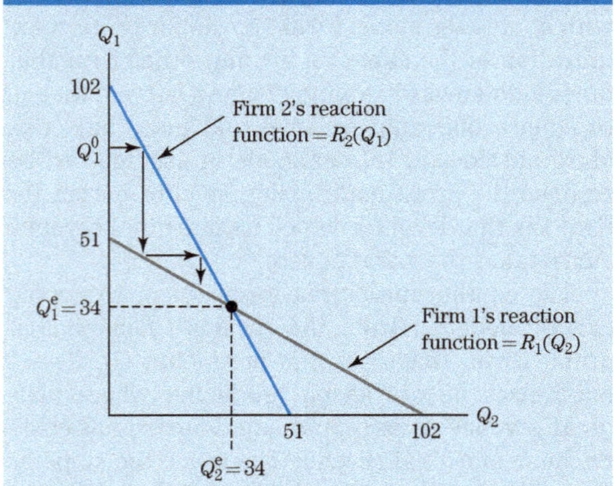

The duopolists are in a stable equilibrium at the point at which their reaction functions intersect. If market demand is $P = 204 - 2Q$, it will be at $Q = 34$.

How profitable are the Cournot duopolists? Since their combined output is 68, the market price will be $P = 204 - 2(68) = 68$. At this price, each will have total revenue equal to $(68)(34) = 2312$. And since neither firm has any production costs, total revenues and economic profits here are one and the same.

Let us now turn to the general algebraic case and assume that the market curve is:

$$P = a - bQ = a - b(Q_1 + Q_2) \tag{11.1}$$

We once again assume there are two firms and that firm 2 will provide Q_2. Based on firm 1's assumption that firm 2's output is fixed at Q_2, we can write firm 1's demand as

$$P_1 = (a - bQ_2) - bQ_1 \tag{11.2}$$

We get firm 1's demand curve by subtracting bQ_2 from the vertical intercept of the market demand curve. In Fig. 11.3, it is as though the vertical R/Q axis of firm 1 shifts Q_2 units to the right.

Like we did with the numerical example, firm 1 will maximize its profit by setting its marginal revenue equal to its marginal cost. Given the demand curve of firm 1 (equation 11.2), we know that total revenue of firm 1 is $TR_1 = (a - bQ_2)Q_1 - bQ_1^2$ and marginal revenue is the first-order derivative of this function, namely, $MR_1 = (a - bQ_2) - 2bQ_1$.

As was the case with the numerical example, if Q_2 is zero, firm 1's demand curve will be

[1] For example, this more general approach is needed if firms are asymmetric (not identical), and thus would not produce the same level of output.

Figure 11.3 The profit-maximizing Cournot duopolist

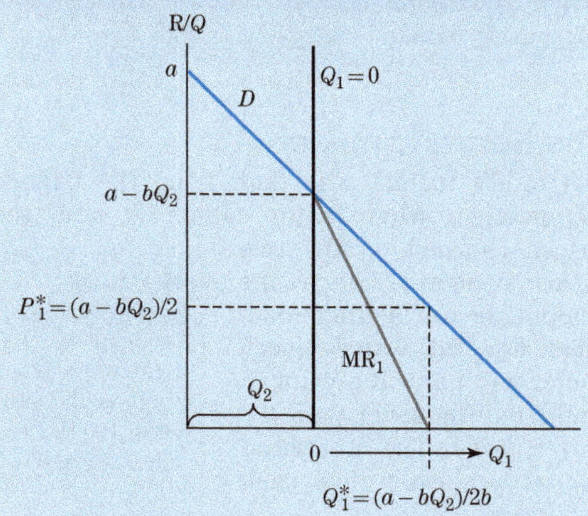

The Cournot duopolist's demand curve is obtained by shifting the vertical axis rightwards by the amount produced by the other duopolist (Q_2 in the diagram). The portion of the original market demand curve that lies to the right of this new vertical axis is the demand curve facing firm 1. Firm 1 then maximizes profit by equating marginal revenue and marginal cost, the latter of which is zero.

illustrated by D in Fig. 11.3. However, if Q_2 is positive, we get firm 1's demand curve by shifting the vertical axis rightwards by Q_2 units. It intersects the quantity axis at $Q_1 = (a - bQ_2)/b$. The associated marginal revenue curve has double the slope of the demand curve, as calculated above. Because we assume that marginal cost is zero, firm 1 will maximize profits where marginal revenue is zero.

Because marginal revenue has a slope that is double the slope of the demand curve, it intersects the quantity axis at half the distance from the $Q_1 = 0$ axis to the horizontal intercept of the demand curve. The firms are identical, which implies $Q_1 = Q_2$, so that each segment in Fig. 11.3 is the same length. The demand curve D in Fig. 11.3 has a horizontal intercept of $Q = a/b$. This means that $Q_1 = Q_2 = a/(3b)$. The same conclusion can be drawn by setting marginal revenue equal to marginal cost, and solving for the output of firm 1 in terms of the output of firm 2:

$$Q_1^* = \frac{a - bQ_2}{2b} \qquad (11.3)$$

We call this the reaction curve of firm 1 and write it as $Q_1^* = R_1(Q_2)$. It tells us how the quantity supplied by firm 1 will react in response to the quantity supplied by firm 2.

The Cournot duopoly problem is symmetrical and therefore we can write firm 2's reaction curve in the same way:

$$Q_2^* = R_2(Q_1) = \frac{a - bQ_1}{2b} \qquad (11.4)$$

The reaction curves are plotted in Fig. 11.4 and, once again (as was explained in the discussion of the numerical problem), if firm 1 initially produces Q_0, firm 2 will respond according to its reaction curve; eventually we will end up with a stable equilibrium where the two reaction curves intersect. The equilibrium level of output for firm 1 can be calculated by substituting $Q_1^* = Q_2^*$ into the reaction curve:

$$\begin{aligned} R_1(Q_2^*) &= \frac{a - bQ_2^*}{2b} \\ &= \frac{a - bQ_1^*}{2b} \\ &= Q_1^* \end{aligned}$$

And when we solve $Q_1^* = \frac{a-bQ_1^*}{2b}$, it yields $Q_1^* = a/3b$. This implies that $Q_2^* = a/3b$ and that these output levels are a Nash equilibrium for the duopolists.

How profitable are the Cournot duopolists? Since their combined output is $2a/3b$, the market price will be $P = a - b(2a/3b) = a/3$. At this price, each will have total revenue equal to $(a/3)(a/3b) = a^2/9b$. And since neither firm has any production

Figure 11.4 Reaction functions for the Cournot duopolists

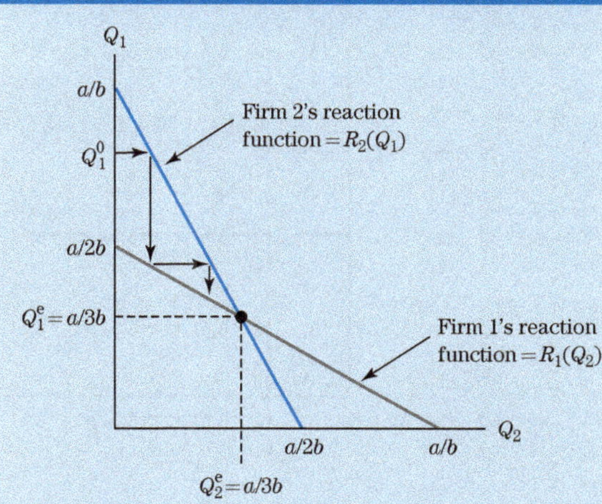

The reaction function for each duopolist gives its profit-maximizing output level as a function of the other firm's output level. The duopolists are in a stable equilibrium at the point at which their reaction functions intersect.

costs, total revenues and economic profits here are one and the same.

To solve the algebraic example, we follow exactly the same procedure that we used to solve the numerical example. In the numerical example, with demand curve $P = 204 - 2Q$ we just know that $a = 204$ and $b = 2$. Work through the generic algebraic example and convince yourself that you get the same values as produced by the numerical example if you substitute a with 204 and b with 2.

You may be wondering why the Cournot duopolists assume that their own production decisions will be ignored by their rivals. If so, you have asked a penetrating question – the same as that posed by Cournot's critic, the French economist Joseph Bertrand. Let's now consider his alternative solution to the duopoly problem.

Exercise 11.1

Repeat Example 11.1 with the two firms facing a market demand curve of $P = 44 - Q$.

The Bertrand model

Bertrand's insight was that, from the buyer's perspective, what really counts is how the prices charged by the two firms compare. Since the duopolists are selling identical mineral water, every buyer will naturally want to buy from the seller with the lower price. The **Bertrand model** proposed that each

Bertrand model An oligopoly model in which each firm assumes that rivals will continue charging their current prices.

Example 11.1

Cournot duopolists face a market demand curve given by $P = 56 - 2Q$, where Q is total market demand. Each can produce output at a constant marginal cost of 20/unit. Graph their reaction functions, and find the equilibrium price and quantity.

Figure 11.5(a) shows the residual demand curve facing firm 1 when firm 2 produces Q_2 units. Firm 1's marginal revenue curve has the same vertical intercept as its demand curve, and is twice as steep. Thus the equation for firm 1's marginal revenue curve is $MR_1 = (56 - 2Q_2) - 4Q_1$. Equating MR_1 to marginal cost (20), we solve for firm 1's reaction function, $Q_1^* = R_1 = 9 - (Q_2/2)$. As a result of symmetry, firm 2's reaction function is $R_2 = 9 - (Q_1/2)$. The two reaction functions are shown in Fig. 11.5(b), where they intersect at $Q_1 = Q_2 = 6$. Total market output will be $Q_1 + Q_2 = 12$. Consulting the market demand curve, we see that the market price will be $P = 56 - 2(12) = 32$.

Figure 11.5 Deriving the reaction functions for specific duopolists

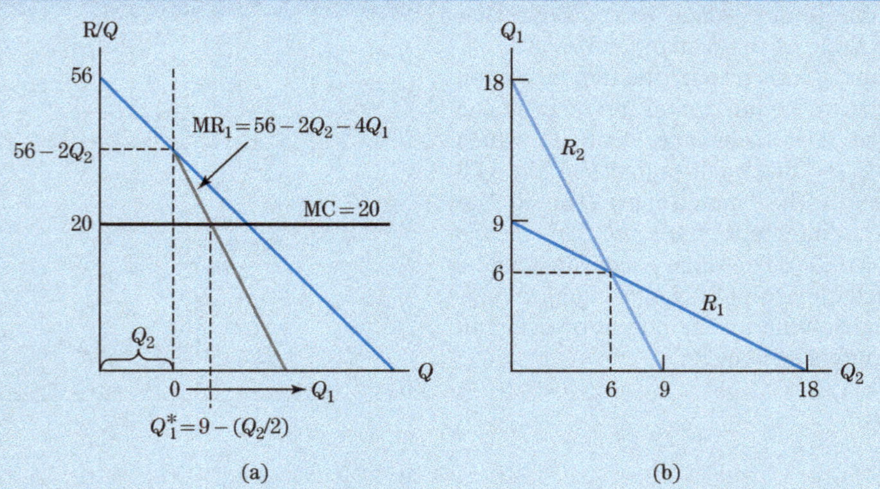

Panel a shows the profit-maximizing output level for firm 1 (Q_1^*) when firm 2 produces Q_2. This, and the parallel expression for firm 2, constitute the reaction functions plotted in panel b.

firm chooses its price on the assumption that its rival's price will remain fixed. On its face, this assumption seems no more plausible than Cournot's, and since prices and quantities correspond uniquely along market demand curves, it may seem natural to wonder whether Bertrand's assumption even leads to a different outcome. On investigation, however, the outcomes turn out to be very different indeed.

To illustrate, suppose the market demand and cost conditions are the same as in the Cournot example. And suppose firm 1 charges an initial price of p_0^1. Firm 2 then faces essentially three choices:

- it can charge more than firm 1, in which case it will sell nothing
- it can charge the same as firm 1, in which case the two firms will split the market demand at that price
- it can sell at a marginally lower price than firm 1, in which case it will capture the entire market demand at that price

The third of these options will always be by far the most profitable.[2]

As in the Cournot model, the situations of the duopolists are completely symmetrical in the Bertrand model, which means that the option of selling at a marginally lower price than the competition will be the strategy of choice for both firms. Needless to say, there can be no stable equilibrium in which each firm undersells the other. The back-and-forth process of price-cutting will continue until it reaches its natural economic limit – namely, marginal cost, which in the mineral spring example is zero. (If instead we had considered an example in which both firms have the same positive marginal cost, price would have fallen to that value.) Once each firm has cut its price to marginal cost, it will have no incentive to cut further. With each firm selling at marginal cost, the duopolists will share the market equally.

Let's continue with our numerical example where market demand is $P = 204 - 2Q$ and marginal cost is equal to zero. Thus the solution is where $P = 204 - 2Q = 0$, which solves for $Q = 102$. Because the firms split the market equally, each firm produces 51. Market price will be $P = 204 - 2(102) = 0$. Industry profit will thus also be zero.

Exercise 11.2

If the market demand curve facing Bertrand duopolists is given by $P = 10 - Q$, and each has a constant marginal cost of 2, what will be the equilibrium price and quantity for each firm?

We thus see that a seemingly minor change in the initial assumptions about firm behaviour – that each duopolist takes its rival's price, not quantity, as given – leads to a sharply different equilibrium. Now we consider how another small change in the initial assumptions about firm behaviour can lead to yet another equilibrium.

The Stackelberg model

In 1934 the German economist Heinrich von Stackelberg asked the simple but provocative question, 'What would a firm do if it knew its only rival were a naive Cournot duopolist?' The answer is that it would want to choose its own output level by taking into account the effect that choice would have on the output level of its rival. We will once again start with the numerical example in which market demand is given by

Example 11.2

Bertrand duopolists face a market demand curve given by $P = 56 - 2Q$. Each can produce output at a constant marginal cost of 20/unit. Find the equilibrium price and quantity.

The solution is that both firms price at marginal cost $P = MC = 20$. Industry output is determined by market demand: $20 = 56 - 2Q$ implies $Q = 18$. The firms split the market equally, so each firm produces half of industry output $Q_1 = Q_2 = Q/2 = 9$.

[2] In the case of a price only infinitesimally smaller than firm 1's price, firm 2's profit will be virtually twice as large under option 3 as under option 2.

Example 11.3

A Stackelberg leader and follower face a market demand curve given by $P = 56 - 2Q$. Each can produce output at a constant marginal cost of 20/unit. Find the equilibrium price and quantity.

The solution is found by substituting firm 2's reaction function $Q_2 = 9 - Q_1/2$ into the demand facing firm 1, $P = (56 - 2Q_2) - 2Q_1$, to find $P = 38 - Q_1$ with corresponding marginal revenue $MR_1 = 38 - 2Q_1$. Setting marginal revenue equal to marginal cost yields firm 1's output $Q_1 = 9$. Inserting firm 1's output into firm 2's reaction function yields firm 2's output $Q_2 = \frac{9}{2}$. Total industry output is $Q = Q_1 + Q_2 = \frac{27}{2}$, with price $P = 56 - 2Q = 56 - 27 = 29$.

$P = 204 - 2Q$ and then work through the generic algebraic example.

Returning to the Cournot model, suppose firm 1 knows that firm 2 will treat firm 1's output level as given. How can it make strategic use of that knowledge? To answer this question, recall that firm 2's reaction function is given by $Q_2^* = R_2(Q_1) = \frac{204-2Q_1}{4} = 51 - ½Q_1$. Knowing that firm 2's output will depend on Q_1 in this fashion, firm 1 can then substitute $R_2(Q_1)$ for Q_2 in the equation for the market demand curve, which yields the following expression for its own demand curve: $P = 204 - 2[Q_1 + R_2(Q_1)] = 204 - 2(Q_1 + 51 - ½Q_1) = 102 - Q_1$. This demand curve and the associated marginal revenue curve are shown as D_1 ($P = 102 - Q_1$) and MR_1 ($P = 102 - 2Q_1$) in Fig. 11.6. Since marginal cost is assumed to be zero in the mineral spring example, firm 1's profit-maximizing output level will be that for which MR_1 is zero ($102 - 2Q_1 = 0$), namely, $Q_1^* = 51$. The market price will be $P = 204 - 2(51) = 51$.

Exercise 11.3

The market demand curve for a Stackelberg leader and follower is given by $P = 10 - Q$. If each has a marginal cost of 2, what will be the equilibrium price and quantity for each?

For obvious reasons, firm 1 is referred to as a *Stackelberg leader*. *Stackelberg follower* is the term used to describe firm 2. To help place the Stackelberg leader's behaviour in clearer perspective, let's again consider the graph of the two firms' Cournot reaction functions, reproduced here as Fig. 11.7. The reaction curves in Fig. 11.7 are identical to those in Fig. 11.2. As we saw in Fig. 11.6, 51 is the best output for firm 1 to produce once it takes into account that firm 2 will respond to its choice according to the reaction function $R_2(Q_1) = 51 - ½Q_1 = 51 - ½(51) = 25.5$. Once firm 1 produces 51, firm 2 will consult R_2 and thus

Figure 11.6 The Stackelberg leader's demand and marginal revenue curves

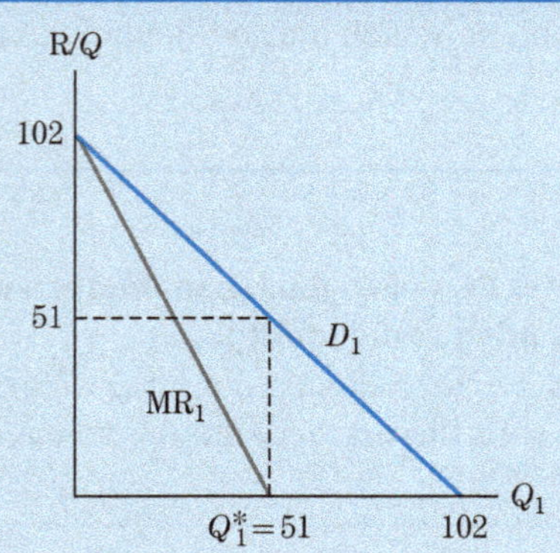

When firm 1 knows firm 2 is a Cournot duopolist, it can take account of the effect of its own behaviour on firm 2's quantity choice. The figure portrays the situation for firm 1 if market demand is given as $P = 201 - 2Q$.

Figure 11.7 The Stackelberg equilibrium

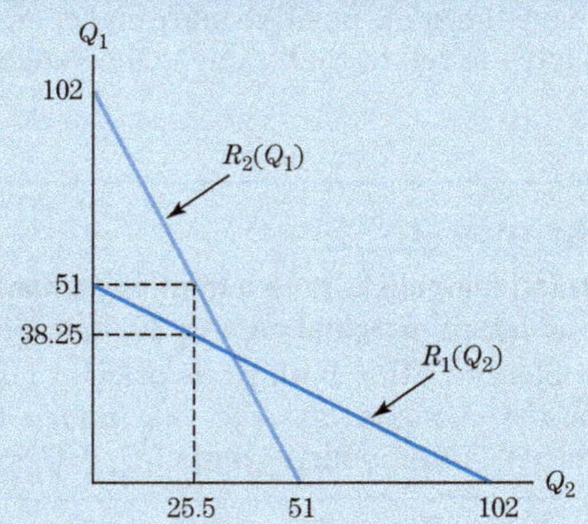

In the Stackelberg model, firm 1 ignores its own reaction function from the Cournot model. If market demand is $P = 204 - 2Q$, firm 1 (the Stackelberg leader) will produce 51 and firm 2 will produce 25.5.

respond by producing 25.5. Now here is the crucial step. If firm 1 thought that firm 2 would stay at 25.5 no matter what, its best bet would be to consult its own reaction function and produce the corresponding quantity, namely, $R_1(Q_2) = 51 - \frac{1}{2}Q_2 = 51 - \frac{1}{2}(25.5) = 38.25$. By doing so, it would earn more than by producing 51. The problem is that firm 1 realizes that if it cuts back to 38.25, this will elicit a further reaction from firm 2, culminating in a downward spiral to the intersection point of the two reaction functions. Firm 1 would do better to move to 38.25 if it could somehow induce firm 2 to remain at 25.5. But it cannot. The best option open to firm 1 is therefore to grit its teeth and stay put at 51.

If firm 1 stays put at 51 and firm 2 produces 25.5, the market price will be $P = 204 - 2(76.5) = 51$. Profit or total revenue (because we assume marginal cost is zero) will be equal to 51(51) [firm 1] + 51(25.5) [firm 2] = 3901.50.

Let us now move to the discussion of the generic model whereby market demand is given as $P = a - bQ = a - bQ_1 - bQ_2$. The Stackelberg leader (firm 1) knows that firm 2 will treat firm 1's output as given. Recall that firm 2's reaction curve is given by $Q_2^* = R_2(Q_1) = (a - bQ_1)/2b$. Firm 1 can thus substitute $R_2(Q_1)$ for Q_2 in the market demand curve, which yields the following demand curve:

$$\begin{aligned} P &= a - b[Q_1 + R_2(Q_1)] \\ &= a - b\left(Q_1 + \frac{a - bQ_1}{2b}\right) \\ &= \frac{a - bQ_1}{2} \end{aligned} \tag{11.5}$$

In Fig. 11.8 the demand and marginal revenue curves of firm 1 are illustrated by D_1 and MR_1, respectively. Firm 1 will maximize its profit where MR_1 is zero (recall that MC = 0). This implies that $MR_1 = \frac{1}{2}a - bQ_1 = 0$; which solves for $Q_1^* = a/2b$.

To place the Stackelberg leader in perspective, let us once again consider the reaction curves of the Cournot duopolist. We reproduce it in Fig. 11.9. As we saw in Fig. 11.8, the best output for firm 1 will be $a/2b$ if it takes into account that firm 2 will react according to its reaction curve $R_2(Q_1) = (a - bQ_1)/2b = [a - b(a/2b)]/2b = a/4b$. If firm 1 assumes that firm 2 will stay at that output level no matter what, firm 1's best bet will be to respond according to its reaction curve. In other words, firm 1 will then produce $R_1(Q_2) = (a - bQ_2)/2b = [a - b(a/4b)]/2b = 3a/8b$. By doing so, it will do better than by producing $a/2b$. However, firm 1 knows that, if it cuts back to $3a/8b$, firm 2 will respond and so a downward spiral to the intersection point of the two reaction curves will begin. Firm 1 would do better to move to $3a/8b$ if it somehow could induce firm 2 to stay at $a/4b$. Because firm 1 cannot do that, it will be in its best interest to stay put at $a/2b$.

In this situation, total output in the industry will be equal to $a/2b + a/4b = 3a/4b$. Market price will be $P = a - b(3a/4b) = a/4$. Total revenue or profit will be equal to $(a/4)(3a/4b) = 3a^2/16b$.

Figure 11.8 The Stackelberg leader's demand and marginal revenue curves

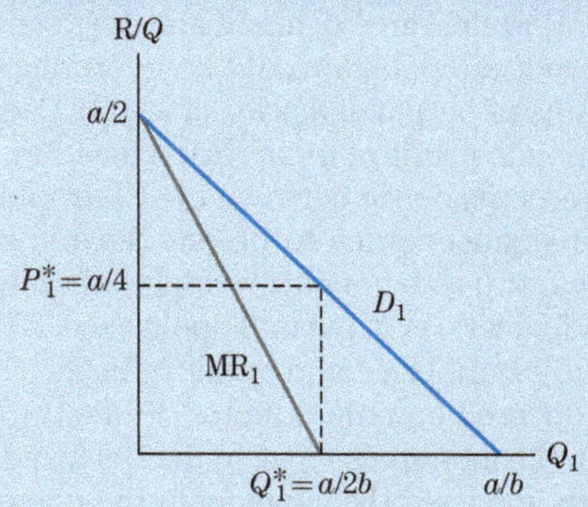

When firm 1 knows that firm 2 is a Cournot duopolist, it can take account of the effect of its own behaviour on firm 2's quantity choice. The result is that it knows exactly what its demand curve will be.

Comparison of outcomes

Now that we have considered three different types of behaviour for duopolists, let's compare the outcomes of the different models. The generic

Figure 11.9 The Stackelberg equilibrium

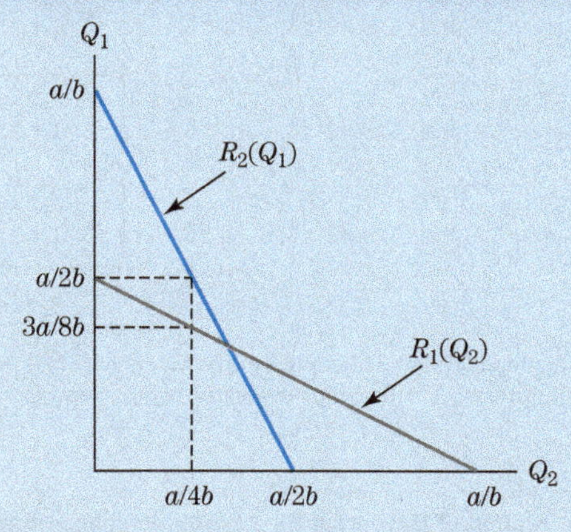

In the Stackelberg model, firm 1 ignores its own reaction function from the Cournot model. It chooses its own quantity to maximize profit, taking into account the effect that its own quantity will have on the quantity offered by firm 2.

algebraic values will be given in the discussion while the numeric values for our function $P = 204 - 2Q$ are written in brackets. A monopoly confronting the same demand and cost conditions as Cournot duopolists would have produced $a/2b$ (102) units of output at a price of $a/2$ (102), earning an economic profit of $a^2/4b$ (5202) (see Fig. 11.10). The interdependence between the Cournot duopolists thus causes price to be one-third lower and total quantity to be one-third higher than the corresponding values in the monopoly case.[3] Whereas the equilibrium price and quantity in the Cournot model differed by only a factor of one-third from those in the monopoly case, in the Bertrand model they are precisely the same as in the competitive case.[4]

How well should the Stackelberg duopolists do? Naturally, the leader fares better, since it is the one strategically manipulating the behaviour of the follower. Referring to Fig. 11.9 (or Fig. 11.7 in the numerical example), we see that firm 1's profit is $a^2/8b$ (2601), which is twice that of firm 2. As it happens, this is exactly what firm 1 would have earned had it and firm 2 colluded to charge the monopoly price, $a/2$ (102), and split the market evenly (see Fig. 11.10). The combined output of the two firms in the Stackelberg case is $3a/4b$ (76.5 units), which is slightly higher than in the Cournot case, with the result that the market price, $a/4$ (51), is slightly lower than in the Cournot case $a/3$ (68). The results of the four possibilities considered thus far are summarized in Table 11.1.

The Stackelberg model represents a clear improvement on the Cournot and Bertrand models in that it allows at least one of the firms to behave strategically. But why should only one firm behave in this fashion? If firm 1 can make strategic use of its rival's reaction function, why can't firm 2 do likewise? Suppose, in fact, that both firms try to be Stackelberg leaders. Each will then ignore its own reaction function and produce $a/2b$ (51 units), with the result that total industry output and price will be a/b (102) and 0, respectively, the same as in the Bertrand model. From the perspective of consumers, of course this is a very desirable outcome. But for the owners of the firms, universal strategic behaviour leads to the worst possible outcome.

Price rigidity

Implicit collusion tends to be fragile, and therefore oligopolistic firms have a strong desire for price stability. This is why price rigidity sometimes characterizes oligopolistic industries, even if costs and demand change. For example, if costs fall or market demand declines, they are reluctant to lower prices in fear of their

Figure 11.10 Comparing equilibrium price and quantity

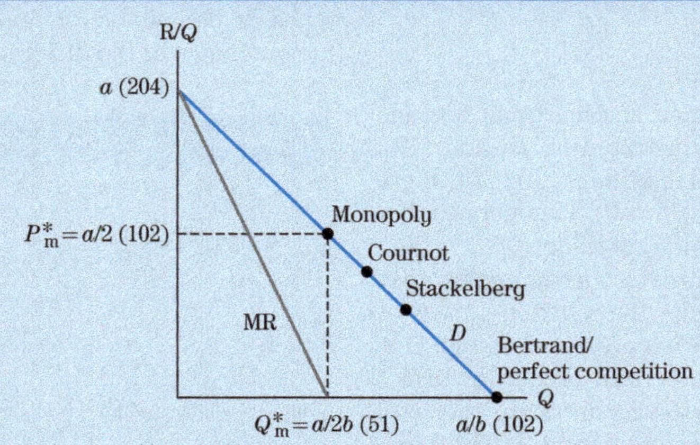

The monopolist would maximize profit where marginal revenue equals zero, since there are no marginal production costs. The equilibrium price will be higher, and the equilibrium quantity lower, than in the Cournot case.

[3] As a fraction of the output for a perfectly competitive industry, industry output under a Cournot duopoly is $N/(N + 1)$ with N firms. As the number of firms, N, becomes large, the Cournot industry output (and therefore price and profit) approaches that of a perfectly competitive industry. In this sense, Cournot duopoly is truly between monopoly and perfect competition.

[4] If firms choose capacity and then price, the outcome matches the Cournot equilibrium. See David Kreps and Jose Scheinkman, 'Quantity precommitment and Bertrand competition yield Cournot outcomes', *Bell Journal of Economics*, 1983, vol. 14, pp. 326–337.

Table 11.1 Comparison of oligopoly models

Model	Industry output, Q	Market price, P	Industry profit, Π
Shared monopoly	$Q_m = a/(2b) = 51$	$P_m = a/(2) = 102$	$\Pi_m = a^2/(4b) = 5202$
Cournot	$(4/3)Q_m = 68$	$(2/3)P_m = 68$	$(8/9)\ \Pi_m\ 4624$
Stackelberg	$(3/2)Q_m = 76.5$	$(1/2)P_m = 51$	$(3/4)\ \Pi_m\ 3901.5$
Bertrand	$2Q_m = 102$	0	0
Perfect competition	$2Q_m = 102$	0	0

All four models assume a market demand curve of $P = a - bQ$ and marginal cost equal to zero. (Of course, if marginal cost is not zero, the entries will all be different from those shown.) Numeric values are given for the function $P = 204 - 2Q$.

competitors interpreting that action as the beginning of a price war. In the same fashion, if costs or demand increase they may not increase their prices because they are afraid that their competitors will not follow suit.

Price rigidity is the basis of the kinked demand curve model that is illustrated in Fig. 11.11. According to this model, each firm faces a demand curve that is kinked at the prevailing price P^*. For prices above P^*, the firm's demand curve is very elastic because the firm believes that, if it raises its price above P^*, its competitors will not follow suit. This means that the firm will lose some of its market share in the process. However, if it lowers its price, the other firms will follow because they do not want to lose part of their own market share. Sales will thus increase only to the extent that a lower market price increases total market demand. A firm's demand curve below a price of P^* is thus less elastic than above P^*.

Because the firm's demand curve is kinked, the marginal revenue curve is discontinuous. For

Figure 11.11 The kinked demand curve

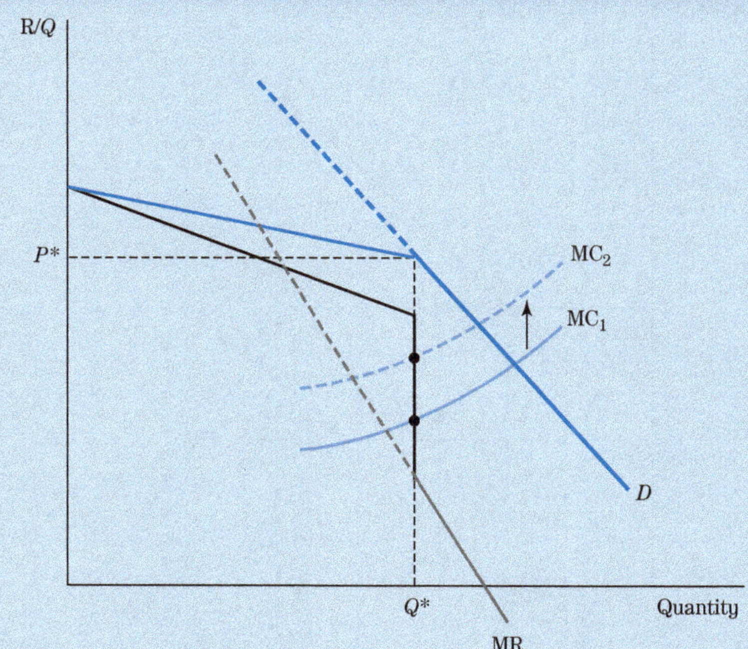

A firm believes that, if it raises its price above P^*, other firms will not follow suit and it will lose much of its sales. If it lowers its price, other firms will follow. The result is that the demand curve is kinked at a price of P^* and marginal revenue is a discontinuous curve at that point. Marginal cost can thus increase from MC_1 to MC_2, while production remains unchanged at Q^* and price remains at P^*.

the price above P^*, the marginal revenue curve is double the slope of the elastic part of the demand curve. For a price below P^*, it is double the slope of the more inelastic part of the demand curve. As illustrated in Fig. 11.11, the firm's marginal cost can increase from MC_1 to MC_2 but still equal marginal revenue at the same quantity, and therefore price remains unchanged. Although this explanation intuitively makes sense, nothing is said about how the firms arrived at the original price of P^* rather than another price. This is thus only a useful *description* of price rigidity, not an explanation of it.

Price setting by a dominant firm

In some oligopolistic markets one large firm has the major share of total sales while the other smaller firms supply the remainder of the market. The large firm can then act as the dominant firm, setting a price that will maximize its profit, while the other firms sell the rest of the demand of that market at the same price. The price of the dominant firm is taken as given, and the other firms set their production accordingly.

In Fig. 11.12 the market demand curve is portrayed by D_M and the supply curve of all the small firms (aggregate of their MC curves) by S_S. The dominant firm must determine its demand curve (D_D) – the difference between the market demand curve and the supply curve of the smaller firms. This is a crucial aspect to understand, otherwise you will struggle to follow the rest of the explanation. At every price, the dominant firm's demand is equal to the market demand minus what all the other smaller firms supply. For example, at price P_1 the small firm's supply is exactly equal to market demand, and the dominant firm will sell nothing at this price. In other words, its demand will be zero. At price P_2, the small firms supply nothing. The dominant firm will thus supply the whole market and its demand curve will be equal to the market demand curve. For prices between P_1 and P_2, the dominant firm faces the demand curve D_D – the difference between market demand (D_M) and what the smaller firms supply (S_S).

The marginal revenue of the dominant firm, MR_D, intersects the marginal cost of the firm, MC_D, at a quantity Q_D. To maximize its profit, the dominant firm should ask a price of P^*. At that price

Figure 11.12 Price setting by a dominant firm

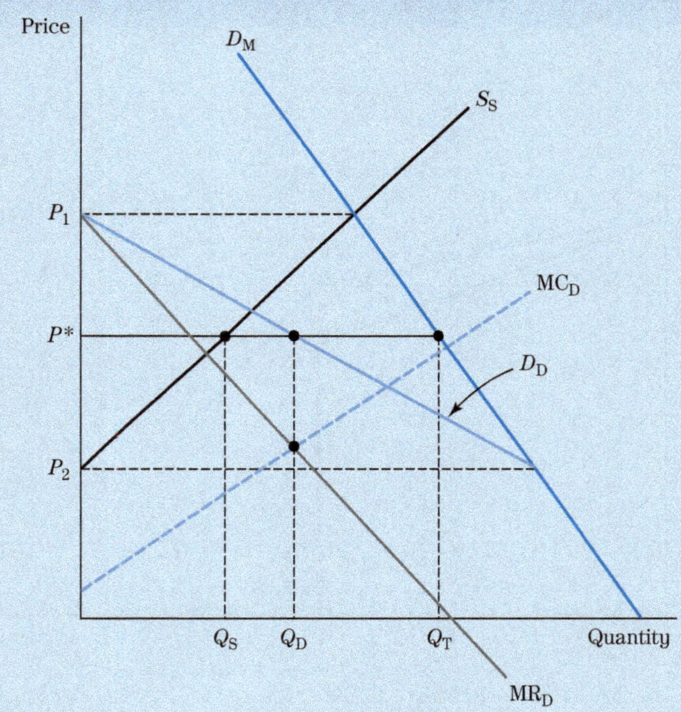

The dominant firm sets the price, and the other firms sell all they can at that price. The dominant firm's demand curve, D_D, is the difference between market demand, D_M, and the supply of all the other small firms, S_S. The dominant firm produces Q_D where its marginal revenue, MR_D, equals its marginal cost, MC_D. The corresponding price is P^*, the small firms sell Q_S and total sales are Q_T.

the small firms will supply Q_S units: thus the total quantity sold is $Q_T = Q_D + Q_S$.

The OPEC oil cartel

Producers in a cartel explicitly agree to co-operate in setting prices and output levels. Only rarely do all producers of a good combine to form a cartel. However, if enough producers adhere to the cartel agreement, and demand is sufficiently inelastic, the cartel may drive prices well above competitive levels. The OPEC cartel is a good example of an international agreement among oil-producing countries that has succeeded in raising world oil prices well above competitive levels.

In Fig. 11.13 the world demand for crude oil is given by D_T, and S_c is the competitive (non-OPEC) supply of oil. The demand for OPEC oil is D_{OPEC}, and is the difference between competitive supply and total demand. MR_{OPEC} is the marginal revenue of the OPEC cartel and MC_{OPEC} is the marginal cost: as you can see, the cost structure of the oil cartel is much lower than that of the non-OPEC producers. The OPEC cartel will maximize its profit by selling Q_{OPEC} (where $MR_{OPEC} = MC_{OPEC}$) at a price of P^*. At that price, the competitive supply will be Q_c.

What would have happened if the oil-producing exporting countries did not form a cartel and instead produced competitively? Price would then equal marginal cost, where D_{OPEC} equals MC_{OPEC}. The price P_c is much lower than the cartel price of P^*. Total demand and non-OPEC supply are inelastic, with the result that the demand for OPEC oil is also fairly inelastic. Therefore the cartel has substantial monopoly power, and has used that power to drive prices well above competitive levels. For example, OPEC's manipulation of oil supply to artificially low levels caused the price of oil price to rise above \$160 per barrel in 2008. However, after the world economy entered a recession at the end of 2008, the oil price dropped to below \$45 per barrel; as the economy recovered, it slowly rose to reach about \$80 a barrel by the end of 2010. Although the cartel has substantial monopoly power, it is thus clearly not free to set prices without taking into consideration what happens in the world economy. By 2011 the price had risen to about \$110 per barrel and since then has fluctuated between \$85 and \$110 per barrel. Clearly, the world has become more price sensitive and increasing

Figure 11.13 The OPEC oil cartel

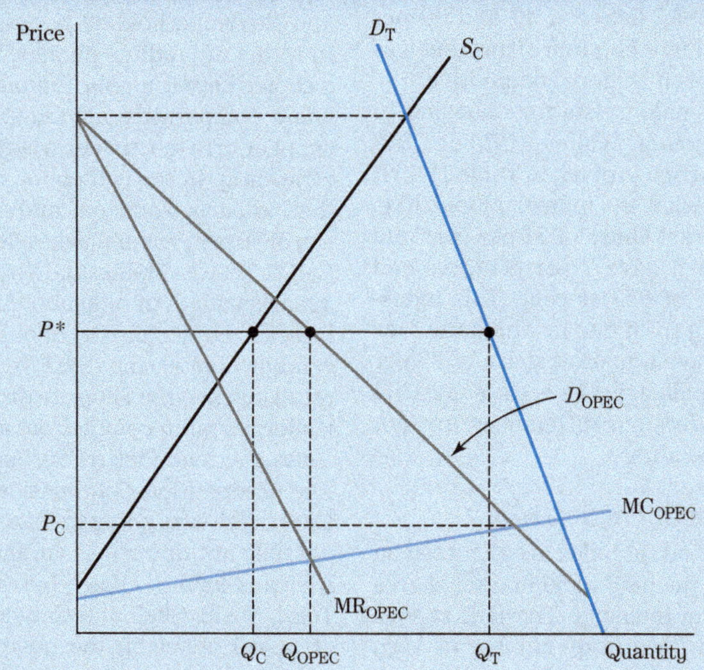

D_T is world demand for oil, S_c is competitive (non-OPEC) supply and D_{OPEC} is the difference between the two. OPEC's maximizing quantity Q_{OPEC} is where MR_{OPEC} equals MC_{OPEC} and then sells at a price P^*. If OPEC producers did not form a cartel, the price would be P_C, where OPEC's demand and marginal cost intersect.

research into alternative energy sources means it will become even more so.

Concentration indexes

We have covered the situation of perfect competition in which there are many firms, then discussed monopoly in which there is only one firm and, in this chapter, considered a market structure in which there are only a few firms in an industry. In an attempt to quantify whether an industry relates more to perfect competition than to monopoly, we devised concentration ratios. Market concentration is a function of the number of firms in a market and their respective market shares. Market share can be measured in terms of revenue, sales output or assets.

Concentration ratio (CR)

A concentration ratio is the percentage of the industry output produced by a specified number of the largest firms. The concentration ratio for n firms is calculated by simply adding up the market shares of these n firms. The commonly used four-firm concentration ratio, or CR4, is the total market share held by the four biggest firms in the industry. A large CR4 value means the industry is very concentrated, while a low CR4 value means it is a more competitive industry. As a rule of thumb, a CR4 value of more than 90 per cent means the industry is a monopoly, between 40 and 90 per cent means it is dominated by four firms and less than 40 per cent means it is more competitive.

No scientific rationale exists for choosing to work with a CR4, however. Why not CR5 or CR6? (The CR5 for South Africa is given in Table 11.6.) It also does not tell us what the industry looks like. If one firm has a market share of 71 per cent and three other firms each have 7 per cent, we end up with a CR4 value of 92 per cent. This industry may differ greatly from one in which the four biggest firms each have a market share of 23 per cent. However, both industries have the same CR4 values and their underlying differences are not picked up by the CR4 value.

Hirschman–Herfindahl Index (HHI)

The Hirschman–Herfindahl Index is calculated by adding the square of the individual market shares of all the firms in the industry. The HHI ranges from 0 in a market with a large number of very small firms, to 10 000 in the case of a pure monopoly (100^2). Normally, an HHI between 0 and 1000 is regarded as an industry with low concentration. Generally speaking, a concentration value of between 0 and 40 per cent corresponds to this HHI value. An HHI value of 1000 to 1800 is regarded as an industry of medium concentration. This level corresponds to concentration values of between 40 and 80 per cent. An HHI of 1800 to 10 000 is a highly concentrated industry. Most industries in South Africa fall within this category. These values correspond to concentration ratios of between 80 and 100 per cent.

The HHI has the advantage that it reflects the distribution of the market shares of the largest firms as well as the composition of the market outside these biggest firms. The HHI gives proportionally greater weight to the market shares of the larger firms. Assume one market in which the largest firm has 71 per cent of market share and three others each have 7 per cent, while in another market four firms each have 23 per cent of market share. Assume for simplicity that in both cases the remaining 8 per cent is divided between two firms with 4 per cent each. In the first case, the HHI gives a value of 5220, but in the second case only 2148. The inequality in firm size gives rise to a larger HHI value.

The South African experience

South Africa's economy is characterized by a couple of oligopolistic industries. In the banking sector the four largest banks, Absa, Standard, FNB and Nedbank, hold 89 per cent of retail deposits. In terms of landline phones, South Africans have a choice between only Telkom and Neotel; Telkom has a comparative advantage as the established supplier, irrespective of whether or not it operates efficiently. In the cell phone market, the giants in the industry, Vodacom and MTN, controlled just shy of 80 per cent of market share in 2014. Although Cell C, Telkom Mobile and Virgin Mobile controlled a market share of only about 20 per cent, they had increased that share by about 25 per cent (or 5 percentage points) since 2011. In the R300 billion food retail market, the Shoprite group is the undisputed leader; its main competitors are Massmart and, to a lesser extent, Pick n Pay, Spar and Woolies Food. The Competition Commission announced in June 2009 that it was going to investigate this sector for possible unfair business practices. For fuel, South Africans have a choice between only BP, Engen, Total, Sasol, Shell and Caltex. However, the price of petrol is set by the government and individual petrol stations have to adhere to it. They *are* allowed to set their own price for diesel. However, we see very little competition between the different garages selling diesel. The cement industry is also heavily concentrated. Four companies – PPC Cement, Lafarge (Pty) Ltd, Alpha (Pty) Ltd and Natal Portland Cement – dominate the cement industry in South Africa. PPC Cement is the largest supplier, with at least 35 per cent market share. Natal Portland Cement supplies more than 65 per cent of the market in Natal. Ash Resources and Slagment are the only other two suppliers of note in this industry.

Table 11.2 shows the C5% Concentration Index for the South African manufacturing industry. The C5% refers to the cumulative percentage of output attributable to the five biggest firms in an industry. From the table it is clear that many industries are dominated by a few firms. The other interesting trend is that, although the number of firms in all industries has increased substantially, the C5% Concentration Index over time did not decrease

Table 11.2 C5% Concentration Index for South African manufacturing industry, 1976 and 2001

Sector	Number of firms		C5% Index	
	1976	2001	1976	2001
Food and food products	76	134	65.29	65.93
Beverages	12	21	55.64	76.27
Textiles	26	51	52.29	36.00
Clothing, except footwear	60	75	46.75	34.18
Leather and leather products	8	12	37.17	27.69
Footwear	6	16	36.73	39.99
Wood, and wood and cork products	32	67	51.35	38.45
Paper and paper products	8	30	53.36	78.13
Printing, publishing and allied industries	56	83	60.99	48.90
Basic chemicals	7	23	69.55	68.55
Rubber products	22	64	55.97	40.33
Plastic products	3	14	36.55	30.22
Glass and glass products	16	58	53.46	69.74
Other non-metals	1	13	69.60	66.07
Basic iron and steel industries	45	56	73.48	76.00
Non-ferrous metal basic industries	6	30	47.60	70.60
Metal products, except machinery and equipment	4	45	58.48	47.49
Machinery, except electrical	119	225	56.14	38.14
Electrical machinery apparatus	54	248	60.77	51.60
Motor vehicles, parts and accessories	29	89	79.42	78.87
Transport equipment	33	120	68.01	58.99
Furniture	37	67	53.39	56.68
Other manufacturing industries	7	30	53.15	50.66
Average	**29**	**68**	**56.31**	**54.34**
Average weighted by output			**60.81**	**61.09**

Source: Johannes Fedderke and Witness Simbanegavi, *South African Manufacturing Industry Structure and its Implications for Competition Policy*, ERSA Working Paper 111, 2008.

very much, and in certain sectors even went up. More recent data for South Africa was unobtainable; indeed, recent reports actually referred back to this table. Clearly, data problems make it very difficult to update these estimates.

Monopolistic competition

Monopolistic competition, a market structure that is close to perfect competition, occurs if many firms serve a market with free entry and exit but one firm's products are not perfect substitutes for the products of other firms. The degree of substitutability between products then determines how closely the industry resembles perfect competition. Firms compete by selling differentiated products that are close substitutes. There is free entry and exit, so new firms can enter the market relatively easily with their own brands, or existing firms can leave the industry easily if their products become unprofitable. The important detail to bear in mind here is that product homogeneity is no longer assumed because we now investigate a market in which products are differentiated.

The Chamberlin model

The traditional economic model of monopolistic competition was developed independently during the 1930s by Edward Chamberlin and Joan Robinson. It begins with the assumption of a clearly defined 'industry group', which consists of a large number of producers of products that are close, but imperfect, substitutes for one another. The market for men's clothing provides a convenient illustration. Clothes made by Givenchy serve essentially the same purpose as those made by Supreme, Woolrich Woolen Mills, Maiden Noir or Adam Kimmel. And yet, for many consumers, it is hardly a matter of indifference which brand they buy. A second assumption is that the number of firms in the specific industry is so large that each firm expects that its actions will go unnoticed by its rivals. The third assumption is that demand and cost curves are the same for all firms in the industry. This is indeed a rather restrictive assumption because you would expect demand and cost curves to be dissimilar if products are dissimilar.

Two important implications follow from these assumptions about industry structure. The first is that, because the products are viewed as close substitutes, each firm will confront a downward-sloping demand schedule. Someone who has a particular liking for Adam Kimmel shirts would be willing to pay more for one than for a shirt made by some other manufacturer. But let Adam Kimmel raise its price sufficiently and even these buyers will eventually switch to another brand. The second implication, which follows from the assumption of a large number of independent firms, is that each firm will act as if its own price and quantity decisions have no effect on the behaviour of other firms in the industry. And because the products are close substitutes, this in turn means that each firm perceives its demand schedule as being highly elastic.

A fundamental feature of the Chamberlin model is the perfect symmetry of the position of all firms in the industry. In metaphorical terms, the Chamberlinian firm may be thought of as one of many fishing boats, each of which has several fishing lines in the water. If any one boat were to set its hooks with a more alluring bait while others used the same bait as before, the effect would be for the innovator to increase its share of the total catch by a substantial margin. After all, its lines have become more attractive not only in absolute terms, but also relative to the lines of other boats. Because the situation is perfectly symmetrical, however, if it makes sense for one boat to use more attractive bait, so it will for others. Yet when all use better bait, the innovator's lines are no more attractive in relative terms than before. Accordingly, the addition to its total catch will be much smaller than if others had held to their original behaviour.

The analogy between the fishing example and pricing behaviour by the Chamberlinian monopolistically competitive firm is complete. In contemplating the demand for its own product, the firm assumes that its competitors do not respond in any way to its price and quantity decisions. Like the operators of the fishing boats, the firm is correct in assuming that a change in its own behaviour will not *cause* others to change theirs. Yet the symmetry between firms ensures that, if it makes sense for one firm to alter its price, it will make sense for all others to do likewise.

The existence of differentiated products in the South African market is vast indeed. For example, Apple, Samsung, Blackberry, Nokia, LG and Motorola mobile phones are available, all of which do basically the same things; each, however, has some unique features. The same is true for cameras (Canon, Nikon, Sony, Panasonic and FujuFilm), laptops (Hewlett-Packard, Acer, Dell, AppleMac and Sony) and GPSs (Garmin, TomTom, Motorola and GlobalSat). And so the list go on.

The result is that the firm really confronts two different demand curves – one that describes what

Figure 11.14 The monopolistic competitor's two demand curves

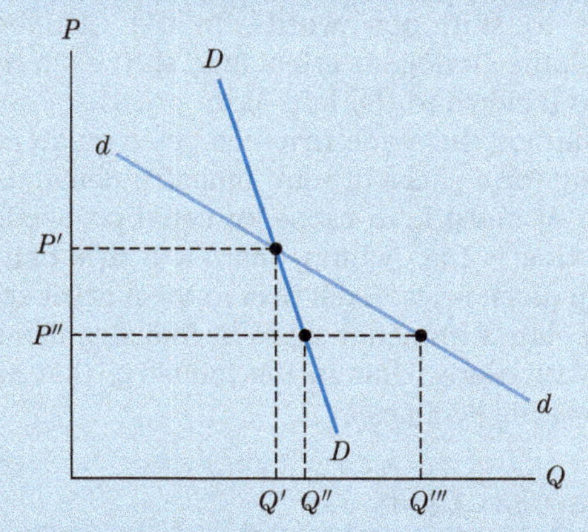

The demand facing any one firm will be more elastic if others hold prices constant (*dd*) than if all firms vary prices in unison (*DD*).

will happen when it alone changes its price, and a second that describes what will happen when all prices change in unison. Thus, for example, the curve *dd* in Fig. 11.14 represents the demand curve facing the Chamberlinian firm if it alone varies its price; the curve *DD* is the demand curve when all firms change prices together. In an initial situation in which all firms charge P', each will sell Q'. If only one firm lowers its price to P'', it will sell Q'''. But if others match its price cut, each will sell only Q''. This is closely related to the kinked demand curve concept that was discussed under the price rigidity of the oligopoly.

It is important to stress that individual firms need not fail to realize that the prices of similarly situated firms tend to move together. On the contrary, each firm may be perfectly aware of that. But it also realizes that its own price movements are not what *cause* other firms to change their behaviour. When it is thinking about the consequences of a price move, therefore, it is forced to think in terms of movements along *dd*, not along the demand curve that describes what happens when all prices change in unison (*DD*). The issue is closely related to that of confronting participants in the prisoners' dilemma. Each person may know that it is rational for the other person to defect, and may even expect him to do so. But each person also knows that his own behaviour will not affect what the other person does.

Chamberlinian equilibrium in the short run

For illustrative purposes, let us consider the monopolistically competitive firm whose demand (the *dd* curve), marginal revenue, average total cost and short-run marginal cost curves are portrayed in Fig. 11.15. Following precisely the same argument we employed in the case of the pure monopoly, we can easily show that the short-run profit-maximizing quantity is Q^*, the one for which the marginal revenue curve intersects the short-run marginal

Figure 11.15 Short-run equilibrium for the Chamberlinian firm

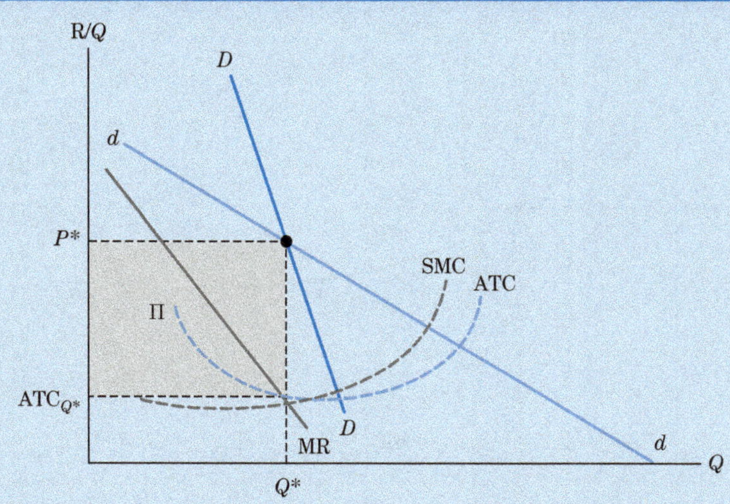

The Chamberlinian monopolistically competitive firm maximizes economic profit in the short run by equating marginal revenue and short-run marginal cost. Economic profit is Π, the area of the shaded rectangle.

cost curve. The profit-maximizing price is P^*, the value that corresponds to Q^* on the demand curve *dd*. This is closely related to the monopoly solution because the Chamberlinian firm is the only seller of a specific brand name, and thus is a monopolist in selling that specific brand of a product.

In Fig. 11.15, note also that the demand curve *DD* intersects the demand curve *dd* at the profit-maximizing price, P^*. This is yet another consequence of the fundamental symmetry that exists within Chamberlinian firms. The *DD* curve, recall, is the locus along which each firm's quantity would move with price if the prices of all firms moved in unison. The *dd* curve, by contrast, is the locus along which the firm's quantity will move with price when the prices of all other firms are fixed. Because the situation confronting each firm is the same, if P^* is the profit-maximizing price for one, it must also be for the rest. The price level at which other firms' prices are fixed along *dd* is thus P^*, which implies that, at P^* on *dd*, the price of *every* firm will be P^*. And this is why *dd* intersects *DD* at P^*.

Chamberlinian equilibrium in the long run

As in the perfectly competitive case, the fact that there are economic profits in the short run will have the effect of luring additional firms into the monopolistically competitive industry. What is the effect of the entry of these firms? In the competitive case, we saw that it was to shift the industry supply curve rightwards, causing a reduction in the short-run equilibrium price. Put another way, the effect of entry in the perfectly competitive model is to cause each firm's horizontal demand curve to shift downwards. In the Chamberlin model, the analogous effect is to shift each firm's demand curve to the left. More precisely, on the assumption that each firm competes on an equal footing for a share of total industry demand, the effect of entry is to cause an equal proportional reduction in the quantity that each firm can sell at any given price. Each firm in the market essentially claims an equal share of industry demand, and with more firms in the industry, that share necessarily declines.

Exercise 11.4

Each of 20 firms in a Chamberlinian monopolistically competitive industry faces a *dd* curve given by $P = 10 - 0.001Q$. What will each firm's *dd* curve be following the entry of five new firms?

Following the leftward shift in demand caused by entry, each firm has the opportunity to readjust the size of its capital stock and choose its new profit-maximizing level of output. If extra-normal profit still remains, entry will continue.

The long-run equilibrium position is one in which the demand curve *dd* has shifted left to the point where it is tangent to the long-run average cost curve (and tangent as well to the associated short-run average cost curve). Note in Fig. 11.16

Figure 11.16 Long-run equilibrium in the Chamberlin model

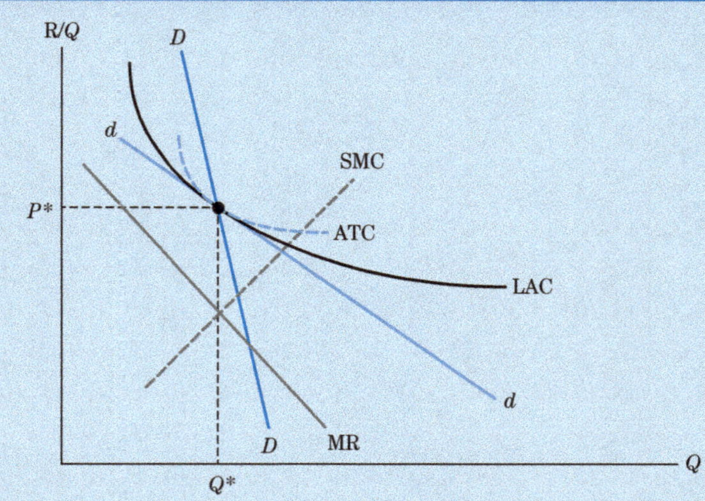

Entry occurs, shifting *dd* leftwards until it becomes tangent to the LAC curve. The firm produces Q^*, sells for P^* and earns zero economic profit.

that Q^*, the profit-maximizing level of output by the MR = MC criterion, is exactly the same as the output level for which the *dd* curve is tangent to the long-run and short-run average cost curves. This is no mere coincidence. We can argue independently of the MR = MC condition that the tangency point must be the maximum-profit point. At that point the firm earns zero economic profit, while at any other output level average cost would exceed average revenue, which means that economic profit would be negative.

Note again in Fig. 11.16 that the demand curve *DD* intersects *dd* at the equilibrium price P^* for the reasons discussed earlier. If all firms raised price from P^*, each would move upwards along *DD*, and each would earn an economic profit. But in the absence of a binding collusive agreement, it would not be in the interest of any firm to maintain its price above P^*, because at any such price its marginal revenue (along the MR curve associated with *dd*) would exceed its marginal cost. At any price above P^*, it could earn higher profits by cutting price and selling more output. The only stable outcome is the tangency point shown in Fig. 11.16. In the long run, all firms will make zero economic profit because new firms will enter as long as certain firms still make economic profit; the individual demand curve of all firms will shift to the left until a situation emerges whereby all firms are making only normal profit and thus zero economic profit.

Perfect competition versus Chamberlinian monopolistic competition

There are several obvious points of comparison between the long-run equilibrium positions of perfect competition and Chamberlinian monopolistic competition. This is clearly illustrated in Fig. 11.17. First, competition meets the test of allocative efficiency, whereas monopolistic competition does not. Under competition, price (P_c) is exactly equal to long-run marginal cost, which means that there are no unexploited possibilities for mutual gain through exchange. Under monopolistic competition, by contrast, price (P_{MC}) will exceed marginal cost, even in the long run. This means that there will be people in society who value an additional unit of output more highly than the value of the resources required to produce it. If monopolistic competitors could come up with a way to cut price to such buyers without cutting price on existing sales, they would gladly do so, making everyone better off in the process. As we saw in the case of the monopolist, such selective price cutting is sometimes possible. But it is inherently imperfect, and on this account monopolistic competition is destined to fall short of perfect competition on the narrow efficiency standard. There is thus a deadweight loss equal to the shaded triangle in Fig. 11.17(b).

Figure 11.17 Monopolistic competition equilibrium and perfectly competitive equilibrium

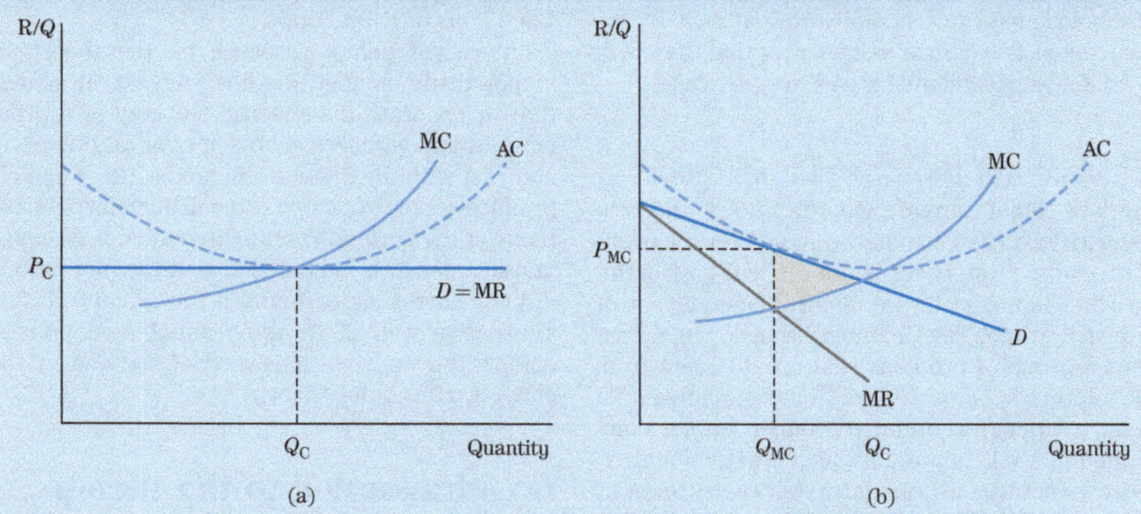

Under perfect competition (panel a) price equals marginal cost, but under monopolistic competition (panel b) price exceeds marginal cost. There is thus a deadweight loss equal to the shaded area in panel b. Under both market formats economic profits are zero, but with monopolistic competition the zero-profit point is to the left of the point of minimum average cost.

Some economists also argue that monopolistic competition is less efficient than perfect competition because in the former case firms do not produce at the minimum points of their long-run average cost (LAC) curves (Q_{MC} versus Q_C in Fig. 11.17). This is not a very telling comparison, however, because other aspects of the two cases are so different. The relevant question is whether people who currently buy from monopolistic competitors would be happier if all products were exactly the same and cost a little less. This is not an easy question, and, lacking an answer to it, we cannot conclude that monopolistic competition is inefficient merely because firms don't produce at the minimum points of their LAC curves.

There is at least one important sense in which the Chamberlin model is strikingly more realistic than the competitive model. In the perfectly competitive case, recall, price and marginal cost are the same in equilibrium. This implies that the firm should react with indifference to an opportunity to fill a new order at the current market price. In the monopolistically competitive case, by contrast, price exceeds marginal cost, which implies that the firm should greet a new order at the current market price with enthusiasm. Periods of temporary shortages apart, we know of very few instances of the former reaction. Almost every businessperson who ever lived is delighted to accept new orders at the current market price, especially if they are making at least normal profits.

In terms of long-run profitability, finally, the equilibrium positions of both the perfect competitor and the Chamberlinian monopolistic competitor are precisely the same. Freedom of entry in each case holds long-run economic profit at zero. By the same token, freedom of exit ensures that there will be no long-run economic losses in either case.

Criticisms of the Chamberlin model

The late Nobel laureate George Stigler and others criticized the Chamberlin model on a variety of grounds. First, there is the difficulty of defining what is meant by the amorphous concept of 'industry group'. The Chamberlinian concept envisions a group of products that are different from one another in some unspecified way, yet equally likely to appeal to any given buyer. Stigler complained that it is impossible, as a practical matter, to draw operational boundaries between groups of products in this fashion. Viewed from one perspective, a product like Coca-Cola is unique unto itself. (Thus buyers reacted angrily when Coke made a slight alteration in its traditional formula, which lead the company to reintroduce 'Coke Classic'.) Viewed slightly differently, however, Coke is a substitute for Pepsi, which can be a substitute for milk, which in turn is a substitute for ice cream. But ice cream is a substitute for chocolate cake, which certainly doesn't *seem* like a substitute for Coca-Cola. Pushed to its logical extreme, Stigler argued, the Chamberlinian product group quickly expands to include virtually every consumer product in the economy.

From a methodological perspective, Stigler joined Milton Friedman in arguing that a theory should be judged not by the descriptive accuracy of its assumptions, but by its ability to predict responses to changes in the economic environment. (See Chapter 1.) Stigler believed that Chamberlin's theory significantly complicates the theory of perfect competition, without appreciably altering its most important predictions. With respect to many specific issues, this charge has clear merit. Both theories, for example, predict that economic profit will attract entry, which will both reduce prices and eliminate profit in the long run.

But the most telling criticism of the Chamberlin model is not that it too closely resembles the competitive model, but that in at least one very important respect it does not depart sufficiently from it. The problem lies with the critical assumption that each firm has an equal chance to attract any of the buyers in an industry. In some cases this description is reasonably accurate, but in many other instances it clearly falls short. In the breakfast cereal industry, for example, the person who buys ProNutro might consider switching to Weet-Bix or Instant Oats, but wouldn't dream of switching to Coco Pops or Fruit Loops.

In recent years, research on the theory of monopolistic competition has focused on models that incorporate the specific features of a product that make buyers choose it over all others. In contrast with the Chamberlin model, these models produce conclusions that often differ sharply from those of the perfectly competitive model. Because market research indicated that most institutions did not have time or found it too advanced, this alternative way of thinking about monopolistic competition will be discussed at the end of the chapter, after game theory.

An introduction to the theory of games

In this section the collusive behaviour of oligopolists will be explained with the aid of game theory.

Let's start the discussion with a simple example. At the market equilibrium price, worldwide demand for coffee is inelastic with respect to price. Thus, when a frost or tornado destroys half the crop in a country that exports a large share of the world's coffee, the price of coffee may rise so much that local farmers actually earn higher profits than if there had been no frost or tornado. If coffee growers could earn more by selling less coffee, why do they need to wait for a frost to kill half their crop? Why not just plant less coffee in the first place?

The answer, of course, is that while it might be in the interests of farmers as a whole to curtail production, no individual farmer would ever have an incentive to do so. Each individual farmer, after all, does best if all others *except* him cut back. In that way he gets to sell the same quantity as before, but now at the new, higher price. In a competitive industry such as coffee farming, the existence of many small independent producers makes it difficult to organize conspiracies to curtail output.

Such collusion might seem less difficult to accomplish among oligopolists – that is, in industries served by only a small number of firms. But although successful collusion sometimes does work to the benefit of firms in such industries, it usually turns out to be surprisingly difficult to sustain. Indeed, a recurring theme in the economics of oligopoly is that what pays each firm to do individually often turns out to be harmful to the industry taken as a whole. Another problem that we shall deal with later in the chapter is the issue of honesty in sticking to the agreement if one of the firms knows it can cheat while the others do not know it, and in the process improve its own situation.

The basic problem confronting colluding oligopolists can be illustrated using the data given in Table 11.3. Let us assume that two prisoners are held in separate cells for a serious crime that they did in fact commit. The prosecutor, however, has only enough hard evidence to convict them of a minor offence, for which the penalty is, say, a year in jail. Each prisoner is told that if one confesses while the other remains silent, the confessor will go scot-free while the other spends 20 years in prison. If both confess, they will get an intermediate sentence of, say, five years. These pay-offs are summarized in Table 11.3. The two prisoners are not allowed to communicate with one another.

Table 11.3 The prisoners' dilemma

		Prisoner Y	
		Confess	**Remain silent**
Prisoner X	**Confess**	5 years for Y 5 years for X	20 years for Y 0 years for X
	Remain silent	0 years for Y 20 years for X	1 year for Y 1 year for X

The dominant strategy for each prisoner is to confess. Yet when each confesses, each does worse than if each had remained silent.

Situations like the prisoners' dilemma may be analysed using the mathematical theory of games, initially developed by John von Neumann and Oskar Morgenstern during the 1940s.[5] This theory begins by describing the three elements common to all games:

- the players
- the list of possible strategies
- the pay-offs that correspond to each combination of strategies

In Table 11.3 the two players in the game are prisoner X and prisoner Y. Each player has two strategies: confess or remain silent. The pay-offs to each combination of strategies are the sentences they receive, which are summarized in the *pay-off matrix* shown in Table 11.3.

> **Dominant strategy** The strategy in a game that produces better results, irrespective of the strategy chosen by one's opponent.

Some games, like the prisoners' dilemma, have a **dominant strategy**, which means a strategy that produces better results no matter what strategy the opposing player follows. The dominant strategy in the prisoners' dilemma is to confess. No matter what Y does, X gets a lighter sentence by speaking out: if Y too confesses, X gets 5 years instead of 20; and if Y remains silent, X goes free instead of spending a year in jail. The pay-offs are perfectly symmetric, so Y also does better to confess, no matter what X does. The difficulty is that, when each behaves in a self-interested way, both do worse than if each had shown restraint. Thus, when both confess, they get 5 years, instead

[5] See John von Neumann and Oskar Morgenstern, *Theory of games and economic behavior*, 3rd edn, Princeton University Press, Princeton, NJ, 1953.

of the 1 year they could have got by remaining silent.

To illustrate the analogy between the prisoners' dilemma and the problem confronting oligopolists who are trying to collude, let us consider two firms that are the sole providers of mineral water in a given market, say, Valpré and Sonaqua. Suppose the market demand curve takes the specific form $P = 20 - Q$, and that each firm can produce mineral water from its own spring at zero marginal cost. Suppose the two firms are considering a collusive agreement under which each produces half the monopoly output and offers it for sale at the monopoly price. For the specific demand curve assumed, the monopoly quantity (that is, the quantity for which MR = MC = 0) is 10, and the monopoly price is also 10. If the firms enter into and abide by this agreement, each will sell 5 units at a price of 10, giving each an economic profit of 50. According to a strict profit criterion, there is no possibility for each firm to do better than that.

Yet this does not ensure that each firm will abide by the agreement. Note that the pay-off to each firm depends on the combination of behaviours they choose. Each firm has two options: to abide by the agreement or to defect. For the sake of discussion, suppose that to defect means to cut price by 1 unit, from 10 to 9. If one firm abides by the agreement while the other defects, what will happen? Since the two firms are selling identical products, the defecting firm will capture the entire market because of its lower price. Selling 11 units at a price of 9, it will earn a profit of 99; the trusting co-operator will sell no output and thus will earn zero profit.

If both firms defect, they will end up splitting the 11 units of output sold at a price of 9, and each will make an economic profit of 49.50. Since each firm has two options – (1) co-operate, by charging 10 as agreed; or (2) defect, by charging 9 – there are four possible combinations of behaviour. These combinations, and the profits that result from each, are summarized in Table 11.4.

Note in the table that it is a dominant strategy for each firm to defect. That is, each firm gets a higher pay-off by defecting, no matter which option the other firm chooses. To illustrate, consider the choice facing firm 2. It says to itself, 'Suppose firm 1 co-operates; which choice is best for me?' By co-operating when firm 1 co-operates, the firms end up in the upper-left cell of the profit matrix in Table 11.4, which means each earns 50. But if firm 2 defects, the result will be the lower-left cell, where it would end up earning 99. Now firm 2 says, 'Suppose firm 1 defects. Which choice is best for me this time?' If firm 2 co-operates, we get the upper-right cell of the profit matrix, where it earns 0. But if firm 2 defects, it earns 49.50. Thus, no matter which choice firm 1 makes, firm 2 earns higher profit by defecting.

Table 11.4 Profits deriving from co-operation and defection

		Firm 1	
		Co-operate ($P = 10$)	**Defect ($P = 9$)**
Firm 2	**Co-operate ($P = 10$)**	$\Pi_1 = 50$	$\Pi_1 = 99$
		$\Pi_2 = 50$	$\Pi_2 = 0$
	Defect ($P = 9$)	$\Pi_1 = 0$	$\Pi_1 = 49.50$
		$\Pi_2 = 99$	$\Pi_2 = 49.50$

The dominant strategy is for each firm to defect, for by so doing it earns higher profit no matter which option its rival chooses. Yet when both defect, each earns less than when each co-operates.

Using exactly parallel reasoning, defection is also a dominant strategy for firm 1. Note, however, that when each firm defects, each does worse than if each had co-operated. In this situation, behaviour that is in the interest of each individual firm adds up to a result that is not in the interest of firms generally.

As this example is set up, the firms don't do much worse when each defects than when each co-operates. But firms that find it in their interest to defect once are likely to find it in their interest to do so again. If one now charges 8 while the other remains at 9, for example, the former will earn a profit of 96, while the latter earns 0. A firm need not feel a compelling desire to outdo its rival in order for defection to be an attractive option. On the contrary, its motive may be purely self-protective, motivated by the rational fear that its rival will defect. The resulting process of competitive price-cutting will terminate only when price has plummeted all the way down to marginal cost. At that point, neither firm earns any profit at all. So the cost of failing to abide by a co-operative agreement can be high indeed.

Oligopolists compete not only along the price dimension, but also through the use of advertising. And here, too, the interests of an individual firm often conflict with the interests of firms taken as a whole, as Economic naturalist 11.1 illustrates.

Economic naturalist 11.1

Why do cigarette companies advertise 'too much'?

When a firm advertises its product, its demand increases for two reasons. First, people who never used that type of product before learn about it, leading some to buy it. In other words, the advertisement creates a want that was not there in the past. Second, other people who already consume a different brand of the same product may switch brands as a result of advertising. The first effect boosts sales for the industry as a whole. The second merely redistributes existing sales among firms.

The South African cigarette industry is one in which the most important effect of advertising is believed to be brand switching. In such industries, the decision whether to advertise often confronts individual firms with a prisoners' dilemma. Table 11.5 shows the profits accruing to a hypothetical pair of cigarette producers under the four possible combinations of their advertise/don't advertise decisions. If both firms advertise (lower-right cell), each earns a profit of only 250, as compared with a profit of 500 each if neither advertises (upper-left cell). So it is clearly better for neither firm to advertise than for both to advertise.

Yet note the incentives confronting the individual firm. Firm 1 sees that, if firm 2 doesn't advertise, it can earn higher profits by advertising (750) than by not advertising (500). Firm 1 also sees that, if firm 2 does advertise, it will again earn more by advertising (250) than by not advertising (0). It is thus a dominant strategy for firm 1 to advertise. And because the pay-offs are symmetric, it is also a dominant strategy for firm 2 to advertise. So here, too, when each firm does what is rational from its own point of view, firms as a group do worse than if they had acted in concert.

The Tobacco Products Control Act No. 83 of 1993 came into effect in 1995. From then on, including health warnings on tobacco products was compulsory, and smoking on public transport and selling cigarettes to children under the age of 16 were both prohibited. This Act was replaced by the Tobacco Control Amendment Act No. 12 of 1999, which banned advertising and promoted clean air. As a result, customers were to be guaranteed a smoke-free venue in which to eat, which meant that restaurants had to either create a smoking room or make smokers go outside. This Act was replaced by the Tobacco Products Control Amendment Bill 24 of 2006, which further regulated smoking in public places, and aimed to protect workers from exposure to pollution created by tobacco smoke. It brought the current law into compliance with the World Health Organization Framework Convention on Tobacco Control. In 2007 the Act was again amended, making it illegal to smoke in a car if a child under 12 years of age is a passenger and prohibiting anyone younger than 18 to enter an area where smoking is allowed. By June 2012 regulations relating to smoking in public places, outdoor eating or drinking areas, health facilities, schools, childcare facilities and stadiums were published for public comment, but no new legislation was passed as a result.

Banning advertising is an attempt to protect people from messages that might persuade them to consume a product proven to be hazardous to human health. Adult (age 15+) smoking rates fell by about 35 per cent, from 31 per cent in 1994 to about 20 per cent in 2013; smoking is still, however, responsible for 44 000 deaths per year. In 1999, 23.0 per cent of pupils in grades 8–10 smoked; by 2011this had fallen to only 16.9 per cent. Between 1993 and 2012 total legal, 'tax paid' cigarette consumption decreased by 39 per cent, down from 1.8 billion packs (36 billion cigarettes) in 1993 to 1.1 billion packs (22 billion cigarettes) in 2012.

The law thus seems to have at least achieved its main purpose. But it has also had an unintended effect, which was solving – at least temporarily – the prisoners' dilemma confronting South African cigarette manufacturers. In 1987 direct tobacco spending was R49 million, but by 1997 (a year before the ban on advertising was enacted) it had increased to no less than R250 million. If sponsorships of sports, arts and cultural organizations are added to this figure, total advertising expenditure amounted to R477 million in 1997. The advertising ban thus accomplished for the cigarette manufacturers what the imperatives of individual profit seeking could not – an effective way of limiting the advertising arms race.

Table 11.5 Advertising as a prisoners' dilemma

		Firm 1	
		Don't advertise	**Advertise**
Firm 2	**Don't advertise**	$\Pi_1 = 500$	$\Pi_1 = 750$
		$\Pi_2 = 500$	$\Pi_2 = 0$
	Advertise	$\Pi_1 = 0$	$\Pi_1 = 250$
		$\Pi_2 = 750$	$\Pi_2 = 250$

When advertising's main effect is brand switching, the dominant strategy is to advertise heavily (lower-right cell), even though firms as a whole would do better by not advertising (upper-left cell).

The Nash equilibrium concept

When, as in the prisoners' dilemma, both parties have a dominant strategy in a game, the equilibrium for the game occurs when each plays the dominant strategy. But there are many games in which not every player has a dominant strategy. Consider, for example, the variation on the advertising game shown in Table 11.6. No matter what firm 2 does, firm 1 does better to advertise; so advertise is the dominant strategy for firm 1. But now the same cannot be said of firm 2. If firm 1 advertises, firm 2 does best also to advertise. But if firm 1 does not advertise, firm 2 does best not to advertise. In contrast to the prisoners' dilemma, here the best strategy for firm 2 depends on the particular strategy chosen by firm 1.

Even though firm 2 does not have a dominant strategy in this game, we can say something about what is likely to happen. In particular, firm 2 is able to predict that firm 1 will advertise because that is a dominant strategy for firm 1. And since firm 2 knows this, it knows that its own best strategy is also to advertise. In this game, the lower-right cell is called a **Nash equilibrium**,[6] which is defined as a combination of strategies such that each player's strategy is the best he can choose, given the strategy chosen by the other player. Thus, at Nash equilibrium, neither player has any incentive to deviate from its current strategy. Note that, when each player follows his dominant strategy in a prisoners' dilemma, the result is a Nash equilibrium. But, as we have seen, a Nash equilibrium does not require both players to have a dominant strategy.

Nash equilibrium
The combination of strategies in a game such that neither player has any incentive to change strategies given the strategy of his opponent.

A good rule of thumb for assessing whether a particular combination of strategies constitutes a Nash equilibrium is to ask whether either player has any incentive to choose a different strategy. Does either player have an incentive to choose a different cell of the pay-off matrix in Table 11.6?

To answer this question, note first that each player has the option of moving to only one other cell in the table. Firm 2, for example, can choose only the top row or the bottom row, and so it cannot move to a cell in a different column. If it wants to move from the upper-left cell, its only option is the lower-left cell. But since its profit (0) would be lower there than in the upper-left cell (400), it would not want to make that move.

Similarly, firm 1 can choose only the left column or the right column, and so it cannot move to a cell in a different row. Starting from the upper-left cell, then, firm 1's only option would be to move to the upper-right cell. And since its profit in that cell (750) would be higher than in the upper-left cell (500), it would want to move. Thus, if we start in the upper-left cell, at least one player (firm 1) would want to move, which means that the upper-left cell cannot be a Nash equilibrium. (The same will apply to the upper-right and lower-left cells. Repeat the above procedure to convince yourself.)

In contrast, consider the lower-right cell of Table 11.6. Firm 2, which chooses only the row, can move only to the upper-right cell, which it would not want to do because its profits there (100) would be lower than in the lower-right cell (200). Similarly, firm 1, which chooses only the column, can move only to the lower-left cell, which it would not want to do because its profit there (200) would be lower than in the lower-right cell (300). And since neither firm would want to move away from the lower-right cell of Table 11.6, that combination of strategies satisfies the definition of a Nash equilibrium.

Table 11.6 A game in which firm 2 has no dominant strategy

		Firm 1	
		Don't advertise	Advertise
Firm 2	Don't advertise	$\Pi_1 = 500$	$\Pi_1 = 750$
		$\Pi_2 = 400$	$\Pi_2 = 100$
	Advertise	$\Pi_1 = 200$	$\Pi_1 = 300$
		$\Pi_2 = 0$	$\Pi_2 = 200$

Firm 1's dominant strategy is to advertise. But firm 2 has no dominant strategy. If firm 1 advertises, firm 2 does best also to advertise, but if firm 1 does not advertise, firm 2 does best not to advertise.

Exercise 11.5

Does either firm have a dominant strategy in the game depicted on page 361? Does the game have a Nash equilibrium?

[6] After John F. Nash, the American mathematician who introduced the concept in 1951. John Nash received the Nobel Prize in Economics in 1994. The film *A Beautiful Mind* about his life was released in 2002, and received four Oscars.

		Firm 1	
		High research budget	Low research budget
Firm 2	High research budget	$\Pi_1 = 200$	$\Pi_1 = 60$
		$\Pi_2 = 40$	$\Pi_2 = 100$
	Low research budget	$\Pi_1 = 0$	$\Pi_1 = 40$
		$\Pi_2 = 30$	$\Pi_2 = 80$

The maximin strategy

In the game shown in Table 11.6, we saw that, if firm 1 follows its dominant strategy by advertising, firm 2 will also do better by advertising. So if firm 2 believes that firm 1 will act rationally, firm 2's best option is to advertise. But firm 2 may not be sure that firm 1 will choose rationally. In that case, firm 2 might want at least to consider the possibility that firm 1 will choose not to advertise. In that case, if firm 2 advertises, it will earn a profit of 0, far worse than the 400 it would earn by not advertising.

When firm 2 does not have a dominant strategy of its own, and is uncertain about firm 1's choice, what should it do? The answer depends both on the likelihood it assigns to firm 1's possible choices and on how its own pay-offs are affected by those choices. Under the circumstances, it is extremely difficult to predict what firm 2 will do.

Suppose, however, that firm 2 takes an extremely cautious approach when confronted with such uncertainty. It might then choose to follow what is called the **maximin strategy**, which means choosing the option that maximizes the lowest possible value of its own pay-off. Referring again to Table 11.6, note that, if firm 2 chooses not to advertise, the lowest pay-off it can receive is 100 (which will happen if firm 1 advertises). But if firm 2 chooses to advertise, the lowest pay-off it can receive is 0 (which will happen if firm 1 chooses not to advertise). So if we know that firm 2 follows the maximin strategy in this situation, we can predict that it will choose not to advertise.

Maximin strategy Choosing the option that makes the lowest pay-off one can receive as large as possible.

Strategies for repeated play in prisoners' dilemmas

The games discussed thus far have involved only two players. But these games are easily extended to cover multiple players. In the multi-player prisoners' dilemma, for example, the two strategy choices are again co-operate and defect, and defecting is again a dominant strategy for every player. And the defining condition of the game continues to be that each player receives a higher pay-off when each co-operates than when each defects.

To say that the costs of failing to co-operate are high in prisoners' dilemmas is simply another way of saying that there are powerful financial incentives to find some way to hold collusive agreements together. What the potential participants in a collusive agreement need is some way to penalize those who defect, thereby making it in their material interests not to do so. When a prisoners' dilemma confronts parties who will interact only once, this turns out to be very difficult to achieve. But when the participants expect to interact repeatedly in the future, new possibilities emerge.

Experimental research in the 1960s identified a very simple strategy that proves remarkably effective at keeping potential defectors in check.[7] The strategy is called *tit-for-tat*, and it works as follows. The first time you interact with someone, you co-operate. In each subsequent interaction you simply do what that person did in the previous interaction. Thus, if your partner defected on your first interaction, you would then defect on your next interaction with her. If she then co-operates, your move next time will be to co-operate too.

Tit-for-tat is described as a 'nice' strategy because of the propensity of players to co-operate on the first interaction. If two tit-for-tat players interact together over a long period of time, the result will be co-operation in each and every interaction. Tit-for-tat is also a 'tough' strategy, however, because those who follow it always stand ready to punish defectors in the next interaction. Finally, it is a 'forgiving' strategy, in the sense that a player is willing to co-operate with a former defector once she shows evidence of willingness to co-operate.

University of Michigan political scientist Robert Axelrod conducted an extensive analysis of how well the tit-for-tat strategy performs against other strategies for playing the repeated

[7] See Anatol Rapoport and A. Chammah, *Prisoner's Dilemma*, University of Michigan Press, Ann Arbor, 1965.

prisoners' dilemma game.[8] In an early round of Axelrod's computer simulations, tit-for-tat was the most successful strategy, in the sense that people who followed it earned more, on average, than those using any of the other strategies tested. Axelrod then published this finding and invited experts from all over the world to try to design a better strategy. His challenge produced a host of ingenious responses. Axelrod found, however, that even these strategies, many of which had been put together for the specific purpose of defeating tit-for-tat, did not survive against it.

The success of tit-for-tat requires a reasonably stable set of players, each of whom can remember what other players have done in previous interactions. It also requires that players have a significant stake in what happens in the future, for it is only the fear of retaliation that keeps people from defecting. When these conditions are met, co-operators can identify one another and discriminate against defectors.

The conditions called for in the tit-for-tat strategy are often met in human populations. Many people do interact repeatedly, and most keep track of how others treat them. Axelrod has assembled persuasive evidence that these forces help explain how people actually behave. Perhaps the most impressive evidence supporting the tit-for-tat strategy is the behaviour of soldiers in the trenches during the First World War – a system of 'live-and-let-live'. Often, the same enemy units lay encamped opposite one another in the trenches over a period of several years. Units were often closely matched, with the result that neither side had much hope of quickly defeating the other. Their choices were to fight intensively, with both sides sustaining heavy casualties, or to exercise restraint. Troops dug in only a few hundred feet from each other would evolve an unspoken understanding. If a sniper killed a soldier on one side, the other could expect an equal retaliation. Conversely, if no one was killed for a period of time, the other side would acknowledge that this implied a 'truce' and act accordingly. A 'separate peace' was thus created between the trenches.

The conditions of interaction described by historian Tony Ashworth in his account of trench warfare closely resemble those required for the success of tit-for-tat.[9] The identities of the players

©Library of Congress/DAL

were more or less stable. Interactions between them were repeated, often several times daily, for extended periods. Each side could easily tell when the other side defected. And each side had a clear stake in keeping its future losses to a minimum.

There is little doubt that tit-for-tat often did emerge as the strategy of choice for both Allied and German fighting units in the First World War. Although strongly discouraged as a matter of official policy, restraint was sometimes conspicuously apparent. Referring to night patrol squads operating out of the trenches, Ashworth writes:

> Both British and Germans on quiet sectors assumed that should a chance face-to-face encounter occur, neither patrol would initiate aggression, but each would move to avoid the other. Each patrol gave peace to the other where aggression was not only possible, but prescribed, provided, of course, the gesture was reciprocated, for if one patrol fired so would the other.[10]

In the words of one of the participants in the conflict:

> We suddenly confronted, round some mound or excavation, a German patrol. ... We were perhaps twenty yards from one another, fully visible. I waved a weary hand, as if to say, what is the use of killing each other? The German officer seemed to understand, and both parties turned and made their way back to their own trenches.[11]

[8] Robert Axelrod, *The Evolution of Cooperation*, Basic Books, New York, 1984.

[9] Tony Ashworth, *Trench Warfare: The Live and Let Live System*, Holmes and Meier, New York, 1980 and Richard Dawkins, *Nice Guys Finish First*, BBC, 1986.

[10] Ashworth, p. 103.

[11] Herbert Read, quoted in Ashworth, p. 104.

Often, bombardments would occur only at specified times of day, and would be directed away from the most vulnerable positions. Mealtimes and hospital tents, for example, were usually tacitly off limits.

The conditions discussed by Axelrod help to explain not only when people will co-operate, but also when they are most likely to *refrain* from co-operation. For example, he notes that mutual restraint in trench warfare began to break down once the end of the war was clearly in sight.

As in warfare, so too in the world of business. Companies pay their bills on time, Axelrod suggests, not because it is the right thing to do but because they require future shipments from the same suppliers. When future interactions appear unlikely, this tendency to co-operate often breaks down: '[An] example is the case where a business is on the edge of bankruptcy and sells its accounts receivable to an outsider called a "factor".' This sale is made at a very substantial discount, because

> once a manufacturer begins to go under, even his best customers begin refusing payment for merchandise, claiming defects in quality, failure to meet specifications, tardy delivery, or what-have-you. The great enforcer of morality in commerce is the continuing relationship, the belief that one will have to do business again with this customer, or this supplier, and when a failing company loses this automatic enforcer, not even a strong-arm factor is likely to find a substitute.[12]

One additional requirement for the success of tit-for-tat is that there not be a known, fixed number of future interactions. Indeed, if players know exactly how many times they will interact, then mutual co-operation on every move cannot be a Nash equilibrium. To see why, suppose each firm knew it was going to interact with its rival for, say, exactly 1000 more times. Each would then know that the other would defect on the last interaction because there would be no possibility of being punished for doing so. But since each firm realizes that, it will also have no reason not to defect on the 999th interaction. After all, a defection will occur on the 1000th interaction, no matter what it does on the round before. The same argument can be applied, step by step, back to the first interaction, with the result that the tit-for-tat strategy completely unravels.

The unravelling problem does not arise if there is not a known, fixed number of interactions.[13] If we suppose, for example, that there is always some positive probability that a further interaction will ensue, then no interaction can ever be identified as being the last one, which means the threat of future punishment will always have at least some force. In the situations in which most firms find themselves (an exception being the bankruptcy case cited earlier), it seems plausible to assume that there will always be some probability of interaction in the future.

Is it inevitable, then, that the tit-for-tat strategy will produce widespread collusion among firms? By no means. One difficulty is that tit-for-tat's effectiveness depends on there being only two players in the game. In competitive and monopolistically competitive industries there are generally many firms, and even in oligopolies there are often several. When there are more than two firms, and one defects in this period, how do the co-operators selectively punish the defector next period? By cutting price? That will penalize everyone, not just the defector. Even if there are only two firms in an industry, the problem remains that some other firm may enter the industry. So the would-be co-operators have to worry not only about each other, but also about the entire list of firms that might decide to compete with them. Each firm may see this as a hopeless task and decide to defect now, hoping to reap at least some extra-normal profit in the short run.

We shall consider the threat of potential entry in greater detail in the sections to follow. For the moment, we may note that, as a purely empirical matter, cartel agreements and other forms of collusion have occurred frequently in the past, but have tended to be highly unstable. Apparently the practical problems involved in implementing tit-for-tat in the environments confronting firms make it very difficult to hold collusive agreements together for long.

Sequential games

The games we have considered so far have been ones in which both players must pick their

[12] Mayer, quoted in Axelrod, op. cit., pp. 59, 60.

[13] Another way in which the unravelling problem is avoided is if there is some positive probability that others will follow the tit-for-tat strategy even though, strictly speaking, it is not rational for them to do so. See David Kreps, Paul Milgrom, John Roberts and Robert Wilson, 'Rational cooperation in finitely repeated prisoner's dilemmas', *Journal of Economic Theory*, 1982, vol. 27, pp. 245–252.

strategies *simultaneously*. Each player had to choose his strategy knowing only the incentives facing his opponent, not the opponent's actual choice of strategy. But in many games one player moves first, and the other is then able to choose his strategy with full knowledge of the first player's choice. What happened during the Cold War between East (the Soviet Union) and West (the USA and Western European nations) following the end of the Second World War until about 1989 and the collapse of the Berlin Wall roughly fits this description.

At that time, the military strategies of both sides were based on the doctrine of mutually assured destruction (MAD). The idea behind MAD was simple: both sides should maintain sufficiently large and well-defended nuclear arsenals to ensure that each would be able to retaliate if the other launched a first strike. The prospect of a devastating counterstrike, according to the MAD theory, is what prevented each side from even considering a first strike.

The fact that neither side ever launched a first strike is interpreted by some people as evidence that the MAD strategy must have worked. And yet there is an apparent logical flaw in the strategy, one that suggests that the real source of restraint must lie elsewhere. To appreciate the problem, put yourself in the shoes of a US president who has just learned that the Russians have launched a first strike. At that moment, you know that the MAD strategy has already failed. For whatever reason, the threat of a counterstrike did not in fact deter the Russian first strike. Do you now order a counterstrike anyway? You realize that to do so will only increase the likelihood of total world destruction. True enough, the US president knows that American interests have been grievously damaged by the attack. But at that point, a counterstrike will only damage them further.

The logical difficulty with MAD is thus that each side knows perfectly well that, once a first strike has already been launched, it will not be in the other side's interest to retaliate. And since each party knows this, the threat of a counterstrike loses all power to deter.

Or at least so it seems in theory. Perhaps the threat deters because each side fears that the other might not respond rationally, once it is the victim of a first strike. But whether or not MAD is an effective defence strategy, its apparent flaw is troubling. The same logic that exposed this flaw suggests a simple way to repair it. It is to install a so-called *doomsday machine* – a tamper-proof device that will *automatically* retaliate once a first strike has been launched. Once each side became aware the other had such a device in place, the MAD strategy would be complete, and a first strike truly would become unthinkable.

To see how economists treat sequential games analytically, suppose the former Soviet Union was considering whether to launch a nuclear strike against the United States. This decision may be portrayed in a *game tree* diagram like the one shown in Fig. 11.18. If the first move is the USSR's, the game starts at point A. The first two branches of the game tree represent the USSR's alternatives of attacking and not attacking. If it attacks, then the United States finds itself at point B on the top branch of the game tree, where it must decide whether or not to strike back. If the United States retaliates, we end up at point D, where the pay-offs are −100 for each country. If the United States does not retaliate, we end up at point E, where the pay-offs are 100 for the USSR and −50 for the United States. (The units of these pay-offs are purely arbitrary. The values chosen are intended to reflect each country's hypothetical relative valuation of the gains and losses of each action.)

The bottom half of the game tree represents the alternative in which the USSR does not attack. If the USSR chooses this alternative, the United States finds itself at point C, where it again faces a decision about whether or not to launch missiles at the USSR. For argument's sake, suppose that the pay-offs to the two countries under each alternative are shown on the bottom two branches of the game tree at points F and G, respectively.

Given the assumed pay-offs for each of the four possible outcomes of the game tree, the USSR can analyse what the United States will do under each alternative. If the USSR attacks (point B), the best option open to the United States is not to retaliate (point E). If the USSR does not attack (point C), the best option for the United States is also not to attack (point G). The USSR thus knows that, if the United States is a pay-off maximizer, the game will end at point E if the USSR attacks, and at point G if the USSR does not attack. And since the USSR has a higher pay-off at point E, it does best to attack. The United States may threaten to retaliate, but as long as its adversaries believe it is a pay-off maximizer, such threats will lack credibility.

Now suppose that the United States could install a doomsday machine – a device that would automatically retaliate in the event of an attack by the USSR. The effect would be to eliminate the bottom half of the top branch of the game tree in Fig. 11.18. The USSR would then know that, if it attacked, the game would end at point D, where

Figure 11.18 Nuclear deterrence as a sequential game

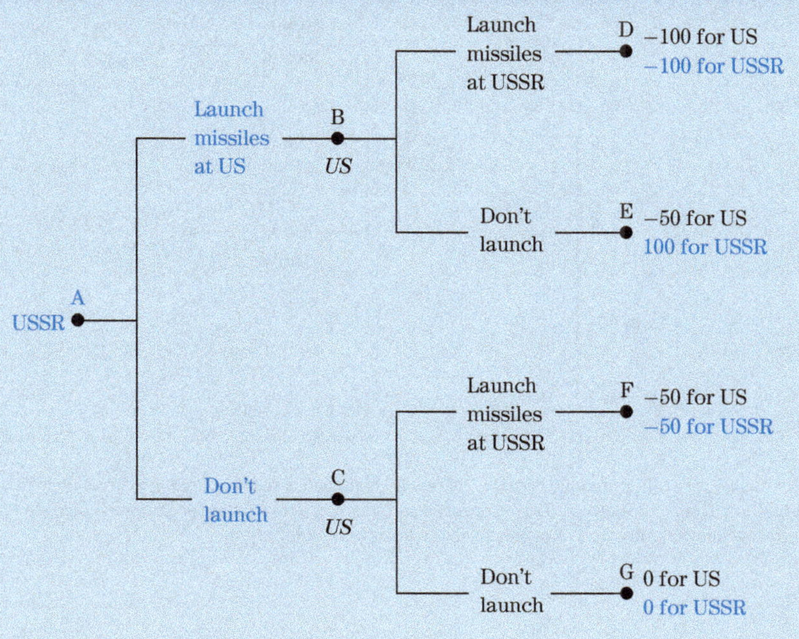

If the USSR attacks, the best option for the United States is not to retaliate (point E). If the USSR doesn't attack, the best option for the United States is also not to attack (point G). Since the USSR gets a higher pay-off at E than at G, it will attack. If the United States is believed to be a pay-off maximizer, its threat to retaliate against a first strike will not be credible.

Economic naturalist 11.2

Why might a company invest in something it knows it will never use?

The 50-floor and 223-metre-tall Carlton Centre in Johannesburg is currently the tallest building in Southern Africa. Officially opened in 1973 and built at a cost of R88 million, it has been the tallest building in Southern Africa for 39 years. (Although the Hillbrow Tower at 269 m and the Sentech Tower at 239 m are taller than the Carlton Centre, they are not, strictly speaking, buildings.) This status endows the building with a special form of prestige, enabling its owners to command higher rents than in otherwise similar office buildings. Now, suppose that company X is considering whether to build an even taller building. (In reality this will demand a huge investment as the replacement cost of the Carlton Centre is estimated at R1.8 billion.) Suppose it knows that any firm that has permanent ownership of the tallest building will earn a large economic profit. Its concern, naturally, is that Transnet (the current owner of the Carlton Centre) or some other firm may build a still-taller building, which would substantially diminish company X's pay-off.

Both Transnet and company X realize that they are participants in a sequential game of the type pictured in Fig. 11.19. The game starts at point A, where X must decide whether to enter with a taller building. If it does not, Transnet will receive a pay-off of 100, X a pay-off of 0. In other words, the status quo will prevail. If X enters, however, the game moves to point B, where Transnet must decide whether to build higher or stand pat. Suppose that, if Transnet builds higher, its pay-off will be 30, while X will earn a pay-off of −50; and that if Transnet does not build higher, its pay-off will be 40, while X will get a pay-off of 60. Transnet naturally wants X not to enter. It may even announce its intention to build a taller building in the event that X enters. But as long as X knows the pay-offs facing Transnet, it can conclude that the best option open once X enters is for Transnet to stand pat. The Nash equilibrium of this sequential game is point E, where X enters and Transnet stands pat.

Now suppose that, before Transnet had originally built its tower, it had the option of building a platform atop the building, on which it could build an addition that would make the building taller. Assume further that to build this platform costs 10 units, but reduces the cost of building a taller building by 20 units. If Transnet had installed this platform, the sequential game between it and company X would then be as portrayed by the game tree in Fig. 11.20. Transnet's pay-off at point D is now 40 (it saves 20 on building costs less the 10-unit cost of the platform). Its pay-offs at C and E are each 10 units less than in Fig. 11.20 (reflecting the 10-unit cost of the platform). Despite the small magnitude of these changes in pay-offs, the presence of the platform dramatically alters the outcome of the

Figure 11.19 The decision to build the tallest building

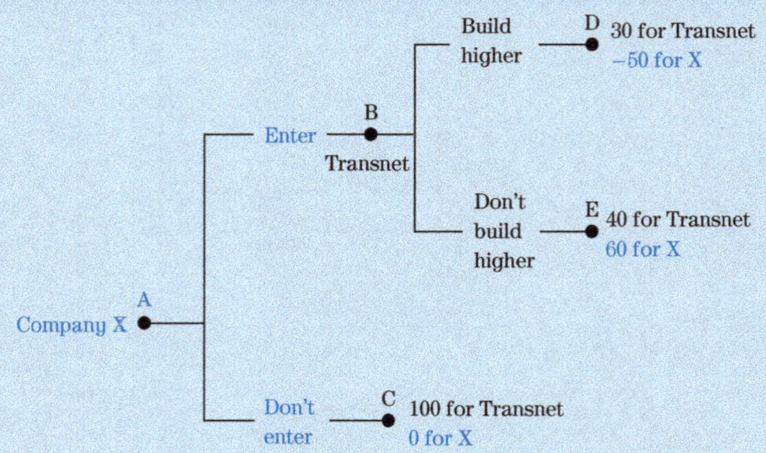

If company X builds a skyscraper taller than the Carlton Centre, Transnet must decide whether to build higher (point D), or yield its status as the tallest building (point E). Because Transnet earns a higher pay-off at E than at D, it will not build higher. And since X knows that, it will enter the market, despite Transnet's threat to build a taller building.

game. This time X can predict that, if it enters with the tallest building, it will be in Transnet's interest to add to its existing building, which means that X will receive a pay-off of −50. As a result, X will not find it worthwhile to enter this market, and so the game will end at point C. The pay-off to Transnet at C is 90 (the original 100 minus the 10-unit cost of building the platform). Its 10-unit investment in the platform thus increases its net pay-off by 50 (the difference between the 90-unit pay-off it receives with the platform and the 40-unit pay-off it would have received without it).[14]

The platform investment just discussed is an example of what economists call *strategic entry deterrence*. When such investments are effective, it is because they change potential rivals' expectations about how the firm will respond when its market position is threatened.

Figure 11.20 Strategic entry deterrence

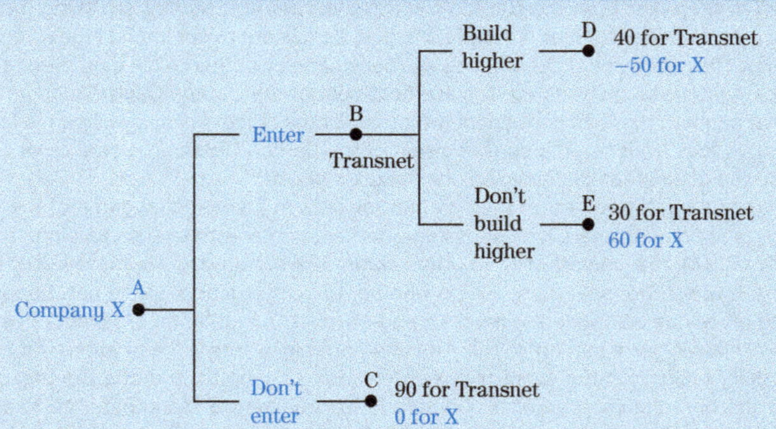

Had it originally built a platform atop its building, at a cost of 10 units, Transnet would have reduced the cost of building a taller building by 20 units. Then company X would have calculated that it would not be worthwhile to build a taller building, because it then would have been in Transnet's interest to respond with an addition. The Nash equilibrium of the altered game occurs at point C.

[14] Microsoft Internet Explorer versus Firefox is one recent example of strategic entry deterrence games.

Economic naturalist 11.3

Why would a firm build a factory with more capacity than it would ever need?

Larger production facilities typically have higher fixed costs and lower marginal costs than smaller ones. So the question can be rephrased as follows: why might it be in a firm's interest to have a factory with very low marginal cost, even if the result were to make its total cost higher than for a smaller facility?

A possible answer is that the larger factory constitutes another example of strategic entry deterrence. If potential entrants knew that an incumbent firm had extremely low marginal cost, they could predict that it would be in the incumbent's interest to remain in business, even at a price level too low for entrants to earn a normal profit. In that case, it would not be rational for rivals to enter the market. And their absence, in turn, would enable the incumbent to charge a price sufficiently high to cover the costs of the larger facility. However, it means that the firm may not maximize its profits – the main goal of firms.

©iStock.com/blinowbl
Why might a firm build a bigger factory than it needs?

the USSR gets a pay-off of −100. And since this is worse than the outcome if the USSR does not attack (point G), the best option open to the USSR would then be to leave its missiles in their silos.

A spatial interpretation of monopolistic competition

This section provides an alternative way of looking at monopolistic competition and deals with new ways of thinking resulting from criticism of the Chamberlinian model of monopolistic competition. As noted earlier, the extent to which one monopolistically competitive firm's product is an effective substitute for another's determines how closely their industry will resemble perfect competition. One concrete way of thinking about lack of complete substitutability is distance. Petrol sold on the other side of town is not a perfect substitute for petrol sold at the nearest corner, especially when your tank is nearly empty.

Imagine yourself a resident of a small island nation with a large lake in the middle of it. Business activity there is naturally restricted to the doughnut-shaped piece of land that constitutes the island's periphery. There is considerable specialization of labour on your island. People toil all day at their respective tasks, and then take their evening meals at restaurants. People on your island lack the customary preference for culinary diversity. Instead, you and your neighbours prefer to eat baked potatoes and grilled beefsteak every night. Meals in any given restaurant are produced under increasing returns to scale – the more meals produced, the lower the average cost per meal.

How many restaurants should there be in this island nation? We are tempted to say only one, thereby keeping the cost per meal to a minimum. If the circumference of the island were, say, only 300 m, this would almost surely be the correct answer. But for a much larger island, the direct cost of meals is not likely to be the only concern to you and your fellow residents. You will also care about the cost of getting to and from the nearest restaurant. If the island were 300 km around, for example, the cost savings from having only a single restaurant could hardly begin to compensate for the travel costs incurred by those who lived on the far side of the island.

The market for evening meals on this island is in one respect the same as the markets we have considered in earlier chapters: a single, standardized meal is served in every restaurant. But the type of food served is not the only important characteristic of a meal. Buyers care also about *where* the meal is served. When products differ along one or more important dimensions – location, size, flavour, quality, and so on – we immediately confront the general question of how much product diversity there should be. How many different kinds of tennis racquet should there be? Should an economy have five different brands of cars, or 10, or 50? Many people say South Africa has too many models available for such a small economy. Is this type of reasoning correct?

To help fix ideas, suppose there are initially two restaurants evenly spaced around the periphery of the island, as represented by the grey squares in Fig. 11.21. Suppose the circumference of the island is 2 km. The distance between adjacent restaurants will then be 1 km, and no one can possibly live more than ½ km away from the nearest restaurant, the one-way trip length required for someone who lives exactly halfway between two restaurants.

To fill out the structure of the environment, suppose there are L consumers scattered uniformly about the circle, and suppose the cost of travel is t rands per km. Thus, for example, if t were equal to R36/km, the transportation cost incurred by someone who lives $d = ½$ km from the nearest restaurant would be the product of the round-trip distance ($2d$) and the unit travel cost (t):

$$2td = 2(\text{R}36/\text{km})(½\text{ km}) = \text{R}36.$$

Figure 11.21 An industry in which location is the important differentiating feature

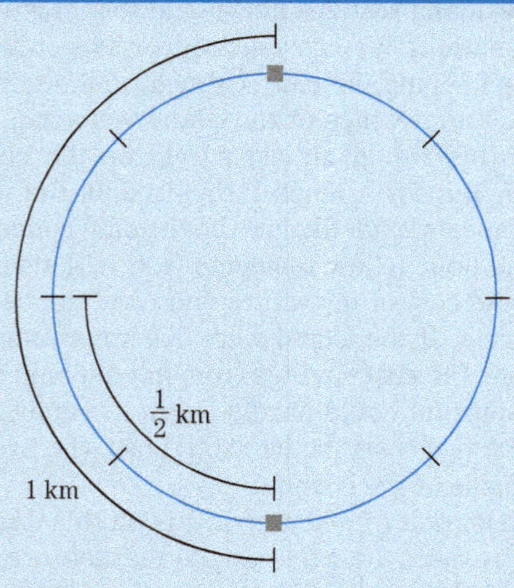

Restaurants (indicated by the squares) are the same except for their geographic location. Each person dines at the restaurant closest to home. If the circumference of the loop is 2 km, this means that the distance between restaurants will be 1 km, giving rise to a maximum one-way trip length of ½ km.

Suppose further that each consumer will eat exactly 1 meal/day at the restaurant for which the total price (which is the price charged for the meal plus transportation costs) is lowest. And suppose, finally, that each restaurant has a total cost curve given by

$$\text{TC} = F + MQ \qquad (11.6)$$

Recall from earlier chapters that the total cost curve in Eq. 11.6 is one in which there is a fixed cost, F, and a constant marginal cost, M. Here, F may be thought of as the sum of equipment rental fees, opportunity costs of invested capital and other fixed costs associated with operating a restaurant; and M is the sum of the labour, raw material and other variable costs incurred in producing an additional meal.

Recall also that average total cost (ATC) is simply total cost divided by output. With a total cost function given by $\text{TC} = F + MQ$, average total cost is thus equal to $F/Q + M$. This means that the more customers who are served in a given location, the lower the average total cost will be.

Suppose, for example, that each of the restaurants has a total cost curve, measured in rands per day, given by $\text{TC} = 500 + 5Q$, where Q is the number of meals it serves each day. If the population, L, is equal to 100 persons, each restaurant will serve $(100/2) = 50$ meals/day, and its total cost will be given by $\text{TC} = 500 + 5(50) =$ R750/day. Average total cost in each restaurant will be $\text{TC}/50 =$ R750/day/(50 meals/day) = R15/meal. By comparison, if there were only one restaurant, it would serve 100 meals/day and have an average total cost of only R10/meal.

What will be the average cost of transportation when there are two restaurants? This cost will depend on unit transportation costs (t), and on how far apart the restaurants are. Recall that the distance between adjacent restaurants will be 1 km when there are two restaurants. Some people will live right next door to a restaurant, and for these people the transportation cost will be zero. With two restaurants, the farthest someone can live from a restaurant is ½ km, the one-way distance for a person who lives halfway between two adjacent restaurants. For this person, the round trip will cover 1 km; and if t is again equal to R36/km, the travel cost for this patron will be (R36/km)(1.0 km) = R36. Since people are uniformly scattered about the loop, the average round trip will be halfway between these two extremes; it will thus cover a distance of ½ km, and its cost will be R18.

The *overall average cost per meal* is the sum of average total cost (R15/meal in the two-restaurant example) and average transportation cost (here, R18/meal), which comes to R33/meal.

The optimal number of locations

If unit transportation cost (t) were zero, it would then clearly be optimal to have only a single restaurant, because that would minimize the overall average cost per meal. But if transportation cost were sufficiently high, a single restaurant would not be optimal because the average patron would have to travel too great a distance. The optimal number of locations is thus the result of a trade-off between the start-up and other fixed costs (F) of opening new locations, on the one hand, and the savings from lower transportation costs, on the other.

What is the best number of outlets to have? Our strategy for answering this question will be to ask whether the overall average cost per meal served (average total cost plus average transportation cost) would decline if we had one more restaurant than we have now. If so, we should add another restaurant and ask the same question again. Once the overall average cost stops declining, we shall have reached the optimal number of restaurants.

To illustrate, suppose we increase the number of restaurants in our earlier example from two to three. How will this affect overall average cost? Again supposing that the restaurants are evenly spaced around the loop, each will now attract only one-third of the island's 100 inhabitants, which means that each will serve (100/3) meals/day. The ATC for each restaurant will thus be [500 + 5(100/3)]/(100/3) = R20/meal – up R5/meal from the previous value. (Recall that ATC with two restaurants was R15/meal.) The distance between adjacent restaurants is ⅔ km when there are three restaurants. This means that the average one-way trip with three restaurants is ⅙ km, which in turn means that the average round-trip length is ⅓ km. Average transportation cost is thus ⅓ km(R36/km) = R12.00. Note that this is R6.00 less than the previous average transportation cost of R18.00, reflecting the decline in average trip length. Adding average total cost and average transportation cost, we see that the overall average cost with three restaurants is R20.00 + R12.00 = R32.00/meal.

Exercise 11.6

In the preceding example, what is the overall average cost per meal if we add a fourth restaurant to the loop?

Your calculation in Exercise 11.6 demonstrates that overall average cost per meal goes up when we increase the number of restaurants from three to four. And since the overall average cost declined when we moved from two to three, this means the optimal number of restaurants for our island nation is three.

We can make the preceding analysis more general by supposing that there are N outlets around the loop, as shown by the grey squares in Fig. 11.22. Now the distance between adjacent outlets will be $2/N$ km, and the maximum one-way trip length will be half that, or $2/2N$ km. If we again suppose that people are uniformly distributed around the loop, it follows that the average one-way distance to the nearest outlet is $2/4N$ km (which is halfway between 0, the distance of the person closest to a given outlet, and $2/2N$ km, the distance of the person farthest from it). The average round-trip distance is twice the average one-way distance, and is thus equal to $2/2N$ (= N) km.

Because the distance between restaurants declines as the number of restaurants grows, the total transportation cost, denoted by C_{trans}, will be a decreasing function of the number of outlets. Since transportation cost is t rands per person per km travelled, total transportation cost will be the product of the cost per km (t), population (L) and average round-trip length $2/2N$:

$$C_{\text{trans}} = tL\frac{2}{2N} = \frac{tL}{N} \tag{11.7}$$

Figure 11.22 Distances with N outlets

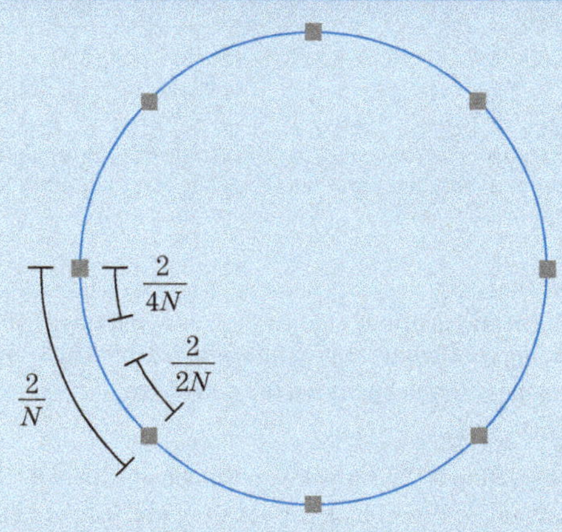

With N outlets, the distance between adjacent outlets will be $2/N$ km. The farthest a person can live from an outlet is $2/2N$ km. And the average one-way distance people must travel to reach the nearest outlet is $2/4N$ km. The average round-trip distance is $2/2N$ km.

The total cost of meals served, denoted C_{meals}, also depends on both population and the number of outlets. It is given by

$$C_{\text{meals}} = LM + NF \tag{11.8}$$

where the first term on the right reflects the fact that each of the L people eats a meal whose marginal cost is M, and the second term is the total fixed cost for N outlets. The object is to choose N to minimize the sum of the two types of cost, $C_{\text{trans}} + C_{\text{meals}}$.

The two cost functions and their sum are shown graphically in Fig. 11.23, where N^* denotes the cost-minimizing number of outlets.[15]

The slope of the C_{meals} curve is equal to F, which represents the cost of an additional outlet. The slope of the C_{trans} curve is equal to $-tL/N^2$, and represents the savings in transportation cost from adding an additional outlet.[16] If the slope of C_{meals} is less than the absolute value of the slope of C_{trans}, the reduction in transportation cost from adding another outlet will more than compensate for the extra fixed cost from adding that outlet. The optimal number of outlets, N^*, is the one for which the slope of the C_{meals} curve is the same as the absolute value of the slope of the C_{trans} curve. N^* must thus satisfy

$$\frac{tL}{N^{*2}} = F \tag{11.9}$$

which yields

$$N^* = \sqrt{\frac{tL}{F}} \tag{11.10}$$

This expression for the optimal number of outlets has a straightforward economic interpretation. Note first that, if transportation cost rises, N^* will also rise. This makes sense, because the whole point of adding additional outlets is to economize on transportation costs. Note that N^* also increases with population density, L. The more people there are who live on each segment of the

Figure 11.23 The optimal number of outlets

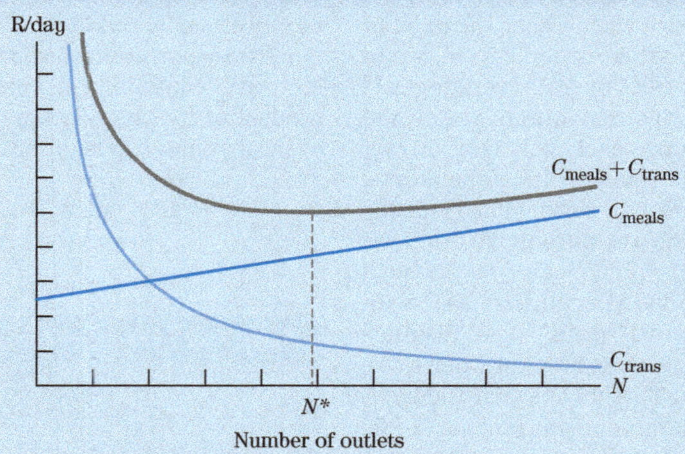

Total transportation cost (C_{trans}) declines with the number of outlets (N), while total cost of meals served (C_{meals}) increases with N. The optimal number of outlets (N^*) is the one that minimizes the sum of these costs.

[15] These functions are plotted as though N were a continuous variable, not an integer. For industries involving large numbers of firms, the continuous approximation will introduce only minimal error.

[16] This slope is found by taking the derivative

$$\frac{d(C_{\text{trans}})}{dN} = \frac{-tL}{N^2}$$

again treating N as if it were continuously variable. Students who haven't studied calculus can convince themselves that this expression is correct by letting ΔN be, say, 0.001 and then calculating the resulting change in C_{trans}:

$$\Delta C_{\text{trans}} = \frac{tL}{N + 0.001} - \frac{tL}{N} = \frac{-0.001tL}{N(N + 0.001)}$$

The ratio $\Delta C_{\text{trans}}/\Delta N$ is thus

$$\frac{\Delta C_{\text{trans}}}{0.001} = \frac{-tL}{N(N + 0.001)} \approx \frac{-tL}{N^2}$$

loop, the more people there are who will benefit if the average distance to the nearest outlet becomes shorter. And note, finally, that N^* declines with F, the start-up cost of an additional outlet, which is also just as expected.

Applying Eq. 11.10 to our restaurant example in which $L = 100$, $t = 36$ and $F = 500$, we get $N^* = \sqrt{(36 \times 100)/500} = 2.7$. Needless to say, it is impossible to have 2.7 restaurants, so we choose the integer nearest to 2.7, namely, 3. And indeed, just as our earlier calculations indicated, having three restaurants results in a lower overall average cost than does having either two or four.

Exercise 11.7

How would N^* change in the preceding example if there were 400 people on the island instead of 100?

Will the independent actions of private, profit-seeking firms result in the optimal number of outlets around the loop? This question sounds very simple, but turns out to be exceedingly difficult to answer. We now know that under some conditions there will tend to be more than the optimal number, while under other conditions there will be fewer. But for the moment let us note that the number of outlets that emerges from the independent actions of profit-seeking firms will in general be related to the optimal number of outlets in the following simple way: any environmental change that leads to a change in the optimal number of outlets (here, any change in population density, transportation cost or fixed cost) will lead to a change in the same direction in the equilibrium number of outlets. For example, a fall in transportation cost will tend to decrease both the optimal number of outlets and the number of outlets we actually observe in practice.

The analogy with product characteristics

The power of the spatial interpretation of monopolistic competition is that it can be applied not only to geographic location, but also to a variety of other product characteristics. Consider, for example, the various airline flights between any two cities on a given day. People have different preferences for travelling at various times of day, just as they have different preferences about where to eat or shop. Figure 11.24 depicts an air-travel market (for

Figure 11.24 A spatial interpretation of airline scheduling

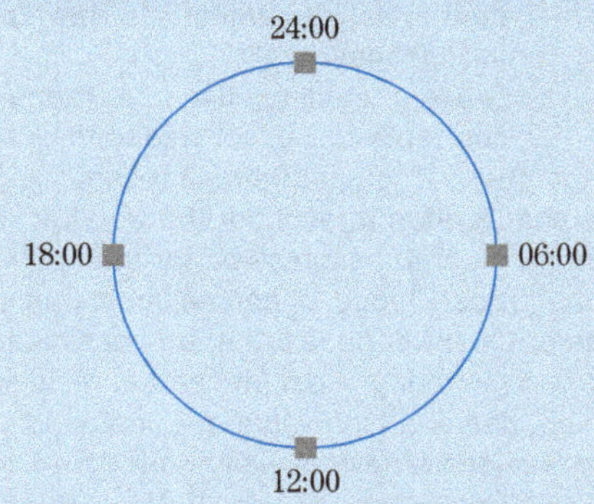

In a market with four flights per day, there is no traveller for whom there is not a flight leaving within three hours of his most preferred departure time.

example, Cape Town to Durban) with four flights per day, scheduled at midnight, 06:00, 12:00 and 18:00. With the choice of an airline flight, just as with the choice of a place to dine, people will tend to select the alternative that lies closest to their most preferred option. Thus a person who would most prefer to go at 19:00 will probably choose the 18:00 flight. In terms of our spatial model, having to wait for a flight is the analogue of having to travel a certain distance in order to get to a shop.

Why not have a flight leaving every five minutes, so that no one would be forced to travel at an inconvenient time? The answer again has to do with the trade-off between cost and convenience. The larger an aircraft is, the lower its average cost per seat. If people want frequent flights, airlines are forced to use smaller planes and charge higher fares. Conversely, if people didn't care when they travelled, the airline could use the largest possible aircraft (in today's fleet, the 853-seat Airbus A380-800) and fly at whatever interval was required to accumulate enough passengers to fill the plane. (On the Calitzdorp to Pofadder route – if we assume the plane can take off and land at the local airports – that would mean one flight every other 29 February!) But most passengers have schedules to keep, and are willing to pay a little extra for more conveniently timed flights. The result is the same sort of compromise we saw in the restaurant and grocery shop examples. However, there are many routes for which it makes sense to use the biggest aeroplane to reap economies of scale. By 2014, 19 airlines were using 123 Airbus A380-800 planes in total; another 181 were still on order. Emirates has 44 of these planes and another 100 on order!

Economic naturalist 11.4

Why are there fewer grocery shops in most cities now than there were in 1930? And why do residential neighbourhoods in New York City have more grocery shops than residential neighbourhoods in Johannesburg?

Grocery retailing, like other forms of retailing, is characterized by strong economies of scale. It thus confronts the usual trade-off between direct production cost, on the one hand, and transportation cost, on the other. Throughout the last century, changing patterns of car ownership affected the pattern of grocery shop size and location throughout the world. In 1920 most families did not own cars, and had to do their shopping on foot. In terms of our expression for the optimal number of outlets (Eq. 11.10), this meant a high value of t, unit transportation cost. Today, of course, most families own a car (especially in the cities), which has lead people to take advantage of the lower prices that are possible in larger shops. One exception to this general pattern is Manhattan in New York. Even today, most Manhattan residents do not own cars. Moreover, population density is extremely high there, which means a high value of L in Eq. 11.10. The combined effect of high values of L and t is that very few Manhattan residents have to walk more than two blocks to get to their nearest grocery shop. The total population in Johannesburg is also very high, but it is spread out over a much larger area, and most families own at least one car. As a result, Johannesburg grocery shops are both larger and further apart than their New York City counterparts.

Virtually every consumer product can be interpreted fruitfully within the context of the spatial model. In the car market, for example, the available permutations of turbo versus non-turbo, automatic versus standard, coupe versus convertible, saloon versus station wagon, two doors versus four doors, SUV versus 4×4, air-conditioned versus climate control, metallic indigo versus forest green and so on, lead to an extraordinarily large number of possibilities. It would be considerably cheaper, of course, if we had only a single standard model. But people are willing to pay a little extra for variety, just as they are willing to pay a little extra for a more conveniently located shop. In the parlance of the spatial model, car manufacturers are said to *locate* their models in a *product space*. Their aim is to see that few buyers are left without a choice that lies *close* to the car that would best suit them. Similar interpretations apply to cameras, mobile phones, holidays, bicycles, navigation equipment, wedding rings and virtually every other good for which people have a taste for variety.

Paying for variety

Variety, as we have seen, is costly. Many critics claim that market economies serve up wastefully high degrees of product variety. Wouldn't the world be a better place, these critics ask, if we had a simpler array of products to choose from, each costing less than the highly specific models we see today? The extra costs of product variety may indeed seem an unnecessary burden imposed on consumers who neither desire nor can easily afford it. In a slightly more detailed model of spatial competition, however, these problems appear much less serious.

In our simple model, we assumed that each buyer faced the same unit transportation cost. This assumption is unrealistic, even in models where the only dimension of variety is geographic location. Buyers who own cars, for example, will have much lower transportation costs than those who don't; likewise, buyers whose time is worth little, in opportunity cost terms, have lower transportation costs than those whose time is more valuable. The issue is the same for product variety. Those who care a lot about special product features will have higher 'transport costs' than those who do not, which means simply that people in the former group are willing to pay more than others for a product whose special features suit their particular tastes.

It is also true, as a general proposition, that the demand for variety increases sharply with income. We can say that variety is a luxury, not a necessity. The association between income and the demand for variety plays a pivotal role in the way most producers market their products. To illustrate, consider the array of cars offered by Toyota SA, ranging from the sub-compact Toyota Yaris 1.05dr (from about R130 000) to the full-sized Toyota Land Cruiser 200 4.5 Twin Turbo VX Diesel (that costs more than R1 million). All these cars incorporate a variety of specialized features, which are the result of costly research and development. The research and development costs are largely fixed, which gives rise to a substantial scale economy in the production of cars. If Toyota (or General Motors, or any other company) could sell more cars in a given year, it could produce each of them at a lower cost.

When marginal cost lies below average cost, it is not possible to charge each buyer a price equal to marginal cost and still earn a normal profit.

(Recall from Chapter 8 that a firm's average cost includes a normal rate of profit.) As we saw in Chapter 10, the firm with a scale economy has an incentive to expand its market by setting price close to marginal cost if it can do that without altering its prices on existing sales. But we also saw that, if some buyers pay prices below average cost, others must pay prices above it.

The car manufacturer's response to this situation is to set the prices of its better models above average cost, while pricing its lesser models below average cost. Panels a and b in Fig. 11.25, for example, show the cost and demand conditions for the Volkswagen Passat and Audi S4, respectively. The marginal cost of producing an Audi is slightly higher than that of producing a Volkswagen. The basic design innovations are available to the company for both cars, and the hardware produced for the Audi is only slightly more costly than that used for the Volkswagen. But because the buyers who care most about variety are willing to pay much more for an Audi than for a Volkswagen, the company can set sharply different prices for the two models. In an average year, the surplus of total revenue above variable cost for all models (which is the sum of the two shaded rectangles in Fig. 11.25) is just about enough to cover the company's research and development and other fixed costs.

Variety is costly, just as the critics claim. But the cost of variety is not distributed evenly among all buyers. In the example above, it was paid by the buyers of Audis not by the buyers of Volkswagens. By the same token, people who buy the Mercedes-Benz C180 enjoy almost all the important advantages of the extensive Mercedes-Benz research programme for about R45 000 less than the people who buy the Mercedes-Benz C200 Blue Tec, which differs from the C180 only in having a slightly more powerful engine. Even by the yardstick used by critics of the market system, this seems a better outcome than the one they urge, which is that all buyers have a standardized 'people's car'. Under current marketing arrangements, people who don't place high value on variety get to enjoy it at the expense of those who care most about having it. The alternative would be to deny variety to the people who care most about it, without producing real cost savings for the buyers who would be satisfied with a standardized product. Even Volkswagen, which once touted the virtues of a single, standardized model, now offers several dozen versions of its Golf, Jetta, Polo and Passat lines. For example, the standard Passat 2.0 TDI Comfortline DSG, which sells for about R400 000, can be topped up with additional extras to the value of R135 000. The same principle applies – those who want variety will have to pay for it.

Similar pricing strategies affect recovery of the costs of variety in virtually every industry. Consider again the restaurant industry. In a city in which most people have cars, which is to say in virtually every city, the cheapest way to provide restaurant meals would be to have a single restaurant with only one item on the menu. An army of chefs would labour over gigantic cauldrons of peas and mashed potatoes, while others operated huge ovens filled with roasting chickens. But

Figure 11.25 Distributing the cost of variety

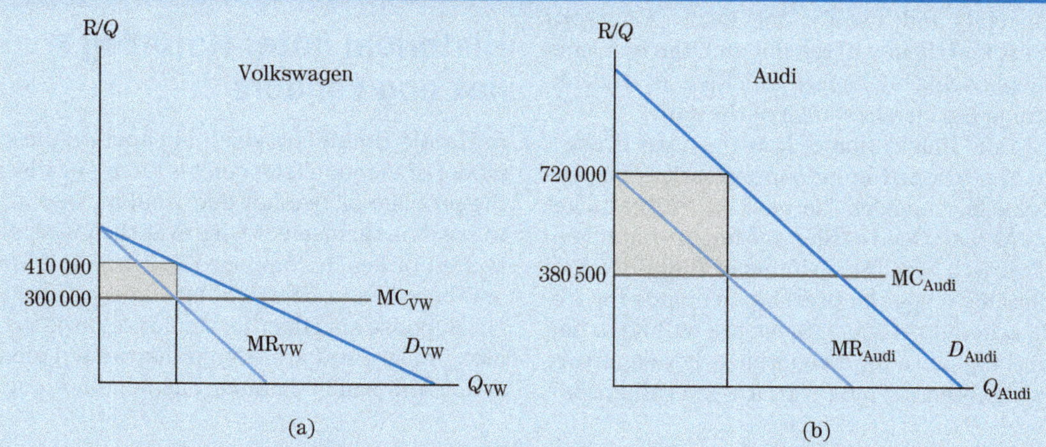

The buyers who care most about variety will generally choose the model with premium features. By pricing its models differently, the seller recovers most of the extra costs of variety from the buyers who are most responsible for their incurrence.

people don't want the same meal every night, any more than they all want the same kind of car. Even in small cities like Port Elizabeth and Bellville, we have Indian, Mexican, Thai, Chinese, Japanese, Korean, Greek, Italian, French and Spanish restaurants in addition to the usual domestic fare and fast-food chains.

How are the extra costs of all this variety apportioned? Most restaurants price the different items on their menus in differing multiples of marginal cost. Alcoholic beverages, desserts and coffee, in particular, are almost always priced at several times marginal cost, whereas the mark-up on most entrées is much smaller. Most restaurants also offer some sort of daily specials, entrées that are priced very close to marginal cost. The result is that the diner who wants to economize on the cost of eating out, whether because she has low income or for any other reason, will order only the basic meal, taking before-dinner drinks and dessert and coffee at home (or doing without those extras). Such diners end up paying a price not much more than the marginal cost of being served. Other diners, who are willing or able to do so, will purchase the more costly option of having the entire package at the restaurant. The diners who pursue the latter strategy are much more likely than others to be the ones who feel strongly about variety (again, because the demand for variety is strongly linked to income). Under current marketing arrangements, they are the ones who end up paying most of its cost. Those who care less about variety are still able to enjoy a crusted chicken breast one night and beef rump the next; and if they don't order drinks and dessert, they pay little more than they would have to in a standardized soup kitchen. In the university town where I live are a number of different restaurants offering daily specials and 'two for one' deals. A cursory glance around them will tell you that the residents of Stellenbosch are as price sensitive as students in sourcing the cheapest dish of the day!

As a final illustration of how the costs of variety are apportioned in monopolistically competitive markets, consider the case of airline ticket pricing. As discussed earlier, the important dimension of variety here is the timing of flights. Not all travellers have equally pressing demands for frequently scheduled flights. Some are willing to pay substantially more for a slightly earlier departure time, while others would wait a week rather than pay even R100 more. To the extent that airlines use smaller, more costly (per seat) aircraft in order to offer more frequent flights, it is to accommodate the needs of the former group.

Who pays the added costs of the smaller flights? Virtually every airline employs the hurdle model of differential pricing described in Chapter 10. The particular variant the airlines use offers substantial discounts to passengers who satisfy two restrictions: (1) they must buy their tickets in advance, usually at least 2 weeks or longer before flight time; and (2) their journey must include a Saturday night. The effect of these two restrictions together is to eliminate most travellers who demand maximum travel flexibility. In particular, business travellers, whose schedules tend to be much tighter than those of vacation travellers, almost always end up paying the regular air fare under the current marketing system. An example is the Cape Town–Johannesburg route for which the Friday afternoon and late Sunday evening/early Monday morning tickets are the most expensive. Many business travellers work in Gauteng during the week and fly home to Cape Town to spend the weekend with their families. By contrast, very few vacation travellers fail to qualify for at least some form of discount.

If it is largely the scheduling demands of business travellers that dictate the use of smaller, more costly aircraft, this apportioning of the costs appears not only fair but also efficient. Discount tickets enable airlines to attract passengers who would not fly otherwise, and these passengers make possible the use of larger, less costly aircraft. Business travellers end up getting the frequent service they want, and leisure travellers are not forced to pay the added costs of it.[17]

Historical note: Hotelling's hot dog vendors

In Harold Hotelling's seminal paper on the spatial model of monopolistic competition,[18] he discussed the problem of two hot dog vendors who are free to position themselves wherever they wish along a stretch of beach. Suppose the beach is 2 km long and bounded at each end by some natural obstacle. Suppose also that the vendors charge the same price, customers are evenly distributed along the beach and each customer buys one hot dog from

[17] For a more detailed discussion of this issue, see R. Frank, 'When are price differentials discriminatory?', *Journal of Policy Analysis and Management*, 1983, vol. 2, Winter, pp. 238–255.

the nearest vendor. If the vendors' goal is to sell as many hot dogs as possible, where should they position themselves?

Suppose, as in Fig. 11.26, that vendor 1 stands at point A and vendor 2 stands at point B, where both A and B are ½ km from the midpoint of the beach, located at C. In this configuration, all customers to the left of C are closest to vendor 1 and will buy from him, while those to the right of C will buy from vendor 2. Each vendor thus gets half the market. The greatest one-way distance any customer has to travel is 0.5 km, and the average one-way distance between customers and their nearest vendor is half that, or 0.25 km.

Mathematically inclined readers can verify that A and B are in fact the locations that minimize average travel distance for all consumers. And yet these locations are clearly not optimal from the perspective of either vendor. To see why, suppose vendor 1 at point A were to move 10 m towards B. The customers to the left of C would continue to find him the closest vendor. But now those customers less than 10 m to the right of C – people who used to be closest to vendor 2 – will suddenly find themselves switching to vendor 1. Moving further to the right will increase vendor 1's sales still further. Vendor 1 will maximize his sales by positioning himself as close as he can get to vendor 2 on the side of vendor 2 that is closer to the centre of the beach.

Vendor 2 can, of course, reason in the same fashion, so his strategy will be perfectly symmetrical: he will try to get as close to vendor 1 on the side of vendor 1 that is closest to the centre. And when both vendors behave in this fashion, the only stable outcome is for each to locate at C, the centre of the beach. At C each gets half of the market, just as he did originally. But the average distance that customers must travel is now 0.5 km, twice what it was when the vendors were located at A and B.

Having both vendors at the middle of the beach is thus not optimal from the vantage point of customers, and yet neither vendor would be better off if he were to move unilaterally. The hot dog vendor location problem is thus not one of those cases in which Adam Smith's invisible hand guides resources so as to produce the greatest good for all.

Consumer preferences and advertising

In perfectly competitive markets it would never pay a producer to advertise her product. Being only one of many producers of identical products, the firm that advertised would attract only an insignificant share of any resulting increase in demand. In monopolistically competitive and oligopolistic markets the incentives are different. Because products are differentiated, producers can often shift their demand curves outwards significantly by advertising.

How does advertising affect the efficiency with which markets allocate resources? In the description of the world offered by rational choice theory, producers are essentially agents of consumers. Consumers vote with their rands, and producers are quick to do their bidding. This description has been called the *traditional sequence*, and the late Harvard economist John Kenneth Galbraith was one of its most prominent critics. In its place, he proposed a *revised sequence* in which the producer, not the consumer, sits in the driver's seat. In Galbraith's scheme, the corporation decides which products are cheapest and most convenient to produce, and then uses advertising and other promotional devices to create demand for them.

Galbraith's revised sequence recasts Adam Smith's invisible hand in an unflattering new light. Smith's story, recall, was that producers motivated only by self-interest would provide the products that best meet consumers' desires. Those who did not would fail to attract customers and go

Figure 11.26 The hot dog vendor location problem

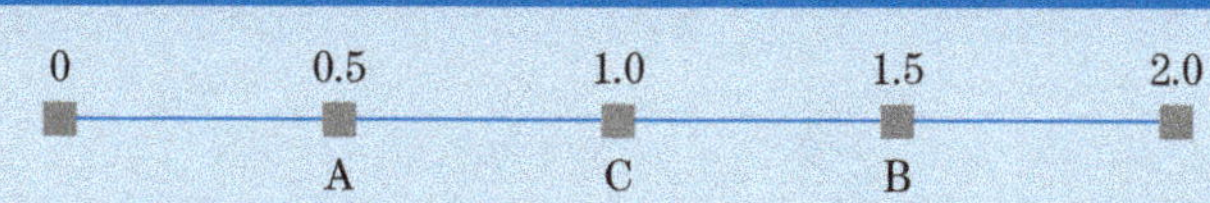

Each hot dog vendor does best by positioning himself at the centre of the beach, even though that location does not minimize the average distance that the vendors' customers must travel.

[18] Harold Hotelling, 'Stability in competition', *Economic Journal*, 1929, vol. 39, pp. 41–57.

out of business. If Galbraith is correct, however, this story is turned on its head: it is like saying that the all-too-visible hand of Adderley Street guides consumers to serve the interests of large corporations.

Galbraith's revised sequence is not without intuitive appeal. Many people are understandably sceptical, for example, when an economist says that the purpose of advertising is to make consumers better informed. The plain fact, after all, is that this is often anything but its intent. For example, the celebrity milk moustache is surely not part of a process whereby we become more knowledgeable about the nutritional merits of milk consumption.

But for all the obvious hype in advertising messages, the Galbraith view of the process overlooks something fundamental: it is easier to sell a good product than a bad one. All an advertisement can reasonably hope to accomplish is to induce the consumer to *try* the product. If it is one she tries and likes, she will probably buy it repeatedly. She will also recommend it to friends. If it is one she doesn't like, however, the process will usually end there. Even if a firm were to succeed in getting *everyone* to try it once, it still wouldn't be able to maintain a profitable, ongoing venture.

Imagine two alternative products, one that meets real human needs but is costly to produce, and another that meets no real need but is somewhat cheaper. Which of these two types would a profit-hungry producer do best to advertise? Given the importance of repeat business and word-of-mouth endorsements, the first will generally be more attractive, often by a compelling margin. The fact that it costs more to produce will not deter consumers unless its extra benefits do not justify those extra costs.

New products go through extensive market testing before they ever land on the shelves. Millions of rands are spent analysing test subjects' reactions to them. In the end, most products that enter this testing process never see the light of day. Only when a firm has concrete evidence that a product is likely to be well received does it dare to commit the millions of rands required for an intensive national advertising campaign.

Firms that fail to adopt this posture often pay sharp penalties. In the late 1990s the Lotus software company, for example, spent more than $10 million advertising Jazz, its spreadsheet program for the Apple Macintosh, even though it had clear evidence that the program lacked specific features that many users deemed vital. The Lotus ads were incredibly sophisticated, and no doubt succeeded in selling a fair number of programs. And yet Jazz's main rival, Microsoft's Excel, a much better product, quickly captured the market with only a small fraction of Lotus' advertising outlay.

Advertising and other efforts to persuade consumers are best viewed as part of a pump-priming process. Given the enormous costs, it usually pays to promote only those products that consumers are likely to want to purchase repeatedly, or to speak well of to their friends. And in fact there is clear evidence that most firms follow precisely this strategy. Frozen-dinner producers advertise their fancy ethnic entrées, not their chicken pot pies. Publishers advertise books that seem likely to become best-sellers, not their titles with more limited appeal. Motion picture studios tout the movies they hope will become blockbusters, not their low-budget films.

Because producers have an incentive to advertise only those products that consumers are most likely to find satisfying, the so-called traditional sequence is more plausible than Galbraith and other critics make it out to be. True enough, where the quality differences between competing goods are small, advertising may have a significant influence on which brand a consumer chooses. But as a first approximation it still makes sense to assume that consumers have reasonably well-defined notions of what they like, and that producers spend much effort on trying to cater to those notions.

This is not to say, however, that market incentives lead to the amount of advertising that is best from society's point of view. As we saw earlier in this chapter, strategic competition between rivals leads firms to spend excessively on advertising.

Summary

- In the Cournot model, each firm takes the *quantities* produced by its rivals as given; in the Bertrand model, by contrast, each firm takes its rivals' *prices* as given. Although the behavioural orientation of firms sounds very much the same in these two cases, the results are strikingly different. The Cournot model yields a slightly lower price and a slightly higher quantity than we would see if the firms colluded to achieve the monopoly outcome. By contrast, the Bertrand model leads to essentially the same outcome we saw under perfect competition.
- A slightly more sophisticated form of interdependence among firms is assumed in the Stackelberg model, in which one firm plays a leadership role and its rivals merely follow. This model is similar in structure to the Cournot model, except that where the Cournot firms take one another's quantities as given, the Stackelberg leader strategically manipulates the quantity decisions of its rivals.
- Monopolistic competition is defined by two simple conditions: (1) the existence of numerous firms, each producing a product that is a close, but imperfect, substitute for the products of other firms; and (2) free entry and exit of firms. In the spatial model of monopolistic competition, customers have particular locations or product characteristics they most prefer. The result is that firms tend to compete most intensively for the consumers of products most similar to their own.
- The characteristic feature of oligopolistic markets is interdependence among firms. The interdependences among oligopolistic firms are often successfully analysed using the mathematical theory of games. The three basic elements of any game are the players, the set of possible strategies and the pay-off matrix. A Nash equilibrium occurs when each player's strategy is optimal, given the other player's choice of strategy. A strategy is called dominant if it is optimal no matter what strategy the other player chooses.
- The incentives facing firms who attempt to collude are similar to those facing participants in the prisoners' dilemma. The difficulty in holding cartels together is that the dominant strategy for each member is to cheat on the agreement. Repeated interactions between a very small number of firms can support collusive behaviour under circumstances in which strategies such as tit-for-tat are effective.
- Incumbent firms may sometimes act strategically to deter potential rivals from entering their markets. Often this involves incurring higher costs than would otherwise be necessary.
- There is not always a strong tendency for natural monopoly to emerge from the interaction of a small number of firms, each of which produces under sharply increasing returns to scale. Here, the role of sunk costs turns out to be important. It may sometimes be necessary for buyers to take certain initiatives if they are to secure the least costly of the potentially available options.
- A central feature of the spatial model of monopolistic competition is the trade-off between the desire for lower cost, on the one hand, and for greater variety or locational convenience, on the other. The optimum degree of product diversity depends on several factors. Greater diversity is expected with greater population density and higher transportation costs (where, in the general case, 'transportation costs' measure willingness to pay for desired product features). Optimal product diversity is negatively related to the start-up costs of adding new product characteristics or locations. The market metes out a certain rough justice, in that the costs of additional variety tend to be borne most heavily by those to whom variety is most important.

Questions for review

1. What is the fundamental difference between the Cournot, Bertrand and Stackelberg models of oligopoly?
2. How is the problem of oligopoly collusion similar in structure to the prisoners' dilemma?
3. What is the difficulty with using the tit-for-tat strategy as a possible solution to the oligopoly collusion problem?
4. Does the equilibrium in the Cournot model satisfy the definition of a Nash equilibrium?
5. Describe the trade-off between cost and variety.
6. How is the optimal degree of product variety related to population density? To transportation cost? To the fixed costs of offering new products?

Problems

1. The market demand curve for mineral water is given by $P = 15 - Q$. If there are two firms that produce mineral water, each with a constant marginal cost of 3 per unit, fill in the entries for each of the four duopoly models indicated in the table. (In the Stackelberg model, assume that firm 1 is the leader.)

Model	Q_1	Q_2	$Q_1 + Q_2$	P	Π_1	Π_2	$\Pi_1\Pi_2$
Shared monopoly							
Cournot							
Bertrand							
Stackelberg							

2. The market demand curve for a pair of Cournot duopolists is given as $P = 36 - 3Q$, where $Q = Q_1 + Q_2$. The constant per unit marginal cost is 18 for each duopolist. Find the Cournot equilibrium price, quantity and profits.
3. Solve the preceding problem for Bertrand duopolists.
4. The market demand curve for a pair of duopolists is given as $P = 36 - 3Q$, where $Q = Q_1 + Q_2$. The constant per unit marginal cost is 18 for each duopolist. Find the equilibrium price, quantity and profit for each firm, assuming the firms act as a Stackelberg leader and follower, with firm 1 as the leader.
5. Because of its unique expertise with explosives, Fireworks for Africa has long enjoyed a monopoly of the South African market for public firework displays, close-proximity pyrotechnics (such as sport meetings) and indoor pyrotechnics. Assume that the annual demand for these firework displays is $P = 140 - Q$. The marginal cost of putting on a firework display is 20. Assume that a business dispute has split the firm in two, and that there are now two firms in operation, Allbright Fireworks and Light Fireworks. They still have the same marginal costs, but now they are Cournot duopolists. How much profit has the industry lost?
6. While grading the final economics exam, a professor discovers that two students have virtually identical answers. He talks to each student separately and tells them that he is sure that they shared answers, but he cannot be sure who copied from whom. He offers each student a deal: if they both sign a statement admitting to the cheating, each will be given an F for the course. If only one signs the statement, he will be allowed to withdraw from the course and the other non-signing student will be expelled from the university. Finally, if neither signs the statement they will both get a C for the course because the professor does not have enough evidence to prove that cheating has occurred. Assuming the students are not allowed to communicate with one another, set up the relevant pay-off matrix. Does each student have a dominant strategy?

7 Suppose A and B know that they will interact in a prisoners' dilemma exactly four times. Explain why the tit-for-tat strategy will not be an effective means for ensuring co-operation.

8 Firm 1 and firm 2 are car manufacturers. Each has the option of producing either a big car or a small car. The pay-offs to each of the four possible combinations of choices are as given in the following pay-off matrix. Each firm must make its choice without knowing what the other has chosen.

		Firm 1	
		Big car	Small car
Firm 2	Big car	$\Pi_1 = 400$	$\Pi_1 = 800$
		$\Pi_2 = 400$	$\Pi_2 = 1000$
	Small car	$\Pi_1 = 1000$	$\Pi_1 = 500$
		$\Pi_2 = 800$	$\Pi_2 = 500$

a Does either firm have a dominant strategy?

b There are two Nash equilibriums for this game. Identify them.

9 Suppose we have the same pay-off matrix as in Problem 8, except that now firm 1 gets to move first, and knows that firm 2 will see the results of this choice before deciding which type of car to build.

a Draw the game tree for this sequential game.

b What is the Nash equilibrium for this game?

10 The state has announced its plans to license two firms to serve a market whose demand curve is given by $P = 100 - Q$. The technology is such that each can produce any given level of output at zero cost, but once each firm's output is chosen, it cannot be altered.

a What is the most you would be willing to pay for one of these licences if you knew you would be able to choose your level of output first (assuming your choice was observable by the rival firm)?

b How much would your rival be willing to pay for the right to choose second?

***11** Firm 1 and firm 2 are competing for a cable television franchise. The present value of the net revenues generated by the franchise is equal to R. Each firm's probability of winning the franchise is given by its proportion of the total spent by the two firms on lobbying the local government committee that awards the franchise. That is, if I_1 and I_2 represent the lobbying expenditures of firms 1 and 2, respectively, then firm 1's probability of winning is given by $I_1/(I_1 + I_2)$, while firm 2's probability of winning is $I_2/(I_1 + I_2)$. If each firm assumes that the other firm's spending is independent of its own, what is the equilibrium level of spending for each firm?

12 State whether *true or false*, and briefly explain why: If a business owner is delighted to accept additional orders at the current price, she cannot have been a profit-maximizing, perfectly competitive producer.

13 A toll road commission is planning to locate garages for tow trucks along the 200 km circular highway between Johannesburg and Pretoria. Each garage has a fixed cost of R5000 per day. Towing jobs are equally likely along any point of the highway, and cost per kilometre towed is R50. If there were 800 towing jobs per day, what number of garages would minimize the sum of the fixed costs and towing costs?

14 The 1000 residents of Velddrift are all fishermen. Every morning they go to the nearest port to launch their fishing boats, and they return in the evening with their catch. The residents are evenly distributed along the 10 km perimeter of the beach. Each port has a fixed cost of R30 000/day. If the optimal number of ports is 2, what must be the per kilometre travel cost?

Answers to in-chapter exercises

11.1 $P_1 = (44 - Q_2) - Q_1$; so $MR_1 = (44 - Q_2) - 2Q_1$. This means $Q_1^* = R_1 = 12 - \frac{Q_2}{2}$ and $Q_2^* = R_2 = 12 - \frac{Q_1}{2}$ and they intersect where $Q_1 = Q_2 = 8$ and total market output will be 16. Market price will be $44 - 16 = 28$. This is illustrated by the figures at the top of page 380.

* This problem requires the use of calculus maximization techniques.

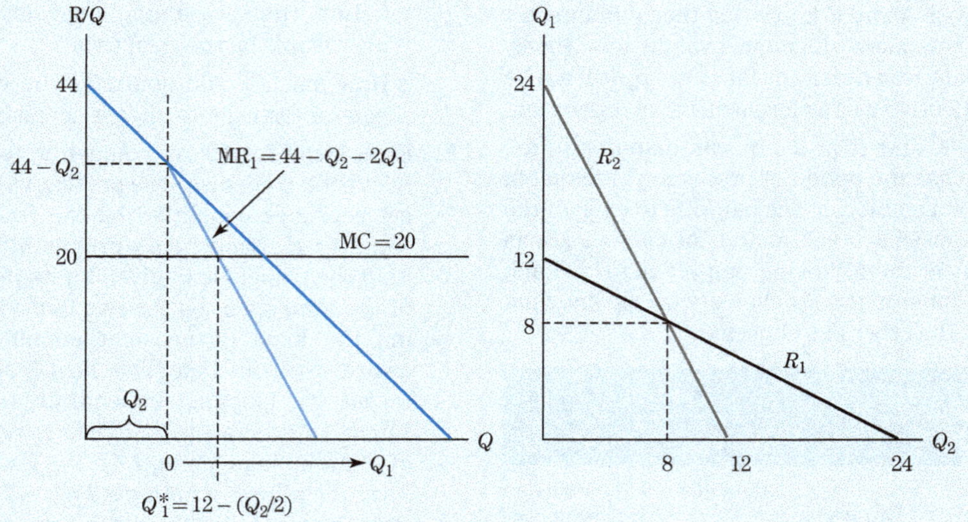

Exercise Answer 11.1

11.2 Price will settle at marginal cost, and so $P = 2$. So $P\ (= 2) = 10 - Q$ and we get the corresponding market demand, $Q = 8$, that will be shared equally by the two firms: $Q_1 = Q_2 = 4$.

11.3 Firm 2's marginal revenue curve is given by $10 - Q_1 - 2Q_2$. Setting MR = MC = 2, we have firm 2's reaction function, $R_2(Q_1) = Q_2^* = 4 - (Q_1/2)$ Substituting into firm 1's demand function, we get $P_1 = 10 - Q_1 - 4 + (Q_1/2) = 6 - (Q_1/2)$, and the corresponding marginal revenue curve, $MR_1 = 6 - Q_1$. $MR_1 = MC = 2$ solves for $Q_1^* = 4$. This means that Q_2 will be 2 units, for a total market output of 6 units. The market price will be $10 - 6 = 4$.

11.4 Each firm initially got $\frac{1}{20} = 5$ per cent of total demand, but will now get only $\frac{1}{25} = 4$ per cent. This means that, at every price, the quantity demanded will be 20 per cent lower than before (see the graph below). The new *dd* curve is $P = 10 - 0.00125Q$.

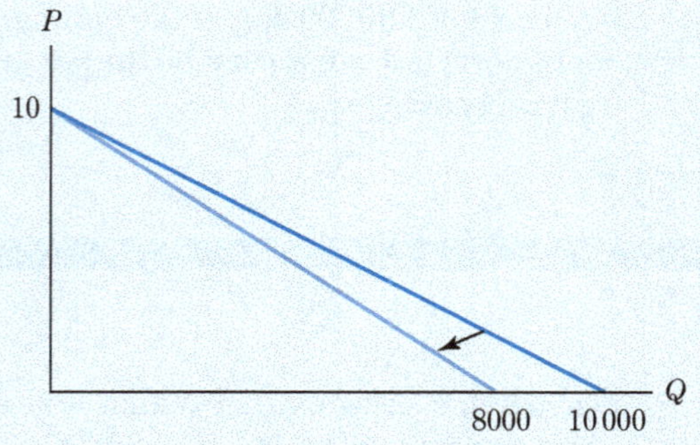

11.5 Regardless of firm 1's strategy, firm 2 does best with a high research budget. The choice of a high research budget is thus a dominant strategy for firm 2. Firm 1 does not have a dominant strategy. If firm 2 chooses a low research budget, then firm 1 does best by choosing a low research budget. But if firm 2 chooses a high research budget, then firm 1 does best by choosing a high research budget. Since firm 1 can predict that firm 2 will choose a high research budget, firm 1's best strategy is to choose a high research budget. The combination of 'high research budget–high research budget' (upper-left cell) is a Nash equilibrium.

11.6 With four restaurants, the average round trip distance is 0.25 km, which yields an average transportation cost of R9. On average, each restaurant will attract 100/4 people per day, which yields an ATC of [500 + 5(25)]/(25) = R25/day. Overall, average cost with four restaurants is thus R34/day.

11.7 N^* will now be $\sqrt{(36 \times 400)/500} \approx 5.4$, so there should now be five restaurants.

Part 4

Factor Markets

Part contents

In the following two chapters we shall examine the workings of markets for productive inputs. In Chapter 12 we shall see that, although the labour market behaves like the market for ordinary goods and services in many respects, in other important ways it is very different. Chapter 13 discusses the markets for real and financial capital. One feature that sets capital apart from other inputs, we shall see, is that while other inputs are usually hired on a period-by-period basis, capital equipment is often owned outright by the firm.

Chapter 12

Labour

Sometimes people earn money that we could argue has something to do with their productivity or what they are worth to their company. However, in many instances the salaries people receive seem to be out of line with their productivity, or their marginal product if we look at the situation from an economic perspective. Let us now look at a few examples of certain people's appearing to be out of line with what 'ordinary' people earn.

According to a PwC report,[1] the highest paid executive in South Africa was Richard Lepeu, paid more than R50 million by Richemont in 2013. Other Richemont executives who were among the 12 best-paid executives include Johan Rupert (R40 million), Gary Saage (R28 million) and Frederick Mostert and Martha Wikstrom (R22 million apiece). Other top earners include Marius Kloppers of BHT Billiton (R31 million), Cynthia Carroll of Anglo American (R24 million), Graham Mackay (R27 million) and Malcolm Wyman (R22 million) of SABMiller. The list of highest-earning executives is dominated by these companies because they are listed outside South Africa and pay their executives in euros, dollars or pounds sterling. Whitey Basson, chief executive of Shoprite, is the only South African-based executive on the list (at more than R40 million). Other executives of companies with a primary listing on the Johannesburg Stock Exchange include Mark Cutifani of AngloGold Ashanti (R16 million), Marius Jooste of Steinhoff (R15 million), Jerome Smith of Cipla Medpro (R14 million) and Thys Visser of Remgro (R12 million). Bear in mind that these packages also include bonuses and other benefits. If we look at the total wealth of South Africans nobody comes near to Bill Gates' estimated R500 billion. Although one must read statistics about individuals' net worth with caution, the following information gives you an idea of

[1] Referenced in article by Carin Smith, 'SA executives still raking it in': http://www.fin24.com/Economy/SA-executives-still-raking-it-in-20130716.

who the richest South Africans were in 2013.[2] Ivan Glasenberg, CEO of Glenmore International, was the richest individual in South Africa, with a net worth of R59.7 billion which put him in 125th position on Forbes World's Billionaire's List. Diamond magnate Nicky Oppenheimer, with a net worth of R55.6 billion, is just a shade behind Gkasenberg. Johan Rupert, chairman of Richemont and Remgro, has a net worth of R41.7 billion and Christo Wiese, chairman of Shoprite, an estimated net worth of R25.4 billion. Mining magnate Patrick Motsepe, of African Rainbow Minerals, is the only black billionaire, with an estimated net worth of R22.1 billion.

Sport stars who are in the limelight frequently earn an income that is not directly related to their 'productivity'. David Beckham, former England soccer captain, used to be in the news every day for at least six months of the year. No question, an eager audience awaited his views. Yet, with an income of $49 million a year in 2008 when he joined Los Angeles Galaxy, he hardly appeared to have made a real economic sacrifice. Plenty of people, probably you included, would have been willing to do Beckham's job for less. Indeed, Beckham himself would surely have been willing to perform for a subsistence wage rather than work in lifelong obscurity in some anonymous job elsewhere in the private sector.

Beckham's lofty salary was the result of two important factors: (1) he could do valuable things that the rest of us can't; and (2) more than one employer could provide him with a place in the spotlight. When Sir Alex Ferguson and Beckham had a difference of opinion when he still played for Manchester United, plenty of other clubs were willing to buy his services. In Beckham's case (or Ronaldinho, Ronaldo or Wayne Rooney), if Los Angeles Galaxy hadn't paid him such a high salary, some other team gladly would have done. Thousands of extra fans were drawn to the stadiums by the prospect of seeing one of the best all-round players in the game. Attendance at Los Angeles Galaxy games went up by 57 per cent in Beckham's first season. Los Angeles Galaxy knows it could hire your economics lecturer for much less, but even for free he'd probably be a bad bargain. Even though he retired after the 2013 season, Beckham still earned more than any other soccer player ($50.6 million). Cristiano Ronaldo of Real Madrid and Lionel Messi of Barcelona earned $43.5 million and $40.3 million, respectively. These players earn more in a week than the South African president in a year! How can we explain these abnormal remuneration packages from an economic perspective? In this chapter we try to answer this question.

Chapter preview

Our goal in this chapter is to examine the economic forces that govern wages and other conditions of employment. Relatively simple models of the labour market shed light on a variety of interesting questions, such as: how much will a worker with a given set of skills earn? Why do working conditions differ from one occupation to another? What do labour unions do? And so on.

We shall begin by deriving the demand curve for labour in both the short and the long run. We shall then approach the supply side of the labour market from the standpoint of an individual worker trying to decide how much to work at a given wage rate.

Our next step will be to take up the issue of compensating wage differentials – differences in wage payments that reflect differences in the environments in which people work. The general result is that the attractiveness of the overall compensation package – wages and environmental factors taken as a whole – tends to equalize across jobs that employ workers of a given skill level. As a further illustration of the concept of compensating differentials, we shall then examine the question of safety levels in the workplace.

We shall also apply the economic theory of labour markets to such topics as discrimination and minimum wage laws. We shall conclude, finally, by looking at why differences in pay sometimes seem to overstate differences in productivity and at other times to understate them.

The perfectly competitive firm's short-run demand for labour

Consider a firm that produces output using two inputs: capital (K) and labour (L). Suppose that, in the short run, its capital stock is fixed. If this firm sells all its output in a perfectly competitive market at the going market price, and if it can hire

[2] 'South Africa's richest people': http://businesstech.co.za/news/general/21775/south-africas-richest-people.

any quantity of labour it wishes at a wage rate of R120/hr, how many units of labour should it hire?

If the manager of the firm is thinking like an economist, she will reason as follows. 'The benefit of hiring an extra unit of labour will be the amount for which I can sell the extra output I will get. The cost will be the wage rate. Thus I should hire an extra unit of labour as long as the former exceeds the latter. If the latter exceeds the former, however, I should reduce the amount of labour I hire.' An important point to remember with the demand for factor inputs is that it is a *derived demand*. This means that the demand for inputs is derived from the firm's level of output and the cost of inputs: for example, the demand for painters is determined by the number of new houses built as well as by the cost of painters. We are so used to working with the market for goods or services that we are tempted to treat the factor market in the same way. Be careful as we now graph factor markets. They are different to those of the goods market and we must make sure that we do not confuse the two sides of the market.

The reasoning above is easily translated into a simple graphical hiring rule. Figure 12.1(a) shows the marginal product curve for labour input when capital is fixed (see Chapter 7). The marginal product curve, recall, tells how much extra output the firm will get when it hires an extra unit of labour. For example, when there are 40 units of labour employed, hiring an extra unit will yield 8 units of output. The downward slope of the marginal product curve reflects the law of diminishing returns (or as it is sometimes called, the law of diminishing marginal product).

Figure 12.1(b) simply multiplies the marginal product curve by the price of output, here $P = $ R20. When we multiply the output price and marginal product, $P \times MP_L$, we get the **value of the marginal product** of labour – denoted VMP_L – which is the extra revenue the firm will get by selling the extra output produced by the extra unit of labour. *The hiring rule for the firm is to choose that amount of labour for which the wage rate is equal to the* VMP_L. In Fig. 12.1(b), the rule thus tells the firm it should hire 80 units of labour when the wage rate is R120. Let us now look at two examples in which that equality does not hold. If we hire 40 workers, the $VMP_L = 160$, but we pay the worker only R120. It thus makes sense to employ more workers because we earn more with the extra output than what we are paying the marginal worker. On the other hand, when we employ 120 workers, the $VMP_L = 80$. Then our additional income from the extra output of the last worker is clearly less than the R120 we pay the worker and it makes sense to reduce the labour force.

Value of marginal product (VMP) The value, at current market price, of the extra output produced by an additional unit of input.

Figure 12.1 The competitive firm's short-run demand for labour

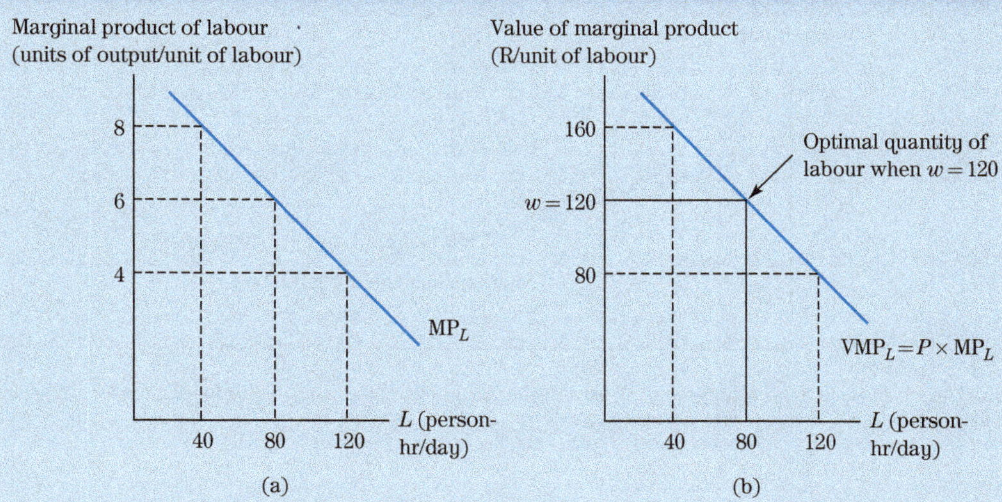

When the wage rate is R120/unit of labour (panel b), the perfectly competitive firm will hire 80 units of labour, the amount for which, VMP_L, and the wage rate are the same.

Only at $L = 80$ will the firm be unable to take additional steps to increase its profit.[3] Figure 12.1(a) is drawn for $MP_L = 10 - (\frac{1}{20})L$. When $P = 20$, the value of the marginal product of labour, depicted in Fig. 12.1(b), is

$$\begin{aligned} \text{VMP}_L &= P(\text{MP}_L) \\ &= 20(10 - 0.05L) \\ &= 200 - L \end{aligned}$$

If the wage is $w = 120$, then the optimum quantity of labour demanded by the firm will be

$$\begin{aligned} w &= \text{VMP}_L \\ &\Rightarrow 120 = 200 - L \\ &\Rightarrow L^* = 80 \end{aligned}$$

Exercise 12.1

At a wage rate of R120/unit of labour, how many units of labour would the firm shown in Fig. 12.1 hire if its product sold not for R20/unit but for R30/unit?

The perfectly competitive firm's long-run demand for labour

In the short run, the only way for the firm to respond to a reduction in the wage rate is to hire more labour. In the long run, however, all inputs are variable. As we saw in Chapter 7, a reduction in the price of labour will cause the firm to substitute labour for capital, reducing its marginal cost still further. This additional cost reduction will cause an even greater expansion of output than before. It follows that the firm's long-run hiring response to a change in the wage rate will be larger than its short-run response. The relationship between the two labour demand curves is portrayed in Fig. 12.2.

The firm's demand for labour will also tend to be more elastic, the more elastic is demand for its product. If a price reduction stimulates a large increase in the quantity of the product demanded, it will also stimulate a large increase in the amount of labour required to produce it. Finally, the firm's demand for labour will tend to be more elastic, the more it is able to substitute the services of labour for those of other inputs. Other things equal, the firm with L-shaped isoquants will have the least-elastic demand curve for labour.

The market demand curve for labour

Recall from Chapter 4 that the technique for deriving a market demand curve for a product is to add the individual consumer demand curves horizontally. The technique for generating the market demand curve for labour is similar, except for one important difference. In Fig. 12.3, the curve

Figure 12.2 Short-run and long-run demand curves for labour

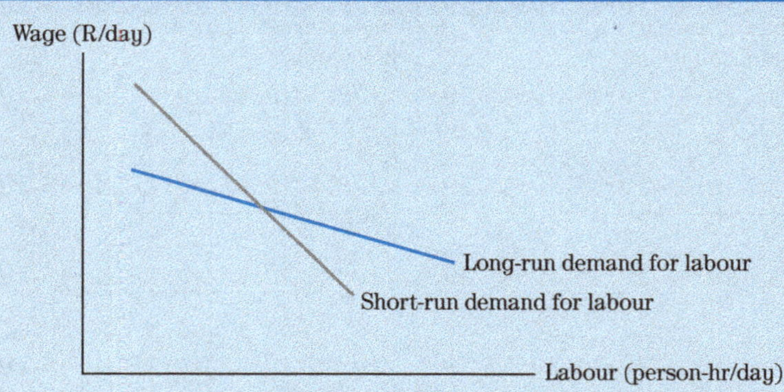

The demand for labour is more elastic in the long run because the firm has the opportunity to substitute labour for capital. In the short run, its only avenue of response is to increase output.

[3] There is one important limitation to the application of the $w = \text{VMP}_L$ rule. Suppose the wage rate were above the value of the average product of labour, which is the product of price and the average product of labour, denoted by VAP_L. If the firm pays a wage higher than VAP_L, it will be paying out more than the total value of what workers produce, which means that it will earn a loss on each worker it hires. For values of w above VAP_L, then, the perfectly competitive firm will demand no labour at all.

labelled $\sum VMP_L$, $P = P_1$ is the horizontal summation of the individual VMP_L curves when the output price is equal to P_1. (This VMP_L curve is thus uniquely related to a product price of P_1.) At that value of the price of output, firms taken as a whole demand L_1 units of labour per time period when the wage rate is equal to w_1. Now let the wage rate fall to w_2. This makes labour more affordable and each firm will hire more labour, in the process moving downwards along its own individual demand curve for labour. As each firm responds in this way, it offers more of its product for sale in the market. Such action by any one firm in a competitive market would leave the price of output unchanged. But the effect of all firms acting in concert is to produce a downward movement along the industry product demand curve.

This increase in output will necessarily involve a reduction in output price. In turn, this will cause the VMP_L curve for each firm to shift downwards. If output price falls from P_1 to P_2, aggregate demand for labour will be given by the point corresponding to w_2 on the curve labelled $\sum VMP_L$, $P = P_2$. For each different price at which the product is sold, we thus get a different $\sum VMP_L$ curve. According to this reasoning, we see that the market demand curve for labour (the curve labelled *DD*) will be steeper than the horizontal summation of the VMP_L curves.

The preceding discussion implicitly assumed that there is only one type of labour, and that all of it is employed by a single competitive industry. In the real world, of course, matters are more complicated. There are almost countless categories of labour – carpenters, electricians, physicists, attorneys, high school teachers, and so on – and any one type finds employment in many different industries. Thus electricians are employed in the residential, construction, automobile, commercial office building, steel, computer and fishing industries, to name but a few. The market demand curve for electricians is therefore made up of the individual demand of firms in not just one industry but many. In other words, there are many types of labour available, but labour with the same educational background is demanded in many different industries.

Suppose payments to electricians by firms in each separate industry constitute only a small fraction – say, 0.1 per cent – of their respective total costs. A small change – say, 10 per cent – in the wage paid to electricians would then produce an all but imperceptible change – namely, 0.01 per cent – in each industry's total costs, and hence no appreciable effect on their respective output prices. Under these circumstances, the demand for electricians will be closely approximated by the horizontal summation of the various individual firm demand curves, and the complication discussed in connection with Fig. 12.3 may be ignored.

The firm's situation in a competitive labour market

The individual firm in a competitive market for labour cannot influence the going wage rate. That

Figure 12.3 The market demand curve for labour

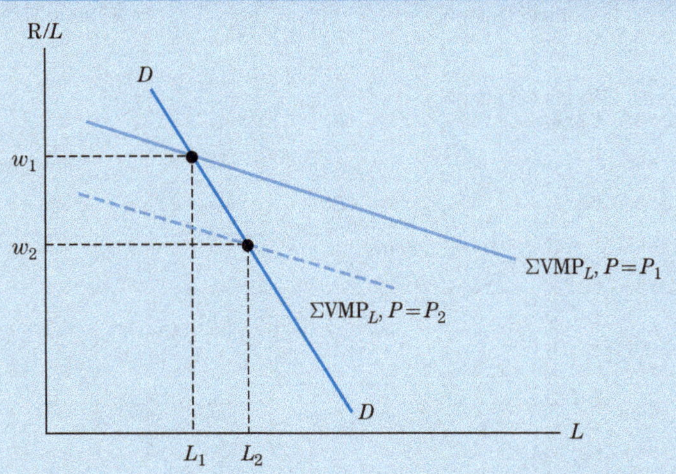

When the wage rate falls from w_1 to w_2, each firm hires more labour and produces more output. The increase in output causes output price to fall, which reduces the value of labour's marginal product. The market demand curve for labour is thus steeper than the horizontal summation of the individual demand curves.

is determined in the total market for labour, and is illustrated in Fig. 12.4. As we would expect, more labour would be supplied at higher wages and more labour demanded at lower wages. Just like in any other market, equilibrium is where demand for labour is equal to supply. In Fig. 12.4 it is at a wage rate of R120/hr.

Because the individual firm in a perfectly competitive labour market cannot affect the price of labour (the wage), the current going wage is a given for the firm. Workers will thus supply their labour at R120/hr and that is what the firm has to pay. The only thing that the firm can decide is how many workers to employ. If the firm employs 40 workers, the MRP_L is R160/hr, but the additional cost of each worker (also known as marginal expenditure or marginal input costs) is only R120/hr. In such a situation, it makes sense to expand and employ additional workers because the additional revenue that the firm gains from hiring another worker is R40/hr more than what it has to pay the worker. By hiring more workers, it can increase its profits. However, if the firm hires 120 workers, the MRP_L is only R80/hr, but the workers must be paid R120/hr. Then the obvious thing to do will be to cut back on production and hire fewer workers. When the firm hires 80 workers the additional income of the last worker is R120/hr and that is equal to the additional cost, namely, the wage of R120/hr that must be paid to the last worker. The rational firm in a competitive labour market will thus hire the number of workers at which MRP equals the wage rate (or marginal expenditure).

An imperfect competitor's demand for labour

Our discussion of the demand for labour has assumed that the firm faces a perfectly elastic demand for its product. Any additional output produced by additional workers could be sold at the same price as existing output. With an imperfect competitor, of course, this will not be so. Such firms face downward-sloping demand curves, and if they hire additional workers, they must cut their prices in order to sell the additional output. If you are uncertain about this concept, reread Chapters 10 and 11, in which imperfect competition are discussed.

We saw that, with a perfect competitor, the value of the extra output obtained by hiring an extra worker is the product of price and the marginal product of labour. With an imperfect competitor, by contrast, it is the product of marginal revenue and marginal product. This product is called the **marginal revenue product** of labour, and is denoted MRP_L. In terms of the definitions of marginal revenue and marginal product, MRP_L is thus given by

Marginal revenue product (MRP) The amount by which total revenue increases with the employment of an additional unit of input.

Figure 12.4 A firm's hiring decision for labour in a competitive market

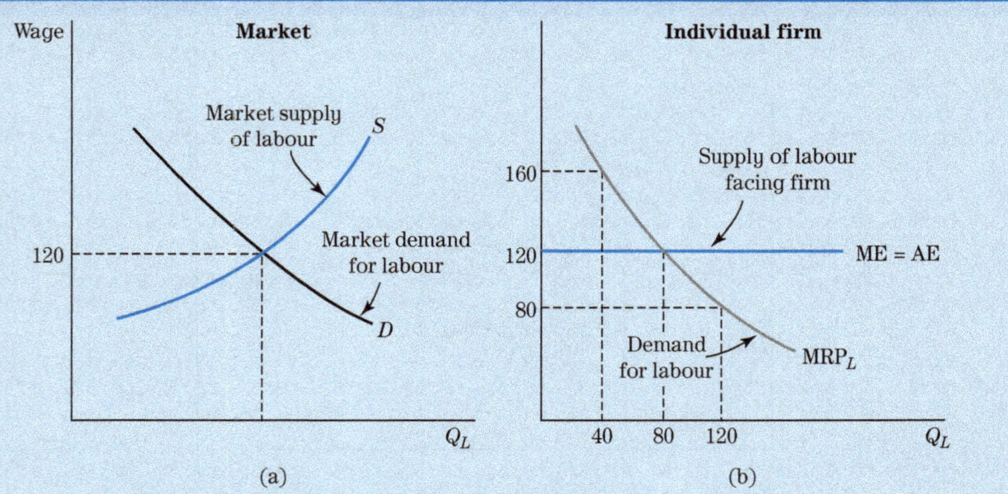

In a perfectly competitive labour market, a firm faces a perfectly elastic supply of labour S_L and can hire as many workers as it wants at a wage of R120. The firm's demand for labour is given by the MRP_L curve. The profit-maximizing firm will hire 80 workers where the marginal revenue product of labour is equal to the wage rate of R120/hr.

$$\text{MRP}_L = \frac{\Delta Q}{\Delta L}\frac{\Delta \text{TR}}{\Delta Q} \text{ or it can be written as } (MP_L) \times (\text{MR}) \tag{12.1}$$

which reduces to

$$\text{MRP}_L = \frac{\Delta \text{TR}}{\Delta L}\left(\text{or } \frac{\text{dTR}}{\text{d}L}\right) \tag{12.2}$$

VMP_L and MRP_L are alike in that each represents the addition to total revenue that results from the addition of a unit of labour. The difference between them is that MRP_L takes into account that the sale of additional output requires a cut in price for the imperfect competitor. VMP_L values the extra output at the existing product price, which is unaffected by variations in the perfect competitor's output. MRP_L values the additional output at its marginal revenue, which is less than its price.

How much labour will a firm hire if it faces a downward-sloping demand curve for its output? The answer is that it will hire that quantity for which the wage rate and MRP_L are equal. The argument for this claim is essentially similar to that offered for the $w = \text{VMP}_L$ condition for the perfect competitor.

In the case of the perfectly competitive firm, the short-run demand for labour is downward sloping because of the law of diminishing returns. The more labour the firm hires, the lower will the MP_L be and hence the lower will the VMP_L be. For the monopolist, too, the law of diminishing returns causes the short-run demand curve for labour to be downward sloping. But there is an additional reason in the case of the monopolist, which is that its marginal revenue curve is also downward sloping (remember that $\text{MRP}_L = \text{MP}_L \times \text{MR}$).

For the same reasons as discussed in the perfectly competitive case, the monopolist's long-run demand for labour will be more elastic than its short-run demand. But we need not make any additional adjustments to the MRP_L curve when moving from the firm to the industry demand curve, in either the long run or the short run. The monopolist's demand for labour *is* the industry demand for labour. It already takes account of the fact that extra output means a lower product price.

The supply of labour

For simplicity, let's again imagine that there is only one category of labour, and that the choice confronting each worker is how many hours to work each day. The alternative to working is to spend time on 'leisure activities', which here include playing, sleeping, eating and any other activity besides paid work in the labour market. If the worker is paid at a constant rate of R150 for each hour she works, how many hours should she work?

On reflection, this turns out to be a simple consumer choice problem of the same sort considered in Chapter 3 when we discussed indifference curves. The choice in this context is between two goods we may call 'income' and 'leisure'. We assume that the consumer's preferences regarding the two goods can be summarized in the form of an indifference map. In Fig. 12.5 the curves labelled I_1, I_2 and I_3 represent three such curves for a hypothetical worker.

The line labelled B in the same diagram represents the individual's budget constraint. If she spent the entire day pursuing leisure activities, she would earn no income, which says that the point (24, 0) must be the horizontal intercept of B. Alternatively, if she worked 24 hr/day at the wage rate $w_0 = \text{R}150/\text{hr}$, her daily income would be $24w_0 = \text{R}3600$, which tells us that the point (0, 3600) must be the vertical intercept of B. The remainder of B is the straight line that joins these two points. Note that h on the leisure axis measures the hours spent on leisure. The hours that she works are thus $(24 - h)$. The equation of line B is $M = w(24 - h) = 150(24 - h) = 3600 - 150h$, where M is daily income in rands. The slope of B is simply the negative of the hourly wage rate, $-w_0 = -150$.

Given her preferences and budget constraint, the best this hypothetical consumer can do is point A in Fig. 12.5, the tangency between B and the indifference curve furthest away from the origin, namely, I_2. Here, the optimal bundle corresponds to spending $h^* = 16$ hr/day on leisure, the remaining $24 - h^* = 8$ hr on paid work. The consumer's daily income in rands will be $(24 - h^*)w_0 = \text{R}1200$. At A, the marginal rate of substitution between leisure and income is exactly w_0, the hourly wage rate. This means that, at the optimal bundle, the marginal value of an extra hour of leisure is exactly equal to the opportunity cost of acquiring it – namely, the R150 the consumer would have earned had she worked that extra hour.

Exercise 12.2

Suppose the wage rate is $w = \text{R}200/\text{hr}$. Find the equation for the income–leisure budget constraint, and graph it. Suppose that, facing this wage, an individual chooses $h = 14$ hr of leisure. Find the worker's income M per day for this amount of leisure.

Figure 12.5 The optimal choice between leisure and income

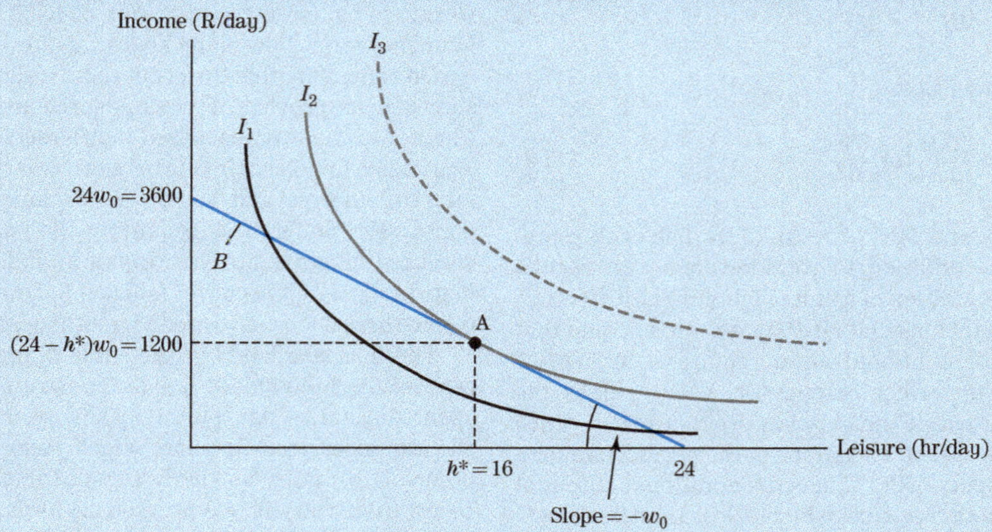

The optimal amount of leisure is $h^* = 16$ hr/day, which corresponds to a point of tangency between the budget constraint, B, and the indifference curve, I_2. The corresponding amount of paid labour is $24 - h^* = 8$ hr/day, which yields a daily wage income of $(24 - h^*) w_0 =$ R1200/day.

To generate a worker's supply curve for labour, we simply ask how the optimal amount of paid work varies as the wage rate varies. Figure 12.6 looks at the optimal leisure choices for three different hourly wage rates: $w = 60$, $w =$ R120 and $w =$ R180. The supply of labour corresponding to $w =$ R60 is $24 - h_1^* = 6$ hr; to $w =$ R120, $24 - h_2^* = 9$ hr; and to $w =$ R180, $24 - h_3^* = 7$ hr.

Figure 12.7 plots the relationship between the wage rate and the hours of work supplied by the hypothetical worker whose indifference map is shown in Fig. 12.6. Calling this person the ith

Figure 12.6 Optimal leisure choices for different wage rates

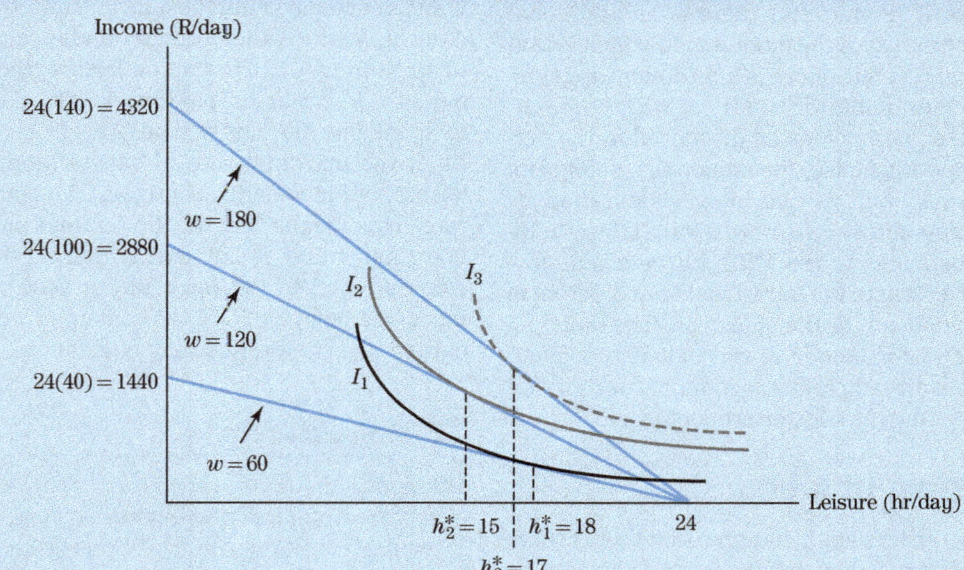

When the hourly wage rises from R60 to R120, the optimal amount of leisure falls from 18 to 15 hr/day. But when the wage rises still further, to R180, the optimal amount of leisure rises to 17 hr/day.

Figure 12.7 The labour supply curve for the *i*th worker

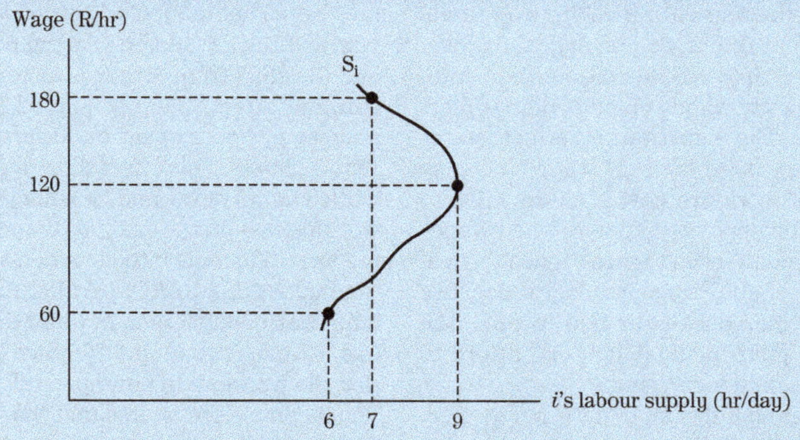

For this worker, an increase in the wage elicits greater labour supply when the wage is less than R120/hr, but smaller labour supply when the wage is above R120/hr.

worker of many, we see that his supply curve is the line denoted S_i. When compared with the other supply curves we have encountered, the salient feature of S_i is that it is not everywhere upward sloping. In particular, it is 'backward bending' for values of w larger than R120/hr, which is another way of saying that, in that region, higher wages lead to fewer hours of work supplied.

We can use the income and substitution effects to explain such behaviour by workers. Let us assume our worker starts off with a wage of R120/hr. In Fig. 12.8 it is clear that the worker will

Figure 12.8 Substitution and income effects of a wage increase

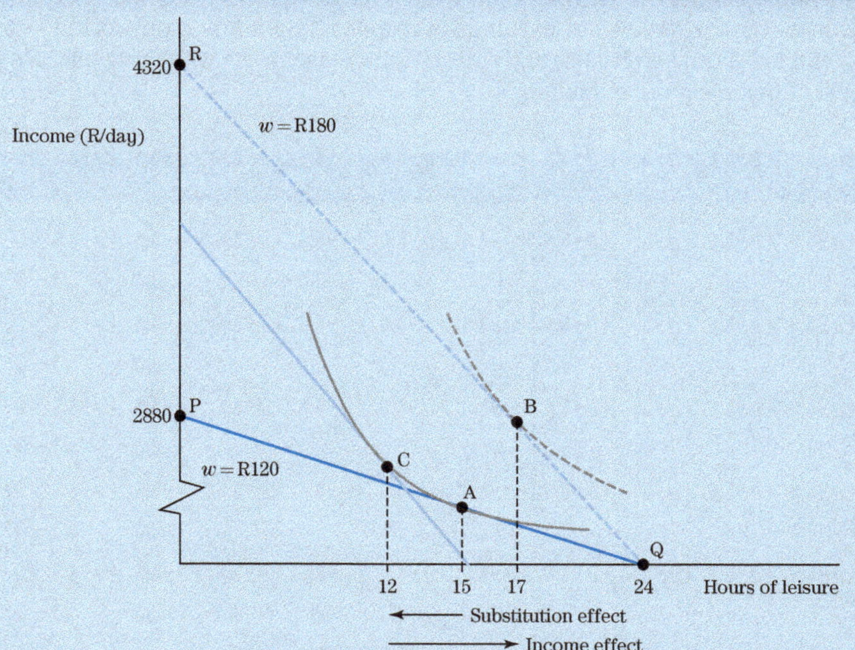

When the wage rate rises from R120/hr to R180/hr, the worker's budget line shifts from *PQ* to *RQ* and the worker moves from point A to point B. Initially, the worker worked 9 hours, but after the wage increase only 7 hours. The income effect outweighs the substitution effect, and in this case gives rise to a backward-bending supply curve for labour.

initially be at point A, where 15 hours are spent on leisure, meaning that he works 9 hours a day. Now assume his wage increases to R180/hr; eventually he will end at point B, but we can split the movement from A to B into an income and substitution effect. Whenever wages change, both effects come into play. The substitution effect states that you will work more hours if wages increase because hours of work are now of more value to you. Of course, the opposite happens when wages decrease. The income effect states that you will work fewer hours if your wage increases. Because a wage increase increases your real income (the buying power of your income), you can afford to work fewer hours, and vice versa.

Let us begin at equilibrium point A in Fig. 12.8, where the worker is initially in equilibrium. Now his wage increases from R120/day to R180/day. With the substitution effect, we take into consideration only what happens to relative prices. Therefore we know that the slope of the budget line becomes steeper. We draw a 'temporary' budget line with the new slope, but tangent to the *original* indifference curve of the consumer. C is the point of tangency, and the shift from A to C is as a result of the substitution effect. Clearly, Fig. 12.8 shows that the number of hours spent on leisure decreases from 15 to 12 hours. This effect thus causes the worker to work 3 hours more, and he will now have a 12-hour working day. In the next step, we take the increase in our real income into consideration, which shifts the budget line to RQ, parallel to the right of the temporary budget line. At point B, this new budget line is tangent to an indifference curve, indicating that the worker will now spend 17 hours on leisure. The income effect states that the worker will work 5 hours (12 – 7) less, and the net effect is that the worker will work 2 hours less as a result of the wage increase. In this example, the income effect was greater than the substitution effect.

Example 12.1

Caster wants to earn R2000/day, because with that amount she can live comfortably and meet all her financial obligations. Graph Caster's labour supply curve.

If L^s denotes the number of hours per day Caster chooses to work, it must satisfy $wL^s = 2000$, where w is Caster's hourly wage rate in rands. Caster's supply curve will thus be given by $L^s = 2000w$, which is shown in Fig. 12.9.

A person who holds this goal will always work less whenever the wage rate rises, and will have a backward-bending supply curve. You might work over the summer holidays to finance your education. As soon as the target level of earnings is reached, you might stop working (or work fewer hours) and spend more time on leisure activities. An increase in the wage rate enables you to reach the target level of income more quickly.

Figure 12.9 The labour supply curve for a worker seeking a target level of income

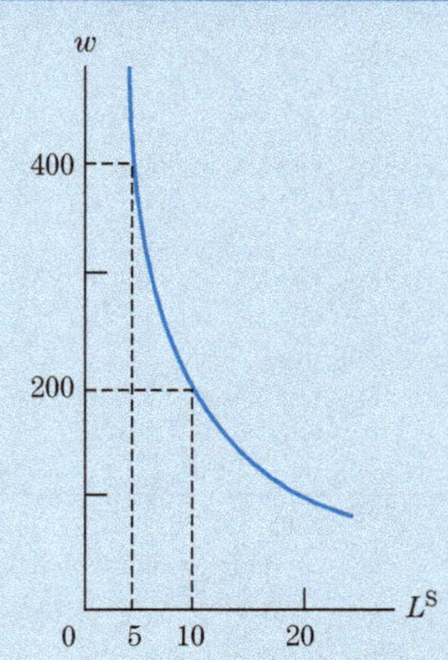

The higher her hourly wage rate, the fewer hours Caster has to work to earn her daily target of R2000.

We can link this to Fig. 12.7. If wages increase from R60/hr to R120/hr, the substitution effect is greater than the income effect, causing the worker to increase his working day from 6 to 9 hours. As his wage increases further, to R180/hr, he shortens his working day by 5 hours because his income effect is greater than his substitution effect, so that his working day is now only 7 hours per day. Whether a worker will work more or fewer hours will be determined by which of the two effects is the biggest. As long as the substitution effect is the biggest, we shall have a normal, positively-sloped supply curve for labour, meaning that the more the employer is paying the worker, the more hours he will work. However, if the income effect is dominant, we get a negatively-sloped supply curve for labour. Remember that, when the wage changes, *both* effects are at play and the net effect will depend on which effect is the greatest.

Exercise 12.3

Draw the labour supply curve for a person with a daily target income of R1200.

Not all individuals exhibit backward-bending supply curves like those in Example 12.1 and Exercise 12.4. An increase in the wage makes leisure (the opportunity cost of working longer hours) more expensive. Only if the income effect dominates the substitution effect over some range of wage rates, do we see a backward-bending labour supply curve over that range. Otherwise, the labour supply curve will be everywhere upward sloping, as Example 12.2 clearly illustrates. In reality, relatively few people reach the point at which they are not willing to work longer hours if their wages increase.

Exercise 12.4

Suppose instead that a cab driver's goal was to earn a target level of earnings not for each day, but rather for each week. The driver also prefers to drive no more hours than necessary to reach his target, and in his city it always rains two days each week. How would this driver's hours driven on rainy days compare with his hours driven on sunny days?

For many people, the wage rate varies with the number of hours they work, as in the case of a higher wage for overtime. People who have the opportunity to earn premium pay by working overtime face a kinked budget constraint, as illustrated in Exercise 12.5.

Exercise 12.5

Find the optimal leisure demand for wage $w = \text{R}200/\text{hr}$ for someone who views income and leisure as perfect substitutes in a 100:1 ratio (willing to sacrifice 1 hour of leisure for R100 of income). *Hint*: This person's indifference curves are straight lines given by the equation $M = a - 100h$ for various values of a.

Often we can judge whether a change in income possibilities leaves people better off or worse off without detailed information about their preferences. Knowing their two budget constraints (before and after) and their initial choice of leisure can suffice. If the initial choice of leisure lies on the new budget constraint, but the wage at that point has changed, the individual must be better off. The individual can be no worse off, since she can still afford the same leisure and income. Now, the worker can adjust leisure choice (more leisure if her wage falls, less leisure if her wage rises) to reach a higher indifference curve. This line of reasoning will help you work through Exercise 12.6.

Exercise 12.6

Karim can work as many hours as he chooses. In his current job, Karim is paid R50/hr for the first 8 hours he works and R200 for each hour over 8. Faced with this payment schedule, Karim chooses to work 12 hours a day. If Karim is offered a new job that pays R100 for every hour he works, will he take the new job? Explain your answer with the aid of indifference curves.

Interestingly, if you take the US labour market as a whole, there has been a steady tendency for the average workweek to decline over time, while at the same time real wages have been rising. (We shall not use South African statistics here because many non-economic factors – especially political ones – have influenced the labour market here for many years.) Manufacturing production workers in the USA, for example, worked 20 per cent fewer hours in 1980 than in 1914, even though their real wage was more than four times as high in 1980 as in 1914. This negative correlation between wage rates and average hours naturally does not establish that rising wages are the sole cause of

Economic naturalist 12.1

Why is it so hard to find a taxi during rush hours?

In South Africa we are used to our minibus taxis. In New York, alone, there are more than 13000 yellow taxi cabs, and London is famous for its black taxis. Normally in the big cities one can generally hail a taxicab within a matter of seconds during good weather. But during rush hours, finding one may be extremely difficult. Why this difference?

© Glow Images
Why do many taxis disappear during rush hours?

The most obvious reason is that roads are very congested in rush hours and, although the taxi drivers would love to pick up more fares, the traffic makes it impossible. That is also the time when demand for taxis is highest. High demand linked with slow-moving traffic creates a situation whereby many people cannot easily find taxis. During bad weather people experience the same problems. Many people who would be willing to walk short distances during good weather prefer to take a cab instead when it rains. But taxi drivers tend to work shorter days during bad weather. A study carried out in New York in the late 1990s revealed that many drivers work only as long as necessary to reach a target level of income each day.[4] On low-demand sunny days, they must spend much of their day cruising for passengers, but on high-demand rainy days they can reach their target income much quicker.

shorter workweeks. But, given our theory of individual labour supply, it seems plausible to suppose that they have played a role. This interpretation is reinforced by the observation that a modest decline in manufacturing wages since 1985 has been accompanied by a small increase in average weekly hours.

The theory of labour supply plays a crucial role in the logic of welfare reform. The goal of welfare is to provide additional income for the poor.

Example 12.2

Find the optimal leisure demand for wage $w = $ R200/hour for someone who views income and leisure as perfect complements in a 100:1 ratio (that is, who requires 1 hour of leisure for every R100 of income).

If we assume that hours spent on leisure are h and hours spent working are w, then the income/leisure budget constraint is

$$\begin{aligned} M &= w(24 - h) \\ &= 200(24 - h) \\ &= 4800 - 200h \end{aligned}$$

Since the individual requires 1 hr of leisure for every R100 of income, the consumption point must lie on the line $M = 100h$. The intersection of the budget constraint and this consumption line (see Fig. 12.10) yields the leisure demand:

$$\begin{aligned} 4800 - 200h &= 100h \\ \Rightarrow 4800 &= 300h \\ \Rightarrow h &= 16 \text{ hr/day} \end{aligned}$$

[4] L. Babcock, C. Camerer, G. Loewenstein and R. Thaler, 'Labour supply of New York City cab drivers: one day at a time', *Quarterly Journal of Economics*, 1997, vol. 111, pp. 408–441.

Figure 12.10 When leisure and income are perfect complements

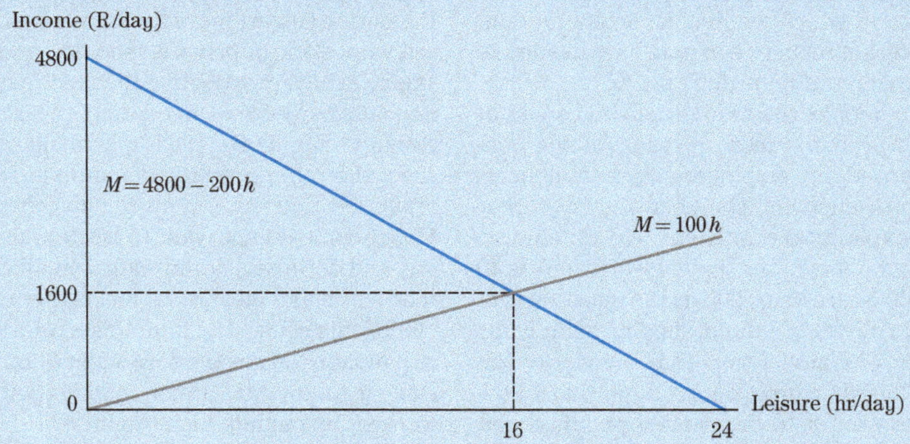

If income and leisure are perfect complements in a 100:1 ratio, an individual will consume leisure at a point on the budget constraint that satisfies $M = 100h$.

One concern, however, is that welfare assistance may weaken incentives to work. In this respect, the specific form taken by welfare assistance is important.

Exercise 12.7

Consider the following two anti-poverty programmes: a payment of R48/day and a payment of 40 per cent of wage income. Assuming that poor people have the option of working at R10/hr, show how each programme would affect the budget constraint of a representative poor worker (who is already working for R10/hr). Which programme would be most likely to reduce the number of hours worked?

The non-economist's reaction to the labour supply model

Seeing the economic model of labour supply for the first time, many non-economists consider it a most unrealistic description of the way people actually allocate their time between labour and leisure. Most jobs, after all, offer little choice in the number of hours to work each day. One can of course choose between part-time and full-time work, but jobs in the part-time category are often so unattractive that many workers view this as a choice not even worth considering.

In part, such criticism of the labour supply model is based on too narrow an understanding of it. The model does not say that people literally choose the number of hours they work each day. Critics are correct that this is simply not a choice open to most workers. But over the span of several months or years, people have considerably more say over the amount of time spent at work. Law school graduates, for example, can go to work for fast-track law firms where associates routinely put in 14-hour days, 7 days a week; or they can choose firms where everyone is out by 17:00. People can choose jobs, such as teaching, which offer long holidays. They can also change jobs frequently, taking time off in between.

Even allowing for all these possible sources of flexibility, however, it is still fair to say that the options for most people are limited. If firms could offer complete flexibility with no loss in productivity, it would be to their advantage to do so. But most firms hire groups of workers who must interact, and things begin to break down if people are not all on the premises during the same hours of the day. This still leaves the possibility of different firms having working days of different lengths, which, as noted, we do see to some extent. But even here there are often limits. If the workers in one firm need to interact with those in other firms, even if only to exchange information over the telephone, there has to be a common span of time when people are reliably at their desks.

Obviously, workers can make contact with customers or their employers through their laptops or cell phones from any place. However, even in the electronic era in which we live, a certain amount of human interaction between parties is needed to ensure misunderstandings don't occur.

For many people, the amount of time spent at work is thus probably more a result of the constraints imposed by employers than a deliberate choice of their own. The need for co-worker interaction explains the existence of a common workweek, but not why the typical workweek is 40 rather than 30 hours long. This is the question that the economic model of labour supply really helps us to answer. The model says that the workweek is 40 hours long because, on average, that's how long workers want it to be. If most people found an extra hour of leisure much more valuable than an extra hour's wage, profit-seeking employers would have an immediate incentive to reduce the length of the workweek. Here, again, we see the power of a simple theory to help explain what people do, even when they themselves correctly perceive that the proximate reasons for their actions are forces beyond their control.

The market supply curve

The market supply curve for any given category of labour is obtained by horizontally adding the individual supply curves for the potential suppliers of labour in that category. Even though many individuals may have backward-bending supply curves – indeed, even though the nation as a whole may have a backward-bending supply curve – the supply curve for any particular category of labour is nonetheless almost certain to be upward sloping. The reason is that wage increases in one category of labour not only change the number of hours worked by people already in that category, but also lure people into that category from other categories. Just as an increase in the price of potatoes causes many cotton farmers to switch to potatoes, so an increase in the wages of hair stylists causes file clerks, department store salespeople and others to try their hand at cutting hair.

Monopsony

The classic illustration of a single-employer labour market is the so-called company town. Workers either cannot or will not leave the area, and new firms cannot enter. A firm in this position is called a *monopsonist* – or 'sole buyer' – in its labour market. In the South African case, the school education market is basically a monopsony. Teachers are demanded only by the Department of Education (if we ignore the small number of teachers who work in private schools), and with fixed salary scales prospective teachers have very limited alternatives to accepting the remuneration package supplied by the Department of Education. Also, the mining sector demands a specific type of worker that is not required by other industries. Most people do not want to work underground all day and definitely not in such a small confinement that will make most of us feel rather claustrophobic. In this sense, the mining sector also operates as a monopsony as the sole buyer of mine workers. Does it follow that a monopsonist will exploit its workers by paying them too little?

Let's consider the question of wages. A firm that hires labour in a perfectly competitive labour market faces a supply curve of labour that is a horizontal line at the market wage. Its own hiring decisions have essentially no effect on the market wage. For the monopsonist, by contrast, the labour supply curve is the market supply curve itself. Suppose, for the sake of discussion, that it is upward sloping, like the curve labelled S in Fig. 12.12. S is also called the **average factor cost**, or AFC, curve, because it tells us the average payment per worker necessary to achieve any given level of employment. The total cost of a given level of employment – called **total factor cost**, or TFC – is simply the product of that employment level and the corresponding value of AFC. Thus the total factor cost of an employment level of 100 workers/hr in Fig. 12.12 is equal to $100 \times$ R70 = R7000/hr.

Average factor cost (AFC) Another name for the supply curve for an input.
Total factor cost (TFC) The product of the employment level of an input and its average factor cost.

Now suppose the firm already has 100 workers (for which it pays R70/hr), and is considering the cost of adding the 101st. To increase its employment by 1 unit, it must raise its wage by R1.00/hr, not only for the additional unit of labour it hires, but for the current 100 units as well. The total factor cost of 101 workers is R71.00 $\times$ 101 = R7171. The **marginal factor cost**, or MFC, of the 101st worker is

Marginal factor cost (MFC) The amount by which total factor cost changes with the employment of an additional unit of input.

Example 12.3

Rising enrolment on MBA programmes has increased the demand for economists in business schools. If most economists are currently teaching in economics and business management faculties at the comprehensive universities, how will this increase in business school demand affect salaries and employment of economists in the two environments?

In Fig. 12.11(c), the market supply curve of economists is the line labelled S. It is upward sloping, on the assumption that higher wage rates for economists will induce some people to choose economics over other professions. The demand curve for economists at the normal economics and business management faculties at the comprehensive universities is shown in Fig. 12.11(a). In Fig. 12.11(b), the original and new demand curves for economists on the part of business schools are labelled D_{B1} and D_{B2}, respectively. Adding the faculties and business school demand curves horizontally (on the assumption that the salaries paid to economists are too small a share of total university costs to affect tuition significantly), we get both the original and new total demand curves for economists in Fig. 12.11(c), labelled $D_U + D_{B1}$ and $D_U + D_{B2}$, respectively.

Note that the increased demand by business schools causes the wage rate for economists in both environments to rise from w_1 to w_2. To see how employment in the two environments is affected, we simply trace w_2 leftwards to the respective demand curves. The increase in business school employment of economists is $Q_{B2} - Q_{B1}$, while the reduction in faculty employment is $Q_{U1} - Q_{U2}$. The gain in business school employment will be equal to the sum of the movements out of faculty positions ($Q_{U1} - Q_{U2}$) and the overall movement into the economics profession from the outside ($Q_2 - Q_1$).

This example illustrates two points of particular interest. First is the tendency of salaries for workers in a given occupation to equalize across sectors of the economy that employ that occupation. When the demand for bricklayers went up because of a boom in commercial construction projects before the 2010 World Cup in South Africa, homeowners who wanted to add a recreation room to their house found themselves paying more as well. The idea here is simple: unless the wages of bricklayers employed in residential construction also rose, many of them would leave that sector for commercial construction. Provided that work in the two environments is in other respects equally desirable, the only stable outcome is for the wage to be the same in each.

The second point suggested by the example is that a small occupational subsector can experience a large proportional rise in demand without appreciably bidding up wages throughout the

Figure 12.11 An increase in demand by one category of employer

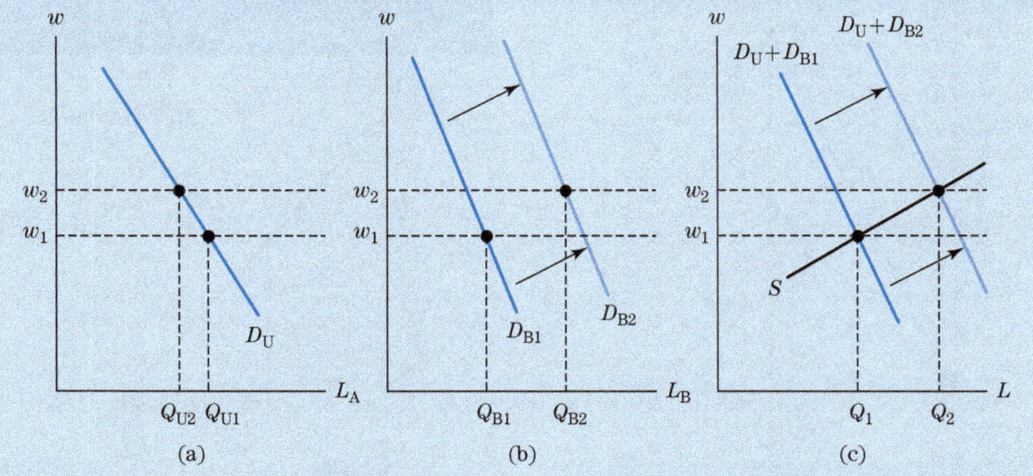

The demand for economists to teach in business schools rises (panel b), causing the total market demand curve for economists to rise (panel c). Employment at the new higher wage is determined by consulting the respective demand curves of the faculties (panel a) and business school sector (panel b).

occupation. Because business schools employed only a small fraction of the total number of academic economists to begin with, these schools could increase their employment substantially without having to pay dramatically higher wages. The general rule is that the effective elasticity of supply to any small occupational subsector will be much higher than to the occupational market taken as a whole.

As a strictly empirical matter, economists who teach in business schools earn about 15 per cent higher salaries than those who teach in normal faculties. This is a large enough difference to suggest that something must be missing from our theory that calls for equal wages in each sector. It is not sufficient merely to observe that business schools are 'richer' and therefore can afford to pay more. The question is why they should have to pay more if the economist's only other alternative is to work at the faculty's salary.

The implicit assumption in our model most likely to be invalid is that economists regard the two working environments as being equally attractive. For reasons we shall explore later in the chapter, it seems to be necessary to pay economists a premium to induce them to move from a faculty to a business school environment.

the amount by which total factor cost changes as a result of hiring that additional worker:

$$\text{MFC} = \frac{\Delta\text{TFC}}{\Delta L}\left(\text{or } \frac{\text{dTFC}}{\text{d}L}\right) \quad (12.3)$$

For the example given in Fig. 12.12, we thus have MFC = R7171 – R7000 = R171/hr. The MFC of the 101st worker is the sum of the R71/hr he is paid directly and the extra R100/hr that must be divided among the existing 100 workers. Because hiring an extra worker always means paying more to existing workers, the MFC curve will always lie above the corresponding AFC curve. If the AFC curve is a straight line with the formula $\text{AFC} = a + 2bL$, then the corresponding MFC curve will be a straight line with the same intercept and twice the slope as the AFC curve: $\text{TFC} = \text{AFC} \times \text{L} = aL + 2bL^2$, which yields $\text{MFC} = a + 4bL$.

Figure 12.13 describes the equilibrium wage and employment levels for a monopsonist. A monopsonist's demand curve for labour is

Figure 12.12 Average and marginal factor cost

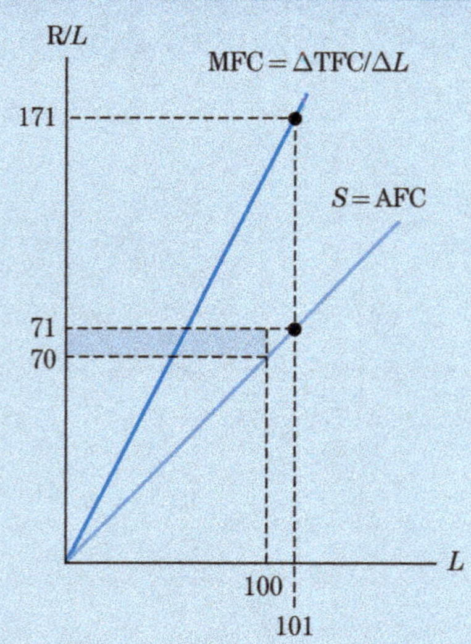

When the supply curve (S) facing a monopsonist is upward sloping, the cost of hiring an additional unit of labour (MFC) is no longer merely the wage he must be paid. To that wage must be added the additional payment that must be made to existing workers (the shaded rectangle).

Figure 12.13 The profit-maximizing wage and employment levels for a monopsonist

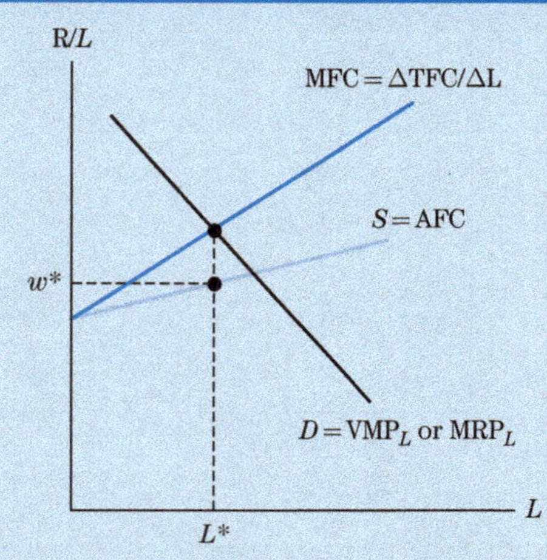

At L^*, the cost of expanding or contracting employment is exactly equal to the benefit. Both exceed the profit-maximizing wage of w^*.

constructed in the same way as that of any firm. If it is a perfect competitor in its product market, its demand for labour will be VMP_L. If its product demand curve is downward sloping, its demand for labour will be MRP_L. Given its demand curve, its optimal level of employment is the level for which MFC and the demand for labour intersect, L^* in Fig. 12.13. At that level of employment, it must pay a wage given by the value on its supply curve, namely, w^*.

The argument that L^* is the profit-maximizing level of employment takes much the same form as the one we saw in the other labour market structures. The demand curve for labour, recall, represents the increase in the firm's total revenue that results from hiring an additional unit of labour, while the MFC curve represents the corresponding addition to its total costs. To the left of L^*, the former exceeds the latter, so the firm's profit will rise if it expands employment. To the right, the latter exceeds the former, so it will do better if it contracts.

Exercise 12.8

A monopsonist's demand for labour is given by $w = 120 - 10L$. If her AFC curve is given by $w = 20 + 20L$, with corresponding $MFC = 20 + 40L$, what wage rate will she offer and how much labour will she hire?

How do the wage and employment levels under monopsony compare with those in competitive labour markets? If the same overall demand were the result of hiring by not one but many firms, the level of employment would rise to L^{**}, the point at which demand intersects the supply curve in Fig. 12.14. The wage rate, too, would rise, from w^* to w^{**}.

In comparison with this competitive norm, the monopsony equilibrium is inefficient in much the same sense that the monopoly equilibrium in the product market is inefficient – it does not exhaust all potential gains from trade. Note in Fig. 12.14 that, when the employment level is L^*, workers would be willing to supply an additional hour of labour for a payment of only w^*, whereas the extra revenue that would be produced by that extra unit is MFC^*. If the firm could somehow increase total employment by 1 unit without paying its existing workers more, both it and the extra worker would be better off. To the extent that such exchanges are blocked by the calculus of profit maximization, the monopsony structure is less efficient than the

Figure 12.14 Comparing monopsony and competition in the labour market

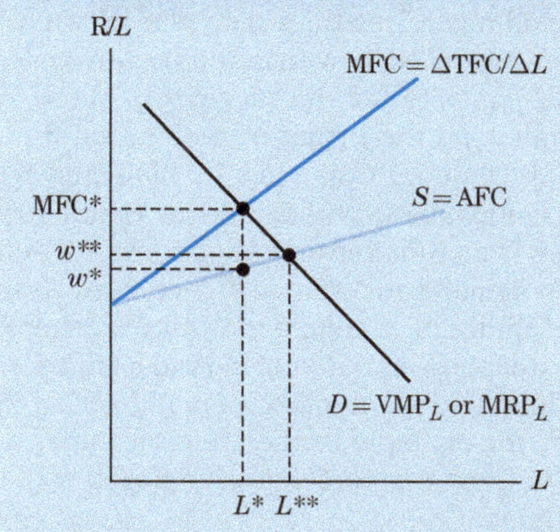

Because the monopsonist takes into account the effect of employment expansions on wages paid to existing workers, it will employ less and pay less than the corresponding values under competition.

competitive ideal. For the monopsony firm, then, wages will indeed be lower than under competition, lending force to the critics' claims of exploitation.

How important is the problem of monopsony? Recall that the requirement for perfect competition in the labour market is that workers be freely mobile. Many workers, especially older ones, have commitments – networks of friends, family close by, mortgage payments, children in school, and so on – that make it difficult to move. It is far less clear, however, that this confers the power to exploit. At the entry level most workers are relatively free to move, and most shop carefully for the jobs they ultimately accept. Since 1991 the urban population in South Africa has grown by 4.1 per cent per annum; between 2000 and 2012, it grew by no less than 9.7 per cent per annum; and, by 2013, 62.4 per cent of the population lived in urban areas. No firm can survive for long without a steady inflow of new workers; and without a competitive compensation package, it would be difficult to attract entry-level workers.

To this observation, critics often respond that firms offer competitive terms to entry-level workers but then cut wages and benefits (or have them grow insufficiently) once these workers have put down roots. But firms develop reputations in the labour market much as they do in the product market. Other things being the same, a firm with a reputation for paying competitive wages to all its workers will be able to lure the best entry-level workers away from firms with reputations for exploiting older workers.

But even if *no* workers were willing or able to move, firms still might not be able to exploit their workers in the long run. If firms in a particular area paid much less than the value of what their workers produced, new firms could move into that area to compete for the services of those workers. Following the lifting of the ban on the ANC (African National Congress) in 1990, and with it the accompanying withdrawal of South African soldiers from Namibia and Angola, the SA Defence Force's demand for weapons decreased dramatically. Hundreds of engineers who were employed in the weapons-manufacturing industry were laid off. Thus a great number of engineering firms moved, for example to the Western Cape, where many of these temporarily unemployed engineers were living.

The most compelling argument against the allegation of widespread exploitation is that the profit rates we observe in practice are too low to be compatible with a significant degree of monopsony power. If we assume that the monopsonist holds wages down by only 10 per cent of the level paid in competitive labour markets, it follows that the rate of return for the monopsonist will be roughly 50 per cent higher than the competitive rate of return.[5] Yet few firms consistently earn profit rates as high as that.

More important, those industries that do have higher-than-average rates of return almost always turn out to be high-wage rather than low-wage industries. Empirical studies have repeatedly found that wage rates are positively, not negatively, influenced by profit rates.[6] To be sure, the Orkney coal miner in a one-mine town earns a relatively low wage. But the mine that employs him probably exists on the margin of economic profitability. To say that exploitation is the cause of the miner's low wages seems strange if the consequence of paying higher wages would be to force the mine into bankruptcy. Whereas the mining sector in South Africa provided jobs for more than 800000 workers in 1985, this number had dropped to less than 389000 in 2013. Perhaps the general public considers that mine workers are exploited, and this may be the reason why most mine workers are members of a trade union. However, with so many marginalized mines in South Africa, it may be world prices of commodities that will determine wages, rather than the pressure of trade unions.

Minimum wage laws

Labour laws in South Africa are perceived by some people as being too restrictive, and they feel that they have a negative effect on foreigners considering investing in the country. How is labour in South Africa governed? To a large extent it is regulated by the Labour Relations Act 66 of 1995, the Basic Conditions of Employment Act of 1997, the Skills Development Act 97 of 1998 and the Employment Equity Act 55 of 1998.[7] Although the Acts have been amended on numerous occasions, they still form the basis on which labour laws and regulations are based. In South Africa, workers are not allowed to work for longer than 45 hours per week, or more than 9 hours on a specific day if a worker works for 5 days or less. If they work more than 5 days a week, they may not work more than 8 hours a day. Workers are not allowed to work more than 12 hours' overtime per week and must be paid 1.5 times their normal wage. In certain circumstances, a collective agreement can increase overtime to 15 hours per week for a period of up

[5] To illustrate this claim, consider the case of a firm that hires labour in a competitive market at an annual wage rate w, and which can borrow at an annual interest rate r. If L denotes this firm's employment level and K the size of its capital stock, and these are its only factors of production, then its total costs, TC, are given by $TC = wL + rK$. Suppose that $r = 0.10$, and that labour costs are 70 per cent of total costs. Then $TC = 0.7TC + 0.1K$, from which it follows that $K = 3TC$ (or, in words, that the value of the firm's capital stock is three times its annual total production costs).

Now consider a firm identical to the one above except that its monopsony power in the labour market enables it to pay its workers only 90 per cent of the competitive wage level. Let Π denote the excess profit it receives as a result of its monopsony power. To calculate Π, note first that the monopsonist's total revenue (which will be the same as the competitor's total costs, TC) will equal its total costs plus its extra-normal profit. Thus we solve

$$(0.9)(0.7)\,TC + (0.1)\,3TC + \Pi = TR = TC$$

for Π, which yields $\Pi = 0.07TC$. Suppose that half of the firm's capital stock (1.5TC) is owned by stockholders; the other half is financed by loans. Its rate of return will then be the sum of the competitive return on capital ($0.10 \times 1.5TC = 0.15TC$) and the excess return (0.07TC) divided by the capital it owns (1.5TC), which yields $0.22TC/1.5TC = 0.147$, a 47 per cent premium over the competitive rate of return.

[6] See, for example, George J. Stigler, 'The economics of minimum wage legislation', *American Economic Review*, 1946, vol. 36, pp. 358–365; Laurence Siedman, 'The return of the profit rate to the wage equation', *Review of Economics and Statistics*, 1979, vol. 61, pp. 139–142; and Alan Krueger and Lawrence Summers, 'Reflections on the interindustry wage structure', http://www.nber.org/papers/w1968.pdf.

[7] For a more detailed summary of labour laws in South Africa, go to http://www.labourlaw.co.za, and also to http://www.labourguide.co.za.

to two months. If workers have to work on public holidays or Sundays they must be paid double their normal remuneration, except if they ordinarily work on Sundays, in which case they must be paid 1.5 times their normal pay. Workers must be granted at least 21 days' annual leave or one day for every 17 days worked. Workers are entitled to 6 weeks' paid sick leave in a period of 36 months. Workers are entitled to a meal break of 60 minutes after 5 hours of work, which can be shortened to 30 minutes or denied if the employee works fewer than 6 hours a day. Pregnant workers are entitled to 4 months' maternity leave, which can start 4 months before the expected date of birth. The correct regulations and procedures must be followed when an employer wants to terminate the employment of a worker as a result of misconduct, incapacity (poor performance or ill health) or retrenchment by the company. It is a criminal offence to employ children under 15 years of age, and children under 18 may be employed only if they perform labour that is not inappropriate for their age and does not put them at risk.

Minimum wages are laid down in the civil engineering, cleaning, hospitality, private security, taxi, wholesale and retail sectors, and for domestic and farm workers. Such employment legislation was intended to elevate the wages of unskilled and low-skilled workers sufficiently to lift them from poverty. Economists have long been sceptical, however, about the power of government to legislate the price of anything. And, indeed, the minimum wage laws seem to have had a variety of unintended, undesired consequences.

Figure 12.15 shows the demand and supply curves for unskilled labour, which intersect at an equilibrium real wage of w_0, at which employment is L_0. If the statutory minimum wage is set at wm, the effect is to reduce employment to D_m, while increasing the quantity of labour supplied to S_m. The difference, $S_m - D_m$, is the unemployment that results from the minimum wage.

According to the simple model in Fig. 12.15, there are both winners (insiders) and losers (outsiders) from the imposition of the minimum wage. The unskilled workers who retain their jobs are known as the *insiders*: they earn more as a result, and obviously gain from the increase in wages. Those who lose their jobs are the *outsiders*: they earn less, and lose out as a result of the wage increase. Whether the net effect is to increase the amount of income earned by unskilled workers depends on the elasticity of demand for that category of labour. If it exceeds 1, earnings will fall; if it is less than 1, they will rise.

Figure 12.15 A statutory minimum wage

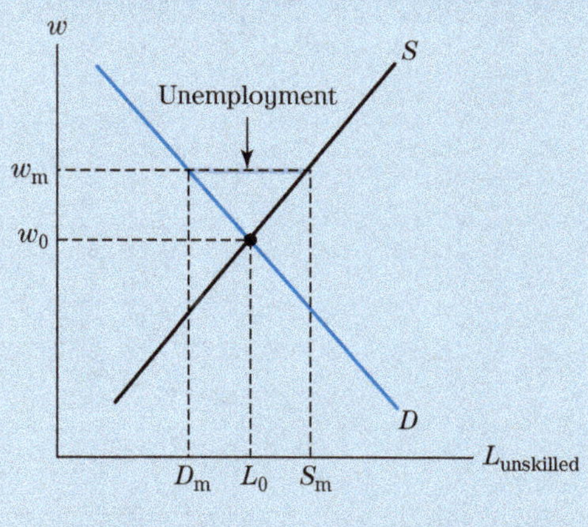

The effect of the minimum wage is to reduce employment of unskilled labour from L_0 to D_m, while increasing supply from L_0 to S_m. The resulting difference, $S_m - D_m$, is the unemployment attributable to the minimum wage.

Proponents of the minimum wage implicitly assume that the demand curve for unskilled labour is nearly vertical. Opponents, by contrast, tend to describe it as highly elastic. Empirical estimates turn out to be highly variable, and depend on whether studies were carried out in developed or developing countries.

There is a strong consensus, however, that minimum wage legislation has reduced the employment of teenagers. The size of any group's employment reduction will depend not only on the elasticity of demand, but also on the extent to which the minimum wage exceeds the market-clearing level. Teenagers as a group are much less productive than adults, if only because they have less education and experience, and so the statutory minimum wage creates a much larger employment gap for them than for other groups. There has been pressure to eliminate teenagers from minimum wage coverage altogether, or else to have a much lower 'sub-minimum' wage apply to them. Opponents of these proposals fear that it will cause some firms to substitute teenagers for adult workers, and these proposals were not accepted.

An interesting exception exists to the general proposition that minimum wages imply a reduction in employment. Figure 12.16 shows the case of a monopsony firm that, without a minimum wage, would hire L^* workers at a wage of w^*. Confronted with a minimum wage of w_m, its marginal factor cost curve suddenly becomes horizontal over the region from 0 to L_1. No matter how much labour it hires in that region, the marginal cost of an additional worker is constant at w_m. If it wants

Figure 12.16 The minimum wage law in the case of monopsony

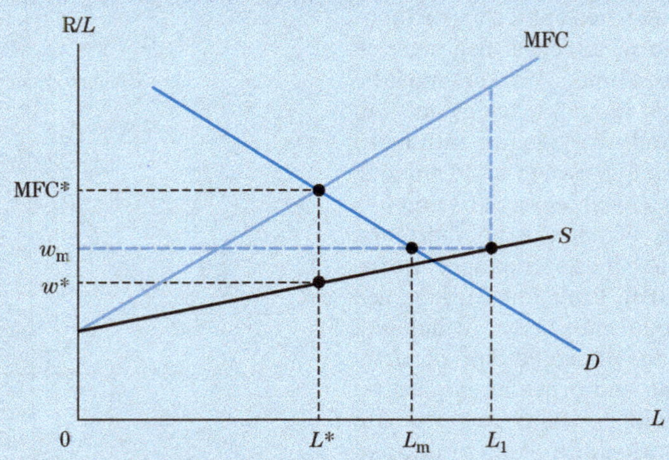

The effect of a minimum wage at w_m is to make the monopsonist's MFC curve horizontal in the region from 0 to L_1, which increases employment from L^* to L_m.

to expand employment beyond L_1, it must offer a higher wage than w_m, as indicated along the original supply curve. With the minimum wage in effect, the monopsonist's demand curve for labour intersects its new MFC curve at L_m. The effect of the law is thus to increase both the wage and the employment level for the monopsonist.

Minimum wages will not always increase employment in monopsony labour markets. If the minimum wage were set above MFC*, for example, the effect would be to reduce employment. And no matter where the minimum wage is set in the region above w^*, the effect will be to reduce the monopsonist's overall rate of return on investment. If the monopsonist's profit were close to normal to begin with, the long-run effect would thus be to induce him to leave the market. Needless to say, this too would result in a reduction of employment for unskilled workers.

Exercise 12.9

A monopsonist's demand curve for labour is given by $w = 120 - 10L$. If she originally faced an AFC curve given by $w = 20 + 20L$, with corresponding MFC $= 20 + 40L$, how will her wage and employment offers be affected by the passage of a law requiring $w \geq 80$? A law requiring $w \geq 100$?

Minimum wage legislation is still a much more hotly debated topic in developing countries such as South Africa than in developed economies such as the USA. Earning a decent living wage in South Africa is just more important than in the USA, where the minimum wage is set below the equilibrium wage level in many unskilled labour markets. In the Boston area, for example, entry-level employees in fast-food restaurants are paid roughly twice the minimum wage. In South Africa, the current minimum wage is so low that many people feel that it is not possible to survive on it. The national poverty line (upon which the minimum wage is based) was created in 2008 and has not been adjusted since then. The minimum wage for a cashier in 2014 was R718.20 per week or R3111.96 per month; for farm workers, R525 per week or R2274.82 per month; for workers in the hospitality sector, R621.45 per week or R2692.72 per month; and for domestic workers, R304.29 per week or R1328.48 per month. The current level of poverty in South Africa, and an official unemployment rate in excess of 23 per cent, means that minimum wages will remain a contentious issue for many years to come.

Labour unions

When considering the South African situation, it is important to see the role of labour movements or trade unions in perspective. The majority of the population had no political power until the first democratic elections in 1994. It was also only after the Wiehahn Commission's recommendations were implemented in 1979 that black labour movements were legalized. The trade unions were to a large extent the political voice of the masses. Over time, we have seen a marked increase in strikes and, especially in the 1980s, these were accompanied by mass action as the unions became more militant and increasingly assertive politically (and were gradually moving closer to the then-banned ANC). At present, South Africa is governed by the Tripartite Alliance, comprising the ANC, the South African Communist Party and COSATU (Congress of South African Trade Unions). There can be little doubt that the organizational power and backing of COSATU strengthened the ANC's political campaign, despite the conflicting political opinions expressed by individual alliance members. The history of the trade union movement in South Africa also partly explains why COSATU is still part of the governing alliance even though serious differences of opinion exist between the alliance members on a couple of issues, of which the economy is one.

Labour movements are very active in South Africa, but lately the popularity of trade unions has decreased. In 2012, there were 3 415 760 trade union members in South Africa, which represented 25.4 per cent of employed workers.[8] However, this is much lower than the 45.2 per cent of employed people who belonged to trade unions in 1998. The number of trade unions also decreased markedly, from more than 500 in 2002 to 191 in 2012. Mining is the most unionized sector, with 86 per cent of workers belonging to trade unions in 2012; however, 97 per cent of mine workers did so in 2000. COSATU, founded in 1985, is the largest labour movement, with 2.2 million members. The Federation of Trade Unions of South Africa (FEDUSA), founded in 1997, with 556 000 members, and the National Union of Metal Workers of South Africa, founded in 1987, with 273 000 members, are also among the largest trade unions. Solidarity, formed in 1990, grew from 37 000 to 140 000 members between 2004 and 2014, and is the largest independent trade union. The South African Democratic Teachers Union (SADTU) is the largest in the education sector, with 251 276 members, and the Transnet Bargaining Council, with 75 000 members, is the largest single employer bargaining council. In a number of economic sectors the number of trade union members has decreased quite substantially. During the period 2000–2012, union members in agriculture decreased from 100 000 to 30 000, in mining from 420 000 to 300 000, in manufacturing from 500 000 to 470 000 and in private households from 30 000 to 10 000. However, in the public sector union membership increased from 1 020 000 to 1 670 000. Almost 60 per cent of trade union members are in the public sector or mining.

The primary difference between unionized and non-unionized employment is simple. Unionized workers bargain collectively over the terms and conditions of employment; to non-unionized workers, the firm simply announces its offer, which the workers can either accept or reject, by staying with or leaving the firm. For much of the last century economists focused almost exclusively on the collective bargaining aspect of union activity and suggested that they act to further their members' interests at the expense of general economic welfare.

To illustrate, consider a simple economy with two sectors, one unionized, the other not. Suppose that the total supply of labour to the two sectors is fixed at S_0, and that the union and non-union labour demand curves are as shown by D_U and D_N in Figs. 12.17(a) and 12.17(b), respectively. Without union bargaining, the same wage, w_0, would prevail in each sector, and employment levels in the two sectors would be L_{U0} and L_{N0}, respectively, where $L_{U0} + L_{N0} = S_0$.

Collective bargaining fixes the wage in the union sector at $w_U > w_0$. The demand for labour is downward sloping, and this causes firms in the union sector to reduce employment from L_{U0} to L_{U1}. The displaced workers in the union sector are then forced to seek employment in the non-union sector, which drives the wage down to w_N in that sector. To make this process easier to understand, think in terms of real wages and not nominal money wages, because workers won't accept a decrease in nominal wages – even if they do not have a trade union to represent them. However, if they receive a wage increase lower than the rate of inflation rate, it means that their real wage has decreased, as shown in Fig. 12.17(b).

At first glance, the process resembles a zero-sum game, one in which the gains of the union workers are exactly offset by the losses of non-union workers. On closer inspection, however, we see that the process actually reduces the value of total output. Recall from Chapter 7 that the condition for output maximization with two production processes is for the value of the marginal product of the resource to be the same in each process. With the wage set initially at w_0 in both sectors, that condition was satisfied. But with the divergence in wages caused by the collective bargaining process, the value of total output can no longer

[8] This section is based on data obtained from the South African Institute of Race Relations, *South Africa Survey 2013*, Paarl Media: Johannesburg.

Figure 12.17 The allocative effects of collective bargaining

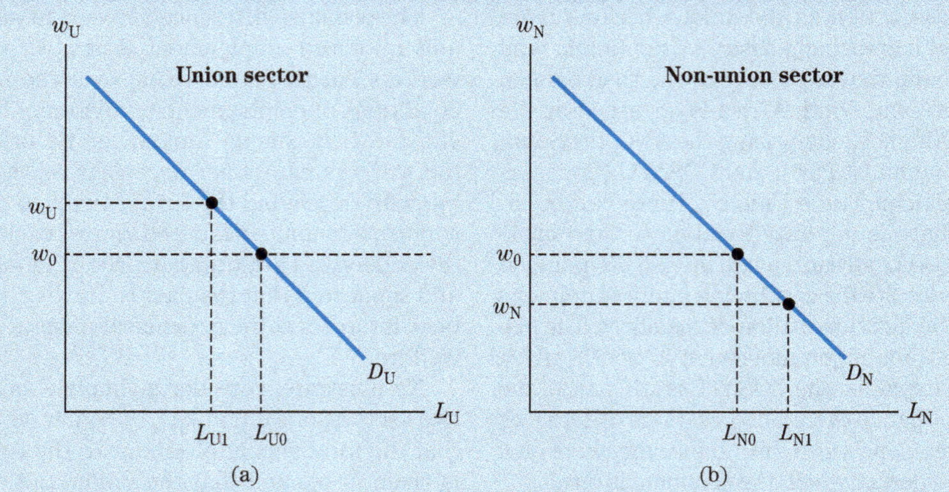

Without collective bargaining, the same wage, w_0, prevails in each sector. With the union wage pegged at w_U, employment falls in the union sector. The displaced workers seek employment in the non-union sector, driving wages down in that sector. The result is a reduction in national output.

be at a maximum. Note that if a worker is taken out of the non-union sector, the reduction in the value of output there will be only w_N, which is less than w_U, the gain in the value of output when that same worker is added to the union sector.

The economic distortion implied by the analysis in Fig. 12.17 is exaggerated. If the unionized firm is required to pay a higher wage, it will attract an excess supply of workers. In practice the skill levels of workers differ a great deal, and the natural response of the unionized firm will be to select the most qualified of its job applicants. The other side of the same coin is that non-unionized firms will be left to hire workers who are less productive than average. Empirical studies have shown that the union premium not accounted for by differences in worker quality is only about 10 per cent. This means that the gain from shifting workers from the non-union to the union sector will be smaller than it first appeared.

Researchers have discovered a variety of ways in which unions may actually boost productivity.[9] The revisionist view stresses their role in communicating worker preferences to management. The union's role is to offer the worker a voice as an alternative to leaving. The organization of formal grievance procedures, combined with the higher level of monetary compensation, boosts morale among union workers, which they claim in turn leads to higher productivity. Rates of attrition in unionized firms, for example, are significantly lower than in non-unionized firms, enabling them to economize on hiring and training costs. Even though monetary wages are higher in unionized firms, labour costs per unit of output may not be. If this conclusion is correct, it resolves the paradox of how unionized firms survive in competition with their non-unionized rivals.

But in so doing, it raises an even more troubling question: if unions lead to higher morale and increased wages, and don't raise unit labour costs, why don't all firms have unions? In South Africa unions played an important political role during the years of apartheid. As mentioned before, this is why COSATU has a main role in the current ANC alliance government. Union membership in South Africa increased by leaps and bounds in the 1980s when it was closely associated with politics, because for the majority of South Africans who did not have the power to vote, trade unions fulfilled the role of political parties. This is exactly what the revisionist theory would lead us to expect. Since the 1990s trade union membership numbers have stagnated to a large extent, or at best have increased very slowly. From the record, it is tempting to conclude that unions may enhance productivity enough to offset wage increases in some industries but not in others. Are South African

[9] See, in particular, Albert O. Hirschman, *Exit, Voice, and Loyalty*, Harvard University Press, Cambridge, MA, 1973; and Richard B. Freeman and James Medoff, *What Do Unions Do?* Basic Books, New York, 1985.

union members really more productive than their non-union counterparts? There are no clear empirical evidence that this is the case and much more research needs to be carried out before we have a clearer picture of just what unions do.

Monopoly power and the wage rate

Just as buyers of inputs can have monopsony power, sellers of inputs can have monopoly power. Let us look at a situation in which a trade union has monopoly power over the wage rate. In Fig. 12.18, D_L portrays the demand for labour (with no monopsony power). It thus aggregates the MRP_L of the firms competing to buy labour. The labour supply curve for members of the trade union, if the union does not exert monopoly power, is given by S_L. In such competitive market conditions, L^* workers will be employed at a wage of w^*, where demand equals supply.

Strangely, South Africa experienced several strikes and lengthy wage negotiations on the part of trade unions following the 2008 financial crisis. An interesting aspect of these labour actions was that the unions negotiated as though South Africa was experiencing rapid economic growth and the labour market was characterized by almost full employment. The result was that wage increases of 10–15 per cent were the order of the day while the inflation rate was only in the region of 7 per cent. This is a good example to illustrate the market power of trade unions in practice. However, we also saw the militant side of union action, not seen since the 1980s. This was highlighted by the Marikana massacre in 2012. On 10 August 2012, rock drillers at the Lonmin platinum mines near Rustenburg initiated a wildcat strike and demanded a pay rise – a tripling of their monthly salary, to R12 500. On 16 August, the police opened fire on a group of strikers, killing 34 people and wounding 78 others. During a week of protests, at least 44 people lost their lives.

If a union has monopoly power it can choose the wage rate and the corresponding number of workers supplied at that rate. This is analogous to the monopolist seller of output who chooses the price and the corresponding quantity of output. If the union wants to maximize the number of workers to be employed, it will choose the competitive outcome at A. However, if the union wants to ensure a higher than competitive wage of w^*, it has two options. It can limit membership to L_2, which will result in a wage of w_2. Although the workers who have jobs are now in a better position, some

Figure 12.18 Monopoly power of sellers of labour

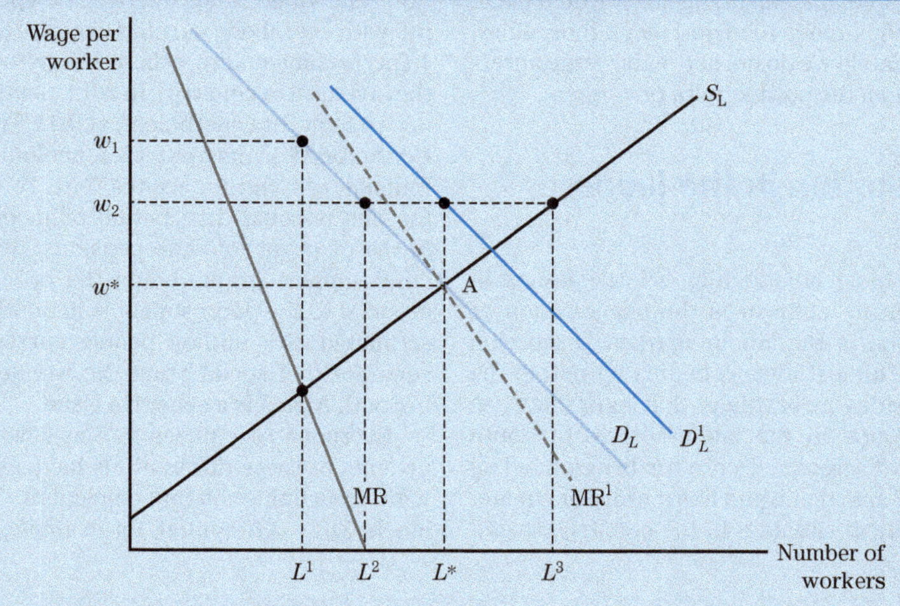

When the trade union is a monopolist, it can decide among points on the buyer's demand curve for labour, D_L. The seller can maximize the number of workers hired at L^* and a wage of w^*. If the seller wants to maximize the rent of employees, L_1 workers will be employed at a wage of w_1. If the union wants to maximize the total wages paid to union members, it should make L_2 workers available to work at a wage rate of w_2.

are worse off. By receiving the higher wage of w_2, there are L_2 workers (the insiders) whose position is now superior to those on a wage of w^*. In the process, $L^* - L_2$ who previously had jobs are now unemployed. They are the outsiders who did not gain from the wage negotiations. In the same way, trade unions may negotiate a wage of w_2. This will give rise to exactly the same situation as discussed above. At a wage rate of w_2, employers are willing to hire only L_2 workers. Union members who retain their jobs will be better off, but those who cannot find a job will be worse off. Strictly speaking, $L_3 - L_2$ workers who want to work at a wage of w_2 are now unemployed.

Another option open to trade unions is to agree on wage increases that are based on productivity increases. This is not a popular negotiating strategy on the part of trade unions in South Africa, and they normally take the inflation rate as the benchmark. However, if the productivity of workers increases, the demand curve for labour shifts to the right (D'_L). When the union now demands a wage of w_2, the firm will be willing to employ L^* workers. Theoretically, it is thus possible that no worker will loses his job, and that everybody will now receive the higher wage, w_2. With such a wage agreement there are only winners; all the workers employed before the wage increase keep their jobs and receive the higher wage. South Africa's high unemployment rate (officially 25.6 per cent in 2013, but 36.8 per cent according to the expanded definition of unemployment) means it would make sense for trade unions to negotiate on these lines, but unfortunately we do not see many wage agreements based on the productivity of workers.

Discrimination in the labour market

One of the most emotionally volatile issues in economics in its entirety is the phenomenon of discrimination in the labour market. Discussion of this issue almost always begins by noting the large disparities in earnings that exist between different groups in the labour force. In South Africa these discrepancies are further clouded by the policy of apartheid, and it is a well-known fact that the political situation in the country created many of these inequalities. The United Nations Development Programme (UNDP) estimated that there were 22 million poor people in South Africa in 2006, of whom 90 per cent were black. If one looks at per capita figures for the different racial groups, the inequality is even more striking.

In 1970 per capita income for Africans was R3134, for coloureds R8184, for Indians R9595 and for whites R39 217. By 2000, in real terms, per capita income had increased to R7283 for Africans, R14 126 for coloureds, R23 938 for Indians and R62 360 for whites. Although the relative difference between white income and the income of the other groups decreased over time, the per capita figure for whites in 2000, for example, was still 8.5 times larger than the corresponding figure for Africans.[10] In 2008, Africans comprised 79.3 per cent of the population, but earned only 43.5 per cent of monthly income.[11] In 2012, annual per capita income for Africans was R24 476, for coloureds R37 948, for Indians R98 729 and for whites R187 136 (in current prices).[12] Whites still earned 7.6 times more per capita than Africans. On the other hand, whites comprised only 9.2 per cent of the population, but earned 40.3 per cent of monthly income. This inequality is further illustrated by the fact that the richest 10 per cent of households earned 57 per cent of income, while the poorest 50 per cent of households earned only 8 per cent. The Gini coefficient is a measure of how unequally income is distributed among a particular population. The value ranges between 0 (perfect equality, with everybody earning exactly the same) and 1 (perfect inequality, where one person earns all the income in a country). In 2012, South Africa had a very high Gini coefficient, at 0.63. The Gini coefficient for Africans was 0.55, for coloureds 0.53, for Indians 0.44 and for whites 0.40. To compensate for this unequal distribution of income, various forms of grant (old-age pensions, disability and child support grants being the most important) are paid to the poorest people in South Africa. An estimated 16.9 million people currently receive some form of social grant. No wonder inequality in South Africa is a sensitive issue.

Everyone recognizes that at least some components of these differentials have nothing to do with discrimination by employers. Part of the black–white differential, for example, reflects the

[10] Servaas van der Berg and Megan Louw, 'Changing patterns of South African income distribution: Towards time series estimates of distribution and poverty', http://www.sarpn.org.za/documents/d000727/p800-Poverty_trends_vdBerg_Louw.pdf.

[11] Arden Finn, Murray Leibbrandt and Ingrid Woolard, *Income and Expenditure Inequality: Analysis of the NIDS Wave 1 Dataset*, National Income Dynamics Study Discussion Paper 5, July 2009.

[12] South African Institute of Race Relations, *South Africa Survey 2013*, Johannesburg: Paarl Media.

fact that whites on average were better educated than Africans, and were appointed in the more skilled occupations. Also, part of the male–female differential reflects the historical pattern whereby women's participation in the labour market was always much more intermittent than men's.

Each effect is almost surely the result of *some* sort of discrimination against the affected groups. Blacks so often grow up in poverty, without the education or health care resources to achieve the same life expectancy as whites. No one denies that these conditions are rooted in society's history of discrimination against blacks. Nor do many people deny that the asymmetric distribution of child care responsibilities between the sexes is at least in part the result of discriminatory social attitudes about gender roles. For present purposes, however, it is important to emphasize that, from any individual employer's point of view, such effects are examples of *non-market* discrimination – effects that lower productivity *before* job applicants even make contact with the employer. The wage differences for which non-market discrimination is responsible cannot logically be attributed to the employer's current hiring behaviour.

Our concern here is with that portion of the wage differential that cannot be attributed to non-market discrimination. In particular, we are concerned with the case in which a firm pays a lower wage to a black worker than it would to an equally productive white worker.

One theory is that the firm's customers do not wish to deal with certain racial groups. This is known as *customer discrimination*. When employment discrimination is the result of attitudes held by a firm's customers, collective action through legislation is one logical way, perhaps even the only practical way, to end the impasse. The reason is that, without the legislation, discrimination may be the only strategy open to firms that is consistent with profit maximization, and hence with survival. Black staff may have been just as productive as white staff, but from the perspective of the employer blacks were less productive because of the racial bias of certain customers.

Similar considerations may apply to a law firm's decision regarding whether to hire female lawyers. If clients, or even judges, are less likely to take the advice of a female attorney seriously, the law firm may think twice before hiring one. Here again, legislation requiring equal treatment in hiring may be the only effective way to end the impasse. Currently, a serious effort is being made to make the professions more demographically representative. Some see this move as reverse discrimination because black workers are now favoured above any other group, particularly following Black Economic Empowerment (BEE) initiatives to increase black ownership of firms.

Customer discrimination is a powerful explanation for employment discrimination in certain cases, but it cannot account for wage differentials in the cases of workers – such as those in the manufacturing industry – who never come into contact with customers. Wage differentials in such cases have sometimes been explained as the result of *co-worker discrimination*. White workers may feel uneasy about working with blacks or the fragile egos of some men may make them unable to deal with the idea of taking orders from a female supervisor.

Such preferences imply employment segregation, but not a pattern of wage differentials for equally productive workers. Blacks may work together in some firms or plants, while whites work together in others. Or men may tend to work in different environments to women. Segregation of just this sort is sometimes observed, and makes using co-worker discrimination theory to explain any significant part of observed wage differentials difficult. An employer in an all-black or all-female establishment who paid lower wages than were received by white males with the same productivity would experience lower costs, and hence higher profits, than all-white-male employers. That situation would provide an incentive for a new firm to bid for that employer's workers, an incentive that should persist until all wage differentials have been eliminated.

Employer discrimination is the term generally used to describe wage differentials that arise from an arbitrary preference on the part of the employer for one group of workers over another. Let us suppose that there are two labour force groups, the *M*s and the *F*s, and that there are no productivity differences between them. More specifically, suppose that the values of their respective marginal products are the same:

$$\mathrm{VMP}_F = \mathrm{VMP}_M = V_0 \tag{12.4}$$

and that discriminating employers pay a wage of V_0 to *M*s, but only $V_0 - d$ to *F*s.

Labour costs for a discriminating employer will be a weighted average of V_0 and $V_0 - d$, where the weights are the respective shares of the two groups in the employer's workforce.

Apart from the isolated cases in which customer discrimination might be a relevant factor, a consumer will be unwilling to pay more for a product produced by an F. If product price is unaffected by the composition of the workforce that produces the product, a firm's profit will be smaller the more Ms it employs. The most profitable firm will be one that employs only Fs.

Given our initial assumption that Ms are paid the value of their marginal product, firms that employ only Ms will earn a normal profit, while those that hire a mix will earn a positive economic profit. The initial wage differential provides an opportunity for employers who hire mostly Fs to grow at the expense of their rivals.

But as profit-seeking firms continue to pursue this strategy, the supply of Fs at the wage rate $V_0 - d$ will not be adequate for further expansion. The short-run solution is to offer the Fs a slightly higher wage. But this strategy works only if other firms do not pursue it. Once they too start offering a higher wage, Fs will again be in short supply. Ultimately, of course, the only solution is for Fs' wage to be bid up all the way to V_0, thereby eliminating further opportunities for profitable expansion by hiring additional Fs.

Any employer who wants to voice a preference for hiring Ms must now do so by paying Ms a wage in excess of V_0. Employers can discriminate against Fs if they want to, but only if they are willing to pay premium wages to the Ms out of their own profits. Few firms could continue to attract capital for long at profit rates much below normal.

The competitive labour market model suggests that the persistence of significant employer discrimination requires the owners of the firm to supply capital at a rate of return substantially below what they could earn by investing their money elsewhere. The theory of competitive labour markets tells us that, unless we can come up with a plausible reason to suppose they might do so, we should concentrate our search for the sources of wage differentials on factors other than employer discrimination. Or else we should look for additional ways in which the theory of competitive labour markets provides an incomplete description of reality.

Statistical discrimination

In Chapter 5 we saw how insurance companies employed data on average claims by various groups to arrive at differential rates for policyholders whose individual claim records were identical. A similar kind of statistical discrimination is pervasive in the labour market. The theory of competitive labour markets tells us that workers will be paid the values of their respective marginal products. But an employee's marginal product is not like a number tattooed on his forehead, there for everyone to observe at a glance. On the contrary, because people often work together in complicated team activities, it is often exceedingly difficult, even after many years on the job, to estimate what any one worker contributes. The problem of estimating the productivity of job applicants, with whom the employer has had no direct experience, is obviously even more difficult.

Still, the task is not hopeless. Insurance companies know from long experience that adolescent males are much more likely than other drivers to file accident claims. Therefore, males under 25 years of age pay the highest premiums. In the same fashion, employers know that applicants from certain groups are likely to be much more productive than others. The average university graduate, for example, may be seen as more productive than the average person who has completed only grade 12,

Economic naturalist 12.2

Why does Steinhoff sponsor the popular Varsity Cup rugby series and why has it extended the idea to include hockey, soccer, netball and athletics?

Steinhoff was founded in 1964 by Bruno Steinhoff to source furniture from Eastern Europe to sell in Western Europe. Manufacturing facilities were established in former East Germany, Hungary, Poland and Ukraine. When the Soviet system collapsed, the company converted from a marketing and distribution company to a manufacturer and distributor of furniture. Over time, it extended its business activities to Africa, Australia and the United Kingdom. Steinhoff Germany, Steinhoff Europe and Steinhoff Africa consolidated under Steinhoff International Holdings limited and was listed on the Johannesburg Stock Exchange on 23 September 1998. It is now doing business in 44 countries. By 2008 (10 years after listing on the stock exchange) its market capitalization had increased from R2.6 billion to R21.5 billion, revenue from R2.8 billion to R45 billion and net asset value per share from R2.16 to R16.37.

Why would this company get involved in sponsoring varsity sports? Because these events are televised and thus gain a great deal of exposure. This type of sponsorship is basically a sound and successful advertising campaign on the part of an international company. As a result, most South Africans are familiar with its name.

even though in reality many learners who have successfully completed high school are much more productive than their university counterparts.

In the insurance case we saw that, even when two people had identical driving records, competitive pressures led to different rates if they happened to belong to groups with differing accident records. We see closely analogous results in the labour market. Even when the employer's information indicates that two individuals have exactly the same productivity, there will be competitive pressure to pay higher wages to the person who belongs to the group with higher average productivity. The problem is, unless the employer's information about individual productivity is perfect, group membership conveys relevant information about likely productivity differences.

To illustrate how group membership influences the estimation of individual productivity, consider a labour market group – call it group A – the VMPs of whose members are *uniformly distributed* between R200/hr and R600/hr, as shown in Fig. 12.19. This means that if we were to choose a person at random from group A, the value of his marginal product would be equally likely to be any number from R200/hr to R600/hr. If we knew nothing about this person other than that he was from group A, the expected value of his productivity would simply be the average for members of that group, which is R400/hr.

If there were no practical way to learn anything about a specific individual's productivity, and if the productivity distribution of his group were known, competitive pressures would require that members of group A be paid R400/hr.[13] Suppose an employer offered less – say, R300/hr – perhaps because it fears being unlucky and hiring the least productive member of group A. This employer would not be able to retain its workers because a competing firm could offer R320/hr and lure them away. And since group A workers are worth an average of R400/hr each, this competing firm would augment its expected profits by R80/hr for each worker it hired. But, for the same reason, it too would eventually lose the workers to yet another competing firm.

Alternatively, consider a firm that paid R500/hr to workers from group A, perhaps because it felt bad about underpaying the more productive members of that group. This firm would lose an average of R100/hr for every worker from group A it hired, and unless it had some source of extra-normal profits, it would sooner or later be forced out of business.

If individual productivity values cannot be measured, the only competitively stable outcome is for members of group A to be paid R400/hr. Some of them will end up being paid more than they are worth, others less. But the firms that hire at this rate will cover all their costs, on average, and can expect to remain in business. Any other policy will result in failure.

Now suppose that employers have a productivity test. This test is not perfect, but it does provide information about individual productivity values. To keep the analysis simple, suppose that the test is 100 per cent accurate half of the time, but has no value the other half of the time; and suppose that employers have no way of knowing when the test is accurate.

Suppose further that the test is administered to a worker from group A and yields a value of R480/hr. What is our best estimate of this worker's true productivity? The test is 100 per cent accurate half of the time, and if we knew this was one of those times, the answer would, of course, be R480. Alternatively, if we knew that this was one of the times the test was worthless, our best estimate would be the expected value of a random number drawn from the uniform distribution between R200/hr and R600/hr, namely, R400/hr, the average productivity value for group A. The problem is that we don't know which particular mode this test result falls into. So the best we can do is to take

Figure 12.19 A hypothetical uniform productivity distribution

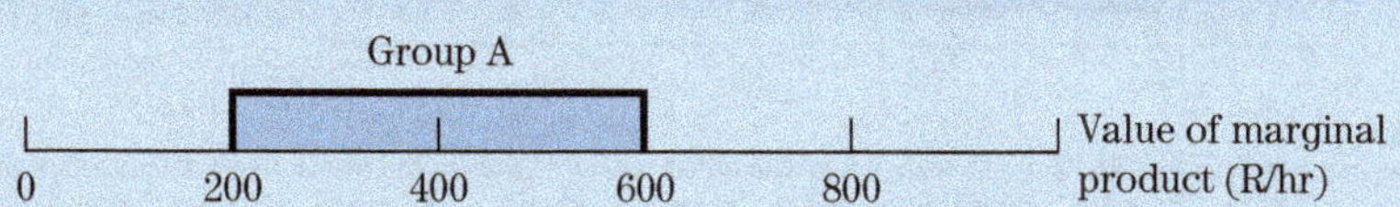

The productivity values for members of this group are uniformly distributed between R200/hr and R600/hr. This means that the VMP of a person chosen at random from the group is equally likely to be any number from R200/hr to R600/hr. The average VMP for members of this group is R400/hr.

[13] This analysis ignores the complication of compensating wage differences for internal rank, discussed in the next section.

a weighted average of the two results (where the weights are the respective probabilities of occurrence). Our best estimate of the VMP of a worker from group A with a test score of R480/hr, denoted VMP(480), is thus given by[14]

$$\text{VMP}(480) = \left(\tfrac{1}{2}\right)(\text{R}480/\text{hr}) + \left(\tfrac{1}{2}\right)(\text{R}400/\text{hr}) = \text{R}440/\text{hr} \quad (12.5)$$

This means that if we took a large number of persons from group A who happened to score R480/hr on the test, their average productivity value would turn out to be R440/hr.

Suppose instead that we had observed a test result of R320/hr for a member of group A. Our best estimate of his VMP would then be

$$\text{VMP}(320) = \left(\tfrac{1}{2}\right)(\text{R}320/\text{hr}) + \left(\tfrac{1}{2}\right)(\text{R}400/\text{hr}) = \text{R}360/\text{hr} \quad (12.6)$$

This time note that the effect of the uncertainty in the test causes us to revise upwards the estimate of the individual's productivity.

In general, the rule is that, when a test is less than completely accurate, our best estimate of a worker's productivity will lie between his actual test score and the average productivity of the group to which he belongs.

And, again, the prediction of competitive labour market theory is that any firm that did not pay its workers according to the best available estimates of their respective VMPs would eventually be driven from the market by the forces of competition.

Exercise 12.10

In the preceding example, what is the best available estimate of the VMP of a person with a test score of 240?

Now suppose an employer confronts job applicants not only from group A but also from group B. And suppose the VMP distribution for group B is uniform between R400/hr and R800/hr, as shown in Fig. 12.20. Suppose, finally, that two applicants come in one morning, one from group A, the other from group B, and that each gets a score of 560 on the test (the same test as before). What are the employer's best estimates of their respective productivity values?

In both cases, the imperfection in the test calls for an adjustment towards the relevant group average. Specifically, the best estimate of the VMP for the worker from group A, denoted $\text{VMP}_A(560)$, is

$$\text{VMP}_A(560) = \left(\tfrac{1}{2}\right)(\text{R}560/\text{hr}) + \left(\tfrac{1}{2}\right)(\text{R}400/\text{hr}) = \text{R}480/\text{hr} \quad (12.7)$$

while the corresponding estimate for the worker from group B is

$$\text{VMP}_B(560) = \left(\tfrac{1}{2}\right)(\text{R}560/\text{hr}) + \left(\tfrac{1}{2}\right)(\text{R}600/\text{hr}) = \text{R}580/\text{hr} \quad (12.8)$$

Thus, even though the two workers earn exactly the same score on the test, the employer adjusts downwards in one case, upwards in the

Figure 12.20 Productivity distributions for two groups

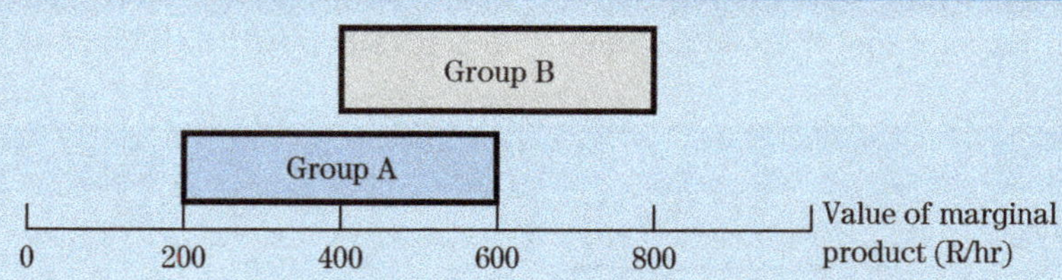

The VMP values of members of group A are uniformly distributed between R200/hr and R600/hr, while those of members of group B are uniformly distributed between R400/hr and R800/hr. If we know only the groups to which people belong, our best estimates of an individual's VMP would be the average VMP for his group – R400/hr for group A, R600/hr for group B.

[14] Note the similarity of this adjustment procedure to that discussed in Chapter 6, whereby we estimated the probability that a given shy person was a librarian.

other. It is a cruel understatement to say that such competitive imperatives have caused great pain for both employees and employers. The many talented and productive members of group A cannot help but feel chagrined when their group identity causes them to be treated differently from the members of other groups. And surely there cannot be many employers who feel comfortable offering different salaries to people whose records look just the same.

Note carefully that statistical discrimination is the result, not the cause, of average productivity differences between groups. Its sole effect is to reduce wage variation within each group.

The internal wage structure

On first examination, the wage structure within many private firms seems much more egalitarian than would be warranted under our marginal productivity theory of wages. Many firms, for example, follow strict salary formulae based on experience, education and length of tenure within the firm, even when there are large visible differences in the productivity of workers paid the same under these formulae. Indeed, pay patterns of the sort predicted by marginal productivity theory are virtually never observed in practice.

A simple amendment to our theory helps to square it with the wage distributions we observe in practice.[15] The amendment rests on two plausible assumptions:

- most people prefer high-ranked to low-ranked positions among their co-workers
- no one can be forced to remain in a firm against her wishes

By the laws of simple arithmetic, not everyone's preference for high rank in the wage distribution of her firm can be satisfied. After all, only 50 per cent of the members of any group can be in the top half. But if people are free to associate with whomever they please, why are the lesser-ranked members of groups content to remain? Why don't they all leave to form new groups of their own in which they would no longer be near the bottom? Many workers undoubtedly do precisely that. And yet we also observe many stable, heterogeneous groups. Not all accountants at General Motors South Africa are equally talented, and in every law firm some partners attract much more new business than others. If everyone prefers to be near the top of her group of co-workers, what holds these heterogeneous groups together?

The apparent answer is that their low-ranked members receive extra compensation. If they were to leave, they would gain by no longer having to endure low status. By the same token, however, the top-ranked members would lose; they would no longer enjoy high status. If their gains from having high rank are larger than the costs borne by members with low rank, it does not make sense for the group to disband. Everyone can do better if the top-ranked workers induce their lesser-ranked colleagues to remain by sharing some of their pay with them.

Of course, not everyone assigns the same value to having high rank. Those who care relatively less about it will do best to join firms in which most workers are more productive than themselves. As lesser-ranked members in these firms, they will receive extra compensation. People who care most strongly about rank, by contrast, will want to join firms in which most other workers are less productive than themselves. For the privilege of occupying top-ranked positions in those firms, they will have to work for less than the value of what they produce. Workers can thus sort themselves among a hierarchy of firms in accordance with their demands for within-firm status.

How large are the compensating wage differentials for rank within the firm? The answer will be different for different occupations. In occupations in which co-workers do not associate closely with one another, people will not be willing to pay much for a high-ranked position. After all, the comparisons that matter most are those between people who interact most intensively. The price paid for high rank (and received for low rank) will be highest in occupations in which co-workers work closely together for extended periods.

The role of concerns about rankings in internal wage distribution helps shed light on the example we considered earlier, in which economists working in business schools often earn 15 per cent more than their counterparts working in faculty. Business schools have to pay their other faculty members – accountants, marketers, financial analysts and the like – high salaries because of the high earning opportunities available in these fields in the private sector. Economists who accept jobs in a business school find themselves at the bottom of the pay scale among their co-workers.

[15] For a more complete development of the argument, see R. Frank, *Choosing the Right Pond*, Oxford University Press, New York, 1985.

The premium salaries they receive in comparison with economists in faculty may be interpreted in part as a compensating differential for occupying a low-ranked position.

Winner-take-all markets

In this section we shall see that differences in rank sometimes cause small differences in ability to translate into large differences in the values of marginal products.[16] The essence of the idea is captured in the following simple example. Imagine that your company, Toyota, has been sued by Volkswagen for R1 billion for patent infringement. On its merits, the case is so close that it is certain to be decided in favour of the side that hires the better lawyer. Suppose Deborah Marcicano and Dario Tanziani are the top two lawyers in the country and that, while they are almost equally talented in every respect, Tanziani is just perceptibly better.

Naturally, both Volkswagen and Toyota will want to hire Tanziani, and so both start bidding vigorously for his services. How much will the winner have to pay him? On a moment's reflection, it should be clear that the answer must be R1 billion. If Volkswagen offered only R999 million, it would be in Toyota's interest to bid still higher, because the alternative would be to lose the lawsuit. But then Volkswagen would respond by raising its own bid, for its alternative is also to lose the lawsuit. Unless Volkswagen and Toyota can collude successfully, the only stable outcome is for Tanziani to be paid R1 billion. Marcicano's value, even though she is only a shade less talented, is exactly zero, for, by assumption, the side that hires her will lose the lawsuit.

The example is a caricature, but it captures the flavour of what happens in a variety of labour market contexts. Consider, for example, the pay structure in professional tennis. Given the limited amount of time most people are willing to spend watching tennis matches on television, it is practical to see only a handful of players in action during any given year. And, given a choice, most fans would be willing to pay a little extra to see the top-ranked players play. A recent broadcast from Indian Wells, one of the more prestigious tournaments on the ATP tennis circuit, of a match between two good players, ranked 23rd and 28th in the world, revealed that the stands were virtually empty. It illustrated the principle that the demand for tennis players ranked in the top 10 is hundreds of times greater than for players ranked around 100. And yet the difference in playing ability between the two categories are often relatively small. Let the 101st-ranked player meet the 102nd-ranked player and fans will see almost as exciting a match as when the 1st-ranked player meets the 2nd-ranked player. The problem, from the perspective of the lower-ranked pair, is that most fans have time to watch only a single match, and would naturally prefer to see the top-ranked pair. The result is that top-ranked players earn millions each year, while those in the second tier earn barely enough to cover their expenses on the tour. For example, Paolo Lorenzi turned pro in 2003 and was ranked number 100 in the world at the beginning of 2014. His accumulated earnings were $1 426 580 by the end of 2013. The accumulated earnings of Kevin Anderson, South Africa's best tennis player, were $3 548 905 by the end of 2013, not bad at all. However, Rafael Nadal, the best tennis player in the world, earned $1 701 492 in January and February 2014 alone (and just over $12 million in 2013) and his career earnings were $66 334 255 by the end of 2013. Roger Federer, arguably the best tennis player of all time, had a total income (including sponsorships and endorsements) of $71.5 million in 2013.

Similar *superstar effects* are observed in virtually every professional sport, in the world of entertainment and even in the ordinary workings of business. Three tenors earn the bulk of the royalties from the CDs purchased by opera lovers. Regulated companies spend vast sums bidding for the services of a handful of expert witnesses. A small number of actors and actresses have their pick of all the best roles.

For the superstar effect to occur, there must be a winner-take-all effect somewhere in the production process. In tennis, it is that the top players capture virtually the entire viewing audience. In the lawsuit example, it was that the better lawyer wins the suit. For the superstar effect to be important, the stakes in the contest must be high, as they are in each of these examples.

The marginal productivity theory of pay determination has been criticized on the ground that workers with nearly identical abilities are often

[16] The discussion in this section draws on R. Frank, *The Economics of Buying the Best*, Cornell University Department of Economics Working Paper, 1978; Sherwin Rosen, 'The economics of superstars', *American Economic Review*, 1981, vol. 71, no. 5, pp. 845–858; and R. Frank and P. Cook, *The Winner-Take-All Society*, Free Press, New York, 1995.

paid vastly different amounts. At first glance such observations do indeed seem to contradict the theory. But a closer look reveals that critics may have been too hasty to condemn the model. The difficulty, as we have seen, is that small differences in ability sometimes translate into very large differences in the values of marginal products. Let's end the chapter with another practical example. In 2013, Tiger Woods was the world's best golfer and earned (including prize money, endorsements, bonuses, speaking engagements, books and instructional videos) a massive R83 million. Adam Scott ended the year as the second-best golfer in the word, but earned 'only' R15.6 million. Although an income of R16 million is very handsome indeed, it was less than a fifth of what the best player in the world earned. However, Phil Mickelson, regarded as the third-best player in the world, earned $7 million in prize money, but product endorsements pushed his earnings up to a very healthy $52 million – still only about 60 per cent of what the best player earned.

Summary

- Our goal in this chapter was to examine the economic forces that govern wages and other conditions of employment. The perfectly competitive firm's hiring rule in the short run is to keep hiring until the value of what the last worker produces – the VMP_L – is exactly equal to the wage rate. In the long run, the firm's demand curve for labour is more elastic than in the short run because the firm faces the additional possibility of substituting labour for capital.
- To aggregate the individual firm demand curves into an industry demand curve for labour involves more than a simple horizontal summation of the individual firm demand curves. An adjustment has to be made for the fact that increasing industry output brings a lower product price.
- The demand curve for labour for a monopolist in the product market is constructed by comparing the wage, not with the value of the output the worker produces, but with the amount by which the worker's output will change total revenue – MRP_L. Unlike the perfectly competitive firm, monopolists must take into account that an increase in output requires them to sell existing output at a lower price.
- We began our approach to the supply side of the labour market by considering the individual worker's decision regarding how much to work at a given wage rate. The more she works, the more she will earn, but the less time she will have available for other activities. In the labour supply context, it is not uncommon for people to supply fewer hours of labour when wage rates rise. To generate the market supply curve, we add the individual supply curves horizontally. The market supply and demand curves intersect to determine the industry wage level and total volume of industry employment.
- The conventional view of labour unions is that they increase labour's bargaining power *vis-à-vis* management, thereby increasing labour's share of a fixed economic pie. Recent research, however, suggests that unions may actually improve the productivity of workers, thereby enlarging not only their slice of the economic pie but also management's.
- Proponents of minimum wage laws say they are needed to protect workers from being exploited by employers with excessive market power. Whether the legislation actually serves this goal, however, turns out to be a difficult empirical question.
- Critics claim that certain firms pay members of certain groups – notably blacks and females – less than they pay white males with the same productivity. Such charges pose a fundamental challenge to the very core of microeconomic theory, for they imply that firms are passing up opportunities to enhance their profits. We saw several reasons, including discrimination by institutions other than firms, why people in the affected groups appear to earn lower salaries.

- An apparent anomaly is the fact that people whose abilities differ only slightly sometimes earn vastly different salaries. This time the key to resolving the contradiction is to observe that, in many contexts, the value of what someone produces depends not only on the absolute level of his skills, but also on how those skills compare with the skills of others. In arm wrestling, being just a little stronger than your opponent means you win just about every time. In the labour market too, being just a little better than the competition sometimes means earning vastly more than it does.

Questions for review

1. What is the difference between the perfect competitor's VMP_L curve and the imperfect competitor's MRP_L curve?
2. If a monopolist bought all the firms in a formerly competitive industry and acquired the legal right to exclude entry, how would the quantity of labour employed be affected?
3. Why might local employers pay workers the value of what they produce even if workers are unable or unwilling to move to another area to accept a better job?
4. Why does economic theory lead us to place more emphasis on discrimination by persons and institutions other than employers as a cause of wage differences that exceed productivity differences?

Problems

1. Given the information in the following table, fill in the value of the marginal product of labour for price $P = 60$. Find the perfectly competitive firm's optimal labour demand for a wage $w =$ R60/hr.

L	MP	VMP
0	4	
10	3	
20	2	
30	1	
40	0	

2. Given the information in the adjacent table, graph the budget constraint (depicted for $w =$ R60/hr, where H is hours of leisure per day and M is income per day). Find and graph the new budget constraint (income per day $= M'$) for $w =$ R120/hr. How do the slopes of the two budget constraints compare, and why?

H	*M*	*M′*
0	1440	
6	1080	
12	720	
18	360	
24	0	

3. Given the information in the following table, find the monopsonist's optimal labour demand and wage paid.

L	AFC	TFC	MFC	VMP
0	0	0	0	160
10	20	200	40	120
20	40	800	80	80
30	60	1800	120	40

4. A perfectly competitive firm has $MP_L = 220 - 10L$. Find and graph the value

of its marginal product of labour at a product price of $P = 50$. Find its optimal quantity demanded of labour at a wage of $w =$ R1000/hr.

5 In his current job, Mandla can work as many hours per day as he chooses, and he will be paid R10/hr for the first 8 hours he works and R25/hr for each hour thereafter. Faced with this payment schedule, Mandla chooses to work 12 hr/day. If Mandla is offered a new job that pays R15/hr for as many hours as he chooses to work, will he take it? Explain.

6 Consider the following two antipoverty programmes: (1) a payment of R150/day is to be given this year to each person who was classified as poor last year; and (2) each person classified as poor will be given a benefit equal to 20 per cent of the wage income he earns each day this year.

a Assuming that poor people have the option of working at R60/hr, show how each programme would affect the daily budget constraint of a representative poor worker during the current year.

b Which programme would be most likely to reduce the number of hours worked?

7 A monopsonist's demand curve for labour is given by $w = 240 - 40L$, where w is the hourly wage rate and L is the number of person-hours hired.

a If the monopsonist's supply (AFC) curve is given by $w = 40L$, which gives rise to a marginal factor cost curve of $\text{MFC} = 80L$, how many units of labour will he employ, and what wage will he pay?

b How would your answers to part (a) be different if the monopsonist were confronted with a minimum wage bill requiring him to pay at least R140/hr?

c How would your answers to parts (a) and (b) be different if the employer in question were not a monopsonist but a perfect competitor in the market for labour?

8 Secury Locks is the sole supplier of security systems in the product market, and the sole employer of locksmiths in the labour market. The demand curve for security systems is given by $P = 1000 - 10Q$, where Q is the number of systems installed per week. The short-run production function for security systems is given by $Q = 40L$, where L is the number of full-time locksmiths employed per week. The supply curve for locksmiths is given by $W = 4000 + 200L$, where W is the weekly wage for each locksmith. How many locksmiths will Secury Locks hire, and what wage will it pay?

9 The demand curve for labour facing a monopsonist is given as $W = 350 - 60L$; the supply curve (AFC) for this monopsonist is $W = 30 + 10L$, where W represents the hourly wage rate and L is the number of person-hours hired.

a Find the optimal quantity of labour and the wage rate for this profit-maximizing monopsonist.

b Suppose a law imposed a R170/hr minimum wage. How would this affect the quantity of labour demanded by this firm?

10 A monopolist can hire any quantity of labour for R100/hr. If her marginal product of labour is currently 2, and her current product price is R50/unit, should she increase or decrease the amount of labour hired?

11 BHP Billiton is the only employer in its area. Its only variable input is labour, which has a constant marginal product equal to 5. Because it is the only employer in the area, the firm faces a supply curve for labour given by $W = 10 + L$, where W is the wage rate and L is the number of person-hours employed. This supply curve yields the marginal factor cost curve $\text{MFC} = 10 + 2L$. Suppose the firm can sell all it wishes at a constant price of 8.

a How much labour does the firm employ, how much output does it produce and what is the wage?

b Suppose now the firm sells a special kind of coal, such that it faces a downward-sloping demand curve for its output. In particular, assume that BHP Billiton faces the demand curve given by $P = 102 - 1.96Q$. How much labour does the firm employ, how much output does it produce, what price does it set for the output and what is the wage?

c Assume that BHP Billiton still faces the demand curve $P = 102 - 1.96Q$, but now further assume that BHP Billiton has five labourers under contract to produce coal at a wage of 15. If BHP Billiton has the option of hiring additional labourers at a higher wage without increasing the wage to the five labourers already hired, will BHP Billiton increase its labour force? Explain.

12 Suppose vacation time comes in one-week intervals, and that the total willingness to pay for total vacation time by younger and older workers in a competitive industry is as given in the following table:

Total vacation time, weeks	Total willingness to pay	
	Younger workers	Older workers
1	600	1000
2	950	1600
3	1200	2100
4	1400	2500
5	1500	2800

Suppose VMP = 300/wk for younger workers, 350/wk for older workers, and that existing firms give all their workers, young and old, 5 weeks per year of vacation time. Can these firms be maximizing their profits? If so, explain why. If not, say what changes they should make, and how much extra profit will result.

13 Members of two groups, the blues and the greens, have productivity values ranging from R150 to R300/hr. The average productivity of the blues is R180/hr, and the corresponding average for the greens is R360/hr. A costless productivity test is known to provide the correct productivity value with probability 1/3, and a random productivity value drawn from the relevant group distribution with probability 2/3.

- **a** Assuming labour markets are competitive, how much will a blue with a test value of 270 be paid?
- **b** How much will a green with the same test value be paid?
- **c** Is it correct to say that statistical discrimination accounts for why the greens, as a group, are paid more than the blues?

14 A firm has a task to carry out that involves opportunities to shirk, with little probability of detection. If it can hire a non-shirking employee for this task, it will make a lot of money. Its strategy for finding a non-shirker is to pay a very low wage at first, and then to increase the wage gradually each year so that, by the time the worker has been with the firm for 10 years, he will be earning more than he could elsewhere. The present value of the wage premiums in the later years is larger than the present value of the shortfall in the early years.

- **a** Explain how this strategy helps to attract a non-shirking employee. Would the same strategy work if the probability of detecting shirking were zero?
- **b** Explain why the ability of the firm to implement this strategy might depend to an extent on its own reputation in the labour market.

15 Consider a two-sector economy that employs a total of 80 units of a single input, labour. N_1 of these units are allocated to sector 1, where the wage is 100 for the top five workers in that sector and zero for all others. (Both the wage for the top workers and the number who receive that wage are invariant to changes in N_1.) The remaining $N_2 = 80 - N_1$ units of labour serve in sector 2, where every worker receives a wage of 10. All workers in sector 1 have an equal probability of being among the top five workers, $5/N_1$, and all workers are risk neutral.

- **a** How many workers will work in sector 1?
- **b** What will be the value of GNP for the economy?
- **c** How would your answers differ if there were a 50 per cent tax on the earnings of workers in sector 1?

***16** A firm produces output according to the production function $Q = K^{\frac{1}{2}} L^{\frac{1}{2}}$. If it sells its output in a perfectly competitive market at a price of 100, and if K is fixed at 16 units, what is this firm's short-run demand curve for labour?

***17** How would your answer to the preceding problem be different if the employer in question sold his product according to the demand schedule $P = 20 - Q$?

* This question requires the calculus definition of the marginal product of labour: $MP_L = \partial Q/\partial L$.

Answers to in-chapter exercises

12.1 When the product price rises to R30, the VMP_L curve is as shown in panel b of the diagram below. The new quantity of labour demanded at $w = R120$ is 120 units.

The value of the marginal product is

$$VMP_L = P(MP_L) = 30(10 - \tfrac{1}{20}L)$$
$$= 300 - \tfrac{30}{20}L$$

The optimal quantity of labour is found by solving

$$w = VMP_L \Rightarrow 120 = 300 - \tfrac{30}{20}L$$
$$\Rightarrow 180 = \tfrac{3}{2}L \Rightarrow L^* = 120$$

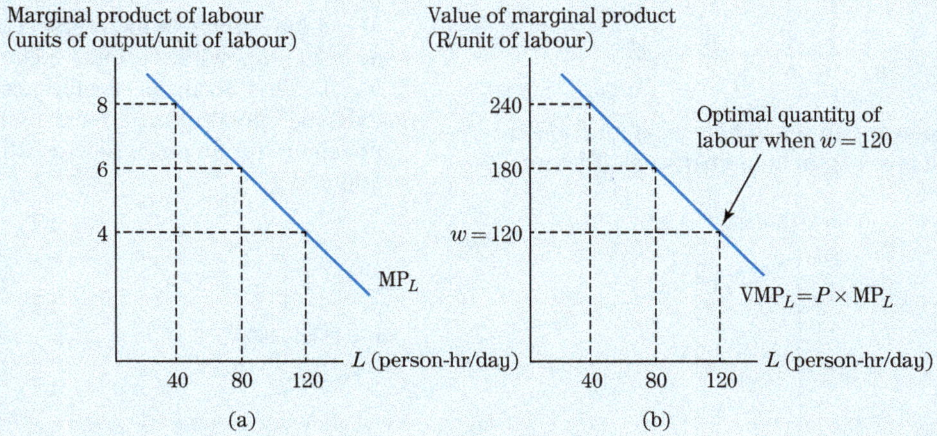

12.2 With $w = R200/hr$, the income/leisure budget constraint is

$$M = w(24 - h) = 200(24 - h) = 4800 - 200h$$

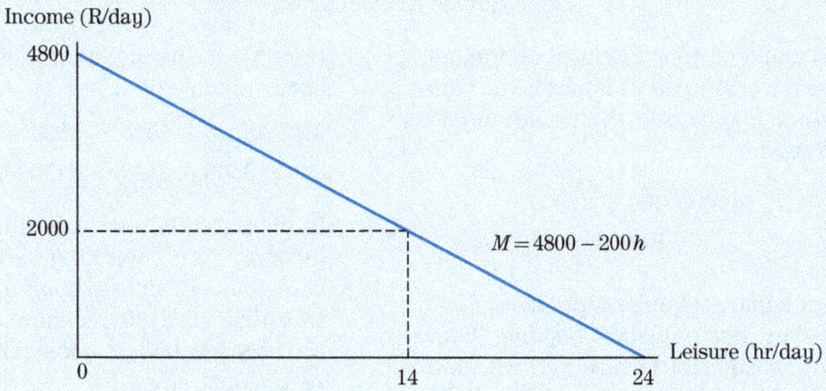

At leisure $h = 14$ hr/day, income per day is

$$M = 200(24 - h) = 200(24 - 14)$$
$$= 200 \times 10 = R2000$$

12.3

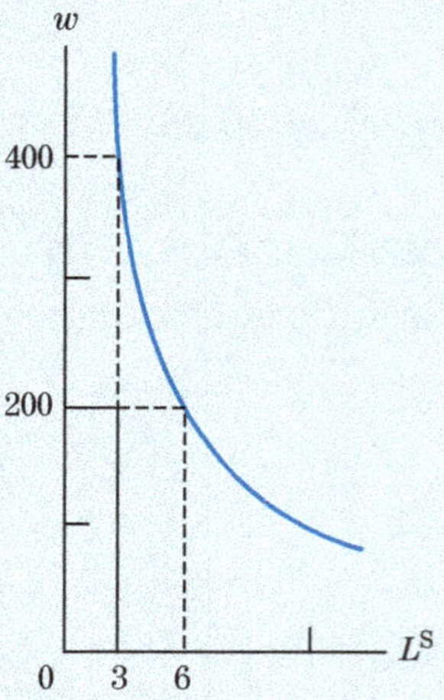

12.4 The driver can reach his weekly income target in fewer total hours per week if he works longer hours during the rainy days and shorter hours during the non-rainy days. During rainy days more people will use taxis instead of walking and it makes sense to work longer on those days.

12.5 The budget constraint remains $M = 4800 - 200h$. As the individual is willing to sacrifice 1 hour of leisure for R100 of income, indifference curves are straight lines of the general form $M = a - 100h$ provided in the hint. The highest indifference curve that shares a point with the income/leisure constraint is $M = 4800 - 100h$ (will intersect the leisure axis at 48), with optimal leisure demand $h = 0$. This form of preferences exhibits extreme substitution effects (will consume no leisure for any $w > 100$ and all leisure for any $w < 100$).

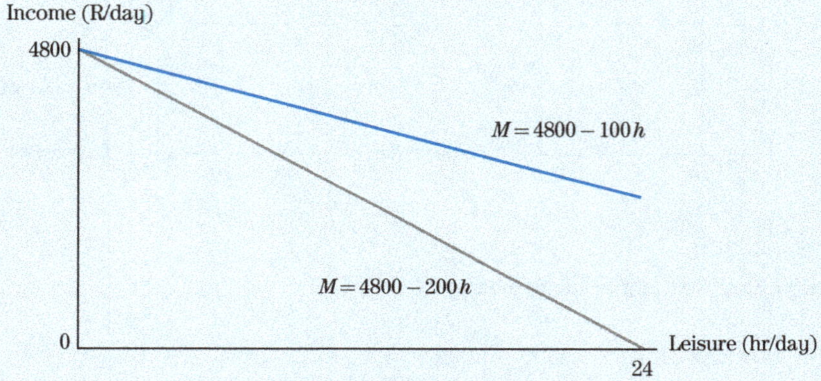

Exercise Answer 12.5

12.6 Under his current job, Karim's maximum income from working all 24 hours is the sum of 8 hours at R50/hr and the remaining 16 hours at R200/hr:

$$(8 \times 50) + (16 \times 200) = 400 + 3200 = \text{R3600/day}$$

Each hour of leisure requires sacrificing R200 up to $h = 16$ hr, but only R50 beyond 16 hr. Consuming $h = 16$ hr of leisure and working $24 - h = 24 - 16 = 8$ hr yields $(8 \times 50) = \text{R400}$ income (at the kink in the budget constraint). Karim's original budget constraint is thus

$$M_1 = \begin{cases} 3600 - 200h; & 0 \le h \le 16 \\ 400 - 50h; & 16 \le h \le 24 \end{cases}$$

The budget constraint has two parts, reflecting the two wages (regular and overtime). If Karim works 12 hours, then he enjoys $h_1 = 12$ hr of leisure per day, and thus with the original budget constraint earns income of

$$M_1 = 3600 - 200h = 3600 - (200 \times 12) = 3600 - 2400 = \text{R1200/day}$$

In his potential new job, Karim's maximum income from working all 24 hours is $24 \times 100 = \text{R2400}$. An hour of leisure requires sacrifice of R100 income up to 24 hours. Karim's new budget constraint is

$$M_2 = 2400 - 100h$$

Here, the budget constraint is a simple straight line. Karim's original optimal labour supply choice would still be feasible with the new budget constraint: Karim could earn the same income with the same amount of leisure time under the new budget constraint:

$$M_2 = 2400 - 100h = 2400 - (100 \times 12) = 2400 - 1200 = \text{R1200/day}$$

Thus Karim can be no worse off with the new budget constraint. However, Karim will have an opportunity cost of leisure time of $w = 100$ with the new budget constraint rather than $w = 200$ with the old budget constraint. Therefore Karim must optimally adjust his labour supply towards more leisure. Karim will be happier at his new optimal labour supply choice: he reaches a higher indifference curve (I_2) between income and leisure, so he will accept the new job.

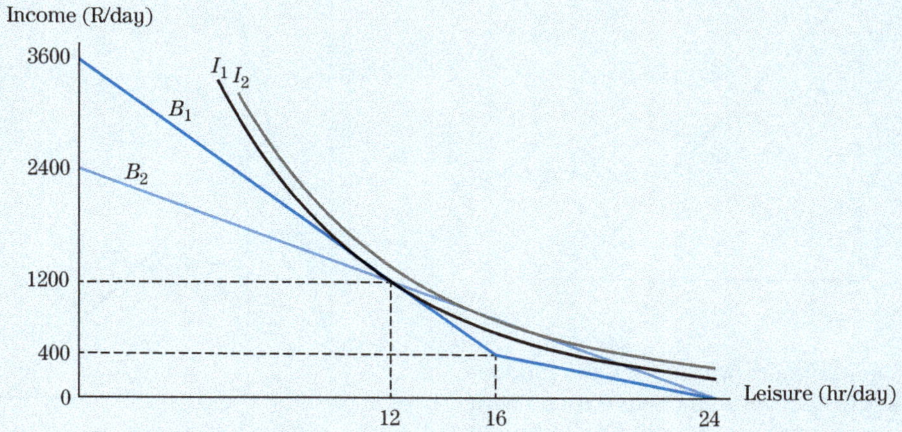

12.7 The original budget constraint is

$M_0 = w(24 - h) = 10(24 - h) = 240 - 10h$

The first programme yields a budget constraint of

$M_1 = S + w(24 - h) = 48 + 10(24 - h)$
$= 288 - 10h$

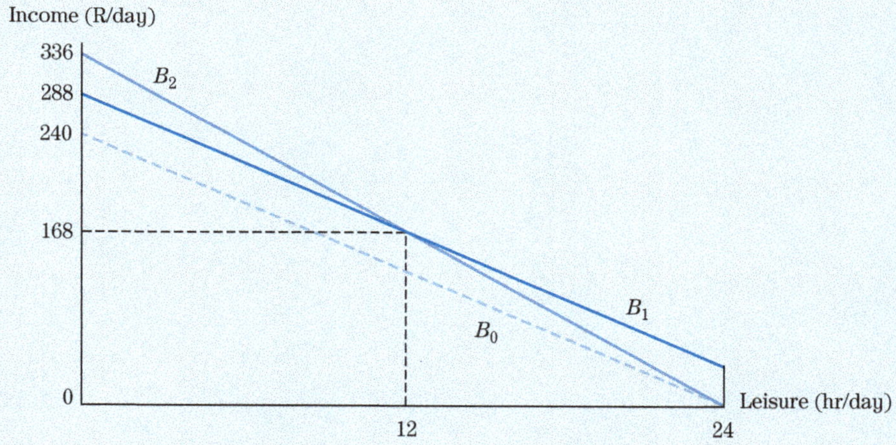

The second programme yields a budget constraint of

$M_2 = (1 + S)\,w\,(24 - h) = (1 + 0.4)10(24 - h)$
$= 14(24 - h) = 336 - 14h$

The first programme is more likely to reduce hours worked, because it increases income but leaves the opportunity cost of leisure unchanged: assuming leisure is a normal good, higher income leads to more leisure consumed. In contrast, the second programme increases the opportunity cost of leisure: for low wage levels, an increase in the wage generally increases labour supply, as the substitution effect dominates the income effect. Thus the poor will probably work less under the first programme and more under the second programme.

12.8 Graphically, it is presented below. The number of workers that the firm will hire will be where $120 - 10L = 20 + 40L$; which solves for

$L = 2$ (as in the graph). The wage will be $w = 120 - 10(2) = 100$.

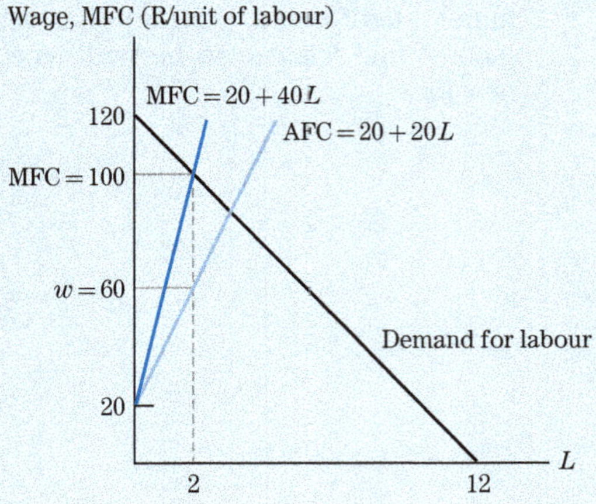

12.9 When the minimum wage is 80, the monopsonist's MFC curve is the heavy locus with the discontinuity at $L = 3$. The demand curve for labour passes through this discontinuity, which means that the monopsonist will hire 3 units of labour at a wage of 80. When the minimum wage is 100, the firm will pay $w = 100$ and hire 2 units of labour, the same quantity she would have hired in the absence of a minimum wage (but now at R100 and not R60).

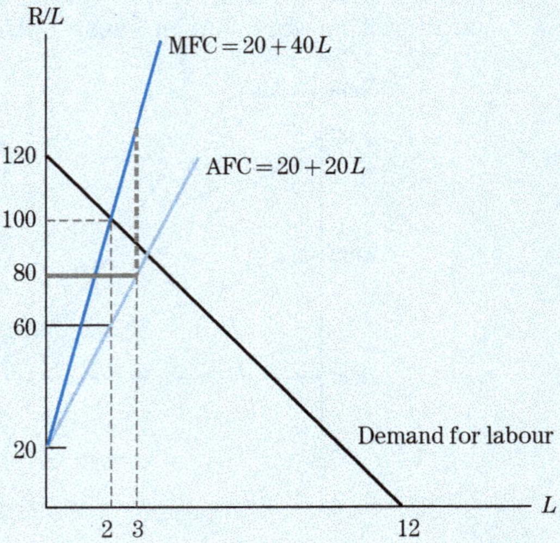

12.10 $VMP(320) = \left(\frac{1}{2}\right)(R240/hr) + \left(\frac{1}{2}\right)(R400/hr)$
$= R320/hr$

Chapter 13

Capital and exhaustible resources

The Topco Media research team, in association with the University of Stellenbosch Business School, runs a yearly competition to determine the top five most well-managed companies in different sectors of the South African economy. For the last 10 years it has provided detailed information on the top five companies in each sector in *Top Performing Companies*. In 2013 the top soft drink companies were Appletiser SA (Pty) Ltd, Ceres Fruits (Pty) Ltd, Coco-Cola SA (Pty) Ltd, Quality Beverages 2000 (Pty) Ltd and Shoreline Beverages cc. The top hotels were Tsonga Sun Hotels, Protea Hospitality Group (Pty) Ltd, City Lodge Ltd, Three Cities Management Ltd and Legacy Hotels and Resorts (Pty) Ltd. The top medical schemes were Discovery Health (Pty) Ltd, Bonitas Medical Fund, Medihelp Medical Fund, Bestmed Medical Scheme and Fedhealth Medical Scheme. These are just a few examples of companies that are rated by experts as the best in South Africa.[1]

The *Financial Mail* also publishes a list of South Africa's leading companies listed on the Johannesburg Stock Exchange. Its top rated company was Coronations, followed by EOH, Famous Brands, Afrocentric and Life Healthcare. The other firms in the top ten were Kumba Iron Ore, Woolworths, Invicta, Adcorp and Discovery. The firms rounding off the top 20 were Truworths, Howden, Naspers, Kagiso Media, Tongaat-Hulett,

[1] For a detailed outline of the latest rankings of the top five companies in South Africa in the resources, manufacturing and services sectors, visit http://www.top500.co.za/index.asp.

Vodacom, Clientele, Clicks, Mix Telematics and Value Group.[2]

The people compiling these rank orders are extremely knowledgeable, and there is every reason to believe that the companies they name are indeed among the most well managed. And yet it is common for people who bought stocks in these companies following publication of each year's *Top Performing Companies* to actually earn slightly less (or at best not notably better) on their investments than the average return for the stock market taken as a whole (especially in the short run).

We see a similar pattern with respect to the advice published in investment newsletters. These newsletters are compiled by the country's leading financial analysts, and often sell for several hundred rands per year. And yet the stocks recommended in most of these newsletters perform no better, on average, than the stocks picked by a monkey throwing darts at the financial pages. With investment newsletters, the anomaly is not that the stocks they recommend do no better than others, but that people continue to pay such high prices for this kind of advice.

Chapter preview

In this chapter we shall examine the market for services of capital inputs. In many respects, the results from our study of labour inputs will carry forward intact. One feature that often sets capital apart from other inputs is that, whereas other inputs are usually hired on a period-by-period basis, capital equipment is often owned outright by the firm.

We shall then examine the distinction between real and nominal rates of interest. This distinction will help make clear why the interest rates charged by banks and other lenders tend to rise hand in hand with the overall rate of inflation.

Next we shall see how interest rates are determined in the market for lendable funds. A topic of special focus will be the market for stocks and bonds, and the apparent anomalies mentioned in the chapter introduction. Additional items on our agenda include economic rent, peak-load pricing and exhaustible resources.

Financial capital and real capital

When people use the term 'capital', they usually mean one of two very different things. They may have in mind **financial capital**, which essentially means money or some other form of paper asset that functions like money. Or they may mean **real capital** (or *physical capital*), which means a piece of productive equipment, such as a robot or a printing press, that generates a flow of productive services over time. When we refer to capital as a factor of production, we are almost always talking about real capital.[3] When people talk about the 'capital market', they generally mean the market for financial capital, such as bank loans, corporate stocks and bonds. Our direct concern in this chapter is with real capital, but because firms require financial capital to purchase real capital, we must consider markets for financial capital as well.

> **Financial capital** Money, or some other paper asset that functions like money.
>
> **Real capital** Productive equipment that generates a flow of services; also called *physical capital*.

The demand for real capital

Our theory of the individual firm's demand for labour developed in Chapter 12 applies without modification to the demand for capital. In the short run, if the firm can acquire the services of as much capital as it wishes at a constant rental rate of r/yr, it should employ capital up to the point at which its marginal revenue product (MRP_K) is exactly equal to the rental rate:

$$MRP_K = MR \times MP_K = r \tag{13.1}$$

where MR is the firm's marginal revenue, and MP_K is the marginal product of capital.

If the firm happens to be a perfect competitor in its product market, so that its marginal revenue is the same as its product price, then Eq. 13.1 reduces to the simpler form

$$VMP_K = P \times MP_K = r \tag{13.2}$$

where VMP_K denotes the value of the marginal product of capital, and P is the price of the firm's output.

[2] See http://cdn.bdlive.co.za/images/pdf/FMTopCompanies2013.pdf for a detailed report on how the top companies were chosen.

[3] The exception is what we call 'working capital' – money the firm keeps on hand to facilitate timely payment of debts when current revenues fall short. By allowing the firm to function more efficiently, this working capital is no less a factor of production than are labour and machines.

For firms in a perfectly competitive industry, aggregation of individual firm demand curves into an industry demand curve for capital involves essentially the same complication we saw for labour. We must take into account that an expansion of industry output involves a reduction in the product price, with attendant moderations in the quantities of capital demanded. Again, as before, this effect is already accounted for in the monopolist's demand curve for capital.

One salient difference between capital and labour markets is that, whereas workers tend to specialize in particular types of activity, new sources of capital (financial capital) are almost completely fungible. Thus a given sum can just as easily fund the construction of a machine to make soft ice cream as it can a printing press or the production by Pixar Animation Studios (currently the undisputed leader in computer-animated films) of a new animated film. Once financial capital has been used to purchase real capital, however, the firm's flexibility is limited. Whereas labour can, at some expense, be retrained to perform new tasks when conditions change, it is much more difficult to transform a drill press into a sewing machine.

The relationship between the rental rate and the interest rate

How is the rental price of a unit of real capital equipment related to the interest rate at which money can be borrowed? Suppose the purchase price of a particular machine is R10 000 and the interest rate is 7 per cent/yr. To cover just the opportunity cost of the R10 000 you have tied up in the machine, you would have to charge R700/yr for it. Suppose further that the machine requires R1 000/yr worth of maintenance. Your break-even rental will then have risen to R1 700/yr. Finally, you must also consider changes in the future price of the machine.

> **Technological obsolescence** The process by which a good loses value not because of physical depreciation, but because improvements in technology make substitute products more attractive.

Even a well-maintained machine will lose some of its value each year as a result of wear and tear. Indeed, if newer, more efficient machines are being designed each year, an existing machine may lose its economic value overnight, even though it continues to function exactly as it did when new. This phenomenon is called **technological obsolescence**. If the net result of these factors is for the price of the machine in our example to fall by R1000/yr, the total cost of supplying it will then be R2700/yr: R700 in forgone interest, R1000 in maintenance and R1000 in lost market value. Any additional costs you incur as a rental business – such as wages for your staff who operate the machine – would have to be added to that figure.

Let m stand for annual maintenance expenses, expressed as a fraction of the price of the capital good, and let δ stand for physical and technological depreciation, similarly expressed. If i denotes the market rate of interest, then the annual rental rate of capital, k, will be the sum of i, m and δ:

$$k = i + m + \delta \qquad (13.3)$$

Sometimes a machine will actually grow in value, rather than depreciate, over time. This can happen, for example, when a key input used in making the machine becomes more expensive. In such cases, the term δ in Eq. 13.3 would be negative. For example, if the rental firm from our earlier example expected the price of a machine to go *up* by R1000 in the year to come, it could break even at a rental fee of only R700, R2000 lower than if the price of the machine went down by R1000.

> ***Exercise 13.1***
>
> Suppose the purchase price of a Coke machine is R300 000. If the annual interest rate is 0.07, the maintenance rate is 0.025 and the rate of physical and technological depreciation is 0.25, how much will the machine's annual rental fee be?

The criterion for buying a capital good

Another factor that sets capital apart from labour is that firms have the option of purchasing capital equipment. Professional athletes are sometimes bought and sold as if they were no different from machines, but even they cannot be forced to play for a team indefinitely against their wishes. Labour contracts in general permit workers to move whenever the terms of employment are no longer attractive, the primary reason being that it is impractical to make a disgruntled employee work effectively on the firm's behalf. For example, JP Peterson asked the Sharks to end his contract prematurely so that he could join the Panasonic

Wild Knights in Japan. The machine, of course, enjoys no such latitude. It goes to the highest bidder.

What factors govern a firm's decision about whether to buy a given piece of capital equipment? As always, the firm will weigh the benefits of owning the machine against its costs. On the benefit side, the machine will bolster the firm's rate of production not only in the current period, but also in the future. Suppose the extra output made possible by the machine will enhance the firm's total revenue by R for each of the next N years. Suppose further that the machine costs M each year to maintain, and that at the end of N years it has a scrap value of S rands. And suppose, finally, that the firm expects the machine to operate for N years, at which point it will sell it for scrap. By how much will the present value of the firm's stream of profits go up?

To answer this question, we must translate net revenues the firm will receive in the future into an equivalent present value. The present value of a rand to be received 1 year from now is R1.00/$(1 + i)$, where i denotes the market rate of interest. The present value of a rand to be received 2 years from now is R1.00/$(1 + i)^2$. The net present value of the stream of returns produced by the machine, including the proceeds from sale for scrap, is therefore given by

$$PV = \frac{R-M}{1+i} + \frac{R-M}{(1+i)^2} + \cdots + \frac{R-M}{(1+i)^N} + \frac{S}{(1+i)^N} \tag{13.4}$$

The cost of the machine is simply its purchase price, P_K. The firm should buy the machine if and only if PV is greater than or equal to P_K.

Exercise 13.2

Suppose a machine generates R60 500 worth of revenue at the end of each of the next 2 years, at which time it can be sold to a salvage company for R121 000. If the annual rate of interest is 0.07, what is the maximum amount a business would pay for this machine?

Interest rate determination

To recapitulate, a firm's demand for capital equipment depends on the rate of interest, the purchase price of capital and the rates of technological and physical depreciation. Interest rates, in turn, are determined by the intersection of the supply and demand curves for lendable funds. Because financial capital is perfectly fungible, the market for lendable funds is an almost literal embodiment of the ideal of a perfectly homogeneous, standardized product. The result is a national – indeed, international – market for lendable funds in which the interest rate charged to a given type of borrower is virtually the same everywhere.

How is the demand for lendable funds related to the demand for capital? A firm's demand for capital tells us how much capital it would like to employ at any given rental rate of capital, k. If it is a firm that has already been in operation for some time, it presumably has already acquired much of the capital it needs.

For simplicity, let us assume that in the current year the firm wishes to bridge the entire gap between the amount of capital it has and the amount it would like to have. This gap then constitutes its demand for lendable funds. At the industry level, similarly, the demand for lendable funds is the difference between the amount of capital firms as a whole would like to have and the amount they already do have. The price that is used to ration money in the lendable funds market is the interest rate.

Firms are not the only borrowers in the lendable funds market. Consumers borrow to finance the purchase of houses, cars and other goods. Governments borrow to build roads and schools, and to finance general budget deficits. The demand curve for lendable funds is the horizontal summation of the demands from all these sources.

On the supply side, there are also multiple sources of lendable funds. Consumer savings supplement funds made available by firms out of profits, and foreign lenders can also actively participate in the market for lendable funds. The theory of consumer behaviour tells us that a rise in interest rates may either raise or lower consumer savings, depending on the size of the income and substitution effects, and theory alone does not tell us which will dominate. Empirical studies suggest that the elasticity of consumer savings with respect to interest rates is very small.

For savings by private firms there is no analogue to the income effect in the consumer case, so the quantity of lendable funds supplied by firms will respond positively to interest rates. Most foreign lenders are happy to supply funds to South African borrowers whenever the interest rate meets or exceeds what they can earn at home. Adding all sources of supply horizontally,

Figure 13.1 Equilibrium in the market for lendable funds

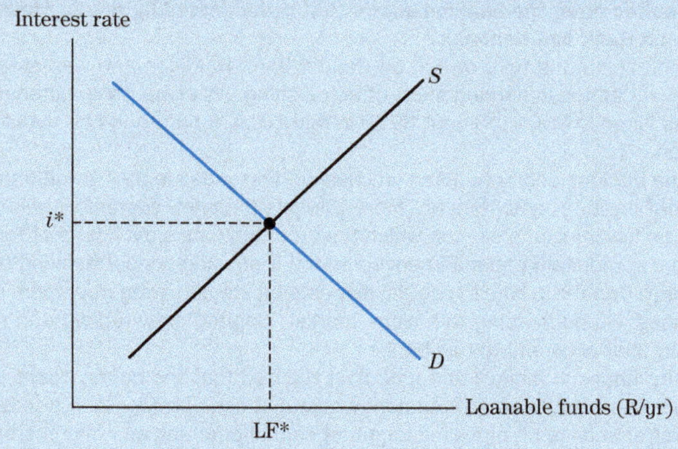

The quantity of lendable funds demanded at any interest rate (*D*) is the difference between the desired stock of capital at that interest rate and the amount of capital stock already in place. The supply of lendable funds (*S*) comes from consumers, firms and international lenders. Normally the supply curve of lendable funds will be upward sloping.

we obtain the aggregate supply curve of lendable funds. The intersection of this curve with the aggregate demand curve for lendable funds, shown in Fig. 13.1, determines both the market rate of interest, i^*, and the total volume of funds exchanged, LF^*.

Real versus nominal interest rates

Suppose you borrow R14 580 from a bank in 2014, which you agree to repay at the same time in 2015 at 7 per cent interest. And suppose that in this year the overall price level in the economy has risen by 10 per cent. What has been the real cost to you of your loan?

To answer this question, let us make use of an example. In 2014 when you borrowed the money, you could buy 1 oz of gold at R14 580/oz. Because the price of gold, like every other price, is assumed to be rising at 10 per cent/yr, this means you can sell your gold for R16 038/oz when your loan is due. The proceeds from this sale of R16 038 will be R438 more than the R16 500 you need to repay the bank. The real cost to you of the loan, measured in rands on its due date, is therefore *minus* R438. Not only did it not cost you any real resources to borrow the money, but you actually came out R438 ahead. On the reciprocal end of this transaction, the bank that lent you the money came out R438 behind.

Needless to say, a bank could hardly hope to remain in business if it continued to lend money on such unfavourable terms. When banks expect the overall level of prices to rise, they will charge an interest premium to counteract the erosion of the real purchasing power of future loan payments. The actual number that appears on the bank loan contract is called the *nominal rate of interest* – 7 per cent in our example. If n denotes the nominal annual rate of interest and q denotes the annual rate of inflation, then the *real rate of interest* is given by

$$i = \frac{n - q}{1 + q} \tag{13.5}$$

Using the values from our hypothetical example, we have $i = (0.07 - 0.10)/1.10 = -0.0273$, or -2.73 per cent. We can see from Eq. 13.5 that, when the rate of inflation is small, the real interest rate is approximately equal to the difference between the nominal rate of interest and the rate of inflation, $n - q$. In all our prior examples, the interest rate has been implicitly assumed to be the real interest rate. In its investment decisions, the firm wants to compare the real costs of capital with the real benefits, and proceeds only if the latter exceeds the former.

The market for stocks and bonds

One common method by which firms raise money for new investments is by issuing *corporate bonds*. A bond is essentially a promissory note issued by the firm. An investor gives the firm

Economic naturalist 13.1

Why did Capitec enter the banking sector that is dominated by the 'big four': Absa, Standard Bank, First National Bank and Nedbank?

Capitec Bank Limited is fully owned by Capital Bank Holdings and was established in March 2001. The growth of Capitec is nothing short of astonishing. Its share price increased from R1.17 per share when it was listed in 2001 to about R220 in mid-2014. It currently has about 500 branches and a client base of about 4 million.

While the 'big four' in the banking sector focused on chasing mortgages in their traditional middle-income market, they failed to recognize that existing customers are more valuable than new customers, which are more expensive to acquire. Capitec focused on lower-income clients, which the other big banks did not cater for. Its operating costs are lower because it works in a completely paperless environment; it provides longer banking hours; and it's supported by good brand management. Capitec is able to contain its costs by staying away from more expensive products such as car loans and mortgages. By addressing this niche market, Capitec grew rapidly and now even middle-income customers are transferring their accounts to this bank.

Capitec saw a gap in the financial market and took it. It realized that the poorer client is very price sensitive in terms of banking fees and thus created an environment whereby it can cater for their needs by charging lower fees. Capitec also provides a better service by providing longer opening hours and allowing customers to withdraw money at retailers such as Shoprite and Pick n Pay – services not provided by the other banks.

some money – say, R100 000 – and in return the firm hands the investor a handsomely engraved certificate that promises to pay the investor a fixed rate of interest – say, 10 per cent – for a specified time. The *face value* of the bond is the amount for which it was sold to the investor who bought it from the firm. *Short-term bonds* often promise to return their face value in full within 90 days. Many *long-term bonds* reach maturity only after 30 years, and some have even longer lifetimes.

Once bought, a bond may be traded in the open market. If it is a short-term bond, its price will almost always be close to its face value. For longer-term bonds, however, the price fetched in the open market can differ substantially from face value.

To see why, suppose the market rate of interest is 10 per cent when an investor buys a R100 000 bond from a corporation; the bond promises to pay her R10 000/yr interest for the next 30 years and then to return her R100 000 in full. As long as the interest rate remains at 10 per cent, the bond will continue to be 'worth' R100 000, in the sense that its R10 000 annual interest payment fully compensates the investor for the opportunity cost of doing without her money. But suppose the interest rate suddenly falls to 5 per cent. Now the opportunity cost of doing without R100 000 suddenly falls from R10 000/yr to only R5000/yr. The investor who holds a bond that promises to give her R10 000/yr would not be willing to sell it for only R100 000, because with the interest rate at 5 per cent, she would need R200 000 in order to earn the R10 000/yr interest she will get by keeping the bond.

The price of the bond in this example will not rise all the way to R200 000, however, because the new buyer knows that the bond will be worth only R100 000 when it reaches maturity. If the due date is imminent, the price will be close to R100 000 no matter what the interest rate is. But the further away is the maturity date of the bond, the less its face value will affect its current market price. Indeed, there is a particular type of bond, a **perpetual bond** or **annuity**, for which the face value does not matter at all. A perpetual bond is a promise to pay its bearer a fixed sum of money each year for ever.

Perpetual bond
A bond that pays a fixed payment each year in perpetuity; also called an *annuity*.

As a close approximation, the current market price of an annuity is the amount of money that would be needed, at the current interest rate, to generate the same amount of interest as is paid by the annuity. Thus, for example, an annuity that promises to pay R10 000/yr will be worth R100 000 when the interest rate is 10 per cent, and R200 000 when the interest rate is 5 per cent. More generally, if I represents the annuity's annual payment and i is the market rate of interest, then the price of the annuity, P_A, will be given by

$$P_A = \frac{I}{i} \tag{13.6}$$

Exercise 13.3

Consider a perpetual bond that pays R15 000/yr to its owner. By how much would the price of this bond rise if the interest rate fell from 10 to 5 per cent?

Corporations are not the only institutions that issue bonds. Governments do so as well. The examples discussed earlier implicitly assumed that there is a single, uniform market rate of interest at any moment, but in fact there are many different interest rates. The general rule is that the greater is the risk that a borrower will not repay a loan, the higher the interest rate that borrower will pay. The RSA Retail Savings Bonds, fully backed by the South African Reserve Bank, carry the lowest risk of default available in the bond market in South Africa, and the government therefore pays lower rates of interest than do the issuers of other bonds. By the end of 2014, the interest paid on a 2-year fixed interest bond was 7.25 per cent, on a 3-year bond 7.75 per cent and on a 5-year bond 8.25 per cent. You can link the bond to inflation and the rate on a 3-year bond is thus 1 per cent, on a 5-year bond is 1.25 per cent and on a 10-year bond is 2.25 per cent. Suppose, for example, a private company issues bonds; one would expect the interest rate to be higher because of the greater risk attached to it. In South Africa, the City of Johannesburg issued R6 billion municipal bonds between April 2004 and May 2006 to meet certain capital expenditure needs. By 2011 Johannesburg, Cape Town and Ekurhuleni had accumulated bond issuances amounting to R12.3 billion. The City of Tswane raised R1.39 billion in 2013 in a debut bond issue. The difference between the higher private interest rate and the lower interest rate offered by the Treasury is called a **risk premium**, and it compensates the investor for the fact that the private company has a higher likelihood of not repaying its loan than does the government.

Risk premium A payment differential necessary to compensate the supplier of a good or service for having to bear risk.

Someone who owns a corporate bond does not have an ownership share in the corporation. The bondholder's financial position is similar to that of a bank that has issued the corporation a loan. The corporation's stockholders are the people who actually own it. A firm that wants to raise money to invest in capital equipment can hire a broker to arrange a new issue of stock certificates. The broker then prepares a description of the firm's investment proposal and, with the co-operation of a network of other brokers, offers the new stock for sale to the public.

If a firm sells 1000000 shares of stock, each share constitutes a claim against 1/1000000 of the current and future profits of the firm. Profits may be distributed to shareholders directly in the form of dividends, or they may be reinvested in the company, which will increase the value of the company's future profits.

What price will each share of stock command? Suppose the present value of the current and future profits of our 1000000-share hypothetical company is known with certainty to be R500 million. Its stock should then trade at exactly R500/share. At a price any lower than that, investors could increase their wealth immediately by buying it. And at any price above R500, no one would have any economic incentive to own it.

Seldom, if ever, is a company's future profit stream known with certainty. The price people are willing to pay for shares depends on their best estimates of the firm's prospects. For new firms, or for firms that are moving into uncharted territory, the risk of low earnings can be very substantial indeed.

In other areas of the economy, the economic prospects of a company are easier to predict. Budget car rental, founded in 1958, has been in the business of renting cars for many decades now, and no major surprises appear to be on the horizon. The company stands almost no chance of hitting a big jackpot. But, by the same token, its odds of continuing to survive are relatively high.

Consider two firms with the same expected value of current and future profits. The present value of firm 1's profit stream is R100 million with certainty. The present value of firm 2's profit stream, by contrast, has a 50:50 chance of being either R200 million or zero. If the stock prices of the two firms were the same, which one would you prefer to buy? If you are like most investors, you are risk averse and therefore prefer firm 1, the safer of the two.

As an investor confronting the stock market, you face a budget constraint something like the curve labelled *BB* in Fig. 13.2. Along *BB*, the safer the investment, the lower its expected return. Investors with relatively low marginal rates of substitution between return and safety will choose risky investments such as A, which offer relatively high expected returns. Those with higher marginal rates of substitution between return and safety will choose safer investments such as C. Virtually everyone would like to own stocks with high expected returns *and* high safety. But the terms available in the market force people to choose between these attributes.

The efficient markets hypothesis

Most economists believe the stock market is efficient. By this we mean that the price of a stock

Figure 13.2 The trade-off between safety and expected return

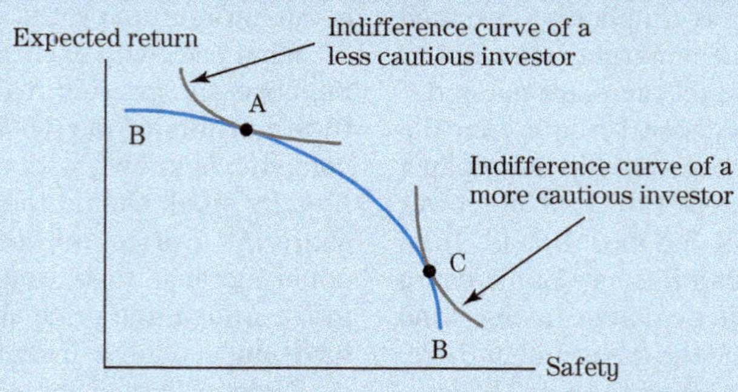

Because most investors are averse to risk, they will not buy a risky stock unless its expected return is greater than that of less risky stocks. Relatively cautious investors will prefer safer stocks such as C. Less cautious investors will give up some safety for the greater expected return on investments such as A.

embodies all available information that is relevant to its current and future earning prospects. To illustrate, consider a hypothetical example involving Genentech, a highly successful genetic engineering company. Although the biotechnology industry would like us to believe that genetically modified (GM) crops are a great success, it is rather surprising that 98 per cent of GM crops are grown in the USA, Argentina, Brazil, Canada and China, while South Africa is the only country in Africa involved in GM production. According to the South African National Seed Organization (SANSOR), in 2011 all cotton seed, 77 per cent of maize seed and 78 per cent of soya beans sold were genetically modified. These three crops account for 94 per cent of all GM crops planted globally.

Whatever may be the case, let us assume that Genentech is currently very successful and that, on the strength of its earnings prospects, the current value of one of its shares is R200. Now suppose that one of Genentech's researchers suddenly stumbles on to a miracle cure for cancer. The discovery is simple, and easy to patent. The company is certain to win government approval for its discovery, at which point its revenues will soar dramatically. However, bureaucratic red tape means the approval process never takes less than three years. You read in *Biophile* about Genentech's discovery, and decide to buy stock in the company. Is this a shrewd move on your part?

The answer is almost certainly no, but not because the company does not have the rosy future that has been forecast for it. By the time you hear about it, the rise in price for which it is responsible will have long since occurred.

Critics of the efficient markets hypothesis argue that it may take a considerable time for new information to disseminate, and so its effect on stock prices may be gradual and protracted. Thus, they conclude, if the news of the Genentech discovery is only a few weeks old, there will still be plenty of room for stock prices to keep growing on the strength of it.

This view is almost certainly wrong. In practice, it would be much more common for the market to learn at first only that a Genentech researcher had a promising lead on a cure for cancer. This more limited information would justify a much smaller boost in the company's stock price, which would then be followed by further increases if the development continued to show promise. But it would be followed by a plunge in stock prices if the development were to fizzle. In either event, however, the full value of the information at hand would be reflected in the stock price of the moment. Unlike the conditions in our hypothetical example, in the real world it is usually hard to quantify exactly what information becomes available at specific times. It is extremely difficult to verify the efficient markets hypothesis empirically. Nonetheless, most economists believe that it is correct. Why?

The answer is that the alternative hypothesis – namely, that stock prices *don't* embody all the available information – leads to conclusions that we find so difficult to accept. To illustrate, consider our cancer cure example again, and suppose the market did not immediately bid up the price of the stock to reflect the higher future profits implied by the new discovery. Then you or I could simply pick up the phone and instruct your stockbroker to buy as many shares in Genentech as you could afford. You could then sit back and wait for the market to bid up your shares to their full market value, reaping a substantial gain in the process.

The one belief that economists hold more deeply than any other is that the only way to reap such gains is by some combination of talent, hard work and luck. But if we deny the efficient markets hypothesis, there can be cash just sitting on the table for the taking. We need no talent; we needn't do any hard work; and because the information is certain, we don't even need to be lucky. We just call our brokers and wait for the money to roll in. There is an ample supply of people who would be delighted to earn their livings in this painless way. That it seems generally impossible to do so is all the confirmation most economists need for the efficient markets hypothesis.

Economic naturalist 13.2 helps us explain one of the apparent anomalies mentioned at the outset of the chapter. Recall that shares in the best-managed companies frequently perform no better than the stock market taken as a whole. Indeed, they can even perform slightly worse. We can now see that this does not mean that the best-managed companies are no more profitable than others. If they do have higher profits because they are better managed, and if investors already know that, then their stock prices will have been high to begin with. There is no reason to expect them to grow more rapidly than the stock prices of other firms. It is important to remember that the above discussion concerned the growth rate in stock prices. However, the dividends paid out by more profitable firms will normally be higher than those of less profitable firms.

The anomaly of the investment newsletter

I am always amused at how often I'm asked to give or receive expert advice on the stock market. For example, when people at parties first learn that I am an economist, they often ask me which stocks they should buy. I duly tell them that if I knew the answer to that question, I wouldn't have to work for a living.

As result of their faith in the efficient markets hypothesis, most economists believe that it is generally fruitless to act on investment advice. The one important exception to this general rule occurs when the advice is based on information not available to other investors. Suppose, for example, that your sister was the Genentech researcher who came up with the miracle cure for cancer. You know that she has been working on this problem in her office in the house you share, and you can tell by the spring in her step that she has just solved it. And because you have learned this before anyone else, you can be sure of making a lot of money from buying Genentech stock. But note that even this example does not violate the rule that substantial gains require talent, hard work or luck. Here, it is simply your good fortune to have learned of the discovery before anyone else could act on it.

But generally the information we get about new profit opportunities is days, weeks or even months old. To illustrate the problem, consider an analyst

Economic naturalist 13.2

Why is owning stock in a monopoly like De Beers no better than owning stock in a perfectly competitive firm?

Many people believe that it is better to buy stock in a highly profitable company than in one with only an average profit level. An important implication of the efficient markets hypothesis, however, is that this belief is wrong. To see why, consider two firms identical in all respects except that one is a monopoly and earns twice the profit earned by the other. If the prices of the two stocks were the same, everyone would naturally want to own stock in the monopoly. But, for that very reason, the prices of the two stocks cannot be the same. The excess profit of the monopoly will result in its stock selling for twice the price of the other firm's stock. From the perspective of the person buying the stock, therefore, the rate of return will be exactly the same for the two firms. True enough, the monopoly is twice as profitable, but its stock will cost twice as much to acquire.

Are stocks in monopoly firms a good deal? ©Jewelrystock/Alamy

who on 1 June discovers in his research that faulty accounting procedures have understated the profits of some company. Because investors thought the company was less profitable than in fact it was, its stock sold for too low a price. The analyst discusses this finding with his colleagues and superiors, who do some additional digging and confirm his conclusion. On 15 June the researcher writes up his findings in an article for the company's newsletter. The newsletter goes to the typesetter on 22 June, comes back for proofreading, errors are corrected, and the printer returns the finished copies by 1 July. The staff prepare the newsletters for mailing, and they are in subscribers' hands by 4 July (or 1 July if they send electronic copies).

Numerous people are in a position to act on the new information during the time that elapses between the initial discovery of the information and the time it reaches subscribers. Of course, many newsletters come out more frequently than once a month, but even with a daily newsletter the problem remains essentially the same. Even on the instantaneous internet, you are unlikely to be the first to come upon an update; after all, someone had to write the web page. It is therefore unlikely that someone will make money based on the information contained in the investment newsletter. Apart from making the reader appear well-informed, it does not make economic sense to pay much for these newsletters.

Sound advice for investors

The preceding discussion may make it appear that investment advisers serve no purpose. On the contrary, there is a clear role for professional investment advice, but of a different sort than many investors hope for. The efficient markets hypothesis suggests that investment advisers will not be able to tell you how to pick stocks that do better than the market as a whole. But they can tell you how to select the kinds of stock that best suit your investment objectives. More specifically, they can help you decide intelligently about what combination of risk and expected return best suits your purposes. If you are a young person trying to save for retirement, it will usually make sense for you to acquire a portfolio of riskier stocks with higher-than-average returns. They may perform poorly during some periods, but if your real concern is to obtain the highest growth over the long run, this is the best mix for you. If you are near retirement, you want to invest in safer stocks to protect your savings against a large drop in value.

Tax policy and the capital market

The government's tax policy towards the income earned from investments often has strong effects on how people allocate their resources. Let us illustrate this situation with a hypothetical example. Let us assume that the interest earned by holders of municipal bonds is exempted from income tax. A municipal bond is in most respects like a corporate bond, except that it is issued by a local government, not a corporation. An investor gives the local government some money – say, R100 000 – and the city pays the investor a fixed rate of interest – say, 6.75 per cent – for a specified period, often 10 years, and then returns the R100 000.

We assume that, in order to make it easier for local governments to raise money, central government has exempted the interest earned on municipal bonds from normal income tax. The holder of the bond in the example would thus receive R6750 of tax-free interest each year. The interest earned on RSA Retail Savings Bonds from National Treasury, by contrast, is fully taxable, as is the interest on bonds issued by corporations.

Hearing about this government policy for the first time, you may wonder why anyone ever buys any kind of bond other than a municipal bond. Why buy an RSA Retail Savings or corporate bond and pay tax on the interest? People would indeed purchase only municipal bonds if the terms they offered were in other respects the same as those of treasury or corporate bonds. Naturally, however, their terms will not be the same. In particular, local governments quickly discover that they do not have to pay as high an interest rate as the issuers of other bonds. Thus a 10-year RSA Retail Savings Bond pays 8.50 per cent interest, whereas a 10-year City of Johannesburg Metropolitan Municipality bond pays (say) only 6.75 per cent.

Which kind of bond you should buy depends on the marginal rate at which your income is taxed. Suppose you are taxed at the 30 per cent rate on any extra income you earn (your marginal tax rate). A Treasury bond that pays R8500/yr interest will leave you with only R5950/yr of interest after taxes. You would do better to purchase the municipal bond with its smaller, but tax-free, interest of R6750/yr. Alternatively, suppose you pay tax at the marginal rate of only 18 per cent. Your after-tax earnings for the Treasury bond (R6970) would then be higher than for the municipal bond (again, R6750).

Tax policy also affects the firm's decision regarding whether to buy or lease its capital equipment. Under income tax law, firms are granted a depreciation allowance for all capital equipment they own. If a firm owns a machine with a 10-year lifespan, say, it is permitted to deduct 10 per cent of the purchase price of the machine from its corporate profit each year in reflection of the machine's depreciation in value.

The depreciation allowance reduces the firm's income tax only if it has to pay income tax in the first place. If a firm experiences not a profit but a loss, or if it is a non-profit firm, then it owes no tax to the central government, and its depreciation allowance essentially goes unclaimed. This fact has opened up an opportunity for entrepreneurs who start companies to lease capital equipment to firms that owe little or no corporate income tax. Because the leasing company can claim the full value of the depreciation allowance, it can essentially supply capital to its clients more cheaply than it can supply it to itself.

Economic rent

In everyday usage, the term 'rent' refers to the payment received by a landlord, a rental car company or some other owner in return for the use of a real economic asset. In economic analysis, **economic rent** is the difference between the payment actually received by the owner of a factor of production and his reservation price (the minimum amount necessary to induce him to employ it in its current use).

Economic rent The difference between what a factor of production is paid and the minimum amount necessary to induce it to remain in its current use.

For example, if a landlord would rather see his land lie fallow than let someone else farm it for a payment of less than R10 000/mth, then only R15 000 of the R25 000 monthly payment he currently gets for his land is economic rent.

If an input is supplied perfectly inelastically (that is, if its owner would supply it no matter how low the price), then the entire payment to the owner is economic rent. This situation is shown in Fig. 13.3(a). Suppose, however, that the owner of an input has an upward-sloping supply curve, which intersects the demand curve for the input at a price of r_1^*, as shown in Fig. 13.3(b). If buyers of the input could collude and make the owner a take-it-or-leave-it offer for K_1^* units of the input, the lowest amount the owner would accept is equal to the area under the supply curve up to K_1^* (the dark shaded area in Fig. 13.3(b)). But if buyers do not collude, the owner receives a price of K_1^* on each unit sold, and thus receives more than this minimum amount. His economic rent is the light shaded area above the supply curve.

Economic rent is the factor market analogue of producer surplus in the goods market. Producer surplus, recall, is the revenue in excess of the minimum required to call forth a given supply of output in the goods market. As with producer surplus, economic rent will be greater, other things being equal, the more inelastic the supply curve of the product.

Whether the payment to a factor of production constitutes an economic rent depends in part on the vantage point from which the transaction is viewed. Consider, for example, the parcel of land on which the McGraw-Hill headquarters sits. From the landowner's point of view, no portion of McGraw-Hill's monthly payment for the site is an economic rent. After all, if the company paid any less than it did for the site, the landowner could rent it for the same amount to some other company. In this sense, McGraw-Hill is not paying a cent more than necessary. But if we view the same transaction from the point of view of the economy as a whole, virtually the entire payment is an economic rent, because the owner of that land will offer it to *someone*, no matter how low the price falls.

Though rent is strongly associated in the public mind with payments to the owners of capital inputs, economic rents are often of even greater importance in the labour market. Recall, in particular, our discussion of the economics of winner-take-all markets at the end of Chapter 12. People of rare talent or ability often command exceptionally high salaries, even though, in many instances, they would be willing to perform their services for much less. The multimillion-dollar salaries of top entertainers and professional athletes, for example, are for the most part economic rent, not compensation for the inconvenience of sacrificing leisure. Robert Downey Jr was the highest-paid actor in 2013, and earned $75 million. Surely he would work for much less than that? Although the highest-paid actress in 2013, Angelina Jolie, earned 'only' $33 million, she would also be willing to work for far less than that. The portion of their earnings that we can classify as economic rent must be substantial.

Figure 13.3 Economic rent

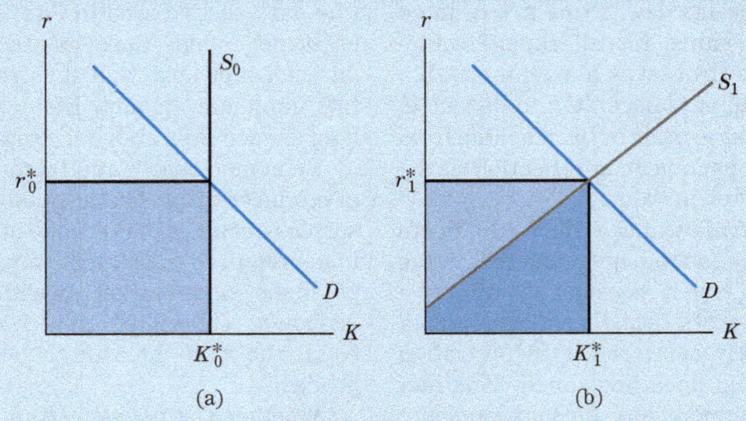

(a) When the supply of an input is perfectly inelastic, the entire payment it receives is an economic rent. (b) The economic rent received by an input with an upward-sloping supply curve is the shaded area above the supply curve.

The same can be said about our own golf superstar, Ernie Els. After winning the British Open in 2012, he was the highest paid South African sportsman in 2012/13, with earnings of $18.2 million. He also featured on the European Tour list, with earnings of €29.93 million. Retief Goosen didn't do badly for himself either; he comes sixth according to all-time career earnings in Europe. Obviously, both of these players would be willing to play for much less.

Peak-load pricing

A firm's demand for capital will depend not only on the rental rate of capital, but also on how it apportions the costs of its capital equipment among the buyers of its product. To illustrate the nature of this relationship, and at the same time help shed light on an extremely important policy issue, let us consider the case of companies such as Eskom, whose demands differ sharply at different times of the day. The historical pattern has been to charge a single, uniform price for electricity sold at different times of the day or year. This price was generally pegged at a level sufficient to enable the company to cover its labour, equipment, fuel and other costs, plus a normal return on its investment. In Eskom's case, provision was not made for proper maintenance, capital outlays, extending the electricity network or building new electricity plants. That is why we saw increases in electricity rates of 31.3 per cent in 2009, 24.8 per cent in 2010, 25.8 per cent in 2011 and 25.9 per cent in 2012. Resistance from consumers and the negative effect this had on the economy forced NERSA (National Energy Regulator of South Africa) to approve further increases only in the region of a maximum 8 per cent per annum until 2016. The rest of the discussion focuses on how electricity supply firms typically transformed their price structure and policy.

Recently, electricity suppliers have begun to alter their policy, implementing rate structures in which prices are directly related to the intensity of overall usage at the time of consumption. (One problem with something like electricity is that it cannot be stored in the off-peak period to make more electricity available in the peak period.) For example, a company whose loads are heaviest during business hours may charge a higher price for electricity used between 08:00 and 20:00 than for electricity used during other hours. Such rate structures are commonly referred to as **peak-load pricing**.

Peak-load pricing The practice whereby higher prices are charged for goods or services during the periods in which they are consumed most intensively.

To illustrate the effects of peak-load pricing, consider an electricity utility that uses only two inputs, generators and coal. Suppose that customer demands for electricity in the short run vary by time of day according to the pattern shown in Fig. 13.4. The demand curve during business hours is labelled 'Peak demand' and the demand curve during the rest of the day is labelled 'Off-peak demand'. Suppose the company initially sells all its power at the same rate, 50 cents/kWh, and that

Figure 13.4 The effect of peak-load pricing

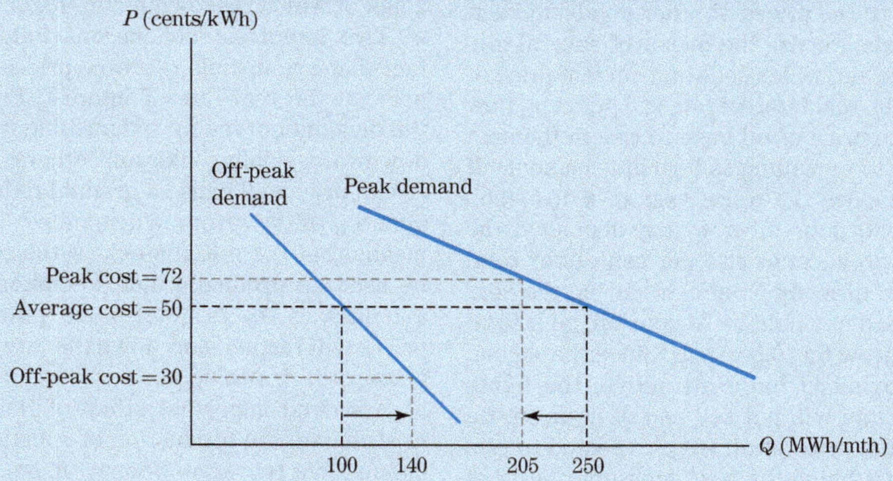

By charging higher prices during peak hours ($P = 72$) and lower prices during off-peak hours ($P = 305$), utilities give their customers an incentive to shift consumption to off-peak hours. The resulting fall in peak-period usage enables the utility to serve its customers with a significantly smaller stock of generating equipment.

its revenues at that rate exactly cover all its costs. Note in the diagram that, when all power sells for 50 cents/kWh, peak demand is 250 MWh/mth.

If the average cost of production is 50 cents/kWh, we know that the marginal cost of serving off-peak users must be less than 50 cents/kWh, while the marginal cost of serving peak users must be more. This follows because we can serve an extra off-peak user without having to add any more generating equipment, whereas we must add new generators to serve additional peak users. The only cost of serving an off-peak user will be the extra coal required to run some of the generating capacity that would otherwise be idle during that period. Suppose this off-peak marginal cost is 30 cents/kWh. The extra cost during the peak period will include not only the cost of fuel, but also the cost of the required extra capital. For purposes of illustration, suppose that these peak-period costs add up to 72 cents/kWh.

And suppose, finally, that the utility charges 72 cents/kWh to peak-period users and only 30 cents/kWh to off-peak users. Note in Fig. 13.4 that the effect is to reduce peak-period consumption by 45 MWh/mth, most of which shifts to the off-peak period. The shift is achieved in a variety of ways. For example, people may buy timers that operate water geysers, air conditioners and security lights only during off-peak hours. Similarly, they may avoid using dishwashers, washing machines and tumble dryers during the peak period. The net result of such consumption shifts is that a utility can serve its customers with much smaller generating capacity.

Airlines also employ peak-load pricing, cancelling some or all of their discount seats during heavy travel periods. Taking the cable car up Table Mountain will cost you more in the summer than in the winter. Seasonal price differences are a common practice among resort hotels, charging you a higher price during the December holidays than on a weekday in the middle of winter. Peak-load pricing, in all of these examples, means that the overall level of capital required can be reduced significantly.

Exhaustible resources as inputs in production

Natural resources are also important inputs in many production processes. An exhaustible resource is one that cannot be replenished by people, such as coal, oil, gold or titanium. How does a competitive market allocate exhaustible resources?

The owner of an exhaustible resource has two options: (1) he can hold the resource; or (2) he can sell it. The opportunity cost implicit in the first option is the interest that could have been earned had the resource been sold and the proceeds deposited in a bank. The only economic reason the owner of an exhaustible resource would have for holding it is the expectation that its price will rise relative to the prices of other goods and services. Suppose you are the owner of several million barrels of oil, which sells at a current price of \$105/bbl. If the real interest rate is 5 per cent, how much will the price of oil have to rise in the next year for you to be willing to hold at least some of your oil? Suppose the price rises to \$115.50/bbl. If you sold all your oil now and deposited the proceeds in an account at 5 per cent, your total wealth would grow by 5 per cent during the next year. If instead you hold on to your oil, your total wealth will grow by 10 per cent. Since the second option is obviously more attractive, the likelihood is that you will not sell any of your oil. By contrast, if the price of oil were expected to rise to only \$107.63/bbl in the next year, your best bet would be to unload all your oil now and invest the proceeds at 5 per cent. A \$2.63 rise in the price of a \$105 barrel oil means that oil you hold will grow by only 2.5 per cent in value.

It should be clear from this example that, for the market for an exhaustible resource to be in equilibrium, its price must be rising at precisely the real rate of interest. A growth in price any smaller than that would result in *all* owners trying to sell, and one any higher would result in a complete shutdown of trading. Suppose P_0 denotes the current price of an exhaustible resource. If this price grows at the rate of i per year, then the mathematical expression for the price after t years will be given by[4]

$$P_t = P_0 (1 + i)^t \qquad (13.7)$$

a plot of which is shown in Fig. 13.5.

Two important conclusions follow from the fact that exhaustible resource prices will tend to grow at the real rate of interest. First, because the demand curves for exhaustible resources are downward sloping, like any others, the gradual rise in price will cause a gradual reduction in the quantity of the resource demanded. This, in turn, means that the initial stock of the resource will be used up gradually, not precipitously. As less and less of the original stock remains, higher prices will further slow down the rate at which the resource is drawn upon.

A second important effect of rising prices is to stimulate the production of substitutes for the exhaustible resource. Sooner or later, the world is going to run out of oil. The activities for which we use oil today will someday have to be carried out using some other means, or else not be done at all. Research to discover alternative ways of carrying out the activities that require oil is on the increase. For example, in 2015 customers had a choice between a Toyota Prius, Ford Fusion, Chevrolet Volt, Nissan Leaf and a Honda Civic if they wanted to buy a hybrid car. In the SUV market, 41 different models were available in 2015; unfortunately, they're still rather expensive. The markets for exhaustible resources in general function smoothly and severe disruptions are normally the result of politically-related cutbacks in supply.

Figure 13.5 The equilibrium price path for an exhaustible resource

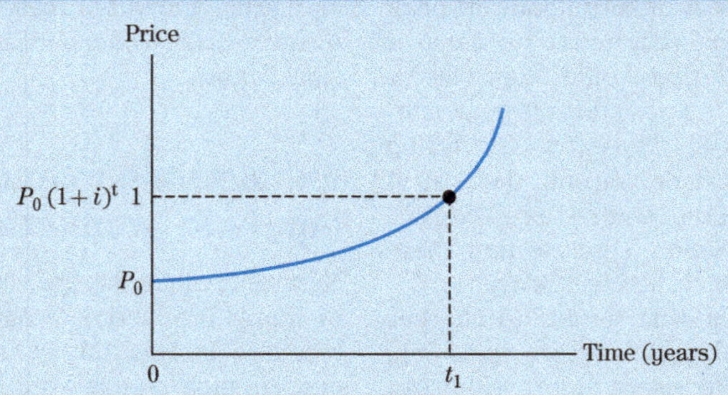

When the market for an exhaustible resource is in equilibrium, its price will grow at the real rate of interest.

[4] If the growth in price is continuous, the exact relationship will be $P_t = P_0e^{it}$, where e denotes the constant, 2.7183. Equation 13.7 provides a close approximation to this relationship.

In South Africa we are also dealing with exhaustible resources, or not enough energy to drive the economy. We have already discussed the problems of Eskom, which uses mainly coal (which is an exhaustible resource) to generate electricity. Examples of attempts to use more environmentally-friendly approaches to energy supply include the introduction of LED bulbs to replace halogen bulbs, which decreased energy consumption from 75 W per head to about 10 W per head; and the use of solar-powered traffic lights in Cape Town. The South African government supports renewable energy developments and was one of 191 states that signed the Kyoto Protocol in 2002 to reduce emissions of greenhouse gases.

Natural resources as inputs in production

We can divide natural resources into two distinct categories:

- renewable resources, such as trees
- exhaustible resources, like oil, that cannot be replaced once expended

Renewable resources

Consider the case of a timber company whose business it is to produce timber from the trees grown on its own land in such a way as to maximize the present value of its current and future profits.

An agricultural specialist advises the firm on how far apart to plant its trees, what fertilizers to apply, and so on. The economist's expertise lies in answering the question of when the trees should be harvested. Each year the firm must decide whether to cut a tree down or let it grow another year. The benefit of cutting it down now is to get the revenue from selling it right away. If the firm waits a year, it loses the use of that revenue for the time being, but in the meantime the tree continues to grow.

Let us assume trees grow over time according to the growth curve labelled B in Fig. 13.6. To keep calculations simple, suppose also that the price of timber remains constant through time, and that the real market rate of interest is constant at i/yr. At what age should a tree then be harvested for its timber?

The slope of the growth curve, $\Delta B/\Delta t$ (or dB/dt), tells us how much extra timber the firm will get by waiting an additional Δt time periods. The rate at which revenue will grow if the tree is left alone is the extra timber divided by the size of the tree, $(\Delta B/\Delta t)/B$. Thus, if Δt is 1 year and if $\Delta B = 0.10B$, then the rate at which timber – and hence total revenue – grows will be 0.10/yr. Because the slope of the B curve eventually declines over time (see Fig. 13.6), it follows that the value of $(\Delta B/\Delta t)/B$ will also eventually decrease over time, as shown in Fig. 13.7.

Figure 13.6 The growth curve for a tree

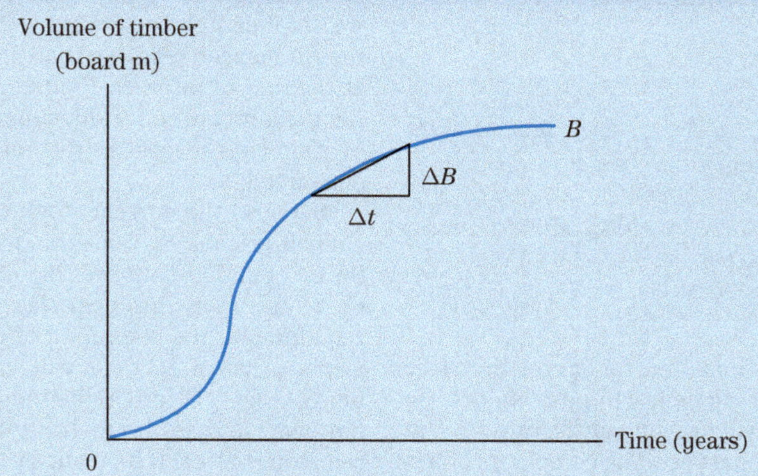

The curve labelled B tells us the volume of timber in the tree as a function of its age in years.

Figure 13.7 The optimal time of harvest

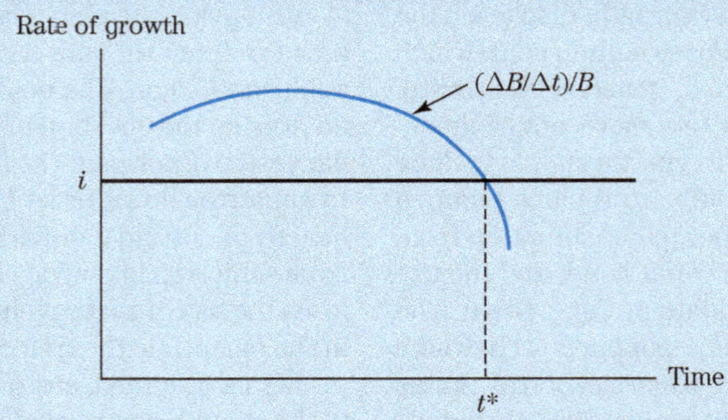

The optimal harvest time, t^*, is when the growth rate of the tree, $(\Delta B/\Delta t)/B$, is exactly equal to the real rate of interest, i. At that point, the extra revenue from leaving the tree in the ground for Δt longer is exactly equal to the interest that could be earned by harvesting the tree and investing the proceeds at i.

If, instead of letting the tree continue to grow, the firm cuts it down now and invests the proceeds at the market rate of interest, its revenue will grow at the rate of i/yr. It follows that the tree should be harvested as soon as

$$\frac{\Delta B/\Delta t}{B} = i \tag{13.8}$$

which will happen for $t = t^*$ in Fig. 13.7. For values of t to the left of t^*, the growth rate of the tree exceeds the growth rate of money deposited at i, which means that the firm should wait a little longer. For values of t greater than t^*, by contrast, money deposited at i will grow faster than the timber in the tree, so the firm should harvest the tree a little sooner.

Exercise 13.4

The volume of timber in a tree is given by $B = 80\sqrt{t}$, the slope of which curve at any point is given by $\Delta B/\Delta t = 40/\sqrt{t}$. If the annual interest rate is 0.05 per cent, at what age should the tree be harvested?

Note that the optimal time for harvesting a tree is not when it is as big as it will possibly get. On the contrary, it is still growing at the rate $i > 0$ at the optimal time of harvest. The company's objective is not to get the maximum possible quantity of timber out of any one tree, but to maximize the net revenues that result from an ongoing process of growing trees. And this will necessarily mean clearing out slower-growing mature trees to make room for faster-growing young ones. If a tree is growing on land owned or controlled by the firm that will harvest it, there is every financial incentive not to harvest it too soon or too late, for to do so would only reduce the present value of the firm's future earnings.

Exhaustible resources

All exhaustible sources of energy will eventually run out, at which point we shall be forced to rely on those that are renewable. Again, for simplicity, assume that oil is the only exhaustible energy source, and that when it is used up we shall switch to solar energy. Equilibrium in the oil market requires that the price of oil rise at the rate of interest. Figure 13.8, in which D is the demand curve for oil, summarizes the effect of rising oil prices on the rate at which oil is consumed.

Suppose the current stock of oil is S_0 and its current price is P_0. Consulting the demand curve for oil (Fig. 13.8), we see that consumers will use Q_0 units of oil this year, leaving $S_0 - Q_0$ units remaining at the beginning of next year. At next year's price of P_1 they will use Q_1 units, leaving $S_0 - Q_0 - Q_1$ at the beginning of the following year; and so on. Plotting the quantity of oil remaining at each moment in time, we have the *stock exhaustion path*, shown in Fig. 13.9.

Suppose that the price of solar energy is P^* per unit and is expected to remain constant through

Figure 13.8 The effect of rising prices on the use of oil

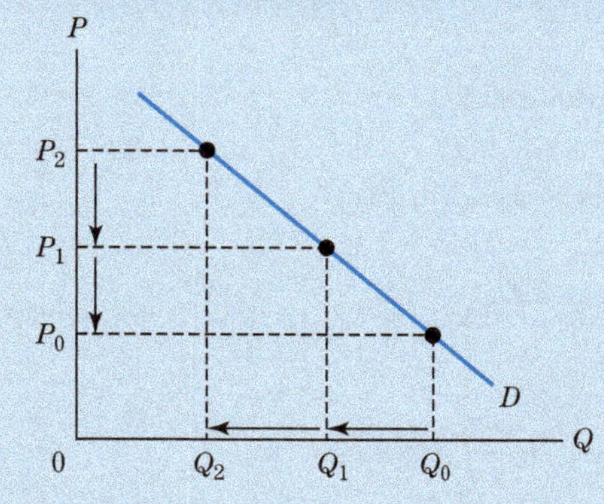

The demand curve for oil is downward sloping. Gradually rising prices thus lead to gradual reductions in the quantities by which the stock is depleted each year.

time. Suppose also that our current stock of oil embodies S_0 units of energy. We have already seen that the theory of exhaustible resource markets tells us that the price of energy in the form of oil will grow at the real rate of interest. But the theory also predicts that the last drop of oil will be used up at the very moment that its price reaches P^*, the level at which it becomes economical to use solar energy.

To see why this second prediction must be expected to hold, suppose that the owners of oil expect that when the price of oil reaches P^*, they will have some additional oil left. The locus labelled SEP_0 in the top panel of Fig. 13.10 depicts the stock exhaustion path corresponding to an initial stock of S_0, with an initial price of P_0. Starting at P_0, price rises at the real rate of interest over time, intersecting P^* when time = t_1 (bottom panel of Fig. 13.10). Note in the top panel that at t_1 there are S_1 units of oil remaining. But the owners of oil know that once its price reaches P^*, it can increase no further. After all, why should anyone be willing to pay more than P^* for oil if solar energy can be had for that price? If the owners have oil left over when the price reaches P^*, they will be able to sell it only at the rate at which people demand energy at that price.

Individual owners can avoid that outcome by selling their oil right now. And since all owners face the same incentive to sell, it follows that the current price will fall – from P_0 to P_0' in the bottom panel of Fig. 13.10. This fall in price will accomplish two things: (1) when price again grows at the real rate of interest, it will take longer than before to reach P^*; and (2) oil use levels will be higher, both now and in the future (because the demand curve for oil is downward sloping). In Fig. 13.10 the first effect is reflected in the fact that $t_2 > t_1$, the second in the fact that the new stock exhaustion locus (SEP_1) lies below the original one. Both effects will tend to reduce the amount of oil left over when the price reaches P^*. As Fig. 13.10 is

Figure 13.9 The stock exhaustion path

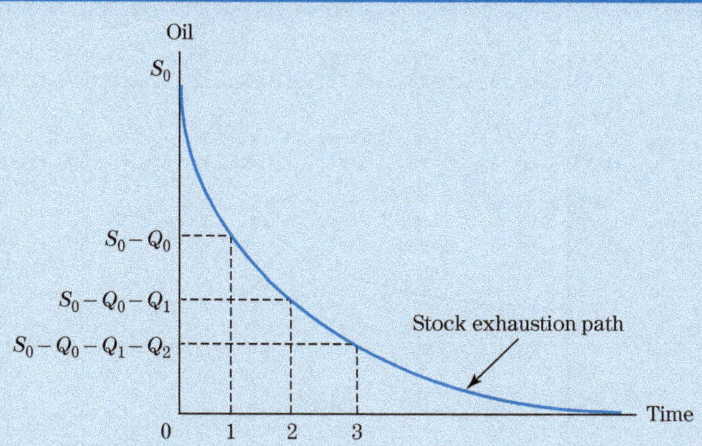

In the current moment ($t = 0$), the stock of oil is S_0 units. Given its current price of P_0, we consult the demand curve (Fig. 13.8) to get this year's consumption (Q_0). The stock remaining at the beginning of next year ($t = 1$) will be $S_0 - Q_0$. At next year's price of $P_0(1 + i) = P_1$ consumption will be Q_1, which means that the stock remaining at the beginning of the following year will be $S_0 - Q_0 - Q_1$; and so on.

Figure 13.10 Adjustment when investors expect to be stuck with excess oil

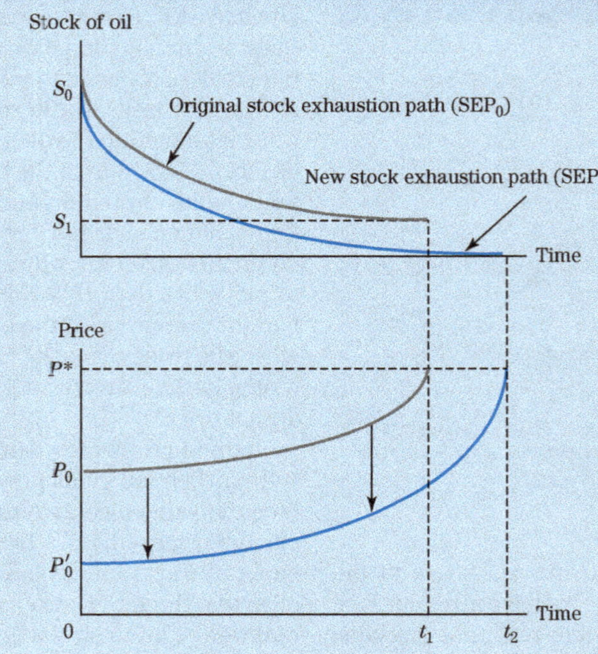

If investors believe they will still be holding some oil when its price reaches P^* (the price of solar energy), they will try to reduce their current holdings. This leads the current price to fall (bottom panel), which causes current and future use to increase. The increased rate of consumption is reflected in the downward shift of the stock exhaustion path (top panel).

Figure 13.11 Adjustment when investors expect oil to run out too soon

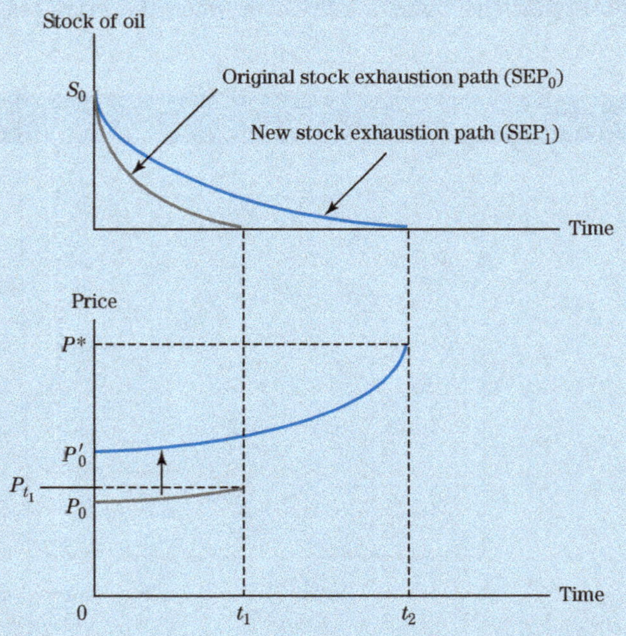

If oil is expected to run out before price reaches P^*, owners will conclude that they can earn more than the real rate of interest by holding on to their oil. This will cause current price to rise (bottom panel), which in turn will cause an upward shift in the stock exhaustion path (top panel). The upward price adjustment will continue until investors expect price to reach P^* at the moment all stocks are exhausted.

drawn, the last drop of oil is used at the exact moment the new price path reaches P^*.

Alternatively, suppose owners think they will run out of oil before its price reaches P^*. That is, suppose, as in Fig. 13.11, that we start with an initial stock of S_0 and price of P_0, and that we run out of oil at t_1, before its price reaches P^*. Once oil runs out, people will have to pay P^* per unit of energy, since solar energy will be the only source available. So owners can foresee that, at t_1, they will be able to charge not P_{t_1} but P^* for their oil. This means that by holding on to their oil until t_1, they can earn more than the real rate of interest. So if the owners of oil expect it to run out before its price reaches P^*, they will have an immediate incentive to stop selling oil right now. This produces an increase in the current price of oil, from P_0 to P_0' in the bottom panel of Fig. 13.11, which in turn causes an upward shift in the stock exhaustion path (top panel). The upward movement in price will continue until owners expect that the new price path will reach P^* at the exact moment the corresponding stock exhaustion path reaches zero.

However, we do not know how much oil remains in the ground at any moment and what solar energy will cost once we run out of oil. If we build these two uncertainties into the equation, it becomes a little more complicated.

Summary

- Our task in this chapter was to examine the market for services of capital inputs. Many of the results from our study of labour inputs apply to capital as well. Thus a firm's demand for the services of a capital input is the marginal revenue product of that input.
- One feature that often sets capital apart from other inputs is that, while other inputs are usually hired on a period-by-period basis, capital equipment is often owned outright by the firm. In considering whether to purchase a machine, the firm must ask how much its output will increase not only in the current period, but also in future periods. The firm's decision rule is to acquire the machine if and only if the present value of the current and future increases in revenue made possible by the machine exceeds its purchase price.
- The real rate of interest measures interest in terms of equivalent quantities of real goods or services. If, for example, a bank lends 100 oz of gold and requires a repayment of 105 oz after 1 yr, the real interest rate would be 5 per cent. When the rate of inflation is small, the nominal rate of interest is approximately equal to the real rate of interest plus the rate of inflation.
- A firm's demand for borrowed money depends on how the amount of capital equipment it would like to have compares with the amount it actually does have. The supply of lendable funds is highly responsive to interest rates because of the importance of foreign lenders in this market. The market interest rate and equilibrium level of borrowing are determined by the intersection of the supply and demand curves for lendable funds.
- The market for stocks and bonds is one of the principal sources of funds to finance new capital equipment. A corporate bond is essentially a loan from the purchaser of the bond to the corporation. As a bond nears maturity, its price must converge to its face value. But for bonds that are far from maturity, there will be a significant inverse relationship between current interest rates and the price of the bond. The price of a given stock is the present value, suitably discounted for risk, of the current and future profits to which it provides claim.
- The efficient markets hypothesis says that, holding risk constant, all available information about current and future earnings of a firm is immediately incorporated into the price of its stock.
- Tax policy has numerous effects on capital market decisions. If municipal bonds are tax-free, their interest rates will generally be lower than for bonds with taxable interest. Tax policy also sometimes induces

firms to lease, rather than buy, their capital equipment.

- The term 'rent' as used by economists has a somewhat different meaning from the one familiar from everyday usage. It is the payment to a factor of production in excess of the minimum value required to keep that factor in its current use. A significant share of the payments received by owners of capital constitutes economic rent under this definition.
- In peak-load pricing schemes, firms and regulatory agencies must decide how much to charge for the use of capital equipment when the intensity of demand varies greatly. As ever, the rule for efficient allocation is to set prices on the basis of marginal cost. Peak-load pricing enables firms to serve their markets while using significantly smaller amounts of capital equipment.
- In competitive markets for exhaustible resources, such as petroleum or titanium, prices tend to rise at the real rate of interest. This not only curtails the rate at which exhaustible resources are used, but also stimulates the rate at which new substitutes are developed. And it also ensures a smooth transition between the use of an exhaustible resource and its eventual substitute.

Questions for review

1 What is the difference between real capital and financial capital? Why does concern with one type of capital invariably involve concern with the other?

2 Explain why depreciation is an economic cost just like any other.

3 Why do higher interest rates make future events economically less important?

4 Why do nominal interest rates rise approximately one-for-one with increases in inflation?

5 Why are bond prices and interest rates inversely related?

6 Why is published investment advice like the investors' newsletter unlikely to be worth very much?

7 Give three examples of peak-load pricing used in your community.

8 Who will typically achieve a higher expected return on their investments: young investors, or older investors with more immediate need for retirement income?

9 Why does equilibrium require the price of exhaustible resources to rise at the real rate of interest?

Problems

1 You are deciding which of two computers to purchase. The interest rate is 0.09 and the maintenance rate of both machines is 0.01. The first computer costs R12 000 and has a rate of physical and technological depreciation of 0.10. The second computer, on the verge of obsolescence, has a rate of physical and technological depreciation of 0.30. If the annual rental payment for the two computers is the same, how much must the purchase price of the second computer be for you to be willing to buy it?

2 A machine that costs R100 000 will yield returns of R30 000 at the end of each of the next 3 years, at which time it will be sold as scrap for R30 000. If the interest rate facing this firm is 10 per cent, should it purchase this machine?

3 Suppose a perpetual bond pays R30 000/yr to its owner. What is the price of the bond at 5 per cent interest? At 6 per cent?

4 If everyone's marginal tax rate is 30 per cent, and if the interest rate on taxable government

bonds is 10 per cent, what will be the interest rate on non-taxable municipal bonds?

5 If the interest rate on taxable government annuities is 10 per cent, what will happen to the price of an existing tax-exempt government annuity if the government reduces everyone's marginal tax rate from 40 to 20 per cent?

6 Suppose a majority of investors do not care whether the companies whose stock they own do business in China. How, if at all, will the rate of return on stocks of companies that do business in China differ from the rate of return on stocks that do not?

7 Tony's barbershop has four chairs and four barbers. Most of the time at least one barber is idle, except on Saturday mornings, when all four are continuously booked. Explain, in terms a non-economist could understand, why the cost of providing a haircut on Saturday morning is higher than at other times of the week.

8 Around 1890 the vineyards in Bordeaux were infected by phylloxera, a louse that attacks the vine's roots. To preserve the original grape varieties, the Bordeaux vines were grafted onto roots taken from South African grape plants. Since 1890 most Bordeaux wines have been made with vines grafted onto South African roots. These wines do not taste the same as the wines made before the phylloxera infection. A bottle of Bordeaux that was made before the infection sells for thousands of euros. Suppose you had a bottle of pre-phylloxera Bordeaux that you could sell today for R20000, and you were interested only in its value as an investment. To make it worthwhile for you to hold on to your investment, what must be the expected price of the bottle in n years if the market rate of interest is i?

9 Suppose solar energy can be produced at a cost of R20 per unit of energy. Suppose the current price of oil is R12.00 per unit of energy, and that there is currently enough oil to last 100 more years at current use levels. If the real interest rate is 5 per cent, what do you expect to happen to the current price of oil?

10 There are two remaining exhaustible energy sources, underground oil and offshore oil, with extraction costs of R20/barrel and R60/barrel, respectively. There is also solar energy, with the price of R120 per energy equivalent of a barrel of oil. Everyone believes that there are currently S_1 barrels of underground oil and S_2 barrels of offshore oil remaining. How would the discovery of A additional barrels of underground oil affect the time and the gross price at which offshore oil will first be extracted? How will the discovery affect the length of the 'offshore oil age' – that is, the length of the time interval during which we use offshore oil?

11 Suppose a certain species of tree grows according to the function $B = 20\sqrt{t}$, where B is the volume of lumber in the tree, measured in board-feet, and t is the tree's age in years. If the interest rate is 0.05, at what age should the trees be cut if the goal is to maximize long-run profit?

12 Suppose there are two kinds of oil left, underground oil and shale oil. The cost of extracting a unit of underground oil is R20/barrel, and that of shale oil R100/barrel. Once extracted from the earth, the two kinds of oil are identical. Explain, in terms a non-economist could understand, why it does not make sense to begin using the shale oil until all the underground oil has been exhausted.

Answers to in-chapter exercises

13.1 Since $k = i + m + \delta$, we have $k = 0.07 + 0.025 + 0.25 = 0.345$. So the annual rental payment will be k (R300000) = R103500.

13.2

$$PV = \frac{60\,500}{1.07} + \frac{60\,500}{1.07^2} + \frac{121\,000}{1.07^2}$$
$$= 56\,542.06 + 52\,843.04 + 105\,686.09$$
$$= \text{R}215\,071.19$$

13.3 The price at 10 per cent is R15000/0.10 = R150000. At 5 per cent the price will be R15000/0.05 = R300000, so the rise in price is R150000.

13.4

$$\frac{\Delta B/\Delta t}{B} = \frac{40/\sqrt{t}}{80\sqrt{t}} = \frac{1}{2t} = 0.05$$

which solves for $t = 10$ years.

Part 5

Externalities, public goods and welfare

Part contents

This part of the text examines in greater detail the conditions under which unregulated markets tend to produce efficient outcomes. Chapter 14 examines the role of a well-defined system of property rights in the functioning of markets and the consequences of externalities, both positive and negative. Chapter 15 examines what microeconomic theory tells us about the role of government. Chapter 16 uses the theory of consumer and firm behaviour to explore the formal theory underlying Adam Smith's invisible hand.

Chapter 14

Externalities, property rights and the Coase theorem

Many of us have probably walked on the seafront and admired the modern houses and, as in the Strand, the multi-storey buildings containing luxury flats. Perhaps you have seen an old little house that looked totally out of place between these modern buildings. Obviously that small house must be worth millions, which developers will be more than willing to pay if the owners of that house are willing to sell it. As time goes on, that house becomes more valuable, because open space on the seafront is a shrinking asset.

In Calle de Cuchilleros 17 in Madrid is the world's oldest restaurant, Sobrino de Botin, which opened its doors in 1725. When developers wanted to build a block of flats on the site, the restaurant was not willing to sell because it had been a family business for generations. Eventually the parties involved came up with a creative solution. They negotiated a multimillion-dollar agreement whereby, without disturbing a single brick in the restaurant, a high-rise structure would be constructed *above* the restaurant. Sobrino de Botin is still open for business, a quaint, old-world restaurant nestled beneath the block of flats. In a similar multimillion-euro transaction, a developer purchased the rights to build the Park Plaza Victoria hotel near Centraal Station in Amsterdam astraddle two small flats when the owners of the flats refused to sell it when the hotel was built in 1895. The hotel was completely refurbished in 2011, but when I visited Amsterdam in 2014 the one single-storey flat and one four-storey flat were still clearly visible on the facade.

In most jurisdictions, owning a piece of property confers the right to exclude anyone from constructing a building in the airspace above it. But a similar right does not extend to all other forms of activity in the same airspace. For example, hundreds of South African houses are located beneath commercial flight paths between major cities, and each day many airliners use the airspace above these houses without paying a cent. This pattern of rights is not a matter of historical accident. It has emerged, as we shall see, as a means of making the most efficient use of property when it is difficult to negotiate agreements on a case-by-case basis.

Chapter preview

Our subjects in this chapter are externalities and property rights. We shall begin with a series of examples illustrating what happens when an action by one party harms another and the parties are able to negotiate costlessly with one another. Next we shall consider a related set of examples in which negotiation is costly. We shall then apply the principles that emerge from these examples to a variety of questions regarding the design of property rights. Should the owner of a dock be allowed to exclude a boater from tying up during a storm? When should a person be allowed to exclude others from walking across her land? Or from blocking her view? Should pastureland be owned privately or in common? Should a developer be allowed to construct an office building over someone else's property without his consent? Should aeroplanes be allowed to fly over houses? The answers to such questions, we shall see, depend on the kinds of agreements people would reach among themselves if they were free to negotiate costlessly with one another.

Next we shall apply the theory of property rights and externalities to the topic of contests for relative position. We shall conclude this chapter with an examination of taxation as a possible solution to the problem of negative externalities.

The reciprocal nature of externalities

In your introductory course in economics you must have touched on externalities. Recall that externalities are spillover costs or benefits. For example, if your economics professor visits the doctor to receive treatment for an infectious disease, the students also benefit because now they will not be infected. Although they did not pay anything, they will benefit. This is an example of a **positive externality**. If someone owns a factory that is responsible for creating air pollution which causes respiratory infections, some people will incur medical expenses as a result of that firm's production activities. The cost that the firm imposes on society without being penalized is known as a **negative externality**.

Positive externality A benefit that you receive for which you did not pay.

Negative externality Harm that you cause to somebody else without being penalized or punished for it.

Ronald H. Coase is the author of one of the most influential and widely cited economics papers of the post-war era. Titled 'The problem of social cost',[1] this paper profoundly changed the way economists, legal scholars, political philosophers and others think about externalities, and the legal and social institutions that have evolved to deal with them.

Coase began his paper with an example involving a doctor whose ability to examine patients was disrupted by the noise of machinery operated by a confectioner in an adjacent building. Historically, the economic and legal view of such a situation was clear and simple: the confectioner's noise was harming the doctor, thus he ought to be held liable for it. Coase's seminal insight was that this view completely overlooks the reciprocal nature of the problem. True enough, the confectioner's noise does harm the doctor. *But if we prevent the noise, we harm the confectioner.* After all, the confectioner makes the noise, not for the purpose of harming the doctor, but in pursuit of his own livelihood. In such situations there will be harm to *someone*, no matter what happens. Whether the harm caused to the doctor by the noise is greater than the harm that would be caused to the confectioner if he were prohibited from making it is strictly an empirical question. The common interest of each party, Coase recognized, is to avoid the larger of these two unpleasant outcomes.

Coase pointed out that if the doctor and the confectioner were able to negotiate costlessly with one another, the most efficient outcome would occur, regardless of whether the confectioner was liable. His simple and elegant argument in support of this claim is illustrated in the following series of numerical examples.

Note that, because the gain to the confectioner of operating his machinery (40) is smaller than the noise damage it imposes on the doctor (60), the most efficient outcome is for the

[1] R.H. Coase, 'The problem of social cost', *Journal of Law and Economics*, 1960, vol. 3, pp. 144–171. Coase received the Nobel Prize in Economics in 1992.

Example 14.1

Suppose the benefit to the confectioner of continuing to make noise is 40, whereas the cost of the noise to the doctor is 60.[2] If the confectioner's only alternative to making the noise is to produce nothing, what will happen if he is made liable for the noise damage? (To be liable for the damage means being required to compensate the doctor for any damage caused by the noise.)

The confectioner will examine his two options – shutting down or compensating the doctor – and choose the one that makes him better off. If he stays open, he will earn 40, but will have to pay 60 to the doctor, for a net loss of 20. If he shuts down, his net gain is 0, and since this is clearly better than losing 20, he will discontinue operation.

Alternatively, suppose the confectioner had not been liable for noise damage. That is, suppose the law grants him the right to continue operating without compensating the doctor. Coase argued that, in this case, the doctor will pay the confectioner to shut down. If the confectioner stays open, he will gain only 40 while the doctor will lose 60. But the doctor can compensate the confectioner for the loss of shutting down and still have enough left over to be better off than if the confectioner had stayed open. Suppose, for example, the doctor pays the confectioner 50 to shut down. The confectioner's net gain will now be 10 more than if he had stayed open. And the doctor's net gain of 10 is 10 more than if the noise had continued.

If P denotes the payment the doctor makes to the confectioner to compensate him for shutting down, we know that P must be at least 40 (what the confectioner would get by staying open) and no larger than 60 (what the doctor would get if there were no noise). The net results under the two legal regimes (confectioner liable versus confectioner not liable) are summarized in Table 14.1.

Table 14.1 Outcome and pay-off summary for Example 14.1

Legal regime	Outcome	Net benefit		
		Doctor	Confectioner	Total
Liable	Confectioner shuts down to avoid liability payment	60	0	60
Not liable	Doctor pays confectioner P to shut down, $40 \leq P \leq 60$	$60 - P$	P	60

The gain to the confectioner from operating is 40. The loss to the doctor from the noise is 60. The efficient outcome is for the confectioner to shut down, and this happens under both legal regimes.

confectioner to shut down. Example 14.1 makes it clear that if both the doctor and confectioner are rational and can negotiate costlessly with one another, this will happen regardless of whether the confectioner is liable for noise damage. On efficiency grounds, the legal regime is thus a matter of complete indifference here. On distributional grounds, however, the parties will be anything but neutral about liability. If the confectioner is not liable, his gain is $P \geq 40$, whereas he will be forced to shut down and earn nothing if he is liable. The doctor's net gain will be 60 if the confectioner is liable, but only $60 - P$ if the confectioner is not liable.

In the preceding examples we assumed that the only alternatives open to the two parties were either to continue operations in the current form or to shut down entirely. Because in practice one or both parties often face a broader range of alternatives, let us now consider other possibilities whereby they can negotiate costlessly and reach efficient outcomes.

The patterns revealed in the preceding examples may be stated formally as:

The Coase theorem: When the parties affected by externalities can negotiate costlessly with one another, an efficient outcome results no matter how the law assigns responsibility for damages.

[2] The numerical cost and benefit values used in this and in the following examples represent the present values of all current and future costs and benefits to the parties in question.

Example 14.2

This is the same as Example 14.1, except that now the benefit to the *confectioner* of operating is 60, the benefit to the doctor in a noise-free environment only 40. Assume that the doctor must shut down if the noise continues.

This time the efficient outcome is for the confectioner to continue operating, since his gain exceeds the cost he imposes on the doctor. If he is not liable for noise damages, the confectioner will stay open, and the doctor's best option will be to shut down. Alternatively, if the confectioner is liable for noise damage, he will again continue to operate, and pay the doctor 40 to compensate him for his losses. The net results for this example are summarized in Table 14.2. Note that, as in Example 14.1, both legal regimes lead to the most efficient outcome, but have very different distributional consequences.

Table 14.2 Outcome and pay-off summary for Example 14.2

Legal regime	Outcome	Net benefit		
		Doctor	Confectioner	Total
Liable	Confectioner stays open and pays doctor 40	40	20	60
Not liable	Confectioner stays open; doctor shuts down	0	60	60

The gain to the confectioner from operating is 60. The loss to the doctor from the confectioner's noise is 40. The efficient outcome is for the confectioner to continue operating, and this happens under both legal regimes.

Example 14.3

This is the same as Example 14.1, except that now the *confectioner* has access to a soundproofing device that will completely eliminate the noise from his machines. The cost of the device is 20, which means that if he installs it, his net gain from operating will fall from 40 to 20. As in Example 14.1, the doctor will gain 60 if there is no noise, 0 if there is noise.

If the confectioner is liable for noise damage, his best option will be to install the soundproofing. His alternatives are either to shut down or to pay the doctor 60 in noise damages, and each of these is clearly worse. If the confectioner is not liable, it will be in the doctor's interest to pay the confectioner to install the soundproofing. His alternative, after all, is to shut down or to endure the noise damage. The minimum payment that would be acceptable to the confectioner to install the soundproofing is 20, its cost. The most the doctor would be willing to pay for him to install it is 60, the amount the doctor would lose if it weren't installed. Again letting P denote the payment from the doctor to the confectioner, the outcomes and pay-offs for the two legal regimes are as summarized in Table 14.3.

Table 14.3 Outcome and pay-off summary for Example 14.3

Legal regime	Outcome	Net benefit		
		Doctor	Confectioner	Total
Liable	Confectioner installs soundproofing at own expense	60	20	80
Not liable	Doctor pays confectioner P to install soundproofing, $20 \leq P \leq 60$	$60 - P$	$20 + P$	80

The gain to the confectioner from operating without soundproofing is 40. Soundproofing costs 20. The loss to the doctor from the confectioner's noise is 60. The efficient outcome is for the confectioner to install soundproofing and to continue operating, and this happens under both legal regimes.

Example 14.4

This is the same as Example 14.3, except that now the doctor can escape the noise damage by moving his examination room to the other side of his office. The noisy room in which he was examining patients can now be used for storage. The cost to the doctor of this rearrangement is 18.

With this new option available, the doctor is the one who is able to eliminate the noise damage at the lowest possible cost. If the confectioner is liable for noise damage, he will offer the doctor a payment P to compensate him for rearranging his office. The payment must be at least 18, or else the doctor would not make the accommodation. And the payment cannot exceed 20, or else the confectioner could install soundproofing and solve the problem on his own. If the confectioner is not liable for noise damage, the doctor will rearrange his office at his own expense. The outcomes and pay-offs for this example are summarized in Table 14.4. Note that we again get the efficient outcome no matter which legal regime we choose. Note also that the choice of legal regime again affects the distribution of costs and benefits, only this time by a much smaller margin than in Example 14.3. The difference is that each party now has a relatively inexpensive method for solving the noise problem unilaterally. In Example 14.3 the doctor lacked such an alternative, making the confectioner's bargaining power very strong when he was not liable for noise damage. In this example, by contrast, the confectioner cannot extract a large payment from the doctor for keeping quiet, because the doctor can solve the noise problem on his own.

Table 14.4 Outcome and pay-off summary for Example 14.4

Legal regime	Outcome	Net benefit		
		Doctor	Confectioner	Total
Liable	Confectioner pays doctor P to rearrange his office, $18 \leq P \leq 20$	$42 + P$	$40 - P$	82
Not liable	Doctor rearranges his office at his own expense	42	40	82

The gain to the confectioner from operating without soundproofing is 40. Soundproofing costs 20. The loss to the doctor from the confectioner's noise is 60. The doctor can rearrange his office to eliminate the noise problem at a cost of 18. The efficient outcome is for the doctor to rearrange his office, and this happens under both legal regimes.

In the wake of its publication, Coase's classic paper became a subject of great controversy. Many took him to be saying that there is no real role for government in solving problems related to pollution, noise and other externalities. According to this interpretation, Coase's message seemed to be that if government stays out of the way, people will always come up with efficient solutions on their own. And yet Coase stated clearly that this conclusion holds only for a world in which parties can negotiate with one another at relatively *low cost.* He recognized that for many important externalities this assumption is not satisfied. At the simplest level, time and energy are required for negotiation, and when the potential benefits are small, it may simply not be worth it. Alternatively, there are situations in which a single polluter causes damage to a large number of people. Negotiating with large groups is inherently difficult and costly, and each person in the group faces strong incentives to escape these costs. When there are negotiating costs, it matters very much indeed which legal regime we choose. Let us now turn to examples in which the parties involved do not negotiate free of costs.

In Example 14.5, the total gain for society as a whole is 80 if the confectioner is liable, and only 60 if he is not liable. But as the following example will illustrate, the existence of barriers to negotiation does not guarantee that we shall always get an efficient outcome by making parties liable for the damage caused by external effects.

Exercise 14.1

How would the entries in Table 14.6 be affected if the cost of negotiation were 20 instead of 25?

Example 14.5

As in Example 14.2, suppose that the gain to the doctor in a noise-free environment is 40, while the gain to the confectioner from unfettered operations is 60. Suppose also that the confectioner has access to a soundproofing device that eliminates all noise damage at a cost of 20. And suppose, finally, that it costs the doctor and confectioner 25 to negotiate a private agreement between themselves. For negotiation to be a worthwhile alternative, they must be able to share this cost in some way that makes each of them better off than if they did not negotiate.

If the confectioner is made liable for noise damage, he will install the soundproofing. His next-best alternative, after all, is to pay the doctor 40 in noise damages,[3] and the installation of soundproofing costs him only 20. Because being liable gives the confectioner an incentive to install the soundproofing on his own, there is no need for him to negotiate an agreement with the doctor, and thus no need to incur the cost of negotiation.

But now suppose that the confectioner is not liable for noise damage. If there were no costs of negotiation, the doctor would pay the confectioner P, where $20 \leq P \leq 40$, to install soundproofing. If it costs 25 to negotiate an agreement, however, then it is no longer possible for the doctor to compensate the confectioner for installing soundproofing. The soundproofing makes it possible for the doctor to gain 40, which is insufficient to cover both the cost of the soundproofing (20) and the cost of negotiating the agreement (25), which total 45. When it is costly to negotiate, we no longer get the efficient outcome irrespective of which legal regime we choose. In this example, for which the relevant data are summarized in Table 14.5, we get the most efficient result only if the confectioner is liable.

Table 14.5 Outcome and pay-off summary for Example 14.5

Legal regime	Outcome	Net benefit		
		Doctor	Confectioner	Total
Liable	Confectioner installs soundproofing at his own expense	40	40	80
Not liable	Confectioner does not install soundproofing; doctor shuts down	0	60	60

The gain to the confectioner from operating without soundproofing is 60. Soundproofing costs 20. The loss to the doctor from the confectioner's noise is 40. The cost of negotiating a private agreement is 25. The efficient outcome is for the confectioner to install soundproofing, but this happens only when he is made liable for noise damage.

Example 14.6

This is the same as Example 14.5, except that the confectioner no longer has a soundproofing option; instead, the doctor has the option of avoiding the noise by rearranging his office, which will cost him 18.

If the confectioner is not liable for noise damage, this is exactly what the doctor will do. But if the confectioner is liable, the cost of negotiation now stands in the way of his paying the doctor to rearrange his office. The sum of negotiating costs (25) and rearrangement costs (18) comes to 43, which is 3 more than the 40 that will be saved by avoiding the noise. So, if he is liable, the best option available to the confectioner is simply to continue operating and pay the doctor 40 for the

[3] For the confectioner to operate and pay noise damages to the doctor, it is not necessary for them to incur the cost of negotiating a private agreement.

noise damage.[4] Here, unlike Example 14.5, we get the efficient outcome when the confectioner is not liable. The data for Example 14.6 are summarized in Table 14.6.

Table 14.6 Outcome and pay-off summary for Example 14.6

Legal regime	Outcome	Net benefit		
		Doctor	Confectioner	Total
Liable	Confectioner operates and pays doctor 40 for noise damage	40	20	60
Not liable	Doctor rearranges his office at his own expense	22	60	82

The gain to the confectioner from operating is 60. The loss to the doctor from the confectioner's noise is 40. The doctor can escape the noise by rearranging his office at a cost of 18. The cost of negotiating a private agreement is 25. The efficient outcome is for the doctor to rearrange his office, but this happens only when the confectioner is not liable for noise damage.

Property rights

Private property laws and their exceptions

No free-market economy can function successfully without laws that govern the use of private property. Among other things, these laws describe how people can lawfully acquire different types of property – by inheriting it, purchasing it or receiving it as a gift, but not by theft or other means that entail the use of force. In most cases, these laws grant owners of property the right to exclude others from using it without permission. Yet hosts of detailed exceptions sharply limit this right to exclude. As the following Economic naturalist examples suggest, these exceptions are not random. Rather, they follow a systematic pattern, one that the insights of Coase help us to understand.

There are exceptions to this general principle, however, and these too provide an illuminating illustration of the Coasian efficiency rule. The most conspicuous exception involves approach and take-off lanes to and from airports near major metropolitan areas. Jets fly low to the ground just

Economic naturalist 14.1

Why does the law permit airlines to operate flights over private land without permission?

Unlimited air rights existed when people began owning real estate. It was not an issue that anyone concerned themselves with before the twentieth century. The first legal limits placed on air rights came about because of the aeroplane. The law states that in congested areas planes must stay 300 m higher than any obstacle (building, antenna, etc.) within a 610 m radius of the aircraft. In 2009 a disaster was narrowly avoided in Durban when an SA Airlink crashed and just missed a populated suburb. However, the law still permits commercial airliners to fly over someone's land without payment whenever they choose.

©Ingram Publishing/Superstock
Should commercial aircraft be allowed to fly over private land without the property owner's permission?

This case involves an externality – the noise from and possible danger posed by planes. The crucial problem in this example is that individual negotiation with the airline using someone's airspace is very difficult. The benefits resulting from an efficient outcome are extremely unlikely to be large enough to justify the costs of negotiation. Because the total benefits of overflight are large relative to the total costs imposed on homeowners, we get an efficient outcome here if property rights do not permit landowners to exclude planes from flying overhead.

[4] Again, making a liability payment does not require the parties to incur the costs of negotiation.

after take-off and just before landing, and the noise that reaches property below is often deafening. In these situations, local ordinances commonly prohibit landing and take-off during the hours when it is most costly (difficult) for property owners to adjust to noise – namely, the hours when most of them are sleeping. Here again, negotiation on an individual basis is impractical, and the best we can do is to define rights to achieve the lowest cost of accommodation.

Most people who grow up in market economies like South Africa take the institution of private property rights for granted. But as the preceding examples make clear, property laws embody sophisticated, if often implicit, calculations about how to reach the most efficient solutions to

Economic naturalist 14.2

Why does the law of trespass not apply to waterfront property?

In many countries, people regard a stranger walking across their land as an intrusion. (Scotland is an exception to this rule; it's illegal to prohibit someone from walking on your property. Perhaps that's why so many Scots are fond of hiking!) The trespasser, in the economist's parlance, confers a negative externality on the property owner. Such externalities might be dealt with in a variety of ways. Many people fence in their gardens to prevent others from taking shortcuts across their property. Some even erect signs warning people to beware of violent dogs. In most jurisdictions it is perfectly lawful to take such steps to exclude others from using your property. However, this right does not extend to people who own houses on the seafront at Clifton – the most expensive properties in South Africa. On the contrary, they explicitly permit any citizen to walk across any parcel of land located along the seafront below the high-tide mark.

©Ingram Publishing
Should trespassing on waterfront property be permitted?

This distinction exists not because the owners of seafront property value their privacy any less than do others. Rather, it is because the cost of not being able to cross a person's land along the beach or dam shore is so much higher than it is elsewhere. To illustrate, suppose that A, B and C in Fig. 14.1 are three dam-shore properties at the Gariep Dam, and that someone at A wants to visit someone at C. Access to dam-shore properties by road involves travel from the main highway down long, steep, often treacherous driveways. Lacking the ability to cross B's property, A would have to ascend his driveway out to the main road, travel to C's driveway and then make the trip down it. Because the costs involved in this circuitous route are so much larger than the costs of the direct path along the dam shore, the law of trespass makes an exception for these types of property. Their owners consider an occasional unwelcome disturbance a small price to pay for the additional convenience of being able to travel freely along the dam shore. The same principle applies to people owning houses on the beachfront, where it is much easier and more convenient to walk along the beach than to go by road with a car.

Figure 14.1 Lakeshore property and the law of trespass

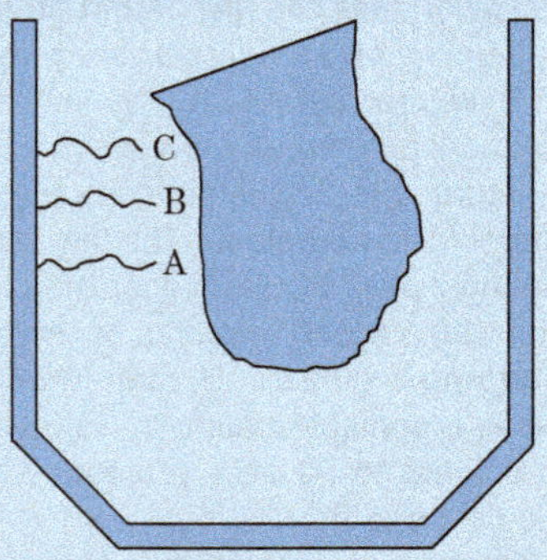

The cost of getting from A to C without crossing B's property is much higher than that by the direct route along the dam shore. For this reason, the law does not allow dam-shore homeowners to exclude people from walking across their property.

By contrast, the right to cross someone's property in an urban residential neighbourhood would be worth relatively little. The streets are all close together, so there is always a relatively easy route available which doesn't require shortcuts. Because negotiation with regard to trespass is prohibitively costly on a case-by-case basis, so the law of property defines rights of access in the way that, on average, leads to an efficient outcome. It gives most property owners the right to exclude, but withholds that right from the owners of dam-shore or beach front property.

Economic naturalist 14.3

Why are property laws often suspended during storms?

On 13 November 1904 Mr Ploof, his wife and two children went sailing on Vermont's Lake Champlain. A sudden violent storm made it impossible for them to sail back to their home port. In desperation, they took refuge by tying up at a dock on an island in the lake. The dock was owned by Mr Putnam, who sent his servant down to order the Ploofs off his property. The Ploofs cast off into the storm, and shortly thereafter their boat was destroyed, injuring family members in the process. In 1908 the Ploofs filed a successful suit for damages against Putnam. The court decided that, although Putnam would ordinarily have the right to exclude people from using his dock, the circumstances of the storm created an exception. Note that, in deciding the case in this way, the Vermont court was mimicking the result that dock and boat owners would generally reach for themselves if it were possible to negotiate costlessly and dispassionately during a storm. The value of the dock to a boater in distress is almost certainly higher than the value to the owner of being able to exclude him, and the Vermont court chose to define the state's laws of property with this observation in mind. The result was that Putnam had to compensate Ploof for the losses experienced by his family.

Economic naturalist 14.4

Why do building height limits vary from city to city?

In the old historic town of Stellenbosch it is almost impossible to get permission for buildings more than three storeys high, but in Johannesburg it will be no issue at all. Why the difference? Consider the situation pictured in Fig. 14.2. Resident A owns a house on a hillside overlooking the sea, and places high value on being able to watch the sunset from his living room window. Now B purchases the piece of land below A, and is considering which of two houses to build. The first is a one-storey house that would leave A's view intact. The second is a two-storey design that would completely block A's view. Suppose the gain to A from an unobstructed view is 100, the gain to B from a one-storey house is 200, and the gain to B from a two-storey house is 280. If property laws let people build houses of any height they choose, and if negotiation between property owners were costless, which of the two houses would B build?

To answer this question, first note that the increase in B's gain from having the taller house is 80, which is 20 less than the cost to A from the loss of his view. The efficient outcome is thus for B to build the one-storey house. And that is exactly what would happen if the two parties could negotiate costlessly. Rather than see B build the taller house, it will be in A's interest to compensate B for choosing the shorter version. To do so, he will have to give B at least 80, for that is what B gives up by not having the two-storey house. The most A would be willing to give B is 100, since that is all the view is worth to A. For some payment P, where $80 \leq P \leq 100$, A will get to keep his view.

Suppose, however, that negotiations between the two parties were impractical. B would then go ahead with the two-storey house, since that is the version he values most. By comparison with the one-storey design, B would gain 80, but A would lose 100. The optimal structure of property rights in this particular example would be to prohibit any building that blocks a neighbour's view.

Of course, if the valuations assigned by the parties were different, a different conclusion might follow. If, for example, B valued the two-storey house at 300 and A's view were again worth 100, the optimal structure of property rights

Figure 14.2 The value of an unobstructed view

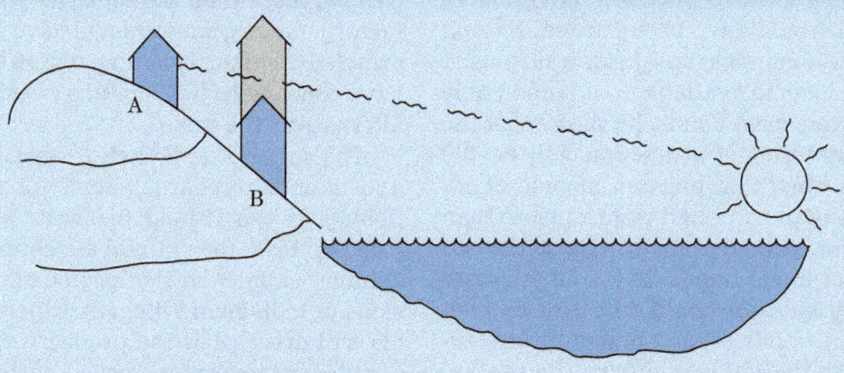

It is efficient for B to build a two-storey house if, and only if, the extra value of the taller house to B is greater than the value to A of maintaining his view.

would be to allow people to build to whatever height they chose. In either case, the optimal structure of property rights is the one that places the burden of adjustment (either the loss of a view or the loss of a preferred building design) on the party that can accomplish it at the lowest cost.

As a practical matter, the laws of property in many jurisdictions often embody precisely this and other similar principles. For example, Stellenbosch, which places a high value on the historical appearance of the town and its buildings, applies strict zoning laws to ensure that new builds complement the existing architecture and to ban skyscrapers from the town centre; Gordon's Bay restricts new builds that block an existing building's line of sight. Zoning laws in cities with less to look at are generally much more liberal in the kinds of building they permit. But even in cities with no special view to protect, zoning laws generally limit the number of man-made structures. Most people value access to at least some sunlight, and ordinances of this sort make it possible for them to get it. The plethora of skyscrapers in the financial districts of many cities, however, makes one wonder whether they're subject to any zoning restrictions at all.

---

practical problems involving externalities. Indeed, as the following section illustrates, the very existence of private property may be traced to early attempts to deal with externalities.

The tragedy of the commons

To explore the origins of the institution of private property, it is instructive to consider, as in Example 14.7, what would happen in a society that lacked a well-developed institution of property rights.

In this example individual households ignored an important externality by not accounting for the fact that sending an extra Boer goat onto the commons would cause existing cattle to gain less weight. Pastureland is a scarce resource in this example, and this community failed to allocate it efficiently because they were allowed to use it for free.

The problem would be solved if individuals could own pastureland and exclude others from using it. Anyone who buys the pastureland has the right to restrict the number of Boer goats to 2, which is the income-maximizing amount. We saw that, if used in this way, the land will generate an annual income of 36 from an annual investment of 200 (the price of two Boer goats). Had the 200 instead been used to purchase government bonds, only 24 would have been earned. Having control over the commons thus yields a surplus of 12/yr over the income available to a person able to buy only government bonds. It follows that the price of the pastureland at auction will be 100 (the price of a bond that pays an income of 12/yr). If the price of pastureland were any less than 100, all investors would want to buy it instead of buying government bonds. If it sold for more than 100, every investor could do better by buying government bonds. The community government could take the 100 raised from the auction of its pastureland and distribute it among the six households, for an average payment of $\frac{100}{6}$.

> **Exercise 14.2**
>
> What grazing fee would solve the commons problem discussed in Example 14.7?

The difficulty with common ownership is that it leads to overexploitation of the resource. Figure 14.3 illustrates the problem of individual villagers who have the option of working in a factory at a wage of W/day, or of keeping all the fish they can catch from the village lake. If fishermen get to keep whatever they catch, their decision rule will be to fish up to X', the point where AP (average catch per fisherman) $= W$. At X', the value of the total catch is exactly equal to the total income that the villagers who fished could have earned by working in the factory.

The socially optimal allocation is to fish only up to X^* in Fig. 14.3, the point at which $W = MP$, and for all remaining villagers to work in the factory. At this allocation, the villagers who fish will earn the shaded area S^* more than they could have earned by working in the factory.

If villagers are given free access to fish in the lake, the allocation that sends X^* out to fish will not be stable. Because each fisherman will be earning more than the villagers who work in the factory, factory workers will have an incentive to switch to fishing. Switching will stop only when X' have gone out to fish, making earnings in the two alternatives the same.

The simplest approach to sustaining efficient allocation is to charge people for the right to go fishing. If the fishing fee were set at $\text{AP}^* - W$ (see Fig. 14.3), the optimal allocation would result automatically from the income-maximizing decisions of individual villagers. Otherwise, individuals will over-utilize the productive resource they are allowed to use for free.

The fishing industry on the West Coast is an example of firms overexploiting an exhaustible

Example 14.7

The Industrial Development Corporation (IDC), the Department of Agriculture and the Kalahari Kid Corporation are trying to stimulate Boer goat farming in the Kamieskroon district. Let's take a subsample from these communities to indicate that increasing the number of animals is not always the best policy. It also depends on the alternatives available to these farmers. Our subsample consists of six households, each of which has wealth of 100. Each household may either invest its money in a government bond, which pays 12 per cent per year, or use it to buy a year-old Boer goat, which will graze on the village commons (there being no individually-owned grazing land in this community). Year-old Boer goats and government bonds each cost exactly 100. Boer goats require no effort to tend, and can be sold for a price that depends on the amount of weight they gain during the year. Yearly weight gain, in turn, depends on the number of Boer goats that graze on the commons. The prices of two-year-old Boer goats are given in Table 14.7 as a function of the total number of Boer goats. If this community's households make their investment decisions independently, how many Boer goats will graze on the commons?

Table 14.7 Boer goat prices as a function of grazing density

Number of Boer goats	Price per 2-year-old Boer goat
1	120
2	118
3	114
4	111
5	108
6	105

As more Boer goats graze on the commons, each goat gains less weight, resulting in a lower price per goat.

As long as each household cannot control access to the commons by cattle owned by others, the income-maximizing strategy will be to send an extra Boer goat out onto the commons if and only if its price next year will be at least 112 (equal to the gain from buying a bond). By this reckoning, there will be 3 Boer goats sent onto the commons, and the rest of the villagers' money will be invested in government bonds. With this pattern of investment, village income from investment will be 14 from each of the 3 steers and 12 from each of the 3 bonds, for a total of 78.

This however is not an optimum policy. From the point of view of the community as a whole, the investment rule for Boer goats should be: send an extra Boer goat onto the commons if, and only if, its marginal contribution to the value of the total herd after 1 year is greater than or equal to 112. Sending the third Boer goat onto the commons resulted in a total herd worth $3 \times 114 = 342$, which is only 106 more than the value of a herd with only 2 Boer goats ($2 \times 118 = 236$). Total community income is maximized by buying 4 bonds and sending 2 Boer goats onto the commons. This pattern results in an income of 48 from bonds and 36 from Boer goats, for a total of 84.

resource. Dwindling fish stocks in the area necessitated the introduction of industry quotas in 2009. These were met with fierce resistance from the fishing community. The irony is that poor communities were hardest hit in the process because they have few opportunities for finding alternative employment. Agriculture, Forestry and Fisheries Minister at the time, Tina Joemat-Pettersson, was forced to reassess the situation. In 2014 she drastically reduced the number of new fishing licences

Figure 14.3 The tragedy of the commons

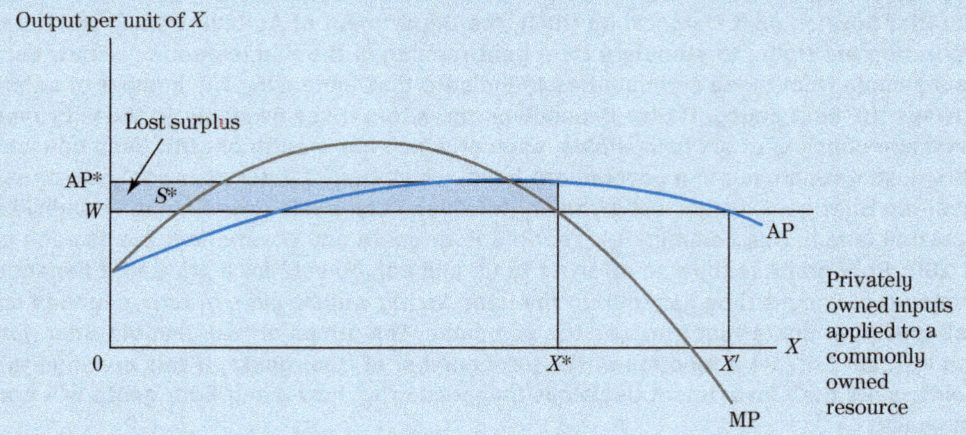

When a resource, such as a fishery or a pasture, is owned in common, each user gets to keep the average product of his own productive inputs that he applies to the resource. Privately owned inputs will be applied to the resource until X', the point at which their average product equals their opportunity cost, W, resulting in an economic surplus of zero. The socially optimal allocation is X^*, the level of input for which W is equal to the marginal product of privately owned inputs, and results in an economic surplus of S^*.

available, a move which again lead to protests and appeals against the ruling. The situation currently remains unresolved.

One of the continuing sources of inefficiency in modern economies involves the allocation of resources that no single nation's property laws can govern. Let us look at the example of global warming. Scientists now estimate that if carbon dioxide and other greenhouse gases continue to accumulate in the atmosphere at current rates, the earth's average temperature will rise by as much as 3.5°C by 2050 – enough to melt the polar ice caps and flood thousands of square kilometres of coastal land. If a single agency had the power to enact globally binding environmental legislation, it would be a straightforward, albeit costly, matter to reduce the build-up of greenhouse gases. But in our world of sovereign nations, this power does not exist.

A country's ecological footprint is the sum of all cropland, grazing land, built-up land, forests and fishing waters required to produce the food, fibre and timber it consumes, to absorb the wastes emitted when it uses energy and to provide space for its infrastructure.[5] At present, the world's total ecological footprint is 18.2 billion global hectares (gha), an average of 2.7 gha per person. The earth's bio-capacity is only 12 billion gha, or 1.8 gha per person. This means that we are using ecological services 1.5 times as quickly as the earth can renew them. The three countries with the highest average gha per person are Qatar (11.7), the United Arab Emirates (9.4) and the USA (9.3). Afghanistan has the lowest recorded average footprint, at 0.5 gha per person. China's large population means that it has a relatively low footprint, 2.2 gha per person. However, taken together the USA and China have the largest total footprint, and each uses 21 per cent of the earth's bio-capacity. As a result, the USA and China are dependent on the resources of other nations to meet their needs. South Africa has a relatively high average ecological footprint for a developing country, 2.5 gha per person, caused by its dependence on coal for generating electricity.

Externalities, efficiency and free speech

As the following discussion illustrates, the Coasian principles of efficiency apply not only to the design of property rights but also to the design of constitutions. In particular, they shed light on the extent to which society has an interest in protecting the right to free speech.

The Constitution of the Republic of South Africa, Act No. 18, Second Amendment Act No. 3

[5] See the *Living Planet Report 2012*, World Wide Fund For Nature, for a detailed discussion on this topic.

of 2003 protects most forms of opinion, association, speech and expression, even those that cause intensely painful effects on others. A man once wrote to a newspaper advice columnist to confess to a cruel act he had committed decades earlier, during his senior year in high school. He and his friends had leafed through the school yearbook and picked out the photograph of the girl they agreed was the ugliest in their class. The letter writer had then called the girl on the telephone to congratulate her on her selection. During the ensuing years, he had never been able to forget her anguished groan in response. He would give anything, he said, if he could turn back the clock and recant that phone call.

Given the choice between receiving such a telephone call and being hit sharply on the arm with a stick, many people would immediately choose the latter. Had the boys hit the girl with a stick, they could have been put in jail. And yet they were perfectly within their constitutional rights to make that phone call.

Why does our constitution prohibit one form of harm but not the other? Within the Coasian framework, the first thing to recognize is that identifying on a case by case basis the effects of harm resulting from psychological as opposed to physical acts is highly impractical. We just cannot imagine a scenario in which the girl states what she would be willing to pay to avoid hearing a painful remark or, for that matter, to avoid being struck with a stick. The structure of the law must therefore be guided by a judgement about which structure of rights will generate the best outcome where case-by-case negotiation is impractical.

Any law that prevented people from making cruel remarks to others would almost surely prohibit a great deal of highly valuable speech as well. Just think how uninteresting politics would be if politicians were no longer allowed to criticize each other! The fear of criticism keeps many an otherwise wayward person in line, much to society's benefit. If it were practical to write a law that would permit justified criticism but prohibit criticism that was unwarranted, or even merely unkind, we might be seriously tempted to implement it. But, so far, no one has come up with such a law.

Smoking rules, public and private

Research shows that exposure to cigarette smoke exhaled by others can be harmful to one's health. Such findings have lent considerable support to the recent implementation of laws banning smoking in public places. On the plausible assumptions that (1) negotiating with strangers in public places is generally impractical, and (2) the harm to non-smokers from undesired exposure to smoke is more important than the harm to smokers from not being able to smoke in public places, such laws make good sense in the Coasian framework.

Although there are many smoke-free buildings in South Africa, thus far no law has been proposed that would disallow smoking in private dwellings. The result is that sometimes people are exposed to smoke by their roommates. On the plausible assumption that the cost of negotiation with prospective roommates is relatively low, the following example illustrates that the lack of such laws is not likely to lead to an undesirable outcome.

Example 14.8 drives home the point that external effects are completely reciprocal. Seziphelele's smoking harms Dominique, but denying Seziphelele the opportunity to smoke will harm her as well. Smoking is a quintessentially shared problem. Because people are free to make whatever living arrangements they find mutually agreeable, Dominique cannot be forced to endure smoke against her wishes. And, by the same token, Seziphelele cannot be forced to give up smoking. If they are to reap the savings from living together, one party must compromise on the smoking issue, and the other must compromise financially.

Exercise 14.3

How would the entries in Table 14.8 be different if an exhaust system were available that completely eliminated secondary damage smoking at a cost of R900/mth?

Positive externalities

The Coase theorem applies not only to negative externalities but also to positive ones. When a beekeeper and an apple grower operate on adjacent properties, the activities of each confer positive externalities on the other. If the beekeeper adds an additional hive, the apple trees in the adjacent orchard will be more fully pollinated, ensuring a larger crop. If the orchard owner plants additional trees, the beekeeper's output of honey will rise. These positive externalities, if ignored, will result in sub-optimally small levels of both apple and honey production.

Example 14.8

Seziphelele and Dominique are trying to decide whether to share a two-bedroom apartment or to live separately in one-bedroom apartments. The rental fees are R4500/mth for one-bedroom and R6300/mth – or R3150/mth per person – for two-bedroom apartments. Seziphelele is a smoker, and would be willing to give up R3750/mth rather than give up being able to smoke at home. Dominique, however, is a non-smoker, and would sacrifice up to R2250/mth rather than live with a smoker. Apart from the issues of smoking and rent, the two find joint living neither more nor less attractive than living alone. Neither has an alternative roommate available. Will they live together or separately?

It is more costly to live alone, but each can have things the way they want on the smoking issue. If they live together, they will save on rent, but one of them will have to compromise on the smoking issue. By living together, each party saves R1350/mth in rent. If we ignore the possibility of negotiation, they will not live together because this saving is less than the cost to Dominique of having to live with a smoker.

But suppose they are able to negotiate costlessly. The total saving in rent is R2700/mth, which is the difference between the R9000/mth total they would pay if they lived alone and the R6300 they will pay living together. And since this saving exceeds the cost to Dominique by R450/mth, it should be possible to negotiate an agreement whereby the two will prefer to live together. Seziphelele will have to give some of her R1350/mth savings to Dominique.

Let X denote the amount that Seziphelele gives to Dominique. Since the cost to Dominique of living with a smoker is R2250/mth, and her saving in rent is only R1350/mth, X must be at least R900/mth. Because Seziphelele gets to continue smoking in the shared living arrangement, her R1350/mth rent saving is pure gain, which means that R1350/mth is the largest possible value for X. The relevant details for this example are summarized in Table 14.8.

Table 14.8 Pay-off summary for Example 14.8

	Net rental payment (R/mth)		Net gain (R/mth)		
	Dominique	Seziphelele	Dominique	Seziphelele	Total
Live separately	4500	4500	–	–	–
Live together; Seziphelele pays Dominique X to compensate for smoke, $900 \leq X \leq 1350$	$3150 - X$	$3150 + X$	$X - 900$	$1350 - X$	450

The cost to Dominique of living with a smoker is R2250/mth. The total saving in rent from living together is R9000/mth – R6300/mth = R2700/mth, which is R450/mth more than the least-costly compromise required by shared living quarters, which is the R2250/mth it costs Dominique to live with a smoker.

Positional externalities

In many areas of endeavour, rewards are determined not by our absolute performance, but by how we perform relative to others. To be a champion swimmer, for example, what counts is not how fast you swim in absolute terms, but how your times compare with those of others. Swimmer Mark Spitz won seven gold medals in the 1972 Olympics, yet his winning times would not even have qualified him for the 2008 team. In 2008 Michael Phelps bettered Mark Spitz's record and won eight gold medals in Beijing; one can only speculate on how his times will compare with those of top swimmers in 2030. Sprinter Carl Lewis provides another example. Regarded as one of the best athletes of all time, he won his first of nine Olympic gold medals for running the 100 m in 9.99 seconds in Los Angeles in 1984. This time would have placed him in only seventh position in 2009 when Usain Bolt ran the 100 m in 9.58 seconds – a new world record.

Situations in which rewards are determined by relative performance are often called *contests*. In virtually every contest, each contestant will take a variety of actions in an attempt to enhance her probability of winning. Indeed, taking such actions is the essence of what it means to be in a contest. Some of these actions entail only minimal cost, such as wearing high-tech swimsuits. That said, when swimmers with the most technologically superior swimwear began winning every event, the sport's governing body intervened. Swimwear length is now closely regulated. Because rewards in contests are distributed according to relative position, the laws of simple arithmetic tell us that any action that increases one contestant's chance of winning must necessarily reduce the chances of others. With this observation in mind, it is instructive to think of performance-enhancing actions as giving rise to *positional externalities*. If A and B are competing for a prize that only one of them can attain, anything that helps A will necessarily harm B.

The result is that, when the stakes are high, unregulated contests almost always lead to costly *positional arms races*. In the absence of effective drug regulations in rugby compared with those in athletics, for example, many forwards apparently now feel compelled to enhance their size and strength by using supplements. It is easy to see why. In an arena where sheer physical bulk plays a central role, failure to use these (sometimes) dangerous hormones might jeopardize a player's position. Some supplements can have dangerous side effects. Anabolic steroids, for example, have been linked to cancer of the liver and other serious health problems; however, many players in the lower leagues (which aren't tested for illegal substances) use them to get a chance at competing in the top league.

In cricket it is nowadays standard procedure for batsmen to use helmets, pads and gloves to protect their bodies from the ball. Bowlers such as Dale Steyn and Mitchell Johnson frequently bowl at speeds in excess of 160 km/h, and a blow to the head may be fatal. In the 1970s the 'terrible four' West Indian fast bowlers, Malcolm Marshall, Curtley Ambrose, Michael Holding and Andy Roberts, created havoc all over the world. It was during their reign that protective clothing was introduced. On objective grounds it seems utter folly for a player to go in to bat and risk being hit in his face by a ball travelling at 160 km/h. And yet few players ever hesitated to do so when the chance arose. The urge to win – to do well in relative terms – is a powerful force of human nature. In situations where the material pay-offs from winning are very large, this is hardly surprising. But even when the stakes are ostensibly low – as, for example, in a non-league high school cricket game in Soweto – people go to extreme lengths to enhance their chances. Given what's at stake, voluntary restraint is rarely an effective solution to positional arms races. It is for this reason that governing bodies in many sports now require strict drug testing.

One of the most important contests people face in life is the task of making sure their children enter the labour market with a good education behind them. This task is a contest because a 'good' education, like an 'effective' lock in rugby, is an inescapably *relative* concept. If an effective lock is one who is bigger, stronger and faster than most other locks, a good education is one that is better than the education that most others receive. This relativistic aspect of our objective is what makes us vulnerable to a positional arms race of the sort we see elsewhere.

In the educational context, what form does this arms race take? Public schools are funded largely by taxes, but educational quality and neighbourhood quality are closely linked in our public school systems. The reason is that people living in wealthier neighbourhoods are able to pay higher school fees to enable the schools to appoint more teachers, buy more equipment, and so on. These schools also attract the best-qualified teachers. Competition for position thus often involves trying to move to the best possible neighbourhoods. Again, however, the laws of simple arithmetic remind us that it is not possible for *everyone* in society to move forward in relative terms. Only 10 per cent of our children can occupy the top tenth of our school seats, no matter how valiantly everyone strives.

Limiting the workweek

As covered in Chapter 12, the laws that govern labour in South Africa require, among other things, that employers pay a 50 per cent wage premium whenever people work more than 9 hours a day or 45 hours a week. On public holidays and Sundays workers must receive double their normal pay. These regulations have been defended on the grounds that, without them, monopsony employers would require unacceptably long hours.

Positional externalities suggest an alternative rationale for regulation of working hours. If someone stays a few extra hours at work, she will increase her earnings, in both absolute and relative terms. One result is that she will be able to afford a house in a better school district. But, again, the problem is that one family's forward movement in relative terms means a backward movement for others. Rather than see their families fall behind, others will feel pressure to work longer hours themselves. In the end, these efforts are largely offsetting. As before, only 10 per cent of our children can get a place in the best schools.

By working until 20:00 each day, we can produce more and enjoy larger incomes than if we work only until 17:00. But, in the process, we have less time to spend with our families and friends. It is easy to see why people might prefer to live in communities where everyone quits work at 17:00. And it is equally easy to see why there might be few such communities in the absence of overtime laws.

Savings

Many observers complain, correctly, that the social security system prevents them from deciding for themselves when and how much to save for retirement. The traditional view that having more options is better than having fewer, means it would appear better for participation in social security to be purely voluntary. Yet most societies have mandatory programmes to supplement retirement incomes. Positional externalities may again help us to understand why.

A parent has the choice of saving some of her current income for retirement, or spending that income now on a house in a better school district. When everyone spends more on a house in a better school district, the result is merely to bid up the prices of those houses. In the process, no one moves forward in the educational hierarchy, and yet parents end up having too little savings for retirement. Acting as individuals, however, their only real alternative is to send their children to less desirable schools. The social security system mitigates this dilemma by making a portion of each person's income unavailable for spending.

Workplace safety

As a final illustration of positional externalities, consider the example of safety regulations in the workplace. As in the case of working hour regulation, proponents of safety regulations often defend them by saying that monopsonists would otherwise force their workers to labour under unacceptably risky conditions. But this argument seriously underestimates the pressures of competition in the labour market. With these pressures in mind, critics of safety regulation say that it deprives workers of the right to decide for themselves how much safety they want to purchase in the workplace.

Once we take positional externalities into account, however, the institution of safety regulation appears less puzzling. One worker's choice of a riskier job makes it difficult for other workers to bid as effectively as before for houses in the best school districts. Feeling this pressure, they too are more likely to opt for riskier jobs. In positional terms, of course, these movements largely offset one another. People may prefer to neutralize this arms race by adopting laws that set minimum standards for workplace safety.

Taxing and subsidizing externalities

Before the appearance of Coase's 1960 paper, the economics profession was wedded to the view, pioneered by the British economist A. C. Pigou, that the best solution to negative externalities is to tax them. The idea is simple. If A carries out an activity that imposes a cost on B, then taxing A by the amount of that cost will provide him with the proper incentive to consider the externality in his production decisions. We will now illustrate the use of Pigouvian taxes and subsidies graphically.

Assume that a coal-fired power station near Graskop pollutes the air and water used by man and animal in the district. This is a typical example of a negative externality. We can illustrate the situation with the aid of Fig. 14.4. In the figure, the demand curve (D) represents the private (= social) benefits and the private supply curve (S_P) for the electricity generated by the power station. It indicates the benefits to the consumers, and the private costs, of the power station. Equilibrium will then occur at E_1, and the electricity will sell at a price of P_1.

However, this does not take into account the full cost to society of the power station. When the external cost of the pollution is added to the private cost of producing the electricity, the negative externality raises the cost of supplying the electricity above the private cost of the supplier. In our figure it is illustrated by the new supply curve (S_S = marginal social costs). If a Pigouvian tax equal to the vertical distance between S_P and S_S (E_1B or AE_2) is levied on the producer, it causes its

Figure 14.4 Negative externality and Pigouvian tax

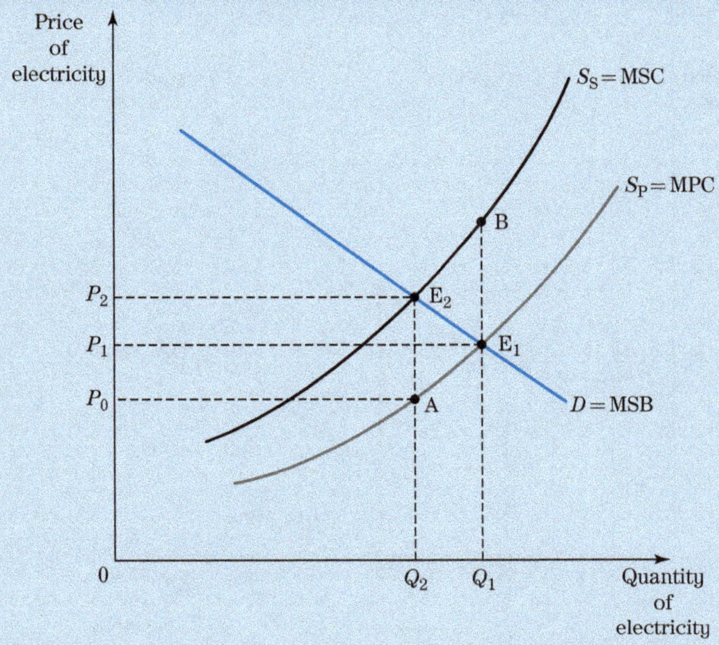

Without a Pigouvian tax, equilibrium will be at E_1, where Q_1 is supplied at a price of P_1. The S_S curve represents the full cost to the society. If a Pigouvian tax equal to the vertical distance between S_P and S_S is levied on the power station, equilibrium will be at E_2, where Q_2 is produced and sold at a price of P_2.

marginal cost curve to shift up to S_S, and the new equilibrium will be at E_2, where Q_2 units are supplied at a price of P_2. Without levying a Pigouvian tax, the effect of the negative externality is that it leads to an oversupply and underpricing of the good in question. The producer does not fully pay for the negative externality, as consumers pay part of the higher price as a result of the tax ($P_2 - P_1$ of $P_2 - P_0$) owing to the benefits they experience from the electricity generation.

Let's take the provision of education to illustrate a positive externality. Education benefits the receiver thereof in the form of skills accumulation, expected higher future earnings, the enjoyment of education, and so on. There is also a spillover effect on the rest of the community. People with more education are normally less involved in criminal activities, their knowledge is passed on to the next generation (their children), they have a positive influence on their neighbours or colleagues at work, and so on. In Fig. 14.5 the supply curve (S) is the social supply of education, or the marginal cost of providing education. The private demand curve (D_P) is an indication of the benefits the recipients of education will receive. Without taking the positive externality into consideration, equilibrium will be at E_1, where Q_1 units of education will be sold at a price of P_1.

However, the full benefits to the community are represented by the D_S curve. If a subsidy equal to the external benefits is paid to consumers, it will shift their demand curve to D_S. New equilibrium is then at E_2, where Q_2 units of education are sold at a price of P_2. Remember that the consumer receives a subsidy equal to $P_2 - P_3$, and actually pays less than before (price was P_1), namely, P_3. In South Africa it is normally the supplier of education that receives the subsidy. That causes the supplier's supply curve to shift to S', and now equilibrium is at E_3, where Q_2 units of education are traded at a price of P_3. Irrespective of who receives the subsidy, the consumer's out-of-pocket expenses decrease from P_1 to P_3, and the quantity of education supplied increases from Q_1 to Q_2. Without a Pigouvian subsidy, positive externalities will lead to an undersupply of a good at too high a price.

As Example 14.9 amply demonstrates, a tax on noise pollution can leave us in a worse position than if there were no tax at all. This is not surprising once we recognize that a tax on pollution has essentially the same effect as making the polluter

Figure 14.5 Positive externality and Pigouvian subsidy

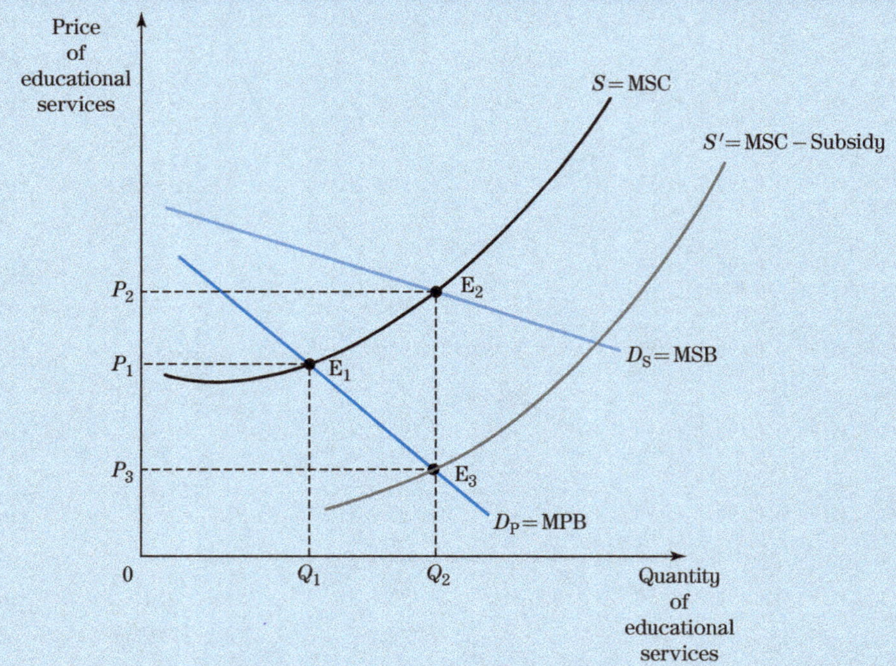

Without a Pigouvian subsidy, equilibrium will be at E_1, where Q_1 is supplied at a price of P_1. The D_S curve represents the full benefit to society. If a subsidy is paid to the consumers to account for all external benefits, the marginal benefits to the community will increase to D_S. Then equilibrium will be at E_2, where Q_2 units of education will be supplied at a price of P_2. Because of the subsidy, consumers pay only P_3. The supplier can also receive the subsidy, shifting the supply curve to S'. Equilibrium will then be at E_3, where Q_2 units are supplied at a price of P_3.

liable for pollution damages. But this same recognition implies that taxation will not *always* be inefficient. It happened to be inefficient in Example 14.9 because the doctor happened to be the party who was best able to deal with the noise problem, and the tax removed all incentive for him to do so. Suppose, on the contrary, that the doctor had not had some inexpensive means of escaping the noise damage. The tax still would have lead the confectioner to shut down, but this would now be the most efficient outcome. (See Example 14.1.)

Alternatively, suppose the confectioner had had some inexpensive means of eliminating the noise problem. Suppose, for example, that he could have installed soundproofing for a cost of 10. Here, too, the tax would have lead to the most efficient outcome. The confectioner would have installed the soundproofing to escape the tax, and the doctor would have operated without disturbance.

Whether it is efficient to tax pollution thus depends on the particular circumstances at hand. If negotiation is costless, taxing will always lead to an efficient outcome. If negotiation is impractical, taxing pollution will still lead to an efficient outcome if the polluter has the least costly way of reducing pollution damage. Only if negotiation is impractical and the victim has the least costly means of avoiding damage will taxing pollution lead to an inefficient outcome. Taxing and not taxing will yield essentially the same outcomes if the costs of limiting pollution damage are roughly the same for both polluter and victim.

More generally, suppose that there are two producers, firm X and firm Y, whose marginal costs of smoke removal are shown by the curves labelled MC_X and MC_Y, respectively, in Fig. 14.6. If the goal is to reduce total smoke emissions by $Q = Q_X^* + Q_Y^*$ tonnes/day, a tax of T^* will accomplish that goal in the least costly way. The characteristic feature of this solution is that the marginal cost of pollution reduction would be exactly the same for all firms. If that were not the case, it would always be possible to reallocate the pollution reduction in such a way as to reduce total costs.

When the government places a tax on a product whose production does not generate externalities, the product will sell for a price that exceeds its marginal cost (see Chapter 2). And when price exceeds marginal cost, output falls short of the

Figure 14.6 The tax approach to pollution reduction

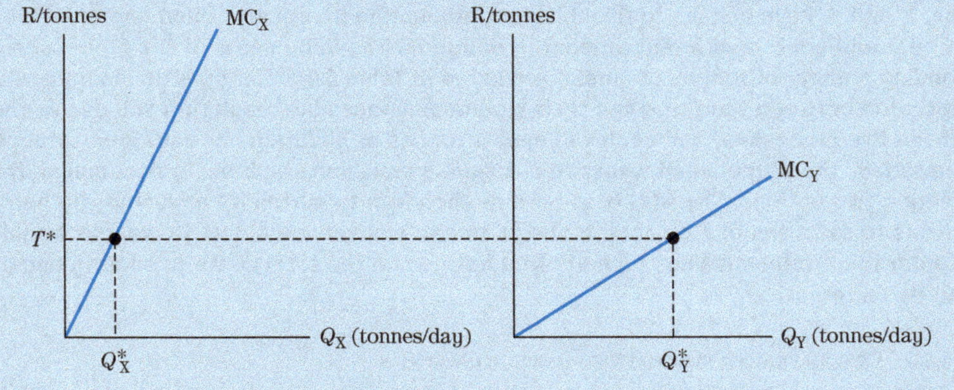

MC_X and MC_Y represent the marginal cost of smoke reduction for firms X and Y, respectively. When pollution is taxed at a fixed rate, each firm reduces its emissions up to the point where the marginal cost of further reduction is exactly equal to the tax. The result is the least costly way of achieving the corresponding aggregate pollution reduction.

Example 14.9

Consider again the doctor and confectioner from Examples 14.1 to 14.6. Suppose that the doctor gains 60 by operating in a noise-free environment, and that the confectioner gains 40 by operating his noisy equipment. Suppose also that the doctor can eliminate the noise problem by rearranging his office at a cost of 18. And suppose, finally, that negotiation between the doctor and confectioner is prohibitively costly. The tax approach calls for a tax on the confectioner equal to the damage his activity would cause, which, in the absence of a response by the doctor, means a tax of 60. How will the outcome under such a tax compare with what would have happened in its absence?

If there were costless negotiation, the confectioner could pay the doctor to rearrange his office and then operate without paying the tax, since his operation would cause no noise damage. But since negotiation is impractical, the doctor has no reason to incur this cost on his own. He knows that, by doing nothing, the confectioner will face a tax of 60 if he operates, which in turn means that the confectioner's best option is to shut down. After all, his operation generates a gain of only 40 to begin with. With the confectioner no longer in operation, the doctor will gain 60 and the confectioner 0.

With no tax, however, the confectioner would have continued operations, for a gain of 40. The doctor's best response would have been to rearrange his office at a cost of 18, leaving him with a net gain of 42. Without the tax, we thus get the most efficient outcome, whereas the total gain with the tax is considerably smaller. The relevant data for this example are summarized in Table 14.9.

Table 14.9 Outcome and pay-off summary for Example 14.9

Legal regime	Outcome	Net benefit		
		Doctor	Confectioner	Total
Tax of 60 on confectioner	Confectioner shuts down	60	0	60
No tax or liability	Doctor rearranges his office at his own expense	42	40	82

The gain to the confectioner from operating is 40. The loss to the doctor from the confectioner's noise is 60. The doctor can rearrange his office to eliminate the noise problem at a cost of 18. The efficient outcome is for the doctor to rearrange his office, and this happens only when there is no tax on the confectioner.

Example 14.10

Two firms, X and Y, have access to five different production processes, each one of which has a different cost and emits a different amount of pollution. The daily costs of the processes and the corresponding number of tonnes of smoke are listed in Table 14.10. If pollution is unregulated, and negotiation between the firms and their victims is impossible, each firm will use A, the least costly of the five processes, and each will emit 4 tonnes of pollution per day, for a total pollution of 8 tonnes/day. The city council wants to cut smoke emissions by half. To accomplish this, it is considering two options. The first is to require each firm to curtail its emissions by half. The alternative is to set a tax of *T* on each tonne of smoke emitted each day. How large would *T* have to be in order to curtail emissions by half? And how would the total costs to society compare under the two alternatives?

Table 14.10 Cost and emissions for five production processes

Process (smoke)	A (4 tonnes/day)	B (3 tonnes/day)	C (2 tonnes/day)	D (1 tonne/day)	E (0 tonnes/day)
Cost to firm X	100	190	600	1200	2000
Cost to firm Y	50	80	140	230	325

Each firm has access to five alternative production processes, A–E, which vary both in cost and in the amount of pollution they produce.

If each firm is required to cut pollution by half, each must switch from process A to process C. The result will be 2 tonnes/day of pollution for each firm. The cost of the switch for firm X will be 600/day − 100/day = 500/day. The cost to Y will be 140/day − 50/day = 90/day, which means a total cost for the two firms of 590/day.

How will each firm respond to a tax of *T* per tonne of pollution? To illustrate, suppose a tax of 50/tonne were levied. Firm X would stick with process A because it costs 90/day less than process B, and produces only 1 tonne/day of extra smoke and thus 50/day in extra taxes. Firm Y, by contrast, will switch to process B, because it costs only 30/day more and will save 50/day in taxes. But firm Y will not continue on to C, because it costs 60/day more than *B* and will save only an additional 50/day in taxes. With firm X staying with A and firm Y switching to B, we get a total pollution reduction of 1 tonne/day. A tax of 50/tonne thus does not produce the desired 50 per cent reduction in pollution.

The solution is to keep increasing the tax until we get the desired result. Consider what happens with a tax of 91/tonne. This tax will lead firm X to adopt process B, and firm Y to adopt process D. Total emissions will be the desired 4 tonnes/day. The cost to firm X will be 190/day − 100/day = 90/day, and the cost to firm Y will be 230/day − 50/day = 180/day. The total cost for both firms is thus only 270/day, or 320/day less than the cost of having each firm cut pollution by half.

The advantage of the tax approach is that it concentrates pollution reduction in the hands of the firms that can accomplish it in the least costly way. With this approach, note that the cost of the last tonne of smoke removed is the same for each firm.

level that would maximize economic surplus. In contrast, when there is no tax on a product whose production generates negative externalities, output of that product exceeds the level that would maximize economic surplus. (This is exactly what is illustrated by Fig. 14.4.)

Taxing positional externalities

There is considerable evidence that the utility that people get from consumption depends not only on absolute consumption levels, but also on relative consumption levels. No one in the nineteenth century felt disadvantaged by not owning a cell phone or a laptop, and yet people who lack these items today are apt to feel strongly dissatisfied indeed. And their dissatisfaction is not merely a matter of envying the possessions of their neighbours. If no one owned a cell phone, then you would not be required to have one to meet the minimal demands of social existence. But because almost everyone has a cell phone today, it is extremely difficult to get along without one.

If relative consumption is important, it follows logically that each person's consumption imposes negative externalities on others. When any one person increases her consumption, he raises, perhaps imperceptibly, the consumption standard for others.

The fact that many forms of consumption generate negative externalities has important implications for tax policy. To illustrate, consider a young man's decision regarding the size of diamond to give his fiancée. Because the function of this gift is to serve as a token of commitment, the one he buys must necessarily cost enough to hurt. His jeweller will probably tell him that it is customary to spend two months' salary on the stone and setting. A solitaire engagement ring with a 0.25-carat diamond costs about R9000 and a 1 carat diamond ring up to R65 000. If the young man earns R120 000/yr, he will have to come up with R20 000.

From the perspective of the economy as a whole, the outcome would be better if there were a 400 per cent tax on jewellery. The after-tax price of what is now only a R4000 diamond would then rise to R20 000. In buying this smaller diamond, the young man would incur the same economic hardship as before. And since this is the essence of the gift's function, his goal would not really be compromised by the tax. Nor would the young man's fiancée suffer any real loss. Because *everyone* would now be buying smaller diamonds, the smaller stone would provide much the same satisfaction as the larger one would have. On the plus side, the government gets an additional R16 000 to finance its expenditures or reduce other taxes. The only loser is the de Beers diamond cartel in South Africa, which would earn R16 000 less than before the tax.

The standards that define acceptable schools, houses, wardrobes, cars, vacations and a host of other important budget items are inextricably linked to the amounts other people spend on them. For the same reasons that it is often efficient to tax pollution, it will be efficient to tax many of these forms of consumption. On efficiency grounds, such taxes would be an attractive substitute for existing taxes that interfere with efficient resource allocation.

Summary

- When an action by one party harms another, and the parties are able to negotiate costlessly with one another, the negative externalities are dealt with efficiently, regardless of whether the law makes people liable for the harmful effects of their actions. This result is known as the Coase theorem.
- When negotiation is costly, it does matter how liability is assigned. In general, the most efficient outcome occurs when the law places the burden of avoiding harmful effects on the party that can accomplish it at the lowest cost.
- This general principle helps explain: why the owner of a dock may not legally exclude a boater from tying up during a storm; when people are allowed to exclude others from walking across their land or from blocking their view; why pastureland is more productive if owned privately rather than in common; why aeroplanes are allowed to fly over someone's property, while developers cannot build above it without permission. In each case, the laws of property are set up to mimic as closely as possible the kinds of accommodation people would reach for themselves if they were free to negotiate costlessly with one another.
- Similar principles apply to a variety of other governmental restraints on behaviour. In the case of free speech, and other constitutional liberties, the best legal solutions turn out to be those that most closely resemble the solutions people would have negotiated

among themselves, had it been practical to do so.

- Similar conclusions apply in situations that involve positive externalities. If negotiation is costless, people will forge agreements that result in efficient outcomes, even in cases in which one party's activities create indirect benefits for the other. And where negotiation is costly, institutions often tend to evolve that encourage activities with positive external effects.
- In contests for relative position, as in all other contests, the efforts by one contestant confer a negative externality on other contestants: anything that increases one party's odds of winning necessarily reduces the odds of others. The theory of externalities and property rights sheds light on the laws by which citizens of modern societies restrict such arms races.
- Taxation is one solution to the problem of negative externalities. Although it is not always an ideal answer, it does offer several important advantages over direct regulation in many situations. Pigou showed that taxes and subsidies can be used to rectify the adverse effects of negative or positive externalities.

Questions for review

1. When negotiation costs are negligible, why is the assignment of liability for externalities irrelevant for efficiency?
2. Does the assignment of liability matter for distributional reasons?
3. Suppose you are the party who can avoid a particular external effect at the lowest cost. Why might you favour a general rule that assigns liability to whichever party can avoid damage at the lowest cost?
4. Why do we permit aeroplanes but not real estate developers to use the airspace over private homes without prior consent?
5. Why do most property laws limit private coastal property to the waterline at high tide?
6. Give three examples of the tragedy of the commons on your campus.

Problems

1. Every November, AB and JP each face the choice between burning their leaves or stuffing them into rubbish bags. Burning the leaves is much easier, but produces noxious smoke. The utility values for each person, measured in utils, are listed in the table for each of the four possible combinations of actions:

		JP	
		Burn	**Bag**
AB	**Burn**	JP: 4	JP: 2
		AB: 4	AB: 8
	Bag	JP: 8	JP: 6
		AB: 2	AB: 6

   a. If AB and JP are utility maximizers, and make their decisions individually, what will they do?
   b. How will your answer to part (a) differ, if at all, if AB and JP can make binding agreements with each other?

   Now suppose the pay-off matrix is as follows:

		JP	
		Burn	**Bag**
AB	**Burn**	JP: 6	JP: 2
		AB: 6	AB: 8
	Bag	JP: 8	JP: 4
		AB: 2	AB: 4

c What will they do this time if they can make binding agreements?

2 AB can produce with or without a filter on his smokestack. Production without a filter results in greater smoke damage to JP. The relevant gains and losses for the two individuals are listed in the table below:

	With filter	Without filter
Gains to AB	R2000/wk	R2450/wk
Damage to JP	R350/wk	R850/wk

a If AB is not liable for smoke damage, and there are no negotiation costs, will he install a filter? Explain carefully.

b How, if at all, would the outcome be different if AB were liable for all smoke damage, and the cost of the filter were R100/wk higher than indicated in the table? Explain carefully.

3 AB can operate his sawmill with or without soundproofing. Operation without soundproofing results in noise damage to his neighbour, JP. The relevant gains and losses for AB and JP are listed in the table:

	Without soundproofing	With soundproofing
Gains to AB	R1500/wk	R340/wk
Damage to JP	R1250/wk	R60/wk

a If AB is not liable for noise damage, and there are no negotiation costs, will he install soundproofing? Explain.

b How, if at all, would your answer differ if the negotiation costs of maintaining an agreement were R40/wk? Explain.

c Now suppose JP can escape the noise damage by moving to a new location, which will cost him R1200/wk. With negotiation costs again assumed to be zero, how, if at all, will your answer to part (a) differ? Explain.

4 Samantha and Julia are trying to decide whether to share an apartment. To live separately, each would have to pay R4500/mth in rent. An apartment large enough to share can be rented for R6750/mth. Costs aside, they are indifferent between living together and living separately, except for these two problems: Samantha likes to play her stereo late at night, which disturbs Julia's sleep; and Julia likes to sing in the shower at 06:00, which awakens Samantha. Julia would sacrifice up to R1200/mth rather than stop singing in the shower, and Samantha would sacrifice up to R2325/mth rather than stop playing her stereo late at night. Samantha would tolerate Julia's singing and Julia would tolerate Samantha's stereo in return for compensation payments not less than R1125/mth and R1200/mth, respectively.

a Should they live together? If so, indicate how they can split the rent so that each does better than by living alone. If not, explain why no such arrangement is feasible.

b Now suppose Samantha wins a free pair of stereo headphones. If she wears them late at night, Julia's sleep is not disturbed. Samantha likes the headphones well enough, but would be willing to pay R600/mth to keep on listening to late-night music through her speakers. How, if at all, does the existence of this new option affect your answer to part (a)? Explain carefully.

5 Ashes and Beugel can live separately at a rent of R4000/mth each, or together at a rent of R6000/mth. Each would be willing to give up R300/mth to avoid having to give up his privacy. In addition to the loss of privacy, joint living produces two other conflicts. Each has a particular behaviour the other finds offensive: Beugel is a trumpet player, and Ashes smokes cigarettes. Beugel would be willing to pay R600/mth rather than tolerate smoking in his house, and R1200/mth to continue playing his trumpet. Ashes, for his part, would pay up to R1000/mth to continue smoking, and up to R900/mth to avoid listening to the trumpet. Will they live together? Explain carefully. Would your answer be different if Ashes didn't mind giving up his privacy?

6 Aggie and Bennie live on adjacent plots of land. Each has two potential uses for her land, the present values of each of which depend on the use adopted by the other, as summarized in the table. All the values in the table are known to both parties.

		Aggie	
		Apple growing	Pig farming
Bennie	Rental housing	Aggie: R2000	Aggie: R4500
		Bennie: R7000	Bennie: R4000
	Bee keeping	Aggie: R4000	Aggie: R4500
		Bennie: R6500	Bennie: R5000

a If there are no negotiation costs, what activities will the two pursue on their land?

b If there are negotiation costs of R1500, what activities will the two pursue on their land?

c What is the maximum net income Aggie can earn in parts (a) and (b) above?

7 A village has six residents, each of whom has R5000. Each resident may either invest his money in a government bond, which pays 11 per cent/yr, or use it to buy a year-old Boer goat, which will graze on the village commons. Year-old Boer goats and government bonds each cost exactly R5000. Boer goats require no effort to tend, and can be sold for a price that depends on the amount of weight they gain during the year. Yearly weight gain, in turn, depends on the number of Boer goats that graze on the commons. The prices of 2-year-old Boer goats are given in the table as a function of the total number of Boer goats.

Number of Boer goats	Price per 2-year-old steer (rands)
1	6000
2	5875
3	5750
4	5625
5	5500
6	5375

a If villagers make their investment decisions independently, how many Boer goats will graze on the commons?

b How many Boer goats would graze on the commons if investment decisions were made collectively?

c What grazing fee per Boer goat would result in the socially optimal number of Boer goats?

8 A competitive fishing industry consists of five independently owned and operated fishing boats working out of the port of Saldanha. Assume that no other fishermen fish in the vicinity, and that the MC of operating a boat for 1 day is equivalent to 70 kg of fish. (A boat left idle generates no costs.) The total catch per shoreline, in kilograms, is given in the following table as a function of the number of boats fishing to the north and to the south of the harbour:

Number of boats per side	Total catch	
	North	South
1	100	85
2	180	150
3	255	210
4	320	260
5	350	300

a If each boat owner decides independently which side of the harbour to fish, and all boats are in plain view of each other, how many boats would you expect to find fishing in each direction on any given day? What is the net catch (that is, the total catch from all boats, less operating costs)?

b Is this distribution of fishing craft optimal from the social point of view? If so, explain why. If not, what is the socially optimal distribution, and the corresponding net catch?

9 Two firms, X and Y, have access to five different production processes, each one of which emits a different amount of pollution. The daily costs of the processes and the corresponding number of tonnes of smoke are listed in the table (top of page 469).

Process (smoke)	A (4 tonnes/ day)	B (3 tonnes/ day)	C (2 tonnes/ day)	D (1 tonne/ day)	E (0 tonnes/ day)
Cost to firm X	1000	1200	1400	1700	2200
Cost to firm Y	600	1000	1500	2550	3750

a If pollution is unregulated, which process will each firm use, and what will be the total daily smoke emissions?

b The city council wants to cut smoke emissions by half. To accomplish this, it requires a municipal permit for each tonne of smoke emitted, and limits the number of permits to the desired level of emissions. The permits are then auctioned off to the highest bidders. If X and Y are the only polluters, how much will each permit cost? How many permits will X buy? How many will Y buy?

c Compare the total cost to society of this permit auction procedure with the total cost of having each firm reduce emissions by half.

10 Suppose the government attempts to restrict pollution by mandating a maximum amount that each firm can pollute. In general, this will result in a higher cost for pollution control than is necessary. Explain why.

***11** A small village has six people. Each can either fish in a nearby lagoon or work in a factory. Wages in the factory are R40/hour. Fish sell in competitive markets for R10 apiece. If L persons fish the lagoon, the total number of fish caught per hour is given by $F = 80L - 20L^2$. People prefer to fish, unless they expect to make more money working in the factory.

a If people decide individually whether to fish or work in the factory, how many will fish? What will be the total earnings per hour for the village?

b What is the socially optimal number of fishermen? With that number, what will the total earnings per hour of the village be?

c Why is there a difference between the equilibrium and socially optimal numbers of fishermen?

12 Once a week Benny purchases a six-pack of Coca-Cola, and puts it in his refrigerator for his two children to drink later. He invariably discovers that all six cans get drunk the first day. Moeketsi also purchases a six-pack of Coca-Cola once a week for his two children but, unlike Benny, he tells them that each may drink no more than three cans. Explain why the Coke lasts much longer at Moeketsi's house than at Benny's.

13 Suppose Devon owns and works in a bakery located next to an outdoor cafe owned by Hendrik. The patrons of the outdoor cafe like the smell that emanates from the bakery. When Devon leaves his windows open, the cafe faces the demand curve $P_c = 30 - 0.2Q_c$, while when the windows are closed, demand is given by $P_c = 25 - 0.2Q_c$. However, Devon doesn't like the street noise he hears when his windows are open, and, the disutility he receives has a monetary value of 5. Assume that the cafe has a constant marginal cost of 10, and that integration (merger) is not a possibility, because each owner greatly enjoys owning and operating his own establishment.

a In the absence of a contract between the parties, do the firms behave in an efficient fashion? If not, describe the range of contracts that might emerge in response to the externality problem present in the environment. In answering this question, assume Devon understands how the bakery odour affects demand at the cafe, and Hendrik knows how much Devon dislikes street noise.

b Suppose now everything is the same as above, except that, given the current seating arrangement in the cafe, the cafe does not face a higher demand when the bakery windows are open. To realize this higher demand, Hendrik needs to make a sunk investment of 50, which moves the tables closer to the bakery. Is it wise for Hendrik to make this investment prior to Devon and Hendrik signing a contract? Explain.

* This problem is most easily solved by making use of the calculus definition of marginal product.

c Go back to the initial set-up, but now assume that Devon's disutility from street noise equals 50 rather than 5. Further, suppose that, prior to the parties agreeing on a contract, Hendrik becomes the mayor and grants himself the property rights concerning whether the bakery windows are left open or closed. Does this have an effect on whether the parties reach an efficient outcome? Explain.

14 Melissa and Jacques face the choice of driving to work early or late. If they both drive to work at the same time, each gets in the way of the other on the road, and so their daily commute takes longer and is more irritating. The monetary pay-offs for each person are listed in the table below for each of the four possible combinations of actions:

		Jacques	
		Early	Late
Melissa	Early	Jacques: 30	Jacques: 20
		Melissa: 30	Melissa: 50
	Late	Jacques: 50	Jacques: 10
		Melissa: 20	Melissa: 10

a If Melissa and Jacques are pay-off maximizers and make their decisions individually, what will they do?

b If Melissa and Jacques can make binding agreements with each other, what will they do?

15 Same as Problem 14, except now the pay-off values of each person are:

		Jacques	
		Early	Late
Melissa	Early	Jacques: 30	Jacques: 20
		Melissa: 30	Melissa: 60
	Late	Jacques: 50	Jacques: 10
		Melissa: 20	Melissa: 10

a If Melissa and Jacques are pay-off maximizers and make their decisions individually, what will they do?

b If Melissa and Jacques can make binding agreements with each other, what will they do?

c How do your answers differ from Problem 14, and why?

16 Matthew loves dogs and has a pair of Staffordshire Bull Terriers. Tumi has an incredible fear of dogs, and cannot stand to be within sight of them. Matthew and Tumi are deciding whether to live in Rondebosch or Sea Point. If they end up living in the same part of Cape Town, Tumi will run into Matthew out walking the Staffies and be frightened. Thus Tumi prefers to be physically separated from Matthew. The pay-offs for each person are listed in the table below for each of the four possible combinations of actions:

		Tumi	
		Rondebosch	Sea Point
Matthew	Rondebosch	Tumi: 0	Tumi: 800
		Matthew: 800	Matthew: 800
	Sea Point	Tumi: 500	Tumi: 0
		Matthew: 900	Matthew: 900

a If Matthew and Tumi are pay-off maximizers and make their decisions individually, what will they do?

b If Matthew and Tumi can make binding agreements with each other, what will they do?

17 Same as Problem 16, except that now the pay-off values of each person are:

		Tumi	
		Rondebosch	Sea Point
Matthew	Rondebosch	Tumi: 0	Tumi: 600
		Matthew: 800	Matthew: 800
	Sea Point	Tumi: 500	Tumi: 0
		Matthew: 1000	Matthew: 900

a If Matthew and Tumi are pay-off maximizers and make their decisions individually, what will they do?

b If Matthew and Tumi can make binding agreements with each other, what will they do?

c How do your answers differ from Problem 16, and why?

Answers to in-chapter exercises

14.1 With a negotiation cost of only 20, it is now practical for the confectioner to pay the doctor to rearrange his office when the confectioner is liable. But note in the table below that it is still more efficient for the confectioner not to be liable:

Legal regime	Outcome	Net benefit		
		Doctor	Confectioner	Total
Liable	Confectioner operates and pays doctor $18 \leq P \leq 20$ to rearrange office	$22 + P$	$40 - P$	62
Not liable	Doctor rearranges his office at his own expense	22	60	82

14.2 Recall that the optimal number of Boer goats is 2. The grazing fee must be more than 2 to prevent a third Boer goat from being sent out to graze. The fee cannot be more than 6 without keeping the second Boer goat from being sent out.

14.3 Now the cost of accommodating to the smoke problem is 900, which is again less than the joint savings in rent. Let X represent Dominique's contribution to the cost of the exhaust system, which means that Seziphelele's contribution is $900 - X$. X cannot exceed 1350, or else Dominique will live separately; and X cannot be less than 450, or else Seziphelele will live separately. The total gain is $2700 - 900 = 1800$.

	Net rental payment (R/mth)		Net gain (R/mth)		
	Dominique	Seziphelele	Dominique	Seziphelele	Total
Live separately	4500	4500	–	–	–
Live together and install exhaust system for smoke, $450 \leq X \leq 1350$	$3150 + X$	$4050 - X$	$1300 - X$	$450 + X$	1800

Chapter

15

Government

Frequently local telephone companies are regulated monopolies, and so government regulators must rule on all their charges to the public. Historically, regulatory agencies prevented charges for directory assistance calls in the belief that such charges would diminish the value of a vital public communications network. Most economists did not agree with this action because directory assistance calls cost the phone company a lot of money to provide, and the economist's immediate fear is that people will be uneconomical in their use of this or any other resource for which they do not have to pay. Currently calls to directory assistance in South Africa are still free of charge.

However, the authorities in New York came up with a brilliant solution to this dilemma that would preserve efficiency gains while at the same time eliminating any adverse effects on the poor. They gave every telephone subscriber a 30-cent credit on her monthly telephone bill and billed each directory assistance call at 10 cents. For example, someone who made one directory assistance call per month would be charged 10 cents, which, when combined with the credit, would make her monthly bill 20 cents less than before. Someone who made three directory assistance calls per month would break even, someone with four would pay 10 cents more than before, and so on. On the plausible assumption that a charge of 10 cents per call would be more likely to induce a low-income person than a high-income person to cut down on directory assistance calls, the net effect of the amended proposal was actually to increase the real purchasing power of the poor.

Chapter preview[1]

The directory assistance episode illustrates two critically important points about government

[1] This chapter is just an introduction to public economics and the role of the government in the economy. See, for example, Philip Black, Estian Calitz and Thaart Steenekamp, *Public Economics for South African Students*, Oxford University Press, Cape Town, 2011, for a much more detailed discussion of everything that is dealt with in this chapter.

economic policy: first, that, distributional concerns permeate discussion of even the most seemingly trivial policies; and, second, that the most efficient solution to a public policy problem is one that enables both rich and poor alike to do better than before. Our task in this chapter is to explore two important functions of government: the provision of public goods, and the direct redistribution of income. Concerns about both fairness and efficiency, we shall see, are inextricably linked in both of these areas.

We shall also see that the mere fact that a good has the characteristics of a public good does not mean that it must necessarily be provided by government. We shall see that problems similar to those that arise in connection with public goods are encountered whenever there are significant indivisibilities or economies of scale in the production of private-consumption goods.

Next we shall take up the question of how societies make choices between competing public projects, with particular focus on cost–benefit analysis as an alternative to majority voting schemes.

We shall also address the problem of rent seeking, namely, that self-interested parties have an incentive to influence outcomes in their own favour.

We shall then turn to the topic of direct income transfer programmes. Here, our focus will be on how such transfers might be accomplished without undermining incentives to work and take risks.

Public goods

Public goods are those goods or services that possess, in varying degrees, the properties of *non-rivalry* and *non-excludability*. The non-rivalry property says that any one person's consumption of a public good has no effect on the amount of it available for others. If you walk underneath a street light at night there is no less light available to all other students reading this text. But if you eat the last hamburger (a private good) in your student centre there are no hamburgers left for others. Non-excludability means that it is either impossible or prohibitively costly to exclude non-payers from consuming the good. If you do not pay your taxes, you can still use the street lights. However, if you do not pay your DStv subscription fees, you cannot watch the non-SABC programmes.

Pure public good A good that has a high degree of non-rivalry and non-excludability.

Goods that have high degrees of both of these properties are often called **pure public goods**, the classic example of which is national defence. If they provide safety for citizen A, they automatically also provide it for citizen B. The fact that they provide safety for A does not decrease the safety available for B. Goods that have only the non-rivalry property are sometimes referred to as **collective goods**. Not all goods provided by government are public goods. Many public goods are financed by government although they do not physically produce them – they pay a private firm to do it on their behalf. An inadequate profit motive means that private firms are unlikely to be involved in the production of public goods unless the government pays them to provide them.

Collective good A good that is excludable and has a high degree only of non-rivalry.

Let's begin our analysis with the case of a government trying to decide what quantity to provide of some pure public good – say, public television programming. In many countries a number of free TV channels exist, but in South Africa you must pay an annual licence fee of about R300 to view SABC broadcasts. For simplicity, imagine that there are only two citizens, A and B, and that each assigns a different value to any given quantity of the public good. In Fig. 15.1, the horizontal axis measures the quantity of programming. The curve labelled AA′ represents the amount A would be willing to pay for an additional unit of programming, and BB′ represents the corresponding curve

Figure 15.1 The aggregate willingness-to-pay curve for a public good

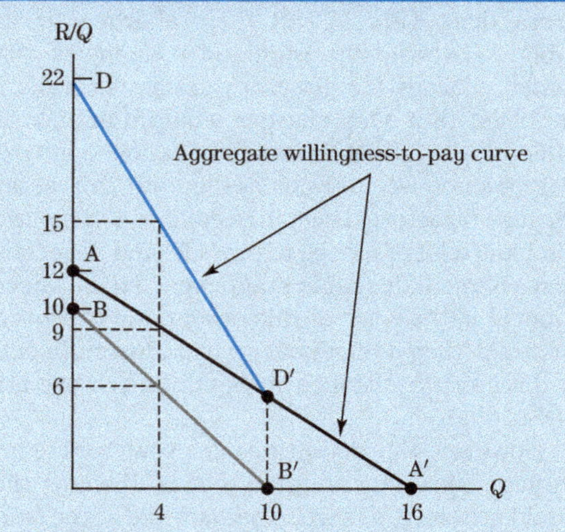

AA′ and BB′ represent the respective amounts that A and B are willing to pay for an additional unit of the public good. The aggregate willingness-to-pay curve is the vertical summation of the individual willingness-to-pay curves, the curve labelled DD′A′.

for B. Thus, at a level of 4 units of programming, A would be willing to pay R9/wk for an additional unit, whereas B would be willing to pay only R6/wk. The fact that the two willingness-to-pay curves are downward sloping reflects the fact that the more programming there already is, the less valuable an additional unit will be.

The central fact about providing any pure public good is that each person must consume the same amount of it. In markets for private goods, by contrast, each person can consume whatever amount she chooses at the prevailing price. To obtain the market demand curve for a private good, we simply added the individual demand curves horizontally. In the case of public goods, the analogue of the market demand curve is the aggregate willingness-to-pay curve. It is obtained by adding the individual willingness-to-pay curves not horizontally but *vertically*. At $Q = 4$ units of programming in Fig. 15.1, for example, A and B together are willing to pay a total of $9 + 6 =$ R15/wk for an additional unit of programming. The curve labelled DD′A′ represents the vertical summation of the two individual willingness-to-pay curves.

Exercise 15.1

Ten homogeneous consumers all have individual willingness-to-pay curves $P = 12 - \frac{1}{5}Q$ for a public good – say, a concert in an open park (where P is measured in rands and Q is measured in minutes). Construct and graph the aggregate willingness-to-pay curve. For a 30-minute concert, what is the maximum each individual would be willing to pay?

The analogy to joint production

In passing, let's note the striking similarity between the procedure for generating the aggregate willingness-to-pay curve for a public good and the procedure whereby the demand curve for a product such as chicken is generated from the demand curves for the various parts of a chicken. For simplicity, suppose chickens are composed of only two parts, wings and drumsticks, the demand curves for which are given by the curves labelled WW′ and DD′ in Fig. 15.2. The horizontal axis in Fig. 15.2 measures three things simultaneously: total pairs of drumsticks, total pairs of wings and total number of chickens – because any given number of chickens will give rise to that same number of pairs of wings and drumsticks. On the simplifying assumption that wings and drumsticks are

Figure 15.2 Equilibrium in a market for jointly produced products

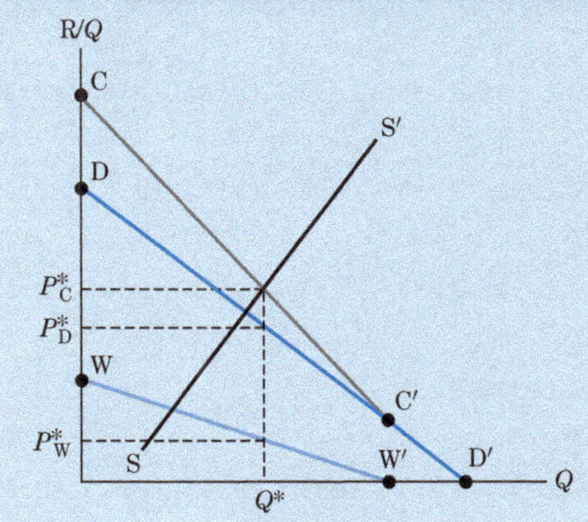

the only two chicken parts, we get the market demand curve for chickens by adding the demand curve for wings and the demand curve for drumsticks vertically. The curve labelled CC′D′ in Fig. 15.2 represents this vertical summation and has a kink at C′.

The curve labelled SS′ in Fig. 15.2 is the supply curve for chickens. Assuming the chicken industry is competitive, it is the horizontal summation of the marginal cost curves of the individual chicken producers. As in any other competitive market, equilibrium in the market for chickens occurs at the intersection of the supply and demand curves. The equilibrium quantity of chickens will be Q^*, and that quantity will give rise to Q^* pairs of drumsticks and Q^* pairs of wings. The market-clearing prices for drumsticks and wings will be P^*_D and P^*_W, respectively. These two prices sum to the equilibrium price of chickens, P^*_C.

At Q^* the cost to society of producing another chicken is P^*_C. Note that the price of each chicken part cannot be determined from cost information alone, even if we know exactly the marginal cost of raising another chicken. Drumsticks and wings sell for their respective prices because those are the prices necessary to clear the market for each.

The optimal quantity of a public good

Let's return to our example of public television programming. Given the aggregate willingness-to-pay curve, what is the optimal quantity of programming? The answer is determined in much the same way as in the market for chickens. In Fig. 15.3, the curve labelled DD′A′ again represents the aggregate willingness-to-pay curve for public

Figure 15.3 Optimal provision of a public good

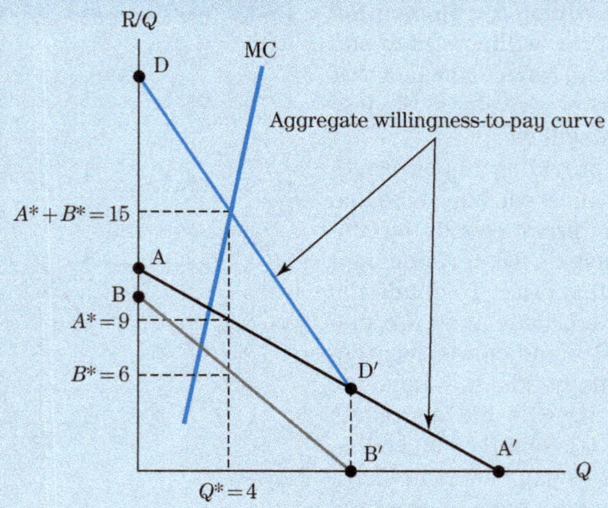

The optimal level of the public good is $Q^* = 4$, the level for which aggregate marginal willingness to pay for the good is exactly equal to its marginal cost.

television programming. The curve labelled MC represents the marginal cost of television programming as a function of its quantity. The intersection of these two curves establishes $Q^* = 4$, the optimal level of public television programming. At $Q^* = 4$, the amounts that A and B would be willing to pay for another unit of programming add to exactly the cost (R15/wk) of producing another unit. If this equality did not hold, we could easily show that society would be better off by either expanding or contracting the amount of programming.

Exercise 15.2

Consider the scenario described in Exercise 15.1, and suppose that the marginal cost of providing the concert is $MC = 2Q$. Determine the optimal length of the concert.

Paying for Q^*

We must make a slight qualification to the claim that Q^* is the optimal level of the public good in Fig. 15.3. The statement is true subject to the provision that the *total* cost of Q^* does not exceed the total amount that the public would be willing to pay for it. The total willingness to pay for Q^* is the area under the aggregate willingness-to-pay curve up to Q^*. The total cost is the area under the marginal cost curve up to Q^*, plus any fixed costs. Provided that the total cost is smaller than the total willingness to pay, Q^* is the optimal level of the public good. This qualification is similar to the requirement that a profit-maximizing firm should produce where $MR = MC$, subject to the proviso that total revenues cover total costs.

If the government is to produce Q^* units of a public good, it must raise sufficient tax revenue to cover the total production costs of that amount. Suppose the government's tax structure requires the collection of equal tax payments from all citizens. In Fig. 15.3, B's willingness to pay for the public good is smaller than A's. For example, if the total cost of the good is 100, and each party must be taxed equally, B will vote for it only if his total willingness to pay exceeds 50. If the amount B is willing to pay for the public good is only, say, 40, this condition will not be satisfied, and so the project will not win approval.

And yet we know that this public good is one whose benefits to all citizens add up to more than its costs. Compared with the alternative, in which the public good is not provided, both A and B can be made better off by providing Q^* of it and then taxing A more heavily than B in order to pay for it. It follows that a tax structure that levies the same tax on all citizens cannot in general be Pareto efficient.

The situation here is analogous to the case in which the incomes of two spouses differ substantially. Suppose Julie earns R500 000/yr while her husband, Bruce, earns only R160 000/yr. Given her income, Julie as an individual would want to spend much more than would Bruce on housing, travel, entertainment and the many other items they consume in common. But suppose the couple adopted a rule that each had to contribute an equal share towards the purchase of such items. The result would be to constrain the couple to live in a small house, to take only inexpensive vacations, to skimp on entertainment and dining out, and so on. However, Julie would find it attractive to pay considerably more than 50 per cent for jointly consumed goods, thereby enabling both of them to consume in the manner their combined income affords.

As in the case of private goods, willingness to pay for public goods is generally an increasing function of income. The rich, on average, assign greater value to public goods than do the poor – not because they have different tastes but because they have more money. A tax system that taxed the poor just as heavily as the rich would result in the rich getting smaller amounts of public goods than they want. Rather than see that happen, the rich would gladly agree to a tax system that assigns them a larger share of the tax burden. Also, the tax payments of the poor, though small, mean the rich end up paying less than if they had to finance public goods all by themselves.

Private provision of public goods

Governments are not the exclusive providers of public goods in any society. Substantial quantities of such goods are routinely provided through a variety of private channels. If it is impractical to exclude people from consuming a public good, the pressing question is: how can the good be paid for, if not by mandatory taxes?

Funding by donation

One method for funding public goods is through voluntary donations. People donate great artworks to museums such as the Mandela Family Museum in Soweto or the Rupert Museum in Stellenbosch, and they make contributions to listener-supported radio stations, to fund animal shelters such as the SPCA, to deal out mosquito nets to combat malaria, and so on. Motives for such donations are as varied as the projects they support. Some see charitable giving as a means of gaining respect and admiration in the community.[2] Others may feel pressure to give in order to avoid social ostracism. These motives are really two sides of the same coin – social reward in the first case and social penalty in the second. Where such social forces are effective, they are a practical way of excluding non-payers from full enjoyment of the public good.

Alternatively, people may donate because the increment to the public good that their contribution will finance is simply worth that much money to them. This motive is most likely to be important in situations in which one person's action can significantly affect the scale of the public good. Someone who lives at the end of a short dirt road in a rural area, for example, may find it worthwhile to pave the entire road at his own expense. He would naturally be happier if everyone who lived on the road chipped in. But rather than do without the road altogether, it may be worthwhile for him to pave it himself. Similarly, a person who plants a flower garden in front of her house provides a public good for neighbours to enjoy. If her own personal enjoyment from the garden exceeds its cost, pure self-interest is a sufficient motive for her to plant it.

But self-interested motives do not seem sufficient to explain why people make anonymous donations that will have no appreciable effect on the benefits they themselves receive. In the case of listener-supported radio stations, no single person's contribution will make a perceptible difference to the nature or quality of programming.

> **Free-riding** Choosing not to donate to a cause but still benefiting from the donations of others.

In such situations, the logic of pure self-interest seems to dictate **free-riding** – abstaining in the hope that others will contribute. And yet millions of people contribute to such enterprises each year. For many of these people, the satisfaction of giving is an end in itself. For some people these donations give them a 'feel good' feeling, and that is why they are willing to do it.

The fact that public goods are often financed through voluntary contributions does not necessarily mean, however, that they are supported at socially optimal levels. Residents might be perfectly willing to pay sufficient taxes to build the socially optimal road. And yet, in the absence of taxes, the road that actually gets built is likely to be considerably smaller. Similarly, many people might strongly want society to invest more in

[2] To achieve the social benefit of charitable giving, the gift must become public knowledge. Most charitable organizations publicize their list of donors.

public television programming, but these same people might be reluctant to give voluntarily as much as they would be willing to pay in taxes.

Sale of by-products

Free-rider problems are sometimes solved by devising novel means to finance the public good. One such way is the sale of an important by-product of the public good. In the case of commercial television, for example, financing comes mainly from sponsors, generally private corporations, who pay for the right to beam advertising messages to the audience attracted by the broadcast. The captive viewing audience is a by-product of the broadcast, and sponsors are willing to pay a lot for access to it. Advertising time is typically much more expensive just before or after an important sporting event such as the World Cup soccer and rugby finals. As the following example makes clear, however, this system does not always ensure an optimal allocation of broadcasting resources.

Development of new means to exclude non-payers

Another way to finance public goods privately is to devise cheap new ways of excluding people who do not pay for the good. In broadcasting, it is now simple to exclude households. If you do not pay your DStv subscription your signal is not encoded, and you cannot watch those programmes. With the ability to charge for specific programmes (and in South Africa, more specifically batches of channels), it is no longer necessary to make programming decisions on the basis of which programme will garner the largest audience. In our *Boots* versus *Telemundo* example (see Example 15.1), a broadcasting company that can exclude non-payers would have every incentive to show *Telemundo* because its proponents now have a practical means of translating their greater willingness to pay into profits for the producer.

But note that, whereas the outcome of pay-per-view TV is more efficient in the sense of selecting the programmes the public most values, it is less efficient in one other important respect. By charging each household a fee for viewing, it discourages some households from tuning in. And since the marginal social cost of an additional household watching a programme is exactly zero, it is inefficient to limit the audience in this way. Which of the two inefficiencies is more important – free TV's inefficiency in choosing between programmes or pay TV's inefficiency in excluding potential beneficiaries – is an empirical question.

Private contracts

Legal contracts among private individuals offer yet another means for overcoming some of the difficulties associated with the free-rider problem. Consider, for example, the public good consisting of residential maintenance and beautification.

Example 15.1

In a given time slot, a television network faces the alternative of broadcasting either *Boots and All* or a *Telemundo* soap opera. If it chooses *Boots*, it will win 23 per cent of the viewing audience; if it chooses *Telemundo*, it will win only 18 per cent. Suppose those choosing *Boots and All* would collectively be willing to pay R12 million for the right to see that programme, while those choosing *Telemundo* would be willing to pay R28 million. And suppose, finally, that the time slot is to be financed by a detergent company. Which programme will the network choose? Which programme would be socially optimal?

The sponsor cares primarily about the number of people who will see its advertisements, and will thus choose the programme that will attract the largest audience – here, *Boots and All*. The fact that those who prefer *Telemundo* would be willing to pay a lot more to see it is of little concern to the sponsor. But this difference in willingness to pay is critical when it comes to determining the optimal result from society's point of view. Because the people who prefer *Telemundo* could more than compensate the *Boots and All* viewers for relinquishing the time slot, *Telemundo* is a Pareto-superior outcome. But unless its supporters happen to buy more soap in total than the *Boots and All* viewers, *Boots and All* will prevail. The difficulty with reliance on advertising and other indirect mechanisms for financing public goods is that there is no assurance that they will reflect the relevant benefits to society.

As neighbourhoods are customarily organized, it is impractical to exclude your neighbours from the benefits they will reap if you keep your house well painted and your garden neatly trimmed. Nor would it be efficient to exclude them, because their consumption of these benefits does not diminish their value to you and others in any way. In this respect, home maintenance and beautification satisfy the definition of a pure public good and, for this reason, will generally be undersupplied by private individuals. If your neighbour's garden is a joy to behold, she clearly gains more pleasure from working in it than the neighbour whose plot is knee-deep in weeds.

We saw in Chapter 14 that if transactions were costless, your neighbours could subsidize your investments in home maintenance and beautification, and you could do likewise for them. But in general it is costly to negotiate such subsidies on a case-by-case basis, and so the level of investment in home maintenance often ends up being well below optimal.

Neighbourhoods in different school districts may pursue different school policies. One district may choose higher spending levels on schools (and higher school fees to fund them) than another district nearby. Households then self-select: families that feel strongly about the upkeep of the neighbourhood choose to live in the high-tax area, and those less concerned choose to live in the other district.

The economics of clubs

A pure public good has the property that an additional person's consumption of the good does not limit the amount of it available to others. Stated another way, the marginal cost of additional consumption of the public good is exactly zero. Many privately produced goods like swimming pools have the property that marginal cost, although not zero, declines sharply with the number of users accommodated. The number of swimmers it can accommodate rises in proportion to its surface area, but its cost rises much more slowly.

When the marginal cost of expanding the capacity of a private good is low relative to its average cost, consumers face an economic incentive to share the purchase and use of the good. If 20 families each buy a swimming pool for R80 000 from Penguin Pools, an established pool manufacturer in South Africa since 1995, the total cost for them will be R1.6 million. However, they could install a slightly bigger pool for R400 000 which all of them will be able to use simultaneously. It also makes sense for households to share goods like ladders, electric drills, saws and grinders.

The disadvantage of sharing, besides the fact that it requires someone to take the initiative in organizing the arrangement, is that it limits both the privacy and flexibility of access to the good. Thus a homeowner might want to use the ladder on a particular Saturday afternoon, only to find it already in use by one of its other co-owners. Sometimes such inconveniences are trivial in relation to the cost savings; at other times, they will not be.

On the plausible assumption that the demand for privacy increases with income, we would predict that high-income consumers would be more likely to purchase their own pools than low-income consumers. But even consumers with very high incomes will find it attractive to participate in sharing arrangements for extremely costly consumption goods. Rather than maintain exclusive rights to operate an aeroplane that would sit idle on the tarmac most hours of the week, for example, even wealthy amateur pilots often choose to become members of flying clubs, the use of whose aircraft is shared with other members.

In the case of very inexpensive goods, by contrast, we would expect the demand for privacy to take precedence over the lure of cost savings, even for consumers of relatively modest means. A privately owned toothbrush, like a privately owned aeroplane or swimming pool, is destined to remain idle for most hours of the day. Its cost per owner could be lowered substantially if it were shared by the members of a teeth-brushing club. But the savings from such a transaction would be far too small to justify the sacrifice in privacy. Virtually everyone, even the poorest citizen, finds it worthwhile to maintain exclusive access to her personal toothbrush, which costs only in the region of R20.

Public choice

Whether public goods are provided by governments, charitable organizations or private clubs, decisions must be made about the types and quantities to provide. The budget constraint confronting the group is often clear enough. The much more difficult aspect of the problem is devising some means for translating the diverse preferences of the group's members into a single voice.

Majority voting

One method of discerning group preferences is the majority vote. By this standard, projects favoured by a majority – in either a direct referendum or a vote taken by elected representatives – are adopted, and all others are abandoned. In recent years much attention has been given to the fact that majority voting often leads to intransitivities in the ranking of alternatives. To illustrate, consider a group with three members – Malema, Barnard and Tutu – each of whom has a well-ordered ranking of three alternative projects: a new missile, a medical research project and more aid to the poor. Malema likes the missile best, medical research next best and aid to the poor least. Barnard likes medical research best, aid to the poor next best and the new missile least. Tutu, finally, likes aid to the poor best, a new missile next best and medical research least. These rankings are summarized in Table 15.1.

Given these rankings, note what happens when each of the three pairs of alternatives is put to a vote. In deciding which of any pair of alternatives to vote for, each voter will naturally choose the one he prefers to the other. Thus, in a vote between a new missile and medical research, the missile will get 2 votes (Malema and Tutu), the research only 1 (Barnard). In a vote between research and aid to the poor, research gets 2 votes (Malema and Barnard), aid only 1 (Tutu). And finally, in a vote between aid and the missile, aid gets 2 votes (Barnard and Tutu), the missile only 1 (Malema). Thus the missile defeats the research programme and the research programme defeats aid to the poor, and yet aid to the poor defeats the missile programme! Such intransitivities were assumed not to occur in individual preference orderings, but can easily happen if social choice takes place by successive majority votes between pairs of alternatives.

Agenda manipulation

The possibility of intransitivities in majority voting makes the order in which alternatives are considered by the electorate critically important. Suppose, for example, that Malema is in charge of setting the agenda for voting. His first priority will be to avoid a direct confrontation between the missile (his most favoured project) and the aid project (which he knows will defeat the missile in a majority vote). He can ensure the missile's success by first conducting a vote between the aid project and the research project, followed by a vote between the winner of that election and the missile. The research project will win the first vote and will then be defeated by the missile in the second. Given power to set the agenda, either Barnard or Tutu could have taken similar steps to ensure victory for either the research project or the aid project.

Table 15.1 Preferences that produce intransitive choices in majority voting

	Malema	Barnard	Tutu
Best	Missile	Research	Aid
Second	Research	Aid	Missile
Third	Aid	Missile	Research

In a majority vote, the missile defeats the research programme, which in turn defeats aid to the poor. And yet aid to the poor wins when paired against the missile. Majority voting schemes can lead to intransitivities, even when individual preference orderings are transitive.

The median voter theorem

Intransitive rankings do not always result when alternatives are considered pairwise in a majority voting system. For example, we shall get no intransitivities when the alternatives represent different quantities of a given public good, and each voter ranks each according to how close it is to what, for her, is the optimal amount of the good. To illustrate, suppose our three voters are now considering what percentage of GDP to devote to national defence; and suppose that, as shown in Fig. 15.4, the ideal percentages for Malema, Barnard and Tutu are 15, 2 and 5, respectively. Suppose, finally, that the percentages being considered for adoption are 1.5, 3.5, 6, 8, 12 and 20.

Does the power to set the order in which pairs of alternatives are considered confer the power to choose the ultimate outcome? This time the answer is no. In any pair of alternatives put to a vote, the winner will always be the one preferred by Tutu. Suppose, for instance, that 1.5 and 3.5 are put to a vote. Malema and Tutu will vote for 3.5 and Barnard for 1.5, making Tutu's choice the winner. If the alternatives are 8 and 20, Barnard and Tutu will vote for 8 and Malema for 20, and Tutu's choice again wins. Because Tutu's most preferred outcome lies between the most preferred choices of the other two, he is the so-called **median voter** in this situation, and his vote will always prevail. The *median voter theorem* states that, whenever alternatives can be ranked according to their closeness to each voter's ideal outcome, majority voting will always select the alternative most preferred by the median voter.

Median voter The voter whose ideal outcome lies above the ideal outcomes of half the voters.

Figure 15.4 The power of the median voter

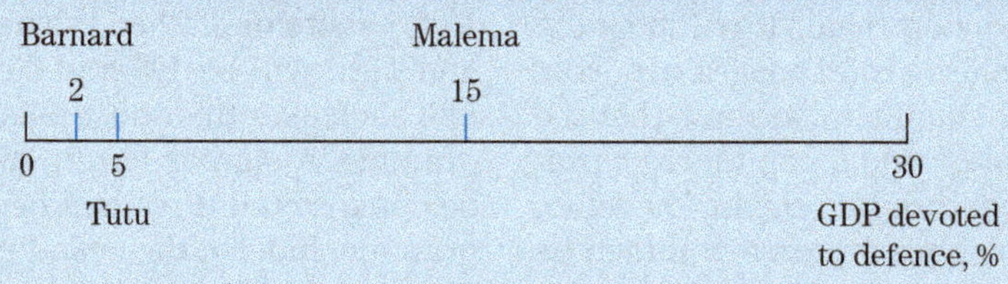

The most preferred options for Barnard, Tutu and Malema are 2, 5 and 15 per cent, respectively, making Tutu the median voter. No matter what pair of proposed percentages for defence is put to a vote, the one closest to Tutu's most preferred option will win.

Exercise 15.3

Given that the percentages of GDP under consideration for spending on national defence are again 1.5, 3.5, 6, 8, 12 and 20, which outcome will be chosen if the most preferred percentages of Barnard, Tutu and Malema are 6, 9 and 12, respectively?

Numerous important examples occur in practice in which majority voting leads to intransitive rankings, making the power to set the agenda tantamount to the power to choose the final outcome.

Cost–benefit analysis

The inherent problem of public choice by majority voting is not just that it sometimes leads to intransitivities. An even more serious problem is that it almost completely obscures important differences in the intensity with which different voters hold their preferences. Suppose, for example, that two alternatives are put to a vote: (1) to allow smoking in public buildings; and (2) to prohibit smoking in public buildings. If 53 per cent of the voters prefer the first alternative and 47 per cent the second, the result will be to allow smoking in public buildings. But suppose the 47 per cent who favour a ban on smoking feel very strongly about it, and collectively would be willing to pay R100 million/yr in order to have it. And suppose the opponents of the ban are only mildly opposed to it. Collectively, the most they would be willing to pay in order to continue smoking in public buildings is only R9 million/yr. Under these circumstances, there is a simple transfer payment that makes the outcome chosen by the majority clearly Pareto inferior to the ban on smoking in public buildings. If those in favour of the ban give the smokers R15 million/yr in exchange for agreeing to the ban, both groups will be better off than if smoking continues – the smokers by R6 million/yr, the non-smokers by R85 million/yr.

Cost–benefit analysis is an alternative to majority voting that attempts to take explicit account of how strongly people feel about each of the alternatives under consideration. In the smoking example, it would immediately rule in favour of the ban on smoking, because its benefits to its supporters (as measured by what they would be willing to pay to have it) strongly outweigh its costs to its opponents (as measured by what they would be willing to pay to avoid it).

Another advantage of cost–benefit analysis is that it would also avoid the intransitivities that often arise under majority voting. To illustrate, let's consider how it would deal with the missile–aid–research decision we discussed earlier. Table 15.2 displays hypothetical valuations assigned by Malema, Barnard and Tutu to each of the three alternatives. Positive entries in the table represent the amounts each person would pay to have a programme he likes. Negative entries represent what someone would pay to avoid a programme he dislikes. Note that each person's ranking of the alternatives is the same in Table 15.2 as it was in Table 15.1.

To keep the discussion simple, suppose that the cost of each programme is 100, but that because

Table 15.2 Willingness to pay for three projects

	Malema	Barnard	Tutu	Total
Missile	100	–25	45	120
Research	10	90	40	140
Aid	–20	50	95	125

Cost–benefit analysis chooses the project with the largest surplus of benefits over costs. If each project costs 100, the surplus will be 20 for the missile, 40 for the research programme and 25 for the aid programme.

of budgetary shortages only one of the three programmes can be undertaken. How will cost–benefit analysis choose among them? It will pick the one for which the surplus of total benefit over cost is greatest. Again, for simplicity, assume that the amounts the three voters would pay for each programme accurately capture all relevant benefits. The total benefit of each programme will then be the sum of what each voter would pay to have (or avoid) it. These totals are listed in the last column of Table 15.2, and reveal that the research programme is the clear winner.

Note also that the research programme would not have won if Malema had been able to set the agenda for a majority voting session. He would first put the research programme against the aid programme, defeating it 2 to 1. And Malema's favoured missile project would then defeat the research programme by the same margin. Tutu, through similar agenda manipulation, could arrange for his favoured aid programme to emerge the winner in a majority voting sequence.

Note, finally, that if the research programme did *not* get adopted, it would always be possible to construct a Pareto-preferred switch to it. Suppose, for example, that Malema set the agenda in a majority voting sequence, with the result that the missile programme was chosen. This outcome yields a loss of 25 for Barnard. By contrast, had the research programme been chosen, Barnard would have had a gain of 90 – a net improvement of 115 for him. This improvement is big enough to enable Barnard to compensate both Malema and Tutu for the losses they would suffer by switching from the missile to the research programme. Suppose, for example, that Barnard gives Malema 95 and Tutu 10 for switching. Then the net benefits to Malema and Tutu will be 105 and 50, respectively, a gain of 5 each over their positions with the missile programme. A similar Pareto-improving move could be constructed if we had begun with the aid programme. Indeed, the cost–benefit test will in general lead to a Pareto-efficient outcome.

One objection to cost–benefit analysis is that, because it measures benefits by what people are willing to pay, it gives insufficient weight to the interests of people with little money. This sounds at first like a serious objection, but as Example 15.2 clearly demonstrates, it does not survive close scrutiny.

Critics of cost–benefit analysis sometimes concede that it would lead to Pareto-optimal outcomes in every case if it were practical to make the needed compensation payments. But they go on to argue that such compensation payments usually are not practical on a case-by-case basis. And so, they conclude, it is unfair to make decisions on the basis of cost–benefit analysis.

This argument also fails on close examination. In most societies literally thousands of decisions are taken each year with respect to public goods and programmes and some help people and hurt others. Almost always the individual magnitudes of the gains and losses in any one decision are extremely small, much less than 1 per cent of even a poor person's annual earnings. If projects are decided by the cost–benefit criterion, the amount that winners gain on any adopted project will

Example 15.2

Suppose there are only two people, Richie (who is rich) and Porchie (who is poor). And suppose that Richie favours a public project that Porchie opposes. In purely psychological terms, their intensity of feeling is the same. But because Richie has much more money, he would be willing to pay 100 to have the project, whereas Porchie would be willing to pay only 10 to avoid it. If each could choose which method to use for deciding on public projects, which would each favour, cost–benefit analysis or majority rule?

At first glance, majority rule sounds attractive to Porchie, because it gives him veto power over any project he does not favour. But the first step Porchie would take if he were given that veto power would be to yield it in exchange for a compensation payment. If Richie values the project at 100 and Porchie would pay only 10 to avoid it, the most efficient outcome here is to go ahead with the project. If Richie gives Porchie a compensation payment of X, where $10 \leq X \leq 100$, then each party will be better off than if Porchie had insisted on exercising his veto. By Porchie's own reckoning, the inconvenience of the project is less than the value to him of the compensation payment. The fact that the cost–benefit test always leads to the greatest economic surplus means that it will always be in the interests of Richie and Porchie alike to use it.

necessarily outweigh the amount that losers lose. The law of large numbers tells us that it is virtually certain that everyone will come out a winner in the end.

The one telling argument in favour of majority voting is its simplicity. It is much easier to take a majority vote than to gather detailed information about what different individuals would be willing to pay for their preferred alternatives. Much progress has been made in recent years in the design of mechanisms that induce people to reveal their valuations truthfully. But these mechanisms remain cumbersome, and it is a lot easier to allow people to reveal their preferences in their voting behaviour. And in many situations, of course, majority voting and cost–benefit analysis will lead to the same outcome anyway.

Local public goods and the Tiebout model

Even with a perfect mechanism for choosing between alternative public goods, it is difficult to escape the need for painful compromise. One group will sincerely believe that it is society's duty to provide complete health care for every citizen; another will believe with equal sincerity that it is each individual's responsibility to provide for his own health care. Given differences of this sort, the result is often some form of compromise – partial public support for health care – that pleases neither group of voters.

With respect to public goods provided at the local level, Professor Charles Tiebout suggested that at least some of these compromises can be avoided if people are free to form communities with others of similar tastes.[3] Those who favour high levels of public goods can group together in communities in which they willingly accept the high tax rates necessary to finance these levels. And others who favour a more limited menu of public goods and services can form groups of their own and have lower tax rates. People thus vote with their feet. In South Africa it is more difficult to behave in this way as a result of the unnatural development of our cities during the years of apartheid.

Rent seeking

As a practical matter, the gains from public choices are often large, and concentrated in the hands of a few, whereas the costs, while also large, are spread among many. The difficulty such situations create for the public is clear. The prospective beneficiaries of a public programme have powerful incentives to lobby government in favour of it, while each of the prospective losers has too little at stake to bother about. The result, all too frequently, is that projects are approved even when their benefits do not exceed their costs.

A related difficulty arises in the case of similar projects whose benefits do exceed their costs. Because there are large gains to be had from one particular project, for example, private parties are willing to spend large sums in order to enhance their odds of being chosen as its beneficiaries. Pursuit of these gains goes by the name of *rent seeking*. One consequence of rent seeking is that the expected gains from government projects are often squandered by the competition among potential beneficiaries. See Example 15.3 for a practical illustration.

Example 15.3

Three firms have met the deadline for applying for the franchise to operate the tollgate at Chapman's Peak during the coming year. The daily cost of operating the system is 25, and the demand curve for its services is given by $P = 50 - Q$, where P is the price per vehicle per trip and Q is the number of vehicles per day. The franchise lasts for exactly 1 year and permits the franchisee to charge whatever price it chooses. The city council will choose the applicant that spends the most money lobbying members of the city council. If the applicants cannot collude, how much will each spend on lobbying?

The winner will set the monopoly price for the service, which is the price that corresponds to the quantity at which marginal revenue equals marginal cost. Marginal revenue for the tollgate is given by $MR = 50 - 2Q$, and marginal cost is zero by assumption. The profit-maximizing quantity will

[3] Charles Tiebout, 'The pure theory of local expenditure', *Journal of Political Economy*, 1956, vol. 64, no. 5, pp. 416–424.

thus be 25, which gives rise to a price of R25. Total revenue will be 25 × 25 = R625, which makes for a profit of 625 − 25 = R600 per day. This gives rise to an annual profit of R219 000. If any applicant spends more on lobbying than the other two, it will win the franchise. If all three spend the same, each applicant will have a 1-in-3 chance of earning R219 000 in profit, which means an expected profit of R73 000. If the lobbyists could collude, each would agree to spend the same amount on lobbying. But in the absence of a binding agreement, each will be strongly tempted to try to outspend the others. If each firm's spending reaches R73 000, each will have expected profits of zero (a one-third chance to earn R219 000, minus the R73 000 spent on lobbying). At this point, it might seem foolish to bid any further because higher spending levels would mean an expected loss. And yet if any one of the three spent R73 001, while the other two stayed at R73 000, it would get the franchise for sure and earn a net profit of R145 999. The losers would each have losses of R73 000. Rather than face a sure loss of R73 000, the losers may well find it attractive to bid R73 001 themselves. Where this process will stop is anyone's guess.[4] The one thing that seems certain is that it will dissipate some or all of the gains that could have been had from the project. From the viewpoint of any individual firm, it is perfectly rational to lobby in this fashion for a chance to win government benefits. From the standpoint of society as a whole, however, such activity is almost completely wasteful. The efficient government is one that takes every feasible step to discourage rent seeking – for example, by selecting contractors on the basis of the price they promise to charge, not on the amount they lobby.

Income distribution

In market economies, the main means of earning income is by selling factors of production.

This system of distributing incomes is far from perfect, but it does have several attractive properties. First, it leads to a determinate outcome: each factor will be paid the value of its marginal product, and in long-run competitive equilibrium these payments will add up to exactly the total product available for distribution.[5] A second attractive feature of the marginal productivity system is that it rewards initiative, effort and risk-taking. The harder, longer and more effectively a person works, the more she will be paid. And if she risks her capital on a venture that happens to succeed, she will reap a handsome dividend.

The Rawlsian criticism of the marginal productivity system

The marginal productivity system is not without flaws, however. The most common criticism is that it often generates a high degree of inequality. In Chapter 12 we focused on inequalities in the South African economy, and indicated that those who do well in the marketplace end up with vastly more than they can spend, while those who fail often cannot meet even their basic needs. Such inequality might be easier to accept if it were strictly the result of differences in effort, but it is frequently a matter of luck.

Even having abundant talent is no guarantee of doing well. It is also necessary to have the *right* talent. Being able to hit a golf ball 400 m with consistency and accuracy will earn you millions annually, while being the best fourth-grade teacher in South Africa will earn you little. The golf star earns so much more, not because he works harder or has more talent, but because he is lucky enough to be good at something people are willing to pay a lot for.

John Rawls, a Harvard moral philosopher, constructed a cogent ethical critique of the marginal productivity system, one based heavily on the microeconomic theory of choice itself.[6] The question he asked was, 'What constitutes

[4] The following experiment provides some relevant evidence. A R100 note is auctioned off subject to the following rules. The note goes to the highest bidder, who must pay the auctioneer the amount he bid. The second-highest bidder gets nothing, but must also pay the auctioneer the amount he bid. In a typical trial of this auction, the bids slowly approach R50, at which point there is a pause. Then the second bidder offers more than R50 and the bids quickly escalate to R100. There is another pause at R100, whereafter the second bidder bids more than R100, and the bids again quickly escalate. It is not uncommon for the winning bid to exceed R100 by a fair margin.

[5] Recall that long-run competitive equilibrium occurs at the minimum point of every firm's long-run average cost curve; at that point, there are constant returns in production. It is a property of production functions with constant returns that $F(K, L) = K\partial F/\partial K + L\partial F/\partial L$, which says that paying each factor its marginal product will exactly exhaust the total product available.

[6] His most influential work is, *A Theory of Justice*, London: Oxford University Press, 1973.

a just distribution of income?' To answer it, he proposed the following thought experiment. Imagine that you and the other citizens of some country have been thrown together in a meeting to choose the rules for distributing income. This meeting takes place behind a 'veil of ignorance', which conceals from each person any knowledge of what talents and abilities he and others possess. No individual knows whether she is smart or dull, strong or weak, fast or slow, and so on – which means that no one knows which particular rules of distribution would work to her own advantage. Rawls argued that the rules people would choose in such a state of ignorance would necessarily be fair; and if the rules are fair, it follows that the distribution to which they give rise will also be fair.

What rules would people choose from behind a veil of ignorance? If the national income to be distributed were a fixed amount every year, it is likely that most would choose to give everyone an equal share. This is likely, Rawls argued, because most people are strongly risk averse. Since an unequal distribution would involve not only a chance of doing well, but also a chance of doing poorly, most people would prefer to eliminate the risk by choosing an equal distribution.

The difficulty, however, is that the total amount of income available for distribution is *not* a fixed amount every year. Rather, it depends on how hard people work, how much initiative and risk they take, and so on. Without rewards for hard work and risk taking, national income would be dramatically smaller than if such rewards existed. Of course, material rewards for effort and risk taking necessarily lead to inequality. But Rawls argues that people would be willing to accept a certain degree of inequality as long as these rewards produced a sufficiently large increase in the total amount of output available for distribution.

How much inequality? Much less than the amount produced by purely competitive factor markets, Rawls argued. The idea is that each person behind the veil of ignorance would rationally fear being in a disadvantaged position, and so each would choose distributional rules that would maximize the income of the poorest citizen. That is, additional inequality would be considered justified as long as it had the effect of raising the income of each and every citizen. Rawls' basic point was that people behind a veil of ignorance would choose rules that would produce a more equal distribution of income than is possible under the marginal productivity system.

Practical reasons for redistribution

The moral argument Rawls outlined has obvious force. But there are also compelling practical reasons for limiting inequality. We saw, for example, that an equal tax levied on every citizen will in general result in an inefficient level of public goods. To the extent that willingness to pay for public goods increases with income, high-income citizens will have every selfish reason to support a tax structure in which they carry a much larger share of the tax burden than do the poor. And to the extent that the public goods financed under such a tax system are equally available to persons of different income levels, the effect will be to reduce inequality.

Recall from Chapter 12 that within any single firm the tendency is for the most productive employees to be paid less than the values of their marginal products, and for the least productive employees to be paid more. The difference between a worker's wage and the value of her marginal product may be interpreted as a compensating differential that reflects her rank within the firm.

These forces in the firm are reflected at the societal level as well. In terms of distribution of income within society, it is obviously advantageous to occupy a higher position. If experience is any guide, social cohesion may simply not be possible without some attempt to compensate people for the implicit burden of occupying low positions in the overall distribution of income.

Fairness and efficiency

No modern economy leaves income distribution entirely to the marketplace. Remember, the market looks after you only if you have money. The fact that the market does not provide what the poor needs is one of the big shortcomings of the market mechanism (capitalism). This underlying commitment to norms of equality is strong, and plays a pivotal role in almost every debate on public policy.

Although the economist's natural advantage lies in answering questions related to efficiency, she also has to get involved in issues related to equity. Virtually every policy change will affect not only efficiency, but also the distribution of income. And we know that most societies seem prepared to reject efficient allocations if they do not pass muster on grounds of fairness.

During an interruption in supply of some important commodity, for example, economists are almost always quick to recommend letting the price rise to market-clearing levels. We know, after all, that this policy will lead to an efficient allocation of the scarce good. The social complaint, however, is that sharply rising prices will impose an unacceptable burden on the poor. And so, in the wake of shortages, governments often reject the free-market path in favour of rationing, queues and other, more cumbersome, methods of distribution.

The unfortunate irony in this response is that inefficient solutions make the economic pie smaller for everyone, rich and poor alike. But merely adopting an efficient policy does not guarantee that everyone will be made better off. So when economists recommend a policy on grounds of efficiency, they must also be prepared to explain how its distributional consequences can be altered to meet social constraints.

Recall the example of local telephone companies in New York that were permitted to charge for calls to directory assistance. Every telephone subscriber was given a 30-cent credit on his telephone bill and each directory assistance call was charged at 10 cents. In Fig. 15.5 the horizontal axis measures directory assistance calls per month, and the vertical axis measures expenditure on all other goods. The horizontal line labelled B_2 represents the budget constraint for a consumer with a monthly income of Y_0 in the event that there is no charge for directory assistance calls. B_1 represents the same person's budget when there is a 10-cent charge for such calls. And B_3 is the budget constraint when there is a 30-cent monthly credit in addition to the 10-cent charge per call. B_3 intersects the B_2 line if three directory assistance calls per month are made. I_1, I_2 and I_3 are indifference curves. They have the conventional shape, except that beyond some number of calls each month they turn upwards, reflecting the fact that most people would not choose to make an unlimited number of calls to directory assistance, even if those calls were free. For the consumer shown, failure to charge for directory assistance calls results in C_3 calls/mth. A simple 10-cent charge results in C_1 calls/mth, a sharply lower number. The 10-cent charge with 30-cent credit results in C_2 calls/mth. On the plausible assumption that 30 cents/mth is a trivial amount of income, even for a poor person, C_2 and C_1 should be almost the same. The 30-cent credit is financed by the cost savings that result when the number of calls falls from C_3 to C_2. This reduction in calls enables the telephone company to run its operations with fewer switchboards and operators – resources that are freed up to do something more useful.

Methods of redistribution

The methods by which society redistributes income are subject to the same kinds of analysis that economists bring to bear on other programmes and institutions. Our principal concern here is that poorly designed redistributive programmes can easily undo the very efficiency gains they were created to facilitate.

Figure 15.5 Charging for directory assistance

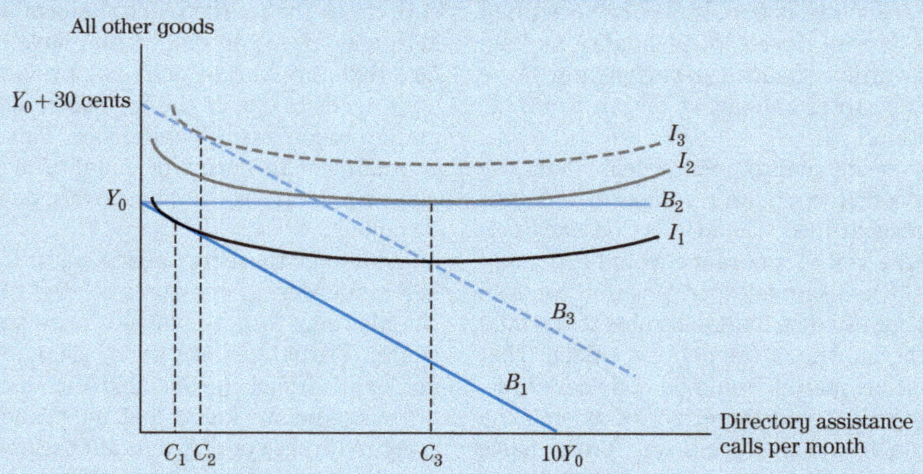

When directory assistance calls are free, the consumer makes C_3 of them each month. Charging 10 cents per call cuts down the volume of these calls to C_1, while a 30-cent credit and a 10-cent per call charge will result in C_2 calls. The new system is more efficient than the old, and places more purchasing power in the hands of the typical customer.

Economic naturalist 15.1

Why are prostitutes worse off today than a century ago?

Tracking the sex trade is difficult because most of the activities are illegal. There are no receipts and researchers have to rely on interviews with lawyers, police, prostitutes and pimps. Some interesting findings of a recent research project undertaken in seven cities in the USA shed some light on the industry.[7] The typical annual income of a street prostitute in 1911 was $25 000 (in 2007 prices); in 2007 it was $18 000. The income of high-end prostitutes/escorts decreased from $430 000 in 1911 to $144 000 in 2007 (again in 2007 prices). In 1911, 69 per cent of white men said they had paid for sex; only 15 per cent did so in 2006. Clearly, the world's oldest profession is far from booming.

Although such statistics must be interpreted with caution as the data may be unreliable, as economists we can analyse this changing trend in terms of demand and supply. A century ago men's demand for commercial sex was higher because non-commercial sex was harder to obtain. Finding a willing partner outside of marriage was much more difficult. At the same time job opportunities for women were much scarcer than today, which is why some were drawn into prostitution. Prostitutes also demanded relatively higher wages to compensate them for the social stigma they experienced. For example, in 1911 street prostitutes earned 385 per cent more than a shop worker; by 2007 that figure was 144 per cent.

Applying the basic principles of demand and supply clearly goes a long way in explaining why a prostitute today is worse off than one working a century ago.

Current welfare programmes

The main problem the poor confront is that they have too little income. The solution may be disarmingly simple: just give them some money. Welfare programmes, however, are much more complicated. In 2015, spending on the more than 17 million South Africans who received some form of social grant accounted for more than 12 per cent of total government spending. The different grants can be summarized as follows. An old age grant (pension) is paid to all South Africans older than 60. For the 2014 financial year, it was pegged at R1280 per month. A disability grant of R1260 per month is paid to citizens older than 18 who have been disabled for more than 6 months and cannot support themselves as a result. War veterans older than 60 who fought in the First or Second World Wars or the Korean War receive R1280 per month. In 2014, 11.9 million people received a child support grant of R290 per month for children under 18. A foster care grant of R800 per month is also paid to foster parents of a child who has been placed in their custody. Parents or foster parents of a child between the ages of 1 and 18 who needs full-time care as a result of severe mental and/or physical disability receive a care dependency grant of R1260 per month. Lastly, institutional grants are paid to welfare organizations, which disburse them to beneficiaries in their care. In 2001, 12.5 million people were employed and 3.8 million people received some form of grant. By 2012, 13.5 million people were employed, but 15.6 million people received grant payments. The increased dependency ratio is obvious.

Costs are obviously attached to ensuring that grants are paid to the people who really qualify for them. High as they are, however, these costs are not the major problem from an efficiency standpoint. Of potentially far greater concern is the effect that current programmes have on work incentives. To illustrate the difficulty, it is necessary first to describe some of the administrative details of such programmes. Once a beneficiary begins to earn more than an established threshold, his benefits are reduced by some fraction of each additional rand earned (or he receives nothing at all). This fraction is called the *marginal benefit reduction rate.* For example, a single parent earning more than R34 800 or a married couple earning more than R69 600 are not eligible for a child support grant. Figure 15.6 shows a hypothetical example of how benefits vary with income for a programme with a full benefit level of R15 000/yr, a threshold income level of R60 000/yr and a marginal benefit reduction rate of 50 per cent.

The real problem emerges when a person participates in several welfare programmes at once, as is common under the current South African system. Consider, for example, a person enrolled in four programmes like the one shown in Fig. 15.7. Once his income reaches R60 000/yr, he will lose R2 in benefits (50 cents from each of the four programmes) for every additional rand he earns. Needless to say, these terms are hardly conducive

[7] 'The economics of prostitution: Sex, lies and statistics', *The Economist*, 22 May 2014.

Figure 15.6 Benefits versus income for a typical welfare programme

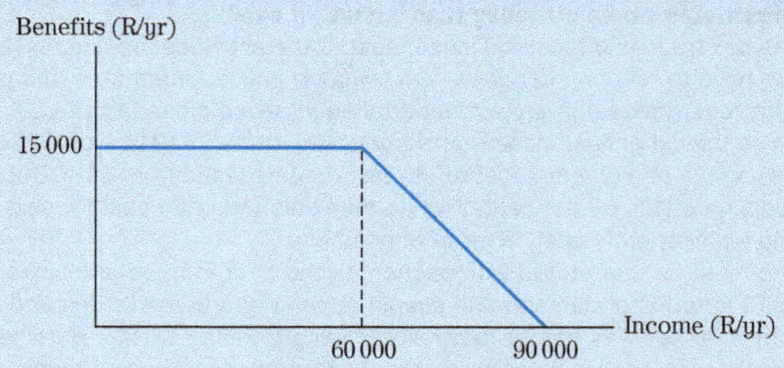

People who earn below R60 000/yr receive the full benefit level of R15 000/yr. For each rand earned above R60 000, benefits go down by 50 cents. Once a person's income reaches R90 000/yr, all benefits cease.

to the expenditure of effort. The adverse effects on labour supply decisions are one of the most serious costs of current welfare systems. Take note that, in South Africa, threshold income levels are applied to almost all grants. If your income is low enough, you receive a grant; if it's too high, you don't. Unfortunately, this system is open to abuse as it provides a clear incentive to either lie about your income or work less hard to ensure you receive a grant.

Negative income tax

In the 2013/2014 financial year more than 16.6 million South Africans (almost a third of the population) received some form of social assistance grant – accounting for R113 billion in total. It implies that for a third of households these state hand-outs are now their biggest source of income. Although we cannot argue against efforts to help the poor, these grants neither offer a way out of poverty nor stimulate economic growth. Based on the data above, on average every recipient of a grant received R6804 in 2014. These high welfare costs, together with the adverse effects on work incentives, lead economist Milton Friedman to propose radical reform in the USA whereby the whole array of welfare programmes would be replaced by a single programme he called the *negative income tax (NIT)*.[8]

Friedman's version of the NIT starts out by giving every man, woman and child – rich or poor – an income tax credit that is large enough to sustain a minimally adequate standard of living. Someone who earned no income would receive this credit in cash. People with earned income would then be taxed on their income at some rate less than 100 per cent. The initial credit and the tax rate combine to determine a break-even income level at which each person's tax liability exactly offsets his initial tax credit. People earning below that level would receive a net benefit payment from the government, while those earning more would make a net tax payment.

Figure 15.7 shows how such a programme would work in South Africa with a tax credit of R60 000/yr and a tax rate of 50 per cent. The break-even income level for these programme values is R120 000/yr. Someone earning R60 000/yr would receive a net benefit payment of R30 000/yr, while someone earning R180 000/yr would make a tax payment of R30 000/yr.

Exercise 15.4

Find the break-even income level for a programme whose tax credit is R60 000 and whose tax rate is 40 per cent. What is the net benefit received by a person who earns R45 000/yr from paid employment?

One strong advantage of the NIT is thus its promise to eliminate the costly overlapping bureaucracies of our current programmes. But the main attraction of the NIT to economists is that it has a much less perverse effect on work incentives than do current programmes. Because the marginal tax rate confronting poor people would

[8] Originally introduced by Milton Friedman in *Capitalism and Freedom*, University of Chicago Press, 1962. More than half a million copies were sold and it was translated into 18 languages.

Figure 15.7 A negative income tax programme

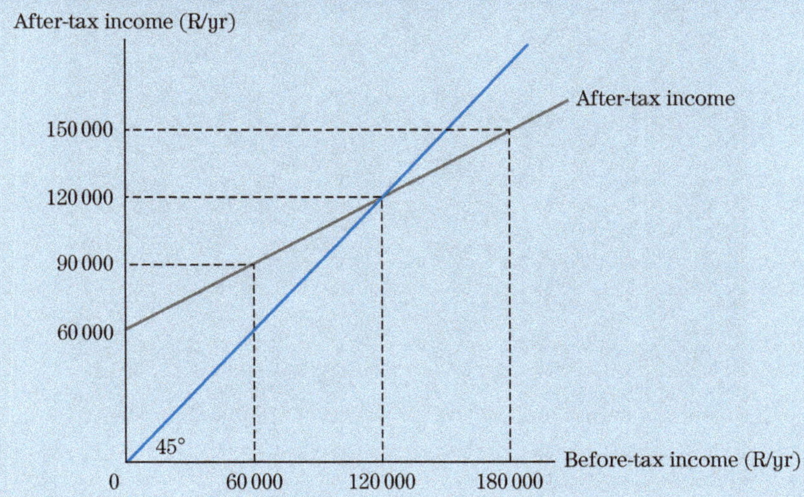

This NIT starts each person off with a tax credit of R60 000/yr. People who earn no income receive that amount in cash. All earned income is then taxed, here at the rate of 50 per cent, resulting in a break-even income level of R120 000/yr. People who earn less than that amount receive a net benefit payment from the government; people who earn more make a net tax payment.

never exceed 100 per cent under the NIT, people would be assured of having more after-tax income if they worked longer hours.

Although the incentive problem is less severe under the NIT than under our current welfare programmes, it remains a serious difficulty. If the NIT is to be the *sole* means of insulating people against poverty, its payment to people with no earned income must be at least as large as the poverty threshold. And if the payment is large enough to live on, it will inevitably induce many people to stop working. In developing countries like South Africa, the NIT would probably also be unaffordable without greatly raising the tax rate, which would obviously be met by fierce resistance.

Public employment for the poor

In 2003, the South African government launched the Expanded Public Works Programme (EPWP) to create more jobs, especially for the poor. These proposals had the obvious appeal of not providing handouts for people who could support themselves. The government planned to create these jobs through public–private investment partnerships, by focusing on labour-intensive sectors and by supporting the Proudly South African campaign to strengthen local businesses. The government also provided skills training, particularly for the unemployed and financially supported black economic empowerment (BEE) programmes. The first phase of the EPWP succeeded in creating 1 million jobs by 2008, a year before the deadline. However, the programme's success must be evaluated in light of the fact that it creates short-term jobs only, not permanent employment.

The second phase of the EPWP was announced by Baleka Mbete, former Deputy President of the Republic of South Africa, in 2009; it aimed to halve unemployment by 2014. This phase put the unemployed to work on labour-intensive public projects such as road building, thereby providing short-term jobs and helping them to learn skills they could use when seeking permanent employment. The programme also aims to provide provinces and municipalities with a fiscal incentive linked to the creation of longer-term stable employment. However, by 2013 the official unemployment rate was still very high, at 25.6 per cent; using the expanded definition it was 36.8 per cent.

A combination of NIT and EPWP

With a few simple changes, however, the EPWP and NIT programmes can be combined in a way that eliminates many of the difficulties we encounter when each is viewed as the sole weapon against poverty.

With EPWP, for example, the government could solicit bids from private contractors to hire unskilled workers at lower-than-normal wages to perform a variety of specified tasks. With the wage set much lower than for private jobs, there would be no reason to fear a massive exodus from the private sector to more comfortable jobs in the public sector.

Workers repairing a road
© iStock.com/eyjafjallajokull

Having public jobs for the poor administered by private contractors chosen through competitive bidding would do much to eliminate the inefficient management that so often plagues government operations. There is general agreement that, given competent management, many useful tasks can be performed by people who lack extensive experience and training. The poor can transport the elderly and disabled in specially equipped vans; fill potholes in city streets; replace burned-out street lamps; transplant seedlings in erosion control projects; remove graffiti from public places; paint government buildings; and recycle newspapers, aluminium and glass containers.

The traditional NIT could be changed by limiting the maximum NIT payment to a figure that, like the EPWP salary, is well below the annual earnings equivalent of full-time employment at the minimum wage. With the payment held below that level, it would not be possible for people to drop out of the labour market to live at taxpayers' expense. Yet when combined with earnings from

Figure 15.8 Income sources in the NIT–EPWP programme

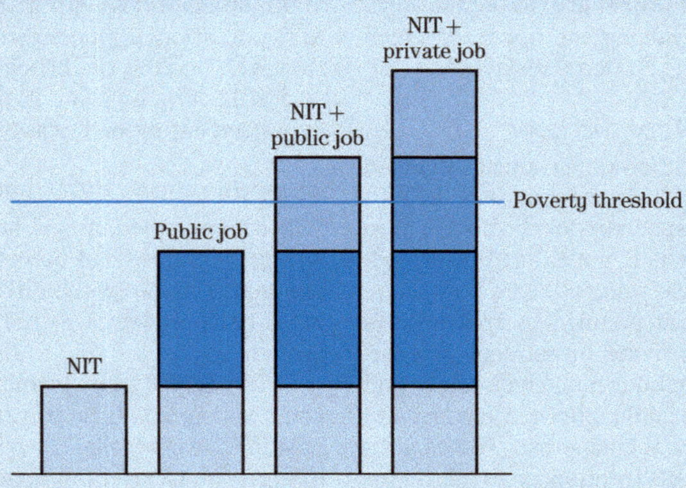

An NIT with a cash grant far too small to live on would not encourage people to drop out of the labour force. Nor would a government-sponsored job at minimum wages lure productively employed workers out of private sector jobs. But the combined income from both programmes would be sufficient to lift people above the poverty threshold. And because of the low pay in public jobs, participants would have strong incentives to continue searching for permanent jobs in the private sector.

the EPWP programme – or, better still, with earnings from a private job – the NIT grant would lift a person above the poverty threshold (see Fig. 15.8). Neither programme alone can accomplish this goal without creating unacceptable side effects; together, however, they can.

The NIT–EPWP combination would not be cheap; but neither is our current system. However, no empirical work on the affordability of such a system has as yet been undertaken for South Africa.

Summary

- Public goods are like other goods in that their value can be measured by what people would be willing to pay to have more of them. But whereas the aggregate demand curve for a private good is formed by adding the individual demand curves horizontally, the aggregate willingness-to-pay curve for a public good is the vertical summation of the corresponding individual curves.
- There is a clear analogy between the demand for public goods and the demand for jointly produced private goods. To produce additional chicken wings, it is necessary to produce additional drumsticks. Just as the quantity of a public good must be the same for all consumers, so must the quantity of chicken wings consumed be exactly equal to the quantity of drumsticks consumed. And just as the price one person is willing to pay for a given quantity of a public good can differ from what another is willing to pay, so will the price of drumsticks generally be different from the price of wings.
- As with private goods, the supply curve of a public good is simply the marginal cost of producing it. The optimal quantity of a public good is the level for which the aggregate willingness-to-pay curve intersects the supply curve. In order to pay for the optimal quantities of public goods, it will generally be necessary for individual tax payments to vary directly with the amounts that individuals are willing to pay for public goods. To the extent that people with higher incomes demand higher quantities of public goods, the result is that both rich and poor will favour a tax system that places a larger share of the total tax burden on the rich.
- The mere fact that a good has the characteristics of a public good does not mean that it must necessarily be provided by government. For example, free commercial television and highly structured collective legal contracts are provided without government involvement.
- Problems similar to those that arise in connection with public goods are encountered whenever there are significant indivisibilities or economies of scale in the production of private-consumption goods. In such situations, we saw, it is common for clubs to form in which members share the costs of important consumption goods.
- Majority voting sometimes produces intransitive rankings among projects. When it does, the power to choose the order in which different pairs of alternatives are considered is often tantamount to the power to determine the final outcome. With respect to single issues in which each voter ranks every alternative in terms of its distance from her ideal choice, the final outcome will be the one most preferred by the median voter, no matter what order the votes are taken in. This result is known as the median voter theorem.
- Cost–benefit analysis is a simple but very powerful alternative to majority voting. Applied in the proper way to a sufficiently large number of small decisions, it almost always satisfies the Pareto criterion.
- Even with a perfect mechanism for revealing public sentiments about the relative desirability of different public goods, there will still be difficult choices about which goods to produce. The problem is that the types of public good strongly favoured by

some groups are often strongly opposed by others. One solution is for voters to group themselves into communities with relatively homogeneous tastes.

- A problem that plagues all mechanisms of public decision making is that self-interested parties have an incentive to influence outcomes in their own favour. This problem goes by the name of rent seeking.
- The primary mechanism for distributing income in market economies is the factor market. People sell their labour in return for a payment equal to the value of their marginal product, and they invest their savings at interest rates that are similarly linked to the marginal productivity of capital. This method of income distribution has several desirable properties on efficiency grounds – in particular, it rewards effort and the willingness to incur risk. But critics, notably John Rawls, have argued that people would never voluntarily choose to live under a process that yields such highly unequal outcomes as we see in untampered factor markets.
- In addition to the moral argument Rawls has offered, there are at least two practical reasons for income redistribution. First, the rich would favour paying more than an equal share of the total tax burden because otherwise they would end up with an inefficiently small provision of public goods. And, second, redistribution may be necessary to maintain a voluntary sense of social cohesion, something in the interests as much of the rich as of the poor.
- Our current array of welfare programmes is costly, not only because of bureaucratic duplication, but also because of its indirect effects on work incentives and on public policies with respect to private markets. A combination of a small negative income tax supplemented by sub-minimum wage public jobs could transfer income to the poor without many of the unintended side effects of the current programmes.

Questions for review

1. Why are the individual willingness-to-pay curves added vertically, not horizontally, to find the aggregate willingness-to-pay curve for a public good?
2. How are jointly produced private goods analogous to public goods?
3. Why would even rich citizens be likely to oppose having equal tax payments by rich and poor alike?
4. In what way does a private good produced under conditions of increasing returns to scale resemble a public good? Describe the trade-off between flexibility and cost that confronts users of such goods.
5. How does majority voting lead to intransitive social rankings?
6. Describe two forms of inefficiency associated with rent seeking.
7. Why is a negative income tax, by itself, unable to solve the redistribution problem?

Problems

1. A government is trying to decide how much of a public good to provide. The willingness-to-pay curves for each of its two citizens are as given in the diagram. The marginal cost curve for the public good is given by $MC = Q/2$, where Q is the quantity of the good. There is also a fixed cost of 10 associated with production of the good.
   - **a** What is the optimal quantity of the public good?
   - **b** If both citizens must be taxed equally to provide the good, will it receive a majority vote?

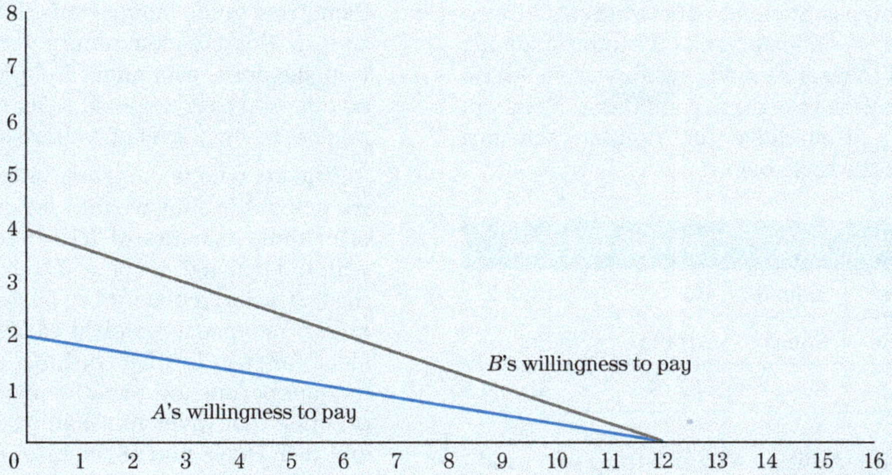

2 On the assumption that the public good described in Problem 1 is provided at the optimal level, how much should the state charge each citizen each time she uses the public good?

3 Ten identical consumers all have individual willingness-to-pay curves $P = 500 - 5Q$ for a public good – say, local parks (where P is measured in rands and Q is measured in hectares). Construct and graph the aggregate willingness-to-pay curve. For 50 ha of parks, what is the maximum each individual would be willing to pay?

4 Consider the scenario described in Problem 3, but now consider that the marginal cost of providing parks measured in rands is $MC = 50Q$. Determine the optimal size of local parks.

5 Chicken wings and chicken drumsticks are jointly produced private goods. The introduction of Ostrich wings – the new fastfood sensation – has lead to a sharp increase in the demand for chicken wings. Show how this affects the equilibrium price and quantity of drumsticks.

6 Lumber and sawdust are joint products, whose demand functions are D_L and D_S, as shown in the diagram. The quantity axis measures the number of trees. Points on the demand schedules indicate demands for the lumber or sawdust equivalents of a given quantity of trees.

   a Provide an economic interpretation of the fact that the demand schedule for sawdust extends below the horizontal axis.

   b If the supply schedule for trees is as given in the diagram, show the equilibrium prices and quantities of sawdust and lumber on a graph.

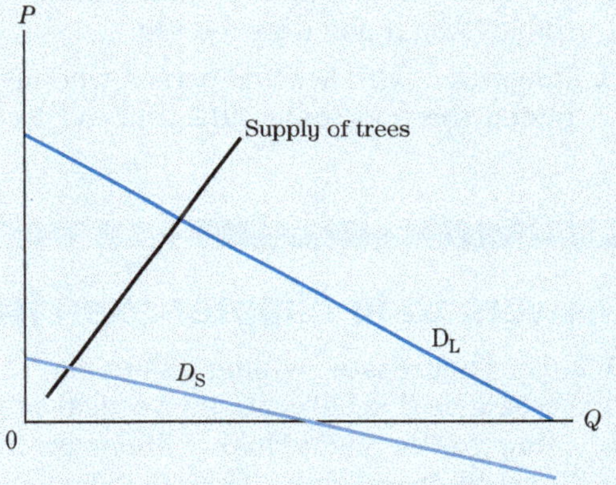

7 Universities commonly name buildings and business or medical schools after substantial donors (witness, for example, the E.G. Malherbe Library at the University of KwaZulu Natal, and later the Carnegie Library on the campus of Stellenbosch University). Meanwhile, few donors care to earmark their gifts for routine maintenance of university buildings. How might the social benefits of charitable giving explain these observations?

8 *True or false*: Because the issues at stake in national elections are much more important than those in local elections, rational choice theory says a much larger proportion of voters will turn out for the former than the latter. Explain.

9 *True or false*: The fact that voter turnout is significantly higher in close rather than one-sided national elections provides clear support for the proposition that voters are rational. Explain.

10 The Business Society, consisting of 20 first-year, 20 second-year and 20 senior students, is about to elect its next president. Arnold, Bo and Chuck are the three candidates. Members of each group have the ranking schemes given in the table below:

Class	Best	Next-best	Last
Seniors	Arnold	Bo	Chuck
Seconds	Chuck	Arnold	Bo
Firsts	Bo	Chuck	Arnold

Fraternity tradition means pitting two candidates against each other, and then pitting the winner of that contest against the third candidate. If you were a second-year student, whom would you pair off in the preliminary round? And if you were a senior?

11 Robyn is a hard-hearted person who favours giving the poor only sufficient aid to keep them from going hungry. Assuming everyone else in Robyn's community feels the same way she does, why might Robyn nonetheless be opposed to a proposal to let each community set its own level of welfare support?

12 A. Katzke, who is currently unemployed, is a participant in four welfare programmes that offer daily benefits of R100 each to people with no earned income. Each programme then curtails its benefits by 50 cents for every rand of income a recipient earns. A. Katzke's identical twin brother, B. Katzke, is enrolled in an experimental negative income tax programme that gives him R400/day in benefits and then taxes him at the rate of 50 per cent on each rand of earned income. Now suppose A. Katzke is offered a job that pays R40/hr, the same wage his brother earns.

a Draw the budget constraint for each twin.

b How many hours would they have to work before A. Katzke ended up with more net cash and benefits than his brother?

Answers to in-chapter exercises

15.1 The aggregate willingness-to-pay curve would be $P = 120 - 2Q$, the vertical summation of the individual willingness-to-pay curves (see graph). For $Q = 30$ min, each individual would be willing to pay up to $P = 12 - 0.2Q = 12 - (0.2 \times 30) = R6$, for a total of R60 from 10 consumers.

15.2 To find the optimal duration of the concert, equate the aggregate willingness-to-pay $P = 120 - 2Q$ and the marginal cost $MC = 2Q$ to find $Q = 30$ min. This is where the MC and willingness-to-pay curves intersect. (See figure below.)

15.3 Again, Tutu is the median voter. The alternative closest to his ideal percentage is 8, and this will win a majority in a vote on any pair of alternatives.

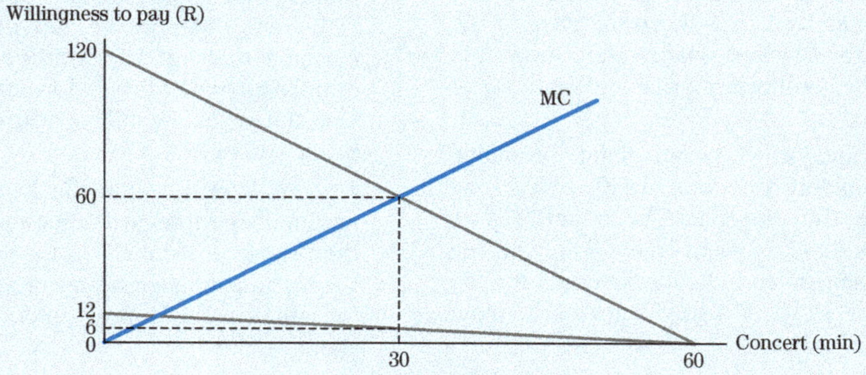

Exercise Answer 15.2

15.4 Let Y^* denote the break-even income level. To calculate Y^*, we solve $60000 + (1 - 0.4)Y^* = Y^*$, which yields $Y^* = R150000$/yr. A person who earns R60000/yr would pay 0.4(R45000) = R18000/yr in taxes, and would thus receive a net annual benefit of R60000 − R18000 = R42000.

Chapter

16

General equilibrium and market efficiency

Hairdressers earn more today than they did 50 years ago, not because they cut hair any faster than they did then, but because productivity has grown so rapidly in the other occupations they could have chosen. By the same token, 210 mm × 297 mm (A4) paper now sells in much greater quantities, not because we have discovered a cheaper way to produce it, but because so many more people now own their own printers, fax machines and photocopiers. And we know that when a frost kills half the coffee crop in Brazil, the price of tea grown in Darjeeling usually rises substantially.

In the preceding chapters we saw occasional glimpses of the rich linkages between markets in the real world. But, for the most part, we ignored these linkages in favour of what economists call *partial equilibrium analysis* – the study of how individual markets function in isolation. One of our tasks in this chapter is to investigate the properties of an interconnected system of markets. This is called *general equilibrium analysis*, and its focus is to make explicit the links that exist between individual markets. It takes into account, for example, the fact that inputs supplied to one market are unavailable for any other, and that an increase in demand in one market implies a reduction in demand in others.

Chapter preview

We shall begin with an illustration of how partial equilibrium analysis differs from general equilibrium analysis. The markets for movie tickets and DVDs (which are substitutes) will be used to illustrate the difference graphically. Then we move on to one of the simplest forms of **general equilibrium analysis**, a pure exchange economy

General equilibrium analysis The study of how conditions in each market in a set of related markets affect equilibrium outcomes in other markets in that set.

with only two consumers and two goods. We shall see that, for any given initial allocation of the two goods between the two consumers, a competitive exchange process always exhausts all possible mutually beneficial gains from trade.

Next we shall add the possibility of production, again using one of the simplest possible models, one with only two inputs, whose total supply is fixed. We shall see that, here too, competitive trading exploits all mutually beneficial gains from exchange.

We shall then add the possibility of international trade, assuming that prices are given externally in world markets. We shall see that even though trade leaves domestic production possibilities unchanged, its immediate effect is to increase the value of goods available for domestic consumption.

From trade, we shall move to the question of how taxes affect the allocation of resources. We shall conclude with a brief discussion of factors that interfere with the efficient allocation of resources.

General equilibrium of two interdependent markets

In our analysis in earlier chapters in the book we did not take into consideration that happenings in one market can influence the working of another market. We briefly touched on substitutes and complementary goods, and on how a change in the price of one good can influence demand for the other good. With general equilibrium analysis, we focus on how more than one market can be in equilibrium simultaneously, and explicitly take feedback effects into account. Assume that the South African government taxes oil imports. The result of that will be that the oil supply curve will shift up and to the left, with an accompanying increase in the price of oil. This may lead to an increase in demand for natural gas (which we can import from Mozambique or produce in small quantities at PetroSA near Mossel Bay), and the demand curve for gas will shift to the right. This will lead to an increase in the price of gas. The effect of the increase in the price of gas will be an increase in the demand for oil, with a resulting increase in the price of oil. Demand for gas will once again increase and its price will rise, leading to an increase in demand for oil . . . and so on. It is difficult to present more than two products (markets) graphically, and we shall restrict ourselves to only two products. However, with mathematics we can extend the example to include as many products as we want to.

Let us work with competitive markets for DVD rentals and movie theatre tickets. These two products are clearly substitute goods, as they satisfy the same consumer want. Let us assume the movie ticket market is initially in equilibrium at a price of R45 where the D_{MOV} and S_{MOV} curves intersect (see Fig. 16.1(a)). Simultaneously, the DVD market is in equilibrium at a price of R24,

Figure 16.1 Two interdependent markets: (a) movie tickets and (b) DVDs

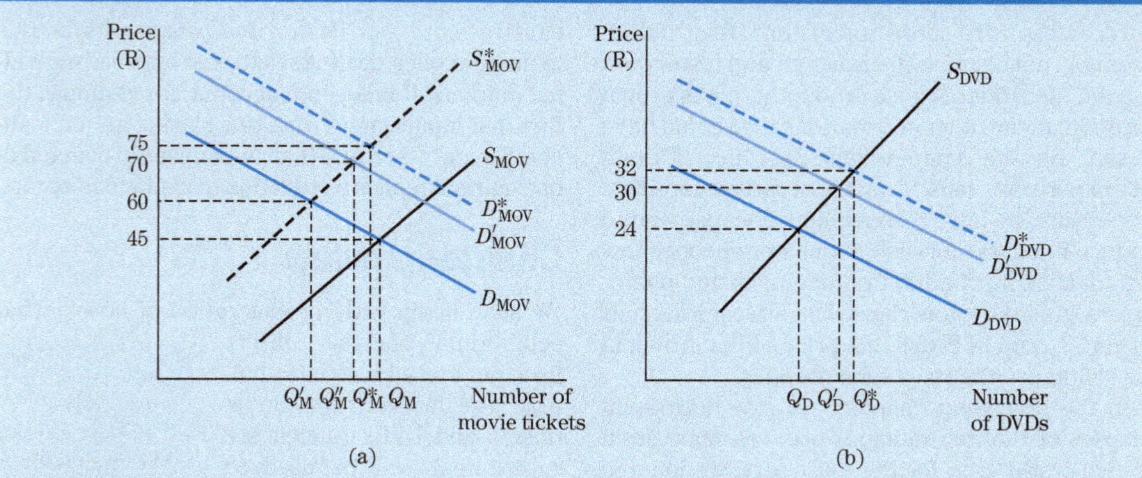

When two markets are interdependent, the activities in one influence the other. Here, a tax on movie tickets shifts the supply of movie tickets from S_{MOV} to S^*_{MOV}, and the price increases from R45 to R60. This causes demand for DVDs to increase to D'_{DVD} and the price to increase to R30, which causes demand for movie tickets to increase to D'_{MOV}, and the price of movies to increase to R70. The process continues until a general equilibrium is reached, where the price of movies is R75 (at the intersection of D^*_{MOV} and S^*_{MOV}) and the price of DVDs is R32 (the intersection of D^*_{DVD} and S_{DVD}).

where the S_{DVD} and D_{DVD} curves intersect (see Fig. 16.1(b)).

Assume that the government levies an entertainment tax of T per movie ticket. The result is that the supply curve of movie tickets shifts vertically up with the size of the tax (or we can say it shifts to the left) to S^*_{MOV}, and the new price of movie tickets is R60. As a result of the price increase, only Q'_M tickets are sold. With partial equilibrium analysis, which we have used throughout the rest of this textbook, everything stops here. However, with general equilibrium analysis we say that the price increase of movie tickets will affect the rental of DVDs. The quality of today's home entertainment systems means that some people may now opt to rent DVDs rather than go to the cinema. The result is an increase in demand for DVDs to D'_{DVD} and an increase in the price of DVDs to R30.

As a result of the increase in the price of DVDs, more people may find it worthwhile to go to the cinema. The demand curve for movie tickets shifts to the right, up to D'_{MOV}, and the price of movies increases to R70. And so the cycle continues until both markets are in equilibrium simultaneously. Movie tickets will cost R75 in equilibrium, where the demand (D^*_{MOV}) for movie tickets equals the supply (S^*_{MOV}) of movie tickets.

The equilibrium price for DVDs of R32 is where the demand and supply curves for DVDs (D^*_{DVD} and S_{DVD}) intersect. These are the correct general equilibrium prices, because the demand and supply curves for DVDs have been drawn on the assumption that the price of movies is R75, and the demand and supply of movies on the assumption that the price of DVDs is R32.

Let us compare the result of the general equilibrium analysis with the equilibrium under partial equilibrium analysis. As was stated above, with partial analysis the introduction of an entertainment tax on movie tickets will result in an increase in the price of movie tickets to R60. With general equilibrium analysis, we concluded that the net result of the entertainment tax will be to increase movie ticket prices to R75. If the two goods are substitutes (as in our example), partial analysis *understates* the effect of the tax. Draw a graph of two complementary goods and convince yourself that partial equilibrium analysis will *overstate* the impact of a tax.

A simple exchange economy

Imagine a simple economy in which there are only two consumers – Julia and Thandi – and two goods, food and clothing. Food and clothing are not produced in this economy. Rather, they arrive in fixed quantities in each time period, just like manna from heaven. To help fix ideas, suppose there is a total of 100 units of food in each time period and a total of 200 units of clothing. An allocation is defined as an assignment of these total amounts between Julia and Thandi; for example, Julia receives 70 units of clothing and 75 units of food and Thandi gets the remaining 130 units of clothing and 25 units of food. In general, if Julia receives F_J units of food and C_J units of clothing,

Economic naturalist 16.1

Why are more people today undertaking research to develop an alternative to gas-guzzling cars than was the case a decade or two ago?

The *Deepwater Horizon* oil disaster in April 2010 was by far the biggest in the history of the petroleum industry. Oil flowed into the Gulf of Mexico for 87 days before the well was capped. Estimates suggest that 4.9 million barrels' worth of oil was discharged. Eleven people died. Although the well was officially declared sealed in September 2010, reports indicate that it continues to leak.

Despite efforts to protect beaches, wetlands and estuaries from the spreading oil, marine and wildlife habitats were extensively damaged and the fishing and tourism industries badly affected. In Louisiana, 4.6 million pounds of oily material was removed from the beaches in 2013, over double the amount collected in 2012. In 2013 it was reported that dolphins and other marine life continued to die in record numbers, with infant dolphins dying at six times the normal rate.

In November 2012, BP and the United States Department of Justice settled federal criminal charges with BP pleading guilty to 11 counts of manslaughter, two misdemeanours and a felony count of lying to Congress. BP was fined a record-breaking $4.525 billion. By February 2013, criminal and civil settlements and payments to a trust fund had cost the company $42.2 billion.

This incident demonstrated the devastating effects on the environment when something goes wrong at an oil well. It was oil on the fire for organizations such as Greenpeace, which demanded that oil companies must be more accountable for their negative impact on the environment. This and the fact that oil is a finite resource means that more research is focused on developing environmental friendly cars than was the case in the recent past.

then Thandi will get 100 – F_J units of food and 200 – C_J units of clothing. The amount of the two goods with which Julia and Thandi begin each time period are called their initial endowments.

In the next section we'll have more to say about where these initial endowments come from, but for now let's take them as externally determined. The question before us here is 'What will Julia and Thandi do with their initial endowments?' One possibility is that they might simply consume them, but only in rare circumstances will that be the best option available. To see why, it is helpful to begin by portraying the initial endowments diagrammatically. Consider again the case in which Julia receives 70 units of clothing and 75 units of food, with the remaining 130 units of clothing and 25 units of food going to Thandi. From earlier chapters, we know how to represent these initial endowments as bundles in two separate food–clothing diagrams. The same allocation can also be represented as a point in a single rectangular diagram – namely, point R in Fig. 16.2. The height of the rectangle corresponds to the total amount of food available per time period, 100 units. Its width is equal to the total amount of clothing, 200 units. O^J is the origin for Julia, and the left and bottom sides of the rectangle are the axes that measure her quantities of food and clothing, respectively. O^T is the origin for Thandi, and movements to the left from O^T correspond to increases in her amount of clothing. Downward movements from O^T correspond to increases in Thandi's amount of food.

Because of the special way the rectangle is constructed, every point that lies within it corresponds to an allocation that exactly exhausts the total quantities of food and clothing available. Thus point R is 70 units to the right of O^J and 130 units to the left of O^T, which means 70 units of clothing for Julia and 130 units for Thandi, for a total of 200. R also lies 75 units above O^J and 25 units below O^T, which means 75 units of food for Julia and 25 for Thandi, for a total of 100. The rectangular diagram in Fig. 16.2 is often referred to as an **Edgeworth exchange box**, after the British economist Francis Y. Edgeworth, who introduced it.

Edgeworth exchange box A diagram used to analyse the general equilibrium of an exchange economy.

Exercise 16.1

Suppose point S in Fig. 16.2 lies 25 units above O^J and 25 units to the right of O^J. Verify that Thandi's initial endowment at S is 75 units of food and 175 units of clothing.

If Julia and Thandi have the initial endowments represented by R, what will they do with them? Their possibilities are either to consume what they already have or to engage in exchange with one another. Exchange is purely voluntary, so trades can take place only if they make *both* parties better off.

Figure 16.2 An Edgeworth exchange box

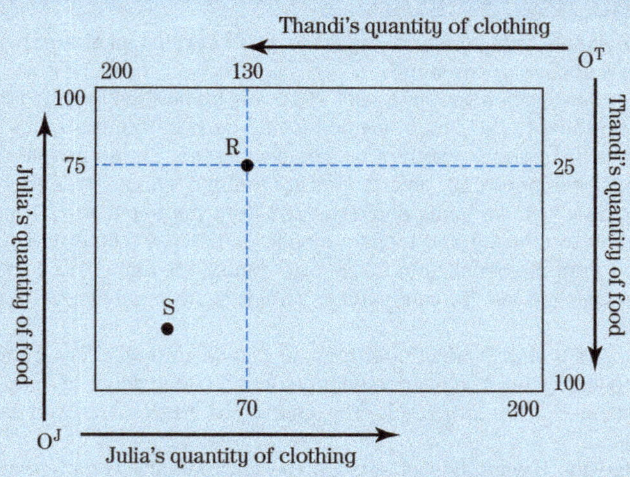

Julia's quantity of food at any point is measured by how far the point lies above O^J. Julia's clothing is measured by how far the point lies to the right of O^J. Thandi's clothing is measured leftwards from O^T, and her food downwards from O^T. At any point within the Edgeworth box, the individual quantities of food and clothing sum to the total amounts available.

Our criterion for saying an exchange makes someone better off is very simple: it must place her on a higher indifference curve. In the Edgeworth box in Fig. 16.3, Julia's indifference map has the conventional orientation, whereas Thandi's is rotated through 180°. (If you have difficulty seeing it, turn the book around by 180° and convince yourself that Thandi's curves are exactly the same as Julia's – just from a different origin.) Thus the curves labelled I_{J1}, I_{J2} and I_{J3} are representative curves from Julia's indifference map, and I_{T1}, I_{T2} and I_{T3} play the corresponding role for Thandi. Julia's satisfaction increases as we move to the northeast in the box; Thandi's as we move to the southwest.

Because we assume that preference orderings are complete, we know that each party will have an indifference curve passing through the initial endowment point R. In Fig. 16.3, these curves are labelled I_{J2} and I_{T2}. Note that Julia's MRS between food and clothing at R (that is, the slope of her indifference curve) is much larger than Thandi's (where the MRS for Thandi is measured with respect to her own food and clothing axes). Suppose, for example, that Julia requires 2 units of food in order to be willing to part with a unit of clothing, whereas Thandi requires only $\frac{1}{2}$ unit of food to make the same exchange. Both parties will then be better off if Julia gives Thandi a unit of food in exchange for a unit of clothing. Indeed, any point in the lens-shaped shaded region in Fig. 16.3 is one for which each party lies on a higher indifference curve than at R. Point T, at which Julia has 65 units of food and 85 units of clothing, is one such point. The two parties can move from R to T by having Julia give Thandi 10 units of food in exchange for 15 units of clothing.

From Fig. 16.4 it is clear that a movement from R to T increased the welfare level of both consumers because they are now on a higher indifference curve. However, the movement from R to T does not exhaust all possible gains from exchange. In Fig. 16.4 there is again a lens-shaped region enclosed by the indifference curves that pass through T by both parties.

Through a process of repeated exchange, Julia and Thandi will finally reach a point at which further mutual gains from trade are no longer possible. The indifference curves for the two parties that pass through any such point will necessarily be tangent to one another, as at point M in Fig. 16.5. (If point M is not a tangent point, they would necessarily enclose yet another lens-shaped region in which further gains from exchange would be possible.) Note that at M the marginal rates of substitution for Julia and Thandi are exactly the same. It was a difference in these rates that provided the original basis for exchange, and once they are the same, all voluntary trading will cease.

Pareto superior allocation An allocation that at least one individual prefers and others like at least as well.

One allocation is said to be **Pareto superior**, or Pareto preferred, to another if at least

Figure 16.3 Gains from exchange

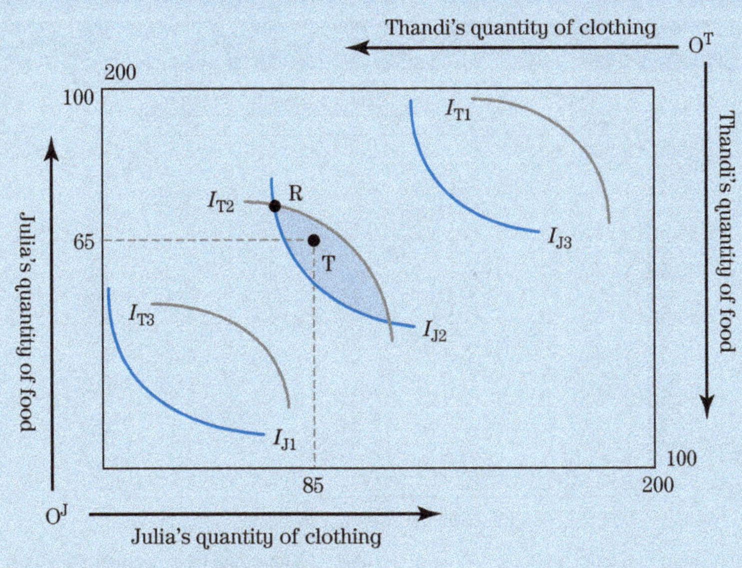

By moving from R to T, each party attains a higher indifference curve.

Figure 16.4 Further gains from exchange

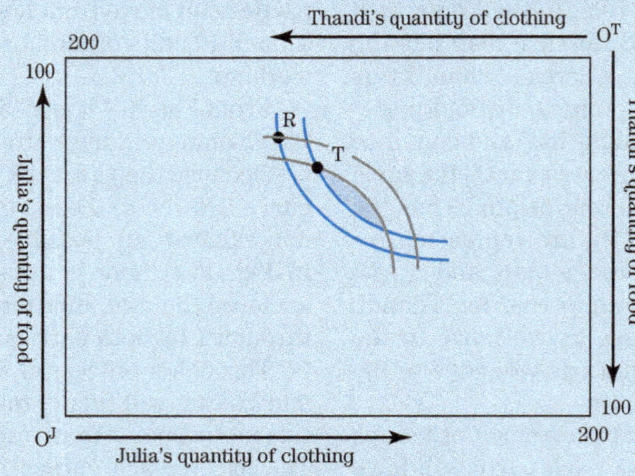

Any point in the shaded region lies on a higher indifference curve for both parties than those that pass through T.

Pareto optimal The term used to describe situations in which it is impossible to make one person better off without making at least some others worse off.

one party prefers it and the other party likes it at least as well. Allocations like the one at M are called **Pareto optimal**. A Pareto-optimal allocation is one for which there is no other feasible reallocation that is preferred by one party and liked at least equally well by the other party. The concept of Pareto optimality was introduced by the nineteenth-century Italian economist Vilfredo Pareto. Pareto-optimal allocations are essentially ones from which further mutually beneficial moves are impossible.

Exercise 16.2

Suppose Julia has an initial allocation of 50 units of food and 100 units of clothing in Fig. 16.5. She regards food and clothing as perfect, one-for-one substitutes. Thandi regards them as perfect, one-for-one complements, always wanting to consume one unit of clothing for every unit of food. Describe the set of allocations that are Pareto preferred to the initial allocation.

In any Edgeworth exchange box, there will be not one but an infinite number of mutual

Figure 16.5 A Pareto-optimal allocation

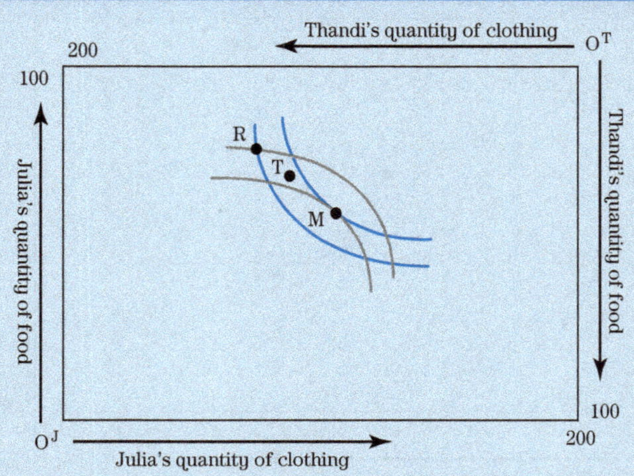

At the allocation M, no further mutually beneficial exchange is possible. The marginal rate of substitution of food for clothing is the same for both parties at M.

Figure 16.6 The contract curve

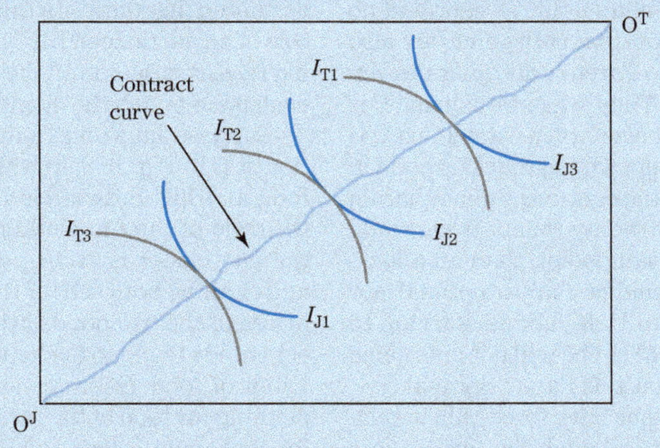

The locus of mutual tangencies in the Edgeworth exchange box is called the contract curve. Any point on the contract curve is an efficient way to divide the two goods between the two consumers.

Contract curve A curve along which all final, voluntary contracts must lie.

tangencies, as illustrated in Fig. 16.6. The locus of these tangencies is called the **contract curve**, a name that was chosen because it describes where all final, voluntary contracts between rational, well-informed persons must lie. Put another way, the contract curve identifies all the efficient ways of dividing the two goods between the two consumers.

Where our consumers end up on the contract curve naturally depends on the initial endowments with which they start. Suppose they start with the one labelled F in Fig. 16.7. We can then say that they will end up somewhere on the contract curve between points U and V. Given that they are starting from F, the best possible outcome from Julia's point of view is to end up at V. Thandi, of course, would most prefer U. Whether they end up closer to U or to V depends on the relative bargaining skills of the two traders. Had they instead started at the allocation G, they would have ended up between W and Z on the contract curve.

The uses and limitations of the two Pareto criteria – Pareto preferred and Pareto optimal – can be seen by an examination of some of the points in Fig. 16.7. Note, for example, that both W and Z are Pareto preferred to the original allocation G. This

Figure 16.7 Initial endowments constrain final outcomes

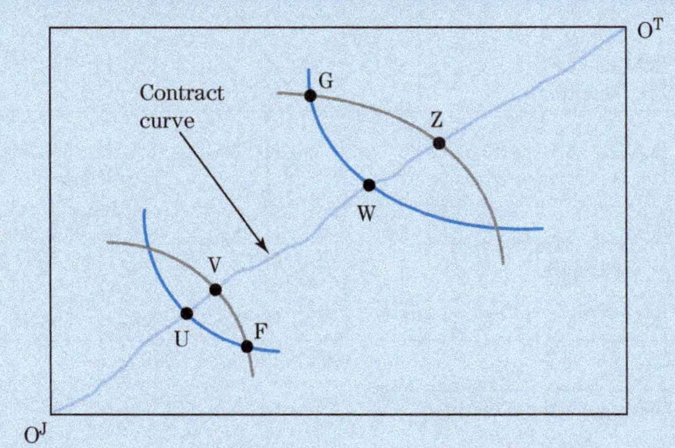

Starting from F, traders will move to a point on the contract curve between U and V. They will land closer to V the better Julia's bargaining skills are relative to Thandi's. If they start at G, they will end up between W and Z on the contract curve.

follows because W is better than G from Thandi's point of view and no worse from Julia's; and, similarly, Z is better from Julia's point of view and no worse from Thandi's. Note that both points are also Pareto optimal. The two Pareto criteria are essentially relative in nature. Thus, when we say that U is Pareto preferred to F, or even when we say that U is Pareto optimal, we are not saying that U is good in any absolute sense. On the contrary, Julia is hardly likely to find U very attractive, and it is certainly much worse, from her standpoint, than an allocation like G, which is neither Pareto optimal nor even Pareto preferred to U. If Julia is starving to death in a tattered coat at U, she will not take much comfort in being told that U is Pareto optimal.

The Pareto criteria thus have force only in relation to the allocation with which the two players begin. Rather than remain at an initial allocation, both will always agree to move to one that is Pareto preferred and, indeed, to keep on moving until they reach one that is Pareto optimal.

In the simple, two-person economy described above, exchange took place through a process of personal bargaining. In market economies, by contrast, most exchanges have a much more impersonal character. People have given endowments and face given prices, and then decide how much of the various goods and services they want to buy and sell. We can introduce market-type exchange into our simple economy by the simple expedient of assuming that there is a third person who plays the role of an auctioneer. His function is to keep adjusting relative prices until the quantities demanded of each good match the quantities supplied.

Suppose Julia and Thandi start with the allocation at E in Fig. 16.8, in which each has 50 units of food and 100 units of clothing. Suppose also that the ratio of food to clothing prices announced by the auctioneer is $P_{C0}/P_{F0} = 1$, meaning that food and clothing both sell for the same price. When the prices of the two goods are the same, the auctioneer stands ready to exchange 1 unit of clothing for 1 unit of food. (More generally, he will exchange clothing for food at the rate of P_{C0}/P_{F0} units of food for each unit of clothing.) Note that, with the given initial endowments, this rate of exchange uniquely determines the budget constraints for both Julia and Thandi. We know that E has to be a point on each person's budget constraint, because each has the option of simply consuming all of her initial endowment. But suppose that Julia wants to sell some food and use the proceeds to buy more clothing. She can do this by moving downwards from E along the line labelled HH′. Alternatively, if she wants to sell clothing to buy more food, she can move upwards along HH′. The same HH′, seen

Figure 16.8 A disequilibrium relative price ratio

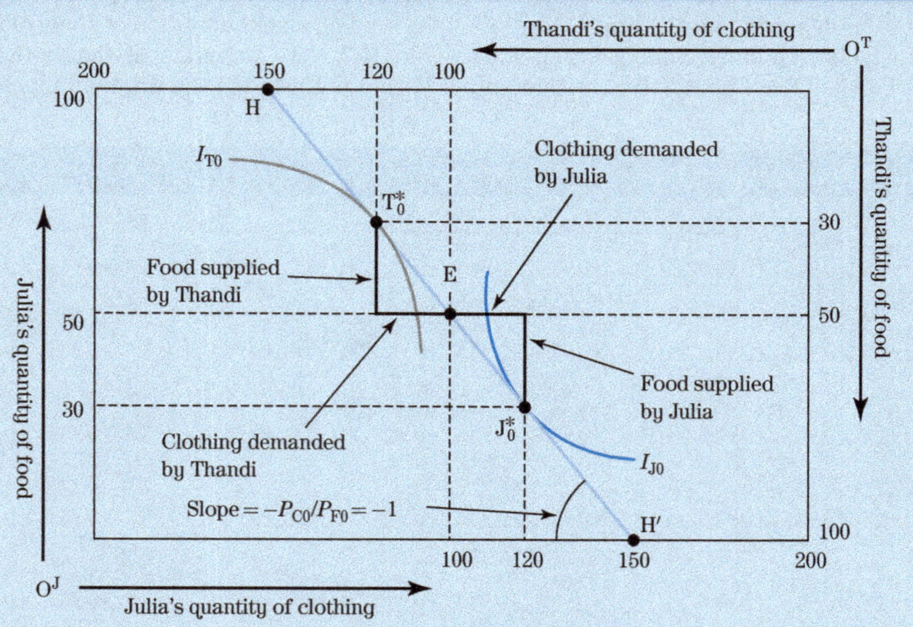

At the price ratio $P_{C0}/P_{F0} = 1$, both Julia and Thandi want to sell 20 units of food and buy 20 more units of clothing. But in general equilibrium, the amount sold by one party must equal the amount bought by the other. Both the food and clothing markets are out of equilibrium here.

from Thandi's point of view, constitutes the budget constraint for Thandi.

Given their budget constraints and preferences, Julia and Thandi face a simple choice problem of the sort we discussed in Chapter 3. The optimal bundle for Julia on the budget HH′ is the one labelled J_0^* in Fig. 16.8, in which she consumes 30 units of food and 120 units of clothing. The corresponding bundle for Thandi is labelled T_0^*, and it too contains 30 units of food and 120 units of clothing. Note that by choosing J_0^*, Julia indicates that she wants to sell 20 units of her initial endowment of food in order to buy 20 units of additional clothing. Similarly, by choosing T_0^*, Thandi indicates that she too wants to sell 20 units of food and buy 20 more units of clothing.

This creates a problem, however. There are only 200 units of clothing to begin with, and the initial endowments of clothing at E add to precisely that amount. It is thus mathematically impossible for each person to have more clothing. By the same token, it is not possible for each person to sell food. The auctioneer in this exercise is a figment, a hypothetical person who calls out relative prices in the hope of stimulating mutually beneficial exchange. He acts as a middleman, arranging for clothing to be exchanged for an equivalent value of food. But if everyone wants to sell food and buy clothing, there is no such exchange he can arrange.

At the price ratio $P_{C0}/P_{F0} = 1$ there is excess demand for clothing and excess supply of food. At this price ratio the markets are not in general equilibrium. The solution to this problem is straightforward: the auctioneer simply calls out a new price ratio, in which the price of clothing relative to food is higher than before. If there is still excess demand for clothing, he calls out a still higher price ratio, and so on, until the excess demand in each market is exactly zero.[1] Starting with the allocation at E, the price ratio $(P_C/P_F)^*$ that produces general equilibrium is shown in Fig. 16.9. On the new budget line H_1H_1' through E with slope $(P_C/P_F)^*$, the highest attainable indifference curves for Julia and Thandi are tangent. In order to move from E to the bundle J*, Julia must purchase exactly the quantity of food (12 units) that Thandi wishes to sell. And for Thandi to move from E to the bundle T*, she must purchase exactly the quantity of clothing

Figure 16.9 General equilibrium

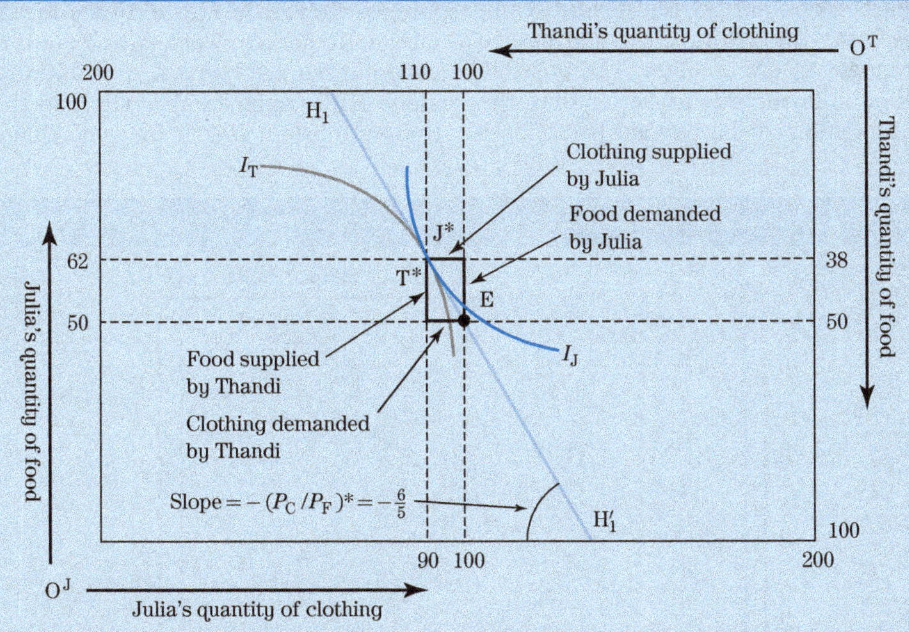

A simple exchange economy is in equilibrium when excess demands for both products are exactly equal to zero. At the price ratio $(P_C/P_F)^* = \frac{6}{5}$, Julia wants to buy 12 units of food, which is exactly the amount Thandi wants to sell; also, Julia wants to sell 10 units of clothing, which is exactly the amount Thandi wants to buy.

[1] In advanced courses, we show that a competitive equilibrium will exist in a simple exchange economy if the sum of all individual excess demands is a continuous function of relative prices. This will always happen whenever individual indifference curves have the conventional convex shape.

(10 units) that Julia wishes to sell. In this illustration, excess demands for both products are exactly equal to zero at the price ratio $(P_C/P_F)^* = \frac{6}{5}$.

Only relative prices are determined

From the information given in our simple exchange model, note that we are able to determine only the ratio of clothing prices to food prices, not the actual value of individual prices. If, for example, $P_C = 6$ and $P_F = 5$ produce a budget constraint with the slope shown in Fig. 16.9, then so will the prices $P_C = 12$ and $P_F = 10$, or indeed any other pair of prices whose ratio is doubling or halving. In real terms, such price movements leave budget constraints unchanged.

Competitive equilibrium in consumption

We are now in a position to consider whether the following statement by Adam Smith is true:

> An equilibrium produced by competitive markets will exhaust all possible gains from exchange.

It basically means that equilibrium in competitive markets is Pareto optimal. At the general equilibrium allocation, the optimizing indifference curves are tangent to one another. The possible allocations that Julia regards as better than the equilibrium allocation all lie beyond her budget constraint, and the same is true for Thandi. And since the two budget constraints coincide in the Edgeworth box, this means that there is no allocation that both prefer to the equilibrium allocation, which is just another way of saying that the equilibrium allocation is Pareto optimal.

According to Smith, every competitive equilibrium allocation – like D in Fig. 16.10 – is efficient. But suppose you are a social critic, and don't like that particular allocation; you feel that Thandi gets too much of each good and Julia too little. The problem, in your view, was that the initial endowment point – J in the diagram – is unjustly favourable to Thandi. Suppose there is some other allocation on the contract curve – such as E – that you find much more equitable. Is there a set of initial endowments and relative prices for which E will be a competitive equilibrium? This brings us to another theorem, that:

> Any allocation on the contract curve can be sustained as a competitive equilibrium.

The basic condition that ensures this result is that consumer indifference curves be convex when viewed from the origin. We know that an allocation such as E, or any other efficient allocation, lies at a point of tangency between indifference curves. In Fig. 16.10 the locus HH′ is the mutual tangent between I_{J2} and I_{T2}. If the indifference curves are convex, any initial endowment along HH′ – such as M – will lead to a competitive equilibrium at E. If we redistribute the initial

Figure 16.10 Sustaining efficient allocations

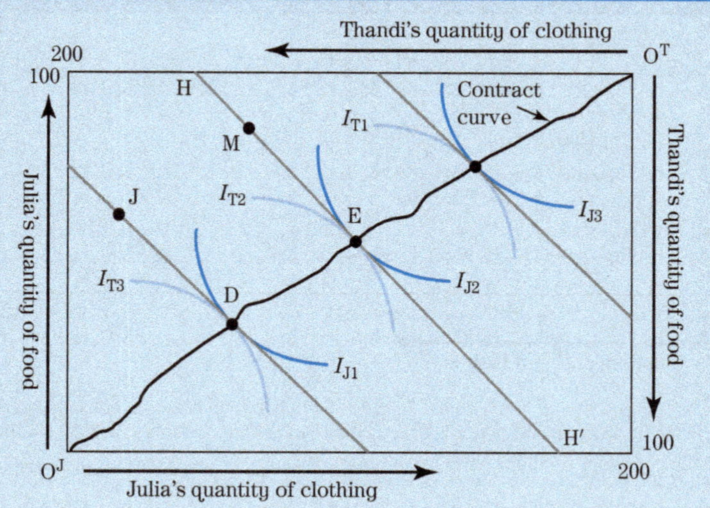

If indifference curves are convex, any efficient allocation can be sustained through a suitable choice of initial endowments and relative prices. To sustain E, for example, we announce a relative price ratio equal to the slope of HH′, the mutual tangent to I_{J2} and I_{T2}, and give consumers an initial endowment bundle that lies anywhere on HH′, such as M.

endowments from J to M, and announce a price ratio equal to the slope of HH′, Julia and Thandi will then be lead by market forces to E. Indeed, any point along the contract curve can be reached in this fashion by a suitable choice of initial endowments and relative prices.

If we are free to move from J to M in Fig. 16.10, then we ought to be able to move directly to E and cut out the intervening steps. Why, then, do we bother with the intermediate steps of announcing prices and allowing people to make trades? The difficulty in practice is that the social institutions responsible for redistributing income have little idea of the shapes and locations of individual consumer indifference curves. People know their own preferences much better than do governments. And for an initial endowment of given value, they will generally achieve a much better result if they are free to make their own purchase decisions. The competitive equilibrium illustrates that the issue of equity in distribution is logically separable from the issue of efficiency in allocation. As the nineteenth-century British economist John Stuart Mill saw clearly, society can redistribute incomes in accordance with whatever norms of justice it deems fitting, at the same time relying on market forces to ensure that those incomes are spent to achieve the most good.

Efficiency in production

In our simple exchange model, the total supply of each good was given externally. We now add a productive sector to our exchange economy, one with two firms, each of which employs two inputs – capital (K) and labour (L) – to produce either of two products, food (F) or clothing (C). Suppose firm C produces clothing and firm F produces food. In order to keep the model simple, suppose that the total quantities of the two inputs are fixed at $K = 50$ and $L = 100$, respectively. Suppose, finally, that the production processes employed by the two firms give rise to conventional, convex-shaped isoquants.

Just as the Edgeworth exchange box provided a convenient way to summarize the conditions required for efficiency in consumption, a similar analysis serves an analogous purpose in the case of production. Figure 16.11 is called an *Edgeworth production box*. O^C represents the origin of the clothing firm's isoquant map, and O^F the origin of the food firm. Any point within the box represents an allocation of the total inputs to firm C and firm F. Firm C's isoquants correspond to increasing quantities of clothing as we move to the northeast in the box; firm F's correspond to increasing quantities of food as we move to the southwest.

Suppose the initial allocation of inputs is at point R in Fig. 16.11. We know that this allocation cannot be efficient, because we can move to any point within the shaded lens-shaped region and obtain both more food and more clothing (or more food while clothing stay the same, or vice versa). As in the consumption case, the contract curve is the locus of efficient allocations, which here is the locus of tangencies between isoquants. Recalling from Chapter 7 that the slope at any point of an isoquant is the marginal rate of technical substitution (MRTS), meaning that it is the ratio at which labour can be exchanged for capital without altering the total amount of output. The MRTS between K and L must be the same for both firms at every point along the contract curve.

Suppose the equilibrium food and clothing prices are P_F^* and P_C^*, respectively. Suppose also that the two firms hire labour and capital in perfectly competitive markets at the hourly rates of w and r, respectively. If the firms maximize their profits the resulting general equilibrium will satisfy the requirements of efficiency in production, namely, that the MRTS between capital and labour will be the same for each firm.

To see why, first note that a firm that maximizes its profits must also be minimizing its costs. Recall from Chapter 8 that the following conditions must be satisfied if the firms are minimizing costs:

$$\frac{\text{MP}_{L_C}}{\text{MP}_{K_C}} = \frac{w}{r} \quad \left(\text{or } \frac{\text{MP}_{L_C}}{w} = \frac{\text{MP}_{K_C}}{r}\right) \tag{16.1}$$

and

$$\frac{\text{MP}_{L_F}}{\text{MP}_{K_F}} = \frac{w}{r} \quad \left(\text{or } \frac{\text{MP}_{L_F}}{w} = \frac{\text{MP}_{K_F}}{r}\right) \tag{16.2}$$

where MP_{L_C} and MP_{K_C} are the marginal products of labour and capital in clothing production, and MP_{L_F} and MP_{K_F} are the corresponding marginal products in food production. Recall, too, that the ratio of marginal products of the two inputs is equal to the marginal rate of technical substitution. Since both firms pay the same prices for labour and capital, Eqs 16.1 and 16.2 tell us that the marginal rates of technical substitution for the two firms will be equal in competitive equilibrium ($\text{MRTS} = \text{MP}_L/\text{MP}_K$ for both firms, and also $\left(\frac{MP_L}{w} = \frac{MP_K}{r}\right)$. And this tells us, finally, that competitive general equilibrium is efficient, not only in

Figure 16.11 An Edgeworth production box

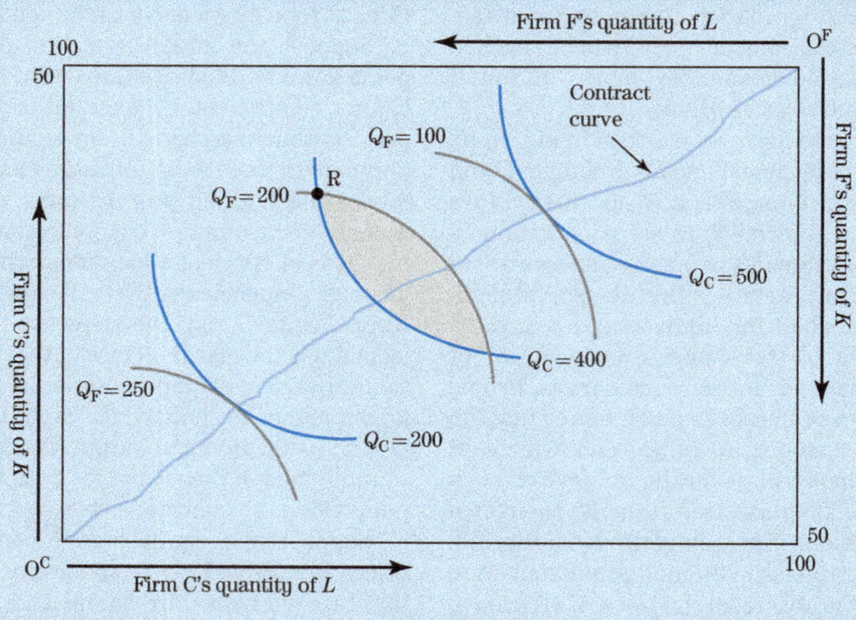

Firm C's quantity of capital at any point is measured by how far the point lies above O^C. Firm C's quantity of labour is measured by how far the point lies to the right of O^C. The corresponding values of firm F's inputs are measured downwards and leftwards, respectively, from O^F. At any point within the Edgeworth production box, the separate input allocations to the two firms add up to the total amounts available, $K = 50$ for capital, $L = 100$ for labour. The contract curve is the locus of tangencies between isoquants.

the allocation of a given endowment of consumption goods, but also in the allocation of the factors used to produce those goods.

Exercise 16.3

For an economy like the one described above, suppose the price per unit of labour and the price per unit of capital are both equal to R40/hr. Suppose also that in clothing production we have $MP_{L_C}/MP_{K_C} = 2$ and that in food production we have $MP_{L_F}/MP_{K_F} = \frac{1}{2}$. Is this economy efficient in production? If not, how should it reallocate its inputs?

Efficiency in product mix

An economy could be efficient in production and at the same time efficient in consumption, and yet do a poor job of satisfying the wants of its members. This could happen if, for example, the economy is producing more clothing than consumers want. The production quantities could be allocated efficiently and the inputs could be allocated efficiently. But everyone would be happier if there were less clothing and more food. There is thus one additional efficiency criterion of concern, namely, whether the economy has an efficient mix of the two products.

To define an efficient product mix, it is helpful first to translate the contract curve from the Edgeworth production box into a **production possibilities frontier**, the set of all possible output combinations that can be produced with given quantities of capital and labour. Every point along the contract curve gives rise to specific quantities of clothing and food. Suppose $F_C(K, L)$ and $F_F(K, L)$ denote the production functions for clothing (firm C) and food (firm F), respectively. Point O^C in the top panel in Fig. 16.12 represents what happens when we allocate all the inputs (50 units of capital, 100 units of labour) to food production and none to clothing. If $F_F(50, 100) = 275$, then the product mix to which this allocation gives rise has zero units of clothing and 275 units of food, and is shown by point O^C in the bottom panel. Point O^F in the top panel in Fig. 16.12 represents what happens when we allocate all the inputs to clothing production and none to food. If $F_C(50, 100) = 575$, then the product mix to which this allocation gives rise has 575 units of clothing

Production possibilities frontier The set of all possible output combinations that can be produced with a given endowment of factor inputs.

Figure 16.12 Generating the production possibilities frontier

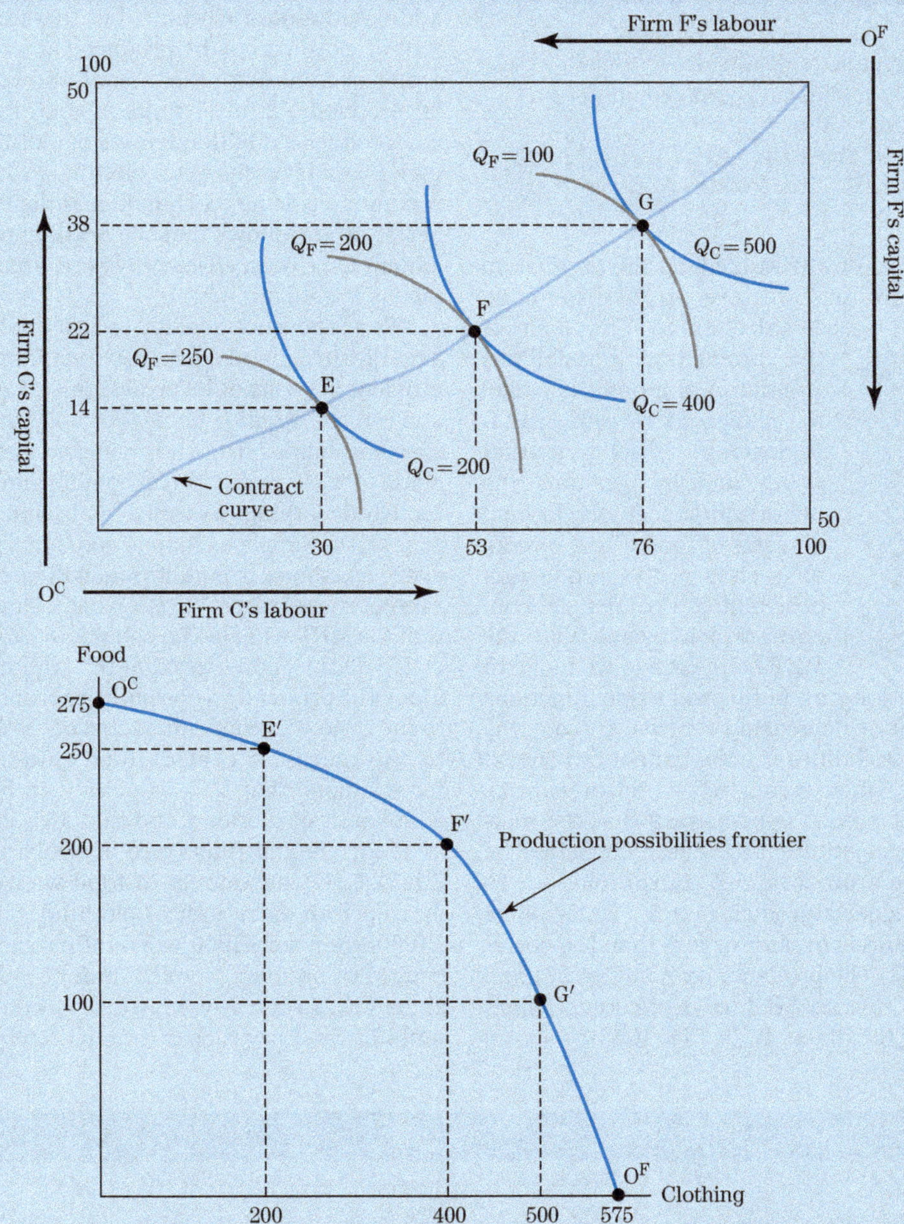

Each point on the contract curve in the Edgeworth production box (top panel) gives rise to specific quantities of food and clothing production. The food–clothing pairs that lie along the contract curve are plotted in the bottom panel, and their locus is called the production possibilities frontier. Movements to the northeast along the contract curve correspond to movements downwards along the production possibilities frontier.

and zero units of food, and is shown by point O^F in the bottom panel. The product mix corresponding to point E in the top panel has $F_C(14, 30) = 200$ units of clothing and $F_F(36, 70) = 250$ units of food, and is shown by point E' in the bottom panel. Similarly, the product mix at F in the top panel has $F_C(22, 53) = 400$ units of clothing and $F_F(28, 47) = 200$ units of food, and corresponds to F′ in the bottom panel. Likewise, G in the top panel has $F_C(38, 76) = 500$ units of clothing and $F_F(12, 24) = 100$ units of food, and corresponds to G′ in the bottom panel. By plotting other correspondences in like fashion, we can generate the entire production possibilities frontier shown in the bottom panel.

Exercise 16.4

In the economy shown in Fig. 16.12, suppose that a technical change occurs in the clothing industry that makes any given combination of labour and capital yield twice as much clothing as before. Show the effect of this change on the production possibilities frontier.

As we move downwards along the production possibilities frontier, we give up food for additional clothing. The slope of the production possibilities frontier at any point is called the **marginal rate of transformation (MRT)** at that point, and it measures the opportunity cost of clothing in terms of food. For the economy shown, the production possibilities frontier is concave, which means that the MRT increases as we move to the right. As long as both production functions have constant or decreasing returns to scale, the production possibilities frontier cannot be convex.

Marginal rate of transformation (MRT) The rate at which one output can be exchanged for another at a point along the production possibilities frontier.

In order for an economy to be efficient in terms of its product mix, it is necessary that the marginal rate of substitution for every consumer be equal to the marginal rate of transformation. To see why, consider a product mix for which some consumer's MRS is greater or less than the corresponding MRT. The product mix Z in Fig. 16.13(a), for instance, has an MRT of 1, whereas Julia's consumption bundle at W in Fig. 16.13(b) shows that her MRS is 2. This means that Julia is willing to give up 2 units of food in order to obtain an additional unit of clothing, but that an additional unit of clothing can be produced at a cost of only 1 unit of food. With the capital and labour saved by producing 2 fewer units of food for Julia, we can produce 2 additional units of clothing. We can give 1.5 units of this extra clothing to Julia and the remaining 0.5 unit to Thandi, making both parties better off. It follows that the original product mix cannot have been efficient (where, again, efficient means Pareto optimal).

We are now in a position to ask, finally, whether a market in general competitive equilibrium will be efficient in terms of its product mix. Here, too, the answer turns out to be yes, provided the production possibilities frontier is concave. Let P_F^* and P_C^* again denote competitive equilibrium prices for food and clothing. As we have already seen in the case of the simple exchange economy, the MRS of every consumer in equilibrium will be equal to the ratio of these prices, P_C^*/P_F^*. What we must show is that the MRT will also be equal to P_C^*/P_F^*.

To do this, note first that the MRT at any point along the production possibilities frontier is equal to the ratio of the marginal cost of clothing (MC_C) to the marginal cost of food (MC_F). Suppose, for example, that MC_C at point Z in Fig. 16.14 is R1000/unit of clothing and that MC_F is R500/unit of food. The marginal rate of transformation at Z is $\Delta F/\Delta C$, the amount of food we have to give up to get an extra unit of clothing. Since MC_C is R1000, we need R1000 worth of extra labour and capital to produce an extra unit of clothing. And since MC_F is R500, we have to produce 2 fewer units of food in order to free up R1000 worth of

Figure 16.13 An inefficient product mix

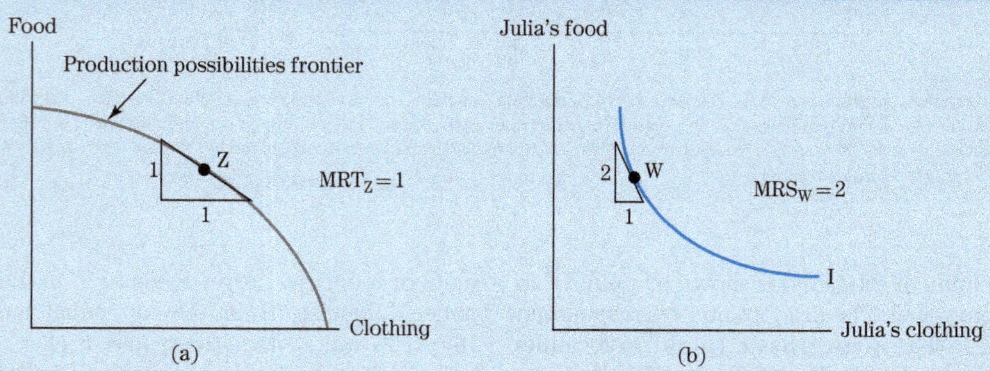

At the product mix Z (panel a), the MRT is smaller than Julia's MRS at W (panel b). By producing 2 fewer units of food, we can produce 2 additional units of clothing. If we give 1.5 of these extra units to Julia and the remaining 0.5 unit to Thandi, both parties will be better off. Efficiency requires that every consumer's MRS be exactly equal to the economy's MRT.

Figure 16.14 MRT equals the ratio of marginal costs

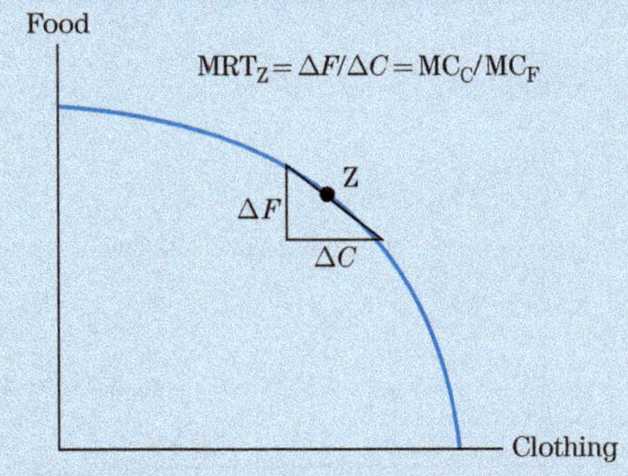

At Z, to produce an extra unit of clothing requires MC_C worth of labour and capital. Each unit less of food we produce at Z frees up MC_F worth of labour and capital. To get an extra unit of C, we must give up MC_C/MC_F units of food, and so the marginal rate of transformation is equal to MC_C/MC_F.

labour and capital. MRT at Z is therefore equal to 2, which is exactly the ratio of MC_C to MC_F:

$$MRT = \frac{MC_C}{MC_F} \tag{16.3}$$

We also know that the equilibrium condition for competitive food and clothing producers is that product prices be equal to the corresponding values of marginal cost:

$$P_F^* = MC_F \tag{16.4}$$

and

$$P_C^* = MC_C \tag{16.5}$$

Dividing Eq. 16.5 by Eq. 16.4, we have

$$\frac{P_C^*}{P_F^*} = \frac{MC_C}{MC_F} \tag{16.6}$$

which establishes that the equilibrium product price ratio is indeed equal to the marginal rate of transformation.

When output and input markets are competitive, production will be efficient if MRS equals MRT. However, if the quantity demanded does not equal the quantity produced, the result is either shortages or surpluses in production. This can be illustrated with the aid of Fig. 16.15. Let us assume that the market generates a price ratio of P_C^1/P_F^1. If producers are producing efficiently, they will produce at point A; in other words, C_1 units of clothing and F_1 units of food. When consumers are faced with this budget constraint they will consume at point B, where they maximize their level of satisfaction by operating on the highest indifference curve, I_2. Producers are producing C_1 units of clothing, but consumers want to consume C_2. There is thus a shortage of clothing. The reverse is true for food. Producers are producing F_1 units of food, but consumers want to consume only F_2 units, leading to an oversupply of food.

Figure 16.15 Competition and output efficiency

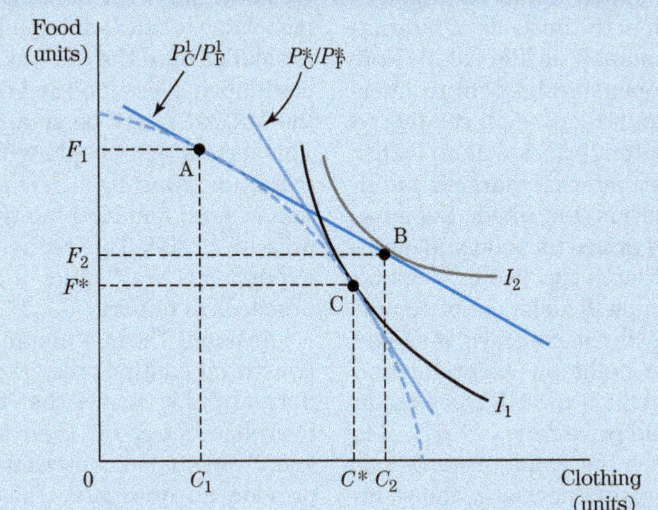

In competitive output and input markets, consumers consume at a point where MRS is equal to the price ratio, and producers choose their output levels so that MRT is equal to the price ratio. If MRS equals MRT, the market is efficient. To be in equilibrium the quantity of each good produced must equal the quantity of those goods consumed.

In competitive markets shortages and surpluses will be corrected by the price mechanism. Because there is a shortage in clothing, the price of clothing will increase. The surplus of food will lead to a reduction in the price of food. The result will be that the slope of the price line will increase and move along the production possibility frontier. The market will be in equilibrium if the price ratio is P_C^*/P_F^* at C. Here, consumers demand F^* units of food, and these are what are being produced. Similarly, C^* units of clothing are produced and consumed. Once again, the MRS equals the MRT and the competitive equilibrium is efficient.

To summarize, we have now established that an economy in competitive general equilibrium will, under certain conditions, be simultaneously efficient (Pareto optimal) in consumption, in production and in the choice of product mix. As we have already seen, a society with a Pareto-optimal allocation of resources is not necessarily a good society. The final equilibrium in the marketplace depends very strongly on the distribution of initial endowments, and if this distribution isn't fair, we have no reason to expect the competitive equilibrium to be fair.

Gains from international trade

In our simple model of exchange and production, we saw why efficiency requires that every consumer's MRS be equal to the economy's MRT. This same requirement must be satisfied even for an economy that is free to engage in foreign trade. To illustrate, consider an economy just like the one we discussed, and suppose that its competitive general equilibrium in the absence of international trade occurs at point V in Fig. 16.16. Now suppose that country opens its borders to international trade. If the country is small relative to the rest of the world, output prices will no longer be determined in its own internal markets, but in the much larger international markets. Suppose, in particular, that world prices for food and clothing are P_F^w and P_C^w, respectively. The best option available to this economy will no longer be to produce and consume at V. On the contrary, it should now produce at Z, the point on its production possibilities frontier at which the MRT is exactly equal to the international price ratio, P_C^w/P_F^w. Z is the point that maximizes the value of its output in world markets. Having produced at Z, the country is then free to choose any consumption point along its *international budget constraint*, BB′. Since the original competitive equilibrium point, V, lies within BB′, we know that it is now possible

Figure 16.16 Gains from international trade

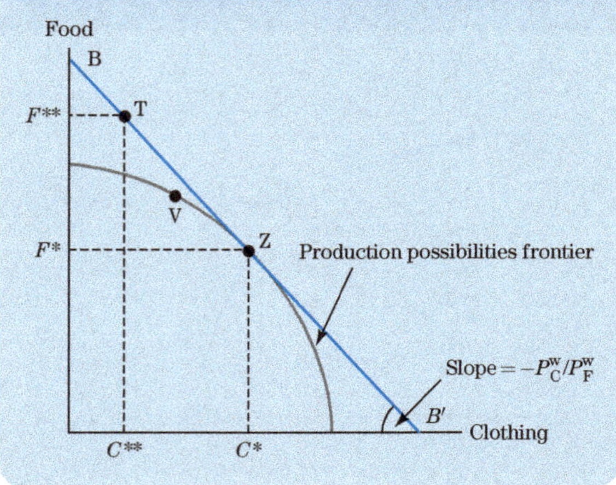

for every person in the economy to have more of each good than before.

Without international trade, the economy's competitive equilibrium was at V. With the possibility of buying or selling in world markets, the economy maximizes the total value of its output by producing at Z, where its MRT is equal to the international price ratio, P_C^w/P_F^w. Along BB′, the international budget constraint, it then chooses the consumption allocation for which every consumer's MRS is equal to P_C^w/P_F^w. If this occurs at T, the country will export $C^* - C^{**}$ units of clothing and import $F^{**} - F^*$ units of food.

Which of the infinitely many bundles along BB′ should be chosen? The best outcome is the one for which P_C^w/P_F^w is equal to every consumer's MRS. We know that without international trade the common value of MRS was equal to the MRT at V, which is smaller than the MRT at Z. Since there is more clothing and less food at Z than at V, it follows that the MRS at Z will be smaller than the MRT at V. This means that people will be better off moving to the northwest from Z. Suppose T is the combination of food and clothing that equates everyone's MRS to P_C^w/P_F^w. This economy will then do best by exporting $C^* - C^{**}$ units of clothing and using the proceeds to import $F^{**} - F^*$ units of food.

As noted, the fact that the international budget constraint contains the original competitive equilibrium point means that it is possible to make everyone better off than before. But the impersonal workings of international trading markets provide no guarantee that every single person will in fact be made better off by trade. In the illustration given, international trading possibilities lead the economy to produce more clothing and less food than it used to. The effect will be to increase the demand for factors of production used in clothing production, and to reduce the demand for those used in food production. If food production is relatively intensive in the use of labour, and clothing production is relatively intensive in the use of capital, the shift in product mix would drive up the price of capital and drive down the price of labour. In this case, the primary beneficiaries from trade would be the owners of capital. People whose incomes derive exclusively from the sale of their own labour would actually do worse than before, even though the value of total output is higher. What our general equilibrium analysis shows is that trade makes it possible to give everyone more of everything. It does not prove that everyone necessarily will get more.

Much has been written about the agonizing trade-off between equity and efficiency, the notion that greater distributional fairness requires some sacrifice in efficiency. The lesson in Example 16.1 is that, when people are able to negotiate costlessly with one another, there is in fact no conflict between equity and efficiency. When the total size of the economic pie grows larger, it is always possible for everyone to have a larger slice than before. Efficiency is achieved when we have made the economic pie as large as possible. Having done that, we are then free to discuss what constitutes a fair division of the pie.

Sources of inefficiency

Taxes

Introducing taxes will have the effect that too little of the product that is taxed will be produced. The problem with taxes is that they cause producers to see a different price ratio to consumers. Consumption decisions are based on gross prices – that is, on prices inclusive of taxes. Production decisions, by contrast, are guided by net prices – the amount producers get to keep after the tax has been paid. When producers confront a different price ratio from the one that guides consumers, the MRS can never be equal to the MRT in equilibrium. By driving a wedge between the price ratios seen by producers and consumers, the tax leads to an inefficient mix.

Subsidies, like taxes, upset the conditions required for efficiency. The problem with a taxed product is that it appears too cheap to its producer. By contrast, the problem with a subsidized product is that it appears too expensive. In general equilibrium, we get too much of the subsidized product and too little of the unsubsidized one. Taxes almost always lead to some sort of inefficiency in the allocation of resources.

Monopoly

Taxes are but one of many factors that stand in the way of achieving Pareto optimality in the allocation of resources. One other source of inefficiency is monopoly. The general equilibrium effects of monopoly are closely analogous to those of a commodity tax. Consider again our simple production economy with two goods, and suppose that food is produced by a monopolist, clothing by a price taker. The competitive producer selects an output level for which marginal cost is equal to the price of clothing; the monopolist, as we saw in Chapter 10, selects one for which marginal cost is equal to

Example 16.1

You are the president of a small island nation that has never engaged in trade with any other nation. You are considering the possibility of opening the economy to international trade. The chief economist of the island's only labour union, to which every worker belongs, tells you that free trade will reduce the real purchasing power of labour, and you have no reason to doubt him. You are determined to remain in office, and need the union's support in order to do so. The union will never support a candidate whose policies adversely affect the welfare of its members. Does this mean you should keep the island closed to trade?

The answer is yes only if there is no way to redistribute the gains that trade will produce. Our general equilibrium analysis establishes that trade will increase the total value of output, which makes it possible for everyone to do better. If the alternative is for the island to remain closed, the owners of capital should readily agree to transfer some of their gains to labour. The only president who would fail to open the island's economy is one who is too lazy or unimaginative to negotiate an agreement under which every party ends up with more of everything than before.

marginal revenue. Because price always exceeds marginal revenue along a downward-sloping demand curve, this means that price will exceed marginal cost for the monopolist.

From the standpoint of efficiency, this wedge between price and marginal cost functions exactly like a tax on the monopolist's product. The marginal rate of transformation, which is the ratio of the marginal cost of clothing to the marginal cost of food, will no longer be equal to the ratio of product prices. Producers will be responding to one set of incentives, consumers to another. The result is that too few of the economy's resources will be devoted to the production of food (the monopolized product), and too many to the production of clothing (the competitive product).

The general equilibrium analysis of the effect of monopoly adds an important dimension to our partial equilibrium analysis from Chapter 10. The partial analysis called our attention to the fact that there would be too little output produced by the monopolist. The general equilibrium analysis forcefully reminds us that there is another side of this coin, which is that the resources not used by the monopolist will be employed by the competitive sector of the economy. Thus, if monopoly output is too small, competitive output is too big. The additional competitive output does not undo the damage caused by monopoly, but it partially compensates for it. Viewed within the framework of general equilibrium analysis, the welfare costs of monopoly are thus smaller than they appeared from our partial equilibrium analysis.

Externalities

Another source of inefficiency occurs when production or consumption activities involve benefits or costs that fall on people not directly involved in the activities. As discussed in Chapter 14, such benefits and costs are usually referred to as *externalities*. A standard example of a negative externality is the case of pollution, in which a production activity results in emissions that adversely affect people other than those who consume the product. The planting of additional apple trees, whose blossoms augment the output of honey in nearby beehives, is an example of a positive externality. And so is the case of the beekeeper who adds bees to his hive, unmindful of the higher pollination rates they will produce in nearby apple orchards.

Externalities are both widespread and important. The problem they create for efficiency stems from the fact that, like taxes, they cause producers and consumers to respond to different sets of relative prices. When the orchard owner decides how many trees to plant, he looks only at the price of apples, not at the price of honey. By the same token, when the consumer decides how much honey to buy, he ignores the effects of his purchases on the quantity and price of apples.

In the case of negative externalities in production, the effect on efficiency is much the same as that of a subsidy. In deciding what quantity of the product to produce, the producer equates price and his own private marginal cost. The problem is that the negative externalities impose additional costs on others, and these are ignored by the producer. As with the subsidized product, we end up with too much of the product with negative externalities and too little of all other products. With positive externalities, the reverse occurs. We end up with too little of such products and too much of others.

As noted earlier, the best tax from an efficiency standpoint is one levied on an activity there would otherwise be too much of. This suggests that the welfare losses from monopoly can be mitigated by placing an excise tax on the good produced in the competitive sector. Properly chosen, such a tax could exactly offset the wedge that is created by the disparity between the monopolist's price and marginal cost.

In the case of negative externalities, the difficulty is that individuals regard the product as being cheaper than it really is from the standpoint of society as a whole. By taxing the product with negative externalities at a suitable rate, the efficiency loss can be undone. For products accompanied by positive externalities, the corresponding solution is a subsidy.

Public goods

One additional factor that stands in the way of achieving efficient allocations through private markets is the existence of public goods. As discussed in Chapter 15, a pure public good is one with two specific properties: (1) non-rivalry, which means that one person's use of the good does not diminish the amount of it available for others; and (2) non-excludability, which means that it is either impossible or prohibitively costly to exclude people who do not pay from using the good. In the days before the invention of channel scramblers, broadcast television signals were an example of a pure public good. Your tuning in to a movie on channel 104, for example, does not make that movie less available to anyone else. And before the advent of decoders, there was no practical way to exclude anyone from making use of a television signal once it was broadcast. In South Africa, in fact, viewers who do not pay their TV licences still cannot be excluded from watching programmes broadcast by SABC 1, 2 and 3 and e-TV. National defence is another example of a pure public good. The fact that Solly enjoys the benefits of national defence does not make those benefits any less available to Janet. And it is exceedingly difficult for the government to protect some of its citizens from foreign attack while denying the same protection to others.

There is no reason to presume that private markets will supply optimal quantities of pure public goods. Indeed, if it is impossible to exclude people from using the good, it might seem impossible for a profit-seeking firm to supply any quantity of it at all. But profit-seeking firms often show great ingenuity in devising schemes for providing pure public goods. Commercial broadcast television, for example, covers its costs by charging advertisers for access to the audience it attracts with its programming. But even in these cases, there is no reason to suppose that the amount and kind of television programming we get under this arrangement are economically efficient.

The problem is less acute in the case of goods that have the non-rivalry but not the non-excludability property. Once every household is wired for DStv, for example, it will be possible to prevent people from watching any given programme if they do not pay for it. But, even here, there are likely to be inefficiencies. Once a TV programme has been produced, it costs society nothing to let an extra person see it. If there is a positive price for watching the programme, however, all those who value seeing it at less than that price will not tune in. It is inefficient to exclude these viewers, since their viewing the programme would not diminish its usefulness for anyone else.

Summary

- One of the simplest possible general equilibrium models is a pure exchange economy with only two consumers and two goods. For any given initial allocation of the two goods between the two consumers in this model, a competitive exchange process will always exhaust all possible mutually beneficial gains from trade. This result is known as the first theorem of welfare economics.
- If consumers have convex indifference curves, any efficient allocation can be sustained as a competitive equilibrium. This result is known as the second theorem of welfare economics. Its significance is that it demonstrates that the issues of efficiency and distributional equity are logically distinct. Society can redistribute initial endowments according to accepted norms of distributive justice, and then rely on markets to assure that endowments are used efficiently.
- An economy is efficient in production if the marginal rate of technical substitution is the same for all producers. In the input market, too, competitive trading exploits all mutually beneficial gains from exchange.
- Even though international trade leaves domestic production possibilities unchanged, its immediate effect is to increase the value of goods available for domestic consumption. With a suitable redistribution of initial endowments, a free-trade economy will always be Pareto superior to a non-free-trade economy.
- Taxes often interfere with efficient resource allocation, usually because they cause consumers and producers to respond to different price ratios.
- Monopoly, externalities and public goods are three other factors that interfere with the efficient allocation of resources.

Questions for review

1 Why does efficiency in consumption require the MRS of all consumers to be the same?

2 Distinguish between the terms 'Pareto superior', 'Pareto preferred' and 'Pareto optimal.'

3 Why might voters in a country choose a non-Pareto optimal allocation over another that is Pareto optimal?

4 How do the initial endowments constrain where we end up on the contract curve?

5 In general equilibrium, can there be excess demand for every good?

6 How might a social critic respond to the claim that government involvement in the economy is unjustified because of the working of the market mechanism?

7 Why is the slope of the production possibilities frontier equal to the ratio of marginal production costs?

8 How might a critic respond to the claim that taxes always make the allocation of resources less efficient?

Problems

1 You regard gold and silver as substitutes because both serve as a hedge against inflation. Assume the supplies of gold ($Q_G = 75$) and silver ($Q_S = 300$) are fixed in the short run. The demands for gold and silver are given by the following functions:

$P_G = 975 - Q_G + 0.5\,P_S$

and

$P_S = 600 - Q_S + 0.5\,P_G$

a What is the equilibrium price of gold and silver?

b Assume that the discovery of new gold increases the supply of gold to 150. How will this affect the price of gold and silver?

2 With general equilibrium analysis we take into account feedback effects. How will the following events influence the market?

a In 2013 there was an outbreak of bird fever in the Southern Cape and thousands of ostriches was shot and burned to prevent the disease from spreading. How would this influence the South African market for chicken and ostrich?

b The government increases the tax levied on airline tickets to Sun City. If we assume you have to fly in, how will this influence the market for airline tickets and hotel rooms in Sun City?

3 Bert has an initial endowment consisting of 10 units of food and 10 units of clothing. Ernie's initial endowment consists of 10 units of food and 20 units of clothing. Represent these initial endowments in an Edgeworth exchange box.

4 Bert regards food and clothing as perfect 1-for-1 substitutes. Ernie regards them as perfect complements, always wanting to consume 3 units of clothing for every 2 units of food.

a Describe the set of allocations that are Pareto preferred to the one given in Problem 3.

b Describe the contract curve for that allocation.

c What price ratio will be required to sustain an allocation on the contract curve?

5 How will your answers to Problem 4 differ if 5 units of Ernie's clothing endowment are given to Bert?

6 Consider a simple economy with two goods, food and clothing, and two consumers, A and B. For a given initial endowment, when the ratio of food to clothing prices in an economy is 3/1, A wants to buy 6 units of clothing while B wants to sell 2 units of food. Is $P_F/P_C = 3$ an equilibrium price ratio? If so, explain why. If not, state in which direction it will tend to change.

7 How will your answer to Problem 6 change if A wants to sell 3 units of clothing and B wants to sell 2 units of food?

8 Suppose Sarah has an endowment of 2 units of X and 4 units of Y, and has indifference curves that satisfy our four basic

assumptions (see Chapter 3). Suppose Brian has an endowment of 4 units of X and 2 units of Y, and has preferences given by the utility function $U(X, Y) = \min\{X, Y\}$, where

$$\min(X,Y) = \begin{cases} X \text{ if } X \leq Y \\ Y \text{ if } Y \leq X \end{cases}.$$

On an Edgeworth box diagram, indicate the set of Pareto-superior bundles.

9 A simple economy produces two goods, food and clothing, with two inputs, capital and labour. Given the current allocation of capital and labour between the two industries, the marginal rate of technical substitution between capital and labour in food production is 4, while the corresponding MRTS in clothing production is 2. Is this economy efficient in production? If so, explain why. If not, describe a reallocation that will lead to a Pareto improvement.

10 Given the current allocation of productive inputs, the marginal rate of transformation of food for clothing in a simple two-good economy is equal to 2. At the current allocation of consumption goods, each consumer's marginal rate of substitution between food and clothing is 1.5. Is this economy efficient in terms of its product mix? If so, explain why. If not, describe a reallocation that will lead to a Pareto improvement.

11 Calvin can make 5 units of food per day if he devotes all his time to food production. He can make 10 units of clothing if he spends the whole day at clothing production. If he divides his time between the two activities, his output of each good will be proportional to the time spent on each. The corresponding figures for Frikkie are 10 units of food and 15 units of clothing. Describe the production possibilities frontier for their economy.

12 If Calvin and Frikkie regard food and clothing as perfect 1-for-1 substitutes, what should each produce?

13 Now suppose a trading ship visits Calvin and Frikkie's island each day and offers to buy or sell food and clothing at the prices $P_F = 4$, $P_C = 1$. How, if at all, will the presence of this ship alter the production and consumption decisions of Calvin and Frikkie?

14 How will your answers to Problems 11, 12 and 13 differ if Frikkie's maximum production figures change to 20 units of food and 50 units of clothing?

15 There are two industries in a simple economy, each of which faces the same marginal cost of production. One of the industries is perfectly competitive, the other is a pure monopoly. Describe a reallocation of resources that will lead to a Pareto improvement for this economy.

16 Suppose capital and labour are perfect substitutes in production for clothing: 2 units of capital or 2 units of labour produce 1 unit of clothing. Suppose capital and labour are perfect complements in production of food: 1 unit of capital and 1 unit of labour produce 1 unit of food. Suppose the economy has an endowment of 100 units of capital and 200 units of labour. Describe the set of efficient allocations of these factors to the two sectors (determine the contract curve in an Edgeworth production box).

17 Construct the production possibilities frontier for the economy described in Problem 16. What is the opportunity cost of food in terms of clothing?

18 Construct the production possibilities frontier for an economy just like the one described in Problem 16, except that its endowment of capital is 200 units.

Answers to in-chapter exercises

16.1 Thandi's endowment of food = 100 – Julia's endowment = 100 – 25 = 75. Thandi's endowment of clothing = 200 – Julia's endowment = 200 – 25 = 175.

16.2 Let M denote the initial allocation. Julia's indifference curve through M is a straight line with slope = –1. (See figure at top of page 516.) Thandi's indifference curve through M is right-angled, as shown in the following diagram. The set of Pareto-superior allocations is indicated by the shaded triangle.

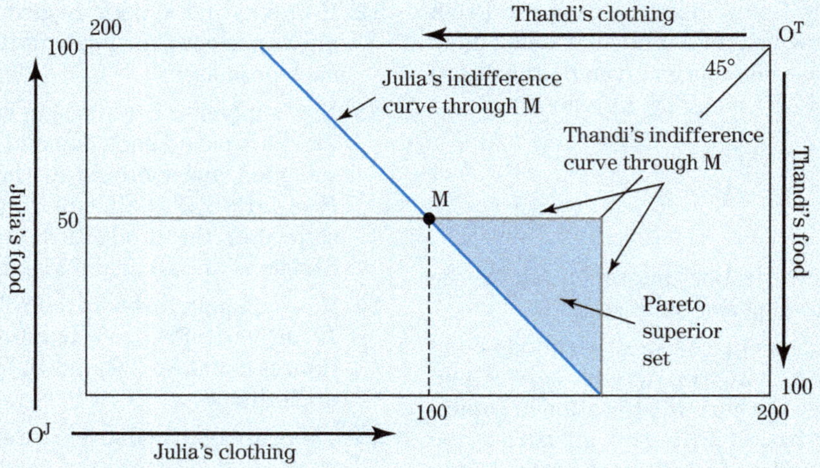

16.3 Here, $P_L/P_K = 1$, which is half as big as MP_{L_C}/MP_{K_C}:

$$\frac{P_L}{P_K} = \frac{1}{2}\frac{MP_{L_C}}{MP_{K_C}}$$

from which it follows that

$$\frac{MP_{K_C}}{P_K} = \frac{1}{2}\frac{MP_{L_C}}{P_L}$$

In words, this says that the last rand spent on capital in clothing production produces only half as much extra output as does the last rand spent on labour in clothing production. It follows that clothing producers can get more output for the same cost by hiring less capital and more labour. Parallel reasoning tells us that food producers can increase food production at no extra cost by hiring less labour and more capital. Only when these producers have reached a cost-minimizing input mix characteristic of a competitive equilibrium will efficiency in production be achieved.

16.4 On the new production possibilities frontier, the maximum quantity of food that can be produced is unchanged. At every level of food production, the corresponding amount of clothing that can be produced is exactly double the original amount.

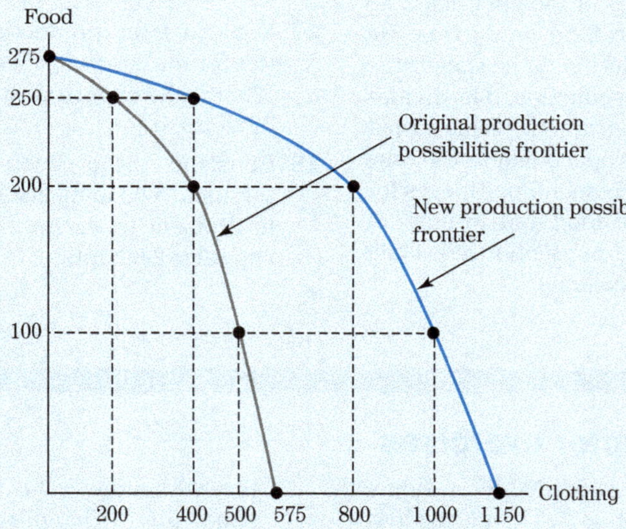

Index

J

K

L